BASEBALL SABERMETRIC 1993

by
Brock J. Hanke
Don Malcolm
David Raglin
Brian Rodewald
Win Murray

cover photo by
L. T. "Jug" Spence
(St. Louis Post-Dispatch)

Mad Aztec Press
in association with
Red Herring Press, Trans-Elven BHTC, Mad AzTech

ISBN: 0-9625846-1-4

Printed in the United States of America by *Mad Aztec Press*
1215 Willow View Drive, Kirkwood, MO 63122-1212
(314) 965-9789.

10 9 8 7 6 5 4 3 2 1

Table of Contents

Introduction for New Readers 5

Introduction for Old Readers 7

I. GENERAL ESSAYS

My Year Underwater as a Bill James Fantasy Freak 10

Walkmen 29

Gary W. Jones 52

Warren Newson 55

II. TEAM ESSAYS

American League East

Toronto Blue Jays 61

Milwaukee Brewers 66

Baltimore Orioles 71

Cleveland Indians 76

New York Yankees 81

Detroit Tigers 86

Boston Red Sox 92

American League West

Oakland Athletics 100

Minnesota Twins 106

ChicagoWhite Sox 111

Texas Rangers 117

California Angels 122

Kansas City Royals 128

Seattle Mariners 133

National League West

Atlanta Braves 141

Cincinnati Reds 146

San Diego Padres 152

Houston Astros 157

San Francisco Giants 163

Los Angeles Dodgers 169

National League East

Pittsburgh Pirates 179

Montreal Expos 183

St. Louis Cardinals 188

Chicago Cubs 193

New York Mets 198

Philadelphia Phillies 202

III. PLAYER SEASON RANKINGS

Starting Pitchers	208
Relief Closers	218
Catchers	223
First Basemen	229
Second Basemen	235
Third Basemen	241
Shortstops	247
Left Fielders	253
Center Fielders	259
Right Fielders	265
Designated Hitters	271

IV. REFERENCE

LISTS

TWAR by WAR	274
TWAR Alphabetical	278
OWAR	282
DWAR	284
Trade Value	286
Base Stealing Profit	290
Ballpark Adjusted ERA	294
Ballpark Adjusted Top Tens	296
Ground Balls / Fly Balls / Strikeouts	298

MAJOR LEAGUE EQUIVALENCIES	299
and Peak Projections	
GLOSSARY	313
ORDER and RESPONSE SHEET	319

Introduction for New Readers

You see, there used to be this book called THE BILL JAMES BASEBALL ABSTRACT. It was written by a man named, you guessed it, Bill James. The ABSTRACT was fun to read and full of controversial pronouncements to excite the blood of any baseball fan. But, more, it was full of statistical analysis, designed to back up the pronouncements, rather than just arguments in support of them. This was - and is - regarded as cheating by much of the sporting press, but many fans found the novel idea of honest and careful analysis most rewarding to read. And thus did the book sell and sell until 1988, when Bill James got tired of writing it, and turned his hand to the material which can now be found in the BILL JAMES BASEBALL BOOK, on sale at good bookstores everywhere.

When Bill gave up writing the ABSTRACT, he was aware that there would be writers who wanted to produce a continuation of the concept. When the inevitable proposals came to his attention, he chose to combine those of Brock J. Hanke and Rob Wood. This book was the 1989 BASEBALL ABSTRACT. Unfortunately, Rob and Brock ("I" am Brock) did not make a good collaborative pair, and thus it came to pass that neither one of them has the right to use the title BASEBALL ABSTRACT any more. This book, BASEBALL SABERMETRIC, is Brock's attempt to continue the concept of the ABSTRACT.

This is not to say that I write the book all by myself. No, what I have done is to put together a team of people who want to write material in the style of the ABSTRACT, and who I think are more than capable of doing so. The advantage of this is that you, the reader, get a much closer focus on each topic than I could possibly generate if I had to examine them all myself. You also get some variety in writing style, which may help in the reading; and some variety also in the ideas, which doubtless helps in the understanding.

My longtime friend Don Malcolm is the main collaborator. David Raglin has been with us for several years now, specializing in the American League East. Don came up with Win Murray, who competes with Don in the Bill James Winter League game (from STATS, Inc.), but who collaborates with him here. And, not at all least, there's Brian Rodewald. Brian does the work involved in producing the Major League Equivalencies you'll find near the end of the book. It's a daunting task, not helped at all by being boring, and I'm sure glad I don't have to do it.

I mentioned STATS, Inc., which provides all the wonderful statistic lists you'll see here. STATS is the brainchild of John Dewan, who followed up on a Bill James suggestion to found an organization called PROJECT SCORESHEET. The Project was formed to score every game in the Major Leagues, so that statistics therefrom could be obtained by analysts for several thousand dollars less than the official statisticians, Elias, will sell them for. Project Scoresheet began as a volunteer organization and has remained so, while John formed STATS, Inc. to do the same thing on a more professional basis. Without STATS, I couldn't even attempt this book, as I couldn't afford the raw material. It is also true that John was the person who believed in my proposal to continue the ABSTRACT enough that he brought it to Bill James' attention....

STATS, Inc. has also gotten into the fantasy league business. With developmental work from Bill James, STATS now has two leagues. One is played during the baseball season, and is sort of an advanced, sabermetric rotisserie league. If you like this book,, you'll love the league. If you're in the league, you'll love this book. The other league is played during the winter, and features players from all times. This is the Winter League's first year; Don is in it, and it sounds like a great fun and learning experience, Unfortunately, I have to produce a book over the winter.

STATS leads to a quick mention of Dick Cramer. Dick was one of the very first sabermetricians, and did the original computer programming for STATS. Fortunately for me, he lives in St. Louis, as do I, and does the programming for all those wonderful statistics lists in the book here. Did I mention that Dick fits this in between his regular job and playing jazz and his wife and... I didn't? Well, he does, and I thank him as often as I can.

So enough of the publishing history. What kind of book do you have here? Well, Bill called what he was doing "sabermetrics," which is where the title comes from. My opinion is that sabermetrics amounts to "systems analysis of baseball." That is, sabermetricians take a look at the game of baseball as a system and attempt to figure out how it is working. That's why all the statistics; in order to analyze a system, you have to have enough mathematical information about it to make a mathematical model.

Needless to say, sabermetrics is not like sportswriting. That activity is inherently relies on "insider" information. Sportswriters, as you doubtless know, talk to players and managers and focus on their personal struggles, both with the game itself and with each other. I know very little about the insider aspect of baseball. I can't tell you how to adjust your swing to hit a curve, or how to correct a pitching motion or how to keep race problems from destroying a ballclub. But, in focusing on such things, insiders often lose the ability to see the proverbial forest through the trees. That is, they lose sight of the whole system in their need to focus on individual parts. Sabermetrics provides the most valuable service of retreating the focus and thereby widening the scope. Also, let's face it, most readers aren't baseball insiders, either. You who are reading this right now will probably get a better grasp of what I am doing than you will ever really have of what, say, Rickey Henderson does.

It may be no little help that the actual mathematics of sabermetrics is not very difficult. I have a degree in mathematics, but you won't be needing one. Even better, we have a nice big glossary of terms and methods in the back of this book, which I have tried to write in layman's language.

Feel free to dip into the SABERMETRIC wherever you want to start. The essays (we don't really have "chapters") are not organized in reading order, but by category. The introductory material, comes first, and then we print the General Essays, then the Team Comments, then the Player Comments, and, finally, the reference material, including the MLEs and the Glossary. So use the Table of Contents to flip right to your favorite essay, team or player, because it's finally come time for me to shut up.

Thanks for Reading,

- Brock J. Hanke

Introduction
for Old Readers

We've got two sorts of old readers, here, you know. There's the old readers who were with us last year, not to mention the previous four years, and then there's the "old" readers who had no idea anyone was doing anything with the BASEBALL ABSTRACT concept. First, a few (well, four) paragraphs for the second category, those who only remember Bill James' book. Those of you who remember last year's edition can skip this; it's the same four paragraphs as last year.

Bill, you will remember, gave up the ABSTRACT with the 1988 edition. Of the proposals he received, he decided to combine mine (I am Brock J. Hanke) with that of Rob Wood. We did produce a 1989 BASEBALL ABSTRACT, but then we found we were unable to continue as partners. So we both lost the right to use the ABSTRACT title. I, Brock, decided to continue doing an ABSTRACT-style book, with my own hand-picked team of collaborators, which was published the next year as BASEBALL SABERMETRIC, 1990, and which is back again as what you have in your hands.

There are two big differences between this book and Bill's work. First, we are not so theoretically oriented as Bill. Bill did a lot of what can only be called groundbreaking analysis, devising new methods and approaches. We don't have nearly as much of that; instead, we rely heavily on Bill's methods, to which he relinquished copyright in the 1988 book. We do have some advancements upon that base, like my own Stolen Base Profit Method, but the basics in this book are going to seem awfully familiar to you old readers.

A lot of this is simply the result of Bill's getting a lot done during his decade of the ABSTRACT. I have always suspected that one of his primary motivations for quitting the book was that he was confronting the Law of Diminishing Returns in original analysis, doing more work for less result. The rest is probably my own personality. I have much more an engineer's background and mindset than Bill does; I like applying the same old methods, year after year, to different raw data, to see what small differences in results arise.

The second difference is that we have many more, and much more sophisticated, stat boxes than Bill ever had. This is the result of STATS, Inc. and their scoring database. Bill, you will recall, kept having to ask teams for whatever stats they'd send him, while I can just go to STATS, Inc. and ask for a report. I have to pay them, of course, but they're well within the reach of even this self-published enterprise. Trust me, STATS, Inc. bears no resemblance whatsoever to Elias.

Back to all the old readers. Last year, you'll remember that I produced a very scanty work-in-progress report on pitchers' workloads and arm troubles. Well, it's still not finished. I want to do something thorough, and I just haven't had the time to finish up. I'm not backing down on anything I've said so far, mind you. I still am quite sure that most pitchers cannot stand workloads over 200 innings. The ones who can seem to be the few hardest throwers in the game. And I'm still sure that 70 innings is the most you should give your closer. Got some support for that one. Dennis Eckersley himself said he liked to keep his innings down to 60 or 70, and he got 80, and he was bad in the postseason, right on schedule. But I'm just not finished examining and testing theories yet, and I'm not printing any more half-assed partial results.

There is a new wrinkle in the Major League Equivalencies of minor league stats. They're in the back, and they're still great, but this year's PEAK Projection lines are more accurate than last year's. That's because I had one of those "how could I have missed that?" revelations. Bill originally billed (heh) the MLEs as "equivalencies" of what the minor league player would have done that year in the Majors. But that's not how Bill tested the method. He tested it by comparing the MLEs to the players' lines in the Majors the NEXT YEAR. Now, that's of only minor interest in using the MLEs themselves, though it is of interest. But, for the PEAK lines, it's crucial. That's because the PEAKs are generated by placing the MLE lines into the BROCK2 projection spreadsheet. BROCK2 generates a better PEAK line for younger players. If you have the age wrong by one year too young, you get a PEAK that is just a bit too hot. That's what we had last year; PEAKs that were too good. This year, we inserted the MLEs into the BROCK2 as if the players were one year older than they were. That gave us very reasonable PEAKs, PEAKs you should trust. You can still use last year's; the shape of the lines is still good, so all you have to do is downgrade the whole just a tad. But this year's PEAKs look really reasonable to me; trust them with your fantasy team's life.

A couple of notes about the contents here. I think that Don Malcolm's fantasy league diary is one of the best items I have been privileged to print here in the SABERMETRIC. Give it a read if you have any interest in fantasy ball at all. It tells you everything you need to know about what it takes to win, and how it feels to play. And yes, Don and I do recommend the Bill James Fantasy game, from STATS, Inc. It's great, and it's realistic.

Don's walkmen article is great, too, a major research essay. However, it is long, and therefore there are no team profiles this year. However, there are lists of Ballpark-Adjusted ERAs in the lists section, along with grounder / fly ball / strikeout data for teams. New wrinkles from Dick Cramer and STATS. There's also new boxes in the team essays, with projected lineups for 1993. Just another SABERMETRIC service here in the Year of Player Movement.

Many of you will remember the Sabermetricians' Hall of Fame balloting. I would have printed final results this year except for two things: I ran out of room, and some of the people who wrote in and asked for ballots haven't returned them yet. If you still want to vote, write for a ballot. But you MUST return it by October 1, 1993! I've got to print results some year.

A real tiny detail. Three of the four section headings have changed. "General Essays" and "Reference" should be self-explanatory. They explain why some items end up in one place, and some in another. "Player Season Rankings" addresses one of the problems Bill James had with my first proposal to continue the ABSTRACT. He didn't want me to "rank players" according to a numerical method, without any common-sense adjustments. I've finally figured out what I should have said then. I'm not in the business of ranking players. I don't know enough to do that; sabermetrics isn't enough to do that by itself. I am, however, in the business of evaluating the seasons the players turned in last year. I may talk about how good the player "is" in a comment, but the listed numerical ranking is an evaluation of his 1992 season, nothing more and nothing less. Sorry I didn't think of that then, Bill.

One last thing. Last year, the book was published through Elysian Fields Press. They are now out of the baseball book business, and I am several thousand dollars in the hole. (If any of you readers know of a publisher looking for a thorough analysis book, please let me know. Self-publishing is fun, but it is also time consuming. I'd get a lot more pitcher studies done if I didn't have to paste the book up every January. Hell, I might even answer my mail.) Last year's book did not appear in bookstores until April, though I had my copies in time to ship in February. What I want to say is that I have no problems with my editor, Steve Lehman. None of this was his fault. He did the best he could with what he had. Thanks for trying, Steve.

And thank all you readers for buying. I sure can use the business this time.

Thanks Once Again for Reading,

Brock J. Hanke

I

General Essays

My Year Underwater as a
Bill James Fantasy Freak

Don Malcolm

You're thinking: that's supposed to be undercover, year undercover. A semi-infamous sabermetrician plunks down his money under an assumed name and is humiliated by aardvark-like baseball freaks from all across the country. An inverted spy story, sort of a dada George Plimpton.

But it's not undercover, it's underwater. Because most of the moves that I made during the course of the 1992 baseball season were done via coaxial cable laid under the Pacific Ocean connecting Hawaii to the mainland. I spent about half of 1992 in Hawaii, and way too much of my time (spare and otherwise) involved in Bill James Fantasy Baseball (BJFB for short). Not that I minded it so much: I did win (after all, sabermetrics is worth something). But I warn you, at the outset of my combination post-mortem and reminiscence about the experience, that one can truly feel submerged by the amount of attention to detail required to be successful in a game as challenging and well-designed as BJFB.

This article has been written, as my still-waterlogged brain can barely process, for three (3) reasons:

1) Because Brock Hanke, the editor and chief crank of this book (I am only a secondary crank, though no less formidable despite my inaccessibility), promised the world that such an article would appear.

2) Because I wanted to give credit to a great group of guys scattered across the country who not only put up with me all year but were exceedingly gracious when they wound up losing to a team with the strange and unfathomable name of the San Antonio Trotters (it's an inside joke, folks: so inside it's outside, if ya know what I'm alluding to).

3) Because—most important now—the BJFB game deserves a plug, and since you are something of a baseball maniac (how can I tell? You're reading this book, aren't you? then you obviously qualify), you may be perfectly suited to play BJFB in '93, which will make the folks at STATS, Inc. very happy, somewhat more prosperous, and possibly more inclined to give Hanke and myself additional arcane statistical breakouts at no extra charge. (And you better believe that we want those breakouts, too.)

This article has not been written to tell you how to win at BJFB. First, it would be incredibly arrogant for me to imply that I have figured out how to win simply because I came in first in my division last season. I might actually believe that I have figured it out, but I am not going to utter such a statement in public, because what if I'm wrong? You guys (and gals: we know you're out there) would lynch me if I advertised a "foolproof" method that was not only not foolproof but not waterproof either. (Glub, glub, glub...got to keep that soggy metaphor floatin' your way....)

In the course of the next few pages, you'll relive the highlights and lowlights of a very eventful 1992 fantasy baseball season, and watch the San Antonio Trotters, fledgling franchise in the Eastern Division of the Juan Marichal League, do battle with Black Irish, the Malibu Mowers, the Iowa Hogheads, the West Des Moines Weevils, and the Winnebago Pork Queens for the division crown. In the meantime, the Western Division will rear up its head late in the season and have an incredible down-to-the-final-day race between the Topanga Thunder, the Pikes Peak Players, and the El Toro Devils, who will be pursued by the Santa Barbara Sun Sox, the Surfers of the Apocalypse (not owned by Keanu Reeves: sorry, Hollywood wave fans, it's a false rumor), and the South Bronx Bombers. You'll see who my main trading partners were, what incredibly smart and dumb moves I made, and how I scammed my way to the top (while all the while wearing scuba gear...).

THE GAME

But first (ca-CHING), let's describe the game itself. Fantasy or rotisserie baseball, as most of you know, is not at all like the real game. It is an accumulation of numbers pure and simple (or, in the case of BJFB, pure and complex). The objective is to have the most points at the end. There are many fantasy baseball games available: I had never played one prior to 1992, but several friends had been in them over the years, so I had a good idea of how they worked.

BJFB is exceptionally thorough, however. Pitching, fielding, and hitting all factor into the game, and have an impact on how well you'll do. Virtually all of the meaningful statistics found in a pitcher's line (BB/SO ratio, baserunners per nine innings, ERA) all weigh heavily in determining how many points are awarded for each pitching performance. The formulas differ for starters and relievers, of course, but the same principle holds: a pitcher like Doug Jones, with 35 saves and a sub-2.00 ERA, is significantly more valuable point-wise than a Randy Myers, who has more saves but an ERA more than twice as high.

Hitters earn points for hits, doubles, triples, homers, walks, runs, RBI, and stolen bases, plus what the BJFB calls "batter effectiveness points." The BEP, as they're known to the anointed, are a function of batting average. You're supposed to balance your team around speed, power, batting average, and on-base. There are limits to the number of each category you're allowed to accumulate before they stop counting for you. I don't remember all of them now, as I sit here in my leaky office in Santa Monica (there's that water thing again...), but the limit for doubles is 330, homers 200, pitchers' wins 100, things like that. If you know the history of baseball at all, you can see immediately that Bill James, Dick Cramer, John Dewan et al have thought carefully about how to structure a fantasy game that brings a great sense of statistical verisimilitude to the way the numbers accumulate over the course of a season.

Fielding is still the sketchiest part of the equation, but the elements that have been incorporated make a lot of sense. Second basemen, shortstops, and third basemen get their double plays added to their totals; catchers get complete-game wins (meaning games that their team wins in which they catch the whole game) and catcher's caught stealing added to their totals. All players lose two points for every error they commit: Dave Endicott of the Iowa Hogheads kept bouncing Jose Offerman (40+ errors at SS) up and down like a buoy in a galestorm (yes! nautical imagery as well!! nauseating, ain't it?) during the stormy—heh, heh— 1992 campaign.

All of this is processed and kept track of by STATS, using their trusty VAX computer (named "Babe"). You don't have to calculate anything. STATS does it for you. You just receive your reports every week, curse or cheer depending on how many points you've accumulated, and plot whatever strategy you need in order to steer you team through the roiling waters (can't help it, it's in the blood) in hopes of reaching the proverbial port of victory (at sea). But most of the time you'll be swabbing the deck, cursing the wind or the Great White Whale or Jack Morris or some other guy on somebody's team that's going apeshit and keeping that lucky sonovabitch several hundred points ahead of you. BJFB ain't no leisurely sea cruise where you get to dance with all the pretty girls on the boat (how long can he keep this up, folks? how long before you ask for a refund?), nosiree: you've got to keep the radar on full time, 'cause you never know what's coming down the seawaves rightatcha under cover of darkness. (Just remember, Vince Lombardi was the second guy to say "Winning isn't everything, it's the only thing"—the first guy was Admiral Nimitz.)

But I digress. (Pick yourself up off the deck—er, floor—at this point, please.) The game is very detailed, and will require a good deal of daily attention from a team owner. If you don't enjoy reading box scores, BJFB may not be for you: you'll become intimately acquainted with all of them throughout the course of a season. I've been told that the league I was put into is one of the best BJFB leagues, and that was borne out by the fact that the Juan Marichal League finished first in total points in 1992 among all BJFB leagues. So prepare yourself, if you decide to enter into BJFB, for a kaleidoscopic free-for-all that begins with your seven "freeze" players in February and ends—hopefully, at least—when the last pitch of the World Series has been thrown.

THE DIARY

(Being nothing more or less than an honest mighty sailor man, I will inform you at the outset that these "diary entries" are recollections, not jottings du jour. So if anything seems forced or suspiciously filigreed for effect, you're right—it's landlubber's license. Now prepare the bathysphere, Captain Nemo...)

FEBRUARY

1st week:

I inherited a mess.

I don't know what crackpot had this team last year, but he (or she: let's be fair, a woman could have screwed this up this bad too) must've been smoking those clove cigarettes that after awhile make a man look like Marlene Dietrich with five o'clock shadow. Yikes!

The fortunate thing is that you only have to freeze seven of these blokes. The rest of the team gets drafted for you by computer from the prioritized lists you supply to the friendly but anonymous (or is that anonymous but friendly?) folks at STATS. Friendly? I'm expecting fan mail from some flounder at any time.

And flounder is what the San Antonio Trotters are likely to do, all right...

3rd week:

After great deliberation, a rash of bad humor, and consultation with a well-known local medium (whose later mysterious disappearance, trust me, was totally coincidental...), I have selected my "freezers," as Dave Endicott calls them. (Yes, some of these players do resemble frozen turkeys, that's true.)

Did I mention Dave Endicott? He's the owner of the Iowa Hogheads, and he is the first member of the Juan Marichal League to call me. He wants to make a trade—Terry Pendleton for Harold Reynolds. I look at my team and decide I'd rather keep Reynolds, since there are precious few second basemen rated better than him last year and I (like many others) expect a collapse from Pendleton in '92. Dave tells me that the league is in its fourth season, and that there are several interesting factions in it— for instance, a couple of high school kids in Orange County named Mike Miller and Dave Schultz, the former a cocksure young brawler with a track record for winning in the Western Division.

Dave lives in Forest City, Iowa, and teaches at a local college there along with his friend Jay Sierszyn, who, like me, will be putting his team—the Winnebago Pork Queens (great name)—into BJFB action for the first time in 1992. It's nice to talk to him, but I'm sure he can tell that I'm really just beginning to feel my way around this Great White Beast of a fantasy baseball game.

Oh, yeah, the seven "freezers" (remember this list, because it'll be very interesting to see which guys are left at the end of the season):

Starting pitchers Bret Saberhagen and Jack McDowell;
First baseman Cecil Fielder (ooh! homers!!);
Second baseman Harold Reynolds;
Shortstop Bill Spiers;
Left fielder Kevin Mitchell (he'll hit 40 for sure in the Kingdome...);
Center fielder Kirby Puckett;

Not frozen, but guaranteed to be mine, is right fielder Danny Tartabull, on my roster and the position in the draft where my team picks first. This permits me to keep those all-important middle infielders. (Or, as they would later be known, the "all-impotent middle infielders.")

In a few weeks, I will see what the computer has selected from my prioritized lists and I'll have my first 25-man roster. I note that the BJFB "major league roster" contains only 20 players instead of 25. As James explains in his writeup about the game, the players that get selected are all regulars in the real game, so instead of permitting a full set of stats from 16 hitters, they only allow for an average of 12 full-time hitters in terms of equivalent at-bats. The maximum is 14, which means that the minimum pitching staff you can carry is six. Theoretically, you can have just the eight position player hitters and 12 pitchers as the other extreme configuration. I am sure I don't have a clue as to what might prompt someone to play such extreme set-ups. (Later, after the many mind-bending permutations of the game made me seasick, I understood why.)

APRIL

1st:

My team is here. I'm going to get killed.

The eight **pitchers** are: freezers Saberhagen and McDowell, plus Bruce Hurst, Bill Wegman and Mike Remlinger, starters; Randy Myers, Jeff Montgomery, and Al Osuna, relievers.
Catchers are Brian Harper and Greg Olson.
First basemen: Fielder and Dave Magadan.
Second basemen: Reynolds and Randy Ready (who's injured).

Shortstops: Spiers and Luis Rivera.
Third basemen: Gary Gaetti and Dave Hollins.
Left fielders: Mitchell and Milt Thompson (good player, but a part-timer).
Center fielders: Puckett and Junior Felix.
Right fielders: Tartabull and Jesse Barfield.
Multi-position player: Larry Walker.

Remlinger, the throw-in with Mitchell in the big off-season trade between the Giants and the Mariners, pitched well in spring training but inexplicably gets cut, making him useless for BJFB purposes. Bill Spiers has a bad back and isn't going to start the season, which leaves me with Rivera, who's no stalwart and might get beaten out for the Boston SS job by Tim Naehring. Barfield and Tartabull play the same position on the same team.

When is that first reentry draft??

5th:

I set my opening day roster, the 20 guys who are going to accumulate points for me, the 20 guys who are going to ruin my reputation forever, who will drag me down into the muck and mire of sabermetric ruin, sullying me as sure as Solomon's cup (or was that his bicuspid?) o'erfloweth with misplaced lust. Or some other mangled image: make up your own, I'm too depressed.

The unholy twenty: Saberhagen, McDowell, Wegman, Hurst, Myers, Montgomery, Osuna, pitchers; Harper and Olson, catchers; Fielder and Magadan, first base; Reynolds, second base; Rivera, shortstop; Gaetti and Hollins, third base; Mitchell, left field; Puckett and Felix, center field, Tartabull, right field; Walker, multi-position (listed in right). In the minors: Remlinger, Ready, Spiers the lame, Thompson, and Barfield.

It's enough to make a guy want to jump overboard. Still, I'm beginning to get some vague sense of this thing that many of my women friends derisively call "male bonding." It's a strange thing, feeling psychically connected to a bunch of guys making millions of dollars. I wonder if BJFB knows which team in the Juan Marichal League has the highest payroll? Thankfully, that's one thing that doesn't really matter in fantasy baseball. Or does it?

As they say in the bigs, it's time to close your eyes and swing...

12th:

Dear STATS:

Your nightly FAX service sucks.

No, there's nothing wrong with it technically. The FAX image is clear. It arrives promptly at 1:15 am every morning, and is well-designed, thorough, accurate, and complete.

And it is full of confirmatory evidence that my team is a piece of shit.

Therefore, your nightly FAX service sucks.

PS: Can I change my team name to the PT Barnum All-Day Suckers? Or to the MIA's? I keep hoping that the box scores will tell me something different than what you've been sending me these last few nights. But I pick up the paper the next morning and, dammit, it's exactly the same.

It's a great service, but it's costing me what little sleep I already get.

Do you need an extra FAX machine for the office?? I'm putting mine up for sale—cheap.

19th:

Two firsts for the league are coming up in the next few days: the first league statistical information printout, which will confirm what I already know about my team (it stinks), and the first re-entry draft.

The re-entry draft is a big deal, because there are a lot of players still unclaimed who can be a big help to someone. My only problem is that I need someone at every position. So far Gary Gaetti has more errors than hits, Kevin Mitchell is hitting bloop singles when he's hitting at all, and I've flip-flopped Milt Thompson the part-timer off and on my major league roster (using the three-day rule for hitters) with such expert timing that I've missed all of his hits so far this season.

On the pitching side: Bret Saberhagen has been bombed, and Jeff Montgomery is never gonna get any saves for the Royals, who've started out the season 1-12. I'm still planning to get a communications package so I can access the STATS computer via "STATS On-Line," but I'm not sure that I want to see the results. They're going to be very ugly.

I'm going to Hawaii for a couple of weeks: maybe the change of scenery will help my team. (I don't know, maybe by osmosis. Or by mass hallucination. The further away I am from those guys, the better. Gary Gaetti doesn't know how close he came to extinction the other night: I was on the freeway headed toward Hollywood, and I had the Angel game on the radio—masochism, OK, that's why. Al Conin, as usual, was doing his best obnoxious Dick Enberg imitation, all nasal and warm as a pitcher of John Nance Garner joy juice—what Gaylord Perry used to put on the baseball, for all you savants out there—and I could hear his inflection cloyingly modulate into the calculated astonishment that passes for true excitement, coupled with the phrase ripped off from Enberg: "OH MY! Gary Gaetti BOOTS ANOTHER ONE!!! That's seven errors in just eleven games!!! Not a lucky combo for Gaetti or for the Angels, and JIM ABBOTT's in TROUBLE again!!!"

A cold coil of terrorist rage began circulating where once my blood had flowed: I was going to buy an AK-47, smuggle it into the Big A, and ritually assassinate Gary Gaetti in front of four thousand disaffected fans, Christians and lions, thus delivering me and countless unknown other victims from his leather-and-bat-induced pestilence. Jail time? Death row? Psychobabble articles in the LA Weekly comparing and contrasting me with Robert Alton Harris, California's Mr. Death Penalty? It'd be worth it, just so that gaggling goon wouldn't kick another goddamn baseball ever again.

Fortunately for Gaetti and for my subsequent criminal record, there was an unexpected traffic jam around the bend at the La Cienega exit, and I was trapped in the slowdown in the fast lane long enough to cool off, reconsider, and stifle my impending entry into the psychoexotic fringe of the rifle rack set. There was a simpler, less law enforcement-intensive way to rid myself of Gaetti. I'd RELEASE the bastard!! After all, I was god of my own little team, my band of infidels, my gaggle of honking miscreants, my collection of worn-out cliches, my denizens of offensive deconstruction—is there any other kind? What position would Jacques Derrida play, anyway? Anybody out there care to guess? Maybe Jacques will write six hundred tortured pages on this sometime, and not give us the answer in four thousand two hundred and fifty-six excruciating excursuses.)

My thoughts about murder having been (at least temporarily) neutralized, I construct a draft list which carefully includes the demotion and release of Gaetti, and prepare for my trip the next day. So on the plane to Hawaii, I get to go first class due to some mileage program, and sitting next to me on the flight to Maui is—no, not Gary Gaetti—JACQUES DERRIDA. (He is, as many of you already know, the Professor of Deconstruction at the University of California, Irvine. It's a big, messy job, but somebody's got to do it, and John Wayne is dead.) The diffident Derrida is charming, a compulsive drinker of Koala sparkling waters—apple and black currant, s'il vous plait—and has a Bill James Fantasy Baseball team of his own—incroyable!! (The lucky frog is in the Susan Sarandon League, but playing, as I understand it later, under an assumed name, like Mallarme or Lautreamont or something like that.)

He, too, has Gary Gaetti, and admits to murderous thoughts of late, but he says that he considers such rages to be therapeutic, like the doctrinal practice of purification propounded by the mad philosopher-poet Empedocles, whose byword—if I can paraphrase Professor Derrida without fear of conflation—was: "If you can't burn 'em, jump into a volcano." (Sort of a self-destructive variant on "If you can't convince 'em, confuse 'em.") It was a fascinating discussion, except that I missed about half of it because I fell asleep. When I awoke, Derrida was still talking, musing about the double play as the missing element in metaphysics. (Yep, you guessed right: Derrida is a second baseman.) All of which is, I have since been told, discussed in detail in his forthcoming book, The Pivot and the Armpit: A New Keystone for Metaphysics (translated by Mike Kopf).

22nd:

Irrefutable logic of the scorned: Gary Gaetti, released by the San Antonio Trotters two days ago, had three hits yesterday.

Changes to the team from the first re-entry draft: relief pitchers Doug Jones and Steve Howe (got to play him now before he gets suspended or banned again); middle infielders Mariano Duncan and Mark Lewis, swing pitcher Jose Melendez. Released to make room for these stalwarts: Gaetti (natch), Randy Ready, Mike Remlinger. Why so few released with so many picked up? Each team is allowed to carry 28 players, 20 in the majors earning points (ostensibly, anyway), and 8 in the "minors" awaiting the call. You just begin with 25 and get to draft up to the full roster two weeks into the season.

For all my moaning, I am not the worst team in the league at this point. That dubious honor goes to Jay Sierszyn's Pork Queens, who have been just killed in terms of hitting in the first two weeks of the season and are low in the league. Jay got to draft first: he took Deion Sanders in the first round. Dave Endicott was kind enough to read me the entire list of draftees the other night (thanks, Dave, it was a long list) and I am beginning to see what one of his strategies is—stockpile a bunch of pitchers and get a solid point-generating combination in place to offset any fluctuation in hitting. That hasn't been the approach that Eastern Division leader Dave Morgan of the Malibu Mowers (how can a team from Malibu be in the Eastern Division??) has taken: Dave has started with 14 hitters and just six pitchers, and he is more than 200 points ahead of the rest of us in terms of hitting. The pitchers he's got (Candiotti, Drabek, Zane Smith) have been hot, so he's looking mighty good at the moment.

26th:

First trade of the season for the San Antonio Trotters has been made. Trading partner: the Winnebago Pork Queens. The deal: Larry Walker and Jeff Montgomery for Bip Roberts and John Wetteland.

(As we go on the chaining effect of making trades will start to become clear. Once I got into trying to make trades, I discovered a serious Frank Lane streak in myself, with an especial taste for the lockbuster—more

than three players per side. Jay Sierszyn was my most frequent trading partner: together we made some pretty amazing deals. But it was just the warmup for the three deals that really put my team on the map.) Roberts gives me some badly needed speed to go with the strangely quiescent Harold Reynolds. I've got enough power without Walker, I think.

27th:

Or should I say I had enough power without Walker for one day. Danny Tartabull is going on the disabled list. I have no other right fielder, since I released Barfield and Thompson. God, this is an infuriating game!!

29th:

Picked up Rob Deer and Dave Martinez in the reentry draft to cover for Tartabull. (I would give up too quickly on Deer, who had a pretty good year overall and could have helped me in the long run. Martinez quickly became a platoon player and was released just as Tartabull came off the DL).

Have brought Doug Jones, Steve Howe, and John Wetteland up and am running a four and four pitching staff. Jack McDowell (6-0) has been awesome, Wegman (2.34 ERA) has been fine, Hurst OK, and Saberhagen is coming around brilliantly after a rocky start. Now that I have Jones, Al Osuna is totally expendable. Looks like I need to start investigating how to put together some backup starting pitching.

MAY

3rd:

The point standings in the Juan Marichal League, as of May 2:

East	Batting	Pitching	Total
Malibu Mowers	783	482	1265
Black Irish	642	506	1147
West Des Moines Weevils	791	349	1140
Iowa Hogheads	737	378	1115
San Antonio Trotters	655	385	1040
Winnebago Pork Queens	492	349	840
West			
Surfers of the Apocalypse	693	493	1185
Pikes Peak Players	739	369	1108
South Bronx Bombers	656	394	1050
Santa Barbara Sun Sox	779	223	1002
El Toro Devils	654	337	991
Topanga Thunder	682	223	905

Not a pretty sight. But it sure looks as though I've wound up in the stronger division.

While we have a minute, let's give just a cursory feel for who was what player on some of these teams. This is just a very brief look at the very best players, and doesn't give a complete view of the teams, but it will help give a little flavor into the league.

Superstar pitchers: Clemens is on the Weevils. Tom Glavine is on the El Toro Devils. Jose Rijo is on the Sun Sox. Bill Swift, off to such a great start for the Giants but doomed to injury problems due to the idiotic managing of Roger Craig, is on the Surfers. Greg Maddux is on the Bombers. David Cone is on the Players.

Relief aces: Tom Henke is on Black Irish. Dennis Eckersley is on the Sun Sox. Lee Smith is on the Hogheads. Bobby Thigpen is on the Thunder. Top catchers: Tettleton is on the Sun Sox. I have Brian Harper, who's the best hitter for average: the fact that he's really an indifferent defensive catcher doesn't matter as much in this game. Ivan Rodriguez is on the Mowers. Hot Chris Hoiles is on the Hogheads.

First basemen: Fred McGriff is on the Surfers. Frank Thomas is on Black Irish. Will Clark is on the Weevils. The rejuvenated Mark McGwire (11 HRs) is on the Players. Young Jeff Bagwell is on the Bombers.

Second basemen: Ryne Sandberg is on the Mowers. Lou Whitaker is on the Bombers.

Shortstops: Cal Ripken is on the Pork Queens. Jay Bell and Travis Fryman (who can be used at SS even though he plays a lot of 3B) are both on Black Irish. Barry Larkin is on the Mowers. Ozzie Smith is on the Thunder.

Third basemen: Edgar Martinez is on Black Irish. Pendleton, the guy I turned down from Endicott's Hogheads in pre-season, got traded to the Thunder. Robin Ventura is on the Sun Sox. The revitalized Gary Sheffield is on the Players. I have a real sleeper on my team, I think, in Dave Hollins. Chris Sabo is on the Pork Queens.

Left fielders: Barry Bonds is on the Sun Sox. Rickey Henderson is on the Thunder. John Kruk is on the Bombers. Brady Anderson, so hot thus far for the Orioles, got drafted by the Pork Queens. I have Kevin Mitchell, who's been making my life sick.

Center fielders: Brett Butler is on the Devils. Mike Devereaux and Andy Van Slyke are on the Surfers. Juan Gonzalez is on the Thunder, though he's playing left. Ray Lankford is also on the Thunder. I have Puckett, as you might remember—and he's one of the few things that's working as expected for me thus far.

Right fielders: Darryl Strawberry is on the Hogheads. Bobby Bonilla and Tony Gwynn are on Black Irish. Dave Winfield is on the Bombers. Shane Mack (now really playing left) is on the Mowers. Joe Carter and Jose Canseco are on the Devils. I have Tartabull, who's not hitting much yet, but he's walking a ton and he'll get it rolling down the line, despite the long list of naysayers. Ruben Sierra is on the Weevils. Larry Walker is on the Pork Queens né the Trotters (you're welcome, Jay). The Queens also have Dave Justice.

9th:

Black Irish has moved past the Mowers into first place. Here's my roster as of today:

```
    Team:     San Antonio Trotters

C HARPER,Brian    SS-LF DUNCAN,Marian
RF TARTABULL,Dan    R WETTELAND,John
1B FIELDER,Cecil  SS-2B LEWIS,Mark
DH DOWNING,Brian    R MYERS,Randy
1B>3B MAGADAN,Dave  SS*SPIERS,Bill
S SABERHAGEN,Br     R JONES,Doug
1B*KARROS,Eric    SS*RIVERA,Luis
 S MCDOWELL,Jack    R*ASSENMACHER,Pa
2B REYNOLDS,Haro   LF MITCHELL,Kevi
S WEGMAN,Bill       R*HENRY,Butch
2B-CF ROBERTS,Bip  CF PUCKETT,Kirby
S HURST,Bruce       R*HOWE,Steve
3B HOLLINS,Dave    CF FELIX,Junior
S*GARDINER,Mike     R*OLIN,Steve
* = Minors   Dash (-) = Multi-Position Player
 > = Irreversible Position Change
```

This listing comes directly from a "captured text" file during my on-line session with Babe, STATS' computer. The on-line services are incredible. When I was in Hawaii, I could log into Chicago at around 9 pm Hawaii time and get all of the day's box scores. I could also get the latest stats for the Juan Marichal League. All of the statistics are updated automatically every night. Owners can handle all of their transactions through the on-line services, which saves you the $1 dollar per player per move transaction fee (though you do have to pay computer time: but if you know what you're doing, you can get on and off in about three minutes, which would cost you about 75 cents instead of $2 to $4 to $6 if you handle it over the phone).

That have been said (ca-CHING), let's look at what my team looks like now. I've jettisoned some more dead wood, and picked up some new guys to try out. Mariano Duncan is really hot right now: I think that I ought to trade him while he's hot (a good maxim). Steve Howe has pitched great, but he's about to get suspended, so I've sent him down and brought up a recent free agent pick, Brian Downing. One big problem with the team is that they just don't walk enough. Tartabull and Hollins are really the only original picks who do. I've got to find a way to correct this situation—walks are as important as any other category, and I love guys who walk.

(Retrospective note: my infatuation with relief pitchers is about to come to a close, to be replaced by the strategy that got my team off the floor: collect, cultivate, and hoard starting pitching. It's coming.)

One other note about the codes at the bottom of the roster listing: the BJFB rulemakers are sneaky, at least as sneaky as the sneakiest BJFB owner. When a player has an "irreversible position change," for example Dave Magadan, it means that once he is switched to third base, he can no longer be switched back to first. When you acquire a player with an irreversible position change symbol in a trade, he is automatically switched to his new position as part of the trade. So if I traded Magadan away, the team receiving him acquires a third baseman only.

13th:

Back in LA and ready to trade again. Having talked with Dave Morgan, I came close to making a one-for-one swap of Mariano Duncan for Darren Lewis, but Dave backed out when STATS revised Duncan's position eligibility to be SS-LF instead of SS-2B. Dave wanted a single backup for both his middle infielders (Sandberg and Larkin): he eventually found it in Mike Bordick, who is leading the AL in hitting at this point.

So, back to the phone and a call to my good buddy Jay Sierszyn. I'm not happy with Cecil Fielder, so I decide to put together a deal that has at least one big name in it to get Jay interested. After a lot of discussion, we finally work out the first big blockbuster deal of my fantasy career: the Trotters send Fielder, Bill Spiers, Junior Felix, and Mariano Duncan for Dave Justice, Brady Anderson, Kal Daniels, and Melido Perez.

Looking back at this deal, it's clear that I got the better of it, because even though I didn't end up keeping any of the players I received, I was able to parlay them into players who turned out to be crucial to my team's success. Two major trends or elements in the trading patterns to be exhibited as the 1992 season evolved first occurred here: 1) trading players while they were hot, and 2) trading up in walks. A key acquisition was Melido Perez, who strengthened and stabilized my pitching rotation for more than two months before being dealt for even higher game. Slowly, ever so slowly, the light bulb was beginning to flicker...

16th:

Looks like Black Irish is starting to cruise. Endicott told me that Tom Cavanagh is a madman, and that he really knows his stuff. I can tell the latter just by looking at his team. He has one pitcher on his roster whom I'd really like to get—Curt Schilling. I think that the kid's a sleeper and is going to really turn things around this year. Plus, he's listed as a relief pitcher, but is about to go into the Phillies' starting rotation. I'm entranced with Endicott's strategy of keeping Seattle lefty Dave Fleming, in the starting rotation all year, listed as a reliever to meet the two reliever minimum. It gives him extra innings, extra pitcher effectiveness points, and probably extra wins, especially since he's sitting on Lee Smith as his closer. If I could get Schilling I could do the same thing.

Unfortunately, Cavanagh is not at home when I call, and I'm in one of those moods where I don't want to leave a message (I mean, the guy's a madman, he's a three-time winner of the game, and I've never even met him: sometimes I just get kind of shy, you know?), so this looks like it's going to be one of those scams that wasn't meant to be.

The Trotters are currently in fifth place, 239 points behind Black Irish. We'd be in second place if we were in the Western Division...

18th:

The following list, extracted from my captured text files, gives the flavor of transactions on a typical Sunday night in the Juan Marichal League:

05/18	Pork Queens	Rel	HABYAN, John
05/18	Pork Queens	Sgn	NEAGLE, Denny
05/18	Trotters	Rel	HENRY, Butch
05/18	Trotters	Sgn	ANTHONY, Eric
05/18	Trotters	Rel	KARROS, Eric
05/18	Trotters	Sgn	GALLEGO, Mike
05/18	Trotters	Rel	GARDINER, Mike
05/18	Trotters	Sgn	CASTILLO, Frank
05/18	Trotters	Rel	CURTIS, Chad
05/18	Trotters	Sgn	MAGRANE, Joe
05/18	Trotters	Dem	SABERHAGEN, Bret
05/18	Trotters	Dem	WETTELAND, John
05/18	Trotters	Pro	DANIELS, Kal
05/18	Trotters	Pro	ASSENMACHER, Paul
05/18	Hogheads	Rel	GORDON, Tom
05/18	Hogheads	Sgn	LIVINGSTONE, Scott
05/18	Hogheads	Dem	STRAWBERRY, Darryl
05/18	Hogheads	Pro	CIANFROCCO, Archi
05/18	Irish	Rel	SCHILLING, Curt
05/18	Irish	Sgn	SLUSARSKI, Joe
05/18	Players	Rel	MASON, Roger
05/18	Players	Sgn	HOWE, Steve
05/18	Players	Rel	MCELROY, Charlie
05/18	Players	Sgn	KING, Jeff
05/18	Thunder	Rel	PENA, Alejandro
05/18	Thunder	Sgn	BECK, Rod
05/18	Sun Sox	Rel	HOWELL, Jay
05/18	Sun Sox	Sgn	GUBICZA, Mark
05/18	Devils	Rel	CHAMBERLAIN, Wes
05/18	Devils	Sgn	GONZALES, Rene
05/18	Apocalypse	Rel	MORANDINI, Mickey
05/18	Apocalypse	Sgn	BURBA, Dave
05/18	Apocalypse	Rel	THOME, Jim
05/18	Apocalypse	Sgn	LEIUS, Scott
05/18	Apocalypse	Rel	TRAMMELL, Alan
05/18	Apocalypse	Sgn	LEE, Manuel
05/18	Apocalypse	Dem	CLARK, Jerald
05/18	Apocalypse	Pro	GREENWELL, Mike

It was the beginning of a very active and fruitful period of acquisition, tinkering, and fine-tuning for the Trotters. Feeling the pinch because of an ill-timed injury to Bret Saberhagen (on an incredible hot streak since mid-April), I was casting about for additional starting pitching. The two Sunday nights of 5/17 and 5/24 would provide me with a great deal of what I needed to get develop a uniquely consistent starting staff.

First, the pickup of Frank Castillo, young Cub righthander, was a good start. I had been following Castillo for a few weeks and decided that he was showing enough consistency to be stuck in the rotation. It was fortunate that he was overlooked so long, for in a league as experienced and sharp as the Juan Marichal there were many instances of players being gone in the first week that they arrived in the majors. Mick Lucero of the Topanga Thunder was particularly adept at tracking players, and beat me to at least half a dozen during the course of the season. Guy Langlo, mastermind of the Santa Barbara Sun Sox, was also good at this. Neil Levy and later Tom Cavanagh himself, two guys who spent a lot of the 1992 season in first place and hence at the bottom of the free agent drafting order, told me that it was almost impossible to get the guys they really wanted from such a vantage point. I was lucky that no one spotted Castillo in the first week of May: he turned into a solid pitcher for me.

Second, did you happen to notice an intriguing name in the transaction list above? You may want to look it over again just to refresh your memory. That's right. Curt Schilling. Black Irish released Curt Schilling. Oh my God. Just keep all twenty digits crossed until next Sunday night, submit a draft list with Schilling at the top of it, and hope like hell that nobody else is on to it.

Another excellent pickup, at least for awhile, was Eric Anthony, the embattled Houston tout who's never lived up to his rep. Jay Sierszyn began the year with Anthony, but dropped him early in May when it looked as though he wasn't going to play much. You have to carefully read the box scores in order to mine the hidden nuggets, plus you have to keep up with the latest scuttlebutt tossed around in the media. By scouring all the available sources, I got wind of the fact that Anthony was on the brink of winning a regular job, and—pounce. He was up and down for me, and I traded him, reacquired him, and eventually traded him back to Jay, but he provided some great moments (I still remember his two pinch hits—one a homer—against the Dodgers that helped beat them in the Astrodome) and was a real catalyst for the Trotters throughout the month of June.

One big name released in this batch of transactions was Alan Trammell, who suffered a knee injury and was likely to be out until at least late August or September. Many teams would have just put Trammell into their group of eight "minor league players," but evidently Surfers owner Ken Lawrence didn't feel that he could afford to do that.

25th:

Curt Schilling is mine.

I'm back in Hawaii, preparing to assist in videotaping a conference that my dad and his organization, the Kapalua Pacific Center, is putting on right after Memorial Day. I almost don't have time to react, but I'm thrilled. I'll get him onto the major league roster as soon as possible.

I do get excited enough to make a late night call to my silent partner Gary Daer. Did I say "silent"? That is not a good term to use when describing Gary. He is not overly talkative, but he has a very barbed tongue and can be gotten on a seemingly endless roll at times. Gary could be a first-class sabermetrician if he'd get his mind off football (which was how we first became friends, as rivals in a fantasy football league that I inexorably took over during the course of three seasons and turned into a fearsomely overwrought celebration of statistical arcana). By the way, Gary loves it when I talk like this, even though he gives me a lot of grief about having an eight-bit vocabulary. I just refer him to Richard Hofstader's classic <u>Anti-Intellectualism in American Life</u> and tell him to go sit on his thesaurus.

If he gives me too much grief, or if he accuses me of being a conniving scumbag (or some similar term of endearment), I just remind him that he's the only guy I know that has a foolproof fallback plan in case he loses his job, that he can just wander into a video arcade and, with his baby face and Pillsbury doughboy complexion, get fought over by innumerable hordes of fourteen year old girls who will wish to secret him in their cellars, feed and care for him, and lose their virginity to him over and over again. Gary's wife Lisa is usually within earshot for some of these exchanges, and she just laughs at the fourteen-year-old gibe, because bits and pieces of the story actually did occur to Gary. He is uncannily appealing to girls who have just reached puberty, and while he still lived in Las Vegas I would always keep his tongue in line by suggesting a trip to the video arcade. Lisa just howls over this, and usually makes some remark about wishing that she was fourteen again so she could understand what all the fuss is about.

So after hearing his face get read over the phone, I tell him that we've got Schilling. He says two things. One, Black Irish's days are numbered. Two, I want Barry Bonds.

I groan. We've had this discussion several times already. I made a pitch to get Bonds from Guy Langlo in mid-May, using Jack McDowell and Kevin Mitchell as trade bait. Guy, who is no dummy, politely declined the offer. (I would spend months trying to unload Mitchell, a man who caused me more grief than anyone on my roster. Nobody wanted the guy.) But Gary, who can be pretty stubborn when the situation demands it (and even when it doesn't), held firm. I could hear that jaw setting into place. I knew what grim, implacable expression (yet still incongruously appealing to thirteen-year-old girls) was settling onto his face. The transformation from silent partner to Pillsbury autocrat was underway. "Get me BONDS!!" he snapped. I felt like I should salute, or something.

So Bonds, that greatest of all, would somehow have to be heisted away from the Sun Sox. It's not as if I didn't want the guy just as much as Gary—I probably wanted him more. From a fantasy standpoint, Barry Bonds is the ultimate: speed, power, batting average, and strike zone judgment just don't get packaged up like that very often. Guy Langlo knew this better than just about anyone. What did I have that could induce to make that trade?

<u>26th:</u>

I did make another trade with Jay, another based on the principle of "trade 'em while they're hot." The other principle involved was to trade down for ERA. The deal was Jack McDowell and Harold Reynolds for Bob Tewksbury and Devon White. Tewksbury, the Cardinals' soft tosser, was having an incredible run that no one had expected or thought would continue: his era was down around 1.60. McDowell was still 7-2, but his ERA had glided up to 3.87. I decided to go for the margin. Trading Harold Reynolds was something of a gamble because I had no other credible backup for Bip Roberts, but I had soured on Reynolds, who was having a lethargic season. I thought that Devon White, who had two of the four things I wanted in a hitter (speed, power), would start to hit for a better average. So Jay and I inked our third trade: two nights later, I dialed in to the STATS computer and found out that Tewksbury had thrown a four-hitter and was now 6-1 on the year.

In order to sign Schilling, I decided to release John Wetteland, who had been struggling. I had been carrying two relievers (Wetteland and Myers) who had very high ERA's, and I was transitioning toward a configuration dominated by starters. With Schilling still listed as a reliever, I could pull the Endicott scam all year if necessary. I didn't like giving up on Wetteland, because I liked him and thought he would eventually put it all together, but I just didn't have the room for him.

A complete look at my team, as provided by the "See My Team" option from the STATS computer:

San Antonio Trotters Thru Sunday MAY-24-1992

BATTING

	BA	AB	R	H	2B	3B	HR	RBI	BB	SB	CS	CWIN E	CWIN DP	C PEN CS	C PEN BNS	PTS
PUCKETT, Kirby CF	.337	175	31	59	11	2	7	29	6	3	1	2	0	0	0	169
HOLLINS, Dave 3B	.270	148	31	40	9	1	5	26	25	3	2	3	7	0	0	142
HARPER, Brian C	.292	137	16	40	8	0	1	23	7	0	0	2	15	12	0	113
ROBERTS, Bip 2B-CF	.309	110	16	34	9	1	0	11	17	9	5	0	4	0	0	94
TARTABULL, Dan RF	.292	89	13	26	5	0	3	15	23	0	0	0	0	0	0	89
MAGADAN, Dave 1B>3B	.279	136	20	38	5	1	1	12	21	1	0	3	0	0	0	87
MITCHELL, Kevi LF	.236	140	16	33	6	0	2	19	12	0	2	0	0	0	0	72
ANDERSON, Brad LF	.239	46	5	11	2	0	2	6	3	2	0	0	0	0	0	31
JUSTICE, Dave RF	.167	42	8	7	1	0	2	3	9	0	2	1	0	0	0	22
RIVERA, Luis SS	.273	33	1	9	2	0	0	1	3	0	0	2	5	0	0	14
ANTHONY, Eric RF	.308	13	0	4	3	0	0	3	0	0	0	0	0	0	0	10
DANIELS, Kal 1B	.227	22	1	5	1	0	0	3	0	0	0	0	0	0	0	7
	BA	AB	R	H	2B	3B	HR	RBI	BB	SB	CS	CWIN E	CWIN DP	C PEN CS	C PEN BNS	PTS
TOTALS	.264	1722	243	455	86	9	42	240	186	30	22	40	69	12	0	1236

San Antonio Trotters Thru Sunday MAY-24-1992

PITCHING

	W	L	PCT	ERA	SV	HD	IP	H	R	ER	BB	K	Q6	Q1	BN	PTS
WEGMAN, Bill S	4	4	.500	2.51	0	0	82.1	70	24	23	17	35	7	0	0	156
MYERS, Randy R	1	1	.500	5.24	11	0	22.1	25	13	13	10	22	0	9	0	102
HURST, Bruce S	3	4	.429	3.97	0	0	68.0	66	32	30	23	44	6	0	0	91
PEREZ, Melido S	2	0	1.000	2.91	0	0	21.2	19	7	7	9	20	2	0	0	51
JONES, Doug R	2	3	.400	5.14	3	0	14.0	18	8	8	3	9	6	0	0	37
CASTILLO, Fran S	1	0	1.000	3.38	0	0	5.1	5	3	2	0	3	0	1	0	16
TEWKSBURY, B S	0	0	.000	0.00	0	0	0.0	0	0	0	0	0	0	0	0	0
	W	L	PCT	ERA	SV	HD	IP	H	R	ER	BB	K	Q6	Q1	BN	PTS
TOTALS	25	19	.568	3.58	20	2	359.2	332	151	143	96	252	24	32	0	798

San Antonio Trotters Thru Sunday MAY-24-1992

BATTING

	BA	AB	R	H	2B	3B	HR	RBI	BB	SB	CS	CWIN E	CWIN DP	C PEN CS	C PEN BNS	PTS
LEWIS, Mark SS-2B	.289	38	4	11	1	0	1	7	4	0	2	11	11	0	0	16
GALLEGO, Mike 2B-SS	.000															
OTHERS	.233	593	81	138	23	4	18	82	56	12	8	16	27	0	0	374

PITCHING

	W	L	PCT	ERA	SV	HD	IP	H	R	ER	BB	K	Q6	Q1	BN	PTS
SABERHAGEN, Br S	3	2	.600	3.81	0	0	52.0	44	23	22	13	54	4	1	0	103
MELENDEZ, Jose R	0	0	0.000	0.00	0	0	0.0	0	0	0	0	0	0	0	0	0
GARDINER, Mike S	0	0	0.000	0.00	0	0	0.0	0	0	0	0	0	0	0	0	0
OLIN, Steve R	0	0	0.000	0.00	0	0	0.0	0	0	0	0	0	0	0	0	0
MAGRANE, Joe S	0	0	0.000	0.00	0	0	0.0	0	0	0	0	0	0	0	0	0
OTHERS	9	5	.643	3.64	2	0	94.0	85	41	38	21	65	5	15	0	244

Some brief explanatory notes are in order. There are three parts to the "see my team" query. The first lets you see the batting statistics for the players on the major league roster (anywhere from 8 to 14 players, depending on how the owner has his or her team structured at any given time.) The second shows the pitching statistics. The third shows the players, both hitters and pitchers, who are currently in the minors.

The statistics show what a player has done while he has been on your major league roster. When you look at Mark Lewis, for example, you see what he did while I had him in the majors up until May 24th. (You can also see why he's back in the minors—he has as many errors as hits.)

The general rule of thumb I evolved over the year was that a hitter was doing well enough if his point total was better than 80% of his listed at bats. When you examine him in this light, you can see why my opinion of Dave Hollins is so high: he's not very far off the pace set by .337-hitting Kirby Puckett. Bip Roberts, Brian Harper, and the often-missing Tartabull are also doing well, but in order to win you need about twice as many players performing at their level. The Trotters' team average at this point in the season is about 72%, which is too low. Walks and stolen bases are still too low, power is just barely adequate. There is still a lot to do to get this team's butt in gear.

For starting pitchers, the eyeball measurement is points per innings pitched. If your starter is over 2 points per inning, he's a god. Anything over 1.5 can be lived with, but the closer to two the better. Big strikeout pitchers can rack up extra points for you, but they often take as many away with the extra walks they allow. A Jekyll-and-Hyde pitcher like Black Irish's Randy Johnson is going to keep a fantasy owner on the edge of his seat. But then again, I'd already gotten something of a notion that Cavanagh was descended from the Flying Wallendas (pun intended).

So of my starters at this point, Perez is super, the injured Saberhagen almost as good, Wegman very fine (and very underrated throughout the league). Hurst had been a little rocky, but I had confidence that the veteran lefty would come around. With Tewksbury, Castillo, and Schilling in the fold, I suddenly had a lot of starting pitching—and would be even better when Saberhagen returned from his weird finger injury (shades of Sandy Koufax?).

The bullpen was a little shaky, but I still had faith that the mercurial Randy Myers would turn it around. Doug Jones' record was deceiving at this point, because he had been lit up in one appearance for five runs and five hits in less than an inning. Take away that outing and his ERA was consistent with his overall performance to date (remember, I selected Jones after the first two weeks, when he was 1-0 with 6 saves; that isn't reflected on his totals here).

The real problem: shortstop. Mark Lewis, Luis Rivera, and Mike Gallego (recently activated by the Yankees) were just not going to cut it over the long haul. Lewis and Gallego at least gave me some versatility in that they could play both 2B and SS.

About two hours a day is going into tracking the team, perusing the box scores, gleaning information, pondering what kind of trades to make. That's about 12% of each day on baseball. Yikes!!

JUNE

8th:

In San Francisco on my way back to Las Vegas, staying at long-time family friends the Dick Ericksons, I sit in front of the TV set watching baseball as my team faces one of its most dramatic nights. Four of my starting pitchers are going to the mound tonight: Wegman, Hurst, Castillo, and Schilling.

The Ericksons are out of town: I have their comfortable, lived-in Berkeley hills home all to myself. It's a very long baseball evening. The Cubs and Cardinals are playing a doubleheader in Busch Stadium that is going on and on and on. Slowly over the course of the evening it becomes clear that Schilling (a three-hit shutout), Wegman, and Hurst have won. I go out to pick up a few grocery items, stop in at an old friend's, and get back to discover that the Cubs are nursing a 6-2 lead in the seventh inning of the nightcap. A procession of Cub relief pitchers proceed to keep me glued to my chair in anxiety as they discover new ways to fritter away a four-run lead. It is still Castillo's game to win—he went 6+ innings and got pulled by Jim "Captain Hook" Lefebvre. (Later examination of Castillo's season indicated that Lefebvre had very good reason to watch him closely in the seventh: going into the seventh inning, Castillo's ERA was 2.40. In the seventh inning, his ERA was—22.25!!)

It is close to midnight when Chuck McElroy gets the final out and Harry (still awake at 2 am CDT) screams, "Cubs win!" The Trotters get four wins in one night, and a save from Doug Jones. The team is now on the move: having slipped past the West Des Moines Weevils into third place as the month of June began, the Trotters move past the Iowa Hogheads into second place. The league totals (also available via the STATS computer) show a much healthier team than the one we saw just two weeks before:

BATTING

EAST	BA	AB	R	H	2B	3B	HR	RBI	BB	SB	CS	C WIN E	C DP	C CS	PEN BNS	PTS
Irish	.271	2534	349	687	125	20	64	343	297	42	26	49	125	15	0	1939
Trotters	.271	2277	330	618	106	13	62	326	244	43	32	51	81	16	0	1706

BATTING

EAST	BA	AB	R	H	2B	3B	HR	RBI	BB	SB	CS	C WIN E	C DP	C CS	PEN BNS	PTS
Hogheads	.269	2264	312	610	101	10	57	273	235	64	38	51	157	23	0	1676
Mowers	.267	2551	340	681	142	9	74	360	226	67	24	52	115	36	0	1888
Weevils	.275	2335	332	642	125	14	57	316	247	74	32	35	100	11	0	1811
Pork Queens	.248	2025	250	503	97	15	47	234	203	58	20	35	124	19	0	1373
WEST																
Players	.272	2360	361	642	124	10	76	293	300	88	34	44	85	20	0	1908
Apocalypse	.265	2196	292	583	117	12	48	279	247	24	26	31	110	16	0	1585
Devils	.262	2198	310	575	90	14	64	267	236	45	29	38	93	15	0	1588
Sun Sox	.257	2331	316	598	122	11	70	309	300	67	21	50	106	27	0	1769
Bombers	.266	1889	281	503	97	11	63	258	254	54	22	22	69	15	0	1560
Thunder	.269	2317	308	621	105	13	66	281	246	89	38	31	93	16	20	1755

PITCHING

EAST	W	L	PCT	ERA	SV	HD	IP	H	R	ER	BB	K	Q6	Q1	BN	PTS
Irish	29	22	.569	3.13	21	4	445.0	379	179	155	191	343	38	41	0	997
Trotters	36	23	.610	3.30	28	2	488.1	439	196	179	133	339	35	41	0	1148
Hogheads	37	36	.507	3.64	23	0	575.2	523	251	233	209	386	46	32	15	1101
Mowers	22	22	.500	3.10	24	1	374.0	343	147	129	113	245	27	33	0	816
Weevils	33	29	.532	4.01	20	0	497.2	481	245	222	155	357	30	30	0	892
Pork Queens	24	34	.414	4.14	16	5	480.2	486	234	221	190	318	32	37	0	720
WEST																
Players	27	22	.551	3.51	14	7	484.2	450	208	189	172	343	33	34	0	924
Apocalypse	36	22	.621	3.43	18	0	538.0	503	219	205	168	303	41	28	0	1064
Devils	31	23	.574	3.70	30	1	516.0	499	241	212	184	321	41	33	0	1015
Sun Sox	19	24	.442	3.85	30	0	402.0	387	190	172	134	300	27	38	0	738
Bombers	30	30	.500	3.48	16	5	494.2	466	203	191	166	306	37	42	0	942
Thunder	20	34	.370	3.90	15	9	441.0	419	206	191	154	292	32	29	0	711

Thanks to this most recent charge, the Trotters have climbed to within a hundred points of division-leading Black Irish.

I call Gary Daer and tell him about the latest developments. He is amazed at the four wins in a night feat, noting that he had known all four pitchers were going and heard that all four games had been wins for the respective teams they pitched for, but that he found it almost inconceivable that we could pull off such a feat. Conceive of it, Bwana, I said, using one of his least-favored nicknames. He was silent for a minute, then grunted GET BONDS. I tell him I'm working on it, that it's going to take some more preparatory trades in order to make it happen. He said you want to win, GET BONDS.

After I got off the phone with him (he even grunted good night), I realized that this was the perfect time to go after Bonds, since he had pulled a rib cage muscle the night earlier and no one seemed to know the extent of the injury. But it was still going to take some other moves to make us solid. We still needed a bonafide shortstop. And if I was going to get Bonds and have to give up a lot in a monster deal, then I wanted to get Jose Rijo in the deal too. So I needed an extra pitcher to trade in some kind of 4-for-2 or 4-for-3 deal. The next day I scratched out about fifteen different options as I flew back to LA, looking for the combination that I could parlay into Bonds.

12th:

The log from STATS tells it all:

```
To identify team, enter (any from among) Owner, League, Team Nickname:
   Owner of team to Trade With->SCHULTZ
   Nickname of team to Trade With->BOMBERS
ID#/Last name of player to Give Up (RETURN if done)->WHITE
ID#/Last name of player to Give Up (RETURN if done)->MAGADAN
ID#/Last name of player to Give Up (RETURN if done)->
ID#/Last name of player to Obtain (RETURN if done)->KEY
ID#/Last name of player to Obtain (RETURN if done)->WALLACH
ID#/Last name of player to Obtain (RETURN if done)->
Jimm.KEY        now in Majors. Keep him there (Y/N)->Y
Tim .WALLACH    now in Minors. Keep him there (Y/N)->Y
Trade OK to post (Y/N)->Y

To identify team, enter (any from among) Owner, League, Team Nickname:
   Owner of team to Trade With->LUCERO
   Nickname of team to Trade With->THUNDER
ID#/Last name of player to Give Up (RETURN if done)->JUSTICE
ID#/Last name of player to Give Up (RETURN if done)->GALLEGO
ID#/Last name of player to Give Up (RETURN if done)->OLIN
ID#/Last name of player to Give Up (RETURN if done)->
ID#/Last name of player to Obtain (RETURN if done)->SMITH
ID#/Last name of player to Obtain (RETURN if done)->PENA
ID#/Last name of player to Obtain (RETURN if done)->RADINSKY
ID#/Last name of player to Obtain (RETURN if done)->
Ozzi.SMITH       now in Majors. Keep him there (Y/N)->Y
Gero.PENA        now in Majors. Keep him there (Y/N)->Y
Scot.RADINSKY    now in Minors. Keep him there (Y/N)->Y
Trade OK to post (Y/N)->Y
```

```
Team:     San Antonio Trotters

     C HARPER,Brian       3B HOLLINS,Dave      RF TARTABULL,Dan      S*SABERHAGEN,Bre
    1B KARROS,Eric        SS SMITH,Ozzie        S TEMKSBURY,Bob      S*BURKETT,John
  1B*WALLACH,Tim       SS-2B LEWIS,Mark         S KEY,Jimmy          S*SEMINARA,Frank
 1B-LF*DANIELS,Kal        LF ANDERSON,Brad       S PEREZ,Melido       R SCHILLING,Curt
    2B PENA,Geronimo      LF MITCHELL,Kevi       S WEGMAN,Bill        R JONES,Doug
 2B-CF ROBERTS,Bip        CF PUCKETT,Kirby       S HURST,Bruce        R*MYERS,Randy
    2B*OQUENDO,Jose       RF ANTHONY,Eric        S CASTILLO,Fran      R*RADINSKY,Scott

 * = Minors   Dash (-) = Multi-Position Player   > = Irreversible Position Change

 Projected roster, not including any free agent signings or releases.
```

Dave Schultz, high school senior from Mission Viejo, is a very personable young fellow who turned out to be a great trading partner. I wish him well as he begins his studies at UC Santa Barbara.

I first talked to Dave on June 12th, with vague notions of getting a pitcher like Andy Benes and Howard Johnson, who was having about as bad of a year as Kevin Mitchell. I soon discovered that Dave was a big fan of the New York teams, and was particularly enamored of HoJo, so I scrapped that idea for the time being. After a couple of interruptions, and a lot of fun talking about baseball in general as we probed trade ideas, we finally settled on the Magadan and White for Key and Wallach deal. I was riding on pitching and Kirby Puckett as an indestructible center fielder. Wallach was having his second bad year in a row, and was temporarily listed as a first baseman, but he would shortly be shifted back to third and thus would function as an emergency backup for Hollins.

I now had the extra pitcher I wanted. Now it was time to go get that shortstop. Mick Lucero of the Topanga Thunder, good friends with Guy Langlo (the man with Bonds) and Dave Morgan (they went to Pepperdine University in Malibu together, hence the Malibu, Topanga, and Santa Barbara location names for their teams), was a great guy with an ample sense of humor. His team had been suffering through a protracted slump, and he was good-naturedly complaining about it all the way through our conversation.

The shortstop I wanted to get from Mick was Craig Grebeck. I wasn't looking for anything incredible, like Smith or Ripken or Larkin: I just wanted someone solid, who would hit decently, take some walks, make a reasonable number of DPs, and not kick the ball as the snakebit Mark Lewis had been doing. Mick had been there ahead of me in early May when Grebeck became desirable after Ozzie Guillen's season-ending injury.

I also wanted to try to pry away Geronimo Pena away from him. Brock Hanke had been hyping me on Pena for awhile, but he hadn't started soon enough, because Mick had beaten me to Pena as well. In a league that was very sharp, Mick might have been the best tracker of players and trends. Having moved up to second place, I was discovering that it was harder to get the top free agents than it had been a few weeks back.

It was a long, looping discussion, with many humorous digressions, and the trade slowly transformed itself into a blockbuster, the first of two big ones that ended up helping both teams a good bit. The final deal that got made sent Dave Justice, Mike Gallego, and Indians closer Steve Olin to the Thunder for Ozzie Smith, Geronimo Pena, and White Sox set-up man Scott Radinsky. For Mick, the key to the deal was Justice. For me, the middle infield depth that I had never really had was finally in place. It took awhile to get both Smith and Pena on the field together permanently in 1992, but when it happened it was spectacular.

Even with these moves, Black Irish, led by the incomparable Juan Guzman (9-1 with an ERA near 1.20), was rolling along with a 200 point lead. I didn't call Daer right away to tell him the news, because I knew what the response would be.

15th:

First base has become a problem. Even though Kal Daniels has finally surfaced with the Cubs, he's still not playing enough to make it worthwhile to bring him up. Eric Karros has gone stone cold since being re-drafted after the Dodgers finally handed him the starting first base job. Even when he is hitting, Karros just isn't going to walk enough to make him somebody I'd want to keep. Seems like everywhere you look on this damn team, another leak just pops open and starts squirting water at you....

Signed Luis Gonzalez today. He's the Astro LF who had such a rotten start this year that he got sent back to Tucson, where he got red hot and slashed his way back to the big leagues. He's starting to hit well and he could be a useful replacement for Mitchell.

19th:

Roster changes. (Retrospective note: I expected Jay Howell to come back and be the Dodgers' closer in the second half of the season. But the Dodgers were so pathetic that no one ended up being particularly useful as a closer, so the pick went nowhere. There are lots of picks like this during the course of a season, good ideas that just don't pan out.)

```
Transactions effective JUN-20-1992
Position Shift  of Bip .ROBERTS     ( CF ) by San Antonio Trotters
Promotion       of Luis.GONZALEZ    ( LF ) by San Antonio Trotters
Promotion       of Jay .HOWELL      ( R1P) by San Antonio Trotters
Demotion        of Tim .WALLACH     (*1B ) by San Antonio Trotters
Demotion        of Kevi.MITCHELL    (*LF ) by San Antonio Trotters
```

Note the continual flip-flopping of Mitchell. I suppose one can get so inside on a game like this that you start thinking that you are actually "punishing" the guy by "benching" him. In the case of Kevin Mitchell, I surely wished that something like that was going on.

21st:

Here it is. The big trade. Finally, Gary Daer will smile and remove the Al Davis "Just Win, Baby" sunglasses. It was the epic blockbuster of the season, the biggest of the year by far, though there were still plenty to come.

```
To identify team, enter (any from among) Owner, League, Team Nickname:
  Owner of team to Trade With->langlo
    Nickname of team to Trade With->sun sox
ID#/Last name of player to Give Up (RETURN if done)->anderson
ID#/Last name of player to Give Up (RETURN if done)->roberts
ID#/Last name of player to Give Up (RETURN if done)->tewksbury
ID#/Last name of player to Give Up (RETURN if done)->key
ID#/Last name of player to Give Up (RETURN if done)->
ID#/Last name of player to Obtain (RETURN if done)->bonds
ID#/Last name of player to Obtain (RETURN if done)->rijo
ID#/Last name of player to Obtain (RETURN if done)->blankenship
ID#/Last name of player to Obtain (RETURN if done)->
Barr.BONDS              now in Minors. Keep him there (Y/N)->n
Jose.RIJO              now in Majors. Keep him there (Y/N)->y
Lanc.BLANKENSHIP       now in Majors. Keep him there (Y/N)->y

Trade OK to post (Y/N)->y
```

It was an intricate trading process. The first offer I had made to Guy was Brady Anderson, a choice of two pitchers from the following four (Tewksbury, Key, Wegman, Hurst), and Mitchell for Bonds and Rijo. Guy pondered that for a day, and then called me back and said it wouldn't work. I was silent for a second, and then asked if he had a counteroffer. I really didn't expect him to say that he did, but he surprised me by saying yes. The counter included Bip Roberts, whom I hadn't planned on losing, and two pitchers, one of them Tewksbury, the other my choice, plus Anderson, for Bonds and Rijo.

I immediately suggested that it would be Jimmy Key as the second pitcher, and, thinking as quickly as I could, noted that by taking Roberts he would be cleaning out my best second baseman and that I would probably need one back. That's when Lance Blankenship entered the picture. As I looked over Blankenship, it struck me that he was almost equal to Roberts: despite a far lower batting average, he walked a ton (more than twice as often as Bip), stole bases about as well, and actually played more second base (since Bip was still shuttling between second, third, and the outfield at this time.) So I said to Guy that I could do the deal if he tossed in Blankenship to cover my 2B hole. He was agreeable, and the deal was done.

Of course, it would be about ten days before Bonds would be back in the lineup, so merely getting him wasn't going to provide an immediate boost to the team's numerical fortunes. I called Gary, talked to him for about fifteen minutes, and then casually said, "Oh, by the way, I made another trade today." Daer: "Who'd you get?". Malcolm: "Somebody named Sdnob." Daer: "Who?" Malcolm: "Yrrab Sdnob." Daer: "Who does he play for?" Malcolm: "Let me spell that for you." I spelled it, then told him to reverse the letters. The tone in his voice when he realized who it actually was made it all worthwhile.

In some ways, though, I considered the key to the deal to be Rijo. This guy is, to my mind at least, a great pitcher. Terrific K/BB ratio, extremely useful in a fantasy league. Not the lowest ERA or BR/9, but in the lower half of the Top 10. And consistent. In order to win the league, you need to have several pitchers like Rijo on your team. The two division winners in the Juan Marichal League had Rijo on their team for good portions of the 1992 season.

The other advantage that I got from the trade was that I opened up a free roster slot on the squad, which I filled by picking up my last sleeper, Cubs' starting pitcher Danny Jackson. As had been the case with Frank Castillo, I had been tracking Jackson for several weeks and it looked to me as though he had gotten his stuff back. I figured that he was going to pitch more like the Danny Jackson who had reeled off 22 wins for the Reds in 1988. The maneuver left me with a seven man staff of Rijo, Schilling, Perez, Hurst, Wegman, Castillo, and Jackson. This evolved into the best overall staff in the Juan Marichal League for the next six weeks, until it came time to evolve it, change it, and dismantle it. It really hummed, and I'm not entirely sure that I could duplicate its success on demand in subsequent seasons.

23rd:

Team rosters as of Monday, June 23rd:

Team: Black Irish   Owner: Thomas J Cavanagh

C PAGNOZZI,Tom   SS-3B FRYMAN,Travis RF-3B BONILLA,Bobby   S DARLING,Ron
1B THOMAS,Frank SS BELL,Jay   RF*SNYDER,Cory   S*RHODES,Arthur
1B HRBEK,Kent   LF POLONIA,Luis   DH>RF*BAINES,Harold   S*BLACK,Bud
1B*MAAS,Kevin   LF*VAUGHN,Greg   S> R BULLINGER,Jim   S*JOHNSON,Randy
2B SAX,Steve   CF BURKS,Ellis   S GUZMAN,Juan   R HENNEMAN,Mike
3B WILLIAMS,Matt CF CUYLER,Milt   S APPIER,Kevin   R CHARLTON,Norm
3B MARTINEZ,Edga RF GWYNN,Tony   S MOORE,Mike   R*WORRELL,Todd

Team: Iowa Hogheads   Owner: Dave Endicott

C HOILES,Chris   3B-2B BAERGA,Carlos RF>CF LOFTON,Kenny   S WILSON,Trevor
C*SANTIAGO,Beni SS FERNANDEZ,Ton   RF*STRAWBERRY,Da   S OSBORNE,Donova
C*VALLE,Dave   SS OFFERMAN,Jose   RF>CF*SOSA,Sammy   S*HAMMOND,Chris
1B PALMEIRO,Rafa LF-CF GANT,Ron   S WITT,Bobby   S*BANKS,Willie
1B-3B*CIANFROCCO,Ar LF MAY,Derrick S SMOLTZ,John   R SMITH,Lee
2B DESHIELDS,Del LF*MALDONADO,Can   S MCDONALD,Ben   R SCHOOLER,Mike
3B BOGGS,Wade   CF YOUNT,Robin   S NAVARRO,Jaime   R> S FLEMING,Dave

Team: Malibu Mowers   Owner: Dave Morgan

C DAULTON,Darre 3B-LF PALMER,Dean   CF>LF DAVIS,Eric   S SMITH,Zane
C*RODRIGUEZ,Iva SS LARKIN,Barry   CF*LEWIS,Darren   S*NABHOLZ,Chris
1B JOYNER,Wally SS*BORDICK,Mike   RF>LF MACK,Shane   S*HESKETH,Joe
1B*GUERRERO,Pedr LF BELL,George   S WELCH,Bob   S*VALERA,Julio
2B SANDBERG,Ryne LF REIMER,Kevin   S DRABEK,Doug   R RUSSELL,Jeff
3B GRUBER,Kelly LF ALOU,Moises   S CANDIOTTI,Tom   R FRANCO,John
3B LANSFORD,Carn CF DYKSTRA,Lenny   S FERNANDEZ,Ale   R*BANKHEAD,Scott

Team: San Antonio Trotters   Owner: Don Malcolm

C HARPER,Brian   3B HOLLINS,Dave   RF ANTHONY,Eric   S CASTILLO,Frank
1B KARROS,Eric   SS-2B LEWIS,Mark   RF TARTABULL,Dan   S*SABERHAGEN,Bre
1B*WALLACH,Tim   SS*SMITH,Ozzie   S RIJO,Jose   R> S SCHILLING,Curt
1B-LF*DANIELS,Kal LF BONDS,Barry   S PEREZ,Melido   R HOWELL,Jay
2B BLANKENSHIP,L LF GONZALEZ,Luis   S JACKSON,Danny   R JONES,Doug
2B PENA,Geronimo LF*MITCHELL,Kevi   S WEGMAN,Bill   R*MYERS,Randy
2B*OQUENDO,Jose CF PUCKETT,Kirby   S HURST,Bruce   R*RIGHETTI,Dave

Team: West Des Moines Weevils   Owner: Jeffrey Lowe

C MACFARLANE,Mi 3B ZEILE,Todd   RF SIERRA,Ruben   S STEWART,Dave
C*NILSSON,Dave   SS OWEN,Spike   RF>LF HALL,Mel   S OLIVARES,Omar
1B CLARK,Will   SS>2B*STILLWELL,Kur DH>1B*CLARK,Jack   S*TAPANI,Kevin
1B MURRAY,Eddie LF>CF NIXON,Otis   S CLEMENS,Roger   S*STOTTLEMYRE,To
1B-3B*COOPER,Scott LF*CALDERON,Ivan S MULHOLLAND,Te   R BELINDA,Stan
2B ALOMAR,Robert LF KELLY,Roberto   S LEIBRANDT,Cha   R MEACHAM,Rusty
2B KNOBLAUCH,Chu CF MCRAE,Brian   S GROSS,Kevin   R*HARVEY,Bryan

Team: Winnebago Pork Queens   Owner: Jay Sierszyn

C PENA,Tony   3B SABO,Chris   CF FELIX,Junior   S BROWNING,Tom
1B GRACE,Mark   3B HAYES,Charlie   LF-RF*WALKER,Larry   S*FINLEY,Chuck
1B FIELDER,Cecil SS RIPKEN,Cal   RF-1B WALKER,Larry   S*FINLEY,Chuck
1B*JEFFERSON,Reg LF-SS DUNCAN,Marian RF-LF*JORDAN,Brian   R DIBBLE,Rob
2B THOMPSON,Robb LF*BELL,Derek   S MCDOWELL,Jack   R WETTELAND,John
2B REYNOLDS,Haro LF>CF*SANDERS,Deion S GOODEN,Dwight   R> S LEITER,Mark
2B-SS*STANKIEWICZ,A LF*GWYNN,Chris   S HERSHISER,Ore   R*MONTGOMERY,Jef

Team: El Toro Devils   Owner: Mike Miller

C STEINBACH,Ter 3B CAMINITI,Ken   RF CARTER,Joe   S BROWN,Kevin
C*PARRISH,Lance SS GAGNE,Greg   RF*BROOKS,Hubie   S*PORTUGAL,Mark
1B MOLITOR,Paul LF-1B KRUK,John   S LEFFERTS,Crai   S*GREENE,Tommy
1B*MARTINEZ,Tino LF*BUTLER,Brett   S MARTINEZ,Ramo   S BOSIO,Chris
2B-LF MILLER,Keith CF JACKSON,Darri S GLAVINE,Tom   R AGUILERA,Rick
2B-3B PHILLIPS,Tony CF>RF MCGEE,Willie S MORGAN,Mike   R REARDON,Jeff
2B*MORANDINI,Mic RF CANSECO,Jose   S HILL,Ken   R*MCDOWELL,Roger

Team: Pikes Peak Players   Owner: Neil Levy

C BORDERS,Pat   3B SHEFFIELD,Gar   LF*STAIRS,Matt   S HARNISCH,Pete
C*FISK,Carlton   3B SEITZER,Kevin   CF GRISSOM,Marqu   S SWINDELL,Greg
1B MCGWIRE,Mark SS WEISS,Walt   CF*GRIFFEY JR,Ke   S AVERY,Steve
1B MILLIGAN,Rand SS>SCHOFIELD,Dic   RF JOSE,Felix   S*MCCASKILL,Kirk
2B BIGGIO,Craig SS*TRAMMELL,Alan   RF BICHETTE,Dant   S PARRETT,Jeff
2B*SAMUEL,Juan   LF RAINES,Tim   S GULLICKSON,Bi   R HENKE,Tom
2B*GONZALES,Rene LF-RF MCREYNOLDS,Ke S CONE,David   R WARD,Duane

Team: Santa Barbara Sun Sox   Owner: Guy Langlo

C TETTLETON,Mic 3B BUECHELE,Stev   CF FINLEY,Steve   S SMILEY,John
C*MANWARING,Kir SS LISTACH,Pat   CF>RF*HAYES,Von   S GUBICZA,Mark
1B OLERUD,John   SS*CEDENO,Anduja   RF O'NEILL,Paul   S*KEY,Jimmy
1B O'BRIEN,Pete LF ANDERSON,Brad   RF MUNOZ,Pedro   S> R*ALVAREZ,Wilson
2B-3B JEFFERIES,Gre LF COLEMAN,Vince S TEWKSBURY,Bob   S*MAHOMES,Pat
2B-1B*DORAN,Billy LF*GLADDEN,Dan   S BELCHER,Tim   R ECKERSLEY,Denn
3B VENTURA,Robin CF-2B ROBERTS,Bip   S GUZMAN,Jose   R HENRY,Doug

Team: South Bronx Bombers   Owner: David Schultz

C NOKES,Matt   SS VIZQUEL,Omar   CF*WHITE,Devon   S ERICKSON,Scott
C*HUNDLEY,Todd   SS THON,Dickie   CF-RF*ESPY,Cecil   S TOMLIN,Randy
1B BAGWELL,Jeff SS>DUNSTON,Shawo   RF WINFIELD,Dave   S KRUEGER,Bill
1B*QUINTANA,Carl LF BELLE,Albert   RF WHITEN,Mark   S*BIELECKI,Mike
2B WHITAKER,Lou LF GILKEY,Bernar   DH DAVIS,Chili   R WILLIAMS,Mitch
3B>CF JOHNSON,Howar CF SANDERS,Reggi S BENES,Andy   R JACKSON,Mike
3B MAGADAN,Dave CF>HENDERSON,Dav   S MADDUX,Greg   R> S*CADARET,Greg

Team: Surfers of the Apocalypse   Owner: Kenneth E. Lawrence

C SURHOFF,B.J.   3B GOMEZ,Leo   CF DEVEREAUX,Mik   S VIOLA,Frank
C*SCIOSCIA,Mike 3B*LEIUS,Scott   RF PLANTIER,Phil   S NAGY,Charles
1B MCGRIFF,Fred SS DISARCINA,Gar   RF BUHNER,Jay   S OJEDA,Bobby
1B MATTINGLY,Don SS*LEE,Manuel   S BLYLEVEN,Bert   S*SUTCLIFFE,Rick
1B*SORRENTO,Paul LF GREENWELL,Mik   S MORRIS,Jack   R OLSON,Gregg
2B FRANCO,Julio LF*CLARK,Jerald   S RYAN,Nolan   R FARR,Steve
2B REED,Jody   CF VAN SLYKE,And   S MUSSINA,Mike   R> S*SWIFT,Bill

Team: Topanga Thunder   Owner: Mick Lucero

C ALOMAR,Sandy   SS-3B GREBECK,Craig RF DEER,Rob   S*STIEB,Dave
1B MORRIS,Hal   SS*CLAYTON,Royce   DH>1B BRETT,George   S*HANSON,Erik
1B*DAVIS,Glenn   LF HENDERSON,Ric   S FERNANDEZ,Sid   S*HARRIS,Greg W.
1B*MERCED,Orland LF>CF GONZALEZ,Juan S ABBOTT,Jim   R THIGPEN,Bobby
2B-SS GALLEGO,Mike   S MARTINEZ,Denn   R BECK,Rod
2B*RANDOLPH,Will RF JUSTICE,Dave   S LANGSTON,Mark   R OLIN,Steve
3B PENDLETON,Ter RF DAWSON,Andre   S GARDNER,Mark   R*WOHLERS,Mark

Yes, this printout also comes from the STATS On-Line services. You can get a complete listing of the league rosters just by selecting an option on the system menu. I have tracked the dispersion of players from the Trotters in the above list, so you can get a feel for how much roster alteration had actually occurred by late June. (When I finally met Guy Langlo in person in late August— thanks again for the tip on the Straits Cafe, Guy, great place to eat—he bemusedly noted that the rest of the league thought my goal was not so much to win but to make sure that I had traded every original player off my team in the course of the season. Not missing a beat, I told him that my goal was to do both.) The players in italics are those who began as members of the Trotters' original roster. The players underlined are players acquired by the Trotters who were themselves used in subsequent trades. A player like Dave Justice, acquired from the Pork Queens and sent on to the Thunder, is an example of this.

29th:

All this pitching isn't getting me much closer to Black Irish. That team just keeps rollin' on:

Juan Marichal League Standings Thru Sunday JUN-28-1992

		W	L	Pct	GB	-Equivalent- Batting	Pitching	Total
East								
1	Black Irish	42	33	.560		2588	1326	3913
2	San Antonio Trotters	40	35	.533	2	2211	1510	3721
3	West Des Moines Weevils	38	37	.507	4	2306	1217	3523
4	Iowa Hogheads	37	38	.493	5	2163	1317	3479
5	Malibu Mowers	37	38	.493	5	2467	1002	3468
6	Winnebago Pork Queens	32	43	.427	10	1965	1064	3029
West								
7	Pikes Peak Players	40	35	.533		2481	1256	3737
8	El Toro Devils	38	37	.507	2	2217	1363	3580
9	Surfers of the Apocalypse	37	38	.493	3	2066	1434	3499
10	Santa Barbara Sun Sox	37	38	.493	3	2347	1108	3455
11	Topanga Thunder	36	39	.480	4	2287	1083	3370
12	South Bronx Bombers	36	39	.480	4	1996	1347	3343

JULY

4th:

Picked up a promising young pitcher in the Astros' Brian Williams, who's started strongly since being recalled from Tucson. I'm trying to press the advantage with respect to pitching, as it appears to be as viable a way to get an edge in the league as hitting. I have to be encouraged that I haven't fallen further back during this hot streak by Black Irish, as I've been without Bonds and Ozzie Smith (the chicken pox!!) for most of the last two weeks. Mark Lewis just doesn't make it as a substitute.

I still have to do something about that first base problem. I'll have to leave that matter for when I get back to Hawaii—not enough time with all the chaos and intrigue at work in Las Vegas.

13th:

Falling further behind the Irish. That slimy Cavanagh got to Dave Schultz and talked him into parting with Andy Benes for Cory Snyder and Kevin Maas. Good Christ! I called Dave up before I left for Hawaii and let him know I wasn't too thrilled about it. It was a brilliant trade for the Irish, I have to admit; and it also tells me that he's worried.
I just wish my team could hit some more. All these trades still haven't gotten the walk total moving in the right direction, and we're still too low in stolen bases. Irish has a 240 point lead and he's gotten it up that high by making a run at me with pitching—the Guzman-Appier 1-2 punch has got him revved up. I can only hope that Benes doesn't put on a 10-1 stretch run the way he did in '91. This is getting serious...

BATTING

EAST	BA	AB	R	H	2B	3B	HR	RBI	BB	SB	CS	CWIN E	C PEN DP	CS	BN	PTS
Irish	.273	3952	550	1080	198	25	106	519	441	82	45	83	185	22	0	3009
Trotters	.270	3495	484	945	172	22	95	465	364	68	44	71	151	27	0	2606
Mowers	.265	3978	527	1053	221	17	110	564	375	110	43	75	177	47	0	2926
Hogheads	.273	3497	474	954	162	26	85	401	355	114	57	77	242	28	-25	2595
Weevils	.276	3510	499	969	197	24	80	461	379	108	51	53	164	13	0	2724
Pork Queens	.255	3387	409	865	155	22	80	392	315	89	36	56	219	28	0	2314
WEST																
Players	.268	3634	514	975	182	16	105	452	448	141	51	68	147	29	0	2815
Devils	.271	3467	509	941	156	25	97	412	384	75	46	56	159	27	0	2646
Sun Sox	.264	3612	491	955	180	19	103	466	469	115	40	76	146	34	0	2760
Apocalypse	.270	3397	437	917	177	19	85	437	352	36	35	51	165	22	0	2480
Bombers	.263	3073	428	808	157	21	93	397	400	80	43	36	111	22	0	2399
Thunder	.268	3492	450	937	165	21	99	433	353	112	46	49	149	26	20	2620

PITCHING

EAST	W	L	PCT	ERA	SV	HD	IP	H	R	ER	BB	K	Q6	Q1	BN	PTS
Irish	46	36	.561	3.16	39	4	679.2	585	276	239	278	518	58	63	0	1558
Trotters	55	42	.567	3.28	33	4	817.1	756	327	298	227	546	60	59	0	1741
Mowers	38	36	.514	2.99	32	2	605.0	556	228	201	168	377	45	50	0	1330
Hogheads	54	57	.486	3.81	34	1	879.2	810	409	372	314	554	65	48	15	1562
Weevils	47	40	.540	3.78	26	5	760.0	707	349	319	238	505	50	44	0	1406
Pork Queens	39	46	.459	3.90	29	5	768.0	764	355	333	284	487	57	55	0	1281
WEST																
Players	43	32	.573	3.23	20	13	762.1	682	301	274	262	553	57	58	0	1576
Devils	52	32	.619	3.33	48	1	784.2	738	339	290	267	497	65	51	0	1708
Sun Sox	35	37	.486	3.50	46	0	661.2	644	281	257	199	492	47	63	0	1352
Apocalypse	55	33	.625	3.52	29	0	831.1	796	345	325	250	473	65	38	0	1625
Bombers	50	40	.556	3.26	22	7	756.2	700	293	274	245	474	59	60	0	1538
Thunder	39	52	.429	3.63	27	9	715.0	679	312	288	240	479	51	53	0	1279

Now I just have to make sure that my seven-man starting staff doesn't get too carried away and get on a track to win a lot more than 100 games, which is the BJFB limit. All wins past 100 will not count, so I've got to be ready to act in case success gets out of hand (!).

16th:

A new crisis: all my second basemen are injured. Lance Blankenship has just gone on the DL with a finger injury. Geronimo Pena has been out for about ten days with a sore shoulder. I'm going to have to dust off Mark Lewis again. Thank God I turned him into a 2B before I demoted him the last time. Arrgh!!

18th:

Black Irish is pulling away (275 point lead). He's just on fire right now. Still, I like the way most of my team has been shaping up. The data below shows that eight of my hitters are over the 80% threshold (see the entry for May 26th). That's double what it used to be.

San Antonio Trotters Thru Saturday JUL-18-1992

BATTING

		BA	AB	R	H	2B	3B	HR	RBI	BB	SB	CS	CWIN E	C PEN DP	CS	BNS	PTS
PUCKETT, Kirby	CF	.336	369	64	124	23	4	14	66	18	10	3	3	0	0	10	376
HOLLINS, Dave	3B	.270	337	58	91	14	3	13	47	43	6	5	11	15	0	0	276
HARPER, Brian	C	.299	284	34	85	15	0	4	42	15	0	0	5	37	27	0	247
TARTABULL, Dan	RF	.249	233	39	58	10	0	13	45	62	2	0	0	0	0	0	235
MITCHELL, Kevi	LF	.269	245	31	66	17	0	3	30	19	0	2	0	0	0	0	150
ANTHONY, Eric	RF	.234	158	21	37	8	1	8	30	11	2	3	0	0	0	0	118
KARROS, Eric	1B	.254	177	17	45	7	1	5	18	7	1	0	3	0	0	0	91
SMITH, Ozzie	SS	.344	61	6	21	2	0	1	11	5	3	2	18	0	10	68
DANIELS, Kal	1B-LF	.263	76	6	20	4	0	3	11	11	0	0	0	0	0	56
BONDS, Barry	LF	.326	43	5	14	6	2	0	7	7	0	1	0	0	0	10	54
LEWIS, Mark	2B-SS	.252	123	9	31	3	1	0	10	6	0	2	14	27	0	0	45
SANDERS, Deion	CF	.500	4	1	2	0	1	0	1	0	0	0	0	0	0	0	8

		BA	AB	R	H	2B	3B	HR	RBI	BB	SB	CS	CWIN E	C PEN DP	CS	BNS	PTS
TOTALS		.271	3609	499	979	176	23	99	483	378	72	45	72	155	27	30	2739

San Antonio Trotters Thru Saturday JUL-18-1992

PITCHING

		W	L	PCT	ERA	SV	HD	IP	H	R	ER	BB	K	Q6	Q1	BN	PTS
WEGMAN, Bill	S	8	7	.533	3.27	0	0	154.0	152	62	56	32	69	13	0	0	247
HURST, Bruce	S	8	6	.571	3.54	0	0	140.0	135	58	55	38	99	13	0	0	241
JONES, Doug	R	5	6	.455	2.58	13	0	45.1	43	13	13	10	34	0	27	10	216
PEREZ, Melido	S	6	5	.545	3.28	0	0	93.1	84	40	34	46	83	7	1	0	151
SCHILLING, Cur	R>S	4	3	.571	2.77	0	0	65.0	53	23	20	16	41	6	0	0	131
CASTILLO, Fran	S	4	4	.500	3.36	0	0	64.1	58	28	24	23	39	6	1	0	104
RIJO, Jose	S	4	0	1.000	2.61	0	0	31.0	28	9	9	8	30	3	1	0	89
JACKSON, Danny	S	1	2	.333	2.96	0	0	27.1	20	9	9	10	8	3	0	0	43

	W	L	PCT	ERA	SV	HD	IP	H	R	ER	BB	K	Q6	Q1	BN	PTS
TOTALS	57	44	.564	3.32	33	4	855.0	793	345	315	241	572	64	60	10	1807

I saw Curt Schilling pitch in LA before I came back to Hawaii to edit the proceedings for the conference held last May. It was part of the monster homestand that the Dodgers had due to the May riots. Schilling looked great, but he was done in by his defense, especially the sieve-like Dale Sveum. It pissed me off to see what was otherwise a really good performance get trashed by defensive miscues. That, and Dave Hollins is in a slump. Come out of it, Dave, I can't afford to play Tim Wallach in place of you...

Ensemble pitching works—if you can find it. These guys (see above) ain't glamorous but they're the best outfit in the league.

Finally pulled the plug on Randy Myers. It just doesn't seem that he's going to get a full shot to be the closer. (A week after I dropped him, Greg Riddoch relented and gave Myers another chance. Randy proceeded to save 23 games over the last half of the season.) I'm livin' or dyin' with Doug Jones as my only true reliever, and the Endicott Scam (Curt Schilling). Lord help me...

24th:

The more I thought about it, the more I got ticked off. That damn Cavanagh had gotten Andy Benes from Dave Schultz when he wouldn't give him to me in a better deal. Hmmph!! I decided that I was going to find a way to talk him out of Greg Maddux, who, after Juan Guzman, was the best pitcher in the game at this point.

I was lucky. Dave Schultz liked me. I'd shipped him some spare Dodger tickets as a thank you for the first trade—if you're reading this, Dave, I'm sorry we never got to meet in person, hope that we'll rectify the situation next year. He didn't want to part with Greg Maddux—he felt that his team was going down the tubes, and he was hoping that Maddux would win the Cy Young award so he'd have something good to remember the season by.

I was relentless, however. Through a long, supremely rational discussion of how I could improve his team by taking his best player away from him, I managed to consummate the following deal, as recorded by STATS On-Line:

```
To identify team, enter (any from among) Owner, League, Team Nickname:
  Owner of team to Trade With->schultz
  Nickname of team to Trade With->bombers
ID#/Last name of player to Give Up (RETURN if done)->perez
ID#/Last name of player to Give Up (RETURN if done)->saberhagen
ID#/Last name of player to Give Up (RETURN if done)->mitchell
ID#/Last name of player to Give Up (RETURN if done)->anthony
ID#/Last name of player to Give Up (RETURN if done)->karros
ID#/Last name of player to Give Up (RETURN if done)->
ID#/Last name of player to Obtain (RETURN if done)->maddux
ID#/Last name of player to Obtain (RETURN if done)->johnson
ID#/Last name of player to Obtain (RETURN if done)->bagwell
ID#/Last name of player to Obtain (RETURN if done)->sanders
ID#/Last name of player to Obtain (RETURN if done)->
Greg.MADDUX           now in Majors. Keep him there (Y/N)->y
Howa.JOHNSON          now in Majors. Keep him there (Y/N)->y
Jeff.BAGWELL          now in Majors. Keep him there (Y/N)->y
Regg.SANDERS          now in Majors. Keep him there (Y/N)->n
Trade OK to post (Y/N)->y
```

```
                    Projected Roster
Team:    San Antonio Trotters

    C HARPER,Brian      3B HOLLINS,Dave      CF SANDERS,Deion      S HURST,Bruce
    1B BAGWELL,Jeff     3B-1B*WALLACH,Tim    CF-LF*SANDERS,Reggi   S CASTILLO,Frank
1B-LF DANIELS,Kal       SS SMITH,Ozzie       RF TARTABULL,Dan      S RIJO,Jose      R> S SCHILLING,Curt
2B-SS STANKIEWICZ,A     LF BONDS,Barry       S MADDUX,Greg         R JONES,Doug
    2B*BLANKENSHIP,L     LF*GONZALEZ,Luis     S JACKSON,Danny       R*HOWELL,Jay
    2B*PENA,Geronimo     CF JOHNSON,Howar     S WEGMAN,Bill
2B-SS*LEWIS,Mark        CF PUCKETT,Kirby

* = Minors   Dash (-) = Multi-Position Player   > = Irreversible Position Change
```

It was a very big trade. Bigger than the Bonds trade, I think. It probably won me the division. Even though Howard Johnson was a total washout, the combination of Maddux, Bagwell, and Reggie Sanders was a devastating addition to the Trotters. My maniacal hoarding of starting

pitchers was paying off: I was able to give up the two New York pitchers (Dave just really liked those guys) to get the Chicago ace. Bagwell was a vast improvement over Karros, who just wouldn't take a walk, and Reggie Sanders proved to be a godsend in center field during August, his 6 homers in 10 games helping me to close the gap on Black Irish. I felt bad that Dave wound up with two injuries out of the deal (Bret Saberhagen, who made a brave return right after the All-Star break, reinjured his finger in just his third start since returning from the DL; and later, Kevin Mitchell). I hated giving up Melido Perez, and I had visions of Kevin Mitchell suddenly hitting fourteen homers in sixteen games once he was finally out of my hair, but I needed to keep pushing the envelope, refining the team, restructuring until I could get strength at every position. Only second base was elusive now, and that would be solved if and when Geronimo Pena could recover from his shoulder miseries.

29th:

Maddux and Schilling are still hot. Still not getting enough walks!! Bagwell and Bonds are still in the doldrums—and I'm still 170 points behind Black Irish.

AUGUST

1st:

The entire month was spent looking for a second baseman, as Blankenship and Pena continued to languish on the DL or on rehab assignments. I tried trading (Andy Stankiewicz for Brian Williams: the diminutive Stankiewicz immediately went into a slump upon becoming a Trotter) and drafting (Mike Sharperson, Eric Young, Jeff Kent: but none of them played well enough or long enough to be useful). Nothing worked. Black Irish just seemed to loom overhead, leering at my sleight-of-hand. Get a real team, he seemed to be saying. So I kept trying to do so...

4th:

We're in the "find anything that play second base" mode. If it moves and even thinks about turning the pivot, we'll sign it up. Pride is not something we're long on as the "dog days" set in. I just wish that one of these guys would start scoring some positive numbers. The Trotter roster as of August 4th:

```
                         Current Roster
Team:    San Antonio Trotters

   C HARPER,Brian       2B*YOUNG,Eric        CF SANDERS,Deion      S WEGMAN,Bill
   1B BAGWELL,Jeff      3B HOLLINS,Dave      CF-LF*SANDERS,Reggi   S HURST,Bruce
1B-LF DANIELS,Kal       3B-2B*KENT,Jeff      RF-1B MERCED,Orland   S CASTILLO,Frank
2B-SS SHARPERSON,Mi     SS SMITH,Ozzie       RF*TARTABULL,Dan      S*HERSHISER,Orel
2B-SS STANKIEWICZ,A     LF BONDS,Barry       S RIJO,Jose       R> S SCHILLING,Curt
   2B*BLANKENSHIP,L     CF JOHNSON,Howar     S MADDUX,Greg         R JONES,Doug
   2B*PENA,Geronimo     CF PUCKETT,Kirby     S JACKSON,Danny       R*YOUNG,Anthony

* = Minors   Dash (-) = Multi-Position Player   > = Irreversible Position Change
```

The concentration of bit players in the middle infield can be seen at this point: note, though, that Mark Lewis is gone. Reggie Sanders is about to come off the DL for the Reds and become a real force in the offense. Eric Anthony, traded away in the Maddux deal, is about to come back for the slumping Stankiewicz, courtesy of Dave Schultz. Howard Johnson is about to get injured. Jeff Kent, who played very well during Kelly Gruber's absence, is about to get benched and become useless in a fantasy context. The team has become somewhat infirm due to all the transactional machinations. If the pitching should falter, we're sunk—but we can only rely on it so much because of the point limits. More hitting is needed. We need Bonds to snap out of his homer slump, and Tartabull back from the DL with some lightning in his bat. Hurry up!!

And so, with that stream of semi-consciousness egging me on, I made the next in a series of blockbuster moves. For some reason, I had this faith that Reggie Sanders could be my center fielder for the rest of the season. Actually, that's a lie, or at least a misstatement. I wanted to get Ray Lankford from Mick Lucero, and I was willing to give up Kirby Puckett. I had decided that Puckett was just not going to be the right type of player to anchor the team. I needed more speed, more on-base. In order to rely on Puckett as a superstar in a fantasy league, Kirby needs to hit at least .340 because he walks so little. I didn't think he'd keep it up, and I decided to cash him in while the other owners still thought of him as a god.

So the negotiations went on, over the phone from Maui to the Denver suburbs. Try as I might, though, Mick was just plain unwilling to give up Ray Lankford. After a long discussion, I finally walked away with the following:

```
To identify team, enter (any from among) Owner, League, Team Nickname:

   Owner of team to Trade With->lucero
   Nickname of team to Trade With->thunder
ID#/Last name of player to Give Up (RETURN if done)->puckett
ID#/Last name of player to Give Up (RETURN if done)->rijo
ID#/Last name of player to Give Up (RETURN if done)->sanders
   ID# FPOS NAME
  4333 CF   Deion SANDERS
  4737 M/D Reggie SANDERS
Enter ID# of Player ->4333
ID#/Last name of player to Give Up (RETURN if done)->
ID#/Last name of player to Obtain (RETURN if done)->abott
'abott' not found on Topanga Thunder roster
ID#/Last name of player to Obtain (RETURN if done)->abbott
ID#/Last name of player to Obtain (RETURN if done)->henderson
ID#/Last name of player to Obtain (RETURN if done)->curtis
ID#/Last name of player to Obtain (RETURN if done)->cordero
ID#/Last name of player to Obtain (RETURN if done)->
Jim .ABBOTT             now in Majors. Keep him there (Y/N)->n
Rick.HENDERSON         now in Majors. Keep him there (Y/N)->y
Chad.CURTIS            now in Minors. Keep him there (Y/N)->n
Wil .CORDERO           now in Minors. Keep him there (Y/N)->n
Trade OK to post (Y/N)->y

ID#/Last name of player to change position of (RETURN if done)->curtis
The following are possible fielding positions:
CODE  FDG.POSITION
  9      RF
  8      CF
  7      LF   (means 10 point penalty for your team)
Enter the CODE (not the FDG.POSITION) of the new fielding position ->8
Fielding Position OK to post (Y/N)->y

              Projected Roster

Team:   San Antonio Trotters

    C HARPER,Brian    3B HOLLINS,Dave   CF-RF CURTIS,Chad     S HURST,Bruce
   1B BAGWELL,Jeff   3B-2B KENT,Jeff      CF*JOHNSON,Howar    S CASTILLO,Frank
 1B-LF DANIELS,Kal   SS SMITH,Ozzie       RF ANTHONY,Eric     S*ABBOTT,Jim
   2B YOUNG,Eric     SS CORDERO,Wil     RF*TARTABULL,Dan    S*HERSHISER,Orel
 2B*BLANKENSHIP,L    LF BONDS,Barry        S MADDUX,Greg  R> S SCHILLING,Curt
 2B*PENA,Geronimo    LF HENDERSON,Ric      S JACKSON,Danny     R JONES,Doug
 2B-3B*SHARPERSON,Mi CF-LF SANDERS,Reggi   S WEGMAN,Bill     R*YOUNG,Anthony
```

Mick had no second baseman to give me: I had taken Pena away from him in June, and his replacement Mike Gallego had gotten injured. So I took Rickey Henderson and Jim Abbott and decided that they would be enough to replace Puckett and Rijo. Chad Curtis would play more than Deion Sanders, and there was some hope that the Expos would give young SS Wil Cordero a long look. It was probably the biggest gamble yet, in the eyes of the league. But Rickey Henderson is a greater player than Kirby Puckett, both in fantasy and real baseball, and if he stayed healthy and part of a stretch drive, I'd probably get the best out of him that anyone would get for the entire season.

So I took the gamble. My pitching was still strong: if I could just hold on 'til Bonds and Tartabull broke loose. I was just 90 points out of first. Mick told me that Cavanagh was worried. It was more fun, more nerve-wracking, not to talk to the Black Irish owner just yet, to leave the battle pitched in mystery, like some mythically overwrought comic book. Will this baseball season ever end???

8th:

Within 63 points of Black Irish, the closest yet to first place. Still looking for middle infielders and hunches. I've decided to try Chris Donnels over John Valentin. (Retrospective note: boy, was that a dumb idea.) Donnels is going to get a lot of playing time now that Magadan is hurt.

10th:

I scored 0 points yesterday. That's right. Zero. I'm now 140 points back. Just like that. I feel as though I've been mugged.

11th:

ANOTHER horrible night!! Now I'm 196 points behind. I feel like the team has suddenly gone into freefall. The Mowers are only 65 points behind me. A lot of the guys in the league think that if Dave Morgan can get some more pitching, he's the one who's going to win. What a revolting development. I need to get away from this team for a few days before I blow a fuse.

16th:

Lance Blankenship is back! Finally some stability at second base.

17th:

Black Irish is slowing down, because of the injury to Juan Guzman. I picked up 50 points last night, and have crawled back to within 140 points. Don't give up. Headed back to San Francisco for a few days before going over to close out the Las Vegas situation: will get a chance to finally meet Guy Langlo and go to a game with him at the Stick (Giants—Pirates). We'll see if our presence can light a fire under Mr. Barry Bonds.

23rd:

Bonds had a big day yesterday, homer, double, four RBI. The Trotters are back to 105 points down to the Irish. Cavanagh was invited to the game but didn't get in touch with Guy, so I guess we'll remain shadowy nemeses until the end of the season.

Guy is in med school, and has a pleasantly sarcastic sense of irony. He's about 6'1 and pretty well-built, and he played some baseball in high school. I think that the Langlo-Morgan-Lucero troika must have been a cut-up during their Pepperdine days. He's headed back to southern California next year for a residency program, so we might touch base again down there with Morgan, whose team is still hanging tough (about 160 points behind the Trotters). He still hasn't quite balanced out to enough pitching, and I've decided that unless he's willing to do one of my patented two-for-one pitcher tradeups (e.g. Perez and Saberhagen for Maddux; in his case, it would have been Wegman and Hurst, my unsung journeymen, for Doug Drabek), I'm not going to make any deals. I still value pitching more than anything. (Of course, with Bonds back on the loose, with Rickey Henderson in high gear, and with Reggie Sanders looking awesome, it's easy to start having delusions of grandeur. Hang on, hang on, the finish line is dimly coming into view...)

28th:

The trading deadline is coming up on August 31st. I have a couple more deals I'd like to make. I really want to get Fred McGriff from the Surfers. I've never talked with Ken Lawrence, but Mick indicates that he's a friendly guy who's open to trading. When I tell Mick I'm interested in McGriff, his reply is "Who isn't?" and wishes me good luck. I decide to wait another couple of days before giving Ken a call.

The other deal is what I think is the absolute final solution. I'm going to trade off two pitchers and a second baseman (Blankenship, Pena, or the recently acquired Bret Boone) for Lou Whitaker and Ken Hill. This deal is made easier since my trading ally Dave Schultz acquired Ken Hill from his friend Mike Miller (El Toro Devils, now making a run at first place in the Western Division against Neil Levy's Pikes Peak Players). If Hill were still on the Devils, it'd be a tougher deal, plus it'd be messier because it would need to be two separate trades. But I can't raise Dave on the phone, and he has his answering machine turned off. Has he gone on to Santa Barbara already? Nah, it's too early: he told me he wasn't due there until late September. Where is he??

30th:

Before I can get to Ken or Dave, I get a call from my first (and still most prolific) trading partner, Jay Sierszyn. The Pork Queens still haven't hit much (they're the lowest rated offensive team in the league), but Jay has done a good job stockpiling pitchers, and he's out to get another one if he can. He wants Jim Abbott, and he's prepared to give me both Robbie Thompson and Andre Dawson. After a little more talking (it's 9:45 pm PDT, which leaves about fifteen minutes to call in the trade before STATS' Live Line closes down for the night), we wind up with the following deal: Abbott and Eric Anthony for Thompson, Dawson, and Brian Williams.

I've got to make a split-second decision. The pitching staff has cracked the 80-win barrier, and I've got to acquire more hitting so as to put the brakes to the win column. (How strange.) Dawson isn't my type of player at all—he never walks—but he's hot, he's motivated to perform in September because he's in his free agent year, and he's a guy who can put some numbers up fast if things go right. Thompson is a real solid little player: I can't believe that Jay is willing to give him up.

I stumble around a bit for a few more seconds, shuffling some papers, and then I finally decide—what the hell, go for it. It's only a game. As I call in the trade (I've hemmed and hawed so long that I have to talk to the STATS guys directly instead of dialing up the computer), I'm struck by the wheels within wheels within wheels that can be applied to the strange microuniverse of baseball. As with anything in life, you have to seize it when it's in front of you, because in another instant, it might be gone forever. (Actually, as you all know, it's not quite that simple, but a good bit of the time it works just like that.) So I did it. Welcome back, Brian Williams. Welcome aboard, Robbie Thompson and Andre Dawson. You ain't seen nothin' yet...

31st:

Holy shit! Black Irish has done it again!! Remember back in May, when he dropped Curt Schilling, thus paving the way for the ascension of the Trotter pitching staff? Well, now he's just up and dropped Mike Moore, who's still in the rotation for the Oakland A's, still a viable pitcher, and a guy who will be a Trotter next Sunday night if I can get there before Mick Lucero.

Which reminds me: ever since the trade that Mick and I made, his Topanga Thunder have been vaulting up the ladder in the Western Division. Four weeks ago he was in fifth place more than 500 points out of first. Now he's third and about 220 points out. I wonder if he's got enough horses to pull it off...

Juan Guzman is back, and the Black Irish, despite dropping Moore, are back to a 200 point lead. But there is one ominous cloud on the horizon: Bobby Bonilla is going to have shoulder surgery in about ten days, and

he's going to miss the rest of the season. That's not going to help Cavanagh.

SEPTEMBER

1st:

The final trade:

```
To identify team, enter (any from among) Owner, League, Team Nickname:
  Owner of team to Trade With->schultz
  Nickname of team to Trade With->bombers
ID#/Last name of player to Give Up (RETURN if done)->wegman
ID#/Last name of player to Give Up (RETURN if done)->jackson
ID#/Last name of player to Give Up (RETURN if done)->boone
ID#/Last name of player to Give Up (RETURN if done)->
ID#/Last name of player to Obtain (RETURN if done)->hill
ID#/Last name of player to Obtain (RETURN if done)->whitaker
ID#/Last name of player to Obtain (RETURN if done)->
Ken .HILL                now in Majors. Keep him there (Y/N)->y
Lou .WHITAKER             now in Majors. Keep him there (Y/N)->y

Trade OK to post (Y/N)->y
```

Lord, what an excruciating, nailbiting set of circumstances surrounded this trade. The evening of August 31st was first spent in a fruitless search trying to locate Ken Lawrence—I still wanted to get Fred McGriff if I could, and I was ready to sacrifice Jeff Bagwell and even Rickey Henderson if necessary. But Ken's number netted me someone who had never heard of Ken Lawrence. I called this poor fellow twice—he must have thought I was a lunatic (a lot of people are probably nodding in agreement right now). No Lawrence. There was no number for Ken Lawrence in any of the adjoining suburbs of Denver. A call to Mick Lucero and a call to Guy Langlo produced only surprised reactions from them: they thought the number was good, but they hadn't tried to call Ken in awhile. It was 9 pm. One hour left.

Dave Schultz had yet to turn up as well. I kept calling, and his machine was back on, but I had a feeling that he just might not return a phone message tonight, so I just kept trying every 15 minutes or so. At 9:30 I called and he answered. He told me he was late for a party—it sounded like an important thing to him—and he didn't have time to talk trade. (Even though he was very polite about it, I got the message that maybe I'd talked to him too long on some other occasions. I also knew that his team had fallen into last place, and that he was thinking about taking a year off from BJFB during his freshman year.)

But I had to have those players. (That's what this league does to you: if you're close to winning, you become relentless, unyielding.) I told him that I knew exactly what deal I wanted to make and that I just wanted to run it by him in thirty seconds and if he was willing to make it, fine, if not, fine. I pitched the deal as shown above, except that I gambled and gave him the option of choosing between Blankenship, Pena, and Bret Boone. He went for Boone. I swallowed hard. He agreed to the deal. He took the ten minutes and called the deal in. I dialed up the computer, typed in the deal, then called to confirm that he'd done his part. He had. Thank you, Dave. You helped me win the Eastern Division. You didn't have to, but you did. We've never met in person, but you helped me, you were generous, you gave me players that were your personal favorites. Why? For some reason you liked me. What an astonishing thing. What an amazingly simple, incredibly straightforward, totally kind gesture. Four months later, I'm still flabbergasted. Four decades from now, I might still be.

Projected Roster

Team: San Antonio Trotters

C HARPER, Brian	SS SMITH, Ozzie	CF-LF SANDERS, Reggi	S HILL, Ken
1B BAGWELL, Jeff	SS BELL, Juan	CF-RF*CURTIS, Chad	S HURST, Bruce
2B BLANKENSHIP, L	SS EASLEY, Damion	RF TARTABULL, Dan	S*HERSHISER, Orel
2B WHITAKER, Lou	SS*CORDERO, Wil	RF DAWSON, Andre	S*CASTILLO, Frank
2B THOMPSON, Robb	LF BONDS, Barry	DH*WEDGE, Eric	R> S SCHILLING, Curt
2B*PENA, Geronimo	LF HENDERSON, Ric	S WILLIAMS, Bria	R JONES, Doug
3B HOLLINS, Dave	LF*GONZALEZ, Luis	S MADDUX, Greg	

* = Minors   Dash (-) = Multi-Position Player   > = Irreversible Position Change

7th:

Got Mike Moore. The transformation is complete. Cardinal callup Rod Brewer—if I can get him this Sunday the 13th—will be the backup first baseman for Bagwell in case he gets hurt. I now have four solid second baseman after having none for nearly two months—Christmas in September. Geronimo Pena is back and is hot. Bonds is on fire. Dawson has been driving in runs like crazy. I'm just 51 points behind Black Irish. Come on, come on!!!

8th:

The team stats as we edge ever closer to the Irish (46 points behind today):

San Antonio Trotters Thru Monday SEP-07-1992

BATTING

		BA	AB	R	H	2B	3B	HR	RBI	BB	SB	CS	E	DP	CWIN CS	C PEN BNS	PTS
HOLLINS,Dave	3B	.263	501	87	132	23	4	22	76	65	9	6	17	22	0	0	422
HARPER,Brian	C	.305	443	52	135	22	0	8	63	21	0	0	9	55	45	0	388
TARTABULL,Dan	RF	.254	342	59	87	17	0	19	65	88	2	1	2	0	0	0	349
BONDS,Barry	LF	.293	184	42	54	15	3	12	40	61	15	3	0	0	0	10	280
SMITH,Ozzie	SS	.300	220	31	66	10	1	0	6	26	17	5	3	44	0	10	191
HENDERSON,Ric	LF	.306	98	18	30	5	0	4	14	27	14	3	1	0	0	0	115
BAGWELL,Jeff	1B	.238	147	19	35	9	2	4	23	25	1	0	1	0	0	0	111
SANDERS,Reggi	CF-LF	.260	100	21	26	7	0	7	11	10	3	2	2	0	0	0	97
PENA,Geronimo	2B	.274	73	11	20	2	1	1	6	6	4	3	1	13	0	0	58
CURTIS,Chad	CF-RF	.186	70	11	13	2	0	1	7	12	3	4	1	0	0	0	31
DAWSON,Andre	RF	.571	21	3	12	3	0	2	1	0	0	0	0	0	0	0	29
THOMPSON,Robb	2B	.348	23	4	8	2	0	1	4	2	0	0	1	4	0	0	27
WHITAKER,Lou	2B	.238	21	1	5	1	0	0	2	1	1	0	1	0	0	0	6
EASLEY,Damion	SS	.214	14	0	3	0	0	0	1	2	1	0	0	0	0	0	5

		BA	AB	R	H	2B	3B	HR	RBI	BB	SB	CS	E	DP	CWIN CS	C PEN BNS	PTS
TOTALS		.267	5378	768	1438	270	29	154	709	639	135	66	103	232	45	30	4165

San Antonio Trotters Thru Monday SEP-07-1992

PITCHING

		W	L	PCT	ERA	SV	HD	IP	H	R	ER	BB	K	Q6	Q1	BN	PTS
JONES,Doug	R	7	8	.467	2.17	25	0	78.2	69	24	19	12	59	0	45	10	394
HURST,Bruce	S	14	7	.667	3.54	0	0	200.2	199	82	79	49	124	20	0	0	364
SCHILLING,Cur	R>S	9	6	.600	2.41	0	0	134.2	105	42	36	35	83	14	0	0	293
MADDUX,Greg	S	4	3	.571	2.24	0	0	72.1	53	18	18	22	53	7	0	0	163
HILL,Ken	S	1	0	1.000	1.50	0	0	6.0	7	2	1	1	3	1	0	0	18
WILLIAMS,Bria	S	1	1	.500	6.10	0	0	10.1	13	7	7	7	3	1	0	3	3

		W	L	PCT	ERA	SV	HD	IP	H	R	ER	BB	K	Q6	Q1	BN	PTS
TOTALS		85	67	.559	3.15	45	4	1324.0	1202	511	463	366	843	107	79	10	2794

San Antonio Trotters Thru Monday SEP-07-1992

BATTING

		BA	AB	R	H	2B	3B	HR	RBI	BB	SB	CS	E	DP	CWIN CS	C PEN BNS	PTS
BLANKENSHIP,L	2B	.234	94	20	22	9	0	1	9	18	5	2	2	9	0	0	76
GONZALEZ,Luis	LF	.276	76	10	21	3	2	3	10	11	3	2	1	0	0	0	66
BELL,Juan	SS	.195	41	3	8	1	0	0	2	3	0	0	1	6	0	0	13
CORDERO,Wil	R>S	9	6	.667	3	1	2	0	0	0	0	0	0	1	0	0	6
LEONARD,Mark	LF	0.000	0	0	0	0	0	0	0	0	0	0	0	0	0	0	0
VELARDE,Randy	SS	0.000	0	0	0	0	0	0	0	0	0	0	0	0	0	0	0
OTHERS		.261	2907	375	759	139	16	71	368	252	57	35	60	78	0	10	1900

PITCHING

		W	L	PCT	ERA	SV	HD	IP	H	R	ER	BB	K	Q6	Q1	BN	PTS
CASTILLO,Fran	S	4	7	.364	3.70	0	0	107.0	95	49	44	36	63	8	1	0	144
MOORE,Mike	S	0	0	.000	0.00	0	0	0.0	0	0	0	0	0	0	0	0	0
OTHERS		45	35	.563	3.26	20	4	714.1	661	287	259	204	455	56	33	0	1417

I keep on shopping up to the final free agent draft. Randy Velarde is a good pickup: he's playing every day for the Yankees, hitting pretty well, and will replace Easley in the majors.

Note that eleven of the hitters are now exceeding the 80% threshold. Also note that, in direct contrast to most of the other teams in the league, I'm down to six pitchers—still milking the Endicott Scam to the very end. Doug Jones might be the MVP of this team—great save stats, of course, but it's the low ERA, fantastic K/W ratio, and the extra wins he's provided that have really propelled the staff ever since he was picked up in the first round of the very first reentry draft. Mike Moore takes over for Brian Williams tout suite.

That bit of French reminds me: I'm sure most of you figured out that Jacques Derrida really didn't sit next to me on that plane ride to Maui (it would have been better if it had been a busride to nowhere, except it would have had to have been Jean-Paul Sartre). But I swear to God that one of the private leagues in BJFB is called the Jacques Derrida League, with team names such as the Upper Derby Deconstructionists, the

Aberdeen Anomie, the West Hartford Heideggerians, etc. Sounds like a bunch of slightly bent Yalies, or a crueler hoax than the story of Sidd Finch. (Hey, STATS! Let's have a Sidd Finch League, with teams all called Paper something—Paper Lions, Paper Tigers, Paper Buddhas, Paper Chasers, Paper Pushers, Paper Trails, etc., etc. Maybe George Plimpton will join, and do an endorsement for you—after all, he's endorsed just about everything else.)

9th:

It happened last night. It happened. The Trotters are in first place.

I logged in and decided to check a few boxscores. (I think I told you about checking box scores from Hawaii. Now I'm back in California, but there's still a time lag from the East Coast, so I decide to dial up STATS and look at the East Coast games.)

The box scores, by the way, are the ones that STATS sends to many of the newspapers around the country. They are the "expanded box score" that you're starting to become familiar with, where walks and strikeouts are posted for individual batter, batting averages and ERAs are updated based on the results of the game, and all kinds of idiosyncratic (but often useful) information is included. It's still not the "account form box score," which would tell you exactly what happened in every inning, but it's a significant advance over what we've been looking at for most of the past century.

Since it is a bit expensive to get box scores over the phone, I've tried to wean myself away from the habit. But this is crunch time: I just can't help it now. I remember the deep commitment to the pennant race that I had in 1969, when I was rooting for the Mets from across the continent, waiting breathlessly for Vin Scully to update us on what was going on in early September. You were hanging on every scrap of news at that point, hoping against hope that the Mets were gonna somehow do it. That's how I feel about this race. Like the Mets in '69, it's got me by the throat.

I nearly go through the roof when this box score comes sailing across my computer screen:

```
9/ 8/92
NEW YORK        ab  r  h bi  w  k  avg    BALTIMORE       ab  r  h bi  w  k  avg
Williams, cf     6  2  2  0  0  0 .248    Orsulak, lf      4  1  1  2  1  0 .298
Velarde, 3b      5  3  3  2  1  1 .284    Milligan, 1b     2  0  0  0  2  1 .251
Mattingly, 1b    4  2  2  0  0  1 .288    Parent, c        1  0  0  0  0  1 .105
  Maas, 1b       2  1  1  0  0  0 .247    Devereaux, cf    4  0  0  0  0  3 .281
Tartabull, rf    5  3  5  9  0  0 .262    Scarsone, ss     1  0  0  0  0  0 .000
James, rf        1  0  1  0  0  0 .264    C.Ripken, ss     2  1  0  0  1  0 .244
R.Kelly, lf      5  2  1  0  1  0 .280    Mercedes, cf     1  1  1  0  0  0 .095
Stanley, c       5  0  1  1  0  1 .257    Horn, dh         3  0  1  0  0  0 .236
Leyritz, dh      2  1  1  0  0  0 .243    Hulett, ph-dh    1  0  0  0  0  0 .274
Hall, ph-dh      3  1  1  0  0  1 .283    Hoiles, c        3  0  1  0  0  0 .286
Stankiewicz, ss  5  0  1  1  0  1 .269    Segui, 1b        1  0  0  0  0  0 .245
P.Kelly, 2b      4  1  1  1  1  1 .239    Martinez, rf     3  0  1  2  0  1 .242
                                          Gomez, 3b        4  0  1  0  0  0 .266
                                          McLemore, 2b     4  1  1  0  0  0 .259

TOTALS          47 16 20 15  3  5        TOTALS          34  4  7  4  4  5
```

```
New York        104 132 050—16
Baltimore       012 000 010— 4
```

E-Mattingly (3). LOB-New York 7, Baltimore 8. Scoring Position-New York, 10 for 16; Baltimore, 2 for 7. 2B-Gomez (22),Mercedes (1), Tartabull (18), Mattingly 2 (36), P.Kelly (21), McLemore (7), Velarde (19). HR-Orsulak (3), Tartabull 2 (21). SF-Martinez. Runners Moved Up-Hall, Stankiewicz. SB-P.Kelly (8), Williams (2).

```
NEW YORK          IP    H  R ER BB  K #Pit  ERA
Sanderson (W 12-9) 7    4  3  3  4  5  126  4.49
Young              1    3  1  1  0  0   21  3.68
Nielsen            1    0  0  0  0  0    8  3.09
BALTIMORE         IP    H  R ER BB  K #Pit  ERA
Rhodes (L 5-5)    2.1   4  4  4  1  2   49  4.36
S.Davis           1.2   4  3  3  0  1   36  3.46
Milacki           2     6  4  4  0  3   34  6.16
Poole             1     0  0  0  0  1    8  0.00
Flanagan          0.2   5  5  5  1  0   28  8.81
Williamson        1.1   1  0  0  1  1   15  0.00
```

WP-Williamson. T-3:17. A-45,861.

That's right. Danny Tartabull—my Danny boy—NINE RBI's. 5-for-5. Two homers and a double. It was—to quote the deep-voiced twit on the

Toyota commercials—epic. Tartabull, that floundering, walk-taking machine, that alleged malingerer, woke up. And announced it to the world like the Norse god Thor, hammering the hell out of everything within reach.

I mailed Daer a copy of the next day's standings because I wasn't sure that we'd still be in first at the end of the week, and I just wanted him to have documentary evidence that for one day at least, the Trotters had clawed their way to the top:

Juan Marishal League Standings Thru Tuesday SEP-08-1992

East	W	L	Pct	GB	Batting	Pitching	Total
1 San Antonio Trotters	74	65	.532		4245	2794	7039
2 Black Irish	74	65	.532		4538	2497	7034
3 Malibu Mowers	71	68	.511	3	4717	1991	6708
4 Iowa Hogheads	69	70	.496	5	4161	2406	6567
5 West Des Moines Weevils	67	72	.482	7	4189	2179	6367
6 Winnebago Pork Queens	62	77	.446	12	3458	2390	5848

Even though he was already deep into football (with a team in STATS' Fantasy Football League as well as our own league to manage), Gary was more than a little pumped up about the Trotters. Looking at the team roster, he noted that there were only four players left from the original team as assembled in April—Tartabull, Dave Hollins, Bruce Hurst, and Brian Harper. Tartabull was the only "freeze" level player we hadn't managed to deal away in the ensuing months. This one indelible night, when five mighty swings of his bat put at least one of the several thousand fantasy teams he appears on into first place, has immortalized him in our eyes.

Now that we've got there, can we hold it??

15th:

Irish has gone flat!! We've opened up a 120 point lead. Rod Brewer joins the roster, and may get a chance to play.

It's too soon to tell, but Cavanagh seems to be getting some additional bad luck. Kevin Appier, Edgar Martinez, and Kent Hrbek all look as though they might miss the rest of the season due to injuries. That might be more than Irish can overcome, unless my guys decide to stumble.

20th:

The lead is holding. Jeff Bagwell has gotten hot. He's hitting over .400 in September. And we're actually closing in on Irish in terms of team offense, as the league totals indicate:

Juan Marichal League Standings Thru Friday SEP-18-1992

East	W	L	Pct	GB	Batting	Pitching	Total
1 San Antonio Trotters	80	68	.541		4637	2927	7563
2 Black Irish	79	69	.534	1	4757	2658	7415
3 Malibu Mowers	75	73	.507	5	4957	2143	7099
4 Iowa Hogheads	74	74	.500	6	4421	2536	6957
5 West Des Moines Weevils	71	77	.480	9	4346	2353	6698
6 Winnebago Pork Queens	66	82	.446	14	3640	2614	6254
West							
7 El Toro Devils	78	70	.527		4629	2772	7400
8 Pikes Peak Players	78	70	.527		4783	2597	7380
9 Topanga Thunder	77	71	.520	1	4523	2736	7259
10 Santa Barbara Sun Sox	74	74	.500	4	4472	2473	6945
11 Surfers of the Apocalypse	72	76	.486	6	4189	2621	6809
12 South Bronx Bombers	64	84	.432	14	3869	2199	6067

Juan Marichal League Thru Friday SEP-18-1992

BATTING

EAST	BA	AB	R	H	2B	3B	HR	RBI	BB	SB	CS	E	DP	CS	BNS	PTS
Trotters	.272	5793	845	1574	293	30	173	793	698	153	75	109	248	49	30	4637
Irish	.268	6462	877	1734	319	37	166	819	680	141	78	133	314	32	40	4757
Mowers	.272	6397	864	1738	344	38	184	879	620	180	62	123	299	81	30	4957
Hogheads	.268	6053	796	1625	270	42	143	699	594	187	83	112	378	45	25	4421
Weevils	.274	5777	789	1582	302	35	120	692	623	183	82	82	259	22	70	4346
Pork Queens	.253	5404	632	1368	240	36	127	635	470	130	55	90	355	52	30	3640

BATTING

WEST	BA	AB	R	H	2B	3B	HR	RBI	BB	SB	CS	E	DP	CS	BNS	PTS
Devils	.276	5835	830	1610	274	40	160	748	631	148	70	87	265	49	60	4629
Players	.277	5793	845	1603	307	32	177	738	681	232	78	103	250	49	50	4783
Thunder	.272	5833	757	1588	286	31	182	769	573	159	77	79	257	54	40	4523
Sun Sox	.269	5863	814	1575	290	32	146	721	763	204	78	115	227	45	30	4472
Apocalypse	.273	5671	720	1546	284	38	150	728	562	59	53	95	284	39	20	4189
Bombers	.260	5159	707	1340	252	30	151	659	619	122	65	61	200	32	0	3869

PITCHING

EAST	W	L	PCT	ERA	SV	HD	IP	H	R	ER	BB	K	Q6	Q1	BN	PTS
Trotters	92	71	.564	3.17	45	4	1396.0	1275	542	491	381	891	111	82	10	2927
Irish	79	61	.564	3.18	58	5	1184.2	1031	476	419	456	862	97	101	35	2658
Mowers	62	60	.508	3.17	46	5	1050.2	979	418	370	314	633	79	80	0	2143
Hogheads	83	91	.477	3.79	60	1	1375.0	1278	635	579	464	897	98	92	35	2536
Weevils	82	74	.526	3.77	33	12	1323.2	1285	609	555	395	885	95	72	10	2353
Pork Queens	76	76	.500	3.67	79	5	1363.2	1352	596	556	478	873	100	103	20	2614
WEST																
Devils	88	59	.599	3.42	75	2	1211.2	1259	566	498	431	787	104	84	30	2772
Players	73	64	.533	3.51	43	26	1346.1	1265	581	525	447	885	93	108	10	2597
Thunder	75	71	.514	3.20	50	16	1264.1	1120	496	450	399	912	95	110	20	2736
Sun Sox	72	71	.503	3.75	74	1	1232.2	1203	556	514	372	862	88	97	20	2473
Apocalypse	79	63	.556	3.50	56	3	1314.1	1251	548	511	414	815	103	82	20	2621
Bombers	70	72	.493	3.41	30	11	1181.2	1112	486	448	392	745	89	90	10	2199

The pitching staff is now on a pace to win exactly 100 games. The hitters' walk totals, anchored by Henderson and Bonds, and supplemented by Bagwell and Whitaker, are soaring. The Trotters are in full flight!!

24th:

The Trotter juggernaut rolls on. We're close to 300 points ahead of Irish now, with just ten days left. Brock Hanke thinks we've got it locked up, but I don't buy it. Not until the final day. Irish is down but not out—he's still getting some amazing occurrences, like big games from Randy Johnson, who's picked the worst freakin' time to get hot (but it's exactly when sabermetrics tells you power pitchers like Johnson do get hot, so what can you do but wail).

Let's look at the in-process Trotter team stats again:

San Antonio Trotters Thru Wednesday SEP-23-1992

BATTING

		BA	AB	R	H	2B	3B	HR	RBI	BB	SB	CS	E	DP	CS	BNS	PTS
HOLLINS,Dave	3B	.263	556	96	146	25	4	25	86	72	9	6	17	22	0	0	469
TARTABULL,Dan	RF	.266	387	67	103	19	0	23	81	94	2	2	0	0	0	0	413
HARPER,Brian	C	.303	475	53	144	23	0	8	70	23	0	0	12	60	52	0	412
BONDS,Barry	LF	.331	242	56	80	23	4	15	51	72	21	3	0	0	0	10	381
SMITH,Ozzie	SS	.304	273	43	83	13	1	0	9	32	25	6	4	51	0	10	243
BAGWELL,Jeff	1B	.293	205	33	60	13	2	8	36	33	2	1	4	0	0	0	194
HENDERSON,Ric	LF	.301	146	28	44	6	1	6	17	37	15	6	2	0	0	0	157
SANDERS,Reggi	CF-LF	.259	135	27	35	8	0	8	15	21	3	2	2	0	0	0	120
PENA,Geronimo	2B	.287	115	18	33	5	1	2	18	14	10	4	2	20	0	0	113
DAWSON,Andre	RF	.361	83	14	30	5	1	3	16	2	1	0	0	0	0	0	83
WHITAKER,Lou	2B	.288	66	9	19	4	0	3	15	9	2	0	1	3	0	0	67
THOMPSON,Robb	2B	.358	53	7	19	4	0	2	7	5	1	2	1	10	0	0	59
VELARDE,Randy	SS	.333	39	8	13	4	0	1	8	6	0	0	1	4	0	0	45
BREWER,Rod	1B	.375	24	5	9	0	0	0	2	3	0	1	0	0	0	0	20
		BA	AB	R	H	2B	3B	HR	RBI	BB	SB	CS	E	DP	CS	BNS	PTS
TOTALS		.273	6026	882	1648	306	32	180	828	724	162	78	113	264	52	30	4867

San Antonio Trotters Thru Wednesday SEP-23-1992

PITCHING

		W	L	PCT	ERA	SV	HD	IP	H	R	ER	BB	K	Q6	Q1	BN	PTS
JONES,Doug	R	10	8	.556	2.07	25	0	87.0	76	26	20	14	65	0	49	10	436
SCHILLING,Cur	R>S	10	7	.588	2.30	0	0	160.2	124	48	41	38	97	17	0	0	355
HURST,Bruce	S	14	9	.609	3.85	0	0	217.1	223	96	93	51	131	20	0	0	354
MADDUX,Greg	S	7	3	.700	2.31	0	0	93.1	76	25	24	26	77	9	0	0	221
HILL,Ken	S	2	2	.500	2.66	0	0	23.2	23	8	7	9	17	3	0	0	44
MOORE,Mike	S	2	1	.667	6.32	0	0	15.2	22	12	11	5	5	0	1	0	9
		W	L	PCT	ERA	SV	HD	IP	H	R	ER	BB	K	Q6	Q1	BN	PTS
TOTALS		95	73	.565	3.19	45	4	1429.1	1313	558	506	390	913	114	84	10	2981

Remember the 80% point to at bat threshold? At this point of the season, all fourteen hitters are exceeding it—exactly what you want to have happen, and exactly at the right time of the year. (The point to AB ratios for the fourteen hitters above: Hollins 84.6, Tartabull 106.7, Harper 86.7, Bonds an incredible 157.4, Ozzie 89.0, the streaking Bagwell 94.6, Rickey Henderson 107.5, Reggie Sanders 88.9, Pena 98.3, Dawson 100.0, Whitaker 101.5, Thompson 111.3, Velarde 115.4, Brewer 83.3.)

As for the pitching, I have three guys to choose from for next year's freeze list: Maddux, Schilling, and the recently-acquired Ken Hill. The fine pitchers that I had on my team—Jack McDowell, Bret Saberhagen, Bob Tewksbury, Melido Perez, Jose Rijo, Jim Abbott, Bill Wegman, Danny Jackson, Jimmy Key, Frank Castillo (still in my minors)—all helped keep the Trotters in the race from June until August. It was the systematic yet still trial-and-error process of cashing them in for hitters, coupled with some timely free agent pickups, that got us to the point where we look like we've got a lock on the division race.

Meanwhile, over in the West, Mick Lucero's Topanga Thunder has closed the gap and has made it into a three-team race to the wire with his brother-in-law Neil Levy's Pikes Peak Players, and Mike Miller's perennially tough El Toro Devils. Seven weeks ago Mick was 500 points back: now he's in second place, just 20 points out of first. A comeback win from him would be a lot more dramatic than my slow, methodical grinddown of the leader (aided by the rash of untimely injuries that made Black Irish's complexion unseasonably pale). Come on, Mick!!

25th:

Latest standings: Trotters up by 320 in the East.

In the West: Devils 7619, Players 7561, Thunder 7550. Don't fold now, Mick!!

27th:

Latest: Trotters by 364 in the East. In the West: Devils 7689, Players 7649, Thunder 7639. What a race!! (Come on, Mick!!)

28th:

Irish's last gasp—or is it?. A big night from Randy Johnson (18 strikeouts). Irish knocked off nearly 100 points from my lead. Holy shit!! Walk the park next time, you big lug. If I get beaten by Randy Johnson and that asshole Jack Morris I'll eat my laptop, connector cables and all. In the West: Devils 7754, Thunder 7747, Players 7725. Three teams within 30 points of each other with one week to go. Come on, Mick!!

30th:

Have almost certainly got it locked up now. The lead has gone back over 300. Greg Maddux' 20th win was a shutout. We have a chance to end with exactly 100 wins (97 to date with four starts left).

In the West: Devils 7826, Players 7819, Thunder 7790. Mick, if you get this close and don't win, I'm really gonna be upset...

OCTOBER

1st:

He's done it!! Mick has moved into first place! Latest standings: Thunder 7862, Players 7843, Devils 7816. Bet there are a lot of phone calls flying back and forth from Denver to Colorado Springs (where Neil Levy lives).

A look at Mick's team (using STATS' "Scout a team" option) shows us that Mick has gotten a lot of help from a certain owner in the Eastern Division. Namely, me. Specifically, three players:

| BATTING | | | | | | | | | | | | CWIN | C PEN | | | |
	BA	AB	R	H	2B	3B	HR	RBI	BB	SB	CS	E	DP	CS	BNS	PTS
JUSTICE,Dave RF	.268	313	50	84	12	4	13	47	50	1	2	4	0	0	0	268
PUCKETT,Kirby CF	.306	196	26	60	11	0	5	32	20	6	1	0	0	0	0	166

| PITCHING | | | | | | | | | | | | | | | |
	W	L	PCT	ERA	SV	HD	IP	H	R	ER	BB	K	Q6	Q1	BN	PTS
RIJO,Jose S	7	1	.875	1.54	0	0	76.0	53	15	13	15	54	10	0	0	226
HERNANDEZ,Rob R	2	1	.667	1.50	9	0	30.0	20	5	5	5	25	0	11	0	151

Messrs. Justice, Puckett, and Rijo, as is obvious from their numbers, have been big factors in Topanga's Thundering Comeback. One of Mick's most brilliant picks (and another guy that he snatched away from me just in the nick of time, goldarn it) was Roberto Hernandez of the

White Sox, who had awesome numbers for an ensemble relief pitcher. If Mick holds on to win, it's because he pays attention to the smallest detail, acts decisively, and has great instincts for fantasy baseball. Even so, it's going to be tough: his two rivals are no slouches. Come on, Mick!!

2nd:

Looks like the Devils may be slipping out of the race. Latest Western Division standings: Thunder 7903, Players 7864, Devils 7833. Only three days left.

3rd:

My last roster moves of the 1992 season. This is what my roster will look like when I take up the Trotters again in February 1993:

```
ID#/Last name of player to Call Up (RETURN if done)->hollins
ID#/Last name of player to Call Up (RETURN if done)->sanders
   ID# FPOS NAME
  4333 CF   Deion SANDERS
  4737 M/D  Reggie SANDERS
Enter ID# of Player ->4333
ID#/Last name of player to Call Up (RETURN if done)->cordero
ID#/Last name of player to Call Up (RETURN if done)->
ID#/Last name of player to Send Down (RETURN if done)->easley
ID#/Last name of player to Send Down (RETURN if done)->brewer
ID#/Last name of player to Send Down (RETURN if done)->velarde
ID#/Last name of player to Send Down (RETURN if done)->
Minor league transaction OK to post (Y/N)->y
```

```
                Projected Roster

Team:    San Antonio Trotters

   C HARPER,Brian    2B*BLANKENSHIP,L   LF BONDS,Barry      S MADDUX,Greg
   C*LAVALLIERE,Mi   3B HOLLINS,Dave    LF HENDERSON,Ric    S HILL,Ken
  1B BAGWELL,Jeff    3B*EASLEY,Damion   CF SANDERS,Deion    S HURST,Bruce
  1B*BREWER,Rod      SS SMITH,Ozzie     CF-LF SANDERS,Reggi S MOORE,Mike
  2B PENA,Geronimo   SS CORDERO,Wil     CF-RF*CURTIS,Chad   S*CASTILLO,Frank
  2B WHITAKER,Lou    SS*LEE,Manuel      RF TARTABULL,Dan  R> S SCHILLING,Curt
  2B THOMPSON,Robb   SS*VELARDE,Randy   RF DAWSON,Andre     R JONES,Doug

* = Minors   Dash (-) = Multi-Position Player   > = Irreversible Position Change
```

The lead over Black Irish is steady at 300. It's over. The San Antonio Trotters, conceived in infamy and weaned on diet soft drinks, are the champions of the Eastern Division of the Juan Marichal League for 1992.

It's going to be interesting trying to figure out which seven players to freeze for the 1993 edition of the Trotters. Bonds, Henderson, Hollins, and Tartabull would appear to be locks, and I'd lean toward keeping Bagwell, too. Part of it will depend on which defensive position winds up being the spot where we pick #1. Where once there was a wasteland, now there is something akin to an embarrassment of riches.

In the West: Mick's lead is now 90 points over Neil (7981 to 7891). The Devils are at 7868. Two days to go. It's too early to say for sure, but I think you can hear the fat lady warming up.

5th:

It's all over—Mick has done it! He's staged an incredible come-from-behind win, winding up with a winning margin of nearly 100 points. I call him and offer my congratulations on a well-earned and extremely hard-fought victory. It was Mick's attention to detail that allowed him to beat two tough and knowledgeable opponents.

The final statistics for the Juan Marichal League:

East		W	L	Pct	GB	-Equivalent- Batting	Pitching	Total
1 San Antonio Trotters		88	74	.543		5138	3151	8288
2 Black Irish		85	77	.525	3	5040	2946	7986
3 Malibu Mowers		82	80	.506	6	5246	2483	7729
4 Iowa Hogheads		82	80	.506	6	4840	2859	7699
5 West Des Moines Weevils		77	85	.475	11	4721	2559	7280
6 Winnebago Pork Queens		73	89	.451	15	3996	2859	6855
West								
7 Topanga Thunder		86	76	.531		4959	3105	8064
8 Pikes Peak Players		85	77	.525	1	5078	2895	7972
9 El Toro Devils		84	78	.519	2	4925	3015	7940
10 Santa Barbara Sun Sox		82	80	.506	4	4863	2891	7754
11 Surfers of the Apocalypse		79	83	.488	7	4469	2974	7443
12 South Bronx Bombers		70	92	.432	16	4183	2441	6624

League MVP of the Year: SANDBERG,Ryne of the Mowers, 672 points
Cy Young of the Year: ECKERSLEY,Dennis of the Sun Sox, 633 points

BATTING

EAST	BA	AB	R	H	2B	3B	HR	RBI	BB	SB	CS	E	DP	CWIN CS	C BNS	PEN	PTS
Trotters	.272	6422	931	1747	324	33	191	872	775	173	84	128	301	52	30		5138
Irish	.267	6947	931	1857	345	37	177	874	719	151	89	117	400	51	29		5040
Mowers	.270	6849	922	1850	367	39	195	937	669	194	66	135	328	89	40		5246
Hogheads	.270	6557	873	1773	297	45	154	760	651	201	89	117	400	55	24		4840
Weevils	.272	6352	865	1726	326	39	132	756	681	199	88	93	286	28	70		4721
Pork Queens	.255	5941	688	1513	263	39	136	694	517	143	61	99	391	62	30		3996
WEST																	
Thunder	.275	6297	831	1733	322	37	196	834	618	165	83	84	269	55	40		4959
Players	.274	6302	905	1729	327	36	186	784	717	248	85	110	274	54	50		5078
Devils	.273	6360	889	1734	297	43	166	804	696	156	77	95	288	54	60		4925
Sun Sox	.269	6388	883	1721	312	39	161	786	836	226	90	121	243	45	30		4863
Apocalypse	.269	6178	779	1660	312	39	158	787	609	67	54	105	313	44	20		4469
Bombers	.261	5565	768	1454	272	34	162	713	660	128	69	71	216	34	0		4183

PITCHING

EAST	W	L	PCT	ERA	SV	HD	IP	H	R	ER	BB	K	Q6	Q1	BN	PTS
Trotters	99	74	.572	3.10	50	4	1500.2	1361	571	517	407	960	122	90	10	3151
Irish	88	70	.557	3.19	60	6	1319.1	1144	529	467	509	978	109	109	53	2946
Mowers	73	68	.518	3.11	47	10	1213.1	1120	471	419	370	742	90	91	0	2483
Hogheads	91	99	.479	3.66	67	1	1510.1	1393	677	614	518	985	109	116	35	2859
Weevils	86	77	.528	3.74	35	15	1419.0	1369	650	590	420	958	103	81	10	2559
Pork Queens	81	83	.494	3.62	88	5	1485.0	1456	641	598	517	957	107	117	20	2859
WEST																
Thunder	84	78	.519	3.15	55	20	1427.0	1250	554	499	447	1040	107	123	20	3105
Players	82	75	.522	3.53	50	27	1512.0	1427	665	593	481	987	104	122	10	2895
Devils	96	67	.589	3.38	77	2	1432.1	1376	614	538	455	865	113	96	30	3015
Sun Sox	83	72	.535	3.61	77	1	1389.2	1322	602	558	420	982	103	101	20	2891
Apocalypse	86	65	.570	3.39	65	7	1435.1	1350	582	541	447	890	114	93	20	2974
Bombers	76	82	.481	3.41	34	11	1315.0	1236	540	498	425	834	96	104	10	2441

The Trotters, with their wild rush at the end of the season, actually managed to catch Black Irish in runs scored and wound up tied for the most runs scored. In terms of overall offensive points, the Trotters managed to pass Black Irish and finish second behind the Mowers, who had many more at-bats than the Trotters.

Remember the point to at-bat threshold, and how I said to have a winning team you should be aiming for 80%? The Trotters came in at 80.00622% for the entire season. How's that for defining a standard and keeping to it? The 80.0 for the Trotters ranked second in the league behind the Players, who hit 80.6. Complete totals for this measurement: Players 80.6, Trotters 80.0, Thunder 78.7, Devils 77.4, Mowers 76.6, Sun Sox 76.1, Bombers 75.2, Weevils 74.3, Hogheads 73.8, Irish 72.5, Surfers 72.3, Pork Queens 67.3. Note to Dave Schultz: your 75.2 indicates that you had good players who just didn't play enough (your AB total was almost 1500 behind the leaders). Note to Jay: it wasn't all just the bad start that hurt your offense. The extremely low totals in walks and the sub-average extra base hit totals must be corrected if next year's squad is going to contend.

As for pitching, the Trotters led in wins, missing the 100 limit by one. They also led in quality starts (Q6) with 122, well ahead of their closest division rivals. They also managed to capture the ERA crown in a squeaker over the Mowers (3.10 to 3.11). The Mowers never did get enough pitching to get back into the race: their IP total was nearly 300 behind the top teams. Remember the 2-to-1 points to IP factor? The league average was 2.02 (34178 pitching points in 16958 IP). The individual team performances: Irish 2.23, Thunder 2.17, Devils 2.11, Trotters 2.10, Sun Sox 2.08, Surfers 2.07, Mowers 2.05, Pork Queens 1.92, Players 1.91, Hogheads 1.89, Bombers 1.86, Weevils 1.80. The

Weevils' total is especially noteworthy because it is a pitching staff anchored by Roger Clemens. Jeff Lowe's squad thus mirrors some of the latter-day real-life difficulties of the Boston Red Sox.

Teams that exploited strikeout pitchers, saves, and holds, and had a low ERA, tended to be the best in this measurement: the Trotters eschewed saves and holds, and concentrated on ERA and control, which explains why they're fourth. Despite an indifferent won-loss record, it's clear that Mick's Thunder team won in large part because of his pitching. Just to give you an idea of how good Mick's pitching staff really was down the stretch, here's a breakout of his first-half and second-half raw pitching stats:

	IP	H	R	ER	BB	SO	W	L	ERA
First half	715	679	312	288	240	479	39	52	3.63
Second half	712	571	242	211	207	561	45	26	2.67

I'd guess it's safe to consider that to be just a little bit of a second-half surge, don't you think?? Just for fun, let's compare those figures to the Trotter pitchers' first and second half:

	IP	H	R	ER	BB	SO	W	L	ERA
First half	817	756	327	298	227	546	55	42	3.28
Second half	684	605	244	219	180	414	44	32	2.88

I was very good—Mick was better. That .634 winning percentage in the second half comes from having a strikeout staff (7.09 K/9) with super control (2.62 W/9) and low hits allowed (7.22 H/9). That second-half baserunners per nine innings average (9.84) is awesome: good as they are, the Trotters (10.33 BR/9 in the second half) just aren't close.

But just as Mick transformed his pitching staff, I was able to develop the type of offensive team that I was looking for. The first half and second half offensive totals for the Trotters bear this out. The Trotters hit about the same: .270 in the first half, .274 in the second, but that's where the similarity ends. Percentage of extra base hits was up 5%, slugging average was up 20 points (.432 vs. .413 in the first half), stolen bases were up over 80% as a function of plate appearances (3.15 per 100 PA in the second half, 1.76 per 100 PA in the first).

But the key jump was in base on balls: the Trotters' BBP (walks per 100 plate appearances) was 9.4 in the first half. In the second half, thorough assiduous acquisition of players with good strike zone judgment, the BBP rose to 12.3, an increase of nearly 31%. The OBP for the first half was .339; in the second half, it was .364. By acquiring Bonds, Henderson, Bagwell, Whitaker, Sanders, and Pena to go along with originals Tartabull, Hollins, and Harper, the Trotters became an offensive machine with as much hum as anyone. It was one part sabermetrics, one part persuasion, and one part luck. Going into 1993 with the players above to choose from as freezers (let's not forget Messers. Maddux, Schilling, and Hill), the Trotters ought to be well positioned to defend their title.

But it ain't going to be easy. Tom Cavanagh (who did, by the way, graciously call me when it became clear that he'd been beaten: sorry it took so long to get to you, Tom, it really has been a helluva year) might very well have won anyway in 1992 if he hadn't lost Kevin Appier, Edgar Martinez, Bobby Bonilla, and Kent Hrbek for the last two-to-three weeks of the season. I figure he lost about 260 points from those guys. That would have left the Trotters with a 42-point margin of victory. It's gonna be tough to hold him off—he has a knack with a pitching staff, and he is a very good trader. And Dave Morgan is also very crafty: his late season trade for Larry Walker sets him up to have an even better nucleus than he started with last year. Likewise, Dave Endicott just needs better luck with his pitchers to be there at the end in '93—you know someone's sharp if he has a fantasy league term (Endicott's Scam) named after him.

As for Jeff and Jay, they have some work to do, but Jeff has been a winner before—in his first year, just like me—so you know he has the potential to put it together; I liked the way Jay built his pitching staff over the second half—his points to IP ratio after the All-Star Break was an excellent 2.20—so it's clear that he's learning on the job pretty fast.

Thanks to all the guys for an incredible introduction to the sweet torture of BJFB, and thanks most of all to Bill James and STATS for making a game that has the three-dimensionality to keep even jaded sabermetricians sweating it out to the bitter end. (You can send me the money for writing you this 30+ page plug to the usual address, guys, or you can put an extra $100,000 into the Tokyo Walkmen account in the Winter Game. Yes, the Winter Game. We'll plug that one next year—if we win, that is...)

One final chart. Remember when we showed the dispersion of players to and from the Trotters earlier in the season? Here are the final team rosters for 1992, with the original Trotter players show in italics, and all players who were on the Trotters at any point but were traded to another team shown underlined. They didn't call me the Trader Jack of the Juan Marichal League for nothing...

Team: Black Irish — Owner: Thomas J Cavanagh

C PAGNOZZI, Tom	SS-3B FRYMAN, Travis	RF BAINES, Harold	S MORRIS, Jack
1B THOMAS, Frank	SS*ARIAS, Alex	RF-3B BONILLA, Bobby	S*HAAS, Dave
1B COLBRUNN, Greg	LF POLONIA, Luis	S DARLING, Ron	S*BLACK, Bud
1B*VAUGHN, Mo	LF VAUGHN, Greg	S BENES, Andy	S*APPIER, Kevin
2B SAX, Steve	LF MEULENS, Hensl	S HARRIS, Greg/W	R ROJAS, Mel
3B WILLIAMS, Matt	CF DEVEREAUX, Mik	S GUZMAN, Juan	R GRAHE, Joe
3B*MARTINEZ, Edga	CF>MP*COLE, Alex	S JOHNSON, Randy	R HENNEMAN, Mike

Team: Iowa Hogheads — Owner: Dave Endicott

C HOILES, Chris	SS FERNANDEZ, Ton	RF>CF LOFTON, Kenny	S*WITT, Bobby
C*ALOMAR, Sandy	SS*OFFERMAN, Jose	RF-LF*ORSULAK, Joe	S*RHODES, Arthur
1B PALMEIRO, Rafa	LF MALDONADO, Can	S BARNES, Brian	S*WILSON, Trevor
1B GRACE, Mark	LF HILL, Glenalle	S CONE, David	S*HANSON, Erik
2B DESHIELDS, Del	LF-RF*CHAMBERLAIN, S	S SMOLTZ, John	R OLIN, Steve
3B BOGGS, Wade	CF WILLIAMS, Bern	S OSBORNE, Donov	R SMITH, Lee
3B-2B BAERGA, Carlos	CF FELIX, Junior	S SMITH, Pete	R> S FLEMING, Dave

Team: Malibu Mowers — Owner: Dave Morgan

C DAULTON, Darre	3B-LF*PALMER, Dean	S WELCH, Bob	S*GOODEN, Dwight
1B-RF WALKER, Larry	SS-2B BORDICK, Mike	S DRABEK, Doug	S*SMITH, Zane
1B*JOYNER, Wally	SS LARKIN, Barry	S CANDIOTTI, Tom	S*MESA, Jose
1B*MARTINEZ, Carl	LF BELL, George	S NABHOLZ, Chris	S WORRELL, Todd
2B SANDBERG, Ryne	CF JOHNSON, Lance	S FINLEY, Chuck	R> S RIVERA, Ben
3B GRUBER, Kelly	CF*DYKSTRA, Lenny	S DARWIN, Danny	R RUSSELL, Jeff
3B LANSFORD, Carn	RF>LF MACK, Shane	S*ASTACIO, Pedro	R SCANLAN, Bob

Team: San Antonio Trotters — Owner: Don Malcolm

C HARPER, Brian	2B*BLANKENSHIP, L	LF BONDS, Barry	S MADDUX, Greg
C*LAVALLIERE, Mi	3B HOLLINS, Dave	LF HENDERSON, Ric	S HILL, Ken
1B BAGWELL, Jeff	3B*EASLEY, Damion	CF SANDERS, Deion	S HURST, Bruce
1B*BREWER, Rod	SS SMITH, Ozzie	CF-LF SANDERS, Reggi	S MOORE, Mike
2B PENA, Geronimo	SS CORDERO, Wil	CF-RF*CURTIS, Chad	S*CASTILLO, Frank
2B WHITAKER, Lou	SS*LEE, Manuel	RF TARTABULL, Dan	R> S SCHILLING, Curt
2B THOMPSON, Robb	SS*VELARDE, Randy	RF DAWSON, Andre	R JONES, Doug

Team: West Des Moines Weevils — Owner: Jeffrey Lowe

C MACFARLANE, Mi	3B-1B COOPER, Scott	RF-1B BRUNANSKY, Tom	S STEWART, Dave
1B CLARK, Will	3B-1B KING, Jeff	RF SIERRA, Ruben	S*LEIBRANDT, Char
1B*MURRAY, Eddie	SS OWEN, Spike	DH>1B*CLARK, Jack	S*OLIVARES, Omar
2B ALOMAR, Robert	LF>CF NIXON, Otis	S CLEMENS, Roger	S HERNANDEZ, Xavi
2B KNOBLAUCH, Chu	LF-RF HALL, Mel	S TAPANI, Kevin	S BELINDA, Stan
2B-SS*LEWIS, Mark	CF-LF KELLY, Roberto	S MULHOLLAND, Te	R*HARVEY, Bryan
3B ZEILE, Todd	CF*MCRAE, Brian	S GROSS, Kevin	R*MEACHAM, Rusty

Team: Winnebago Pork Queens — Owner: Jay Sierszyn

C RODRIGUEZ, Iva	3B*LIVINGSTONE, S	CF YOUNT, Robin	S ELDRED, Cal
C OLIVER, Joe	SS RIPKEN, Cal	CF-RF HAMILTON, Dary	S HIBBARD, Greg
1B FIELDER, Cecil	SS*GUILLEN, Ozzie	CF*BURKS, Ellis	S*VALERA, Julio
1B*JORDAN, Ricky	LF MAY, Derrick	RF ANTHONY, Eric	S*GARDNER, Mark
2B SOJO, Luis	LF-CF XUPCIC, Bob	S MCDOWELL, Jack	R NETTLAND, John
3B BARBERIE, Bret	LF REIMER, Kevin	S ABBOTT, Jim	R MONTGOMERY, Jef
3B*SABO, Chris	LF*BELL, Derek	S NAVARRO, Jaime	R MYERS, Randy

Team: El Toro Devils — Owner: Mike Miller

C STEINBACH, Ter	SS GAGNE, Greg	RF WINFIELD, Dave	S TOMLIN, Randy
1B MOLITOR, Paul	SS*BELLIARD, Rafa	RF CARTER, Joe	S BROWN, Kevin
2B-LF MILLER, Keith	LF BELLE, Albert	RF*CANSECO, Jose	S*MARTINEZ, Ramon
2B-3B PHILLIPS, Tony	CF BUTLER, Brett	DH>DOWNING, Brian	R MCDOWELL, Roger
2B LEMKE, Mark	CF JACKSON, Darri	S BOSIO, Chris	R AGUILERA, Rick
2B*LIND, Jose	CF*HENDERSON, Dav	S GLAVINE, Tom	R REARDON, Jeff
3B CAMINITI, Ken	CF*WILSON, Willie	S MORGAN, Mike	

Team: Pikes Peak Players — Owner: Neil Levy

C BORDERS, Pat	LF-CF GANT, Ron	S GULLICKSON, Bi	S*SWINDELL, Greg
C KARKOVICE, Ron	LF-RF*MCREYNOLDS, Ke	S RASMUSSEN, Den	S*AVERY, Steve
1B BIGGIO, Craig	CF GRIFFEY JR, Ke	S HARNISCH, Pete	R BECK, Rod
2B BIGGIO, Craig	CF GRISSOM, Marqu	S MCCASKILL, Kir	R HENKE, Tom
3B SEITZER, Kevin	RF JOSE, Felix	S BULLINGER, Jim	R RADINSKY, Scott
3B*SHEFFIELD, Gar	S PUGH, Tim	S*SEMINARA, Fran	R*THIGPEN, Bobby
SS BELL, Jay	S DESHAIES, Jim	S*STOTTLEMYRE, T	R*YOUNG, Anthony

Team: Santa Barbara Sun Sox — Owner: Guy Langlo

C TETTLETON, Mic	SS LISTACH, Pat	RF O'NEILL, Paul	S SMILEY, John
1B OLERUD, John	SS*CEDENO, Anduja	RF MUNOZ, Pedro	S*PICHARDO, Hipol
1B*MARTINEZ, Tino	LF CALDERON, Ivan	S WAKEFIELD, Tim	R ALVAREZ, Wilson
2B-LF ROBERTS, Bip	LF ANDERSON, Brad	S KEY, Jimmy	R ECKERSLEY, Denn
2B-3B JEFFERIES, Gre	LF-CF*COLEMAN, Vince	S TEWKSBURY, Bob	R*HENRY, Doug
3B VENTURA, Robin	CF FINLEY, Steve	S BELCHER, Tim	R*PENA, Alejandro
3B*BUECHELE, Stev	CF>RF*SALMON, Tim	S GUZMAN, Jose	

Team: South Bronx Bombers — Owner: David Schultz

C NOKES, Matt	SS-2B*STANKIEWICZ, A	RF WHITEN, Mark	S KRUEGER, Bill
C*HUNDLEY, Todd	SS*THON, Dickie	RF*STRAWBERRY, Da	S SABERHAGEN, Bre
1B KARROS, Eric	LF GILKEY, Bernar	DH DAVIS, Chili	S*JACKSON, Danny
1B MAAS, Kevin	LF-1B KRUK, John	S WEGMAN, Bill	R WILLIAMS, Mitch
2B BOONE, Bret	LF*MITCHELL, Kevi	S PEREZ, Melido	R JACKSON, Mike
3B MAGADAN, Dave	CF WHITE, Devon	S ERICKSON, Scot	R*CADARET, Greg
SS VIZQUEL, Omar	RF-LF SNYDER, Cory	S LEFFERTS, Crai	R*CADARET, Greg

Team: Surfers of the Apocalypse — Owner: Kenneth E. Lawrence

C SURHOFF, B.J.	3B GOMEZ, Leo	RF BUHNER, Jay	S NAGY, Charles
C*SCIOSCIA, Mike	3B*LEIUS, Scott	RF*GWYNN, Tony	S*OJEDA, Bobby
1B MCGRIFF, Fred	SS VALENTIN, John	RF*PLANTIER, Phil	R CHARLTON, Norm
1B MATTINGLY, Don	SS DISARCINA, Gar	R RYAN, Nolan	R OLSON, Gregg
1B SORRENTO, Paul	LF CLARK, Jerald	S MUSSINA, Mike	R> S SWIFT, Bill
2B REED, Jody	LF*GREENWELL, Mik	S VIOLA, Frank	R FARR, Steve
2B*FRANCO, Julio	CF VAN SLYKE, And	S SUTCLIFFE, Ric	R*MILLS, Alan

Team: Topanga Thunder — Owner: Mick Lucero

C WALTERS, Dan	LF>CF GONZALEZ, Juan	RF DEER, Rob	S*FERNANDEZ, Sid
C*SANTIAGO, Beni	LF RAINES, Tim	S GREENE, Tommy	S*RIJO, Jose
1B BRETT, George	LF ALOU, Moises	S FERNANDEZ, Ale	S*MARTINEZ, Denni
2B-SS BLAUSER, Jeff	CF PUCKETT, Kirby	S MAHOMES, Pat	S*LANGSTON, Mark
3B PENDLETON, Ter	CF LANKFORD, Ray	S MCDONALD, Ben	R DIBBLE, Rob
SS-2B FLETCHER, Scot	CF>JOHNSON, Howar	S WICKMAN, Bob	R HERNANDEZ, Robe
SS CLAYTON, Royce	RF JUSTICE, Dave	S*TROMBLEY, Mike	R*WARD, Duane

This, of course, doesn't include all the players I picked up and dropped over the course of the season. A complete wiring diagram of all the trades and other acquisitions made over the course of the season would be visually overwhelming.

And I was the major culprit: it is fitting to conclude with the note that of the 25 players I began the season with in April, only four remained on my roster at season's end: Dave Hollins, Danny Tartabull, Brian Harper, and Bruce Hurst. I suspect that, after a season of frenetic trading in order to establish competitiveness, the Trotters' roster will prove to be more stable in 1993. Stay tuned...

Walkmen

Don Malcolm

This article is dedicated to Gary Jones, who should have been the next Eddie Stanky, and to Warren Newson, who ought to be leading off for somebody on a full-time basis in 1993, but probably won't.

A few years back some of you read the saga of Big Ed (1989 Baseball Abstract, Cincinnati Reds). Ed's exploits occurred during the hazy daze of college, almost half a lifetime ago, where Brock Hanke, Harold Karabell, Chris Mooney, Ed and yours truly spent hours of leisure time (the type uniquely afforded to students even in that era of protest, "free love", and social strife) in pursuit of baseball Nirvana.

We had our own "Winter Game", except that it was not simulated via computer, as is Bill James' latest creation. Our game was All Star Baseball, the hoary old chestnut developed by ex-major leaguer Ethan Allen (who couldn't crack any of our starting lineups, by the way), which featured circular disks of players with their offensive statistics represented via numerical codes.

There was an empty storage room one level above the top floor of the dormitory (all male: we had to wait a couple of years before the dorms were dual gender) where late at night, while other residents slept, some or all of the All Star Crew would face each other down with their disks. We prayed for the numbers 1, 5, 7, 9, 11, and 13, which were apportioned irregularly across the disks according to the players' career (or sometimes single season) stats.

Brock had played All Star for many years prior to college, with a friend named Ronnie Welch, who was tragically killed in a automobile accident in 1969. Ronnie and Brock played All Star together in junior high and on into high school, and had an impressive collection of player disks that reached back into the fifties. Those disks were the most dramatic, because the display format was simpler and there was less segmentation into separate numbers. I can still remember the unique heft and weight of those old disks: when Ed discovered the legacy of the Negro League players, he devised a set that mimicked the format and the feel of the old cardboard, in order to make it seem that the disks had been created during the Negro Leaguers' playing days.

So the old disks, in particular, did not break up the "9" area. Did I forget to tell you what "9" stood for? Let me explain all of the "good" numbers: 1 is a home run, which varied from a big fat swatch for Babe Ruth and Ralph Kiner to the barest dotted line for singles hitters like Nellie Fox or Richie Ashburn; 5 is a triple, which was invariably a dotted line unless you had a Ty Cobb or Sam Crawford card (or unless, like Ed, you made a single season disk for Owen "Chief" Wilson in 1912); 11 is a double, which looked very inviting on the Tris Speaker disk; 7 and 13 were singles, which were disproportionately large on the Lloyd Waner disk (primarily because everything else was so small...); and 9 is—well, you guess what's left.

That's right. 9 is walks. The old free pass. The base on balls. The thing that, according to players from the majors on down to slow pitch softball, real men aren't supposed to want to settle for. The "9" on the old Eddie Yost disk, rendered in uninterrupted space, was enormous. It seemed like it was half the disk. (In reality it was .1801 x 360, or 64.836 degrees, as measured and logged by Big Ed.) When Brock played Ronnie's team, which was called the Combine, Yost would walk once or twice every game.

It was while I watched Brock play Ronnie's team, which had several players with enormous "9" areas, that I began to get seriously fascinated with guys who walked a lot. (So, too, did Ed, who seemed to live for the generation of new player disks, all of whom he originally planned to seed his Deity team with in the interest of world domination.) I latched onto the Ferris Fain disk, which was even more impressive in terms of its "9" size than Yost's, and calmly batted it second between Nap Lajoie and Rogers Hornsby (who played short—look it up, he played 356 games there—for my Cynic team). Fain proceeded to lead our league in runs scored, something that—strangely, I thought at the time—he never did in the big leagues.

Ed's research was extremely thorough (and remember, this all happened in the early seventies, or several years B.B.J.—Before Bill James) and he identified all of the players who walked like crazy. All of the names that you will be getting familiar with—Yost, Fain, Max Bishop, Eddie Stanky, Roy Cullenbine, just to name a few—were spotted in The Baseball Encyclopedia (1st edition, thank you) and turned into player disks. One of my favorites was the Bill Joyce disk—lots of walks, excellent extra-base power, and a third baseman to boot. (We were unfazed by the discovery that he was one of the greatest butchers in the field ever—it didn't matter in All Star.)

Brock and I were sufficiently entranced by batters who walked a lot to model the "Hanke" and "Malcolm" players who appeared in our own baseball simulation game after the Fains and Stankys and Bishops of the world. And in fast pitch intramural softball we practiced what we preached—although we found it difficult to convince most of our teammates that taking walks was a good idea. (Big Ed, who understood the value of walks, was unable to make our team into a walking troika due to nerves: he would get up to the plate and worry about falling behind two strikes, and start swinging. The results, for the most part, were feeble. As Brock says, if you can't hit, WALK!!)

In the course of our (pre-sabermetric) research, Ed and Brock and I had become dimly aware that there were two rough classes of ballplayers who walked a lot. There were the big sluggers with good strike-zone judgement who received excess walks due to pitchers' fear (in order of propensity to walk: Ted Williams, Babe Ruth, Mickey Mantle, Ralph Kiner, Lou Gehrig, Mel Ott, Jimmie Foxx, Eddie Mathews; from recent and still-active players, you can add Mike Schmidt, Darrell Evans, Frank Thomas and Barry Bonds).

But then there were the gnats, the pests, the non-slugger types who worked the count, took the walks, and usually scored a ton of runs, especially in relation to the number of hits they produced. Guys like Max Bishop, Eddie Stanky, Ferris Fain, Eddie Yost. Roy Thomas. Elmer

Valo. Eddie Lake. Eddie Joost. Lu Blue. Miller Huggins. These were the guys that really intrigued us, the ones with otherwise indifferent offensive skills who survived, even thrived, due to their batting eye.

And now, admiration for these unusual players has belatedly led to study. In a fit of sabermetric zeal, I have dipped deeply into Macmillan and Total Baseball to compile a list of all the players who drew 100 walks or more in a single season. It's one of the most interesting lists one can imagine, as it cuts across the entire history of baseball from the 1880's to the present, and includes both the well-known superstar and the incredibly obscure journeyman. For purposes of introduction, we will profile all of the 141 players who have achieved this milestone at least once in their career. We will meet them in chronological order, from the first instance of 100 walks in a season (George Gore in 1886) to the present-day walkmen (Frank Thomas, Brett Butler, Mickey Tettleton, Tony Phillips, Rickey Henderson).

100 WALKS—DECADE BY DECADE

THE 1880's

THE PLAYERS:

George Gore
Jim McTamany
Paul Radford
Yank Robinson

George Gore, Chicago White Stockings center fielder, has the distinction of being the first player in the history of professional baseball to draw 100 or more walks in a single season. It's a distinction that is a bit misleading: while Gore was a fine player (lifetime .301 hitter, seven seasons over .300, led the NL in batting and slugging average in 1880), his lifetime walks per 100 plate appearances (hereafter referred to as BBP) is just 11.8, slightly below the average of all the walking men. There must have been rule changes in the mid 1880's as well, for Gore's walk totals, which were in the high 20's in 1881-83 (and are at or near the league lead during those years) suddenly jump into the 60's in 1884, peaking at 102 in 1886. League walk totals more than doubled from 1883 (2.95 walks per game, both teams) to 1889 (6.97).

This surge, which was contemporaneous in the American Association, is reflected in the appearance of the first true "walkmen" in 1887-89, all of whom achieved their 100+ walk seasons in the AA prior to its demise in 1891. Jim McTamany, born in Philadelphia while the Battle of Gettysburg was being fought, was a light-hitting outfielder who exceeded 100 walks in each of the last three seasons of the AA in 1889. He obviously batted leadoff (Run Element Ratio of over 2.5 and more than four times as many runs scored as RBI), but had some trouble making contact (92 strikeouts in 1891). In the hard-hitting climate of the 1890s, and with job scarcity created by the collapse of the American Association, McTamany was unable to remain in the big leagues, and thus becomes the first of four players in the history of baseball to draw 100+ walks in his final season in the majors.

Paul Radford, the second man to walk 100+ times in a season (in 1887, with 106; he did it again in 1893) was one of the most well-traveled players of the pre-1900 era, playing with nine different teams in a twelve year career. He primarily played right field, but was skilled enough defensively to play both center field and shortstop, which was the position he mostly played for the league champion New York Mutuals of the American Association in 1887. It's clear that Radford (who had

a lifetime BA of just .242) managed to hang around because of his defense and secondary offensive skills. He shows a similar jump in walks during the mid-1880's seen earlier in Gore. From 1887 to the end of his career with the lowly Washington club in 1894, Radford averaged slightly under 16 walks per 100 plate appearances.

Yank Robinson hit even less than Radford (.241 lifetime) and was an indifferent fielder, but was good enough to hold down the starting second base job for one of the most successful franchises ever, the St. Louis Browns of the mid-to-late 1880's. Robinson's best season came in 1887, the year before he began the first three-year streak of 100+ walk seasons, when he hit .305, with 92 walks, 75 stolen bases, and 102 runs scored. As we will soon discover, the year after a player's best overall offensive season is often the one where he cracks the 100 BB barrier, accompanied by a drop in other offensive totals. Yank Robinson's 1888 was the first example of this pattern: while his walk total leaped to 116, his BA dropped 74 points (to .231), and he lost 91 points off his slugging average, primarily because his doubles power was cut in half (from 32 in 1887 to 17 in 1888). Robinson's offensive skills didn't just atrophy, they went permanently AWOL: in the last five years of his career beginning in 1888, Robinson batted just .208 (compared with .276 through 1887). He stayed in the big leagues only because his walk ratio nearly doubled (11.9 BBP from 1882-87; 19.9 from 1888-92). His single season BBP of 24.82 in 1890 is second all time, eclipsed only by Ted Williams (26.05 in 1954).

THE 1890's

THE PLAYERS:

Cap Anson
Cupid Childs
Roger Connor
John Crooks
Billy Hamilton
Dummy Hoy
Bill Joyce
Joe Kelley
John McGraw
Jim McTamany
Paul Radford
Yank Robinson
Roy Thomas

In the 1890s we begin to see the "cross-section" effect that is the predominant feature of the 100BB list. Superstars, stars, and obscure journeymen co-inhabit and, save for the catching position, could field a credible starting eight (Anson or Connor at first, Childs, Crooks or Robinson at second, Radford or McGraw at SS, McGraw or Joyce at third; nobody would sneeze at an outfield of Billy Hamilton in left, Joe Kelley in center, and Dummy Hoy switched over to right, with Radford, Roy Thomas, and Jim McTamany as reserves). It'd be a hard team to beat.

Cap Anson was one of the oldest players to crack the 100-walk barrier: he did it at the age of 39. John McGraw was the youngest man to do it—20 years old, a month younger than his protege Mel Ott was in 1929. (The other 20-year old to crack 100 walks? Ted Williams in 1939.) Joe Kelley was also quite young (22) when he peaked at 107 walks in 1894. For Kelley, it was the only time he broke the barrier: his next best BB total was 91 in 1896. Somewhat uncharacteristically, Kelley's 1894 represented the coincidence of peak walk and peak RC27 totals, something that usually happens to the greatest of superstars. Kelley's 1894 season looks very comparable to Norm Cash's 1961.

Cupid Childs is one of the best players not elected to the Hall of Fame. He and Joe Kelley are the only nineteenth-century members of the Triple 100 Club (100 or more runs, runs batted in, and walks in a single season: see the 1990 Baseball Sabermetric for more details). Actually, Childs' triple hundred in 1896 was a bit of a fluke: originally a leadoff man, he had been switched in the batting order with Jesse Burkett, who was on his way to his second straight .400 season for the Cleveland Spiders, and was the beneficary of the Crab's .455 OBP. The Baseball Maniacs' Hall of Fame poll/research experiment put Childs in their "Outer Circle" of the Hall; the reason why he has been overlooked by the BBWAA is due to the fact that he faded so quickly after the age of 30. This is a signature characteristic for one subclass of "walkmen," who emerge in the big leagues with what Bill James termed "old players' skills": they tend to have a narrower skill range, and once it begins to fade, they are not able to compensate for its loss, with the result being that the bottom drops out of their career.

CUPID CHILDS	BA	BBP
BEFORE 30	.321	15.9
AFTER 30	.255	11.4

BBP: bases on balls per 100 plate appearances

Roger Connor was a huge man for his time (6'3", 220 lbs.), and was one of the best hitters in the 1880's, winning a batting title in 1885 (.371). His prime walk seasons coincide with a general downturn in his batting average, and his one 100+ walk season in 1892, at the age of 35, went along with a subpar .294 BA. His lifetime BBP of 11.39 is the second lowest of all the pre-1900 "walkmen." Connor was belatedly elected to the Hall of Fame in 1976; the Baseball Maniacs placed him toward the low end of their "Inner Circle" (among the top 100 players of all time).

John (Jack) Crooks is next in the lineage of Robinson-Radford-McTamany type players (.240 lifetime average). Crooks had a short but colorful career which was marked by several year-long interruptions. His BBP in 1892 (23.41) ranks 12th all-time for single seasons. A good second baseman who led two leagues in fielding percentage, Crooks had three consecutive 100+ walk seasons, but (like many in his subclass of player) was through at 31.

Few baseball historians argue with the notion that Billy Hamilton is the greatest leadoff hitter in the history of the game. His credentials for the 100+ walk club are as impeccable as his other offensive stats: five 100+ plus seasons, a peak single-season BBP of 18.39, lifetime of 15.89.

Dummy Hoy was a much-travelled centerfielder of the 1890's, a solid .290 hitter with good but not great plate discipline (12.35 BBP lifetime). His career started a bit late (26) due his deaf-mute condition, but he overcame it sufficiently to record 2054 hits, 1004 walks, and 597 stolen bases. His one 100+ walk season came in 1891, his only year in the American Association. He is the only player in history to lead both the American Association and the American League in walks. (Now there's a barroom bet-winner for sure...)

Bill Joyce, known as Scrappy Bill, was described by Baseball Maniac Hall of Fame mastermind Tom Hull as "a sabermetrician's wet dream." Joyce, whose fielding abilities at third base could charitably be called "non-existent," has the most impressive combination of plate discipline and power in the pre-1900 era. His peak walk season is 1890, his rookie year, when he led the Players' League with 123, and he topped 100 again in 1896. His lifetime 17.82 BBP is second highest in the era behind Crooks, and 11th all-time.

John McGraw hit .321 and walked 101 times at the age of 20, statistics that would place him on Bill James' All-Time All-Star Team for Age 20 if he were counting pre-1900 players. Before becoming one of the game's greatest and most infamous managers, McGraw hit .334 lifetime, and teamed with Willie Keeler to form one of the greatest hit-and-run combos ever. Due to the Orioles' dirty style of play, McGraw was often injured, but he managed to turn in two more 100+ walk seasons in 1898-99, the latter season ranking 9th all-time in single season BBP (23.71). After McGraw became a manager, he brought much of his personal offensive style to the construction of his teams. McGraw teams averaged 85.6% of the aggregate league leading total of walks for the years 1902-32, which must be fairly high on the list of managers (I haven't researched this comparison thoroughly, but I suspect that Joe McCarthy's Cubs, Yankees, and Red Sox would pull a higher percentage than McGraw's). As the numbers below indicate, there is definitely some correlation between winning and drawing walks. Oddly, though, McGraw never had a man who drew 100+ walks on any of his pennant winning teams; only Mel Ott (1929, 1930, 1932) ever broke the barrier as a McGraw protege.

PERCENTAGE OF LEAGUE LEADING WALKS, NEW YORK GIANTS, SORTED BY FINISH IN STANDINGS

BBNYG	BBNLLead	Pct	Finish
4691	5041	93.1	1
4714	5578	84.5	2
4021	5054	79.6	>2

period covered: 1902-32

The quintessential comment about Roy Thomas was made by Bill James in his superb special edition Baseball Abstract Newsletter "Leaders, Lasters, and Lists" (Volume 2, Special Edition, 1985): "If all the great leadoff men in history got together and formed a ballclub, Roy Thomas would bat leadoff." Thomas, who played most of his career with the Phillies, had six consecutive 100+ walk seasons from 1899-1904 and thus really belongs in the next section.

THE 1900's

THE PLAYERS:

Topsy Hartsel
Miller Huggins
Roy Thomas

So since he does, let's talk about him some more. Roy Thomas had virtually no power (only 10.4% of his hits went for extra-bases, the all-time low for a player appearing in more than 1400 games). He was an indifferent base stealer for a leadoff man (25 per 154 games in the dead ball era), but he had a batting strategy—fouling off pitches— that ultimately forced a major rule change (see Jim Baker's piece on Thomas in the Bill James Historical Baseball Abstract, 2nd edition, p. 413, for details). Like many of the players in his subclass, Thomas faded early. His career average up to the age of 31 is .310; after 31, .248. Seven seasons of 100+ walks, however, represent the best achievement prior to the lively ball, and his six consecutive 100+ seasons is tied for second all-time.

Once the dead ball era took hold, the type of player able to draw 100+ walks per season reverted back to those few who took pitches as an extreme strategy. In the pitcher-rich environment, walks bottomed out in the early years of the 1900's, especially in the AL. In 1905, Philadelphia Athletics left fielder Topsy Hartsel set a record for the largest gap between first and second place in walks when he drew 121 walks, 48 more than the second place finisher. (It lasted until 1923, when Babe Ruth eclipsed it with a mark that is likely never to be broken—his margin in 1923 was 72 walks!!) Hartsel was a good leadoff man, and shows up well in the Palmer-Thorn linear weights measurements during the years 1903-1907 due to his .382 OBP (compared to the 03-07 AL average of .295). Hartsel got a late start, possibly due to his size (5'5", 135 lbs.) and had what amounts to the standard eight year career for a low power, leadoff type walkman. His other big claim to fame: he scored one of the three runs that the A's managed off the Giants in the 1905 World Series.

The other walkman from the era is much better known today as the manager of the 1927 New York Yankees. Miller Huggins had three 100+ seasons, the first coming in his sophomore year with Cincinnati. After his batting average had fallen to .214 and he was sent back to the minors in 1909, he got lucky and was hooked up with Roger Bresnahan, who had left John McGraw's Giants the year before to become playing manager in St. Louis. Bresnahan had a good batting eye and was emphasizing plate discipline as a key feature of his offense: the Cardinals doubled their 1908 team walk total in Roger's first year. With Huggins installed as the leadoff man (116 walks) in 1910, St. Louis set what was then the NL record for team BB (655). Huggins took over as playing manager in 1913, had his third and last 100+ BB season in 1914, and moved to the Yankees in 1918. Babe Ruth and immortality followed him there in 1920.

THE 1910's

THE PLAYERS:

Johnny Bates
Bob Bescher
Donie Bush
Ty Cobb
Eddie Collins
Jack Graney
Miller Huggins
Babe Ruth
Jimmy Sheckard
Burt Shotton

In the full flowering of the dead ball era, a few new practitioners of the art of the walk appeared, due in no small amount to the brief offensive surge in 1911-1912. The first pair of teammates to walk 100+ times in the same year occurs in 1911, when Cincinnati outfielders Johnny Bates and Bob Bescher pull off the feat. Bescher was the leadoff man and had four effective years with the Reds, setting what was the NL record for stolen bases (81) in the same season. Oddly, Bescher stopped walking in 1914, the year he was traded to John McGraw's Giants. And once the central skills had atrophied (Bescher averaged 68 stolen bases from 1909-1912 and 90 walks from 1910-1913, his 1914 totals for New York were 38 SB and 45 BB), the slide was quick.

Johnny Bates, who batted second and hit .292 for the Reds in 1911, is one of the "fluke" members of the 100BB club: his total of 103 walks is 35 more than his next best total. Bates was a solid defender at any of the three outfield positions (he led the NL in outfield double plays in 1910), but he jumped to the Federal League in the middle of the 1914 season and wound up out of baseball at 32.

Donie Bush was the Tigers' light-hitting, slick fielding, walk-taking shortstop for more than a dozen years. Like Roy Thomas, he had very little power (14.9% of his hits were for extra bases). Bush's best walking seasons were clustered around 1911-15, when he averaged 105 walks a season. Again, the central skill faded early: at the age of 28, his walk-

taking skills declined into the 70s (average in 1916-20: 76 BB). Traded to Washington in 1922, he could not compete with the keystone combo of Harris and Peckinpaugh, and essentially retired to manage the Senators in 1923, the year before Bucky Harris led them to a World Championship.

Ty Cobb's 1915 season (118 walks) is totally out of context with the rest of his career (lifetime BBP of just 9.85). It was just another of Cobb's peachy offensive seasons, one in which he set what was for more than 45 years the stolen base record (96), and missed a Triple 100 by one RBI.

Eddie Collins had a stretch of walk-taking beginning in 1912, when he walked 101 times, through 1917 (average number of walks for the six - year period: 97). His best walk season was 1915, his first year with the White Sox, but his BA would go through its lowest five year average in the years 1915-19 before picking up again with the lively ball in the 20s.

Jack Graney, journeyman outfielder for Cleveland from 1910-1922, would be an interesting case study in how a batter can retrain himself to take walks. After averaging around 10 BBP in his first six seasons in the majors, Graney suddenly leaps to a new plateau in 1916, at the age of 30. There had been a premonition of such a jump in Graney's 1912 season (50 BB in 314 PA), but the reasons for Graney's sudden transformation are unclear. Unusually, his power totals went up along with the walks; but his BA went down, which cost him a regular job for most of 1918. He bounced back in 1919 to walk 105 times and lead the league, but it was his last full season at 33.

Jimmy Sheckard set the NL record for walks (147) in 1911, a mark that stood for more than thirty years until Eddie Stanky broke it in 1945. Sheckard's career is one of the wildest and most unpredictable of the dead ball era, with incredible peak achievements and roller coaster stats (77 SB in 1899, followed by 30, 35, and 25, then back up to 67 SB in 1903, followed by 21, 23, 30; a .353 BA in 1901, followed by .265, .332, .239, .292; 21 triples in 1901, a league leading total, followed by no more than 11 in any of the next 12 seasons). The only constant in Sheckard's career was a continuing growth in his ability to draw walks. Nothing quite prepares us for the incredible leap that Sheckard takes (an increase of 64 walks from 1910 to 1911), but at least the chart below, which shows the cumulative four year averages, clearly shows us his inexorable upward trend. Once Sheckard acquired his walk-taking skills, he lost the ability to hit for contact and average, and his speed went. By 1913, he had nothing left but walk-taking skills (.194 BA, .366 OBP), and he was finished.

Before he became well known as the man who replaced Leo Durocher as manager of the Brooklyn Dodgers in 1947, Burt Shotton was a speedy center fielder for the St. Louis Browns who had back-to-back 100+ walk seasons in 1915 and 1916. (We will see that the back-to-back phenomenon is quite common, and cuts across all classes of walkmen.) What happened to Burt is within the classic pattern. After his two big walk seasons, he lost a lot of batting average (down sixty points), lost power (just 12.4% XBH in 1917 compared to 18% in 1915-16), and lost speed (just 16 SB, down from an average of 42 SB the previous two years). Shotton was 32 when the bottom dropped out of his game. Sound familiar?

Babe Ruth had the first triple hundred in twenty-three years in 1919. Turns out that he merely pulled the pin on a very big grenade that was about to shower baseball with offense the likes of which had never been seen, not even in the middle 1890's. The Babe pulled the pin in 1919; in 1920 he exploded. As we all know, baseball hasn't been the same since.

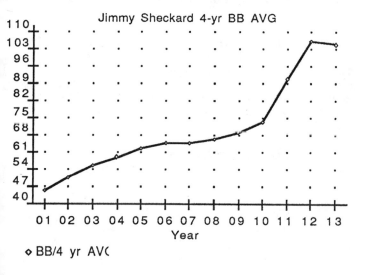

Jimmy Sheckard 4-yr BB AVG

Year

◊ BB/4 yr AVG

remaining effective into their mid-thirties. Due to the offensive explosion that began in the early 20s, though, players like Bishop and Blue had a tougher time reaching the majors at an early age: both were nearly 25 when they first made it. Blue, a personal favorite (like me, he switch-hits, but throws left, a very rare occurrence), had four 100+ walk seasons spread out between 1921 (his rookie year) and 1931. He is the first of what will become an avalanche of first basemen to belong to the BB100 club (30 total out of 141 qualifiers).

George Burns is the only player from a John McGraw pennant winning team (he played on the 1913, 1917, and 1921 Giants) to exceed a hundred walks—except that he did it after being traded to Cincinnati. He led the NL that year (1923) with 101. Previously he led the NL four times with the Giants, but with totals in the 70s and 80s. His lifetime BBP is among the lowest of the group at 10.75 (only nine members of the BB100 club have lower lifetime BBPs), and his 100+ season ranks 374th out of 377 100+ walk seasons in terms of BBP.

Before we get to the sluggers, let's talk about the most obscure and unusual of the 20s walkmen, shortstop Emory Elmo (Topper) Rigney. Bill James notes that the Topper Rigney for Buddy Myer trade, made between the Red Sox and the Senators on May 2, 1927, was one of the most lopsided in history (BJHBA, p. 133). But he didn't explore the matter past the fact that Rigney played only 45 more major league games after the trade, while Myer (also a member of the BB100 Club: he did it in 1934) became a star. His career, all 694 games of it, is strange for several reasons in addition to the 1927 trade.

Rigney came up with Detroit in 1922 (Ty Cobb was the player-manager of the Tigers) at the age of 25, and proceeded to average .301 in his first three years. 1924 was the first of his 100+ walk seasons, and what is most interesting about it is that it's clear that Rigney was not the leadoff man despite leading the team in walks. Rigney drove in 93 runs, second highest on the Tigers behind Harry Heilmann: it appears he batted fifth behind Lu Blue and Fred Haney, Heinie Manush, Cobb, and Heilmann, and was followed by Johnny Bassler, Del Pratt and Les Burke (platooning at second), and Bob (Ducky) Jones, a good-field, no-hit third baseman. (Jose Francisco Cabrera, who may or may not be the Braves' starting catcher in 1993, states in his blurb on Rigney in The Ballplayers that he batted seventh, but the run/RBI data suggests otherwise, at least for '24.) The 1924 Tigers, by the way, led the AL in runs (849), hits, doubles (their total of 315 is 26th highest all-time), BA, and walks: their pitching was nearly a run a game worse than the Senators, though, and they finished third, six games back.

The next season Rigney was benched for a shortstop named John (Jackie) Tavener, whose main skills were defensive (led the AL in double plays and in total chances per game, but not until 1926 and 1927 respectively). Rigney, only one year older than the .245 hitter Tavener, hit the pine, playing just 62 games with less than 150 ABs. He was sold to the Red Sox after the 1925 season, presumably because he was making Cobb's life miserable (which appears to be vice-versa as well, to quote Yogi Berra). The lowly Red Sox, who sold everything to the Yankees earlier in the decade and had hit rock bottom (though they will still cough up Red Ruffing to the Bronxters a few years later just for old times' sake), promptly installed Rigney at short and batted him leadoff, where he proceeded to walk 108 times, hit .270, and lead the league in assists, total chances per game, and fielding average.

So when the Senators (who had won two pennants in 1924-25, had finished eight games back in 1926, and may have still thought that they had a chance to be in the pennant race in 1927) traded Myer for Rigney, they probably thought they were getting an established shortstop to take the place of an erratic but talented youngster (Myer was a poor big league shortstop and was switched to 3B, and finally to 2B, when he was traded

THE 1920's

THE PLAYERS:

Max Bishop
Lu Blue
George Burns
Jimmie Foxx
Lou Gehrig
Rogers Hornsby
Mel Ott
Topper Rigney
Babe Ruth

The 1920's mark a return to the diversity of player type experienced in the 1890's, as the pendulum of emphasis swung wildly in the direction of offense. Over time, sluggers will start to provide the greater share of the BB100 population; in the 20's, though, there is an interesting transition toward a subclass of leadoff man whose career is sustained longer than the six-to-eight year effectiveness range seen earlier.

Max Bishop is the greatest pure walkman in the history of baseball. Only Ted Williams and Babe Ruth compare in terms of the number of single year totals in the Top 40 of 100+ walk seasons, and those two were obviously beneficiaries of many more intentional passes or walks-by-avoidance than Bishop, who had a career total of 41 homers. Five of Bishop's seven 100+ seasons rank in the Top 40; a sixth is ranked 41st—only Williams is more prevalent in the Top 40. Leading off for the powerful Philadelphia A's from 1924-33, preceding such hitters as Jimmie Foxx, Al Simmons, and Mickey Cochrane, Bishop compiled the highest ratio of runs scored per hit in 20th century baseball (.794 runs per hit) with the estimable disadvantage of hitting 673 less home runs than Babe Ruth (second at .757 runs per hit). Bishop's highest walk ratio actually came in 1934, after being traded to the Red Sox with Jimmie Foxx and Rube Walberg for immortals Bob (Junior) Kline (5.05 lifetime ERA) and Rabbit Warstler (.229 lifetime BA), but it didn't qualify for inclusion in the study due to it being a partial season (82 BB in 355 PA, 23.10 BBP). Bishop's nickname? "Camera Eye."

Both Bishop and Lu Blue, who both exceeded 100 walks in 1929 and 1931, had longer careers than the previous generation of leadoff walkmen, back to the Senators). But what happened to Rigney? As James notes, he played just 45 games for the Senators, but there is no indication why this occurred in 1927. The shortstop who replaced him, Bobby Reeves, was erratic defensively (fielding averages of .923 and .909) and was included in the deal with Boston after the 1928 season that got Myer back. The Senators didn't care: they had Joe Cronin to replace Reeves, and they wisely switched Myer to second, where he quickly turned into a standout defensive player.

But—I repeat—what happened to Rigney? He was only 30, and he was coming off a year in which he was arguably the second-best SS in the AL behind Joe Sewell. Anybody got the bug to do some research on this one??

Now to the sluggers. We'll discuss Gehrig, Foxx and Ott in the next section: most of their 100+ BB season occur in the 30s. Although we don't have the statistics to prove it, the 20s certainly saw the development of a burgeoning new strategy—intentionally walking a feared hitter. And there is no question that such a practice had a signficant impact on walk totals. The upward arc of walks allowed began in response to Babe Ruth and Rogers Hornsby, the two most devastating hitters of the 20s, and continued virtually unabated until the early 50s (save for the war years and the 1931-35 NL: there was something about the strike zone in the NL during those years, in reaction to 1930).

Hornsby, for all the terror he induced, only had one 100+ season, in 1928, when he was playing with—and subsequently managing—the lowly Boston Braves (one of the worst seventh place teams ever—50-103—saved from the cellar by a Phillies team that was even worse). I'd love to know how many intentional walks Hornsby received that year, since the Braves were not a strong hitting team by 1928 standards, especially when you take away Hornsby's .387 BA. Hornsby had evolved into a more patient hitter by this time (he led the league with 86 walks in 1927, with the third place Giants; he had 87 walks in 1929 with the pennant-winning Cubs), but the extra twenty walks probably came from the weak offensive context on the Braves.

Based on this thesis, it is interesting to look at Babe Ruth's thirteen 100+ walk seasons (of course it's the most: did you even have to ask?) in the light of BBP. Ruth's two highest BBP figures, both over 24, come in 1923 and 1920, years in which he set records for walks, the 1923 season having yet to be broken. In the 22 range are 1926, 1932, and 1934, which add credence to the "old player's skills" theory: at 37 and 39, with overall offensive skills deteriorating, the Babe becomes more selective. In the 21 range: 1924 and 1921 (we're going in descending order of BBP, not chronologically, in case you're wondering). In the 20 range: 1930, 1927, 1928. In the 19 range: 1933, 1931. Below 19 (actually, 18.95): 1919. Many people forget that Ruth actually missed 12 games in 1920, and so might have had even bigger numbers in that first incredible season with the Yankees. As it stood, Ruth's 1920 season was arguably the best ever—the OINX rating, which divides runs created per game (RC27) by batting average, rates it first at 48.64, followed by his 1921 and 1923 seasons. (Ted Williams' 1941 season rates fourth. Ruth and Williams are the only players with OINX ratings over 40: Ruth did it six times, Williams twice.)

The offensive contexts of the early 20s, if not creating the strategy of intentional walks, certainly brought it into a great deal more prominence. And it seems likely that Babe Ruth was the first target of this strategy. Ruth's BBP figures before Lou Gehrig are noticeably higher than they were with Gehrig batting behind him, which makes perfect sense, doesn't it? Prior to 1927, when Gehrig permanently became the cleanup hitter, pitchers could try to pitch around Ruth more (not that it worked, mind you). After 1927, when Ruth began to slowly decline (most sabermetricians would settle for a guy who's "fallen" from 15 RC per

game to 12, however), the BBP percentage declines due to the dropoff in IBB's.

Ruth's top five BBP seasons, by the way, are 1923 (3rd all time); 1920 (6th), 1926 (17th), 1932 (25th), and 1934 (31st). Three more (1924, 1921, and 1930) rank in the Top 50. Speaking of the Top 50, since we're roughly halfway through the biographical discussion of walkmen, let's list the Top 50 BBP seasons. This will provide a review of the ground we've just covered, and will offer a preview of some of the highlights left to come:

TOP 50 WALK-PER-100 PLATE APPEARANCE (BBP) SEASONS, 1876-1992

Year	Player	Team	L	BBP	Age
1954	Williams, Ted	BOS	A	26.05	35
1890	Robinson, Yank	PIT	P	24.82	30
1923	Ruth, Babe	NY	A	24.57	28
1987	Clark, Jack	StL	N	24.50	31
1962	Mantle, Mickey	NY	A	24.45	30
1920	Ruth, Babe	NY	A	24.42	25
1941	Williams, Ted	BOS	A	24.13	22
1990	Clark, Jack	SD	N	23.74	34
1899	McGraw, John	BAL	N	23.71	26
1957	Mantle, Mickey	NY	A	23.55	25
1947	Williams, Ted	BOS	A	23.48	28
1892	Crooks, John	StL	N	23.41	25
1946	Williams, Ted	BOS	A	23.28	27
1969	Wynn, Jim	HOU	N	23.02	27
1947	Cullenbine, Roy	DET	A	22.80	31
1956	Yost, Eddie	WAS	A	22.67	29
1926	Ruth, Babe	NY	A	22.54	31
1930	Bishop, Max	PHI	A	22.50	29
1989	Clark, Jack	SD	N	22.49	33
1926	Bishop, Max	PHI	A	22.48	26
1951	Westrum, Wes	NY	N	22.37	28
1949	Williams, Ted	BOS	A	22.25	30
1977	Tenace, Gene	SD	N	22.24	30
1985	Harrah, Toby	TEX	A	22.20	36
1932	Ruth, Babe	NY	A	22.15	37
1949	Joost, Eddie	PHI	A	22.11	33
1946	Stanky, Eddie	BKN	N	22.10	29
1957	Williams, Ted	BOS	A	22.08	38
1976	Wynn, Jim	ATL	N	22.05	34
1927	Bishop, Max	PHI	A	22.01	27
1934	Ruth, Babe	NY	A	22.01	39
1942	Williams, Ted	BOS	A	21.74	23
1970	McCovey, Willie	SF	N	21.68	32
1973	McCovey, Willie	SF	N	21.52	35
1950	Stanky, Eddie	NY	N	21.46	33
1911	Sheckard, Jimmy	CHI	N	21.43	32
1951	Williams, Ted	BOS	A	21.33	32
1933	Bishop, Max	PHI	A	21.33	32
1893	Crooks, John	StL	N	21.27	26
1929	Bishop, Max	PHI	A	21.23	28

1932	Bishop, Max	PHI	A	21.19	31
1971	Mays, Willie	SF	N	21.17	40
1992	Bonds, Barry	PIT	N	21.17	27
1924	Ruth, Babe	NY	A	21.16	29
1975	Wynn, Jim	LA	N	21.07	33
1921	Ruth, Babe	NY	A	21.05	26
1945	Stanky, Eddie	BKN	N	21.05	28
1975	Morgan, Joe	CIN	N	20.95	31
1930	Ruth, Babe	NY	A	20.80	35
1969	Killebrew, Harmon	MIN	A	20.71	33

The average age of the Top 50 100+ walk BBP players is 30.4, which is several years later than what Bill James has defined as "prime seasons" (26-29), and about a year and half older than the average of all 377 100+ walk seasons (average age: 28.9). The list certainly helps put a player like Jack Clark into sharper historical perspective, and introduces several very interesting players (Roy Cullenbine, Eddie Joost, Wes Westrum, Eddie Yost, just to name a few) whom you'll get to know better.

THE 1930's

THE PLAYERS

Luke Appling
Max Bishop
Lu Blue
Dolf Camilli
Harlond Clift
Mickey Cochrane
Frank Crosetti
Woody English
Jimmie Foxx
Lou Gehrig
Charlie Gehringer
Hank Greenberg
Buddy Myer
Mel Ott
Babe Ruth
George Selkirk
Arky Vaughan
Ted Williams
Hack Wilson

The list of walkmen has been overlapped for those players who straddle decades, so that an idea of the overall prevalence of such players can be compared from era to era. The two most plentiful decades per capita are, of course, the 30s and the 40s, with the 70s a close third due to a boost from two expansions. The thirties were the greatest hitting decade in baseball history, and this emphasis for the most part overwhelmed an admittedly secondary offensive strategy such as drawing walks.

Of the 19 players who topped 100 walks in the 30s, only five could be considered less than fearsome (Bishop, Blue, Crosetti, English, and Myer). All the rest were either great hitters for average (Appling, Gehringer, and Vaughan), various subclasses of sluggers (Camilli, Clift, Foxx, Gehrig, Greenberg, Ott, Ruth, Williams, and Wilson), or an unclassifiable hybrid (Cochrane, Selkirk). Drawing walks as an art form—as an extreme offensive strategy— went into hibernation when Max Bishop retired in 1935.

The year before Luke Appling hit .388 (1936), he drew 122 walks. Appling was considered a much more robust hitter than Max Bishop due

to his .310 lifetime average, but in fact his isolated power is less than Bishop's by nearly ten points (.088 to .097). Due to his longevity, Appling ranks 24th on the all time walk list, but his 12.82 BBP is in the bottom 4th of the walkmen group. His 1939 season is 78th on the all-time BBP list for 100+ walk seasons. Appling is also the oldest man to make the BB100 Club: the great walk spike of 1949 helped to boost him over for a third 100+ walk year at the age of 42. (It was his last full season.)

Dolf Camilli was the catalyst for what became an extended renaissance of baseball in Brooklyn. He had four 100+ seasons, three with the Dodgers (including 1941, when the Dodgers won their first pennant since 1920). Camilli was shorter than the prototypical slugger (5'10"), and made up for it by swinging hard (he also exceeded 100 strikeouts in four seasons, an unheard-of occurrence in those days). His career was shortened due not to premature aging but because he took longer to reach the majors (Camilli came up in the Cubs' organization, and they had player-manager Charlie Grimm at first). He had three triple 100s (1936, 1938, 1939), and led the NL in HR and RBI in 1941, his last 100+ walk season.

Harlond Clift is well known to the readers of BJHBA, where he was touted as one of the great lost players in the history of the game. Clift is not obscure in the pantheon of the walkmen: he had six 100+ walk seasons, five in a row from 1938-1942. Oddly, Clift is one of the few power hitters to evidence the early fade, a phenomenon almost exclusively associated with the Punch-and-Judy class of walkmen. Illnesses certainly had much to do with it, but Clift had lost most of his home run power in 1942, and may have been affected psychologically by an adversarial relationship with Luke Sewell, who became manager of the Browns modway through 1941 and was not fond of players who took too many pitches.

It would be interesting to see where in the batting order Clift was placed throughout his career. Runs/RBI data from his 1934-36 seasons suggest that he was batting leadoff; from 1937-41 it looks as though he was hitting fourth; and 1942 appears to be a return to the #1 slot.

Mickey Cochrane is one of two catchers in the history of the game to have a triple 100 to his credit. (I'll keep you guessing as to the identity of the second one for awhile.) He is also only one of two catchers to have had multiple 100+ walk seasons (yes, you're gonna have to guess this one two).

Frank Crosetti had three big walk seasons in 1936-38, culminating with 105 in '38. After that year, Crosetti had a carrer average of just .225— except that the Yankees, unlike other teams who jettisoned their fading walkmen, kept playing him.

Woody English had his lone 100+ walk season in the Year of the Hitter (1930), a season which was by far his best in the majors. English scored 152 runs partially due to his fluke walk season, but also because he had hitters like Riggs Stephenson and Hack Wilson (also a 100+ walkman for the only time in 1930) batting behind him. English is another of the "fluke" players on the list: his second best walk total is 68, and even the lone 100+ walk season (exactly 100) ranks 376th out of 377 player seasons in terms of BBP.

Jimmie Foxx was plenty scary enough at the plate to get his walk totals over a hundred almost perennially (he made it seven times, and was in the 90s four more times). Foxx had three 100+ walk seasons in a row ('34-'36) and missed by one walk in 1937 of making it five in a row.

Lou Gehrig was not the walker Babe Ruth was: only one of his 100+ seasons ranks in the Top 100 (1935, the first year Ruth was no longer in the lineup). Gehrig's highest BBP figues all occur in the first three seasons after the Babe. Stands to reason, doesn't it? It's hard to downplay a man who exceeded 100 walks eleven times, but the majority of Gehrig's 100+ years rank in the bottom fourth of all walkmen.

Charlie Gehringer took to walking late in his career (his first 100+ season came at the age of 35). Neither season was among his best from a total offensive standpoint, but I wouldn't mind having a season like 1938, with 133 runs scored, 107 RBI, 57 extra base hits—pluz the man could play some second base, too.

Hank Greenberg had back-to-back walk seasons in 1937 and 1938, two years that couldn't have been more different despite being just a fifteenth of a run apart in terms of RC27. In 1937 Greenberg still had speed and his secondary power (ability to hit doubles and triples—49 and 14, respectively). In 1938 Hammerin' Hank had just 23 doubles, 4 triples, and 58 homers. The only thing consistent about the two years was that no one really wanted to pitch to him (102 and 119 walks). Greenberg's third 100+ BB season occurred nine years later in Pittsburgh, which makes him one of four players to walk 100 or more times in their last season in the majors. (Who are the other three? One is Jim McTamany. The other two we have yet to meet: but a clue for one of them is that he achieved this curious feat in the same year as Greenberg.)

When we last saw Buddy Myer, he was an erratic young shortstop. By the time we see him in the BB100 Club he has long since become the second best second basemen of the decade (hard to go against Gehringer, as Bill James suggests). Myer suddenly turns on the strike-zone judgement at the age of 30: from 1934 on, his BBP is over 15. What was that phrase—"old players' skills"?

Mel Ott, the smallest big slugger in baseball history at 5'9", 170 lbs, took advantage of his size in a way similar to that of Jimmie Wynn. He had ten 100+ walks seasons from 1929 to 1942, and came close (95 and 90) in the war years. By the end of the thirties the Giants are beginning to run out of steam, and are entering into a fourteen year lull between pennants. Ott didn't have much behind him after 1938: a lot of those records where he was walked seven times in a doubleheader happened in this time frame.

George Selkirk's fame as a player stemmed from being the man who replaced Babe Ruth. He should also be remembered as the only platoon player ever to score a Triple 100 (in 1939, also his only 100+ walk season). Selkirk, with the mystifying nickname of "Twinkletoes," started demonstrating strike-zone judgement in his sophomore year (1936), and hit the jackpot in 1939. But Selkirk, like Harlond Clift, faded early: after his great 1939, he stalled, then crashed to earth in 1941 (.220). He went into the military service in the middle of 1942 and never came back to the big leagues as a player. His lone 100+ walk season is good for 76th on the all-time list.

Arky Vaughan topped 100 walks for the first time the year after he hit .385 (is it any surprise?). Bill James rightly lists him as the best shortstop of the thirties. His walk totals peaked in the mid-thirties, when he led the NL three straight years (1934-36), although only one of those seasons ('36) was above 100. Vaughn is pretty much an exception to the rule that players walk more as they get older: his last three full seasons before temporarily retiring in 1944 are back at the level of his first two seasons in 1932-33.

You would think that a fellow Hack Wilson's size (5'6") would be able to draw a lot of walks. But with the exception of 1930, the year of 191 RBI, the original Hackman (take that, Jeffrey Leonard) had no better than above average walk totals. His lone 100+ season ranks 346th in BBP.

Ted Williams? One of only three men to exceed 100 walks in three decades. (Who do you think the other two are? I'll tell you—in the next decade...)

THE 1940's

THE PLAYERS:

Luke Appling
Dolf Camilli
Harlond Clift
Roy Cullenbine
Dom DiMaggio
Bob Elliott
Ferris Fain
Elbie Fletcher
Jimmie Foxx
Augie Galan
Charlie Gehringer
Eddie Joost
Charlie Keller
Ralph Kiner
Eddie Lake
Cass Michaels
Stan Musial
Mel Ott
Johnny Pesky
Pee Wee Reese
Eddie Stanky
Vern Stephens
Elmer Valo
Ted Williams

The forties, especially the late forties, were the halcyon days of the base on balls. Particularly in the American League. In 1949 the American League as a whole averaged 703 walks per team, which is the highest league average in the history of baseball. The 1992 Oakland A's, who walked a ton by present-day standards, led the AL with 707 walks. They would have been just about average in 1949.

What caused the "walk spike" of the late forties? Craig Wright and Bill James have offered some ideas, but they don't seem particularly convincing. Craig suggested that the AL pitchers became excessively cautious in light of the rise in home runs that occurred right after the war, which would explain the difference in walks. Except that the walk totals in the AL had been consistently higher than the NL since the middle of the dead ball era (except for 1928-29 and during the Second World War). When the AL went on its three year spike (654, 703, and 675 league average in '48-'50), the NL stayed flat (around 550 per team).

The NL HR total nearly doubled from 1946 to 1950 as a new style of hitting emerged, coupled with the fact that the post-war player could reach the seats more often in the 20-to-40 year old ballparks. The AL HR total increased earlier (the big jump, as can be seen in the figure below, came a year earlier in the AL than in the NL), and didn't quite get as out of control as in the NL. Was it because of the extra walks?

Well, maybe. But the figure below also shows that such a strategy, if it was in fact employed, was a resounding failure in terms of preventing runs. In the four years between 1948-1951, the NL outhomered the AL by more than 600 homers, an average of 150+ more per year. The AL drew 3461 more walks in those same four years, an average of 865 more walks per year. Who scored more runs in those four years? The AL, by about 275 runs per year.

HOME RUNS, WALKS, & RUNS SCORED
NL VS. AL, 1945-1952

Year	HR NL	HR AL	BB NL	BB AL	R NL	R AL
1945	577	430	4151	4145	5512	4774
1946	562	653	4379	4404	4916	5037
1947	886	679	4464	4745	5666	5161
1948	845	710	4396	5232	5487	5841
1949	935	769	4393	5627	5650	5776
1950	1100	973	4537	5418	5760	6253
1951	1024	839	4379	4889	5552	5716
1952	907	794	4147	4630	5158	5191

NOTE: League totals for 8 teams

James surmises (BJHBA, pp. 180-82) a generational shift in pitchers from the Bob Feller-type (high walks) to the Robin Roberts type (less smoke, more control). This suggestion, which tries to cover the development of a trend and its ebbing away, is very sketchy at best, doesn't address the difference between the two leagues, and simply doesn't hold up if you go back and look at Roberts' BB/9 numbers from the same time period. As a rookie in 1948, Roberts walked nearly 4 men a game; by 1952 he was down to less than 2 per game. So Robin Roberts himself did not start out as a "Robin Roberts-type of pitcher," which kind of shoots Bill's thesis in the foot.

The general trend toward hitting more and more homers, as Bill does note, is probably the key to the reversal, added to the fact that a lot of managers didn't like it when their hitters took so many pitches and worked for walks. It wasn't macho to take pitches, you're supposed to want to hit. (I hear this in slow-pitch softball all the time: stud or not, I'll take the walk if the pitcher gives it to me.) The home run craze may have gotten the better of the hitters, plus the consistent increase in night games as the fifties proceeded must have taken its toll on walks (not only can you not hit what you can't see, as Honus Wagner suggested, but you can't take what you can't see either). The "close your eyes and swing" approach began to prevail more and more, until even 155-lb. second basemen were shooting for the fences when they should have been keeping their bats on their shoulders.

But all that was in the future. The forties were it for depth, breadth, and sheer variety of walkmen. The transitional nature of the game allowed for the brief flowering of an alternate offensive strategy; as with some of the players we encountered in the dead ball era, the flexibility of the offensive context allowed certain hitters to survive and thrive in ways that would have been far less likely in the twenties and thirties.

But managers were still not enamored with the strategy. Roy Cullenbine was called the "laziest human being you ever saw" by Bill DeWitt, owner of the St. Louis Browns from 1936 to 1951. "[Luke] Sewell (manager of the Browns from 1941 to 1946) would give him the hit sign and he'd take it, trying to get the base on balls." Bill Mead, who quoted De Witt in Even the Browns, goes on to note that Cullenbine drew "an astounding number of walks for a man who was neither a leadoff hitter not the kind of power hitter than frightened pitchers."

Obviously, DeWitt is engaging in standard baseball-style exaggeration when he states that Cullenbine "wouldn't swing the bat": Cullenbine's lifetime BBP is 18.01, which means that he did swing the bat more than 80% of the time. There is, as noted earlier, a macho aversion to taking pitches. (You've heard it on the sandlot—"He doesn't want to swing", "He's a looker"—and from the broadcast booth—"You can't walk off

the island"—explaining, with more than a bit of approval in the tone of voice, why players from the Dominican Republic tend to swing at anything.) Cullenbine appears to have suffered from that aversion during his career; it is probably the reason why his career ended prematurely at 33. In his ten year career, Cullenbine played for six different teams (including one team, the Tigers, twice: he started and ended his big league career in Detroit).

As with many of the "misfit" players with strike zone judgement, Cullenbine had hot and cold years, but from 1941 to 1946 he was an extremely potent hitter, averaging .294 with 28 doubles, four triples, and twelve homers, scoring and driving in 75 runs per year, and averaging 101 walks per season. But the type of response to Cullenbine's hitting style that was prevalent even in an AL environment that was beginning to permit, even encourage, the drawing of bases on balls, is summed up by his 1945 season, where he was traded by the Indians to the Tigers in late April after just eight games. At that point in time, Cullenbine was hitting .077 (1-for-13), but he had drawn 11 walks and so was the possessor of a .500 OBP. Evidently it was important to get the immortal Felix Mackiewicz (?) into the lineup, plus there was a hole at third base that developed in 1945 when Ken Keltner went into military service. (Never mind that Cullenbine had led the team in runs and homers in 1944.)

Cullenbine's biggest walk season was both his strangest and his last. Brock Hanke made an interesting point when we discussed the bizarre 1947 season, in which he wondered how many players hit their highest number of home runs in what ends up being their final season. For that is exactly what Roy Cullenbine did: he hit 24 homers for the Tigers in 1947, but hit just .224 and was cut loose, never playing another game in the majors. When one looks at his line in Macmillan, one sees that he hit .335 the year before, so one probably concludes that the Tigers decided he was washed up. But Cullenbine also drove in 78 runs, scored 82, and drew 137 walks (second behind Ted Williams' 162). His OBP, even with the low BA, was .401!! How could anyone decide that he was so completely through that they wouldn't even give him another chance at the major league level, especially when he had hit over .300 the year before? The only explanation is the age-old prejudice against secondary offensive skills, as examplified by Bill DeWitt's evaluation of Cullenbine quoted above.

Maybe Cullenbine was a pop-off: maybe he reacted even more strongly to the prevailing prejudice than I do when playing slow-pitch softball. (When I walked seven times in one doubleheader, there were a lot of guys looking daggers at me: I looked them right back.) Maybe he was derisive about the ribbings he got—I don't know. But I don't think I would have been as hasty as the Tigers seem to have been in letting Cullenbine go after the 1947 season. (But, then again, I have the hindsight to know that the next three years in the AL were the three greatest seasons for walks in the history of baseball, and that the Tigers would play the following immortals at first base in 1948-50: George Vico, Paul Campbell, and Don Kolloway.)

Of the three DiMaggio brothers, only Dominic (the runt of the family at 5'9") was inclined toward serious plate discipline. Big brother Joe's highest walk total was 80, coming in his second-to-last season (1950)—though if he'd been healthy for the entire 1949 season, he might have cracked the 100 barrier (55 BB in 76 games during that record BB year). Dom walked 90 times in his sophomore season (1941), but didn't approach 100 again until he cracked the barrier in 1948 with 101. He probably would have repeated in '49, but he missed 10 games and wound up with 96. After that, his walk totals receded as the league totals declined: in 1952, his last full season, he had only 57 walks in 543 plate appearances. Dom's 1948 season ranks 378th, or dead last, among the 141 walkmen.

- 37 -

Bob Elliott's walk totals took a sudden leap when he was traded from the Pittsburgh Pirates to the Boston Braves after the 1946 season. Part of it doubtless had to do with the increased power that Elliott acquired due to playing in Boston's Braves Field (Elliott averaged 6 homers per season in his 7 years with the Pirates; his five-year average for Boston was 20). In 1948, Elliott was as instrumental as Spahn, Sain, and the two days of rain in getting the Braves into the World Series, as he hit 23 home runs, had 113 RBI, and drew a league-leading 131 walks. It was a one-year peak good enough to rank 85th all-time in BBP, but Elliott's lifetime BBP (11.93) is undistinguished in this rarefied company.

Ferris Fain, however, was totally rarefied in this group: ol' Burrhead, as he was called, has the sixth highest lifetime BBP in major league history (fifth if we discount Frank Thomas). He had five 100+ BB seasons, three of them in a row from 1948-50 (during the AL walk spike). Strangely, he was not a leadoff hitter, for he came up for a team (the Philadelphia Athletics) already possessed of walkmen (Eddie Joost and Elmer Valo, whom we'll meet shortly).

In 1948, the numbers tell us that Joost, Valo, and veteran leadoff man Barney McCosky (.326 with 68 BB) were the top of the lineup hitters. Fain probably batted fifth behind Hank Majeski (120 RBI—but who knows how many runs Majeski would have driven in if Mack had flip-flopped him with Fain). In 1949, it appears that Mack moved rookie Nellie Fox into the leadoff role midway through the year, with Valo and Joost each dropping down a notch. Fain, with 136 walks, probably batted fifth again. In 1950, the A's crashed, losing 29 more games than the year before: Fain, with 133 walks, had exactly the same number of runs scored as RBI (83). The leadoff men? Probably third baseman Bob Dillinger, before he was sold to the Pittsburgh Pirates for $35,000 in July, and 39-year-old Wally Moses. (Mack, in a fit of senility, had traded Nellie Fox to the White Sox for the unforgettable Joe Tipton.)

Fain won the first of his two batting titles in 1951, hitting .344, and would have had a sixth 100+ BB season except that he broke a foot and missed 37 games. He repeated as batting champ in 1952 (.327), drawing 105 walks and batting leadoff (!!) at least part of the time. He was rewarded for this by being traded to the White Sox, who probably thought that they could win the pennant. But Fain slumped to .256, although he did walk 108 times.

A knee injury limited him to just 65 games in 1954, and he was traded to Detroit. There Fain began a season that should be reconstructed if only to savor its ineffable strangeness. In 58 games with Detroit (but only appearing part-time due to the effects of the knee injury), Fain walked 52 times in 192 plate appearances, or a little over 27% of the time—slightly higher than the all-time record BBP (Ted Williams in the previous season—1954—26.05). Fain is on base at least 89 times for the Tigers and scores 23 runs. Despite an OBP of .464, he is released. Released!!

He hooks on with the Indians, who are struggling to keep pace with the Yankees after their 111-win season the year before and have a hole at first due to Vic Wertz' illness. Fain, platooned with Al Rosen (we'll meet him later) and then with 23-year old Joe Altobelli, walks 40 times in 158 plate appearances. He reaches base 72 times for the Indians—and scores 9 runs. That is no misprint. N-I-N-E. For the year, Fain has been on base 161 times and has scored 32 runs. After a season like that, I think I would have retired, too. (Where did they bat him? Probably seventh—in front of good-field, no-hit eighth hitters like George Strickland—.209 for the Indians—and Fred Hatfield—.232 for the Tigers. The box scores for the 1955 season must have been priceless.)

Part of Fain's problem, as was the case for several other walkmen, was that he was a first baseman with little power in an age that was increasingly demanding power from that position. Another player whose career was curtailed in this way was Elbie Fletcher, who had four 100+ walk seasons for the Pittsburgh Pirates from 1940 to 1946, including three in a row (1940-42). Fletcher's best all-around year was probably 1940, when he also hit 16 HR and drove in 104 runs; but he wasn't able to sustain such power, falling back into single figures in 1942-3 before spending the next two years in the military. Fletcher slumped to .256 with just 4 homers in 1946, and despite 111 walks, he was made into a part-time player the next season and wound up in the minors in 1948. A shoulder injury to Earl Torgeson (another future walkman) gave Fletcher a last lease on life in the big leagues in 1949, and he turned in a representative Fletcher season (.262, 11 homers, 84 walks in 497 plate appearances), but there was no work in the big leagues for the 33-year old the next year.

Another first baseman who ran into this difficulty was Les Fleming, whose entire career was squeezed by the war. Fleming came up in the Detroit organization, which made it hard to get much attention at first base (a couple of fellows named Greenberg and York saw to that). It wasn't until 1942, when he was 26, that Fleming got a chance to play full-time—but with the Indians. He hit .292, with 14 homers and 82 RBI, and drew 106 walks. But then military service got in the way: Fleming returned late in the 1945 season and hit .329 in 40 games, but in 1946 he didn't get to play full time, for reasons that are difficult to isolate. His partial season numbers in '46 are not far off from his 1942 season, but something wasn't right. The next season Fleming was pushed aside by Eddie Robinson (the same Eddie Robinson traded for Cass Michaels in 1950), who had a better home run stroke. Fleming's average skidded to .242, and he wound up in the minors the next year, resurfacing only for a brief cup of coffee with the Pirates in 1949. Fleming was one of those players who was really hurt by the war, as it took his prime seasons away from him, the years that might have established his reputation.

As we have seen earlier, some walkmen have pronounced tendencies for up-and-down seasons. Augie Galan qualifies as a member of this subclass. One can discount some of Galan's rollercoaster stats to injuries (he suffered a broken foot in 1940 that took three years to really mend), but he was up-and-down before that, going from .314 and 203 hits in his first full year (1935) to .252 two years later. It is only after the Cubs have given up on him that he becomes part of our story. In 1943, finally recovered from his injuries and playing full-time for the Dodgers in a war-weakened National League, Galan returns to form and has the first of three consecutive 100+ BB seasons. It appears that he batted third in the Dodgers' war year lineups.

Eddie Joost you may remember from the earlier discussion about Ferris Fain. Joost was an embattled player who didn't find himself until he was after 30: his early years with the Reds and Braves were nightmarish (45 errors at SS in 1941 and 1942, .185 BA for Boston in 1943). After voluntarily retiring in 1944, and a comeback aborted by injuries in 1945, Joost escaped the minors in 1947 and landed with the Philadelphia A's. Although he hit only .206 in 1947, Joost drew 114 walks, the first of six consecutive 100+ walk seasons he would have for the A's. In 1948, Joost, Fain, Valo, McCosky, and Hank Majeski kept the A's afloat in the pennant race until mid-August; the Mackmen eventually finished fourth. Joost, Fain, and Valo twice drew 100+ walks in the same season (1949 and 1952), the only trio to do it more than once. Joost's best all-around season, in opposition to one prominent walkman pattern, came at the age of 35 (1951), when he hit .289, with 19 HR, 78 RBI, 107 runs, and 106 walks.

Charlie (King Kong) Keller was a terror for about six and a half seasons for the New York Yankees, primarily in the early '40s. Keller had back-to-back triple 100's in 1941-42, and just missed in 1946, his last full season before back miseries curtailed his career. Bill James ranked him

52nd in peak value for all players in baseball history (BJHBA, p. 449), although he erroneously lists him among the right fielders. Because of his congenital back problem, Keller only had 759 plate appearances after the age of 30. When you take a look at Keller's seasons, and you stack DiMaggio, Tommy Henrich, Joe Gordon, Phil Rizzuto, and Bill Dickey next to him, it's little wonder that the Yankees won by 17 games in 1941, 10 games in 1942, and 14 games in 1943. James considers the outfield of Keller, DiMaggio and Henrich the greatest to ever play together; it's hard to disagree. Keller, who had five 100+ BB seasons (four in a row between 1940-43), never had any monster BBP's—just a solid 17% in virtually every season. He'd be an Inner Circle Hall of Famer if he'd stayed healthy; as it is, I think he should be in the Hall just on what he did before he was hurt.

The great Pirate slugger Ralph Kiner straddles the late forties and early fifties. It would be interesting to see how many times Kiner was walked intentionally, especially when you take into account that during the eight seasons that Kiner was with the Pirates (1946-1953) their record was 492-739 (.400). Kiner's best BBP came in a year (1951) when the Pirates managed to finish seventh; his best overall season in 1949 (.310, 54 homers) saw the Bucs leap all the way to sixth place. You have to figure that a quarter of his walks were intentional.

The second of the four Eddie guys in the walkmen club is a fellow with the last name of Lake. Like Joost, Lake had a terrible time getting started: some memorable batting averages dot his record, such as .105 (8-for-76) with the Cardinals in 1941, and .199 with the Red Sox in 1943. The Red Sox were so concerned about his hitting that they experimented with making him into a pitcher the next year. In 1945, however, when Bobby Doerr, the last of the Red Sox stars, was drafted, Lake finally got a full shot and made the most of it, hitting .279. He also drew 106 walks. The Detroit Tigers were sufficiently impressed to trade Rudy York to the Red Sox over the offseason to acquire Lake. York drove in 119 runs as Boston went to the World Series; Lake walked 103 times, but his BA dropped to .254, and Detroit, World Champs the year before, finished second, 12 games back. Lake added a third 100+ walk season in 1947 (teaming with Roy Cullenbine), but his average fell back to .211. Switched to second base the next year, he suffered a broken finger and missed more than half the season; in 1949, he lost his hitting stroke entirely (.196) and was released early in 1950 at the age of 34.

Cass Michaels is a fluke member of the walkmen, cracking the 100 BB barrier in 1949, the year of the spike. Michaels had begun as a teenaged shortstop for the White Sox, debuting at 17 during the height of World War II. He bounced around for about five years as a utility man for the Pale Hose, but in 1949 new manager Jack Onslow handed him the second base job and Michaels responded with a performance that is the epitome of the term "career year." Michaels achieved personal highs in hits, doubles, triples, runs scored, RBI (83), BB (101), BA (.308), SA, and OBP. But over the winter of 1949, the White Sox acquired Nellie Fox. The Pale Hose needed some punch at first base (their top two first sackers had combined for a grand total of two homers in 1949), and so on May 31, 1950, they packed up Michaels (hitting .312 at the time) and sent him to Washington for Eddie Robinson.

It turned out to be a good deal for the White Sox: Robinson hit 20 homers after joining the Pale Hose in 1950, hit 29 homers the next year, had 22 homers and 104 RBI in 1952 as Chicago moved up to third under Paul Richards. Michaels just sort of faded back to the level he had been at prior to his career year, and—ironically—wound up back with the Sox in 1954 as their third baseman, only to have his career ended prematurely when he was beaned by the Philadelphia A's Marion Fricano on August 27, 1954. Michaels sustained a double fracture of the skull and suffered from impaired vision as a result of the beaning: he was only 28 when he was forced to retire.

The first of Stan Musial's three 100+ walk seasons came—not surprisingly—the year after his career season in 1948, when he hit .376 and narrowly missed the Triple Crown. 1949 brought the Man's walk totals to a new plateau, and he averaged 99 walks a year from 1949 to 1954 before his totals dipped back into the 70s and 80s. Musial was not a great walkman—his individual BBP's for his 100+ walk seasons all rank in the bottom 50 of the walkmen, and were doubtless inflated due to pitcher fear.

Johnny Pesky was the reason why the Red Sox were so willing to part with Eddie Lake. Pesky's first three years in the big leagues were all 200-hit seasons—the only other person to do it was Lloyd Waner. Unlike Waner, though, Pesky could also draw a walk: his totals improved dramatically until he peaked with two 100+ seasons in 1949-50 (a natural enough point in time to do it, as you doubtless understand by now). By this point Pesky had been shifted to third to make room for Vern Stephens, but he was moved back in 1951. The bottom fell out of his hitting in the following year and he was traded to Detroit, where he stopped walking and stopped hitting: he was finished at 35 (in 1954).

The first inkling that Pee Wee Reese was going to turn into a good hitter came in 1942, when he walked 82 times and nudged his batting average back over .250. After three years off for the war, Reese returned as a solid, crafty hitter, leading the league in walks with 104 in 1947 while batting low in the order (Jackie Robinson and Eddie Stanky batted 1-2 for the Dodgers that year). Shifted to leadoff in 1949, Reese responded with his second 100+ walk season (116) and led the league in runs scored with 132. He turned into a steady, long-lived hitter who averaged .275 with 85 walks and 90-100 runs scored for about another decade—a definite Middle Circle Hall of Famer.

The third Eddie—Eddie Stanky—shares the record for the most number of teams played for while drawing 100+ walks. The number is three, and the other recordholders are Roy Cullenbine, Bill Joyce, Darrell Evans, and Jimmie Wynn. He still shares the NL record for walks (148) with Wynn. Three of his individual season BBPs rank in the top 50 all time (1945—the record walk year; 1946; and 1950). His lifetime BBP ranks fourth all-time behind Williams, Bishop, and Ruth. Like many of the leadoff class of walkmen, he arrived in the majors late (26 in his rookie season of 1945); unlike some in this class who faded early, Stanky chose to curtail his career when he became manager of the Cardinals in 1952, the year after he helped the Giants overcome a 13 1/2 game deficit by drawing 127 walks in his sixth 100+ BB season.

Vern Stephens is another member of the "fluke" group of walkmen: his walk totals jumped up dramatically just as the AL walk spike was beginning (in 1947) and fell back down with equal drama as the walk mania began to subside in 1950. His 1949 season, with 101 walks in 711 plate appearances, ranks 371st out of 377 100+ walk seasons. At 5'10", he should have walked more than he did.

Elmer Valo probably could have had several more 100+ walk seasons if he hadn't been platooned so much during his career. In twenty seasons, Valo had more than 500 plate appearances in only four years. In 1952, Valo had less than 500 plate appearances (489 to be exact), but still managed to draw 101 walks: his BBP for that year ranks 52nd all-time. Fittingly, Valo had more walks (91) than hits (90) as a pinch-hitter. He twice combined with Eddie Joost and Ferris Fain to comprise a trio of 100+ walkers on a single team (1949, 1952). Valo's career was extremely consistent: when you break it down by decades, he hit .284 in the 40s, and .285 in the 50s. He had 689 hits in the 40s, with 436 walks; in the 50s, he had 700 hits and 477 walks. The only unusual thing is that he walked a bit more frequently in the walk-declining 50s (16.26 BBP vs. 15.21 in the 40s), but we can attribute the "old player's skills" component of career dynamics to be the cause of this.

The greatest walker of all time? There is no doubt: Theodore Samuel Williams. Ruth may have had more 100+ walk seasons (13 to 11), but he didn't miss five years out of his prime, either. (It is hard to say what Ruth's batting numbers might have looked like had he began his career as an outfielder in, say, 1915: but it is likely that he would have added only one or two more 100+ walk seasons during that four-year span. Williams was a virtual lock for 100+ BB in 43-45 and 52-53, was a lock in 1950 and 1955 until injured, and just missed in 1940 and 1958, so we can project him for a hypothetical minimum of sixteen 100+ seasons, at least one more than what we can reasonably project for Ruth).

Eight of Williams' 11 100+ BB seasons rank in the Top 40 for BBP, including #1 (1954, the year the rules cheated him out of an seventh batting title), #7 (1941—you know about that year); #11 (1947—162 walks); #13 (1946— 156 walks to go with 37 doubles, 7 triples, and 38 homers: is it any wonder they walked him?). Nine of Williams' 100+ BB seasons are over 20% BBP (Ruth had ten). Williams ranks first in lifetime BBP at 20.76, a figure that would place him 49th on the single-season BBP list.

Williams' 162 walks was the anchor for the greatest walking team of all time: the 1949 Boston Red Sox, one of four teams to ever have three 100+ walk players in a single season. (Vern Stephens and Johnny Pesky were the other two; Dom DiMaggio had 96 and missed nine games during the year—if he'd made it over 100, the Red Sox would be the only team in history to have four 100+ walkers.) The Red Sox' 835 walks exceeded their own record of 823 set the previous year. No one else has ever cracked the 800 barrier.

As mentioned earlier, the manager most attuned to the value of the base on balls was Joe McCarthy (the honorary manager of the Bill James Winter Game entry the Tokyo Walkmen—more about them later). McCarthy's teams led the league in walks 14 times in 23 seasons. He won pennants with seven of those teams (two non-leaders in BB—1941 and 1942 Yankees—also won), and came damn close with three others (1930 Cubs, 1948-49 Red Sox). His "percentage of league leading walks" (see the discussion concerning John McGraw above) is a little over 90%, which must be the all-time high for managers with more than 1000 games managed. There is little question that the 1948-49 Red Sox were encouraged to be patient at the plate: the results can be seen in the record book.

Oh yeah—I promised to tell you who the other players who drew 100+ walks in three decades are, didn't I? The answers: Jimmie Foxx and Mel Ott.

THE 1950's

THE PLAYERS:

Richie Ashburn
Larry Doby
Ferris Fain
Jim Gilliam
Gil Hodges
Eddie Joost
Ralph Kiner
Mickey Mantle
Eddie Mathews
Stan Musial
Jackie Robinson
Al Rosen
Roy Sievers
Duke Snider
Eddie Stanky
Earl Torgeson
Wes Westrum
Ted Williams
Eddie Yost

While there was a notable overall decline in walks during the 50s, we must put this in the context of the walk spike of the late 40s and note that the 50s were still a pretty fair walking decade. Many of the players who are on the BB100 list in the fifties began their careers in the immediate post-war years, when walking was a major rage. Ashburn, Doby, Hodges, Robinson, Rosen, Sievers, Snider, Torgeson, Westrum and Yost, players who first crack the 100 BB list in the 50s, all began their major league careers in the late 40s, and so can be considered holdovers from that era. Only Mantle, Mathews, and Gilliam are players who begin their careers in the fifties; Gilliam, who was a good but not great walker, cracked 100 BB only once, in his rookie year (another singular occurrence).

Ashburn and Yost, the alphabetical bookends of the 50s list, are the only long-term leadoff men on the list. (Gilliam spent only the early years of his career batting leadoff, eventually becoming a leadoff-style #2 hitter for the LA incarnation of the Dodgers). All of the rest of these players are sluggers, even Westrum, who might be considered as the evolutionary precursor to Gene Tenace.

The big new walk stars of the decade are Mantle and Mathews. Mantle's ten 100+ walk seasons are evenly split between the 50s and 60s, though there isn't much question as to which decade is better in an overall offensive sense (the 50s, by a wide margin). Mantle's biggest walk seasons come in 1962 (5th highest BBP all-time) and 1957 (146 walks, 10th highest BBP all-time.) Because he batted third on a Yankee team that in the late fifties was not blessed with good leadoff men, he missed many chances to have Triple 100's due to subpar RBI totals (he made it in 1954, 1956, and 1961; his near misses, all due to sub-100 RBI totals, occur in 1955, 1957, 1958, and 1960). Mantle's ability to draw walks was not solely due to pitcher fear: his last two 100+ walk seasons occur in his last two seasons, when the rest of his offensive skills had clearly atrophied. He is the fourth player to draw 100+ walks in his final season in the big leagues (the other three were—remember?—McTamany, Greenberg, and Cullenbine). His lifetime BBP of 17.63 ranks twelfth all-time.

Mathews was not as prolific a walker as Mantle, but he was no slouch. His biggest walk seasons come before the advent of Henry Aaron (1954-55). Consistently in the 80s and 90s through the fifties, Mathews led the NL in walks for three straight seasons (1961-63), the last two producing his final 100+ seasons. One suspects that the emergence of Darrell Evans as a walking man might have had something to do with the influence of Mathews, who managed him during his breakout years (1972-74).

The other major walkman of the period is Eddie Yost—the fourth Eddie. Yost compiled eight 100+ BB seasons between 1950 and 1960, thus earning his well-known nickname ("The Walking Man"). Yost didn't show much propensity for walking in his rookie season (1947), but his totals shot up in conjunction with the walk spike (82 in '48, 92 in '49), and he perfected his technique in 1950, beginning a string of five straight 100+ seasons. His all-time high in walks (151) came in 1956, which is also his high mark for single-season BBP (22.67, 16th all time). Traded from the Senators to Detroit in 1959, he responded with two more 100+ BB seasons for the Tigers in 1959-60. Drafted by the Los Angeles Angels in 1961, he fell apart, partially due to a broken hand, hit just .202, and was finished at the age of 35. But his lifetime BBP (18.01) ranks eighth all-time, and it is his name more than any other individual which has become synonymous with drawing walks. (What else did they have to write about the Senators in the early to mid-fifties, anyway? From 1950-56, they were 461-615, a .428 winning percentage.)

Richie Ashburn is unusual in that his walk totals do not shoot up until well into the fifties. 1954 marks a turning point for Ashburn: he begins to walk significantly more often. From 1948 to 1953, Ashburn's BBP is 9.26; from 1954 to 1962, it's 14.84. His three 100+ seasons all occur in the fifties, two of them back-to-back in 1954-55 (there's that repeating pattern again). Ashburn has a profile quite similar to modern-day walkman Brett Butler, who's a bit overrated by sabermetricians who haven't done their homework. Ashburn has twenty points of BA and OBP on Butler, and he was a better center fielder. Ashburn retired early at 35 with 2574 hits; if he'd been motivated, he had a real good shot at 3000.

Most of the remaining members of the BB100 list in the 50s are one-shots, with the exception of Kiner, Fain, Joost, Musial, Stanky, and Williams, all holdovers from the 40s. One exception is Larry Doby, who started his career in 1947 but didn't crack the 100 barrier until 1951 (he had 91 in 1949, and 98 in 1950). Doby had two 100+ walk seasons, and a total of four in the 90s.

The other is Earl Torgeson, a big (6'3"), hulking (220 lbs.) first baseman who walked a ton for the Boston Braves in the late forties and early fifties. Torgeson put two 100+ walk years together back-to-back in 1950 and 1951. These two seasons, coming at the ages of 26 and 27, were easily his best years; by the middle of 1952, he had lost a good bit of his hitting edge and became a platoon player for the rest of his career. His most bizarre season came late in his career, in 1959, when he platooned with Ted Kluszewski and a young Norm Cash on the Go-Go White Sox. Torgeson hit just .220, but had an RBI/TB ratio of .460 (incredibly high) and drew 62 walks in 339 plate appearances (18.28 BBP). His 1960 season as a pinch hitter was even wilder: he drew 21 walks in 78 plate appearances (26.92%), right up at the theoretical limit as defined by the database. From 1956-60 he was one of the best pinch-hitters in the game (44-for-144, .305). An interesting character...

The one-shot wonders? They include several justly enshrined Brooklyn Dodgers (Duke Snider, Jackie Robinson, Gil Hodges), the fascinatingly strange journeyman Roy Sievers (whose lone 100-walk season came in an off-year before his two-season homer explosion in 1957-58), and the underrated, career-shortened-by-injury Al Rosen.

But the most interesting of the one-shots is undoubtedly Wes Westrum, the .217 hitting catcher mentioned earlier as the prototype for Gene Tenace. Westrum was not much of a hitter, but he had tremendous strike zone judgement: his lifetime BBP is 17.40, which ranks 15th all-time.

Brock Hanke named a new statistic after him: the Westrum Ratio measures the amount of a player's runs created that is generated through homers and walks. Westrum's ratio is the highest of all the walkmen at 5.99. Nobody is even close, partially because Westrum's lifetime BA is so low.

Westrum was a great defensive catcher, and played regularly for the Giants from 1950-54 despite his low BA (including a .187 season in 1954). His lone 100+ BB season came in 1951, when the Giants came back from 13 1/2 back to overtake the Dodgers. He teamed with Eddie Stanky that year as one of baseball's 39 teammate pairs who have both walked 100 or more times in the same season.

THE 1960's

THE PLAYERS:

Bob Allison
Richie Ashburn
Sal Bando
Norm Cash
Rocky Colavito
Joe Cunningham
Frank Howard
Reggie Jackson
Harmon Killebrew
Mickey Mantle
Eddie Matthews
Dick McAuliffe
Willie McCovey
Joe Morgan
Norm Siebern
Rusty Staub
Jim Wynn
Carl Yastrzemski
Eddie Yost

In the 1960s we see the effects of expansion on the base on balls. After expansion, there was a surge in offense in each league. Baseball quickly remedied this problem after the 1962 season by enlarging the strike zone, with the result that only eight players managed 100+ walks from 1963-68, as opposed to 19 in the immediately previous six year period (1957-62). In 1969 alone, partly due to the effects of another expansion and the re-shrinking of the strike zone, there were nine players who cracked the 100 BB barrier.

Who are the new names? Bob Allison, who was a big hitter for the Twins in their first few seasons in Minneapolis, averaging 32 homers a year from 1961-64, along with 90+ walks. His lone 100+ season came in the year of expansion, when he teamed with Harmon Killebrew, the next great walkman. The Killer had seven 100+ seasons, and dominates the sixties with five. His best walk season, 1969 (also an expansion year), rates 50th best all-time in BBP; two other seasons (1967 and 1970) rate in the Top 100.

Another duo that you think of as seventies ballplayers reached early fruition in the expansion season of 1969. Sal Bando and Reggie Jackson each walked more than 100 times that year, Jackson in large part because he was on a pace to break Ruth's homer record until the middle of August. He finished with 47, his highest total in his career, as were the 114 walks. Bando repeated in 1970, but Jackson never got over 86 in his subsequent career.

There was another 100+ walk duo in 1961: the Tigers' Norm Cash and

Rocky Colavito. Raw batting average (.361) propelled Cash; raw power (45 HR) gave Colavito the push. Cash repeated in 1962, primarily because everyone was treating him with kid gloves; Colavito came very close (96), but started to fade as a big homer threat and his walk totals declined into the 80s as the sixties progressed.

Another two-time member is Norm Siebern, whose career is a bit reminiscent of the Mariners' fine 1B-DH of the mid-eighties, Alvin Davis. Siebern's career year came at 28, when he had a Triple 100 as the cleanup hitter on the 1962 Kansas City A's. Traded to Baltimore in 1964, he faded as a hitter but retained his batting eye enough to snag a second 100+ season. Like Davis, his skill base just sort of eroded overnight and he never got it back. He was unable to get his BA above .256 for the rest of his career and was finished at the age of 34.

A throwback to the Ferris Fain school of walkman was Joe Cunningham, who was a solid hitter and an underrated walker for the Cardinals in the late fifties, but was never able to land a full-time job over six seasons, despite hitting .345 in 1959. Part of his problem was that he couldn't play anywhere but first, and the Cardinals had installed Stan Musial there in 1955, blocking Cunningham's path. He played the outfield a lot in 1959-61 (by this time the Cards had Bill White at first), but wasn't much of an outfielder and was dealt to the White Sox in 1962 for Minnie Minoso. The Cards got screwed, because Minoso, who was 38 to begin with, got hurt and hit just .196, while Cunningham was installed at first by the Pale Hose and had his lone 100+ BB season, hitting .295. It looked like a match made in heaven, but Cunningham broke his collarbone midway through the 1963 season and just suddenly lost his offensive abilities. Like so many walkmen, he just sort of disintegrated before your eyes. He was through at the age of 34.

Expansion helped two very big men become walkmen in 1969. Frank Howard was in the second of three consecutive 40+ HR seasons in 1969, and the pitchers just started walking him a ton. His walk totals just exploded (from 54 in 1968 to 102 in 1969, then up to 132 in 1970). Howard, though, was in his mid-thirties by this time and faded fairly fast, hitting just 26 homers in 1971, then falling apart completely when the Senators moved to Texas the following year.

Willie McCovey was the best hitter in the NL in 1968; the smaller strike zone helped him take another step the next year, when he led the league in homers, RBI and slugging average. His 121 walks were by far his best total to date, but he topped it in 1970 with 137, as pitchers just quaked with fear when they saw Stretch in the batter's box. His 1970 season ranks 33rd in all-time BBP; his 1973 season, the last of his first tour with the Giants, is right behind it at 34th. He was just as feared in his first year with the Padres (1974): even though he didn't crack 100 walks, his 96 BB in 440 PA represented the highest BBP of his career (21.81).

Dick McAuliffe was a steady middle infielder for the Tigers whose first of two 100+ BB seasons came in the Tigers' unsuccessful pennant bid in 1967. McAuliffe's distinctive open stance produced 197 homers, a fine total for a middle infielder, and he topped 100 walks again in 1970.

The Houston Astros were unable to build a winning team around three exceptional talents that they developed in their organization during the sixties: Joe Morgan, Jimmie Wynn, and Rusty Staub. All three walked more than 100 times in 1969. Staub had been sent to the Expos in that strange trade where Donn Clendenon retired, then "un-retired," and he had a fine year in Jarry Park, hitting .302 with 29 homers and 110 walks. He cracked 100 walks again in 1970, and eventually wound up as a mainstay of the Mets' improbable pennant drive in 1973.

Morgan and Wynn teamed up to be the first teammates on an expansion team to walk 100+ times in a year. Wynn tied the NL record (set by Eddie Stanky in 1945, an "expansion"-like year due to WW2) that year. In 1970, they did it again, becoming the first duo to repeat since Fain and Joost's threepeat in 1948-50. But the Astros gave up on little Joe in 1972, which resulted in a lot of pennants for the Big Red Machine and six more 100+ BB seasons for Morgan. The Astros sent Wynn packing after the 1973 season, resulting in the Dodgers' pennant in 1974 and three more 100+ BB seasons for the Toy Cannon.

After the Impossible Dream year in 1967, Carl Yastrzemski found it impossible to get a good pitch from AL hurlers: his walk totals, which had always been good (70s, 80s, low 90s from 1961-67), jumped up to a new level in 1968. Yaz walked 119 times that season and began a string of four consecutive 100+ seasons. After missing in 1972, he added two more in 1973-74 before his skills began to fade. Even though his lifetime BBP is not among the leaders (it's still a very respectable 13.34), due to his longevity Yaz ranks fourth all-time in lifetime walks behind Ruth, Williams, and Joe Morgan.

THE 1970's

THE PLAYERS:

Bob Bailey
Sal Bando
Johnny Bench
Don Buford
Jeff Burroughs
Dick Dietz
Darrell Evans
Bobby Grich
Mike Hargrove
Toby Harrah
Frank Howard
Harmon Killebrew
Greg Luzinski
Willie Mays
John Mayberry
Dick McAuliffe
Willie McCovey
Joe Morgan
Darrell Porter
Boog Powell
Pete Rose
Paul Schaal
Mike Schmidt
Ken Singleton
Reggie Smith
Rusty Staub
Gene Tenace
Jim Wynn
Carl Yastrzemski

More players broke the 100 walk barrier in the 1970s than in any other decade (29); this is due in part to the fact that there was another expansion in the AL in 1977, bringing the total number of teams up to 26. Per capita, the 40s are still the greatest period for walkmen, but the 70s was a very good period in its own right, with a fine mix of players.

1970 saw 12 players crack the 100 walk barrier; this ties it with 1949 for the most players. Not only did Wynn and Morgan repeat as teammates, but another duo occurred in the American League, an odd couple on the three-time AL champion Baltimore Orioles—leadoff man Don Buford and cleanup hitter Boog Powell. Buford, a versatile player who played second, third, and the outfield in a ten-year major league career, added some power to his skill mix when he arrived in Baltimore in 1968. 1970 was the second of three straight years that he scored 99 runs as the Birds' leadoff man; during the three Oriole pennant seasons, he averaged 98 walks per year, peaking in '70 with 109.

For Boog Powell, 1970 was his last great season, his fourth and last 30+ homer campaign; he hit .297 and walked 104 times, driving in 114 runs. The 104 walks was twenty more than he managed in any other season, but he ended his career with 1001 lifetime walks and a very creditable 13.03 BBP.

The usual cast of sluggers dominates the rest of the 1970 crop of walkmen, all players we're already familiar with (Howard, Yaz, Killebrew, Bando, McAuliffe, McCovey, Staub, Morgan, and Wynn). All except one. Catcher Dick Dietz teamed with McCovey to give the Giants a fantastic team total of 729. Dietz, at 28, stepped up and had a magnificent season, hitting .300, slugging .515, walking 109 times, hitting 36 doubles, 22 homers, and driving in 107. He lost a lot on his BA in the following year (down to .252), but the same mix of skills—good power (19 homers), high walks (97 BB)—was still intact, and the Giants won their division. Dietz is a great sleeper pick in the Bill James Winter League: he has good power, and a super lifetime BBP of 17.24. His career was short, and I'm surprised that he didn't get another chance after an amazing partial season with the Braves in 1973 that contains one of the highest BBPs I've seen: 49 walks in 188 plate appearances (26.06, up there in Williams territory). Dietz hit .295, and played some first base for Eddie Mathews' Braves that year. Why he wasn't given a shot to play regularly I don't know: John Oates was hitting .220 with no power and was sharing the catching job with Vic Correll. Anybody know the answer?

Parenthetical note about that 1970 Giants club. It had five guys who really could get on base that year: Bobby Bonds (77 walks) leading off, followed by Ken Henderson (87 walks), Willie Mays (79 in his last really good hitting season), McCovey (137 walks, 126 RBI), and then Dietz (109 BB, 82 runs). They led the NL with 831 runs, a total that hadn't been exceeded since before the strike zone adjustment (the '62 Giants and Dodgers were the last teams to exceed 831 runs in the NL).

In 1971 Killebrew and Yaz continue their walking ways, but they are joined by journeyman third baseman Paul Schaal, who blossomed at 28 on a third-year Royals team that finished second in the AL West (16 games behind the first of five consecutive Oakland pennant winners). Schaal came up with the Angels and was typecast early as a failed power hitter. After struggling with the Angels for four years, he was taken in the draft by the Royals and turned his hitting around to the point where he was handed the full-time third base job by manager Bob Lemon. Schaal responded with a season in which he set personal highs in hits, doubles, homers, runs, RBI, walks, and stolen bases. He slumped badly in '72, bounced back in '73 and hit .288 with 63 walks in 460 plate appearances, but the advent of a 21-year old player named George Brett made him expendable. Traded back to the Angels, he faded quickly, and reportedly retired due to a recurrence of equilibrium problems resulting from a beaning in 1968.

The other walkman in 1971, and the only one in the NL, was 40-year old Willie Mays. The Say Hey senior citizen had begun to play a lot of games at first base that year (48), and with the absence of McCovey for more than a third of the season was pitched around a lot more than usual. Mays had several seasons of walking in the 80s (1961, 1964), but he was not a player who looked to walk. Still, his 1971 season ranks 42nd all time in BBP; and he is the second oldest man in history to walk 100 times in a year.

The rise in offense associated with expansion was a brief one: pitching

reasserted itself in 1972 to enough of a degree that the AL voted to infuse additional punch into the game with the designated hitter rule. Only three players walked 100 or more times in 1972, just one more than in "the pitcher's year" of 1968. All three were National Leaguers; two were members of the offensive powerhouse of the decade, the Cincinnati Reds. Those two: Joe Morgan (his third of eight 100+ BB seasons) and Johnny Bench. For Bench, it was his only 100+ walk season; his other peak seasons were in the low 80s. The other 1972 NL walkman? Why, Jimmie Wynn, of course.

Perhaps it was the DH, perhaps not, but the AL certainly returned to walking in 1973: in conjunction with a 20 point rise in batting average (from .239 to .259), AL batters drew 900 more walks. (Some of this increase is due to the seven-to-nine fewer games played in 1972 due to the players' strike, but the walk level did legitimately rise about 50 per team in '73.) Accompanying this rise were four walkmen, one familiar face and three newcomers—one of whom became a significant force in the lore of taking a pitch.

The familiar face: Yaz. The newcomers: John Mayberry, Bobby Grich, and Gene Tenace. Mayberry and Grich both repeated the 100+ BB feat in 1975. Tenace began a skein of 100+ walk seasons that dominated the 70s. Only Joe Morgan had more 100+ BB seasons in the decade than Tenace, who put together two streaks of three consecutive seasons over 100, one with Oakland (1973-75) and the other with San Diego (1977-79). The Padres, who had a weak hitting team throughout the late 70s, weren't able to build a successful offensive context around Tenace, whose low batting average did not make him an ideal middle of the lineup hitter. Tenace's best BBP (22.24, 23rd best for a single season) came in his first year with the Padres: his 125 walks led the league. He cracked the BBP Top 100 again in 1978 (20.12, 62nd best).

Over in the NL, Little Joe and Stretch, regulars at the BB100 bar, are joined by two newcomers who become significant names in the pantheon of pitch-taking: Darrell Evans and Ken Singleton. Singleton began a streak of four odd-year 100+ BB performances, the first occurring with the Montreal Expos, the last three with the Baltimore Orioles. People tend to forget what a fine hitter Singleton was: lifetime he hit .282, slugged .436 (246 homers), and reached base a shade under 39% of the time. There are worse players in the Hall of Fame. Evans is one of four players who had 100+ BB seasons for three different teams, and he shares the record with Hank Greenberg for length of time between 100+ seasons (nine years: 1978, 1987). A big dip in the middle of his career dropped his totals out of Hall of Fame consideration, but he hung around long enough to wind up eighth on the all-time walk list with 1605. (Of the Top 20 in number of lifetime walks, by the way, only five are not presently in the Hall of Fame: Evans, Yost, Mike Schmidt, Dwight Evans, and Pete Rose—who isn't there for more compelling reasons.)

1974 demonstrated that a consistent level of achievement had been created for walking in the decade, as five repeaters (Wynn, Morgan, Yaz, Evans, and Tenace) topped the list, along with one soon-to-be-repeater in Mike Schmidt. It was Schmidt's first great season, and the first of seven 100+ BB seasons for the great Phillie third baseman.

The one-shot wonders: 1) the aforementioned Pete Rose, whose 106 walk season was also his first sub-.300 year since 1964. His next best season for walks came in 1979, when he drew 95. Rose's lifetime total of 1566 walks looks impressive until you notice that his lifetime BBP is 10.03. 2) Bob Bailey, who began drawing walks when he got to the more inviting power alleys at Montreal's Jarry Park. In the five years from 1970-74, Bailey averaged 21 HR, 77 RBI, and 83 walks, while hitting a respectable .264 and slugging a very creditable .447.

There are no new members of the BB100 club until 1977, the year of the third AL expansion. Fittingly, perhaps, the two new members came from the same original expansion team (Senators, now the Texas Rangers). Toby Harrah and Mike Hargrove played together on the most successful Texas team in history that season: the Rangers won 94 games and finished second to the Royals, who were in the midst of a three-year domination of the AL West. Hargrove hit .305 that year and had the best HR total of his career (18). It was the first of four 100+ BB seasons for the man they called The Human Rain Delay. Harrah's 1977 is among his best in terms fo power and overall production; but it is his 1985 that commands all the attention from BB aficionados. Stripped of much of his power by this point, Harrah turned on the "old players' skills" and drew 113 walks in 509 plate appearances. The resulting BBP (22.20) places him 24th on the all-time BB100 List.

In the NL, the only new member of the club is slugger Reggie Smith, whom the Dodgers had shamelessly stolen away from the Cardinals the year before in a deal that should have been listed in Joe Reichler's list of best trades made by a team. (Wake up, Joe!! Reggie Smith for Joe Ferguson and Bobby Detherage is just a ridiculous ripoff and should be at the top of the freakin' list already.) It was a fluke season, since Smith's next highest total was 71. Reggie's RC27 was 9.10 that year, so it's no wonder that the pitchers gave him a wide berth, even on a team with four 30+ HR hitters.

1978 and 1979 bring three new walkmen to the ranks: Jeff Burroughs, Greg Luzinski, and Darrell Porter. All are one-shot members: Burroughs and Luzinski slow-footed sluggers, Porter a catcher whose peak season was a Triple 100 year (which answers our other Mickey Cochrane question about catchers and Triple Hundreds). Burroughs was a good walker (13.05 BBP) who had several other years where he was over 90 BB; he leaped into the club because pitchers became very leery of him after he had hit 41 homers in his first season with the Braves. Luzinski made it primarily because Mike Schmidt had an off-year, and the Bull was the more feared hitter over the course of 1978.

Note that what is missing from the list of walkmen in the 70s is the classic leadoff hitter type that we saw frequently until the 60s. The leadoff men who make the list (Buford, Grich, McAuliffe, Rose) are, in general, more powerful hitters than the earlier leadoff-hitter type (Stanky, Bishop et al). The leadoff hitters are also not the ones who repeat: this is left to the big sluggers, or to hybrid players like Joe Morgan, who began as leadoff hitters but developed enough power to drop down in the order.

THE PLAYERS:

Wade Boggs
George Brett
Jack Clark
Alvin Davis
Brian Downing
Darrell Evans
Dwight Evans
Mike Hargrove
Toby Harrah
Von Hayes
Rickey Henderson
Gary Matthews
Fred McGriff
Dale Murphy
Dwayne Murphy
Eddie Murray
Willie Randolph
Cal Ripken
Mike Schmidt
Kevin Seitzer
Jason Thompson
Andre Thornton

In the 80s we begin to see the return of the classic leadoff walkman, in addition to the slugger types that predominated in the 60s and 70s. Players like Wade Boggs, Rickey Henderson, Kevin Seitzer, and Willie Randolph proved that the Bishops and Blues and Stankys of the game were not yet extinct.

Or are they? When we examine that quartet more closely, we see that only Henderson was unequivocally a leadoff man. Boggs was shifted around a lot between the 1, 2, and 3 slots in the order; Randolph and Seitzer batted #2 a lot. Hence the nostalgic paeans to Brett Butler (who cracked the walkman list in 1991 after three seasons in the 90s during this decade), who is the closest thing to Roy Thomas we've got. Close, but no cigar: Butler's average walks per year in the last nine seasons is 84. Nobody seems to want to give a low-power, high on-base guy a chance. And nobody, or at least a very small minority of managers, is encouraging leadoff hitters to take walks. (We'll get back to this issue in the discussion accompanying the 90s walkmen.)

The most dramatic walker of the 80s, not in terms of frequency of occurrence but in BBP rate, was Jack Clark. Without the shoulder injury that sidelined him in early September, Clark would have set an new NL record for walks in 1987. His BBP for that season (24.50) ranks fourth all-time. Three of Jack's four 100+ BB seasons all rank in the Top 20 all time. One of the big reasons why the Cardinals haven't gotten back to the World Series since 1987 is because they haven't had anything like the colossal force in their lineup that Clark provided. The OINX rating ranks Clark's 1987 season 33rd among the 377 individual 100+ BB years in the database, just slightly ahead in "bang for the buck" than Barry Bonds' 1992 season, and in the vicinity of more conventionally understood "big seasons" such as Hank Greenberg's 58 HR season in 1938, Norm Cash's .361, 41 HR 1961, and Ralph Kiner's 54 HR year in 1949.

There is no telling how many times Rickey Henderson might have made the 100+ BB list if it were not for injuries. The chart below shows that, in addition to the four times Rickey has cracked the 100 walk barrier in his career, there are six more seasons in which he was on a pace to exceed 100 walks in a 690 plate appearance season (about right for a healthy leadoff man). That would make for a total of ten 100+ BB seasons, which would put Henderson in the upper reaches of the walkman pantheon. Looking at these numbers, and then factoring in the rest of Rickey's skills, there is no way to dispute the assertion that he is the greatest leadoff man in the history of modern baseball.

RICKEY HENDERSON—ADJUSTED BB TOTALS*

YEAR	G	AB	BB	BBP	ADJ BB
1979	89	351	34	8.8	61
1980	158	591	117	16.5	114
1981	108	423	64	13.1	91
1982	149	536	116	17.8	123
1983	145	513	103	16.7	115
1984	142	502	86	14.6	*101*
1985	143	547	99	15.3	*106*
1986	153	608	89	12.8	88
1987	95	358	80	18.3	*126*
1988	140	554	82	12.9	89
1989	150	541	126	18.9	130
1990	136	489	97	16.6	*114*
1991	134	470	98	17.3	*119*
1992	117	396	95	19.3	*134*

* based on 690 PA per full season

Figures in italics represent projected additional years over 100 BB

Henderson's early eighties teammate Dwayne Murphy is one of the more interesting walkmen. He and Henderson were a devastating 1-2 batting order combination for the "Billyball" Oakland A's. Murphy was on a pace to drive in 90 runs from the #2 slot in 1981, and projects to a second 100+ BB season at 104 sans strike. When Billy Martin was let go as manager after the 1982 season, Murphy stopped batting behind Rickey, and took serious aim at being a power hitter, with less than salutary effect to his batting average. The original idea was better, and, with Tony Armas batting #3, it made for a three-man offense at the top of the A's lineup that, for a little while at least, was very hard to beat.

Wade Boggs is the other significant "old style" walkman to emerge in the eighties, posting four consecutive 100+ BB seasons from 1986-89. In mid-1988 new Red Sox manager Joe Morgan installed Boggs as the permanent leadoff man: the move helped Boston stage a come-from-behind division championship.

Boggs' teammate Dwight Evans staged a remarkable—and unusual—offensive transformation in 1981, and sustained it throughout the rest of the decade, posting three 100+ BB seasons during that time. His finest overall season was probably 1987, when he rolled a Triple 100 and set personal bests in doubles, homers, RBI, SA, OBP, and RC27.

Alvin Davis came up with a bang in 1984 (27 HR, 116 RBI, 97 BB) and at 23 looked like a big star for the Seattle Mariners. As is sometimes the case for players who arrive with "old players' skills," Davis did not develop any further: he had arrived at the peak of his offensive capabilities. His walk totals were consistently in the 90s in his first six seasons, except for the years when Dick Williams—no fan of the walk—was his manager from mid-1986 to mid-1988. I can just hear the crusty, irascible Williams (who had a lifetime BBP of just 7.1 as a utility player) sniping at Davis, whom he probably saw as a 30-to-35 HR man: "Quit taking so many pitches—be more *&%$#ing aggressive up there." In 1987, when everybody was doin' it, Davis hit 29 homers, but as soon as Williams was gone, Davis reverted back to what got him there. In 1989, Davis cracked the 100 BB barrier and hit .305, but it was his last really good year. He slumped badly in 1991 and was never given much of a chance to bounce

back: the Angels sold him to Japan in the middle of 1992 to give the immortal Lee Stevens (!!) more playing time.

Von Hayes had two 100+ seasons for the Phillies in the late 80s, but he too seems to have faded early. Jason Thompson was criticized for not having sufficient dedication, and that may have been a factor in his early demise. His 1982 season, however, was mighty sweet. Cal Ripken's big walk season came in the Orioles' season of doom in 1988: without anyone to bat behind him, he just stopped swinging for a year. He's never come close to 100 walks before or since. His longtime teammate, Eddie Murray, has always shown good strike zone judgement, but cracked the 100 BB barrier primarily due to the lack of a hitter behind him in the Orioles' fall to earth in 1984. Ripken was batting in front of Murray that season, as the O's fell from the World Championship to fifth place en route to 1988's 21-game season-opening losing streak.

Andre Thornton was a slugger with fine plate discipline who never quite got a shot with the Cubs, though everything he could have been for them is writ large in his 1975 numbers (19.1 BBP, .516 SA). When he slumped early the next year, the Cubs panicked and unloaded him to the Expos for the laughable combo of Steve Renko and Larry Biittner. By mid-1977, when Thornton had reemerged with the Indians, it was clear how foolish the Cubs had been. Thornton had two 90+ BB seasons in 1978-79, missed all of 1980 with a knee injury, and finally broke into the 100+ BB category in 1982. His lifetime BBP is a solid 14.20, and I'll take his RBI/TB ratio (.375) any day.

Possibly the most notable walker to emerge late in the decade is Fred McGriff, who is one of a handful of players to exceed 100 walks in both leagues. McGriff has a very good chance to a perennial member of the 100+ BB club as long as he remains on the Padres, though we'll have to see if Jim Riggleman can work the same magic with Phil Plantier that Greg Riddoch was able to do with Gary Sheffield. McGriff's current lifetime BBP is 15.55, and he is just 29; we may see him move up in the pantheon a good bit over the next 4-to-6 years.

Other one-shots to note: George Brett, who really did carry the Royals to the World Series in 1985, a really unsung great year in a great career; Gary Matthews, who saved his best for just about last and nearly helped get the Cubs into that elusive World Series in 1984; Brian Downing, an overlooked gem of a season in 1987 at the age of 36, in a career that has to rank among the best post-30 performances of the past forty years; and Dale Murphy, who had a true career year in 1987.

THE 1990's

THE PLAYERS:

Barry Bonds
Brett Butler
Jack Clark
Fred McGriff
Mark McGwire
Randy Milligan
Tony Phillips
Danny Tartabull
Mickey Tettleton
Frank Thomas

There are two new walk kings as we await the fourth season of the 1990s. Those two are, in order of BBP, Frank Thomas and Mickey Tettleton. Both have already cracked the Top 100 for BBP (Thomas' 1991 ranks 72nd; Tettleton's 1990 ranks 95th). Both seem likely to go on racking up 100+ walk seasons for some time: Tettleton is 32 this season, Thomas just 25. (Tettleton, by the way, is the second answer to the question "What two catchers have had multiple 100+ BB seasons?". The first, as you doubtless remember, is—you do remember, don't you?—Mickey Cochrane.)

Joining them at the top is Barry Bonds, who has cracked 100 walks in each of the last two seasons and is likely to get serious kid gloves treatment in San Francisco in 1993 (assuming that they bat him fourth behind Will Clark: it probably makes the most sense, if you think about it, because Bonds can use the extra walks he gets to fuel his running game, which might be cut down if he were to be on base in front of the Thrill). One suspects that Bonds' discipline as a hitter would get him close to 100 walks on his own (his non-intentional walk totals over the past four seasons are 71, 78, 82, and 95) regardless of where he bats.

Another slugger with demonstrated strike-zone judgement is Mark McGwire, who cracked 100 walks in 1990 and, like teammate Rickey Henderson, would have made it easily in 1992 were it not for injuries. (Oakland was the first team since the 1970 Giants and Orioles to crack the 700 team walk barrier last year; that total could increase next year with full years from Henderson, McGwire, and walking pests like Lance Blankenship and Jerry Browne.)

Danny Tartabull has always shown good strike zone judgement, and cracked the 100 walk barrier last season while playing in only 123 games. Unless the Yankees can come up with a hitter in the lineup to protect him, it's likely that Tartabull will have several more 100+ BB seasons over the next few years. Some people seem to think that 1992 was a disappointing year from Tartabull: I think that the numbers (7 runs created per game, .410 OBP) are just fine, and that the Colorado Rockies should have taken him in a blink instead of Charlie Hayes. He could have hit 45 homers playing in that thin air (and that's not counting the road games...).

Brett Butler we talked about in the last section. Butler has been given a lot of recognition (I call it "nostalgic recognition") for being an incredible leadoff hitter, and he has been excellent: a notch below the Bishop/Stanky/Morgan class in terms of drawing walks, to be sure, but better in terms of speed (though it's tricky comparing across eras on SB because they just weren't emphasized in the 20s, 30s, 40s, and 50s). Still, Rickey Henderson he's not—nor is he as good as Tim Raines, who hasn't walked quite as much (three seasons in the 90s, four in the eighties) but has more power and more speed.

But one question that we have to address is whether it makes that much of a difference whether the guy occupying the #1 slot in the batting order takes a lot of walks, or if there are other combinations that stil promote an effective offense. The answer is that of course there are other combinations: the Toronto Blue Jays, for example, the 1992 World Champions, have a #1 slot hitter, Devon White, who does not take many walks. They work around this deficiency rather well by having their best all-around hitter, Roberto Alomar, who has everything (except HR power) White has and much more, batting #2. It's like having a leadoff man and a real leadoff man: an interesting—and so far successful—approach.

I'm wondering if the Dodgers might be about to stumble on a similar strategy in the way they're using Butler and Jose Offerman. I've written more about this in the Dodger article, so I'll just note that last year, when Butler was shifted to the #2 slot, he hit .362, was on base .460, and had a higher BBP (16.39 to 14.06) than when batting #1. If Offerman can improve enough to be a decent leadoff man, and Butler is truly more effective batting #2, then the Dodgers could score a lot more runs just from the structural difference in the lineup. That, and the return of a healthy Darryl Strawberry: there is no way to really prove the hypothesis using last year's Dodger lineup.

Where you place your walkman in the lineup is important: Butler's (and Alomar's) ability to hit as a "real" leadoff hitter (when there is no one on, but not no one out), and to hit well with men on first (Butler hit .394 in that situation last year) might be as important to the offense than just the raw ability to get on base. It will be interesting to see if the Dodgers keep the Offerman-Butler 1-2 configuration intact in '93.

Finally, our last two walkmen: the semi-unclassifiables Randy Milligan (power hitter? breath mint?) and Tony Phillips (outfielder? infielder? power hitter? candy mint?). Both have shown strong propensities for drawing walks: Milligan's lifetime BBP of 17.53 ranks 14th all-time. Phillips is the only true utility man to ever become a great leadoff hitter, and those people who like to characterize Sparky Anderson as brain-dead need to take a look at the players he's collected over the years (Morgan, Lou Whitaker, Darrell Evans, Tettleton). Sparky may be too glib for words but he knows the value of a walk. Phillips' role is probably assured for a couple years, or for as long as he can stay close to his production in 1992; Milligan is sort of the Les Fleming/Elbie Fletcher type (yeah, he can walk, but I got three first basemen who'll hit more homers or for a higher average). I wouldn't be surprised if he ends up on an expansion team, or—hell—maybe in Detroit, next year. It'd sure beat the hell out of Rico Brogna, Sparky, and he'd fit right in with Phillips and Tettleton and Lou Whitaker.

ANALYSIS AND FURTHER COMMENTARY

Before we try to make sense out of the data that can be culled from a sample of 141 players and 378 player-seasons, let's start with a frequency distribution of walkmen. The following figure shows the number of 100+ BB seasons achieved, the amount of players who have achieved that number of seasons, and the players' names.

# 100+	# Players	Who
13	1	Babe Ruth
11	2	Lou Gehrig, Ted Williams
10	2	Mickey Mantle, Mel Ott
8	2	Joe Morgan, Eddie Yost
7	5	Max Bishop, Jimmie Foxx, Harmon Killebrew, Mike Schmidt, Roy Thomas
6	7	Harlond Clift, Eddie Joost, Ralph Kiner, Eddie Stanky, Gene Tenace, Jimmy Wynn, Carl Yastrzemski
5	5	Darrell Evans, Ferris Fain, Billy Hamilton, Charlie Keller, Eddie Mathews
4	9	Lu Blue, Wade Boggs, Dolf Camilli, Cupid Childs, Jack Clark, Elbie Fletcher, Mike Hargrove, Rickey Henderson, Ken Singleton
3	15	Luke Appling, Richie Ashburn, Donie Bush, Jack Clark, Jack Crooks, Roy Cullenbine, Dwight Evans, Augie Galan, Hank Greenberg, Miller Huggins, Eddie Lake, Willie McCovey, John McGraw, Jim McTamany, Stan Musial, Yank Robinson, Mickey Tettleton
2	29	Sal Bando, Barry Bonds, Norm Cash, Mickey Cochrane, Eddie Collins, Larry Doby, Charlie Gehringer, Jack Graney, Bobby Grich, Toby Harrah, Topsy Hartsel, Von Hayes, Frank Howard, Bill Joyce, John Mayberry, Dick McAuliffe, Fred McGriff, Johnny Pesky, Paul Radford, Pee Wee Reese, Topper Rigney, Jimmy Sheckard, Burt Shotton, Norm Siebern, Rusty Staub, Frank Thomas, Earl Torgeson, Elmer Valo, Arky Vaughan
1	63	Bob Allison, Cap Anson, Bob Bailey, Johnny Bates, Johnny Bench, Bob Bescher, George Brett, Don Buford, George Burns, Jeff Burroughs, Brett Butler, Will Clark, Ty Cobb, Rocky Colavito, Roger Connor, Frank Crosetti, Joe Cunningham, Alvin Davis, Dick Dietz, Dom DiMaggio, Brian Downing, Bob Elliott, Woody English, Johnny Evers, Les Fleming, Jim Gilliam, George Gore, Gil Hodges, Rogers Hornsby, Dummy Hoy, Reggie Jackson, Joe Kelley, Lyn Lary, Greg Luzinski, Gary Matthews, Willie Mays, Mark McGwire, Cass Michaels, Randy

Milligan, Dale Murphy, Dwayne Murphy, Eddie Murray, Buddy Myer, Tony Phillips, Darrell Porter, Boog Powell, Willie Randolph, Cal Ripken, Jackie Robinson, Pete Rose, Al Rosen, Paul Schaal, Kevin Seitzer, George Selkirk, Roy Sievers, Reggie Smith, Duke Snider, Vern Stephens, Danny Tartabull, Jason Thompson, Andre Thornton, Wes Westrum, Hack Wilson

Now let's run a list of the players in terms of how old they were when they had their first 100+ BB season (asterisks indicate that the season was the only 100+ season the player had, daggers indicate the only 100+ season for a still-active player):

20: John McGraw, Mel Ott, Ted Williams

21: Jimmie Foxx, Rickey Henderson

22: Reggie Jackson*, Joe Kelley*, Mickey Mantle, Eddie Mathews.

23: Harlond Clift, Cupid Childs, Woody English*, Lou Gehrig, Charlie Keller, John Mayberry, Cass Michaels*, Frank Thomas, Eddie Yost

24: Johnny Bench*, Lu Blue, Donie Bush, Will Clark*, Jack Crooks, Elbie Fletcher, Jim Gilliam*, Bobby Grich, Bill Joyce, Babe Ruth, Mike Schmidt, Arky Vaughan

25: Sal Bando, Eddie Collins, Roy Cullenbine, Ralph Kiner, Fred McGriff, Jim McTamany, Joe Morgan, Dwayne Murphy*, Paul Radford, Willie Randolph*, Rusty Staub, Roy Thomas

26: Bob Allison*, Max Bishop, Barry Bonds, Norm Cash, Darrell Evans, Les Fleming*, Hank Greenberg, Miller Huggins, Harmon Killebrew, Mark McGwire†, Al Rosen*, Ken Singleton, Gene Tenace, Earl Torgeson

27: Richie Ashburn, Bob Bescher*, Jeff Burroughs*, Rocky Colavito*, Frank Crosetti*, Larry Doby, Ferris Fain, Mike Hargrove, Greg Luzinski*, Dick McAuliffe, Darrell Porter*, Topper Rigney, Cal Ripken†, Kevin Seitzer†, Jason Thompson*, Jimmy Wynn

28: Luke Appling, Wade Boggs, Ty Cobb*, Alvin Davis†, Dick Dietz*, Toby Harrah, Von Hayes, Gil Hodges*, Eddie Murray†, Stan Musial, Boog Powell*, Pee Wee Reese, Yank Robinson, Paul Schaal*, Norm Siebern, Duke Snider*, Eddie Stanky, Vern Stephens*, Elmer Valo, Wes Westrum*, Carl Yastrzemski

29: Johnny Bates*, Dolf Camilli, Mickey Cochrane, Dummy Hoy*, Eddie Lake, Johnny Pesky, Roy Sievers*, Danny Tartabull†,

Mickey Tettleton
30: Joe Cunningham*, Dwight Evans, Jack Graney, Lyn Lary*, Randy Milligan†, Buddy Myer*, Burt Shotton, Hack Wilson*
31: Bob Bailey*, Jack Clark, Dom DiMaggio*, Bob Elliott*, Augie Galan, Topsy Hartsell, Eddie Joost, Willie McCovey, Dale Murphy†, George Selkirk
32: George Brett†, Rogers Hornsby*, Frank Howard, Jimmy Sheckard, Reggie Smith*, Andre Thornton*
33: Don Buford*, George Burns*, Gary Matthews*, Tony Phillips†, Jackie Robinson, Pete Rose
34: Brett Butler†, George Gore*
35: Roger Connor*, Charlie Gehringer
36: Brian Downing†.
39: Cap Anson*
40: Willie Mays*

The distribution curve for 100+ BB seasons looks like this:

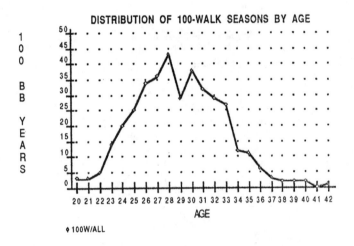

DISTRIBUTION OF 100-WALK SEASONS BY AGE

100 BB YEARS / AGE

◆ 100W/ALL

This would look fairly similar to a distribution by age of seasons greater than six runs created per game, I would suspect, except that the decline phase would be a bit quicker after the age of 30. Walkmen also probably are a bit low on the front end, since one subclass tends to languish in the minors longer because their power and BA stats are not sufficiently impressive to get them to the majors as fast as someone who hits .300 or hits homers.

Since there are only 378 100+ walk seasons in the 106 years where it has been theoretically feasible to draw 100 walks, it is difficult to break any of this age data down into eras or decades and see if we have any new trends in terms of distribution by age. It should be noted, though, that there are only three players who have ever drawn 100 walks at the age of 20, and they span 100 years of baseball (John McGraw, 1892; Ted Williams, 1939; and Rickey Henderson, 1980 and still quite active as 1993 begins). At the opposite end of the spectrum, the 40-42 year-olds also span from the pre-1900 era to the close to present-day (Anson, 1894; Appling, 1949; Mays, 1971—and if we drop down to 39-year olds we pick up Darrell Evans as recently as 1987).

So walking—despite the AL spike in 1947-51—is not a phenomenon isolated to a particular era, like low ERAs to the deadball era or high batting averages to the 1920-45 period. About three players a year (both leagues) will crack the 100 walk barrier—although there is a big difference between leagues, as can be seen in the distribution by decade figures below:

100 WALKS—DISTRIBUTION BY DECADES (ALL, AL, NL)

ALL

DECADE	TOT	0	1	2	3	4	5	6	7	8	9
1880	5	—	—	—	—	—	—	1	1	1	2
1890	25	4	4	3	4	3	0	3	1	1	2
1900	10	2	1	1	1	1	2	1	1	0	0
1910	18	2	3	3	0	2	4	2	0	0	2
1920	22	1	2	0	2	2	0	4	3	3	5
1930	51	6	4	6	3	4	3	7	3	9	6
1940	56	6	7	6	2	1	4	5	7	6	12
1950	47	8	8	7	5	6	4	5	2	1	1
1960	32	4	5	6	1	1	0	1	3	2	9
1970	62	12	4	3	8	8	8	3	7	5	4
1980	35	4	0	6	2	2	3	1	7	4	7
1990	14	3	5	6							
377											

AL

DECADE	TOT	0	1	2	3	4	5	6	7	8	9
1900	2	—	0	0	0	0	1	0	1	0	0
1910	11	0	0	2	0	1	4	2	0	0	2
1920	19	1	2	0	1	2	0	4	3	2	4
1930	38	3	4	5	3	4	3	4	2	6	4
1940	34	4	4	4	1	0	2	3	4	4	8
1950	28	5	4	4	2	3	1	5	2	1	1
1960	24	2	5	5	0	1	0	1	3	2	5
1970	26	7	3	0	4	2	4	0	3	1	2
1980	25	4	0	4	1	1	3	1	4	3	5
1990	9	2	2	5							
216											

NL

DECADE	TOT	0	1	2	3	4	5	6	7	8	9
1900	8	2	1	1	1	1	1	1	0	0	0
1910	7	2	3	1	0	1	0	0	0	0	0
1920	3	0	0	0	1	0	0	0	0	1	1
1930	13	3	0	1	0	0	0	3	1	3	2
1940	22	2	3	2	1	1	2	2	3	2	4
1950	19	3	4	3	3	3	3	0	0	0	0
1960	8	2	0	1	1	0	0	0	0	0	4
1970	36	5	1	3	4	6	4	3	4	4	2
1980	10	0	0	2	1	1	0	0	3	1	2
1990	5	1	3	1							
131											

PRE-1900 DISTRIBUTION: —NL 20, AA 8, PL 2.

Looking at this data tells us that walking has shown a pronounced tendency to be an American League trait (62.2% of 100+ BB seasons since 1900 have occurred in the AL), and that the ten-year period right after WW2 was, as alluded to earlier, the halcyon days of the base on balls (72 100+ seasons, nearly 20 percent of the total number, occurred between 1946—1955).

Some other salient statistics:

—Greatest number of 100+ BB seasons in a single year: 12 (1949, 1970)
—Greatest two-year total: 21 (1969-70).
        Next highest is 20 (1949-50).
—Greatest three year total: 28 (1949-51).
        Next highest: 26 (1948-50), 25 (1970-72).
—Greatest four year total: 35 (1949-52).
        Next highest: 34 (1948-51).

You see why I call the 1948-52 period the "great walk spike"....

The AL is still more of a walking league than the NL, though nothing like what was seen from the 20s to the 60s. During those five decades, the AL had 143 100+ seasons to the NL's 65 (69%/31%). The NL's best decade by far came in the 70s, with Morgan, Wynn, Schmidt, and Darrell Evans leading the way, but the AL/NL pattern seems to have reasserted itself in the 80s and 90s (the AL has had 34 in the last thirteen years to the NL's 15, that same 69/31 breakdown seen from 1920-69).

Now the real question for such a pronounced tendency (as Brock Hanke knows) is "Why?" As noted before, the AL has historically had higher walk totals. This goes back to the middle of the deadball era, around 1912, when the two leagues just flip-flopped in terms of walks, with the AL becoming the walking league. NL walk totals jumped significantly at the end of the twenties, and for two years—1928-29—the leagues were almost even (partly because there was an accompanying downturn in the AL).

Ironically, the juice ball of 1930 seemed to signal a new decline in walking in the NL, a slide that bottomed out in 1933. For much of the 30s, AL teams averaged 150 more walks per year than their NL counterparts, a phenomenon that ebbed during World War II. The explanantion might be that the NL lost more good pitchers to the war, the AL more good hitters, causing walk totals to rise in the NL, and fall in the AL.

After the war came the great walk spike, predominantly an AL phenomenon, although NL totals rose to their highest levels ever. Those totals begin to sag in the mid-fifties in both leagues, with the NL beginning a long slide toward deadball era walk totals in 1956.

The answer to "Why?" is still unknown. Craig Wright and Bill James, as noted earlier, have not been especially illuminating on this one. The historical tendency for one league to walk more than the other, though far less pronounced in the post-expansion era, is hardly traceable to the scenarios posited by either of the two most renowned sabermetricians, or by more prosaic explanations offered by many concerning differences in umpiring tendencies. One can accept that there are differences in umpiring between leagues, but a fifty-year difference that creates more walks? I think not. The answer to "Why?" is quite complex, and is probably beyond the current reach of sabermetrics as a science: we'll need an anthropological element to it before we get the full explanation.

Expansion years created a boom in 100+ walk seasons. The AL had just 6 100+ BB seasons from 1957-60; the next two years produced 10. The NL did not have such a boom in 1962, but they did have a big jump in the first two years following the 1969 expansion, which led them into their big 70s decade. From 1956 to 1968, only four NL hitters cracked the 100 BB barrier: four players did it in 1969 alone, five more in 1970. The AL experienced a similar jump in 1969-70, going from seven 100+ BB seasons in the previous six years (1963-68) to twelve in the first two expansion years. The single league expansion in 1977 did not produce a similar effect, although the AL did go from a drought year in '76 to three in the expansion year.

Based on this data, one would anticipate that there will be an increase in 100+ walk seasons in 1993, especially in the NL, where only one (Barry Bonds) occurred in 1992. Candidates to join Bonds are Fred McGriff, Brett Butler, Dave Justice, Jeff Bagwell, Craig Biggio, Darren Daulton, John Kruk, and Dave Hollins.

The fact that I've just name two sets of teammates with shots at making the 100+ BB club in '93 brings us to another list, namely "Teammates Who Have Walked 100+ Times in The Same Season." It's a fun list, trust me, and if you strain your eyes downward you can read it for yourself:

TEAMMATES WHO WALKED 100+ TIMES IN THE SAME SEASON

Year	Team	Players
1911	CIN N	Bates 103, Bescher 102
1915	DET A	Cobb 118, Bush 118
1926	NY A	Ruth 144, Gehrig 105
1927	NY A	Ruth 138, Gehrig 109
1929	PHI A	Bishop 128, Foxx 103
1930	CHI N	Wilson 105, English 100
1931	NY A	Ruth 128, Gehrig 117
1932	PHI A	Foxx 116, Bishop 110, Cochrane 100
1932	NY A	Ruth 130, Gehrig 108
1933	PHI A	Bishop 106, Cochrane 106
1934	NY A	Gehrig 109, Ruth 103
1936	StL A	Lary 117, Clift 115
1938	NY A	Gehrig 107, Crosetti 106
1938	DET A	Greenberg 119, Gehringer 112
1941	StL A	Cullenbine 121, Clift 113
1945	BKN N	Stanky 148, Galan 114
1947	DET A	Cullenbine 137, Lake 120
1947	BKN N	Reese 104, Stanky 103
1948	BOS A	Williams 126, D. DiMaggio 101
1948	PHI A	Joost 119, Fain 113
1949	BOS A	Williams 162, Stephens 101, Pesky 100
1949	PHI A	Joost 149, Fain 136, Valo 119
1949	CHI A	Appling 121, Michaels 101
1950	PHI A	Fain 133, Joost 102
1951	NY N	Stanky 127, Westrum 104
1952	PHI A	Joost 122, Fain 105, Valo 101
1952	BKN N	Hodges 107, Robinson 106
1956	WAS A	Yost 151, Sievers 100
1961	DET A	Cash 124, Colavito 113
1961	MIN A	Killebrew 107, Allison 103
1969	OAK A	Jackson 114, Bando 111
1969	HOU N	Wynn 148, Morgan 110
1970	BAL A	Buford 109, Powell 104
1970	SF N	McCovey 137, Dietz 109
1970	HOU N	Wynn 106, Morgan 102
1972	CIN N*	Morgan 115, Bench 100
1974	CIN N	Morgan 120, Rose 106
1975	BAL A	Singleton 116, Grich 107
1977	TEX A	Harrah 109, Hargrove 103
1980	OAK A	Henderson 117, Murphy 102
1982	CLE A	Thornton 109, Hargrove 101
1987	BOS A	Evans 106, Boggs 105
1992	DET A	Tettleton 122, Phillips 114

* Team won Pennant or Division Title

I mentioned earlier that there have been just four instances where three teammates have each walked 100 or more times in the same year: it's a list dominated by A's teams. Joost, Fain, and Valo were quite a walkman law firm for the aging Connie Mack; a more successful trio in terms of pennants was the Foxx, Bishop, Cochrane tag team (but not in the year that they all drew 100+ BB). The other troika (Williams, Pesky, Stephens) was nearly a quartet, as discussed during the section on 40s walkmen (Dom DiMaggio amassing 96).

As with many lists, it's one dominated by Ruth and Gehrig, who managed five 100+ pairings, one more than Joost and Fain. Joe Morgan teamed up with three different partners to appear on the pairs list four times; Eddie Stanky and Max Bishop each made a pairs list three times.

The "fluke" pairs (instances where both players walked way over their next best BB season): Bescher and Bates in 1911, Wilson and English in 1930, possibly Hodges and Robinson in 1952.

The most number of walking pairs in any given year? Why, 1949—of course, with three (tied with 1970).

Most number of consecutive seasons for a single team to have walking pairs? Three, the 1948-50 Philadelphia A's. Back to back walking pairs seasons are a bit more common: five teams have managed this—the 1926-27 Yankees, 31-32 Yankees, 32-33 A's, 48-49 Red Sox, and 69-70 Astros.

Walking pair seasons occur with sufficient regularity for us to predict that we'll see somewhere between three and five in the 90s. Were it not for injuries that kept Rickey Henderson and Mark McGwire out of the lineup for more than twenty games each, there would have been two sets of walking pairs in the AL last season. (And, if McGwire stays with the A's and Lance Blankenship plays full time, the A's have a shot at having only the fifth trio to crack 100 BB in a single season).

That's a lot of "ifs." And a question that needs answering about walkmen is just how "iffy" they are. (The conventional wisdom of baseball would have you believe that walking is a random phenomenon. To which I say: macho myths are extremely hard to kill.) Are walkmen "fickle"? Do they have a big walk year and then nosedive due to an inability to remain disciplined, or because pitchers decide to throw them strikes?

Macho men, eat your heart out. Because the year after a 100+ walk season, 40.5% of the walkmen crack 100 walks again (153 out of 378). An additional 14.8% walk between 90 and 99 times the following season. That exact same percentage walk 80 to 89 teams in the next year. All told, 70% of walkmen get back at least 80% of their BB achievement in the following year. Nearly 20% of the the group draw more walks in the season after a 100+ BB performance. In short, there is an art and a science to walking that can be learned and applied, and it is a skill with sufficient stability to serve as an identifying agent for a player's offensive profile.

However, it is more fragile than some of the other identifiers. It is more difficult to maintain a high walk ratio than it is to maintain an extra-base hit level, for example. Third season correlations indicate that players remain within 20% of their extra-base totals (+/-) about 75% of the time; the figure is down at around 45% for walks, and rises only to about 55% for our walkmen (third season, remember, not second or "following" season).

For walking is a tricky art. Baseball players are trained to be aggressive: they are indoctrinated to put the ball in play. They are seduced by the forty-year overemphasis on hitting the long ball. There is pressure placed on most hitters to be less patient at the plate than they might be otherwise. ("He doesn't want to hit." "He's a looker." "You can't walk

your way off the island.") Only a few swim upsteam, against the torrents of propaganda which would bid them swing. The true walkman—the Rickey Hendersons, the Max Bishops, the Roy Thomases, the four Eddies (Lake, Joost, Stanky, and Yost)—are rare in any generation. When someone like Rickey comes along who can hit for average and power, steal a record number of bases, and walk a ton, he's among the ten best players in the history of the game. The rest of the crop had to walk even more frequently than a Henderson just to get to the big leagues, and they starred there despite the fact that their big skill was underappreciated.

But are walkmen born and not made? The answer is "yes and no." Some are born, some are made. The first-time age of walkmen mirrors the distribution for all walkman seasons, as shown in the chart below. Walking increases as a player gets older, and players tend to cluster their highest walking seasons together in patterns of two to four years. The variations within the pattern of walking indicate that it is very much an acquired capability, and that players who have demonstrated the innate tendency can exploit it further, e.g. the late-blooming tendencies of hitters like Jimmy Sheckard, Eddie Joost, and Dolf Camilli.

Primarily, walking is a mental activity that requires discipline and encouragement. The two 800-walk teams in history, the 1948-49 Red Sox, coincided with three elements: an anchoring slugger with tremendous plate discipline in Ted Williams, two selective hitters (Pesky and Dom DiMaggio) coupled with a "fluke" walker (Vern Stephens), and a manager who actively encouraged walks (Joe McCarthy). In 1992, Tony LaRussa made walking an active element in his offensive strategy, and the A's became the first team in more than twenty years to crack the 700 walk barrier. It helped them win a division that no one thought they could win when the season began.

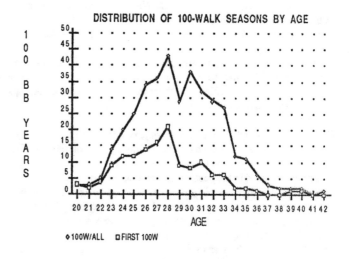

What is the difference between the walkman type and the average hitter? It's pretty simple: he takes more pitches. The listing of "pitches seen per plate appearance" that STATS provides shows that the Top Ten list in each league is dominated by players who walk a lot. On the AL list, four of the five 100+ BB hitters appear: Tettleton is first, Tartabull 3rd, Milligan 4th, and Frank Thomas 9th. In the NL, Brett Butler (95 walks) is first.

There is also a difference between "pitches seen" and "pitches taken," especially early in the count. Four big-walk leadoff men (Brady Anderson, Brett Butler, Rickey Henderson, and Tony Phillips) were compared against the league average in terms of BBP for plate appearances after the count is 0-1 and 1-0, and also in terms of frequency of occurrence of the 0-1 and 1-0 counts. The findings showed that after an 0-1 count, the four walkmen had an 89% increase in BBP over the league; the gain after the 1-0 count was lower but still significant (69%). The percentage of 1-0 counts was about 10% higher for the walkmen than the league, which means that the walkmen take more first pitches (9% of walkmen plate appearances end on the first pitch, as opposed to over 14% for the AL and NL as a whole). The conundrum for managers is that the first-pitch batting average is .302. What they overlook is that the true on-base average for this count situation is also .302, while the on-base average after a 1-0 count is .370.

What isn't known from the STATS data is the frequency of batters swinging and missing the first pitch. This would be an interesting piece of comparative data, but we can use common sense and extrapolate from the fact that walkmen receive 10% more 1-0 counts to see that walkmen are taking a lot more first pitches in general.

And what this means, of course, is that anyone can decide to try to work the count more. In short, anyone can decide to be a walkman. What is so strange and disconcerting is to discover how few decide to do so. My favorite players—and the ones I try to collect on fantasy teams—are those who work the count, who draw walks. My especial favorites are the guys who do this almost as a way of life, in some cases (see the sidebar on Warren Newson) as a means of major league survival.

WALKMEN DREAM TEAMS

I'd love to see a modern-day team load up with walkmen and make a run for it. The Tigers and the A's are the two teams with the best shot at putting these teams together. If the Tigers would sign Milligan, and trade for Newson, they could have a pretty amazing lineup in 1993. I'd bat it like this:

1. Phillips, cf
2. Newson, lf
3. Whitaker, 2b
4. Fielder, 1b
5. Tettleton, c
6. Milligan, dh
7. Fryman, 3b
8. Deer, rf
9. Trammell, ss

Despite the dud in the #7 slot (Fryman never walks), this team could probably crank out about 750 walks. If the A's added Milligan and Newson, and keep McGwire, they'd look pretty scary in the walk department too:

1. Henderson, lf
2. Blankenship, 2b
3. Sierra, rf
4. McGwire, 1b
5. Milligan, dh
6. Steinbach, c
7. Newson, cf
8. Bordick, ss
9. Browne, 3b

Not nearly as much power here, and the A's might be ready to try someone like Troy Neel at DH this season, but this team could get close to the Detroit total. The best option would be if Detroit signed McGwire, then traded Fielder and Fryman to the Phillies for Kruk and Hollins. Then you'd have a real walkin' team:

1. Phillips, cf
2. Newson, rf
3. Hollins, 3b
4. McGwire, 1b
5. Tettleton, c
6. Kruk, lf
7. Whitaker, 2b
8. Milligan, dh
9. Trammell, ss

Of course the Tigers aren't going to trade Fryman, but this lineup would definitely make a serious run at 800 walks in a season. Maybe the best collection of walkmen ever can be simulated in a competition like Bill James' Winter Game, which is what I've done for the sake of experimentation this winter. The Tokyo Walkmen are entered in the Hardball Association League: they aren't the absolute optimum walkers (Ruth and Williams are way too expensive to allow anyone to build a team of walkers—or any other players—around them), but they're pretty damn close. The optimum starting lineup from the team I picked:

1. Billy Hamilton, cf (5 100+ BB seasons, lifetime BBP 15.86)
2. John McGraw, ss (3 100+ BB seasons, lifetime BBP 17.53)
3. Charlie Keller, lf (5 100+ BB seasons, lifetime BBP 17.24)
4. Dolf Camilli, 1b (4 100+ BB seasons, lifetime BBP 15.01)
5. Al Rosen, 3b (1 100+ BB season, lifetime BBP 13.61)
6. Roy Cullenbine, rf (3 100+ BB seasons, lifetime BBP 18.01)
7. Max Bishop, 2b (7 100+ BB seasons, lifetime BBP 20.42)
8. Dick Dietz, c (1 100+ BB season, lifetime BBP 17.14)

Bench players are: Wes Westrum, Joe Collins, Don Buford, Hank Thompson, and Wayne Causey (Buford and Westrum are members of the BB100 Club; Collins, Thompson, and Causey were the best talent at the price to fit the definitions and fill the required backup positions). The pitchers are Dazzy Vance, Wes Ferrell, Bob Caruthers, Jesse Tannehill, Rube Foster, Dick Radatz, and Tom Hall.

We'll do a complete rundown on how the Walkmen fared in the Winter Game in next year's book. A warning, though: the simulation, at least though the early weeks of the simulated season, doesn't appear to give the walkmen their due (even sabermetricians can ignore the value of a walk and—more important conceptually—the continuity of walking skills across eras). The fate of the Walkmen may be a spectacular, controversial, and contentious matter—just like this article, which is dedicated to the proposition that the macho bias against taking pitches must come to an end. Make those pitchers WORK for those outs!!

The Next Eddie Stanky - Victimized by the Arms Race
Gary W. Jones

Don Malcolm

Odds are that you haven't heard of Gary W. Jones. Why should you? He never made it to the majors. He is just one of several thousand gifted athletes who wind up with chump change instead of the fattened money clip. Over the course of baseball history, there have been many more flagrant cases of players who have never gotten the shot they deserved in the majors. Negro Leaguers suffered more virulent discrimination. But Gary W. Jones was also discriminated against, and in ways no less invidious for their subtlety and seeming lack of harm.

For you see, Gary W. Jones is a walkman. During an eight-year career in the minors that saw him reach AAA ball, he drew 783 walks in 899 games. His lifetime BBP (walks per 100 plate appearances) was 21.32—higher than anyone in the history of baseball at any level. Higher than Ted Williams or Babe Ruth— or Max Bishop, the man Jones most closely resembled. His MLE's indicated that he would have been a perennial 100+ BB man in the majors. Whether he would have hit much higher than .250 is hard to say, but the walk totals would have kept his OBP close to .400—in short, the type of leadoff man that most managers say they're looking for, but rarely choose to use when one materializes from wherever walkmen come from.

I blame World War II for Gary Jones' plight. It brought us nuclear weapons, which destroyed the concept of a global land-based war. Since all global wars could now be fought by men in bunkers firing warheads at each other, there would never be a scenario where a high proportion of major league baseball talent would find itself in uniform fighting overseas. Hence there would never be a situation permitting marginal players to establish themselves as major leaguers, as had occurred in 1943-45.

Eddie Stanky was one of the players who came up during World War II. He was 26. If it hadn't been for the war, Stanky's fiery temperament and walk-taking skills would remain unknown. Gary Jones needed a war like that one—not some limited conflict in a banana republic, but a grueling, labor-intensive, protracted war that siphoned off the bigger, the stronger. You know, all the guys that look like jocks.

That's the crime against Gary Jones. Baseball is a small place, and like most closed shops there are rules that don't necessarily stand up to scrutiny but continue to be applied. Rules that work against short players with little power. Assumptions that damn with faint praise a player who makes taking pitches into a central offensive strategy.

I first encountered Gary Jones in a Baseball Guide, the 1984 one. He was at that point in the Cubs organization and was playing second base in the California League. His keystone companion at that point was Shawon Dunston. I was struck by the diametric opposition in the two players' offensive strategies. Dunston drew 7 walks during his 1983 stay in the Midwest league: Jones drew 126 walks, had a .466 OBP, and had 58 stolen bases. Dunston gets bumped up to the Texas League; Jones moves on to a second year of A-ball.

Jones has another fine year offensively at Lodi. His walk total remains outrageously high (138). By this point I can't stand it. During the winter of 1984 I do the first research on walk levels, discovering the "walk spike" in the 1948-50 American League. I have begun a brief correspondence with Craig Wright, precipitated by a misattribution that I made in an article. Craig turned out to be pretty gracious about it, and I learned never to publish something that I hadn't verified myself.

Since I have gone a bit batty over walks, I bring up the subject of Gary Jones to Craig. At that point in time, Craig was working for the Texas Rangers as a sabermetrician—still the only one ever hired directly by a major league baseball club—so it was his business to know everything, including the details on Gary Jones' career. His letter gives us the full perspective on the challenges facing a 5'9" converted outfielder in his effort to overcome long odds and make it to the big leagues:

```
7 March 1985

Dear Don,

I thought you'd like to know more about Jones. He is
a Texas boy from Henderson. Played college ball for
Arkansas U. as an outfielder. We had one scout who
liked him based on:


+

Plus speed
Above avg. range in OF
Good eye, draws walks
Good build for little guy, bowlegged
Left-hand batter


-

Small: 5'9", 162, no growth left
Below avg power (way below for OF)
Below average arm
Near-sighted, contacts, may
deteriorate
```

This scout recommended him for draft and $10,000 signing bonus. No one ended up drafting him. Signed by Cubs as a free agent in July 1982. Now every team would be willing to have him, but that is a long way from seeing him as a major league prospect. These facts must temper your enthusiasm:

1) He is 24 and has yet to play above high A-ball.

2) His conversion to the infield is not a success yet. His range is not as strong as it first appears. In California League his range was strictly middle of the pack and he was below average on DP. He is extremely error-prone. In 1983 he fielded .953 and led the second basemen with 30 errors. In 1984 he fielded .945 and led again with 39 errors, 14 more than any other second baseman. I still have hope for him though.

3) In 1984, relative to the league average, he hit for less average, walked less, and was less successful as a stealer than in 1983.

Still, I believe he is a major league prospect like Eddie Stanky was. Stanky didn't get to the majors until he was 26. Jones could do it. Maybe we'll get a chance to acquire him. That's more difficult than you would think.

Best wishes,
Craig

So the facts about Gary Jones dovetail neatly into the dilemma for walkmen. A small player is rarely paid much attention, even if he has significant offensive talent, if he plays somewhere other than the middle infield. Gary Jones played the outfield in college. He wanted to play pro baseball pretty badly—a lot of 5'9" guys want it a lot more than their six-footer counterparts. He got a tryout with the Cubs, who decided that he would never make it as an outfielder, and kept him in Class A ball an extra year to work on his conversion to second base.

The rest of the story gets more interesting—and more agonizing. Jones was promoted to Pittsfield, the Cubs' Eastern League (AA) affiliate, in 1985. The Eastern League is known for being a pitcher's league, so Jones had his work cut out for him. He started slowly, got hurt, but hit about .330 in the last four weeks to inch his batting average over .250. His BBP was down, but it was still the league's best at over 18%. (Remember that the average player walks about 9% of the time.)

At this point, the Cubs gave up on him, or decided that they wanted another prospect more, for they included Jones in a swap of minor league prospects. Jones was traded to the Oakland A's organization during the 1985-86 off-season. He winds up at Huntsville, the A's Southern League (AA) farm team, and has a helluva year with the bat. He hits .311, walks 128 times, scores 116 runs, steals 34 bases. His on-base percentage is .464; his BBP is slightly over 22%. His MLE projects him to hit .270 with 105 walks.

The A's, however, have 5'10" Tony Phillips already at 2B, so there is not much chance that Jones is going to crack the A's lineup in 1987. He is sent to Tacoma in the Pacific Coast League

(AAA). He has another fine year. His average is down a bit (.277), but the walks remain constant (a league-leading 123). His OBP is .426, his BBP is 20.64%. Tony Phillips breaks an ankle in late July. But the A's are in a pennant race (sort of) and trade for Tony Bernazard instead of giving Jones a shot. He doesn't even get a September call-up.

In 1988, the bottom begins to drop out of Jones' chances to make it with the A's. First, Oakland signs veteran second baseman Glenn Hubbard, a 5'8" banjo hitter whose profile is similar to Jones. Well, they're both short. Jones goes back to Tacoma and has a bad year—hits just .234, misses about 30 games either due to injury or because his BA was too low. But the killing blow isn't Hubbard or the bad season. It's the emergence of a younger player with a similar profile.

Who is that man? Lance Blankenship. The man who might become the third 100+ walkman on the A's. (Belatedly, of course—it took Lance several years to get his shot, and he showed just enough in 1992 to get a full opportunity this year.) Blankenship, a tenth round draft pick for the A's in 1986, made it to Tacoma in 1988 and, shifted from third base (his original position, the one he played at Cal), he led all PCL second basemen in total chances and also led the league in walks with 96. Blankenship was a better infielder than Jones, he walked about 75% as much and he had a little more pop in his bat (due in part to being 6', 185 instead of 5'9", 165): it stands to reason that he would move ahead of Jones.

All of which makes sense in context. If we want to assume that baseball teams value walks at the appropriate level, we can say that Gary Jones got incredibly unlucky. He signed with the Cubs, who had Ryne Sandberg. He was traded to the A's organization, where a procession of players with skills bearing a pale resemblance to his outrageous walk-taking skill were either already on the big league club, acquired by the big league club, or were drafted by the organization. He got lost in the shuffle.

But if we begin with the notion that baseball teams don't value walks sufficiently, we see that Gary Jones' central skill was never seen as a consistently valuable offensive resource. Certainly not in the way that speed, power, and hitting for average are prized. The well-known joke "Those who can't do, teach" translates into baseball epistemology as "Those who can't hit, walk." The bias against walks runs very deep. Jack Clark was constantly criticized for taking too many pitches even during his career year in 1987. As he aged, and lost a significant amount of his batting average, the criticism escalated. Due to Clark's previously established reputation as an offensive force, baseball dimly seemed to realize that Jack Clark hitting .240 and walking 20% of the time was worth at least as much as someone else hitting .285 and walking half as much.

The key word in that last sentence is "dimly." Players with Gary Jones' profile—good but not great speed, little power, good but not great batting average—are all over the place. The farm system is supposed to sift them out, to see who's got what it takes to make it at that most intense level of competition. The three elements we just listed are common attributes of erstwhile major leaguers. There are two others that come into play—defensive ability, especially in the middle infield; and ability to take walks. If we ranked these five elements in terms of baseball's decision making practice for advancing players through the farm system to the majors, allowing for 100 points (representing 100% of the process), the figures would look something like this:

1. Batting average   30
2. Power   25
3. Speed   20
4. Defense   20
5. Walk-taking   5

In a structure such as this, Gary Jones could walk 30% of the time and still not get a look. And that's just about what he did in 1989, his last season in organized baseball. Sent back to Huntsville after 11 games with Tacoma (no room for him in the outfield there, what with Dann Howitt, Doug Jennings, and Felix Jose), Jones responded with 107 walks in 96 games. The BBP for Jones' second stint at Huntsville: 27.16%. That rate is higher than any single season BBP turned in during the history of major league baseball.

Baseball's lack of science is lamentable enough in general, but its performance with respect to players with an extreme skill centered around strike zone judgment is abominable. The great walkmen who have made it to the big leagues at a young age had exceptional skills in the other areas of the game, and those are the skills that got them there. Can you think of a single player at the age of 21 who made it to the majors because the big league club liked the way he worked the count for walks?

It's common knowledge that hitters walk less the higher they go in organized baseball. Pulling out any Baseball Guide (for example, the 1988 Guide) will demonstrate that. There were no 100+ walkmen in any of the three AAA leagues in the U.S., though Blankenship was close with 96. Likewise, there were no 100+ walkers in AA either: Ed Whited, veteran catcher in the Braves system on his way back down from the majors, had the

highest total (97). But when we get to the full-season Class A leagues, things change. In the California League in 1988 there were no less than seven 100+ walkers. Some of these names will be familiar, some won't: Carlos Montoyo (156), Mark Leonard (118), Greg Ritchie (116), Paul Sorrento (110), Warren Newson (107), Mike Brocki (107), Ruben Amaro (105). Four of these seven are in the majors right now, but only one has a regular job (Sorrento). Only Amaro has yet to show a pronounced ability to draw walks at the major league level.

Of the other three, one (Brocki) is no longer in baseball. The other two (Montoyo and Ritchie) have made it to AAA. Montoyo is a second baseman in the Brewers organization who hit .324 in 89 games at Denver last season. His lifetime BBP is 19.5%, though it was down to 15.4% last season. Still, Montoyo's MLE for '92 shows a solid .283 BA with a .371 OBP. He could play for someone—but probably not the Brewers, who seem committed to playing Bill Spiers or Bill Doran at second. Ritchie is a 29-year-old left-handed slap-hitting outfielder who has been stalled at Phoenix for the past three seasons. He played less than half the time in '92, but he still knows how to walk (19.03 BBP). He has even less of a chance than Montoyo, though, because he's an outfielder without power, plus the Giants have all these outfield prospects (Leonard, Darren Lewis, Ted Wood, Steve Hosey) to cram into no spare slot, since there's still Willie McGee, plus free agents Barry Bonds and Dave Martinez.

It's easy to get trapped in a farm system. But Gary Jones was special. His lifetime BBP was over 21%—higher, as I said earlier, than anyone else in the history of the game. There is no reason to believe that he wouldn't have retained 85% of that walking ability in the majors. That works out to a projected major league BBP of slightly over 18%. Add a .250 batting average and you wind up with an OBP hovering slightly above .390. He would have been another Eddie Stanky. But Stanky needed World War II to get his shot. There was no such attrition of talent to force the majors to quit ignoring Gary Jones' magnificent talents. If he is bitter and haunted by his experience in professional baseball, he has every right to be.

Jones' complete minor league record:

Year	Team	Lea	G	AB	R	H	TB	D	T	HR	RBI	BB	SO	SB	BA	SA	OBP	BBP
1982	Chicago-NL	Fla. St.	29	106	29	37	42	3	1	0	12	17	16	18	.349	.396	.439	13.82
1982	Geneva	NY-P	2	5	1	1	4	0	0	1	1	1	1	0	.200	.800	.333	16.67
1983	Quad Cty	Mid	133	428	105	132	179	23	3	6	34	126	105	58	.308	.418	.466	22.74
1984	Lodi	Cal	138	471	111	137	184	17	6	6	44	138	94	38	.291	.391	.452	22.66
1985	Pittsfield	East	111	325	56	82	99	7	5	0	30	72	51	17	.252	.305	.388	18.14
1986	Huntsville	So	130	450	116	140	177	23	4	2	49	128	60	34	.311	.393	.464	22.15
1987	Tacoma	PCL	135	473	102	131	174	22	6	3	49	123	83	30	.277	.368	.426	20.64
1988	Tacoma	PCL	114	312	50	73	95	8	4	2	22	68	61	13	.234	.304	.371	17.89
1989	Tacoma	PCL	11	32	5	7	16	1	1	2	5	3	10	1	.219	.500	.286	8.57
1989	Huntsville	So	96	287	67	79	98	10	3	1	45	107	61	16	.275	.341	.472	27.16
TOTAL			899	2889	642	819	1068	114	33	23	291	783	542	225	.283	.370	.436	21.32

Who the Hell is
Warren Newson

And Why is   Don Malcolm   Ranting about Him Anyway?

1) He's a 5'7", 190 lb. outfielder for the Chicago White Sox who could be the next great walkman;

2) Because it's my job (to rant about guys like this).

You might recall Newson's name from the sidebar on Gary Jones. He was one of seven players in the California League during 1988 who drew more than 100 walks (107 to be exact). Unlike Gary Jones, Warren Newson has some pop in his bat (doubtless because he looks like a left-handed version of Kirby Puckett). At Riverside in 1988, he hit .297, with 23 doubles, 7 triples, and 22 home runs. He slugged .532, got on base .432.

The Padres, who owned him at the time, were dutifully impressed enough to send him up to Wichita in the Texas League in 1989. Newson essentially duplicated his performance at Riverside: .304 BA, 103 walks, 20 doubles, 6 triples, 18 homers, .505 SA, .438 OBP. This was, again, reasonably impressive to the Padres, so they moved Newson up to Las Vegas.

At AAA Newson veered just a bit off track. He hit .304 (about .275 elsewhere), slugged .465 (about .420 elsewhere), but his on-base remained constant (.421 with 83 walks). The Padres, filled with holes in the outfield big enough to drive a tank through, decided he wasn't going to make it and traded him to the White Sox. (After all, how many guys that look like Tony Gwynn could you stand to have on the same team? We've got to be fashion conscious, for Chrissakes. Too many guys who look like fire hydrants could cause a serious pissing contest to break out in the clubhouse, and you know what that leads to.)

The Sox, ever cautious, and because they hadn't quite finished flagellating themselves with the lost potential of Dan Pasqua, start Newson out at Vancouver in 1991. Warren proceeds to seriously mangle the PCL for about six weeks, hitting .369 and getting on-base half the time (.497). The Sox, smelling smoke from the northwest woods, recall Newson but decide that they shouldn't rush him into a starting job too fast (after all, there's still Pasqua's ghost to be exorcised). Newson, in limited action, is extremely impressive: he hits .295, is on base .419, and even hits 4 homers in 160 PA (works out to about 16 in a full season).

It looks like Newson might get a chance to be a #2 hitter (leadoff is out of the question, 'cause the Sox have Tim Raines), but—

NO! The Sox "go for a pennant" and sign Steve Sax, who is erroneously installed as the #2 hitter and promptly has one of his lousiest years. Newson is relegated to a backup role and slides downward, hitting .221 and even getting farmed out for some regular playing time at Vancouver. The on-base capability, however, remains intact. Warren's BBP for 1992 is 21.4. He has more walks (37) than hits (30). Retreads Mike Huff and Shawn Abner get more playing time than he does, despite the fact that neither one can walk much at all.

Newson's slump in 1992 may signal the end of his chance to be a prominent member of the White Sox' offense. The handwriting appears to be writ large: over the winter the Sox have signed Ellis Burks. You see, they're still "going for a pennant" and they can't afford to have a guy in right field who gets on base .387 even when he's hitting .221. Ellis Burks is two months younger than Warren Newson, is 6'2, 205, and looks like a ballplayer. In the past two seasons, Burks has hit just .252, and has gotten on base just .314. His BBP is 8.4. He has lost his base stealing ability (last three years he's had a less than 50% success rate). He clearly isn't the ballplayer he once was, but he's only 28 and he has this nice set of stats, so the White Sox were more than willing to toss a contract at him worth $500,000 and lots of incentives.

Meanwhile, of course, Newson collects splinters. It wouldn't be so bad to gamble on Burks if the Sox would think about putting him in center and getting Lance Johnson out of there. But the White Sox aren't likely to do that, because Johnson is considered to be a fine center fielder and has just enough batting average and speed to fool them into believing that he's an effective offensive performer. His BBP last year was 5.7. Jeff Torborg discovered in 1991 that Johnson just couldn't cut it as a #2 hitter: hence Steve Sax, who couldn't cut it either. The #2 hitter the Sox need is right under their noses, but will they ever give Newson 300 AB's to prove it to them?

If I were the general manager of the Colorado Rockies, I would have drafted Warren Newson in the expansion draft. Failing that, I would trade for him—I'd give the Sox a pitching prospect, a Mo Sanford, for instance. Then I'd put Warren at the top of my lineup and tell him to work the count and try to get on base .400. Bill James' projection for Newson in 1993—even with last season—shows his OBP at .395. Here's the full projection, recalculated to show a full season (640 plate appearances):

AB	R	H	TB	D	T	HR	RBI	BB	SO	SB	CS	BA	SA	OBP	RC27	BBP
532	79	144	213	23	3	13	66	108	141	13	10	.272	.401	.395	5.87	16.9

This is one helluva leadoff man. And you can figure that these totals are a little low, because Denver ought to be a hitter's park. Only the stolen base totals are marginal: but Newson has stolen as many as 36 in the minors and can probably reach 20-25 with a 65-70% success rate.

The above projection is why I am ranting about Warren Newson. He is so much better than what most teams customarily lead off that it makes me sick to see him languishing in obscurity. The following teams should line up and bid for Warren's services: Boston, Detroit, Milwaukee, California, Kansas City, Minnesota, Texas in the AL; Chicago, Florida, New York, Philadelphia, Pittsburgh, St. Louis, Colorado, Los Angeles, San Diego in the NL. That's 16 teams out of 28 that have no excuse for not giving Newson a shot except the Jerome Waltons and Brian McRaes that they keep trotting out there. There's got to be one of you sixteen willing to take a gamble: he's not going to cost you much, for Crissakes, just a pitching prospect, probably (the White Sox need starting pitching so badly it ain't funny). Somebody—anybody— show some imagination. Keep Warren Newson from becoming another Gary Jones. Give him a full time job. As Al Franken used to say, you'll be glad you did.

II

Team
Comments

Eastern Division

1. Toronto Blue Jays
2. Milwaukee Brewers
3. Baltimore Orioles
4. Cleveland Indians
5. New York Yankees
6. Detroit Tigers
7. Boston Red Sox

AL Eastern Division Team Batting

	G	AB	Run	Hit	2B	3B	HR	TB	RBI	W	K	IW	HB	SB	CS	BRng Eff	GI DP	SH	SF	Avg	Slug	OBP	Runs Ctd
Baltimore	1734	5485	705	1423	243	36	148	2182	680	647	827	55	51	89	48	.432	139	50	59	.259	.398	.340	758
Boston	1741	5461	599	1343	259	21	84	1896	567	591	865	46	31	44	48	.405	116	60	43	.246	.347	.321	621
Cleveland	1723	5620	674	1495	227	24	127	2151	637	448	885	46	45	144	67	.457	140	42	44	.266	.383	.323	689
Detroit	1677	5515	791	1411	256	16	182	2245	746	675	1055	42	24	66	45	.385	124	43	53	.256	.407	.337	772
Milwaukee	1644	5504	740	1477	272	35	82	2065	683	511	779	45	33	256	115	.440	100	61	72	.268	.375	.330	704
New York	1670	5593	733	1462	281	18	163	2268	703	536	903	51	42	78	37	.439	138	26	55	.261	.406	.328	746
Toronto	1645	5536	780	1458	265	40	163	2292	737	561	933	41	47	129	39	.429	121	26	54	.263	.414	.333	784

AL Eastern Division Sabermetric Team Batting

	AB	Run	Hit	2B	3B	HR	RBI	W	SO	Avg	Ball Park Adjusted Slug	OBP	Runs Ctd	Outs	Run/ 27o	OW%	OG	OWAR
Baltimore	5462	709	1448	259	34	140	682	649	841	.265	.402	.345	772	4333	4.81	.567	160	34.88
Boston	5544	588	1309	241	21	89	554	606	903	.236	.335	.313	592	4517	3.54	.450	167	16.70
Cleveland	5706	649	1471	217	26	122	616	448	895	.258	.369	.316	664	4525	3.96	.450	168	16.71
Detroit	5526	785	1419	251	17	170	745	648	1026	.257	.401	.334	753	4376	4.65	.474	162	20.13
Milwaukee	5325	782	1470	292	42	89	719	492	772	.276	.397	.337	732	4189	4.72	.564	155	33.20
New York	5678	725	1482	289	20	158	693	528	941	.261	.402	.326	745	4454	4.52	.495	165	23.86
Toronto	5506	783	1464	254	36	164	735	537	927	.266	.414	.333	775	4277	4.89	.540	158	30.15

AL Eastern Division Team Pitching

	ERA	W	L	Pct	G	GS	CG	ShO	GF	Sv	IP	R	ER	H	2B	3B	HR	BB	IW	SO	HB	WP	BK
Baltimore	3.79	89	73	.549	452	162	20	9	142	48	1464.0	656	617	1419	250	31	124	518	38	846	36	45	6
Boston	3.63	73	89	.451	490	162	22	6	140	39	1448.2	669	585	1403	260	28	107	535	56	943	41	50	6
Cleveland	4.11	76	86	.469	541	162	13	4	149	46	1470.0	746	672	1507	245	27	159	566	31	890	34	53	12
Detroit	4.61	75	87	.463	517	162	10	2	152	36	1435.2	794	736	1534	254	26	155	564	88	693	29	57	3
Milwaukee	3.43	92	70	.568	500	162	19	6	143	39	1457.0	604	556	1344	250	26	127	435	33	793	47	37	8
New York	4.22	76	86	.469	470	162	20	4	142	44	1452.2	746	681	1453	270	33	129	612	49	851	35	52	7
Toronto	3.92	96	66	.593	446	162	18	5	144	49	1440.2	682	627	1346	260	18	124	541	37	954	45	66	6

AL Eastern Division Sabermetric Team Pitching

	Adj ERA	Expected W	L	Pct	BFP	Avg	Opposing Batters Slg	OBA	RC/G	GDP	SB	CS	PK	PKE	SH	SF	Supported RSup	RSp/G	W	L	Pct
Baltimore	3.82	83	79	.514	6193	.257	.380	.322	4.22	138	131	44	5	6	59	47	705	4.33	83	79	.515
Boston	3.55	89	73	.549	6173	.255	.371	.323	4.15	138	115	51	5	6	51	49	599	3.72	77	85	.475
Cleveland	3.96	80	82	.495	6330	.268	.407	.336	4.67	154	109	64	5	6	56	56	674	4.13	76	86	.472
Detroit	4.58	69	93	.424	6254	.277	.416	.343	4.99	131	102	61	5	6	52	63	791	4.96	80	82	.492
Milwaukee	3.60	88	74	.543	6040	.246	.371	.305	3.79	124	95	53	5	6	47	42	740	4.57	92	70	.570
New York	4.16	76	86	.470	6256	.263	.394	.338	4.66	139	164	62	5	6	39	53	733	4.54	80	82	.495
Toronto	3.92	81	81	.500	6108	.248	.371	.318	4.18	85	144	62	5	6	32	55	780	4.87	91	71	.560

```
AL Eastern Division Catchers
            G    PO    A   Er    TC   DP  PB   SB   CS  CS%   FPct     DI    DG   DW%   DWAR   ERA
Baltimore  162   897   72    5   974   12  15  131   44 .251  .995   1464.0  10.0  .396   0.46  3.79
Boston     162   988   72   11  1071   14   8  115   51 .307  .990   1448.1  10.0  .389   0.39  3.63
Cleveland  162   938   83    8  1029    7   9  109   64 .370  .992   1470.0  10.0  .322  -0.28  4.11
Detroit    162   752   69    7   828   17   8  102   61 .374  .992   1435.2  10.0  .240  -1.10  4.61
Milwaukee  162   853   83   11   947    8   5   95   53 .358  .988   1457.0  10.0  .415   0.65  3.43
New York   162   906   87   11  1004   10  16  164   62 .274  .989   1452.1  10.0  .283  -0.67  4.22
Toronto    162   973  106   10  1089    8  15  144   62 .301  .991   1440.0  10.0  .367   0.17  3.92
LG.AVG     162   916   84   11  1011   11  11  121   61 .335  .989   1440.2
```

```
AL Eastern Division First Base
            G    PO    A   Er    TC   DP  FPct     DI    DG   DW%   DWAR
Baltimore  162  1402  110    8  1520  152 .995   1464.0   3.0  .551   0.60
Boston     162  1526  110   23  1659  148 .986   1448.1   3.0  .408   0.17
Cleveland  162  1435  110   10  1555  165 .994   1470.0   3.0  .476   0.38
Detroit    162  1455  123   17  1595  144 .989   1435.2   3.0  .495   0.43
Milwaukee  162  1481  129   10  1620  136 .994   1457.0   3.0  .507   0.47
New York   162  1453  123    6  1582  157 .996   1452.1   3.0  .637   0.86
Toronto    162  1400  107    8  1515   99 .995   1440.0   3.0  .528   0.53
LG.AVG     162  1443  115   11  1569  142 .993   1440.2
```

```
AL Eastern Division Second Base
            G    PO    A   Er    TC   DP  FPct     DI    DG   DW%   DWAR
Baltimore  162   357  524   12   893  116 .987   1464.0   8.0  .649   2.40
Boston     162   362  542   15   919  124 .984   1448.1   8.0  .653   2.43
Cleveland  162   407  483   19   909  140 .979   1470.0   8.0  .630   2.24
Detroit    162   370  482   13   865  111 .985   1435.2   8.0  .546   1.57
Milwaukee  162   361  530    8   899  117 .991   1457.0   8.0  .750   3.20
New York   162   344  504   15   863  115 .983   1452.1   8.0  .552   1.62
Toronto    162   326  442   10   778   72 .987   1440.0   8.0  .427   0.62
LG.AVG     162   357  489   14   860  112 .984   1440.2
```

```
AL Eastern Division Third Base
            G    PO    A   Er    TC   DP  FPct     DI    DG   DW%   DWAR
Baltimore  162   122  318   25   465   27 .946   1464.0   6.0  .442   0.55
Boston     162   102  351   20   473   29 .958   1448.1   6.0  .483   0.80
Cleveland  162   101  330   33   464   30 .929   1470.0   6.0  .349  -0.01
Detroit    162   127  328   22   477   30 .954   1435.2   6.0  .470   0.72
Milwaukee  162   123  303   13   439   21 .970   1457.0   6.0  .511   0.97
New York   162   110  291   18   419   40 .957   1452.1   6.0  .468   0.71
Toronto    162   141  295   28   464   14 .940   1440.0   6.0  .363   0.08
LG.AVG     162   119  327   23   469   28 .951   1440.2
```

```
AL Eastern Division Shortstop
            G    PO    A   Er    TC   DP   FPct      DI    DG   DW%    DWAR
Baltimore  162  293  452   13   758  120  .983   1464.0  11.0  .635   3.13
Boston     162  232  552   25   809  118  .969   1448.1  11.0  .592   2.66
Cleveland  162  255  475   33   763  108  .957   1470.0  11.0  .451   1.11
Detroit    162  251  524   23   798  104  .971   1435.2  11.0  .532   2.00
Milwaukee  162  268  516   29   813  103  .964   1457.0  11.0  .617   2.93
New York   162  290  517   26   833  111  .969   1452.1  11.0  .571   2.44
Toronto    162  233  448   11   692   83  .984   1440.0  11.0  .496   1.60
LG.AVG     162  259  499   24   782  106  .969   1440.2
```

```
AL Eastern Division Left Field
            G    PO    A   Er    TC   DP   FPct      DI    DG   DW%    DWAR
Baltimore  162  391   11    8   410    4  .980   1464.0   4.0  .610   1.04
Boston     162  320   14    8   342    2  .977   1448.1   4.0  .548   0.79
Cleveland  162  347   10   12   369    2  .967   1470.0   4.0  .463   0.45
Detroit    162  390   14    9   413    3  .978   1435.2   4.0  .639   1.15
Milwaukee  162  357    8    3   368    0  .992   1457.0   4.0  .600   1.00
New York   162  372   14    4   390    1  .990   1452.1   4.0  .687   1.35
Toronto    162  324   15    6   345    2  .983   1440.0   4.0  .621   1.08
LG.AVG     162  357   11    7   375    1  .981   1440.2
```

```
AL Eastern Division Center Field
            G    PO    A   Er    TC   DP   FPct      DI    DG   DW%    DWAR
Baltimore  162  451    5    6   462    3  .987   1464.0   6.0  .502   0.91
Boston     162  376   12   10   398    1  .975   1448.1   6.0  .395   0.27
Cleveland  162  467   15    8   490    4  .984   1470.0   6.0  .588   1.43
Detroit    162  457    8    6   471    2  .987   1435.2   6.0  .521   1.03
Milwaukee  162  460    6    2   468    0  .996   1457.0   6.0  .638   1.73
New York   162  471    9    6   486    4  .988   1452.1   6.0  .559   1.26
Toronto    162  491   10    7   508    2  .986   1440.0   6.0  .613   1.58
LG.AVG     162  458    9    6   473    2  .987   1440.2
```

```
AL Eastern Division Right Field
            G    PO    A   Er    TC   DP   FPct      DI    DG   DW%    DWAR
Baltimore  162  374   15    8   397    2  .980   1464.0   5.0  .665   1.57
Boston     162  350   13    6   369    4  .984   1448.1   5.0  .590   1.20
Cleveland  162  367   15    7   389    2  .982   1470.0   5.0  .635   1.43
Detroit    162  393   10   10   413    1  .976   1435.2   5.0  .555   1.03
Milwaukee  162  341   14    2   357    3  .994   1457.0   5.0  .722   1.86
New York   162  334   10    8   352    3  .977   1452.1   5.0  .492   0.71
Toronto    162  337   12    8   357    3  .978   1440.0   5.0  .562   1.06
LG.AVG     162  346   12    6   364    2  .984   1440.2
```

Toronto Blue Jays

David Raglin

TORONTO										
YEAR	1983	1984	1985	1986	1987	1988	1989	1990	1991	1992
W	89	89	99	86	96	87	89	86	91	96
L	73	73	62	76	66	75	73	76	71	66
WPCT	0.549	0.549	0.615	0.531	0.593	0.537	0.549	0.531	0.562	0.593
R	795	750	759	809	845	763	731	767	684	780
RA	726	696	588	733	655	680	651	661	622	682
PWPT	0.545	0.537	0.625	0.549	0.625	0.557	0.558	0.574	0.547	0.567
PythW	88	87	101	89	101	90	90	93	89	92
PythL	74	75	61	73	61	72	72	69	73	70
LUCK	1	2	-2	-3	-5	-3	-1	-7	2	4

Defensive Efficiency Record: .7102

What was different about this Blue Jay team than the Blue Jay teams of the last few years? After all, this team won 96 games, the most for Toronto since 1987, only trailing the 1985 Jays (99-92) in team history. From 1988 to 1991, the American League East was a wasteland, basically serving as cannon fodder for the West in the playoffs, but the Jays won just as many games as Oakland during the regular season.

Let's start with the basic building blocks of baseball: runs. Here are the runs scored and allowed by the Blue Jays in 1991 and 1992 along with their win-loss records (league ranks in parenthesis):

	RF	RA	W-L
1991	684 (12th)	622 (1st)	91-71 (2nd)
1992	780 (2nd)	682 (8th)	96-66 (1st)
Difference	+96 (2nd)	-60 (13th)	+5 (5th T)

They actually allowed many more runs in 1992 than they did in 1991; only the Mariners had a bigger dropoff in runs allowed. The offense made up for it, though, scoring 96 more runs in 1992 than they did in 1991. Only Cleveland had a bigger jump (98 runs), and they had the advantage of a reconfigured ball park.

Where did all of the extra runs come from? Let's look at the Blue Jays offense by defensive position to help get the answer. The Bill James statistics Runs Created (RC) and Runs Created Per Game (RC/G), figured using the stolen base method, are provided for comparison purposes. The "Difference" columns are the change from 1991 to 1992; a positive number indicates an improvement.

Position	92 Starter	TWAR	93 Starter	TWAR
Catcher	Borders	1.06	Borders	1.06
First base	Olerud	4.75	Olerud	4.75
Second base	Alomar, R.	6.26	Alomar, R.	6.26
Third base	Gruber	-0.54	Sojo	1.53
Shortstop	Lee, M.	2.44	Zosky	-0.01
Left field	Maldonado	4.48	Bell, D.	0.77
Center field	White	3.76	White	3.76
Right field	Carter, J.	4.64	Carter, J.	4.64
DH	Winfield	5.59	Molitor	6.79

1991 and 1992 Toronto Blue Jays By Defensive Position

1991	AB	BB	R	H	HR	RBI	BA	RC	RC/G
C	576	30	46	147	13	67	.255	65	4.0
1B	563	87	75	135	19	77	.240	76	4.6
2B	647	60	88	190	9	69	.294	105	5.8
3B	602	44	71	150	23	82	.249	73	4.1
SS	539	32	54	120	0	36	.223	40	2.5
LF	590	55	71	159	16	75	.269	84	5.0
CF	679	57	111	189	17	61	.278	102	5.3
RF	623	46	82	158	30	108	.254	87	4.8
DH	581	80	67	144	5	57	.248	68	4.0
PH	89	8	14	20	1	17	.225	8	2.8
Tot	5489	499	684	1412	133	—	.257	707	4.4

Difference 1992	AB	BB	R	H	HR	RBI	BA	RC	RC/G	RC	RC/G
C	587	41	53	137	16	72	.233	62	3.6	-4	-0.4
1B	587	81	77	161	18	79	.274	89	5.5	+13	+0.9
2B	628	90	110	187	8	80	.298	106	6.1	+2	+0.3
3B	609	44	77	140	18	74	.230	63	3.4	-10	-0.7
SS	524	57	66	135	3	47	.258	55	3.6	+14	+1.1
LF	590	67	75	159	22	77	.269	91	5.5	+7	+0.4
CF	696	49	108	175	17	64	.251	87	4.3	-15	-1.0
RF	648	48	108	187	32	125	.289	113	6.3	+25	+1.4
DH	619	78	95	165	29	112	.267	100	5.7	+31	+1.6
PH	48	6	11	12	0	7	.250	5	3.6	-3	+0.8
Total	5536	561	780	1458	163	737	.263	767	4.8	+60	+0.4

Difference 1992	AB	BB	R	H	HR	RBI	BA	RC	RC/G	RC	RC/G
Carter	622	36	97	164	34	119	.264	94	5.3	-10	-0.4
White	641	47	98	159	17	60	.248	79	4.2	-21	-1.3
Winfld	583	82	92	169	26	108	.290	107	6.7	+46	+2.7
Other	707	77	99	194	23	91	.274	109	5.5	+32	+1.4
Total	2553	242	386	686	100	378	.269	390	5.4	+46	+2.4

The runs created formula accounts for 60 of the 96 run increase. In 1991 they scored 23 less runs than the formula said they should, and in 1992, they scored 13 more than the formula predicted. We can use Runs Created to, at least, find out where those 60 runs came from.

Notice where the big changes are. Center field and third base (Devon White and Kelly Gruber/Jeff Kent in 1992) actually dropped off, but the losses were made up there by first base (John Olerud/Pat Tabler) and shortstop (Manny Lee and change). The big changes were in right field and designated hitter.

Designated hitter was a big problem for the 1991 Jays. Their DHs were about equal to their catchers in productivity. Bill James said something in the 1983 Abstract to the effect that if a team is missing a DH, that is relatively good news (compared to, for example, missing a shortstop), because there are always good hitters standing around looking for a job, and anybody can DH.

The Blue Jays realized this, and as soon as the Angels let Dave Winfield go, they outmuscled the Tigers to sign him. He made a huge difference; they went from a catcher's offense to a Top Ten MVP level.

About right field though, didn't Joe Carter play right both years? Did he have a much better 1992, or what else is going on here? Actually in 1991, Carter DHed and played left a bit too. Instead of looking at the outfield/DH in terms of LF/CF/RF/DH, let's look at it in terms of the constants (Carter, White), the big change (1991 DHs/Winfield), and everybody else. Looking at it that way, it becomes much clearer (Carter, White, and Winfield's statistics are for every position):

1991 and 1992 Blue Jay Outfielders/DH

1991	AB	BB	R	H	HR	RBI	BA	RC	RC/G
Carter	638	49	89	174	33	108	.273	103	5.7
White	642	55	110	181	17	60	.282	101	5.6
DH	535	75	61	131	4	53	.245	61	3.9
Oth	658	59	71	164	14	80	.249	78	4.0
Tot	2473	238	331	650	68	301	.263	344	4.8

The improvement between the 1991 DHs and Dave Winfield we know about, but this chart indicates that it is larger than previously indicated (because Joe Carter hit better as a DH in 1991 than 1992, and Winfield hit .355 playing right field in 1992).

The other big improvement is among the "others". Who are those mysterious others. In 1991, there were a mix of schleps (a lot of Mookie Wilson, some Glenallen Hill and Mark Whiten before Cleveland took them off their hands, some good play from Candy Maldonaldo after they got him from Milwaukee, Rob Ducey, Cory Snyder, Dave Parker, Derek Bell, and Turner Ward). In 1992, it was mostly Candy Maldonado, with a little bit of mediocre play from players like Derek Bell thrown in).

The unsung hero of the 1992 Blue Jays was Candy Maldonado. He created 79 runs in 1992, at a 5.7 runs created per game pace. That wasn't a fluke, either. In 1990 for Cleveland, he created 84 runs at a 5.4 pace. He had a disastrous first half of 1991 for the Brewers, but after he was traded to Toronto, he created 29 runs at a 5.9 pace.

So what did the Jays do about Maldonado? They let him go to the Cubs as a free agent. Proper attention has been paid to the loss in pitching depth the Jays have suffered this off-season (Cone, Key, and Henke, adding only Stewart), and the loss of Winfield has been covered by the signing of Molitor, but the loss of Maldonado will hurt too because they don't have a replacement, unless Derek Bell comes through.

It could end up being like the Walt Terrell/Howard Johnson trade the Tigers made after 1984. Even if HoJo hadn't developed into a star, it was a bad trade for the Tigers because it forced them into making Tom Brookens a regular again; they had nobody better.

So much of the 1993 success or failure of the 1993 Toronto Blue Jays will fall on Derek Bell's shoulders. Bell is a great prospect, but the road of the late 1980s is filled with failed Blue Jay outfield can't miss top prospects (Sil Campusano, Rob Ducey, Junior Felix, Glenallen Hill, and Mark Whiten). None of them are stars, or even solid regulars. In 1993, we will see if Derek Bell is added to that list.

Toronto Blue Jays Home Park Performance Factors

	Outs	Runs	Hits	2b	3b	HR	W	K	SH	SF	HBP	IBB	SB	CS	GDP
Home LH Batters	1.020	1.223	1.067	.882	7.334	1.901	.936	1.043	7.334	1.367	2.934	.972	7.334	1.048	.825
Home RH Batters	.954	.926	.970	1.039	.733	.851	.891	.959	.709	.832	.802	.691	.884	1.199	.911
All Home Batters	.967	.948	.983	.969	.783	.953	.894	.979	.846	.897	.868	.741	.929	1.144	.881
Opp LH Batters	1.054	1.071	1.031	.860	1.311	1.086	1.037	1.044	1.086	1.057	1.403	.805	.998	.960	1.086
Opp RH Batters	.999	1.070	1.019	1.020	.937	1.039	.980	.976	1.089	.908	.848	.920	.979	.890	1.043
All Opp Batters	1.016	1.060	1.026	.950	1.032	1.060	1.023	1.008	1.023	.995	.954	.866	1.001	1.036	1.077
All LH Batters	1.043	1.124	1.042	.870	1.503	1.306	.997	1.043	1.296	1.168	1.650	.875	1.045	.956	.948
All RH Batters	.973	.986	.992	1.028	.786	.922	.930	.965	.891	.865	.823	.757	.926	1.010	.964
All Batters	.990	1.002	1.005	.958	.863	1.005	.955	.992	.936	.945	.910	.798	.963	1.061	.964

Conventional Batting Records for Toronto Blue Jays

	G	AB	Run	Hit	2B	3B	HR	TB	RBI	W	K	IW	HB	SB	CS	BRng Eff	GI DP	SH	SF	Avg	Slug	OBP	Runs Ctd
Borders	138	480	47	116	26	2	13	185	53	33	75	3	2	1	1	.392	11	1	5	.242	.385	.290	53
Olerud	138	458	68	130	28	0	16	206	66	70	61	11	1	1	0	.364	15	1	7	.284	.450	.375	79
Alomar R	152	571	105	177	27	8	8	244	76	87	52	5	5	49	9	.436	8	6	2	.310	.427	.405	112
Gruber	120	446	42	102	16	3	11	157	43	26	72	3	4	7	7	.655	14	1	4	.229	.352	.275	39
Lee M	128	396	49	104	10	1	3	125	39	50	73	0	0	6	2	.456	8	8	3	.263	.316	.343	46
Maldonado	137	489	64	133	25	4	20	226	66	59	112	3	7	2	2	.325	13	2	3	.272	.462	.357	81
White D	153	641	98	159	26	7	17	250	60	47	133	0	5	37	4	.464	8	0	3	.248	.390	.303	81
Carter J	158	622	97	164	30	7	34	310	119	36	109	4	11	12	5	.425	14	1	13	.264	.498	.309	94
Winfield	156	583	92	169	33	3	26	286	108	82	89	10	1	2	3	.386	10	1	3	.290	.491	.377	111
Kent	65	192	36	46	13	1	8	85	35	20	47	0	6	2	1	.432	3	0	4	.240	.443	.324	29
Bell D	61	161	23	39	6	3	2	57	15	15	34	1	5	7	2	.536	6	2	1	.242	.354	.324	19
Griffin Alf	63	150	21	35	7	0	0	42	10	9	19	0	0	3	1	.591	3	3	2	.233	.280	.273	12
Tabler	49	135	11	34	5	0	0	39	16	11	14	0	0	0	0	.368	6	0	1	.252	.289	.306	11
Myers G	22	61	4	14	6	0	1	23	13	5	5	0	0	0	0	.556	1	0	2	.230	.377	.279	7
Sprague	22	47	6	11	2	0	1	16	7	3	7	0	0	0	0	.429	0	0	0	.234	.340	.280	5
Ward T	18	29	7	10	3	0	1	16	3	4	4	0	0	0	1	.200	1	0	0	.345	.552	.424	6
Ducey	23	21	3	1	1	0	0	2	0	0	10	0	0	0	1	.250	0	0	0	.048	.095	.048	0
Knorr	8	19	1	5	0	0	1	8	2	1	5	1	0	0	0	.000	0	0	0	.263	.421	.300	2
Quinlan	13	15	2	1	1	0	0	2	2	2	9	0	0	0	0	.333	0	0	0	.067	.133	.176	0
Martinez D	7	8	2	5	0	0	1	8	3	0	1	0	0	0	0	.625	1.000	0	0	.625	1.000	.625	5
Zosky	8	7	1	2	0	1	0	4	1	0	2	0	0	0	0	.000	0	0	1	.286	.571	.250	1
Maksudian	3	3	0	0	0	0	0	0	0	0	0	0	0	0	0	.000	0	0	0	.000	.000	.000	0
Mulliniks	3	2	1	1	0	0	0	1	0	1	0	0	0	0	0	.000	0	0	0	.500	.500	.667	1
Cone	0	0	0	0	0	0	0	0	0	0	0	0	0	0	0	.000	0	0	0	.000	.000	.000	0
Stottlemyre	0	0	0	0	0	0	0	0	0	0	0	0	0	0	0	.000	0	0	0	.000	.000	.000	0
Wells	0	0	0	0	0	0	0	0	0	0	0	0	0	0	0	.000	0	0	0	.000	.000	.000	0
Ward D	0	0	0	0	0	0	0	0	0	0	0	0	0	0	0	.000	0	0	0	.000	.000	.000	0
Henke	0	0	0	0	0	0	0	0	0	0	0	0	0	0	0	.000	0	0	0	.000	.000	.000	0
Key	0	0	0	0	0	0	0	0	0	0	0	0	0	0	0	.000	0	0	0	.000	.000	.000	0
Timlin	0	0	0	0	0	0	0	0	0	0	0	0	0	0	0	.000	0	0	0	.000	.000	.000	0
TOTALS	1645	5536	780	1458	265	40	163	2292	737	561	933	41	47	129	39	.429	121	26	54	.263	.414	.333	784

Sabermetric Batting Records for Toronto Blue Jays

	AB	Run	Hit	2B	3B	HR	RBI	W	SO	Avg	Slug	OBP	Ctd	Outs	27o	OW%	OG	OWAR	DWAR	TWAR
					Ball Park Adjusted				Runs		Run/									
Alomar R	567	105	177	25	7	8	75	83	51	.312	.423	.403	109	412	7.14	.715	15	5.57	0.69	6.26
Bell D	157	22	38	6	2	1	14	14	32	.242	.325	.320	17	127	3.61	.391	5	0.19	0.58	0.77
Borders	470	46	115	26	1	12	52	30	72	.245	.381	.289	51	370	3.72	.405	14	0.75	0.31	1.06
Carter J	610	96	163	30	5	32	118	33	105	.267	.490	.309	91	476	5.16	.567	18	3.82	0.82	4.64
Ducey	21	3	1	0	0	0	0	0	10	.048	.048	.048	0	21	0.00	.000	1	-0.27	0.09	-0.18
Griffin Alf	149	21	35	6	0	0	9	8	18	.235	.275	.272	11	120	2.47	.231	4	-0.53	0.14	-0.39
Gruber	436	41	101	16	2	10	42	24	69	.232	.346	.275	38	358	2.87	.287	13	-0.83	0.29	-0.54
Kent	187	35	45	13	0	7	34	18	45	.241	.422	.316	26	148	4.74	.525	5	0.96	-0.08	0.88
Knorr	17	0	4	0	0	0	1	0	4	.235	.235	.235	1	13	2.08	.175	0	-0.08	-0.01	-0.10
Lee M	393	49	104	9	0	3	38	47	72	.265	.310	.342	45	307	3.96	.435	11	0.96	1.48	2.44
Maksudian	3	0	0	0	0	0	0	0	0	.000	.000	.000	0	3	0.00	.000	0	-0.04	-0.00	-0.04
Maldonado	479	63	132	25	3	18	65	55	108	.276	.453	.355	77	364	5.71	.616	13	3.58	0.89	4.48
Martinez D	6	1	4	0	0	0	2	0	0	.667	.667	.667	3	2	40.50	.988	0	0.05	0.00	0.05
Mulliniks	2	1	1	0	0	0	0	0	0	.500	.500	.500	1	1	27.00	.973	0	0.02	0.00	0.02
Myers G	62	4	14	5	0	1	14	4	5	.226	.355	.265	6	50	3.24	.340	2	-0.02	-0.14	-0.16
Olerud	476	78	136	24	0	23	75	69	63	.286	.481	.373	88	366	6.49	.674	14	4.40	0.36	4.75
Quinlan	13	1	0	1	0	0	1	1	8	.000	.077	.071	0	13	0.00	.000	0	-0.17	-0.03	-0.20
Sprague	45	5	10	2	0	0	6	2	6	.222	.267	.255	3	35	2.31	.208	1	-0.18	0.07	-0.11
Tabler	131	10	33	5	0	0	15	10	13	.252	.290	.305	11	103	2.88	.290	4	-0.23	0.18	-0.05
Ward T	28	7	10	2	0	1	2	3	3	.357	.536	.419	6	19	8.53	.781	1	0.30	0.10	0.40
White D	636	98	159	24	6	17	59	45	132	.250	.387	.303	80	490	4.41	.488	18	2.51	1.25	3.76
Winfield	572	91	168	33	2	24	107	76	86	.294	.484	.375	106	418	6.85	.697	15	5.38	0.22	5.59
Zosky	5	0	1	0	0	0	0	0	1	.200	.200	.200	0	4	0.00	.000	0	-0.05	0.02	-0.04
TOTALS	5506	783	1464	254	36	164	735	537	927	.266	.414	.333	775	4277	4.89	.540	158	30.15	7.21	37.37

Pitching Records for Toronto Blue Jays

	ERA	W	L	Pct	G	GS	CG	ShO	GF	Sv	IP	R	ER	H	2B	3B	HR	BB	IW	SO	HB	WP	BK
Morris Jk	4.04	21	6	.778	34	34	6	1	0	0	240.2	114	108	222	41	3	18	80	2	132	10	9	2
Key	3.53	13	13	.500	33	33	4	2	0	0	216.2	88	85	205	45	1	24	59	0	117	4	5	0
Guzman J	2.64	16	5	.762	28	28	1	0	0	0	180.2	56	53	135	24	1	6	72	2	165	1	14	2
Stottlemyre	4.50	12	11	.522	28	27	6	2	0	0	174.0	99	87	175	31	0	20	63	4	98	10	7	0
Stieb	5.04	4	6	.400	21	14	1	0	3	0	96.1	58	54	98	21	2	9	43	3	45	4	4	0
Cone	2.55	4	3	.571	8	7	0	0	0	0	53.0	16	15	39	6	2	3	29	2	47	3	3	0
Wells	5.40	7	9	.438	41	14	0	0	14	2	120.0	84	72	138	35	2	16	36	6	62	8	3	1
Ward D	1.95	7	4	.636	79	0	0	0	35	12	101.1	27	22	76	10	2	5	39	3	103	1	7	0
Henke	2.26	3	2	.600	57	0	0	0	50	34	55.2	19	14	40	9	0	5	22	2	46	0	4	0
Hentgen	5.36	5	2	.714	28	2	0	0	10	0	50.1	30	30	49	11	1	7	32	5	39	0	2	1
MacDonald	4.37	1	0	1.000	27	0	0	0	9	0	47.1	24	23	50	12	2	4	16	3	26	1	0	0
Timlin	4.12	0	2	.000	26	0	0	0	14	1	43.2	23	20	45	6	0	0	20	5	35	1	0	0
Eichhorn	4.35	2	0	1.000	23	0	0	0	7	0	31.0	15	15	35	4	2	1	7	0	19	2	6	0
Linton	8.63	1	3	.250	8	3	0	0	2	0	24.0	23	23	31	5	0	5	17	0	16	0	2	0
Weathers	8.10	0	0	.000	2	0	0	0	0	0	3.1	3	3	5	0	0	1	2	0	3	0	0	0
Trlicek	10.80	0	0	.000	2	0	0	0	0	0	1.2	2	2	2	0	0	0	2	0	1	0	0	0
Leiter	9.00	0	0	.000	1	0	0	0	0	0	1.0	1	1	1	0	0	0	2	0	0	0	0	0
TOTALS	3.92	96	66	.593	446	162	18	5	144	49	1440.2	682	627	1346	260	18	124	541	37	954	45	66	6

	Adj ERA	Expected W	L	Pct	BFP	Avg	Slg	OBA	RC/G	GDP	SB	CS	PK	PKE	SH	SF	RSup	RSp/G	W	L	Pct
Cone	2.55	5	2	.704	224	.207	.309	.318	3.81	1	15	4	0	0	0	3	23	3.91	5	2	.660
Eichhorn	4.35	1	1	.448	135	.285	.374	.328	4.65	2	3	0	0	0	1	2	14	4.06	1	1	.418
Guzman J	2.64	14	7	.688	733	.207	.275	.286	2.84	7	27	8	2	0	5	3	98	4.88	15	6	.738
Henke	2.26	4	1	.750	228	.197	.315	.272	2.98	3	2	1	0	0	0	3	9	1.46	1	4	.254
Hentgen	5.36	2	5	.349	229	.254	.430	.357	5.70	5	5	0	0	0	2	2	31	5.54	3	4	.468
Key	3.53	14	12	.553	900	.248	.391	.298	4.03	11	14	9	0	3	2	7	129	5.36	17	9	.655
Leiter	9.00	0	0	.160	7	.200	.200	.429	6.03	0	0	0	0	0	0	0	1	9.00	0	0	.452
Linton	8.63	1	3	.171	116	.323	.531	.417	8.11	2	0	2	0	0	1	2	8	3.00	0	4	.091
MacDonald	4.37	0	1	.446	204	.270	.422	.330	5.27	1	4	0	0	0	1	1	27	5.13	1	0	.532
Morris Jk	4.04	13	14	.486	1005	.246	.358	.312	3.81	15	22	16	0	0	4	7	160	5.98	17	10	.644
Stieb	5.04	4	6	.377	415	.275	.420	.355	4.92	10	3	6	2	0	6	5	35	3.27	3	7	.257
Stottlemyre	4.50	10	13	.432	755	.262	.398	.329	4.88	8	17	0	0	0	2	11	114	5.90	13	10	.586
Timlin	4.12	1	1	.475	190	.271	.307	.351	3.85	4	4	3	0	0	2	1	21	4.33	1	1	.476
Trlicek	10.80	0	0	.117	9	.286	.286	.444	4.64	1	0	0	0	0	0	0	0	0.00	0	0	.000
Ward D	1.95	9	2	.801	414	.207	.286	.282	2.90	5	14	4	0	0	3	4	39	3.46	8	3	.721
Weathers	8.10	0	0	.190	15	.385	.615	.467	7.72	2	0	0	0	0	0	0	0	0.00	0	0	.000
Wells	5.40	6	10	.346	529	.289	.471	.346	5.89	8	14	6	1	3	3	4	71	5.33	7	9	.445
TOTALS	3.92	81	81	.500	6108	.248	.371	.318	4.18	85	144	62	5	6	32	55	780	4.87	91	71	.560

Batting 'Splits' Records for Toronto Blue Jays

SPLITS for Alomar R

	G	AB	Run	Hit	2B	3B	HR	TB	RBI	W	K	IW	HB	SB	CS	DP	SH	SF	Avg	Slug	OBP	RC
vs LHP	74	156	27	48	5	0	5	68	23	25	17	1	4	9	4	2	2	1	.308	.436	.414	31
vs RHP	151	415	78	129	22	8	3	176	53	62	35	4	1	40	5	6	4	1	.311	.424	.401	81
Home	75	268	55	95	14	5	5	134	49	42	22	5	3	30	4	5	2	2	.354	.500	.444	68
Away	77	303	50	82	13	3	3	110	27	45	30	0	2	19	5	3	4	0	.271	.363	.369	46
Grass	60	238	39	64	11	3	2	87	19	31	24	0	0	15	3	2	4	0	.269	.366	.353	35
Turf	92	333	66	113	16	5	6	157	57	56	28	5	5	34	6	6	2	2	.339	.471	.439	78
April/June	68	262	45	88	9	4	6	123	42	33	22	3	3	14	6	5	2	0	.336	.469	.416	53
July/October	84	309	60	89	18	4	2	121	34	54	30	2	2	35	3	3	4	2	.288	.392	.395	59

SPLITS for Maldonado

	G	AB	Run	Hit	2B	3B	HR	TB	RBI	W	K	IW	HB	SB	CS	DP	SH	SF	Avg	Slug	OBP	RC
vs LHP	64	117	18	34	4	1	4	52	16	22	26	1	0	1	1	6	1	1	.291	.444	.400	21
vs RHP	136	372	46	99	21	3	16	174	50	37	86	2	7	1	1	7	1	2	.266	.468	.342	60
Home	64	219	25	55	10	3	8	95	32	27	50	1	4	0	1	8	2	1	.251	.434	.343	32
Away	73	270	39	78	15	1	12	131	34	32	62	2	3	2	1	5	0	2	.289	.485	.368	50
Grass	58	212	31	61	8	1	11	104	27	27	46	2	3	2	1	5	0	1	.288	.491	.374	40
Turf	79	277	33	72	17	3	9	122	39	32	66	1	4	0	1	8	2	2	.260	.440	.343	42
April/June	56	202	24	50	15	1	5	82	25	19	51	0	2	0	1	9	1	2	.248	.406	.316	24
July/October	81	287	40	83	10	3	15	144	41	40	61	3	5	2	1	4	1	1	.289	.502	.384	58
July/October	78	329	50	83	16	3	8	129	30	22	71	0	1	19	1	3	0	2	.252	.392	.299	42

SPLITS for Winfield

	G	AB	Run	Hit	2B	3B	HR	TB	RBI	W	K	IW	HB	SB	CS	DP	SH	SF	Avg	Slug	OBP	RC
vs LHP	71	146	25	44	7	1	8	77	28	24	21	4	0	1	1	2	0	2	.301	.527	.395	32
vs RHP	156	437	67	125	26	2	18	209	80	58	68	6	1	1	2	8	1	1	.286	.478	.370	79
Home	77	268	44	81	10	2	13	134	47	47	37	6	0	2	2	4	1	3	.302	.500	.403	57
Away	79	315	48	88	23	1	13	152	61	35	52	4	1	0	1	6	0	0	.279	.483	.353	54
Grass	61	240	37	65	17	0	11	115	46	26	44	3	1	0	1	5	0	0	.271	.479	.345	39
Turf	95	343	55	104	16	3	15	171	62	56	45	7	0	2	2	5	1	3	.303	.499	.398	72
April/June	75	280	46	85	17	1	13	143	44	41	39	5	0	2	1	6	0	2	.304	.511	.390	57
July/October	81	303	46	84	16	2	13	143	64	41	50	5	1	0	2	4	1	1	.277	.472	.364	54

SPLITS for Toronto Blue Jays (all batters except pitchers)

	G	AB	Run	Hit	2B	3B	HR	TB	RBI	W	K	IW	HB	SB	CS	DP	SH	SF	Avg	Slug	OBP	RC
vs LHP	729	1435	208	388	69	4	41	588	193	183	230	10	13	28	15	41	7	19	.270	.410	.354	213
vs RHP	1554	4101	572	1070	196	36	122	1704	544	378	703	31	34	101	24	80	19	35	.261	.416	.326	571
Home	830	2641	390	688	129	24	79	1102	366	295	439	27	26	65	16	65	14	29	.261	.417	.337	383
Away	815	2895	390	770	136	16	84	1190	371	266	494	14	21	64	23	56	12	25	.266	.411	.330	400
Grass	635	2237	306	598	106	14	72	948	292	204	380	13	14	52	19	43	10	16	.267	.424	.330	318
Turf	1010	3299	474	860	159	26	91	1344	445	357	553	28	33	77	21	78	16	38	.261	.407	.335	465
April/June	758	2610	357	681	125	18	81	1085	339	260	438	17	23	47	20	66	12	24	.261	.416	.330	360
July/October	887	2926	423	777	140	22	82	1207	398	301	495	24	24	82	19	55	14	30	.266	.413	.336	423

Milwaukee Brewers

Brock J. Hanke

MILWAUKEE										
YEAR	1983	1984	1985	1986	1987	1988	1989	1990	1991	1992
W	87	67	71	77	91	87	81	74	83	92
L	75	94	90	84	71	75	81	88	79	70
WPCT	0.537	0.416	0.441	0.478	0.562	0.537	0.500	0.457	0.512	0.568
R	764	641	690	667	862	682	707	732	799	740
RA	708	734	802	734	817	616	679	760	744	604
PWPT	0.538	0.433	0.425	0.452	0.527	0.551	0.520	0.481	0.536	0.600
PythW	87	70	69	73	85	89	84	78	87	97
PythL	75	92	93	89	77	73	78	84	75	65
LUCK	0	-3	2	4	6	-2	-3	-4	-4	-5

Defensive Efficiency Record: .7237

You know, if you took this team as it is, and just signed Paul Molitor, Chris Bosio, Kevin Seitzer, and Dan Plesac as free agents, you'd have a hell of a team. This would be the lineup:

Listach   ss
Yount   cf
Molitor   DH
Jaha   1b
Vaughn   lf
Reimer   rf
Seitzer   3b
Surhoff   c
Doran or Gantner 2b

This would be the rotation:

Wegman
Navarro
Bosio
Bones
Aldred

And Dan Plesac would compete with Doug Henry for the closer spot, with the other one moving to setup.

Yes, there's less power than you would like, and yes, John Jaha would have to come through for the Brewers to actually beat out the Blue Jays, but still, it's a good, balanced team, with good people everywhere, and great people in enough places, and John Jaha looks ready, and he's turning 27 this year. The Brewer Contender Profile, from the Philadelphia Phillie essay, would be:

SUPERSTARS

Molitor
Listach

Position	92 Starter	TWAR	93 Starter	TWAR
Catcher	Surhoff	1.94	Nilsson	0.68
First base	Stubbs	1.02	Jaha	0.63
Second base	Fletcher	4.50	Spiers	0.01
Third base	Seitzer	3.60	Surhoff	1.94
Shortstop	Listach	6.63	Listach	6.63
Left field	Vaughn, G.	3.56	Vaughn, G.	3.56
Center field	Yount	4.95	Yount	4.95
Right field	Hamilton	5.24	Hamilton	5.24
	Bichette	2.80		
DH	Molitor	6.79	Reimer	3.63

STARS

Wegman
Navarro
Bosio
Aldred (probably)
Seitzer
Yount

CHAMPIONSHIP QUALITY

Surhoff
Jaha (probably)
Vaughn
Reimer

BULK

Doran and Gantner
Plesac and Henry

HOLES

- 66 -

That's a 2 / 6 / 4 / 2 / 0 profile. A normal American League contender would have a profile of about 2 / 5 / 5 / 1 / 1. If one of the starting pitchers got hot and moved up to superstar class (Wegman finished 11th, while superstar extends only to 10th, and Aldred was out of sight in his limited trial), the Brewers would look just like the 1992 A's or Jays.

But it's not to be. Molitor, the only reliable superstar, is gone. I suppose Cranklin Stubbs could DH, if he makes the ballclub at all. And the Brewers did pick up Larry Sheets and Tom Brunansky. Darryl Hamilton looks pretty good to me, but he just finished being 27, and in any case, he's no Paul Molitor. Bosio, one of the stars, is gone, too, and there is no candidate for his job of even championship quality. Seitzer is gone, and there's no obvious player for his position at all, of any quality. And Dan Plesac is gone, too, which means the closer spot looks like a hole. Well, what else am I to say, when the incumbent posted a 4.02 ERA. Forget the saves, Henry was horrid.

So let's say Henry recovers and is bulk pitching on his own. Let's say that the Brewers can come up with a #4 starter who is better than a hole, although I don't know who that would be. Let's say that Aldred is for real, and so is Jaha, and that Darryl Hamilton is a championship quality ballplayer. What does that leave?

SUPERSTARS

Listach

STARS

Wegman
Navarro
Aldred (probably)
Yount

CHAMPIONSHIP QUALITY

Surhoff
Jaha (probably)
Vaughn
Reimer
Hamilton

BULK

Doran and Gantner
the unknown starting pitcher
Henry

HOLES

third base

That's 1 / 4 / 5 / 3 / 1, and it's the rosy picture, and it isn't enough to contend with.

So, how did this happen? Has poor, broken Bud Selig been forced to sell off his contending team just to stay in business and avoid the welfare rolls? Is this the first sign that the owners really are going bankrupt, and that the smaller cities' teams are going to turn into a sort of junior league, outspent and outplayed by the fat cats in New York and L.A.? Are the Brewers just the first wave in a flood of teams forced to sell off their stars to stay out of bankruptcy court? Well, I've got a few things to say about that.

First, there's a man here in St. Louis named Charles Korr. He teaches at the University of Missouri in St. Louis, and he's working on a book about the players' union. He just gave a little talk at the university, and had the following research to reveal. In 1939, player salaries constituted 32% of Major League Baseball's gross revenues. By the 1980's, it was 39%. But, in 1991, it was right back to 32%, due to merchandising and television.

Now, have the owners been contending all along that their problem was that expenses other than player salaries were completely out of control, rising at a pace that outstripped wages? No, they have not; they have been saying the exact opposite. Well, then, if player salaries are no greater a percentage of revenue than they used to be, and other expenses are not outstripping wages, then the percentage of gross revenues that goes into the owners' pockets as profits MUST BE NO LESS than it was in 1939!

Let's make a list here. Here's a list of expenses as a percentage of gross revenue, circa 1939, with an estimated profit margin of 5%:

Salaries 32%
Other Expenses 63%
Profit 5%

The owners have been claiming that salaries have been going wild, outstripping all other expenses, and that they have been losing money. Sprots media all over the country have been buying into this. The claim would indicate, and the media believe, that the list looks something like this:

Salaires 50%
Other Expenses 55%
Profit -5%

That is, salaires are way up, other expenses are severely down, as a percentage of gross receipts, and profit has disappeared. However, what Charles Korr is claiming is that the list actually looks something like this:

Salaires 32%
Other Expenses 55%
Profit 13%

To argue with that, you have to insist that 1) Charles Korr has the salary percentage of gross receipts wrong, or 2) expenses other than salaries have been rising faster than salaries have. The second item is in disagreement with what the owners themselves have been contending. As for the first, well, Charles Korr has done the research, and you and I haven't.

Now, all this is just the percentage, not the actual dollar amount. The dollar amount of profit must be much greater; in fact, it must have been growing at least as fast as player salaries have. In fact, since the owners claim that the salaries are the fastest-growing segment of expenses, it stands to reason that the profit percentage of revenue has been increasing, because other expenses have not been keeping pace with salaries, and salaries are not eating up any higher percentage than they were in 1939. That is, as in the chart above, profit is something like 13% of the much higher gross revenues. And that's not counting those hot new expansion franchise fees.

All this is to say that the owners, gripe as they will, are making money hand over fist. It can't all be going into George Steinbrenner's pockets. No, even the owners of the smallest cities' franchises are making money. All this owner complaining is just another negotiating ploy against the union. Don't swallow a bit of it.

And what's more, even all of this is not to mention that the ownership of the Brewers does have an option, if Bud Selig really is going bankrupt, and it really is the ballclub's fault, instead of some other enterprise he's in that collapsed at the end of Ronald Reagan's 1980s. They could always sell. Wayne Huizenga is waiting, checkbook in hand. It's a pitiful $130 million or so: fire sale prices, really; but maybe Bud Selig could pay his heating bill

for this winter with that poor sum. And yes, Huizenga would move the team to Tampa, but so what? This is America, land of free enterprise. If you're going bankrupt in one place, you move to another, if that will result in your making money and avoiding bankruptcy. Why should the Lords of Baseball be immune to the concept of free enterprise?

More to the point, why should the players' union subsidize the Lords' immunity to free enterprise? If Wayne Huizenga would pay more in player salaries than Bud Selig will, why shouldn't the players in the union get that money? Is there another business in America, other than sports, where the employees are forced to work for less money than they could get in a free market?

Let's face it, Bud Selig is not going bankrupt. He is not hurting for money. He is playing politics, and he is union-busting. He thinks that he can stampede the fans of the game into pressuring the players' union to settle for an unfair contract. Do you want to be a part of Bud Selig's little scam here? Do you really? What has Bud Selig done for you lately? Why do you want to help this multimillionaire? And besides, if you really do buy all his propaganda, take a look at the 1950's. This was when the owners had full control of player salaries. Who won the pennants? Do you see the names "Yankees" and "Dodgers" and "Giants" out there with depressingly frequency? Do you remember that, at the time, these were the teams in New York? Do you really believe that, if the owners do break the players' union, you in Milwaukee will have a better chance at the pennant? Do you really?

Milwaukee Brewers Home Park Performance Factors														
	Outs	Runs	Hits	2b	3b	HR	W	K	SH	SF	HBP	IBB	SB	CS	GDP
Home LH Batters	.931	.968	.923	1.074	1.202	1.049	.832	1.013	.765	.828	.567	.701	.892	1.036	.808
Home RH Batters	.951	.985	.988	1.058	.854	1.054	.864	.934	.993	.833	.834	.777	1.045	.940	.903
All Home Batters	.947	.977	.977	1.068	.921	1.043	.858	.960	.902	.839	.797	.780	.987	.960	.893
Opp LH Batters	.994	1.222	1.033	1.176	1.499	1.181	.976	.999	1.279	.847	2.344	1.166	.917	1.070	.976
Opp RH Batters	.952	1.083	.985	1.029	1.508	1.047	1.115	1.040	.751	1.843	1.174	4.094	.966	.937	.940
All Opp Batters	.968	1.136	1.014	1.083	1.487	1.142	1.070	1.024	.869	1.269	1.293	1.518	.943	1.013	.964
All LH Batters	.965	1.101	.983	1.124	1.356	1.117	.910	1.007	.938	.843	1.254	.938	.932	1.077	.899
All RH Batters	.950	1.026	.987	1.048	1.051	1.042	.955	.984	.885	.997	1.000	1.000	1.037	.946	.919
All Batters	.956	1.049	.995	1.076	1.119	1.092	.950	.991	.893	.972	1.032	.994	.993	.991	.927

Conventional Batting Records for Milwaukee Brewers

	G	AB	Run	Hit	2B	3B	HR	TB	RBI	W	K	IW	HB	SB	CS	BRng Eff	GI DP	SH	SF	Avg	Slug	OBP	Runs Ctd
Surhoff BJ	139	480	63	121	19	1	4	154	62	46	41	8	2	14	8	.365	8	5	10	.252	.321	.314	51
Stubbs	92	288	37	66	11	1	9	106	42	27	68	3	1	11	8	.610	2	5	1	.229	.368	.297	32
Fletcher S	123	386	53	106	18	3	3	139	51	30	33	1	7	17	10	.452	4	6	4	.275	.360	.335	48
Seitzer	148	540	74	146	35	1	5	198	71	57	44	4	2	13	11	.385	16	7	9	.270	.367	.337	66
Listach	149	579	93	168	19	6	1	202	47	55	124	0	1	54	18	.533	3	12	2	.290	.349	.352	79
Vaughn G	141	501	77	114	18	2	23	205	78	60	123	1	5	15	15	.506	8	2	5	.228	.409	.313	64
Yount	150	557	71	147	40	3	8	217	77	53	81	9	3	15	6	.453	9	4	12	.264	.390	.325	74
Bichette	112	387	37	111	27	2	5	157	41	16	74	3	3	10	7	.329	13	2	3	.287	.406	.318	47
Molitor	158	609	89	195	36	7	12	281	89	73	66	12	3	31	6	.456	12	4	11	.320	.461	.389	117
Hamilton	128	470	67	140	19	7	5	188	62	45	42	0	1	41	14	.477	10	4	7	.298	.400	.356	70
Gantner	101	256	22	63	12	1	1	80	18	12	17	2	0	6	2	.314	9	3	2	.246	.313	.278	21
Nilsson	51	164	15	38	8	0	4	58	25	17	18	1	0	2	2	.188	1	2	0	.232	.354	.304	18
Jaha	47	133	17	30	3	1	2	41	10	12	30	1	2	10	0	.323	1	1	4	.226	.308	.291	15
McIntosh	35	77	7	14	3	0	0	17	6	3	9	0	2	1	3	.500	1	1	1	.182	.221	.229	4
Allanson	9	25	6	8	1	0	0	9	0	1	2	0	0	3	1	.286	1	2	0	.320	.360	.346	3
Suero	18	16	4	3	1	0	0	4	0	2	1	0	1	1	1	.600	2	0	0	.188	.250	.316	1
Spiers	12	16	2	5	2	0	0	7	2	1	4	0	0	1	1	.667	0	1	0	.313	.438	.353	2
Diaz A	22	9	5	1	0	0	0	1	1	0	0	0	0	3	2	.571	0	0	0	.111	.111	.111	0
Tatum	5	8	0	1	0	0	0	1	0	1	2	0	0	0	0	.000	0	0	0	.125	.125	.222	0
Valentin J	4	3	1	0	0	0	0	0	0	1	0	0	0	0	0	.000	0	0	1	.000	.000	.000	0
TOTALS	1644	5504	740	1477	272	35	82	2065	683	511	779	45	33	256	115	.440	100	61	72	.268	.375	.330	704

Sabermetric Batting Records for Milwaukee Brewers

	Ball Park Adjusted								Runs				Run/								
	AB	Run	Hit	2B	3B	HR	RBI	W	SO	Avg	Slug	OBP	Ctd	Outs	27o	OW%	OG	OWAR	DWAR	TWAR
Allanson	23	6	7	1	0	0	0	0	1	.304	.348	.304	3	17	4.76	.569	1	0.14	-0.13	0.01
Bichette	371	38	109	28	2	5	42	15	73	.294	.420	.323	48	284	4.56	.548	11	2.08	0.72	2.80
Diaz A	7	5	0	0	0	0	1	0	0	.000	.000	.000	0	8	0.00	.000	0	-0.10	0.04	-0.06
Fletcher S	370	54	104	18	3	3	52	29	32	.281	.370	.341	49	288	4.59	.551	11	2.14	2.36	4.50
Gantner	246	24	61	13	1	1	19	10	17	.248	.321	.276	20	199	2.71	.300	7	-0.37	1.35	0.98
Hamilton	453	73	136	21	9	5	66	40	42	.300	.419	.355	69	348	5.35	.625	13	3.54	1.70	5.24
Jaha	126	17	29	3	1	2	10	11	29	.230	.317	.292	15	102	3.97	.478	4	0.48	0.14	0.63
Listach	560	98	167	20	7	1	49	53	122	.298	.364	.359	81	424	5.16	.607	16	4.04	2.59	6.63
McIntosh	72	7	13	3	0	0	6	2	8	.181	.222	.221	4	62	1.74	.150	2	-0.46	0.11	-0.35
Molitor	585	92	192	37	8	12	91	72	65	.328	.480	.396	121	426	7.67	.774	16	6.68	0.10	6.79
Nilsson	158	16	37	8	0	4	26	15	18	.234	.361	.301	18	125	3.89	.468	5	0.54	0.14	0.68
Seitzer	518	76	144	36	1	5	72	56	43	.278	.380	.344	68	416	4.41	.531	15	2.79	0.81	3.60
Spiers	14	2	4	2	0	0	2	0	4	.286	.429	.286	1	12	2.25	.227	0	-0.05	0.00	-0.05
Stubbs	277	40	64	12	1	10	44	24	68	.231	.390	.295	32	227	3.81	.457	8	0.90	0.12	1.02
Suero	14	4	2	1	0	0	0	1	0	.143	.214	.250	1	12	3.08	.200	0	-0.07	0.11	0.04
Surhoff BJ	463	69	118	21	1	4	66	41	41	.255	.330	.313	50	373	3.62	.432	14	1.14	0.80	1.94
Tatum	6	0	0	0	0	0	0	0	1	.000	.000	.000	0	6	0.00	.000	0	-0.08	0.03	-0.05
Valentin J	2	1	0	0	0	0	1	0	0	.000	.000	.000	0	3	0.00	.000	0	-0.04	-0.01	-0.05
Vaughn G	480	79	112	18	2	24	80	59	121	.233	.429	.320	66	396	4.50	.541	15	2.80	0.77	3.56
Yount	533	73	144	41	3	8	79	52	79	.270	.403	.329	76	421	4.87	.580	16	3.59	1.37	4.95
TOTALS	5325	782	1470	292	42	89	719	492	772	.276	.397	.337	732	4189	4.72	.564	155	33.20	13.13	46.33

Pitching Records for Milwaukee Brewers

	ERA	W	L	Pct	G	GS	CG	ShO	GF	Sv	IP	R	ER	H	2B	3B	HR	BB	IW	SO	HB	WP	BK
Wegman	3.20	13	14	.481	35	35	7	0	0	0	261.2	104	93	251	50	2	28	55	3	127	9	1	2
Navarro	3.33	17	11	.607	34	34	5	3	0	0	246.0	98	91	224	42	6	14	64	4	100	6	6	0
Bosio	3.62	16	6	.727	33	33	4	2	0	0	231.1	100	93	223	38	3	21	44	1	120	4	8	2
Bones	4.57	9	10	.474	31	28	0	0	0	0	163.1	90	83	169	27	5	27	48	0	65	9	3	2
Eldred	1.79	11	2	.846	14	14	2	1	0	0	100.1	21	20	76	10	3	4	23	0	62	2	3	0
Robinson R	5.86	1	4	.200	8	8	0	0	0	0	35.1	26	23	51	12	1	3	14	0	12	2	0	0
Plesac	2.96	5	4	.556	44	4	0	0	13	1	79.0	28	26	64	17	0	5	35	5	54	3	3	1
Henry D	4.02	1	4	.200	68	0	0	0	56	29	65.0	34	29	64	14	2	6	24	4	52	0	4	0
Fetters	1.87	5	1	.833	50	0	0	0	11	2	62.2	15	13	38	8	0	3	24	2	43	7	4	1
Austin	1.85	5	2	.714	47	0	0	0	12	0	58.1	13	12	38	9	0	2	32	6	30	2	1	0
Ruffin	6.67	1	6	.143	25	6	1	0	6	0	58.0	43	43	66	11	2	7	41	3	45	0	2	0
Holmes	2.55	4	4	.500	41	0	0	0	25	6	42.1	12	12	35	6	2	1	11	4	31	2	0	0
Orosco	3.23	3	1	.750	59	0	0	0	14	1	39.0	15	14	33	4	0	5	13	1	40	1	2	0
Nunez E	2.63	1	1	.500	10	0	0	0	5	0	13.2	5	4	12	2	0	1	6	0	10	0	0	0
Heaton	0.00	0	0	.000	1	0	0	0	1	0	1.0	0	0	0	0	0	0	1	0	2	0	0	0
TOTALS	3.43	92	70	.568	500	162	19	6	143	39	1457.0	604	556	1344	250	26	127	435	33	793	47	37	8

Sabermetric Pitching Records for Milwaukee Brewers

	Adj ERA	Expected W	L	Pct	BFP	Avg	Slg	OBA	RC/G	GDP	SB	CS	PK	PKE	SH	SF	RSup	RSp/G	Supported W	L	Pct
Austin	1.85	6	1	.818	235	.191	.266	.308	2.56	7	2	4	0	0	1	1	30	4.63	6	1	.837
Bones	4.79	8	11	.401	705	.264	.448	.321	5.20	11	13	2	1	1	2	5	75	4.13	7	12	.380
Bosio	3.77	11	11	.519	937	.254	.376	.291	3.52	25	12	7	0	0	6	5	134	5.21	13	9	.611
Eldred	1.79	11	2	.827	394	.207	.283	.258	2.42	5	8	4	1	0	1	0	73	6.55	12	1	.917
Fetters	1.87	5	1	.815	243	.185	.268	.290	2.36	8	4	3	0	0	5	2	38	5.46	5	1	.876
Heaton	0.00	0	0	.000	4	.000	.000	.250	0.75	0	0	0	0	0	0	0	0	0.00	0	0	.000
Henry D	4.15	2	3	.472	277	.256	.400	.319	4.56	2	4	3	0	0	1	2	5	0.69	0	5	.022
Holmes	2.55	6	2	.703	173	.224	.308	.284	3.01	3	4	1	0	0	4	0	16	3.40	5	3	.594
Navarro	3.48	16	12	.560	1004	.246	.351	.295	3.40	23	17	11	0	2	9	13	127	4.65	17	11	.596
Nunez E	2.63	1	1	.689	58	.231	.327	.310	3.59	0	0	1	0	0	0	0	8	5.27	2	0	.767
Orosco	3.23	2	2	.596	158	.232	.366	.297	3.41	3	3	4	0	2	0	2	17	3.92	2	2	.549
Plesac	3.08	6	3	.619	330	.229	.343	.317	3.64	6	2	3	0	2	8	4	37	4.22	5	4	.608
Robinson R	6.11	1	4	.292	171	.331	.481	.392	7.77	1	3	1	0	1	0	1	23	5.86	2	3	.431
Ruffin	6.98	2	5	.240	272	.293	.453	.398	6.49	8	5	3	0	0	3	3	16	2.48	1	6	.094
Wegman	3.34	16	11	.580	1079	.250	.387	.294	3.85	22	18	6	2	0	7	4	141	4.85	17	10	.635
TOTALS	3.60	88	74	.543	6040	.246	.371	.305	3.79	124	95	53	4	8	47	42	740	4.57	92	70	.570

Batting 'Splits' Records for Milwaukee Brewers

SPLITS for Listach

	G	AB	Run	Hit	2B	3B	HR	TB	RBI	W	K	IW	HB	SB	CS	DP	SH	SF	Avg	Slug	OBP	RC
vs LHP	63	148	37	51	7	3	1	67	18	8	25	0	1	18	4	0	4	0	.345	.453	.382	28
vs RHP	148	431	56	117	12	3	0	135	29	47	99	0	0	36	14	3	8	2	.271	.313	.342	52
Home	73	267	38	67	9	1	0	78	26	22	53	0	1	19	8	0	8	2	.251	.292	.308	27
Away	76	312	55	101	10	5	1	124	21	33	71	0	0	35	10	3	4	0	.324	.397	.388	53
Grass	125	483	71	140	17	2	1	164	37	41	97	0	1	41	17	2	12	2	.290	.340	.345	62
Turf	24	96	22	28	2	4	0	38	10	14	27	0	0	13	1	1	0	0	.292	.396	.382	18
April/June	62	233	36	66	4	3	0	76	17	19	48	0	0	24	7	1	4	2	.283	.326	.335	29
July/October	87	346	57	102	15	3	1	126	30	36	76	0	1	30	11	2	8	0	.295	.364	.363	50

SPLITS for Molitor

	G	AB	Run	Hit	2B	3B	HR	TB	RBI	W	K	IW	HB	SB	CS	DP	SH	SF	Avg	Slug	OBP	RC
vs LHP	58	132	28	56	11	1	6	87	32	14	11	5	0	16	2	1	0	5	.424	.659	.464	45
vs RHP	158	477	61	139	25	6	4	194	57	59	55	7	3	15	4	11	4	6	.291	.407	.369	76
Home	80	286	39	87	13	4	4	120	36	43	34	9	1	12	3	4	1	6	.304	.420	.390	52
Away	78	323	50	108	23	3	8	161	53	30	32	3	2	19	3	8	3	5	.334	.498	.389	65
Grass	134	507	73	157	27	5	10	224	68	64	52	11	1	20	6	10	3	8	.310	.442	.383	91
Turf	24	102	16	38	9	2	2	57	21	9	14	1	2	11	0	2	1	3	.373	.559	.422	27
April/June	71	273	50	88	16	2	10	138	40	33	30	5	2	13	2	6	2	7	.322	.505	.390	58
July/October	87	336	39	107	20	5	2	143	49	40	36	7	1	18	4	6	2	4	.318	.426	.388	60

SPLITS for Yount

	G	AB	Run	Hit	2B	3B	HR	TB	RBI	W	K	IW	HB	SB	CS	DP	SH	SF	Avg	Slug	OBP	RC
vs LHP	61	125	23	35	10	1	2	53	18	16	24	4	0	4	1	3	0	1	.280	.424	.359	20
vs RHP	149	432	48	112	30	2	6	164	59	37	57	5	3	11	5	6	4	11	.259	.380	.315	54
Home	75	269	33	72	17	2	3	102	35	25	35	4	2	8	5	6	2	7	.268	.379	.327	34
Away	75	288	38	75	23	1	5	115	42	28	46	5	1	7	1	3	2	5	.260	.399	.323	40
Grass	127	465	55	122	30	2	7	177	68	42	67	7	3	13	5	9	4	12	.262	.381	.320	59
Turf	23	92	16	25	10	1	1	40	9	11	14	2	0	2	1	0	0	0	.272	.435	.350	15
April/June	70	257	40	72	20	0	5	107	33	27	39	6	2	5	4	4	0	4	.280	.416	.348	38
July/October	80	300	31	75	20	3	3	110	44	26	42	3	1	10	2	5	4	8	.250	.367	.304	36

SPLITS for Milwaukee Brewers (all batters except pitchers)

	G	AB	Run	Hit	2B	3B	HR	TB	RBI	W	K	IW	HB	SB	CS	DP	SH	SF	Avg	Slug	OBP	RC
vs LHP	663	1283	226	372	68	13	23	535	209	134	182	14	8	88	24	22	19	21	.290	.417	.355	204
vs RHP	1553	4221	514	1105	204	22	59	1530	474	377	597	31	25	168	91	78	42	51	.262	.362	.322	502
Home	808	2580	339	671	111	17	35	921	313	271	361	26	19	117	54	50	31	39	.260	.357	.330	319
Away	836	2924	401	806	161	18	47	1144	370	240	418	19	14	139	61	50	30	33	.276	.391	.330	385
Grass	1404	4628	596	1219	212	23	73	1696	549	424	656	38	26	199	103	84	51	62	.263	.366	.325	564
Turf	240	876	144	258	60	12	9	369	134	87	123	7	7	57	12	16	10	10	.295	.421	.359	142
April/June	736	2535	352	685	122	16	46	977	323	227	339	23	13	99	46	51	24	34	.270	.385	.329	328

Baltimore Orioles

David Raglin

BALTIMORE										
YEAR	1983	1984	1985	1986	1987	1988	1989	1990	1991	1992
W	98	85	83	73	67	54	87	76	67	89
L	64	77	78	89	95	107	75	85	95	73
WPCT	0.605	0.525	0.516	0.451	0.414	0.335	0.537	0.472	0.414	0.549
R	799	681	818	708	729	550	708	669	686	705
RA	652	667	764	760	880	789	686	698	796	656
PWPT	0.6	0.51	0.534	0.465	0.407	0.327	0.516	0.479	0.426	0.536
PythW	97	83	87	75	66	53	84	78	69	87
PythL	65	79	75	87	96	109	78	84	93	75
LUCK	1	2	-4	-2	1	1	3	-2	-2	2

Defensive Efficiency Record: .7083

It's not often that a club can jump 22 games in the standings and still not have that be the big story of the year for the team. In Baltimore, 1992 will be remembered as the year that Camden Yards opened for business. As the first park in what looks to be a new burst of ballpark construction, Camden Yards really is the beginning of an era. After attending about 30 games in the new park, I have a few observations about it and the new generation of ballparks coming up.

First, Camden Yards is the most beautiful building in the majors. "Yeah", you might say, "what about Tiger Stadium, or Fenway, or Wrigley?" I'm not talking about the view of the field here, or history, or anything like that. I'm talking about beautiful architectural structures. Those old ballparks are not beautiful buildings. Fenway looks like an office building of the era in which it was built. Tiger Stadium is a big aluminum can. Wrigley is another old brick building. They're great for watching baseball, and they hold
a lot of memories, but as buildings...

Camden Yards was chosen as one of the top ten designs (of anything, not just buildings) for 1992 by Time magazine. Coming on the highway from Washington and the Baltimore Beltway, you pass over a bridge; and there, staring right at you, is the park. It is an impressive sight - and site. Camden is within walking distance of the beautiful Inner Harbor complex that has been a tourist site for several years now. It looks like it's been there for years. By now, you know about the old warehouse beyond the right field wall that they saved. They built the park into the ground so that the top of it is the same height as the warehouse. Instead of making it a overbearing concrete shell, they made it as open as possible. It's not so good when it rains, but it provides a nice, unobstructed look to the park. The secret was using steel girders instead of all concrete.

The other thing that makes Camden so beautiful is the consistency of the look. So many stadiums open half-finished, and never look

Position	92 Starter	TWAR	93 Starter	TWAR
Catcher	Hoiles	3.54	Hoiles	3.54
First base	Davis, G.	2.54	Davis, G.	2.54
Second base	Ripken, B.	0.73	Reynolds	0.84
Third base	Gomez	3.95	Gomez	3.95
Shortstop	Ripken, C.	5.79	Ripken, C.	5.79
Left field	Anderson, B.	8.21	Anderson, B.	8.21
Center field	Devereaux	5.49	Devereaux	5.49
Right field	Orsulak	3.96	Martinez, Ch.	1.82
DH	Milligan	3.83	Baines	2.04

quite right. Camden Yards looked perfect the first day. The builders wanted to capture the old-fashioned look, and they didn't miss a spot. The facade on the outside is brick, matching the warehouse bricks, with huge steel gates that open to let you in (with the Oriole logo painted on the middle of the gate). The old-fashioned Coke sign on the back of the scoreboard, facing a main entrance to the park, harkens back to a previous era, and above it is a sign saying "Welcome to Oriole Park at Camden Yards". On the front of the scoreboard, the Coke and Bud ads are also done in a classic mode, and the big Baltimore Sun clock on the scoreboard fits the mood perfectly. Even the ushers are dressed in old-fashioned garb. Everything is either in Oriole orange and black or Camden Yards forest green. The same bricks that are used in the facade are found in the sidewalks and walkway approaches to the park.

However, in the upper deck at Camden Yards, you are a lonnnnng way from home plate. Mind you, the Orioles had the taxpayers of the State of Maryland build them this park because they had to have the revenue from corporate tax-deductible outrageously-priced luxury seating. And so, there is a middle deck of about eighteen rows of "Club" seating ($25 a game, but you get waitress service), and then there are the luxury boxes, and all of this is built so there is a minimum of overhang. Therefore, the upper deck is way, way up there. Even in the first few rows, you are a lot farther away than you were in Memorial Stadium.

This is not just my imagination - the upper deck in Camden Yards is in point of fact farther back than at Memorial Stadium. A great article about the new wave of ballparks recently appeared in the SABR Baseball Research Journal 21. If you're a SABR member, go back and reread that article. If you're not a SABR member, join now and find out how you can get a copy of the piece. Author John Pastier said, in a chart accompanying the article, that in old Memorial, the distance from home plate to a seat behind home but a third of the way up the upper deck was 161 feet. The same measurement is 182 feet in the "new, improved" ballpark.

They say that Camden Yards has an "intimate" feel to it. Yeah, if you're in the lower deck or the "club" seats between first and third. Upper deck, you're in Siberia. The contrast with a truly intimate park was striking the week I went to games in both Camden Yards and Tiger Stadium. I have to commend Tom Boswell of the Washington Post here. While other sportswriters were gushing over the park, falling over each other to praise it, Boswell was the only sportswriter I read who thought enough of the fans to go to the upper deck, see how far away the seats are, and write about it. Not to say he didn't like the stadium, but at least his report had a little balance and feeling for the average fan.

So the Average Joe taxpayer of Maryland foots the bill and is rewarded with a worse seat than he or she had at Memorial so that the business people can sit in the doubly-taxpayer-subsidized "Club" and luxury box seats (doubly subsidized because they are tax deductible. "Business" is being done there). The Orioles didn't have to be so greedy. They could have had the luxury boxes all the way around the stadium, rather than the eighteen rows of "Club" seats, and brought the upper deck way down. Maybe then the people who paid for the park could see the game.

I wonder how long these "Club" seat ideas will last. Of all of the good things Mike Ilitch is doing in Detroit, the awful thing he has done is to make the lower boxes of Tiger Stadium similar to Baltimore's "Club" seats. They're called the "Tiger Den", and the people who buy them, loyalists for years, are being rewarded with a ticket increase from $12.50 a seat to $20.00. Of course they will have waiter and waitress service. Big deal. Ilitch has taken a lot of heat in the Detroit papers for his 60% increase for those fans, and some people have canceled their seats altogether.

Baltimore seems to be having trouble keeping their fans happy too. After the successful 1992 season, without an unsold seat in the house, the Orioles raised the price of a good number of their seats. They deceptively advertised it as a "price adjustment" by lowering the prices of a few seats that were mostly obstructed view. (Funny, I thought that this perfect stadium had no obstructed view seats.) We were also told that they were going to limit the number of season and partial season tickets sold and start a season ticket waiting list. They had a big party in early January when single seats went on sale for 1993, but reportedly did much less business than expected.

They also seem to be losing more season ticket holders than they thought. I had a 29-game plan for 1992, but am dropping it for 1993 because I will be buying some games from a friend who has full season tickets. The Orioles informed me, in an ominous letter I received in November, that if my money wasn't in by December 11th, I'd lose my seats. (Oh, no, Mr. Bill!) That day passed and, in early January, the Orioles sent me a letter saying that I now had until January 14th to get my money in to save my seat location. A few days later, I received a call from them wondering if I was going to renew. This sounds like an organization that overplayed its hand, and found out that a lot of these people who bought tickets in 1992 were not long term customers, at least not after the team got greedy and bumped their prices.

A lot of people probably got the 29-game plan (the other plans are for 13 games) because it included the initial Opening Day. Considering that the Orioles had trouble selling the "Club" seats at first, and given the problems they are having selling seats for 1993 at this time, I wonder what the long term potential is for seats like these - very expensive non-luxury box seats. After all, aside from the waiter and waitress service and the carpeted hallways, the "Club" seats are no better than many of the lower deck seats below them, but they cost a lot more.

Another negative note: the fans at Camden Yards are dead. Not that Oriole fans were the loudest in baseball before this, but they were dead in 1992. There were a lot of people at Camden Yards who weren't there to see baseball, at least Oriole baseball. The crowd would arrive by the second inning, usually, and they seemed to think that the "Take Me Out To The Ballgame" in the seventh-inning stretch meant the game was over. There seemed to be more fans of visiting teams there, too, especially from Eastern cities for the weekend series. We learned that if you encourage non-baseball fans to go to baseball games, they are very quiet. I've never been to games on the West Coast, but I've heard that it's similar there. In the East, though, we're used to real fans making real noise.

Conclusion: Camden Yards was billed as the perfect baseball stadium, combining the best of the old and the new. It falls disappointingly short of that goal. When the team management designed it, they forgot that what we fans disliked the most about the new stadiums was the distance from the field. Camden Yards does not solve that problem. It's a beautiful building, but just an okay place to watch a ballgame. In 1992, people looked at the park. As the years go on, people will look less and less at the matching bricks in the facade and the iron fences and more at the field, and they will be less and less satisfied.

Unfortunately, it seems that, like it or not, Camden Yards is the model of the forseeable future. Cleveland, Texas, and possibly Atlanta, will build new parks on the Camden Yards model, including the "Club" seats. The new park in Milwaukee that has been discussed might be the one that breaks the mold. That park has not been designed yet, and they reportedly have had trouble just selling the luxury boxes. It seems unlikely that "Club" seats will sell there. Plus, by the time they come up with a final design for that new park, we may find out that the "Club" seats, with their waitresses, will have gone as out of fashion as the player under a million dollars. Maybe then, we will have the perfect stadium.

Now on to the team on the field. How did the O's improve so much in 1992? It's an easy answer; as important as Brady Anderson was, and he was our sabermetric MVP for the American League, just look at the starting pitching:

Orioles Starting Pitching, 1992

Name	W	L	ERA	GS	IP	IP/GS	ER
Sutcliffe	16	15	4.47	36	237.3	6.6	118
McDonald	13	13	4.24	35	227.0	6.5	107
Mussina	18	5	2.54	32	241.0	7.5	68
Milacki	6	8	5.92	20	106.3	5.3	70
Rhodes	7	5	3.63	15	94.3	6.3	38
Mesa	3	8	5.35	12	65.7	5.5	39
Lefferts	1	3	4.09	5	33.0	6.6	15
Mills	1	1	5.40	3	13.3	4.4	8
Davis	0	0	1.86	2	9.7	4.8	2
Lewis	1	1	10.80	2	6.7	3.3	8
92 Totals	66	59	4.12	162	1034.3	6.4	473

Orioles Starting Pitching, 1991

Name	W	L	ERA	GS	IP	IP/GS	ER
Milacki	9	9	4.25	26	163.0	6.3	77
Mesa	6	11	5.97	23	123.7	5.4	82
Ballard	6	12	5.48	22	116.7	5.3	71
Mcdonald	6	8	4.84	21	126.3	6.0	68
Robinson	4	9	5.44	19	97.7	5.1	59
Johnson	2	8	8.13	14	62.0	4.4	56
Smith	5	3	5.23	14	75.7	5.4	44
Mussina	4	5	2.87	12	87.7	7.3	28
Rhodes	0	3	8.00	8	36.0	4.5	32
Flanagan	0	1	11.25	1	4.0	4.0	5
Telford	0	0	8.31	1	4.3	4.3	4
Jones	0	0	9.00	1	3.0	3.0	3
91 Totals	42	69	5.29	162	900.0	5.6	529

Note: Statistics only as starting pitchers for Baltimore.

The Orioles starting pitching in 1991 was a disaster. How did they fix it? Seven pitchers who started for the O's in 1991 were not allowed back in 1992: Jeff Ballard, Jeff M. Robinson, Dave Johnson, Roy Smith, Mike Flanagan, Anthony Telford, and Stacy Jones (Flanagan started one game in 1991 and none in 1992). Those seven pitchers, in 72 starts, had an ERA of 5.99. Can you believe that Dave Johnson was given 14 starts to show that he could accumulate an 8.10 ERA? Two other pitchers, Bob Milacki and Jose Mesa, pitched the 1991 season and most of 1992 before the O's dumped them. They combined for a 4.99 ERA in 1991 and a 5.70 ERA in 1992. Only three of the 12 starters in 1991 are still Orioles, and one of the three, Arthur Rhodes, was an disaster in 1991. Only two solid starters, Ben McDonald, and Mike Mussina, are still in town, and neither pitched a full season in 1991. McDonald was hurt, and Mussina spent most of the season down on the farm.

To make up for the seven departed starters, the Orioles got full seasons from McDonald and Mussina and Rick Sutcliffe. In 1991, McDonald, Mussina, and the seven bums had 105 starts; in 1992, Sutcliffe, McDonald, and Mussina combined for 107. The Orioles replaced the starts lost when Milacki and Mesa were shot by Rhodes and Craig Lefferts.

That's the big difference. What about the bullpen? Actually, the Orioles' pen in 1991 was pretty good; a 3.48 ERA despite having to come in so early because of the starters. That shows how important Rick Sutcliffe is to this team; there's nobody behind him. That's scary, to be so dependent on a pitcher with a history of arm trouble who will turn 37 years old in June.

```
Baltimore Orioles Home Park Performance Factors
                 Outs  Runs  Hits    2b    3b    HR     W     K    SH    SF   HBP   IBB    SB    CS   GDP
Home LH Batters  .981  .991 1.032 1.213 1.014  .964  .937 1.029 1.135 1.353 1.229  .921 1.045  .925 1.057
Home RH Batters  .968 1.010  .969  .959  .691 1.011  .995 1.020  .910 1.173  .952 1.242  .952  .705 1.136
All Home Batters .971  .993  .993 1.056  .877  .964  .960 1.010  .950 1.206 1.030 1.029 1.047  .828 1.078
Opp LH Batters   .975  .991 1.038 1.139 2.565  .789 1.022  .964  .773 1.308 2.784 1.361 1.303  .947 1.526
Opp RH Batters  1.020 1.032 1.043 1.072  .926 1.016 1.051 1.031 1.122 1.032 1.177 1.472  .884 1.031 1.125
All Opp Batters 1.006 1.021 1.043 1.083 1.043  .937 1.047 1.026 1.039 1.128 1.232 1.370 1.006 1.046 1.198
All LH Batters   .979  .991 1.034 1.185 1.144  .891  .965 1.004  .969 1.336 1.362 1.093 1.132  .932 1.230
All RH Batters   .993 1.020 1.005 1.015  .812 1.016 1.025 1.022 1.019 1.108 1.057 1.328  .865  .872 1.131
All Batters      .987 1.007 1.017 1.067  .950  .954 1.000 1.016  .993 1.173 1.112 1.154 1.011  .924 1.134
```

Conventional Batting Records for Baltimore Orioles

	G	AB	Run	Hit	2B	3B	HR	TB	RBI	W	K	IW	HB	SB	CS	BRng Eff	GI DP	SH	SF	Avg	Slug	OBP	Runs Ctd
Hoiles	96	310	49	85	10	1	20	157	40	55	60	2	2	0	2	.356	8	1	3	.274	.506	.384	62
Milligan	137	462	71	111	21	1	11	167	53	106	81	0	4	0	1	.337	15	0	5	.240	.361	.383	70
Ripken B	111	330	35	76	15	0	4	103	36	18	26	1	3	2	3	.383	10	10	2	.230	.312	.275	27
Gomez L	137	468	62	124	24	0	17	199	64	63	78	4	8	2	3	.398	14	5	8	.265	.425	.356	73
Ripken C	162	637	73	160	29	1	14	233	72	64	50	14	7	4	3	.476	13	0	7	.251	.366	.323	77
Anderson B	159	623	100	169	28	10	21	280	80	98	98	14	9	53	16	.527	2	10	9	.271	.449	.373	119
Devereaux	156	653	76	180	29	11	24	303	107	44	94	1	4	10	8	.417	14	0	9	.276	.464	.321	94
Orsulak	117	391	45	113	18	3	4	149	39	28	34	5	4	5	4	.421	3	4	1	.289	.381	.342	52
Davis G	106	398	46	110	15	2	13	168	48	37	65	2	2	1	0	.358	12	1	4	.276	.422	.338	56
McLemore	101	228	40	56	7	2	0	67	27	21	26	1	0	11	5	.674	6	6	1	.246	.294	.308	21
Martinez C	83	198	26	53	10	1	5	80	25	31	47	4	2	0	1	.474	9	0	4	.268	.404	.366	29
Segui	115	189	21	44	9	0	1	56	17	20	23	3	0	1	0	.362	4	2	0	.233	.296	.306	18
Tackett	65	179	21	43	8	1	5	68	24	17	28	1	2	0	0	.514	11	6	4	.240	.380	.307	19
Horn	63	162	13	38	10	1	5	65	19	21	60	2	1	0	0	.313	8	0	1	.235	.401	.324	20
Hulett	57	142	11	41	7	2	2	58	21	10	31	1	1	0	1	.217	7	0	0	.289	.408	.340	18
Mercedes	23	50	7	7	2	0	0	9	4	8	9	0	1	0	1	.400	2	2	1	.140	.180	.267	3
Parent	17	34	4	8	1	0	2	15	4	3	7	0	1	0	0	1.000	0	2	0	.235	.441	.316	5
Scarsone S	11	17	2	3	0	0	0	3	0	1	6	0	0	0	0	.750	0	0	0	.176	.176	.222	1
Dempsey	8	9	2	1	0	0	0	1	0	2	1	0	0	0	0	.667	1	0	0	.111	.111	.273	0
Alexander M	4	5	1	1	0	0	0	1	0	0	3	0	0	0	0	.000	0	0	0	.200	.200	.200	0
Shields T	2	0	0	0	0	0	0	0	0	0	0	0	0	0	0	.000	0	0	0	.000	.000	.000	0
Voigt	1	0	0	0	0	0	0	0	0	0	0	0	0	0	0	.000	0	0	0	.000	.000	.000	0
Olson Gregg	1	0	0	0	0	0	0	0	0	0	0	0	0	0	0	.000	0	0	0	.000	.000	.000	0
Mills A	1	0	0	0	0	0	0	0	0	0	0	0	0	0	0	.000	0	0	0	.000	.000	.000	0
Milacki	1	0	0	0	0	0	0	0	0	0	0	0	0	0	0	.000	0	0	0	.000	.000	.000	0
TOTALS	1734	5485	705	1423	243	36	148	2182	680	647	827	55	51	89	48	.432	139	50	59	.259	.398	.340	758

Sabermetric Batting Records for Baltimore Orioles

	Ball Park Adjusted								SO	Avg	Slug	OBP	Runs Ctd	Outs	27o	OW%	OG	OWAR	DWAR	TWAR
	AB	Run	Hit	2B	3B	HR	RBI	W												
Alexander M	4	1	1	0	0	0	0	0	3	.250	.250	.250	0	3	0.00	.000	0	-0.04	0.02	-0.02
Anderson B	618	99	174	32	17	18	79	95	97	.282	.476	.387	132	480	7.43	.758	18	7.25	0.97	8.21
Davis G	396	46	110	15	1	13	48	37	66	.278	.419	.339	55	304	4.88	.575	11	2.53	0.01	2.54
Dempsey	8	2	1	0	0	0	0	2	1	.125	.125	.300	0	8	0.00	.000	0	-0.10	0.04	-0.06
Devereaux	651	77	181	29	8	24	108	45	96	.278	.458	.324	94	500	5.08	.594	19	4.51	0.98	5.49
Gomez L	465	63	124	24	0	17	64	64	79	.267	.428	.360	73	371	5.31	.615	14	3.65	0.31	3.95
Hoiles	308	50	85	10	1	20	40	56	61	.276	.503	.388	62	237	7.06	.739	9	3.41	0.13	3.54
Horn	160	12	39	11	1	4	18	20	59	.244	.400	.333	20	132	4.09	.487	5	0.67	0.00	0.67
Hulett	141	11	41	7	1	2	21	10	31	.291	.397	.342	17	107	4.29	.510	4	0.64	0.37	1.00
Martinez C	195	25	54	11	1	4	24	30	46	.277	.405	.360	30	157	5.16	.601	6	1.46	0.36	1.82
McLemore	226	40	57	7	1	0	27	21	26	.252	.292	.315	22	185	3.21	.369	7	0.13	0.86	0.99
Mercedes	49	7	7	2	0	0	4	8	9	.143	.184	.271	3	47	1.72	.144	2	-0.36	0.17	-0.18
Milligan	459	72	111	21	0	11	53	108	83	.242	.359	.387	71	369	5.20	.605	14	3.48	0.35	3.83
Orsulak	387	44	116	21	5	3	38	27	33	.300	.403	.357	58	281	5.57	.638	10	2.99	0.97	3.96
Parent	33	4	8	1	0	2	4	3	7	.242	.455	.324	5	27	5.16	.586	1	0.24	-0.05	0.18
Ripken B	328	35	76	15	0	4	36	18	26	.232	.314	.276	27	277	2.63	.282	10	-0.70	1.43	0.73
Ripken C	634	74	160	29	0	14	72	65	51	.252	.364	.325	77	497	4.18	.498	18	2.72	3.07	5.79
Scarsone S	16	2	3	0	0	0	0	1	6	.188	.188	.235	1	14	1.93	.174	1	-0.09	0.02	-0.07
Segui	187	21	44	9	0	0	17	20	23	.235	.283	.309	17	148	3.10	.353	5	0.02	0.40	0.41
Shields T	0	0	0	0	0	0	0	0	0	.000	.000	.000	0	0	0.00	.000	0	0.00	0.00	0.00
Tackett	178	21	43	8	0	5	24	17	28	.242	.371	.308	18	157	3.10	.352	6	0.01	0.32	0.34
Voigt	0	0	0	0	0	0	0	0	0	.000	.000	.000	0	0	0.00	.000	0	0.00	0.00	0.00
TOTALS	5462	709	1448	259	34	140	682	649	841	.265	.402	.345	772	4333	4.81	.567	160	34.88	10.72	45.61

Pitching Records for Baltimore Orioles

	ERA	W	L	Pct	G	GS	CG	ShO	GF	Sv	IP	R	ER	H	2B	3B	HR	BB	IW	SO	HB	WP	BK
Mussina	2.54	18	5	.783	32	32	8	4	0	0	241.0	70	68	212	39	5	16	48	2	130	2	6	1
Sutcliffe	4.47	16	15	.516	36	36	5	2	0	0	237.1	123	118	251	37	7	20	74	4	109	7	7	2
McDonald	4.24	13	13	.500	35	35	4	2	0	0	227.0	113	107	213	44	5	32	74	5	158	9	3	2
Milacki	5.84	6	8	.429	23	20	0	0	1	1	115.2	78	75	140	31	4	16	44	2	51	2	7	1
Rhodes A	3.63	7	5	.583	15	15	2	1	0	0	94.1	39	38	87	20	4	6	38	2	77	1	2	1
Mesa	5.19	3	8	.273	13	12	0	0	1	0	67.2	41	39	77	19	0	9	27	1	22	2	2	0
Lefferts	4.09	1	3	.250	5	5	1	0	0	0	33.0	19	15	34	4	0	3	6	0	23	0	1	0
Lewis R	10.80	1	1	.500	2	2	0	0	0	0	6.2	8	8	13	3	0	1	7	0	4	0	0	0
Frohwirth	2.46	4	3	.571	65	0	0	0	23	4	106.0	33	29	97	15	0	4	41	4	58	3	1	0
Mills A	2.61	10	4	.714	35	3	0	0	12	2	103.1	33	30	78	16	2	5	54	10	60	1	2	0
Davis Storm	3.43	7	3	.700	48	2	0	0	24	4	89.1	35	34	79	8	1	5	36	6	53	2	4	0
Olson Gregg	2.05	1	5	.167	60	0	0	0	56	36	61.1	14	14	46	4	1	3	24	0	58	0	4	0
Flanagan	8.05	0	0	.000	42	0	0	0	15	0	34.2	34	31	50	6	1	3	23	1	17	5	4	0
Clements P	3.28	2	0	1.000	23	0	0	0	4	0	24.2	10	9	23	3	0	0	11	0	9	2	1	0
Williamson	0.96	0	0	.000	12	0	0	0	5	1	18.2	3	2	16	1	1	1	10	1	14	0	1	0
Poole	0.00	0	0	.000	6	0	0	0	1	0	3.1	3	0	3	0	0	0	1	0	3	0	0	0
TOTALS	3.79	89	73	.549	452	162	20	9	142	48	1464.0	656	617	1419	250	31	124	518	38	846	36	45	6

Sabermetric Pitching Records for Baltimore Orioles

	Adj ERA	Expected W	Expected L	Pct	BFP	Opposing Batters Avg	Slg	OBA	RC/G	GDP	SB	CS	PK	PKE	SH	SF	Supported RSup	RSp/G	W	L	Pct
Clements P	3.28	1	1	.588	105	.258	.292	.350	3.55	3	0	0	0	0	2	1	19	6.93	2	0	.786
Davis Storm	3.43	6	4	.568	372	.244	.321	.320	3.52	10	9	2	0	0	6	4	46	4.63	6	4	.601
Flanagan	8.05	0	0	.192	180	.338	.453	.438	8.15	5	2	0	0	0	2	2	20	5.19	0	0	.255
Frohwirth	2.46	5	2	.717	444	.247	.316	.323	3.48	14	11	2	0	1	7	1	41	3.48	4	3	.622
Lefferts	4.09	2	2	.479	136	.268	.370	.299	3.64	4	6	2	0	0	2	1	10	2.73	1	3	.268
Lewis R	10.80	0	2	.117	40	.406	.594	.500	15.48	0	3	0	0	0	0	1	7	9.45	1	1	.387
McDonald	4.24	12	14	.461	958	.247	.421	.311	4.55	14	20	8	0	1	6	6	117	4.64	13	13	.496
Mesa	5.19	4	7	.364	300	.287	.459	.353	5.80	5	8	5	0	1	0	3	32	4.26	4	7	.357
Milacki	5.84	4	10	.311	525	.297	.481	.357	6.33	13	11	1	0	0	3	3	64	4.98	5	9	.375
Mills A	2.61	10	4	.693	428	.215	.312	.315	3.35	11	12	4	0	0	6	5	48	4.18	9	5	.678
Mussina	2.54	16	7	.705	957	.239	.348	.278	3.09	18	9	9	1	1	13	6	128	4.78	17	6	.745
Olson Gregg	2.05	5	1	.785	244	.211	.280	.287	2.74	8	10	0	2	0	0	2	4	0.59	0	6	.063
Poole	0.00	0	0	.000	14	.231	.231	.286	2.54	0	2	1	0	1	0	0	0	0.00	0	0	.000
Rhodes A	3.63	6	6	.539	394	.250	.382	.325	4.04	10	4	4	0	1	5	1	49	4.67	7	5	.578
Sutcliffe	4.47	13	18	.435	1018	.273	.393	.328	4.61	20	22	5	0	5	6	11	111	4.21	13	18	.422
Williamson	0.96	0	0	.943	78	.239	.328	.338	3.57	3	2	1	0	0	1	0	9	4.34	0	0	.943
TOTALS	3.82	83	79	.514	6193	.257	.380	.322	4.22	138	131	44	3	11	59	47	705	4.33	83	79	.515

Batting 'Splits' Records for Baltimore Orioles

SPLITS for Anderson B

	G	AB	Run	Hit	2B	3B	HR	TB	RBI	W	K	IW	HB	SB	CS	DP	SH	SF	Avg	Slug	OBP	RC
vs LHP	97	190	22	43	8	2	5	70	26	31	35	0	5	6	3	0	5	3	.226	.368	.345	28
vs RHP	159	433	78	126	20	8	16	210	54	67	63	14	4	47	13	2	5	6	.291	.485	.386	91
Home	79	313	50	82	14	2	15	145	46	48	54	7	4	24	8	2	2	3	.262	.463	.364	58
Away	80	310	50	87	14	8	6	135	34	50	44	7	5	29	8	0	8	6	.281	.435	.383	61
Grass	134	530	86	143	22	5	19	232	65	80	88	13	6	42	14	2	5	6	.270	.438	.368	96
Turf	25	93	14	26	6	5	2	48	15	18	10	1	3	11	2	0	5	3	.280	.516	.402	23
April/June	75	301	44	85	18	6	13	154	48	39	43	6	5	24	7	2	4	4	.282	.512	.370	62
July/October	84	322	56	84	10	4	8	126	32	59	55	8	4	29	9	0	6	5	.261	.391	.377	57

SPLITS for Baltimore Orioles (all batters except pitchers)

	G	AB	Run	Hit	2B	3B	HR	TB	RBI	W	K	IW	HB	SB	CS	DP	SH	SF	Avg	Slug	OBP	RC
vs LHP	765	1459	200	377	65	7	40	576	191	181	215	11	20	13	16	35	13	16	.258	.395	.345	203
vs RHP	1599	4026	505	1046	178	29	108	1606	489	466	612	44	31	76	32	104	37	43	.260	.399	.338	555
Home	865	2679	339	681	108	19	75	1052	327	323	392	26	24	39	28	62	26	23	.254	.393	.337	362
Away	869	2806	366	742	135	17	73	1130	353	324	435	29	27	50	20	77	24	36	.264	.403	.342	396
Grass	1478	4624	598	1208	195	29	136	1869	574	538	686	47	40	73	41	121	44	47	.261	.404	.340	646
Turf	256	861	107	215	48	7	12	313	106	109	141	8	11	16	7	18	6	12	.250	.364	.337	112
April/June	795	2542	364	681	122	19	82	1087	353	314	379	29	26	42	23	60	20	22	.268	.428	.352	391
July/October	939	2943	341	742	121	17	66	1095	327	333	448	26	25	47	25	79	30	37	.252	.372	.330	369

Cleveland Indians

Brock J. Hanke

CLEVELAND										
YEAR	1983	1984	1985	1986	1987	1988	1989	1990	1991	1992
W	70	75	60	84	61	78	73	77	57	76
L	92	87	102	78	101	84	89	85	105	86
WPCT	0.432	0.463	0.370	0.519	0.377	0.481	0.451	0.475	0.352	0.469
R	704	761	729	831	742	666	604	732	576	674
RA	785	766	861	841	957	731	654	737	759	746
PWPT	0.446	0.497	0.418	0.494	0.375	0.454	0.460	0.497	0.365	0.449
PythW	72	80	68	80	61	73	75	80	59	73
PythL	90	82	94	82	101	89	87	82	103	89
LUCK	-2	-5	-8	4	0	5	-2	-3	-2	3

Defensive Efficiency Record: .6908

It's been over a year now that the national press, not to mention the Cleveland Indian promotional machine, has claimed that the Indians were on the verge of moving up into contention. The arrival of Carlos Baerga, coupled with the acquisition of several kid outfielders from other organizations, has gone straight to the Lake Erie head. But aren't those kid outfielders the ones the other organizations wanted to give away? And didn't the Indians give away their starting rotation to get them? Are the Indians, in actual fact, likely to be contenders in 1993?

To deal with that question, I'm going to use the method I invented for the Philadelphia Phillies essay elsewhere in this book. In fact, I copied that essay over here, and am replacing the Philly paragraphs with the Indians'. I considered rewriting rather than cut-and-paste, but eventually decided that the parallel structure would pay off more than original writing would. So sue me.

What we're going to do is divide the world of Major League baseball players into five classes: superstars, stars, championship-quality players, bulk players, and holes. We're going to see how many of each the Indians have got among their starters, and how those numbers compare to what last year's contenders had. Then we're going to take a look at the three components of a bench: the bullpen, the pinch hitting, and the backups at the skill positions.

First, you need to understand what I mean by "starters". I figure that a National League team has 13 of these, while AL teams have 14. The eight front line position players, plus the DH in the AL, are obvious, as is the closer on the pitching staff. Then, I figure that each team has four starting pitchers who are actually in a real rotation. The #5 guy gets swapped in and out, according to the vagaries of the schedule, and so is not given regular work, in the sense that the front four are. In support of this, I offer that, when I compile the player rankings section, I rank only those starters who have had 20 or more starts. In both leagues, that number is very close to four times the number of teams; teams have four real rotation starters.

Position	92 Starter	TWAR	93 Starter	TWAR
Catcher	Alomar, S.	-0.30	Alomar, S.	-0.30
First base	Sorrento	3.18	Sorrento	3.18
Second base	Baerga	7.16	Baerga	7.16
Third base	Jacoby	-0.06	Thome	-0.52
	Martinez, Ca.	-0.07		
Shortstop	Lewis	0.51	Lewis	0.51
Left field	Hill, G.	0.62	Hill, G.	0.62
	Howard, T.	0.77		
Center field	Lofton	5.80	Lofton	5.80
Right field	Whiten	2.94	Whiten	2.94
DH	Belle	3.14	Belle	3.14

All right, let's talk superstars. In this class, I include only those position players and relief closers who can regularly be counted upon to finish in the top two at their position, if they get a full year's play. For starting pitchers, the top ten. At shortstop, for example, Barry Larkin, Ozzie Smith and Cal Ripken, Jr. are the superstars. Jay Bell is not, though he could finish ahead of either Larkin or Smith in any given year. But to do that, Ozzie or Barry would have to get hurt or have an off year. Bell really isn't in their class of player, injuries being equal. No one but Ripken is really like that in the American League, so there are only three real superstars at shortstop. At second base, there are rather more.

SUPERSTARS:

I figure that the Indians have two superstars, Carlos Baerga and Charles Nagy. Carlos is probably not really better than Roberto Alomar, and may not be better than Julio Franco will come back to be, but that's OK. Second base is producing some horses right now, and there is room for three superstars at the position in the American League. Nagy has only done this for one year now, and he pitched far too many innings for my taste, but let's give the Indians the benefit of the doubt here.

As to the four postseason participants for 1992, they all have two or more superstars. Toronto has Roberto Alomar and Juan Guzman. Last year they had Dave Winfield, and they've replaced him with Paul Molitor. The Oakland A's have Rickey Henderson, albeit on an off year, and they had Jose Canseco, not to mention Dennis Eckersley. The Braves have, as a minimum, Terry Pendelton and Tom Glavine. And the Pirates used to have Barry Bonds and Doug Drabek. That's not to mention the Pittsburgh catching platoon. If you rate the entire catching position for each team, that's the top combo in the league. However, it's not one superstar player, so let's count the 'Rats in for only the two superstars. The Indians can hold their own here, as long as you believe in Charles Nagy.

STARS:

One reason for giving the Indians the benefit of the doubt above is that they only have two players in what I call the "star" category. One is Kenny Lofton, but he's also on his first year of top play. The other is Albert Belle. If you look at our rankings, you won't find Belle, as he did not play the most on the Indians at any one position. But he is actually the player who will take Thomas Howard's place. Howard you would find down in the "holes" category. I'm sure that the Indians want to believe that Mark Whiten and Glenallen Hill will be stars in 1993, but they have done nothing so far to suggest that. As for totals, the Indians have only four players who are stars or better. As you'll see, that's not enough.

The Blue Jays have four stars. Their names are Carter, Olerud, Henke and Key, now replaced by Stewart. Candy Maldonado was just on a hot year. Jack Morris did not pitch as well as his Won/Lost record. Duane Ward will probably be a star next year, now that Henke is gone. That gives the Jays a total of seven stars and superstars. The A's had five stars: Steinbach, McGwire, Dave Henderson, Dave Stewart, and whichever of Bob Welch and Mike Moore was healthy in a given year. You don't count both Ruben Sierra and Jose Canseco. Nor do you count Pat Bordick, on the basis of one career year. In any case, the total of stars and superstars is eight. That's how you win 96 games.

The Braves have Smoltz, Avery, Justice, Nixon, and Gant. No wonder they win. And they've added Greg Maddux, too. Well, the 1992 total is, one more time, seven stars and above. the Pirates have Jay Bell, Andy Van Slyke, and Zane Smith. You count Smith for the same reason you count Dave Henderson but not Pat Bordick or Tim Wakefield. We're talking about the talent core of the team, not it's unproven luck. The total, given that we've already counted the catchers, is six stars or above. There is nothing that even remotely resembles a postseason team that has only two star players behind the two superstars.

CHAMPIONSHIP-QUALITY

A championship-quality player will finish somewhere in the middle of the pack of starters at his position in his league. That's still a good player. Remember, only about half the league's players are starters. If you're in the middle there, you're at about the 75% point in talent over the whole league. You're helping your team, not hurting it. The Phillies have four players of this caliber: Paul Sorrento, Mark Whiten, Dennis Cook, and Steve Olin. Sorrento might develop into a star. He took a big stride forward in 1992, after moving over from an organization that did not really want him around. Also, he's going to be 27, and might turn in a career year. Still, the Indians need more than for some of their championship-quality players to turn into stars. That's because, as you'll see below, postseason teams have as many of them as the Indians do, and have the stars, too. For the record, the Indians have only eight players of championship quality or above.

The Jays have, or had five championship-quality players. They are Pat Borders, Candy Maldonado, Devon White, Jack Morris, and Manny Lee backing up Eddie Zosky. The cumulative total is 12. The A's have Borders / Blankenship, Baines and Ron Darling, for a total of 11. The Braves have the first basemen, the catchers, and Charlie Leibrandt, for a total of ten. That's if you don't count the shortstop platoon. The Pirates have, or had, the right field group, Steve Buechele, Randy Tomlin, and the committee bullpen. That's ten again.

BULK

The Indians have three bulk players. They are Mark Lewis (or Felix Fermin or whoever is going to play short in 1993), the aforementioned Glenallen Hill at DH, and Jack Armstrong the All-American Bust. What the Indians need is for all three of them to turn into stars. Along with me, Don Malcolm, and you, gentle reader. That is to say, no chance. "No chance" is also the term for the star qualities of Sandy Alomar, Jr., Brook Jacoby, and Scott Scudder. They're holes, and filling them is the main priority for the Indians. What's that you say? Sandy Alomar, Jr. is supposed to be a star someday? Well, how many years to you intend to wait for this to happen? Face it, the Indians lost this gamble. Of course, Brook Jacoby used to be at least championship quality, but he's too old now. But, then, the good teams replace their aging players before they get quite this bad, don't they?

The Blue Jays have 12 positions manned with championship quality or above. That leaves third base and #4 starter. I'm sure that the Jays were expecting at least championship quality from Kelly Gruber, but they didn't get it. They got a hole. The #4 starter was either Todd Stottlemyre or Dave Stieb, and both were awful. But the Jays reacted in mid-season, with David Cone. That upgrades the hole to at least bulk. One bulk starter, for a total of thirteen out of fourteen. The A's have three places left. Walt Weiss was awful. The #4 starter, Mike Moore, was certainly bulk. The Lansford / Browne platoon was, too. That's 13 for 14, with the only hole being at short.

The Braves have a hole at second base, with the collapse of Jeff Treadway. Their bullpen was a hole as well. But the shortstops were certainly at least bulk players. That's 11 positions out of 13. The Pirates had at least bulk play out of every position other than Jose Lind's absent bat at second base. That's 12 out of 13.

STARTERS OVERALL:

You can see that the Indians are several pieces short of a contender. they have six starters who are bulk or holes, while the postseason teams have about two each. What's worse, they need to turn those bad starters into stars, not just decent players. The huge gap in star players is absolutely critical to the Indians. Unfortunately, stars cost money, and the Indians don't have that. They also don't have any trade surplus to use to get the stars. Simply put, they are not going into contention any time soon.

I want to emphasize this. All the 1992 contenders, all four of them, share a basic profile. They have a couple or three true superstars, about five stars behind them, and mostly championship quality everywhere else. They just don't have holes. The basic profile of superstars / stars / champs / bulk / holes is 2 / 5 / 4 / 1 / 1. Let's check this against reality. Instead of discussing who "is" a superstar, let's say a team had a superstar in 1992 if the player finished first or second in his league at his position, or the equivalent for starting pitchers. Third through fifth, he was a star. Sixth through tenth was championship quality. Eleventh or twelfth was bulk play, and thirteenth or fourteenth was a hole. In the NL, bulk was 10-11, and only 12 was a real hole. Remember, this is tough criteria; Dennis Eckersley is only a "star" here, as he finished third among AL closers in our rankings. So is Rickey Henderson, and Willie Wilson is the Oakland center fielder.

Using this mechanical system, Toronto had a ridiculous four superstars: Roberto Alomar, Joe Carter, Dave Winfield, and Juan Guzman. They had only two regular stars: John Olerud and Candy Maldonado. But they had five championship-quality ballplayers, only two bulk players, and only Kelly Gruber was a hole. The profile is 4 / 2 / 5 / 2 / 1. Oakland's profile is 2 / 4 / 6 / 1 / 1. In the NL, with only 13 starters, the Braves are 3 / 4 / 4 / 2 / 0, and Pittsburgh fielded 2 / 4 / 3 / 3 / 1. If anything, these profiles are even stronger than the theoretical ones developed above.

The Indians, on the other hand, figure to be more like 2 / 2 / 4 / 3 / 3. So let's take a look at the bench, and see if they can make it up.

PINCH HITTING:

The Indian pinch hitting corps can be summed up in one simple phrase: they used Thomas Howard as a starter in the outfield. Now, your first backup starter in the outfield is usually considered to be your best pinch hitter. Thomas Howard. The man who Jerald Clark ran out of town in San Diego.

Of the contenders above, none are quite that bad off. The Pirates had the sort of hitting bench you dream about, because only they had the sort of outfield platoon that leaves bats on the bench in any given game. The Jays traded all their bulk outfielders away, and were a little thin on the bench, but not as thin as the Indians are. The A's didn't have much behind Willie Wilson, but Wilson was supposed to be on the bench. The Braves platoon in the infield, where the hitters are few, but they do have Deion Sanders and a couple of backup first basemen. Francisco Cabrera you may recall.

BULK BULLPEN:

The Indians started Scott Scudder. That's what happens when you have to dispose of all your expensive star pitchers to get kid outfielders.

SKILL REPLACEMENTS:

The Phils do OK. They have Milt Thompson, who can play a fine reserve center field. They also have just a raft of decent good-glove infielders. The problem, like in the bullpen, is that they have to start them. But they do have enough such people that they won't have troubles with injuries to the keystone combination. The one thing they don't have is a real backup for Darren Daulton. They let Steve Lake go, which a real contender shouldn't do.

The Indians can't decide whether to start Mark Lewis or Felix Fermin at short. Either one would be a decent backup. However, that's about it for the Tribe, in terms of hot gloves on the bench. Well, Thomas Howard can play center field. He just can't hit. The Jays and A's actually lived off their infield replacements, and the A's had to play their backup center fielder all year. They still won 96 games. The Braves have deep platooning at the keystone, and Deion Sanders in center and Damon Berryhill behind the plate. They didn't lose a step in defense up the middle. Only the Pirates were questionable. They had Cecil Espy behind Andy Van Slyke, and a platoon at catcher, but not much to try around the keystone. On balance, though, the Phils don't look any better than the contenders do.

FINAL ANALYSIS:

The Indians need a real right side of the infield, a real pitching staff, and a catcher. They need some stars to extend the offensive sequence. Their kid outfielders show no signs of becoming these people. This is just not a contending team. The management is blowing smoke. The real use of this essay and the Philly one is to take a look at how similar the profiles of the contenders were. Use that info the next time someone tells you his favorite team is on the verge of winning. 2 / 5 / 4 / 1 / 1. One hole, no more, and the team shouldn't really be expecting it. That's the ticket, and nothing else.

```
Cleveland Indians Home Park Performance Factors
                 Outs  Runs  Hits   2b    3b    HR     W     K    SH    SF   HBP   IBB    SB    CS   GDP
Home LH Batters  1.045 .955 1.000  .964  .979 1.034  .949 1.066  .805  .652  .783 1.034  .981  .955  .858
Home RH Batters  1.008 .868  .917  .919  .620 1.046  .886 1.012  .911  .892 1.099  .880 1.125  .828  .970
All Home Batters 1.021 .914  .949  .953  .803 1.020  .924 1.023  .873  .851 1.054  .929  .989  .883  .927
Opp LH Batters   1.069 1.094 1.061 1.095 1.878 .966 1.245  .987 1.459 1.533 1.216 1.326 1.181 1.184 1.084
Opp RH Batters   1.006 .976  .995  .883 1.375  .873 1.025  .984  .985 1.089 1.417  .987 1.216 1.089 1.094
All Opp Batters  1.033 1.013 1.019 .967 1.425  .915 1.077 1.001 1.072 1.156 1.392 1.031 1.242 1.106 1.074
All LH Batters   1.055 1.017 1.028 1.024 1.251 1.008 1.077 1.036 1.124  .912  .954 1.155 1.049 1.055  .955
All RH Batters   1.007 .927  .958  .898 1.010  .921  .965  .995  .950  .995 1.222  .935 1.175  .957 1.035
All Batters      1.027 .963  .984  .959 1.064  .954 1.003 1.012  .975  .998 1.189  .977 1.095  .986  .999
```

Conventional Batting Records for Cleveland Indians

	G	AB	Run	Hit	2B	3B	HR	TB	RBI	W	K	IW	HB	SB	CS	BRng Eff	GI DP	SH	SF	Avg	Slug	OBP	Runs Ctd
Alomar S	89	299	22	75	16	0	2	97	26	13	32	3	5	3	3	.313	7	3	0	.251	.324	.293	27
Sorrento	140	458	52	123	24	1	18	203	60	51	89	7	1	0	3	.367	13	1	3	.269	.443	.341	68
Baerga	161	657	92	205	32	1	20	299	105	35	76	10	13	10	2	.517	15	2	9	.312	.455	.354	106
Jacoby	120	291	30	76	7	0	4	95	36	28	54	2	1	0	3	.425	13	3	4	.261	.326	.324	29
Lewis M	122	413	44	109	21	0	5	145	30	25	69	1	3	4	5	.377	12	1	4	.264	.351	.308	42
Belle	153	585	81	152	23	1	34	279	112	52	128	5	4	8	2	.425	18	1	8	.260	.477	.320	87
Lofton	148	576	96	164	15	8	5	210	42	68	54	3	2	66	12	.621	7	4	1	.285	.365	.362	88
Whiten	148	508	73	129	19	4	9	183	43	72	102	10	2	16	12	.587	12	3	3	.254	.360	.347	65
Hill G	102	369	38	89	16	1	18	161	49	20	73	0	4	9	6	.349	11	0	1	.241	.436	.287	42
Howard T	117	358	36	99	15	2	2	124	32	17	60	1	0	15	8	.441	4	10	2	.277	.346	.308	38
Ortiz	86	244	20	61	7	0	0	68	24	12	23	0	4	1	3	.361	7	2	0	.250	.279	.296	19
Martinez Crl	69	228	23	60	9	1	5	86	35	7	21	0	1	1	2	.440	5	1	4	.263	.377	.283	23
Fermin	79	215	27	58	7	2	0	69	13	18	10	1	1	0	0	.444	7	9	2	.270	.321	.326	23
Thome	40	117	8	24	3	1	2	35	12	10	34	2	2	2	0	.500	3	0	2	.205	.299	.275	10
Cole	41	97	11	20	1	0	0	21	5	10	21	0	1	9	2	.400	2	0	1	.206	.216	.284	7
Jefferson R	24	89	8	30	6	2	1	43	6	1	17	0	1	0	0	.308	2	0	0	.337	.483	.352	14
Levis	28	43	2	12	4	0	1	19	3	0	5	0	0	0	0	.143	1	0	0	.279	.442	.279	5
Worthington	9	24	0	4	0	0	0	4	2	2	4	0	0	0	0	1.000	0	0	0	.167	.167	.231	1
Perezchica	18	20	2	2	1	0	0	3	1	2	6	0	0	0	0	.400	0	2	0	.100	.150	.182	1
Kirby	21	18	9	3	1	0	1	7	1	3	2	0	0	0	3	.667	1	0	0	.167	.389	.286	1
Rohde	5	7	0	0	0	0	0	0	0	2	3	1	0	0	0	.000	0	0	0	.000	.000	.222	0
Hernandez J	3	4	0	0	0	0	0	0	0	0	2	0	0	0	0	.000	0	0	0	.000	.000	.000	0
TOTALS	1723	5620	674	1495	227	24	127	2151	637	448	885	46	45	144	67	.457	140	42	44	.266	.383	.323	689

Sabermetric Batting Records for Cleveland Indians

	Ball Park Adjusted								Runs				Run/							
	AB	Run	Hit	2B	3B	HR	RBI	W	SO	Avg	Slug	OBP	Ctd	Outs	27o	OW%	OG	OWAR	DWAR	TWAR
Alomar S	296	20	71	14	0	1	23	12	31	.240	.297	.283	24	236	2.75	.282	9	-0.60	0.30	-0.30
Baerga	665	88	201	30	1	19	101	35	76	.302	.436	.347	102	490	5.62	.622	18	4.93	2.22	7.16
Belle	580	74	145	20	0	32	103	49	127	.250	.450	.310	80	461	4.69	.533	17	3.13	0.01	3.14
Cole	101	11	20	1	0	0	5	10	21	.198	.208	.268	7	85	2.22	.205	3	-0.46	0.05	-0.41
Fermin	213	24	55	6	1	0	11	17	9	.258	.296	.315	20	174	3.10	.334	6	-0.10	0.53	0.42
Hernandez J	4	0	0	0	0	0	0	0	1	.000	.000	.000	0	4	0.00	.000	0	-0.05	0.01	-0.04
Hill G	366	35	85	14	0	17	45	19	72	.232	.410	.279	38	297	3.45	.383	11	0.37	0.26	0.62
Howard T	362	34	97	14	2	1	30	17	60	.268	.326	.299	36	287	3.39	.374	11	0.25	0.52	0.77
Jacoby	288	27	72	6	0	3	33	26	53	.250	.302	.311	25	236	2.86	.299	9	-0.45	0.39	-0.06
Jefferson R	89	7	29	5	2	0	5	1	17	.326	.427	.341	12	62	5.23	.587	2	0.54	0.05	0.59
Kirby	18	9	3	1	0	1	1	3	2	.167	.389	.286	1	18	1.50	.105	1	-0.16	0.01	-0.15
Levis	44	2	12	4	0	1	3	0	5	.273	.432	.273	5	32	4.22	.481	1	0.16	-0.06	0.10
Lewis M	410	40	104	18	0	4	27	23	68	.254	.327	.296	37	325	3.07	.330	12	-0.24	0.75	0.51
Lofton	604	98	169	15	11	5	42	74	55	.280	.366	.359	93	458	5.48	.610	17	4.41	1.39	5.80
Martinez Crl	226	21	57	8	0	4	32	6	20	.252	.341	.271	20	178	3.03	.324	7	-0.17	0.11	-0.07
Ortiz	242	18	58	6	0	0	22	11	22	.240	.264	.287	17	194	2.37	.226	7	-0.89	-0.42	-1.31
Perezchica	19	1	1	0	0	0	0	1	5	.053	.053	.100	0	19	0.00	.000	1	-0.25	-0.04	-0.29
Rohde	7	0	0	0	0	0	0	2	3	.000	.000	.222	0	7	0.00	.000	0	-0.09	0.03	-0.06
Sorrento	479	53	126	24	1	18	61	55	91	.263	.430	.337	69	372	5.01	.566	14	2.98	0.20	3.18
Thome	122	8	24	3	1	2	12	10	34	.197	.287	.259	10	102	2.65	.267	4	-0.31	-0.21	-0.52
Whiten	515	70	126	18	4	8	41	72	103	.245	.342	.338	62	417	4.01	.456	15	1.64	1.30	2.94
Worthington	23	0	3	0	0	0	1	1	3	.130	.130	.167	1	20	1.35	.087	1	-0.20	0.01	-0.18
TOTALS	5706	649	1471	217	26	122	616	448	895	.258	.369	.316	664	4525	3.96	.450	168	16.71	7.41	24.12

Pitching Records for Cleveland Indians

	ERA	W	L	Pct	G	GS	CG	ShO	GF	Sv	IP	R	ER	H	2B	3B	HR	BB	IW	SO	HB	WP	BK
Nagy	2.96	17	10	.630	33	33	10	3	0	0	252.0	91	83	245	41	4	11	57	1	169	2	7	0
Armstrong	4.64	6	15	.286	35	23	1	0	5	0	166.2	100	86	176	28	4	23	67	0	114	3	6	3
Cook D	3.82	5	7	.417	32	25	1	0	1	0	158.0	79	67	156	34	3	29	50	2	96	2	4	5
Scudder	5.28	6	10	.375	23	22	0	0	0	0	109.0	80	64	134	23	2	10	55	0	66	2	7	0
Mesa	4.16	4	4	.500	15	15	1	1	0	0	93.0	45	43	92	14	1	5	43	0	40	2	0	0
Otto	7.06	5	9	.357	18	16	0	0	0	0	80.1	64	63	110	17	0	12	33	0	32	1	5	0
Boucher	6.37	2	2	.500	8	7	0	0	0	0	41.0	29	29	48	5	1	9	20	0	17	1	1	0
Mlicki	4.98	0	2	.000	4	4	0	0	0	0	21.2	14	12	23	3	1	3	16	0	16	1	1	0
Embree	7.00	0	2	.000	4	4	0	0	0	0	18.0	14	14	19	5	0	3	8	0	12	1	1	1
Mutis	9.53	0	2	.000	3	2	0	0	0	0	11.1	14	12	24	3	2	4	6	0	8	0	2	0
Shaw	8.22	0	1	.000	2	1	0	0	1	0	7.2	7	7	7	0	0	2	4	0	3	0	0	0
Nichols Rod	4.53	4	3	.571	30	9	0	0	5	0	105.1	58	53	114	16	5	13	31	1	56	2	3	0
Power	2.54	3	3	.500	64	0	0	0	16	6	99.1	33	28	88	14	0	7	35	9	51	4	2	1
Olin	2.34	8	5	.615	72	0	0	0	62	29	88.1	25	23	80	8	1	8	27	6	47	4	1	1
Plunk	3.64	9	6	.600	58	0	0	0	20	4	71.2	31	29	61	9	0	5	38	2	50	0	5	0
Lilliquist	1.75	5	3	.625	71	0	0	0	22	6	61.2	13	12	39	10	0	5	18	6	47	2	2	0
Wickander	3.07	2	0	1.000	44	0	0	0	10	1	41.0	14	14	39	5	1	1	28	3	38	4	1	1
Christopher	3.00	0	0	.000	10	0	0	0	4	0	18.0	8	6	17	4	2	2	10	1	13	0	2	0
Bell E	7.63	0	2	.000	7	1	0	0	2	0	15.1	13	13	22	5	0	1	9	0	10	1	1	0
Arnsberg	11.81	0	0	.000	8	0	0	0	1	0	10.2	14	14	13	1	0	6	11	0	5	2	2	0
TOTALS	4.11	76	86	.469	541	162	13	4	149	46	1470.0	746	672	1507	245	27	159	566	31	890	34	53	12

Sabermetric Pitching Records for Cleveland Indians

	Adj ERA	Expected W	L	Pct	BFP	Avg	Slg	OBA	RC/G	GDP	SB	CS	PK	PKE	SH	SF	RSup	RSp/G	Supported W	L	Pct
Armstrong	4.43	9	12	.440	735	.269	.430	.337	5.26	8	15	9	2	3	6	5	77	4.16	9	12	.421
Arnsberg	10.97	0	0	.113	54	.317	.780	.481	12.18	4	0	0	0	0	0	0	0	0.00	0	0	.000
Bell E	7.04	0	2	.237	75	.349	.476	.432	8.12	2	4	1	0	0	1	1	3	1.76	0	2	.049
Boucher	5.93	1	3	.305	184	.302	.516	.377	6.52	7	0	1	1	0	1	3	31	6.81	2	2	.521
Christopher	2.50	0	0	.711	79	.254	.463	.346	5.43	1	2	2	0	0	1	1	9	4.50	0	0	.728
Cook D	3.65	6	6	.537	669	.255	.463	.312	4.94	7	8	10	2	4	3	3	72	4.10	6	6	.511
Embree	6.50	1	1	.267	81	.271	.471	.346	6.33	1	3	0	0	1	0	2	7	3.50	0	2	.193
Lilliquist	1.61	7	1	.857	239	.187	.306	.253	2.47	4	4	2	0	0	5	4	12	1.75	4	4	.495
Mesa	3.97	4	4	.494	400	.262	.350	.344	4.20	10	6	3	1	0	2	2	49	4.74	4	4	.541
Mlicki	4.57	1	1	.424	101	.280	.451	.404	7.02	2	7	1	0	0	2	0	13	5.40	1	1	.535
Mutis	8.74	0	2	.168	64	.429	.768	.469	16.99	0	0	0	0	0	0	2	4	3.18	0	2	.098
Nagy	2.82	18	9	.659	1018	.260	.346	.300	3.19	34	12	15	0	3	6	9	122	4.36	18	9	.663
Nichols Rod	4.36	3	4	.448	456	.273	.429	.323	5.05	6	6	2	1	0	1	5	65	5.55	4	3	.572
Olin	2.24	10	3	.754	360	.249	.355	.314	3.31	15	2	4	0	0	5	2	28	2.85	7	6	.572
Otto	6.72	4	10	.254	368	.333	.494	.395	6.89	16	11	2	0	1	3	1	32	3.59	3	11	.190
Plunk	3.39	9	6	.572	309	.229	.320	.324	3.75	4	3	2	1	0	3	2	39	4.90	9	6	.632
Power	2.36	4	2	.735	409	.248	.346	.316	3.57	13	5	3	0	0	7	8	41	3.71	4	2	.672
Scudder	5.04	6	10	.378	509	.303	.432	.380	6.02	14	14	7	0	0	6	4	51	4.21	6	10	.366
Shaw	7.04	0	1	.237	33	.259	.481	.355	5.57	1	1	0	0	0	2	0	3	3.52	0	1	.171
Wickander	2.85	1	1	.654	187	.260	.327	.386	4.75	5	3	0	0	0	2	2	16	3.51	1	1	.555
TOTALS	3.96	80	82	.495	6330	.268	.407	.336	4.67	154	109	64	8	13	56	56	674	4.13	76	86	.472

Batting 'Splits' Records for Cleveland Indians

SPLITS for Cleveland Indians (all batters except pitchers)

	G	AB	Run	Hit	2B	3B	HR	TB	RBI	W	K	IW	HB	SB	CS	DP	SH	SF	Avg	Slug	OBP	RC
vs LHP	670	1353	182	386	71	3	30	553	172	123	220	10	13	50	23	31	10	16	.285	.409	.347	194
vs RHP	1611	4267	492	1109	156	21	97	1598	465	325	665	36	32	94	44	109	32	28	.260	.375	.315	496
Home	873	2781	366	786	117	15	62	1119	344	240	429	25	20	73	38	76	25	25	.283	.402	.341	377
Away	850	2839	308	709	110	9	65	1032	293	208	456	21	25	71	29	64	17	19	.250	.364	.305	314
Grass	1457	4771	584	1287	192	22	108	1847	549	390	742	40	34	118	61	124	36	36	.270	.387	.327	596
Turf	266	849	90	208	35	2	19	304	88	58	143	6	11	26	6	16	6	8	.245	.358	.299	94
April/June	798	2621	299	680	94	9	56	960	284	200	418	13	22	75	31	62	22	20	.259	.366	.315	302
July/October	925	2999	375	815	133	15	71	1191	353	248	467	33	23	69	36	78	20	24	.272	.397	.330	387

New York Yankees

Don Malcolm

NEW YORK YEAR	1983	1984	1985	1986	1987	1988	1989	1990	1991	1992
W	91	87	97	90	89	85	74	67	71	76
L	71	75	64	72	73	76	87	95	91	86
WPCT	0.562	0.537	0.602	0.556	0.549	0.528	0.460	0.414	0.438	0.469
R	770	758	839	790	788	772	698	603	674	733
RA	703	679	660	738	758	748	792	749	777	746
PWPT	0.545	0.555	0.618	0.534	0.519	0.516	0.437	0.393	0.429	0.491
PythW	88	90	100	87	84	84	71	64	70	80
PythL	74	72	62	75	78	78	91	98	92	82
LUCK	3	-3	-3	3	5	1	3	3	1	-4

Defensive Efficiency Record: .6971

Every day was an eternity, a mounting collection of ceaseless tickings on a slow, grinning clock, melting in the Florida sun like an orange juice commercial by Dali. Every moment called out its passing, drops of water splashed against his forehead in the ritual of oblivion. It would not be much longer. It would be forever.

He tried to douse his mind, he tried an internal divination, memory drowning him in tears that pre-empted the water flicking into his reddened eyes. The slight salt content was slowly creating a rift zone of pain that forced him to blink continuously, almost involuntarily, spreading the salt further into the recesses of his lids. He could hear his breathing quicken and slow, he could feel the failing muscles in his arms lengthen and contract as the cords swayed him, suspended in mid-air over the diamond-shaped pit, high above the black, roaring waters below, their torrent a distant, throbbing growl.

For months, maybe years he had been suspended in this way. At incalculable intervals there would be nourishment extended across to him, by a curious man who had the face and hands of a dwarf, but whom he knew to be seven feet tall. Or so he thought. The long wooden rod dangled teasingly for some time, as the feeder tortured him with anticipation before finally permitting him to eat.

Occasionally, because he knew himself to be clairvoyant—how he had argued with his subjects over this point—he received a vision of what was occurring in his kingdom while he was absent. He saw small men dividing up his riches, consolidating his vast wealth into parcels for their own use. The faces always looked up, startled, and began to scurry away with whatever it was they held in their hands as they saw him approach. He heard his voice rising with anger, scorn, and the presentiment of divine revenge, the power of retribution stirring him to a laughter wilder than the hyena's. As he felt the glow of vengeance spread throughout his body, he would invariably awaken to find himself suspended over the pit, his eyes still puffy and stained. The pain in his back

Position	92 Starter	TWAR	93 Starter	TWAR
Catcher	Nokes	-0.09	Nokes	-0.09
First base	Mattingly	3.73	Mattingly	3.73
Second base	Stankiewicz	2.57	Stankiewicz	2.57
Third base	Hayes, C.	1.95	Boggs	3.34
Shortstop	Velarde	2.83	Owen	3.77
Left field	Hall	3.11	O'Neill	4.80
Center field	Kelly, R.	2.94	Williams, B.	2.20
Right field	Williams, B.	2.20	Tartabull	5.05
DH	Tartabull	5.05	Maas	2.86

was the ache of Prometheus: he felt his stomach, his liver, his spleen as they sagged and shifted, twisting into each other like sadistic dancers, each bent on bringing their partners to their knees.

He had recalled the instructions he gave his lords as he took his leave. "If I am not back in a few months, consider me to be dead, and do not look for me." He had made sure that they could not break up his wealth until an appointed period of time had past. For three years after his disappearance, his kingdom would remain intact, unpillaged. But now he could no longer keep count of how long he had been imprisoned.

At times he thought that he might be inside a larger dream, for he felt the tossing and turning, the to and from of dull, inchoate, darkened aches and moans, and try as he might he could never quite grasp the features of the feeder, the only face that he saw, but that face only intermittently. It never seemed to be exactly the same twice, except for a single characteristic: it was always too small for its body. Slowly he began to see patterns in the appearance of the face, as if various times of the day, or various cycles in his ability to see, produced the mutations, the whimsical, grating deformities who seemed to laugh without expression, speak without moving their lips, supplying to him a silent, telepathetic derision.

The dream would slowly mutate, as he'd see glimpses of an iron horse, a magnificent steed, riderless, that would magically come to life, and gallop for miles without tiring, until it would come to a cliff and run straight over it, whinnying with terrified delight as it fell, turning and gyrating as it picked up speed. And then while in mid-air it would slow its fall, and while it slowed itself it began to disintegrate, to shrivel up, to shrink and dessicate, to age in alarming rapidity even as its fall was suspended, until the magnificent torso collapsed in on itself. Before the moment of death his dream would jump cut: he would never actually see the horse die, but at times he would see a closeup of its eyes, frozen in a wild stare, glazed, glaring at the world in feeble, useless defiance.

Sometimes he would see brief snippets of the gatherings of his fellow monarchs, who, though they were bound by the terms that he had set forth for disposition of his kingdom in case of catastrophe, were conspiring—as he had always known they would—to invade and occupy his territories, in the name of stability, of continuity, in the false claim that such would be in the best interests of his people. Often these snippets would contain by a shadowy man who would speak to the assembled monarchs from behind a veil. As the dream continued, he would frantically attempt to count the other monarchs in the room, which was framed in a doorway. But as he reached the count of fourteen, the door was suddenly allowed to shut. No amount of knocking would ever induce the door to be reopened.

And then, further inside the dream, would come additional faces: swirling, spiralling faces that cascaded before his eyes for an instant, strange and wistful hallucinations that dissolved into one another, accelerating like the winds of an approaching hurricane. They were all men in uniform, wearing caps, all with names and numbers assigned, bold colors accompanying their featureless smiles, their dizzying sameness of expression. But as each image began to fade, as each man started to dissolve into his successor, he could see the men mouth an epithet, a parting gesture in recognition of his bellicosity, his warlord mentality. And the epithet was uniform: "Screw you," "up yours," "step in it," "bend over." As the montage continued, the men stopped mouthing their crudities, and replaced them with a more economic gesture sometimes known as "the shipbuilder's greeting" or "the naval salute," but one universally understood across the eons of hated dynasties.

It was no longer possible for him to tell which was the dream. As his eyes continued to blink, the images of the men and the high, dank walls began to mingle and spin, whirling until he lost all sense of light, shadow or image. Silence, blackness, the slow sense of unconciousness was attached to him only by the dim tautness that still somehow pervaded his limbs, that sense which radiated back to him like a very distant, almost inaudible voice...

* * * *

—"George! George!" The voice was saying. "Are you all right?"

He raised his head groggily from the conference table. Slowly the room came into focus. Fourteen men whose faces had been part of the early shards of dream were standing in various phases of concern. The men had worn medieval costumes when he had last seen their faces: now they were dressed in the uniform of predators, their entrepreneurially wide lapels belied by their narrow, monopolistic ties.

He summoned some of that brash Henry Fonda with a rasp and a double chin that he thought was a trademark inflection. "Why, sure I'm all right. I just was trying to keep a low profile. I've been so busy lately that I haven't been getting a lot of sleep."

"We know that it's taken a lot out of you, George."

"We just wanted you to clear up a few things in your personal life."

"We thought the time off would do you a lot of good."

"We've been following in your footsteps while you've been gone."

He was still a little dazed, and the affected tributes which issued from his companions' lips did not reveal their true meanings to him as he sat in his chair in the large conference room, as absorbent as a single-ply paper towel. He felt like a Surrealist landscape, but looked like a Cubist bandit: a multitude of disconnected hands armed with unrecognizable weaponry.

"Am I back?" he asked hesitantly, as if looping dialogue to his own image on a movie screen.

The faces smiled bravely. But not without some trepidation did they all begin to nod their heads.

"Yessss!" he hissed, an Alex Keating in age makeup. He got up from the table, but had to catch his balance: his head was still swimming. But there was so much to do: so many free agents, so little time. There were prospects to trade away, havoc to wreak, Ivanas and Marlas and innumerable wannabes to flirt with, organizational dissension to recreate: it was a whole new era, with his brethren more in control than ever, and more room for him to insult, outrage, and scheme than ever before. His head finally clear, he strode purposely to the door, but before he could exit he was stopped by a tug on his sleeve.

"George—," a new face said, haltingly.

He flashed the Tyrone Power-with-omnivorous-jowls smile, the knockout fourth of July fireworks dazzler at the timid new peer.

"We wanted you to have this memento," he said. He handed him a box wrapped in pinstriped gift paper.

He thanked all of those in attendance. Profusely. And then with a needless flourish, he opened the package.

Inside were a set of long stout cords, pieces of rope that had been stretched to the straining point by a strong, agitated prisoner. Sets of metal ankle and wrist shackles were also in the box, still with flecks of dried skin that the prisoner had ground into them as he had stretched across a dim, distantly remembered abyss.

He looked down at the implements for a moment, looked back at his fellow peers, and then began to laugh maniacally. As each man in turn joined in the laughter and backslapping welcome, the following closing credits roll across your TV screen:

Produced by Major League Baseball.

Any use of these pictures and images without express written permission of
George Steinbrenner, his psychiatrist, the (vacant) Office of the Commissioner,
and Major League Baseball, is strictly prohibited.

The New York Yankees:

Free agent signings—Spike Owen, Jimmy Key, Wade Boggs.

Players acquired in trade—Jim Abbott, Paul O'Neill.

Players traded away—Roberto Kelly.

Prospects dealt away—J.T. Snow, Russ Springer, Jerry Nielsen. (And many more to come...)

Projected starting rotation—Abbott, Key, Melido (Mr. Tough Loss) Perez, Sam Militello, Bob Wickman.

Co-starring—Steve Howe as Mr. Cocaine, DEA agent.

With—Steve Farr, John Habyan, Rich Monteleone, Scott Kamieniecki.

Catcher—Matt Nokes, Mike Stanley.

First base—Don Mattingly.

Second base—Andy Stankiewicz, Pat Kelly, Mike Gallego.

Shortstop—Owen, Stankiewicz, Gallego, Randy Velarde.

Third base—Boggs, Kelly, Velarde, Hensley Meulens.

Left field—O'Neill, Meulens, Dion James.

Center field—Bernie Williams, Gerald Williams, Esther Williams.

Right field—Danny (K.C.) Tartabull.

Designated hitter—Kevin Maas.

Directed, produced, written, gnawed on, worried over, reviewed, revisited,
and refried by—George Steinbrenner.

Assistant camerman—Gene Michael.

Gaffer—Buck Showalter.

Technical adviser—Toots Shor.

Executive producer—Vincent Spira.

Fine print—prognosis:

With miminal involvement from George—87-90 wins.

With normal involvement from George—75-80 wins.

New York Yankees Home Park Performance Factors														
	Outs	Runs	Hits	2b	3b	HR	W	K	SH	SF	HBP	IBB	SB	CS	GDP
Home LH Batters	.968	.857	.976	1.031	2.035	.866	.810	1.121	1.295	.996	.498	.765	.824	.858	1.039
Home RH Batters	1.015	1.005	1.022	1.011	.876	1.010	1.012	1.045	.945	.823	1.043	1.045	.932	.963	1.026
All Home Batters	.996	.939	.997	1.014	1.076	.929	.934	1.041	.922	.907	.836	.921	.894	.917	1.025
Opp LH Batters	.975	.959	.976	.894	1.263	.899	.962	.974	.581	.843	1.423	.994	.850	.858	1.145
Opp RH Batters	1.055	1.086	1.052	1.098	1.183	1.097	1.079	1.067	1.033	1.523	1.168	1.004	1.236	.891	1.053
All Opp Batters	1.036	1.041	1.031	1.046	1.179	1.010	1.037	1.045	.918	1.188	1.219	1.044	1.112	.917	1.088
All LH Batters	.971	.898	.977	.973	1.504	.880	.886	1.041	.674	.937	.772	.871	.835	.851	1.086
All RH Batters	1.034	1.043	1.035	1.052	1.025	1.050	1.044	1.057	.986	1.093	1.095	1.031	1.077	.923	1.038
All Batters	1.015	.987	1.013	1.029	1.126	.967	.983	1.043	.912	1.027	.979	.978	1.013	.908	1.054

Conventional Batting Records for New York Yankees

	G	AB	Run	Hit	2B	3B	HR	TB	RBI	W	K	IW	HB	SB	CS	BRng Eff	GI DP	SH	SF	Avg	Slug	OBP	Runs Ctd
Nokes	121	384	42	86	9	1	22	163	59	37	62	11	3	0	1	.146	14	0	6	.224	.424	.293	46
Mattingly	157	640	89	184	40	0	14	266	86	39	43	7	1	3	0	.422	11	0	6	.287	.416	.327	87
Kelly P	106	318	38	72	22	2	7	119	27	25	72	1	10	8	5	.491	6	6	3	.226	.374	.301	36
Hayes C	142	509	52	131	19	2	18	208	66	28	100	0	3	3	5	.404	12	3	6	.257	.409	.297	59
Stankiewicz	116	400	42	107	22	2	2	139	25	38	42	0	5	9	5	.539	13	7	1	.268	.347	.338	47
Hall M	152	583	67	163	36	3	15	250	81	29	53	4	1	4	2	.400	12	0	9	.280	.429	.310	76
Kelly	152	580	81	158	31	2	10	223	66	41	96	4	4	28	5	.510	19	1	6	.272	.384	.322	72
Tartabull	123	421	72	112	19	0	25	206	85	103	115	14	0	2	2	.390	7	0	2	.266	.489	.409	92
Maas	98	286	35	71	12	0	11	116	35	25	63	4	0	3	1	.424	1	0	4	.248	.406	.305	38
Velarde	121	412	57	112	24	1	7	159	46	38	78	1	2	7	2	.460	13	4	5	.272	.386	.333	53
Williams B	62	261	39	73	14	2	5	106	26	29	36	1	1	7	6	.492	5	2	0	.280	.406	.354	37
Stanley M	68	173	24	43	7	0	8	74	27	33	45	0	1	0	0	.222	6	0	0	.249	.428	.372	28
Gallego	53	173	24	44	7	1	3	62	14	20	22	0	4	0	1	.500	5	3	1	.254	.358	.343	22
James D	67	145	24	38	8	0	3	55	17	22	15	0	1	1	0	.556	3	0	2	.262	.379	.359	21
Leyritz	63	144	17	37	6	0	7	64	26	14	22	1	6	0	1	.263	2	0	3	.257	.444	.341	23
Barfield Je	30	95	8	13	2	0	2	21	7	9	27	2	0	1	1	.667	5	0	1	.137	.221	.210	4
Williams G	15	27	7	8	2	0	3	19	6	0	3	0	0	2	0	.500	0	0	0	.296	.704	.296	6
Snow	7	14	1	2	1	0	0	3	2	5	5	1	0	0	0	.000	0	0	0	.143	.214	.368	2
Silvestri	7	13	3	4	0	2	0	8	1	0	3	0	0	0	0	.667	1	0	0	.308	.615	.308	2
Humphreys	4	10	0	1	0	0	0	1	0	0	1	0	0	0	0	.000	2	0	0	.100	.100	.100	0
Meulens	2	5	1	3	0	0	1	6	1	1	0	0	0	0	0	.000	1	0	0	.600	1.200	.667	3
Farr	2	0	0	0	0	0	0	0	0	0	0	0	0	0	0	.000	0	0	0	.000	.000	.000	0
Cadaret	1	0	0	0	0	0	0	0	0	0	0	0	0	0	0	.000	0	0	0	.000	.000	.000	0
Habyan	1	0	0	0	0	0	0	0	0	0	0	0	0	0	0	.000	0	0	0	.000	.000	.000	0
TOTALS	1670	5593	733	1462	281	18	163	2268	703	536	903	51	42	78	37	.439	138	26	55	.261	.406	.328	746

Sabermetric Batting Records for New York Yankees

	Ball Park Adjusted AB	Run	Hit	2B	3B	HR	RBI	W	SO	Avg	Slug	OBP	Runs Ctd	Outs	Run/ 27o	OW%	OG	OWAR	DWAR	TWAR
Barfield Je	97	8	13	2	0	2	7	9	28	.134	.216	.206	4	90	1.20	.065	3	-0.95	0.19	-0.76
Gallego	178	25	45	7	1	3	14	20	23	.253	.354	.340	22	141	4.21	.460	5	0.57	0.77	1.34
Hall M	567	60	159	34	4	13	76	25	55	.280	.423	.307	71	430	4.46	.488	16	2.20	0.91	3.11
Hayes C	526	54	135	20	2	18	67	29	105	.257	.405	.296	61	416	3.96	.429	15	1.22	0.73	1.95
Humphreys	10	0	1	0	0	0	0	0	1	.100	.100	.100	0	11	0.00	.000	0	-0.14	0.03	-0.11
James D	140	21	37	7	0	2	16	19	15	.264	.357	.350	18	107	4.54	.498	4	0.58	0.18	0.77
Kelly P	328	39	74	23	2	7	27	26	76	.226	.372	.302	38	272	3.77	.406	10	0.56	0.69	1.25
Kelly	599	84	163	32	2	10	67	42	101	.272	.382	.321	74	466	4.29	.469	17	2.05	0.89	2.94
Leyritz	148	17	38	6	0	7	26	14	23	.257	.439	.339	24	115	5.63	.604	4	1.08	-0.03	1.05
Maas	277	31	69	11	0	9	33	22	66	.249	.386	.301	34	212	4.33	.474	8	0.97	-0.01	0.96
Mattingly	621	80	179	38	0	12	81	34	45	.288	.407	.323	81	459	4.76	.521	17	2.91	0.82	3.73
Meulens	5	1	3	0	0	1	1	1	0	.600	1.200	.667	3		327.00	.972	0	0.07	0.01	0.08
Nokes	372	38	83	8	1	19	56	32	64	.223	.403	.285	40	309	3.50	.370	11	0.22	-0.31	-0.09
Silvestri	13	3	4	0	2	0	1	0	3	.308	.615	.308	2	10	5.40	.583	0	0.09	0.03	0.12
Snow	14	0	2	1	0	0	1	4	5	.143	.214	.333	1	12	2.25	.195	0	-0.07	0.02	-0.05
Stankiewicz	413	54	110	23	2	2	25	39	44	.266	.346	.336	48	327	3.96	.430	12	0.97	1.60	2.57
Stanley M	178	25	44	7	0	8	27													

Pitching Records for New York Yankees

	ERA	W	L	Pct	G	GS	CG	ShO	GF	Sv	IP	R	ER	H	2B	3B	HR	BB	IW	SO	HB	WP	BK
Perez M	2.87	13	16	.448	33	33	10	1	0	0	247.2	94	79	212	33	3	16	93	5	218	5	13	0
Sanderson	4.93	12	11	.522	33	33	2	1	0	0	193.1	116	106	220	35	9	28	64	5	104	4	4	1
Kamieniecki	4.36	6	14	.300	28	28	4	0	0	0	188.0	100	91	193	38	1	13	74	9	88	5	9	1
Leary	5.57	5	6	.455	18	15	2	0	2	0	97.0	62	60	84	19	0	9	57	2	34	4	7	0
Militello	3.45	3	3	.500	9	9	0	0	0	0	60.0	24	23	43	13	0	6	32	1	42	2	1	0
Johnson J	6.66	2	3	.400	13	8	0	0	3	0	52.2	44	39	71	17	2	4	23	0	14	2	1	0
Wickman	4.11	6	1	.857	8	8	0	0	0	0	50.1	25	23	51	9	3	2	20	0	21	2	3	0
Hitchcock	8.31	0	2	.000	3	3	0	0	0	0	13.0	12	12	23	5	0	2	6	0	6	1	0	0
Cadaret	4.25	4	8	.333	46	11	1	1	9	1	103.2	53	49	104	17	2	12	74	7	73	2	5	1
Monteleone	3.30	7	3	.700	47	0	0	0	15	0	92.2	35	34	82	13	4	7	27	3	62	0	0	3
Hillegas	5.51	1	8	.111	21	9	1	1	4	0	78.1	52	48	96	17	4	12	33	1	46	0	2	0
Habyan	3.84	5	6	.455	56	0	0	0	20	7	72.2	32	31	84	13	2	6	21	5	44	2	2	1
Farr	1.56	2	2	.500	50	0	0	0	42	30	52.0	10	9	34	4	0	2	19	0	37	2	0	0
Young C	3.32	3	0	1.000	13	5	0	0	3	0	43.1	21	16	51	13	0	1	10	1	13	2	0	0
Burke	3.25	2	2	.500	23	0	0	0	10	0	27.2	14	10	26	11	0	2	15	4	8	1	2	0
Howe S	2.45	3	0	1.000	20	0	0	0	10	6	22.0	7	6	9	0	0	1	3	1	12	0	1	0
Guetterman	9.53	1	1	.500	15	0	0	0	7	0	22.2	24	24	35	7	1	5	13	3	5	0	1	0
Nielsen J	4.58	1	0	1.000	20	0	0	0	12	0	19.2	10	10	17	2	1	1	18	2	12	0	1	0
Springer R	6.19	0	0	.000	14	0	0	0	5	0	16.0	11	11	18	4	1	0	10	0	12	1	0	0
TOTALS	4.22	76	86	.469	470	162	20	4	142	44	1452.2	746	681	1453	270	33	129	612	49	851	35	52	7

Sabermetric Pitching Records for New York Yankees

	Adj ERA	Expected W	L	Pct	BFP	Avg	Slg	OBA	RC/G	GDP	SB	CS	PK	PKE	SH	SF	Supported RSup	RSp/G	W	L	Pct
Burke	2.93	3	1	.642	122	.250	.413	.350	5.23	2	4	1	1	0	2	0	14	4.55	3	1	.666
Cadaret	4.17	6	6	.470	471	.267	.414	.385	5.86	9	19	7	0	5	3	3	54	4.69	6	6	.511
Farr	1.38	4	0	.889	207	.186	.240	.267	2.38	3	7	0	0	0	1	2	10	1.73	2	2	.563
Guetterman	9.13	0	2	.156	114	.354	.596	.421	10.25	2	1	0	0	0	0	2	20	7.94	1	1	.384
Habyan	3.72	6	5	.527	316	.295	.418	.344	4.96	11	5	0	3	0	5	3	20	2.48	3	8	.268
Hillegas	5.40	3	6	.346	351	.306	.500	.369	6.66	7	15	6	1	3	1	3	33	3.79	3	6	.289
Hitchcock	7.62	0	2	.210	68	.377	.557	.441	10.37	1	1	1	0	1	0	0	8	5.54	1	1	.304
Howe S	2.05	2	1	.786	79	.122	.162	.154	0.79	1	0	0	0	0	1	1	10	4.09	2	1	.767
Johnson J	6.49	1	4	.267	245	.329	.481	.395	6.80	9	4	2	1	1	2	2	25	4.27	1	4	.263
Kamieniecki	4.26	9	11	.459	804	.269	.379	.340	4.59	19	29	6	1	1	3	5	92	4.40	9	11	.468
Leary	5.47	4	7	.339	414	.245	.379	.354	4.55	14	17	4	0	0	4	6	49	4.55	4	7	.362
Militello	3.30	4	2	.586	255	.195	.335	.302	3.72	4	7	0	1	2	0	0	27	4.05	3	3	.554
Monteleone	3.21	6	4	.600	380	.235	.355	.289	3.48	3	3	5	0	0	3	1	40	3.88	5	5	.548
Nielsen J	4.12	0	1	.476	90	.243	.343	.393	4.86	2	2	2	0	2	1	1	11	5.03	1	0	.552
Perez M	2.80	19	10	.663	1013	.235	.332	.308	3.34	19	18	18	9	7	6	8	112	4.07	18	11	.636
Sanderson	4.84	9	14	.396	851	.286	.464	.340	5.63	17	18	8	1	1	3	11	134	6.24	13	10	.578
Springer R	5.63	0	0	.327	75	.281	.375	.387	5.77	2	3	0	0	0	0	0	5	2.81	0	0	.171
Wickman	3.93	3	4	.499	213	.273	.385	.344	4.44	9	8	1	1	0	1	3	39	6.97	5	2	.721
Young C	3.12	2	1	.613	188	.298	.392	.341	4.68	5	3	1	0	1	3	2	30	6.23	2	1	.767
TOTALS	4.16	76	86	.470	6256	.263	.394	.338	4.66	139	164	62	19	24	39	53	733	4.54	80	82	.495

Batting 'Splits' Records for New York Yankees

SPLITS for New York Yankees (all batters except pitchers)

	G	AB	Run	Hit	2B	3B	HR	TB	RBI	W	K	IW	HB	SB	CS	DP	SH	SF	Avg	Slug	OBP	RC
vs LHP	925	1764	252	452	85	6	53	708	242	203	284	23	16	42	10	45	5	17	.256	.401	.336	245
vs RHP	1579	3829	481	1010	196	12	110	1560	461	333	619	28	26	36	27	93	21	38	.264	.407	.324	501
Home	831	2735	385	717	135	8	88	1132	373	283	422	27	26	43	20	65	14	30	.262	.414	.334	383
Away	839	2858	348	745	146	10	75	1136	330	253	481	24	16	35	17	73	12	25	.261	.397	.322	363
Grass	1393	4700	626	1221	219	14	145	1903	600	463	757	45	39	65	31	116	23	44	.260	.405	.328	629
Turf	277	893	107	241	62	4	18	365	103	73	146	6	3	13	6	22	3	11	.270	.409	.323	117
April/June	772	2607	336	659	138	7	81	1054	324	250	448	24	20	35	14	62	9	25	.253	.404	.320	340
July/October	898	2986	397	803	143	11	82	1214	379	286	455	27	22	43	23	76	17	30	.269	.407	.334	406

Detroit Tigers

David Raglin

DETROIT YEAR	1983	1984	1985	1986	1987	1988	1989	1990	1991	1992
W	92	104	84	87	98	88	59	79	84	75
L	70	58	77	75	64	74	103	83	78	87
WPCT	0.568	0.642	0.522	0.537	0.605	0.543	0.364	0.488	0.519	0.463
R	789	829	729	798	896	703	617	750	817	791
RA	679	643	688	714	735	658	816	754	794	794
PWPT	0.575	0.624	0.529	0.555	0.598	0.533	0.364	0.497	0.514	0.498
PythW	93	101	86	90	97	86	59	81	83	81
PythL	69	61	76	72	65	76	103	81	79	81
LUCK	-1	3	-2	-3	1	2	0	-2	1	-6

Defensive Efficiency Record: .6966

Last August, the prayers of Tigers' fans everywhere were answered with the change in ownership to Mike Ilitch. I was lucky enough to be at the first home game of the Ilitch era, and I wrote a piece on the experience for the Mayo Smith Society (a Detroit Tiger fan club) newsletter Tigers Stripes, for which I am the main writer. I think the piece is worth rerunning here:

THE FEELING IS BACK

Happy days are here again.

As we walked into Tiger Stadium on Friday night August 28th at what will be forever known as Ilitch Game One, we heard that song coming from the organ that had been silenced earlier in the year. It's amazing how perfect that was, how much one song can say, because happy days were here again. The feeling was back; the pall that had gripped the corner of Michigan and Trumbull for the last few years had been lifted.

It had often been depressing the last few years, and I didn't know how depressing it had been until it was over. It wasn't just the losing; only in 1989 were the Tigers that bad. It was the decisions, the obviously bad decisions like losing so many stars to free agency while the owner bought million dollar cars, the Ernie mess, the belligerent stadium attitude, the lack of promotion which lead to the tiny crowds. Even during the pennant race of 1987, one of the most exciting in Tiger history, the stadium was mostly empty until the final weekend. Friends either pitied or laughed at me for sticking with them. I'd come home from Washington, DC, and nobody would be talking Tigers.

I gave up defending their decisions; I tried to separate my love for the team from my dislike for the things the team was doing, much as someone still loves a person close to them even when they mess up. When I got to visit the park, it felt so empty, like Tiger Stadium was not the "place to be". That was so sad, after so many years that Tiger Stadium was the "place to be". Detroit was

Position	92 Starter	TWAR	93 Starter	TWAR
Catcher	Tettleton	3.72	Tettleton	3.72
First base	Fielder	3.43	Fielder	3.43
Second base	Whitaker	4.11	Whitaker	4.11
Third base	Livingstone	0.47	Fryman	4.07
Shortstop	Fryman	4.07	Trammell	0.49
Left field	Gladden	0.96	Phillips	4.86
Center field	Cuyler	-0.69	Cuyler	-0.69
Right field	Deer	3.88	Deer	3.88
DH	Phillips	4.86		

getting the reputation of being a "bad baseball town". It hurt.

That is what made Friday night so special. It didn't hurt anymore. There were about 25,000 people there, quite a few considering it was so cold that by the end of the game, I had three layers of clothes on. I overheard many people saying that this was the first time they'd been to the park in a long time. Mr. Ilitch had told us that there wouldn't be a big show, just a few touches, and he was right, but the touches were nice.

As we walked up to the Stadium, we were greeted by the sounds of a live jazz ensemble setting a festive tone. When we entered the stadium, we were handed "Homer Hankies", with the date and a "Thank You For Your Support" from "The Ilitch Family". Our new family. In the beginning, the scoreboard kept teasing us with "Dog Row", which turned out to be the fan in a chosen seat location and those ten to the left and ten to the right were treated to those fabulous Tiger Stadium hot dogs (the best in the game). The "Take Me Out To The Ballgame" in the seventh-inning stretch even received a new twist as it was led by a local celebrity on the roof of the Tigers' dugout. "Dog Row" and the celebrity sing-a-long are promotions which are going to continue to be a part of the Ilitch Tigers.

The game lived up to the moment. The Tigers fell behind early 2©0, but tied with two in the seventh. In the eighth, with the homer hankies out in full force, Cecil singled and Mickey Tettleton flied out. The fans put away the homer hankies with singles-hitter Dan Gladden at the plate, but Gladden became the one to conquer the stiff wind blowing in with a liner into the lower deck in left for the game-winning home run. Mike Henneman came in to nail down the game in the ninth.

As we left the stadium, they played the song again. Yes, happy days were here again. The feeling was back again. The pall was gone. The nightmare was over. It didn't hurt anymore. I had never had more pride in my baseball team than at that moment. Walking through the halls of Tiger Stadium, I couldn't help but singing that song to myself silently, and I suspect I wasn't the only one:

Happy days are here again.
The skies above are clear again.
So let's sing a song a cheer again.
Happy days are here again.

When I got my copy of the newsletter in the mail, I reread the article. I was taken aback at the emotion there. "I never had more pride in my baseball team than at that moment." That is a strong statement; as a Tiger fan since the early 1970s, I have had a lot of exciting players and some great teams to watch.

I thought about it a great deal, about why I had written that statement. My conclusion was that Ilitch Game One showed that the Tigers were alive again. The team, and baseball in Detroit, had been dying, but that night showed that Tom Monaghan and Bo Schembechler could not kill this franchise. Even their worst actions could not kill the tradition; the Tigers were stronger than those who had been ruining it.

Maybe I was overstating the problems under Monaghan/ Schembechler. The ownership follies in cities like Seattle and Houston have had make what has happened in Detroit seem like nothing. Still, we've been spoiled with stability in Detroit, and we are not used to.

One more point to close the Tom Monaghan Era in Detroit. When Monoghan bought the Tigers in 1983, we were heartened to hear that he wouldn't interfere in the day-to-day affairs of the team, similar to the policy of previous owner John Fetzer. This was the era of Steinbrenner firing managers every other day, Ted Turner making himself manager, and not long after Charlie Finley had gotten rid of the A's. We didn't want one of these ego-crazed guys changing the Tigers.

However, we learned that the other extreme isn't always so great all the time either. In the 1980s, the Tigers were only able to win one Series and finish first only twice despite a deep talent base. Part of the problem was that the Tigers were the Pirates of the 1980s, letting core players Lance Parrish, Jack Morris, and Kirk Gibson leave as free agents. Later, Monaghan made the only major decision of his ownership, and it was a disastrous one,

hiring his hero, Bo Schembechler, to run the team. When the Tigers fired Ernie and demanded that the taxpayers of the area give the Tigers a new ballpark, Monaghan. Through it all, the Tigers refused to promote the team in the community and attendance died; the 1987 team with the best record in baseball and a participant in one of the greatest pennant races in history barely drew the major league average number of fans.

There did not seem to be any accountability in the Tiger front office. The Tigers lived in the 1960s, led by the team President Jim Campbell, as baseball moved into the 1980s, but Campbell was still allowed to run the team. At some point, the owner has to say, "Hey, you're letting some of our best players to get away for nothing, you don't promote the team, and the team deteriorated. It's time for you to get out of there." Monaghan finally let Campbell have it (at the same time as Bo), but only weeks before he let the team go.

It looks like Ilitch, given his experience with the Red Wings, will be a good compromise. He lets the pros make the on-the-ice decisions, but he retains control of the rest of the operation and holds the on-the-ice accountable for their failings. We're looking forward to a new era in Tiger baseball. We're coming back.

If I told you that John Doherty was one of the most interesting Tigers, and a prospect to be a fine starting pitcher, you might either think I'm too much of a homer or have had too many sticks of Crazy Bread. After all, Doherty was a rookie pitcher up from AA who gave up 131 hits in 116 hits with only 37 strikeouts (and 25 walks).

Doherty first stood out in spring training 1992 when Sparky Anderson touted him as a young player to watch. He had not pitched above Double A, so considering Sparky's reputation for picking out young players in spring training (Chris Pittaro and Torey Lovullo, among others), we didn't pay a lot of attention. At least, not until we kept reading in the press that scouts for several teams agreed with Sparky, something that we didn't hear much with the others.

He made the team and pitched middle relief for the first two thirds of the season, but we kept hearing how Sparky had him pegged for the rotation. The day finally came, August 3rd against Baltimore, and he threw six shutout innings, although the O's came back to win after Doherty left. He started ten other games, ending up with a 5-2 record as a starter with a 3.67 ERA despite allowing 77 hits in 61 1/3 innings. A mirage? Let's look at the stats. The top line is Doherty (full season) and the bottom is the league average per 116 innings:

John Doherty Compared to the AL League Average, 1992

1992	AB	H	2B	3B	HR	RBI	BA	OBP	SLG
Doherty	457	131	13	1	4	51	.287	.328	.346
AL Pit	440	114	20	2	10	53	.259	.328	.384

1992	IP	SB	CS	DP	BB	SO	RF	NB	ERA	G/F
Doherty	116	4	4	14	25	37	22	138	3.88	3.02
AL Pit	116	10	5	10	44	70	42	138	3.94	1.22

DP estimated for Doherty; there were 12 DP in Doherty's 11 starts, a pace of 14 for 116 innings. This is probably a low estimate of Doherty's DPs.

RF (Runners Past First): 2B+3B+HR+SB
NB (Net Runners On Base): H+BB-CS-GIDP

Now we see how he did it. He allowed a .287 batting average versus a .259 mark for the league, but his low number of walks meant that the on-base percentage against him was at exactly the league average, .328. He also allowed extra base hits at a much lower rate than the league average, so the slugging percentage against him was .038 lower than the league mark. The .346 slugging percentage against his wouldn't have qualified him among the five lowest in the league, even if he had the 162 innings to qualify, but the isolated power (SLG/AB) figure against him (.059) was lower that the isolated power figure of the five lowest in slugging percentage allowed (Juan Guzman, Johnson, Clemens, Appier, and Viola).

Looking at some of the more obscure statistics on the second set of lines, he was very good at stopping the running game and at getting the double play ball. His stolen base allowed percentage of 50% would have been tied for third in the league if he had qualified, and his 1.1 estimated double plays per nine innings would have put him in a virtual tie for fifth in the league. He struck out very few people, but walked few too, so his SO/BB ratio of 1.52 was just about the AL average of 1.22. What does that all mean?

Look at the RPF, runners past first figure. Doherty allowed only 22 runners past first base compared to the average AL pitcher, who allowed 42 past first per 116 innings pitched. Despite the high batting average against Doherty, his few walks, ability to stop the running game, and ability to get the double play ball meant that his net runners on base was the same as the league mean.

Was this just random chance? How did he post such unique numbers? The last numbers on the second set of lines say it all. Doherty allowed over three ground balls for every fly ball he gave up, compared to the 1.22 league average. Among pitchers with 162 innings, the major league leader was Billy Swift with a 2.62 mark. Suddenly, all of the numbers make more sense. He allowed a lot of hits because ground balls are more likely to go through than fly balls are to fall in, but ground balls are very rarely for extra bases. A ground ball pitcher is also more likely to get double plays. Despite what you may think from the strikeout/ walk numbers, Doherty is not a soft tosser. His best pitch is a hard slider/sinking fastball that really moves up there. It's not hard enough or moves enough that batters can't hit it, but they can't hit it well.

Several more points about Doherty:

He is the classic "Tommy John" pitcher, as defined by Bill James.

Ground ball pitcher. Doesn't strike out a lot of hitters, but walks very few either. Gives up a lot of hits, but he doesn't give up many for power. Controls the number of baserunners by stopping the running game and getting double plays. He's left handed. (Okay, so Doherty is not left handed, but you can't tell by looking at the numbers: .240 BA against lefthanders, .323 against righties.)

"Tommy John" pitchers are very dependent on their defense (which makes sense, since they don't get the outs themselves). Would it make sense, then, to do a defensive platoon the days Doherty starts? With all of the ground balls, especially to the right side with a righthander on the mound, maybe those would be the days you would tend to have Cecil DH. Sparky didn't do that last year; Fielder was a fielder for nine of Doherty's eleven starts.

Tiger Stadium is the ideal park for him to pitch in, with the tall grass slowing down those grounders, but he actually pitched about the same at home as on the road, with actually a few more hits allowed at home.

He threw 7 quality starts in 11 games, 63.7%. I don't have the 1992 figures, but according to the STATS Scoreboard book, the major league average was 52.6% for 1991. A couple of the quality starts were exactly three earned runs in six innings but he just missed a quality start on August 10th with three runs allowed in 5.2 innings, so it all balances out.

I would be a little surprised if Doherty doesn't develop into a solid starter. I'm not predicting he will become a star, I'm just saying that you have to look past the standard statistics when rating a player. Bill James has taught us to do that for hitters, but less attention has been paid to pitchers' statistics over the years. Doherty will not be a good rotisserie player, because what he does well doesn't show up in those games, but I think he will continue to get better. Given the state of the Tigers' pitching, he'll get the chance.

In 1992, a young Tiger outfielder, Phil Clark, hit .407. He did it, though, in only 54 at-bats, getting 22 hits. Does it mean anything to hit for such a high average, even it is in such a few number of at-bats? Let's look at the young players who have hit at least .400 in at least 40 but less than 150 at-bats to see. There are 17 players who have hit at least .400 in with 40 -150 at-bats. Surprisingly, only five of them don't fit the definition of a young hitter. I would have expected that more of the players are guys who got hurt, or had to go into military service, or something else). Two of them were pitchers (Walter Johnson in 1925 and Jack Bentley in 1923), and three were veteran hitters who had a low number of at-bats for a special reason (Ted Williams in 1953, Jerry Coleman in 1952, and Duke Farrell in 1903). The other thirteen were players who had not established themselves yet. Here is a list of them, with stats for that season and for their career:

The 13 Prospect Hitters With Over a .400 Season Average

Player	Team	Year	H/AB	BA	Career	H/AB	BA
Gil Coan	Giants	1947	21/42	.500	1946-56	731/2877	.254
Gary Ward	Twins	1980	19/41	.463	1979-90	1236/4479	.276
Monte Cross	Pirates	1894	19/43	.442	1894-07	1364/5817	.292
Babe Ganzel	Senators	1927	21/48	.438	1927-28	23/74	.311
Dale Mitchell	Indians	1946	19/44	.432	1946-56	1244/3984	.312
Stan Musial*	Cardinals	1941	20/47	.426	1941-63	3630/10972	.331
Elmer Valo	Athletics	1941	21/50	.420	1940-61	1420/5029	.282
Fred Lynn	Red Sox	1974	18/43	.419	1974-90	1960/6925	.283
Joe Judge	Senators	1915	17/41	.415	1915-34	2352/7898	.298
Bob Hazel	Braves	1953	54/134	.403	1955-58	81/261	.310
M. Archdeacon	White Sox	1923	35/87	.402	1923-25	128/384	.333
Mike Davis	Athletics	1982	30/75	.400	1980-89	778/2999	.259
Frank Laporte	Highlanders	1905	16/40	.400	1905-15	1185/4212	.281

*I think I've heard of him before.

These players ended up turning out to be pretty good. I really didn't expect that; I expected to see a lot more Hurricane Hazels than Fred Lynns. Ten of the thirteen had at least 2,877 at-bats, and eight had at least 1,000 hits. One thousand hits is not that common. Stan the Man, nothing more need be said. Joe Judge came this close to being qualified for the Hall of Fame. Fred Lynn won the Rookie of the Year and MVP the next year. You might not recognize names like Monte Cross and Frank Laporte, but fans fifty years from now won't recognize Gary Ward and Mike Davis, but they turned out to be valuable players for several seasons. That's not a bad list to fall into.

Where does Phil Clark fall into it? He was the Tigers' top draft choice in 1986 as a catcher and was making progress up the scale as a high-average low-power catcher (like B. J. Surhoff when he came up) before an injury took him away from behind the plate. He moved to the outfield, but his lack of either very good speed or power stalled him. The Tigers brought him up in the middle of 1992 to provide bench strength in the wake of several injuries, but he was sent back down despite the fact he was doing well precisely because Sparky didn't have a role for him given the fact that he didn't have the power or speed to define a role for him. He was exposed in the expansion draft in at least the first round (and probably the second) and not taken; that doesn't bode well for his future.

One clue to a role for him is the fact that he hit .487, 19/39, against southpaws but only .200, 3/15, against northpaws (well, if lefthanders are southpaws...). Look for him to make it as a platoon player, most likely not in Detroit, and to last several years. If things turn out well, he could get a fair chance against righthanders, and if he hits them, get a more regular role.

I wish him well. One reason I did the piece on him is that I met him a few years ago in Double A and I was very impressed by him as a person. He was a nice guy to talk to, and I've rooted for him since. I hope he gets the chance to make it. He certainly is off to a good start.

Detroit Tigers Home Park Performance Factors														
	Outs	Runs	Hits	2b	3b	HR	W	K	SH	SF	HBP	IBB	SB	CS	GDP
Home LH Batters	1.059	1.002	1.019	.893	1.000	.926	.946	.941	.876	1.120	7.445	1.212	1.191	.987	.931
Home RH Batters	.939	.899	.994	.916	.699	.951	.854	.921	.792	.899	.767	.669	1.002	1.133	.905
All Home Batters	.974	.944	.989	.936	.863	.946	.886	.946	.804	.937	.804	.902	1.031	1.085	.924
Opp LH Batters	1.015	.978	.977	1.009	.892	.858	.948	.978	.914	1.224	1.209	.878	1.125	.832	1.107
Opp RH Batters	1.039	1.064	1.052	1.053	2.091	.964	1.057	1.002	1.162	1.112	1.008	1.200	1.169	1.165	1.107
All Opp Batters	1.028	1.040	1.023	1.032	1.286	.924	1.035	1.001	1.072	1.156	1.050	1.042	1.123	1.059	1.120
All LH Batters	1.033	.988	.994	.950	.914	.884	.943	.962	.876	1.189	1.622	.944	1.152	.884	1.035
All RH Batters	.990	.982	1.020	.986	1.207	.962	.956	.971	.980	1.006	.887	1.006	1.083	1.123	1.006
All Batters	1.001	.993	1.004	.984	1.093	.937	.959	.979	.935	1.048	.926	.979	1.075	1.057	1.020

Conventional Batting Records for Detroit Tigers

	G	AB	Run	Hit	2B	3B	HR	TB	RBI	W	K	IW	HB	SB	CS	BRng Eff	GI DP	SH	SF	Avg	Slug	OBP	Runs Ctd
Tettleton	157	525	82	125	25	0	32	246	83	122	137	18	1	0	6	.280	5	0	6	.238	.469	.379	102
Fielder	155	594	80	145	22	0	35	272	124	73	151	8	2	0	0	.241	14	0	7	.244	.458	.325	90
Whitaker	130	453	77	126	26	0	19	209	71	81	46	5	1	6	4	.386	9	5	4	.278	.461	.386	85
Livingstone	117	354	43	100	21	0	4	133	46	21	36	1	0	1	3	.417	8	3	4	.282	.376	.319	41
Fryman T	161	659	87	175	31	4	20	274	96	45	144	1	6	8	4	.452	13	5	6	.266	.416	.316	86
Gladden	113	417	57	106	20	1	7	149	42	30	64	0	2	4	2	.467	10	5	5	.254	.357	.304	45
Cuyler	89	291	39	70	11	1	3	92	28	10	62	0	4	8	5	.405	4	8	0	.241	.316	.275	25
Deer	110	393	66	97	20	1	32	215	64	51	131	1	3	4	2	.319	8	0	1	.247	.547	.337	73
Phillips	159	606	114	167	32	3	10	235	64	114	93	2	1	12	10	.507	13	5	7	.276	.388	.387	98
Carreon	101	336	34	78	11	1	10	121	41	22	57	2	1	3	1	.313	12	1	4	.232	.360	.278	32
Kreuter	67	190	22	48	9	0	2	63	16	20	38	1	0	0	1	.343	8	3	2	.253	.332	.321	19
Bergman	87	181	17	42	3	0	1	48	10	20	19	1	0	1	0	.194	4	1	2	.232	.265	.305	16
Barnes	95	165	27	45	8	1	3	64	25	10	18	1	2	3	1	.412	4	2	2	.273	.388	.318	20
Pettis	48	129	27	26	4	3	1	39	12	27	34	0	0	13	4	.531	3	3	1	.202	.302	.338	16
Trammell	29	102	11	28	7	1	1	40	11	15	4	0	1	2	2	.412	6	1	1	.275	.392	.370	14
Clark P	23	54	3	22	4	0	1	29	5	6	9	1	0	1	0	.000	2	1	0	.407	.537	.467	13
Hare	15	26	0	3	1	0	0	4	5	2	4	0	0	0	0	.000	0	0	1	.115	.154	.172	1
Brogna	9	26	3	5	1	0	1	9	3	3	5	0	0	0	0	.500	0	0	0	.192	.346	.276	3
Rowland	6	14	2	3	0	0	0	3	0	3	3	0	0	0	0	.500	1	0	0	.214	.214	.353	1
Munoz	1	0	0	0	0	0	0	0	0	0	0	0	0	0	0	.000	0	0	0	.000	.000	.000	0
Tanana	1	0	0	0	0	0	0	0	0	0	0	0	0	0	0	.000	0	0	0	.000	.000	.000	0
Henneman	2	0	0	0	0	0	0	0	0	0	0	0	0	0	0	.000	0	0	0	.000	.000	.000	0
Aldred	1	0	0	0	0	0	0	0	0	0	0	0	0	0	0	.000	0	0	0	.000	.000	.000	0
Leiter M	1	0	0	0	0	0	0	0	0	0	0	0	0	0	0	.000	0	0	0	.000	.000	.000	0
TOTALS	1677	5515	791	1411	256	16	182	2245	746	675	1055	42	24	66	45	.385	124	43	53	.256	.407	.337	772

Sabermetric Batting Records for Detroit Tigers

	Ball Park Adjusted								Runs				Run/						
	AB	Run	Hit	2B	3B	HR	RBI	W	SO	Avg	Slug	OBP	Ctd	Outs	27o	OW%	OG	OWAR	DWAR	TWAR
Barnes	164	26	46	7	1	2	24	9	17	.280	.372	.318	19	126	4.07	.409	5	0.28	0.25	0.52
Bergman	185	16	41	2	0	0	10	18	18	.222	.232	.288	13	150	2.34	.186	6	-0.91	0.03	-0.88
Brogna	25	2	4	0	0	0	3	2	4	.160	.160	.222	1	21	1.29	.065	1	-0.22	0.01	-0.21
Carreon	334	33	79	10	1	9	40	21	54	.237	.353	.279	31	272	3.08	.284	10	-0.67	0.49	-0.18
Clark P	53	2	22	3	0	0	4	5	8	.415	.472	.466	12	33	9.82	.801	1	0.55	0.03	0.58
Cuyler	291	38	70	10	1	2	27	9	60	.241	.302	.271	23	237	2.62	.223	9	-1.12	0.43	-0.69
Deer	391	64	99	19	1	30	63	48	125	.253	.537	.337	71	303	6.33	.626	11	3.10	0.79	3.88
Fielder	591	78	148	21	0	33	123	69	145	.250	.453	.326	89	464	5.18	.528	17	3.07	0.37	3.43
Fryman T	657	85	179	30	5	19	95	42	138	.272	.420	.318	87	505	4.65	.475	19	2.33	1.73	4.07
Gladden	415	55	108	19	1	6	41	28	61	.260	.354	.305	45	328	3.70	.364	12	0.18	0.79	0.96
Hare	25	0	2	0	0	0	5	1	3	.080	.080	.111	0	24	0.00	.000	1	-0.31	0.06	-0.25
Kreuter	190	21	48	8	0	1	15	19	36	.253	.311	.318	18	155	3.14	.291	6	-0.34	-0.55	-0.89
Livingstone	362	42	99	19	0	3	46	19	34	.273	.351	.306	38	279	3.68	.361	10	0.11	0.36	0.47
Pettis	129	26	26	3	3	0	11	25	33	.202	.271	.329	14	113	3.35	.319	4	-0.13	0.52	0.39
Phillips	607	113	168	31	3	9	63	109	90	.277	.382	.383	95	473	5.42	.551	18	3.53	1.33	4.86
Rowland	13	1	3	0	0	0	0	2	2	.231	.231	.333	1	11	2.45	.201	0	-0.06	-0.01	-0.07
Tettleton	525	81	125	24	0	29	82	117	133	.238	.450	.373	96	417	6.22	.618	15	4.13	-0.42	3.72
Trammell	101	10	28	6	1	0	10	14	3	.277	.356	.362	12	82	3.95	.395	3	0.14	0.36	0.49
Whitaker	464	76	125	24	0	16	71	76	44	.269	.425	.374	79	359	5.94	.596	13	3.27	0.84	4.11
TOTALS	5526	785	1419	251	17	170	745	648	1026	.257	.401	.334	753	4376	4.65	.474	162	20.13	7.39	27.52

Pitching Records for Detroit Tigers

	ERA	W	L	Pct	G	GS	CG	ShO	GF	Sv	IP	R	ER	H	2B	3B	HR	BB	IW	SO	HB	WP	BK
Gullickson	4.34	14	13	.519	34	34	4	1	0	0	221.2	109	107	228	38	5	35	50	5	64	0	6	0
Tanana	4.39	13	11	.542	32	31	3	0	0	0	186.2	102	91	188	34	2	22	90	9	91	7	11	1
King E	5.22	4	6	.400	17	14	0	0	2	1	79.1	47	46	90	12	2	12	28	1	45	1	3	0
Aldred	6.78	3	8	.273	16	13	0	0	0	0	65.0	51	49	80	17	1	12	33	4	34	3	1	0
Haas D	3.94	5	3	.625	12	11	1	1	1	0	61.2	30	27	68	9	1	8	16	1	29	1	2	0
Groom	5.82	0	5	.000	12	7	0	0	3	1	38.2	28	25	48	10	2	4	22	4	15	0	0	1
Terrell	5.20	7	10	.412	36	14	1	0	7	0	136.2	86	79	163	27	2	14	48	10	61	3	3	0
Doherty	3.88	7	4	.636	47	11	0	0	9	3	116.0	61	50	131	13	1	4	25	5	37	4	5	0
Leiter M	4.18	8	5	.615	35	14	1	0	7	0	112.0	57	52	116	19	6	9	43	5	75	3	3	0
Lancaster	6.33	3	4	.429	41	1	0	0	17	0	86.2	66	61	101	21	0	11	51	12	35	3	2	0
Ritz	5.60	2	5	.286	23	11	0	0	4	0	80.1	52	50	88	14	0	4	44	4	57	3	7	1
Henneman	3.96	2	6	.250	60	0	0	0	53	24	77.1	36	34	75	11	2	6	20	10	58	0	7	0
Knudsen	4.58	2	3	.400	48	1	0	0	14	5	70.2	39	36	70	13	1	9	41	9	51	1	5	0
Kiely	2.13	4	2	.667	39	0	0	0	20	0	55.0	14	13	44	10	0	2	28	3	18	0	0	0
Munoz	3.00	1	2	.333	65	0	0	0	15	2	48.0	16	16	44	6	1	3	25	6	23	0	2	0
TOTALS	4.61	75	87	.463	517	162	10	2	152	36	1435.2	794	736	1534	254	26	155	564	88	693	29	57	3

Sabermetric Pitching Records for Detroit Tigers

	Adj ERA	Expected W	L	Pct	BFP	Avg	Slg	OBA	RC/G	GDP	SB	CS	PK	PKE	SH	SF	Supported RSup	RSp/G	W	L	Pct
Aldred	6.65	3	8	.258	304	.307	.517	.387	7.39	5	7	4	0	2	4	3	37	5.12	4	7	.329
Doherty	3.80	6	5	.516	491	.287	.346	.328	3.61	22	4	4	0	0	3	2	86	6.67	8	3	.717
Groom	5.59	2	3	.330	177	.320	.493	.402	6.93	4	0	2	0	1	3	2	18	4.19	2	3	.317
Gullickson	4.30	12	15	.454	919	.267	.447	.305	4.65	15	20	8	0	1	7	9	131	5.32	15	12	.557
Haas D	3.79	4	4	.517	264	.276	.419	.323	4.80	4	1	1	0	0	1	0	43	6.28	6	2	.693
Henneman	3.84	4	4	.511	321	.256	.369	.299	3.74	7	2	1	0	0	3	5	10	1.16	1	7	.070
Kiely	1.96	5	1	.800	231	.224	.306	.317	3.27	7	2	1	0	0	4	3	37	6.05	5	1	.887
King E	5.11	4	6	.371	348	.285	.449	.343	5.62	5	8	3	0	0	1	2	48	5.45	5	5	.484
Knudsen	4.46	2	3	.437	313	.264	.423	.362	5.42	4	6	5	0	1	4	2	44	5.60	3	2	.566
Lancaster	6.23	2	5	.284	404	.294	.451	.386	6.43	8	3	3	0	0	2	4	47	4.88	2	5	.336
Leiter M	4.10	6	7	.478	475	.277	.415	.342	4.68	11	7	9	3	2	2	8	66	5.30	8	5	.580
Munoz	2.81	2	1	.661	210	.246	.341	.335	4.13	4	3	1	0	0	4	2	10	1.88	1	2	.268
Ritz	5.49	2	5	.338	368	.278	.361	.368	5.20	3	11	5	0	0	1	4	38	4.26	2	5	.331
Tanana	4.34	11	13	.450	818	.267	.415	.351	5.03	21	21	11	1	9	7	10	89	4.29	11	13	.446
Terrell	5.14	6	11	.368	611	.298	.431	.354	5.60	11	7	3	0	0	6	7	87	5.73	9	8	.506
TOTALS	4.58	69	93	.424	6254	.277	.416	.343	4.99	131	102	61	4	16	52	63	791	4.96	80	82	.492

Batting 'Splits' Records for Detroit Tigers

SPLITS for Phillips

	G	AB	Run	Hit	2B	3B	HR	TB	RBI	W	K	IW	HB	SB	CS	DP	SH	SF	Avg	Slug	OBP	RC
vs LHP	84	174	34	47	9	1	5	73	23	37	21	0	1	3	2	6	0	0	.270	.420	.401	31
vs RHP	159	432	80	120	23	2	5	162	41	77	72	2	0	9	8	7	5	7	.278	.375	.382	67
Home	79	289	47	79	12	1	3	102	31	64	42	2	0	4	6	4	3	6	.273	.353	.398	46
Away	80	317	67	88	20	2	7	133	33	50	51	0	1	8	4	9	2	1	.278	.420	.377	52
Grass	136	517	96	139	25	2	7	189	45	98	81	2	1	9	8	12	5	7	.269	.366	.382	78
Turf	23	89	18	28	7	1	3	46	19	16	12	0	0	3	2	1	0	0	.315	.517	.419	20
April/June	74	262	53	63	12	2	7	100	36	66	45	1	0	6	6	3	1	4	.240	.382	.389	44
July/October	85	344	61	104	20	1	3	135	28	48	48	1	1	6	4	10	4	3	.302	.392	.386	54

SPLITS for Detroit Tigers (all batters except pitchers)

	G	AB	Run	Hit	2B	3B	HR	TB	RBI	W	K	IW	HB	SB	CS	DP	SH	SF	Avg	Slug	OBP	RC
vs LHP	750	1442	241	394	72	7	59	657	228	181	264	13	8	17	13	36	18	9	.273	.456	.355	235
vs RHP	1572	4073	550	1017	184	9	123	1588	518	494	791	29	16	49	32	88	25	44	.250	.390	.330	539
Home	845	2640	389	671	126	8	91	1086	366	359	523	21	15	30	19	63	26	27	.254	.411	.344	385
Away	832	2875	402	740	130	8	91	1159	380	316	532	21	9	36	26	61	17	26	.257	.403	.330	387
Grass	1430	4673	673	1191	207	14	164	1918	633	596	886	35	19	54	36	113	37	44	.255	.410	.339	663
Turf	247	842	118	220	49	2	18	327	113	79	169	7	5	12	9	11	6	9	.261	.388	.325	110
April/June	789	2625	391	675	129	10	100	1124	373	314	508	18	15	26	28	51	18	19	.257	.428	.338	384
July/October	888	2890	400	736	127	6	82	1121	373	361	547	24	9	40	17	73	25	34	.255	.388	.336	388

Boston Dead Sox

Brock J. Hanke

BOSTON YEAR	1983	1984	1985	1986	1987	1988	1989	1990	1991	1992
W	78	86	81	95	78	89	83	88	84	73
L	84	76	81	66	84	73	79	74	78	89
WPCT	0.481	0.531	0.500	0.59	0.481	0.549	0.512	0.543	0.519	0.451
R	724	810	800	794	842	813	774	699	731	599
RA	775	764	720	696	825	689	735	664	712	669
PWPT	0.466	0.529	0.552	0.565	0.51	0.582	0.526	0.526	0.513	0.445
PythW	75	86	90	92	83	94	85	85	83	72
PythL	87	76	72	70	79	68	77	77	79	90
LUCK	3	0	-9	3	-5	-5	-2	3	1	1

Defensive Efficiency Record: .6930

This year's Red Sox essay is being written in conjunction with the Chicago Cubs comment. That's because I said similar things about the two teams last year, and they both at least addressed the main issue that I thought confronted them, and it didn't do either team much good. Sort of leaves me with the job of explaining why or making excuses or something like that there.

First, here's a quick précis of last year's comments, for those of you who haven't yet ordered your back issues of last year's SABERMETRIC.

CHICAGO CUBS:

I noted that most of the Wrigley Field pennant winners had been teams driven by their pitching, with a special emphasis on teams that led the National League in ERA. I noted that the opposite is true of old Comiskey Park, where the White Sox did well when they had a hot offense. You will note that the Cubs' team ERA was fifth in the National League. Their team Runs Scored total was tenth. They didn't win anything.

RED SOX:

I noted that the Red Sox have managed to win their division every year that they have had a team ERA under 4.00. I noted that this is because they always seem to have about the same offense, and they always have Roger Clemens, and so they win if they get anything else, and anything else pretty much has to come from the pitching staff. You will note that the Red Sox 1992 team ERA was 3.63, and they led the American League in Ballpark-Adjusted ERA, and they still finished last in their division.

Now, what happened to these two teams was not the same thing. What happened to the Cubs is discussed in their essay. Here's what happened in Boston.

The lineup fell apart. It did that for three reasons. First, a lot of

Position	92 Starter	TWAR	93 Starter	TWAR
Catcher	Pena, T.	-0.26	Pena, T.	-0.26
First base	Vaughn, M.	1.95	Vaughn, M.	1.95
			Quintana	inj.
Second base	Naehring	1.27	Naehring	1.27
Third base	Boggs	3.34	Cooper	2.55
Shortstop	Rivera	0.32	Valentin, Jn.	2.14
Left field	Hatcher	-0.63	Greenwell	-0.44
Center field	Zupcic	2.06	Zupcic	2.06
Right field	Brunansky	4.22	Dawson	5.33
DH	Clark, Jack	1.09	Calderon	0.99

the position players were old. Boggs, Clark, Brunansky; they were a lot of the Boston offense. Tony Pena was worthless with the bat; he's 36 and he's through as anything but an offensive hole. Second, the guys who weren't old were hurt. Greenwell, Burks and Reed. Only Reed played 75 games, and he was on a true off year. I mean, you're supposed to come down a little from age 27 to age 29, but not this much. Third, the projected replacements for the old guys did not come through as desired. That's Vaughn, Plantier and Cooper.

So, OK, that's a pretty impressive collapse. Everyone went into the tank for one reason or another, except Tom Brunansky. He can't carry an offense by himself. So, OK, write it off. Don't panic. Right? Use the bad year to experiment; develop a coherent plan. Right?

Well, wrong. Without knowing any of the people involved, I hate to say this, but the Red Sox response to the problems of 1992 looks like Butch Hobson's personality at its very worst. During the season, the team dumped all the pressure of failure on the shoulders of the kids. Cooper, Vaughn and Plantier took the fall for failings that were not entirely theirs. Actually, it wasn't their fault at all. Cooper was pretty good; I'd have to say he was ready for the big time. Vaughn recovered from his early slump and was certainly not awful on balance. He surely did not deserve a trip to Pawtucket. Plantier was not as good as Cooper or Vaughn, but he wasn't awful, either. If the team had been going well, I think everyone would have been satisfied, if not pleased. On balance, the kids were a help, not a hindrance. They just weren't the forces of nature that the Red Sox hoped they would become, and that the system is used to producing. And the team just didn't have the patience to write a single year down to bad luck. They kept swapping the kids in and out of the lineup, rather than using the year to give them solid experience.

After the season, the panic got worse. I cannot imagine shipping Phil Plantier out of town on the basis of one year, especially a year in which the whole team collapsed. You've got to write that year off and give the player a real chance. Oh, well, the Padres' gain. As for letting Wade Boggs go, well, people have been expecting that for years, and not on the grounds of player value, either. Wade is just difficult to deal with. But previous Red Sox managements have been able to deal with the problem and keep the player. This one failed. Sure, I think Scott Cooper is ready, but why only keep the one of them? Don't the Red Sox have enough question marks to want to have backups? Cooper plays the infield, where the Red Sox options are fewest. Why strip yourself of your one failsafe?

And then there's Jody Reed. The official term for this is, "There's something here that doesn't meet the eye." As of right now, the Red Sox middle infield consists of Luis Rivera, Tim Naehring, John Valentin, and, to replace Reed, Scott Fletcher. Valentin's a decent prospect, although a little long in the tooth for a rookie. He's going to be 26, and he's going to hit .260, with only some power. He'll get on base some, too. At shortstop, that's enough. With Jody Reed, it's a real good double play combination. But, with Scott Fletcher, at age 34.... I don't get it. Jody Reed had an off year, not a career-threatening injury or anything. If the Sox had kept Boggs, and were converting Cooper to second base, I could see the idea. But Scott Fletcher...?

Gee, Ellis Burks had a horrid year. Why, his Offensive Winning Percentage was only .556. Billy Hatcher plays center, too, and had a hot, hot .267 OW%. And the Sox are backed up. Herm Winningham turned in a .237 OW%. Not as good as Hatcher, but close enough that the Sox won't lose anything when giving Billy a rest. Seriously, neither of these two turkeys is going to play center. Bob Zupcic is. The immortal Bob Zupcic is going to be 26. He hit .276, with 3 home runs and 25 walks in 392 at-bats. His On-Base Percentage was .322, and his Slugging Percentage was .352. He did, however, have better defensive stats than Ellis Burks did. Not that Zupcic was really good or anything, but the injured Burks was right at Replacement level in the field. When healthy, you may recall that Burks was a Gold Glove man.

Enough sarcasm. What the whole collection of moves looks like is a fire sale of people that someone in the management can't get along with. Hobson, as you may know, is one of those "work ethic" guys. He judged himself by how many hours of work he was willing to do, and by how hard he was willing to throw his body into the fray. The result was an injury-riddled career, and

a short one. In other words, he's exactly the type of manager that you'd expect to suddenly have a bunch of disabled veterans. And he's also the sort of gung-ho guy that you'd expect to react by wanting to get rid of them as a bunch of babies who won't work. Like I say, I don't know, but that's what it looks like. The old men the Sox did keep were Brunansky, who didn't get hurt, Jack Clark, who's even crazier than Hobson, and Tony Pena, who works as hard as anyone. Just the people you'd expect Butch Hobson to want to keep.

And then there's the guys the Sox picked up. Andre Dawson and Ivan Calderon, indeed. The Calderon move has a real chance to be that famous trade that hurts both teams. The Expos now have a power core of Larry Walker, whereas they had three shots at RBI last year, with Ivan, Larry and Tim Wallach, or his ghost. As for Andre Dawson, well, his notorious inability to take a pitch ain't gonna help the Sox any more than it helped the Cubbies. Fenway is no more a pitchers' park than Wrigley Field. At least Andre has a true lineup spot; even the Red Sox don't have any more specialized a #5 hitter than Andre is.

So, what do the 1993 Red Sox look like? Well, let's assume that Mo Vaughn and Scott Cooper come through. Let's assume that Cooper turns out to be everything Wade Boggs used to be. What the hell, let's assume that Carlos Quintana comes back in full, too. That leaves the Red Sox with Vaughn and Quintana to share first base and DH, with Jack Clark in reserve. Let's say that, between Greenwell and Andre Dawson and Tom Brunansky and Ivan Calderon, the Sox get a left fielder and a right fielder that are as good as Greenwell and Bruno used to be. That's likely; there are four of them. And let's assume that John Valentin is for real, so the shortstop position registers a big, fat plus for the Sox. That's a bit more queasy, and Luis Rivera is what lurks in wait.

What does that leave? Well, it leaves the 1990 Red Sox, without Jody Reed and without Ellis Burks, replaced by Scott Fletcher and Bob Zupcic. I guess you can figure out that's a worse offense, especially as Tony Pena has lost about as much to age as Valentin figures to be better than Rivera. The bottom of that lineup, Fletcher, Valentin, Zupcic, and Pena, leaves a lot on the shoulders of the Front Five. The official term for this is "short offensive sequence"; it's no better for the Red Sox to have only five hitters than it is for the San Diego Padres to have four in a league with no DH.

In addition, it's an offense that has lost its invaluable asset of great On-Base skills at the top of the order. There's just no overemphasizing the importance of the Boggs and Reed "patience, Butch, patience" show to the Bosox run production. Now, take a look at the 1993 Sox, and tell me who's the leadoff man? Scott Fletcher? Jack Clark? Who's the #2? Quintana? Cooper? There's nobody out there who takes those walks; who's going to get on base over 40%. Instead, there's Ivan Calderon batting #3, with Mo Vaughn and Mike Greenwell and Andre Dawson competing for the #4 and #5 slots, and Brunansky and Quintana and Clark wondering what they're doing hitting in the slots that are left, not to mention the playing positions that are left. I mean, the Sox don't even have anybody who's going to steal bases in the leadoff slot.

What they have is a team of Butch Hobsons, or, rather, a team of Butch Hobson's dreams. And a team core composed of slow sluggers, where they used to have a infield-driven lineup. It's almost like they traded Jody Reed and Wade Boggs for Andre Dawson and Ivan Calderon. Would you make that trade? If you already had Mo Vaughn and Mike Greenwell and Carlos Quintana and Tom Brunansky and Jack Clark?

And still, the pitching staff may save them. You see, the other difference between the Red Sox and the Cubs is that the Cubs' pitching was only average, not dominant. It looked good, if you made the normal adjustment for the ballpark, but the ballpark was weird. Well, Fenway was Fenway, and Roger Clemens and Frank Viola were, in fact, Clemens and Viola. The rest of the starting rotation was what is usually is, but at least Roger didn't have to go it alone.

What's more, the Bosox probably have a real bullpen. Only six Boston pitchers had ERAs under the team figure of 3.63, which is what happens when Roger Clemens ruins the curve. But only Clemens and Viola were starters. The rest were a crew of relievers, one a real prospect. Paul Quantrill was the best of them, and he was only 23. No, he's never done anything in the minors to make anyone think he can pitch like this, but he was a starter at Pawtucket. There are a lot of pitchers who can do a lot better with two innings than they can do with six. Tony Fossas was next in the ERA parade, but he's nothing like the prospect Quantrill is. In fact, at age 35 in 1993, he's no prospect at all, unless he's suddenly discovered a trick pitch.

Greg Harris is old too, older than Fossas. But he's pitched well before. In fact, Greg has usually pitched well when used in relief. It's those seasons when some dumb team insists on starting him when he gets hammered. If Hobson has the sense to keep him in the bullpen, I bet he and Quantrill can manage a closer between them. Tom Bolton also pitched well in relief for the Sox, until he got sent to Cincinnati.

OK, so Bolton won't help and Fossas probably won't. But Quantrill and Harris, if Greg stays in the bullpen, do have a real chance to improve on Jeff Reardon, and give Frank Viola a chance to pile up some wins to go with his ERA. This is not to mention Jose Melendez, who the Padres gave for Phil Plantier. Skip, for the moment, whether you'd trade Plantier and pick up Andre Dawson to avoid re-signing Jody Reed. At least the Bosox got pitching for slugging, which is the right direction. Melendez is in fact a decent prospect. There is also Scott Bankhead, who might resurrect his career any year now. He's at least as good a gamble as the Sox usually take on the mound.

And that gives the Sox a chance. As last year's Cubbie comment suggests, the real and true method for regular contention in ballparks like Fenway is to amass a dominant pitching staff. You see, if you amass a dominant offense, you have the trouble of keeping the hitters hungry. Their stats are going to look great if they just cruise along. They're going to think they're at the top of their game when, in reality, they're just coasting along. That doesn't happen on the mound. The pitchers are going to have those inflated ERAs. You can threaten them. You can suggest that they really could do better, and show them the rest of the league's ERAs as proof. Or, if you can't show them any lower ERAs, then they're all Roger Clemens, and you're going to win 130 games no matter how few runs you score.

And frankly, to be honest, I'm going to be rooting for the Blue Jays all year. Butch Hobson doesn't deserve to win the division and keep his job because the team lucked into the correct plan. What he deserves - or what whoever really did orchestrate this fiasco deserves - is for everyone to come back, but for the short-sequence offense to hamstring the team anyway. He deserves for Clemens and Viola to be fine, and Quantrill to come through, and Harris to be solid, and Bankhead to come back, and the rest of them to be what they are, and for the offense to just score too few runs to win with. This year, Butch or whoever could blame it on the kids and the injuries. What he deserves is to lose the excuses, along with Boggs and Reed.

Boston Red Sox Home Park Performance Factors														
	Outs	Runs	Hits	2b	3b	HR	W	K	SH	SF	HBP	IBB	SB	CS	GDP
Home LH Batters	1.076	.928	1.050	1.022	.756	.943	1.000	1.139	1.547	.931	.882	.926	.910	1.432	1.034
Home RH Batters	.984	.900	.894	.776	1.161	.887	.909	1.007	1.010	1.013	1.028	.924	.905	.980	1.031
All Home Batters	1.012	.905	.949	.861	.940	.914	.941	1.048	1.099	.971	.933	.854	.906	1.110	1.036
Opp LH Batters	1.057	1.100	.990	1.017	1.013	1.293	1.105	1.080	1.080	1.303	.975	1.131	1.320	.780	1.381
Opp RH Batters	1.040	1.059	1.020	1.028	1.224	1.205	1.116	1.029	1.018	.967	1.239	1.122	.958	1.283	1.042
All Opp Batters	1.045	1.059	1.002	1.001	1.129	1.221	1.110	1.041	1.087	1.016	1.147	1.091	1.018	1.035	1.115
All LH Batters	1.068	.995	1.023	1.021	.866	1.094	1.036	1.112	1.160	1.047	.926	.992	1.111	1.020	1.177
All RH Batters	1.010	.974	.953	.888	1.200	1.041	1.004	1.016	1.033	.972	1.129	1.025	.909	1.115	1.025
All Batters	1.028	.978	.974	.926	1.030	1.062	1.017	1.042	1.097	.991	1.038	.965	.965	1.067	1.073

	G	AB	Run	Hit	2B	3B	HR	TB	RBI	W	K	IW	HB	SB	CS	BRng Eff	GI DP	SH	SF	Avg	Slug	OBP	Runs Ctd
Pena T	133	410	39	99	21	1	1	125	38	24	61	0	1	3	2	.417	11	13	2	.241	.305	.284	35
Vaughn M	113	355	42	83	16	2	13	142	57	47	67	7	3	3	3	.388	8	0	3	.234	.400	.326	47
Reed Jd	143	550	64	136	27	1	3	174	40	62	44	2	0	7	8	.505	17	10	4	.247	.316	.321	56
Boggs W	143	514	62	133	22	4	7	184	50	74	31	19	4	1	3	.340	10	0	6	.259	.358	.353	69
Rivera L	102	288	17	62	11	1	0	75	29	26	56	0	3	4	3	.300	5	5	0	.215	.260	.287	22
Hatcher B	75	315	37	75	16	2	1	98	23	17	41	1	3	4	6	.580	9	6	1	.238	.311	.283	25
Zupcic	124	392	46	108	19	1	3	138	43	25	60	1	4	2	2	.516	6	7	4	.276	.352	.322	45
Brunansky	138	458	47	122	31	3	15	204	74	66	96	2	0	2	5	.284	11	2	7	.266	.445	.354	73
Clark Jk	81	257	32	54	11	0	5	80	33	56	87	3	2	1	1	.463	4	0	5	.210	.311	.350	33
Plantier	108	349	46	86	19	0	7	126	30	44	83	8	2	2	3	.371	8	2	2	.246	.361	.332	43
Cooper S	123	337	34	93	21	0	5	129	33	37	33	0	0	1	1	.354	5	2	4	.276	.383	.346	46
Burks	66	235	35	60	8	3	8	98	30	25	48	2	1	5	2	.500	5	0	2	.255	.417	.327	33
Winningham	105	234	27	55	8	1	1	68	14	10	53	0	0	6	5	.389	3	0	0	.235	.291	.266	17
Naehring	72	186	12	43	8	0	3	60	14	18	31	0	3	0	0	.323	1	6	1	.231	.323	.308	20
Valentin	58	185	21	51	13	0	5	79	25	20	17	0	2	1	0	.324	5	4	1	.276	.427	.351	28
Greenwell	49	180	16	42	2	0	2	50	18	18	19	1	2	2	3	.310	8	0	2	.233	.278	.307	14
Wedge	27	68	11	17	2	0	5	34	11	13	18	0	0	0	0	.250	0	0	0	.250	.500	.370	14
Flaherty	35	66	3	13	2	0	0	15	2	3	7	0	0	0	0	.571	0	1	1	.197	.227	.229	4
Marzano	19	50	4	4	2	1	0	8	1	2	12	0	1	0	0	.800	0	1	0	.080	.160	.132	1
Lyons S	21	28	3	7	0	1	0	9	2	2	1	0	0	0	1	.600	0	0	0	.250	.321	.300	3
Barrett Tom	4	3	1	0	0	0	0	0	0	2	0	0	0	0	0	.400	0	1	0	.000	.000	.400	0
Brumley	2	1	0	0	0	0	0	0	0	0	0	0	0	0	0	.000	0	0	0	.000	.000	.000	0
TOTALS	1741	5461	599	1343	259	21	84	1896	567	591	865	46	31	44	48	.405	116	60	43	.246	.347	.321	621

	Ball Park Adjusted								Runs		Run/									
	AB	Run	Hit	2B	3B	HR	RBI	W	SO	Avg	Slug	OBP	Ctd	Outs	27o	OW%	OG	OWAR	DWAR	TWAR
Barrett Tom	3	0	0	0	0	0	0	2	0	.000	.000	.400	0	4	0.00	.000	0	-0.05	-0.00	-0.05
Boggs W	541	62	135	22	3	7	51	77	34	.250	.340	.343	66	427	4.17	.532	16	2.88	0.46	3.34
Brumley	1	0	0	0	0	0	0	0	0	.000	.000	.000	0	1	0.00	.000	0	-0.01	0.00	-0.01
Brunansky	456	46	116	27	3	15	70	66	97	.254	.425	.345	68	364	5.04	.624	13	3.70	0.53	4.22
Burks	234	34	57	7	3	8	28	25	48	.244	.402	.318	30	185	4.38	.556	7	1.41	-0.05	1.36
Clark Jk	256	31	51	9	0	5	31	56	88	.199	.293	.343	30	214	3.79	.483	8	1.06	0.03	1.09
Cooper S	354	34	94	21	0	5	33	38	36	.266	.367	.335	45	271	4.48	.568	10	2.18	0.37	2.55
Flaherty	65	2	12	1	0	0	1	3	7	.185	.200	.221	3	54	1.50	.128	2	-0.44	-0.17	-0.61
Greenwell	189	16	42	2	0	2	18	18	21	.222	.265	.290	13	161	2.18	.237	6	-0.67	0.23	-0.44
Hatcher B	313	36	71	14	2	1	21	17	41	.227	.294	.273	23	263	2.36	.267	10	-0.81	0.18	-0.63
Lyons S	29	3	7	0	0	0	2	2	1	.241	.241	.290	2	23	2.35	.265	1	-0.07	0.06	-0.01
Marzano	49	3	3	1	1	0	0	2	12	.061	.122	.115	1	47	0.57	.021	2	-0.57	-0.09	-0.66
Naehring	185	11	41	7	0	3	13	18	31	.222	.308	.301	19	151	3.40	.430	6	0.45	0.83	1.27
Pena T	408	38	94	18	1	1	36	24	62	.230	.287	.274	31	341	2.45	.282	13	-0.85	0.59	-0.26
Plantier	367	46	87	19	0	7	30	46	92	.237	.346	.322	42	296	3.83	.489	11	1.53	0.53	2.05
Reed Jd	549	62	130	24	1	3	38	62	44	.237	.301	.313	51	458	3.01	.371	17	0.36	2.13	2.49
Rivera L	287	16	59	9	1	0	27	26	57	.206	.244	.278	20	241	2.24	.247	9	-0.92	1.24	0.32
Valentin	183	20	48	11	0	5	23	20	17	.262	.404	.341	25	144	4.69	.589	5	1.28	0.86	2.14
Vaughn M	374	42	84	16	1	14	58	49	74	.225	.385	.315	46	305	4.07	.520	11	1.92	0.03	1.95
Wedge	67	10	16	1	0	5	10	13	18	.239	.478	.363	13	51	6.88	.756	2	0.77	-0.00	0.76
Winningham	246	27	56	8	0	1	14	10	58	.228	.272	.258	16	198	2.18	.237	7	-0.83	0.29	-0.54
Zupcic	390	45	103	17	1	3	41	25	61	.264	.336	.313	42	305	3.72	.474	11	1.41	0.65	2.06
TOTALS	5544	588	1309	241	21	89	554	606	903	.236	.335	.313	592	4517	3.54	.450	167	16.70	8.68	25.38

Pitching Records for Boston Red Sox

	ERA	W	L	Pct	G	GS	CG	ShO	GF	Sv	IP	R	ER	H	2B	3B	HR	BB	IW	SO	HB	WP	BK
Clemens	2.41	18	11	.621	32	32	11	5	0	0	246.2	80	66	203	39	2	11	62	5	208	9	3	0
Viola	3.44	13	12	.520	35	35	6	1	0	0	238.0	99	91	214	40	0	13	89	4	121	7	12	2
Hesketh	4.36	8	9	.471	30	25	1	0	1	1	148.2	84	72	162	39	2	15	58	9	104	2	6	0
Dopson	4.08	7	11	.389	25	25	0	0	0	0	141.1	78	64	159	30	1	17	38	2	55	2	3	3
Gardiner	4.75	4	10	.286	28	18	0	0	3	0	130.2	78	69	126	15	6	12	58	2	79	2	8	0
Darwin	3.96	9	9	.500	51	15	2	0	21	3	161.1	76	71	159	31	6	11	53	9	124	5	5	0
Harris GA	2.51	4	9	.308	70	2	1	0	22	4	107.2	38	30	82	11	4	6	60	11	73	4	5	0
Young Mt	4.58	0	4	.000	28	8	1	0	4	0	70.2	42	36	69	12	0	7	42	2	57	3	2	0
Quantrill	2.19	2	3	.400	27	0	0	0	10	1	49.1	18	12	55	6	1	1	15	5	24	1	1	0
Reardon	4.25	2	2	.500	46	0	0	0	39	27	42.1	20	20	53	11	1	6	7	0	32	1	0	0
Bolton	3.41	1	2	.333	21	1	0	0	6	0	29.0	11	11	34	8	1	0	14	1	23	2	2	1
Fossas	2.43	1	2	.333	60	0	0	0	17	2	29.2	9	8	31	10	1	1	14	3	19	1	0	0
Irvine	6.11	3	4	.429	21	0	0	0	8	0	28.0	20	19	31	4	1	1	14	2	10	2	3	0
Taylor S	4.91	1	1	.500	4	1	0	0	1	0	14.2	8	8	13	2	2	4	4	0	7	0	0	0
Ryan K	6.43	0	0	.000	7	0	0	0	6	1	7.0	5	5	4	0	0	2	5	0	5	0	0	0
Hoy	7.36	0	0	.000	5	0	0	0	2	0	3.2	3	3	8	2	0	0	2	1	2	0	0	0
TOTALS	3.63	73	89	.451	490	162	22	6	140	39	1448.2	669	585	1403	260	28	107	535	56	943	41	50	6

Sabermetric Pitching Records for Boston Red Sox

	Adj ERA	Expected W	L	Pct	BFP	Avg	Slg	OBA	RC/G	GDP	SB	CS	PK	PKE	SH	SF	Supported RSup	RSp/G	W	L	Pct
Bolton	3.10	2	1	.615	135	.286	.370	.370	5.43	3	4	0	0	0	0	0	15	4.66	2	1	.650
Clemens	2.34	21	8	.738	989	.224	.308	.279	2.72	28	24	12	1	2	5	5	116	4.23	21	8	.730
Darwin	3.85	9	9	.510	688	.257	.380	.319	4.36	7	14	6	0	0	7	5	69	3.85	8	10	.452
Dopson	3.95	9	9	.497	598	.287	.437	.334	4.91	17	17	7	0	1	2	2	63	4.01	8	10	.460
Fossas	2.12	2	1	.773	129	.279	.414	.365	5.29	2	4	2	0	1	3	0	3	0.91	0	3	.131
Gardiner	4.61	6	8	.420	566	.253	.380	.330	4.40	12	3	2	1	1	3	5	47	3.24	4	10	.289
Harris GA	2.42	9	4	.724	459	.215	.312	.324	3.38	11	3	6	0	2	8	5	29	2.42	6	7	.452
Hesketh	4.24	8	9	.462	659	.276	.425	.339	5.35	10	17	4	0	5	5	6	83	5.02	9	8	.537
Hoy	4.91	0	0	.390	19	.471	.588	.526	11.99	2	2	0	0	0	0	0	0	0.00	0	0	.000
Irvine	5.79	2	5	.315	128	.287	.370	.370	5.23	1	0	1	0	0	1	3	13	4.18	2	5	.301
Quantrill	2.01	4	1	.793	213	.288	.346	.340	4.17	4	3	2	0	0	4	2	27	4.93	4	1	.832
Reardon	4.04	2	2	.485	183	.308	.488	.335	5.77	5	2	0	0	0	1	2	3	0.64	0	4	.020
Ryan K	5.14	0	0	.368	30	.174	.435	.310	4.25	1	0	0	0	0	1	1	2	2.57	0	0	.171
Taylor S	4.30	1	1	.455	57	.245	.585	.298	5.53	0	0	1	1	1	0	0	6	3.68	1	1	.377
Viola	3.37	14	11	.576	999	.242	.331	.313	3.48	29	12	5	1	2	7	10	96	3.63	12	13	.490
Young Mt	4.46	2	2	.437	321	.257	.379	.360	5.11	6	10	3	0	5	4	3	27	3.44	1	3	.329
TOTALS	3.55	89	73	.549	6173	.255	.371	.323	4.15	138	115	51	4	20	51	49	599	3.72	77	85	.475

Batting 'Splits' Records for Boston Red Sox

SPLITS for Vaughn M

	G	AB	Run	Hit	2B	3B	HR	TB	RBI	W	K	IW	HB	SB	CS	DP	SH	SF	Avg	Slug	OBP	RC
vs LHP	43	79	14	15	3	0	5	33	14	10	17	0	0	0	1	1	0	0	.190	.418	.281	9
vs RHP	111	276	28	68	13	2	8	109	43	37	50	7	3	3	2	7	0	3	.246	.395	.339	38
Home	62	202	30	53	11	2	8	92	37	24	38	3	2	3	0	4	0	2	.262	.455	.343	33
Away	51	153	12	30	5	0	5	50	20	23	29	4	1	0	3	4	0	1	.196	.327	.303	15
Grass	102	321	40	77	15	2	11	129	51	42	56	6	3	3	2	7	0	2	.240	.402	.332	44
Turf	11	34	2	6	1	0	2	13	6	5	11	1	0	0	1	1	0	1	.176	.382	.275	3
April/June	31	93	13	21	3	0	3	33	14	24	23	2	0	0	2	3	0	1	.226	.355	.381	13
July/October	82	262	29	62	13	2	10	109	43	23	44	5	3	3	1	5	0	2	.237	.416	.303	33

SPLITS for Boston Red Sox (all batters except pitchers)

	G	AB	Run	Hit	2B	3B	HR	TB	RBI	W	K	IW	HB	SB	CS	DP	SH	SF	Avg	Slug	OBP	RC
vs LHP	730	1445	156	344	79	5	27	514	152	175	220	7	9	10	18	31	12	12	.238	.356	.322	168
vs RHP	1616	4016	443	999	180	16	57	1382	415	416	645	39	22	34	30	85	48	31	.249	.344	.320	453
Home	874	2684	328	696	149	11	45	1002	308	309	402	27	17	24	21	54	26	22	.259	.373	.337	348
Away	867	2777	271	647	110	10	39	894	259	282	463	19	14	20	27	62	34	21	.233	.322	.305	276
Grass	1486	4650	519	1157	222	20	70	1629	489	519	726	41	26	37	44	106	55	38	.249	.350	.325	540
Turf	255	811	80	186	37	1	14	267	78	72	139	5	5	7	4	10	5	5	.229	.329	.295	82
April/June	776	2450	269	602	124	7	34	842	248	290	409	25	14	25	24	50	25	26	.246	.344	.326	285
July/October	965	3011	330	741	135	14	50	1054	319	301	456	21	17	19	24	66	35	17	.246	.350	.316	336

American League
Western Division

1. Oakland Athletics
2. Minnesota Twins
3. Chicago White Sox
4. Texas Rangers
5. California Angels
6. Kansas City Royals
7. Seattle Mariners

AL Western Division Team Batting

	G	AB	Run	Hit	2B	3B	HR	TB	RBI	W	K	IW	HB	SB	CS	BRng Eff	GI DP	SH	SF	Avg	Slug	OBP	Runs Ctd
California	1752	5364	579	1306	202	20	88	1812	537	416	882	40	40	160	101	.452	136	56	40	.243	.338	.301	532
Chicago	1724	5498	738	1434	269	36	110	2105	686	622	784	48	31	160	57	.451	134	47	69	.261	.383	.336	732
Kansas City	1691	5501	610	1411	284	42	75	2004	568	439	741	30	51	131	71	.455	121	45	46	.256	.364	.315	631
Minnesota	1819	5582	747	1544	275	27	104	2185	701	527	834	53	53	123	74	.454	132	46	59	.277	.391	.341	751
Oakland	1748	5387	745	1389	219	24	142	2082	693	707	831	46	49	143	59	.422	139	72	59	.258	.386	.346	751
Seattle	1799	5564	679	1466	278	24	149	2239	638	474	841	47	38	100	55	.358	147	52	51	.263	.402	.323	712
Texas	1863	5537	682	1387	266	23	159	2176	646	550	1036	36	50	81	44	.423	114	56	45	.250	.393	.321	711

AL Western Division Sabermetric Team Batting

	Ball Park Adjusted												Runs	Run/				
	AB	Run	Hit	2B	3B	HR	RBI	W	SO	Avg	Slug	OBP	Ctd	Outs	27o	OW%	OG	OWAR
California	5361	562	1288	211	21	92	520	434	909	.240	.339	.301	537	4392	3.30	.423	163	11.83
Chicago	5512	773	1470	307	40	110	720	632	805	.267	.397	.342	733	4333	4.86	.549	160	31.90
Kansas City	5449	596	1402	272	35	102	563	473	775	.257	.376	.319	650	4353	4.03	.511	161	26.01
Minnesota	5590	745	1526	268	21	106	704	526	804	.273	.385	.338	733	4374	4.52	.523	162	28.03
Oakland	5351	745	1421	241	26	126	691	692	797	.266	.391	.351	764	4233	4.87	.554	157	31.96
Seattle	5627	682	1456	250	27	149	637	493	831	.259	.392	.320	704	4485	4.24	.463	166	18.82
Texas	5554	709	1398	268	24	162	667	560	991	.252	.396	.324	723	4428	4.41	.498	164	24.22

AL Western Division Team Pitching

	ERA	W	L	Pct	G	GS	CG	ShO	GF	Sv	IP	R	ER	H	2B	3B	HR	BB	IW	SO	HB	WP	BK
California	3.84	72	90	.444	459	162	26	6	136	42	1446.0	671	617	1449	221	17	130	532	40	888	39	42	5
Chicago	3.84	86	76	.531	454	162	21	3	141	52	1461.2	690	623	1400	224	34	123	550	48	810	55	35	6
Kansas City	3.81	72	90	.444	502	162	9	5	153	44	1447.1	667	613	1426	265	28	106	512	50	834	39	42	10
Minnesota	3.72	90	72	.556	485	162	16	8	146	50	1453.0	653	600	1391	272	33	121	479	30	923	36	52	5
Oakland	3.73	96	66	.593	562	162	8	3	154	58	1447.0	672	599	1396	235	31	129	601	46	843	41	67	4
Seattle	4.55	64	98	.395	534	162	21	7	141	30	1445.0	799	730	1467	303	25	129	661	50	894	60	61	6
Texas	4.10	77	85	.475	521	162	19	1	143	42	1460.1	753	665	1471	287	29	113	598	30	1034	48	72	6

AL Western Division Sabermetric Team Pitching

	Adj ERA	Expected W	L	Pct	Opposing Batters BFP	Avg	Slg	OBA	RC/G	GDP	SB	CS	PK	PKE	SH	SF	Supported RSup	RSp/G	W	L	Pct
California	3.72	85	77	.526	6154	.264	.382	.331	4.31	143	120	70	5	6	47	50	579	3.60	71	91	.436
Chicago	4.01	79	83	.489	6244	.252	.371	.323	4.21	112	120	57	5	6	43	45	738	4.54	83	79	.514
Kansas City	3.73	85	77	.525	6171	.259	.375	.323	4.18	139	107	52	5	6	50	67	610	3.79	75	87	.460
Minnesota	3.70	86	76	.530	6086	.254	.382	.316	4.13	121	152	62	5	6	50	49	747	4.63	91	71	.563
Oakland	3.72	85	77	.527	6204	.256	.382	.332	4.36	127	118	76	5	6	56	56	745	4.63	91	71	.561
Seattle	4.57	69	93	.424	6349	.266	.400	.348	4.95	128	140	62	5	6	56	53	679	4.23	67	95	.414
Texas	4.25	74	88	.460	6325	.264	.387	.337	4.52	122	87	84	5	6	44	64	682	4.20	72	90	.446

```
AL Western Division Catchers
             G    PO    A   Er    TC   DP   PB    SB   CS   CS%   FPct      DI   DG    DW%   DWAR   ERA
California   162  939   88  15   1042  12    5   120   70  .368  .986   1446.0 10.0  .338  -0.12  3.84
Chicago      162  852   82  10    944  11   13   120   57  .322  .989   1461.2 10.0  .358   0.08  3.84
Kansas City  162  881   73   7    961  10   14   107   52  .327  .993   1447.1 10.0  .379   0.29  3.81
Minnesota    162  952   70  14   1036  12   14   152   62  .290  .986   1453.0 10.0  .355   0.05  3.72
Oakland      162  873   99  19    991   9    8   118   76  .392  .981   1446.1 10.0  .342  -0.08  3.73
Seattle      162  928   87   8   1023  16    9   140   62  .307  .992   1445.0 10.0  .262  -0.88  4.55
Texas        162 1093  112  18   1223  18   19    87   84  .491  .985   1460.1 10.0  .304  -0.46  4.10
LG.AVG       162  916   84  11   1011  11   11   121   61  .335  .989   1452.0
```

```
AL Western Division First Base
             G    PO    A   Er    TC   DP   FPct      DI   DG    DW%   DWAR
California   162 1506  107  11   1624  158  .993   1446.0  3.0  .522   0.52
Chicago      162 1473   99  14   1586  118  .991   1461.2  3.0  .420   0.21
Kansas City  162 1434  150  13   1597  152  .992   1447.1  3.0  .603   0.76
Minnesota    162 1525  104   7   1636  140  .996   1453.0  3.0  .547   0.59
Oakland      162 1371   83  13   1467  146  .991   1446.1  3.0  .382   0.09
Seattle      162 1443  119   9   1571  148  .994   1445.0  3.0  .597   0.74
Texas        162 1306  148   7   1461  133  .995   1460.1  3.0  .671   0.96
LG.AVG       162 1443  115  11   1569  142  .993   1452.0
```

```
AL Western Division Second Base
             G    PO    A   Er    TC   DP   FPct      DI   DG    DW%   DWAR
California   162  349  486  16    851  124  .981   1446.0  8.0  .571   1.77
Chicago      162  356  462  22    840   92  .974   1461.2  8.0  .450   0.80
Kansas City  162  332  465  22    819  115  .973   1447.1  8.0  .495   1.16
Minnesota    162  339  459   8    806  113  .990   1453.0  8.0  .600   2.00
Oakland      162  384  515  10    909  119  .989   1446.1  8.0  .665   2.52
Seattle      162  386  477  18    881  117  .980   1445.0  8.0  .532   1.46
Texas        162  334  479  16    829  103  .981   1460.1  8.0  .442   0.74
LG.AVG       162  357  489  14    860  112  .984   1452.0
```

```
AL Western Division Third Base
             G    PO    A   Er    TC   DP   FPct      DI   DG    DW%   DWAR
California   162  116  394  29    539   38  .946   1446.0  6.0  .556   1.24
Chicago      162  144  385  24    553   27  .957   1461.2  6.0  .593   1.46
Kansas City  162  115  340  30    485   27  .938   1447.1  6.0  .421   0.43
Minnesota    162   89  375  21    485   21  .957   1453.0  6.0  .476   0.76
Oakland      162  138  253  15    406   17  .963   1446.1  6.0  .386   0.22
Seattle      162  113  345  30    488   41  .939   1445.0  6.0  .459   0.65
Texas        162  138  283  23    444   32  .948   1460.1  6.0  .392   0.25
LG.AVG       162  119  327  23    469   28  .951   1452.0
```

```
AL Western Division Shortstop
              G    PO    A   Er    TC   DP  FPct      DI   DG   DW%   DWAR
California   162   265  509   28   802  115  .965   1446.0  11.0  .548   2.18
Chicago      162   231  507   28   766   87  .963   1461.2  11.0  .479   1.42
Kansas City  162   257  481   23   761  116  .970   1447.1  11.0  .559   2.30
Minnesota    162   259  565   24   848  109  .972   1453.0  11.0  .638   3.16
Oakland      162   256  454   30   740  106  .959   1446.1  11.0  .474   1.36
Seattle      162   271  508   16   795  108  .980   1445.0  11.0  .561   2.32
Texas        162   277  479   30   786   98  .962   1460.1  11.0  .447   1.07
LG.AVG       162   259  499   24   782  106  .969   1452.0
```

```
AL Western Division Left Field
              G    PO    A   Er    TC   DP  FPct      DI   DG   DW%   DWAR
California   162   320   13    9   342    4  .974   1446.0   4.0  .514   0.65
Chicago      162   387   16    3   406    2  .993   1461.2   4.0  .777   1.71
Kansas City  162   354    6    4   364    0  .989   1447.1   4.0  .515   0.66
Minnesota    162   347    8    6   361    1  .983   1453.0   4.0  .497   0.59
Oakland      162   383   11    8   402    2  .980   1446.1   4.0  .596   0.99
Seattle      162   353    7    1   361    0  .997   1445.0   4.0  .565   0.86
Texas        162   360   12   19   391    1  .951   1460.1   4.0  .450   0.40
LG.AVG       162   357   11    7   375    1  .981   1452.0
```

```
AL Western Division Center Field
              G    PO    A   Er    TC   DP  FPct      DI   DG   DW%   DWAR
California   162   443   12    8   463    3  .983   1446.0   6.0  .524   1.04
Chicago      162   482   11    6   499    4  .988   1461.2   6.0  .630   1.68
Kansas City  162   488    9    4   501    2  .992   1447.1   6.0  .631   1.68
Minnesota    162   442   12    3   457    4  .993   1453.0   6.0  .635   1.71
Oakland      162   515    3   11   529    1  .979   1446.1   6.0  .521   1.03
Seattle      162   433    8    3   444    4  .993   1445.0   6.0  .539   1.14
Texas        162   436    9   10   455    3  .978   1460.1   6.0  .429   0.47
LG.AVG       162   458    9    6   473    2  .987   1452.0
```

```
AL Western Division Right Field
              G    PO    A   Er    TC   DP  FPct      DI   DG   DW%   DWAR
California   162   332   13    6   351    4  .983   1446.0   5.0  .560   1.05
Chicago      162   361   10    7   378    0  .981   1461.2   5.0  .562   1.06
Kansas City  162   348   11    7   366    1  .981   1447.1   5.0  .551   1.00
Minnesota    162   324   13    5   342    4  .985   1453.0   5.0  .591   1.21
Oakland      162   346   11    4   361    6  .989   1446.1   5.0  .602   1.26
Seattle      162   335   18    5   358    5  .986   1445.0   5.0  .655   1.53
Texas        162   312    7    9   328    0  .973   1460.1   5.0  .362   0.06
LG.AVG       162   346   12    6   364    2  .984   1452.0
```

Oakland A's

Don Malcolm

OAKLAND YEAR	1983	1984	1985	1986	1987	1988	1989	1990	1991	1992
W	74	77	77	76	81	104	99	103	84	96
L	88	85	85	86	81	58	63	59	78	66
WPCT	0.457	0.475	0.475	0.469	0.500	0.642	0.611	0.636	0.519	0.593
R/OAK	708	738	757	731	806	800	712	733	760	745
RA/OAK	782	796	787	760	789	620	576	570	776	672
PWPT	0.450	0.462	0.481	0.481	0.511	0.625	0.604	0.623	0.490	0.551
PythW	73	75	78	78	83	101	98	101	79	89
PythL	89	87	84	84	79	61	64	61	83	73
LUCK	1	2	-1	-2	-2	3	1	2	5	7

Defensive Efficiency Record: .7048

Nobody thinks that the A's can do it again.

Not even George Will.

(Actually, I wish that George Will would write a baseball column. It'd be a lot more entertainingly wrongheaded than his political commentary, and we could find out a lot more revealing things about received wisdom and its misapplications if he were to apply his theories to the minutiae of baseball than to the macroscopic vagaries of social and political issues. For example: term limits for managers. Get 'em outta there before they get senile.)

I suspect that even most A's fans are at a loss as to how Tony LaRussa (one manager who should not be subjected to term limits) is gonna scrape together enough pitching to keep his team in contention.

Actually, I think it's going to be relatively easy for Tony to do that.

The first thing he has to do is to keep his starters healthy enough so that the Big Four (who those guys will be we'll get to later) can give him 115-120 starts.

That hasn't been a simple task in the past two seasons.

In 1991, the year the A's tumbled to fourth place after three straight World Series appearances, the starting pitching did not succumb to injuries. It succumbed to overwork. Stewart and Welch, the mainstays of the rotation, both lost their edge and pitched well below their previously established standards. The top four starters gave LaRussa 120 starts.

But the A's didn't win in '91. (You object. Well, it was bound to happen sometime during this article. We might as well get it over with.) So how can the first thing LaRussa needs to do be to get

Position	92 Starter	TWAR	93 Starter	TWAR
Catcher	Steinbach	0.35	Steinbach	0.35
First base	McGwire	6.10	McGwire	6.10
Second base	Blankenship	4.12	Blankenship	4.12
	Browne	2.50		
Third base	Lansford	2.34	Seitzer	3.60
Shortstop	Bordick	5.60	Bordick	5.60
	Weiss			
Left field	Henderson, R.	5.58	Henderson, R.	5.58
Center field	Wilson	2.17	Henderson, D.	-0.06
Right field	Canseco, J.	3.62	Sierra	4.11
DH	Baines	2.04	Neel	0.33

115-120 starts out of his pitchers? It matters which pitchers, doesn't it?

The answer to that is yes and no. The Oakland ballpark has made a number of journeymen pitchers into terrific won-loss performers. Storm Davis, for one. Scott Sanderson, for another. To a lesser extent, the A's have been successful with Ron Darling, who turned in a journeymen year in '92 (15-10, 3.66 ERA) that helped the A's return to the top.

The first thing is to keep the pitchers healthy enough to make the starts. The second thing is to know when to pull them. Generally, Tony has been pulling his starters a lot earlier than in the past—his quick hook total has been rising, and last year it reached 29, the highest it's been since he joined the A's. (It was second only to Hal McRae's 45.)

The quick hook was made possible in 1992 by a deeper and more varied bullpen than ever before. Jim Corsi, Vince Horsman, Goose Gossage, Rick Honeycutt, Jeff Parrett and, in September, Jeff Russell, did an admirable job setting up Dennis Eckersley. And Eckersley was, until Game 5 of the playoffs, simply incomparable.

The top four starters on the A's gave LaRussa 120 starts—same as 1991.

So how hard is it to get this 115-120 start total, anyway? Why is it significant if it is so easy to achieve?

It's only easy to achieve if a manager knows what roles he wants his pitchers to play. Even with injuries up in 1992, LaRussa did not succumb to flip-flopping pitchers from starting to relieving—unlike his Bay Area counterpart. His ex-Bay Area counterpart, I might add.

What Tony does is that he decides what role the pitcher is going to play, starter or reliever. Once he's made that decision, he then breaks down the assignments in greater specificity. Then—and this is the most important part—he only deviates from the plan if injury or a complete collapse in efficiency occurs. If a pitcher simply can't cut it in the role he's been assigned, Tony usually sends him back to the minors to work on getting his edge back or to change roles.

It's significant because it reveals that a manager has a real plan, and is not an obsessive tinkerer, or a hapless revisionist. Most teams seem to be able to get about 110-115 starts from their top four rotation pitchers each year—good, bad, or indifferent. The teams that get more than this usually win.

Even Toronto, which gets accused of renting pitchers in order to win division titles, got 121 starts from its Big Four last season.

Let's look at the AL last season and see what this simple little truism might reveal.

East—Toronto, 96 wins overall, 121 starts from top four, 62 wins, 45 losses; Milwaukee, 92 wins, 130 starts, 55-41; Baltimore, 89, 123, 54-42; New York, 76, 109, 36-47; Cleveland, 76, 108, 35-44; Detroit, 75, 103, 38-40; Boston 73, 117, 46-43.

West—Oakland, 96, 120, 55-39; Minnesota, 90, 127, 55-39; Chicago, 86, 125, 50-41; Texas, 77, 120, 51-44; California, 72, 120, 35-52; Kansas City, 72, 90, 33-27; Seattle, 64, 108, 33-44.

The average team got 116 starts from its Big Four, with three-quarters of the decisions going to the starter. The average team got 46 wins directly credited to one of the top four, for an average of 11.5 wins per starter. Non-top four starters accounted for 43.7% of all team wins. The complete chart for the AL is shown below:

TEAM	W	L	4S	4SW	4SL	4SWPCT	OW	OL	OWPCT	DEC/4S	OW/W
TOR	96	66	121	62	45	.579	34	21	.618	88.4	35.4
MIL	92	70	130	55	41	.573	37	29	.561	73.8	40.2
BAL	89	73	123	54	42	.563	35	31	.530	78.0	39.3
NY	76	86	109	36	47	.434	40	39	.506	76.1	52.6
CLE	76	86	108	35	44	.443	41	42	.494	73.1	53.9
DET	75	87	103	38	40	.487	37	47	.440	75.7	49.3
BOS	73	89	117	46	43	.517	27	46	.370	76.1	37.0
OAK	96	66	120	55	39	.585	41	27	.603	78.3	42.7
MIN	90	72	127	55	39	.585	35	33	.515	74.0	38.9
CHI	86	76	125	50	41	.549	36	35	.507	72.8	41.9
TEX	77	85	120	51	44	.537	26	41	.388	79.2	33.8
CAL	72	90	120	35	52	.402	37	38	.493	72.5	51.4
KC	72	90	90	33	27	.550	39	63	.382	66.7	54.2
SEA	64	98	108	33	44	.429	31	54	.365	71.3	48.4
AVG/AL	81	81	116	46	42	.520	35	39	.476	75.4	43.7

LEGEND:
W—WINS   L—LOSSES   4S—NUMBER OF STARTS BY TOP FOUR STARTERS   4SW—WINS BY TOP FOUR
4SL—LOSSES BY TOP FOUR   4SWPCT—WIN PCT, TOP FOUR   OW—WINS BY OTHER PITCHERS
OL—LOSSES BY OTHER PITCHERS   OWPCT—OTHER PITCHERS' WIN PCT
DEC/4S—PERCENT OF DECISIONS, TOP FOUR STARTERS (4SW+4SL/4S)
OW/W—PERCENT OF TEAM WINS BY OTHER PITCHERS (OW/W)

The data for 1992 looks fairly representative for any old single season. We see the instability produced in the Royals' pitching staff with the loss of Saberhagen, and we see one of the reasons Milwaukee got so close to Toronto—four iron men and Cal Eldred.

What comes through about the A's on this chart is that they have the most wins from pitchers other than their top four starters (actually tied with the Indians). Unlike the Indians, though, the A's have a .600+ win percentage from these pitchers. Only Toronto had a better win percentage from the non-Big Four.

When we look at both Oakland and Toronto, it is easy to see that these two teams keep a nucleus of pitchers together for a few years and add pitchers around the edges of that rotation. The A's have had Stewart, Welch, and Moore operate as the anchor of their staff over the past five years, while adding pitchers like Davis, Sanderson, Darling, and Kelly Downs from other teams. Their homegrown starters, the Dressendorfers and Slusarskis, have not panned out. The Blue Jays have used a similar strategy, except that their nucleus came from within their own system.

But what they both do is quite similar. Find four guys who can keep you in the game, build an offense around them, and support this edifice with a strong bullpen. The A's have the most depth, and the best closer in Dennis Eckersley, but that didn't prevent the Blue Jays from finally breaking through last season. That depth should serve the A's well in 1993: LaRussa used the bullpen in 80 more innings than the Blue Jays, but the distribution was evened out sufficiently that one expects no adverse effects from last year's higher-than-average workload.

So Tony LaRussa, unlike many managers, can devise a plan. Not only that, he can stick to it. This is just the most basic reason why he has been so successful. He has also learned to adapt to changing conditions: he has been through two cycles of "burn them out and nurse them" with his starting pitchers, first with the White Sox and now with the A's. It's significant to note that, in 1992, the "nurse them" approach, supported by a deep and well-structured bullpen, brought the A's back to the top.

This season, there may be a little more help coming from the farm system. Lefties Johnny Guzman and Gavin Osteen might be able to make a dent in the Oakland rotation in the spring, and 1990 #1 pick Todd Van Poppel will be at AAA this year. An outside chance belongs to Roger Smithberg, a right-hander salvaged from the Padres last year. The A's used him exclusively in relief last season to help build his arm up, and he's being converted back to starting this winter at Mayaguez in the Puerto Rican Winter League. So there's a little extra in the pipeline for LaRussa this year in case the starting five (Welch, Darling, Witt, Davis, and Kelly Downs) run into difficulty.

WALKMEN

Another reason for not raising one's anxiety over the A's chances is to be found in their offense. Among their other feats in 1992, the A's became the first team in more than 20 years to draw more than 700 walks in a season.

This is, obviously, a rare accomplishment; and the A's did it without so much as one man drawing 100 walks, which is usually the prerequisite for a team performance that exceeds 700. Paced by Rickey Henderson and Mark McGwire, both of whom have exceeded 100 walks in a single season in other years, the A's came up with a third walking man in Lance Blankenship, who drew 82 walks in just over 400 plate appearances and looks like a solid bet for the 100 club.

Oakland became the 28th team in major league history to break the 700 walk barrier, and only the fifth to do so without one of the members of its offense exceeding 100. (For the record 22 of the 28 teams with 700 or more walks had one hitter with 100 or more; 14 of those teams had two hitters with 100+.) The A's were the first team since 1970 to make it, which means they're the first AL team since the introduction of the DH to enter this elite little pantheon. I thought it would be interesting to look at the entire list, plus see who the major contributors to the team's walk totals were:

TEAMS WITH 700 OR MORE WALKS IN A SEASON

Team	L	Year	BB	Players
NY	A	1931	748	Ruth 128, Gehrig 117, Lary 88, Lazzeri 79, B. Chapman 75
NY	A	1932	766	Ruth 130, Gehrig 108, Lazzeri 82, Combs 81, B. Chapman 71
NY	A	1933	700	Ruth 114, Gehrig 92, Lazzeri 73, B. Chapman 72
NY	A	1934	700	Gehrig 109, Ruth 103, Lazzeri 71, B. Chapman 67, Crosetti 61
NY	A	1936	700	Gehrig 130, Lazzeri 97, Selkirk 94, Crosetti 90, Rolfe 68
NY	A	1937	709	Gehrig 127, Rolfe 90, Crosetti 86. Dickey 73, Lazzeri 71
NY	A	1938	749	Gehrig 107, Crosetti 106, Henrich 92, Dickey 75, Rolfe 74, Selkirk 68
NY	A	1939	701	Selkirk 103, Keller 81, Rolfe 81, Dickey 77, Gordon 75, Crosetti 65
StL	A	1941	775	Cullenbine 121, Clift 113, Judnich 80, McQuinn 74, Grace 57
DET	A	1947	762	Cullenbine 137, Lake 120, Wakefield 80, Mullin 63, Kell 61
BKN	N	1947	732	Reese 104, Stanky 103, Walker 97, J. Robinson 74, Reiser 68
BOS	A	1948	823	Williams 126, DiMaggio 101, Pesky 99, Doerr 83, Spence 82, Stephens 77, Goodman 74
PHI	A	1948	726	Joost 119, Fain 113, Valo 81, McCosky 68, Suder 60
BOS	A	1949	835	Williams 162, Stephens 101, Pesky 100, DiMaggio 96, Doerr 75, Tebbetts 62
PHI	A	1949	783	Joost 149, Fain 126, Valo 119, S. Chapman 80
DET	A	1949	751	Wertz 80, Lipon 75, A. Robinson 73, Kell 71, Evers 70, Lake 61
NY	A	1949	731	Henrich 86, Rizzuto 73, Coleman 63, Mapes 58, DiMaggio 55
CHI	A	1949	702	Appling 121, Michaels 101, Baker 81, Philley 54

DET	A	1950	722	Priddy 95, Groth 95, Wertz 91, Lipon 81, A. Robinson 75, Evers 71, Kell 66
BOS	A	1950	719	Pesky 104, DiMaggio 82, Williams 82, Zarilla 76, Doerr 67, Stephens 65
BOS	A	1951	756	Williams 144, Pesky 84, Goodman 79, Doerr 57, Vollmer 54
CLE	A	1955	723	A. Smith 93, Rosen 92, Avila 82, Kiner 65, Doby 61
BOS	A	1955	707	Goodman 99, Williams 91, Jensen 89, Hatton 76, Zauchin 69, Piersall 67
BOS	A	1956	729	Williams 102, Klaus 90, Jensen 89, Buddin 65
SF	N	1969	711	McCovey 121, Bonds 81, Dietz 53, Hart 51, Mays 49, Hiatt 48
SF	N	1970	729	McCovey 137, Dietz 109, Henderson 87, Mays 79, Bonds 77
BAL	A	1970	717	Buford 109, Powell 104, F. Robinson 69, Johnson 66
OAK	A	1992	707	Henderson 95, McGwire 90, Blankenship 82, Baines 59, Canseco 48, Steinbach 45

This list covers just about all of the great walkmen, though a few aren't here (like Mickey Mantle, Eddie Mathews, Joe Morgan, and Jimmy Wynn, who toiled for teams who didn't have any depth of players with good strike-zone judgment). There are also some names here that would never come up even in the most informed conversation between baseball experts: catcher Aaron Robinson, for example, or the "Z-boys," Al Zarilla and Norm Zauchin, journeymen or downright marginal players who were briefly touched by an offensive environment that encouraged strike zone judgement.

When you look at the list, it becomes clear that there are two major types of "walkman" teams: the types driven by one or two walkmen with base on balls percentages (BBP) at or above 20%, and the "ensemble" teams where the walks are more evenly distributed, with five or six players in the 13-16% range. The greatest walking team of all time, the 1949 Boston Red Sox, was a combination of the two types, and its record hasn't been seriously challenged in forty years.

The A's were, of course, helped out by the DH rule (74 of their 707 came from this position), but the rarity of the accomplishment seems more significant than the fact that the DH rule skewed the results (after all, the other 27 teams didn't have nine hitters in their lineup, which makes the 1948 Red Sox feat of having seven of eight lineup slots contribute 70 or more walks in a single season look downright incredible.) Trivia question: who was the eighth guy, the one who didn't walk more than 70 times? Answer: catcher Birdie Tebbetts, who managed "only" 62 walks.

From this list we can see that the A's have a pretty good chance at repeating their feat in 1993. There are three instances of a team exceeding 700 walks in four straight seasons (Joe McCarthy's Yankee teams of the thirties did it twice, first in 1931-34—with Ruth; and next in 1936-39, with Gehrig and an impressive ensemble of players who took pitches. The other four in a row run was achieved by the 1948-51 Boston Red Sox, anchored by Ted Williams.) Other teams that have had back-to-back 700+ walk seasons include the 1955-56 Red Sox, the 1949-50 Tigers, and the 1969-70 Giants.

The A's, alas, are not in the same class as truly astonishing ensemble walking teams as the 1950 Tigers or the 1955 Red Sox, but with Henderson, McGwire and Blankenship all on hand for '93 and Troy Neel waiting in the wings to become the A's new DH, Oakland is looking like a 50-50 shot to become a member of the back-to-back 700 club.

The A's chances depend on LaRussa's decision about using Jerry Browne as a full-time player in 1993. Browne's been around for so long that people forget that he's just turning 27 this year. I suspect that Browne will be given the full-time third base job and will contribute 70-75 walks along with his .280 BA.

Neel had a monster season in the PCL last year (.351, 17 HRs, 36 doubles, .586 slugging average, .439 OBP) and will probably be the DH now that Harold Baines has been dealt to the Orioles. He looks good for around 70 walks, which would give the A's the greatest depth in walkmen (defined for this discussion as 70+ BB per season) in some time.

It looks like this as far as the free pass goes for the A's probable starting lineup in 93: Rickey Henderson 100, Blankenship 105, Sierra 60, McGwire 100, Dave Henderson 55, Neel 70, Steinbach 50, Browne 75, Bordick 45. That's 660 walks, which puts them in shouting range for 700 when you add in reserves. It will be interesting to see if LaRussa tries to emphasize walking as an ensemble feature of his offense: this tendency did not fully materialize even with last year's club, which had Jose Canseco for four-fifths of the year. If an ensemble trend is going to emerge, then Sierra and Bordick are the guys to watch. Sierra has never been much of a walker (56 in 1991 is his highest to date), but his BB rate went up markedly last year after being dealt to the A's (12.1% with Oakland, 5.8% with Texas). It's not out of the realm of possibility that Sierra will exceed the 60 I've projected for him. Bordick hasn't shown much of a penchant for walking in the majors, but he did draw walks in the minors, including 87 in 1988 at Huntsville.

It is easy to forget that the A's won last season despite having Rickey out of the lineup for 45 games. The increase in walks since the A's World Championship in 1989 (yearly totals from 1989 on: 562, 651, 642, 707) is no accident, and its meaning is unmistakable. LaRussa is exploiting every margin, every subtle advantage, every avenue or alley of offensive production available to him in order to give his team a better chance to win. The big question is how permanent an element walkmen will be for him: he has somewhat belatedly embraced one of the key trademarks of legendary managers such as Joe McCarthy and Earl Weaver—and whether it is by necessity or as part of an evolving design is what the next several years will reveal.

```
Oakland Athletics Home Park Performance Factors
                  Outs   Runs  Hits    2b    3b    HR     W     K    SH    SF   HBP   IBB    SB    CS   GDP
Home LH Batters   .966   .881  .943 1.017  .571  .757  .930  .972 .703  .920  .715  .715  .876 1.803  .920
Home RH Batters   .979   .966 1.040 1.102  .670  .903  .896  .982 .691  .732  .827  .765  .745  .926  .950
All Home Batters  .970   .947 1.001 1.053  .751  .866  .905  .976 .711  .866  .788  .744  .765  .997  .928
Opp LH Batters    .954  1.039  .992 1.061 1.044  .892 1.010  .863 .944  .907  .944 1.006  .841 1.038  .911
Opp RH Batters   1.017  1.077 1.083 1.201 1.955  .916 1.072  .992 1.095 .976  .926  .920  .999  .884  .940
All Opp Batters   .996  1.054 1.045 1.156 1.451  .911 1.054  .944 1.049 .974  .939  .972  .932  .960  .929
All LH Batters    .960   .956  .968 1.040  .768  .809  .971  .916 .785  .917  .796  .817  .845 1.162  .914
All RH Batters    .997  1.021 1.061 1.152 1.187  .911  .976  .983 .883  .842  .876  .842  .841  .898  .944
All Batters       .982   .999 1.023 1.104 1.053  .889  .974  .957 .845  .918  .857  .846  .839  .968  .928
```

```
                       Conventional Batting Records for Oakland Athletics

                                                             BRng  GI                        Runs
                G    AB  Run  Hit  2B  3B  HR   TB  RBI   W    K  IW  HB  SB  CS  Eff  DP  SH SF  Avg  Slug  OBP  Ctd
Steinbach      128  438   48  122  20   1  12  180   53  45   58   3   1   2   3 .371  20   0  3 .279 .411 .345   58
McGwire        139  467   87  125  22   0  42  273  104  90  105  12   5   0   1 .306  10   0  9 .268 .585 .385  111
Bordick        154  504   62  151  19   4   3  187   48  40   59   2   9  12   6 .398  10  14  5 .300 .371 .358   69
Lansford       135  496   65  130  30   1   7  183   75  43   39   0   7   7   2 .516  14   7  8 .262 .369 .325   61
Weiss          103  316   36   67   5   2   0   76   21  43   39   1   1   6   3 .417  10  11  4 .212 .241 .305   26
Henderson R    117  396   77  112  18   3  15  181   46  95   56   5   6  48  11 .465   5   0  3 .283 .457 .426   92
Wilson W       132  396   38  107  15   5   0  132   37  35   65   2   1  28   4 .436  11   2  3 .270 .333 .329   45
Canseco         97  366   66   90  11   0  22  167   72  48  104   1   3   5   7 .490  15   0  6 .246 .456 .335   52
Baines         140  478   58  121  18   0  16  187   76  59   61   6   0   1   3 .306  11   0  6 .253 .391 .331   63

Blankenship L  123  349   59   84  24   1   3  119   34  82   57   2   6  21   7 .553  10   8  1 .241 .341 .393   55
Browne J       111  324   43   93  12   2   3  118   40  40   40   0   4   3   3 .352   7  16  6 .287 .364 .366   46
Quirk           78  177   13   39   7   1   2   54   11  16   28   3   3   0   0 .400   4   5  1 .220 .305 .294   17
Fox             51  143   24   34   5   2   3   52   13  13   29   0   1   0   3 .650   1   6  1 .238 .364 .299   16
Ready           61  125   17   25   2   0   3   36   17  25   23   1   0   1   0 .438   1   2  2 .200 .288 .329   14
Sierra          27  101   17   28   4   1   3   43   17  14    9   6   0   2   0 .529   2   0  2 .277 .426 .359   17
Brosius         38   87   13   19   2   0   4   33   13   3   13   1   2   3   0 .400   0   0  1 .218 .379 .258    9
Henderson D     20   63    1    9   1   0   0   10    2   2   16   0   0   0   0 .333   0   0  0 .143 .159 .169    2
Neel            24   53    8   14   3   0   3   26    9   5   15   0   1   0   1 .273   1   0  0 .264 .491 .339    8
Howitt          22   48    1    6   0   0   1    9    2   5    4   1   0   0   0 .333   4   1  0 .125 .188 .208    1
Kingery         12   28    3    3   0   0   0    3    1   1    3   0   0   0   0 .250   1   0  0 .107 .107 .138    0
Hemond          17   27    7    6   1   0   0    7    1   3    7   0   0   1   0 .833   2   0  0 .222 .259 .300    2
Mercedes H       9    5    1    4   0   1   0    6    1   0    1   0   0   0   0 .000   0   0  0 .800 1.200 .800    5
Nelson G         2    0    1    0   0   0   0    0    0   0    0   0   0   0   0 .000   0   0  0 .000 .000 .000    0
Slusarski        1    0    0    0   0   0   0    0    0   0    0   0   0   0   0 .000   0   0  0 .000 .000 .000    0
Parrett          1    0    0    0   0   0   0    0    0   0    0   0   0   0   0 .000   0   0  0 .000 .000 .000    0
Darling          1    0    0    0   0   0   0    0    0   0    0   0   0   0   0 .000   0   0  0 .000 .000 .000    0
Corsi            4    0    0    0   0   0   0    0    0   0    0   0   0   0   0 .000   0   0  0 .000 .000 .000    0
Raczka           1    0    0    0   0   0   0    0    0   0    0   0   0   0   0 .000   0   0  0 .000 .000 .000    0

TOTALS        1748 5387  745 1389 219  24 142 2082  693 707  831  46  49 143  59 .422 139  72 59 .258 .386 .346  751
```

```
                       Sabermetric Batting Records for Oakland Athletics

              |————— Ball Park Adjusted —————|  Runs      Run/
               AB  Run  Hit  2B  3B  HR  RBI   W   SO  Avg  Slug  OBP  Ctd  Outs  27o   OW%   OG   OWAR   DWAR   TWAR
Baines        459   55  117  18   0  13   69  57   55 .255 .379 .334   59   361  4.41  .504   13  2.07  -0.02   2.04
Blankenship L 353   60   89  27   1   2   35  80   56 .252 .351 .397   57   286  5.38  .602   11  2.67   1.45   4.12
Bordick       512   63  160  21   5   2   49  39   58 .313 .385 .367   74   382  5.23  .589   14  3.37   2.22   5.60
Brosius        87   13   20   2   0   3   13   2   12 .230 .356 .256    8    67  3.22  .352    2  0.01   0.13   0.14
Browne J      322   43   95  13   2   2   39  39   38 .295 .366 .371   47   254  5.00  .566    9  2.03   0.47   2.50
Canseco       370   67   95  12   0  20   74  47  102 .257 .451 .341   54   298  4.89  .556   11  2.27   0.60   2.87
Fox           141   24   34   5   2   2   12  12   27 .241 .348 .301   15   115  3.52  .393    4  0.18   0.38   0.56
Hemond         26    7    6   1   0   0    1   2    6 .231 .269 .286    2    21  2.57  .257    1 -0.07   0.02  -0.05
Henderson D    62    1    9   1   0   0    2   1   15 .145 .161 .159    2    53  1.02  .051    2 -0.59  -0.04  -0.63
Henderson R   401   78  118  20   3  13   47  93   55 .294 .456 .431   94   298  8.52  .791   11  4.87   0.71   5.58
Howitt         45    0    5   0   0   0    1   4    3 .111 .111 .184    1    43  0.63  .020    2 -0.53   0.14  -0.38
Kingery        25    2    2   0   0   0    0   0    2 .080 .080 .080    0    23  0.00  .000    1 -0.30   0.04  -0.26
Lansford      502   66  137  34   1   6   77  42   38 .273 .380 .333   65   391  4.49  .513   14  2.36  -0.02   2.34
McGwire       473   88  132  25   0  38  107  88  103 .279 .573 .392  112   357  8.47  .790   13  5.81   0.29   6.10
Mercedes H      4    1    4   0   1   0    1   0    0 1.000 1.500 1.000   6   0  ?????  .000    0  ???????  -0.01 ???????
Neel           50    7   13   3   0   2    8   4   13 .260 .440 .315    7    38  4.97  .564    1  0.30   0.03   0.33
Quirk         169   12   37   7   0   1   10  15   25 .219 .278 .290   14   139  2.72  .279    5 -0.37  -0.42  -0.78
Ready         125   17   26   2   0   2   17  24   22 .208 .272 .333   14   101  3.74  .423    4  0.27   0.20   0.47
Sierra         99   17   28   4   1   2   16  13    8 .283 .404 .363   16    73  5.92  .647    3  0.23   0.80   1.03
Steinbach     444   49  129  23   1  10   54  44   57 .291 .414 .353   62   337  4.97  .563   12  2.66   0.35   3.01
Weiss         312   36   68   5   2   0   20  42   37 .218 .247 .308   26   267  2.63  .265   10 -0.84   0.47  -0.37
Wilson W      393   38  109  16   5   0   36  34   62 .277 .344 .333   46   304  4.09  .466   11  1.31   0.87   2.17

TOTALS       5351  745 1421 241  26 126  691 692  797 .266 .391 .351  764  4233 4.87  .554  157 31.96   8.08  40.04
```

Pitching Records for Oakland Athletics

	ERA	W	L	Pct	G	GS	CG	ShO	GF	Sv	IP	R	ER	H	2B	3B	HR	BB	IW	SO	HB	WP	BK
Moore M	4.12	17	12	.586	36	36	2	0	0	0	223.0	113	102	229	43	4	20	103	5	117	8	22	0
Darling	3.66	15	10	.600	33	33	4	3	0	0	206.1	98	84	198	44	5	15	72	5	99	4	13	0
Stewart D	3.66	12	10	.545	31	31	2	0	0	0	199.1	96	81	175	28	6	25	79	1	130	8	3	1
Welch	3.27	11	7	.611	20	20	0	0	0	0	123.2	47	45	114	11	1	13	43	0	47	2	1	0
Downs	3.29	5	5	.500	18	13	0	0	2	0	82.0	36	30	72	13	1	4	46	3	38	4	3	1
Slusarski	5.45	5	5	.500	15	14	0	0	1	0	76.0	52	46	85	17	3	15	27	0	38	6	0	1
Witt B	3.41	1	1	.500	6	6	0	0	0	0	31.2	12	12	31	2	0	2	19	1	25	0	3	0
Briscoe	6.43	0	1	.000	2	2	0	0	0	0	7.0	6	5	12	2	0	0	9	0	4	0	2	0
Parrett	3.02	9	1	.900	66	0	0	0	14	0	98.1	35	33	81	17	2	7	42	3	78	2	13	0
Eckersley	1.91	7	1	.875	69	0	0	0	65	51	80.0	17	17	62	11	1	5	11	6	93	1	0	0
Campbell K	5.12	2	3	.400	32	5	0	0	6	1	65.0	39	37	66	12	1	4	45	3	38	0	2	0
Nelson G	6.45	3	1	.750	28	2	0	0	8	0	51.2	37	37	68	8	3	5	22	5	23	0	2	0
Corsi	1.43	4	2	.667	32	0	0	0	16	0	44.0	12	7	44	4	1	2	18	2	19	0	0	0
Horsman	2.49	2	1	.667	58	0	0	0	9	1	43.1	13	12	39	4	0	3	21	4	18	0	1	0
Honeycutt	3.69	1	4	.200	54	0	0	0	7	3	39.0	19	16	41	5	2	2	10	3	32	3	2	0
Gossage	2.84	0	2	.000	30	0	0	0	13	0	38.0	13	12	32	2	0	5	19	4	26	2	0	0
Walton B	9.90	0	0	.000	7	0	0	0	2	0	10.0	11	11	17	4	0	1	3	0	7	0	0	1
Russell Jf	0.00	2	0	1.000	8	0	0	0	4	2	9.2	0	0	4	1	0	0	3	0	5	0	0	0
Hillegas	2.35	0	0	.000	5	0	0	0	2	0	7.2	5	2	8	2	0	1	4	1	3	0	0	0
Raczka	8.53	0	0	.000	8	0	0	0	1	0	6.1	7	6	8	2	1	0	5	0	2	0	0	0
Guzman R	12.00	0	0	.000	2	0	0	0	2	0	3.0	4	4	8	2	0	0	0	0	0	1	0	0
Revenig	0.00	0	0	.000	2	0	0	0	2	0	2.0	0	0	2	1	0	0	0	0	1	0	0	0
TOTALS	3.73	96	66	.593	562	162	8	3	154	58	1447.0	672	599	1396	235	31	129	601	46	843	41	67	4

Sabermetric Pitching Records for Oakland Athletics

	Adj ERA	Expected W	Expected L	Pct	BFP	Avg	Slg	OBA	RC/G	GDP	SB	CS	PK	PKE	SH	SF	RSup	RSp/G	W	L	Pct
Briscoe	5.14	0	1	.368	40	.400	.467	.538	10.32	1	0	1	0	1	1	0	3	3.86	0	1	.317
Campbell K	4.98	2	3	.383	297	.267	.372	.378	5.06	5	2	5	0	1	3	2	26	3.60	2	3	.301
Corsi	1.23	5	1	.911	185	.275	.350	.344	3.69	7	5	5	0	0	4	2	19	3.89	5	1	.892
Darling	3.62	14	11	.540	866	.253	.379	.318	4.04	15	10	13	1	5	4	3	112	4.89	15	10	.600
Downs	3.18	6	4	.603	364	.237	.326	.341	4.17	6	12	4	0	0	6	4	33	3.62	5	5	.516
Eckersley	1.80	7	1	.826	309	.211	.306	.242	2.53	3	9	1	0	0	3	0	19	2.14	4	4	.538
Gossage	2.61	1	1	.694	163	.230	.353	.327	4.14	2	4	2	0	0	1	2	13	3.08	1	1	.535
Guzman R	9.00	0	0	.160	18	.471	.588	.500	13.74	1	0	0	0	0	0	0	0	0.00	0	0	.000
Hillegas	1.17	0	0	.918	34	.276	.448	.364	5.23	2	1	0	0	0	1	0	6	7.04	0	0	.967
Honeycutt	3.46	3	2	.562	169	.272	.371	.327	4.38	3	4	1	0	0	4	1	18	4.15	3	2	.543
Horsman	2.28	2	1	.747	180	.252	.335	.339	3.37	9	4	2	0	0	3	1	32	6.65	3	0	.875
Moore M	4.08	14	15	.481	982	.269	.399	.349	4.81	26	19	13	0	1	7	11	123	4.96	16	13	.550
Nelson G	6.27	1	3	.281	234	.335	.478	.391	6.60	6	4	3	0	0	4	5	31	5.40	2	2	.379
Parrett	2.93	6	4	.642	410	.226	.344	.308	3.81	4	14	4	0	0	4	4	55	5.03	7	3	.709
Raczka	7.11	0	0	.234	33	.308	.462	.394	8.05	0	0	0	0	0	0	2	6	8.53	0	0	.543
Revenig	0.00	0	0	.000	7	.286	.429	.286	2.01	1	0	0	0	0	0	0	5	4.66	0	0	.000
Russell Jf	0.00	0	0	.000	35	.125	.156	.200	0.79	1	0	1	0	0	0	0	5	4.66	0	0	.000
Slusarski	5.33	4	6	.352	338	.284	.512	.350	6.41	5	6	4	2	0	1	5	44	5.21	4	6	.441
Stewart D	3.61	12	10	.541	838	.237	.393	.315	4.20	14	15	10	1	0	5	8	102	4.61	13	9	.573
Walton B	9.00	0	0	.160	49	.378	.533	.408	9.31	0	0	0	0	0	0	1	13	11.70	0	0	.582
Welch	3.20	11	7	.600	513	.247	.360	.312	3.71	13	8	5	0	1	3	3	73	5.31	12	6	.694
Witt B	3.13	1	1	.612	140	.265	.333	.362	4.45	3	5	2	0	0	2	2	12	3.41	1	1	.495
TOTALS	3.72	85	77	.527	6204	.256	.382	.332	4.36	127	118	76	4	9	56	56	745	4.63	91	71	.561

Batting 'Splits' Records for Oakland Athletics

SPLITS for Oakland Athletics (all batters except pitchers)

	G	AB	Run	Hit	2B	3B	HR	TB	RBI	W	K	IW	HB	SB	CS	DP	SH	SF	Avg	Slug	OBP	RC
vs LHP	662	1246	183	335	55	4	43	527	175	171	205	12	9	36	21	41	20	12	.269	.423	.358	189
vs RHP	1625	4141	562	1054	164	20	99	1555	518	536	626	34	40	107	38	98	52	47	.255	.376	.342	562
Home	868	2574	365	645	97	14	76	998	334	369	398	30	30	89	28	71	49	30	.251	.388	.348	368
Away	880	2813	380	744	122	10	66	1084	359	338	433	16	19	54	31	68	23	29	.264	.385	.344	383
Grass	1483	4493	618	1137	174	19	116	1697	574	608	691	41	39	126	49	114	65	48	.253	.378	.344	614
Turf	265	894	127	252	45	5	26	385	119	99	140	5	10	17	10	25	7	11	.282	.431	.356	138
April/June	798	2558	356	662	97	7	72	989	327	349	396	19	13	68	30	69	29	25	.259	.387	.348	357
July/October	950	2829	389	727	122	17	70	1093	366	358	435	27	36	75	29	70	43	34	.257	.386	.344	395

Minnesota Twins

Win Murray

MINNESOTA										
YEAR	1983	1984	1985	1986	1987	1988	1989	1990	1991	1992
W	70	81	77	71	85	91	80	74	95	90
L	92	81	85	91	77	71	82	88	67	72
WPCT	0.432	0.500	0.475	0.438	0.525	0.562	0.494	0.457	0.586	0.556
R	709	673	705	741	786	759	740	666	776	747
RA	822	675	782	839	806	672	738	729	652	653
PWPT	0.427	0.499	0.448	0.438	0.487	0.561	0.501	0.455	0.586	0.567
PythW	69	81	73	71	79	91	81	74	95	92
PythL	93	81	89	91	83	71	81	88	67	70
LUCK	1	0	4	0	6	0	-1	0	0	-2

Defensive Efficiency Record: .7044

The 1992 Minnesota Twins were a truly incredible team.

—They were third in the AL in runs scored—and second in runs allowed.

—They led the league in batting average and were second in OBP.

—Their pitchers allowed the second fewest walks in the league, while striking out the
fourth most number of batters.

So, with all that balance, all that strength, why didn't they win a second consecutive division championship?

Timing. The team's timing was off. It was a case of great parts, no gears. A beautiful engine, a broken drive train.

In April, the offense was absolutely bludgeoning the opposition. Unfortunately, staff aces Kevin Tapani, Scott Erickson, and John Smiley were sporting tattoos bestowed on them by opposition batters (repective ERA's: 4.81, 5.10, 6.84).

In August and September, the pitching was well nigh unhittable, but the team offense took a long weekend (with Kent Hrbek as the ringleader).

The Twins were the champions of May, June, and July. Lamentably, only once (in 1981) has that distinction been rewarded with post-season play.

As 1993 begins, the Twins have lost John Smiley, Chili Davis, and Greg Gagne; added Dave Winfield; and aged another year at the rest of the positions. The either/or question structure fits the Twins best this year: will the team put its pieces together as was the case in 1991, or is the offense too old and/or the pitching too thin?

Position	92 Starter	TWAR	93 Starter	TWAR
Catcher	Harper	2.76	Harper	2.76
First base	Hrbek	2.69	Hrbek	2.69
	Larkin, G.	1.05		
Second base	Knoblauch	6.21	Knoblauch	6.21
Third base	Leius	0.25	Jorgensen	0.07
Shortstop	Gagne	2.36	Leius	0.25
Left field	Mack	6.69	Mack	6.69
Center field	Puckett	7.51	Puckett	7.51
Right field	Munoz	1.52	Munoz	1.52
DH	Davis, C.	3.93	Winfield	5.59

Should the Twins fail to win 90 games again this season, it will not be the fault of their offense. The hitting is still deep and strong, led by a very underrated Shane Mack. Last year, overshadowed by Kirby Puckett's unsuccessful bid for a second batting title, Mack had an outstanding season. He hit .315, with an OBP of .394, and a slugging average of .467. Over the past five years, his numbers are .310/.380/.468, so it was really a representative kind of year for Shane, who will be 29 this season and may have a shot at a batting title himself. After the All-Star Break last season, he hit .348 and got on base a little more than 43% of the time. Shane is a hitter with one of the most consistently solid profiles to be found (good doubles power, 15-20 homers, intelligent baserunner with SB speed, and a solid if unspectacular outfielder). He began '92 batting leadoff, but hit an astounding .387 when he was moved to the #2 slot midway through the year.

If Mack continues to hit second, then Chuck Knoblauch will remain as a very effective leadoff man. Many people thought Chuck's '91 season was a bit of a fluke (despite MLE's that projected him to be a quality player) and predicted a downturn in '92. But all of his numbers actually improved over his rookie season. He is just 24, and has already proven to be a solid .290 hitter with good strike zone judgement (BBP of 12%). With superb speed and great range at second, Knoblauch appears to have at least a six-year career in the Twin Cities cinched.

Last year, with Knoblauch and Mack in front of him, Kirby Puckett came to the plate with men on base 62% of the time. Runners were in scoring position in 29% of his plate appearances. By having a typical Puckett year, he amassed 110 RBI. Just how typical was this "typical" Puckett year? Very typical. Last year he hit .329, with an OBP of .374 and a slugging average of .490. Over the past five years, those numbers are: .329/.369/.483. Kirby received very serious MVP consideration for a year in which his production was only slightly above his average season. That is the sign of a truly great hitter. He will turn 32 this season and may begin to dip a little below his norms, but it is unlikely that Tom Kelly will be complaining.

Cleanup was a real trouble spot after the break last year, when Hrbek hit only .172. This year, Big Dave will take over. Big Dave is slowly transforming himself into Old Dave, but to render the transformation visible, time-lapse photography may be required. Winfield is still producing at the rate of a 27-year old. Consider David Justice's career numbers: .269 BA, .366 OBP, .488 SA. Over the past five years, Winfield's numbers are: .286/.361/.487. And when Winfield's clubhouse attitude is taken into consideration, there's no question who will be more valuable in '93.

The next three hitters in the lineup (Kent Hrbek, Brian Harper, and Pedro Munoz) will determine whether the Twins' offense is unstoppable or simply above average. In 1992, Hrbek's walk percentage was 15.3, among the top five in the league. If he reproduces that number this year, he'll remain valuable even with another .244 batting average. He projects to hit around 20 homers, hit .270, and walk about 12% of the time— if his shoulder allows him to play. Waiting in the wings is recent Stanford grad Dave McCarty, who could probably produce similar power numbers, but with fewer walks. If McCarty isn't deemed ready, then the fallback is dependable but dull Gene Larkin, who will never get any more famous than he was whn he drove in the winning run in game seven of the '91 series. Full time play is not going to augment his fame, and the Twins will probably rue the trading of Paul Sorrento to the Tribe.

Brian Harper had another solid season last year, and has proven himself to be the best hitter for average among AL catchers. He will be 33 this season and has caught an extraordinary number of games in the past few seasons, and it is possible that his bat will begin to show the effects. Still, one expects at least a .285 average with moderate power. Brian is an incredible contact hitter and is very difficult to walk or to strike out. If he weren't so slow, he'd be an ideal hit-and-run man: the only real knock on Harper is the number of double plays he grounds into (72 in the last five years).

This is the year in which Pedro Munoz needs to live up to his advance billing. His MLE's show him to be a hitter with a profile similar to that of Shane Mack: high average, moderate power, good speed. All he has managed to produce thus far, however, is decent average and moderate power, combined with poor plate judgement (.302 OBP). He slumped badly after the break last season (.247 BA with a 120 point loss in SA), and Tom Kelly

started benching him and even pinch-hitting for him in key situations. Still, he's only 24, and there is some incentive for Kelly to speed along his development rather than using part-time play as an motivational device. The ultimate projection for Munoz is that he'll be a .290 hitter, with double-digit steals and homers. But that might not be what he does in 1993—stay tuned.

If the first seven hitters in the Twins' lineup can perform up to expectations, then it will hardly matter what the last two do. One of that bring-up-the-rear pair will be new shortstop/ex-third baseman Scott Leius (the guy Bill James made up the off-color Chris Berman-style nickname for: sabermetrics misses you, Bill). Leius was, in fact, a shortstop throughout the minors and should be adequate there defensively (perhaps his gangly build will look a bit more natural at short). Still, Leius will not be nearly as accomplished as the departed Greg Gagne, though he's got an excellent chance to up the offensive production from the SS position.

The new number nine hitter will probably be 26-year old rookie third basemen Terry Jorgenson. His career average is currently over .300, but he's likely to really be about a .260 hitter, with moderate doubles power (20-25), and no speed. Kelly has repeatedly denied that he's looking for any additional help at third base, so it appears that Jorgenson is going to get a long look.

The Twins' pitching has always tended to be underrated. In '91 the Twins rode three big starters (Jack Morris, Kevin Tapani, Scott Erickson) to a World Series win. Last season, their three big starters (Tapani, Erickson, John Smiley) got them back to 90 wins despite a terrible start. This season, the Twins will begin with only two big starters (Tapani and Erickson), and if a third man doesn't emerge in the way that Erickson stepped forward in '91, then the Twins are going to fall short again.

Tapani and Erickson are much better pitchers than they are given credit for. Kevin had an off-year, but he finished with 16 wins, an ERA under 4.00, and only 48 walks in 222 innings. While it's true that he received an inordinate amount of offensive support (over six runs per start), he showed some strong signs of his old form during the middle of the season (7-2, 2.98 ERA). His K/BB ratio is still in the neighborhood of 3-to-1, so one expects that he'll right himself and become a bonafide staff ace.

Erickson's start was the worst of the Twins' Big Three, but he finished the year strongly, posting a 2.69 ERA after the break. Erickson was much more effective with 5 days rest (2.79 with 5 days, 3.80 for less than 5 days), so it is important that the Twins find three other strong rotation pitchers. Gagne's departure may affect Erickson the most, since he is an extreme ground ball pitcher (2.46 GB/FB ratio).

About those other three starters: they'll likely emerge from a pool of pitchers which includes Pat Mahomes, Willie Banks, Mike Trombley, Bert Blyleven, and Mark Guthrie. Guthrie has had some success as a starter for the Twins in the past, but he was so good out of the pen last season (1.93 ERA in the second half) that it is unlikely that Tom Kelly will decide to switch him.

That fact alone may assure Blyleven a rotation slot at the opening of the season, but his continued effectiveness is becoming a start-by-start decision process. His ERA over the past five years is 4.35—and that includes his "last hurrah" season of 1989 (2.73). Bert wants to win 300 games badly, but it's hard to see him providing the kind of sustained performance that the Twins will need to remain in contention.

The other three candidates are all unproven prospects, and the Twins are in the unenviable position of needing good years from two of them. Willie Banks, the perennial phenom, is now 24. He had a 4.43 ERA last season in 12 starts. He walked 37 and struck out 37. The Twins have to be worried about his strikeout pitch, which seems to have disappeared between Orlando and Portland.

Mahomes is 22 and people are in love with his arm. A classic wildman power pitcher, Pat started '92 with the big club but was struggling with his control and spent most of the year at Portland. He regained his strikeout pitch in the minors, but didn't really demonstrate that he'd gotten his control together. If he does, though, he's the one member of the trio who can really move up to Big Three status in a hurry.

Trombley, 26, has had an orderly rise through the Twins' system since being drafted in 1989 (43-23 career minor league record). He was impressive in his seven late-season starts, compiling a 3-2 record with a 3.30 ERA. His out pitch is a slow curve, which would be more effective if he were left-handed, but it's likely to

keep him in the majors for a number of years. The gopher ball may prove to be Trombley's biggest weakness.

It's possible that the Twins will try to nurture all three of their rookie starters at once, but if anyone is going to get a full shot this year, it's likely to be Banks. The Twins have a lot invested in him (former #1 draft pick and a recipient of mucho hype).

The bullpen? Carl Willis has put together two killer seasons back-to-back, but the odds of a pitcher relying on off-speed junk and motion putting together three years at that level of performance just aren't that good (ask the White Sox' Donn Pall about that). Mark Guthrie appears to be mastering his control, however, and he could be the dominant set-up man in the AL season. He's capable of being the closer if Rick Aguilera, who was unusually erratic last season, starts to seriously slip. Kelly is likely to stay with Rick for a long time, however: the former Met is an unabashed favorite of the Twins' skipper.

To sum up: any team with as much offense as the Twins have must at least be considered a contender. But the fact is that the Metrodome is not a forgiving place for young pitchers. If Blyleven has anything left, and Trombley continues his September performance into '93, the Twins can win the West again. If none of the young pitchers take any significant steps forward, then the team is going to fall into the 85-90 range. They're definitely close, but the young pitchers might need a full year of learning on the job before they can hold up for a serious pennant run.

```
Minnesota Twins Home Park Performance Factors
                  Outs  Runs  Hits    2b    3b    HR     W     K    SH    SF   HBP   IBB    SB    CS   GDP
Home LH Batters   .949  .813  .861  .900 1.217  .742  .901  .935 1.014  .991  .869  .841  .752  .705  .832
Home RH Batters  1.001  .978  .979 1.086  .769 1.014  .902  .990 1.019  .977  .964  .996 1.002 1.105  .854
All Home Batters  .991  .954  .962 1.018  .760  .924  .912  .981 1.005  .932 1.044  .973  .976 1.067  .842
Opp LH Batters    .995  .977  .967  .901  .724 1.068 1.106  .866  .745  .990  .929  .929  .871 1.083 1.003
Opp RH Batters   1.023 1.049 1.039  .960 1.057 1.178 1.094  .964 1.108 1.263  .862 1.008 1.003 1.245 1.009
All Opp Batters  1.022 1.041 1.016  .934  .862 1.130 1.087  .947 1.013 1.125  .900 1.020  .942 1.118 1.040
All LH Batters    .976  .912  .924  .895  .732  .925 1.014  .887  .854  .982  .905  .901  .825  .916  .934
All RH Batters   1.009 1.008 1.004 1.023  .862 1.085  .981  .973 1.056 1.075  .925  .999 1.004 1.157  .913
All Batters      1.005  .995  .988  .971  .809 1.023  .991  .959 1.007 1.016  .983  .999  .953 1.094  .929
```

Conventional Batting Records for Minnesota Twins

	G	AB	Run	Hit	2B	3B	HR	TB	RBI	W	K	IW	HB	SB	CS	BRng Eff	GI DP	SH	SF	Avg	Slug	OBP	Runs Ctd
Harper B	140	502	58	154	25	0	9	206	73	26	22	7	7	0	1	.378	15	1	10	.307	.410	.343	69
Hrbek	112	394	52	96	20	0	15	161	58	71	56	9	0	5	2	.375	13	2	3	.244	.409	.357	60
Knoblauch	155	600	104	178	19	6	2	215	56	88	60	1	5	34	13	.528	8	2	12	.297	.358	.384	93
Leius	129	409	50	102	18	2	2	130	35	34	61	0	1	6	5	.452	10	5	0	.249	.318	.309	39
Gagne	146	439	53	108	23	0	7	152	39	19	83	0	2	6	7	.571	11	12	1	.246	.346	.280	39
Mack	156	600	101	189	31	6	16	280	75	64	106	1	15	26	14	.476	9	11	2	.315	.467	.394	114
Puckett	160	639	104	210	38	4	19	313	110	44	97	13	6	17	7	.562	17	1	6	.329	.490	.374	115
Munoz P	127	418	44	113	16	3	12	171	71	17	90	1	1	4	5	.381	18	0	3	.270	.409	.298	44
Davis C	138	444	63	128	27	2	12	195	66	73	76	11	3	4	5	.380	11	0	9	.288	.439	.386	79

Batting Records

	G	AB	Run	Hit	2B	3B	HR	TB	RBI	W	K	IW	HB	SB	CS	BRng Eff	GI DP	SH	SF	Avg	Slug	OBP	Runs Ctd
Larkin G	115	337	38	83	18	1	6	121	42	28	43	6	4	7	2	.340	7	0	4	.246	.359	.308	38
Bush	100	182	14	39	8	1	2	55	22	11	37	3	2	1	1	.182	5	0	3	.214	.302	.263	14
Reboulet	73	137	15	26	7	1	1	38	16	23	26	0	1	3	2	.519	0	7	0	.190	.277	.311	14
Webster L	53	118	10	33	10	1	1	48	13	9	11	0	0	0	2	.500	3	2	0	.280	.407	.331	15
Pagliarulo	42	105	10	21	4	0	0	25	9	1	17	0	1	1	0	.714	1	0	1	.200	.238	.213	5
Bruett	56	76	7	19	4	0	0	23	2	6	12	1	1	6	3	.333	0	1	0	.250	.303	.313	8
Jorgensen	22	58	5	18	1	0	0	19	5	3	11	0	1	1	2	.500	4	0	1	.310	.328	.349	5
Hill D	25	51	7	15	3	0	0	18	2	5	6	0	1	0	0	.231	0	2	0	.294	.353	.368	7
Reed D	14	33	2	6	2	0	0	8	4	2	11	0	0	0	0	.000	0	0	2	.182	.242	.216	2
Brown J	35	15	8	1	0	0	0	1	0	2	4	0	1	2	2	.529	0	0	0	.067	.067	.222	0
Brito	8	14	1	2	1	0	0	3	2	0	4	0	0	0		1.000	0	0	1	.143	.214	.133	0
Parks	7	6	1	2	0	0	0	2	0	1	1	0	1	0	0	.250	0	0	0	.333	.333	.500	1
Quinones L	3	5	0	1	0	0	0	1	1	0	0	0	0	0	0	.000	0	0	1	.200	.200	.167	0
Guthrie	1	0	0	0	0	0	0	0	0	0	0	0	0	0	0	.000	0	0	0	.000	.000	.000	0
Aguilera	1	0	0	0	0	0	0	0	0	0	0	0	0	0	0	.000	0	0	0	.000	.000	.000	0
Willis	1	0	0	0	0	0	0	0	0	0	0	0	0	0	0	.000	0	0	0	.000	.000	.000	0
TOTALS	1819	5582	747	1544	275	27	104	2185	701	527	834	53	53	123	74	.454	132	46	59	.277	.391	.341	751

Sabermetric Batting Records for Minnesota Twins

	Ball Park Adjusted								Runs		Run/								
	AB	Run	Hit	2B	3B	HR	RBI	W	SO	Avg	Slug	OBP	Ctd	Outs	27o	OW%	OG	OWAR	DWAR	TWAR
Brito	14	1	2	1	0	0	2	0	3	.143	.214	.133	0	14	0.00	.000	1	-0.18	-0.00	-0.19
Brown J	15	8	1	0	0	0	0	1	3	.067	.067	.125	0	16	0.00	.000	1	-0.21	0.06	-0.15
Bruett	72	7	19	3	0	0	1	6	10	.236	.278	.295	6	57	2.84	.302	2	-0.10	0.16	0.05
Bush	173	12	35	7	0	1	20	11	33	.202	.260	.251	11	144	2.06	.186	5	-0.88	0.13	-0.75
Davis C	444	62	126	26	1	12	66	72	73	.284	.428	.380	76	342	6.00	.658	13	3.91	0.02	3.93
Gagne	443	53	108	23	0	7	40	18	81	.244	.343	.274	38	366	2.80	.296	14	-0.73	2.36	1.63
Harper B	507	58	155	25	0	9	75	25	21	.306	.408	.339	69	378	4.93	.565	14	3.02	-0.25	2.76
Hill D	50	6	14	2	0	0	2	4	5	.280	.320	.333	6	38	4.26	.493	1	0.20	0.07	0.27
Hrbek	376	46	87	18	0	13	54	71	50	.231	.383	.352	54	304	4.80	.552	11	2.27	0.42	2.69
Jorgensen	58	5	18	1	0	0	5	2	10	.310	.328	.328	5	46	2.93	.316	2	-0.06	0.13	0.07
Knoblauch	606	105	179	19	5	2	58	87	58	.295	.353	.380	92	464	5.35	.606	17	4.39	1.82	6.21
Larkin G	337	37	82	17	0	6	42	27	41	.243	.347	.302	36	267	3.64	.415	10	0.64	0.40	1.05
Leius	412	50	102	18	1	2	36	33	59	.248	.311	.303	38	329	3.12	.342	12	-0.09	0.34	0.25
Mack	605	102	190	31	5	17	77	63	103	.314	.466	.389	112	452	6.69	.706	17	5.95	0.73	6.69
Munoz P	421	44	113	16	2	13	73	16	87	.268	.409	.293	44	332	3.58	.407	12	0.70	0.82	1.52
Pagliarulo	100	8	19	3	0	0	8	1	15	.190	.220	.198	4	81	1.33	.087	3	-0.79	0.14	-0.65
Parks	6	1	2	0	0	0	0	0	0	.333	.333	.333	1	4	6.75	.709	0	0.05	0.03	0.08
Puckett	645	105	211	38	3	20	114	43	94	.327	.488	.371	115	464	6.69	.706	17	6.11	1.40	7.51
Quinones L	4	0	0	0	0	0	0	1	0	.000	.000	.000	0	5	0.00	.000	0	-0.06	0.01	-0.05
Reboulet	138	15	26	7	0	1	16	22	25	.188	.261	.300	13	121	2.90	.311	4	-0.18	1.08	0.91
Reed D	33	2	6	2	0	0	4	1	10	.182	.242	.194	2	29	1.86	.157	1	-0.21	0.08	-0.13
Webster L	119	10	33	10	0	1	13	8	10	.277	.387	.323	14	92	4.11	.475	3	0.43	0.22	0.64
TOTALS	5590	745	1526	268	21	106	704	526	804	.273	.385	.338	733	4374	4.52	.523	162	28.03	10.16	38.19

Pitching Records for Minnesota Twins

	ERA	W	L	Pct	G	GS	CG	ShO	GF	Sv	IP	R	ER	H	2B	3B	HR	BB	IW	SO	HB	WP	BK
Smiley	3.21	16	9	.640	34	34	5	2	0	0	241.0	93	86	205	51	4	17	65	0	163	6	4	0
Tapani	3.97	16	11	.593	34	34	4	1	0	0	220.0	103	97	226	53	5	17	48	2	138	5	4	0
Erickson S	3.40	13	12	.520	32	32	5	3	0	0	212.0	86	80	197	29	5	18	83	3	101	8	6	1
Krueger	4.30	10	6	.625	27	27	2	2	0	0	161.1	82	77	166	33	1	18	46	2	86	3	11	0
Banks	5.70	4	4	.500	16	12	0	0	2	0	71.0	46	45	80	15	3	6	37	0	37	2	5	1
Mahomes	5.04	3	4	.429	14	13	0	0	1	0	69.2	41	39	73	19	4	5	37	0	44	0	2	1
Trombley	3.30	3	2	.600	10	7	0	0	0	0	46.1	20	17	43	12	0	5	17	0	38	1	0	0
Willis	2.72	7	3	.700	59	0	0	0	21	1	79.1	25	24	73	12	3	4	11	1	45	0	2	1
Edens	2.83	6	3	.667	52	0	0	0	14	3	76.1	26	24	65	8	3	1	36	3	57	2	5	0
Guthrie	2.88	2	3	.400	54	0	0	0	15	5	75.0	27	24	59	6	1	7	23	7	76	0	2	0
Aguilera	2.84	2	6	.250	64	0	0	0	61	41	66.2	28	21	60	8	0	7	17	4	52	1	5	0
Wayne	2.63	3	3	.500	41	0	0	0	13	0	48.0	18	14	46	11	3	2	19	5	29	3	1	1
Kipper	4.42	3	3	.500	25	0	0	0	12	0	38.2	23	19	40	5	0	8	14	3	22	3	1	0
West	6.99	1	3	.250	9	3	0	0	1	0	28.1	24	22	32	5	0	3	20	0	19	1	2	0
Abbott P	3.27	0	0	.000	6	0	0	0	5	0	11.0	4	4	12	2	1	1	5	0	13	1	1	0
Casian	2.70	1	0	1.000	6	0	0	0	1	0	6.2	2	2	7	1	0	0	1	0	2	0	0	0
Gozzo	27.00	0	0	.000	2	0	0	0	0	0	1.2	5	5	7	2	0	2	0	0	1	0	1	0
TOTALS	3.72	90	72	.556	485	162	16	8	146	50	1453.0	653	600	1391	272	33	121	479	30	923	36	52	5

Sabermetric Pitching Records for Minnesota Twins

	Adj ERA	Expected W	L	Pct	BFP	Avg	Slg	OBA	RC/G	GDP	SB	CS	PK	PKE	SH	SF	Supported RSup	RSp/G	W	L	Pct
Abbott P	2.45	0	0	.719	50	.279	.442	.360	6.53	0	2	0	1	0	0	1	2	1.63	0	0	.268
Aguilera	2.70	5	3	.679	273	.238	.353	.287	3.44	7	5	0	0	0	1	2	11	1.49	2	6	.200
Banks	5.58	3	5	.331	324	.288	.428	.370	6.06	2	8	4	0	0	2	5	31	3.93	2	6	.290
Casian	1.35	1	0	.894	28	.259	.296	.286	3.21	0	0	0	0	0	0	0	2	2.70	1	0	.767
Edens	2.71	6	3	.677	317	.236	.298	.329	3.37	9	15	5	0	2	4	0	33	3.89	6	3	.629
Erickson S	3.35	14	11	.578	888	.252	.371	.328	3.99	31	23	7	0	0	9	7	103	4.37	15	10	.584
Gozzo	21.60	0	0	.032	12	.583	1.250	.583	47.35	0	0	0	0	0	0	0	1	5.40	0	0	.049
Guthrie	2.76	3	2	.669	303	.215	.321	.274	3.02	4	6	2	0	2	4	2	38	4.56	3	2	.692
Kipper	4.19	3	3	.467	168	.268	.463	.343	5.41	3	1	2	0	2	2	0	21	4.89	3	3	.529
Krueger	4.24	7	9	.461	684	.263	.405	.316	4.57	13	21	3	1	2	4	1	108	6.02	10	6	.625
Mahomes	4.91	3	4	.390	302	.279	.439	.364	5.38	6	9	8	1	1	0	3	38	4.91	3	4	.452
Smiley	3.17	15	10	.604	970	.231	.356	.286	3.35	14	25	16	0	10	4	9	119	4.44	15	10	.618
Tapani	3.93	13	14	.500	911	.269	.405	.309	4.25	17	26	11	0	0	8	11	148	6.05	18	9	.662
Trombley	3.11	3	2	.614	194	.247	.402	.318	4.31	2	2	3	1	0	2	0	18	3.50	3	2	.511
Wayne	2.44	4	2	.722	210	.260	.390	.337	4.90	2	5	0	0	0	8	3	22	4.13	4	2	.702
West	6.67	1	3	.257	139	.276	.397	.381	6.37	1	2	0	0	0	0	2	14	4.45	1	3	.268
Willis	2.61	7	3	.693	313	.246	.347	.270	2.90	10	2	1	0	0	2	3	38	4.31	7	3	.692
TOTALS	3.70	86	76	.530	6086	.254	.382	.316	4.13	121	152	62	4	19	50	49	747	4.63	91	71	.563

Batting 'Splits' Records for Minnesota Twins

SPLITS for Mack

	G	AB	Run	Hit	2B	3B	HR	TB	RBI	W	K	IW	HB	SB	CS	DP	SH	SF	Avg	Slug	OBP	RC
vs LHP	58	128	25	38	10	3	4	66	24	11	21	0	1	6	4	1	1	0	.297	.516	.357	23
vs RHP	153	472	76	151	21	3	12	214	51	53	85	1	14	20	10	8	10	2	.320	.453	.403	90
Home	76	286	46	87	14	5	10	141	41	36	53	0	5	12	4	5	6	1	.304	.493	.390	58
Away	80	314	55	102	17	1	6	139	34	28	53	1	10	14	10	4	5	1	.325	.443	.397	56
Grass	61	237	42	79	15	0	6	112	26	22	42	1	8	11	6	2	4	0	.333	.473	.408	48
Turf	95	363	59	110	16	6	10	168	49	42	64	0	7	15	8	7	7	2	.303	.463	.384	66
April/June	74	299	54	89	17	3	9	139	39	27	54	0	7	12	7	3	4	0	.298	.465	.369	52
July/October	82	301	47	100	14	3	7	141	36	37	52	1	8	14	7	6	7	2	.332	.468	.417	61

SPLITS for Munoz P

	G	AB	Run	Hit	2B	3B	HR	TB	RBI	W	K	IW	HB	SB	CS	DP	SH	SF	Avg	Slug	OBP	RC
vs LHP	60	122	16	36	6	1	3	53	21	6	23	1	0	0	2	4	0	1	.295	.434	.326	15
vs RHP	118	296	28	77	10	2	9	118	50	11	67	0	1	4	3	14	0	2	.260	.399	.287	29
Home	61	193	21	53	10	1	8	89	36	10	39	1	1	2	0	8	0	0	.275	.461	.314	26
Away	66	225	23	60	6	2	4	82	35	7	51	0	0	2	5	10	0	3	.267	.364	.285	19
Grass	51	179	18	44	5	1	3	60	30	6	38	0	0	1	2	8	0	3	.246	.335	.266	14
Turf	76	239	26	69	11	2	9	111	41	11	52	1	1	3	3	10	0	0	.289	.464	.323	31
April/June	59	202	22	59	10	0	8	93	41	9	40	0	0	2	3	7	0	1	.292	.460	.321	27
July/October	68	216	22	54	6	3	4	78	30	8	50	1	1	2	2	11	0	2	.250	.361	.278	18

SPLITS for Puckett

	G	AB	Run	Hit	2B	3B	HR	TB	RBI	W	K	IW	HB	SB	CS	DP	SH	SF	Avg	Slug	OBP	RC
vs LHP	59	125	19	41	7	0	3	57	22	12	23	6	0	10	3	4	0	2	.328	.456	.381	22
vs RHP	159	514	85	169	31	4	16	256	88	32	74	7	6	7	4	13	1	4	.329	.498	.372	93
Home	81	325	58	113	17	4	9	165	54	22	53	6	4	10	2	10	0	4	.348	.508	.392	64
Away	79	314	46	97	21	0	10	148	56	22	44	7	2	7	5	7	1	2	.309	.471	.356	51
Grass	60	238	37	73	16	0	8	113	39	15	35	4	2	6	4	7	1	2	.307	.475	.350	37
Turf	100	401	67	137	22	4	11	200	71	29	62	9	4	11	3	10	0	4	.342	.499	.388	78
April/June	75	314	60	107	20	4	14	177	61	13	29	4	1	8	3	10	1	3	.341	.564	.366	61
July/October	85	325	44	103	18	0	5	136	49	31	68	9	5	9	4	7	0	3	.317	.418	.382	53

SPLITS for Minnesota Twins (all batters except pitchers)

	G	AB	Run	Hit	2B	3B	HR	TB	RBI	W	K	IW	HB	SB	CS	DP	SH	SF	Avg	Slug	OBP	RC
vs LHP	660	1227	165	337	68	6	19	474	158	116	194	14	6	38	20	31	10	19	.275	.386	.336	160
vs RHP	1671	4355	582	1207	207	21	85	1711	543	411	640	39	47	85	54	101	36	40	.277	.393	.343	591
Home	908	2723	375	769	132	18	56	1105	352	281	408	26	22	60	32	78	22	32	.282	.406	.351	388
Away	911	2859	372	775	143	9	48	1080	349	246	426	27	31	63	42	54	24	27	.271	.378	.333	363
Grass	695	2166	276	586	107	4	33	800	259	183	318	19	25	50	30	43	20	23	.271	.369	.331	269
Turf	1124	3416	471	958	168	23	71	1385	442	344	516	34	28	73	44	89	26	36	.280	.405	.348	483
April/June	832	2645	407	753	137	15	63	1109	380	256	334	27	23	65	28	65	20	27	.285	.419	.350	392
July/October	987	2937	340	791	138	12	41	1076	321	271	500	26	30	58	46	67	26	32	.269	.366	.334	361

Chicago White Sox

Don Malcolm

CHICAGO YEAR	1983	1984	1985	1986	1987	1988	1989	1990	1991	1992
W	99	74	85	72	77	71	69	94	87	86
L	63	88	77	90	85	90	92	68	75	76
WPCT	0.611	0.457	0.525	0.444	0.475	0.441	0.429	0.58	0.537	0.531
R	800	679	736	644	748	631	693	682	758	738
RA	650	736	720	699	746	757	750	633	681	690
PWPT	0.602	0.460	0.511	0.459	0.501	0.410	0.461	0.537	0.553	0.534
PythW	98	74	83	74	81	66	75	87	90	86
PythL	64	88	79	88	81	96	87	75	72	76
LUCK	1	0	2	-2	-4	5	-6	7	-3	0

Defensive Efficiency Record: .7095

I LOVE A PARADE

Yes, I do. Especially if it's accompanied by a merry-go-round. Two things that are inherently incompatible, you say? This is not a surprise to my friends. They've been saying that I'm inherently incompatible with myself. I can't disagree. I've been that way as long as I can remember.

But a parade can be a merry-go-round. Just ask Gene Lamont after this season. After he will have finished parading in new starting pitchers, old starting pitchers, young starting pitchers, bad starting pitchers. His head will be swimming. He will be walking in circles. Talking in riddles. Organ grinders, hurdy-gurdys, and concertinas will ring incessantly in his ears.

—Step right up, three throws for a quarter. Win a prize for your girlfriend. Just aim it at Karkovice, our dancing bear, and see if you can get within three city blocks of the strike zone. Don't be bashful, son, it's easy. Just aim and throw! Pay no attention to the man behind the screen, he's just calling balls and strikes. Out of purely scientific interest. No, no, no, now, aim at the dancing bear. Yes, that's right. Aim, take aim, now rear back and—throw!! No, no, son, you gotta keep the ball on the fairgrounds at least. Somewhere within reach of the quivering dancing bear. You can do it, you look so big and strong, how can you miss? OK, easy now, relax, no pressure (your girlfriend looks a little worried there son, come on now, you wouldn't want to disappoint her now, would you??), no pressure, easy, aim, wind, and—well, son, maybe you better try lawn bowling or tiddlywinks or something.

Yes, yes indeed. The parade is going to start early, the carnival of dead souls (Nikolai Gogol and Candace Hilligloss fans, allow me to introduce you) will rise up and create the most mordantly festive atmosphere ever seen on the south side of Chicago. After all, a funeral is a kind of parade. Gene Lamont, the Christmas baby, will not have a friend in Jesus as he endures this season in

Position	92 Starter	TWAR	93 Starter	TWAR
Catcher	Karkovice	1.66	Karkovice	1.66
First base	Thomas	7.63	Thomas	7.63
Second base	Sax	0.32	Sax	0.32
Third base	Ventura	6.66	Ventura	6.66
Shortstop	Grebeck	2.90	Guillen	0.12
Left field	Raines	6.89	Raines	6.89
Center field	Johnson, L.	3.24	Johnson, L.	3.24
Right field	Abner	1.46	Burks	1.36
	Newson	0.83		
DH	Bell, G.	1.88	Bell, G.	1.88
	Pasqua	1.03	Pasqua	1.03

hell.

The ex-catcher, ex-Detroit Tiger, ex-coach with the Pirates (where some managerial fairy dust was supposed to have rubbed off from Jim Leyland) is going to be seeing an endless procession (the term that those of you who don't love parades sometimes use to describe them) of home runs and walks. His team is going to be hitting homers and taking walks, but the opposition is going to be hitting homers and taking walks even more frequently. Which is not so good for the old job security, Gino my man.

But don't worry. They're holding that carnival barker's position at the Illinois State Fair open for you. You're a hometown boy, and there's always a place for a hometown boy—even if it is at the very tail end of the parade. And when that's over you'll be ever so helpful making sure the kids get on and off the painted ponies safely. No pushing, and remember only one ride per admission. No credit cards, either.

THE DOCTOR IS ON THE LAM

The Pitch Doctor removes his stethoscope after having examined all of the pitchers on the White Sox forty man roster. He dismisses all of them: after they have all marched out, manager Gene Lamont enters through a side door. The Pitch Doctor turns to him with a funereal expression.

—So how, um, bad is it, doc?

—Bad.

—Yes, I know that. (annoyed) That's why we brought them to you. You're the pitching doctor. You're supposed to take dead arms and graft them onto live bodies and make Frankenstein's monster into Cy Young. So what's this bad? Of course it's bad. Can't you do something?

—I can't fix them any faster than you guys can maim them.

—What do our chances look like? Can we keep a staff together?

—There's not a chance that you'll keep those arms together for more than half the season. That big guy...

—McDowell? Oh, no: what? He's my best pitcher!

—Yes, and you've been pitching him an awful lot over the last two years.

—Not just me—that other guy who had the job before I did. Dimbulb, I think, was his name.

—Torborg. Dimbulb is your nickname, I've been told.

—Who said that?

—Your bosses.

—Oh. Now about McDowell...

—Almost certain to experience arm problems this season. Too many innings. Too many pitches.

—Well, he likes to go all the way.

—That is outmoded thinking.

—You go to the mound and tell him that!

—Who's in charge, you or him? We've long since past the point in time when a pitcher just spat tobacco juice on his sore arm and kept throwing until he couldn't lift it.

—Aw, damn, you've been reading Ball Four again.

—Yes, and Bouton was right. It's much better to throw the knuckleball. You should have kept Charlie Hough.

—But he's so old! He's 45—

—And still pitching. He'll still be pitching long after you've

reduced Jack McDowell's arm to hamburger.

—Don't say that!! Our chances to win the division are riding on him.

—Then you'd better get another horse. The rest of your staff isn't exactly in the pink, either.

—I know that Stieb and McCaskill have had arm troubles.

—And to their detriment.

—But we really think they can win for us.

—They'll be wildly inconsistent, and rarely get through six innings without giving up at least three runs.

—That's not inconsistent, that's—that's BAD.

—They are one and the same to the Pitch Doctor.

—But Fernandez and Alvarez are gonna be OK, right?

—One is wild in the strike zone, the other is just plain wild. You'll be visiting the mound so often that you'll want to get a golf cart. But don't! I can tell that you need all the cardiovascular stimulation you can get.

—I get enough just having to watch these guys pitch. But what about the bullpen?

—Thigpen is shot.

—I've often thought he should be. But what about the other two—you know, Radinsky and Hernandez?

—Likely to be your two best pitchers again. But if the bullpen has no leads to protect, what good will they do you?

—Say, are you a pitching doctor or a stand-up comic? I detect a whiff of cynicism in the air here.

—That's isopropyl rubbing alcohol. It's a common error. As are the terrible things that you and your ilk do to pitcher's arms.

—So what about the rest of the guys, the prospects. Any chance they can help out??

—Hmm...let me see. (consults his chart) Bolton. Yes, I think that's the one. He's not much of a singer, but he looks like he might be able to help you out. Just don't overuse him.

—OK, OK!! No need to get testy. What about Jason Bere?

—Too green.

—Ramon Garcia?

—Maybe as a long reliever. You haven't had much luck with long relievers, have you?

—Most of 'em can't pitch well enough to last long enough to be called a long reliever. Anybody else? Jason Bere, maybe, or Jeff Schwarz?

—Bere is a prospect. Bring him along slowly. A full year at Triple-A—and no more than 180 innings, do you hear me?? Schwarz is wilder than David Lynch's fantasy life. You'd better let him loose in the north woods with a sign saying "I killed Laura Palmer with a wayward breaking ball." Because he did, you know...it's true.

—You're a sick pup, Doc.

—And you should quit treating your pitchers like horses. Or else start taking them to a veterinarian.

BAN THE SAX

I mean it. Let's steal Bill Clinton's so that this hip trip can come to an end. I know that Rhodes scholars aren't really highbrows, but this is too much. I think that Fats Waller should've been president.

Oh, sorry—wrong Sax. (Don't know how I get off on these tangents.) Bill's isn't really that bad—it's just that a little of it goes a long way. Which is not the case with Steve Sax. A lot of him goes a very little way. Can you spell overrated? They oughta run him outta Chicago dressed in nothing more than his stupid little jockstrap. (Am I getting down enough for you? Tired of me holding back?)

OK, here goes. The White Sox would be better off if they just up and released Steve Sax right now. I mean right this minute. Just call up the media and say: boy, were we DUMB. This guy is toothy and cute and as articulate as a dead fish and he can't hit, either. We should've seen it coming. But we were fools. We're eating the money because having him around any longer is going to cost us a fortune in Mylanta.

The White Sox have a much better player on their bench. His name is Craig Grebeck. You might remember him from last year. He played shortstop for about seven-twelfths of the season (give or take a twelfth) after Ozzie Guillen tore up his knee. He played the position quite well (his zone rating at short was .935, a nice hike up from the league average of .889). He can hit, too: his lifetime doubles per 100 PA is 5.5, which is well above the league average of 4.2. Not bad for a guy who's only 5'8".

Prior to the arrival of Sax, Grebeck played second base. And played it well. He played it well enough to have earned the right to the job in 1992. The White Sox, however, decided they were one sparkplug away from a humming engine. Hence Steve Sax. Thus the cracked block where the offense used to be.

OK, if you don't want to eat his salary, trade him. Send him to Florida or Colorado for some pitching prospects. Toss him to the Red Sox for Jose Melendez. Put him in a rickshaw and wheel him toward the Mets: they just love retread second basemen. Take Jeff Kent. He can hit some homers for you. But just get rid of him.

Steve Sax is one of the most overrated players in the history of baseball. Yep, right up there with Freddy Lindstrom and Travis Jackson (two fellas in the Hall of Fame who shouldn't be). There are people that think of him as one of the great leadoff men. Those people, as Brock Hanke is fond of saying, have mush for brains. A great leadoff man gets on base: .380 or higher is about right for greatness. Sax has a lifetime OBP of .336. Not good enough. A great leadoff man, at least by the partial thought process that passes for theory in baseball, is a high percentage stealer (i.e. upwards of 80%, like, for example, Tim Raines—85%). Sax has a lifetime SB success rate of 71%. Not good enough. Great leadoff men work the count and take walks (like Rickey Henderson—15.8%). Steve Sax has a lifetime walk percentage of 7.5%. Not even CLOSE to good enough.

Any sportswriter who casts a Hall of Fame vote for this guy should be drummed out of the BBWAA.

Yo, White Sox! Dump this guy! Make the south side a safer place to live. Give yourself a fighting chance to at least surface in the pennant race for a couple months. Cash him in while there are still some suckers out there willing to take him. Don't make the Pitching Doctor switch smocks and show you how the vital signs of your offense are putting your chances of contending on the critical list. Get on the phone! Get it done! Take out the trash!!

WHY THE WHITE SOX WON'T WIN WITHOUT WARREN

Alliteration is awfully annoying, ain't it? But in this age of short attention spans, there's just no other way. Forgive me later, first read this.

The White Sox have four players who walk a ton. Three of them you've heard of.

These four players combined for 333 of the White Sox' 622 bases on balls in 1992. 622 is a good total, but it could be even better. (The White Sox are in the upper echelon of AL teams with respect to bases on balls: Oakland, Detroit, and Baltimore are their companions.)

It could be even better, because one of the four White Sox walkmen only played about 25% of the season last year. The three you've heard of (Frank Thomas, 122 walks; Robin Ventura, 93 walks; Tim Raines 81 walks) played full-time. If the fourth man got to play full time, he'd add another 70 walks to the team total, which would produce a net gain of 50-60 all by itself and would help the offense.

But it probably won't happen. You see, the White Sox want more power in their outfield. The fourth player is a 5'7", 190 lb. right fielder named Warren Newson (see, I told you that you haven't heard of him). Warren is not most people's idea of a power hitter, although he has a lot more power than you'd first think.

But the White Sox want real power. They want someone who's proven they can hit 20 homers. This walking thing? Too intangible. They want to see those dingers. They want double figures there. The fact that triple figures in walks is really worth more hasn't quite registered with them.

Oh, it's OK that Frank and Robin and Tim walk as far as the White Sox are concerned. Just so it doesn't interfere with their hitting. (Just so it doesn't—?) Yikes. Players like Thomas and Ventura and Raines are special. They are walkmen. Just because you can hit .300 or hit 35-50 doubles, or steal 40-70 bases, just because you have significant offensive talents doesn't mean that you have the mental abilities needed to work the count and draw lots of walks. Baseball seldom nurtures a player who hits .220 but can walk. They don't often seem to understand that a .380 OBP from a guy hitting .230 is worth more than a .310 OBP from a guy hitting .270.

Warren Newson is a walkman. He drew 37 walks in 173 plate appearances for the White Sox last year. His lifetime major league walk percentage is 19.5%. Warren Newson is a serious walkman.

Yes, he hit just .221 last year. He was on base .380. Instead of playing him full time, the White Sox shuttled him in and out, playing Dan Pasqua (.211 last year, but he can hit homers), Shawn Abner (.227 lifetime average and a 4.9% walk average), and Mike Huff (.209 last year, with a .273 OBP).

I've written a lot about Newson's minor league stats and the situation on the White Sox in a sidebar that accompanies my "Walkmen" article, which you'll find in the General Essay section of the book. Suffice it to say that I think Warren Newson is the perfect #2 hitter for this team. His ability to take pitches and work the count will aid Tim Raines in stealing bases (not that Raines needs a lot of help, mind you). His OBP will cause him to score a lot of runs, especially when he'd be preceding Ventura,

Thomas, and George Bell in the Sox lineup. Newson could probably score 120 runs in the #2 slot, if the Sox would play him there all year.

(Those of you with research skills are leaping up at this point. "Aha!" you say. "But the #2 hitters for the White Sox scored 111 runs last season. They're already doing well there! So why Newson?" Glad to see you're doing your homework, but the fact is that the White Sox cheated last year and used both Raines—their ostensible #1 hitter—and Ventura—the #3 hitter—in the #2 slot. They both did fabulously there, as they both should. Raines hit .355 batting second. The batting order slot stats reflect their presence, and if you examine the rest of their batting order positions—or BOPs, as I like to call 'em—you'll see that the rest of them don't look as good, because Gene Lamont was tinkering too much with his batting order.

You solve that problem, Gene, by dedicating 1993 as the year that you will give Warren Newson a full shot to play. Yes, I know you've signed up Ellis Burks. He had some very good years for the Red Sox before he lost the bubble, and then he got hurt. But in truth he's just as much of a gamble as Newson. Split the difference. Play Burks in center, Warren in right, and make Lance Johnson the fourth outfielder. Johnson is not good enough at getting on base to help in the #2 slot. All he has is speed and defense. Use him as a tactical, not a strategic weapon. The first job of a team is to score runs. After you've got a lead, you can employ the other skills to defend it.

You will not win with Raines, Johnson, and Burks in the outfield. You might win with Raines, Burks, and Newson, with Johnson as a floating sub. That pitching is pretty dire, as the Pitch Doctor so sourly noted. And Newson won't hit .221 if you play him full time. Bill James' projection has him at around .270, with an OBP near .400.

Do you want to win, White Sox? Then just do it. (No, Bo, no royalties to you or to Nike for the use of the phrase.) You can pay me later. (I'm not as much of a hardass as the Pitch M.D.) Make the world safe for walkmen. Adopt Warren Newson today.

Chicago White Sox Home Park Performance Factors															
	Outs	Runs	Hits	2b	3b	HR	W	K	SH	SF	HBP	IBB	SB	CS	GDP
Home LH Batters	.971	.924	.996	1.001	1.128	1.001	.879	1.118	.684	.763	.727	1.378	.952	.824	.884
Home RH Batters	1.005	1.011	1.034	1.055	.698	.962	.976	1.081	1.015	1.031	.971	1.292	1.248	1.164	.979
All Home Batters	.991	.981	1.010	1.022	.907	.980	.943	1.081	.915	.959	.914	1.233	1.077	.955	.944
Opp LH Batters	1.001	1.169	1.042	1.263	1.556	.929	1.129	.947	.978	1.201	1.361	.944	1.136	1.043	1.120
Opp RH Batters	.992	1.084	1.030	1.246	1.247	1.056	1.093	.981	.895	.997	1.327	1.894	1.060	1.058	.815
All Opp Batters	.998	1.116	1.041	1.267	1.358	1.021	1.091	.975	.930	1.037	1.315	1.083	1.091	1.051	.894
All LH Batters	.988	1.060	1.023	1.149	1.322	.939	1.015	.997	.852	.980	1.205	1.014	1.049	.939	1.007
All RH Batters	.998	1.048	1.032	1.139	.984	1.010	1.035	1.028	.956	1.018	1.166	1.456	1.145	1.108	.897
All Batters	.995	1.047	1.026	1.131	1.103	1.001	1.014	1.021	.924	.996	1.138	1.151	1.086	1.003	.922

	G	AB	Run	Hit	2B	3B	HR	TB	RBI	W	K	IW	HB	SB	CS	BRng Eff	GI DP	SH	SF	Avg	Slug	OBP	Runs Ctd
Karkovice	123	342	39	81	12	1	13	134	50	30	89	1	3	10	4	.338	3	4	2	.237	.392	.302	42
Thomas F	160	573	108	185	46	2	24	307	115	122	88	6	5	6	3	.472	19	0	11	.323	.536	.439	142
Sax S	143	567	74	134	26	4	4	180	47	43	42	4	2	30	12	.476	15	12	6	.236	.317	.290	52
Ventura	157	592	85	167	38	1	16	255	93	93	71	9	0	2	4	.377	16	1	8	.282	.431	.375	99
Grebeck	88	287	24	77	21	2	3	111	35	30	34	0	3	0	3	.339	5	10	3	.268	.387	.341	39
Raines	144	551	102	162	22	9	7	223	54	81	48	4	0	45	6	.507	5	4	8	.294	.405	.380	99
Johnson L	157	567	67	158	15	12	3	206	47	34	33	4	1	41	14	.543	20	4	5	.279	.363	.318	63
Pasqua	93	265	26	56	16	1	6	92	33	36	57	1	1	0	1	.429	4	1	3	.211	.347	.305	30
Bell Geo	155	627	74	160	27	0	25	262	112	31	97	8	6	5	2	.373	29	0	6	.255	.418	.294	69
Abner	97	208	21	58	10	1	1	73	16	12	35	2	3	1	2	.424	3	2	3	.279	.351	.323	24
Fisk	62	188	12	43	4	1	3	58	21	23	38	5	1	3	0	.357	2	0	2	.229	.309	.313	20
Newson	63	136	19	30	3	0	1	36	11	37	38	2	0	3	0	.567	4	0	0	.221	.265	.387	17
Cora	68	122	27	30	7	1	0	39	9	22	13	1	4	10	3	.576	2	2	3	.246	.320	.371	18
Huff	60	115	13	24	5	0	0	29	8	10	24	1	1	1	2	.474	2	2	2	.209	.252	.273	8
Sveum	40	114	15	25	9	0	2	40	12	12	29	0	0	1	1	.500	1	2	3	.219	.351	.287	12
Beltre	49	110	21	21	2	0	1	26	10	3	18	0	0	1	0	.533	3	2	1	.191	.236	.211	5
Merullo	24	50	3	9	1	1	0	12	3	1	8	0	1	0	0	.167	0	0	1	.180	.240	.208	3
Guillen	12	40	5	8	4	0	0	12	7	1	5	0	0	1	0	.429	1	1	1	.200	.300	.214	3
Jeter	13	18	1	2	0	0	0	2	0	0	7	0	0	0	0	1.000	0	0	0	.111	.111	.111	0
Hemond	8	13	1	3	1	0	0	4	1	1	6	0	0	0	0	.250	0	0	1	.231	.308	.267	1
Cron	6	10	0	0	0	0	0	0	0	0	4	0	0	0	0	.000	0	0	0	.000	.000	.000	0
Santovenia	2	3	1	1	0	0	1	4	2	0	0	0	0	0	0	.000	0	0	0	.333	1.333	.333	1
TOTALS	1724	5498	738	1434	269	36	110	2105	686	622	784	48	31	160	57	.451	134	47	69	.261	.383	.336	732

Sabermetric Batting Records for Chicago White Sox

	Ball Park Adjusted								Runs		Run/									
	AB	Run	Hit	2B	3B	HR	RBI	W	SO	Avg	Slug	OBP	Ctd	Outs	27o	OW%	OG	OWAR	DWAR	TWAR
Abner	208	21	59	11	0	1	16	12	36	.284	.351	.327	25	157	4.30	.488	6	0.80	0.66	1.46
Bell Geo	631	77	165	31	0	25	118	32	100	.261	.429	.301	74	500	4.00	.451	19	1.87	0.00	1.88
Beltre	109	21	21	2	0	1	10	3	18	.193	.239	.212	5	92	1.47	.100	3	-0.85	-0.16	-1.01
Cora	121	28	30	8	1	0	9	22	13	.248	.331	.376	19	98	5.23	.585	4	0.85	0.43	1.28
Cron	9	0	0	0	0	0	0	0	4	.000	.000	.000	0	9	0.00	.000	0	-0.12	0.00	-0.11
Fisk	188	12	44	4	0	3	22	23	39	.234	.303	.318	21	147	3.86	.434	5	0.46	0.01	0.47
Grebeck	288	25	79	24	1	3	37	31	35	.274	.396	.348	41	228	4.86	.548	8	1.67	1.22	2.90
Guillen	39	5	8	4	0	0	7	1	5	.205	.308	.225	3	32	2.53	.248	1	-0.12	0.24	0.12
Hemond	12	1	3	1	0	0	1	1	6	.250	.333	.286	1	10	2.70	.273	0	-0.03	0.02	-0.01
Huff	114	13	24	5	0	0	8	10	24	.211	.254	.276	8	96	2.25	.207	4	-0.51	0.36	-0.14
Jeter	17	1	2	0	0	0	0	0	7	.118	.118	.118	0	15	0.00	.000	0	-0.19	0.01	-0.19
Johnson L	563	70	160	16	16	2	48	34	34	.284	.380	.324	67	443	4.08	.462	16	1.84	1.41	3.24
Karkovice	343	40	83	13	0	13	53	31	91	.242	.394	.309	44	271	4.38	.497	10	1.48	0.18	1.66
Merullo	49	3	9	1	1	0	3	1	8	.184	.245	.216	3	40	2.03	.174	1	-0.26	-0.03	-0.29
Newson	134	19	30	3	0	1	11	37	39	.224	.246	.392	16	108	4.00	.452	4	0.41	0.42	0.83
Pasqua	263	27	57	18	1	5	33	36	58	.217	.350	.311	31	212	3.95	.445	8	0.75	0.28	1.03
Raines	552	106	166	25	10	7	56	82	49	.301	.420	.387	105	406	6.98	.715	15	5.49	1.40	6.89
Santovenia	2	1	1	0	0	1	2	0	0	.500	2.000	.500	2	1	54.00	.993	0	0.02	-0.01	0.02
Sax S	570	77	138	29	3	4	49	44	43	.242	.325	.296	56	475	3.18	.343	18	-0.13	0.45	0.32
Sveum	113	15	25	10	0	2	12	12	29	.221	.363	.291	13	92	3.82	.428	3	0.27	0.09	0.36
Thomas F	578	113	191	52	1	24	122	126	90	.330	.548	.447	151	418	9.75	.830	15	7.44	0.19	7.63
Ventura	589	88	170	43	1	15	94	93	73	.289	.441	.382	102	445	6.19	.663	16	5.17	1.50	6.66
TOTALS	5512	773	1470	307	40	110	720	632	805	.267	.397	.342	780	4333	4.86	.549	160	31.90	8.69	40.59

Pitching Records for Chicago White Sox

	ERA	W	L	Pct	G	GS	CG	ShO	GF	Sv	IP	R	ER	H	2B	3B	HR	BB	IW	SO	HB	WP	BK
McDowell J	3.18	20	10	.667	34	34	13	1	0	0	260.2	95	92	247	45	9	21	75	9	178	7	6	0
McCaskill	4.18	12	13	.480	34	34	0	0	0	0	209.0	116	97	193	31	8	11	95	5	109	6	6	2
Fernandez A	4.27	8	11	.421	29	29	4	2	0	0	187.2	100	89	199	30	3	21	50	3	95	8	3	0
Hibbard	4.40	10	7	.588	31	28	0	0	2	1	176.0	92	86	187	25	5	17	57	2	69	7	1	1
Hough	3.93	7	12	.368	27	27	4	0	0	0	176.1	88	77	160	25	4	19	66	2	76	7	10	1
Alvarez W	5.20	5	3	.625	34	9	0	0	4	1	100.1	64	58	103	13	0	12	65	2	66	4	2	0
Pall	4.93	5	2	.714	39	0	0	0	12	1	73.0	43	40	79	13	0	9	27	8	27	2	1	2
Leach T	1.95	6	5	.545	51	0	0	0	21	0	73.2	17	16	57	9	3	2	20	5	22	4	0	0
Hernandez R	1.65	7	3	.700	43	0	0	0	27	12	71.0	15	13	45	11	0	4	20	1	68	4	2	0
Radinsky	2.73	3	7	.300	68	0	0	0	33	15	59.1	21	18	54	11	2	3	34	5	48	2	3	0
Thigpen	4.75	1	3	.250	55	0	0	0	40	22	55.0	29	29	58	9	0	4	33	5	45	3	0	0
Dunne	4.26	2	0	1.000	4	1	0	0	0	0	12.2	7	6	12	1	0	0	6	1	6	1	0	0
Drahman	2.57	0	0	.000	5	0	0	0	2	0	7.0	3	2	6	1	0	0	2	0	1	0	1	0
TOTALS	3.84	86	76	.531	454	162	21	3	141	52	1461.2	690	623	1400	224	34	123	550	48	810	55	35	6

Sabermetric Pitching Records for Chicago White Sox

	Adj ERA	-Expected- W	L	Pct	BFP	Opposing Batters Avg	Slg	OBA	RC/G	GDP	SB	CS	PK	PKE	SH	SF	Supported RSup	RSp/G	W	L	Pct
Alvarez W	5.38	3	5	.347	455	.272	.401	.381	5.31	13	9	8	1	6	3	4	84	7.53	5	3	.618
Drahman	2.57	0	0	.700	29	.222	.259	.276	2.52	1	1	0	0	0	0	1	1	1.28	0	0	.171
Dunne	4.26	1	1	.459	54	.255	.277	.352	3.89	1	3	0	0	0	0	0	14	9.95	2	0	.818
Fernandez A	4.46	8	11	.436	804	.270	.405	.322	4.63	15	15	4	0	1	6	4	87	4.17	8	11	.419
Hernandez R	1.65	9	1	.850	277	.180	.272	.249	2.25	2	4	4	0	0	0	3	26	3.30	8	2	.767
Hibbard	4.60	7	10	.421	755	.277	.404	.337	4.61	20	9	6	0	1	10	6	77	3.94	6	11	.376
Hough	4.08	9	10	.480	751	.239	.373	.311	4.16	13	17	3	1	1	2	6	73	3.73	8	11	.407
Leach T	1.95	9	2	.801	292	.215	.294	.279	2.77	4	7	3	1	1	2	1	30	3.67	8	3	.743
McCaskill	4.35	11	14	.449	911	.242	.343	.325	4.04	12	12	9	3	2	7	7	110	4.74	12	13	.494
McDowell J	3.31	18	12	.584	1079	.251	.379	.307	4.01	12	29	16	4	4	8	6	158	5.46	21	9	.691
Pall	5.05	3	4	.376	323	.272	.410	.335	4.96	10	10	1	0	1	1	3	43	5.30	3	4	.476
Radinsky	2.73	7	3	.674	261	.243	.351	.347	4.32	4	1	3	0	0	2	1	22	3.34	6	4	.552
Thigpen	4.91	2	2	.390	253	.275	.374	.375	5.36	5	3	0	0	0	2	4	13	2.13	1	3	.134
TOTALS	4.01	79	83	.489	6244	.252	.371	.323	4.21	112	120	57	10	17	43	45	738	4.54	83	79	.514

Batting 'Splits' Records for Chicago White Sox

SPLITS for Grebeck

	G	AB	Run	Hit	2B	3B	HR	TB	RBI	W	K	IW	HB	SB	CS	DP	SH	SF	Avg	Slug	OBP	RC
vs LHP	44	86	3	25	8	0	0	33	9	6	8	0	1	0	2	1	1	0	.291	.384	.344	11
vs RHP	85	201	21	52	13	2	3	78	26	24	26	0	2	0	1	4	9	3	.259	.388	.339	28
Home	43	134	11	36	11	1	2	55	23	18	13	0	2	0	1	4	5	3	.269	.410	.357	20
Away	45	153	13	41	10	1	1	56	12	12	21	0	1	0	2	1	5	0	.268	.366	.325	18
Grass	75	246	24	71	18	2	3	102	32	26	29	0	3	0	1	5	9	3	.289	.415	.360	38
Turf	13	41	0	6	3	0	0	9	3	4	5	0	0	0	2	0	1	0	.146	.220	.222	2
April/June	61	191	15	49	15	1	2	72	21	21	21	0	1	0	3	4	8	2	.257	.377	.330	24
July/October	27	96	9	28	6	1	1	39	14	9	13	0	2	0	0	1	2	1	.292	.406	.361	15

SPLITS for Chicago White Sox (all batters except pitchers)

	G	AB	Run	Hit	2B	3B	HR	TB	RBI	W	K	IW	HB	SB	CS	DP	SH	SF	Avg	Slug	OBP	RC
vs LHP	806	1513	180	391	82	7	24	559	168	171	215	20	7	33	17	34	18	18	.258	.369	.333	192
vs RHP	1596	3985	558	1043	187	29	86	1546	518	451	569	28	24	127	40	100	29	51	.262	.388	.337	539
Home	873	2694	368	695	129	19	54	1024	341	325	348	19	17	74	31	70	26	35	.258	.380	.338	358
Away	851	2804	370	739	140	17	56	1081	345	297	436	29	14	86	26	64	21	34	.264	.386	.333	374
Grass	1423	4578	639	1210	217	31	97	1780	589	546	635	40	28	140	49	119	42	62	.264	.389	.342	632
Turf	301	920	99	224	52	5	13	325	97	76	149	8	3	20	8	15	5	7	.243	.353	.301	100
April/June	775	2463	310	623	119	14	42	896	284	299	366	20	12	71	36	59	30	33	.253	.364	.333	309
July/October	949	3035	428	811	150	22	68	1209	402	323	418	28	19	89	21	75	17	36	.267	.398	.338	423

Texas Rangers

Win Murray

TEXAS YEAR	1983	1984	1985	1986	1987	1988	1989	1990	1991	1992
W	77	69	62	87	75	70	83	83	85	77
L	85	92	99	75	87	91	79	79	77	85
WPCT	0.475	0.429	0.385	0.537	0.463	0.435	0.512	0.512	0.525	0.475
R	639	656	617	771	823	637	695	676	829	682
RA	609	714	785	743	849	735	714	696	814	753
PWPT	0.524	0.458	0.382	0.518	0.484	0.429	0.487	0.485	0.509	0.451
PythW	85	74	62	84	78	69	79	79	82	73
PythL	77	88	100	78	84	93	83	83	80	89
LUCK	-8	-5	0	3	-3	1	4	4	3	4

Defensive Efficiency Record: .6768

Adjectives with evocative qualities rarely surface when one is describing a baseball team. Flat, utilitarian words like "speedy" or "powerful" tend to pop into the mind, and, indeed, get used most frequently by laymen, sportswriters, and insiders alike. Even the occasionally overwrought phrase, like Thomas Boswell's "shaggy, laid-back, suck up a brew and hit two homers crew," used to describe his second favorite team of 1982, the Milwaukee Brewers, tends to be grounded in readily apprehendible imagery.

But neither Boswell nor anyone else has had to contend with the Texas Rangers. They are, well, enigmatic. This is a term usually reserved for young actors with dark looks and self-destructive tendencies. The Baseball Sabermetric, which I am honored to be joining, has championed the use of these types of unorthodox terms to describe attributes of a baseball team, following in the footsteps of Bill James, who once described the other Texas team as being like jazz ("jazz is usually played indoors," "jazz uses few instruments...the Astros use few weapons..."). Don Malcolm's description of the Rangers as an ungainly weimaraner (last year's edition) is still apt, even if the acquisition of Jose Canseco makes you want to change breeds; they're still ungainly, and boy are they enigmatic.

Some samplings from an enigma:

Three years ago many observers were raving about the Rangers' talented young starters: Kevin Brown, Bobby Witt, Jose Guzman, and Scott Chiamparino. That staff then promptly fell apart through injuries, ineffectiveness, and the sudden penchant for walking home the winning run.

Last winter the baseball press was raving about how the Rangers had the best young offensive lineup in recent memory, with Julio Franco, Rafael Palmeiro, Ruben Sierra, Dean Palmer, and Juan Gonzalez leading the way. That fearsome lineup then proceeded to fall to ninth in runs scored in the AL as Franco got injured and the veteran players slumped. Meanwhile, Kevin Brown and Jose Guzman combined for 37 wins, while the rest of the Ranger staff managed 40.

Position	92 Starter	TWAR	93 Starter	TWAR
Catcher	Rodriguez	0.13	Rodriguez	0.13
First base	Palmeiro	5.94	Palmeiro	5.94
Second base	Huson	2.65	Huson	2.65
Third base	Palmer	2.71	Palmer	2.71
Shortstop	Thon	0.98	Lee, M.	2.44
Left field	Reimer	3.63	Gonzalez, Ju.	4.56
Center field	Gonzalez, Ju.	4.56	Hulse	0.42
Right field	Sierra	4.11	Canseco, J.	3.62
DH	Downing	3.09	Franco	0.24

Nobody is raving this winter, except ex-manager Bobby Valentine, who's distancing himself from the enigma he created through misdirection and is probably looking for some butcher knives to start carving up Tony Perez. The questions about the Rangers are approaching bold type:

1) Can the offense return to its 1991 level of production?

2) Can the starting staff withstand the loss of 385 innings (Witt and Guzman) and produce an effective season?

3) Can the bullpen, one of the least effective over the past three seasons, finally become adequate?

There are no answers, just riddles. The Rangers have the benefit of having a very young offensive lineup. It seems as though Canseco and Palmeiro have been around forever, but they will only be 28 this year. In fact, other than Julio Franco, the Rangers have no offensive regular over that age. Palmer, Gonzalez, and Ivan Rodriguez are all still extremely young (24, 23, and 21 respectively), yet have collectively accumulated nearly 3000 at bats in their careers. Obviously, the Rangers' offense will very likely be better this year than last—but what kind of an offense can it be without a true leadoff hitter?

If Franco is healthy again, this problem might well be solved. His career OBP is .382, he was a fine basestealer prior to the knee injury, and he has good doubles power. The leadership factor also seems to be important: Palmeiro confirmed Julio's influence, especially with the younger Latin players, when he was quoted as saying that the team's offensive slump could be traced directly to Franco's physical and psychological absence from the team.

Should Franco not be ready, the leadoff slot and second base will be a big hole for the club. Jeff Frye, who played second for much of '92, is an adequate fielder, but his hitting is still a question mark. His OBP (.320) and his lack of speed (one lifetime SB) make him far less than ideal as a replacement for Franco in the leadoff role.

Another possibility that the Rangers have been contemplating is to have rookie center fielder David Hulse lead off. Hulse, who will be 25 this season, has excellent speed and showed good range in CF during his September callup, but he walked in only three of 97 plate appearances. The left-handed hitting Hulse has yet to play a full season above double-A, so his .304 average in 32 games for the Rangers must be taken lightly. If Hulse sticks, he should bat ninth, not first.

With the retirement of Brian Downing (a truly great hitter), the only player on the Rangers' roster with experience batting leadoff is free agent signee Gary Redus. The former Pirate has always had those good secondary averages, but he is 36 and his OBP last year was down to just .320. The vague notion of a complex platoon may be forming in new manager Kevin Kennedy's mind, with Redus in left and Gonzalez in center against lefties, and Hulse in center and Gonzalez in left against righties. Gonzalez seems to prefer staying in center, however.

One of the most intriguing things about the Rangers is that their batting order positions in the middle of their lineup seem virtually interchangeable. Not counting Franco, who could bat 1st, 2nd, or 3rd, we have Palmer capable of batting 2nd or 6th; Palmeiro 2nd or 3rd; Canseco 3rd, 4th, or 5th; and Gonzalez 4th or 5th. Most of the batting order variation will probably depend on the handedness of the opposing pitcher, but certain trends have emerged that might help maximize the Rangers' offensive production.

Palmeiro is a natural number two hitter for this team. He is a good contact, high average doubles hitter who will take a walk if the pitcher gives it to him. But last year he became fixated with pulling the team out of its slump by himself and began to try to hit homers instead of doubles. He did hit more homers, but his batting average plummeted, his strikeout totals soared, and his slugging percentage actually dropped due to the sharp decline in his doubles totals (only 10 after the break). Having Franco batting directly ahead or behind him should snap Palmeiro back to something close to his '91 form.

Canseco had a bad year by his own standards, but it was still an effective offensive peformance. Jose may never repeat his monster 1988, or even 1991, but he was so far below his career norms that it seems unlikely that he'll do anything but bounce back strongly. Let's not forget that Arlington Stadium should be something of a better home run and batting average park for Canseco, who hit just 45% of his homers at home while with the A's.

Gonzalez is one of the very few major league players whose OBP can hover around .300 while remaining extremely valuable to his team due to the rest of his offensive contributions. As long as his HR production stays up enough to keep his slugging average over .500, and his BA stays above .250, he's an acceptable, if unorthodox, cleanup hitter. (Most players with his profile bat fifth.) The disturbing trend is that his walk and doubles totals decreased from less-than-stellar totals in 1991. Part of that problem seems to stem from the fact that Gonzalez has discovered that he can hit an ankle-high pitch into the opposite field bleachers. This discovery tends to make him swing at just about anything, and he has connected just enough to keep a strict disciplinarian like Bobby Valentine (NOT!!!) from getting on his case. Hopefully Kennedy can be tougher on him without causing the 23-year old wunderkind to sulk.

Dean Palmer is another slugger, but he has more plate discipline than Gonzalez. Unfortunately, he's had a tough time keeping his batting average over .200 due to the big cut that he takes when he does swing. He had a good first half, but hit just .197 with only 19 RBI after the All-Star Break. Intriguingly, he hit much better when batting #2 in the order (.265, .490 SA, .365 OBP), but it is hard to see him in the #2 slot with the other hitters on this team. He's a natural #5 hitter if he can get his average to .250; that's still a big if, though...

At the bottom of the order, we have Ivan Rodriguez (becoming known around the baseball world as "Baby Pudge" due to his youth and his arm), former Blue Jay Manny Lee, and either Frye or Redus, at least until Jeff Huson, who did so well last year shuttling between short and second, can recover fully from his injuries. The Rangers are looking for big, big things out of Rodriguez, but they've got to remember that he's still just 21, and they must take care not to expect too much or overwork him. Last season, even though he missed a month due to a rib injury, Rodriguez caught in 116 games, and the wear and tear took its toll on his hitting, especially his power (.435 SA before the break; just .294 after).

The Rangers would be thrilled if Manny Lee can match his offensive performance with the Blue Jays last year. His OBP was .343, and he hit .295 after the All-Star Break. Career data indicates that he'll probably drop back to around .250, with an OBP of .310, but his glove can probably carry that, at least until Huson returns and some kind of platoon arrangement can be devised.

Another intangible that must be factored into the Ranger enigma is new manager Kevin Kennedy. Having managed in the Dodger and Brewer organizations over the past six seasons, Kennedy has gone on record as saying he prefers a team that places a large emphasis on the running game. He will probably see the error of this notion early on. The only Ranger with demonstrated basestealing ability is Franco, the man coming off a knee injury. Huson had 18 steals last year and led the team, but he's not likely to be back until mid-season. Canseco's totals have dwindled due to his bad back, and the rest of the team has little speed. If Hulse makes the team, he will probably be made into the team's designated basestealer: his SB totals at double-A last year, though, were way off his numbers in the low minors.

The Rangers' pitching was, um, enigmatic last year. Brown and Guzman, as noted, had 37 of the team's 77 wins. Priority #1, however, was sealing the leaks in an embattled and controversial bullpen. It appears that this task has ben accomplished. Tom Henke, late of the Blue Jays, will be 35 this year, but he showed no sign of slowing down last year and ought to be at least as effective as Jeff Russell—assuming no overwork. Kenny Rogers will almost certainly continue to be the chief set up man, and he did an excellent job last season despite some periods of overwork. Free agent Bob Patterson adds a second reliable left-hander to the pen for the first time in what seems a millenium, and Matt Whiteside raced through the Ranger farm system last year to assume the closer role when Russell was traded to the A's. He looks like he'll stick as the right-handed set up man this year, and may get some chances to close: the Rangers want to develop him into their closer of the future.

With Guzman allowed to slip away to the Cubs (and wild man Bobby Witt included in the Sierra for Canseco deal), Brown and the ageless Nolan Ryan are the only holdovers from the Rangers' '92 rotation. Lefties Charlie Leibrandt (acquired from the Braves for third base prospect Jose Oliva) and Craig Lefferts (signed as a free agent) will take up two of the vacated slots.

Brown finally reached his potential and sustained a consistently good level of pitching throughout the year. His secondary skills—denying the stolen base, not giving up the gopher ball—all played a part in his 21-win season. He wasn't as effective after the Break (7-7, 3.71) but most of that can be attributed to a poor July. His ERA was 3.11 from August 1st to the end of the season. If the Rangers return to their hitting ways and Brown can duplicate last year's performance, he might win 25 games this season. Only a recurrence of arm miseries, a danger due to his 265 inning workload, cloud his future.

There can't be too much future left for Nolan Ryan, but at 46 the Express still has to be reckoned with. He was extremely erratic last year, with monthly ERAs that ping-ponged from 1.96 (July) to 7.16 (August) to 0.99 (September). All of his averages against were significantly higher than in recent years, but all of them were still better than the league norms. There isn't much precedent for determining when a 46-year old pitcher is losing his stuff, but Ryan's dominating months seem to show that he still has the ability to pitch effectively. Don't be surprised if there's one more no-hitter left in the Advil man.

Leibrandt could have a good year with Texas. He's out of the Launching Pad and will be a good fit with his right-handed flamethrowing counterparts. He had a very fine second half (8-4, 3.09) and was especially good on the road (6-3, 2.82) last year. Charlie was especially effective at not giving up the home run ball last year (only 9), and if he can carry that over into Arlington Stadium (which slightly suppresses homers by RHB), he could equal or surpass last year's win total.

Lefferts may not be best suited to be a starter, but his K/BB ratio was 2.5-1 in '92, so he was up to the task. He gives up a lot of hits per inning, though, and he'll really require a top-notch defense up the middle. Dan Smith and Roger Pavlik are the candidates for the fifth starter job, with the edge going to Pavlik at this point. Smith was rushed to AAA in '91 and had a horrible year there (4-17, 5.52) but rebounded strongly at Tulsa this season; he is likely to start the year in AAA again. He's a big, gangly southpaw who reminds people of Joe Magrane. If he's ready at any time during the season, it's possible that Lefferts will go back to the bullpen; this would give the Rangers a depth in relief staff that can only be termed unprecedented.

Despite the ungainly enigma that has been Texas Rangers baseball, particularly during the Valentine era, the team has strong audience appeal. They're never dull. The great young hitters provide constant excitement (after a homer, the theme from "Star Wars" is played while the batter is circling the bases) and there is the continuing wonder of Nolan Ryan. The fans also get to see Baby Pudge gun down would-be base stealers, and often try to goad opposing men on first into trying to steal. The scoreboard even has a great Baby Pudge graphic which is shown every time Rodriguez nails a runner. And now Canseco is here, adding a strange mystique and allure that is irresistably, er, enigmatic.

The word in Dallas is that the Rangers' management is working hard to time a winning season for 1994, the first year in the new ballpark. That would be fortuitous timing, and it's possible that they'll meet that schedule. The lack of starting pitching depth is the only thing that could seriously derail them. This season should be another one of contrasts and entertaining contradictions, but if the offense can move back into the upper 700's in runs scored, the Rangers have a chance.

Texas Rangers Home Park Performance Factors														
	Outs	Runs	Hits	2b	3b	HR	W	K	SH	SF	HBP	IBB	SB	CS	GDP
Home LH Batters	.960	.996	.964	1.049	.883	1.039	.983	.964	1.205	.967	.797	.905	1.117	1.218	.860
Home RH Batters	1.031	1.083	.987	.965	.618	1.116	1.010	.958	1.030	.902	.987	1.093	1.090	.999	1.070
All Home Batters	.990	1.037	.974	.985	.742	1.071	.998	.944	1.091	.923	.908	1.016	1.089	1.123	.998
Opp LH Batters	1.020	1.098	1.047	.978	1.158	1.054	1.120	.966	1.495	1.148	2.350	1.651	1.143	1.326	.998
Opp RH Batters	1.024	1.038	1.045	1.072	1.594	.985	.999	.997	1.193	.985	1.064	.780	.930	1.001	1.171
All Opp Batters	1.013	1.043	1.043	1.038	1.406	.968	1.041	.971	1.249	1.005	1.164	.942	1.009	1.129	1.034
All LH Batters	.988	1.044	1.003	1.011	.996	1.050	1.046	.964	1.337	1.054	1.046	1.128	1.131	1.257	.924
All RH Batters	1.028	1.059	1.016	1.018	.915	1.060	1.005	.978	1.108	.949	1.024	.909	.992	.997	1.122
All Batters	1.002	1.039	1.008	1.011	.998	1.029	1.019	.957	1.164	.965	1.018	.983	1.043	1.114	1.015

Conventional Batting Records for Texas Rangers

	G	AB	Run	Hit	2B	3B	HR	TB	RBI	W	K	IW	HB	SB	CS	BRng Eff	GI DP	SH	SF	Avg	Slug	OBP	Runs Ctd
Rodriguez I	123	420	39	109	16	1	8	151	37	24	73	2	1	0	0	.469	15	7	2	.260	.360	.300	43
Palmeiro	159	608	84	163	27	4	22	264	85	72	83	8	10	2	3	.443	10	5	6	.268	.434	.352	97
Frye	67	199	24	51	9	1	1	65	12	16	27	0	3	1	3	.467	2	11	1	.256	.327	.320	22
Palmer Dn	152	541	74	124	25	0	26	227	72	62	154	2	4	10	4	.346	8	2	4	.229	.420	.311	73
Thon	95	275	30	68	15	3	4	101	37	20	40	1	0	12	2	.409	2	3	5	.247	.367	.293	32
Reimer	148	494	56	132	32	2	16	216	58	42	103	5	10	2	4	.329	10	0	1	.267	.437	.336	72
Gonzalez Juan	155	584	77	152	24	2	43	309	109	35	143	1	5	0	1	.471	16	0	8	.260	.529	.304	90
Sierra	124	500	66	139	30	6	14	223	70	31	59	6	0	12	4	.470	9	0	8	.278	.446	.315	70
Downing	107	320	53	89	18	0	10	137	39	62	58	2	8	1	0	.371	7	0	1	.278	.428	.407	61
Huson	123	318	49	83	14	3	4	115	24	41	43	2	1	18	6	.556	7	8	6	.261	.362	.342	43
Newman A	116	246	25	54	5	0	0	59	12	34	26	0	1	9	6	.581	5	8	0	.220	.240	.317	21
Petralli	94	192	11	38	12	0	1	53	18	20	34	2	0	0	0	.263	8	1	0	.198	.276	.274	14
Fariss	67	166	13	36	7	1	3	54	21	17	51	0	2	0	2	.318	3	2	0	.217	.325	.297	16
Daugherty	59	127	13	26	9	0	0	35	9	16	21	1	1	2	1	.211	3	0	2	.205	.276	.295	11
Franco Ju	35	107	19	25	7	0	2	38	8	15	17	2	0	1	1	.370	3	1	0	.234	.355	.328	13
Hulse	32	92	14	28	4	0	0	32	2	3	18	0	0	3	1	.632	0	2	0	.304	.348	.326	11
Cangelosi	73	85	12	16	2	0	1	21	6	18	16	0	0	6	5	.429	0	3	0	.188	.247	.330	8
Canseco	22	73	8	17	4	0	4	33	15	15	24	1	3	1	0	.500	1	0	0	.233	.452	.385	14
Colon	14	36	5	6	0	0	0	6	1	1	8	0	0	0	0	.222	2	1	0	.167	.167	.189	1
Mcginnis	14	33	2	8	4	0	0	12	4	3	7	0	0	0	0	.000	1	0	0	.242	.364	.306	4
Harris D	24	33	3	6	1	0	0	7	1	0	15	0	0	1	0	.750	0	0	0	.182	.212	.182	1
Diaz Mar	19	31	2	7	1	0	0	8	1	1	2	1	0	0	0	.200	2	1	0	.226	.258	.250	1
Peltier	12	24	1	4	0	0	0	4	2	0	3	0	0	0	0	.500	0	0	0	.167	.167	.167	1
Stephens	8	13	0	2	0	0	0	2	0	0	5	0	0	0	0	.000	0	0	1	.154	.154	.154	0
Russell Jn	7	10	1	1	0	0	0	1	2	1	4	0	1	0	0	.000	0	0	1	.100	.100	.231	0
Maurer	8	9	1	2	0	0	0	2	1	1	2	0	0	0	0	.000	0	0	0	.222	.222	.300	1
Davis	1	1	0	1	0	0	0	1	0	0	0	0	0	0	0	.000	0	0	0	1.000	1.000	1.000	1
Russell Jf	1	0	0	0	0	0	0	0	0	0	0	0	0	0	0	.000	0	0	0	.000	.000	.000	0
Bannister F	1	0	0	0	0	0	0	0	0	0	0	0	0	0	0	.000	0	0	0	.000	.000	.000	0
Robinson JM	1	0	0	0	0	0	0	0	0	0	0	0	0	0	0	.000	0	0	0	.000	.000	.000	0
Mathews T	2	0	0	0	0	0	0	0	0	0	0	0	0	0	0	.000	0	0	0	.000	.000	.000	0
Springer	0	0	0	0	0	0	0	0	0	0	0	0	0	0	0	.000	0	0	0	.000	.000	.000	0
TOTALS	1863	5537	682	1387	266	23	159	2176	646	550	1036	36	50	81	44	.423	114	56	45	.250	.393	.321	711

Sabermetric Batting Records for Texas Rangers

	Ball Park Adjusted								Runs		Run/									
	AB	Run	Hit	2B	3B	HR	RBI	W	SO	Avg	Slug	OBP	Ctd	Outs	27o	OW%	OG	OWAR	DWAR	TWAR
Cangelosi	85	12	16	2	0	1	6	18	15	.188	.247	.330	8	77	2.81	.286	3	-0.18	0.35	0.17
Canseco	74	8	17	4	0	4	15	15	23	.230	.446	.380	14	58	6.52	.684	2	0.72	0.63	1.35
Colon	36	5	6	0	0	0	1	1	7	.167	.167	.189	1	33	0.82	.033	1	-0.39	-0.01	-0.40
Daugherty	127	13	26	9	0	0	9	16	20	.205	.276	.297	11	106	2.80	.286	4	-0.25	0.04	-0.21
Davis	1	0	1	0	0	0	0	0	0	1.000	1.000	1.000	1	0	?????	.000	0	???????	0.00	???????
Diaz Mar	31	2	7	1	0	0	1	1	1	.226	.258	.250	2	27	2.00	.169	1	-0.18	0.00	-0.18
Downing	327	56	90	18	0	10	41	62	56	.275	.422	.403	60	244	6.64	.692	9	3.09	0.00	3.09
Fariss	169	13	36	7	1	3	22	17	49	.213	.320	.293	16	139	3.11	.330	5	-0.10	0.15	0.05
Franco Ju	109	20	25	7	0	2	8	15	16	.229	.349	.323	13	88	3.99	.448	3	0.32	-0.08	0.24
Frye	203	25	51	9	1	1	12	16	26	.251	.320	.315	22	168	3.54	.389	6	0.24	0.39	0.63
Gonzalez Juan	598	81	154	24	2	45	116	35	139	.258	.530	.301	91	468	5.25	.584	17	4.06	0.50	4.56
Harris D	33	3	6	1	0	0	1	0	14	.182	.212	.182	1	27	1.00	.049	1	-0.30	0.08	-0.22
Hulse	91	14	28	4	0	0	2	3	17	.308	.352	.330	11	66	4.50	.508	2	0.39	0.03	0.42
Huson	315	51	83	14	3	4	24	43	41	.263	.365	.348	44	261	4.55	.514	10	1.58	1.06	2.65
Maurer	8	1	2	0	0	0	1	1	1	.250	.250	.333	1	6	4.50	.508	0	0.04	0.01	0.04
Mcginnis	33	2	8	4	0	0	4	3	6	.242	.364	.306	4	26	4.15	.468	1	0.11	-0.03	0.08
Newman A	246	26	54	5	0	0	12	34	24	.220	.240	.317	21	212	2.67	.267	8	-0.65	0.57	-0.08
Palmeiro	603	87	163	27	4	23	85	75	80	.270	.443	.362	102	464	5.94	.642	17	5.02	0.91	5.94
Palmer Dn	553	78	125	25	0	27	76	62	150	.226	.418	.307	74	444	4.50	.508	16	2.60	0.11	2.71
Peltier	23	1	4	0	0	0	2	0	2	.174	.174	.174	1	19	1.42	.093	1	-0.18	-0.01	-0.19
Petralli	190	11	38	12	0	1	18	21	32	.200	.279	.280	14	160	2.36	.222	6	-0.76	-0.29	-1.05
Reimer	490	58	132	32	2	16	58	44	99	.269	.441	.347	75	373	5.43	.600	14	3.46	0.17	3.63
Rodriguez I	429	41	110	16	1	8	39	24	71	.256	.354	.297	42	343	3.31	.358	13	0.10	0.03	0.13
Russell Jn	10	1	1	0	0	0	2	1	3	.100	.100	.250	0	9	0.00	.000	0	-0.12	0.02	-0.09
Sierra	501	68	140	30	6	14	72	31	56	.279	.447	.317	71	381	5.03	.563	14	3.01	0.30	3.31
Springer	0	0	0	0	0	0	0	0	0	.000	.000	.000	0	0	0.00	.000	0	0.00	0.00	0.00
Stephens	13	0	2	0	0	0	0	0	4	.154	.154	.154	0	12	0.00	.000	0	-0.16	-0.01	-0.17
Thon	281	31	69	15	3	4	39	20	39	.246	.363	.292	33	222	4.01	.451	8	0.83	0.15	0.98
TOTALS	5554	709	1398	268	24	162	667	560	991	.252	.396	.324	723	4428	4.41	.498	164	24.22	5.11	29.33

Pitching Records for Texas Rangers

	ERA	W	L	Pct	G	GS	CG	ShO	GF	Sv	IP	R	ER	H	2B	3B	HR	BB	IW	SO	HB	WP	BK
Brown Kev	3.32	21	11	.656	35	35	11	1	0	0	265.2	117	98	262	40	1	11	76	2	173	10	8	2
Guzman	3.66	16	11	.593	33	33	5	0	0	0	224.0	103	91	229	52	4	17	73	0	179	4	6	0
Witt B	4.46	9	13	.409	25	25	0	0	0	0	161.1	87	80	152	26	3	14	95	1	100	2	6	1
Ryan	3.72	5	9	.357	27	27	2	0	0	0	157.1	75	65	138	27	3	9	69	0	157	12	9	0
Pavlik	4.21	4	4	.500	13	12	1	0	0	0	62.0	32	29	66	7	4	3	34	0	45	3	9	0
Chiamparino	3.55	0	4	.000	4	4	0	0	0	0	25.1	11	10	25	5	1	2	5	0	13	0	1	0
Jeffcoat	7.32	0	1	.000	6	3	0	0	2	0	19.2	17	16	28	6	2	2	5	0	6	0	0	0
Smith Dan	5.02	0	3	.000	4	2	0	0	1	0	14.1	8	8	18	7	0	1	8	1	5	0	0	0
Burns	3.84	3	5	.375	35	10	0	0	9	1	103.0	54	44	97	26	2	8	32	1	55	4	5	0
Rogers	3.09	3	6	.333	81	0	0	0	38	6	78.2	32	27	80	17	1	7	26	8	70	0	4	1
Russell Jf	1.91	2	3	.400	51	0	0	0	42	28	56.2	14	12	51	9	1	3	22	3	43	2	3	0
Robinson JM	5.72	4	4	.500	16	4	0	0	2	0	45.2	30	29	50	10	0	6	21	1	18	0	6	1
Bohanon	6.31	1	1	.500	18	7	0	0	3	0	45.2	38	32	57	7	2	7	25	0	29	1	2	0
Nunez E	5.52	0	2	.000	39	0	0	0	11	3	45.2	29	28	51	11	3	5	16	0	39	2	5	0
Mathews T	5.95	2	4	.333	40	0	0	0	11	0	42.1	29	28	48	13	0	4	31	3	26	1	2	1
Bannister F	6.32	1	1	.500	36	0	0	0	8	0	37.0	27	26	39	11	0	3	21	6	30	3	3	0
Whiteside	1.93	1	1	.500	20	0	0	0	8	4	28.0	8	6	26	6	0	1	11	2	13	0	2	0
Leon D	5.89	1	1	.500	15	0	0	0	3	0	18.1	14	12	18	2	1	5	10	0	15	3	0	0
Fireovid	4.05	1	0	1.000	3	0	0	0	0	0	6.2	5	3	10	1	1	0	4	2	0	0	0	0
Manuel	4.76	1	0	1.000	3	0	0	0	0	0	5.2	3	3	6	1	0	2	1	0	9	1	0	0
McCullers	5.40	1	0	1.000	5	0	0	0	1	0	5.0	4	3	1	0	0	0	8	0	3	0	0	0
Rosenthal	7.71	0	0	.000	6	0	0	0	2	0	4.2	4	4	7	1	0	1	2	0	1	0	1	0
Campbell	9.82	0	1	.000	1	0	0	0	0	0	3.2	4	4	3	1	0	1	2	0	2	0	0	0
Carman	7.71	0	0	.000	2	0	0	0	1	0	2.1	3	2	4	0	0	0	0	0	2	0	0	0
Alexander G	27.00	1	0	1.000	3	0	0	0	1	0	1.2	5	5	5	1	0	1	1	0	1	0	0	0
TOTALS	4.10	77	85	.475	521	162	19	1	143	42	1460.1	753	665	1471	287	29	113	598	30	1034	48	72	6

Sabermetric Pitching Records for Texas Rangers

	Adj ERA	Expected W	Expected L	Expected Pct	BFP	Avg	Slg	OBA	RC/G	GDP	SB	CS	PK	PKE	SH	SF	Supported RSup	Supported RSp/G	W	L	Pct
Alexander G	27.00	0	1	.021	12	.500	.900	.500	26.51	0	0	0	0	0	0	1	1	5.40	0	1	.032
Bannister F	6.57	1	1	.263	173	.281	.424	.371	6.18	1	3	1	0	1	3	7	16	3.89	0	2	.224
Bohanon	6.50	1	1	.267	220	.297	.464	.377	6.59	4	0	3	0	1	0	2	18	3.55	0	2	.197
Brown Kev	3.42	18	14	.568	1108	.260	.335	.316	3.49	28	7	12	2	5	7	8	140	4.74	20	12	.613
Burns	3.93	4	4	.499	433	.249	.387	.309	3.95	7	1	7	0	0	2	4	30	2.62	2	6	.268
Campbell	9.82	0	1	.138	15	.231	.538	.333	5.31	1	1	0	0	0	0	0	3	7.36	0	1	.317
Carman	7.71	0	0	.206	11	.364	.364	.364	5.68	0	0	0	0	0	0	0	0	0.00	0	0	.000
Chiamparino	3.55	2	2	.550	102	.260	.396	.294	3.38	5	1	1	0	1	0	1	6	2.13	1	3	.229
Fireovid	4.05	0	0	.484	31	.370	.481	.452	6.14	2	0	2	0	0	0	0	14	18.90	1	0	.947
Guzman	3.78	14	13	.519	947	.268	.399	.327	4.34	20	16	15	0	1	9	7	136	5.46	17	10	.633
Jeffcoat	7.32	0	1	.223	89	.350	.550	.379	7.56	1	0	1	0	0	2	2	8	3.66	0	1	.171
Leon D	5.89	1	1	.307	84	.254	.521	.369	6.70	2	1	1	0	0	0	0	9	4.42	1	1	.317
Manuel	4.76	1	0	.404	25	.261	.565	.320	7.43	0	2	0	0	0	0	0	7	11.12	1	0	.818
Mathews T	6.17	2	4	.288	199	.294	.448	.404	6.33	5	0	4	0	0	1	3	10	2.13	1	5	.089
McCullers	5.40	0	1	.346	23	.067	.067	.391	2.29	1	1	0	0	0	0	0	3	5.40	0	1	.452
Nunez E	5.72	1	1	.320	205	.279	.454	.337	5.82	1	1	1	0	0	0	4	11	2.17	0	2	.106
Pavlik	4.35	4	4	.448	275	.280	.381	.375	4.86	5	3	8	1	1	0	2	27	3.92	3	5	.400
Robinson JM	5.91	2	6	.306	203	.281	.438	.351	5.43	5	1	1	0	0	1	8	41	8.08	5	3	.606
Rogers	3.20	5	5	.600	337	.261	.392	.318	4.43	3	2	3	1	4	4	1	23	2.63	3	6	.357
Rosenthal	7.71	0	0	.206	24	.333	.524	.391	9.12	0	1	0	0	0	1	0	0	0.00	0	0	.000
Russell Jf	1.91	4	1	.809	241	.238	.332	.313	3.66	3	1	2	0	0	1	2	11	1.75	2	3	.409
Ryan	3.83	7	7	.512	675	.238	.341	.328	4.10	5	26	12	1	3	6	7	72	4.12	7	7	.488
Smith Dan	5.02	1	2	.379	67	.321	.500	.400	6.94	1	1	2	0	1	2	1	4	2.51	1	2	.171
Whiteside	1.93	2	0	.805	118	.245	.330	.314	3.61	3	1	0	0	1	0	1	13	4.18	2	0	.795
Witt B	4.63	9	13	.418	708	.254	.378	.354	4.67	19	17	8	0	1	5	8	79	4.41	9	13	.427
TOTALS	4.25	74	88	.460	6325	.264	.387	.337	4.52	122	87	84	5	20	44	64	682	4.20	72	90	.446

Batting 'Splits' Records for Texas Rangers

SPLITS for Texas Rangers (all batters except pitchers)

	G	AB	Run	Hit	2B	3B	HR	TB	RBI	W	K	IW	HB	SB	CS	DP	SH	SF	Avg	Slug	OBP	RC
vs LHP	830	1507	199	400	71	8	40	607	185	171	329	12	13	13	13	30	16	10	.265	.403	.343	213
vs RHP	1685	4030	483	987	195	15	119	1569	461	379	707	24	37	68	31	84	40	35	.245	.389	.313	499
Home	945	2727	317	689	131	15	71	1063	302	265	541	17	27	36	16	54	24	24	.253	.390	.322	350
Away	918	2810	365	698	135	8	88	1113	344	285	495	19	23	45	26	60	32	21	.248	.396	.320	361
Grass	1567	4602	539	1133	209	19	127	1761	511	445	861	33	38	63	35	89	47	38	.246	.383	.315	567
Turf	296	935	143	254	57	4	32	415	135	105	175	3	12	18	9	25	9	7	.272	.444	.350	146
April/June	901	2701	363	688	144	12	78	1090	345	290	476	19	24	47	23	57	22	27	.255	.404	.329	368
July/October	962	2836	319	699	122	11	81	1086	301	260	560	17	26	34	21	57	34	18	.246	.383	.314	344

California Angels

Don Malcolm

CALIFORNIA										
YEAR	1983	1984	1985	1986	1987	1988	1989	1990	1991	1992
W	70	81	90	92	75	75	91	80	81	72
L	92	81	72	70	87	87	71	82	81	90
WPCT	0.432	0.5	0.556	0.568	0.463	0.463	0.562	0.494	0.500	0.444
R	722	696	732	786	770	714	669	690	653	579
RA	779	697	703	684	803	771	578	706	649	671
PWPT	0.462	0.499	0.520	0.569	0.479	0.462	0.573	0.489	0.503	0.427
PythW	75	81	84	92	78	75	93	79	81	69
PythL	87	81	78	70	84	87	69	83	81	93
LUCK	-5	0	6	0	-3	0	-2	1	0	3

Defensive Efficiency Record: .6908

IT'S GOT TO BE A RECORD

And I certainly don't think that anyone is going to step up and claim it. The Angels are going to have to live with this one for a long, long time.

What the hell am I talking about? What record?

The record for the lowest batting average ever recorded by the batters hitting in the #4 slot in the batting order.

Are you ready? Remember now, this is the cleanup slot we're talking about.

It's—

No, you'd better sit down. Maybe take a tranquilizer. Check with your doctor (preferably not the Pitch Doctor) to see if your cardiovascular system is stronger than Gene Lamont's.

Yes, it's that bad.

Boy, is it bad.

It's—

Man, I gotta sit down. I'm feeling a little faint myself. Like an arrythmia or something. I think I'll go back and check the stats once more just to make sure it's not a misprint or something.

The Angels' #4 hitters made 128 hits in 640 at bats last season.

That is exactly a .200 batting average.

To make it worse, they walked only 29 times, for an on-base percentage of .235.

Position	92 Starter	TWAR	93 Starter	TWAR
Catcher	Fitzgerald	0.14	Tingley	-0.03
			Orton	-0.16
First base	Stevens	1.48	Snow	0.02
Second base	Sojo	1.53	Gonzales	3.01
Third base	Gaetti	0.77	Gruber	-0.54
	Gonzales	3.01		
Shortstop	Disarcina	1.27	Disarcina	1.27
Left field	Polonia	3.72	Polonia	3.72
Center field	Felix	2.16	Curtis	3.30
Right field	Curtis	3.30	Salmon	-0.20
	Hayes, V.	1.25		
DH	Brooks	-0.96	Davis, C.	3.93

As I said, no organization is likely to step up and say: "Oh, no, Don, we had a year where our cleanup hitters hit .188."

In the immortal words of Jim Gosger: yeah, surre.

Now you can imagine what the impact of this little debacle was on the Angel offense. The #7 slot had the highest number of RBI's (76). #3 and #4 each had 74. Oakland, on the other hand, got more RBI from its leadoff spot (77). The A's #3 slot drove in 114 runs, its #4 slot 105.

Here are the legendary fellows who helped set what is certainly the record for futility in the cleanup slot:

You gotta hand it to 'em, though: they were consistent.

The Angels' #3 hitters weren't exactly stellar, either. They managed to hit just .223, which can't be far from a record, too. The combined average for the #3 and #4 hitters was .211, which is incredible, to say the least. I wish I could say that I was making this up, but I'm not. (I seem to recall saying something about the lack of #3 and #4 hitters in that little romp of a piece last year, where Hanke and I were in the Matterhorn pool discussing why

| CALIFORNIA ANGELS #4 HITTERS, 1992 | | | | | | | | | | | |
Player	AB	H	D	T	HR	RBI	BB	SO	BA	SA	OBP
Brooks	274	59	12	0	8	34	11	38	.215	.347	.246
Gaetti	151	28	1	1	6	19	5	25	.185	.325	.212
Hayes	87	15	4	0	1	10	4	18	.172	.253	.209
OTHERS	128	26	2	0	1	11	9	32	.203	.242	.255
TOTALS	640	128	19	1	16	74	29	113	.200	.308	.235

the Angels were at least as waterlogged as we were. Give me credit for nailing this one right between the cross-hairs.)

RELIEF YOURSELF ON SOMEBODY ELSE'S LAWN

The two teams at the top and bottom of the list for relief innings pitched finished in a flat-footed tie for fifth in the AL West. The Kansas City Royals needed 551 innings from their relievers. Their second line starting staff had a record of 14-32. The bullpen spent most of its time on their feet.

The Angels used the second lowest number of relief innings in 1992 (388 2/3). Only the Brewers used less (385). The Angels' top four starters went 35-52, primarily because they got so little support from Angel hitters (particularly the #3 and #4 batters). Manager Buck Rogers got a little more than 6 1/3 innings out of every start.

The AL average for relief innings was 447 in 1992, or roughly 30.8% of all innings pitched. The Angels were at 26.9%, which means that they used their relievers at 87% of the league average. The Royals, by contrast, used their relievers at 123% of the league average.

It's kind of nice that two teams at such opposite ends of the spectrum would wind up with exactly the same won-loss records. It allows us to take a look at how these teams stack up in terms of the other clubs who have similar IP totals for relievers.

For the Angels, those teams are (AL only, remember): Milwaukee, Chicago, and Toronto. For the Royals, those teams are: Seattle, Oakland, Cleveland, and Detroit. The teams in the middle: New York, Boston, Texas, Baltimore, and Minnesota.

The figures aren't ironclad by any means, but I'd much rather be in the company that the Angels are keeping than the Royals. The average number of wins for a team that gives 90% or less of the league average in relief innings is (excluding the Angels) 91. The average for the teams in the middle is exactly .500 (81-81). The teams that use relievers more average 78 wins (not counting the Royals).

Don't bet the farm on figures like these, since they're only for one season, but the findings tend to make sense. The better your starters are, the less you'll need to go to the pen for long relief. An interesting breakout that could be done (with a little work) would

be the distribution of relief innings. There are 162 1st innings, 162 2nd innings, 162 3rd innings, etc., with maybe two or three lost from inning #5 on out due to rainouts. Then there are probably around 105-120 9th innings, depending on how many road losses there are, plus 10-15 10 innings, 7-10 11th innings, etc. How many of each of those innings, for a given team, are pitched by relievers?

I don't know, but the distribution of the Royals and Angels would be interesting to see.

Another thing that needs to be measured is what, if any, ping-pong effect there might be in relief innings. Does it hold steady from year to year for certain teams, or do the teams at the high and low end change places? A lot of this depends on the managerial style: if you're Roger Craig, you live for the quick hook, plus you like to change your pitchers' roles capriciously. If you're Tony LaRussa, you use the quick hook, but you keep the roles defined and separated clearly from day one. If you're Buck Rodgers, the quick hook is used far less, and the slow hook is among the league's highest.

(In case you've forgotten the definitions for quick hook and slow hook, here they are:

—A quick hook is the removal of a pitcher who has pitched less than six innings and given up three runs or less;

—A slow hook is when a pitcher has more than nine innings pitched in a game, or gives us seven or more runs, or when the combined number of innings pitched and runs allowed is greater than or equal to 13.)

The point of the above was that a team managed by Craig might always have high relief innings; a Tony LaRussa team could go either way; and a Buck Rodgers team might tend to show up with a below average number of relief innings. That data is not readily available at this time, but the research could be done to determine if there are managers who consistently ride their starters.

In 1992, it makes sense that Rodgers would have tried to do so. The injury to closer Brian Harvey took a lot of starch out of his bullpen. A makeshift bullpen was created with Joe Grahe and Steve Frey, but despite their 25 saves they cannot be considered a reliable bullpen. Grahe was much better in relief (1.80) than in his 7 starts, but his strikeout ratio (3.6 per 9 innings) is extremely low for a closer. One of the reasons Rodgers stayed with his starters so long is that his middle relief was spectacularly bad last year: Chuck Crim (7-6, 5.17) and Scott Bailes (3-1, 7.45) must have made him cringe every time they warmed up. Their combined BR/9 in '92 was 15.47. Somehow, Crim and Bailes logged 125 innings between them last year.

THE BIG TRADE

In 1993 the Angels won't have as much starting pitching, since over the winter they unloaded Jim Abbott to the Yankees for first basemen J.T. Snow and pitchers Jerry Nielsen and Russ Springer. All three players are going to have to be counted on to contribute.

Snow is a first basemen whose hitting credentials seem first-rate. Moderate power, good strike zone judgement, high average: it all looks good, but so did Lee Stevens at one point, and now look where he is. The STATS projection for Snow, extrapolated out to full playing time, gives Snow a 15 HR, 80 RBI season with a batting average around .270. The Angels would take that right about now.

Nielsen is a lefty reliever, something that the Halos really need. Unfortunately, the 26-year old proved to be very wild in his September callup with the Yanks (18 BB in 20 IP). He was extremely effective at AA and AAA last season, however (a combined 1.24 ERA).

Springer, a 24-year old right hander, is going to take Abbott's spot in the rotation whether he's ready or not. He was jumped up into AAA after just a couple of starts in AA, but more than held his own (8-5, 2.69 ERA). He has averaged 8.2 strikeouts per nine innings in slightly less than 400 minor league IP. The Yankees used him in relief last year, a role he had never experienced in the minors, so it's hard to judge his performance. The Angels will just have to trot him out there and hope that he brings his strikeout pitch with him to the majors.

That's the big deal, a standard one for a team in trouble: stars for prospects, one able body for three willing ones. Snow does not look like he'll be the cleanup hitter that the Angels need, but he might evolve into the #3 hitter. (Actually, based on what we saw earlier, he'd do just fine as the cleanup hitter.)

However, the #4 slot will probably be occupied by Chili Davis, now entering his second tour of duty with the Halos after a two-year hiatus in Minnesota. Chili has been in an on and off power pattern for the past four seasons, so the Angels are hoping that this will again prove to be an "on year." They'd be thrilled if he had a season like the one he came up with in 1991 (64 extrabase hits, 29 HR, 93 RBI, 95 walks, .277 BA, .385 OBP). One encouraging thing about Davis' recent offensive profile is that he's continuing to draw walks: he kept his OBP up in the .380s again last season, despite a drop in power, and it is on-base that the Angels really need.

One suspects that the Angels will field an opening day lineup that looks like this:

1. Polonia, lf
2. Curtis, cf
3. Snow, 1b
4. Davis, dh
5. Salmon, rf
6. Gruber, 3b
7. Gonzales, 2b
8. Disarcina, ss
9. Myers/Tingley, c

And, surprisingly to some, perhaps, this isn't really all that bad of an offensive team. It's got a chance to be significantly better than what the Angels trotted (read: limped) out there in '92. As a matter of fact, the STATS projections for this team, when added up and slightly tinkered with for batting order position variations, show a reasonably robust offense: 700 runs, 232 doubles, 20 triples, 110 homers, 554 walks, 156 stolen bases. This translates to a .251 team BA, .359 SA, and .318 OBP.

Now these numbers aren't going to knock anyone's socks off (what an image: has anybody stopped to think what something like that really means, anyway? What was it, a personal thermonuclear device used in the bedroom? I mean, what??). But Whitey Herzog and Buck Rodgers will be dancing under the shadow of the Big A (raze it guys, it's an eyesore) if this comes to pass, because it will represent a significant upturn from last year's offensive debacle (.243, 579 runs, 88 homers, 416 walks). The 700 runs figure is probably somewhat high, because the RBI figure is only 603, and runs and RBI are usually about 45-60 apart. So if we give the Angels credit for a little more speed, we can say that the difference will be the maximum, and recalibrate the runs scored to around 665. This is still roughly a 90 run improvement over last year, and it might be better than that because Davis' projection seems a little on the low side.

But what this means is that both Snow and Tim Salmon have to pretty much deliver as advertised. And in order to do that, they'll need to be just handed their jobs and told to make the necessary adjustments.

STAN IS A MAN

But if any of the outfielders falter, the Angels have made one of those subtle acquisitions that can work miracles—well, maybe just a minor miracle. Many of you remember my affection for Stan Javier, the speedy son of Cardinal second baseman Julian Javier. You may also recall my chagrin when the Dodgers signed Brett Butler in 1991, leaving no place for Stan to play. The results for Stan were about what could be expected: with limited playing time, and having felt that he'd proved his worth with a fine 1990 seaon, Stan slumped badly.

Even with massive injuries to the Dodgers outfield last season, Stan remained in the doghouse and was relegated to spot duty. He caught a break in July when the Phillies' Lenny Dykstra, ever injury-prone, got hurt again. The Dodgers sent Javier to the Phillies while they were visiting Dodger Stadium, and Stan promptly went to work on his old team, collecting nine hits in the four games.

Stan hit a little over .260 with the Phillies (a slump in September dropped him from the solid .280 he'd been hitting) and showed that he still had something to offer. An accomplished outfielder who can play all three positions well, Stan is an ideal fourth outfielder who is probably at his best if he gets 350-400 at bats a season. The Angels will probably use him to spell all three of their starters, plus Chili Davis (by moving Salmon to DH and having Javier play right). In this way, Stan could start about 100 games, and either pinch-hit or come in as a late-inning defensive replacement for his old Oakland buddy, Luis Polonia (not so gifted with the glove).

It's a perfect fit for Stan, and I couldn't be happier. It might make it possible to listen to the Angels' games on the radio again.

California Angels Home Park Performance Factors

	Outs	Runs	Hits	2b	3b	HR	W	K	SH	SF	HBP	IBB	SB	CS	GDP
Home LH Batters	1.014	.996	1.014	.928	.644	1.289	.983	1.010	1.251	.720	.787	1.819	1.072	.936	.834
Home RH Batters	.989	.867	.935	.986	1.343	.929	.981	1.056	.895	.894	1.102	1.060	.852	.967	1.117
All Home Batters	.992	.904	.958	.971	.997	.967	.982	1.031	.962	.841	1.048	1.416	.943	.923	1.030
Opp LH Batters	.960	1.132	1.047	1.044	1.204	1.131	1.145	.978	1.082	1.746	1.343	1.186	.822	.572	.815
Opp RH Batters	1.034	1.020	1.011	1.198	1.007	1.139	1.113	1.044	.908	1.116	1.258	1.040	.900	.874	1.087
All Opp Batters	1.016	1.038	1.014	1.120	1.162	1.126	1.108	1.032	.984	1.154	1.295	1.096	.906	.832	1.013
All LH Batters	.985	1.069	1.032	.983	.907	1.167	1.057	.993	1.179	.981	1.235	1.448	.959	.800	.824
All RH Batters	1.010	.937	.969	1.083	1.157	1.026	1.042	1.046	.905	1.007	1.169	1.035	.879	.934	1.100
All Batters	1.004	.970	.985	1.044	1.074	1.050	1.045	1.031	.976	.992	1.159	1.224	.933	.891	1.020

Conventional Batting Records for California Angels

	G	AB	Run	Hit	2B	3B	HR	TB	RBI	W	K	IW	HB	SB	CS	BRng Eff	GI DP	SH	SF	Avg	Slug	OBP	Runs Ctd
Fitzgerald	95	189	19	40	2	0	6	60	17	22	34	0	0	2	2	.300	4	3	0	.212	.317	.294	18
Stevens	106	312	25	69	19	0	7	109	37	29	64	6	1	1	4	.314	4	1	2	.221	.349	.288	31
Sojo	106	368	37	100	12	3	7	139	43	14	24	0	1	7	11	.472	14	7	1	.272	.378	.299	35
Gaetti	130	456	41	103	13	2	12	156	48	21	79	4	6	3	1	.365	9	0	3	.226	.342	.267	41
Disarcina	157	518	48	128	19	0	3	156	42	20	50	0	7	9	7	.538	15	5	3	.247	.301	.283	41
Polonia	149	577	83	165	17	4	0	190	35	45	64	6	1	51	21	.533	17	8	4	.286	.329	.337	64
Felix	139	509	63	125	22	5	9	184	72	33	128	5	2	8	8	.493	9	5	9	.246	.361	.289	52
Hayes V	94	307	35	69	17	1	4	100	29	37	54	4	0	11	6	.473	9	3	3	.225	.326	.305	31
Brooks	82	306	28	66	13	0	8	103	36	12	46	3	1	3	3	.409	10	0	1	.216	.337	.247	22
Curtis C	139	441	59	114	16	2	10	164	46	51	71	2	6	43	18	.539	10	5	4	.259	.372	.341	58
Gonzales R	104	329	47	91	17	1	7	131	38	41	46	1	4	7	4	.432	17	5	1	.277	.398	.363	45
Easley D	47	151	14	39	5	0	1	47	12	8	26	0	3	9	5	.346	2	2	1	.258	.311	.307	15
Tingley	71	127	15	25	2	1	3	38	8	13	35	0	2	0	1	.250	4	5	0	.197	.299	.282	11
Orton	43	114	11	25	3	0	2	34	12	7	32	0	2	1	1	.375	1	2	0	.219	.298	.276	10
Davis A	40	104	5	26	8	0	0	34	16	13	9	2	0	0	0	.200	2	0	1	.250	.327	.331	12
Oberkfell	41	91	6	24	1	0	0	25	10	8	5	2	0	0	1	.545	2	0	2	.264	.275	.317	8
Rose	30	84	10	18	5	0	2	29	10	8	9	1	2	1	1	.412	2	1	1	.214	.345	.295	9
Parrish Ln	24	83	7	19	2	0	4	33	11	5	22	1	0	0	0	.000	1	1	1	.229	.398	.270	9
Salmon	23	79	8	14	1	0	2	21	6	11	23	1	1	1	1	.333	1	0	1	.177	.266	.283	7
Ducey	31	59	4	14	3	0	0	17	2	5	12	0	0	2	3	.444	1	0	1	.237	.288	.292	5
Morris Jn	43	57	4	11	1	0	1	15	3	4	11	1	1	1	0	.375	0	1	0	.193	.263	.258	4
Gonzalez Jo	33	55	4	10	2	0	0	12	2	7	20	1	0	0	1	.417	2	1	1	.182	.218	.270	3
Rb Williams	14	26	5	6	1	1	0	9	2	1	10	0	0	0	2	.750	0	0	0	.231	.346	.259	2
Myers G	8	17	0	4	1	0	0	5	0	5	6	0	0	0	0	.000	0	1	0	.235	.294	.235	1
Schofield	1	3	0	1	0	0	0	1	0	1	0	0	0	0	0	.000	0	0	0	.333	.333	.500	1
Langston	2	2	1	0	0	0	0	0	0	0	2	0	0	0	0	01.000	0	0	0	.000	.000	.000	0
TOTALS	1752	5364	579	1306	202	20	88	1812	537	416	882	40	40	160	101	.452	136	56	40	.243	.338	.301	532

Sabermetric Batting Records for California Angels

			Ball Park Adjusted					Runs			Run/									
	AB	Run	Hit	2B	3B	HR	RBI	W	SO	Avg	Slug	OBP	Ctd	Outs	27o	OW%	OG	OWAR	DWAR	TWAR
Brooks	306	26	64	14	0	8	34	12	48	.209	.333	.241	21	256	2.21	.248	9	-0.97	0.01	-0.96
Curtis C	440	55	110	17	2	10	44	53	74	.250	.366	.337	56	365	4.14	.536	14	2.51	0.79	3.30
Davis A	102	5	26	7	0	0	15	13	8	.255	.324	.336	12	78	4.15	.537	3	0.54	0.07	0.61
Disarcina	518	45	124	20	0	3	40	20	52	.239	.295	.277	39	423	2.49	.294	16	-0.88	2.15	1.27
Ducey	58	4	14	2	0	0	1	5	11	.241	.276	.297	5	47	2.87	.357	2	0.01	0.06	0.07
Easley D	150	13	37	5	0	1	11	8	27	.247	.300	.296	14	121	3.12	.396	4	0.21	0.44	0.65
Felix	508	61	123	23	5	9	69	34	132	.242	.360	.288	52	413	3.40	.437	15	1.33	0.83	2.16
Fitzgerald	188	17	38	2	0	6	16	23	35	.202	.309	.289	17	157	2.92	.365	6	0.09	0.06	0.14
Gaetti	457	38	100	14	2	12	46	21	82	.219	.337	.262	40	369	2.93	.365	14	0.21	0.56	0.77
Gonzales R	328	44	88	18	1	7	36	42	48	.268	.393	.357	44	266	4.47	.573	10	2.19	0.82	3.01
Gonzalez Jo	54	3	9	2	0	0	1	7	20	.167	.204	.258	3	48	1.69	.161	2	-0.34	0.12	-0.22
Hayes V	305	37	71	16	0	4	27	39	53	.233	.325	.317	33	251	3.55	.458	9	1.01	0.24	1.25
Morris Jn	56	4	11	0	0	1	2	4	10	.196	.250	.262	4	46	2.35	.270	2	-0.14	0.03	-0.10
Myers G	16	0	4	0	0	0	0	0	5	.250	.250	.250	1	13	2.08	.225	0	-0.06	-0.02	-0.08
Oberkfell	90	6	24	0	0	0	9	8	4	.267	.267	.320	8	69	3.13	.397	3	0.12	-0.06	0.06
Orton	114	10	24	3	0	2	11	7	33	.211	.289	.268	9	92	2.64	.319	3	-0.11	-0.05	-0.16
Parrish Ln	82	6	18	2	0	4	10	5	23	.220	.390	.261	8	66	3.27	.418	2	0.17	-0.26	-0.09
Polonia	576	88	170	16	3	0	33	47	63	.295	.333	.347	70	448	4.22	.545	17	3.23	0.49	3.72
Rose	83	9	17	5	0	2	9	8	9	.205	.337	.287	8	69	3.13	.397	3	0.12	0.27	0.39
Salmon	78	7	13	1	0	2	5	11	24	.167	.256	.275	6	67	2.42	.282	2	-0.17	-0.03	-0.20
Schofield	2	0	0	0	0	0	0	1	0	.000	.000	.333	0	2	0.00	.000	0	-0.03	0.01	-0.02
Sojo	368	34	97	13	3	7	41	14	25	.264	.372	.292	33	303	2.94	.367	11	0.20	1.34	1.53
Stevens	310	26	71	18	0	8	35	30	63	.229	.365	.297	34	248	3.70	.479	9	1.19	0.29	1.48
Tingley	127	14	24	2	1	3	7	13	36	.189	.291	.275	10	111	2.43	.284	4	-0.27	0.24	-0.03
Rb Williams	25	4	5	1	1	0	1	1	10	.200	.320	.231	2	21	2.57	.308	1	-0.03	0.09	0.06
TOTALS	5361	562	1288	211	21	92	520	434	909	.240	.339	.301	537	4392	3.30	.423	163	11.83	8.48	20.31

Pitching Records for California Angels

	ERA	W	L	Pct	G	GS	CG	ShO	GF	Sv	IP	R	ER	H	2B	3B	HR	BB	IW	SO	HB	WP	BK
Langston	3.66	13	14	.481	32	32	9	2	0	0	229.0	103	93	206	38	3	14	74	2	174	6	5	0
Abbott	2.77	7	15	.318	29	29	7	0	0	0	211.0	73	65	208	28	2	12	68	3	130	4	2	0
Finley C	3.96	7	12	.368	31	31	4	1	0	0	204.1	99	90	212	34	3	24	98	2	124	3	6	0
Valera	3.73	8	11	.421	30	28	4	2	0	0	188.0	82	78	188	38	3	15	64	5	113	2	5	0
Blyleven	4.74	8	12	.400	25	24	1	0	0	0	133.0	76	70	150	24	3	17	29	2	70	5	3	1
Robinson D	2.20	1	0	1.000	3	3	0	0	0	0	16.1	4	4	19	3	0	1	3	0	9	0	1	0
Hathaway	7.94	0	0	.000	2	1	0	0	0	0	5.2	5	5	8	1	0	1	3	0	1	0	0	0
Grahe	3.52	5	6	.455	46	7	0	0	31	21	94.2	37	37	85	12	0	5	39	2	39	6	3	0
Crim	5.17	7	6	.538	57	0	0	0	16	1	87.0	56	50	100	15	1	11	29	6	30	6	4	0
Eichhorn	2.38	2	4	.333	42	0	0	0	19	2	56.2	19	15	51	7	2	2	18	8	42	0	3	1
Frey	3.57	4	2	.667	51	0	0	0	20	4	45.1	18	18	39	4	0	6	22	3	24	2	1	0
Fortugno	5.18	1	1	.500	14	5	1	1	5	1	41.2	24	24	37	4	0	5	19	0	31	0	2	1
Bailes	7.45	3	1	.750	32	0	0	0	10	0	38.2	34	32	59	7	0	7	28	4	25	1	2	1
Lewis S	3.99	4	0	1.000	21	2	0	0	7	0	38.1	18	17	36	2	0	3	14	1	18	2	1	1
Harvey	2.83	0	0	.000	25	0	0	0	22	13	28.2	12	9	22	2	0	4	11	1	34	0	4	0
Butcher M	3.25	2	2	.500	19	0	0	0	6	0	27.2	11	10	29	2	0	3	13	1	24	2	0	0
TOTALS	3.84	72	90	.444	459	162	26	6	136	42	1446.0	671	617	1449	221	17	130	532	40	888	39	42	5

Sabermetric Pitching Records for California Angels

	Adj ERA	Expected W	L	Pct	Opposing Batters BFP	Avg	Slg	OBA	RC/G	GDP	SB	CS	PK	PKE	SH	SF	Supported RSup	RSp/G	W	L	Pct
Abbott	2.69	15	7	.681	874	.263	.349	.323	3.69	22	14	13	1	9	8	4	62	2.64	10	12	.444
Bailes	7.22	1	3	.228	200	.351	.518	.442	9.49	4	4	1	0	1	2	16	3.72	1	3	.180
Blyleven	4.53	9	11	.428	568	.285	.439	.326	5.02	11	10	4	0	0	3	5	55	3.72	7	13	.357
Butcher M	2.93	3	1	.642	125	.264	.364	.352	4.97	2	3	0	1	0	0	0	8	2.60	2	2	.394
Crim	4.97	5	8	.384	383	.293	.440	.355	5.48	8	7	5	0	2	3	4	30	3.10	3	10	.244
Eichhorn	2.22	5	1	.757	237	.238	.318	.294	3.25	4	3	2	0	0	2	3	22	3.49	4	2	.671
Finley C	3.83	10	9	.512	885	.278	.425	.359	4.95	28	21	18	1	5	10	10	85	3.74	8	11	.440
Fortugno	4.97	1	1	.384	177	.236	.357	.316	4.07	2	5	2	1	1	0	1	23	4.97	1	1	.452
Frey	3.38	3	3	.575	193	.238	.372	.330	4.19	3	3	3	0	2	2	3	32	6.35	4	2	.745
Grahe	3.33	6	5	.582	399	.246	.324	.329	3.54	12	7	5	0	0	4	4	37	3.52	5	6	.479
Harvey	2.51	3	1	.709	122	.208	.340	.275	3.51	1	2	0	0	0	2	3	2	0.63	0	4	.049
Hathaway	6.35	0	0	.276	29	.333	.500	.393	8.36	0	0	0	0	0	1	1	4	6.35	0	0	.452
Langston	3.54	15	12	.552	941	.242	.343	.305	3.47	23	21	10	5	9	4	5	94	3.69	13	14	.473
Lewis S	3.76	2	2	.522	160	.255	.333	.325	3.55	4	2	3	0	0	0	3	21	4.93	2	2	.587
Robinson D	1.65	1	0	.849	69	.292	.385	.324	4.09	4	4	0	0	0	1	0	7	3.86	1	0	.818
Valera	3.59	10	9	.544	792	.262	.386	.323	4.34	15	14	4	1	1	6	2	81	3.88	9	10	.490
TOTALS	3.72	85	77	.526	6154	.264	.382	.331	4.31	143	120	70	10	29	47	50	579	3.60	71	91	.436

Batting 'Splits' Records for California Angels

SPLITS for Curtis C

	G	AB	Run	Hit	2B	3B	HR	TB	RBI	W	K	IW	HB	SB	CS	DP	SH	SF	Avg	Slug	OBP	RC
vs LHP	58	122	16	33	6	1	6	59	22	26	18	1	0	13	5	2	0	2	.270	.484	.393	26
vs RHP	132	319	43	81	10	1	4	105	24	25	53	1	6	30	13	8	5	2	.254	.329	.318	34
Home	67	201	32	53	6	1	5	76	20	24	32	1	4	25	9	3	3	3	.264	.378	.349	29
Away	72	240	27	61	10	1	5	88	26	27	39	1	2	18	9	7	2	1	.254	.367	.333	29
Grass	117	367	47	93	13	1	7	129	31	39	60	2	4	36	17	8	5	3	.253	.351	.329	43
Turf	22	74	12	21	3	1	3	35	15	12	11	0	2	7	1	2	0	1	.284	.473	.393	15
April/June	57	169	20	45	6	2	4	67	21	20	24	1	1	10	7	2	1	1	.266	.396	.346	23
July/October	82	272	39	69	10	0	6	97	25	31	47	1	5	33	11	8	4	3	.254	.357	.338	35

SPLITS for Fitzgerald

	G	AB	Run	Hit	2B	3B	HR	TB	RBI	W	K	IW	HB	SB	CS	DP	SH	SF	Avg	Slug	OBP	RC
vs LHP	41	69	6	21	2	0	3	32	12	10	13	0	0	2	2	2	0	0	.304	.464	.392	12
vs RHP	68	120	13	19	0	0	3	28	5	12	21	0	0	0	0	2	3	0	.158	.233	.235	7
Home	46	92	11	19	0	0	3	28	7	11	17	0	0	1	0	3	0	0	.207	.304	.291	8
Away	49	97	8	21	2	0	3	32	10	11	17	0	0	1	2	1	3	0	.216	.330	.296	10
Grass	82	173	17	35	1	0	6	54	14	20	30	0	0	2	1	4	3	0	.202	.312	.285	16
Turf	13	16	2	5	1	0	0	6	3	2	4	0	0	0	1	0	0	0	.313	.375	.389	2
April/June	46	94	10	18	0	0	4	30	8	13	16	0	0	2	1	1	2	0	.191	.319	.290	9
July/October	49	95	9	22	2	0	2	30	9	9	18	0	0	0	1	3	1	0	.232	.316	.298	8

SPLITS for Gaetti

	G	AB	Run	Hit	2B	3B	HR	TB	RBI	W	K	IW	HB	SB	CS	DP	SH	SF	Avg	Slug	OBP	RC
vs LHP	54	124	12	31	6	0	5	52	15	8	13	2	1	1	0	2	0	1	.250	.419	.299	16
vs RHP	128	332	29	72	7	2	7	104	33	13	66	2	5	2	1	7	0	2	.217	.313	.256	26
Home	68	231	27	60	7	1	8	93	30	7	40	1	3	1	1	2	0	1	.260	.403	.289	27
Away	62	225	14	43	6	1	4	63	18	14	39	3	3	2	0	7	0	2	.191	.280	.246	15
Grass	110	378	35	89	12	1	10	133	41	17	66	2	3	2	1	7	0	2	.235	.352	.273	35
Turf	20	78	6	14	1	1	2	23	7	4	13	2	3	1	0	2	0	1	.179	.295	.244	6
April/June	66	240	20	55	7	1	5	79	19	13	42	3	3	3	0	5	0	1	.229	.329	.276	22
July/October	64	216	21	48	6	1	7	77	29	8	37	1	3	0	1	4	0	2	.222	.356	.258	19

SPLITS for Hayes V

	G	AB	Run	Hit	2B	3B	HR	TB	RBI	W	K	IW	HB	SB	CS	DP	SH	SF	Avg	Slug	OBP	RC
vs LHP	31	42	4	5	1	0	0	6	4	5	11	1	0	0	1	1	0	1	.119	.143	.208	1
vs RHP	92	265	31	64	16	1	4	94	25	32	43	3	0	11	5	8	3	2	.242	.355	.321	30
Home	50	162	20	39	9	1	2	56	22	19	28	2	0	7	2	6	1	3	.241	.346	.315	18
Away	44	145	15	30	8	0	2	44	7	18	26	2	0	4	4	3	2	0	.207	.303	.294	13
Grass	85	276	31	60	15	1	4	89	27	34	45	4	0	11	5	8	2	3	.217	.322	.300	27
Turf	9	31	4	9	2	0	0	11	2	3	9	0	0	0	1	1	1	0	.290	.355	.353	4
April/June	57	187	24	48	12	1	3	71	15	27	31	3	0	10	2	5	1	2	.257	.380	.347	27
July/October	37	120	11	21	5	0	1	29	14	10	23	1	0	1	4	4	2	1	.175	.242	.237	6

SPLITS for Polonia

	G	AB	Run	Hit	2B	3B	HR	TB	RBI	W	K	IW	HB	SB	CS	DP	SH	SF	Avg	Slug	OBP	RC
vs LHP	68	132	18	30	3	0	0	33	5	9	25	0	1	9	3	3	3	1	.227	.250	.280	10
vs RHP	147	445	65	135	14	4	0	157	30	36	39	6	0	42	18	14	5	3	.303	.353	.353	55
Home	69	266	38	76	11	3	0	93	19	22	32	3	1	21	13	11	3	2	.286	.350	.340	29
Away	80	311	45	89	6	1	0	97	16	23	32	3	0	30	8	6	5	2	.286	.312	.333	35
Grass	125	478	66	136	16	4	0	160	29	39	49	4	1	38	18	15	8	4	.285	.335	.337	53
Turf	24	99	17	29	1	0	0	30	6	6	15	2	0	13	3	2	0	0	.293	.303	.333	11
April/June	75	281	42	82	6	3	0	94	21	25	28	1	0	27	9	7	2	3	.292	.335	.346	34
July/October	74	296	41	83	11	1	0	96	14	20	36	5	1	24	12	10	6	1	.280	.324	.327	30

SPLITS for California Angels (all batters except pitchers)

	G	AB	Run	Hit	2B	3B	HR	TB	RBI	W	K	IW	HB	SB	CS	DP	SH	SF	Avg	Slug	OBP	RC
vs LHP	655	1250	137	289	44	2	25	412	129	112	222	9	9	35	21	29	14	10	.231	.330	.297	122
vs RHP	1628	4114	442	1017	158	18	63	1400	408	304	660	31	31	125	80	107	42	30	.247	.340	.302	410
Home	875	2637	311	658	100	10	44	910	289	204	415	12	19	80	55	64	28	23	.250	.345	.306	271
Away	877	2727	268	648	102	10	44	902	248	212	467	28	21	80	46	72	28	17	.238	.331	.296	261
Grass	1492	4545	490	1105	165	18	78	1540	454	358	726	34	29	129	88	115	48	35	.243	.339	.300	450
Turf	260	819	89	201	37	2	10	272	83	58	156	6	11	31	13	21	8	5	.245	.332	.302	82
April/June	819	2521	277	616	101	9	52	891	265	213	393	20	14	68	38	68	19	19	.244	.353	.305	266
July/October	933	2843	302	690	101	11	36	921	272	203	489	20	26	92	63	68	37	21	.243	.324	.297	266

Kansas City Royals

Win Murray

KANSAS CITY										
YEAR	1983	1984	1985	1986	1987	1988	1989	1990	1991	1992
W	79	84	91	76	83	84	92	75	82	72
L	83	78	71	86	79	77	70	86	80	90
WPCT	0.488	0.519	0.562	0.469	0.512	0.522	0.568	0.466	0.506	0.444
R	696	673	687	654	715	704	690	707	727	610
RA	767	686	639	673	691	648	635	709	722	667
PWPT	0.452	0.49	0.536	0.486	0.517	0.541	0.541	0.499	0.503	0.455
PythW	73	79	87	79	84	88	88	81	82	74
PythL	89	83	75	83	78	74	74	81	80	88
LUCK	6	5	4	-3	-1	-4	4	-6	0	-2

Defensive Efficiency Record: .6992

General Manager Herk Robinson still seems convinced that his Royals are just one or two players away from winning the pennant. It appears, though, that the more he trades and signs based on this assumption, the more players away from a pennant he gets.

After the 1991 season, Robinson decided it was time to trade longtime staff ace Bret Saberhagen, presumably because the Royals had not finished above fifth in the past two seasons with him. In 1992, the Royals proved to everyone's satisfaction that they didn't need Saberhagen to finish fifth.

This offseason, Robinson targeted one big starter and one big bat as being the way back to the top. They got David Cone—whom they traded away some years back, in a deal that was not Herk's fault—but didn't land Joe Carter. Robinson has been quoted as saying they still need a real power hitter. Someone like Danny Tartabull, perhaps?

The bad news that Mr. Herk Robinson still isn't prepared to accept is that the Royals are a good deal more than "one big bat" away from winning the AL West. I will attempt to quantify the distance as we proceed, but remember that winning pennants is not like making chicken soup: even if you have the right ingredients, you still have to know how to cook.

First, let's accentuate the positives. Kansas City has a very talented and very deep pitching staff, one that has the potential to be among the best in baseball. Kevin Appier is one of the top five starters in the AL, and he will be only 25 this season. His health is still somewhat in question, but even if he should miss the first part of the year, he is still a formidable asset. The Royals should take every imaginable precaution to protect his arm.

David Cone has proven to be a very consistent pitcher and should have an excellent season, even if he is not dominant. Mark Gubicza is such an intelligent pitcher that, even if his skills have

Position	92 Starter	TWAR	93 Starter	TWAR
Catcher	Macfarlane	2.53	Macfarlane	2.53
First base	Joyner	5.17	Joyner	5.17
Second base	Miller	3.74	Lind	0.44
Third base	Jefferies	3.79	Jefferies	3.79
Shortstop	Howard, D.	0.67	Gagne	2.36
Left field	Eisenreich	2.02	Miller	3.74
Center field	McRae	1.83	McRae	1.83
Right field	McReynolds	3.87	McReynolds	3.87
DH	Brett	4.36	Brett	4.36

been somewhat diminished by injuries, he should be able to keep his ERA under 3.80 and be an effective third starter.

After the top three, the Royals have a tremendous (and almost bewildering) array of pitchers who range from serviceable to promising at their disposal. Last year, the choices afforded to manager Hal McRae, coupled with injuries, caused the Royals to scatter their starts among ten different pitchers. Their total of 90 starts from the top four pitchers used as starters was by far the lowest figure in baseball. McRae needs to address this issue, but the continuing influx of pitching via the farm system and trades has created an intriguing glut for him to sort through.

Mark Gardner and Chris Haney (from Montreal), Rick Reed (from the Pirate organization), Dennis Rasmussen (from you name it), Mike Boddicker (from the Orioles via the Red Sox), and farm system products Tom Gordon, Mike Magnante, and Hipolito Pichardo can all start. Barring the invention of a radical new pitching strategy (anyone for the eleven-man rotation?), McRae will likely settle on the two Expo acquisitions at the outset. Their K/BB performance, plus Haney's left-handedness, will likely be the deciding element. The three youngest of this group—Gordon, Haney, and Pichardo, all 25 or younger—will bear the most scrutiny. Any of them could show sudden improvement. People are beginning to give up on Flash's potential, but he has a world of stuff and was a little better as a reliever in the second half of the year (3.50 ERA).

The losers in the starter derby will look to join Jeff Montgomery and Rusty Meachem in the bullpen. Meachem doesn't appear to be a fluke: his K/BB ratio was 3 to 1 and remained consistent throughout the season. The man he is setting up, Montgomery, has quietly become one of the best in the business. Unlike most closers, his effectiveness does not stem from an overpowering fastball. Rather, he has mastered four out pitches and uses them the way a top starter would. Over the past five years, he's been particularly impressive after the All-Star Break (2.12 ERA, 68 of his 115 saves).

The Royals' defense wasn't bad at all last year, and should be improved in '93. Center fielder Brian McRae, the new keystone duo of Greg Gagne and Jose Lind, and first sacker Wally Joyner are all excellent defensively, and Kevin McReynolds isn't as bad as his reputation (he just looks so phlegmatic). Mike Macfarlane is adequate behind the plate, though his caught stealing rate is quite ordinary. The defensive trouble spots are third base (Gregg Jefferies) and left field (Keith Miller and a cast of hundreds beginning with Chris Gwynn—not particularly fleet—and Jim Eisenreich—slowing down markedly). Overall, though, the Royals defense is going to be reasonably good at avoiding unearned runs, which gives the pitching staff an added boost.

However, the old adage remains true: you win by scoring more runs than your opposition. And to score more runs than the opposition, you must have the ability to score runs.

Last year the Royals scored the third fewest runs in the AL, hit the fewest homers (only the Dodgers hit fewer in all of baseball), had the second worst OBP in the AL, and received the fewest intentional walks in the league (a full 16% less than the next worse team, the Rangers). How have the Royals addressed these deficiencies? They've added offensive juggernauts Gagne and Lind, while the rest of the team has merely gotten a year older.

It is hard to see how the Royals can possibly score more runs than they did last season. Even if the pitchers can improve enough to allow, say, 600 runs (an improvement of 67 from last year), they'll still need to add 15%, or 90 runs, to last season's offense to get in the neighborhood of 93 wins, the lowest figure that I see being the division champion's total at the end of the year. 93 in '93 is a laudable goal, but the Royals are probably 10-15 games away from that.

Why is the offense so anemic (and likely to stay that way)? Royals Stadium cuts down homers but improves batting average, doubles, and triples, so it isn't to blame. Let's look at the Royals' offensive players, the ones who are likely to start: Miller, Jefferies, Joyner, McReynolds, Brett, Macfarlane, McRae, Gagne, and Lind. Here are some very quick, and very basic facts:

Average age: 30.3
Without Brett: 29.1

Highest OB+ slugging: .775 (McReynolds)

This basic data tell us that the Royals are, as a team, just past their prime. Offensively, Robinson and Hal McRae are expecting an offensive "last hurrah" from a team that is primarily a "never was." Only Brett, now way in the twilight of his career, can really be considered to ever have been a dominating player. McReynolds OB+ is not that much higher than the Blue Jays' team total (.747).

The Royals have only two starters under the age of 29: Gregg Jefferies and Brian McRae. Jefferies will probably end up justifying the Saberhagen trade, although he didn't have a particularly good '92. He hit .298 in the second half, which is still a bit under what his true ability ought to be. He is a good baserunner, his line drive stroke is well suited to the home park, and he is difficult to strike out. Why the continuing underachievemet? Impatience at the plate might be one reason: working the count more might have a beneficial effect, especially if he is going to bat high in the order. I think that '93 is likely to be the year that Jefferies finally hits .300, which may get the monkey off his back and push his career upward in the way that people have been long expecting.

McRae, on the other hand, may never justify his father's continuing patience with him. His career numbers: .249 BA, .291 OBP, .350 SA. In '92: .223/.285/.308. After the All-Star Break in '92: .219/.280/.299. His walk totals increased a good deal last year (from wretched to poor), but his power disappeared. He is an excellent center fielder, which is valuable in a spacious park like Royals Stadium, but his offensive production is nowhere close to acceptable even for a brilliant outfielder. Not only are the Royals suffering due to McRae's lack of production, they are also losing punch in a defensive position where hitting is traditionally more robust: any old replacement player would significantly upgrade the team's attack. He may eventually become a major league hitter (he's only 25), but having him learn how on a major league roster is killing the Royals' offense.

McReynolds and Miller are likely to be the other two outfielders. Miller is not much of an outfielder (his natural position is second base), and the Royals would really like to sign a power hitter, but I think it would be a mistake to bench him. He was easily the Royals' best leadoff man last year (.352 OBP, good speed, reasonable doubles power). Miller is a late bloomer, however, and is already 30, so he's not likely to get much better. He's also prone to injury, partially because his batting stance tends to induce getting hit by pitches (14 last season, including one that knocked him out for a good bit of the second half).

McReynolds is beginning to display what Bill James called "old players' skills": his 1992 was quietly productive, with a markedly higher walk percentage than in previous seasons (15.2% in '92 vs. 8.6% lifetime). Sometimes changes like that presage a total offensive collapse in a player McReynolds' age (33). The other warning signals are also present: power down (though that should be expected in KC), average down. If the average keeps drifting down at the rate it has fallen over the past five years (between 10 and 11 points per season), then Kevin will have to walk even more to retain his offensive value.

Speaking of old players, George Brett's decision to keep playing after picking up his 3,000th hit was a little surprising. Brett's lifetime BA is .307 and I guess he figured that he'd have to hit .150 to drop it below .300. Last season, Brett hit .285, but his power continued to decay and his walk totals dropped alarmingly (especially for a man who once walked more than 100 times). Brett at 40 is no longer one of the top five hitters on the team, which means that whatever intangibles he brings to the Royals need to be a lot less intangible than usual.

For the Royals to have any kind of chance in '93, it is crucial that Joyner and Macfarlane have better years. Everyone expected Joyner to enjoy hitting in KC, and to increase his average at the expense of some power. Instead, he had downright poor year at home (hitting just .266, with a shockingly low .358 SA and just one homer). Wally is only 31, so he shouldn't be incapable of bouncing back, but he's going to have to stop swinging for the fences.

Macfarlane, however, is most valuable when he tries to jack the ball out of the park. Last season, he hit 7 of the 24 homers hit by the Royals at home. After the All-Star Break, he broke out of an extended slump and slugged .528. From August to the end of the year, Macfarlane had 11 homers in 155 at bats, slugging almost .550. If the Royals had a few more high average doubles hitters to get on base for him, Macfarlane would be a very valuable #6 hitter. As it is, he at least provides the team with some punch at home, something no one else on the team does. The Royals tried to let Brent Mayne tale the number one catching job last year, but Mayne's bat was dreadful, much worse than even McRae's. Macfarlane should start all year in '93: the Royals would be better off for it.

In the middle of the infield, the Royals now have defensive proficiency, but neither Gagne nor Lind approach average major league hitting ability. Lind's career OBP is .298, which might be acceptable if he slugged like Will Clark. Unfortunately, the only Clark he resembles is Horace (Clarke), whose lifetime slugging average was .313, which is six points lower than Lind's. The shrewd manager would let Cone hit for himself and DH for Lind. Gagne has a bit more power and may be able to shorten his stroke for the Stadium, but he is 31 already and has a mortal fear of the base on balls (he walked just 4% of the time last year). An inordinate amount of defensive wizardry is going to be required to offset the chasms in the batting order that these two represent.

So rather than being one hitter away, the Royals are more like three to four. One defensive whiz who can't get on more than .300 can be carried on a team. The Royals have three (McRae, Gagne, Lind). Brett is 40, McReynolds 33, and Kevin is the only player on the team who'll take a walk. The best hope for the Royals would be that Joyner gets hurt and either Jeff Conine or Bob Hamelin gets hot enough to displace him. But since the Royals signed Wally to that big four-year deal (before he hit .250 from June 1st to the end of the season), they've got a problem moving him. If anyone gets displaced, it's probably going to be Brett, and probably by Hamelin, who could be the power hitter the Royals so desperately need if he can lick his back injuries.

Let's pull the curtain on the Royals by gently informing Mr. Herk Robinson that the year is 1993, not 1968. One cannot expect to win by emphasizing pitching and defense to the virtual exclusion of offense. And even the Royals' pitching, despite the addition of Cone, is not a dominating type of staff, since it is predominantly composed of finesse pitchers. So banking on an ensemble pitching performance like a 1968 Cardinals or a 1988 Dodgers is a spectacular leap of faith. The Royals' offense scored 727 runs in 1991 (Danny Tartabull had much to do with that); last season, they scored 610. Is this the bottom of the trough, or can Kansas City fall even further? Herk and Hal may be waiting for a cyclone to take them over the rainbow to Oz, because halfway through '93 they're going to wish that they never see home again.

Kansas City Royals Home Park Performance Factors														
	Outs	Runs	Hits	2b	3b	HR	W	K	SH	SF	HBP	IBB	SB	CS	GDP
Home LH Batters	1.000	.971	1.040	1.008	.782	2.212	1.090	1.147	.828	.821	.735	.846	.880	.948	1.207
Home RH Batters	.915	.874	.903	.892	1.051	1.209	.886	.981	.780	.764	.726	.572	.864	1.139	1.028
All Home Batters	.972	.928	.976	.983	.834	1.454	.975	1.062	.927	.815	.771	.736	.868	.900	1.154
Opp LH Batters	1.010	1.072	1.027	.977	.761	1.655	1.136	1.014	1.150	.993	1.040	1.066	1.396	.976	1.040
Opp RH Batters	1.004	1.001	1.010	.907	.932	1.143	1.204	1.021	1.496	1.302	.972	1.302	1.192	1.386	1.084
All Opp Batters	1.008	1.027	1.012	.937	.871	1.286	1.180	1.031	1.355	1.169	1.027	1.164	1.228	1.258	1.075
All LH Batters	1.004	1.011	1.035	.997	.776	1.841	1.110	1.081	.948	.908	.831	.953	1.021	.957	1.124
All RH Batters	.972	.957	.971	.906	1.005	1.157	1.084	1.006	1.192	1.120	.879	1.014	1.066	1.301	1.051
All Batters	.990	.979	.994	.960	.857	1.333	1.078	1.040	1.133	1.003	.884	.959	1.020	1.043	1.101

Conventional Batting Records for Kansas City Royals

	G	AB	Run	Hit	2B	3B	HR	TB	RBI	W	K	IW	HB	SB	CS	BRng Eff	GI DP	SH	SF	Avg	Slug	OBP	Runs Ctd
Macfarlane	129	402	51	94	28	3	17	179	48	30	89	2	15	1	5	.357	8	1	2	.234	.445	.310	54
Joyner	149	572	66	154	36	2	9	221	66	55	50	4	4	11	5	.468	19	0	2	.269	.386	.336	73
Miller K	106	416	57	118	24	4	4	162	38	31	46	0	14	16	6	.532	1	1	2	.284	.389	.352	62
Jefferies	152	604	66	172	36	3	10	244	75	43	29	4	1	19	9	.504	24	0	9	.285	.404	.329	75
Howard D	74	219	19	49	6	2	1	62	18	15	43	0	0	3	4	.406	3	8	2	.224	.283	.271	17
McReynolds	109	373	45	92	25	0	13	156	49	67	48	3	0	7	1	.380	6	0	5	.247	.418	.357	61
McRae B	149	533	63	119	23	5	4	164	52	42	88	1	6	18	5	.488	10	7	4	.223	.308	.285	49
Eisenreich	113	353	31	95	13	3	2	120	28	24	36	4	0	11	6	.542	6	0	3	.269	.340	.313	38
Brett	152	592	55	169	35	5	7	235	61	35	69	6	6	8	6	.370	15	0	4	.285	.397	.330	75
Wilkerson	111	296	27	74	10	1	2	92	29	18	47	3	1	18	7	.488	4	7	4	.250	.311	.292	28
Mayne	82	213	16	48	10	0	0	58	18	11	26	0	0	0	4	.286	5	2	3	.225	.272	.260	14
Thurman	88	200	25	49	6	3	0	61	20	9	34	0	1	9	6	.618	3	6	0	.245	.305	.281	17
Rossy	59	149	21	32	8	1	1	45	12	20	20	1	1	0	3	.529	6	7	1	.215	.302	.310	14
Koslofski	55	133	20	33	0	2	3	46	13	12	23	0	1	2	1	.500	2	3	1	.248	.346	.313	15
Samuel	29	102	15	29	5	3	0	40	8	7	27	1	1	6	1	.450	2	0	0	.284	.392	.336	14
Shumpert	36	94	6	14	5	1	1	24	11	3	17	0	0	2	2	.375	2	2	0	.149	.255	.175	4
Conine	28	91	10	23	5	2	0	32	9	8	23	1	0	0	0	.563	1	0	0	.253	.352	.313	10
Gwynn C	34	84	10	24	3	2	1	34	7	3	10	0	0	0	0	.300	1	1	2	.286	.405	.303	10
Melvin	32	70	5	22	5	0	0	27	6	5	13	0	0	0	0	.167	3	0	2	.314	.386	.351	9
Pulliam	4	5	2	1	1	0	0	2	0	1	3	0	0	0	0	.000	0	0	0	.200	.400	.333	1
TOTALS	1691	5501	610	1411	284	42	75	2004	568	439	741	30	51	131	71	.455	121	45	46	.256	.364	.315	631

Sabermetric Batting Records for Kansas City Royals

	Ball Park Adjusted								Runs										
	AB	Run	Hit	2B	3B	HR	RBI	W	SO	Avg	Slug	OBP	Ctd	Outs	27o	OW%	OG	OWAR	DWAR	TWAR
Brett	599	56	174	34	3	13	64	38	74	.290	.422	.336	82	449	4.93	.610	17	4.33	0.04	4.36
Conine	86	9	21	4	1	0	8	8	23	.244	.314	.309	9	66	3.68	.466	2	0.28	0.14	0.43
Eisenreich	357	31	98	12	2	3	29	26	38	.275	.345	.322	40	272	3.97	.504	10	1.55	0.47	2.02
Gwynn C	84	10	24	2	1	1	7	3	10	.286	.369	.307	10	62	4.35	.550	2	0.46	0.08	0.54
Howard D	216	18	48	5	1	1	17	16	45	.222	.269	.275	16	185	2.34	.260	7	-0.62	1.28	0.67
Jefferies	597	64	170	34	2	13	74	46	30	.285	.414	.332	76	470	4.37	.551	17	3.50	0.29	3.79
Joyner	579	67	159	35	1	17	69	61	54	.275	.427	.346	83	446	5.02	.619	17	4.44	0.72	5.17
Koslofski	134	20	34	0	1	5	13	13	24	.254	.381	.320	17	104	4.41	.556	4	0.79	0.56	1.36
Macfarlane	384	47	89	25	2	19	47	31	89	.232	.456	.308	52	312	4.50	.566	12	2.49	0.04	2.53
Mayne	214	16	49	9	0	0	18	12	28	.229	.271	.268	15	176	2.30	.254	7	-0.62	0.33	-0.30
McRae B	527	61	118	22	4	5	51	45	92	.224	.309	.290	49	435	3.04	.373	16	0.37	1.46	1.83
McReynolds	356	42	87	22	0	15	48	70	48	.244	.433	.364	62	281	5.96	.696	10	3.60	0.27	3.87
Melvin	67	4	21	4	0	0	5	5	13	.313	.373	.351	8	51	4.24	.536	2	0.35	-0.05	0.30
Miller K	397	53	112	21	3	4	37	32	46	.282	.380	.351	57	296	5.20	.635	11	3.13	0.61	3.74
Pulliam	3	1	0	0	0	0	0	1	3	.000	.000	.250	0	3	0.00	.000	0	-0.04	0.01	-0.03
Rossy	142	19	30	7	0	1	11	20	20	.211	.282	.307	12	129	2.51	.289	5	-0.29	0.70	0.41
Samuel	97	14	27	4	2	0	7	7	27	.278	.361	.327	12	73	4.44	.559	3	0.57	0.14	0.71
Shumpert	89	5	13	4	0	1	10	3	17	.146	.225	.174	3	82	0.99	.059	3	-0.88	-0.05	-0.93
Thurman	190	23	46	5	2	0	19	9	34	.242	.289	.276	14	160	2.36	.264	6	-0.51	0.63	0.13
Wilkerson	292	26	73	9	0	2	28	19	49	.250	.301	.293	27	240	3.04	.373	9	0.20	0.92	1.12
TOTALS	5449	596	1402	272	35	102	563	473	775	.257	.376	.319	650	4353	4.03	.511	161	26.01	8.62	34.63

Pitching Records for Kansas City Royals

	ERA	W	L	Pct	G	GS	CG	ShO	GF	Sv	IP	R	ER	H	2B	3B	HR	BB	IW	SO	HB	WP	BK
Appier	2.46	15	8	.652	30	30	3	0	0	0	208.1	59	57	167	37	6	10	68	5	150	2	4	0
Pichardo	3.95	9	6	.600	31	24	1	1	0	0	143.2	71	63	148	31	2	9	49	1	59	3	3	1
Gubicza	3.72	7	6	.538	18	18	2	1	0	0	111.1	47	46	110	19	3	8	36	3	81	1	5	1
Reed Rk	3.68	3	7	.300	19	18	1	1	0	0	100.1	47	41	105	21	2	10	20	3	49	5	0	0
Aquino	4.52	3	6	.333	15	13	0	0	1	0	67.2	35	34	81	14	0	5	20	1	11	1	1	1
Haney	3.86	2	3	.400	7	7	1	1	0	0	42.0	18	18	35	9	1	5	16	2	27	0	0	0
Rasmussen D	1.43	4	1	.800	5	5	1	1	0	0	37.2	7	6	25	3	0	0	6	0	12	0	3	0
Moeller	7.00	0	3	.000	5	4	0	0	1	0	18.0	17	14	24	4	0	5	11	2	6	0	1	1
Pierce	3.38	0	0	.000	2	1	0	0	0	0	5.1	2	2	9	0	0	1	4	0	3	0	0	0
Gordon	4.59	6	10	.375	40	11	0	0	13	0	117.2	67	60	116	23	2	9	55	4	98	4	5	2
Meacham R	2.74	10	4	.714	64	0	0	0	20	2	101.2	39	31	88	15	3	5	21	5	64	1	4	0
Magnante	4.94	4	9	.308	44	12	0	0	11	0	89.1	53	49	115	17	2	5	35	5	31	2	2	0
Boddicker	4.98	1	4	.200	29	8	0	0	8	3	86.2	50	48	92	22	2	5	37	3	47	8	2	0
Montgomery	2.18	1	6	.143	65	0	0	0	62	39	82.2	23	20	61	7	0	5	27	2	69	3	2	0
Shifflett	2.60	1	4	.200	34	0	0	0	15	0	52.0	15	15	55	8	1	6	17	6	25	2	2	1
Berenguer	5.64	1	4	.200	19	2	0	0	2	0	44.2	30	28	42	10	1	3	20	3	26	1	2	1
Heaton	4.17	3	1	.750	31	0	0	0	8	0	41.0	21	19	43	6	0	5	22	2	29	1	3	1
Davis Mrk	7.18	1	3	.250	13	6	0	0	4	0	36.1	31	29	42	10	1	6	28	0	19	0	1	0
Young C	5.18	1	2	.333	10	2	0	0	2	0	24.1	14	14	29	7	1	1	7	1	7	0	0	0
Sampen	3.66	0	2	.000	8	1	0	0	3	0	19.2	10	8	21	1	1	0	3	1	14	3	1	0
Sauveur	4.40	0	1	.000	8	0	0	0	2	0	14.1	7	7	15	1	0	1	8	1	7	2	0	1
Johnston	13.50	0	0	.000	5	0	0	0	1	0	2.2	4	4	3	0	0	0	2	0	0	0	1	0
TOTALS	3.81	72	90	.444	502	162	9	5	153	44	1447.1	667	613	1426	265	28	106	512	50	834	39	42	10

Sabermetric Pitching Records for Kansas City Royals

	Adj ERA	Expected W	Expected L	Pct	BFP	Avg	Slg	OBA	RC/G	GDP	SB	CS	PK	PKE	SH	SF	RSup	RSp/G	W	L	Pct
Appier	2.38	17	6	.732	852	.217	.319	.281	3.07	11	18	9	1	0	8	3	93	4.02	16	7	.702
Aquino	4.39	4	5	.444	293	.303	.412	.351	4.90	8	1	3	0	1	2	3	19	2.53	2	7	.215
Berenguer	5.44	2	3	.342	195	.247	.371	.325	4.47	2	3	1	1	2	1	3	30	3.12	1	4	.102
Boddicker	4.78	2	3	.403	392	.270	.390	.352	5.16	9	13	2	0	1	2	0	26	3.12	1	4	.260
Davis Mrk	6.94	1	3	.242	176	.294	.503	.400	8.12	2	8	1	0	0	1	4	26	6.44	2	2	.415
Gordon	4.44	7	9	.439	516	.258	.379	.340	4.44	12	5	7	0	1	2	6	52	3.98	6	10	.399
Gubicza	3.64	7	6	.538	470	.259	.374	.316	4.00	10	4	4	0	1	5	3	48	3.88	6	7	.484
Haney	3.64	3	2	.537	174	.226	.394	.293	3.96	1	3	3	0	0	0	3	14	3.00	2	3	.359
Heaton	3.95	2	2	.497	185	.274	.408	.361	5.60	5	9	0	0	0	2	3	23	5.05	2	2	.574
Johnston	10.13	0	0	.131	13	.273	.818	.385	12.42	0	0	0	0	0	0	0	2	6.75	0	0	.268
Magnante	4.74	5	8	.407	403	.325	.427	.382	5.83	13	9	3	0	0	5	7	44	4.43	5	8	.419
Meacham R	2.66	10	4	.686	412	.233	.328	.269	2.92	9	0	1	0	0	3	9	42	3.72	9	5	.618
Moeller	6.50	1	2	.267	89	.333	.597	.407	9.00	3	2	0	0	3	3	3	6	3.00	0	3	.149
Montgomery	2.07	5	2	.783	333	.205	.279	.277	2.59	7	5	2	0	0	4	2	10	1.09	1	6	.186
Pichardo	3.82	8	7	.513	615	.267	.379	.327	4.34	15	11	3	0	1	4	5	91	5.70	10	5	.647
Pierce	1.69	0	0	.844	26	.429	.571	.500	9.71	1	0	1	0	1	0	1	4	6.75	0	0	.930
Rasmussen D	1.19	5	0	.915	134	.197	.220	.233	1.26	2	1	6	0	6	1	0	12	2.87	4	1	.826
Reed Rk	3.59	5	5	.545	419	.271	.413	.312	4.30	11	6	3	3	0	2	5	39	3.50	4	6	.439
Sampen	3.20	1	1	.600	81	.292	.333	.338	3.64	4	4	1	0	0	1	2	6	2.75	1	1	.377
Sauveur	3.77	1	0	.520	65	.273	.345	.385	4.60	3	0	0	0	0	0	0	8	5.02	1	0	.594
Shifflett	2.42	4	1	.724	221	.279	.421	.341	4.62	9	3	1	0	2	4	1	23	3.98	3	2	.690
Young C	4.81	1	2	.400	107	.293	.414	.336	5.07	2	2	1	0	0	0	1	8	2.96	1	2	.238
TOTALS	3.73	85	77	.525	6171	.259	.375	.323	4.18	139	107	52	5	16	50	67	610	3.79	75	87	.460

Batting 'Splits' Records for Kansas City Royals

SPLITS for Kansas City Royals (all batters except pitchers)

	G	AB	Run	Hit	2B	3B	HR	TB	RBI	W	K	IW	HB	SB	CS	DP	SH	SF	Avg	Slug	OBP	RC
vs LHP	878	1655	190	431	101	13	23	627	178	135	241	11	15	30	27	29	20	10	.260	.379	.320	199
vs RHP	1592	3846	420	980	183	29	52	1377	390	304	500	19	36	101	44	92	25	36	.255	.358	.313	432
Home	837	2656	314	684	134	25	24	940	288	217	327	20	32	73	40	47	22	27	.258	.354	.318	306
Away	854	2845	296	727	150	17	51	1064	280	222	414	10	19	58	31	74	23	19	.256	.374	.312	325
Grass	656	2214	231	571	104	12	41	822	222	165	304	7	15	45	23	56	19	16	.258	.371	.312	252
Turf	1035	3287	379	840	180	30	34	1182	346	274	437	23	36	86	48	65	26	30	.256	.360	.317	379
April/June	787	2505	284	628	156	16	36	924	263	210	337	9	23	52	32	61	27	24	.251	.369	.312	286
July/October	904	2996	326	783	128	26	39	1080	305	229	404	21	28	79	39	60	18	22	.261	.360	.318	345

Seattle Mariners

Brock J. Hanke

SEATTLE										
YEAR	1983	1984	1985	1986	1987	1988	1989	1990	1991	1992
W	60	74	74	67	78	68	73	77	83	64
L	102	88	88	95	84	93	89	85	79	98
WPCT	0.370	0.457	0.457	0.414	0.481	0.422	0.451	0.475	0.512	0.395
R	558	682	719	718	760	664	694	640	702	679
RA	740	774	818	835	801	744	728	680	674	799
PWPT	0.362	0.437	0.436	0.425	0.474	0.443	0.476	0.470	0.520	0.419
PythW	59	71	71	69	77	72	77	76	84	68
PythL	103	91	91	93	85	90	85	86	78	94
LUCK	1	3	3	-2	1	-4	-4	1	-1	-4

Defensive Efficiency Record: .6917

I was sanguine about the Mariners last year, as you long-time readers know, and I'm sanguine about them again, lousy year or no lousy year. The reasons, on the other hand, are completely different between the two years. Last year, I thought the M's might put together a good offense to go with a tolerable pitching staff. That didn't happen, partially because the M's never did shore up the roster with backup ballplayers. They had given up their bullpen to get a cleanup hitter, and never did do anything about that. This year, they have more money, and it's beginning to show. They've picked up some serious roster bulk, and the only front-line player they've given up is Kevin Mitchell. No, I don't count Harold Reynolds as a player given up, for reasons I guess I should discuss first.

To be blunt, Harold hasn't been much of a player for about three years now. In fact, his is a typical sad story. At age 26, he began to show his absolute peak of ability. He hit .275 and, while he took no walks, he did manage to hit 331 doubles. He also stole 60 bases, with a good .75 stolen base percentage. It was only his second full year, and he sure looked like a hell of a sophomore, until you remembered he was already 26. The next year, he was on schedule for his age-27 career year. He upped the batting ante to .283, and powered up for 11 triples, leading the league. At that point, he had led the league in two offensive categories: stolen bases and triples. Those categories don't amount to much, but they will give you a reputation as a star, if you're an infielder, and people think you're a young one.

In 1989, Harold was 28, and still holding his peak value. In fact, he hit .300 on the nose, which is, don't you know, much, much better than hitting .299 or something. The next year, Harold did some things that would normally be signs of real improvement. First, he upped his walk total from 55 to 81. For a top-of-the-order guy, that's a big help. Second, the influx of times on base pushed his runs scored total to an even 100. Again, people's perceptions of someone who scores 100 runs are much higher than they are of someone who scores 99, and Harold reaped the

Position	92 Starter	TWAR	93 Starter	TWAR
Catcher	Valle	-0.26	Sasser	-0.42
			Valle	-0.26
First base	Martinez, T.	0.82	Martinez, T.	0.82
Second base	Reynolds	0.84	Boone	-0.62
Third base	Martinez, E.	6.33	Martinez, E.	6.33
Shortstop	Vizquel	3.00	Vizquel	3.00
Left field	Mitchell	2.91	Felder	2.81
Center field	Griffey	5.88	Griffey	5.88
Right field	Buhner	4.21	Buhner	4.21
DH	O'Brien	0.15	O'Brien	0.15

reputation reward. And third, Harold got back the 30+ doubles. But his batting average had dropped to .252, and he was, in fact, not as good as he had been before. Over the last two years, Harold's walks have drifted down, his batting average hasn't moved, and his runs scored have slowly waned as well. In fact, his base hitting stats don't really support the runs scored total; he's been scoring runs because Ken Griffey, Jr. and Edgar Martinez are so good around him.

Now, I don't want to suggest that Harold Reynolds is an offensive hole. He's not. But, on a team with Griffey and Martinez, he absolutely should not be hitting at the top of the batting order. His reputation has kept him there, and the Mariners have suffered. Losing Harold to free agency does two things for the M's. First, it makes way naturally for Bret Boone, who looks pretty ready to me. Boone's MLE has him down for .268, with 8 homers and 21 doubles. He doesn't take more than an average number of walks, but the conversion of about 5 doubles to homers, and the 15 added batting points, make him a better hitter than Reynolds is. And he's 24, not 30. Second, losing Harold removes him from the top of the order; Bret Boone has no reputation to force his hitting there. Overall, the M's have not lost a thing, and they've gained youth and a vital batting order spot.

Kevin Mitchell is another question. He was, in fact, the only real cleanup hitter the Mariners had. Jay Buhner, coming down off his age-27 season, did not hold the value that made him look like a cleanup prospect; he's a #5 hitter, and nothing else. Tino Martinez has another step to take before he becomes a #4 man. Pete O'Brien is finished as that sort of offensive force. There's no one in the minors. So, what makes me sanguine about the team, without Mitchell? Doesn't it seem like they're doing the same sort of wheel-spinning as the Cleveland Indians do, trading pitching for power one year, reversing the trade the next year, but never cleaning up the hole?

Well, maybe. But, then, there's Chris Bosio. He's the first real free agent for the Mariners in years, and he really changes the complexion of the team. Before Bosio, the Mariner rotation was Randy Johnson, Eric Hanson and rookie Dave Fleming. Now, you know what's going to happen there. Johnson is going to pitch his normal, erratic, .500 season, with a ton of strikeouts. Either Fleming is going to collapse from the stress of pitching 228 innings as a rookie, or Hanson is not going to come back fully. The other one would pitch fine, and the Mariners might come up with a New Kid on the Rubber (Roger Salkeld or Mike Remlinger, most likely), but that would leave them with a three-man rotation. That would force the manager to give too many innings to someone, and the chain of failures would remain unbroken again.

But, with Bosio, the M's should have a full 4-man, solid starting corps composed of the three above and Chris. The manager won't have to give anyone a ruinous workload. What's more, the #5 slot will be filled with the worse of Fleming and Hanson. That is, the probable rotation will be Bosio, Johnson, Hanson, Salkeld and Fleming. Last year, the M's split the #5 slot among four pitchers who were awful. They went 3 / 10 with the 21 starts. Even on an off year, Fleming or Hanson will pitch better than that. It's amazing what a difference one man can make.

On top of that, the M's finally have a few options in the outfield, at first base, and at DH. They've lost Mitchell, true, but they've also picked up Mike Felder and Mackey Sasser. Neither one is as good as Mitchell, but they will certainly be better than Mitchell's 1992. Sasser is the real find. He's a first-rate hitter who the Mets were trying to force to play catcher. Unfortunately for that plan, Mackey has developed a phobia about throwing the ball back to the pitcher (yeah, AL fans, it's that guy). With the M's, Mackey won't be asked to catch; he'll be asked to DH or play first, or maybe the outfield. He's going to be better than Pete O'Brien was, and the two of them will be better still. Felder is a good bench outfielder. He can play center and hit a little; he's a real good glove in left or right. And so, Griffey gets some rest, and there's someone behind Henry Cotto and Jay Buhner, as well. Overall, you've got the following platoon possibilities:

Against lefties, you want to bat right handed hitters,

Griffey   cf
E. Martinez   3b
Cotto   lf
T. Martinez   1b

Buhner   rf
Sasser   DH
Vizquel   ss
Boone   2b
Valle   c

Against righties,

Griffey   cf
E. Martinez   3b
Sasser   lf
T. Martinez   1b
Buhner   rf
O'Brien DH
Vizquel   ss
Boone   2b
Valle   c

Those aren't great lineups, and they may not be what the Mariners will actually use, but they're OK if they are used. The offensive sequence lacks a power core, but it extends at least to the #7 man, listed here as Vizquel, but open for grabs to Boone or a catcher who can hit. On balance, that offense should be able to score an average number of runs, to go with the well-above-average pitching rotation and Norm Charlton as closer. If the M's could come up with one decent kid, or a free agent hitter, they'd get tough.

You've possibly seen my contenders profile elsewhere in the book; if not, read the Philly essay. Here's a breakdown of the 1993 M's, according to what I expect of the various starters:

SUPERSTARS

Griffey
E. Martinez

STARS

Bosio
Charlton
Vizquel (yes, Omar)

CHAMPIONSHIP QUALITY

T. Martinez
Cotto
Buhner
R. Johnson
Hanson or Fleming

BULK

Fleming or Hanson
Boone

HOLE

Valle

That's not far off the contender profile. In fact, it's exactly one switch from Championship Quality to Star from modeling the profile exactly. Tino Martinez? If Bosio gets hot, or Norm Charlton responds to freedom from Rob Dibble with an explosion of talent, the M's could be right up there.

Now, I admit that it's an odd distribution of talent. The superstars are those leadoff guys. But so what? Are you going to deny the offensive value of Griffey and Edgar? If anything, the distribution of Mariner talent makes the team easier to improve. After all, look at the DH platoon. Don't you think you could improve on that, if your team found itself in contention and you had money? Well, the M's have that, now. And, with that money, they have acquired a chance.

The one thing I really should mention is the listing of Omar Vizquel as a star. A couple of years ago - hell, one year ago - Omar looked like a man who would never learn to hit AAA pitching, much less the sort that's in the Major Leagues. But last year, he hit just fine, for a shortstop. He doesn't take many walks, and he has now power, and the average was only .289, but this is shortstop, and Omar's defensive stats are wonderful. In 1991, Omar hit .230, and had no power nor walks, giving him an Offensive Winning Percentage just below Replacement Rate. But his 3 Defensive Wins moved him to #2 overall, behind Cal Ripken, Jr.

This year, he was able to contribute some offense. In fact, his OWAR were in about the middle of the shortstop pack. What's more, it was consistent. Omar did not have one hot month that pushed his stats to a silly one-year high. His batting splits are remarkably consistent; there is not just one sort of pitching he learned how to hit. Nor was he 27 years old. He had a drop in offense late in the year, which indicates that he was overworked, but he was hitting .300 until then. His defense was down a little, and the position had some good new players in it, but he still finished #4. Now a star is someone who can be expected to finish third through fifth at his position. Omar Vizquel has finished second and fourth. He could lose a little of that offense and still finish fifth. What am I supposed to call him except a star?

On top of the starter profile, the new management has started to spend the money needed to acquire the backups that fill out a contending team. I make more of the signings of Mike Fitzgerald and Greg Litton than is readily apparent. Fitzgerald, I've liked for years. He has every chance to beat out Dave Valle. On the other hand, he is getting old, and he has been both hurt and bad recently. Still, he's a fine backup catcher who can actually do some pinch hitting without killing the team. That's more than they've had.

Greg Litton has never been as good as Fitzgerald has, but he's just fine as a backup middle infielder. If Bret Boone has a bad month, the M's now have an option. Omar Vizquel had a big drop in offense last August and September, a sign that he's playing a little too much. Litton is capable of spelling Omar. Overall, including the new outfield bats, it's by far the best Mariner bench in years. And it's come from the management not pinching pennies.

Now, I can't tell you the Mariners should be considered up there with the big-time teams or anything like that. I doubt that they can really keep pace with the White Sox or the Twins without a cleanup batter. But the Oakland monster is gone; the fire sale just completed with the departure of Harold Baines, the A's own cleanup batter. The Sox are woefully weak in the pitching staff, and Jack McDowell has been overworked. The Twins look great, and I have to pick them as front runners, but they are counting for a lot out of Dave Winfield and some questionable pitching arms. The M's could get lucky. And, this time, if they do get lucky, they have enough for it to be 90 wins, not 83. At the very least, I think they're finally on the right track.

Seattle Mariners Home Park Performance Factors															
	Outs	Runs	Hits	2b	3b	HR	W	K	SH	SF	HBP	IBB	SB	CS	GDP
Home LH Batters	.990	.903	.964	.836	1.029	.909	.965	1.076	6.729	.862	.658	1.206	.922	1.553	.874
Home RH Batters	1.012	.983	.996	.801	1.558	.907	.975	.991	1.357	.866	1.072	.794	1.106	.886	.962
All Home Batters	1.003	.950	.982	.812	1.034	.930	.974	.998	1.437	.876	.875	.988	.980	1.015	.970
Opp LH Batters	1.026	1.013	.920	.964	.954	1.053	1.121	.894	1.008	.886	.817	1.296	1.197	1.283	1.026
Opp RH Batters	1.033	1.069	1.027	.994	1.729	1.085	1.117	1.010	1.418	1.241	.969	1.304	1.239	.895	.887
All Opp Batters	1.033	1.061	1.005	.987	1.223	1.082	1.110	.981	1.359	1.100	.977	1.391	1.215	.941	.923
All LH Batters	1.007	.955	.942	.892	.983	.963	1.043	.978	1.428	.873	.724	1.242	1.054	1.409	.930
All RH Batters	1.023	1.027	1.013	.894	1.645	.988	1.052	1.001	1.389	1.040	.993	1.018	1.178	.885	.920
All Batters	1.018	1.005	.993	.895	1.125	.999	1.045	.988	1.391	.980	.929	1.155	1.102	.968	.949

Conventional Batting Records for Seattle Mariners

	G	AB	Run	Hit	2B	3B	HR	TB	RBI	W	K	IW	HB	SB	CS	BRng Eff	GI DP	SH	SF	Avg	Slug	OBP	Runs Ctd
Valle	124	367	39	88	16	1	9	133	30	27	58	1	8	0	0	.238	7	7	1	.240	.362	.305	41
Martinez Tino	136	460	53	118	19	2	16	189	66	42	77	9	2	2	1	.354	24	1	8	.257	.411	.316	55
Reynolds H	140	458	55	113	23	3	3	151	33	45	41	1	3	15	12	.429	12	11	4	.247	.330	.316	47
Martinez E	135	528	100	181	46	3	18	287	73	54	61	2	4	14	4	.403	15	1	5	.343	.544	.404	116
Vizquel	136	483	49	142	20	4	0	170	21	32	38	0	2	15	13	.370	14	9	1	.294	.352	.340	54
Mitchell K	99	360	48	103	24	0	9	154	67	35	46	4	3	0	4	.351	4	0	4	.286	.428	.351	56
Griffey Jr	142	565	83	174	39	4	27	302	103	44	67	15	5	10	5	.531	14	0	4	.308	.535	.361	106
Buhner	152	543	69	132	16	3	25	229	79	71	146	2	6	0	6	.257	12	1	8	.243	.422	.333	77
O'Brien P	134	396	40	88	15	1	14	147	52	40	27	8	0	2	1	.308	8	1	7	.222	.371	.289	44
Cotto	108	294	42	76	11	1	5	104	27	14	49	3	1	23	2	.426	2	3	1	.259	.354	.294	34
Briley	86	200	18	55	10	0	5	80	12	4	31	0	1	9	2	.194	4	0	2	.275	.400	.290	23
Parrish Ln	69	192	19	45	11	1	8	82	21	19	48	2	1	1	1	.172	6	0	2	.234	.427	.304	24
Cochrane	65	152	10	38	5	0	2	49	12	12	34	0	1	1	0	.250	3	2	0	.250	.322	.309	16
Boone B	33	129	15	25	4	0	4	41	15	4	34	0	1	1	1	.438	4	1	0	.194	.318	.224	8
Amaral	35	100	9	24	3	0	1	30	7	5	16	0	0	4	2	.333	4	4	0	.240	.300	.276	7
Turner	34	74	8	20	5	0	0	25	5	9	15	0	0	2	1	.278	4	2	2	.270	.338	.341	8
Blowers	31	73	7	14	3	0	1	20	2	6	20	0	0	0	0	.071	3	1	0	.192	.274	.253	5
Schaefer	65	70	5	8	2	0	1	13	3	2	10	0	0	1	1	.583	2	6	0	.114	.186	.139	1
Howitt	13	37	6	10	4	1	1	19	8	3	5	0	0	1	1	.500	2	0	3	.270	.514	.302	5
Sinatro	18	28	0	3	0	0	0	3	0	0	5	0	0	0	0	.500	1	0	0	.107	.107	.107	0
Moses	21	22	3	3	1	0	0	4	1	5	4	0	0	0	0	.000	0	2	0	.136	.182	.296	2
Haselman	8	19	1	5	0	0	0	5	0	0	7	0	0	0	0	.250	1	0	0	.263	.263	.263	1
Heffernan	8	11	0	1	1	0	0	2	1	0	1	0	0	0	0	.000	1	0	0	.091	.182	.091	0
Lennon	1	2	0	0	0	0	0	0	0	0	0	0	0	0	0	.000	0	0	0	.000	.000	.000	0
Bradley S	2	1	0	0	0	0	0	0	0	1	1	0	0	0	0	.000	0	0	0	.000	.000	.500	0
Delucia	1	0	0	0	0	0	0	0	0	0	0	0	0	0	0	.000	0	0	0	.000	.000	.000	0
Acker	1	0	0	0	0	0	0	0	0	0	0	0	0	0	0	.000	0	0	0	.000	.000	.000	0
Powell	1	0	0	0	0	0	0	0	0	0	0	0	0	0	0	.000	0	0	0	.000	.000	.000	0
Nelson J	1	0	0	0	0	0	0	0	0	0	0	0	0	0	0	.000	0	0	0	.000	.000	.000	0
TOTALS	1799	5564	679	1466	278	24	149	2239	638	474	841	47	38	100	55	.358	147	52	51	.263	.402	.323	712

Sabermetric Batting Records for Seattle Mariners

	AB	Run	Hit	2B	3B	HR	RBI	W	SO	Avg	Slug	OBP	Runs Ctd	Outs	27o	OW%	OG	OWAR	DWAR	TWAR
Amaral	101	9	24	2	0	0	6	5	16	.238	.257	.274	7	86	2.20	.188	3	-0.51	0.26	-0.25
Blowers	74	7	14	2	0	0	1	6	20	.189	.216	.250	4	63	1.71	.124	2	-0.53	0.23	-0.30
Boone B	131	15	25	3	0	3	14	4	34	.191	.282	.221	8	110	1.96	.156	4	-0.79	0.17	-0.62
Bradley S	1	0	0	0	0	0	0	1	0	.000	.000	.500	0	1	0.00	.000	0	-0.01	0.01	0.00
Briley	197	17	51	9	0	4	11	4	30	.259	.365	.272	19	152	3.38	.354	6	0.02	0.07	0.09
Buhner	553	70	133	14	4	24	78	74	146	.241	.410	.332	77	445	4.67	.512	16	2.67	1.54	4.21
Cochrane	153	10	37	4	0	2	11	12	33	.242	.307	.297	15	120	3.38	.354	4	0.02	-0.01	0.01
Cotto	298	43	76	9	1	4	26	14	49	.255	.332	.290	33	229	3.89	.421	8	0.60	0.55	1.15
Griffey Jr	557	79	163	35	3	26	102	45	65	.293	.506	.348	95	416	6.17	.646	15	4.56	1.31	5.88
Haselman	19	1	5	0	0	0	0	0	7	.263	.263	.263	1	14	1.93	.152	1	-0.10	0.07	-0.03
Heffernan	10	0	0	0	0	0	0	0	0	.000	.000	.000	0	10	0.00	.000	0	-0.13	-0.02	-0.15
Howitt	36	5	9	3	0	0	7	3	4	.250	.333	.293	3	31	2.61	.247	1	-0.12	0.26	0.15
Lennon	2	0	0	0	0	0	0	0	0	.000	.000	.000	0	2	0.00	.000	0	-0.03	0.00	-0.02
Martinez E	537	102	183	41	4	17	72	56	61	.341	.527	.404	117	376	8.40	.772	14	5.88	0.45	6.33
Martinez Tino	455	50	111	17	1	15	65	43	75	.244	.385	.307	50	376	3.59	.383	14	0.45	0.37	0.82
Mitchell K	366	49	104	21	0	8	66	36	46	.284	.407	.350	55	270	5.50	.592	10	2.42	0.48	2.91
Moses	21	3	2	0	0	0	0	5	3	.095	.095	.269	1	21	1.29	.074	1	-0.21	0.05	-0.17
O'Brien P	392	38	82	13	0	13	51	41	26	.209	.342	.280	39	327	3.22	.333	12	-0.21	0.37	0.15
Parrish Ln	195	19	45	9	1	7	20	19	48	.231	.395	.300	23	157	3.96	.429	6	0.46	-0.12	0.34
Reynolds H	463	55	112	20	3	3	32	46	40	.242	.317	.311	46	391	3.18	.327	14	-0.34	1.18	0.84
Schaefer	71	5	8	1	0	0	2	2	10	.113	.127	.137	2	72	0.75	.026	3	-0.86	0.01	-0.85
Sinatro	28	0	3	0	0	0	0	0	5	.107	.107	.107	0	25	0.00	.000	1	-0.32	-0.05	-0.37
Turner	72	7	18	4	0	0	4	9	14	.250	.306	.329	8	66	3.27	.340	2	-0.02	0.04	0.02
Valle	374	40	89	14	1	8	29	28	58	.238	.345	.304	41	301	3.68	.394	11	0.49	-0.75	-0.26
Vizquel	488	49	141	17	4	0	20	33	37	.289	.340	.335	53	384	3.73	.400	14	0.71	2.28	3.00
TOTALS	5627	682	1456	250	27	149	637	493	831	.259	.392	.320	704	4485	4.24	.463	166	18.82	8.77	27.59

Pitching Records for Seattle Mariners

	ERA	W	L	Pct	G	GS	CG	ShO	GF	Sv	IP	R	ER	H	2B	3B	HR	BB	IW	SO	HB	WP	BK
Fleming	3.39	17	10	.630	33	33	7	4	0	0	228.1	95	86	225	53	4	13	60	3	112	4	8	1
Johnson R	3.77	12	14	.462	31	31	6	2	0	0	210.1	104	88	154	33	2	13	144	1	241	18	13	1
Hanson	4.82	8	17	.320	31	30	6	1	0	0	186.2	110	100	209	34	4	14	57	1	112	7	6	0
Fisher	4.53	4	3	.571	22	14	0	0	2	1	91.1	49	46	80	20	0	9	47	2	26	1	3	1
Leary	4.91	3	4	.429	8	8	1	0	0	0	44.0	27	24	47	7	2	3	30	3	12	5	2	0
Parker C	7.56	0	2	.000	8	6	0	0	1	0	33.1	28	28	47	12	0	6	11	0	20	2	1	0
Kramer	7.71	0	1	.000	4	4	0	0	0	0	16.1	14	14	30	6	0	2	7	0	6	1	0	0
Walker MA	7.36	0	3	.000	5	3	0	0	1	0	14.2	14	12	21	4	0	4	9	3	5	0	1	0
Swan	4.74	3	10	.231	55	9	1	0	26	9	104.1	60	55	104	22	4	8	45	7	45	3	6	0
Delucia	5.49	3	6	.333	30	11	0	0	6	1	83.2	55	51	100	26	1	13	35	1	66	2	1	0
Nelson J	3.44	1	7	.125	66	0	0	0	27	6	81.0	34	31	71	10	3	7	44	12	46	6	2	0
Grant	3.89	2	4	.333	23	10	0	0	4	0	81.0	39	35	100	22	1	6	22	2	42	2	2	0
Jones Cd	5.69	3	5	.375	38	1	0	0	14	0	61.2	39	39	50	9	1	8	47	1	49	2	10	0
Powell	4.58	4	2	.667	49	0	0	0	11	0	57.0	30	29	49	13	0	5	29	2	35	3	2	0
Schooler	4.70	2	7	.222	53	0	0	0	36	13	51.2	29	27	55	6	1	7	24	6	33	1	0	0
Acker	5.28	0	0	.000	17	0	0	0	3	0	30.2	19	18	45	11	0	4	12	1	11	0	1	0
Agosto	5.89	0	0	.000	17	1	0	0	2	0	18.1	12	12	27	5	0	0	3	0	12	0	0	0
Woodson K	3.29	0	1	.000	8	1	0	0	0	0	13.2	7	5	12	2	0	0	11	0	6	2	1	0
Barton	2.92	0	1	.000	14	0	0	0	2	0	12.1	5	4	10	2	1	1	7	2	4	0	2	0
Harris Ge	7.00	0	0	.000	8	0	0	0	2	0	9.0	7	7	8	1	0	3	6	0	6	0	0	1
Gunderson	8.68	2	1	.667	9	0	0	0	4	0	9.1	12	9	12	3	0	1	5	3	2	1	0	2
Brown K	9.00	0	0	.000	2	0	0	0	0	0	3.0	3	3	4	1	1	1	3	0	2	0	0	0
Schmidt D	18.90	0	0	.000	3	0	0	0	0	0	3.1	7	7	7	1	0	1	3	0	1	0	0	0
TOTALS	4.55	64	98	.395	534	162	21	7	141	30	1445.0	799	730	1467	303	25	129	661	50	894	60	61	6

Sabermetric Pitching Records for Seattle Mariners

	Adj ERA	-Expected- W	L	Pct	BFP	Avg	Slg	OBA	RC/G	GDP	SB	CS	PK	PKE	SH	SF	RSup	RSp/G	W	L	Pct
Acker	5.28	0	0	.356	148	.338	.511	.388	7.99	1	1	1	0	0	1	2	13	3.82	0	0	.301
Agosto	5.89	0	0	.307	84	.346	.410	.366	5.88	2	3	0	0	0	2	1	13	6.38	0	0	.492
Barton	2.92	1	0	.644	50	.238	.405	.347	3.68	1	0	3	0	2	1	0	6	4.38	1	0	.650
Brown K	9.00	0	0	.160	15	.333	.833	.467	12.99	1	0	0	0	0	0	0	0	0.00	0	0	.000
Delucia	5.49	3	6	.338	382	.293	.490	.361	6.59	6	5	2	1	0	2	2	48	5.16	4	5	.422
Fisher	4.53	3	4	.428	394	.234	.371	.326	4.38	4	6	3	1	0	1	3	53	5.22	4	3	.522
Fleming	3.39	15	12	.573	946	.257	.371	.306	3.82	16	18	14	0	5	3	2	110	4.34	16	11	.574
Grant	3.89	3	3	.504	352	.311	.441	.357	5.38	11	4	2	0	2	5	1	40	4.44	3	3	.518
Gunderson	8.68	1	2	.170	45	.324	.486	.400	6.81	0	1	3	0	1	0	2	7	6.75	1	2	.333
Hanson	4.82	10	15	.398	809	.287	.402	.341	4.75	25	15	4	0	1	8	9	81	3.91	9	16	.351
Harris Ge	7.00	0	0	.239	40	.235	.529	.350	6.38	1	0	0	0	2	0	0	10	10.00	0	0	.627
Johnson R	3.77	14	12	.521	922	.206	.307	.344	3.98	14	42	16	0	10	3	8	101	4.32	14	12	.521
Jones Cd	5.69	3	5	.322	275	.226	.385	.361	5.00	5	6	3	0	2	1	4	32	4.67	3	5	.357
Kramer	7.71	0	1	.206	84	.400	.560	.458	10.91	2	3	0	0	0	1	0	11	6.06	0	1	.337
Leary	4.91	3	4	.390	210	.280	.399	.394	6.37	4	10	1	0	0	2	5	27	5.52	4	3	.511
Nelson J	3.44	5	3	.565	352	.245	.372	.353	4.45	9	4	3	0	2	9	3	33	3.67	4	4	.483
Parker C	7.56	0	2	.212	154	.338	.554	.390	8.01	4	3	1	0	1	0	2	15	4.05	0	2	.191
Powell	4.58	3	3	.423	243	.238	.374	.340	4.13	7	3	3	0	0	5	0	22	3.47	2	4	.322
Schmidt D	18.90	0	0	.041	19	.438	.688	.526	16.79	0	0	0	0	0	0	0	1	2.70	0	0	.017
Schooler	4.70	4	5	.410	232	.275	.420	.351	5.61	3	8	1	0	0	4	3	16	2.79	2	7	.224
Swan	4.74	5	8	.406	457	.262	.398	.338	4.77	9	5	2	0	1	7	5	32	2.76	3	10	.218
Walker MA	7.36	1	2	.221	74	.333	.587	.411	10.10	1	3	0	0	0	1	1	2	1.23	0	3	.022
Woodson K	3.29	1	0	.587	62	.245	.286	.403	4.26	2	0	0	0	0	0	0	6	3.95	1	0	.543
TOTALS	4.57	69	93	.424	6349	.266	.400	.348	4.95	128	140	62	2	29	56	53	679	4.23	67	95	.414

Batting 'Splits' Records for Seattle Mariners

SPLITS for Seattle Mariners (all batters except pitchers)

	G	AB	Run	Hit	2B	3B	HR	TB	RBI	W	K	IW	HB	SB	CS	DP	SH	SF	Avg	Slug	OBP	RC
vs LHP	792	1506	204	420	77	1	49	646	196	146	220	15	10	27	12	40	22	13	.279	.429	.344	222
vs RHP	1645	4058	475	1046	201	23	100	1593	442	328	621	32	28	73	43	107	30	38	.258	.393	.315	491
Home	881	2742	355	736	173	13	78	1169	338	239	417	24	23	52	27	72	17	29	.268	.426	.329	380
Away	918	2822	324	730	105	11	71	1070	300	235	424	23	15	48	28	75	35	22	.259	.379	.317	333
Grass	713	2205	279	592	85	9	59	872	260	197	333	20	13	38	22	55	28	18	.268	.395	.330	286
Turf	1086	3359	400	874	193	15	90	1367	378	277	508	27	25	62	33	92	24	33	.260	.407	.318	426
April/June	837	2570	315	659	128	11	78	1043	299	211	364	21	16	52	25	67	29	20	.256	.406	.315	322
July/October	962	2994	364	807	150	13	71	1196	339	263	477	26	22	48	30	80	23	31	.270	.399	.330	390

National League
Western Division

1. Atlanta Braves
2. Cincinnati Reds
3. San Diego Padres
4. Houston Astros
5. San Francisco Giants
6. Los Angeles Dodgers

NL Western Division Team Batting

	G	AB	Run	Hit	2B	3B	HR	TB	RBI	W	K	IW	HB	SB	CS	BRng Eff	GI DP	SH	SF	Avg	Slug	OBP	Runs Ctd
Atlanta	2277	5480	682	1391	223	48	138	2124	641	493	924	58	26	126	60	.425	82 93	50		.254	.388	.316	691
Cincinnati	2208	5460	660	1418	281	44	99	2084	606	563	888	83	21	125	65	.422	124 66	52		.260	.382	.328	695
Houston	2398	5480	608	1350	255	38	96	1969	582	506	1025	65	48	139	54	.438	96 88	40		.246	.359	.313	641
Los Angeles	2337	5368	548	1333	201	34	72	1818	499	503	899	36	24	142	78	.362	108102	40		.248	.339	.313	583
San Diego	2186	5476	617	1396	255	30	135	2116	576	453	864	67	26	69	52	.368	126 78	41		.255	.386	.313	653
San Francisco	2298	5456	574	1330	220	36	105	1937	532	435	1067	53	39	112	64	.426	111101	39		.244	.355	.302	588

NL Western Division Sabermetric Team Batting

	AB	Run	Hit	2B	3B	HR	RBI	W	SO	Avg	Slug	OBP	Runs Ctd	Outs	Run/ 27o	OW%	OG	OWAR
Atlanta	5467	669	1367	226	61	135	624	487	944	.250	.388	.312	679	4375	4.19	.541	162	30.92
Cincinnati	5413	641	1427	277	47	86	592	548	866	.264	.380	.330	690	4290	4.34	.551	159	32.01
Houston	5617	668	1406	272	40	113	640	510	1002	.250	.373	.315	681	4501	4.09	.518	167	28.06
Los Angeles	5311	563	1315	208	33	90	525	531	907	.248	.350	.317	603	4317	3.77	.516	160	26.50
San Diego	5474	578	1350	261	32	113	538	438	895	.247	.368	.303	602	4418	3.68	.475	164	20.47
San Francisco	5354	578	1319	219	36	102	526	463	1106	.246	.358	.309	600	4356	3.72	.493	161	23.13

NL Western Division Team Pitching

	ERA	W	L	Pct	G	GS	CG	ShO	GF	Sv	IP	R	ER	H	2B	3B	HR	BB	IW	SO	HB	WP	BK
Atlanta	3.14	98	64	.605	500	162	26	14	136	41	1460.0	569	510	1321	236	30	89	489	55	948	26	58	10
Cincinnati	3.46	90	72	.556	519	162	9	4	153	55	1449.2	609	558	1362	249	48	109	470	51	1060	28	54	6
Houston	3.74	81	81	.500	584	162	5	2	157	45	1459.1	668	606	1386	255	49	114	539	60	978	38	45	14
Los Angeles	3.41	63	99	.389	515	162	18	11	144	29	1438.0	636	545	1401	226	33	82	553	95	981	28	64	10
San Diego	3.58	82	80	.506	525	162	9	6	153	46	1461.1	636	581	1444	220	27	111	439	53	971	21	25	15
San Francisco	3.61	72	90	.444	548	162	9	5	153	30	1461.0	647	586	1385	243	37	128	502	61	927	35	34	22

NL Western Division Sabermetric Team Pitching

	Adj ERA	Expected W	L	Pct	BFP	Opposing Batters Avg	Slg	OBA	RC/G	GDP	SB	CS	PK	PKE	SH	SF	Supported RSup	RSp/G	W	L	Pct
Atlanta	3.09	91	71	.563	6072	.242	.345	.305	3.64	95	149	66	4	16	53	37	682	4.20	98	64	.602
Cincinnati	3.35	85	77	.523	6042	.251	.375	.312	4.00	100	103	54	4	16	78	47	660	4.10	89	73	.550
Houston	4.09	69	93	.423	6213	.252	.378	.320	4.26	97	129	54	4	16	87	46	608	3.75	66	96	.407
Los Angeles ·	3.50	81	81	.501	6192	.257	.355	.326	4.10	113	141	62	4	16	109	44	548	3.43	71	91	.440
San Diego	3.35	85	77	.522	6132	.261	.371	.315	4.06	89	141	69	4	16	93	43	617	3.80	83	79	.512
San Francisco	3.65	78	84	.480	6134	.253	.382	.318	4.03	137	75	64	4	16	88	42	574	3.54	70	92	.434

```
NL Western Division Catchers
               G    PO   A   Er   TC   DP  PB   SB  CS  CS%   FPct      DI   DG   DW%   DWAR  ERA
Atlanta       162  979   75   2  1056  15  13  149  66 .307  .998  1459.2 10.0  .457   1.07  3.14
Cincinnati    162 1104   76  10  1190  11   8  103  54 .344  .992  1449.1 10.0  .356   0.06  3.46
Houston       162 1018   99   9  1126  11  13  129  54 .295  .992  1459.1 10.0  .318  -0.32  3.74
Los Angeles   162 1031  118  17  1166  14  20  141  62 .305  .985  1438.0 10.0  .354   0.04  3.41
San Diego     162 1015   90  15  1120  14   2  141  69 .329  .987  1461.0 10.0  .309  -0.41  3.58
San Francisco 162  961   95   6  1062  18  17   75  64 .460  .994  1460.2 10.0  .360   0.10  3.61
LG.AVG        162  987   92  10  1089  11  11  130  61 .319  .991  1458.1
```

```
NL Western Division First Base
               G    PO    A   Er   TC   DP   FPct     DI    DG   DW%   DWAR
Atlanta       162 1408  120  12  1540  108  .992  1459.2  3.0  .460   0.33
Cincinnati    162 1365  117   5  1487  113  .997  1449.1  3.0  .549   0.60
Houston       162 1385  133   8  1526  114  .995  1459.1  3.0  .617   0.80
Los Angeles   162 1449  149  10  1608  120  .994  1438.0  3.0  .594   0.73
San Diego     162 1351  112  14  1477  102  .991  1461.0  3.0  .386   0.11
San Francisco 162 1473  127  12  1612  149  .993  1460.2  3.0  .513   0.49
LG.AVG        162 1456  121  10  1587  119  .994  1458.1
```

```
NL Western Division Second Base
               G    PO    A   Er   TC   DP   FPct     DI    DG   DW%   DWAR
Atlanta       162  323  452  15   790   90  .981  1459.2  8.0  .475   1.00
Cincinnati    162  314  447  12   773   91  .984  1449.1  8.0  .461   0.89
Houston       162  359  429  12   800   83  .985  1459.1  8.0  .445   0.76
Los Angeles   162  425  530  32   987   99  .968  1438.0  8.0  .510   1.28
San Diego     162  379  437  19   835   92  .977  1461.0  8.0  .451   0.80
San Francisco 162  395  509  20   924  132  .978  1460.2  8.0  .685   2.68
LG.AVG        162  349  488  16   853   98  .981  1458.1
```

```
NL Western Division Third Base
               G    PO    A   Er   TC   DP   FPct     DI    DG   DW%   DWAR
Atlanta       162  135  340  20   495   29  .960  1459.2  6.0  .562   1.27
Cincinnati    162  105  304  18   427   24  .958  1449.1  6.0  .423   0.44
Houston       162  131  279  16   426   22  .962  1459.1  6.0  .425   0.45
Los Angeles   162  101  318  22   441   27  .950  1438.0  6.0  .388   0.23
San Diego     162  117  343  20   480   27  .958  1461.0  6.0  .488   0.83
San Francisco 162  119  325  26   470   36  .945  1460.2  6.0  .489   0.83
LG.AVG        162  114  317  21   452   26  .954  1458.1
```

```
NL Western Division Shortstop
                G    PO    A   Er    TC   DP  FPct       DI   DG    DW%    DWAR
Atlanta        162  237  476   23   736   77  .969   1459.2 11.0   .471    1.33
Cincinnati     162  266  476   17   759   87  .978   1449.1 11.0   .531    1.99
Houston        162  238  463   26   727   80  .964   1459.1 11.0   .423    0.80
Los Angeles    162  234  448   52   734   89  .929   1438.0 11.0   .306   -0.49
San Diego      162  270  444   12   726   76  .983   1461.0 11.0   .475    1.37
San Francisco  162  254  487   22   763  103  .971   1460.2 11.0   .551    2.21
LG.AVG         162  264  479   23   766   89  .970   1458.1
```

```
NL Western Division Left Field
                G    PO    A   Er    TC   DP  FPct       DI   DG    DW%    DWAR
Atlanta        162  331    5    8   344    0  .977   1459.2  4.0   .432    0.33
Cincinnati     162  294    9    3   306    1  .990   1449.1  4.0   .481    0.52
Houston        162  419    8    7   434    2  .984   1459.1  4.0   .577    0.91
Los Angeles    162  306    9   10   325    3  .969   1438.0  4.0   .370    0.08
San Diego      162  362   12    8   382    2  .979   1461.0  4.0   .566    0.86
San Francisco  162  338    6    5   349    3  .986   1460.2  4.0   .480    0.52
LG.AVG         162  340    8    7   355    1  .980   1458.1
```

```
NL Western Division Center Field
                G    PO    A   Er    TC   DP  FPct       DI   DG    DW%    DWAR
Atlanta        162  475   10    4   489    3  .992   1459.2  6.0   .648    1.79
Cincinnati     162  455   14    9   478    4  .981   1449.1  6.0   .563    1.28
Houston        162  453    8    5   466    3  .989   1459.1  6.0   .544    1.17
Los Angeles    162  389    9    3   401    2  .993   1438.0  6.0   .471    0.73
San Diego      162  463   18    4   485    7  .992   1461.0  6.0   .679    1.97
San Francisco  162  440    7    1   448    3  .998   1460.2  6.0   .610    1.56
LG.AVG         162  443    9    5   457    3  .989   1458.1
```

```
NL Western Division Right Field
                G    PO    A   Er    TC   DP  FPct       DI   DG    DW%    DWAR
Atlanta        162  391   12   14   417    3  .966   1459.2  5.0   .584    1.17
Cincinnati     162  346   15    6   367    4  .984   1449.1  5.0   .630    1.40
Houston        162  284   14    8   306    0  .974   1459.1  5.0   .504    0.77
Los Angeles    162  271    5   12   288    0  .958   1438.0  5.0   .227   -0.62
San Diego      162  348   11    7   366    4  .981   1461.0  5.0   .535    0.93
San Francisco  162  327   15   10   352    2  .972   1460.2  5.0   .576    1.13
LG.AVG         162  325   11    7   343    2  .980   1458.1
```

Atlanta Braves

Win Murray

ATLANTA YEAR	1983	1984	1985	1986	1987	1988	1989	1990	1991	1992
W	88	80	66	72	69	54	63	65	94	98
L	74	82	96	89	92	106	97	97	68	64
WPCT	0.543	0.494	0.407	0.447	0.429	0.338	0.394	0.401	0.580	0.605
R	746	632	632	615	747	555	584	682	749	682
RA	640	655	781	719	829	741	680	821	644	569
PWPT	0.576	0.482	0.396	0.423	0.448	0.359	0.424	0.408	0.575	0.590
PythW	93	78	64	68	73	58	69	66	93	96
PythL	69	84	98	94	89	104	93	96	69	66
LUCK	-5	2	2	4	-4	-4	-6	-1	1	2

Defensive Efficiency Record: .7104

In these days of free agency and accelerating roster turnover, the Atlanta Braves are the only team positioned to be a dynasty. Thanks to no front-line free agent losses and a bold move to create the best starting staff in recent memory, the Braves' far-flung fans can be comfortable in the knowledge that the Braves look at least as solid as their deal-making NL West rivals (the Reds and the surprising Astros). The Braves, with their powerful starting pitching and well-stocked farm system, have been anointed by the media as a lock to win ninety games a year for the next half-decade.

Lest the other teams in the division sink into a five-year depression, however, let's take a longer look at the team that Bobby Cox will field in 1993. There is no truth-stretching to be found in the statement that the Braves have the best starting rotation in the majors. Tom Glavine and Greg Maddux are the NL's past two Cy Young Award winners; John Smoltz led the NL in strikeouts in '92 (albeit by forfeit, but he's a strong shot to do it again in '93 now that David Cone is a Royal); Steve Avery is still only 23; and Pete Smith seems to have overcome arm miseries to become the best #5 pitcher in the NL.

Of course, there's more to a pitching staff than just the starters. The Braves clearly have had ongoing bullpen problems, but these haven't stemmed from lack of talent. Cox has been frustrated by the lack of a consistent right-handed closer, and has shown a marked tendency to ride the hot hand among his lefties. Kent Mercker and Mike Stanton are still young (25 and 26 respectively), but they've been around long enough to be seen as suspects instead of prospects. Cox seems to use them like a bank robber uses dynamite. Mercker had a great first half (2.08 ERA, 36-19 K/BB), but developed a sore arm and had a dreadful second half (4.25 ERA, 13-16 K/BB). He wound up in Cox' doghouse by season's end, and was left off the World Series roster. Cox said he was taken off due to injury, but Mercker claims that his arm was fine. Mercker was quite upset at not being taken in the expansion draft. He appears to need constant work to stay sharp

Position	92 Starter	TWAR	93 Starter	TWAR
Catcher	Berryhill	1.14	Berryhill	1.14
	Olson	1.19	Olson	1.19
First base	Bream	3.24	Bream	3.24
Second base	Lemke	1.04	Lemke	1.04
Third base	Pendleton	7.01	Pendleton	7.01
Shortstop	Blauser	3.78	Blauser	3.78
Left field	Gant	4.43	Gant	4.43
Center field	Nixon	4.05	Nixon	4.05
Right field	Justice	5.78	Justice	5.78

(career ERA, 1-2 days rest: 2.24; > 3 days, 4.92; in '92: 1.57/6.46), but I doubt that Cox will give it to him.

On the basis of last year, Stanton will almost certainly be the number one lefty out of the pen. While Mike also had dramatic differences between first-half and second-half ERA (6.10/2.20), his K/BB ratio was more consistent: the difference appears to have been the gopher ball (6 HR allowed in the first half, 0 in the second). Cox went with Stanton as a co-closer with Reardon down the stretch: given his habit of riding the hot hand, one expects to see Stanton used as a combination set-up man and co-closer with Mark Wohlers. This scenario could easily create a climate for overuse: a similar situation occurred when Russ Nixon was managing the Braves, and cost Stanton most of the 1990 season due to arm problems.

Despite being seen as a disappointment thus far, Wohlers is only 23 and is the only viable candidate to be the Braves' right-handed closer in '93. The Cox hot-hand bullpen pattern will likely favor him early due to a strong finish in '92 (1.65 ERA after the All-Star break). Cox appeared hesitant to go to him in save situations last year; but if the Braves are unable to trade for a closer, it's likely that Wohlers will get a shot at being the primary man. What may be worrying Cox is that Wohlers has yet to come close to duplicating his minor-league strikeout ratios (11.48 K/9 in the minors from '90-'92; 4.91 in the majors). Commitment to a course of action can have intangible benefits, however: the Expos saw John Wetteland bloom in the second half of '92 thanks in part to their patience with him in the closer role. Cox might do the Braves and Wohlers a big favor by copying the Expos' behavior with Wetteland.

The rest of the Braves bullpen is very thin. Marvin Freeman is a passable long reliever, but he has never mastered his stuff and remains painfully inconsistent. The Braves were hit hard over the winter, and the attrition rate has seriously eroded their perceived "limitless" pitching depth (Leibrandt was traded to Texas; Ben Rivera was lost last year via waivers; Alejandro Pena and Jeff Reardon, failed closers, were allowed to go free agent, as was Mike Bielecki, who pitched awfully well for the Braves in between stints on the DL). In the short term, this lack of depth may not prove to be very important, but as the year goes on, it could have a devastating effect on the Braves' starters.

Bobby Cox is already well-known as the type of manager who likes to stay with his starters as long as he can; he'd rather start the seventh inning of a close game with a tired Glavine than a rested Freeman. Cox knows that his pitchers hit very well; he knows he has little depth in the pen; and he knows that he has ridden these starters for a few years with an absolutely incredible record of health. All of this, coupled with the amount of mileage already put on young arms, points to some kind of injury to one or more starters during '93. Likely candidates: Maddux or Smoltz (fastballers with more than 900 IP before the age of 27). Of course, it is possible that Cox' good fortune will hold, and that nothing major will happen. But the scenario exists based on widespread occurrence elsewhere, and if a starter or two develops arm trouble, the Braves are not in a good position to replace them.

Questions concerning potential storm clouds for the Braves' pitching staff are purely speculative. Concerns about possible problems with the Braves' offense, however, are much more real. The following players should be regulars/platoon starters this year:

1. Nixon/Sanders, cf
2. Blauser, ss
3. Pendleton, 3b
4. Justice, rf
5. Gant, lf
6. Bream/Hunter, 1b
7. Berryhill/Olson, c
8. Lemke, 2b

Looking at the last five years of these players' careers, who has the highest batting average? Pendleton, at .280. No one else is better than Justice's .269. Highest OBP? Justice, at .366. No one else is higher than .339 (Blauser). The team does have consistent power, with Justice, Gant, and Hunter hitting at least one homer every 23 AB's, and Bream, Blauser, Sanders, and Pendleton slamming one at least per 40 ABs.

Sanders, however, might not come to terms with the team; and even if he does he might get on the bad side of management through continuing insubordination. Another storm signal is Deion's lack of patience at the plate, especially in the second half, when he was in the midst of controversy (just two walks in 86 plate appearances and a .302 OBP). If Sanders is not available or is ineffective, then Nixon and Gant become the only regulars with any discernable speed. Otis will be 34 this season and may be starting to revert to his previous offensive form: he hit only .266 after the All-Star break in '92 (with an OBP of .318, too low for a leadoff man). Despite the fact that he has played well as a Brave (like many, he is helped by hitting in the Pad), he just can't be counted on to remain at this level for much longer. His SB percentage declined significantly last year, which might mean that he has lost a step. Any further slippage in his performance will push him below the margin of effectiveness as a leadoff man. All of this tends to indicate that the Braves' leadoff slot, so strong for the past two seasons, may be far less effective in '93.

Mark Lemke, Greg Olson, and Damon Berryhill must be viewed for what they are—below average offensive players, even at their positions. It is still unclear whether Olson will be able to return from his ankle injury, but even if he does, his playing career is not far from being over. He hit .238 last year with 14 doubles and 3 homers in 302 AB, had an OBP of .316. After the break: .216 BA, .287 OBP. Olson is 32, and at that age there is little to look forward to but decline, and offensively he is already marginal. Berryhill is only 29, but he is less selective than Olson (walks in just 5.3% of his plate appearances, .268 OBP). He had a career high 10 HR (again, helped by the Pad: he hit .291 in Atlanta, just .170 on the road), but his career OBP is so anemic (.277) that he cannot continue to placed in the lineup on the merits of occasional power. Lemke will only be 27 this year, so there is some hope for his bat, though he has shown little growth over the past four years. One possible ray of hope: in the second half last year, Lemke showed a signficant jump in walks (14.1% vs. his lifetime 9.4%). How much of this is due to intentional passes from batting 8th is hard to quantify, but the 5'9" Lemke could be more effective with a higher OBP (just .297 lifetime).

Bream and Pendleton have both turned 32, but I believe that they will continue to be productive. Bream's numbers were slightly down in '92, but his second-half stats were better (he had a memorable hot streak in August, driving in 22 runs). Cox has also gotten savvier about how to platoon Sid, playing him much more selectively and saving him for pinch-hitting, where he was quite effective last year (.333 BA, .529 OBP). Sid has a good eye at the plate and still produces a healthy number of doubles (25.3% of his hits in '92, in the Top Ten in the NL; 25.1% over the last five years). He's painfully slow due to bad knees, but runs intelligently and has enough intangibles that even if his numbers do slip some more, he'll still make a positive contribution to the offense.

Pendleton will also remain productive in '93, though no one should expect him to hit .300 with 20 HRs again. It will become very imporant for him to start taking some days off: he played in 160 games last season. Utility man Bill Pecota, recently signed as a free agent, should allow Cox to rest Terry more often during the next year.

Gant, Justice, and Blauser are all entering their peak years (Gant will be 28, Justice and Blauser 27). Justice is a true talent, slugging over .500 in the second half after a slow start. Historically, he's a killer in September (lifetime .571 SA), but there has not always been smooth sailing prior to the stretch drive. Justice is continually cited in the local press as a poor influence in the clubhouse. He and Sanders seem to have especial difficulties in getting along. Justice has shown a bit of the Strawberry persona: mercurial attitude, a tendency to milk injuries, prone to back problems, but if he's healthy physically and mentally, he can carry a team all by himself. By the end of '92, most of the fans seemed to have forgotten about his slow start, and if he begins '93 well, it might be his best season to date.

Gant also struggled at the plate last year; unlike Justice, he never quite broke out of it. Ronnie's career profile does not contain the standard week or month-long slump-and-surge pattern, but has instead many long, extended periods of either exceptional or downright poor offensive performance. Last year his BA and OBP were almost identical to his career norm, but his slugging was way down. When Gant is in an offensive surge, he becomes an extreme pull hitter, but last year he tended to spray the ball more. I suspect that he will bounce back: a sure way to tell will be if most of his foul ball are landing in the seats just to the left of the LF foul pole. If so, then he is very likely to return to his 30+ HR ways.

Jeff Blauser has always been a moderately productive player, but last year, as Cox gained confidence in his defensive ability at SS, he started to become more of a free swinger at the plate. The result was a marked increase in power and a related rise in OBP (.354 for the year, .402 in the second half). Blauser might be a better leadoff man than Nixon simply due to the OBP: he certainly would be if Nixon's production should slide.

So let's sum up the Braves' offense in light of these thoughts. With dead weight at both catcher and second base, a questionable center fielder, and probable offensive decline imminent at the corners, the Braves could very well have only four or five truly productive slots in the lineup this year. When a team's offense looks like this, it can only group those hitters together at the top of the lineup and hope for synergy. Can that type of offense win games? Yes, with the Braves' starters. Can that offense win 95 games? Probably not.

Is there any help ready to come up from the farm? Possibly. I believe that catcher Javier Lopez could play in the majors right now. He's a legitimate .300 hitter with 10-15 HR power. In fact, I think that every effort should be made to start him in the bigs this year. Maddux would like Berryhill to be his personal catcher, but if Lopez can catch two or three of the other other big starters, it would help his career immensely. The Braves could really use a bat like his in the lineup, as they have virtually no high average hitters.

Ryan Klesko, the highly-touted first base prospect, isn't ready. He could probably hit 13-18 HRs in the NL, but with a very low BA (in the .220s), and with few walks (about 7%). Outfield prospect Melvin Nieves, on the other hand, could help the team halfway through the season if Nixon slumps and Deion goes to football camp. His MLE shows that he has a lot of potential pop (20+ doubles, 15+ homers), and he's just 21.

Francisco Cabrera has proven time and again that he can hit, and hit with power. The Braves' handling of their playoff hero has, frankly, been baffling. Not considered to be acceptable defensively as a catcher, Cabrera has languished in the minors when it is clear from his MLE's that he could be a fourth 20+ HR man for the Braves right now. It would make a lot more sense for the Braves to move Gant back to center, platoon Sanders and Hunter in left, and give Cabrera the right-hand spot in the first base platoon with Bream. The Braves' power would improve signficantly, and there would still be room for Nixon as a roving replacement outfielder—especially given Justice's history of injuries.

Make no mistake: Ted Turner, whose effect on the business of baseball is insufficiently understood by insiders and outsiders alike, has built himself quite a team in Atlanta. Baseball fans from all over the country can tune in every night and see one of his four number one starters try to shut down the opposition. They can watch what is certain to be another pennant chase for the Braves in the NL West, the new "toughest division" in baseball. This year, however, may just be the one that the division rivals have waited for: a thin relief corps, an aging Pendleton, subpar offensive production up the middle, and a starting staff overdue for adversity through injury all cast a shadow over the Braves' colorized grins. Those grins in the team picture might also have gotten a trifle self-satisfied after two consecutive titles. This much is for certain: there will be hungrier teams in the NL West, and the Reds and Astros will be two of them. The Braves may well end up averaging 90 wins a year over the next half-decade; but they'll probably need at least 95 to make it back to the post-season this year.

Atlanta Braves Home Park Performance Factors														
	Outs	Runs	Hits	2b	3b	HR	W	K	SH	SF	HBP	IBB	SB	CS	GDP
Home LH Batters	.997	1.050	1.034	1.062	1.142	.977	.919	1.035	.988	.759	.774	1.249	1.398	.988	.805
Home RH Batters	.970	.942	.934	.981	.958	.943	.827	1.015	.974	.790	.768	.905	1.017	.905	.905
All Home Batters	.984	.959	.969	.999	1.104	.932	.872	1.010	.994	.876	.787	1.032	1.070	.983	.906
Opp LH Batters	1.001	.874	.909	.837	.911	1.033	1.019	1.013	.905	1.083	1.561	1.190	.890	1.012	1.147
Opp RH Batters	1.059	1.078	1.058	1.176	1.729	1.074	1.186	1.060	.997	.828	.982	1.466	1.049	.953	1.102
All Opp Batters	1.022	1.004	.997	1.035	1.458	1.031	1.106	1.033	.970	.863	1.104	1.300	1.021	.998	1.101
All LH Batters	.999	.960	.972	.951	1.060	.994	.967	1.025	.941	.866	.980	1.216	1.105	1.005	.928
All RH Batters	1.016	1.018	.999	1.083	1.269	1.023	.997	1.038	1.019	.824	.874	1.133	1.008	.923	1.008
All Batters	1.002	.983	.983	1.016	1.239	.980	.980	1.021	.994	.876	.918	1.156	1.035	.987	1.004

Conventional Batting Records for Atlanta Braves

	G	AB	Run	Hit	2B	3B	HR	TB	RBI	W	K	IW	HB	SB	CS	BRng Eff	GI DP	SH	SF	Avg	Slug	OBP	Runs Ctd
Olson Greg	95	302	27	72	14	2	3	99	27	34	31	4	1	2	1	.405	8	1	2	.238	.328	.316	32
Bream	125	372	30	97	25	1	10	154	61	46	51	2	1	6	0	.345	3	3	4	.261	.414	.340	57
Lemke	155	427	38	97	7	4	6	130	26	50	39	11	0	0	3	.247	9	12	2	.227	.304	.307	41
Pendleton	160	640	98	199	39	1	21	303	105	37	67	8	0	5	2	.453	16	5	7	.311	.473	.345	102
Belliard	144	285	20	60	6	1	0	68	14	14	43	4	3	0	1	.302	6	13	0	.211	.239	.255	18
Gant	153	544	74	141	22	6	17	226	80	45	101	5	7	32	10	.557	10	0	6	.259	.415	.321	75
Nixon O	120	456	79	134	14	2	2	158	22	39	54	0	0	41	18	.505	4	5	2	.294	.346	.348	58
Justice	144	484	78	124	19	5	21	216	72	79	85	8	2	2	4	.418	1	0	6	.256	.446	.359	84
Blauser	123	343	61	90	19	3	14	157	46	46	82	2	4	5	5	.517	2	7	3	.262	.458	.354	59
Berryhill	101	307	21	70	16	1	10	118	43	17	67	4	1	0	2	.345	4	0	3	.228	.384	.268	31
Sanders	97	303	54	92	6	14	8	150	28	18	52	0	2	26	9	.486	5	1	1	.304	.495	.346	51
Hunter B	102	238	34	57	13	2	14	116	41	21	50	3	0	1	2	.463	2	1	8	.239	.487	.292	35
Smith Lo	84	158	23	39	8	2	6	69	33	17	37	1	3	4	0	.515	1	0	4	.247	.437	.324	25
Treadway	61	126	5	28	6	1	0	36	5	9	16	4	0	1	2	.222	3	1	0	.222	.286	.274	9
Glavine	35	77	11	19	1	1	0	22	7	3	10	0	0	0	0	.500	0	9	1	.247	.286	.272	7
Avery	35	76	8	13	2	1	0	17	4	3	22	0	0	0	0	.385	0	9	0	.171	.224	.203	4
Smoltz	36	75	7	12	0	0	1	15	4	6	32	0	0	0	0	.375	1	10	0	.160	.200	.222	4
Leibrandt	32	58	1	7	1	0	0	8	4	1	12	0	0	0	0	.222	1	8	1	.121	.138	.133	1
Smith P	12	26	1	1	0	0	0	1	2	2	11	0	0	0	0	.500	0	3	0	.038	.038	.107	0
Bielecki	19	24	1	3	0	0	0	3	0	0	13	0	0	0	0	.000	1	4	0	.125	.125	.125	0
Willard	26	23	2	8	1	0	2	15	7	1	3	1	0	0	0	.000	3	0	0	.348	.652	.375	4
Nieves M	12	19	0	4	1	0	0	5	1	2	7	0	0	0	0	.000	0	0	0	.211	.263	.286	2
Gregg	18	19	1	5	0	0	1	8	1	1	7	0	0	1	0	.250	1	0	0	.263	.421	.300	2
Castilla	9	16	1	4	1	0	0	5	1	1	4	1	1	0	0	.000	0	0	0	.250	.313	.333	2
Lopez J	9	16	3	6	2	0	0	8	2	0	1	0	0	0	0	.000	0	0	0	.375	.500	.375	3
Lyons S	11	14	0	1	0	1	0	3	1	0	4	0	0	0	0	.000	1	0	0	.071	.214	.071	0
Klesko	13	14	0	0	0	0	0	0	1	0	5	0	1	0	0	.000	0	0	0	.000	.000	.067	0
Cabrera	12	10	2	3	0	0	2	9	3	1	1	0	0	0	0	.000	0	0	0	.300	.900	.364	3
Nied	6	7	1	2	0	0	0	2	0	0	2	0	0	0	0	.000	0	0	0	.286	.286	.286	1
Mercker	53	5	0	0	0	0	0	0	0	0	5	0	0	0	0	.000	0	0	0	.000	.000	.000	0
Freeman M	58	4	0	2	0	0	0	2	0	0	2	0	0	0	0	.000	0	0	0	.500	.500	.500	1
Pena A	41	2	0	0	0	0	0	0	0	0	2	0	0	0	0	.000	0	0	0	.000	.000	.000	0
Berenguer	28	2	0	0	0	0	0	0	0	0	1	0	0	0	0	.000	0	0	0	.000	.000	.000	0
Stanton M	65	2	1	1	0	0	0	1	0	0	0	0	0	0	0	.000	0	0	0	.500	.500	.500	1
Wohlers	32	2	0	0	0	0	0	0	0	0	2	0	0	0	0	.000	0	0	0	.000	.000	.000	0
Reynoso	3	2	0	0	0	0	0	0	0	0	1	0	0	0	0	.000	0	1	0	.000	.000	.000	0
Rivera B	8	1	0	0	0	0	0	0	0	0	1	0	0	0	0	.000	0	0	0	.000	.000	.000	0
Davis Mrk	14	1	0	0	0	0	0	0	0	0	1	0	0	0	0	.000	0	0	0	.000	.000	.000	0
St.Claire	10	0	0	0	0	0	0	0	0	0	0	0	0	0	0	.000	0	0	0	.000	.000	.000	0
Reardon	14	0	0	0	0	0	0	0	0	0	0	0	0	0	0	.000	0	0	0	.000	.000	.000	0
Borbon	2	0	0	0	0	0	0	0	0	0	0	0	0	0	0	.000	0	0	0	.000	.000	.000	0
TOTALS	2277	5480	682	1391	223	48	138	2124	641	493	924	58	26	126	60	.425	82	93	50	.254	.388	.316	691

Sabermetric Batting Records for Atlanta Braves

	Ball Park Adjusted								Runs						Run/					
	AB	Run	Hit	2B	3B	HR	RBI	W	SO	Avg	Slug	OBP	Ctd	Outs	27o	OW%	OG	OWAR	DWAR	TWAR
Belliard	287	20	59	6	1	0	13	14	44	.206	.233	.248	17	246	1.87	.189	9	-1.46	1.05	-0.41
Berryhill	305	20	68	16	1	9	41	16	68	.223	.370	.260	29	244	3.21	.409	9	0.53	0.61	1.14
Blauser	345	61	89	20	4	14	45	46	85	.258	.461	.348	59	270	5.90	.700	10	3.50	0.27	3.78
Bream	368	28	94	23	1	10	60	44	52	.255	.405	.334	55	281	5.28	.652	10	3.14	0.10	3.24
Cabrera	9	2	2	0	0	2	2	1	1	.222	.889	.300	2	7	7.71	.800	0	0.12	0.00	0.12
Castilla	15	1	3	1	0	0	0	1	4	.200	.267	.250	1	12	2.25	.253	0	-0.04	0.02	-0.02
Gant	548	74	140	23	8	17	79	45	104	.255	.420	.317	75	431	4.70	.597	16	3.94	0.48	4.43
Gregg	17	0	4	0	0	1	0	0	7	.235	.412	.235	2	13	4.15	.536	0	0.09	0.06	0.15
Hunter B	239	34	56	14	2	14	40	21	51	.234	.485	.289	35	192	4.92	.619	7	1.91	0.29	2.21
Justice	479	75	120	18	5	21	71	76	87	.251	.441	.352	81	368	5.94	.703	14	4.81	0.97	5.78
Klesko	13	0	0	0	0	0	0	0	5	.000	.000	.071	0	13	0.00	.000	0	-0.17	0.00	-0.16
Lemke	425	37	95	7	5	5	25	49	39	.224	.299	.303	40	353	3.06	.386	13	0.47	0.57	1.04
Lopez J	15	3	5	2	0	0	1	0	1	.333	.467	.333	2	10	5.40	.662	0	0.12	0.05	0.16
Lyons S	12	0	0	0	1	0	0	0	4	.000	.167	.000	0	12	0.00	.000	0	-0.16	0.01	-0.14
Nieves M	18	0	3	1	0	0	0	1	7	.167	.222	.211	1	15	1.80	.179	1	-0.10	-0.01	-0.10
Nixon O	453	77	131	14	2	1	21	38	55	.289	.336	.343	56	348	4.34	.559	13	2.69	1.36	4.05
Olson Greg	304	27	71	15	2	3	26	34	32	.234	.326	.310	31	242	3.46	.445	9	0.85	0.34	1.19
Pendleton	637	96	195	39	1	20	102	36	68	.306	.465	.340	98	469	5.64	.681	17	5.75	1.26	7.01
Sanders	299	51	89	5	14	8	27	17	53	.298	.488	.340	50	223	6.05	.711	8	2.98	0.36	3.34
Smith Lo	158	23	38	8	2	6	32	17	38	.241	.430	.317	24	124	5.23	.647	5	1.36	0.12	1.48
Treadway	124	4	27	5	1	0	4	8	16	.218	.274	.265	9	101	2.41	.280	4	-0.26	0.48	0.22
Willard	21	1	7	0	0	2	6	0	3	.333	.619	.333	3	16	5.06	.632	1	0.17	0.00	0.17
TOTALS	5467	669	1367	226	61	135	624	487	944	.250	.388	.312	679	4375	4.19	.541	162	30.92	8.40	39.32

Pitching Records for Atlanta Braves

	ERA	W	L	Pct	G	GS	CG	ShO	GF	Sv	IP	R	ER	H	2B	3B	HR	BB	IW	SO	HB	WP	BK
Smoltz	2.85	15	12	.556	35	35	9	3	0	0	246.2	90	78	206	39	5	17	80	5	215	5	17	1
Avery	3.20	11	11	.500	35	35	2	2	0	0	233.2	95	83	216	31	6	14	71	3	129	0	7	3
Glavine	2.76	20	8	.714	33	33	7	5	0	0	225.0	81	69	197	37	4	6	70	7	129	2	5	0
Leibrandt	3.36	15	7	.682	32	31	5	2	0	0	193.0	78	72	191	34	4	9	42	4	104	5	3	2
Bielecki	2.57	2	4	.333	19	14	1	1	0	0	80.2	27	23	77	16	5	2	27	1	62	1	4	0
Smith P	2.05	7	0	1.000	12	11	2	1	0	0	79.0	19	18	63	11	2	3	28	2	43	0	2	1
Mercker	3.42	3	2	.600	53	0	0	0	18	6	68.1	27	26	51	10	0	4	35	1	49	3	6	0
Freeman M	3.22	7	5	.583	58	0	0	0	15	3	64.1	26	23	61	9	1	7	29	7	41	1	4	0
Stanton M	4.10	5	4	.556	65	0	0	0	23	8	63.2	32	29	59	11	0	6	20	2	44	2	3	0
Pena A	4.07	1	6	.143	41	0	0	0	31	15	42.0	19	19	40	5	0	7	13	5	34	0	0	0
Wohlers	2.55	1	2	.333	32	0	0	0	16	4	35.1	11	10	28	3	0	0	14	4	17	1	1	0
Berenguer	5.13	3	1	.750	28	0	0	0	8	1	33.1	22	19	35	8	2	7	16	4	19	1	2	2
Nied	1.17	3	0	1.000	6	2	0	0	0	0	23.0	3	3	10	5	0	0	5	0	19	0	0	0
Davis Mrk	7.02	1	0	1.000	14	0	0	0	7	0	16.2	13	13	22	5	0	3	13	2	15	1	4	1
Rivera B	4.70	0	1	.000	8	0	0	0	3	0	15.1	8	8	21	2	1	1	13	2	11	2	0	0
St.Claire	5.87	0	0	.000	10	0	0	0	1	0	15.1	11	10	17	5	0	1	8	3	7	0	0	0
Reardon	1.15	3	0	1.000	14	0	0	0	11	3	15.2	2	2	14	0	0	0	2	1	7	1	0	0
Reynoso	4.70	1	0	1.000	3	1	0	0	1	1	7.2	4	4	11	4	0	2	2	1	2	1	0	0
Borbon	6.75	0	1	.000	2	0	0	0	2	0	1.1	1	1	2	1	0	0	1	1	1	0	0	0
TOTALS	3.14	98	64	.605	500	162	26	14	136	41	1460.0	569	510	1321	236	30	89	489	55	948	26	58	10

Sabermetric Pitching Records for Atlanta Braves

	Adj ERA	-Expected- W	L	Pct	BFP	Avg	Slg	OBA	RC/G	GDP	SB	CS	PK	PKE	SH	SF	RSup	RSp/G	W	L	Pct
Avery	3.12	12	10	.558	969	.246	.343	.300	3.59	16	42	14	0	6	12	8	102	3.93	12	10	.564
Berenguer	4.86	1	3	.342	148	.269	.523	.354	6.62	3	5	1	1	0	2	0	22	5.94	2	2	.549
Bielecki	2.45	4	2	.671	336	.254	.360	.315	3.92	7	8	2	1	0	3	2	37	4.13	4	2	.698
Borbon	0.00	0	0	.000	7	.333	.500	.429	9.56	0	0	0	0	0	0	0	0	0.00	0	0	.000
Davis Mrk	6.48	0	1	.226	85	.314	.514	.424	8.94	1	0	0	0	1	0	1	12	6.48	0	1	.449
Freeman M	3.08	7	5	.564	276	.251	.383	.332	4.30	6	7	5	0	0	2	1	13	1.82	3	2	.222
Glavine	2.68	18	10	.631	919	.235	.310	.293	3.04	18	13	10	0	4	2	6	133	5.32	21	7	.763
Leibrandt	3.26	12	10	.535	799	.258	.351	.301	3.69	6	28	16	3	14	7	4	92	4.29	13	9	.585
Mercker	3.29	3	2	.531	289	.207	.297	.312	3.47	4	12	2	0	0	4	1	18	2.37	1	4	.297
Nied	0.78	3	0	.952	83	.130	.195	.183	1.19	1	2	0	0	0	1	0	14	5.48	3	0	.976
Pena A	3.86	3	4	.452	173	.255	.420	.310	4.29	5	5	1	0	0	2	1	6	1.29	1	6	.083
Reardon	0.57	3	0	.974	62	.241	.241	.279	2.43	1	2	0	0	0	1	0	6	3.45	1	0	.967
Reynoso	3.52	0	1	.497	32	.393	.750	.452	9.02	2	0	1	1	0	1	0	10	11.74	1	0	.901
Rivera B	4.11	0	1	.421	78	.339	.452	.462	8.07	2	2	2	0	1	0	1	11	6.46	1	0	.668
Smith P	1.94	5	2	.766	323	.217	.300	.285	3.14	1	8	2	2	0	4	1	39	4.44	6	1	.811
Smoltz	2.77	17	10	.615	1021	.224	.332	.287	3.35	10	11	7	2	0	7	8	117	4.27	18	9	.659
St.Claire	5.28	0	0	.305	68	.283	.417	.368	5.39	2	0	1	0	0	0	0	2	1.17	0	0	.039
Stanton M	3.96	4	5	.439	264	.247	.368	.308	3.80	5	1	2	2	1	1	2	43	6.08	6	3	.658
Wohlers	2.29	2	1	.700	140	.235	.261	.319	2.67	5	3	1	0	0	5	1	5	1.27	1	2	.201
TOTALS	3.09	91	71	.563	6072	.242	.345	.305	3.64	95	149	66	13	27	53	37	682	4.20	98	64	.602

Batting 'Splits' Records for Atlanta Braves

SPLITS for Sanders

	G	AB	Run	Hit	2B	3B	HR	TB	RBI	W	K	IW	HB	SB	CS	DP	SH	SF	Avg	Slug	OBP	RC
vs LHP	35	48	10	13	1	4	2	28	5	2	12	0	0	4	0	0	1	0	.271	.583	.300	9
vs RHP	92	255	44	79	5	10	6	122	23	16	40	0	2	22	9	5	0	1	.310	.478	.354	42
Home	48	138	21	36	2	4	5	61	14	13	27	0	1	7	4	2	1	0	.261	.442	.329	20
Away	49	165	33	56	4	10	3	89	14	5	25	0	1	19	5	3	0	1	.339	.539	.360	32
Grass	69	213	39	60	3	9	7	102	19	17	38	0	1	17	7	4	1	1	.282	.479	.336	34
Turf	28	90	15	32	3	5	1	48	9	1	14	0	1	9	2	1	0	0	.356	.533	.370	18
April/June	57	191	35	65	4	11	6	109	16	15	31	0	0	18	8	3	0	0	.340	.571	.388	41
July/October	40	112	19	27	2	3	2	41	12	3	21	0	2	8	1	2	1	1	.241	.366	.271	12

SPLITS for Atlanta Braves (all batters except pitchers)

	G	AB	Run	Hit	2B	3B	HR	TB	RBI	W	K	IW	HB	SB	CS	DP	SH	SF	Avg	Slug	OBP	RC
vs LHP	924	1719	247	465	76	15	56	739	234	140	265	21	5	37	17	22	20	25	.271	.430	.323	245
vs RHP	1768	3761	435	926	147	33	82	1385	407	353	659	37	21	89	43	60	73	25	.246	.368	.313	447
Home	1153	2636	343	681	106	19	72	1041	326	271	434	26	16	58	28	42	44	25	.258	.395	.328	355
Away	1124	2844	339	710	117	29	66	1083	315	222	490	32	10	68	32	40	49	25	.250	.381	.304	336
Grass	1685	4008	497	1024	158	32	107	1567	469	379	694	41	20	90	46	64	68	36	.255	.391	.320	516
Turf	592	1472	185	367	65	16	31	557	172	114	230	17	6	36	14	18	25	14	.249	.378	.303	175
April/June	996	2531	304	652	102	25	64	996	287	212	429	19	12	66	32	36	38	22	.258	.394	.315	321
July/October	1281	2949	378	739	121	23	74	1128	354	281	495	39	14	60	28	46	55	28	.251	.383	.316	369

Cincinnati Reds

Don Malcolm

CINCINNATI YEAR	1983	1984	1985	1986	1987	1988	1989	1990	1991	1992
W	74	70	89	86	84	87	75	91	74	90
L	88	92	72	76	78	74	87	71	88	72
WPCT	0.457	0.432	0.553	0.531	0.519	0.54	0.463	0.562	0.457	0.556
R	623	627	677	732	783	641	632	693	689	660
RA	710	747	666	717	752	596	691	597	691	609
PWPT	0.435	0.413	0.508	0.51	0.52	0.536	0.455	0.574	0.499	0.540
PythW	70	67	82	83	84	87	74	93	81	88
PythL	92	95	80	79	78	75	88	69	81	74
LUCK	4	3	7	3	0	0	1	-2	-7	2

Defensive Efficiency Record: .6985

SOME NOTES ON RACISM AND MARGE SCHOTT

Baseball as an institution is the most pathetic construction in the history of western civilization, which is saying a lot. It is a small-minded, money-grubbing, sycophantic throwback to the age of the robber barons. Owners with corporate smarts learn to use it to siphon off untold millions while complaining loudly about operating losses. Those with a less suave business sense tend to make more of a spectacle of themselves, creating bizarre cults of personality that look like medicine ball caravans and fundamentalist knockoffs of nineteenth-century minstrel shows.

Baseball's racism is at best unabashed: everything it does with respect to race relations is heavily tinged with tokenism. Brock Hanke is right that eventually there will a black-owned and operated team in baseball. But it won't happen in this century, and it might not happen in the existing two leagues. There is still too much oligopoly floating around in the minds of the movers and shakers of the game. As longer as they can continue their profit-taking without concession to any other set of social issues that touch upon the operation of the game, they will do so.

The charges against Marge Schott amount to nothing more than baseball attempting to find a scapegoat for the larger problem of racism that exists within the game. It's become clear that the owners, as they are on every issue of importance that touches the game, are hopelessly confused. The unfortunate Mrs. Schott is not one to be defended for her views on blacks, Jews, or other social and historical issues. She is a peculiarly American phenomenon—the product of a culture that places most of its emphasis on material acquisition and whatever means are necessary to accomplish it. The fact that the baseball ownership saw fit to admit her to their queer fraternity places her into the continuum of the game's own social contradictions, and speaks as much about the Bud Seligs and Peter O'Malleys of the game as it does about Marge Schott.

Of her many offenses, Schott's most damaging one is simply being voluble and doddering. Her alleged verbal railings against blacks and Jews are probably no more heinous or systematically held than by a large plurality of her fellow Americans. This does not make her views acceptable, but neither does it mean that she should be tarred and feathered for unseemly and despicable acts. Her views may be reprehensible, but she has the right to her own mind, addled and misguided as that mind may be.

The Cincinnati Reds do not show signs of any greater amount of institutional racism than any other team in baseball. The game has been slow to respond to the escalating charges of discrimination in its corporate structure that stemmed from the legendary performance of Al

Position	92 Starter	TWAR	93 Starter	TWAR
Catcher	Oliver	2.76	Oliver	2.76
First base	Morris, H.	2.83	Morris, H.	2.83
Second base	Doran	2.64	Roberts	6.08
Third base	Sabo	1.67	Sabo	1.67
Shortstop	Larkin	7.46	Larkin	7.46
Left field	Roberts	6.08	Mitchell	2.91
Center field	Sanders, R.	4.77	Kelly, R.	2.94
Right field	O'Neill	4.80	Sanders, R.	4.77

Campanis on Nightline. (The ultimate irony is that Campanis was one of Jackie Robinson's defenders during his 1946 season at Montreal: Jules Tygiel in Baseball's Great Experiment relates several incidents where Campanis went out of his way to easy Robinson's burden during that crucial year before major league integration.) The Reds have over the off-season (prior to the charges that surfaced about Schott's remarks) acquired two black starting outfielders, and have hired a black Cuban manager (Tony Perez). The Reds will start 1993 with five blacks in their starting offensive lineup; the Dodgers, the original team to integrate (and they still love to remind you), will have only three.

The charges against Schott and, by extension, her organization, are really directed at her generation and its retrograde world view. We must be careful to distinguish between people's private thoughts and their public actions. Despite the appalling nature of her alleged statement about Adolf Hitler, Marge Schott has not evidenced any focused activity in support of these private views. It is easy to magnify the impact of statements when they are taken out of context, and this appears to be part of the effort of baseball and the media to make her into a scapegoat.

For baseball, this is a convenient way to deflect the issue, and one suspects that they are counting heavily on the almost mindless aggression of the media. Political correctness is not in and of itself the primary criterion for holding positions of influence, no matter how much the media and others would like it to be so. There is a watered-down, aberrant strain of utopianism that has infected the American media in terms of its dealings with people responsible for public policy: their demands for instant justice (just add water), instant solutions to complex problems that have plagued the nation (and many institutions in similar states of imperfection as baseball), and instant vindication for the suffering of people they also exploit via media exposure, have a less salutary effect than they realize. A permanent solution to the problem of racism does not happen by banishing the Marge Schotts of the world; the solution begins by finding a way to make all people look deep into their hearts and minds, and confront their own fears and ignorances.

By victimizing Marge Schott, baseball would not redress the victimization of blacks who have been deprived of the same opportunity for career advancement that whites have had. This "eye for an eye" psychology is one of humankind's most durable and unfortunate characteristics; it is not for us to hope that by returning to it that we can solve complex problems, or absolve ourselves from our own point of entry into transgressions against others.

Part of the institutional problem that baseball has is that it doesn't have any requirement for ownership of a franchise except sufficient capital. In this respect it is like most corporations, and it is clear that those organizations have slowly started to become more cognizant of their social and ethical responsibilities. A great deal of that awareness, however, has come through severe pressure and threat of competitive decline, or through legislation.

What baseball needs so that it might put its own house in order (the entire house, not just the set of rooms that Marge Schott occupies) is a challenge to its competitiveness. Nothing else in America is likely to work. Are there really only twenty-eight ownership groups that can sustain a major league baseball franchise? Isn't it possible that a set of ten or twelve new investors could, with the right planning and appropriate adjustments in business operations which accommodate the needs and rights of non-whites, create a sustain a new major league? Wouldn't that be the way to force the existing establishment to change its ways? If a sizeable number of professional athletes would choose their conscience, and settle for a little less money, they could make a difference. That would be the greatest legacy that all athletes could leave behind, no matter their race. Organize a league where the business is run in a way open for all, where the old notion of pluralism could truly flourish. The entrepreneurial spirit, if wedded properly to progressive social policies, can triumph—even over the most malevolent motivations of the human heart.

So don't censure Marge Schott. Hit her where it hurts: in her wallet. Boycotting Opening Day? Nice symbolism. But it's the children of the game, the athletes who have reaped the benefits of the scramble for talent, who are in the only position to advance the cause of reform. A new Player's League is how the Marge Schotts of the world will become obsolete—because the marketplace will no longer silently condone her ideas. And it doesn't take ninety five million dollars to start a new baseball team, my friends, just a few wealthy men willing to make money in order to effect real change.

Year	BOP	OINX	AB	R	H	TB	D	T	HR	RBI	BB	SO	SB	CS	BA	SA	OBP	RC27	BBP	XBH
1991	1	15.61	680	92	180	252	28	1	14	59	57	103	21	10	.265	.371	.322	4.13	7.7	43
1992	1	20.09	662	107	208	289	43	7	8	57	81	75	52	20	.314	.437	.389	6.31	10.9	58
1991	2	20.42	641	105	184	294	28	5	24	76	70	92	20	10	.287	.459	.357	5.86	9.8	57
1992	2	14.90	652	84	157	227	29	7	9	56	62	101	11	13	.241	.348	.307	3.59	8.7	45
1991	3	19.26	634	97	179	275	34	4	18	84	69	94	22	6	.282	.434	.353	5.44	9.8	56
1992	3	20.41	627	87	186	279	36	6	15	95	79	81	17	3	.297	.445	.375	6.06	11.2	57
1991	4	22.93	605	94	173	300	41	1	28	98	81	123	25	6	.286	.496	.370	6.56	11.8	70
1992	4	18.80	613	73	159	251	27	4	19	89	81	96	11	5	.259	.409	.346	4.88	11.7	50
1991	5	18.84	616	76	163	276	32	3	25	100	51	103	14	6	.265	.448	.321	4.98	7.6	60
1992	5	18.79	614	83	154	262	34	7	20	76	67	97	10	7	.251	.427	.325	4.71	9.8	61
1991	6	16.47	614	64	164	248	26	5	16	77	41	108	11	9	.267	.404	.313	4.40	6.3	47
1992	6	18.67	600	66	176	256	37	5	11	73	58	95	13	10	.293	.427	.356	5.48	8.8	53
1991	7	16.15	590	58	142	226	26	5	16	71	52	115	8	7	.241	.383	.302	3.89	8.1	47
1992	7	15.49	581	65	145	208	35	5	6	57	58	90	6	2	.250	.358	.318	3.86	9.1	46
1991	8	14.74	575	60	138	207	21	3	14	58	43	97	2	0	.240	.360	.293	3.54	7.0	38
1992	8	14.78	559	53	137	191	21	3	9	57	56	97	3	4	.245	.342	.314	3.62	9.1	33
1991	9	9.30	546	43	96	137	14	0	9	31	24	171	1	2	.176	.251	.211	1.63	4.2	23
1992	9	7.94	552	42	96	121	19	0	2	46	21	156	2	1	.174	.219	.204	1.38	3.7	21

		OINX	AB	R	H	TB	D	T	HR	RBI	BB	SO	SB	CS	BA	SA	OBP	RC27	BBP	XBH
DIFF	1	129	97	116	116	115	154	700	57	97	142	73	248	200	119	118	121	153	141	135
	2	73	102	80	85	77	104	140	38	74	89	110	55	130	84	76	86	61	88	79
	3	106	99	90	104	101	106	150	83	113	114	86	77	50	105	103	106	111	114	102
	4	82	101	78	92	84	66	400	68	91	100	78	44	83	91	83	93	74	99	71
	5	100	100	109	94	95	106	233	80	76	131	94	71	117	95	95	101	95	129	102
	6	113	98	103	107	103	142	100	69	95	141	88	118	111	110	106	114	124	141	113
	7	96	98	112	102	92	135	100	38	80	112	78	75	29	104	93	105	99	112	98
	8	100	97	88	99	92	100	100	64	98	130	100	150	—	102	95	107	102	131	87
	9	85	101	98	100	88	136	—	22	148	88	91	200	50	99	87	97	85	87	91
AVG		97.5		96	100	94	112	163	60	93	115	88	101	116				98.7	114.6	96.1

GOIN' DOWNTOWN

That "60" in the AVG DIFF column under home runs is one of the major elements in the Reds' inability to stay with the Braves, and it is the major offensive area they have attempted to address during the off-season. Lou Piniella never did learn to put a lineup together worth a damn, and the Reds managed to underutilize some excellent offensive production from their #1 and #3 slots by batting a collection of nimrods in the #2 slot.

That situation may come to an end now that Tony Perez is in charge. Perhaps Atanasio will see that his starting eight is the best unit in the NL, and it can function exactly as most expect it to if he will just put the lineup together properly. Last year I told you that I didn't think Bip Roberts should bat leadoff, but this year I've changed my mind: the Reds' personnel has changed in significant ways that really affect the structure of the batting order.

These changes are: Kevin Mitchell and Roberto Kelly in the outfield for Dave Martinez, Glenn Braggs, and Paul O'Neill; Bip Roberts to second base full-time in place of Billy Doran. It doesn't sound as dramatic as other off-season facelifts, but it's fairly profound. Let's look at the moves in more detail, and examine what changes they imply for the batting order:

1) Without the power supplied in the eighties by Davis and Daniels, the Reds tried to bank on Chris Sabo and Paul O'Neill as their main power hitters in '91-'92. This worked well enough in '91; the Reds' pitching, particularly their starting pitching, let them down badly that year. Last season, Sabo was hurt and missed more than sixty games; O'Neill started strongly, but just faded from view in June and had a terrible second half in all offensive categories, winding up with just 14 homers.
Mitchell and Kelly should solve this problem. Kelly has never played in a home park that favored homers: Yankee Stadium suppresses HRs by right-handed batters. Playing in Riverfront, he's a legitimate 25 HR man. Mitchell, of course, had the strange year in Seattle last year. People see the 9 HRs and think he was a total flop, but the fact is that Kevin hit .286 and drove in 67 runs in 99 games, which works out to 110 RBI in a full season. You've got to figure that he's going to like being back in the NL, and this revived state of mind is probably worth 30-35 HRs. That works out to a net gain of around 35 homers over last year's starters right there.

2) Bip Roberts had a marvelous season for the Reds, and proved that he belongs as the leadoff hitter on this team, producing excellent doubles power and a consistent stolen base threat. It wasn't his fault that he didn't score more runs than his team-leading total of 92: he was at second base under his own power at least 88 times last season. Last season, on a team that projected to spread its power around the batting order, it made sense to bat Bip sixth, where he could act as a second singles hitter and ignite the bottom part of the Reds' lineup. On a team that leans toward a more conventional distribution of power, Bip's talents should be used to get him on base in front of the big power guys.

Closing the #2 gap shouldn't be much of a problem if Tony evaluates his personnel properly, and decides to bat Barry Larkin #2. The principle we've been espousing is that you should get as much power into the top part of your lineup as you can without sacrificing it in the #5 and #6 slots. If you have to sacrifice it, make the #6 batter the one who can fulfill the functions of a secondary leadoff man. Larkin has excellent doubles power, can hit 15-20 homers, and is also capable of stealing 25-30 bases. He doesn't have the same power potential as Reggie Sanders, so I'd bat him #2 and Sanders #3. One suspects that Tony will do it the opposite way opening up the season.

We'll know soon if Tony has a future as a manager by two things. First, if he bats Kelly second, he's a nimrod and the lineup will be less efficient: Roberto just doesn't draw walks, and this lack of selectivity is just not good in a #2 hitter. Second, if he leaves Sanders in the #2 spot all year, he's not paying attention to the subtle differences between his offensive performers. Sanders' isolated power as a rookie was .192; Larkin's, as a veteran, was .150. It is likely that Sanders could hit 40 doubles and 25 homers this season. While I like power at the top of the lineup, that's too much power in the #2 slot unless you have five more hitters that can do that for you.

So my tout for the 1993 Reds lineup looks like this:

1. Roberts, 2b
2. Larkin, ss
3. Sanders, cf
4. Mitchell, lf
5. Sabo, 3b
6. Kelly, rf
7. Morris, 1b
8. Oliver, c

That's a lineup a little bit heavy on right-handed hitting (only Bip, who switch-hits, and Morris will provide left-handed hitting). Morris really faded away in the second half: he and O'Neill really dampened what could have been an offensive charge after the All-Star Break. This might be a crossroads year for Morris: if the Reds hadn't bungled the waiver rules with Reggie Jefferson, Hal would be on very thin ice. As it is, 21-year old Willie Greene has an outside shot to take at least part of the first base job away from Morris this season.

So how many more homers should the Reds hit this year? Let's pencil Mitchell in for 30, Sanders, Kelly, and Sabo 70 among the three of them. That's 100, one more than the Reds hit all last year. Then let's add Larkin's 15, and figure Morris for 10, Oliver for 12, and Bip for six. Then there are reserves like Greene (5-10) and Juan Samuel (5-7). We're edging toward a top limit of around 160 HRs, or right around the 1991 total. And the Reds are going to need every one of those taters to stay close to the Braves.

DEALING DOWN TO WIN

It's Brock Hanke's insight, derived from watching Whitey Herzog at work with the early 80s Cardinals. You deal down in talent in an area where you were overly abundant, and make it up on the margins of the defensive spectrum. It looks to be a tried and true method, and it has lots of variations. The Reds' variant is particularly interesting.

In 1990 the Reds had a ridiculously deep bullpen. By "deep" I don't just mean a lot of bodies. The Reds had Myers, Charlton, and Dibble, all legitimate closers, in the same bullpen. Since then, the Reds have dealt down this strength to just Dibble, and have received Bip Roberts and Kevin Mitchell. It was similar to the move the Reds made in late 1987 that helped to set up their World Championship year: they traded away Dave Parker for Jose Rijo.

What this means, though, is that the Reds must feel that they have sufficient replacements for Myers and Charlton, both of whom are now gone. They may think that they have a new setup man in Milt Hill, who has yet to have an ERA higher than 2.70 in the minors. He had 18 saves with Nashvile last season. Steve Foster also appears ready to assume a significant amount of responsibility in the Reds' bullpen: he was especially strong during the second half (2.13 ERA, 9.47 baserunners per nine innings). The righty contingent looks strong enough to make the Reds forget about Scott Bankhead, who logged a lot of good innings for them as a setup man last year.

For the left side, the Reds signed veteran Greg Cadaret. He's awfully wild (4.87 BB/9), but he's pretty effective against lefties (.236 opposition batting average over the past five years) and could be helpful if used properly.

The starting pitching was improved significantly in the "swap" of Swindell for Smiley. John's opposition BA figures are quite a bit better, plus he's a much stronger finisher (.234 opposition BA from the seventh on compared to Swindell's .299 in 1992). Rijo, Smiley and Belcher are a fine Big Three, and the Reds can piece together a serviceable bsck two-fifths of a rotation by choosing from Tom Browning, Chris Hammond, and Tim Pugh. It ain't the Braves Big Four, but it's just as strong at the top and longer at the bottom.

I expect the Reds to be a lot closer to the Braves this season, and the result of the race might depend on whether they can seize the advantage in head to head play. The reduced number of games between the teams might work in the Reds' favor; the bad news is that the Braves get the extra home contest this season.

And no, I don't think the Reds will be distracted by any goings on regarding Marge Schott. They have managed to work around Marge before. I think a certain amount of turmoil between the players and the team ownership is actually healthy: it can often serve as subliminal motivation. A change from a fiery manager to one who is more laid-back is often a success, too: witness the 1978 Yankees with Bob Lemon taking over for Billy Martin, or the 1982 Brewers with Harvey Kuenn for Buck Rodgers. One suspects that Perez will be a "let them play" manager, which might be the best thing for a team with Mitchell and Dibble in the same clubhouse. The Reds have enough hitting to actually run away from the Braves—if everyone can stay in the lineup. If they can't, the bench strength is low—no credible backup shortstop, no solid fourth outfielder (Juan Samuel and Tommy Gregg, each picked up off the slag heap, are the best contenders here for supersub-type roles).

Last year the Reds lost the pennant in July and August—they went 27-29 in those two months, while the Braves went 35-19. That's nine games' difference: the Braves won the division by eight. If the Reds can play up to the level they achieved in April-June and in September last season (.613 winning percentage), they'll dislodge the Braves. If they can't, they won't. It's a simple as that, sabermetrics notwithstanding.

The other breakout which mirrors the above is the Reds' record against lefties in '92: 28-29, while the Braves were 34-19. But the Reds will lucky to see more than 40 lefty starters in '92 due to their adjustment for this defect in their offense. They'll probably need to go about 28-12 against lefties to make it past the Braves. Keep your eye on the USA Today breakouts on Wednesdays to see if they're matching these goals.

```
Cincinnati Reds Home Park Performance Factors
                 Outs  Runs  Hits   2b    3b    HR    W     K     SH    SF    HBP   IBB   SB    CS    GDP
Home LH Batters  1.002 .955  .965  .983  .983  .852  .975 1.058  .983 1.207  .536  .983 1.242 1.073  .818
Home RH Batters   .964 .862  .969  .887 1.066  .808  .894  .958  .753  .798  .724  .925 1.063  .960  .860
All Home Batters  .975 .886  .968  .912 1.086  .808  .917  .983  .824  .902  .692  .973  .992 1.020  .877
Opp LH Batters    .953 1.113 .990  .870  .937 1.253  .937  .904 1.124 1.548 1.213 1.022  .809  .733 1.178
Opp RH Batters   1.021 1.007 1.086 1.228 1.321  .855 1.081 1.001 1.084 1.377 1.197 1.125 1.041 1.177 1.083
All Opp Batters   .997 1.059 1.045 1.064 1.085  .939 1.031  .968 1.051 1.322 1.171 1.130  .990 1.023 1.060
All LH Batters    .973 1.041 .980  .915  .956 1.057  .953  .960 1.064 1.352  .906  .989  .933  .851  .993
All RH Batters    .990 .931 1.026 1.027 1.181  .829  .981  .974  .904 1.031  .951 1.012 1.051 1.062  .960
All Batters       .986 .967 1.006  .983 1.082  .873  .972  .970  .935 1.077  .918 1.040  .993 1.023  .960
```

```
                            Conventional Batting Records for Cincinnati Reds

                                                                     BRng  GI                      Runs
             G    AB   Run  Hit  2B   3B   HR   TB   RBI  W    K   IW HB  SB  CS  Eff   DP SH SF  Avg  Slug OBP  Ctd
Oliver      143  485   42  131   25   1   10  188   57   35   75  19  1   2   3  .324  12  6  7  .270 .388 .316  58
Morris H    115  395   41  107   21   3    6  152   53   45   53   8  2   6   6  .303  12  2  2  .271 .385 .347  52
Doran       132  387   48   91   16   2    8  135   47   64   40   9  0   7   4  .356  11  3  2  .235 .349 .342  48
Sabo         96  344   42   84   19   3   12  145   43   30   54   1  1   4   5  .457  12  1  6  .244 .422 .302  41
Larkin B    140  533   76  162   32   6   12  242   78   63   58   8  4  15   4  .461  13  2  7  .304 .454 .377  95
Roberts Bip 147  532   92  172   34   6    4  230   45   62   54   4  2  44  16  .529   7  1  4  .323 .432 .393  96
Martinez Da 135  393   47  100   20   5    3  139   31   42   54   4  0  12   8  .523   6  6  4  .254 .354 .323  46
O'Neill     148  496   59  122   19   1   14  185   66   77   85  15  2   6   3  .376  11  3  6  .246 .373 .346  68

Sanders R   116  385   62  104   26   6   12  178   36   48   98   2  4  16   7  .494   6  0  1  .270 .462 .356  65
Braggs       92  266   40   63   16   3    8  109   38   36   48   5  2   3   1  .509  10  1  2  .237 .410 .330  36
Benavides    74  173   14   40   10   1    1   55   17   10   34   4  1   0   0  .545   3  2  0  .231 .318 .277  15
Coles        55  141   16   44   11   2    3   68   18    3   15   0  1   0   1  .423   1  3  2  .312 .482 .322  22
Branson      72  115   12   34    7   1    0   43   15    5   16   2  0   0   1  .423   4  2  1  .296 .374 .322  13
Hatcher B    43   94   10   27    3   0    2   36   10    5   11   0  0   0   2  .308   2  0  3  .287 .383 .314  11
Greene W     29   93   10   25    5   2    2   40   13   10   23   0  0   0   2  .529   1  0  1  .269 .430 .337  13
Swindell     31   80    2   10    2   0    0   12    4    1   15   0  0   0   0  .077   0  5  1  .125 .150 .134   2
Belcher      35   76    3    8    1   0    1   12    4    0   28   0  0   0   0  .000   1  7  0  .105 .158 .105   1
Rijo         33   72    3   14    2   0    0   16    6    0   18   0  0   0   0  .429   1  6  0  .194 .222 .194   3
Hernandez Ce 34   51    6   14    4   0    0   18    4    0   10   0  0   3   1  .357   1  0  0  .275 .353 .275   5
Hammond      30   44    7    6    1   0    1   10    4    6   20   0  0   0   0  .143   0  3  1  .136 .227 .235   3
Costo        12   36    3    8    2   0    0   10    2    5    6   0  0   0   0  .167   4  0  1  .222 .278 .310   3
Afenir       16   34    3    6    1   2    0   11    4    5   12   0  0   0   0  .143   0  1  0  .176 .324 .282   4
Browning     16   31    4    7    1   0    0    8    2    1    6   0  0   0   0  .125   1  2  1  .226 .258 .242   2
Brumfield    24   30    6    4    0   0    0    4    2    2    4   1  1   6   0  .429   0  0  0  .133 .133 .212   2
Reed Jf      15   25    2    4    0   0    0    4    2    1    4   1  0   0   0  .500   1  0  0  .160 .160 .192   1
Wilson D     12   25    2    9    1   0    0   10    3    0    8   0  0   0   0  .250   2  0  0  .360 .400 .429   4
Wrona        11   23    0    4    0   0    0    4    0    0    3   0  0   0   0  .000   2  0  0  .174 .174 .174   0
Berroa       13   15    2    4    1   0    0    5    0    2    1   0  1   0   1  .500   1  0  0  .267 .333 .389   2
Bolton       16   14    0    0    0   0    0    0    0    0    5   0  0   0   0  .000   0  1  0  .000 .000 .000   0
Pugh          7   13    0    1    0   0    0    1    0    1    4   0  0   0   0  .000   0  1  0  .077 .077 .143   0
Green G       8   12    3    4    1   0    0    5    0    0    2   0  0   0   0  .500   0  0  0  .333 .417 .333   0
Bankhead     54    9    0    2    0   0    0    2    0    0    7   0  0   0   0  .000   0  2  0  .222 .222 .222   1
Ayala B       5    9    1    0    0   0    0    0    0    0    6   0  0   0   0  .000   0  1  0  .000 .000 .000   0
Charlton     64    5    0    1    0   0    0    1    0    0    3   0  0   0   0  .000   0  2  0  .200 .200 .200   0
Foster S     31    5    0    1    0   0    0    1    0    0    1   0  0   0   0  .000   0  0  0  .200 .200 .200   0
Dibble       63    5    0    2    0   0    0    2    1    0    0   0  0   0   0  .000   0  0  0  .400 .400 .400   1
Bradley S     5    5    1    2    0   0    0    2    1    1    0   0  0   0   0  .500   0  0  0  .400 .400 .500   1
Henry        60    4    1    1    0   0    0    1    0    0    3   0  0   0   0  .500   0  0  0  .250 .250 .250   0
Ruskin       57    3    0    0    0   0    0    0    0    0    3   0  0   0   0  .000   0  0  0  .000 .000 .000   0
Brown Kth     2    2    0    0    0   0    0    0    0    0    1   0  0   0   0  .000   0  1  0  .000 .000 .000   0
Hillmi       14    0    0    0    0   0    0    0    0    0    0   0  0   0   0  .000   0  0  0  .000 .000 .000   0
Menendez      3    0    0    0    0   0    0    0    0    0    0   0  0   0   0  .000   0  0  0  .000 .000 .000   0

TOTALS     2208 5460  660 1418  281  44   99 2084  606  563  888  83 21 125  65  .422 124 66 52 .260 .382 .328 695
```

Sabermetric Batting Records for Cincinnati Reds

		——— Ball Park Adjusted ———						Runs		Run/									
	AB	Run	Hit	2B	3B	HR	RBI	W	SO	Avg	Slug	OBP	Ctd	Outs	27o	OW%	OG	OWAR	DWAR	TWAR
Afenir	33	2	6	1	2	0	3	4	11	.182	.333	.270	3	27	3.00	.370	1	0.02	0.09	0.11
Benavides	172	13	41	10	1	0	16	9	33	.238	.308	.276	14	135	2.80	.338	5	-0.06	0.32	0.26
Berroa	14	1	4	1	0	0	0	1	0	.286	.357	.333	1	11	2.45	.282	0	-0.03	0.02	-0.01
Bradley S	3	1	1	0	0	0	1	0	0	.333	.333	.333	0	2	0.00	.000	0	-0.03	-0.00	-0.03
Braggs	265	37	64	16	3	6	36	35	47	.242	.392	.330	34	213	4.31	.548	8	1.56	-0.11	1.45
Branson	112	12	33	6	0	0	15	4	15	.295	.348	.316	12	85	3.81	.486	3	0.43	0.21	0.64
Brumfield	29	5	4	0	0	0	1	1	3	.138	.138	.167	1	25	1.08	.071	1	-0.26	0.07	-0.19
Coles	141	14	45	11	2	2	17	2	14	.319	.468	.324	22	100	5.94	.697	4	1.29	0.17	1.46
Costo	35	2	8	2	0	0	1	4	5	.229	.286	.300	3	31	2.61	.308	1	-0.05	0.05	0.00
Doran	382	46	91	15	2	6	45	62	39	.238	.335	.343	46	309	4.02	.513	11	1.86	0.77	2.64
Green G	11	2	4	1	0	0	0	0	1	.364	.455	.364	2	7	7.71	.795	0	0.12	-0.01	0.11
Greene W	90	10	24	4	1	2	13	9	22	.267	.400	.330	12	68	4.76	.597	3	0.62	0.05	0.68
Hatcher B	93	9	27	3	0	1	9	4	10	.290	.355	.310	10	72	3.75	.478	3	0.34	-0.04	0.31
Hernandez Ce	50	5	14	4	0	0	3	0	9	.280	.360	.280	5	37	3.65	.465	1	0.16	0.06	0.21
Larkin B	534	71	166	33	7	9	75	62	56	.311	.449	.381	95	392	6.54	.736	15	5.61	1.86	7.46
Martinez Da	383	48	97	18	4	3	31	40	52	.253	.345	.320	44	309	3.84	.491	11	1.61	0.70	2.31
Morris H	385	42	104	19	2	6	53	43	52	.270	.377	.343	49	301	4.40	.557	11	2.31	0.52	2.83
O'Neill	484	61	119	17	0	14	66	73	83	.246	.368	.341	66	388	4.59	.579	14	3.29	1.51	4.80
Oliver	485	39	134	26	1	8	55	34	73	.276	.384	.319	59	377	4.23	.538	14	2.62	0.14	2.76
Reed Jf	23	2	3	0	0	0	2	0	3	.130	.130	.130	0	20	0.00	.000	1	-0.26	-0.02	-0.28
Roberts Bip	528	89	173	33	6	3	43	60	52	.328	.430	.395	96	381	6.80	.751	14	5.66	0.43	6.08
Sabo	344	39	86	20	3	9	41	29	52	.250	.404	.303	40	280	3.86	.492	10	1.48	0.19	1.67
Sanders R	384	57	106	27	7	9	34	47	95	.276	.453	.359	65	291	6.03	.703	11	3.81	0.96	4.77
Wilson D	24	1	9	1	0	0	2	2	7	.375	.417	.423	4	16	6.75	.748	1	0.24	0.07	0.31
Wrona	22	0	4	0	0	0	0	0	2	.182	.182	.182	1	19	1.42	.116	1	-0.16	-0.08	-0.24
TOTALS	5413	641	1427	277	47	86	592	548	866	.264	.380	.330	690	4290	4.34	.551	159	32.01	7.93	39.94

Pitching Records for Cincinnati Reds

	ERA	W	L	Pct	G	GS	CG	ShO	GF	Sv	IP	R	ER	H	2B	3B	HR	BB	IW	SO	HB	WP	BK
Belcher	3.91	15	14	.517	35	34	2	1	1	0	227.2	104	99	201	42	8	17	80	2	149	3	3	1
Swindell	2.70	12	8	.600	31	30	5	3	0	0	213.2	72	64	210	37	3	14	41	4	138	2	3	2
Rijo	2.56	15	10	.600	33	33	0	0	0	0	211.0	67	60	185	26	4	15	44	1	171	3	2	1
Hammond	4.21	7	10	.412	28	26	0	0	1	0	147.1	75	69	149	20	8	13	55	6	79	3	6	0
Browning	5.07	6	5	.545	16	16	0	0	0	0	87.0	49	49	108	28	7	6	28	7	33	2	3	1
Bolton	5.24	3	3	.500	16	8	0	0	3	0	46.1	28	27	52	4	1	9	23	2	27	2	3	1
Pugh	2.58	4	2	.667	7	7	0	0	0	0	45.1	15	13	47	11	2	2	13	3	18	1	0	0
Ayala B	4.34	2	1	.667	5	5	0	0	0	0	29.0	15	14	33	10	0	1	13	2	23	1	0	0
Brown Kth	4.50	0	1	.000	2	2	0	0	0	0	8.0	5	4	10	3	0	2	5	0	5	0	0	0
Henry	3.33	3	3	.500	60	0	0	0	11	0	83.2	31	31	59	14	4	4	44	6	72	1	12	0
Charlton	2.99	4	2	.667	64	0	0	0	46	26	81.1	39	27	79	18	1	7	26	4	90	3	8	0
Bankhead	2.93	10	4	.714	54	0	0	0	10	1	70.2	26	23	57	10	4	4	29	5	53	3	6	0
Dibble	3.07	3	5	.375	63	0	0	0	49	25	70.1	26	24	48	5	2	3	31	2	110	2	6	0
Ruskin	5.03	4	3	.571	57	0	0	0	19	0	53.2	31	30	56	10	0	6	20	4	43	1	1	0
Foster S	2.88	1	1	.500	31	1	0	0	7	2	50.0	16	16	52	8	3	4	13	1	34	0	1	0
Hillmi	3.15	0	0	.000	14	0	0	0	5	1	20.0	9	7	15	3	1	1	5	2	10	1	0	0
Menendez	1.93	1	0	1.000	3	0	0	0	1	0	4.2	1	1	1	0	0	1	0	0	5	0	0	0
TOTALS	3.46	90	72	.556	519	162	9	4	153	55	1449.2	609	558	1362	249	48	109	470	51	1060	28	54	6

Sabermetric Pitching Records for Cincinnati Reds

	Adj		-Expected-				———Opposing Batters———											Supported				
	ERA	W	L	Pct	BFP	Avg	Slg	OBA	RC/G	GDP	SB	CS	PK	PKE	SH	SF	RSup	RSp/G	W	L	Pct
Ayala B	4.03	1	2	.430	127	.297	.414	.376	5.06	4	2	3	1	0	2	0	15	4.66	2	1	.521
Bankhead	2.80	9	5	.610	299	.218	.333	.301	3.70	3	5	0	0	2	3	3	33	4.20	9	5	.647
Belcher	3.76	13	16	.465	949	.238	.368	.303	3.81	9	6	11	1	0	12	11	113	4.47	16	13	.536
Bolton	5.05	2	4	.325	210	.284	.464	.368	6.12	5	1	1	0	0	1	1	31	6.02	3	3	.537
Brown Kth	3.38	1	0	.519	37	.313	.594	.405	8.04	2	0	0	0	1	0	0	5	5.63	1	0	.694
Browning	4.86	4	7	.342	386	.311	.484	.362	6.34	10	11	1	2	0	5	4	52	5.38	5	6	.500
Charlton	2.88	4	2	.597	341	.262	.397	.323	4.43	7	15	4	0	3	7	3	22	2.43	2	4	.369
Dibble	2.94	5	3	.586	286	.193	.265	.285	2.75	3	8	2	1	1	2	2	20	2.56	3	5	.382
Foster S	2.70	1	1	.627	209	.275	.413	.319	4.42	4	1	1	0	0	5	2	21	3.78	1	1	.615
Hammond	4.03	7	10	.430	627	.266	.399	.333	4.62	11	7	4	4	1	5	3	63	3.85	7	10	.427
Henry	3.12	3	3	.558	352	.199	.313	.301	3.42	3	6	2	0	1	7	3	34	3.66	3	3	.529
Hillmi	2.70	0	0	.627	80	.211	.324	.269	3.01	1	1	0	0	0	2	1	5	2.25	0	0	.362
Menendez	0.00	0	0	.000	15	.067	.267	.067	0.55	0	0	0	0	0	0	0	2	3.86	0	0	.000
Pugh	2.38	4	2	.684	187	.276	.400	.330	4.31	5	1	1	1	0	2	1	14	2.78	3	3	.526
Rijo	2.47	17	8	.667	836	.238	.340	.281	3.04	16	17	12	2	2	9	4	101	4.31	18	7	.712
Ruskin	4.86	2	5	.342	234	.275	.412	.339	4.99	2	5	3	0	2	7	2	12	2.01	1	6	.123
Swindell	2.57	13	7	.650	867	.260	.365	.295	3.60	15	17	9	1	7	9	7	117	4.93	15	5	.750
TOTALS	3.35	85	77	.523	6042	.251	.375	.312	4.00	100	103	54	13	20	78	47	660	4.10	89	73	.550

SPLITS for Larkin B

	G	AB	Run	Hit	2B	3B	HR	TB	RBI	W	K	IW	HB	SB	CS	DP	SH	SF	Avg	Slug	OBP	RC
vs LHP	96	200	37	71	20	4	6	117	29	33	18	6	0	4	2	6	0	2	.355	.585	.443	53
vs RHP	140	333	39	91	12	2	6	125	49	30	40	2	4	11	2	7	2	5	.273	.375	.336	44
Home	70	254	45	78	14	2	8	120	53	34	29	2	4	11	3	8	1	6	.307	.472	.389	49
Away	70	279	31	84	18	4	4	122	25	29	29	6	0	4	1	5	1	1	.301	.437	.366	46
Grass	39	154	19	38	8	2	2	56	12	13	17	2	0	0	0	3	1	1	.247	.364	.304	17
Turf	101	379	57	124	24	4	10	186	66	50	41	6	4	15	4	10	1	6	.327	.491	.405	79
April/June	57	228	34	58	11	1	4	83	30	21	33	2	2	6	2	6	1	1	.254	.364	.321	27
July/October	83	305	42	104	21	5	8	159	48	42	25	6	2	9	2	7	1	6	.341	.521	.417	70

SPLITS for O'Neill

	G	AB	Run	Hit	2B	3B	HR	TB	RBI	W	K	IW	HB	SB	CS	DP	SH	SF	Avg	Slug	OBP	RC
vs LHP	101	173	13	39	6	0	2	51	26	14	46	1	0	0	2	5	3	3	.225	.295	.279	14
vs RHP	144	323	46	83	13	1	12	134	40	63	39	14	2	6	1	6	0	3	.257	.415	.379	56
Home	75	245	30	58	10	1	6	88	33	43	39	6	2	3	0	7	1	1	.237	.359	.354	34
Away	73	251	29	64	9	0	8	97	33	34	46	9	0	3	3	4	2	5	.255	.386	.338	35
Grass	42	146	17	41	5	0	5	61	20	17	27	6	0	2	2	3	2	2	.281	.418	.352	22
Turf	106	350	42	81	14	1	9	124	46	60	58	9	2	4	1	8	1	4	.231	.354	.344	47
April/June	67	227	30	59	10	1	9	98	37	39	43	10	2	4	2	4	2	1	.260	.432	.372	39
July/October	81	269	29	63	9	0	5	87	29	38	42	5	0	2	1	7	1	5	.234	.323	.324	30

SPLITS for Roberts Bip

	G	AB	Run	Hit	2B	3B	HR	TB	RBI	W	K	IW	HB	SB	CS	DP	SH	SF	Avg	Slug	OBP	RC
vs LHP	87	185	32	54	7	0	3	70	15	17	20	1	0	9	4	4	0	1	.292	.378	.350	25
vs RHP	142	347	60	118	27	6	1	160	30	45	34	3	2	35	12	3	1	3	.340	.461	.416	73
Home	72	252	56	89	22	3	3	126	23	36	24	2	1	26	5	3	0	3	.353	.500	.432	61
Away	75	280	36	83	12	3	1	104	22	26	30	2	1	18	11	4	1	1	.296	.371	.357	37
Grass	44	173	22	54	6	3	1	69	16	15	19	2	0	7	7	2	1	0	.312	.399	.367	24
Turf	103	359	70	118	28	3	3	161	29	47	35	2	2	37	9	5	0	4	.329	.448	.405	72
April/June	72	277	49	84	17	2	0	105	20	32	30	2	1	22	9	3	1	3	.303	.379	.374	43
July/October	75	255	43	88	17	4	4	125	25	30	24	2	1	22	7	4	0	1	.345	.490	.415	55

SPLITS for Sabo

	G	AB	Run	Hit	2B	3B	HR	TB	RBI	W	K	IW	HB	SB	CS	DP	SH	SF	Avg	Slug	OBP	RC
vs LHP	67	146	16	36	8	1	6	64	21	14	23	0	0	1	1	8	0	1	.247	.438	.311	17
vs RHP	94	198	26	48	11	2	6	81	22	16	31	1	1	3	4	4	1	5	.242	.409	.295	23
Home	43	148	23	35	11	0	8	70	22	11	27	1	0	2	2	5	0	4	.236	.473	.282	18
Away	53	196	19	49	8	3	4	75	21	19	27	0	1	2	3	7	1	2	.250	.383	.317	22
Grass	30	114	10	24	5	1	1	34	8	10	16	0	0	1	1	4	1	1	.211	.298	.272	9
Turf	66	230	32	60	14	2	11	111	35	20	38	1	1	3	4	8	0	5	.261	.483	.316	33
April/June	55	205	28	52	12	3	7	91	26	18	31	1	0	3	3	7	1	2	.254	.444	.311	26
July/October	41	139	14	32	7	0	5	54	17	12	23	0	1	1	2	5	0	4	.230	.388	.288	15

SPLITS for Sanders R

	G	AB	Run	Hit	2B	3B	HR	TB	RBI	W	K	IW	HB	SB	CS	DP	SH	SF	Avg	Slug	OBP	RC
vs LHP	74	175	30	55	15	4	7	99	18	19	30	2	3	8	4	3	0	0	.314	.566	.391	39
vs RHP	109	210	32	49	11	2	5	79	18	29	68	0	1	8	3	3	0	1	.233	.376	.328	28
Home	64	205	32	50	14	3	6	88	22	32	51	2	3	5	4	5	0	1	.244	.429	.353	32
Away	52	180	30	54	12	3	6	90	14	16	47	0	1	11	3	1	0	0	.300	.500	.360	34
Grass	34	118	18	32	6	2	3	51	7	8	24	0	1	7	2	0	0	0	.271	.432	.323	17
Turf	82	267	44	72	20	4	9	127	29	40	74	2	3	9	5	6	0	1	.270	.476	.370	48
April/June	56	192	24	54	13	3	4	85	21	18	46	0	1	13	4	4	0	1	.281	.443	.344	30
July/October	60	193	38	50	13	3	8	93	15	30	52	2	3	3	3	2	0	0	.259	.482	.367	36

SPLITS for Cincinnati Reds (all batters except pitchers)

	G	AB	Run	Hit	2B	3B	HR	TB	RBI	W	K	IW	HB	SB	CS	DP	SH	SF	Avg	Slug	OBP	RC
vs LHP	1109	2074	263	552	120	14	41	823	240	212	349	31	9	31	21	57	30	17	.266	.397	.334	273
vs RHP	1707	3386	397	866	161	30	58	1261	366	351	539	52	12	94	44	67	36	35	.256	.372	.325	422
Home	1098	2625	355	687	146	18	60	1049	327	291	422	39	15	62	29	66	38	27	.262	.400	.336	358
Away	1110	2835	305	731	135	26	39	1035	279	272	466	44	6	63	36	58	28	25	.258	.365	.322	337
Grass	663	1675	172	429	77	16	20	598	158	139	278	21	2	30	22	39	15	16	.256	.357	.311	184
Turf	1545	3785	488	989	204	28	79	1486	448	424	610	62	19	95	43	85	51	36	.261	.393	.336	512
April/June	989	2500	325	646	127	22	44	949	294	257	414	43	10	72	36	58	29	20	.258	.380	.328	314
July/October	1219	2960	335	772	154	22	55	1135	312	306	474	40	11	53	29	66	37	32	.261	.383	.329	381

San Diego Padres

Don Malcolm

SAN DIEGO										
YEAR	1983	1984	1985	1986	1987	1988	1989	1990	1991	1992
W	81	92	83	74	65	83	89	75	84	82
L	81	70	79	88	97	78	73	87	78	80
WPCT	0.500	0.568	0.512	0.457	0.401	0.516	0.549	0.463	0.519	0.506
R	653	686	650	656	668	594	642	673	636	617
RA	653	634	622	722	763	583	626	673	646	636
PWPT	0.5	0.539	0.522	0.452	0.434	0.509	0.513	0.5	0.492	0.485
PythW	81	87	85	73	70	83	83	81	80	79
PythL	81	75	77	89	92	79	79	81	82	83
LUCK	0	5	-2	1	-5	0	6	-6	4	3

Defensive Efficiency Record: .6918

Last year we told you that the Padres could contend if they signed Danny Tartabull and moved their fences back. They did neither. They didn't contend.

But not so fast. It wasn't that simple. The Padres sort of acquired Danny Tartabull. They picked up Gary Sheffield from the Brewers for a song (I don't remember the name of it, but hum a few bars and I'll have you arrested for impersonating Roseanne Arnold) and suddenly had POWER in the middle of their lineup.

Acquiring Sheffield was not quite like having Tartabull, except that he plays third base (the Padres position of doom ever since jaunty Dave Roberts didn't pan out in the mid-seventies), so it was a superb move, albeit a trifle lucky. Sheffield hit 23 of his 33 homers at the Launching Pad West. (Jack Murphy Stadium), hit .365 there, slugged a mind-bending .684. And Malcolm wanted them to move their fences back??

Well—yes. As a matter of fact I still think they should. But we'll get back to that. What I want to discuss first is a more urgent matter, an ominous trend which the Padres are in the forefront of, a coming practice in the smaller market cities of baseball that we here at Baseball Sabermetric term, in homage to the great but long-forgotten Peter Falk TV character Daniel J. O'Brien:

BARGAIN DAY ON THE STREET OF REGRET

So I'm obscure. But ya gotta admit it's a great title. As I recall the show (I only saw it once, when I was thirteen, when all the other kids in junior high were watching The Man From U.N.C.L.E. and thought—no, actually, they knew—I was weird), lawyer O'Brien winds up defending a slumlord unjustly accused of throwing destitute old people out on the freezing winter streets of New York. His untrustworthy private investigator McGonigle (played by the late, great David Burns) goes undercover to get at the truth, with surprising results. I forget how they worked O'Brien's ex-wife (this might have been the first TV show to acknowledge divorce) into the episode, but I seem to remember the presence of the witty, stylish, and more than occasionally caustic Joanna Barnes.

Anyway, it was a great episode, even if it's not so clear in my mind. The show, which by the way was called The Trials of O'Brien, should be re-run on cable somewhere, since just about everything else that's infinitely worse has been already. I suspect it would hold up just fine after twenty-five years. It was definitely ahead of its time.

Position	92 Starter	TWAR	93 Starter	TWAR
Catcher	Santiago	-0.82	Walters	0.34
First base	McGriff	6.53	McGriff	6.53
Second base	Stillwell	-0.04	Gardner	-0.01
Third base	Sheffield	6.90	Sheffield	6.90
Shortstop	Fernandez	3.79	Stillwell	-0.04
Left field	Clark, Je.	1.57	Plantier	2.05
Center field	Jackson, D.	2.15	Jackson, D.	2.15
Right field	Gwynn	5.07	Gwynn	5.07

So "Bargain Day" is what the small market teams are gonna be looking for, a way to exist in the cold economic winter of a game that resists revenue sharing. "The street of regret" is that every success, every Gary Sheffield, is going to engender five to ten failures.

Am I knocking the strategy? Not particularly. What I don't like about it is that when a team adopts this approach, they are tending to leave unexamined more fundamental issues about how their team should be constructed. They don't take into account the successes in player development that they've had, and then attempt to build on those successes.

The Padres have on their team, as we enter 1993, exactly one position player and three stating pitchers of palpable worth who came up through their system. Those players: Tony Gwynn, Andy Benes, Greg Harris, Frank Seminara. Oh, there are some other prospects who might pan out—Dan Walters, Guillermo Velasquez—but the lack of home-grown talent is pretty appalling.

Of course, the Padres have produced some highly-regarded talent: the problem is that most of it has wound up playing for someone else. The Padres have a pretty good record in producing middle infielders—Ozzie Smith, Ozzie Guillen, Roberto Alomar, Carlos Baerga—but, alas, none of them are playing for the Padres anymore. The Padres have let all of that talent get away in one way or another—Alomar and Baerga basically were dealt to end up with Fred McGriff, Wally Whitehurst, D.J. Dozier, and Raul Casanova—none of whom is a middle infielder.

Barring any other developments, the Padres appear to be going with a middle infield combo of Kurt Stillwell at short and Jeff Gardner at second. This is an impressively weak duo. Stillwell's initial season in the NL could charitably be described as shaky: after May, Kurt hit just .198, got on base about .250. Joe MacIlvaine described the Tony Fernandez trade (the one which netted Whitehurst, Dozier, and Casanova) as "a gamble." Now we understand why the Padres' top farm club is in Las Vegas...

Gardner is a guy who was backed up in the Mets' system forever (three straight seasons at Tidewater before being traded to the Padres last year). At Las Vegas, where just about everybody hits .300, Gardner hit .335, with a walk percentage of 13.2%, not too far below his lifetime average. He's a left handed hitter with little power (only 15.5% of his hits go for

extra bases, with just three lifetime HRs). He comes to the dance as sort of the Padres' only hope from within: new manager Jim Riggleman managed him at Las Vegas last year, though, so we can probably expect that Gardner will get a fairly long look.

(Interestingly, the STATS books provide us with two projections for Gardner's 1993 season: the first, in the red Major League Handbook, gives us a projection based on the mystical factors that somehow go beyond the Major League Equivalence (MLE) system. The second, in the green Minor League Handbook, is the straight MLE itself. We reprint them here without permission because we're puzzled by them, and wanted you to be too:

		G	AB	R	H	TB	D	T	HR	RBI	BB	SO	SB	CS	BA	SA	OBP
Gardner	MLE/Green book	120	402	50	110	136	22	2	0	31	40	50	4	1	.274	.338	.339
Gardner	Proj./Red book	114	373	40	92	106	12	1	0	28	49	40	3	2	.247	.284	.334

Maybe Bill and John and the rest of the crew at STATS will enlighten the reading populace as to how they've come up with two such disparate totals. It's not like they're incredibly far off, guys, but we're just curious out here what other things you do past the MLE to arrive at the bottom projection. If we split the difference between the two projections, which seems reasonable, we have kind of a poor man's Wally Backman, which is historically what the Mets organization has turned out at second base: remember Brian Giles? Sorry—I'll warn you before I do that the next time.)

Oh, yes, the point of all this? To demonstrate how assiduous use of the "bargain day" approach can produce a team with serious structural weaknesses, and undo the player development strength of the organization.

Which leads us to the Padres' next bargain day manuever. It's actually a rather brilliant one, I think, and might prove to be just as successful as the Sheffield move. Acquiring Phil Plantier from the Red Sox for Jose Melendez has the same scenario in mind—take a highly touted young player who didn't pan out and fell out of favor and give him a new start. It's a great idea. It's a good fit—the Padres need outfielders (actually, given the fact that Tony Gwynn has been seen around San Diego this winter looking like a left-handed version of Orson Welles, they may still need outfielders) and the ballpark helps power hitters of all types (lefties somewhat less than righties, though), so—fanfare, please!

The problem with the idea is that you can't find enough of these guys every year to fill out a team that isn't getting useful talent from the farm system. As mentioned earlier, the Padres have maybe two position players capable of helping the team this season who came from their own farm system: Dan Walters and Guillermo Velasquez. Walters will almost certainly be the starting catcher, but Velasaquez is a first baseman and is, of course, blocked there by McGriff. So he'll have to become an outfielder, a position that was never previously on his resume, if he's going to make much of a contribution this year.

Don't expect it. With Plantier in left, Darrin Jackson in center, and the blimp-like Gwynn scheduled to waddle around in right, the Padres will probably postpone such tinkering, or at least relegate it to the AAA level. Dozier is likely to get a shot, since it always behooves a team to make their trades look as good as possible. So that's four outfield slots, with the last one probably to be filled by Jim Vatcher.

If the Padres get lucky, Plantier will hit 25 homers and the Padres will have about 80-85 in the 3-4-5 slot. The big problem is: who's going to be on base when the ball leaves the park? This could be the slowest team of all time: stolen base totals were down 32% from 1991, to a league low of 69. There's no way that the Padres will be close to that total in '93: Fernandez, their best (and worst) base stealer (20 steals, 20 times caught) is gone. The projected replacements for lost starters—Plantier and Gardner—aren't bringing any speed to the dance. While I don't think that the Padres can seriously challenge the all-time low for stolen bases

by a team in a single season (the 1957 Senators, with the incredible total of 13, probably have that one locked up for all time), they will probably be the lowest team in the NL since 1985, when another Padres outfit swiped just 60.

If the Padres get unlucky, Plantier will be a dud, Gardner and Stillwell will remind long-time Padre fans (you know who you are) of Enzo Hernandez and Dave Campbell, and the team will finish sixth. I think that Jim Riggleman has little choice but to try the following lineup—

1. Gardner, 2b
2. the Blimp, rf
3. Sheffield, 3b
4. McGriff, 1b
5. Plantier, lf
6. Jackson, cf
7. Walters, c
8. Stillwell, ss

—and hold his breath. Bargain day could be a lot less than the incautious shopper had bargained for, and filled with a lot more regret.

WHILE WE'RE AT IT, THE BATTING ORDER

The superficial figures for the Padres batting order look good: homers and doubles up, RC27 up 12%. But the OINX figures tell a different story: the Padres had little real offensive value at the top of their lineup. The numbers you see for the #1 and #2 slot are not good enough to allow the Padres to compete in the NL West with the Braves, Reds, and Astros. Despite the addition of Sheffield, the #1 and #2 slots each scored 15-17% less runs.

Notice that the OINX DIFF figures for the #1 and #2 slots are flat. This is in spite of the fact that the Padres moved their #3 hitter from 1991 (Gwynn) to the #2 slot. When Gwynn went out with an injury in mid-September, the team's lack of depth was exposed more flagrantly than porno star Christy Canyon: the #2 hitters other than Gwynn hit just .156. It's no wonder that Sheffield couldn't gain ground in the RBI race late in the season: he had absolutely no one to drive in.

The Padres' dearth of walk-taking conspired to make their vaunted four man offense far less potent than what was generally perceived. Hampered by the hole in the #5 slot, McGriff received 23 intentional walks, second only to Barry Bonds. Relative to his runs created, his runs scored and RBI totals were down the most on the team, which means that his offensive contributions were not adequately accommodated in the team's overall offensive context.

And the improvement in the #7 slot is worth less to the offense that it initially appears. The 51% increase in runs created looks impressive, until you see what the RC27 figure was in 1991—2.84. That figure was

Year	BOP	OINX	AB	R	H	TB	D	T	HR	RBI	BB	SO	SB	CS	BA	SA	OBP	RC27	BBP	XBH
1991	1	14.68	673	102	176	238	23	6	9	52	52	110	34	19	.262	.354	.314	3.84	7.2	38
1992	1	14.63	673	87	180	233	33	4	4	38	57	68	20	20	.267	.346	.325	3.91	7.8	41
1991	2	15.79	647	100	168	236	30	7	8	44	64	95	18	7	.260	.365	.326	4.10	9.0	45
1992	2	15.65	666	87	188	245	33	3	6	47	56	42	4	7	.282	.368	.338	4.42	7.8	42
1991	3	18.33	648	89	202	279	32	12	7	78	47	37	13	9	.312	.431	.358	5.72	6.8	51
1992	3	22.04	650	96	195	338	36	4	33	101	49	66	4	7	.300	.520	.349	6.61	7.0	73
1991	4	24.00	577	94	158	280	21	1	33	113	105	142	7	2	.274	.485	.386	6.57	15.4	55
1992	4	27.31	579	89	168	320	33	4	37	112	105	114	11	6	.290	.553	.399	7.92	15.4	74
1991	5	16.50	623	61	163	246	22	2	19	100	50	130	10	10	.262	.395	.316	4.32	7.4	43
1992	5	14.14	631	59	156	229	34	3	11	75	33	98	9	5	.247	.363	.285	3.50	5.0	48
1991	6	14.63	611	57	138	226	25	3	19	64	38	140	7	7	.226	.370	.271	3.30	5.9	47
1992	6	14.77	595	61	134	215	26	2	17	60	45	100	7	3	.225	.361	.280	3.33	7.0	45
1991	7	13.78	567	45	117	183	23	2	13	63	53	132	5	9	.206	.323	.274	2.84	8.5	38
1992	7	16.39	593	60	155	246	27	8	16	74	32	102	10	3	.261	.415	.299	4.29	5.1	51
1991	8	14.15	543	56	132	178	18	2	8	41	54	100	7	0	.243	.328	.312	3.44	9.0	28
1992	8	13.31	566	50	136	182	21	2	7	41	45	111	2	0	.240	.322	.296	3.20	7.4	30
1991	9	7.74	519	32	67	94	10	1	5	36	38	183	0	1	.129	.181	.189	1.00	6.8	16
1992	9	8.11	523	28	84	108	12	0	4	28	31	163	2	1	.161	.207	.208	1.30	5.6	16

		OINX	AB	R	H	TB	D	T	HR	RBI	BB	SO	SB	CS	BA	SA	OBP	RC27	BBP	XBH
DIFF	1	100	100	85	102	98	143	67	44	73	110	62	59	105	102	98	103	102	109	108
	2	99	103	87	112	104	110	43	75	107	88	44	22	100	109	101	104	108	86	93
	3	120	100	108	97	121	113	33	471	129	104	178	31	78	96	121	97	116	104	143
	4	114	100	95	106	114	157	400	112	99	100	80	157	300	106	114	103	121	100	135
	5	86	101	97	96	93	155	150	58	75	66	75	90	50	94	92	90	81	67	112
	6	101	97	107	97	95	104	67	89	94	118	71	100	43	100	98	103	101	120	96
	7	119	105	133	132	134	117	400	123	117	60	77	200	33	127	129	109	151	60	134
	8	94	104	89	103	102	117	100	88	100	83	111	29	—	99	98	95	93	81	107
	9	105	101	88	125	115	120	—	80	78	82	89	—	100	124	114	110	130	82	100
AVG		104.8		97	106	108	125	83	112	97	90	81	68	81				109.5	89.4	116.3

the worst for all #7 slots in the NL West in '91, and was third worst among non-pitching slots. The gain in the #7 slot was more than offset by the decline in the #5 slot, which lost 25 RBI despite the presence of Sheffield and McGriff in the #3 and #4 slots.

If Plantier makes a Sheffield-style transformation, the Padres will have a solid power center, but they won't have an on-base engine to fuel it, unless Gardner exceeds his projection and Gwynn can hit .350 while wearing all four tires instead of the spare. The most likely scenario is that the Padre offense will remain out of whack. Trading away Bip Roberts, their last bonafide leadoff man, for the mercurial (and now long gone) Randy Myers has brought them to the state of being "three nuts in search of a bolt." (One thinks that watching the mid-fiftyish Mamie Van Doren reenact the beer bath scene from the movie of the same name would somehow be preferable to seeing the Padres' frequent three-solo-homer 4-3 losses this season.)

A PITCH FOR THE HEAVENS, or PENNY-PITCH

Yes, it's another bad TV reference. Ed Wynn, the Twilight Zone, you remember: the pitch to save the little girl? It was pretty hokey—which must be why I made the connection with the '93 Padre pitching staff. Last season the Padres redefined and stretched the elastic limits of the term "replacement value," as they trotted out converted relievers and retread starters from under every available rock. It was an impressive performance, but it didn't save Greg Riddoch's job.

A good number of these journeymen have moved on. Craig Lefferts left before the season was over, and Mike Maddux, Jose Melendez, Jim Deshaies, Larry Andersen, Randy Myers, and Dave Eiland have followed suit. The replacements for this pack of assorted flavors are, so far: Wally

Whitehurst, who just has to keep breathing to be in the starting rotation; Roger Mason, ex-Pirate committeeman who may be the closest thing to a closer on the staff; and Jim Pena, whose qualifications are that he was a late bloomer in the Giants' organization (a bad, bad sign). But he's left-handed, and the only other ones on the staff are Bruce Hurst and Rich Rodriguez, so I suspect that Pena will stick, and might even get a chance to start some games. (Remember, he came over in a trade after Riggleman, who managed in the PCL last season and—ostensibly—saw Pena pitch for Phoenix, was named Padre skipper.)

It was a fine ensemble bullpen last year; excellent, in fact, if you throw out Myers' totals (2.79 ERA). The reason for that performance—depth—is gone now. We're looking at Mason and Rodriguez as closers, Jeremy Hernandez and Pena as set-up men, with the enigmatic Gene Harris as a long reliever-clubhouse lawyer. This is about as blue-collar as you can get in a bullpen. The only other true reliever who's even close to cracking this tool-and-die quintet is big (6'9"), wild (4.97 BB/9 ratio in five minor league seasons) Terry Bross, who was also with Riggleman at Las Vegas last year and might get dragged along as a pet project.

Starters? This team had some good low opposition batting average hurlers at one time, but they've all aged, changed, or moved on. The rotation that one reads about in the trade papers contains Andy Benes, Bruce Hurst, Greg Harris, Wally Whitehurst, and Frank Seminara. Benes is the ace at 25, but it's not the kind of compliment that will get you invited back to dinner.

Benes has never pitched as well at home as he has on the road: previously, it seemed to be the park and its penchant for allowing homers that was hurting him there, but last year he cut down on the homers and still had a 13% higher ERA at home. I suggested in last year's article that removing the inner wall, which produces about 40-45% of all the homers hit in Jack Murphy, would help the Padres' staff in general and Benes in particular. I still believe it would, but there's obviously more at work here in terms of Benes' problems. It may just be that he needs another pitch that would bring him up one more notch. If he can make that jump, there is no question that he can be a franchise pitcher—though it probably won't happen until he's traded or goes elsewhere as a free agent.

There have been trade rumors swirling around Bruce Hurst for the past year and a half. So far, however, nothing, and it probably won't happen until the Padres decide to cash him in to the Red Sox for less than what they wanted to get. He was supposed to be in the Plantier deal, but when the Padres wanted more than just Phil for Bruce, the Sox balked and they wound up swapping Melendez instead. Hurst probably won't leave unless he can go back to Boston, so expect a deal in spring training that will send a shortstop (Tim Naehring or John Valentin) and some kind of starting pitcher (Paul Quantrill, perhaps, or a prospect like Brian Conroy) to the Padres. If Hurst goes, look for the Padres to give Erik Schullstrom, the right-hander they got from the Orioles for Craig Lefferts, a long look. He's considered to be something of a Benes clone.

Harris, Whitehurst, and Seminara are not known quantities at this point, but they are going to do a lot of pitching this year in cost-conscious San Diego. Harris got his arm hurt being converted from a reliever to a starter and hasn't been able to stay off the DL in two years; Whitehurst was buried in the Mets chain for many years and has the potential to give up a lot of home runs in Jack Murphy; Seminara went 9-4 after being recalled from Las Vegas, but has a wild streak that may not stay under control. For poorer, for worse, in sickness and in debt, till arbitration do we part, the Padres are going to assemble the cheapest pitching staff possible: it's the plat du jour in San Diego, a town where frogmen are not French, and on any given day in El Cajon the Padres management can be found looking for ballplayers in thrift shops.

```
San Diego Padres Home Park Performance Factors
                   Outs  Runs  Hits   2b    3b    HR     W     K    SH    SF   HBP   IBB    SB    CS   GDP
Home LH Batters    .952  .866  .967  .980 1.274  .762  .917  .977  .860 1.274  .920  .775 2.070 1.014  .683
Home RH Batters   1.015  .893  .894  .966  .842  .781  .954 1.128  .871 1.262  .999 1.304  .990  .970 1.025
All Home Batters  1.000  .891  .928  .975  .998  .778  .930 1.060  .888 1.104 1.058  .958 1.052  .931  .914
Opp LH Batters     .991  .943 1.016  .915 1.083  .897  .913  .958  .735 1.180 1.180  .900  .930 1.116 1.329
Opp RH Batters    1.022  .971  .984 1.071 1.115  .878 1.019 1.018 1.069 1.047  .979 1.071  .913  .968 1.189
All Opp Batters   1.022  .986 1.007 1.073 1.178  .908 1.004 1.013  .951 1.016 1.055 1.055  .969  .982 1.168
All LH Batters     .971  .902  .989  .950 1.140  .826  .914  .962  .808 1.211 1.078  .823 1.015 1.065  .860
All RH Batters    1.018  .932  .939 1.017  .958  .825  .987 1.067  .990 1.144  .996 1.151  .922  .963 1.091
All Batters       1.011  .937  .967 1.022 1.082  .836  .966 1.032  .920 1.054 1.060 1.004  .978  .955 1.012
```

Conventional Batting Records for San Diego Padres

	G	AB	Run	Hit	2B	3B	HR	TB	RBI	W	K	IW	HB	SB	CS	BRng Eff	GI DP	SH	SF	Avg	Slug	OBP	Runs Ctd
Santiago	106	386	37	97	21	0	10	148	42	21	52	1	0	2	5	.340	14	0	4	.251	.383	.287	38
McGriff F	152	531	79	152	30	4	35	295	104	96	108	23	1	8	6	.264	14	0	4	.286	.556	.394	118
Stillwell	114	379	35	86	15	3	2	113	24	26	58	9	1	4	1	.349	6	4	6	.227	.298	.274	32
Sheffield	146	557	87	184	34	4	33	323	100	48	40	5	6	5	6	.487	19	0	7	.330	.580	.385	118
Fernandez T	155	622	84	171	32	4	4	223	37	56	62	4	4	20	20	.454	5	9	3	.275	.359	.337	76
Clark Je	146	496	45	120	22	6	12	190	58	22	97	3	4	3	0	.257	7	1	3	.242	.383	.278	53
Jackson Dar	155	587	72	146	23	5	17	230	70	26	106	4	4	14	3	.386	21	6	5	.249	.392	.283	61
Gwynn T	128	520	77	165	27	3	6	216	41	46	16	12	0	3	6	.423	13	0	3	.317	.415	.371	78
Teufel	101	246	23	55	10	0	6	83	25	31	45	3	1	2	1	.294	7	0	1	.224	.337	.312	26
Walters D	57	179	14	45	11	1	4	70	22	10	28	0	2	1	0	.348	3	1	2	.251	.391	.295	21
Azocar	99	168	15	32	6	0	0	38	8	9	12	1	0	1	0	.563	3	4	1	.190	.226	.230	9
Ward K	81	147	12	29	5	0	3	43	12	14	38	0	2	2	3	.294	8	1	1	.197	.293	.274	10
Shipley	52	105	7	26	6	0	0	32	7	2	21	1	0	1	1	.182	2	1	0	.248	.305	.262	8
Stephenson	53	71	5	11	2	1	0	15	8	10	11	0	0	0	0	.400	0	3	0	.155	.211	.259	5
Hurst	33	69	2	11	4	0	0	15	1	3	27	0	0	0	0	.182	0	9	0	.159	.217	.194	4
Benes	34	67	3	10	2	0	1	15	5	5	29	0	0	0	0	.143	1	5	1	.149	.224	.205	3
Lefferts	27	52	0	4	0	0	0	4	0	0	21	0	0	0	0	.000	0	9	0	.077	.077	.077	1
Seminara	19	34	3	4	0	0	0	4	0	1	9	0	0	0	0	.286	0	2	0	.118	.118	.143	1
Bilardello	17	33	2	4	1	0	0	5	1	4	8	1	0	0	0	1.000	1	3	0	.121	.152	.216	1
Harris GW	20	31	1	4	1	0	0	5	1	5	13	0	0	0	0	.250	0	5	0	.129	.161	.250	2
Pettis	30	30	0	6	1	0	0	7	0	2	11	0	0	1	0	.250	0	0	0	.200	.233	.250	2
Deshaies	15	29	3	6	0	0	0	6	0	1	9	0	0	0	0	.400	0	5	0	.207	.207	.233	2
Velasquez	15	23	1	7	0	0	1	10	5	1	7	0	0	0	0	.000	0	0	0	.304	.435	.333	3
Gardner J	15	19	0	2	0	0	0	2	0	1	8	0	0	0	0	.000	0	0	0	.105	.105	.150	0
Lampkin	9	17	3	4	0	0	0	4	0	6	1	0	1	2	0	1.000	0	0	0	.235	.235	.458	3
Vatcher	13	16	1	4	1	0	0	5	2	3	6	0	0	0	0	.667	0	1	0	.250	.313	.368	2
Faries	10	11	3	5	1	0	0	6	1	1	2	0	0	0	0	1.000	0	0	0	.455	.545	.500	3
Eiland	7	9	1	1	0	0	1	4	2	0	4	0	0	0	0	.000	0	1	0	.111	.444	.111	0
Maddux M	50	9	0	1	0	0	0	1	0	1	4	0	0	0	0	.000	0	3	0	.111	.111	.200	0
Myers R	66	7	0	1	0	0	0	1	0	0	5	0	0	0	0	.000	1	1	0	.143	.143	.143	0
Rodriguez Rich	61	6	0	0	0	0	0	0	0	1	0	0	0	0	0	.000	1	2	0	.000	.000	.143	0
Melendez J	56	5	0	0	0	0	0	0	0	0	4	0	0	0	0	.000	0	1	0	.000	.000	.000	0
Brocail	3	5	0	1	0	0	0	1	0	0	0	0	0	0	0	.000	0	0	0	.200	.200	.200	0
Howard T	5	3	1	1	0	0	0	1	0	0	1	0	0	0	0	.000	0	1	0	.333	.333	.333	0
Harris Ge	15	3	0	1	0	0	0	1	0	0	1	0	0	0	0	.000	0	0	0	.333	.333	.333	0
Hernandez Jer	26	2	0	0	0	0	0	0	0	0	0	0	0	0	0	.000	0	0	0	.000	.000	.000	0
Clements P	27	1	0	0	0	0	0	0	0	0	0	0	0	0	0	.000	0	0	0	.000	.000	.000	0
Andersen L	34	1	1	0	0	0	0	0	0	1	1	0	0	0	0	.000	0	0	0	.000	.000	.500	0
Scott Tim	34	0	0	0	0	0	0	0	0	0	0	0	0	0	0	.000	0	0	0	.000	.000	.000	0
TOTALS		2186	5476	617	1396	255	30	135	2116	576	453	864	67	26	69	52	.368	126	78	41	.255	.386	.313	653

Sabermetric Batting Records for San Diego Padres

	AB	Run	Hit	2B	3B	HR	RBI	W	SO	Avg	Slug	OBP	Ctd	Outs	27o	OW%	OG	OWAR	DWAR	TWAR
Azocar	163	13	31	5	0	0	7	8	11	.190	.221	.227	8	139	1.55	.139	5	-1.09	0.04	-1.05
Bilardello	32	1	3	1	0	0	0	3	8	.094	.125	.171	1	32	0.84	.045	1	-0.36	0.15	-0.22
Clark Je	494	41	112	22	5	9	53	21	104	.227	.346	.261	45	392	3.10	.391	15	0.60	0.98	1.57
Faries	10	2	4	1	0	0	0	0	2	.400	.500	.400	2	6	9.00	.844	0	0.11	0.01	0.12
Fernandez T	620	78	165	32	4	3	34	54	64	.266	.345	.327	71	490	3.91	.506	18	2.83	0.96	3.79
Gardner J	17	0	1	0	0	0	0	0	7	.059	.059	.059	0	16	0.00	.000	1	-0.21	0.09	-0.12
Gwynn T	507	69	163	25	3	4	39	42	15	.321	.406	.371	74	366	5.46	.666	14	4.28	0.79	5.07
Howard T	2	0	0	0	0	0	0	0	0	.000	.000	.000	0	2	0.00	.000	0	-0.03	0.00	-0.03
Jackson Dar	586	67	137	23	4	14	64	25	113	.234	.358	.267	51	484	2.85	.351	18	0.02	2.13	2.15
Lampkin	15	2	3	0	0	0	0	5	0	.200	.200	.429	3	12	6.75	.753	0	0.18	0.00	0.18
McGriff F	518	71	150	28	4	29	99	87	104	.290	.527	.390	109	392	7.51	.790	15	6.39	0.13	6.53
Pettis	29	0	5	1	0	0	1	1	11	.172	.207	.200	1	24	1.13	.078	1	-0.24	0.02	-0.22
Santiago	385	34	91	21	4	8	38	20	55	.236	.353	.271	32	317	2.73	.332	12	-0.21	-0.61	-0.82
Sheffield	551	81	172	34	2	27	91	47	42	.312	.528	.367	101	413	6.60	.745	15	6.04	0.86	6.90
Shipley	104	6	24	6	0	0	6	1	22	.231	.288	.238	7	82	2.30	.262	3	-0.27	0.55	0.29
Stephenson	68	4	10	1	1	0	7	9	10	.147	.191	.247	4	60	1.80	.178	2	-0.38	0.03	-0.35
Stillwell	379	32	83	15	3	1	22	25	60	.219	.282	.265	30	311	2.60	.312	12	-0.44	0.39	-0.04
Teufel	245	21	51	10	0	4	22	30	48	.208	.298	.293	22	202	2.94	.366	7	0.12	0.16	0.29
Vatcher	15	0	3	1	0	0	1	2	6	.200	.267	.294	1	12	2.25	.253	0	-0.04	0.09	0.05
Velasquez	21	0	6	0	0	0	4	0	6	.286	.286	.286	2	15	3.60	.464	1	0.06	0.00	0.06
Walters D	178	13	42	11	0	3	20	9	30	.236	.348	.274	17	141	3.26	.415	5	0.34	0.01	0.34
Ward K	147	11	27	5	0	2	11	13	40	.184	.259	.253	8	131	1.65	.154	5	-0.95	0.08	-0.88
TOTALS	5474	578	1350	261	32	113	538	438	895	.247	.368	.303	602	4418	3.68	.475	164	20.47	6.87	27.34

Pitching Records for San Diego Padres

	ERA	W	L	Pct	G	GS	CG	ShO	GF	Sv	IP	R	ER	H	2B	3B	HR	BB	IW	SO	HB	WP	BK
Benes	3.35	13	14	.481	34	34	2	2	0	0	231.1	90	86	230	39	6	14	61	6	169	5	1	1
Hurst	3.85	14	9	.609	32	32	6	4	0	0	217.1	96	93	223	31	3	22	51	3	131	0	4	3
Lefferts	3.69	13	9	.591	27	27	0	0	0	0	163.1	76	67	180	29	4	16	35	2	81	0	4	1
Harris GW	4.12	4	8	.333	20	20	1	0	0	0	118.0	62	54	113	18	1	13	35	2	66	2	2	1
Seminara	3.68	9	4	.692	19	18	0	0	0	0	100.1	46	41	98	12	3	5	46	3	61	3	1	1
Deshaies	3.28	4	7	.364	15	15	0	0	0	0	96.0	40	35	92	16	1	6	33	2	46	1	1	2
Eiland	5.67	0	2	.000	7	7	0	0	0	0	27.0	21	17	33	8	2	1	5	0	10	0	0	1
Brocail	6.43	0	0	.000	3	3	0	0	0	0	14.0	10	10	17	5	0	2	5	0	15	0	0	0
Rodriguez Ric	2.37	6	3	.667	61	1	0	0	15	0	91.0	28	24	77	14	1	4	29	4	64	0	1	1
Melendez J	2.92	6	7	.462	56	3	0	0	18	0	89.1	32	29	82	9	0	9	20	7	82	3	1	1
Myers R	4.29	3	6	.333	66	0	0	0	57	38	79.2	38	38	84	16	0	7	34	3	66	1	5	0
Maddux M	2.37	2	2	.500	50	1	0	0	14	5	79.2	25	21	71	7	2	2	24	4	60	0	4	1
Scott Tim	5.26	4	1	.800	34	0	0	0	16	0	37.2	24	22	39	5	3	4	21	6	30	1	0	1
Hernandez Jer	4.17	1	4	.200	26	0	0	0	11	1	36.2	17	17	39	3	1	4	11	5	25	1	0	0
Andersen L	3.34	1	1	.500	34	0	0	0	13	2	35.0	14	13	26	2	0	2	8	2	35	1	0	0
Clements P	2.66	2	1	.667	27	0	0	0	7	0	23.2	9	7	25	4	0	0	12	4	11	2	0	0
Harris Ge	2.95	0	2	.000	14	1	0	0	2	0	21.1	8	7	15	2	0	0	9	0	19	1	1	1
TOTALS	3.58	82	80	.506	525	162	9	6	153	46	1461.1	636	581	1444	220	27	111	439	53	971	21	25	15

Sabermetric Pitching Records for San Diego Padres

	Adj ERA	Expected W	Expected L	Pct	BFP	Avg	Slg	OBA	RC/G	GDP	SB	CS	PK	PKE	SH	SF	RSup	RSp/G	W	L	Pct
Andersen L	3.09	1	1	.563	140	.202	.264	.252	2.49	1	7	1	0	0	1	1	15	3.86	1	1	.560
Benes	3.11	15	12	.559	961	.264	.371	.314	4.02	12	20	11	2	0	19	6	78	3.03	12	15	.437
Brocail	5.79	0	0	.268	64	.298	.491	.355	6.72	0	0	0	0	0	2	0	4	2.57	0	0	.139
Clements P	2.28	2	1	.702	105	.281	.326	.379	4.61	3	5	1	0	0	2	0	12	4.56	2	1	.766
Deshaies	3.00	6	5	.577	395	.258	.360	.321	3.69	7	6	10	2	5	3	2	30	2.81	5	6	.418
Eiland	5.00	1	1	.329	120	.287	.417	.317	5.14	2	4	0	0	0	0	0	15	5.00	1	1	.449
Harris Ge	2.53	1	1	.657	90	.195	.221	.287	2.62	1	4	0	0	0	3	0	9	3.80	1	1	.647
Harris GW	3.81	5	7	.458	496	.252	.384	.307	4.27	4	18	5	1	4	8	3	57	4.35	6	6	.515
Hernandez Jer	3.68	2	3	.475	157	.291	.418	.338	5.09	1	3	1	0	0	3	3	8	1.96	1	4	.188
Hurst	3.60	11	12	.486	902	.267	.390	.308	4.20	8	18	10	2	2	12	4	92	3.81	11	12	.477
Lefferts	3.42	11	11	.513	684	.285	.419	.320	4.54	13	14	8	1	4	12	5	87	4.79	14	8	.616
Maddux M	2.15	3	1	.727	330	.236	.292	.290	3.12	5	15	3	0	2	2	3	43	4.86	3	1	.807
Melendez J	2.72	8	5	.624	363	.249	.359	.295	3.50	5	3	4	1	0	7	4	32	3.22	7	6	.534
Myers R	3.95	4	5	.440	348	.279	.402	.349	4.91	6	2	3	0	1	7	5	15	1.69	1	8	.130
Rodriguez Rich	2.18	6	3	.722	369	.229	.313	.289	2.97	7	6	5	0	2	2	2	38	3.76	6	3	.709
Scott Tim	4.78	2	3	.350	173	.267	.425	.361	5.79	3	6	1	0	0	4	1	20	4.78	2	3	.449
Seminara	3.41	7	6	.514	435	.258	.345	.341	4.07	11	10	6	1	3	3	2	62	5.56	9	4	.685
TOTALS	3.35	85	77	.522	6132	.261	.371	.315	4.06	89	141	69	10	23	93	43	617	3.80	83	79	.512

Batting 'Splits' Records for Houston Astros
SPLITS for San Diego Padres (all batters except pitchers)

	G	AB	Run	Hit	2B	3B	HR	TB	RBI	W	K	IW	HB	SB	CS	DP	SH	SF	Avg	Slug	OBP	RC
vs LHP	903	1812	236	491	77	14	61	779	223	145	289	16	5	17	18	41	23	11	.271	.430	.325	246
vs RHP	1731	3664	381	905	178	16	74	1337	353	308	575	51	21	52	34	85	55	30	.247	.365	.307	408
Home	1109	2689	339	730	126	14	87	1145	320	241	394	33	11	33	28	67	43	19	.271	.426	.332	372
Away	1077	2787	278	666	129	16	48	971	256	212	470	34	15	36	24	59	35	22	.239	.348	.294	284
Grass	1635	4047	469	1041	186	22	113	1610	437	353	605	53	17	50	40	96	63	29	.257	.398	.317	503
Turf	551	1429	148	355	69	8	22	506	139	100	259	14	9	19	12	30	15	12	.248	.354	.299	151
April/June	1028	2627	324	689	122	15	60	1021	294	234	415	36	15	40	29	60	39	24	.262	.389	.323	329
July/October	1158	2849	293	707	133	15	75	1095	282	219	449	31	11	29	23	66	39	17	.248	.384	.303	324

Houston Astros

Don Malcolm

HOUSTON										
YEAR	1983	1984	1985	1986	1987	1988	1989	1990	1991	1992
W	85	80	83	96	76	82	86	75	65	81
L	77	82	79	66	86	80	76	87	97	81
WPCT	0.525	0.494	0.512	0.593	0.469	0.506	0.531	0.463	0.401	0.500
R	643	693	706	654	648	617	647	573	605	608
RA	646	630	691	569	678	631	669	656	717	668
PWPT	0.498	0.548	0.511	0.569	0.477	0.489	0.483	0.433	0.416	0.453
PythW	81	89	83	92	77	79	78	70	67	73
PythL	81	73	79	70	85	83	84	92	95	89
LUCK	4	-9	0	4	-1	3	8	5	-2	8

Defensive Efficiency Record: .7023

GOING FOR THE PUMP

Actually, I'm not sure that this section header has all that much to do with the Astros, but I've always liked the image (for reasons that might prove impervious to decades of psychoanalysis), so here 'tis. My best guess as to what it means is that there are an awful lot of teams trying to buy their way into contention, to pump themselves up, to become the Arnold Schwarzenegger of their division with a protein-rich diet of free agents. It's as though general manager's offices have become workout rooms, where the guys peel off their suits and ties and assume bodybuilding poses around displays of the high-priced talent they've just acquired. With dollar signs taking the place of pecs and triceps.

The Astros are the latest team to get into the "buy your way into fitness," and now that I get over the shock, I realize that I should have seen it coming. The signings of Doug Drabek and Greg Swindell resonate deep into the history of the Houston franchise, which has turned out only three top starters in its thirty-one year history, and only one since the dawning of free agency. Who are those masked men, you ask? For those of you who didn't catch the surreal wordplay that stood in for analysis in the 1989 Baseball Abstract, the answer is: Larry Dierker, Don Wilson, and J. R. Richard.

That's it. It's an incredible record, and of course there is a logical sabermetric explanantion for it. It's the park. Among the other effects that the Astrodome has had on the makeup of the team, it has made pitching appear to be less valuable. But that's nuts, you say. The Astrodome is the most extreme pitcher's park in all of baseball. How could it devalue pitching—that's what helps the team most, that's what they attempt to build the team around.

Now here's where that standard reply, the one I've made for you—I can handle two or three sides of a conversation at once, which is a lot of fun at parties, especially when some of the guests have been rendered mute by excessive alcohol consumption—is ninety degrees off. The value that a baseball organization places on components of the game is proportional to the offensive context of the ballpark in which they play. Since it's easier to generate a lower ERA in an extreme pitcher's park, one tends to get numbed over by the fact that even mediocre pitchers have good ERA's in the Dome. Hence a team's management starts thinking that it should turn its attention to developing an offense that can complement pitching—speed, defense, hit-and-run—when it should be doing the opposite.

Since pitching is a given due to the park, there is less emphasis on

Position	92 Starter	TWAR	93 Starter	TWAR
Catcher	Taubensee	0.19	Taubensee	0.19
First base	Bagwell	7.18	Bagwell	7.18
Second base	Biggio	6.56	Biggio	6.56
Third base	Caminiti	5.11	Caminiti	5.11
Shortstop	Cedeno	-0.79	Uribe	1.35
Left field	Gonzalez, L.	1.97	Gonzalez, L.	1.97
Center field	Finley	6.47	Finley	6.47
Right field	Anthony	2.39	Anthony	2.39

developing pitching talent within the organization. Hence signing big free agents or trading for established pitchers is easier than maintaining a coherent, conscientious, and focused program for developing pitchers through the farm system.

Now I'm not saying that the Astros are without a program to develop pitchers. It's just that the program they have isn't emphasized in comparison with their program for developing hitters. The Astros have had many more great hitters come out of their system than great pitchers. They've also traded most of them away, but that's something that all organizations are prone to do. That's baseball—shrewdness and idiocy are Siamese twins connected at the head.

So the Astros haven't changed a whole lot, and that's OK with me—I like a certain amount of continuity (read: boring predictability) as much as the next guy. But what effect will this continuing continuity have on the Astros? Can they rise up and pump iron with the Braves this year? Does buying a pitching staff work?

Well, obviously it can work, because several teams have been doing it in addition to the Astros. Nobody has made it into an obsession the way Houston has, but it's been done by some pretty successful franchises. People tend to overlook the fact that three-fifths of the starting staff that the Braves began the year with in 1992 came from outside their organization (Smoltz, Leibrandt, Bielecki).

The Astros have themselves bought sufficient quantities of starting pitching to make it into the playoffs twice, in 1980 and 1986. The 1980 squad had the following store-bought or bartered merchandise: Joe Niekro (acquired from Atlanta in 1976), Vern Ruhle (acquired from

Detroit in 1978), Nolan Ryan (signed as a free agent in 1980), and Joaquin Andujar (acquired as a AAA minor leaguer from Cincinnati in 1976). Only Ken Forsch and the ill-fated J.R. Richard came up through the farm system, J.R. being, of course, the third and last great pitcher ever developed by the Astros.

In 1986 the story was even more the same. Ryan was still there, of course, and by this time he had been surrounded by: Mike Scott (from the Mets in 1984), Bob Knepper (from the Giants in 1981), Jim Deshaies (from the Yankees in 1985). Those four outsiders accounted for 131 of the Astros' starts. Thirteen more came from pitchers acquired during the season, Danny Darwin (from Milwaukee for farm system pitcher Mark Knudsen) and Matt Keough (acquired from the Cubs). So that's a total of 144 starts by non-farmhands. That's 89% of the starts, folks. I haven't done a systematic study to see how much higher this figure is than for the average major league team, but it's got to be at least an order of magnitude greater.

So there's a great deal of history behind the Astros' signing of Drabek and Swindell, much more than what one might first think. These signings are as good as any that could be made during this off-season, to be sure, and it means that the Astros will likely have a rotation in 1993 that is eighty per cent store-bought rather than home grown. In addition to Drabek and Swindell, you have Pete Harnisch (acquired from Baltimore) and Mark Portugal (from the Twins). The two most highly regarded and/ or successful-in-the-majors farmhands, Brian Williams and Darryl Kile, will most likely be battling it out for the final spot in the rotation.

As I said, these are as good as could be done if you're going to buy a staff, except maybe if David Cone had been in there somewhere. Swindell had a 3.10 road ERA last year, and a 2.19 ERA on turf, so he's looking like a sound investment. Drabek's record on turf over the last five years is 64-29, with a 2.39 ERA. The Astros play 111 games on turf in 1993: if managed properly, Drabek and Swindell could get as many as three-quarters of their starts on turf, which further enhances their value.

What makes Drabek and Swindell so attractive is that they have a history of pitching well on the road, something not shared by the other four potential starters. The home/road breakouts for Harnisch and Portugal, the established starters, aren't so hot (Portugal 2.67 at home, 4.63 away; Harnisch 3.14/4.37). Harnisch clearly had some conditioning problems last year (batters hit .226 against him in innings 1-6, .298 from the seventh inning on), and his ERA jumped a full run from his fine 1991 season. Portugal pitched extremely well last season, especially for a man who has a lifetime ERA of 4.01. He's a question mark not just due to his checkered past, but also due to the elbow problems that forced him to miss half the season.

Of the two farmhands vying for the fifth spot, you'd have to give the nod to Darryl Kile if for no other reason than he's a power pitcher. He has a moderately serious control problem (4.74 BB/9 in 59 major league games, 4.92 BB/9 in the minors), but his control was a lot better when he returned from Tucson in August (3.30). At Maganalles in the Venezuelan League this winter, Kile's BBP has improved to 2.83, another promising sign. He seems to pitch much better on 5 days rest, so maybe the Astros will give him the swing role and see if it helps him. Williams came up like a house afire in the middle of last season, but faded badly in September. He's one of those pitchers who hasn't been able to retain his K/9 ratio in the transition to the majors (7.08 in the minors, 4.82 in the majors), and he doesn't have a history of allowing a low opposition batting average. Interestingly, though, he pitched better away from the Dome, which might be something to figure into rotation planning. Whoever has the best spring will get the job, of course: all this science is getting us off track.

It's a bold move, no question about it. But how many extra games will it put in the win column for the Astros? They were a dead-even team last year, but they played eight games over their Pythagorean projection. If we split the difference and say that the Astros were roughly a 77-85 team last year, that means that they've got to get about 18 more wins from their

two new staff aces to have a shot at the flag. Since the highest total of wins generated by any two Astro starters last season was 19, and Drabek and Swindell combined for 27 last year, you have to give 'em a +8 right off the bat, which gets the 'Stros to 85 wins if everything else is even. Since the Houston bullpen was indisputably magnificent last year (39-21, 2.89 ERA), you've either got to assume that they'll exceed +8 easily or that the pen will backslide and counteract some of the effects of signing the two aces.

BULLPENITENTIARY

Inside a pen inside a dome seems like a bad variation on a Chinese puzzle: it was a puzzle that Art Howe solved exceptionally well in 1992, however. The bullpen clearly got the Astros the lion's share of those eight extra wins over the Pythagorean projection. The credit can be doled out to illustrious inmates Doug Jones and Xavier Hernandez, who went 19-9 and were about as magnificent as it is possible for two relievers to be.

But there are these problems. Both men pitched 111 innings last season. This was necessitated by the Butch Henrys and Ryan Bowens and Willie Blairs of the world, who made it necessary for the Astros to log 535 relief innings in 1992, second highest in the league. Only that well-known arm abuser Roger Craig used his relievers more, and just by one IP. So Jones and Hernandez have some serious mileage on them, kind of like a cab ride from Houston to New Orleans.

The bottom line, like the bill from the cabbie, is somewhat more prohibitive in expense than one likes to contemplate. One of these guys is almost certain to collapse this season, more likely Hernandez than Jones, since Doug is 36 and is reasonably used to a big workload. But there's Joe Boever, you say brightly—you've been reading the stats with your third eye again: I've told you how distracting that is for me—the Astros are very deep in the pen. Yes, there's Joe Boever. Isn't it interesting to note that Joe also pitched 111 innings last season. (Did Art do this on purpose? Is there some secret numerological cabal at work here??) So all three of these guys have been worked at least 15 IP more in the past year than in any previous season in their career. You make the prognosis while I go sneak a look at the stats. (Numerological factoid of the week: both the individual totals and the combined totals add up to the number 9. What does it mean? As close to nothing as is humanly possible, I suspect. After all, it's a factoid: it doesn't have to mean anything.)

As before, the section header (like the offending factoid) is only of marginal reference to the material contained within it. (So sue me.) A study should be done examining relief innings and the effect on multi-season bullpen effectiveness. How many innings are optimal? And is there a hard threshold between having a bullpen that is a long term escape hatch, or a slamming door that makes the warden one of the inmates. (I knew I could get that reference in there if I just stuck at it long enough. Can we settle out of court?)

Seriously, it's a complex question. Art Howe didn't have much choice last season: he had the least stable starting staff in the NL West. The Astros had the least number of starts from any four starting pitchers in the division. The full breakout:

Atlanta	134
Cincinnati	123
Los Angeles	122
San Diego	113
San Francisco	108
Houston	107

Howe did a better job of assigning roles to his pitchers than Roger Craig, which isn't giving Art much credit: a blind taxidermist with a malfunctioning ouija board and a year's supply of rancid formaldehyde could do a better job than ol' Humm Baby. The downside to Howe's precise role definition: three overworked relievers. What is freedom-inducing and innovative in the short run might be imprisoning and destructive over the long haul. Performances like the ones Jones and Hernandez turned in last season aren't especially abundant, even when you work in an extreme pitcher's park. (The other reason to be optimistic about Jones, by the way, is because he actually pitched better on the road last year—how's a 1.12 ERA grab you?) The performance of the Astros' bullpen will be interesting to watch just from a sabermetric point of view, regardless of its likely impact on the team's chances in '93.

NOTHING THAT A FEW RUNS WOULDN'T CURE

Finally, a section heading that makes sense. In and of itself. Every baseball team needs to score runs to win: one of the great truisms of the game, mastered by general managers and nine year olds alike. What we want to know is: how many runs are enough?

The answer: 608 (the total that the Astros scored in 1992) is not going to be enough. For all the movement upward in the standings (sixteen games worth), the Astros managed to score just three more runs in 1992 than they did the previous year. This despite good seasons from Craig Biggio, Steve Finley, Jeff Bagwell, and Ken Caminiti, plus promising work from Eric Anthony and Luis Gonzalez, and fine part-time support from Pete Incaviglia. (Incaviglia, by the way, is a great sleeper pick in Fantasy Leagues for '93; he's moving to a good hitter's park and just might be ready to explode for 25-30 homers.)

The problem is: in order to win, the Astros are going to need 50-75 more runs with a corresponding drop in runs allowed. (You can't play fast and loose with the Pythagorean formula forever.) Where are these runs going to come from? When we look at the batting order breakouts, we see a lot of improvement in the leadoff spot in terms of on-base, but no change in runs scored. The Astros suffered from a very slow first half of the year from sophomore Jeff Bagwell, 1991's best rookie, and from Luis Gonzalez, who actually had to be farmed out for several weeks in late May to get his stroke back on track.

So the leadoff slot (occupied almost exclusively by Biggio) suffered somewhat in terms of runs scored in the first half. Eric Anthony came alive in late May and picked up some of the slack from Bagwell, but he was injured, then he began to backslide after the All-Star Break. Ken Caminiti batted cleanup part of the time in August. It seemed that whenever Howe would make a lineup adjustment and solve one problem, another one would crop up.

The across-the-board improvement in the #2 slot (a underrated year by Steve Finley) helped stabilize the batting order somewhat, but the Astros might actually be better off if Biggio followed Finley, as Craig is the one with the good batting eye and it would produce more none on, none out situations for the #3 and #4 hitters, thus maximizing the potential for a big first inning.

The Astros' power totals in the 3-6 slots improved significantly enough to produce a 22% overall increase in home runs from the previous year. The 3-4-5-6 slot increase, however, was much greater (52%). The Astros actually hit more homers at home than on the road for the first time in recent memory. (The other thing that contributed to the Astros' ability to exceed their Pythagorean projection was their marked improvement in late-inning offense. They hit 15 points higher, slugged and got on base 31 points higher. Only the Pirates and the Expos scored more runs from the seventh inning on.)

Year	BOP	OINX	AB	R	H	TB	D	T	HR	RBI	BB	SO	SB	CS	BA	SA	OBP	RC27	BBP	XBH
1991	1	15.01	684	93	175	247	30	9	8	51	54	98	29	17	.256	.361	.310	3.84	7.3	47
1992	1	17.07	635	94	173	229	32	3	6	40	96	100	38	16	.272	.361	.368	4.65	13.1	41
1991	2	13.73	658	77	171	215	18	7	4	55	55	82	29	12	.260	.327	.317	3.57	7.7	29
1992	2	17.30	650	89	189	260	30	13	5	56	59	70	45	11	.291	.400	.350	5.03	8.3	48
1991	3	18.01	631	89	177	258	30	6	13	77	66	98	16	7	.281	.409	.349	5.05	9.5	49
1992	3	17.33	648	80	167	262	36	4	17	98	61	97	13	5	.258	.404	.322	4.47	8.6	57
1991	4	15.62	627	65	153	230	28	5	13	80	58	124	6	6	.244	.367	.308	3.81	8.5	46
1992	4	19.28	624	80	169	272	37	3	20	103	68	120	9	5	.271	.436	.342	5.22	9.8	60
1991	5	17.64	610	78	162	244	41	4	11	91	66	124	10	4	.266	.400	.337	4.68	9.8	56
1992	5	16.52	622	70	152	241	26	3	19	73	58	133	8	8	.244	.387	.309	4.04	8.5	48
1991	6	14.33	610	58	145	208	24	3	11	68	53	134	10	7	.238	.341	.299	3.41	8.0	38
1992	6	16.68	610	64	160	245	26	4	17	72	47	102	12	3	.262	.402	.315	4.37	7.2	47
1991	7	15.62	596	53	151	222	28	5	11	68	50	125	12	10	.253	.372	.311	3.96	7.7	44
1992	7	11.13	593	45	129	168	26	2	3	46	36	123	5	4	.218	.283	.262	2.42	5.7	31
1991	8	13.17	572	48	131	180	26	4	5	51	49	97	9	3	.229	.315	.290	3.02	7.9	35
1992	8	13.53	564	45	128	184	30	4	6	53	46	116	6	1	.227	.326	.285	3.07	7.5	40
1991	9	9.06	516	44	80	104	15	0	3	29	51	145	4	2	.155	.202	.231	1.41	9.0	18
1992	9	8.16	533	41	83	108	12	2	3	42	35	164	3	1	.156	.203	.208	1.27	6.2	17

		OINX	AB	R	H	TB	D	T	HR	RBI	BB	SO	SB	CS	BA	SA	OBP	RC27	BBP	XBH
DIFF	1	114	93	101	99	93	107	33	75	78	178	102	131	94	106	100	119	121	179	87
	2	126	99	116	111	121	167	186	125	102	107	85	155	92	112	122	110	141	108	166
	3	96	103	90	94	102	120	67	131	127	92	99	81	71	92	99	92	88	91	116
	4	123	100	123	110	118	132	60	154	129	117	97	150	83	111	119	111	137	116	130
	5	94	102	90	94	99	63	75	173	80	88	107	80	200	92	97	92	86	87	86
	6	116	100	110	110	118	108	133	155	106	89	76	120	43	110	118	106	128	89	124
	7	71	99	85	85	76	93	40	27	68	72	98	42	40	86	76	84	61	74	70
	8	103	99	94	98	102	115	100	120	104	94	120	67	33	99	104	98	102	96	114
	9	90	103	93	104	104	80	—	100	145	69	113	75	50	100	101	90	90	69	94
AVG		103.6		100	100	103	106	88	122	102	101	100	111	79				107.7	101.0	107.5

It's easy to tell from the DIFF chart where the black hole was in the Astros offense last season. The unlucky #7 hole just stopped the offense dead in its tracks. Rookie catchers, Andujar Cedeno, and other retreads produced the worst performance in the NL West from any non-#9 slot except for the Braves' #8 slot (roll over, Rafael Belliard).

FIVE WORST BOP SLOTS, NL WEST 1992*

Team	BOP	RC27
ATL	8	2.20
HOU	7	2.42
LA	6	2.72
LA	3	3.04
HOU	8	3.07

*non #9 (pitching) slots

As the chart indicates, the Astros' #8 slot wasn't so swift, either. It doesn't show up so bad on the DIFF chart because the #8 slot was even worse in '91. Clearly those areas will have to improve in order for the Astros to win enough road games to stay in a pennant race.

But the Astros really haven't done much to help out those areas. The catching position is still in the hands of Eddie Taubensee and Scott Servais, major contributors to the malaise in the 7-8 slots last year. The best thing you can say about them is that they comprise a left-right platoon.

Speaking of platoons, the other winter signings seem geared around finding bats to cover the weaknesses of incumbent players. Hence Kevin Bass and Chris James to spell Gonzalez and Anthony against lefties, and Jose Uribe to platoon with young Andujar Cedeno, whose offense fell through the floor at a velocity not far from the speed of light last year.

Odd thing about that, though: Gonzalez hit .350 against lefties last year, while Bass hit just .222 against them. That's going to be a very interesting platoon. James, who was part of Roger Craig's "complex" (read: semi-conscious) platoon in San Francisco last year, hit .302 against lefties and might be acceptable as a platoon surrogate for Anthony, who still hasn't solved lefties (lifetime .201 average against them, just .212 in '92).

Neither one of these guys figures to provide as much firepower as the departed Incaviglia. And there's very little in the farm system that can be much help. Gary Cooper and Trent Hubbard are old (28 and 29) infield prospects who could be serviceable backups, but they'll see action only if something catastrophic happens to Caminiti or Biggio. Neither can play short, so the coddling of Cedeno will continue with Uribe, who'll probably get to play against all of the tough righthanders, though he's not really an answer there either (.224 against righties in the last five years).

So what do the tea leaves say for the Astros this year? They're going to have to try to win with a six-man offense. Their starting pitching will be vastly improved (Kile looks like a good bet to be a pleasant surprise); the bullpen might hold up, might not. The best scenario, really, looks like about 86-90 wins, maybe 52-29 at home, 38-43 on the road (with the boost that Drabek and Swindell will provide as good turf pitchers). The Astros were 34-47 on the road last year, which is the best they've been on the road since 1986: the fantastic bullpen work is the reason for this, and it will be needed again if the Astros are going to be a real factor this year.

Bottom line: if this team can play .500 on the road, they'll have a shot. But I suspect that will require career years from both Drabek and Swindell and a big step forward from Kile, plus extra pop from Bagwell (who probably can) and Anthony (a lot less likely). It's a long shot, to be sure, but then so were the Braves in 1991...

```
Houston Astros Home Park Performance Factors
                  Outs  Runs  Hits   2b    3b    HR    W     K    SH    SF    HBP   IBB    SB    CS   GDP
Home LH Batters  1.005  .975  .997 1.079  .894  .938  .893  .932 1.002 1.147  .810  .682  .875 1.074 1.304
Home RH Batters  1.009 1.018  .985  .848  .826  .987  .950  .982  .917 1.159  .998  .762  .870  .846 1.044
All Home Batters 1.013 1.010  .994  .909  .881  .982  .937  .966  .953 1.120  .941  .735  .871  .937 1.077
Opp LH Batters   1.036 1.084 1.093 1.184  .950 1.320  .944  .986  .930 1.111  .726  .858  .893 1.099 1.333
Opp RH Batters   1.042 1.276 1.082 1.214 1.615 1.402 1.253 1.015 1.198 1.239  .890 1.652 1.058 1.110  .898
All Opp Batters  1.027 1.190 1.089 1.226 1.264 1.383 1.080  .990 1.133 1.135  .845 1.027 1.012 1.103 1.001
All LH Batters   1.019 1.025 1.041 1.128  .921 1.100  .915  .957  .973 1.112  .788  .775  .892 1.087 1.320
All RH Batters   1.023 1.129 1.029  .990 1.152 1.181 1.070  .997 1.038 1.195  .949  .983  .944  .949  .953
All Batters      1.019 1.095 1.040 1.045 1.053 1.167 1.004  .978 1.035 1.124  .899  .856  .932 1.012 1.035
```

Conventional Batting Records for Houston Astros

	G	AB	Run	Hit	2B	3B	HR	TB	RBI	W	K	IW	HB	SB	CS	BRng Eff	GI DP	SH	SF	Avg	Slug	OBP	Runs Ctd
Taubensee	104	297	23	66	15	0	5	96	28	31	78	3	2	2	1	.326	4	0	1	.222	.323	.299	30
Bagwell	162	586	87	160	34	6	18	260	96	84	97	13	12	10	6	.447	17	2	13	.273	.444	.368	100
Biggio	162	613	96	170	32	3	6	226	39	94	95	9	7	38	15	.404	5	5	2	.277	.369	.378	96
Caminiti	135	506	68	149	31	2	13	223	62	44	68	13	1	10	4	.494	14	2	4	.294	.441	.350	77
Cedeno A	71	220	15	38	13	2	2	61	13	14	71	2	3	2	0	.545	1	0	0	.173	.277	.232	15
Gonzalez L	122	387	40	94	19	3	10	149	55	24	52	3	2	7	7	.429	6	1	2	.243	.385	.289	41
Finley S	162	607	84	177	29	13	5	247	55	58	63	6	3	44	9	.496	10	16	4	.292	.407	.355	94
Anthony	137	440	45	105	15	1	19	179	80	38	98	5	1	5	4	.377	6	0	4	.239	.407	.298	54
Incaviglia	113	349	31	93	22	1	11	150	44	25	99	2	3	2	2	.541	6	0	2	.266	.430	.319	48
Candaele	135	320	19	68	12	1	1	85	18	24	36	3	3	7	1	.333	5	7	6	.213	.266	.269	25
Servais	77	205	12	49	9	0	0	58	15	11	25	2	5	0	0	.321	7	6	0	.239	.283	.283	17
Ramirez R	73	176	17	44	6	0	1	53	13	7	24	1	1	0	0	.359	5	1	0	.250	.301	.283	14
Guerrero J	79	125	8	25	4	2	1	36	14	10	32	2	1	1	0	.333	0	1	2	.200	.288	.261	11
Young G	74	76	14	14	1	1	0	17	4	10	11	0	0	6	2	.933	2	4	0	.184	.224	.279	6
Harnisch	34	67	7	11	5	0	0	16	8	2	12	0	0	0	1	.429	1	5	0	.164	.239	.188	3
Jones Chris	54	63	7	12	2	1	1	19	4	7	21	0	0	3	0	.429	1	3	0	.190	.302	.271	6
Riles	39	61	5	16	1	0	1	20	4	2	11	0	0	1	0	.500	0	0	1	.262	.328	.281	6
Distefano	52	60	4	14	0	2	0	18	7	5	14	1	1	0	0	.800	1	0	0	.233	.300	.303	6
Henry B	28	54	3	8	0	0	1	11	7	1	10	0	0	0	0	.667	1	5	0	.148	.204	.164	2
Tucker	20	50	5	6	1	0	0	7	3	3	13	0	2	1	1	.545	2	1	0	.120	.140	.200	1
Jones Jim	26	36	5	6	1	0	0	7	4	6	13	0	0	0	0	.333	1	9	0	.167	.194	.286	3
Kile	22	32	2	5	0	0	0	5	2	3	15	0	0	0	0	.000	0	5	0	.156	.156	.229	2
Br. Williams	20	30	2	4	1	0	0	5	4	0	13	0	0	0	0	.500	0	5	1	.133	.167	.129	1
Portugal	18	28	1	3	0	0	0	3	0	0	12	0	0	0	0	.000	0	6	0	.107	.107	.107	1
Sims	15	24	1	6	1	0	1	10	3	2	9	0	1	0	0	.000	1	0	0	.250	.417	.333	3
Blair	29	17	0	1	0	0	0	1	0	1	14	0	0	0	0	.000	0	1	0	.059	.059	.111	0
Hernandez X	77	9	1	0	0	0	0	0	0	0	5	0	0	0	0	.500	0	0	0	.000	.000	.000	0
Bowen R	15	9	1	1	0	0	0	1	0	0	3	0	0	0	1	.000	0	0	0	.111	.111	.111	0
Yelding	9	8	1	2	0	0	0	2	0	0	3	0	0	0	0	.000	0	0	0	.250	.250	.250	1
Boever	81	7	0	0	0	0	0	0	0	0	3	0	0	0	0	.000	0	0	0	.000	.000	.000	0
Jones D	80	4	0	0	0	0	0	0	0	0	2	0	0	0	0	.000	0	0	0	.000	.000	.000	0
Rhodes	5	4	0	0	0	0	0	0	0	0	2	0	0	0	0	.000	0	0	0	.000	.000	.000	0
Reynolds S	8	4	1	2	1	0	0	3	0	0	0	0	0	0	0	.000	0	2	0	.500	.750	.500	1
Walling	3	3	1	1	0	0	0	1	0	0	0	0	0	0	0	.000	0	0	0	.333	.333	.333	0
Murphy R	59	1	1	0	0	0	0	0	0	0	0	0	0	0	0	.000	0	1	0	.000	.000	.000	0
Mallicoat	25	1	1	0	0	0	0	0	0	0	0	0	0	0	0	.000	0	0	0	.000	.000	.000	0
Scheid	7	1	0	0	0	0	0	0	0	0	1	0	0	0	0	.000	0	0	0	.000	.000	.000	0
Osuna	66	0	0	0	0	0	0	0	0	0	0	0	0	0	0	.000	0	0	0	.000	.000	.000	0
TOTALS	2398	5480	608	1350	255	38	96	1969	582	506	1025	65	48	139	54	.438	96	88	40	.246	.359	.313	641

Sabermetric Batting Records for Houston Astros

	Ball Park Adjusted								Runs		Run/								
	AB	Run	Hit	2B	3B	HR	RBI	W	SO	Avg	Slug	OBP	Ctd	Outs	27o	OW%	OG	OWAR	DWAR	TWAR
Anthony	450	46	109	16	0	21	86	34	93	.242	.418	.293	54	356	4.10	.520	13	2.24	0.15	2.39
Bagwell	601	99	165	35	7	21	106	92	96	.275	.461	.373	109	474	6.21	.713	18	6.37	0.80	7.18
Biggio	629	110	175	32	3	7	43	103	94	.278	.372	.384	102	479	5.75	.681	18	5.87	0.70	6.56
Caminiti	519	74	155	33	2	15	68	44	66	.299	.457	.351	82	388	5.71	.677	14	4.70	0.41	5.11
Candaele	326	20	70	12	1	1	19	24	35	.215	.267	.268	26	275	2.55	.296	10	-0.55	0.94	0.39
Cedeno A	225	17	39	13	2	2	14	15	70	.173	.276	.231	15	186	2.18	.234	7	-0.80	0.01	-0.79
Distefano	60	4	14	0	1	0	7	4	13	.233	.267	.281	5	47	2.87	.347	2	-0.00	0.09	0.08
Finley S	622	86	184	32	11	5	59	53	60	.296	.407	.352	93	477	5.26	.641	18	5.14	1.33	6.47
Gonzalez L	397	41	98	21	2	11	59	22	49	.247	.393	.287	42	315	3.60	.455	12	1.23	0.74	1.97
Guerrero J	127	9	25	4	2	1	15	11	31	.197	.283	.257	10	105	2.57	.299	4	-0.20	-0.12	-0.32
Incaviglia	358	35	96	22	1	13	49	27	98	.268	.444	.321	51	270	5.10	.626	10	2.76	0.56	3.32
Jones Chris	64	8	12	2	1	1	4	7	20	.188	.297	.268	6	55	2.95	.359	2	0.02	-0.00	0.01
Ramirez R	180	19	45	6	0	1	14	7	23	.250	.300	.278	14	140	2.70	.320	5	-0.16	0.11	-0.04
Rhodes	4	0	0	0	0	0	0	0	1	.000	.000	.000	0	4	0.00	.000	0	-0.05	-0.00	-0.05
Riles	61	5	16	1	0	1	4	1	10	.262	.328	.270	6	46	3.52	.444	2	0.16	0.05	0.21
Servais	209	13	50	9	0	0	16	12	24	.239	.282	.293	17	171	2.68	.317	6	-0.21	0.16	-0.05
Sims	24	1	6	1	0	1	3	2	8	.250	.417	.308	3	18	4.50	.566	1	0.14	0.06	0.21
Taubensee	303	23	68	16	0	5	30	28	74	.224	.327	.291	29	242	3.24	.403	9	0.47	-0.29	0.19
Tucker	51	5	6	1	0	0	3	3	12	.118	.137	.182	1	47	0.57	.021	2	-0.57	-0.10	-0.68
Walling	3	1	1	0	0	0	0	0	0	.333	.333	.333	0	2	0.00	.000	0	-0.03	-0.00	-0.03
Yelding	8	1	2	0	0	0	0	0	2	.250	.250	.250	1	6	4.50	.566	0	0.05	-0.00	0.04
Young G	77	15	14	1	1	0	4	10	10	.182	.221	.276	5	71	1.90	.189	3	-0.42	0.10	-0.32
TOTALS	5617	668	1406	272	40	113	640	510	1002	.250	.373	.315	681	4501	4.09	.518	167	28.06	5.69	33.75

Pitching Records for Houston Astros

	ERA	W	L	Pct	G	GS	CG	ShO	GF	Sv	IP	R	ER	H	2B	3B	HR	BB	IW	SO	HB	WP	BK
Harnisch	3.70	9	10	.474	34	34	0	0	0	0	206.2	92	85	182	37	8	18	64	3	164	5	4	1
Henry B	4.02	6	9	.400	28	28	2	1	0	0	165.2	81	74	185	38	5	16	41	7	96	1	2	2
Jones Jim	4.07	10	6	.625	25	23	0	0	1	0	139.1	64	63	135	27	5	13	39	3	69	5	4	1
Kile	3.95	5	10	.333	22	22	2	0	0	0	125.1	61	55	124	26	6	8	63	4	90	4	3	4
Portugal	2.66	6	3	.667	18	16	1	1	0	0	101.1	32	30	76	13	4	7	41	3	62	1	1	1
Br. Williams	3.92	7	6	.538	16	16	0	0	0	0	96.1	44	42	92	16	2	10	42	1	54	0	2	1
Bowen R	10.96	0	7	.000	11	9	0	0	2	0	33.2	43	41	48	9	1	8	30	3	22	2	5	0
Reynolds S	7.11	1	3	.250	8	5	0	0	0	0	25.1	22	20	42	11	3	2	6	1	10	0	1	1
Boever	2.51	3	6	.333	81	0	0	0	26	2	111.1	38	31	103	13	2	3	45	9	67	4	4	0
Hernandez X	2.11	9	1	.900	77	0	0	0	25	7	111.0	31	26	81	11	2	5	42	7	96	3	5	0
Jones D	1.85	11	8	.579	80	0	0	0	70	36	111.2	29	23	96	14	3	5	17	5	93	5	2	1
Blair	4.00	5	7	.417	29	8	0	0	1	0	78.2	47	35	74	16	3	5	25	2	48	2	3	0
Osuna	4.23	6	3	.667	66	0	0	0	17	0	61.2	29	29	52	7	0	8	38	5	37	1	3	1
Murphy R	4.04	3	1	.750	59	0	0	0	6	0	55.2	28	25	56	8	3	2	21	4	42	0	4	0
Mallicoat	7.23	0	0	.000	23	0	0	0	6	0	23.2	19	19	26	6	2	2	19	2	20	5	2	0
Scheid	6.00	0	1	.000	7	1	0	0	3	0	12.0	8	8	14	3	0	2	6	1	8	0	1	1
TOTALS	3.74	81	81	.500	584	162	5	2	157	45	1459.1	668	606	1386	255	49	114	539	60	978	38	45	14

Sabermetric Pitching Records for Houston Astros

	Adj ERA	Expected W	Expected L	Expected Pct	BFP	Avg	Slg	OBA	RC/G	GDP	SB	CS	PK	PKE	SH	SF	RSup	RSp/G	W	L	Pct
Blair	4.35	5	7	.394	331	.249	.374	.309	3.88	7	6	4	1	1	4	3	42	4.81	6	6	.499
Boever	2.67	6	3	.633	479	.248	.310	.324	3.61	7	7	5	0	1	10	4	36	2.91	4	5	.493
Bowen R	11.76	1	6	.081	179	.333	.576	.455	10.70	2	5	3	1	0	3	0	12	3.21	0	7	.057
Harnisch	4.05	8	11	.428	859	.234	.371	.294	3.92	8	27	6	0	2	5	5	98	4.27	9	10	.475
Henry B	4.40	6	9	.388	710	.285	.433	.325	4.93	10	10	7	0	5	12	7	62	3.37	5	10	.324
Hernandez X	2.27	7	3	.704	454	.200	.275	.279	2.73	5	10	4	0	0	3	2	67	5.43	8	2	.824
Jones D	2.01	14	5	.751	440	.235	.320	.274	2.82	7	5	4	0	0	9	0	30	2.42	10	9	.540
Jones Jim	4.39	6	10	.389	579	.258	.403	.313	4.34	11	20	5	0	0	7	4	72	4.65	8	8	.478
Kile	4.31	6	9	.398	554	.261	.391	.348	4.95	8	6	3	1	2	5	6	45	3.23	5	10	.315
Mallicoat	7.61	0	0	.175	120	.283	.457	.427	7.73	2	3	1	0	0	3	1	2	0.76	0	0	.008
Murphy R	4.37	2	2	.392	242	.260	.353	.322	4.23	3	4	1	0	0	3	3	25	4.04	2	2	.412
Osuna	4.52	3	6	.375	270	.236	.377	.343	4.70	4	4	1	0	1	5	6	26	3.79	3	6	.365
Portugal	2.84	5	4	.603	405	.213	.331	.295	3.04	10	7	6	0	3	5	1	38	3.38	5	4	.535
Reynolds S	7.46	1	3	.181	122	.385	.596	.414	9.61	2	6	1	0	2	6	1	8	2.84	0	4	.106
Scheid	6.00	0	1	.254	56	.280	.460	.357	6.19	2	2	0	0	0	0	0	0	0.00	0	1	.000
Br. Williams	4.20	5	8	.410	413	.255	.393	.330	4.47	9	7	3	0	0	7	3	45	4.20	6	7	.449
TOTALS	4.09	69	93	.423	6213	.252	.378	.320	4.26	97	129	54	3	17	87	46	608	3.75	66	96	.407

Batting 'Splits' Records for Houston Astros

SPLITS for Bagwell

	G	AB	Run	Hit	2B	3B	HR	TB	RBI	W	K	IW	HB	SB	CS	DP	SH	SF	Avg	Slug	OBP	RC
vs LHP	96	210	44	61	13	3	10	110	34	38	31	9	1	7	4	7	1	5	.290	.524	.394	44
vs RHP	161	376	43	99	21	3	8	150	62	46	66	4	11	3	2	10	1	8	.263	.399	.354	56
Home	81	294	40	76	21	3	8	127	48	42	50	9	4	5	4	10	2	4	.259	.432	.355	45
Away	81	292	47	84	13	3	10	133	48	42	47	4	8	5	2	7	0	9	.288	.455	.382	55
Grass	48	172	30	56	4	1	6	80	33	24	23	3	5	2	1	4	0	8	.326	.465	.407	35
Turf	114	414	57	104	30	5	12	180	63	60	74	10	7	8	5	13	2	5	.251	.435	.352	64
April/June	77	280	41	70	14	1	9	113	44	41	52	8	5	6	5	11	0	2	.250	.404	.354	39
July/October	85	306	46	90	20	5	9	147	52	43	45	5	7	4	1	6	2	11	.294	.480	.381	61

SPLITS for Houston Astros (all batters except pitchers)

	G	AB	Run	Hit	2B	3B	HR	TB	RBI	W	K	IW	HB	SB	CS	DP	SH	SF	Avg	Slug	OBP	RC
vs LHP	1035	2035	248	522	105	15	39	774	233	222	368	33	14	58	24	40	36	16	.257	.380	.331	267
vs RHP	1758	3445	360	828	150	23	57	1195	349	284	657	32	34	81	30	56	52	24	.240	.347	.303	375
Home	1220	2733	302	685	145	22	49	1021	288	275	540	47	26	83	29	46	47	18	.251	.374	.323	346
Away	1178	2747	306	665	110	16	47	948	294	231	485	18	22	56	25	50	41	22	.242	.345	.304	296
Grass	700	1634	178	402	57	6	26	549	173	130	279	15	15	31	14	30	29	17	.246	.336	.305	173
Turf	1698	3846	430	948	198	32	70	1420	409	376	746	50	33	108	40	66	59	23	.246	.369	.317	469
April/June	1128	2584	284	619	127	18	43	911	270	233	522	34	23	56	28	43	41	15	.240	.353	.306	288
July/October	1270	2896	324	731	128	20	53	1058	312	273	503	31	25	83	26	53	47	25	.252	.365	.320	354

San Francisco Giants

Don Malcolm

SAN FRANCISCO										
YEAR	1983	1984	1985	1986	1987	1988	1989	1990	1991	1992
W	79	66	62	83	90	83	92	85	75	72
L	83	96	100	79	72	79	70	77	87	90
WPCT	0.488	0.407	0.383	0.512	0.556	0.512	0.568	0.525	0.463	0.444
R	687	682	556	698	783	670	699	719	649	574
RA	697	807	674	618	669	626	600	710	697	647
PWPT	0.493	0.417	0.405	0.561	0.578	0.534	0.576	0.506	0.464	0.440
PythW	80	67	66	91	94	86	93	82	75	71
PythL	82	95	96	71	68	76	69	80	87	91
LUCK	-1	-1	-4	-8	-4	-3	-1	3	0	1

Defensive Efficiency Record: .7052

Position	92 Starter	TWAR	93 Starter	TWAR
Catcher	Manwaring	1.07	Manwaring	1.07
First base	Clark, W.	6.67	Clark, W.	6.67
Second base	Thompson, R.	5.60	Thompson, R.	5.60
Third base	Williams, M.	2.46	Williams, M.	2.46
Shortstop	Clayton	0.92	Clayton	0.92
Left field	Felder	2.81	Bonds	7.63
Center field	McGee	4.03	Martinez, Da.	2.31
Right field	Snyder	3.44	McGee	4.03

They're gone.

After seven tumultuous years, Al Rosen and Roger Craig are no longer running the Giants. There are pitchers in every major league farm system breathing sighs of relief.

It's not yet safe to be traded to the Giants if you're a pitcher, but at least there's no longer a decontamination period required during the first six weeks of the off-season.

Pitchers that glow in the dark are one thing, but pitchers who burn bright and fizzle before you very eyes are something else.

Back in the mid-sixties, the Giants had a Japanese left-hander named Masanori Murakami, who was forced to return to Japan after his rookie season and was stigmatized for several years afterward.

I think of Murakami because the Giants use their pitchers like kamikaze pilots.

They are launched at supersonic speeds. The cockpit strains to remain intact as they race toward the appointed doom. They keep their eye on the target, only on the target.

They flame out spectacularly, taking down with them whatever they can get to, proud suicides for the cause, exhorted into sacrifice of life and limb by an old guard convinced of its utter command of history and knowledge.

And so it is with the Giants staff. Their charismatic, cud-chewing coaxer, their General Patton in cowboy boots, spits in direct proportion to the number of pitching arms currently on the disabled list.

It's a wonder of nature that, as he retires to his ranch in Poway, he has a single drop of saliva left.

Some people are blessed even as they dole out curses. They bask in a reflected glow, pictures hide their facial flaws, people listen to their hokey platitudes and think they've heard something profound.

It's one part mysticism, two parts P.T. Barnum, and several too many parts per million in the local drinking water. The local population builds bonfires on midsummer nights and exhibits a dim green glow emanating from their nostrils. One by one they disappear, later to turn up in a mass grave across the bay near Helgenberger Boulevard.

While the mysterious sacrifice continues, part plague, part murder conspiracy, the legacy of annihilated young arms is spin doctored out of public consciousness. The press, those cloven-hooved camp followers of monosyllabic outrage, dish up lumpy yellowed pudding that's passed off as editorial stewardship. Mass quantities of this nervous system-imploding nourishment are dispensed, using the same methods by which defective medical supplies manage to inundate the third world.

In the midst of this mute carnage, an ex-pitcher and an ex-third basemen survey the wreckage. They don't quite grasp what their eyes take in. One likes the other because he thinks he's smart. The other likes the first because he knows that the other guy thinks he's smart. Each thinks that he's the first guy of the pair.

Their lives are no less strange for being charmed. Infinitesimal particles soar, then crash at the behest of their synapses—irrelevant details, like the mantle with a clock placed with its hands and face reflected in a mirror, so that time might magically run backwards when a young maiden spies the singular discrepancy, cascade from their lips like a lost opportunity, the dream fixating on the maiden, who's showing a lot of leg and a willingness to debase herself for a morsel of celebrity.

But time fools them. The young maiden is really a hag: the clock was not running backwards in the mirror because it had stopped, grinding the magic to a halt before it could begin to take effect. As they turn to regain their bearings they discover that the landscape has been obliterated, all the familiar landmarks are no longer in view. They do not feel the shock wave until it is far too late.

And everywhere, in the underworld at least, everyone is smiling. That strange green glow has slowly returned, is dulling the inhabitant's eyes, and they seem to look through the two old men as they stroll by, oblivious to the tsunami behind them, cresting in the silent promise of destruction, the giant wave ridden by a lone surfer, a youthful body with a face disfigured by premature age, the lone samurai, the silent kamikaze.

A ghost? There is no time to find out. The wave hits: silence overwhelms them. The smiling faces have vanished. The two men can no longer see each other. They cannot see their own hands in front of their faces. All that they can see is the rapidly permeating green glow, the color of unknowing, the color of the lost. As they begin to dematerialize they both sense that the place they are going to is neither San Francisco nor Kansas, not Oz or Shangri-La or even Freedonia.

Fate is a split-finger fast ball. Its forked tongue darts in and out of the chamber, still roiling with the waters of an angry bay, not quieted (not by a long shot) by its reprieve. The final phase has begun, it will be fatal, but no one wants to know. They marvel at the raging waters from their perches on the light-towers. The sea continues to rise.

The truth somehow never seems to sink in. . .

* * *

Wow. Is that strange stuff, or what? That tight chain of allusion, the centripetal motion of the imagery (I told you somewhere else that Brock pays double for it, but he keeps saying that the check is in the mail) is downright disturbing, or maybe just downright disturbed. (I was going to say that it was downright upright, but only a few of you aficionados would catch the sly but stoopid reference to the salacious innuendo in the old Harvey's Bristol Cream commercial.)

Harvey's Bristol Cream? The Bailey's of the Hugh Hefner generation? Aw, shucks...

What did the above have to do with the Giants? Everything—and nothing. (Yes, I do like to have it both ways. No, there's nothing you can do to stop me. Not even if you stop reading.) The most amazing story of the past baseball year is the incredible fight to keep the Giants in San Francisco despite mounting evidence that the team would be better off anywhere else.

This sad state of affairs, as the heavily symbolic material above unplainly says, is in a spiral of decline that a man with a swollen vocabulary would call monotonic. The most surreal insight from the above narrative, one that is well-hidden indeed, is that the Giants were kept in San Francisco just to allow superstar Barry Bonds to follow in his father's footsteps. (It's the bit about the ghost on the surfboard, in case you were having trouble with the knotty problems of metaphor.) It sounds far fetched, I know, but—trust me—anything can happen in baseball these days just so long as it happens behind the scenes. We've reached the stage of meta-collusion, kind of a variation on stagnant inflation where everybody has something to hide.

Perhaps this sounds like nothing more than another waterlogged conspiracy theory to you, a kind of "Rush to Horsehide." (Jim Garrison and Mark Lane fans please exercize your middle finger now.) But I ask you: a team who can't get a new stadium built in the city it's been in for thirty-five years; an owner who has spent ten years trying to get that done and has threatened to move the team, or sell it to those who would move it elsewhere; a final showdown that allows baseball to flex its insider muscles to force one of its own to take less money not to move the team; and then that franchise, fragile and all but packed up and gone from a metropolitan area that can't decide if it wants the team or not, suddenly can go out and sign the MOST EXPENSIVE FREE AGENT IN THE HISTORY OF BASEBALL???

Something's mighty funny about this, folks. And that's funny peculiar, just in case there was any doubt. Jim Bouton wrote in Ball Four that the

pecking order on a ball team was owner, general manager, superstar, manager, established player, coaches, traveling secretary, trainer, clubhouse man, marginal player (which was where Bouton was in 1969). Judging by what has happened in baseball since the writing of Ball Four, and these latest developments over the winter of 1992-93, I'd have to say that the new pecking order for baseball is as follows: owners, superstars, agents, general managers, stars, managers, journeymen, coaches, traveling secretaries, trainers, clubhouse men, marginal players, commissioner.

What it really points up is something that Andrew Zimbalist so cogently notes in his book Baseball and Billions, which, by the way, is must reading for any serious baseball fan. The economic fakery indulged in by the corporate ownership in baseball has become more of an art form that learning to throw a split-finger fastball (we'll get back to the Giants somehow). All of the subtlety has been removed from the shell game, is all. The Giants were a struggling franchise headed for a new city late in the summer. On December 1st they were a struggling franchise with no known home. On December 10th they were back in San Francisco and the owners of a $43 million free agent. I think this deal was wired sometime after the World Series, and that Bonds was the key to the Giants staying in San Francisco. You make up your own minds...

* * *

All right, already. Let's talk a little sabermetrics before you throw the book against the wall. Before the surreal side trip into conspiracy, we were referring to Roger Craig and his unique skill at mangling pitchers.

Now there appear to be two main ways that a manager can do horrendous damage to the arms of his pitchers. The first is familiar to all of us: it's simple overwork. Brock Hanke has been developing some research materials which show the escalating decline of starting pitcher innings pitched since the brief surge in the '70s. The key feature of this research is to show that the "overwork" threshold is dropping faster than the concomitant actual drop.

Overwork is a constant factor, and it is not a simple thing to judge: Craig Wright has come closest to giving us a definitive rule of thumb, however, when he asserts that young pitchers must not be given more than 200 innings until they're 25. Most managers—not just Craig and Tom Lasorda, the two most flagrant offenders—subject their young pitchers to overwork. And most young pitchers—Don Drysdale, Don Gullett, Dwight Gooden—wind up paying for it in terms of career interruptions and/or premature retirement.

The other way to slash up a pitching staff is the Craig way. It's sort of the analogue to Mayan agriculture. You might have heard of that: the historians call it "slash and burn." Craig's slash and burn technique is to keep juggling the roles of his pitchers between starter and reliever. What juggling does is mess up the way a pitcher prepares for a game. Not only does it add strain physically, it also adds strain mentally. This combination of added stress is deadly on pitchers' arms.

Craig was never able to establish a starting rotation where four men managed to make thirty starts in a season. In his seven years with the Giants, he never once had a team that averaged thirty starts from his four most heavily used starters. The complete data is shown in the following figure:

It wasn't just injuries that forced Craig to bring in new starters. It was his willful decision to flip-flop his pitchers from bullpen to starter and back again, sometimes three or four times in the course of a season. In 1991, the year when he got the most number of games from his big four, Craig had three pitchers—Trevor Wilson, Don Robinson, and Kelly Downs—who were shuttled between the bullpen and starting assignments, ranging between starting one-fifth of the time and two-thirds of the time. Four other pitchers (Scott Garrelts, Gil Heredia, Bryan Hickerson, and Mike LaCoss) had similar profiles with less than 20 appearances.

Team	86	87	88	89	90	91	92	TOT	AVG
ATL	123	108	122	115	114	141	134	857	122
CIN	127	124	106	107	112	108	123	807	115
HOU	130	131	123	112	130	110	107	843	120
LA	130	124	117	113	123	130	122	859	123
SD	108	110	127	118	128	108	113	812	116
SF	111	109	101	111	105	113	108	758	108

That was Craig's most stable year. In the Giants' World Series year—another relatively stable year (for the Giants, at least)—four pitchers (Wilson, LaCoss, Atlee Hammaker, and Bob Knepper) were slapdashed. The pattern of slapdashing became more and more pronounced in later years—'91 and '92 represent the highest use of this deadly practice (everybody on the team except Rod Beck and Mike Jackson got at least one start last year: true slapdashers numbered four—Swift, Downs, Oliveras, and Burba).

My most memorable moment of the 1992 season occurred on Opening Day. The Giants were playing the Dodgers in Los Angeles. Brock Hanke and I were there in person to see Bill Swift face Ramon Martinez (another abused pitcher, but that's another story). Martinez had little—as was the case for most of the year—and departed early, though not before throwing 85 pitches. The Giants had a 7-1 lead behind Swift in the seventh. I turned to Brock and offered the thought that Swift had done a good job, he'd really looked sharp, and that surely Craig would rest him now. Brock shook his head. This is Roger pitch-'em-'till-they-drop Craig running the team, he explained. Swift will pitch until he gets in real trouble.

Swift put a couple of men on in the seventh, and had to do a lot of fancy pitching, including some work from behind in the count, to escape unscathed. His pitch count had exceeded 100. Surely he'd be pulled after the seventh, I opined. He had some trouble, but the lead is still intact: the bullpen can easily hold it. Hanke just shook his head again. That wasn't "real trouble," he said. It's going to take something much more serious to get Swift out of there. Swift pitched the eighth.

It wasn't till the ninth that Swift finally got lifted, after giving up another run and putting two more men on base. His pitch count for the day: 118. The Giants ended up winning 7-2, and Bill Swift was off on his fast start that got so much attention early in the year. As we left the game, Brock and I traded predictions as to what day Bill Swift would end up on the disabled list. Our guesses were within two weeks of each other, and they were sandwiched around the actual day that Swift was put on the DL.

The above isn't really meant to show how smart we are, but rather how dumb Roger really is. This is the insidious charisma that I referred to in the literary licentiousness: Craig can convince pitchers to run through walls for him. He built up Bill Swift to be an iron man ace, and slashed up his shoulder in the process. He had Swift on a 272 IP pace at the end of April—about 35 innings too high for an established starter, about 60 innings too high for a pitcher transitioning from reliever to starter, and about 90 innings too high for a guy with Swift's build.

It certainly isn't Bill Swift's job to tell Roger Craig or any other manager that he's pitching him too many innings. He's supposed to go out and do the best he can whenever he's asked to and he isn't hurt. But the key thing is not getting hurt. It's the manager's job to determine how best to utilize his players, and that includes the responsibility for ensuring their health. Craig's record in this area over his seven year span as Giants' skipper is among the worst in baseball. Worse still, he has shown virtually no capability for developing young pitchers, and this leaves the Giants in a desperate position for additional mound strength in the next few seasons. It will be a bitter legacy for Dusty Baker to inherit.

* * *

It's a wonder the Giants didn't lose more games than they did in 1992. As was the case in Houston last year, good work from the bullpen kept the Giants from competing for last place with the downtrodden Dodgers. The pen logged more innings than any other team in the NL last year, though, so there's something to worry about right off the top.

But the major concern has to be the offense. The dropoff with the loss of Mitchell was thunderous: home run totals declined 26%, runs scored by 12%. A poor performance in the #2 slot took a big gouge out of the Giants' attack, resulting in 48 less RBI from the #3 slot—the largest dropoff in production in a before-and-after BOP slot breakout for all teams in '91-92. Despite the loss in RBI, the #3 slot really wasn't very much worse in '92: the big dropoff came in the #4 slot, where Matt Williams really struggled (.173). One of the better performers in that slot was Cory Snyder, who has moved on to the Dodgers. Bonds will solve this problem, and his presence in the lineup may help snap Williams out of his doldrums.

Bonds can't do anything but help this offense, but there's a serious question as to what will be on base for him to drive in. The leadoff slot has been plagued by poor OBP ever since Butler left: the 1992 performance was its most listless to date. Last year there were three players that Craig tried in the #1 slot: Darren Lewis, Mike Felder, and Willie McGee. All of them were found wanting: Lewis started the season as the leadoff man, had a fine April (.319, .398 OBP), and then just lost everything, hitting just .166 from May through August (not counting his time in Phoenix looking for his swing). Felder wasn't too bad with the bat (.282), but he couldn't walk enough to really be effective. McGee could hit for average, but he walked even less than Felder (3.7%).

The new leadoff man, apparently, is Dave Martinez, late of the Reds. He comes with a sizable platoon differential (just .229 against left-handers), and not much of an ability to walk (just 7.1 over the last five years). This projects to improve the #1 slot's RC27 by about six to eight percent, not enough to really help kick-start the offense.

And that #2 slot is troublesome as well. Robby Thompson and McGee hit there for most of '92, with neither man producing his best in that BOP. Thompson seems most comfortable batting #6, The quirkiest solution might be to bunch the hitters, starting with Martinez (perhaps platooning him with Lewis against lefties) and following with Clark, Bonds, Williams, and Thompson, with McGee sixth. Thompson just doesn't walk enough when he bats #2 to make it feasible to bat him there; he's a better hitter lower in the order. The #7 and #8 slots (most likely Kirt Manwaring and Royce Clayon) are not exactly going to instill fear. There was some talk of the Giants signing Mike Scioscia: the veteran ex-Dodger is coming off his worst offensive season, though, and might not even be able to get back enough to make a solid platoon with Manwaring feasible. (Kirt is a much better hitter against lefties: .305 last season vs. .206 against righties, .260/.209 lifetime.)

Can this team compete this year? There's enough strength in the middle of the lineup for the Giants to stay in the race, but they'll need a complete overhaul in their handling of pitchers in order to have enough arms healthy not to just get blitzed in good hitting parks like Atlanta and Cincinnati. The Giants have some very talented pitchers: Dusty Baker just has to decide how he wants to structure his staff, and then—unlike Roger Craig—stick with it.

A rotation of Wilson, Swift, Brantley, Bryan Hickerson, and Burkett could be very effective in a blue collar kind of way, with veteran Bud Black used as the only—ecouter s'il vous plait, Dusty, ONLY—swing man. (Black had a September that would have sent the New York Stock Exchange reeling, and it remains to be seen if he's got enough left to be useful, but I think he just was asked to pitch too much. Three starts and four relief appearances a month would be about right: let's see, that's three times six plus four times two equals 27 innings per month, or 162

I know that Dusty and Roger Craig are probably laughing if they've read this far (doubtful). But this is the type of planning that needs to be made, especially with a staff that has no iron man. The bullpen just can't be used as much as it was in 1992. There's still a good nucleus there, what with Beck and Jackson and Dave Burba, who was a bust as a starter last year but struck out a man per inning as a reliever. Hickerson could be left in the pen if lefty Kevin Rogers is ready to join the rotation: his ERA at Phoenix last season was 4.00, which is about 3.30 normalized for the PCL, and he's shown good K/BB ratios all the way up the chain, so he's worth a gamble.

The Giants—in the race? What have I been smoking, you say. But remember—please—that this team was in contention or close until they let Butler get away. There's still a good nucleus, and adding Bonds gets back a lot more than what was given up when the Giants traded away Mitchell. What it will take is Dusty Baker being able to develop a knack with blue collar pitchers in the way that Jim Leyland has over the past five years with the Pirates. The Giants ought to win about 85 games on the strength of Bonds added to what they have—the rest will take some managing. Let's get busy, Dusty—your chance to chat with Arsenio is riding on it.

Year	BOP	OINX	AB	R	H	TB	D	T	HR	RBI	BB	SO	SB	CS	BA	SA	OBP	RC27	BBP	XBH
1991	1	14.77	661	107	165	227	23	12	5	36	64	93	32	10	.250	.343	.316	3.69	8.8	40
1992	1	13.67	682	84	180	226	21	2	7	47	50	96	41	10	.264	.331	.314	3.61	6.8	30
1991	2	16.07	668	89	183	261	38	5	10	64	46	115	17	12	.274	.391	.321	4.40	6.4	53
1992	2	14.05	670	76	173	235	35	3	7	43	41	109	14	14	.258	.351	.301	3.63	5.8	45
1991	3	22.38	659	96	204	346	35	7	31	133	49	105	7	4	.310	.525	.357	6.93	6.9	73
1992	3	22.03	617	84	188	295	45	4	18	85	78	103	14	8	.305	.478	.383	6.71	11.2	67
1991	4	21.52	615	89	159	302	23	3	38	105	65	107	7	5	.259	.491	.329	5.56	9.6	64
1992	4	15.24	645	60	154	253	35	5	18	94	34	139	6	5	.239	.392	.277	3.64	5.0	58
1991	5	18.78	610	66	153	269	20	6	28	89	56	123	8	8	.251	.441	.314	4.71	8.4	54
1992	5	16.52	627	72	160	254	27	5	19	68	44	136	12	11	.255	.405	.304	4.22	6.6	51
1991	6	15.71	599	65	141	220	21	5	16	45	57	107	12	7	.235	.367	.302	3.70	8.7	42
1992	6	15.56	570	64	136	201	21	4	12	54	63	104	9	8	.239	.353	.314	3.71	10.0	37
1991	7	13.47	570	47	131	187	25	2	9	62	44	87	3	3	.230	.328	.285	3.10	7.2	36
1992	7	14.14	584	45	137	201	23	7	9	61	45	101	7	2	.235	.344	.289	3.32	7.2	39
1991	8	10.98	567	45	110	150	15	8	3	39	46	98	7	6	.194	.265	.254	2.13	7.5	26
1992	8	14.04	554	55	133	183	14	6	8	46	51	101	6	5	.240	.330	.304	3.37	8.4	28
1991	9	9.57	514	45	99	117	15	0	1	32	44	138	2	2	.193	.228	.256	1.84	7.9	16
1992	9	7.58	517	34	69	99	9	0	7	34	29	178	3	1	.133	.191	.179	1.01	5.3	16

		OINX	AB	R	H	TB	D	T	HR	RBI	BB	SO	SB	CS	BA	SA	OBP	RC27	BBP	XBH
DIFF	1	93	103	79	109	100	91	17	140	131	78	103	128	100	106	96	99	98	77	75
	2	87	100	85	95	90	92	60	70	67	89	95	82	117	94	90	94	82	90	85
	3	98	94	88	92	85	129	57	58	64	159	98	200	200	98	91	107	97	162	92
	4	71	105	67	97	84	152	167	47	90	52	130	86	100	92	80	84	65	52	91
	5	88	103	109	105	94	135	83	68	76	79	111	150	138	102	92	97	90	78	94
	6	99	95	98	96	91	100	80	75	120	111	97	75	114	101	96	104	100	115	88
	7	105	102	96	105	107	92	350	100	98	102	116	233	67	102	105	102	107	100	108
	8	128	98	122	121	122	93	75	267	118	111	103	86	83	124	125	120	158	112	108
	9	79	101	76	70	85	60	—	700	106	66	129	150	50	69	84	70	55	67	100
AVG		92.7		88	99	94	107	75	74	88	92	110	118	112				92.1	92.8	91.8

```
San Francisco Giants Home Park Performance Factors
                  Outs  Runs  Hits   2b    3b    HR     W     K    SH    SF   HBP   IBB    SB    CS   GDP
Home LH Batters  1.051  .932  .965 1.033  .907  .784 1.036 1.176 1.113 1.121 1.704 1.003 1.155  .888 1.058
Home RH Batters   .949  .929  .946  .830  .761  .894  .967 1.051  .962  .855 1.145  .915  .958  .840 1.169
All Home Batters  .983  .917  .950  .852  .830  .883  .991 1.079  .995  .941 1.219 1.004  .940  .868 1.093
Opp LH Batters    .968 1.199 1.026 1.097 1.866 1.186 1.224 1.028  .985 1.387 1.002 2.004 1.387 1.254 1.016
Opp RH Batters    .960 1.055 1.023 1.143  .882  .998 1.109  .956  .978 1.173 1.319 1.241 1.473  .878 1.150
All Opp Batters   .973 1.098 1.034 1.143 1.212 1.061 1.138  .995 1.009 1.183 1.054 1.350 1.359  .985 1.081
All LH Batters    .997 1.099 1.005 1.073 1.609 1.004 1.140 1.085 1.040 1.254 1.209 1.273 1.285 1.110 1.032
All RH Batters    .955  .997  .987  .994  .818  .953 1.045  .999  .972 1.011 1.232 1.127 1.123  .861 1.156
All Batters       .978 1.010  .994  .995 1.003  .978 1.068 1.037 1.004 1.059 1.131 1.177 1.087  .927 1.084
```

Conventional Batting Records for San Francisco Giants

	G	AB	Run	Hit	2B	3B	HR	TB	RBI	W	K	IW	HB	SB	CS	BRng Eff	GI DP	SH	SF	Avg	Slug	OBP	Runs Ctd
Manwaring	109	349	24	85	10	5	4	117	26	29	42	0	5	2	1	.268	12	6	0	.244	.335	.311	35
Clark W	144	513	69	154	40	1	16	244	73	73	82	23	4	12	7	.425	5	0	11	.300	.476	.384	101
Thompson Ro	128	443	54	115	25	1	14	184	49	43	75	1	8	5	9	.557	8	7	4	.260	.415	.333	61
Williams MD	146	529	58	120	13	5	20	203	66	39	109	11	6	7	7	.531	15	0	2	.227	.384	.286	54
Clayton	98	321	31	72	7	4	4	99	24	26	63	3	0	8	4	.429	11	3	2	.224	.308	.281	27
James C	111	248	25	60	10	4	5	93	32	14	45	2	2	2	3	.333	2	0	3	.242	.375	.285	27
Lewis D	100	320	38	74	8	1	1	87	18	29	46	0	1	28	4	.441	3	10	2	.231	.272	.295	30
McGee	138	474	56	141	20	2	1	168	36	29	88	3	1	13	4	.464	7	5	1	.297	.354	.339	58
Snyder C	124	390	48	105	22	2	14	173	57	23	96	2	2	4	4	.419	10	2	3	.269	.444	.311	51
Felder	145	322	44	92	13	3	4	123	23	21	29	1	2	14	4	.519	3	3	3	.286	.382	.330	43
Bass K	89	265	25	71	11	3	7	109	30	16	53	1	1	7	7	.280	6	1	2	.268	.411	.310	31
Uribe	66	162	24	39	9	1	2	56	13	14	25	3	0	2	2	.483	3	4	1	.241	.346	.299	17
Litton	68	140	9	32	5	0	4	49	15	11	33	0	0	1	1	.357	2	3	0	.229	.350	.285	14
Leonard M	55	128	13	30	7	0	4	49	16	16	31	0	3	0	1	.250	3	0	1	.234	.383	.331	17
Colbert	49	126	10	29	5	2	1	41	16	9	22	0	0	1	0	.227	8	2	2	.230	.325	.277	10
Patterson J	32	103	10	19	1	1	0	22	4	5	24	0	1	5	1	.538	2	0	0	.184	.214	.229	5
Benjamin	40	75	4	13	2	1	1	20	3	4	15	1	0	1	0	.200	1	3	0	.173	.267	.215	5
Mcnamara	30	74	6	16	1	0	1	20	9	6	25	2	0	0	0	.333	1	2	0	.216	.270	.275	6
Wood	24	58	5	12	2	0	1	17	3	6	15	0	1	0	0	.222	4	2	0	.207	.293	.292	4
Hosey	21	56	6	14	1	0	1	18	6	0	15	0	0	1	1	.200	1	0	2	.250	.321	.241	4
Burkett	32	55	2	1	1	0	0	2	2	4	24	0	0	0	0	.600	1	8	0	.018	.036	.085	0
Black	28	54	1	3	1	0	0	4	2	2	16	0	0	0	0	.500	0	10	0	.056	.074	.089	1
Swift	34	51	3	8	3	0	0	11	3	1	18	0	0	0	0	.286	0	5	0	.157	.216	.173	2
Decker S	15	43	3	7	1	0	0	8	1	6	7	0	1	0	0	.333	1	2	0	.163	.186	.283	3
Wilson Tr	27	39	3	3	1	0	0	4	3	3	21	0	0	2	7	.500	0	0	0	.077	.103	.143	1
Bailey	13	26	0	4	1	0	0	5	1	3	7	0	0	0	0	01.000	0	0	0	.154	.192	.241	1
Burba	23	15	0	1	0	0	0	1	1	1	8	0	0	0	0	.000	0	3	0	.067	.067	.125	0
Downs	19	14	0	0	0	0	0	0	0	0	5	0	0	0	0	.000	0	2	0	.000	.000	.000	0
Carter L	6	10	1	2	0	0	0	2	0	0	5	0	1	0	0	.000	0	1	0	.200	.200	.273	1
Brantley J	56	9	2	1	0	0	0	1	0	1	2	0	0	0	0	01.000	0	0	0	.111	.111	.200	0
Rogers K	6	9	0	2	0	0	0	2	0	0	6	0	0	0	0	.000	1	3	0	.222	.222	.222	0
Righetti	54	7	0	1	0	0	0	1	0	0	4	0	0	0	0	.000	0	4	0	.143	.143	.143	0
Oliveras	16	7	0	1	0	0	0	1	0	1	2	0	0	0	0	.000	0	0	0	.143	.143	.250	0
Heredia G	13	6	0	1	0	0	0	1	0	0	1	0	0	0	0	.000	0	1	0	.167	.167	.167	0
Pena J	25	5	0	1	0	0	0	1	0	0	2	0	0	0	0	.000	0	3	0	.200	.200	.200	0
Hickerson	61	4	0	0	0	0	0	0	0	0	3	0	0	0	0	.000	0	0	0	.000	.000	.000	0
Beck	65	2	0	1	0	0	0	1	0	0	1	0	0	0	0	.000	0	0	0	.500	.500	.500	1
Jackson M	67	2	0	0	0	0	0	0	0	0	0	0	0	0	0	.000	0	0	0	.000	.000	.000	0
Rapp	3	2	0	0	0	0	0	0	0	0	2	0	0	0	0	.000	0	1	0	.000	.000	.000	0
Reed S	18	0	0	0	0	0	0	0	0	0	0	0	0	0	0	.000	0	0	0	.000	.000	.000	0
TOTALS		2298	5456	574	1330	220	36	105	1937	532	435	1067	53	39	112	64	.426	111	101	39	.244	.355	.302	588

Sabermetric Batting Records for San Francisco Giants

	Ball Park Adjusted							Runs	Run/										
	AB	Run	Hit	2B	3B	HR	RBI	W	SO	Avg	Slug	OBP	Ctd	Outs	27o	OW%	OG	OWAR	DWAR	TWAR
Bailey	24	0	3	0	0	0	0	3	7	.125	.125	.222	1	21	1.29	.104	1	-0.19	0.06	-0.13
Bass K	259	25	70	10	3	6	29	17	54	.270	.402	.315	31	204	4.10	.542	8	1.45	0.33	1.78
Benjamin	71	3	12	1	0	0	2	4	15	.169	.183	.213	3	62	1.31	.107	2	-0.56	0.30	-0.25
Clark W	515	73	153	42	1	15	73	82	90	.297	.470	.390	104	387	7.26	.788	14	6.27	0.40	6.67
Clayton	307	30	70	6	3	3	22	26	63	.228	.296	.287	25	256	2.64	.329	9	-0.20	1.12	0.92
Colbert	120	9	28	4	1	0	15	9	22	.233	.283	.282	8	104	2.08	.233	4	-0.45	-0.04	-0.49
Decker S	40	2	6	0	0	0	0	6	7	.150	.150	.277	2	34	1.59	.151	1	-0.25	0.00	-0.25
Felder	315	44	91	12	3	3	22	22	30	.289	.375	.336	43	236	4.92	.630	9	2.45	0.36	2.81
Hosey	53	5	13	0	0	0	5	0	15	.245	.245	.200	3	43	1.88	.200	2	-0.24	-0.04	-0.28
James C	238	24	59	9	3	4	30	14	45	.248	.361	.292	26	186	3.77	.501	7	1.04	0.15	1.19
Leonard M	127	13	29	7	0	3	16	18	34	.228	.354	.340	16	103	4.19	.553	4	0.78	0.15	0.92
Lewis D	306	37	72	7	0	0	17	30	46	.235	.258	.304	30	254	3.19	.417	9	0.63	0.88	1.51
Litton	134	8	31	4	0	3	14	11	33	.231	.328	.290	13	107	3.28	.431	4	0.32	0.39	0.72
Manwaring	334	23	83	9	4	3	24	30	42	.249	.326	.322	34	269	3.41	.451	10	1.00	0.07	1.07
McGee	464	56	139	19	2	0	35	30	91	.300	.349	.343	58	341	4.59	.598	13	3.13	0.90	4.03
Mcnamara	73	6	15	1	0	0	9	6	27	.205	.219	.266	5	61	2.21	.256	2	-0.21	0.08	-0.14
Patterson J	100	10	18	0	1	0	3	5	24	.180	.200	.226	5	84	1.61	.154	3	-0.61	0.29	-0.32
Snyder C	374	47	103	21	2	13	54	23	96	.275	.441	.318	50	289	4.67	.606	11	2.74	0.70	3.44
Thompson Ro	425	53	113	24	0	13	46	44	75	.266	.414	.344	61	338	4.87	.626	13	3.45	2.15	5.60
Uribe	158	24	38	8	1	1	12	14	25	.241	.323	.301	16	129	3.35	.441	5	0.44	0.91	1.35
Williams MD	508	57	118	12	4	18	62	40	109	.232	.378	.296	53	415	3.45	.456	15	1.62	0.83	2.46
Wood	57	5	11	2	0	0	3	6	16	.193	.228	.281	3	52	1.56	.146	2	-0.39	0.06	-0.33
TOTALS	5354	578	1319	219	36	102	526	463	1106	.246	.358	.309	600	4356	3.72	.493	161	23.13	10.05	33.18

Pitching Records for San Francisco Giants

	ERA	W	L	Pct	G	GS	CG	ShO	GF	Sv	IP	R	ER	H	2B	3B	HR	BB	IW	SO	HB	WP	BK
Burkett	3.84	13	9	.591	32	32	3	1	0	0	189.2	96	81	194	34	7	13	45	6	107	4	0	0
Black	3.97	10	12	.455	28	28	2	1	0	0	177.0	88	78	178	27	6	23	59	11	82	1	3	7
Swift	2.08	10	4	.714	30	22	3	2	2	1	164.2	41	38	144	19	4	6	43	3	77	3	0	1
Wilson Tr	4.21	8	14	.364	26	26	1	1	0	0	154.0	82	72	152	25	4	18	64	5	88	6	2	7
Rogers K	4.24	0	2	.000	6	6	0	0	0	0	34.0	17	16	37	2	0	4	13	1	26	1	2	0
Carter L	4.64	1	5	.167	6	6	0	0	0	0	33.0	17	17	34	9	3	6	18	0	21	0	2	0
Rapp	7.20	0	2	.000	3	2	0	0	1	0	10.0	8	8	8	3	1	0	6	1	3	1	0	0
Beck	1.76	3	3	.500	65	0	0	0	42	17	92.0	20	18	62	8	1	4	15	2	87	2	5	2
Brantley J	2.95	7	7	.500	56	4	0	0	32	7	91.2	32	30	67	12	0	8	45	5	86	3	3	1
Hickerson	3.09	5	3	.625	61	1	0	0	8	0	87.1	31	30	74	19	1	7	21	2	68	1	4	1
Jackson M	3.73	6	6	.500	67	0	0	0	24	2	82.0	35	34	76	14	3	7	33	10	80	4	1	0
Righetti	5.06	2	7	.222	54	4	0	0	23	3	78.1	47	44	79	13	3	4	36	5	47	0	6	2
Burba	4.97	2	7	.222	23	11	0	0	4	0	70.2	43	39	80	15	2	4	31	2	47	2	1	1
Downs	3.47	1	2	.333	19	7	0	0	5	0	62.1	27	24	65	10	1	4	24	0	33	3	4	0
Oliveras	3.63	0	3	.000	16	7	0	0	4	0	44.2	19	18	41	10	0	11	10	2	17	1	0	0
Pena J	3.48	1	1	.500	25	2	0	0	4	0	44.0	19	17	49	13	1	4	20	5	32	1	0	0
Heredia G	5.40	2	3	.400	13	4	0	0	3	0	30.0	20	18	32	6	0	3	16	1	15	1	1	0
Reed S	2.30	1	0	1.000	18	0	0	0	2	0	15.2	5	4	13	4	0	2	3	0	11	1	0	0
TOTALS	3.61	72	90	.444	548	162	9	5	153	30	1461.0	647	586	1385	243	37	128	502	61	927	35	34	22

Sabermetric Pitching Records for San Francisco Giants

	Adj ERA	-Expected- W	L	Pct	BFP	Avg	Slg	OBA	RC/G	GDP	SB	CS	PK	PKE	SH	SF	RSup	Supported RSp/G	W	L	Pct
Beck	1.76	5	1	.798	352	.190	.257	.228	1.90	2	2	4	0	0	6	2	32	3.13	4	2	.721
Black	3.97	10	12	.438	749	.263	.422	.321	4.40	16	7	14	2	6	8	4	67	3.41	8	14	.376
Brantley J	2.95	8	6	.586	381	.207	.319	.307	3.42	6	4	1	0	0	7	3	29	2.85	6	8	.433
Burba	4.97	3	6	.332	318	.287	.398	.358	5.25	7	4	1	0	0	2	4	36	4.59	4	5	.410
Burkett	3.84	10	12	.454	799	.264	.382	.308	4.11	13	17	7	0	1	11	4	99	4.70	12	10	.549
Carter L	4.64	2	4	.363	147	.270	.532	.359	6.57	3	1	1	0	0	2	1	11	3.00	2	4	.255
Downs	3.47	2	1	.506	272	.275	.377	.347	4.66	3	5	4	0	0	7	2	13	1.88	1	2	.193
Heredia G	5.40	1	4	.296	132	.278	.409	.371	5.18	4	3	2	0	0	0	0	17	5.10	2	3	.421
Hickerson	3.09	4	4	.562	345	.236	.369	.282	3.11	8	1	6	0	2	4	5	37	3.81	4	4	.554
Jackson M	3.73	6	6	.469	346	.252	.387	.331	4.28	9	6	3	1	1	5	2	35	3.84	6	6	.464
Oliveras	3.63	1	2	.483	179	.250	.512	.294	4.31	6	0	3	0	0	2	2	11	2.22	1	2	.234
Pena J	3.48	1	1	.504	204	.282	.437	.357	5.91	2	1	0	1	0	8	1	19	3.89	1	1	.505
Rapp	7.20	0	2	.191	43	.235	.382	.366	4.90	1	4	1	0	0	2	0	1	0.90	0	2	.013
Reed S	2.30	1	0	.699	63	.220	.390	.270	3.37	2	1	0	0	0	0	0	5	2.87	1	0	.560
Righetti	5.06	3	6	.324	340	.269	.374	.344	4.51	7	7	4	0	1	6	4	28	3.22	2	7	.248
Rogers K	4.24	1	1	.406	148	.280	.386	.349	4.63	3	1	2	0	2	2	0	12	3.18	1	1	.315
Swift	2.08	10	4	.740	655	.239	.314	.292	2.77	26	5	4	0	1	5	2	74	4.04	11	3	.756
Wilson Tr	4.21	9	13	.409	661	.265	.416	.342	4.67	19	6	7	0	2	11	6	48	2.81	6	16	.266
TOTALS	3.65	78	84	.480	6134	.253	.382	.318	4.03	137	75	64	4	16	88	42	574	3.54	70	92	.434

Batting 'Splits' Records for San Francisco Giants

SPLITS for Lewis D

	G	AB	Run	Hit	2B	3B	HR	TB	RBI	W	K	IW	HB	SB	CS	DP	SH	SF	Avg	Slug	OBP	RC
vs LHP	55	125	17	27	3	0	1	33	5	12	16	0	0	11	5	1	3	0	.216	.264	.285	10
vs RHP	90	195	21	47	5	1	0	54	13	17	30	0	1	17	3	2	7	2	.241	.277	.302	20
Home	48	142	16	25	2	0	1	30	8	13	18	0	1	13	4	0	5	1	.176	.211	.248	9
Away	52	178	22	49	6	1	0	57	10	16	28	0	0	15	4	3	5	1	.275	.320	.333	21
Grass	71	214	27	44	5	0	1	52	11	22	27	0	1	17	8	2	8	1	.206	.243	.282	17
Turf	29	106	11	30	3	1	0	35	7	7	19	0	0	11	0	1	2	1	.283	.330	.325	14
April/June	68	229	28	53	4	1	1	62	14	23	36	0	1	20	6	2	6	2	.231	.271	.302	22
July/October	32	91	10	21	4	0	0	25	4	6	10	0	0	8	2	1	4	0	.231	.275	.278	8

SPLITS for San Francisco Giants (all batters except pitchers)

	G	AB	Run	Hit	2B	3B	HR	TB	RBI	W	K	IW	HB	SB	CS	DP	SH	SF	Avg	Slug	OBP	RC
vs LHP	934	1919	199	493	85	14	35	711	184	129	340	15	5	44	26	37	34	15	.257	.371	.303	213
vs RHP	1776	3537	375	837	135	22	70	1226	348	306	727	38	34	68	38	74	67	24	.237	.347	.302	375
Home	1124	2687	307	677	130	21	57	1020	285	209	467	24	15	60	36	49	49	20	.252	.380	.307	314
Away	1174	2769	267	653	90	15	48	917	247	226	600	29	24	52	28	62	52	19	.236	.331	.297	275
Grass	1678	3982	420	974	163	25	76	1415	391	322	734	39	21	86	52	74	68	29	.245	.355	.302	431
Turf	620	1474	154	356	57	11	29	522	141	113	333	14	18	26	12	37	33	10	.242	.354	.302	157
April/June	1047	2485	280	605	101	21	47	889	260	226	498	29	15	67	29	37	51	29	.243	.358	.308	285
July/October	1251	2971	294	725	119	15	58	1048	272	209	569	24	24	45	35	74	50	17	.244	.353	.297	303

Los Angeles Dodgers

Don Malcolm

LOS ANGELES										
YEAR	1983	1984	1985	1986	1987	1988	1989	1990	1991	1992
W	91	79	95	73	73	94	77	86	93	63
L	71	83	67	89	89	67	83	76	69	99
WPCT	0.562	0.488	0.586	0.451	0.451	0.584	0.481	0.531	0.574	0.389
R	654	580	682	638	635	628	554	728	665	548
RA	609	600	579	679	675	544	536	685	565	636
PWPT	0.536	0.483	0.581	0.469	0.469	0.571	0.517	0.53	0.581	0.426
PythW	87	78	94	76	76	93	84	86	94	69
PythL	75	84	68	86	86	69	78	76	68	93
LUCK	4	1	1	-3	-3	1	-7	0	-1	-6

Defensive Efficiency Record: .6830

THE FIFTEEN YEAR BLIP

The Dodgers want their fans to believe that 1992 was one of those once-in-a-century nightmares that happen to otherwise strong franchises. They are attempting to convince their supporters (and, no doubt, themselves) that once they reassemble the broken pieces of the 1992 season, once they repair their damaged merchandise, once they add some selected spare parts from Wile E. Coyote's favorite mail-order house, they will be operating at Roadrunner-like speed.

The newspaper ads have been carefully designed to radiate a sun-bleached optimism, but underneath a heart of darkness is skipping several beats. Fred Claire, the foursquare general manager, continues to earn high marks for public relations, but most of the moves he's made this winter look like someone building a sandcastle in the shadow of a tsunami.

What is ironic about the situation that Claire finds himself in is that he is doing exactly what the Dodgers would have done prior to free agency or the draft. The problem is that such a methodology is at odds with the realities of nineties baseball. The Dodgers have squandered their farm system over the past fifteen years, and what they wish to represent as a single-year aberration is really a fifteen-year blip. Teams cannot win without playing both the player development and player acquisition games: the Dodgers have not really done either one well since the late seventies. In order to better understand what has happened, it's necessary to take a longer look at the Dodgers from the player development perspective.

What saved the Dodgers from a disastrous decade after the retirement of Koufax and the banishment of Wills was the miracle of the 1968 draft. The Dodgers stocked several championship teams out of this draft (Steve Garvey, Ron Cey, Bill Buckner, Dave Lopes, Bobby Valentine, Geoff Zahn, Joe Ferguson, Doyle Alexander). It was the perfect draft at the most opportune time. Even those who didn't make significant contributions to the Dodgers in the seventies helped bring in players who did: Frank Robinson, Andy Messersmith, Reggie Smith, and Burt Hooton.

The Dodgers' subsequent drafts haven't netted them a number of quality players equal to those acquired through or because of the 1968 draft. The drafts since 1969 have netted them Rick Sutcliffe, Dave Stewart, Bob Welch, Mike Scioscia, Steve Sax, Steve Howe, and Orel Hershiser. Only Welch, Scioscia, Sax, and Hershiser made significant contributions to winning Dodger teams. Due to free agency, the "parlay value" for the

Position	92 Starter	TWAR	93 Starter	TWAR
Catcher	Scioscia	0.56	Piazza	0.09
			Hernandez. Ca.	0.26
First base	Karros	4.52	Karros	4.52
Second base	Sharperson	3.55	Reed, Jo.	2.49
Third base	Hansen	0.95	Wallach	1.85
Shortstop	Offerman	2.37	Offerman	2.37
Left field	Webster	2.64	Davis, E.	1.44
	Davis, E.	1.44		
Center field	Butler	7.58	Butler	7.58
Right field	Strawberry	1.24	Strawberry	1.24

players offered in trade has dropped like a stone.

But even when we factor in free agency, we see that the Dodger organization no longer commands the instantaneous respect of the rest of baseball. There are no more Geoff Zahn and Eddie Solomon for Burt Hooton trades happening for the Fred Claire Dodgers. No more Bruce Ellingsen for Pedro Guerrero deals, either. The high expectations and disappointing careers of highly hyped prospects such as Mike Marshall, Greg Brock, Sid Bream, Franklin Stubbs, Dave Anderson, and Candy Maldonado began the Dodgers' slide even before they knew they were in it. (And there is good reason to believe that the Dodgers still don't know they're in a slide: their capacity for denial ranks first among the now 28 major league franchises.)

As the eighties wore on, the Dodgers slid into a morass of bad fundamental baseball; the two 73-89 teams in 1986 and 1987 were propped up by a killing toll on the top starting pitchers' arms, specifically Fernando Valenzuela and Orel Hershiser. The team had to sign Kirk Gibson and trade for additional pitching in 1988 in order to pull off its Mets-like "miracle" against the A's. That team promptly backslid in 1989, a phenomenon originally blamed on the departure of Steve Sax, but more accurately traced to the loss of Pedro Guerrero and the collapse of the entire outfield.

In 1990, the Dodgers surfaced young (22) Ramon Martinez, whose hard-throwing style was packaged in a fragile physique. He won 20, but the rest of the staff was weak, primarily because Orel Hershiser's overworked arm had finally given way: it cost the Dodgers a chance at a pennant, for they had their best offensive team in 20 years, led by Eddie Murray, Kal Daniels, and marvelous part-time work by Stan Javier. Darryl Strawberry and Brett Butler were signed in 1991, but the offense declined, scoring sixty fewer runs despite the high-priced free agents. The toll on Martinez' arm became clear in the second half of '91, when he lost most of his stuff and has never really regained it.

The Dodgers entered 1992 with a newly acquired slugger (Eric Davis). They tried to shift Kal Daniels to first base in order to keep all three of their big hitters (Strawberry, Davis, and Daniels) in the same lineup. But, as noted last season, there was a division amongst the players. Darryl Strawberry, the titular leader of the Dodgers, sounded off about Daniels and suggested that he should be sent packing. Both Claire and Dodger manager Tom Lasorda found themselves with a internicine struggle that suddenly threatened to dwarf their own incompatibilities.

As it turned out, the Dodgers made a half-hearted attempt to keep the lid on their simmering situation. But friction between Daniels and Strawberry was never resolved: it was exacerbated by the arrival of Davis, who had not exactly been bosom buddies with Daniels during their years together in Cincinnati. Rumors of an altercation during spring training surfaced, but were never confirmed: the entire matter was handled with extreme kid gloves, which makes one figure that such an altercation did occur, and that it led to Daniels' release and Strawberry's injury.

With Daniels' unceremonious departure, the Dodgers turned to their farm system for a hitter. (They had not installed a home-grown player as a starter since third baseman Jeff Hamilton in 1989: like most every Dodger hitter hyped due to the offensive distortions caused by the high altitude at Albuquerque, LA's AAA farm team, he had proven to be a major disappointment.) That hitter was first basemen Eric Karros, who became the second farmhand to start in 1992: the other was shortstop Jose Offerman, who managed to endure a fiery and error-filled baptism. Karros is an ugly-looking player, but he has legitimate extra-base power, and must be judged as the first success the Dodgers have had from the farm system in a long time. That this success must still be viewed as a qualified one is not as important as noting that it came only because the Dodgers had no other choice but to play Karros once the Daniels affair reached its ugly and mysterious denouement.

The Dodgers crashed and burned startlingly from June 1st on, compiling a 41-76 mark. The Dodgers' line on the 1992 season is that the injuries ravaged the Dodger attack, but remarkably, the LA attack was just slightly less efficient without the so-called Big Three as it had been prior to their individual and collective demise. Measuring scoring effectivenss by dividing runs scored by "bases created" (total bases plus bases on balls), the Dodgers scored 23.9 runs for every 100 bases created in April and May, and 23.6 for every 100 created from June to the end of the season.

There is also the disturbing fact that the Dodger pitchers were dramatically less effective in the second half of the season (3.69 ERA vs. 3.18 in the first half). Using the runs per bases created ratio, we see a big decline in effectiveness in the second half (27.5 runs per 100 bases created vs. 23.8 in the first: the NL average was, as you might have suspected, 25 runs for every 100 bases, or one run for every four bases—amazing how it works out like that, ain't it??).

The runs per bases created ratio also tells us about the defensive health of a team. Teams with higher aggregate ERAs than the Dodgers have lower runs per bases created ratios—for example the Astros (3.85 ERA, 26.2 runs per 100 bases in the second half of 1992). The higher ratio reflects the number of unearned runs the team is allowing. The Dodgers' total of 91 unearned runs was the worst in the league, and stemmed directly from their league-leading total of 174 errors. The Dodgers lapped the field in errors: their infield error total alone (118) was more than ten other team's total miscues.

And this lack of Dodger fundamentals, the cruelly concrete contradiction of the once-proud credo called the "Dodger way to play baseball", has been in existence ever since the breakup of the Garvey-Lopes-Russell-Cey infield in 1982. For the Dodgers to claim that the team was

bad last year simply due to the catastrophic loss of their two biggest hitters is to defiantly ignore the implacable tendencies and characteristics of the Dodgers for the past fifteen years. The Dodgers have been on a slowly increasing downward slope in terms of real productivity ever since Tom Lasorda's takeover as manager, and they will not come out of it until he steps down or is replaced.

The key area where productivity is declining is in pitching. The Dodgers have lived off their pitching since their move into Dodger Stadium (Chavez Ravine) in 1962. The extreme pitcher's park tendency has held up, and the Dodgers have taken that to the bank as often as humanly possible. But since Lasorda has been manager, there have been lapses in the Dodger pitching dominance which have cropped up from time to time and are now escalating.

The first lapse occurred in 1979, when Tommy John split for New York and Andy Messersmith washed up on the shores of Palos Verdes with a seagull wing instead of a pitching arm. The Dodgers' bullpen also began its long-term pattern of instability.

The next lapse occurred in 1986, when Fernando was overworked, Hershiser slumped, and the bullpen disintegrated. The beginnings of chronic #1 starter abuse had surfaced in 1982-83, and had been cemented in 1984, when Fernando led the league in innings and had his third straight season over 250 IP. Lasorda was, somewhat uncharacteristically, indecisive in pitcher role definition in 1984, splitting Hershiser and Reuss between the bullpen and the starting rotation ("slapdashing": see the Giants article for a definition). The long term effects of "slapdashing" have yet to be quantified, but the effect of overwork on Valenzuela's arm became evident in 1988, and the Dodgers had to scramble for more pitching (trading Guerrero for John Tudor) in order to bring off their "miracle" pennant and Series victory.

The next lapse occurred in 1990, when Hershiser, seriously overworked in 1987-89, missed the entire season, and only Ramon Martinez was an effective starter. (Jim Neidlinger, given 12 starts down the stretch of a season in which the Dodgers blew many chances to get back into the pennant race, compiled a creditable 3.28 ERA and was rewarded by being sent back to Albuquerque the next season, never to return again.) Lasorda let Martinez complete 12 games, which had a catastrophic effect on Ramon's subsequent career.

The latest lapse came last year, as the patchwork staff of Candiotti, Ojeda, Gross, Hershiser, Martinez, and Astacio went up and down—mostly down after the All-Star Break. The bullpen was an even bigger mess than usual: even the casual fan and the Dodger organization could see how ineffective it was (.274 opponent's BA). Martinez' career is still seriously in doubt, and Hershiser is still not close to being the kind of pitcher he was in 1985-88.

Perhaps the trend is becoming clear to you. The lapses are cycling in with greater frequency. Instead of a six-year plague, the periodicity has dropped to four, and now two. It seems extremely unlikely that the 1993 Dodger pitching staff can rebound to the top of the league ERA. The key pitchers—Gross and Hershiser—are 32 and 34 respectively. Ramon Martinez is a huge question mark: to assume that he can return to his 1990 form is serious wishful thinking. Candiotti is in his second season in the NL, and while he has been a reliable pitcher for the past three seasons, one hesitates to bank on a knuckleball pitcher as the staff ace. Teams that have done that have usually been second division clubs: Candiotti was certainly the Dodgers' ace in 1992, and we remember where they finished.

The only move the Dodgers made over the off-season that related to pitching centered around their bedraggled bullpen. They signed Todd Worrell, the hard-throwing Bible thumper whose arm is still considered a risk, to be their closer. But Worrell has already been diagnosed this winter with tendinitis, and the prognosis for his future pitching health is guarded at present. If Worrell can pitch the way he did last year for St. Louis, the Dodgers would have a bonafide closer, but at this point their bullpen situation is as unsettled as ever.

Significantly, the Dodgers did not consider any serious attempts to add to their starting staff, despite the presence of some extremely valuable free agents, four of whom—Greg Maddux, Doug Drabek, Greg Swindell, and John Smiley—were signed by the Dodgers' NL West rivals. The Dodgers are clearly relying on the aging Hershiser, the mercurial Gross, and the fragile Ramon Martinez, plus rookies Pedro Astacio and Pedro Martinez, to form the traditional Dodger staff behind unorthodox staff ace Candiotti. The signing of a Maddux or a Smiley would have given the Dodgers a real chance to rebound, as these two are proven aces who would thrive in Dodger Stadium. The loss of Mike Scioscia, whose catcher ERA was 3.14 (compared to the other catchers' 3.81) is going to cripple the Dodgers' chances for turning around their latest pitching lapse.

The offensive moves might best be deemed a contradiction in terms. I wonder if the Dodgers took a look at what Jody Reed hit away from Fenway Park last season (answer: .218). I wonder if they noticed how much of his doubles power was lost last season (down 36%), and how much more of that he's likely to lose coming from a park that increases doubles by 23% to one that suppresses them 20%. The Dodgers gave up on Eric Young in just 140 plate appearances: I predict that this will come back to haunt them. Young has great speed and has shown a reasonable amount of strike-zone judgment in the minors, and the Colorado Rockies are going to be something like playing in Albuqerque, where Young hit .337 last season. Reed is 30, has no speed, will hit no better than .260 with maybe 25 doubles, and will be an engine for the Dodgers' continuing mediocrity.

Signing Cory Snyder will do the Dodgers very little good, except that they've gotten smart enough to realize that either Davis or Strawberry is going to be out for some extended period and it's best to have a backup who can at least swing for the fences, even if he doesn't reach them (or connect with the ball very often). The STATS folks project Snyder to hit .235 this year and slug .404, with 14 HR and 49 RBI, with an OBP of .274. The Dodgers may well be forced to play Snyder this much because of their "In Yo' Whirpool" duo (Davis and Strawberry), plus the fact that they've acquired the clearly faltering Tim Wallach (.225 and .223 the past two years).

This acquisition clearly demonstrates that Fred Claire and his staff are reading four-year old copies of the Baseball Sabermetric when they go out and make deals. Wallach was a fine player four years ago, but he has lost almost everything that he once had offensively and doesn't figure to get anything back playing in Dodger Stadium. Rather than give Dave Hansen one more chance after a year of disaster, Fred has acquiesced to Lasorda and brought in another burnt-out veteran who will ensure that whatever chance Hansen has to develop will be squandered. The STATS projections predict a .247 average for Hansen, .244 for Wallach. Hansen will have less power, but more on-base, so the change looks like a complete wash—in short, a worthless, needless move except for the purposes of creating better working relations between manager and general manager as they both go numbly into that good night.

Foursquare Fred has done the only thing that an American executive is trained to do: deny the problem until it is time to abandon ship. The Dodgers will tell you that last year was just an aberration, a blip on the screen, an annoying and terribly embarrassing stain on Dodger blue. They will tell you that they've surrounded their erratic young shortstop with soothing veterans who will help him relax. (Perhaps they'll be fielding ground balls for him as well.) They will spin sirens' tales of Davis and Strawberry, and what a murderer's row they'll have with these two and Karros and Wallach and young catcher Mike Piazza. And a lot of people are going to swallow this fishy story tail first.

But don't be fooled. This is the seventeenth year of an ongoing blip that is embodied in the O'Malley prescription for the Dodgers: pretend that you're still the team than dominated the fifties. Deny that anything has really changed. Deny to yourselves that the changes in your behavior, in

your marketing strategies, in your player acquisition methods are real: convince yourself that the Dodger way is still unsullied, unspoiled, and unrivalled. And don't forget to forcefully assert, along with the aforementioned, that the world is flat.

SOME BATTING ORDER, EH?

Perhaps the only interesting thing the Dodgers managed to do last season was switch the top of their batting order around. Right after the All-Star Break, as the Boys in Blue began to demonstrate unmistakable signs of aspyhixiation in the smog-laced LA moonscape, Tom Lasorda moved Jose Offerman into the leadoff slot, and dropped Brett Butler to #2.

The effect on the team was minimal: it kept right on coasting toward its inevitable crash-and-burn in the low foothills. The effect on Offerman was also minimal: he hit about the same, fielded about the same batting #1 as he did #8. Butler, however, went bananas: Brett hit .362 batting #2, which led the way for the Dodgers to have the unlikely honor of the highest BA in any batting order position (BOP) for the NL in '92.

It was a curious move on the Dodgers' part, and uncharacteristically gutsy. I remember having a discussion with Brock Hanke about the move at Dodger Stadium in September, where I started to articulate the reasoning behind the move. Brock tends toward more classical lineup functions than I do, and so he was initially quite skeptical of what I was saying, but as I've refined the argument somewhat and developed both present-day and historical parallels, he's come around somewhat to the ideas expressed, even if he would not see fit to operate his lineup that way.

The original idea was: since the Dodgers know they're going nowhere (in '92), why not give Offerman a chance to bat leadoff in a year where it doesn't matter much? If you want him to eventually learn how to be an acceptable leadoff man, then give him some time there and bat Butler #2, where he can function as a leadoff man if Offerman goes out. While Offerman is no Butler, the fact is that he's 24 and Butler is 35: he's got a lot more career left and the sooner he gets experience as the #1 hitter, the better.

As I recall, the original difference of opinion hinged around the disparities of ability. Brock initially had difficulty accepting the reasoning that you'd sacrifice your leadoff spot in any case, even if you knew the season was down the tubes, which to my mind was the cornerstone of my argument. The idea of evolving Offerman into a good leadoff man seemed alien to Brock, who thought that the MLE data for Jose pretty much ruled that out.

Make no mistake: Jose Offerman will never be a Brett Butler. But the fact is that Butler will be 36 this year, and is a free agent after the 1994 season. The maximum benefit that the Dodgers can get out of Butler is what he can produce and what he can impart to younger players. Unless the Dodgers want to go out and buy another great leadoff man, they have to develop one. There are two ways to develop a great leadoff man: draft Rickey Henderson or Tim Raines, or attempt to evolve a player like Jose Offerman into an acceptable surrogate.

The Dodgers are clearly going to make this attempt. And there are, as I alluded to above, several parallels. A present-day parallel is the Devon White-Roberto Alomar tandem at Toronto. That dynamic is not an exact match for what the Dodgers are up to, but it has several points of overlap. White has more power but less on-base than Alomar and is about as good of a base stealer. But the same principle is in effect for the Blue Jays: if White makes out to start the first, Toronto then puts up an even better leadoff man with one out.

A parallel from the past comes from the sixties Dodgers. Maury Wills was a .280 hitter who didn't walk much (7%), but who was effective as a leadoff hitter due to his prolific and high percentage base stealing. The classic leadoff hitter on the Dodgers, Jim Gilliam (12.7% BBP), batted

#2 from 1960-65. If Wills went out, then Gilliam, with his 86 walks per 162 games, would have an even better chance of getting on base. That's one reason why the Dodgers were able to bunch runs better than their raw statistics seemed to indicate during the early sixties. It also was a perfect first-inning strategy for a team built around dominant starting pitching.

So perhaps the Dodgers, remembering this approach, felt that Offerman could be the next Maury Wills. As far as fielding goes, they may be a good match: Wills made 40 errors in 1960, his first full year as the Dodger shortstop. His subsequent totals were 29, 36, 21, 27, 25, and 23 before he was packed off to Pittsburgh with his guitar. The Dodgers managed to more or less thrive with Wills' higher-than-average error totals.

What is much more problematic is whether Offerman can become a .280-.290 hitter and a high percentage base stealer. The Dodgers would be much happier if these two things happened than if he remained a .260 hitter but cut his errors in half. Or at least they should be. If Offerman can steal 50 bases at a 75% success rate, get on base .350, and hit .285, the gamble would be well worth it, even if he made the same number of errors.

The other question about the switch revolves around Butler. How permanent will the boost to his offensive totals that evidenced itself last season really be? Does hitting with a man on first add a new wrinkle to Butler's slap and bunt tactics that translates into a twenty to thirty point jump in his batting average? Butler hit .394 last season with runners on first: does the infield have to defense him differently when he's up in these situations? He hit .313 with runners on first in 1991, when most of the runners were #8 or #9 hitters. How significant is the offensive context? What was the difference in the distribution of plate appearances with runners on first between 1991 and 1992? How many occurred early in the game (innings 1-3) vs. later? How much of a gain in first inning scoring is possible from a switch like the one described?

The answer is that we don't really know, but we can try to gather the data and study it more closely, especially if the Dodgers decide to continue this lineup arrangement in 1993. The top two slots in the Dodger batting order scored 13% less runs in 1992 than in 1991, but this decline was less than the overall team decline, so you could say that in the context of the team the experiment was successful. But I agree with Brock's cautionary rebuttal: if Offerman cannot evolve to better totals than what he showed during the second half of '92, the approach is not viable for a team expecting to contend.

But I don't expect the Dodgers to contend, and I think the Dodgers would do a lot better this season if they didn't expect to contend and let a lot of things just happen. Lead Offerman off. At least platoon Hansen with Wallach. Don't make an iron man out of Jody Reed, and don't bat him #2 behind Butler—bat him seventh, where his .260 average and 25 doubles might be reasonably useful. Develop a complex platoon which gets two days of rest a week for Davis and Strawberry while finding some structured playing time for Tom Goodwin amidst the Websters and Snyders. Make Piazza and Hernandez compete for the #1 catching job right into the season, and see who rises to the occasion, both offensively and defensively.

As for the pitching, make Astacio into the closer if Worrell can't go, with Gott, Wilson, McDowell and Wally Ritchie as the set up men. Skip Kip Gross as the long man and give the job to the journeyman Neidlinger, who at least has some control. Start Candiotti, the two Martinezes, Gross, and Hershiser. If Worrell can go, keep Astacio in the rotation and make Pedro Martinez into a sixth swing starter in a complex rotation that gives his brother Ramon the extra rest. (Ramon has pitched significantly better with five or more days of rest.) If the staff is nurtured properly, and the big hitters are taken care of, the Dodgers can get back over .500—but not much else. If they go for a pennant, they can wind up in the 90s—90 or more losses.

THE RATING SYSTEM DOESN'T LIE

Brock Hanke devised a team profile rating system that provides a very accurate snapshot of a team's strengths and weaknesses (see his Cleveland and Montreal essays for a more detailed explanation of it). By breaking a team down into five categories of player (superstar, star, championship level player, bulk player, and hole), Brock has provided us a glimpse as to how teams build around their strengths and try to minimize their weaknesses. A more thorough application of the system will probably reveal how fitfully successful teams tend to be.

The distribution of player talent (we're looking at the eight position players, plus the first four starters and the closer) varies, of course, but Brock found that the division champs all tended to cluster around a pattern of 2-5-4-1-1. Meaning two superstars, five stars, four championship level players, one bulk player, and one hole.

I applied the system to the Dodgers, then added one little twist. I added rough point values for each category: 10 for a superstar, 7 for a star, five for a championship level player, four for bulk, and two for a hole. The average division champ, with the 2-5-4-1-1 distribution, comes out with 81 points. The Dodger profile: 1 superstar (Strawberry, by reputation); 2 stars (Butler and Candiotti); 8 championship players (Davis, Reed, Karros, Offerman, Worrell, Hershiser, Gross, and Martinez), 1 bulk player (Wallach) and 1 hole (Piazza and Hernandez as the catching tandem).

You might quibble with a couple of placements; it really doesn't matter much, as you'll see. When we assign the point values, the Dodgers wind up with 62 points, well below the division champ level. Even if you bumped two players up into the "star" category, the total only goes up to 68, still way too low to consider the team a viable contender. Hanke's rating system confirms that the Dodgers would be better off forgetting about first place.

Los Angeles Dodgers Home Park Performance Factors															
	Outs	Runs	Hits	2b	3b	HR	W	K	SH	SF	HBP	IBB	SB	CS	GDP
Home LH Batters	1.002	1.008	.966	1.146	.810	1.180	1.041	1.075	1.060	.888	.934	1.505	.864	.922	.968
Home RH Batters	.971	.872	.951	.952	.726	1.365	.888	.989	.907	.776	.928	.806	.852	1.083	.993
All Home Batters	.986	.947	.963	1.012	.838	1.278	.964	1.042	.980	.861	.952	1.040	.840	.933	.992
Opp LH Batters	1.035	1.171	1.085	1.100	1.550	1.163	1.261	.965	1.211	1.155	.959	1.279	1.008	1.052	1.182
Opp RH Batters	.995	1.072	.987	1.033	1.090	1.446	1.097	.984	1.015	.903	1.094	1.384	.982	1.064	.885
All Opp Batters	.995	1.111	1.010	1.064	1.148	1.230	1.150	.977	1.067	.977	1.066	1.229	.985	1.006	.979
All LH Batters	1.015	1.072	1.013	1.111	.995	1.150	1.129	1.011	1.119	1.008	.941	1.271	.920	.972	1.052
All RH Batters	.983	.976	.969	.994	.965	1.410	.990	.986	.965	.840	1.013	1.110	.924	1.067	.938
All Batters	.990	1.027	.986	1.037	.970	1.252	1.052	1.005	1.022	.918	1.008	1.157	.908	.968	.985

Year	BOP	OINX	AB	R	H	TB	D	T	HR	RBI	BB	SO	SB	CS	BA	SA	OBP	RC27	BBP	XBH
1991	1	16.80	640	114	190	220	14	5	2	39	110	83	39	28	.297	.344	.400	4.99	14.7	21
1992	1	15.12	642	90	169	213	18	10	2	39	82	102	33	25	.263	.332	.347	3.98	11.3	30
1991	2	17.36	655	93	191	263	30	6	10	68	59	113	21	9	.292	.402	.350	5.06	8.3	46
1992	2	20.03	616	89	208	260	28	6	4	60	83	56	32	20	.338	.422	.416	6.77	11.9	38
1991	3	17.96	634	94	156	255	22	4	23	97	74	138	17	6	.246	.402	.325	4.42	10.5	49
1992	3	12.96	640	52	150	200	27	1	7	66	52	99	23	4	.234	.313	.292	3.04	7.5	35
1991	4	18.67	622	76	156	262	29	1	25	110	70	110	12	5	.251	.421	.327	4.68	10.1	55
1992	4	16.47	623	70	147	237	35	2	17	98	63	132	18	6	.236	.380	.306	3.89	9.2	54
1991	5	19.38	599	84	162	254	17	3	23	86	77	115	4	3	.270	.424	.354	5.24	11.4	43
1992	5	14.31	618	59	139	217	25	4	15	71	46	124	8	7	.225	.351	.279	3.22	6.9	44
1991	6	14.97	599	61	159	215	27	4	7	59	47	67	13	6	.265	.359	.319	3.97	7.3	38
1992	6	12.12	593	46	133	175	17	2	7	44	46	96	4	8	.224	.295	.280	2.72	7.2	26
1991	7	15.29	561	60	136	195	24	1	11	54	61	90	7	4	.242	.348	.317	3.71	9.8	36
1992	7	15.24	557	49	143	197	18	3	10	48	54	74	4	3	.257	.354	.322	3.91	8.8	31
1991	8	12.06	554	40	129	152	16	2	1	47	60	92	8	6	.233	.274	.308	2.81	9.8	19
1992	8	13.17	556	46	138	176	13	5	5	38	45	83	13	4	.248	.317	.304	3.27	7.5	23
1991	9	8.45	544	43	87	123	12	3	6	54	25	149	5	1	.160	.226	.197	1.35	4.4	21
1992	9	10.73	523	47	106	143	20	1	5	35	32	133	7	1	.203	.273	.249	2.17	5.8	26

		OINX	AB	R	H	TB	D	T	HR	RBI	BB	SO	SB	CS	BA	SA	OBP	RC27	BBP	XBH
DIFF	1	90	100	79	89	97	129	200	100	100	75	123	85	89	89	97	87	80	77	143
	2	115	94	96	109	99	93	100	40	88	141	50	152	222	116	105	119	134	144	83
	3	72	101	55	96	78	123	25	30	68	70	72	135	67	95	78	90	69	72	71
	4	88	100	92	94	90	121	200	68	89	90	120	150	120	94	90	94	83	91	98
	5	74	103	70	86	85	147	133	65	83	60	108	200	233	83	83	79	61	61	102
	6	81	99	75	84	81	63	50	100	75	98	143	31	133	84	82	88	68	99	68
	7	100	99	82	105	101	75	300	91	89	89	82	57	75	106	102	102	106	90	86
	8	109	100	115	107	116	81	250	500	81	75	90	163	67	107	115	99	116	77	121
	9	127	96	109	122	116	167	33	83	65	128	89	140	100	127	121	126	161	131	124
AVG		92.4		82	98	94	105	117	67	82	87	94	113	115				91.0	88.4	93.6

Sabermetric Batting Records for Los Angeles Dodgers

			Ball Park Adjusted					Runs		Run/									
	AB	Run	Hit	2B	3B	HR	RBI	W	SO	Avg	Slug	OBP	Ctd	Outs	27o	OW%	OG	OWAR	DWAR	TWAR
Anderson D	81	9	23	3	0	4	8	3	10	.284	.469	.306	9	65	3.74	.511	2	0.39	0.08	0.47
Ashley	92	5	20	4	0	2	6	4	33	.217	.326	.250	7	73	2.59	.334	3	-0.04	-0.16	-0.20
Benzinger	289	24	69	16	1	5	32	15	54	.239	.353	.273	27	232	3.14	.425	9	0.65	0.26	0.91
Bournigal	18	0	2	0	0	0	0	0	1	.111	.111	.158	0	16	0.00	.000	1	-0.21	0.07	-0.13
Butler	564	93	175	15	12	3	41	109	68	.310	.395	.423	107	441	6.55	.763	16	6.74	0.84	7.58
Daniels	105	9	24	5	0	2	8	11	30	.229	.333	.299	9	89	2.73	.358	3	0.03	0.15	0.18
Davis E	261	20	59	7	0	7	33	35	70	.226	.333	.323	32	211	4.09	.557	8	1.61	-0.18	1.44
Goodwin	74	16	17	1	1	0	3	6	10	.230	.270	.287	6	59	2.75	.361	2	0.02	0.09	0.11
Hansen	346	32	74	12	0	7	23	39	49	.214	.309	.292	32	282	3.06	.413	10	0.66	0.30	0.95
Harris L	353	30	96	12	0	0	32	27	24	.272	.306	.322	35	281	3.36	.459	10	1.13	0.65	1.78
Hernandez C	168	10	43	3	0	4	18	10	20	.256	.345	.311	17	134	3.43	.468	5	0.58	-0.33	0.26
Javier	56	6	10	3	0	1	5	6	11	.179	.286	.270	5	48	2.81	.372	2	0.04	0.03	0.07
Karros	533	61	135	29	0	28	93	36	101	.253	.465	.301	70	420	4.50	.603	16	3.93	0.59	4.52
Offerman	528	68	137	20	7	1	31	60	98	.259	.330	.334	61	417	3.95	.539	15	2.92	-0.55	2.37
Piazza	67	4	15	2	0	1	7	3	11	.224	.299	.268	6	52	3.12	.421	2	0.14	-0.05	0.09
Rodriguez H	148	11	32	7	0	3	14	9	30	.216	.324	.259	13	120	2.92	.390	4	0.18	-0.01	0.17
Samuel	119	6	31	2	0	0	15	6	21	.261	.277	.299	10	94	2.87	.382	3	0.11	0.05	0.16
Scioscia	353	20	78	6	3	3	25	36	31	.221	.280	.291	30	292	2.77	.366	11	0.17	0.39	0.56
Sharperson	310	46	92	20	0	4	38	46	32	.297	.400	.385	49	234	5.65	.705	9	3.08	0.47	3.55
Strawberry	158	21	37	8	0	5	26	21	34	.234	.380	.322	21	124	4.57	.610	5	1.20	0.04	1.24
Webster M	259	33	69	12	4	7	36	28	49	.266	.425	.338	41	206	5.37	.684	8	2.55	0.10	2.64
Young E	128	8	32	0	0	1	11	7	8	.250	.273	.289	11	102	2.91	.388	4	0.14	0.14	0.28
TOTALS	5311	563	1315	208	33	90	525	531	907	.248	.350	.317	603	4317	3.77	.516	160	26.50	2.98	29.49

Conventional Batting Records for Los Angeles Dodgers

	G	AB	Run	Hit	2B	3B	HR	TB	RBI	W	K	IW	HB	SB	CS	BRng Eff	GI DP	SH	SF	Avg	Slug	OBP	Runs Ctd
Scioscia	117	348	19	77	6	3	3	98	24	32	31	4	1	3	2	.359	8	5	3	.221	.282	.286	29
Karros	149	545	63	140	30	1	20	232	88	37	103	3	2	2	4	.400	15	0	5	.257	.426	.304	67
Harris L	135	347	28	94	11	0	0	105	30	24	24	3	1	19	7	.362	10	6	2	.271	.303	.318	34
Hansen	132	341	30	73	11	0	6	102	22	34	49	3	1	0	2	.222	7	0	2	.214	.299	.286	29
Offerman	149	534	67	139	20	8	1	178	30	57	98	4	0	23	16	.356	6	5	2	.260	.333	.331	61
Davis E	76	267	21	61	8	1	5	86	32	36	71	2	3	19	1	.333	8	0	2	.228	.322	.325	32
Butler	157	553	86	171	14	11	3	216	39	95	67	2	3	41	21	.417	4	24	1	.309	.391	.413	100
Strawberry	43	156	20	37	8	0	5	60	25	19	34	4	1	3	1	.407	2	0	1	.237	.385	.322	21
Sharperson	128	317	48	95	21	0	3	125	36	47	33	1	0	2	2	.446	9	5	3	.300	.394	.387	50
Benzinger	121	293	24	70	16	2	4	102	31	15	54	1	0	2	4	.333	6	0	5	.239	.348	.272	26
Webster M	135	262	33	70	12	5	6	110	35	27	49	3	2	11	5	.341	1	8	5	.267	.420	.334	40
Hernandez C	69	173	11	45	4	0	3	58	17	11	21	1	4	0	1	.115	8	0	2	.260	.335	.316	17
Rodriguez H	53	146	11	32	7	0	3	48	14	8	30	0	0	0	0	.412	2	1	1	.219	.329	.258	12
Young E	49	132	9	34	1	0	1	38	11	8	9	0	0	6	1	.381	3	4	0	.258	.288	.300	12
Samuel	47	122	7	32	3	1	0	37	15	7	22	3	1	2	2	.368	0	4	2	.262	.303	.303	12
Daniels	35	104	9	24	5	0	2	35	8	10	30	0	1	0	0	.500	7	0	1	.231	.337	.302	9
Ashley	29	95	6	21	5	0	2	32	6	5	34	0	0	0	0	.417	2	0	0	.221	.337	.260	8
Anderson D	51	84	10	24	4	0	3	37	8	4	11	0	0	0	4	.400	3	1	2	.286	.440	.311	9
Goodwin	57	73	15	17	1	1	0	20	3	6	10	0	0	7	3	.444	0	0	0	.233	.274	.291	6
Piazza	21	69	5	16	3	0	1	22	7	4	12	0	1	0	0	.333	1	0	0	.232	.319	.284	6
Hershiser	35	68	6	15	5	0	0	20	5	1	10	0	0	1	0	.091	0	6	1	.221	.294	.229	5
Gross K	34	63	3	6	1	0	0	7	0	4	26	0	0	0	0	.143	0	3	0	.095	.111	.149	1
Javier	56	58	6	11	3	0	1	17	5	6	11	2	1	1	2	.556	1	0	1	.190	.293	.277	5
Candiotti	32	56	3	6	1	0	0	7	1	1	9	0	0	0	0	.000	5	12	0	.107	.125	.123	0
Martinez R	26	50	1	6	0	0	0	6	2	0	14	0	0	0	0	01.000	0	5	0	.120	.120	.120	1
Ojeda	29	49	1	5	0	1	0	7	3	1	11	0	0	0	0	.250	1	5	0	.102	.143	.120	1
Astacio	11	24	2	3	0	0	0	3	1	0	14	0	0	0	0	.250	0	5	0	.125	.125	.125	1
Bournigal	10	20	1	3	1	0	0	4	0	1	2	0	1	0	0	.333	0	0	0	.150	.200	.227	1
Crews	49	7	1	2	0	0	0	2	0	0	4	0	0	0	0	01.000	0	0	0	.286	.286	.286	1
Wilson S	60	3	0	1	0	0	0	1	0	0	2	0	0	0	0	.000	0	0	0	.333	.333	.333	0
McDowell R	65	3	1	0	0	0	0	0	0	2	3	0	1	0	0	.000	0	1	0	.000	.000	.500	1
Gott	68	2	0	1	0	0	0	1	0	0	1	0	0	0	0	.000	0	0	0	.500	.500	.500	1
Gross Kip	16	2	1	2	0	0	0	2	1	0	0	0	0	0	0	.000	0	1	01.000	1.000	1.000		2
MartinezP	2	2	0	0	0	0	0	0	0	0	0	0	0	0	0	.000	0	0	0	.000	.000	.000	0
Candelaria	50	0	0	0	0	0	0	0	0	1	0	0	0	0	0	.000	0	0	0	.000	.000	1.000	0
Howell Jay	41	0	0	0	0	0	0	0	0	0	0	0	0	0	0	.000	0	0	0	.000	.000	.000	0
TOTALS	2337	5368	548	1333	201	34	72	1818	499	503	899	36	24	142	78	.362	108	102	40	.248	.339	.313	583

Pitching Records for Los Angeles Dodgers

	ERA	W	L	Pct	G	GS	CG	ShO	GF	Sv	IP	R	ER	H	2B	3B	HR	BB	IW	SO	HB	WP	BK
Hershiser	3.67	10	15	.400	33	33	1	0	0	0	210.2	101	86	209	42	3	15	69	13	130	8	10	0
Gross K	3.17	8	13	.381	34	30	4	3	0	0	204.2	82	72	182	30	5	11	77	10	158	3	4	2
Candiotti	3.00	11	15	.423	32	30	6	2	1	0	203.2	78	68	177	35	4	13	63	5	152	3	9	2
Ojeda	3.63	6	9	.400	29	29	2	1	0	0	166.1	80	67	169	29	6	8	81	8	94	1	3	0
Martinez R	4.00	8	11	.421	25	25	1	1	0	0	150.2	82	67	141	30	2	11	69	4	101	5	9	0
Astacio	1.98	5	5	.500	11	11	4	4	0	0	82.0	23	18	80	8	2	1	20	4	43	2	1	0
MartinezP	2.25	0	1	.000	2	1	0	0	1	0	8.0	2	2	6	3	0	0	1	0	8	0,	0	0
Gott	2.45	3	3	.500	68	0	0	0	28	6	88.0	27	24	72	6	1	4	41	13	75	1	9	3
McDowell R	4.09	6	10	.375	65	0	0	0	39	14	83.2	46	38	103	10	2	3	42	13	50	1	4	1
Crews	5.19	0	3	.000	49	2	0	0	13	0	78.0	46	45	95	10	3	6	20	9	43	2	3	0
Wilson S	4.18	2	5	.286	60	0	0	0	18	0	66.2	37	31	74	13	3	6	29	7	54	1	7	0
Howell Jay	1.54	1	3	.250	41	0	0	0	26	4	46.2	9	8	41	3	0	2	18	5	36	1	3	1
Candelaria	2.84	2	5	.286	50	0	0	0	11	5	25.1	9	8	20	2	1	1	13	3	23	0	1	0
Gross Kip	4.18	1	1	.500	16	1	0	0	7	0	23.2	14	11	32	5	1	1	10	1	14	0	1	1
TOTALS	3.41	63	99	.389	515	162	18	11	144	29	1438.0	636	545	1401	226	33	82	553	95	981	28	64	10

Sabermetric Pitching Records for Los Angeles Dodgers

	Adj ERA	W	L	Pct	BFP	Avg	Slg	OBA	RC/G	GDP	SB	CS	PK	PKE	SH	SF	RSup	RSp/G	W	L	Pct
Astacio	1.98	8	2	.759	341	.255	.303	.302	2.97	12	5	3	0	1	3	2	27	2.96	6	4	.647
Candelaria	2.84	4	3	.603	108	.220	.297	.311	3.64	0	2	0	0	0	2	2	11	3.91	4	3	.607
Candiotti	3.05	15	11	.569	839	.237	.347	.297	3.56	17	30	5	1	1	20	6	73	3.23	12	14	.477
Crews	5.31	1	2	.303	339	.310	.422	.351	5.39	3	12	6	0	0	6	5	34	3.92	1	2	.308
Gott	2.45	4	2	.671	369	.225	.287	.314	3.13	6	6	5	0	0	6	1	24	2.45	3	2	.449
Gross K	3.21	11	10	.544	856	.241	.337	.311	3.66	12	18	9	0	1	14	6	80	3.52	10	11	.495
Gross Kip	4.18	1	1	.412	109	.323	.424	.385	6.06	3	2	1	0	0	0	0	12	4.56	1	1	.493
Hershiser	3.76	12	13	.465	910	.257	.372	.320	4.15	19	13	7	0	3	15	6	77	3.29	10	15	.385
Howell Jay	1.54	3	1	.838	203	.230	.281	.303	3.40	1	7	1	0	0	5	1	13	2.51	3	1	.683
MartinezP	2.25	1	0	.708	31	.200	.300	.226	2.37	0	0	0	0	0	0	0	1	1.12	0	1	.169
Martinez R	4.06	8	11	.427	662	.245	.362	.331	4.42	7	19	7	0	1	12	1	59	3.52	7	12	.381
McDowell R	4.20	7	9	.411	393	.306	.374	.381	5.38	9	3	2	0	1	10	3	31	3.33	5	11	.340
Ojeda	3.68	7	8	.476	731	.268	.371	.349	4.50	15	20	15	1	8	11	7	72	3.90	7	8	.478
Wilson S	4.18	3	4	.412	301	.282	.424	.351	5.30	9	4	1	0	2	5	4	34	4.59	3	4	.495
TOTALS	3.50	81	81	.501	6192	.257	.355	.326	4.10	113	141	62	2	18	109	44	548	3.43	71	91	.440

Batting 'Splits' Records for Los Angeles Dodgers

SPLITS for Butler

	G	AB	Run	Hit	2B	3B	HR	TB	RBI	W	K	IW	HB	SB	CS	DP	SH	SF	Avg	Slug	OBP	RC
vs LHP	104	223	29	66	2	3	1	77	17	39	31	0	1	14	9	3	8	1	.296	.345	.402	34
vs RHP	156	330	57	105	12	8	2	139	22	56	36	2	2	27	12	1	16	0	.318	.421	.420	66
Home	77	267	42	81	4	6	1	100	19	48	28	1	1	22	10	2	10	0	.303	.375	.411	47
Away	80	286	44	90	10	5	2	116	20	47	39	1	2	19	11	2	14	1	.315	.406	.414	53
Grass	116	411	64	131	11	9	3	169	31	72	45	1	1	29	15	2	18	1	.319	.411	.421	79
Turf	41	142	22	40	3	2	0	47	8	23	22	1	2	12	6	2	6	0	.282	.331	.389	21
April/June	72	268	38	72	6	7	1	95	18	42	40	0	2	10	9	2	7	1	.269	.354	.371	38
July/October	85	285	48	99	8	4	2	121	21	53	27	2	1	31	12	2	17	0	.347	.425	.451	62

SPLITS for Karros

	G	AB	Run	Hit	2B	3B	HR	TB	RBI	W	K	IW	HB	SB	CS	DP	SH	SF	Avg	Slug	OBP	RC
vs LHP	90	213	23	59	10	0	8	93	32	16	26	2	0	2	1	7	0	2	.277	.437	.325	29
vs RHP	144	332	40	81	20	1	12	139	56	21	77	1	2	0	3	8	0	3	.244	.419	.291	38
Home	72	251	35	65	14	1	6	99	35	23	45	3	1	1	2	6	0	3	.259	.394	.320	31
Away	77	294	28	75	16	0	14	133	53	14	58	0	1	1	2	9	0	2	.255	.452	.289	35
Grass	109	388	45	102	23	1	13	166	62	30	72	3	2	1	3	9	0	4	.263	.428	.316	51
Turf	40	157	18	38	7	0	7	66	26	7	31	0	0	1	1	6	0	1	.242	.420	.273	16
April/June	59	199	24	54	10	0	9	91	27	11	38	0	0	1	1	7	0	4	.271	.457	.304	26
July/October	90	346	39	86	20	1	11	141	61	26	65	3	2	1	3	8	0	1	.249	.408	.304	41

SPLITS for Sharperson

	G	AB	Run	Hit	2B	3B	HR	TB	RBI	W	K	IW	HB	SB	CS	DP	SH	SF	Avg	Slug	OBP	RC
vs LHP	93	199	23	62	13	0	3	84	22	27	15	1	0	1	2	6	3	2	.312	.422	.390	33
vs RHP	95	118	25	33	8	0	0	41	14	20	18	0	0	1	0	3	2	1	.280	.347	.381	17
Home	61	159	28	50	11	0	2	67	19	18	18	0	0	0	0	6	2	1	.314	.421	.382	25
Away	67	158	20	45	10	0	1	58	17	29	15	1	0	2	2	3	3	2	.285	.367	.392	25
Grass	98	250	39	76	19	0	2	101	32	35	29	0	1	1	1	8	3	2	.304	.404	.387	40
Turf	30	67	9	19	2	0	1	24	4	12	4	1	0	1	1	1	2	1	.284	.358	.387	10
April/June	64	157	26	53	13	0	1	69	21	29	12	1	0	0	2	1	2	2	.338	.439	.436	33
July/October	64	160	22	42	8	0	2	56	15	18	21	0	0	2	0	8	3	1	.262	.350	.335	18

SPLITS for Los Angeles Dodgers (all batters except pitchers)

	G	AB	Run	Hit	2B	3B	HR	TB	RBI	W	K	IW	HB	SB	CS	DP	SH	SF	Avg	Slug	OBP	RC
vs LHP	1026	2007	206	531	74	9	33	722	189	197	286	16	5	44	33	48	37	16	.265	.360	.329	238
vs RHP	1748	3361	342	802	127	25	39	1096	310	306	613	20	19	98	45	60	65	24	.239	.326	.304	346
Home	1136	2627	277	664	96	19	26	876	247	251	404	17	12	84	41	52	50	22	.253	.333	.318	289
Away	1201	2741	271	669	105	15	46	942	252	252	495	19	12	58	37	56	52	18	.244	.344	.309	294
Grass	1728	3965	417	999	144	25	49	1340	380	380	634	25	18	108	61	72	78	36	.252	.338	.318	440
Turf	609	1403	131	334	57	9	23	478	119	123	265	11	6	34	17	36	24	4	.238	.341	.301	143
April/June	1064	2387	253	590	94	18	37	831	235	244	422	22	12	51	36	42	41	22	.247	.348	.317	272
July/October	1273	2981	295	743	107	16	35	987	264	259	477	14	12	91	42	66	61	18	.249	.331	.310	312

National League
Eastern Division

1. Pittsburgh Pirates
2. Montreal Expos
3. St. Louis Cardinals
4. Chicago Cubs
5. New York Mets
6. Philadelphia Phillies

NL Eastern Division Team Batting

	G	AB	Run	Hit	2B	3B	HR	TB	RBI	W	K	IW	HB	SB	CS	BRng Eff	GI DP	SH	SF	Avg	Slug	OBP	Runs Ctd
Chicago	2258	5590	593	1420	221	41	104	2035	566	417	816	49	31	77	51	.410	119	78	40	.254	.364	.307	621
Montreal	2233	5477	648	1381	263	37	102	2024	601	463	976	43	43	196	63	.437	103	82	55	.252	.370	.313	655
New York	2343	5340	599	1254	259	17	93	1826	564	572	956	53	28	129	52	.424	114	74	45	.235	.342	.310	588
Philadelphia	2121	5500	686	1392	255	36	118	2073	638	509	1059	45	52	127	31	.422	111	64	46	.253	.377	.320	687
Pittsburgh	2255	5527	693	1409	272	54	106	2107	656	569	872	88	25	110	53	.455	102	89	56	.255	.381	.324	706
St. Louis	2298	5594	631	1464	262	44	94	2096	599	495	996	49	32	208	118	.418	97	68	41	.262	.375	.323	684

NL Eastern Division Sabermetric Team Batting

	Ball Park Adjusted								Runs				Run/					
	AB	Run	Hit	2B	3B	HR	RBI	W	SO	Avg	Slug	OBP	Ctd	Outs	27o	OW%	OG	OWAR
Chicago	5718	608	1466	226	36	105	588	414	820	.256	.364	.310	641	4538	3.81	.508	168	26.49
Montreal	5353	578	1328	232	33	96	539	466	976	.248	.358	.310	616	4318	3.85	.508	160	25.21
New York	5296	620	1263	260	16	95	583	588	945	.238	.347	.315	611	4316	3.82	.495	160	23.11
Philadelphia	5502	694	1405	263	31	120	649	497	1011	.255	.380	.321	692	4360	4.29	.495	161	23.38
Pittsburgh	5559	709	1396	258	53	125	664	546	861	.251	.384	.319	700	4462	4.24	.532	165	30.03
St. Louis	5701	647	1504	273	48	95	612	502	1020	.264	.379	.324	702	4534	4.18	.546	168	32.92

NL Eastern Division Team Pitching

	ERA	W	L	Pct	G	GS	CG	ShO	GF	Sv	IP	R	ER	H	2B	3B	HR	BB	IW	SO	HB	WP	BK
Chicago	3.39	78	84	.481	534	162	16	5	146	37	1469.0	624	554	1337	261	35	107	575	75	901	44	68	11
Montreal	3.25	87	75	.537	511	162	11	5	151	49	1468.0	581	530	1296	231	34	92	525	41	1014	50	48	11
New York	3.68	72	90	.444	495	162	17	8	145	34	1446.2	653	591	1404	267	56	98	482	54	1025	36	34	9
Philadelphia	4.13	70	92	.432	485	162	27	7	135	34	1428.0	717	655	1387	263	42	113	549	37	851	27	43	9
Pittsburgh	3.35	96	66	.593	516	162	20	9	142	43	1479.2	595	551	1410	264	34	101	455	61	844	30	52	9
St. Louis	3.38	83	79	.512	586	162	10	1	152	47	1480.0	604	556	1405	252	34	118	400	46	842	32	41	3

NL Eastern Division Sabermetric Team Pitching

	Adj ERA	Expected W	L	Pct	Opposing Batters BFP	Avg	Slg	OBA	RC/G	GDP	SB	CS	PK	PKE	SH	SF	Supported RSup	RSp/G	W	L	Pct
Chicago	3.46	82	80	.507	6201	.246	.366	.320	4.00	110	116	72	4	16	88	52	593	3.63	77	85	.474
Montreal	2.91	96	66	.592	6139	.238	.343	.309	3.72	95	199	68	4	16	77	35	648	3.97	98	64	.604
New York	3.81	74	88	.458	6118	.256	.379	.318	4.16	116	148	67	4	16	72	52	599	3.73	71	91	.438
Philadelphia	4.15	67	95	.416	6113	.257	.384	.326	4.39	99	111	53	4	16	81	53	686	4.32	76	86	.470
Pittsburgh	3.39	84	78	.517	6162	.254	.369	.312	3.88	115	124	73	4	16	80	48	693	4.22	90	72	.558
St. Louis	3.47	82	80	.505	6140	.252	.372	.303	3.84	127	124	39	4	16	77	46	631	3.84	81	81	.500

```
NL Eastern Division Catchers
              G    PO   A  Er   TC  DP  PB   SB  CS  CS%  FPct    DI    DG  DW%   DWAR  ERA
Chicago      162  936  118  11 1065  12  14  116  72 .383 .990 1469.0 10.0 .385   0.35  3.39
Montreal     162 1060   97  10 1167   7   9  199  68 .255 .991 1468.0 10.0 .408   0.58  3.25
New York     162 1073   95  11 1179   6  10  148  67 .312 .991 1446.2 10.0 .318  -0.32  3.68
Philadelphia 162  899   81  15  995  10  13  111  53 .323 .985 1428.0 10.0 .213  -1.37  4.13
Pittsburgh   162  862  102  10  974  10  11  124  73 .371 .990 1479.2 10.0 .383   0.33  3.35
St. Louis    162  915   65   4  984  12   8  124  39 .239 .996 1480.0 10.0 .395   0.45  3.38
LG.AVG       162  987   92  10 1089  11  11  130  61 .319 .991 1458.1
```

```
NL Eastern Division First Base
              G    PO    A  Er    TC  DP  FPct    DI   DG  DW%   DWAR
Chicago      162 1638  146   4  1788 126 .998 1469.0 3.0 .675   0.97
Montreal     162 1463  141  14  1618 101 .991 1468.0 3.0 .487   0.41
New York     162 1434   99  15  1548 121 .990 1446.2 3.0 .351   0.00
Philadelphia 162 1418   89   9  1516 112 .994 1428.0 3.0 .451   0.30
Pittsburgh   162 1570  124   8  1702 128 .995 1479.2 3.0 .582   0.70
St. Louis    162 1524  103  16  1643 135 .990 1480.0 3.0 .409   0.18
LG.AVG       162 1456  121  10  1587 119 .994 1458.1
```

```
NL Eastern Division Second Base
              G   PO    A  Er   TC  DP  FPct    DI   DG  DW%   DWAR
Chicago      162 304  566   9  879  96 .990 1469.0 8.0 .600   2.00
Montreal     162 308  459  18  785  81 .977 1468.0 8.0 .413   0.50
New York     162 322  486  22  830 107 .973 1446.2 8.0 .477   1.01
Philadelphia 162 344  484  13  841  97 .985 1428.0 8.0 .520   1.36
Pittsburgh   162 379  518   7  904 103 .992 1479.2 8.0 .662   2.50
St. Louis    162 347  547  15  909 107 .983 1480.0 8.0 .657   2.45
LG.AVG       162 349  488  16  853  98 .981 1458.1
```

```
NL Eastern Division Third Base
              G   PO    A  Er   TC  DP  FPct    DI   DG  DW%   DWAR
Chicago      162 123  317  27  467  23 .942 1469.0 6.0 .417   0.40
Montreal     162 110  355  30  495  29 .939 1468.0 6.0 .480   0.78
New York     162  83  300  24  407  22 .941 1446.2 6.0 .306  -0.26
Philadelphia 162 124  261  19  404  23 .953 1428.0 6.0 .370   0.12
Pittsburgh   162 113  367  23  503  32 .954 1479.2 6.0 .558   1.25
St. Louis    162 108  302  18  428  27 .958 1480.0 6.0 .471   0.73
LG.AVG       162 114  317  21  452  26 .954 1458.1
```

```
NL Eastern Division Shortstop
               G    PO    A   Er    TC   DP  FPct       DI   DG   DW%   DWAR
Chicago       162  307  495   21   823  103  .974   1469.0  11.0  .620  2.98
Montreal      162  265  454   19   738   71  .974   1468.0  11.0  .476  1.39
New York      162  257  490   13   760   97  .983   1446.2  11.0  .554  2.24
Philadelphia  162  279  470   36   785   87  .954   1428.0  11.0  .449  1.09
Pittsburgh    162  278  544   24   846   98  .972   1479.2  11.0  .614  2.90
St. Louis     162  288  506   18   812  102  .978   1480.0  11.0  .645  3.24
LG.AVG        162  264  479   23   766   89  .970   1458.1
```

```
NL Eastern Division Left Field
               G    PO    A   Er    TC   DP  FPct       DI   DG   DW%   DWAR
Chicago       162  318   10   10   338    0  .970   1469.0   4.0  .479  0.52
Montreal      162  323    8    6   337    0  .982   1468.0   4.0  .475  0.50
New York      162  310   11    8   329    4  .976   1446.2   4.0  .467  0.47
Philadelphia  162  369    6    8   383    1  .979   1428.0   4.0  .479  0.52
Pittsburgh    162  362    5    6   373    0  .984   1479.2   4.0  .492  0.57
St. Louis     162  356   14    9   379    5  .976   1480.0   4.0  .620  1.08
LG.AVG        162  340    8    7   355    1  .980   1458.1
```

```
NL Eastern Division Center Field
               G    PO    A   Er    TC   DP  FPct       DI   DG   DW%   DWAR
Chicago       162  390    6   10   406    1  .975   1469.0   6.0  .369  0.11
Montreal      162  425    9    7   441    3  .984   1468.0   6.0  .498  0.89
New York      162  419    5    4   428    1  .991   1446.2   6.0  .468  0.71
Philadelphia  162  477   12    7   496    5  .986   1428.0   6.0  .599  1.49
Pittsburgh    162  455   11    5   471    3  .989   1479.2   6.0  .608  1.55
St. Louis     162  483    5    2   490    1  .996   1480.0   6.0  .645  1.77
LG.AVG        162  443    9    5   457    3  .989   1458.1
```

```
NL Eastern Division Right Field
               G    PO    A   Er    TC   DP  FPct       DI   DG   DW%   DWAR
Chicago       162  276   12    2   290    5  .993   1469.0   5.0  .563  1.06
Montreal      162  330   17    4   351    2  .989   1468.0   5.0  .696  1.73
New York      162  348   10    2   360    2  .994   1446.2   5.0  .595  1.22
Philadelphia  162  320    4    6   330    1  .982   1428.0   5.0  .417  0.34
Pittsburgh    162  318    9    7   334    2  .979   1479.2   5.0  .467  0.58
St. Louis     162  341   13    7   361    1  .981   1480.0   5.0  .605  1.28
LG.AVG        162  325   11    7   343    2  .980   1458.1
```

Pittsburgh Pirates

Brock J. Hanke

PITTSBURGH YEAR	1983	1984	1985	1986	1987	1988	1989	1990	1991	1992
W	84	75	57	64	80	85	74	95	98	96
L	78	87	104	98	82	75	88	67	64	66
WPCT	0.519	0.463	0.354	0.395	0.494	0.531	0.457	0.586	0.605	0.593
R	659	615	568	663	723	651	637	733	768	693
RA	648	567	708	700	744	616	680	619	632	595
PWPT	0.508	0.541	0.392	0.473	0.486	0.528	0.467	0.584	0.596	0.576
PythW	82	88	63	77	79	85	76	95	97	93
PythL	80	74	99	85	83	77	86	67	65	69
LUCK	2	-13	-6	-13	1	0	-2	0	1	3

Defensive Efficiency Record: .7082

Position	92 Starter	TWAR	93 Starter	TWAR
Catcher	Slaught	2.35	Slaught	2.35
	Lavaillere	1.57	Lavaillere	1.57
First base	Merced	2.94	Merced	2.94
Second base	Lind	0.44	Garcia	-0.08
Third base	King	1.77	King	1.77
Shortstop	Bell, Ja.	6.55	Bell, Ja.	6.55
Left field	Bonds	7.63	Smith, L.	1.48
			Martin, A.	0.01
Center field	Van Slyke	8.12	Van Slyke	8.12
Right field	McClendon	0.93	McClendon	0.93
	A. Cole	1.20		

Now lemme get this straight. You can't afford Barry Bonds, who pays for himself in extra tickets and merchandise sold, but you can afford Lonnie Smith and Alejandro Pena, who will sell you not two tickets between them, but who might help you win 72 games instead of 70.

Now lemme get this straight. For three years, you have been a contender, but your team did have three advertised weak points. First, it had a closer-by-committee bullpen. Second, it had a right-field by committee. Third, it had a leadoff-man-by-committee in front of the great power core. So you finally get around to signing a projected full-time closer, in Alejandro Pena, and a full-time outfielder / leadoff man, Lonnie Smith. So why didn't you do that when it might have helped you win the pennant, instead of just the division? Why did you wait until you've gutted the rest of your team? Why did you wait until Pena and Lonnie are suspiciously near being finished?

Now, lemme get this straight. You had to slough off the stars on your division-winning ensemble. You claim it's because you can't get enough people to buy tickets. You also claim that the players are ruining the game by demanding too much money. You claim that this keeps you from competing with the teams in the bigger cities that have higher revenues. In fact, you insist that the players' union should make you concessions because of this competitive disparity, as though teams in New York, Chicago, and Los Angeles had been winning all the recent division titles. But you also claim, in conjunction with the other Lords of Baseball, that you can't move your team to a city that might produce more revenue - let's say Tampa - because it's "not good for baseball". And you want an anti-trust exemption to support this wonderful system of baseball. You want that exemption because teams in baseball are all independent entities who are all trying to win the pennant independently, and who are all able to do so.

Uh, huh. I don't suppose anyone is Pittsburgh is going to love me for saying this, but in any reasonable, antitrust-controlled system, the Pirates would have to leave Pittsburgh. The league would determine that the current ownership was not capable of paying the established salaries of a Major League baseball team. It would also determine that there was an available ownership that could. It would discover that the capable ownership insisted on moving the team to Tampa, on the perfectly sound grounds that the people of Pittsburgh were not buying enough tickets to pay the salaries, whereas the people of Tampa would do so cheerfully.

It would understand that the players have the right to be paid the best salaries they can get, from the ownership most willing to and capable of paying. Since that could only happen with the transfer of ownership, the ownership would have to be transferred.

Let's phrase this another way. Let's look at the situation of the ballplayer Barry Bonds. Bonds wants, naturally, to get as much money for his services as he can. He has a right to do that. That right does not disappear just because any owner will pay him enough in one year for me to live on for the rest of my life. He has the right to get the most he can. Anything that restrains that right is in restraint of trade. That's what the antitrust laws are designed to prevent.

And there exists an ownership out there that would pay him more than he can get in Pittsburgh. Possibly, it would pay him more than he can get in San Francisco. But he is not allowed to get that money, because the ownership is not allowed to own a team. Instead, an ownership that baldfacedly claims to be unable to pay Bonds is allowed to own a team that the Tampa ownership would be delighted to have. That's wrong. It's wrong ethically, and it's wrong morally. It is exactly what the antitrust laws are designed to prevent.

And, not only does this situation exist, but the same ownerships that established the situation are proudly claiming their inability to pay Barry Bonds. They are out there in the press, campaigning for the players' union to make concessions to them on the subject of arbitration, so that they can avoid paying Barry Bonds the sort of money he could command under ideal circumstances. That is, they are saying that the ownership of the Pittsburgh franchise should be subsidized by Barry Bonds. They're saying that Wayne Huizinga cannot employ Barry Bonds to play Major League baseball, because their teams won't play his. He's got the money and the Pittsburgh outfit doesn't. He's got all the stadium he needs, too, so that argument is not available. All that is available as an argument is that the Pittsburgh ownership has the right to a Major League franchise, in perpetuity, regardless of monetary feasibility, and that Barry Bonds and his like are to be required to pay for the Pittsburgh shortfall.

Now do you understand why labor negotiations in baseball are so angry? The Lords of Baseball say "We can't pay." The players say, "So sell to someone who can, like any other ownership of any other business in free enterprise has to." the Lords say, "Oh, no, we don't have to do that. We're baseball franchise owners. We get to manage our businesses as badly as we please, and put all our relatives on the payroll, and you all just have to lump it if we go bankrupt." The players say, "That has to be illegal." The Lords say, "Nope, we have an antitrust exemption." Well, I've got news for the Lords. Every time they do this - every time they sell off a franchise full of players or stop a sale to one ownership and force one to a poorer group - they chip away at that exemption. And, when they compound that with the sort of labor practices they currently use, they're pushing the envelope pretty hard. I doubt - I bet - the exemption will not last five years, much less the decade.

OK, so you didn't like that collection of rant. You think I can keep my unreconstructed-hippie opinions to myself. OK, so you write a reasonable sabermetric essay about the Pirates. I mean, what am I supposed to say that's supposed to be enlightening? The Pirates have a two-man offense left, and that's not enough? It's not enough even if Lonnie Smith makes it a three-man? Even if Slaught and Lavalliere make it four? Zane Smith and Tim Wakefield cannot win a division title with that offense even if Alejandro Pena comes completely back? I don't care if Jim Leyland's a genius, he's not a magician? OK, I just wrote it. Now what?

The problem, you see, is that my ability to write a decent sabermetric essay is dependent on the Pirates fielding a legitimate team. That is, it is dependent on the ownership's ability to pay competitive salaries. Which is dependent on the Lords' ability to get rid of ownerships that can't. Which is dependent on the Lords' willingness to put themselves under the same microscope. Which is, in our American free enterprise system, dependent on the government's ability to enforce the antitrust laws. In the absence of that, I have nothing sabermetric to say, at least about the 1993 Pirates.

About the 1992 Pirates, I do have something for you. It's about the postseason, but it is something about baseball on the field. You may remember the final inning of the NLCS. You may remember that Jose Lind made a miscue on a difficult, but not impossible grounder. You may remember that the Braves got lucky with their pinch hitter there. But do you remember who started pitching the inning? Doug Drabek.

Why was Doug Drabek pitching? Because the Pirates did not have a closer that Jim Leyland trusted, when the chips were down. Now, that's not to say that the Pirates did not have any pitchers who could give up fewer than two runs an inning. They had plenty of those. What they did not have was a single closer who Jim Leyland trusted.

If you look at the top of the essay here, you'll note that I wonder about that. Why, if the team knew enough about their bullpen to want to sign Alejandro Pena now, did they not know it then? I mean, the Braves managed to pick up Jeff Reardon. Reardon didn't come through, but they did address the problem. The Pirates did nothing, and I just can't believe that they were that short of money.

What I think they were short of was desire to complete the team. Look at the other signing I wondered about. The Pirates have been to the NLCS for three years now, and they never have had a true leadoff man. Not since they moved Barry down to the power core have they had one. They've tried platooning Gary Redus with everyone, and they tried Alex Cole for a while, but they never were willing to put out the cash or trade value to complete the lineup. Just as they were never willing to complete the bullpen with a finisher.

I mean, I have no real objection to a committee bullpen. I live in St. Louis, after all. But you've got to trust that committee. You've got to have at least one guy for every situation who you're willing to trust. Especially, you've got to have a guy to trust to pitch the ninth inning of the last game of the NLCS with a one-run lead. If you don't trust your committee members, you've got to get a closer. That's what Whitey did. He had Todd Worrell in there before the 1985 season was over, because he just did not trust the members of his committee with pressure pitching.

This sort of thing never happens to Bobby Cox, either. Bobby took over a Braves team with no fewer holes than the Pirates had. They didn't have a real third baseman. They didn't have a real leadoff man. They didn't have a real closer. Bobby promptly picked up Terry Pendelton. He picked up Otis Nixon, rather than gamble on Deion Sanders or a platoon. He picked up Alejandro Pena and then he picked up Jeff Reardon. All the time, he could have fielded a leadoff platoon as good as the Pirates', and also a committee bullpen just as good, and Bobby Cox loves to platoon. This year, he added Greg Maddux to his starting rotation, because it just didn't look complete enough to him.

But that lack of completeness did happen to Jim Leyland, and it cost him in the end. He had the pennant - had the war - if he just had the horseshoe. And that's why I'm reluctant to place him in the class of Earl Weaver, Whitey Herzog and Bobby Cox. All three of those men were notorious for their complete teams. They always had a plan that they were willing to trust. They never ended up in a pennant situation where they simply did not have an option available, unless someone had recently been hurt. Jim Leyland, as of now, lacks that ability to complete his team. And that's why I'm not with the people who think that the Pirates will somehow be competitive this year just because of Jim Leyland. I think they will be hard pressed to win 70 games, and might fall short of 65, even with Bell and Van Slyke and Zane Smith and Tim Wakefield.

Pittsburgh Pirates Home Park Performance Factors														
	Outs	Runs	Hits	2b	3b	HR	W	K	SH	SF	HBP	IBB	SB	CS	GDP
Home LH Batters	.977	.922	.941	.939	.815	.977	.893	.997	.820	.799	1.226	.904	.856	.724	.940
Home RH Batters	1.009	.938	.982	.928	.991	1.067	.913	1.037	.966	.831	1.269	.813	.796	.802	1.074
All Home Batters	.995	.927	.959	.932	.881	1.004	.902	1.010	.907	.853	1.251	.917	.843	.835	1.022
Opp LH Batters	1.000	1.109	.988	.884	.734	1.495	.925	.944	1.194	1.036	1.364	.845	1.232	1.072	1.091
Opp RH Batters	1.050	1.171	1.056	1.004	1.403	1.399	1.053	.968	1.279	1.166	1.151	1.113	1.133	1.047	1.083
All Opp Batters	1.028	1.121	1.022	.969	1.085	1.372	1.019	.965	1.180	1.094	1.165	1.055	1.123	1.039	1.032
All LH Batters	.986	.985	.960	.919	.795	1.125	.907	.972	1.011	.864	1.273	.895	.974	.860	1.001
All RH Batters	1.030	1.052	1.020	.967	1.183	1.232	.983	.998	1.092	.979	1.177	.954	.979	.931	1.074
All Batters	1.010	1.013	.990	.950	.963	1.160	.956	.986	1.025	.953	1.196	.977	.972	.937	1.024

Conventional Batting Records for Pittsburgh Pirates

	G	AB	Run	Hit	2B	3B	HR	TB	RBI	W	K	IW	HB	SB	CS	BRng Eff	GI DP	SH	SF	Avg	Slug	OBP	Runs Ctd
LaValliere	95	293	22	75	13	1	2	96	29	44	21	14	1	0	3	.186	8	0	5	.256	.328	.350	35
Merced	134	405	50	100	28	5	6	156	60	52	63	8	2	5	4	.531	6	1	5	.247	.385	.332	54
Lind	135	468	38	110	14	1	0	126	39	26	29	12	1	3	1	.431	14	7	4	.235	.269	.275	34
Buechele	80	285	27	71	14	1	8	111	43	34	61	4	2	0	2	.439	5	2	2	.249	.389	.331	38
Bell Jay	159	632	87	167	36	6	9	242	55	55	103	0	4	7	5	.473	12	19	2	.264	.383	.326	80
Bonds	140	473	109	147	36	5	34	295	103	127	69	32	5	39	8	.481	9	0	7	.311	.624	.456	151
Van Slyke	154	614	103	199	45	12	14	310	89	58	99	4	4	12	3	.463	9	0	4	.324	.505	.381	123
Cole	64	205	33	57	3	7	0	74	10	18	46	1	0	7	4	.477	2	1	1	.278	.361	.335	26
King J	130	480	56	111	21	2	14	178	65	27	56	3	2	4	6	.525	8	8	5	.231	.371	.272	47
Slaught	87	255	26	88	17	3	4	123	37	17	23	5	2	2	2	.405	6	6	5	.345	.482	.384	47
Espy	112	194	21	50	7	3	1	66	20	15	40	2	0	6	3	.407	3	1	1	.258	.340	.310	21
McClendon	84	190	26	48	8	1	3	67	20	28	24	0	2	1	5	.514	5	1	3	.253	.353	.350	24
Redus	76	176	26	45	7	3	3	67	12	17	25	0	0	11	4	.513	1	0	0	.256	.381	.321	23
Varsho	103	162	22	36	6	3	4	60	22	10	32	1	0	5	2	.444	2	0	1	.222	.370	.266	16
Wehner	55	123	11	22	6	0	0	28	4	12	22	2	0	3	0	.375	4	2	0	.179	.228	.252	7
Drabek	35	89	5	14	3	0	0	17	6	2	28	0	0	0	0	.444	0	8	0	.157	.191	.176	4
Tomlin R	35	65	4	9	0	0	0	9	1	3	15	0	0	0	0	.333	1	7	0	.138	.138	.176	2
Gibson K	16	56	6	11	0	0	2	17	5	3	12	0	0	3	1	.400	1	1	0	.196	.304	.237	4
Smith Z	26	49	2	6	2	0	0	8	3	2	11	0	0	0	0	.500	0	3	0	.122	.163	.157	1
Prince	27	44	1	4	2	0	0	6	5	6	9	0	0	1	1	.333	2	0	2	.091	.136	.192	1
Walk	36	43	2	4	1	0	0	5	2	0	11	0	0	0	0	.000	1	1	0	.093	.116	.093	0
Garcia C	22	39	4	8	1	0	0	9	4	0	9	0	0	0	0	.375	1	1	2	.205	.231	.195	2
Clark D	23	33	3	7	0	0	2	13	7	6	8	0	0	0	0	.250	0	0	1	.212	.394	.325	5
Wakefield	14	28	0	2	0	0	0	2	0	1	9	0	0	0	0	.000	0	4	0	.071	.071	.103	0
Jackson Dan	15	24	2	2	0	0	0	2	1	1	12	0	0	0	0	.500	0	5	0	.083	.083	.120	0
Palacios	20	14	0	1	0	0	0	1	0	0	6	0	0	0	0	.000	0	2	0	.071	.071	.071	0
Martin A	12	12	1	2	0	1	0	4	2	0	5	0	0	0	0	.000	0	0	1	.167	.333	.154	1
Neagle	56	11	0	0	0	0	0	0	0	0	2	0	0	0	1	.000	0	2	0	.000	.000	.000	0
Robinson JM	8	11	0	1	0	0	0	1	1	0	8	0	0	0	0	.091	0	0	0	.091	.091	.091	0
Mason R	65	10	0	0	0	0	0	0	0	1	5	0	0	0	0	.000	1	0	0	.000	.000	.091	0
Pennyfeather	15	9	2	2	0	0	0	2	0	0	0	0	0	0	0	01.000	1	1	0	.222	.222	.222	0
Young K	10	7	2	4	0	0	0	4	4	2	0	0	0	1	0	.667	0	0	0	.571	.571	.667	3
Patterson B	60	6	1	2	1	0	0	3	4	1	3	0	0	0	0	01.000	0	0	0	.333	.500	.429	1
Cole V	8	4	0	0	0	0	0	0	0	0	0	0	0	0	0	.000	0	1	0	.000	.000	.000	0
Belinda	59	3	1	2	1	0	0	3	2	0	0	0	0	0	0	01.000	0	0	0	.6671.000	.667		2
Miller P	6	3	0	0	0	0	0	0	0	0	3	0	0	0	0	.000	0	0	0	.000	.000	.000	0
Wagner P	6	3	0	1	0	0	0	1	0	0	1	0	0	0	0	.000	0	0	0	.333	.333	.333	0
Cooke	11	3	0	1	0	0	0	1	1	0	0	0	0	0	0	.000	0	2	0	.333	.333	.333	0
Cox	16	3	0	0	0	0	0	0	0	0	1	0	0	0	0	.000	0	0	0	.000	.000	.000	0
Gleaton	23	2	0	0	0	0	0	0	0	1	1	0	0	0	0	.000	0	1	0	.000	.000	.333	0
Lamp	21	1	0	0	0	0	0	0	0	0	0	0	0	0	0	.000	0	0	0	.000	.000	.000	0
Batista	1	0	0	0	0	0	0	0	0	0	0	0	0	0	0	.000	0	0	0	.000	.000	.000	0
Minor	1	0	0	0	0	0	0	0	0	0	0	0	0	0	0	.000	0	0	0	.000	.000	.000	0
TOTALS	2255	5527	693	1409	272	54	106	2107	656	569	872	88	25	110	53	.455	102	89	56	.255	.381	.324	706

Sabermetric Batting Records for Pittsburgh Pirates

	AB	Run	Hit	2B	3B	HR	RBI	W	SO	Avg	Slug	OBP	Runs Ctd	Outs	27o	OW%	OG	OWAR	DWAR	TWAR
Bell Jay	648	91	170	34	7	11	56	54	103	.262	.387	.322	82	516	4.29	.538	19	3.59	2.95	6.55
Bonds	463	110	141	32	3	42	102	115	66	.305	.659	.444	150	344	11.77	.898	13	6.98	0.66	7.63
Buechele	292	28	72	13	1	9	44	33	61	.247	.390	.326	229	4.48	.560	8	1.78	0.64	2.42	
Clark D	31	3	6	0	0	2	6	5	7	.194	.387	.306	4	25	4.32	.541	1	0.18	0.02	0.20
Cole	200	33	54	2	5	0	9	16	44	.270	.330	.324	22	152	3.91	.491	6	0.80	0.40	1.20
Espy	194	21	49	6	2	1	20	14	39	.253	.320	.303	19	151	3.40	.422	6	0.40	0.09	0.49
Garcia C	39	4	8	0	0	0	4	0	9	.205	.205	.200	2	34	1.59	.138	1	-0.27	0.19	-0.08
Gibson K	54	6	10	0	0	2	4	2	11	.185	.296	.214	4	46	2.35	.259	2	-0.16	0.14	-0.01
King J	492	59	113	20	2	17	66	26	56	.230	.382	.269	49	404	3.27	.404	15	0.81	0.96	1.77
LaValliere	287	22	72	11	0	2	28	39	20	.251	.310	.338	31	229	3.66	.458	8	0.92	0.65	1.57
Lind	480	40	112	13	1	0	39	25	29	.233	.265	.271	33	393	2.27	.245	15	-1.52	1.97	0.44
Martin A	10	1	1	0	0	0	1	0	4	.100	.100	.100	0	9	0.00	.000	0	-0.12	0.02	-0.10
McClendon	194	27	48	7	1	3	20	27	24	.247	.340	.342	23	156	3.98	.501	6	0.87	0.06	0.93
Merced	407	51	99	26	4	7	60	49	62	.243	.378	.325	52	322	4.36	.546	12	2.34	0.60	2.94
Pennyfeather	9	2	2	0	0	0	0	0	0	.222	.222	.222	0	9	0.00	.000	0	-0.12	0.03	-0.09
Prince	45	1	4	1	0	0	5	5	9	.089	.111	.176	1	44	0.61	.023	2	-0.53	-0.07	-0.61
Redus	179	27	45	6	3	3	12	16	25	.251	.369	.313	22	138	4.30	.540	5	0.97	0.14	1.11
Slaught	260	27	89	16	3	4	37	16	23	.342	.473	.379	46	188	6.61	.734	7	2.67	-0.33	2.35
Van Slyke	601	104	191	41	9	17	88	52	96	.318	.501	.372	116	429	7.30	.771	16	6.69	1.43	8.12
Varsho	158	22	34	5	2	4	21	9	31	.215	.348	.257	14	127	2.98	.359	5	0.04	0.18	0.22
Wehner	125	11	22	5	0	0	4	11	22	.176	.216	.243	7	109	1.73	.160	4	-0.77	0.28	-0.49
Young K	7	2	4	0	0	0	4	1	0	.571	.571	.625	3		3	27.00	.979	0	0.07	-0.02	0.05
TOTALS	5559	709	1396	258	53	125	664	546	861	.251	.384	.319	700	4462	4.24	.532	165	30.03	10.98	41.01

Pitching Records for Pittsburgh Pirates

	ERA	W	L	Pct	G	GS	CG	ShO	GF	Sv	IP	R	ER	H	2B	3B	HR	BB	IW	SO	HB	WP	BK
Drabek	2.77	15	11	.577	34	34	10	4	0	0	256.2	84	79	218	35	4	17	54	8	177	6	11	1
Tomlin R	3.41	14	9	.609	35	33	1	1	0	0	208.2	85	79	226	45	7	11	42	4	90	5	7	2
Smith Z	3.06	8	8	.500	23	22	4	3	0	0	141.0	56	48	138	23	4	8	19	3	56	2	0	0
Walk	3.20	10	6	.625	36	19	1	0	7	2	135.0	54	48	132	26	3	10	43	5	60	6	7	2
Wakefield	2.15	8	1	.889	13	13	4	1	0	0	92.0	26	22	76	12	2	3	35	1	51	1	3	1
Jackson Dan	3.36	4	4	.500	15	15	0	0	0	0	88.1	40	33	94	18	2	1	29	3	46	1	1	0
Robinson JM	4.46	3	1	.750	8	7	0	0	0	0	36.1	18	18	33	5	1	2	15	0	14	1	0	0
Cole V	5.48	0	2	.000	8	4	0	0	2	0	23.0	14	14	23	6	0	1	14	0	12	0	1	0
Mason R	4.09	5	7	.417	65	0	0	0	26	8	88.0	41	40	80	14	3	11	33	8	56	4	3	0
Neagle	4.48	4	6	.400	55	6	0	0	8	2	86.1	46	43	81	17	1	9	43	8	77	2	3	2
Belinda	3.15	6	4	.600	59	0	0	0	42	18	71.1	26	25	58	13	2	8	29	5	57	0	1	0
Patterson B	2.92	6	3	.667	60	0	0	0	26	9	64.2	22	21	59	12	2	7	23	6	43	0	3	0
Palacios	4.25	3	2	.600	20	8	0	0	4	0	53.0	25	25	56	10	1	1	27	1	33	0	7	0
Gleaton	4.26	1	0	1.000	23	0	0	0	6	0	31.2	16	15	34	6	0	4	19	3	18	0	1	0
Lamp	5.14	1	1	.500	21	0	0	0	2	0	28.0	16	16	33	3	1	3	9	4	15	2	0	1
Cox	3.33	3	1	.750	16	0	0	0	8	3	24.1	9	9	20	4	0	2	8	1	18	0	1	0
Cooke	3.52	2	0	1.000	11	0	0	0	8	1	23.0	9	9	22	6	0	2	4	1	10	0	0	0
Wagner P	0.69	2	0	1.000	6	1	0	0	1	0	13.0	1	1	9	3	0	0	5	0	5	0	1	0
Miller P	2.38	1	0	1.000	6	0	0	0	1	0	11.1	3	3	11	5	0	0	1	0	5	0	1	0
Batista	9.00	0	0	.000	1	0	0	0	1	0	2.0	2	2	4	0	0	1	3	0	1	0	0	0
Minor	4.50	0	0	.000	1	0	0	0	0	0	2.0	2	1	3	1	1	0	0	0	0	0	1	0
TOTALS	3.35	96	66	.593	516	162	20	9	142	43	1479.2	595	551	1410	264	34	101	455	61	844	30	52	9

Sabermetric Pitching Records for Pittsburgh Pirates

	Adj ERA	-Expected-			Opposing Batters												Supported				
		W	L	Pct	BFP	Avg	Slg	OBA	RC/G	GDP	SB	CS	PK	PKE	SH	SF	RSup	RSp/G	W	L	Pct
Batista	9.00	0	0	.132	13	.400	.700	.538	18.93	0	0	0	0	0	0	0	3	13.50	0	0	.647
Belinda	3.15	6	4	.552	299	.223	.381	.295	4.18	1	12	2	0	0	4	6	30	3.79	5	5	.540
Cole V	5.48	1	1	.290	104	.261	.364	.359	4.97	1	2	1	0	0	1	1	5	1.96	0	2	.094
Cooke	3.52	1	1	.497	91	.253	.391	.286	3.47	3	0	0	0	0	0	0	8	3.13	1	1	.392
Cox	3.33	2	2	.526	100	.225	.337	.286	3.54	0	1	0	0	0	2	1	18	6.66	3	1	.766
Drabek	2.77	16	10	.615	1021	.231	.330	.274	2.91	19	18	14	3	0	8	8	112	3.93	16	10	.621
Gleaton	4.26	0	1	.403	142	.283	.433	.379	5.66	3	3	3	0	1	2	1	16	4.55	0	1	.482
Jackson Dan	3.36	4	4	.521	382	.276	.349	.330	4.13	6	6	4	0	1	6	5	44	4.48	5	3	.592
Lamp	5.14	1	1	.317	125	.292	.416	.355	5.29	2	2	2	0	0	1	0	31	9.96	2	0	.754
Mason R	4.09	5	7	.423	374	.246	.409	.320	4.50	3	4	5	1	0	8	4	26	2.66	3	9	.256
Miller P	2.38	1	0	.684	46	.256	.372	.267	3.30	0	0	1	0	0	1	1	6	4.77	1	0	.766
Minor	4.50	0	0	.377	9	.333	.667	.333	6.08	1	0	0	0	0	0	0	0	0.00	0	0	.000
Neagle	4.48	4	6	.379	380	.247	.387	.335	4.97	2	14	3	0	2	4	3	36	3.75	4	6	.364
Palacios	4.25	2	3	.405	232	.280	.355	.364	4.37	6	2	4	0	1	4	1	25	4.25	2	3	.449
Patterson B	2.92	5	4	.590	268	.246	.400	.309	4.04	5	1	3	0	1	3	2	29	4.04	5	4	.609
Robinson JM	4.46	2	2	.382	152	.244	.341	.322	3.86	1	6	4	0	1	0	1	23	5.70	2	2	.571
Smith Z	3.06	9	7	.567	566	.261	.365	.287	3.24	19	9	4	1	1	12	4	58	3.70	9	7	.544
Tomlin R	3.41	12	11	.514	866	.282	.397	.320	4.16	27	21	8	0	8	13	5	92	3.97	12	11	.525
Wagner P	0.69	2	0	.962	52	.191	.255	.269	2.31	0	0	1	0	0	0	0	5	3.46	2	0	.953
Wakefield	2.15	7	2	.726	373	.232	.309	.305	3.09	3	4	3	1	6	4	4	44	4.30	7	2	.766
Walk	3.20	9	7	.545	567	.258	.379	.322	4.21	13	19	5	1	1	5	1	82	5.47	11	5	.704
TOTALS	3.39	84	78	.517	6162	.254	.369	.312	3.88	115	124	73	9	18	80	48	693	4.22	90	72	.558

Batting 'Splits' Records for Pittsburgh Pirates

SPLITS for Pittsburgh Pirates (all batters except pitchers)

	G	AB	Run	Hit	2B	3B	HR	TB	RBI	W	K	IW	HB	SB	CS	DP	SH	SF	Avg	Slug	OBP	RC
vs LHP	1119	2193	264	563	121	22	37	839	250	233	329	24	11	47	26	52	25	21	.257	.383	.328	279
vs RHP	1748	3334	429	846	151	32	69	1268	406	336	543	64	14	63	27	50	64	35	.254	.380	.322	427
Home	1102	2676	363	707	141	30	51	1061	343	308	413	45	9	64	29	47	48	31	.264	.396	.339	376
Away	1153	2851	330	702	131	24	55	1046	313	261	459	43	16	46	24	55	41	25	.246	.367	.310	331
Grass	609	1467	159	372	76	6	27	541	154	131	236	24	5	24	14	29	24	14	.254	.369	.314	172
Turf	1646	4060	534	1037	196	48	79	1566	502	438	636	64	20	86	39	73	65	42	.255	.386	.328	534
April/June	1037	2554	326	640	120	23	46	944	306	294	405	37	12	51	24	53	40	23	.251	.370	.328	322
July/October	1218	2973	367	769	152	31	60	1163	350	275	467	51	13	59	29	49	49	33	.259	.391	.321	384

Montreal Expos

Brock J. Hanke

MONTREAL										
YEAR	1983	1984	1985	1986	1987	1988	1989	1990	1991	1992
W	82	78	84	78	91	81	81	85	71	87
L	80	83	77	83	71	81	81	77	90	75
WPCT	0.506	0.484	0.522	0.484	0.562	0.500	0.500	0.525	0.441	0.537
R	677	593	633	637	741	628	632	662	579	648
RA	646	585	636	688	720	592	630	598	655	581
PWPT	0.523	0.507	0.498	0.462	0.514	0.529	0.502	0.551	0.439	0.554
PythW	85	82	81	75	83	86	81	89	71	90
PythL	77	80	81	87	79	76	81	73	91	72
LUCK	-3	-4	3	3	8	-5	0	-4	0	-3

Defensive Efficiency Record: .7105

Two themes permeate this year's comments on the NL East. One is the obvious: who will rise up to replace the Pirates as champions? The other is related, and a bit more controversial: if these owners can't afford their teams, why aren't they forced to sell them to the people who are willing to buy them and who can afford them? Montreal is at the center of both questions.

Those of you who read last year's SABERMETRIC will remember that I saw the Expos coming. I wrote about the completion and balance of their lineup, and predicted that they would contend if they could come up with just decent pitching. Well, they did, and they did, to the extent that anyone actually contended with the Pirates in 1992. I'm proud of that comment, and of the insight behind it, and would really like to wish the Expos well and join the sportswriters of the world in anointing them as frontrunners for the NL East crown this coming year.

However, I can't do that. I don't evaluate teams on the basis of last year's Won/Lost record. I evaluate them on the basis of the team's structure, and the Expos have lost the balance and depth that they had last year. Frankly, I don't think they're going to win in 1993, although the division is hardly so strong as to prohibit it. And, if I am correct and they don't, it's going to be the questionable money policies of the ownership that did the team in.

Let's review the 1992 Expos. Their projected lineup was:

De Shields	2b
Grissom	cf
Calderon	lf
Walker	rf
Wallach	3b
platoon	1b
Owen	ss
platoon	c

That's not only a strong lineup, it's a complete one. It has two people who get on base well and steal bases well, and they're batting first and second. It has a complete hitter in the three hole. Larry Walker is a fine cleanup man. Tim Wallach was a proven RBI man, with a prototype #5 hitter's profile. If you have first base open, you can always find someone who can bat #6. Spike Owen is a real help hitting seventh, and the Expo

Position	92 Starter	TWAR	93 Starter	TWAR
Catcher	Carter, G.	0.68	Fletcher	0.35
First base	Wallach	1.85	Colbrunn	0.39
Second base	DeShields	4.70	DeShields	4.70
Third base	Barberie	1.21	Berry	0.19
Shortstop	Owen	3.77	Cordero	0.67
Left field	Alou	3.18	Alou	3.18
Center field	Grissom	5.30	Grissom	5.30
Right field	Walker, L.	7.08	Walker, L.	7.08

catchers weren't any worse than anyone else's, except the Pirates.

That lineup can beat you in any type of game. If it's a low-scoring affair, the 1992 Expos could win using the stolen base game or the one-big-homer game. They scored enough runs to win the blowouts and to come from behind. They had a long offensive sequence to pile up those big innings that put away a pitcher who's on the ropes.

In addition, the 1992 Expos had depth, and they had it behind everyone in the lineup. If one of the first two men went down, they had Bret Barberie, a fast man who lives to take walks. If it was Calderon or Walker or Wallach, they had a horde of young hitters, listed as the first base "platoon". Since Barberie could play center field or second or third base (albeit not that well), they were covered from losses in the skill positions. They even had a hot kid shortstop prospect in Wil Cordero. The 1992 Montreal Expo lineup was just plain well put together.

In actual fact, the Expos did not score that many runs. Their total of 648 was only third in the division, and the team Offensive Winning Percentage was only .508. But remember, the team was without Ivan Calderon for almost the entire season, and Bret Barberie had an awful Sophomore Slump. Felipe Alou was able to juggle the kids pretty well in the #3 hole, but he could not use Barberie there to just overpower those pitchers who throw hard, but wildly. And, of course, Tim Wallach was awful too, even after Tom Runnels was fired and Tim was returned to third base. All in all, the Expo lineup took very serious hits, and still was better than average.

But all that is gone now. Ivan Calderon is gone, and Moises Alou just isn't Ivan, not yet. Tim Wallach is gone, too. That wouldn't be such a big deal, except that Calderon is also missing. The combined loss means that the kiddie corps does not have to generate one hot bat among them, but two. That is geometrically harder to do, and I have my doubts. Essentially, John Van Der Wal absolutely must come through. He and Archi Cianfrocco have the only power bat, and Archi can't do anything but hit homers. The Expos really can't expect to pile up runs with Alou batting third and no power bat in the five hole.

And the depth is gone, too. Spike Owen has departed, leaving nothing behind the still-unproven Cordero. So is Tim Wallach, which means that Bret Barberie has to play third base all year with no defense and no late-inning backup. That's not to mention that Barberie has no power, either, and Calderon is gone, and Wallach's loss is from the #5 slot. Bret Barberie. Ahem. That is the Bret Barberie that the Expos Exposed in the expansion draft and promptly lost, isn't it? That does mean that the Expos have no third baseman at all, as well as no #5 hitter, right?

You can see the problems. The Expos lineup, as of this writing, is:

De Shields	2b
Grissom	cf
Alou	lf
Walker	rf
Van Der Wal	1b
Cordero	ss
Tim Spehr	c
no one	3b

If the Expos get lucky, that's the Padres' usual four-man offense, except that it's not really Tony Gwynn, and it's not really Fred McGriff, and it's certainly not a MVP candidate hitting third, and it's not really even the proven mediocrity of Darrin Jackson at #5. The 1992 offense lost Ivan Calderon and watched Tim Wallach collapse and still kept pace with the Cubs, who had Sandberg and Grace both on monster years. This 1993 edition can't hope to do that. It has very little chance of coming up with an OW% over .500, unless it somehow locates the next Gary Sheffield before the signing season is quite over.

Now, let's consider how this happened to the Expos. I mean, they had to know they were on the verge of a title. Every sportswriter in North America is writing about it, after all. So you have to wonder how they could let even one short-term asset depart. One year. That's all. That's all they had to keep Spike Owen for, to insure Wil Cordero. That's all they had to keep Ivan Calderon for, to hit third and provide that hot bat any lineup needs. That's all they had to get out of Tim Wallach, as depth and insurance against Barberie's collapse being for real. It's only one year, and the management knew it, and they couldn't manage to do the absolute obvious. Why?

Well, the answer the ownership gives is "money". Unfortunately, I have reason to doubt them. I doubt that any of the Major League franchises is in any real money trouble under its won name. Not by the time the merchandising is factored in. Now, if the Montreal ownership is experiencing difficulties unrelated to the ballclub, and is leaching money from the Expos to pay off other debts, that's different. That's real money trouble. That's what happened to George Steinbrenner for a while there. But I don't think that's what's going on here.

This is what I think is going on. I think several teams, the Expos among them, are acting like this as a negotiating point against the players' union.

As you doubtless know, the owners are claiming that the teams in the smaller media markets can't afford the current levels of player salaries. The union doubts this. Now, if the Expos manage to find a way to keep all the high-priced players they need to finish off the division in 1993, or if the Pirates were to suddenly find the funds to sign Barry Bonds and Doug Drabek, the owners' case would look pretty silly, wouldn't it? So, those teams absolutely must demonstrate their inability to pay. And thus the Expo sell-off of all free agents plus the salaries of Calderon and Wallach.

For you Montreal fans, this is sad. If the 'Spos had been able to hold off for one more year, or if the Pirates had collapsed one year earlier, you'd have gotten to see a division title. You do deserve to see one, after all the work your farm system has done developing all those hot kids.

What I want to know is at what point this stops being sad for Expo fans and starts being "bad for baseball". I do not mean by this that there is a point where the players should start signing lousy contracts in order to support the Montreal and Pittsburgh franchises. I mean that there is a point where somebody should say, "Look, Montreal ownership. You have this franchise on the grounds that you are legitimately competing in this league for its title. If you can't ever pay for a competitive team, you can't do that. There are people out there who can pay for contending teams who would be more than happy to pay you fair value for your franchise. You've got to sell."

I mean this. In ordinary businesses, if the ownership becomes uncompetitive, it goes bankrupt and loses its company. That's called "free enterprise". It's how our American system of business is supposed to work. But not in baseball. In baseball, all your supposed "competitors" get together with you and attempt to bully your employees into accepting low wages so that you can stay in business, paying whatever salaries you want to pay. And it's all legal.

Why is this legal? Well, it's legal because the owners of baseball teams have this scam that allows them to dodge the laws that our fair country has to prevent this sort of thing. You see, this sort of backroom dealing among competitors, where they actually don't compete with each other, but instead put together a collective monopoly in their field of business, is called a cartel, or "trust". America has laws against doing this; they're called "anti-trust" laws. And baseball has an exemption.

Baseball got this exemption many years ago, when the idea of making business owners play fair with their employees was in its infancy. The reasoning baseball used to get the exemption was that baseball teams are inherently competitive. Since they are all trying to win the pennant, they can't possibly get together into a trust. They have to bid high for the best players, because they're trying to win.

What I'm saying here is that the baseball owners were lying when they said that. They did not then, nor have they ever intended to behave in a competitive fashion. They have always intended to behave like a cartel or trust. And the fans in Pittsburgh are paying for it right now, because the owners of the Pittsburgh franchise cannot be made to go bankrupt and sell to that nice man in Tampa who would have been happy to pay Barry Bonds what he got in San Francisco. Now, you may not have too much sympathy for the fans in Pittsburgh. After all, they have just seen three straight division titles, if no pennants. But Montreal is a different question. Montreal has seen precious few titles. And, in 1993, the fans in Montreal are very likely to pay for the exact same sin. This is wrong, folks, and the players' union is right.

Montreal Expos Home Park Performance Factors

	Outs	Runs	Hits	2b	3b	HR	W	K	SH	SF	HBP	IBB	SB	CS	GDP
Home LH Batters	.937	.860	.978	1.000	.842	1.008	1.005	.970	1.086	1.162	.974	1.409	.950	.949	.732
Home RH Batters	.963	.901	.911	.825	1.016	.872	.979	1.012	.907	.979	.835	1.364	.962	1.234	.717
All Home Batters	.953	.897	.933	.877	.965	.918	.971	.998	.949	.976	.883	1.323	.966	1.089	.738
Opp LH Batters	1.006	.843	.939	.867	.880	.882	1.159	.944	.711	1.042	.685	.958	.950	1.664	1.196
Opp RH Batters	1.008	.876	1.002	.913	.771	1.033	.992	1.042	.998	.973	.947	1.008	.964	1.144	1.053
All Opp Batters	1.012	.889	.990	.891	.820	.978	1.046	1.002	.930	.917	.815	.927	.983	1.159	1.098
All LH Batters	.972	.850	.956	.926	.862	.931	1.086	.956	.919	1.109	.768	1.151	.946	1.223	.857
All RH Batters	.982	.893	.950	.862	.912	.934	.980	1.023	.946	.988	.884	1.147	.967	1.191	.858
All Batters	.981	.895	.961	.886	.891	.948	1.006	.998	.940	.961	.839	1.085	.974	1.122	.882

Conventional Batting Records for Montreal Expos

	G	AB	Run	Hit	2B	3B	HR	TB	RBI	W	K	IW	HB	SB	CS	BRng Eff	GI DP	SH	SF	Avg	Slug	OBP	Runs Ctd
Carter G	95	285	24	62	18	1	5	97	29	33	37	4	2	0	4	.267	4	1	4	.218	.340	.299	30
Wallach	150	537	53	120	29	1	9	178	59	50	90	2	8	2	2	.382	10	0	7	.223	.331	.296	55
DeShields	135	530	82	155	19	8	7	211	56	54	108	4	3	46	15	.496	10	9	3	.292	.398	.359	80
Barberie	111	285	26	66	11	0	1	80	24	47	62	3	8	9	5	.304	4	1	2	.232	.281	.354	33
Owen S	122	386	52	104	16	3	7	147	40	50	30	3	0	9	4	.515	10	4	6	.269	.381	.348	53
Alou	115	341	53	96	28	2	9	155	56	25	46	0	1	16	2	.600	5	5	5	.282	.455	.328	53
Grissom	159	653	99	180	39	6	14	273	66	42	81	6	5	78	13	.569	12	3	4	.276	.418	.322	94
Walker L	143	528	85	159	31	4	23	267	93	41	97	10	6	18	6	.554	9	0	8	.301	.506	.353	96
Cianfrocco	86	232	25	56	5	2	6	83	30	11	66	0	1	3	0	.455	2	1	2	.241	.358	.276	24
Fletcher D	83	222	13	54	10	2	2	74	26	14	28	3	2	0	2	.185	8	2	4	.243	.333	.289	20
Vanderwal	105	213	21	51	8	2	4	75	20	24	36	2	0	3	0	.351	2	0	0	.239	.352	.316	26
Calderon	48	170	19	45	14	2	3	72	24	14	22	1	1	1	2	.478	4	0	1	.265	.424	.323	22
Colbrunn	52	168	12	45	8	0	2	59	18	6	34	1	2	3	2	.333	1	0	4	.268	.351	.294	18
Cordero	45	126	17	38	4	1	2	50	8	9	31	0	1	0	0	.400	2	1	0	.302	.397	.353	18
Foley T	72	115	7	20	3	1	0	25	5	8	21	2	1	3	0	.111	6	3	2	.174	.217	.230	6
Reed D	42	81	10	14	2	0	5	31	10	6	23	2	1	0	0	.286	3	0	0	.173	.383	.239	7
Martinez De	32	74	3	14	0	0	0	14	2	0	20	0	0	0	0	.143	1	10	0	.189	.189	.189	3
Nabholz	32	65	3	8	3	0	0	11	2	1	12	0	0	0	0	.222	3	7	0	.123	.169	.136	1
Cerone	33	63	10	17	4	0	1	24	7	3	5	0	1	1	2	.467	0	1	0	.270	.381	.313	7
Hill K	33	62	10	11	3	1	1	19	4	8	13	0	0	0	0	.500	0	10	0	.177	.306	.271	6
Berry	24	57	5	19	1	0	1	23	4	1	11	0	0	2	1	.273	1	0	0	.333	.404	.345	8
Gardner M	33	50	4	7	0	1	0	9	2	3	18	0	0	0	0	.111	0	8	2	.140	.180	.182	2
Laker	28	46	8	10	3	0	0	13	4	2	14	0	0	1	1	.400	1	0	0	.217	.283	.250	3
Stairs M	13	30	2	5	2	0	0	7	5	7	7	0	0	0	0	.182	0	0	1	.167	.233	.316	3
Barnes B	21	29	1	8	0	0	0	8	1	1	15	0	0	0	0	.000	0	6	0	.276	.276	.300	3
Willard	21	25	0	3	0	0	0	3	1	1	7	0	0	0	0	.000	2	0	0	.120	.120	.154	0
Rojas	68	15	0	1	0	0	0	1	0	0	10	0	0	0	0	.000	1	0	0	.067	.067	.067	0
Lyons S	16	13	2	3	0	0	0	3	1	1	3	0	0	1	2	.000	1	1	0	.231	.231	.286	0
Haney T	7	10	0	3	1	0	0	4	1	0	0	0	0	0	0	.000	1	1	0	.300	.400	.300	1
Haney	10	9	1	2	0	0	0	2	3	0	1	0	0	0	0	01.000	0	1	0	.222	.222	.222	1
Bottenfield	10	8	1	3	0	0	0	3	0	0	3	0	0	0	0	01.000	0	1	0	.375	.375	.375	1
Fassero	70	7	0	1	1	0	0	2	0	0	3	0	0	0	0	.000	0	1	0	.143	.286	.143	0
Sampen	44	6	0	0	0	0	0	0	0	0	5	0	0	0	0	.000	0	1	0	.000	.000	.000	0
Natal	5	6	0	0	0	0	0	0	0	1	1	0	0	0	0	.000	1	0	0	.000	.000	.143	0
Wetteland	67	5	0	1	0	0	0	1	0	0	4	0	0	0	0	.000	0	1	0	.200	.200	.200	0
Bullock	8	5	0	0	0	0	0	0	0	0	1	0	0	0	0	.000	0	0	0	.000	.000	.000	0
Hurst J	3	4	0	0	0	0	0	0	0	0	2	0	0	0	0	.000	0	2	0	.000	.000	.000	0
Goff	3	3	0	0	0	0	0	0	0	0	3	0	0	0	0	.000	0	0	0	.000	.000	.000	0
Valdez	27	3	0	0	0	0	0	0	0	0	0	0	0	0	0	.000	0	0	0	.000	.000	.000	0
Heredia G	7	3	0	0	0	0	0	0	0	0	0	0	0	0	0	.000	0	0	0	.000	.000	.000	0
Krueger	9	3	0	0	0	0	0	0	0	0	2	0	0	0	0	.000	0	1	0	.000	.000	.000	0
Service	5	2	0	0	0	0	0	0	0	0	2	0	0	0	0	.000	0	0	0	.000	.000	.000	0
Risley	1	2	0	0	0	0	0	0	0	0	0	0	0	0	0	.000	0	0	0	.000	.000	.000	0
Simons	7	0	0	0	0	0	0	0	0	0	0	0	0	0	0	.000	0	0	0	.000	.000	.000	0
Landrum B	18	0	0	0	0	0	0	0	0	0	0	0	0	0	0	.000	0	0	0	.000	.000	.000	0
Young P	13	0	0	0	0	0	0	0	0	0	0	0	0	0	0	.000	0	0	0	.000	.000	.000	0
Maysey	2	0	0	0	0	0	0	0	0	0	0	0	0	0	0	.000	0	0	0	.000	.000	.000	0
TOTALS	2233	5477	648	1381	263	37	102	2024	601	463	976	43	43	196	63	.437	103	82	55	.252	.370	.313	655

Sabermetric Batting Records for Montreal Expos

				Ball Park Adjusted						Runs			Run/							
	AB	Run	Hit	2B	3B	HR	RBI	W	SO	Avg	Slug	OBP	Ctd	Outs	27o	OW%	OG	OWAR	DWAR	TWAR
Alou	332	47	91	24	1	8	49	24	47	.274	.425	.319	48	255	5.08	.642	9	2.76	0.42	3.18
Barberie	278	23	63	9	0	0	21	47	62	.227	.259	.349	29	224	3.50	.459	8	0.91	0.30	1.21
Berry	55	4	18	0	0	0	3	0	11	.327	.327	.327	6	38	4.26	.558	1	0.29	-0.10	0.19
Bullock	4	0	0	0	0	0	0	0	0	.000	.000	.000	0	4	0.00	.000	0	-0.05	0.00	-0.05
Calderon	166	16	43	12	1	2	21	13	22	.259	.380	.313	19	128	4.01	.527	5	0.84	0.15	0.99
Carter G	278	21	59	15	0	4	25	32	37	.212	.309	.293	26	229	3.07	.395	8	0.38	0.30	0.68
Cerone	61	8	16	3	0	0	6	2	5	.262	.311	.286	5	47	2.87	.364	2	0.03	-0.06	-0.04
Cianfrocco	226	22	53	4	1	5	26	10	67	.235	.327	.266	20	175	3.09	.398	6	0.31	0.09	0.40
Colbrunn	164	10	43	6	0	1	15	5	34	.262	.317	.283	15	126	3.21	.418	5	0.32	0.08	0.39
Cordero	122	15	36	3	0	1	7	8	31	.295	.344	.338	15	87	4.66	.601	3	0.81	-0.14	0.67
DeShields	512	69	148	17	6	6	54	58	103	.289	.381	.362	74	403	4.96	.631	15	4.19	0.51	4.70
Fletcher D	214	11	51	9	1	1	25	15	26	.238	.304	.286	18	177	2.75	.344	7	-0.04	0.40	0.35
Foley T	111	5	19	2	0	0	4	8	20	.171	.189	.223	5	101	1.34	.110	4	-0.90	0.33	-0.56
Goff	2	0	0	0	0	0	0	0	2	.000	.000	.000	0	2	0.00	.000	0	-0.03	0.00	-0.03
Grissom	638	87	172	33	5	13	57	41	83	.270	.398	.316	86	496	4.68	.604	18	4.66	0.64	5.30
Haney T	8	0	2	0	0	0	0	0	0	.250	.250	.250	1	6	4.50	.585	0	0.05	0.01	0.06
Laker	44	7	9	2	0	0	3	1	14	.205	.250	.222	2	36	1.50	.135	1	-0.29	0.05	-0.23
Lyons S	11	1	2	0	0	0	0	1	2	.182	.182	.250	0	11	0.00	.000	0	-0.14	0.03	-0.11
Natal	5	0	0	0	0	0	0	0	1	.000	.000	.000	0	5	0.00	.000	0	-0.06	-0.03	-0.09
Owen S	377	46	100	14	2	6	35	50	30	.265	.361	.347	50	298	4.53	.588	11	2.63	1.14	3.77
Reed D	79	8	13	1	0	4	8	5	23	.165	.329	.214	5	68	1.99	.215	3	-0.34	0.18	-0.16
Stairs M	28	1	4	1	0	0	4	7	6	.143	.179	.306	2	25	2.16	.245	1	-0.10	-0.01	-0.11
Vanderwal	205	17	48	7	1	3	19	25	34	.234	.322	.317	23	158	3.93	.518	6	0.98	0.22	1.20
Walker L	510	72	152	28	3	21	90	44	92	.298	.488	.353	90	381	6.38	.739	14	5.49	1.59	7.08
Wallach	524	47	114	25	0	8	51	49	92	.218	.311	.290	49	426	3.11	.401	16	0.81	1.04	1.85
Willard	23	0	2	0	0	0	0	1	6	.087	.087	.125	0	22	0.00	.000	1	-0.29	0.00	-0.28
TOTALS	5353	578	1328	232	33	96	539	466	976	.248	.358	.310	616	4318	3.85	.508	160	25.21	7.13	32.34

Pitching Records for Montreal Expos

	ERA	W	L	Pct	G	GS	CG	ShO	GF	Sv	IP	R	ER	H	2B	3B	HR	BB	IW	SO	HB	WP	BK
Martinez De	2.47	16	11	.593	32	32	6	0	0	0	226.1	75	62	172	26	0	12	60	3	147	9	2	0
Hill K	2.68	16	9	.640	33	33	3	3	0	0	218.0	76	65	187	36	5	13	75	4	150	3	11	4
Nabholz	3.32	11	12	.478	32	32	1	1	0	0	195.0	80	72	176	29	7	11	74	2	130	5	5	1
Gardner M	4.36	12	10	.545	33	30	0	0	1	0	179.2	91	87	179	36	3	15	60	2	132	9	2	0
Barnes B	2.97	6	6	.500	21	17	0	0	2	0	100.0	34	33	77	15	0	9	46	1	65	3	1	2
Haney	5.45	2	3	.400	9	6	1	1	2	0	38.0	25	23	40	12	2	6	10	0	27	4	5	1
Hurst J	5.51	1	1	.500	3	3	0	0	0	0	16.1	10	10	18	3	1	1	7	0	4	1	1	0
Risley	1.80	1	0	1.000	1	1	0	0	0	0	5.0	1	1	4	1	0	0	1	0	2	0	0	0
Rojas	1.43	7	1	.875	68	0	0	0	26	10	100.2	17	16	71	15	2	2	34	8	70	2	2	0
Fassero	2.84	8	7	.533	70	0	0	0	22	1	85.2	35	27	81	12	5	1	34	6	63	2	7	1
Wetteland	2.92	4	4	.500	67	0	0	0	58	37	83.1	27	27	64	8	1	6	36	3	99	4	4	0
Sampen	3.13	1	4	.200	44	1	0	0	10	0	63.1	22	22	62	9	1	4	29	6	23	1	1	2
Valdez	2.41	0	0	.000	27	0	0	0	9	0	37.1	12	10	25	5	1	2	12	1	32	0	4	0
Bottenfield	2.23	1	2	.333	10	4	0	0	2	1	32.1	9	8	26	5	1	1	11	1	14	1	0	0
Landrum B	7.20	1	1	.500	18	0	0	0	6	0	20.0	16	16	27	4	1	3	9	2	7	2	0	0
Young P	3.98	0	0	.000	13	0	0	0	6	0	20.1	9	9	18	5	2	0	9	2	11	1	1	0
Krueger	6.75	0	2	.000	9	2	0	0	3	0	17.1	13	13	23	4	1	0	7	0	13	1	1	0
Heredia G	1.84	0	0	.000	7	1	0	0	1	0	14.2	3	3	12	2	0	1	4	0	7	0	0	0
Service	14.14	0	0	.000	5	0	0	0	0	0	7.0	11	11	15	1	1	1	5	0	11	0	0	0
Simons	23.63	0	0	.000	7	0	0	0	2	0	5.1	14	14	15	3	0	3	2	0	6	1	1	0
Maysey	3.86	0	0	.000	2	0	0	0	1	0	2.1	1	1	4	0	0	1	0	0	1	1	0	0
TOTALS	3.25	87	75	.537	511	162	11	5	151	49	1468.0	581	530	1296	231	34	92	525	41	1014	50	48	11

Sabermetric Pitching Records for Montreal Expos

	Adj ERA	W	L	Pct	BFP	Avg	Slg	OBA	RC/G	GDP	SB	CS	PK	PKE	SH	SF	RSup	RSp/G	W	L	Pct
			-Expected-				———Opposing Batters———											Supported				
Barnes B	2.61	8	4	.643	417	.213	.329	.306	3.44	7	14	7	0	4	5	1	42	3.78	8	4	.631
Bottenfield	1.95	2	1	.764	135	.217	.300	.284	3.14	2	3	0	1	0	1	2	17	4.73	2	1	.828
Fassero	2.52	10	5	.659	368	.249	.326	.322	3.90	6	12	2	0	0	5	2	33	3.47	9	6	.607
Gardner M	3.86	10	12	.452	778	.259	.386	.324	4.67	2	29	11	0	4	12	7	87	4.36	11	11	.510
Haney	4.74	2	3	.354	165	.270	.500	.327	5.68	5	6	1	0	1	0	3	21	4.97	2	3	.474
Heredia G	1.23	0	0	.891	55	.250	.354	.302	2.77	3	2	1	1	0	2	1	4	2.45	0	0	.766
Hill K	2.39	17	8	.682	908	.230	.335	.297	3.53	12	30	8	2	2	15	3	109	4.50	19	6	.742
Hurst J	4.41	1	1	.387	72	.281	.406	.361	5.04	0	1	3	0	1	0	0	6	3.31	1	1	.315
Krueger	5.71	1	1	.273	81	.315	.397	.383	6.09	0	1	1	0	1	0	0	9	4.67	1	1	.353
Landrum B	6.30	0	2	.236	95	.325	.506	.404	7.88	2	4	1	0	0	1	0	9	4.05	1	1	.252
Martinez De	2.19	19	8	.720	900	.211	.287	.271	2.59	9	22	17	3	1	12	5	101	4.02	20	7	.734
Maysey	0.00	0	0	.000	12	.364	.636	.417	9.41	0	0	1	0	0	0	0	3	11.60	0	0	.000
Nabholz	2.95	13	10	.585	812	.244	.349	.317	3.76	21	23	6	1	5	7	4	93	4.29	15	8	.633
Risley	0.00	0	0	.000	19	.235	.294	.278	3.26	0	2	0	0	0	1	0	2	3.60	0	0	.000
Rojas	1.25	7	1	.887	399	.199	.269	.271	2.50	7	12	3	0	1	4	2	49	4.38	7	1	.909
Sampen	2.70	3	2	.627	267	.268	.368	.351	4.33	11	11	1	0	0	5	1	21	2.98	2	3	.499
Service	11.57	0	0	.084	41	.417	.583	.488	14.66	0	2	0	0	0	0	0	4	5.14	0	0	.139
Simons	20.25	0	0	.029	35	.500	.900	.529	25.04	0	0	0	0	0	1	1	0	0.00	0	0	.029
Valdez	1.93	2	0	.767	148	.185	.281	.252	2.57	2	9	1	0	0	1	0	6	1.45	1	1	.315
Wetteland	2.59	5	3	.646	347	.213	.306	.304	3.41	4	14	3	0	0	5	1	27	2.92	4	4	.508
Young P	3.54	0	0	.495	85	.247	.370	.329	4.13	2	2	1	0	0	0	2	5	2.21	0	0	.242
TOTALS	2.91	96	66	.592	6139	.238	.343	.309	3.72	95	199	68	8	16	77	35	648	3.97	98	64	.604

Batting 'Splits' Records for Montreal Expos

SPLITS for Barberie

	G	AB	Run	Hit	2B	3B	HR	TB	RBI	W	K	IW	HB	SB	CS	DP	SH	SF	Avg	Slug	OBP	RC
vs LHP	42	67	5	11	3	0	0	14	7	9	18	1	3	3	3	0	1	1	.164	.209	.287	5
vs RHP	102	218	21	55	8	0	1	66	17	38	44	2	5	6	2	4	0	1	.252	.303	.374	28
Home	59	132	14	38	4	0	0	42	15	26	23	2	3	4	2	2	1	1	.288	.318	.414	20
Away	52	153	12	28	7	0	1	38	9	21	39	1	5	5	3	2	0	1	.183	.248	.300	13
Grass	28	93	9	18	3	0	1	24	6	10	27	0	2	3	1	0	0	0	.194	.258	.286	8
Turf	83	192	17	48	8	0	0	56	18	37	35	3	6	6	4	4	1	2	.250	.292	.384	25
April/June	49	119	10	25	4	0	0	29	9	24	33	3	3	3	1	0	1	0	.210	.244	.354	13
July/October	62	166	16	41	7	0	1	51	15	23	29	0	5	6	4	4	0	1	.247	.307	.354	19

SPLITS for DeShields

	G	AB	Run	Hit	2B	3B	HR	TB	RBI	W	K	IW	HB	SB	CS	DP	SH	SF	Avg	Slug	OBP	RC
vs LHP	80	185	31	58	6	2	2	74	21	22	33	0	2	15	5	3	1	2	.314	.400	.389	31
vs RHP	135	345	51	97	13	6	5	137	35	32	75	4	1	31	10	7	8	1	.281	.397	.343	49
Home	71	271	46	75	9	4	1	95	19	23	56	0	2	25	7	6	5	0	.277	.351	.338	34
Away	64	259	36	80	10	4	6	116	37	31	52	4	1	21	8	4	4	3	.309	.448	.381	47
Grass	37	146	20	47	8	2	2	65	24	23	29	4	0	14	6	1	3	2	.322	.445	.409	29
Turf	98	384	62	108	11	6	5	146	32	31	79	0	3	32	9	9	6	1	.281	.380	.339	51
April/June	71	277	44	79	10	5	2	105	22	33	64	1	1	27	10	8	3	3	.285	.379	.360	39
July/October	64	253	38	76	9	3	5	106	34	21	44	3	2	19	5	2	6	0	.300	.419	.359	41

SPLITS for Walker L

	G	AB	Run	Hit	2B	3B	HR	TB	RBI	W	K	IW	HB	SB	CS	DP	SH	SF	Avg	Slug	OBP	RC
vs LHP	98	209	29	66	8	2	10	108	42	10	38	0	4	8	3	3	0	3	.316	.517	.354	38
vs RHP	140	319	56	93	23	2	13	159	51	31	59	10	2	10	3	6	0	5	.292	.498	.353	57
Home	73	257	47	73	12	3	13	130	43	23	47	5	5	5	4	5	0	4	.284	.506	.349	45
Away	70	271	38	86	19	1	10	137	50	18	50	5	1	13	2	4	0	4	.317	.506	.357	51
Grass	40	163	25	52	11	1	8	89	30	9	34	2	1	11	1	4	0	1	.319	.546	.356	32
Turf	103	365	60	107	20	3	15	178	63	32	63	8	5	7	5	5	0	7	.293	.488	.352	64
April/June	63	224	36	63	11	1	14	118	44	21	45	3	2	8	4	3	0	4	.281	.527	.343	41
July/October	80	304	49	96	20	3	9	149	49	20	52	7	4	10	2	6	0	4	.316	.490	.361	55

SPLITS for Montreal Expos (all batters except pitchers)

	G	AB	Run	Hit	2B	3B	HR	TB	RBI	W	K	IW	HB	SB	CS	DP	SH	SF	Avg	Slug	OBP	RC
vs LHP	913	1857	241	498	95	15	42	749	223	155	306	11	16	71	23	27	27	22	.268	.403	.326	255
vs RHP	1763	3620	407	883	168	22	60	1275	378	308	670	32	27	125	40	76	55	33	.244	.352	.305	401
Home	1151	2624	331	673	136	17	50	993	306	218	438	14	22	91	26	65	40	27	.256	.378	.316	319
Away	1082	2853	317	708	127	20	52	1031	295	245	538	29	21	105	37	38	42	28	.248	.361	.310	336
Grass	560	1474	166	372	63	12	26	537	156	132	288	17	13	63	22	22	25	11	.252	.364	.317	179
Turf	1673	4003	482	1009	200	25	76	1487	445	331	688	26	30	133	41	81	57	44	.252	.371	.311	476
April/June	978	2440	311	611	125	15	52	922	289	221	446	13	18	94	31	48	35	26	.250	.378	.314	300
July/October	1255	3037	337	770	138	22	50	1102	312	242	530	30	25	102	32	55	47	29	.254	.363	.311	355

St. Louis Cardinals

Brock J. Hanke

ST. LOUIS										
YEAR	1983	1984	1985	1986	1987	1988	1989	1990	1991	1992
W	79	84	101	79	95	76	86	70	84	83
L	83	78	61	82	67	86	76	92	78	79
WPCT	0.488	0.519	0.623	0.491	0.586	0.469	0.531	0.432	0.519	0.512
R	679	652	747	601	798	578	632	599	651	631
RA	710	645	572	611	693	633	608	698	648	604
PWPT	0.478	0.505	0.63	0.492	0.57	0.455	0.519	0.424	0.502	0.522
PythW	77	82	102	80	92	74	84	69	81	85
PythL	85	80	60	82	70	88	78	93	81	77
LUCK	2	2	-1	-1	3	2	2	1	3	-2

Defensive Efficiency Record: .7145

Several years ago, in 1985 to be exact, Bill James wrote one of the essays that most served to cement his reputation. It was an essay about the Cardinals, in the 1985 ABSTRACT, which covered the 1984 season, just as we do here in the SABERMETRIC. What the essay said was that the St. Louis team, coming off a mediocre 84-78 season, had every chance of winning the NL East division. This, you will recall, was a team that had just lost Bruce Sutter, and had traded away Keith Hernandez and George Hendrick. It had not picked up Jack Clark, as of the writing of the essay. Most people thought the 84-78 of 1984 was an unreachable goal. Well, the Cardinals replaced Sutter with the famous Committee Bullpen, and replaced David Green with Jack Clark, and proceeded to win the National League pennant. Bill James got a lot of press for the "prediction" that the Cards would win. (Bill did not predict that; he just said that he saw no reason that it should be impossible.)

In that vein, and fully aware of the current reputation of the Montreal Expos, and proud as I am of the fact that I was the first analyst to see the Expos coming, I have this to say: there is no reason that the St. Louis Cardinals cannot win the NL East in 1993. In fact, they should be established as the favorites to do this.

Here is a summary of my reasoning. The Pirates have sold off too much to repeat. The Expos have sold off too much to succeed. The Mets have suffered a death in the family (the farm system) and no longer have the star players needed to dominate. The Cubs have no more offense than they had last year, and one fewer superstar pitcher. The Phillies are one superstar and a middle infield away from contention. The Cardinals, on the other hand, are supposed to be in need of a first baseman who can bat cleanup. However, they in fact have so much talent in the critical skill positions that they can afford to bat their first baseman seventh if they need to do so. Their farm system has just kicked out a phenomenal crop of players, and they're loaded with bats. They have nothing like the pitching staff of the Braves, but the Braves are not in their division. In the East, they're the best, right now and on paper.

Here is the lineup I think the Cardinals will probably put together. I could be wrong, but this is my current guess. Within the chart, the third entry for a player is his ranking at his position in 1992. If it's in parentheses, he was not a full-time player in 1992, and it's what I think his ranking will be in 1993. The fourth entry is the same, except that it's his ranking within the NL East, instead of the whole league.

Position	92 Starter	TWAR	93 Starter	TWAR
Catcher	Pagnozzi	1.75	Pagnozzi	1.75
First base	Galarraga	1.26	Brewer	0.94
			Canseco, O.	0.18
Second base	Alicea	2.17	Pena, G.	3.53
Third base	Zeile	3.70	Zeile	3.70
Shortstop	Smith, O.	7.20	Smith, O.	7.20
Left field	Gilkey	4.38	Gilkey	4.38
Center field	Lankford	8.29	Lankford	8.29
Right field	Jose	5.65	Jose	5.65

Bernard Gilkey	lf	3rd	1st
Ozzie Smith	ss	2nd	1st
Ray Lankford	cf	1st	1st
Geronimo Pena	2b	(2nd)	(2nd)
Felix Jose	rf	3rd	2nd
Todd Zeile	3b	6th	3rd
Ozzie Canseco	1b	(6th)	(3rd)
Tom Pagnozzi	c	5th	4th

Looking at this, you can see three things very quickly. First, that's a lot of good ballplayers out there. Within the division, the first five hitters are either #1 or #2. Todd Zeile is #3 only because he had a illness-riddled off season; he is really a better player than Steve Buechele, though not Dave Hollins.

Second, a lot depends on my predictions regarding Geronimo Pena. But not everything. I'm not willing to back down if you tell me that Canseco or Zeile is going to have to bat cleanup. One of the three of them is going to be able to do the job. And, at second base, Pena is backed up by Jose Oquendo and Luis Alicea. Both of them would be in the top three at this spot in this division, behind Ryne Sandberg and Delino De Shields. What makes my predictions regarding Pena unusual among analysts is that I think he's a better player than DeShields is. I'll bother to defend that assertion later.

Third, there is some slack value here. Todd Zeile was way off in 1992. If you pencil him in for the .280 with 15 homers that he's most likely to hit, you see that he's one hell of a #6 bat. If you just pencil him in for .270 and 13, he's still hot in that slot. And Ozzie Canseco is just more hitter than you expect to see in anyone's seventh position.

In addition, there's depth behind that lineup. The aforementioned Oquendo and Alicea are surely the best backup middle infield anyone's had in years, and both of them can play third. If Canseco should falter, the Cardinals have Rod Brewer to back him up, and Tracy Woodson in back of Brewer. Woodson's no prize first baseman, but we're talking about a #7 hitter here. The only real problem is at catcher, where Tom Pagnozzi has proven unable to handle 130 games without falling apart in August, and Hector Villanueva is the only backup. Still, who has top catching any more? Only the Pirates. Right now, there is no true backup for Ray Lankford in center, but Bernard Gilkey could play if he had to, and there are backups for left. Still, a season injury to Lankford is the biggest threat by far.

The pitching rotation looks as follows, again with rankings. For the division rankings, I deleted the pitchers who have moved out of the division, and added Jose Guzman.

Bob Tewksbury	3rd	2nd
Rheal Cormier	27th	12th
Donovan Osborne	34th	16th
Omar Olivares	38th	19th
Joe Magrane	-	-

This is not nearly as good as the offense, but it should still serve. I don't expect Cormier, Osborne, and Olivares to finish in a clump again in 1993, but I expect them to turn in about the same .500 performance overall. The problem here is depth. Magrane is a question mark, coming off a truly severe injury. The #5 starter in 1992 was Mark Clark, and he was not ready. The rest of the starters got deleted, leaving Rene Arocha as the real rotation backup. Arocha is actually being groomed as a reliever, and the Cards could use a bulk starter here.

The bullpen is good and deep. Lee Smith is not what he once was, but he's still in the top third of NL closers. Actually, his 1992 ranking was 8th, Rolaids Award or no; 4th in the division. But he is reliable, and Mike Perez was wonderful behind him, and Arocha is going to be on the roster. The Cards have actually bothered to shore this crew up some, with Rob Murphy and Les Lancaster. They're bulk, but bulk is all the Cardinals need.

On balance, this pitching staff is as good as any in the division, though not in a class with the Braves or the Reds or - gulp - the Astros. The Expos have two top starters, but the Cards have a better 3-5 grouping. Rojas and Wetteland are a wash against Perez and Smith, but the Cards have more bulk. With David Cone gone, Bret Saberhagen and John Franco off injuries, Doc Gooden worn down to mortality, and little depth, the Mets are no better off. The Pirates have no real bullpen, and a rotation of Zane Smith, Randy Tomlin, Tim Wakefield and two warm bodies. The Cubs and Phillies you doubtless know about.

Let's talk about Geronimo Pena. After all, I promised. Bill James has a 1993 prediction for Pena in the Stats, Inc. 1993 MAJOR LEAGUE HANDBOOK. This is a first rate reference book, and Bill James is, well, Bill James, but I disagree on this one. Bill has Geronimo down for a .258 Batting Average, with some line drive power and some on-base skills. But the predicted On-Base Percentage is only .342, while the Slugging Percentage is .385. Compared to Delino DeShields, Pena is predicted to have just a tad more power, but to not get on base as much, by the difference in predicted Batting Average.

The reason that I don't agree with the prediction is that I think Geronimo

Pena got all messed up in 1991, which produced an unnaturally bad season. His current year, 1992, is completely out of line with the prediction. In 1992, Geronimo hit .305, with 7 Home Runs in only 203 At-Bats. Bill predicts Pena for only 11 homers in 496 AB. Geronimo also hit 12 doubles, and Bill has him down for only 20 in those 496 trips. The reason for this is that Bill is factoring in 1991. That year, Pena only hit .243, with 5 homers in 185 AB. this was consistent with his cup of coffee in 1990, but not with 1992. Which are we to believe. Bill believes an average, which is hard to argue with.

But 1991 was an odd year for Geronimo. He did not belong on the Major League roster at all. By this I do not mean that he could not play well enough for the big time; he could. But he was backed up behind Jose Oquendo, and was not going to get a chance to play. The only reason he was on the roster was that he was out of options. The playing time he got was heavily weighted towards pinch-hitting and pinch-running (he was Oquendo's designated base stealer late in the year). The irregularity of the assignment cannot have helped Geronimo, not to mention the frustration of knowing he could play and not getting a chance.

I write that year off, and go with the 1992 campaign, especially as that year is much more in line with Pena's minor league equivalencies and Peak Projections. In fact, when I did the TOP 150 MINOR LEAGUE PROSPECTS book with Rob Rains in 1990, I had Pena down for a Peak Prediction of .292, with 16-homer/30-double power. That would be for the 1994 season, but it's in line with the 1992. It's not in line with the 1991.

In any case, as I said earlier, the Cards do not have to have Pena to have a top offense. A quick look at the NL East Division sheets show what's going on. The Cardinals only scored 631 runs, which was third best in the league, behind Pittsburgh, Philly, and Montreal. Ballpark adjustment produces a Runs total in the Sabermetric batting line of 647, which is better than the Expos, with the gas taken out of the Montreal ballpark. But the real story is in the Runs Created column. There the Cards are credited with 684 RC, which passes the Expos and almost catches the Phillies. None of the other RC totals is anything like that much greater than the actual.

The reason for this disparity of 53 runs was the Cardinal cleanup spot. Even into September that was one of the ten worst batting order spots in the National League. The rest, of course, were teams' 8th and 7th slots. That collapse of the vital cleanup batter, fueled by the Cards' injury problems and the real ability of Andres Galarraga, caused the Cardinal offense to perform very inefficiently. In 1993, that's not going to happen, unless everyone gets hurt again. With the Pirates gone, the Cards will have as much offense as anyone, and probably more. After all, they aren't very likely to have Pena and Oquendo both hurt for most of the year. Nor are they going to be waiting out Galarraga's problems with the bat. No, they're going to have Pena for most of the year, and Oquendo for the rest. They're going to have a couple of first basemen who will both hit better than Andres did. Todd Zeile is very likely to recover to his previous cruising speed; his problems last year seem to have been caused by illness. That means that the Cards will have three options for cleanup, and the two who don't bat there will hit 6th and 7th. An offense that is good enough to bat Todd Zeile 6th and Ozzie Canseco 7th is going to score some runs.

Another way of looking at this is to run a Contender Profile on the Cardinals, from the Phillie essay. That profile considers a team to have 13 starters: the eight position players, the four regular pitchers and the closer. It classifies these people into superstars, stars, championship-quality players, bulk players and holes. Then it takes a look at the pinch hitting bench, the skill position bench and the bullpen.

The criterion for a Superstar player is that he regularly finishes in the top two at his position in his league. The Cards have one of these for sure in Ozzie Smith. Last year, Ray Lankford was in that class, but it's his first year. Bob Tewksbury was also that good, and it's his second year at it. Let's give Ray and Bob half credit each, and say the Cards have two superstars.

Stars are the people who might finish in the top two, but who usually finish 3-5. That describes Felix Jose, and it also describes the one of Tewksbury and Lankford that we don't count as a superstar. Let's say that, between Bernard Gilkey's 1992 and Geronimo Pena's 1992 and Lee Smith's overall reputation, we have two more stars out of three. That's four stars and two superstars.

Todd Zeile and Tom Pagnozzi have to be considered as championship-quality players at least. Joe Magrane has won an ERA title, and the other three finished in a clump right around championship quality. Let's say that at least two of the pitchers will be this good, as well as Lee Smith, for a total of five.

Between Ozzie Canseco and Rod Brewer, the Cardinals will come up with at least bulk play at first base. The two pitchers who aren't championship quality must contend with Rene Arocha for their jobs. Since we're only considering the #4 pitcher as a starter here, the question is whether these three pitchers can produce one bulk starter. Of course, that will happen. That's the other two starting spots, which produces a profile of

2 superstars
4 stars
5 championship quality
2 bulk
0 holes.

The Philly essay claims that the profile of 1992's four postseason teams was 2 / 5 / 4 / 1 / 1. The Cards should, at a conservative estimate, be 2

/ 4 / 5 / 2 / 0. They fit the starter profile of a contending team going to the postseason.

As for pinch hitting, the Cardinal pinch hitters will consist of Rob Brewer, Tracy Woodson, Gerald Perry, Jose Oquendo and Luis Alicea. Perry is the worst of these, and he's a professional pinch hitter.

Oquendo and Alicea also man the skill positions. Oquendo, in particular, can play top glove shortstop, and everywhere else as well. Alicea plays all three infield spots and the outfield. Tim Jones will be carried as insurance, and he can use a glove, although he cannot hit any more. The only skill spots that are not covered well are center field (Gilkey would move over if Lankford got hurt) and catcher, where Hector Villanueva ain't great, but he's as good as anyone else but the Bucs have got.

The bullpen will feature either Rene Arocha, or one of the cluster, or Joe Magrane in middle relief. Mike Perez is a fine setup man. Rob Murphy and Les Lancaster are there for bulk. The Cards are covered.

In sum, the Cardinals fit the profile of a contending team, and no one else in the division does, after the Expo fire sale. The only thing that could really hurt them is a season injury to Lankford early. That won't kill the offense, but Bernard Gilkey is not really a center fielder. Given that as the only weakness, the Cards should be favored to win. Remember, you read it here first, in the SABERMETRIC.

As a final note, I want to say that I am not pleased to be writing this. For the last couple of years - hell, since the times of Richard Nixon - the Cardinals have been in the forefront of the "we don't sign free agents no matter how much money we have" crowd of owners. They've known they needed a first baseman for two years now, and have tried only the cheapest attempts at solving the problem. It's cost them Ken Hill, and they deserve that. For the Pirates and Expos to just hand this management a division title they have not earned burns my ass. But I have to call it as I see it. And that's they way it is.

St. Louis Cardinals Home Park Performance Factors	Outs	Runs	Hits	2b	3b	HR	W	K	SH	SF	HBP	IBB	SB	CS	GDP
Home LH Batters	1.037	1.039	.993	1.063	.866	.912	1.041	1.025	.997	.877	1.215	.789	1.056	1.226	.803
Home RH Batters	.959	.942	.970	1.018	.990	.830	.931	.960	.978	1.147	.832	.767	.844	1.165	.854
All Home Batters	.997	.965	.977	1.059	.889	.866	.981	.998	1.035	1.054	.944	.797	.905	1.140	.897
Opp LH Batters	1.094	1.055	1.102	.952	1.224	1.213	1.024	1.066	1.002	1.196	.905	1.086	1.193	.948	.935
Opp RH Batters	1.031	1.124	1.093	1.159	1.574	1.148	1.077	1.074	1.050	1.340	.857	.950	.955	1.257	1.066
All Opp Batters	1.036	1.087	1.079	1.028	1.318	1.175	1.051	1.050	1.046	1.194	.835	.976	.987	1.058	1.016
All LH Batters	1.067	1.049	1.051	.992	1.066	1.074	1.035	1.051	1.008	1.058	1.033	.930	1.124	1.160	.880
All RH Batters	.996	1.036	1.034	1.092	1.253	.991	1.007	1.021	1.010	1.247	.836	.853	.904	1.241	.963
All Batters	1.016	1.026	1.028	1.042	1.066	1.019	1.017	1.026	1.037	1.125	.877	.880	.947	1.144	.958

Conventional Batting Records for St. Louis Cardinals

	G	AB	Run	Hit	2B	3B	HR	TB	RBI	W	K	IW	HB	SB	CS	BRng Eff	GI DP	SH	SF	Avg	Slug	OBP	Runs Ctd
Pagnozzi	139	485	33	121	26	3	7	174	44	28	64	9	1	2	5	.292	15	6	3	.249	.359	.290	47
Galarraga	95	325	38	79	14	2	10	127	39	11	69	0	8	5	4	.531	8	0	3	.243	.391	.282	34
Alicea	85	265	26	65	9	11	2	102	32	27	40	1	4	2	5	.333	5	2	4	.245	.385	.320	33
Zeile	126	439	51	113	18	4	7	160	48	68	70	4	0	7	10	.327	11	0	7	.257	.364	.352	58
Smith O	132	518	73	153	20	2	0	177	31	59	34	4	0	43	9	.417	11	12	1	.295	.342	.367	72
Gilkey	131	384	56	116	19	4	7	164	43	39	52	1	1	18	12	.506	5	3	4	.302	.427	.364	60
Lankford	153	598	87	175	40	6	20	287	86	72	147	6	5	42	24	.528	6	2	5	.293	.480	.371	108
Jose	131	509	62	150	22	3	14	220	75	40	100	8	1	28	12	.417	9	0	1	.295	.432	.347	76

	G	AB	Run	Hit	2B	3B	HR	TB	RBI	W	K	IW	HB	SB	CS	BRng Eff	GI DP	SH	SF	Avg	Slug	OBP	Runs Ctd
Thompson M	109	208	31	61	9	1	4	84	17	16	39	3	2	18	6	.400	3	0	0	.293	.404	.350	30
Pena G	62	203	31	62	12	1	7	97	31	24	37	0	5	13	8	.537	1	0	4	.305	.478	.386	39
Jordan B	55	193	17	40	9	4	5	72	22	10	48	1	1	7	2	.533	6	0	0	.207	.373	.250	17
Guerrero	43	146	10	32	6	1	1	43	16	11	25	3	0	2	2	.200	4	0	2	.219	.295	.270	11
Jones Tim	67	145	9	29	4	0	0	33	3	11	29	1	0	5	2	.316	1	2	0	.200	.228	.256	9
Perry G	87	143	13	34	8	0	1	45	18	15	23	4	1	3	6	.611	3	0	2	.238	.315	.311	13
Woodson	31	114	9	35	8	0	1	46	22	3	10	0	1	0	0	.333	1	1	0	.307	.404	.331	15
Wilson C	61	106	6	33	6	0	0	39	13	10	18	2	0	1	2	.556	4	2	1	.311	.368	.368	14
Gedman	41	105	5	23	4	0	1	30	8	11	22	1	0	0	0	.000	0	0	1	.219	.286	.291	10
Brewer R	29	103	11	31	6	0	0	37	10	8	12	0	1	0	1	.357	1	0	1	.301	.359	.354	13
Hudler	61	98	17	24	4	0	3	37	5	2	23	0	1	2	6	.476	0	1	1	.245	.378	.265	8
Tewksbury	33	70	4	6	1	0	0	7	3	4	29	0	0	0	0	.000	1	6	0	.086	.100	.135	1
Olivares	36	68	7	16	1	0	1	20	4	1	19	0	0	0	0	.444	0	3	0	.235	.294	.246	5
Carr	22	64	8	14	3	0	0	17	3	9	6	0	0	10	2	.350	0	3	0	.219	.266	.315	7
Cormier	31	59	3	6	2	0	0	8	2	0	13	0	0	0	0	.500	0	10	0	.102	.136	.102	1
Osborne	34	58	4	7	0	1	0	9	0	0	21	0	0	0	0	.400	0	2	0	.121	.155	.121	1
Clark M	20	36	0	5	0	0	0	5	1	0	18	0	0	0	0	.000	0	3	0	.139	.139	.139	1
Oquendo	14	35	3	9	3	1	0	14	3	5	3	1	0	0	0	.500	0	0	0	.257	.400	.350	5
Royer	13	31	6	10	2	0	2	18	9	1	4	0	0	0	0	.667	0	0	1	.323	.581	.333	6
Canseco O	9	29	7	8	5	0	0	13	3	7	4	0	0	0	0	.538	1	0	0	.276	.448	.417	6
DeLeon J	29	21	2	1	0	0	0	1	0	2	8	0	0	0	0	.000	0	4	0	.048	.048	.130	0
Figueroa	12	11	1	2	1	0	0	3	4	1	2	0	0	0	0	.000	0	0	0	.182	.273	.250	1
Magrane	5	10	1	2	0	0	1	5	2	0	2	0	0	0	0	.000	0	1	0	.200	.500	.200	1
Agosto	22	4	0	0	0	0	0	0	0	0	2	0	0	0	0	.000	0	0	0	.000	.000	.000	0
Perez Mk	77	4	0	0	0	0	0	0	0	0	2	0	0	0	0	.000	1	2	0	.000	.000	.000	0
Carpenter	73	3	0	1	0	0	0	1	2	0	1	0	0	0	0	.000	0	1	0	.333	.333	.333	0
Smith B	13	3	0	0	0	0	0	0	0	0	0	0	0	0	0	.000	0	1	0	.000	.000	.000	0
DiPino	9	1	0	1	0	0	0	1	0	0	0	0	0	0	0	.000	0	0	0	1.000	1.000	1.000	1
Worrell	67	0	0	0	0	0	0	0	0	0	0	0	0	0	0	.000	0	0	0	.000	.000	.000	0
Smith Le	70	0	0	0	0	0	0	0	0	0	0	0	0	0	0	.000	0	0	0	.000	.000	.000	0
McClure	71	0	0	0	0	0	0	0	0	0	0	0	0	0	0	.000	0	0	0	.000	.000	.000	0
TOTALS	2298	5594	631	1464	262	44	94	2096	599	495	996	49	32	208	118	.418	97	68	41	.262	.375	.323	684

Sabermetric Batting Records for St. Louis Cardinals

	Ball Park Adjusted								Runs		Run/									
	AB	Run	Hit	2B	3B	HR	RBI	W	SO	Avg	Slug	OBP	Ctd	Outs	27o	OW%	OG	OWAR	DWAR	TWAR
Alicea	269	26	66	9	12	2	32	27	40	.245	.390	.317	33	218	4.09	.535	8	1.49	0.68	2.17
Brewer R	108	11	32	6	0	0	10	8	12	.296	.352	.347	14	78	4.85	.618	3	0.77	0.17	0.94
Canseco O	28	7	8	5	0	0	3	7	4	.286	.464	.429	6	20	8.10	.819	1	0.35	-0.02	0.32
Carr	64	8	14	3	0	0	3	9	6	.219	.266	.315	7	55	3.44	.448	2	0.20	0.19	0.39
Figueroa	10	1	2	1	0	0	4	1	2	.200	.300	.273	1	8	3.38	.439	0	0.03	0.01	0.04
Galarraga	325	39	81	15	2	9	39	11	70	.249	.391	.284	34	258	3.56	.466	10	1.10	0.16	1.26
Gedman	111	5	24	4	0	1	8	11	22	.216	.279	.285	10	88	3.07	.393	3	0.14	-0.06	0.08
Gilkey	385	57	119	20	5	6	43	39	52	.309	.434	.369	61	291	5.66	.688	11	3.64	0.74	4.38
Guerrero	145	10	32	6	1	0	16	11	25	.221	.276	.272	11	120	2.47	.297	4	-0.24	-0.04	-0.28
Hudler	97	17	24	4	0	2	5	2	23	.247	.351	.260	7	82	2.30	.268	3	-0.25	0.10	-0.15
Jones Tim	153	9	30	4	0	0	3	11	30	.196	.222	.250	9	126	1.93	.204	5	-0.68	0.52	-0.16
Jordan B	193	17	41	9	5	4	22	10	48	.212	.373	.251	10	159	2.89	.365	6	0.09	0.42	0.50
Jose	518	63	154	22	3	14	76	40	102	.297	.432	.347	77	386	5.39	.666	14	4.52	1.13	5.65
Lankford	633	91	183	40	6	21	89	74	153	.289	.471	.365	111	487	6.15	.723	18	6.72	1.57	8.29
Oquendo	35	3	9	3	1	0	3	5	3	.257	.400	.350	5	26	5.19	.650	1	0.29	0.16	0.44
Pagnozzi	486	34	124	28	3	6	44	28	65	.255	.362	.294	48	391	3.31	.431	14	1.17	0.59	1.75
Pena G	206	31	63	12	1	7	31	24	37	.306	.476	.382	40	155	6.97	.770	6	2.41	1.12	3.53
Perry G	151	13	35	8	0	1	18	15	24	.232	.305	.302	13	126	2.79	.348	5	-0.01	-0.01	-0.02
Royer	30	6	10	2	0	1	9	1	4	.333	.500	.344	5	21	6.43	.740	1	0.30	0.01	0.31
Smith O	527	74	157	20	2	0	31	59	34	.298	.343	.368	74	402	4.97	.630	15	4.16	3.04	7.20
Thompson M	219	32	63	9	1	4	17	16	40	.288	.393	.342	31	164	5.10	.642	6	1.77	0.04	1.82
Wilson C	106	6	34	6	0	0	13	10	18	.321	.377	.376	18	80	4.72	.606	3	0.76	0.14	0.90
Woodson	114	9	36	8	0	0	22	3	10	.316	.386	.333	15	79	5.13	.644	3	0.86	0.02	0.88
Zeile	440	52	116	19	5	6	49	68	71	.264	.370	.357	59	354	4.50	.582	13	3.04	0.66	3.70
TOTALS	5701	647	1504	273	48	95	612	502	1020	.264	.379	.324	702	4534	4.18	.546	168	32.92	11.30	44.22

Pitching Records for St. Louis Cardinals

	ERA	W	L	Pct	G	GS	CG	ShO	GF	Sv	IP	R	ER	H	2B	3B	HR	BB	IW	SO	HB	WP	BK
Tewksbury	2.16	16	5	.762	33	32	5	0	1	0	233.0	63	56	217	39	4	15	20	0	91	3	2	0
Olivares	3.84	9	9	.500	32	30	1	0	1	0	197.0	84	84	189	35	3	20	63	5	124	4	2	0
Cormier	3.68	10	10	.500	31	30	3	0	1	0	186.0	83	76	194	34	3	15	33	2	117	5	4	2
Osborne	3.77	11	9	.550	34	29	0	0	2	0	179.0	91	75	193	39	5	14	38	2	104	2	6	0
Clark M	4.45	3	10	.231	20	20	1	1	0	0	113.1	59	56	117	18	4	12	36	2	44	0	4	0
DeLeon J	4.57	2	7	.222	29	15	0	0	3	0	102.1	56	52	95	25	4	7	43	1	72	2	3	0
Magrane	4.02	1	2	.333	5	5	0	0	0	0	31.1	15	14	34	3	2	2	15	0	20	2	4	0
Perez Mk	1.84	9	3	.750	77	0	0	0	22	0	93.0	23	19	70	6	2	4	32	9	46	1	4	0
Carpenter	2.97	5	4	.556	73	0	0	0	21	1	88.0	29	29	69	13	2	10	27	8	46	4	5	0
Smith Le	3.12	4	9	.308	70	0	0	0	55	43	75.0	28	26	62	8	4	4	26	4	60	0	2	0
Worrell	2.11	5	3	.625	67	0	0	0	14	3	64.0	15	15	45	7	0	4	25	5	64	1	1	1
McClure	3.17	2	2	.500	71	0	0	0	16	0	54.0	21	19	52	13	0	6	25	5	24	2	1	0
Agosto	6.25	2	4	.333	22	0	0	0	10	0	31.2	24	22	39	8	1	2	9	2	13	3	2	0
Smith B	4.64	4	2	.667	13	1	0	0	3	0	21.1	11	11	20	2	0	3	5	1	9	3	1	0
DiPino	1.64	0	0	.000	9	0	0	0	3	0	11.0	2	2	9	2	0	0	3	0	8	0	0	0
TOTALS	3.38	83	79	.512	586	162	10	1	152	47	1480.0	604	556	1405	252	34	118	400	46	842	32	41	3

Sabermetric Pitching Records for St. Louis Cardinals

	Adj ERA	Expected W	Expected L	Pct	BFP	Avg	Slg	OBA	RC/G	GDP	SB	CS	PK	PKE	SH	SF	RSup	RSp/G	W	L	Pct
Agosto	6.25	1	5	.239	143	.312	.440	.364	5.75	5	3	0	0	0	3	3	16	4.55	2	4	.302
Carpenter	2.97	5	4	.583	355	.220	.371	.288	3.52	7	11	3	0	0	8	3	54	5.52	7	2	.739
Clark M	4.53	5	8	.375	488	.265	.406	.318	4.72	8	17	2	2	1	7	4	40	3.18	4	9	.287
Cormier	3.73	9	11	.469	772	.269	.387	.305	3.96	19	11	4	0	1	11	3	81	3.92	9	11	.475
DeLeon J	4.66	3	6	.361	443	.245	.385	.320	4.53	4	12	4	0	0	5	6	40	3.52	3	6	.317
DiPino	1.64	0	0	.821	45	.220	.268	.273	2.70	0	0	0	0	0	1	0	7	5.73	0	0	.909
Magrane	4.02	1	2	.432	143	.279	.385	.364	5.26	2	2	1	0	0	3	1	7	2.01	1	2	.169
McClure	3.17	2	2	.550	230	.261	.417	.345	4.63	8	1	2	1	1	1	3	29	4.83	3	1	.655
Olivares	3.93	8	10	.443	818	.257	.394	.316	4.07	16	11	13	2	1	8	7	85	3.88	8	10	.444
Osborne	3.82	9	11	.457	754	.275	.404	.312	4.35	18	15	3	0	1	7	4	72	3.62	8	12	.423
Perez Mk	1.84	9	3	.784	377	.210	.276	.278	2.66	6	5	2	1	0	7	4	46	4.45	10	2	.827
Smith B	4.64	2	4	.363	91	.247	.383	.315	4.37	2	4	0	0	0	2	0	20	8.44	4	2	.730
Smith Le	3.12	7	6	.558	310	.221	.320	.286	3.36	4	12	1	0	1	2	1	7	0.84	1	12	.056
Tewksbury	2.20	15	6	.717	915	.248	.353	.265	2.91	25	7	4	0	0	9	7	106	4.09	16	5	.738
Worrell	2.11	6	2	.734	256	.198	.282	.281	2.96	3	13	0	0	0	3	0	21	2.95	5	3	.615
TOTALS	3.47	82	80	.505	6140	.252	.372	.303	3.84	127	124	39	6	6	77	46	631	3.84	81	81	.500

Batting 'Splits' Records for St. Louis Cardinals

SPLITS for Lankford

	G	AB	Run	Hit	2B	3B	HR	TB	RBI	W	K	IW	HB	SB	CS	DP	SH	SF	Avg	Slug	OBP	RC
vs LHP	98	216	28	55	11	2	4	82	32	27	61	0	4	13	6	2	2	2	.255	.380	.345	31
vs RHP	151	382	59	120	29	4	16	205	54	45	86	6	1	29	18	4	0	3	.314	.537	.385	78
Home	78	314	45	97	18	3	13	160	54	35	70	6	0	21	15	2	0	3	.309	.510	.375	59
Away	75	284	42	78	22	3	7	127	32	37	77	0	5	21	9	4	2	2	.275	.447	.366	49
Grass	39	151	22	44	13	2	3	70	17	20	39	0	1	9	6	3	0	1	.291	.464	.376	26
Turf	114	447	65	131	27	4	17	217	69	52	108	6	4	33	18	3	2	4	.293	.485	.369	82
April/June	73	295	42	84	15	4	8	131	30	37	69	3	3	24	11	2	0	1	.285	.444	.369	51
July/October	80	303	45	91	25	2	12	156	56	35	78	3	2	18	13	4	2	4	.300	.515	.372	57

SPLITS for St. Louis Cardinals (all batters except pitchers)

	G	AB	Run	Hit	2B	3B	HR	TB	RBI	W	K	IW	HB	SB	CS	DP	SH	SF	Avg	Slug	OBP	RC
vs LHP	945	1903	224	535	94	13	36	763	215	171	323	20	10	70	41	36	25	14	.281	.401	.341	261
vs RHP	1720	3691	407	929	168	31	58	1333	384	324	673	29	22	138	77	61	43	27	.252	.361	.314	424
Home	1159	2786	328	746	119	26	55	1082	312	249	489	31	17	117	51	53	31	19	.268	.388	.330	362
Away	1139	2808	303	718	143	18	39	1014	287	246	507	18	15	91	67	44	37	22	.256	.361	.317	322
Grass	589	1473	158	379	79	9	19	533	152	129	268	13	4	43	38	20	23	12	.257	.362	.316	168
Turf	1709	4121	473	1085	183	35	75	1563	447	366	728	36	28	165	80	77	45	29	.263	.379	.325	516
April/June	1057	2598	286	677	122	28	37	966	271	220	488	24	18	103	51	48	32	18	.261	.372	.321	313
July/October	1241	2996	345	787	140	16	57	1130	328	275	508	25	14	105	67	49	36	23	.263	.377	.325	370

Chicago Cubs

Brock J. Hanke

CHICAGO										
YEAR	1983	1984	1985	1986	1987	1988	1989	1990	1991	1992
W	71	96	77	70	76	77	93	77	77	78
L	91	65	84	90	85	85	69	85	83	84
WPCT	0.438	0.596	0.478	0.438	0.472	0.475	0.574	0.475	0.481	0.481
R	701	762	686	680	720	660	702	690	695	593
RA	719	658	729	781	801	694	623	774	734	624
PWPT	0.487	0.573	0.47	0.431	0.447	0.475	0.559	0.443	0.473	0.475
PythW	79	93	76	70	72	77	91	72	77	77
PythL	83	69	86	92	90	85	71	90	85	85
LUCK	-8	3	1	0	4	0	2	5	0	1

Defensive Efficiency Record: .7134

This year's Cubs essay is being written in conjunction with the Boston Red Sox comment. That's because I said similar things about the two teams last year, and they both at least addressed the main issue that I thought confronted them, and it didn't do either team much good. Sort of leaves me with the job of explaining why or making excuses or something like that there.

First, here's a quick précis of last year's comments, for those of you who haven't yet ordered your back issues of last year's SABERMETRIC.

BOSTON:

I noted that the Red Sox have managed to win their division every year that they have had a team ERA under 4.00. I noted that this is because they always seem to have about the same offense, and they always have Roger Clemens, and so they win if they get anything else, and anything else pretty much has to come from the pitching staff. You will note that the Red Sox 1992 team ERA was 3.63, and their Ballpark-Adjusted ERA led the American League, and they still finished last in their division.

CHICAGO CUBS:

I noted that most of the Wrigley Field pennant winners had been teams driven by their pitching, with a special emphasis on teams that led the National League in ERA. I noted that the opposite is true of old Comiskey Park, where the White Sox did well when they had a hot offense. You will note that the Cubs' team ERA was fifth in the National League. Their team Runs Scored total was tenth. They, too, didn't win anything.

Now, what happened to these two teams was not the same thing. What happened to the Red Sox is discussed in their essay. Here's what happened in Chicago.

First, the ballpark did not behave normally at all. Normally, Wrigley Field is a hitters' haven. It is not all that small, in terms of fair territory, but the foul ground is small, and the park is open. By that, I mean that the walls of Wrigley are not solid, and the stands do not reach terribly high, especially in back of the famed bleachers, which is, in fact, a very small section of seats. The result is to allow air to pass through the ballpark readily, carrying the baseball with it. That's the norm. But it

Position	92 Starter	TWAR	93 Starter	TWAR
Catcher	Girardi	0.45	Wilkins	2.30
First base	Grace	7.76	Grace	7.76
Second base	Sandberg	9.19	Sandberg	9.19
Third base	Buechele	3.79	Buechele	3.79
Shortstop	Sanchez	2.01	Dunston	0.61
Left field	May	1.87	Maldonado	4.48
Center field	Dascenzo	1.12	Wilson, W.	2.17
Right field	Dawson	5.33	Sosa	1.51
			May	1.87

is possible for the wind in Chicago to behave abnormally, blowing back towards the plate instead of out towards the fences. That's not the usual Chicago air current, but it is possible. It is very likely what happened in 1992.

A check of the ballpark adjustments (the first stat box following the essay here) shows that Wrigley had just a bit below normal effect on offense; 1.9% deflation, to be precise. It also shows that the effect was very pronounced against left handed hitters (10.9%), which means that the prevailing 1992 wind in Wrigley Field blew across from left to right field. Righty hitters, like Ryne Sandberg, got the normal amount of help from Wrigley, but the lefties, like Mark Grace, suffered.

But it's the effect on the pitchers that is important. Normally, if the Cubbie pitching staff finished fifth in team ERA, you would expect them to finish about third or so in ballpark-adjusted ERA. Instead, they finished sixth. Essentially, their pitching staff was tied with the Cardinals'. The two team ERAs were 3.39 (Cubs) and 3.38. After ballpark adjustment, they were 3.46 and 3.47. So, not only were the staffs almost even, but so were the ballparks. I guess you can figure out that, any time Busch Stadium and Wrigley Field have the same ballpark adjustment, something is wrong. What is wrong in this case is that the Cub pitching staff was not as good as it looked, because most people just assumed that the pitchers were better than their raw ERAs.

The other thing that happened to the Cubs was that their offense was ridiculously thin. I commented last year that the 1991 Cubs had a four-man offense of Grace, Sandberg, Dawson and Bell, with part-time help from Hector Villanueva. For 1992, the Cubs let Bell go in a trade that did not provide offense, and Hector collapsed. They did pick up Steve Buechele, in an attempt to find another big hitter, but that plan failed under the weight of Buechele's actual ability, as opposed to his rep for RBIs hitting behind Barry Bonds and Andy Van Slyke and Bobby Bonilla. They finally picked up Kal Daniels, too; a move that I have been advocating for about three years. Daniels was bad, for Kal Daniels, but he did outhit Steve Buechele, as he does have some power. The overall Cubbie result was a three-man offense, and Andre Dawson is not that strong an offensive force any more.

In terms of our Total Wins Above Replacement, Ryne Sandberg is our Sabermetric MVP for the National League, and he is the best-hitting second baseman by plenty. Ryne created 117 runs for the year, which is great. Mark Grace, too, heads the first base rankings, both in total and in offense. He created 102 runs on offense. Andre Dawson is fourth among the right fielders, as is Rick Wilkins at catcher. But Andre is the last Cub to create as many as 40 runs, with his 76. Wilkins did not play most of the Cubs' games at catcher, and created only 34. Steve Buechele comes in fifth at third base, but only created 29 runs for the Cubs in his half a year. He is probably a 50- or 60-RC man for the future, but right now we're discussing what happened in 1992. Behind Buechele, it's Rey Sanchez, ninth at shortstop (24 RC), Derrick May ninth at left field (his 38 RC is the most behind Dawson), and Doug Dascenzo, dead last in center field, with 36 RC.

Overall, that's mediocrity, not a good offense. Doug Dascenzo and Rey Sanchez hurt the Cubs just as much as Sandberg and Grace helped them. The assumption about Chicago and Boston both is that they will always have at least a good offense, because they know they have to have hitting. But the Chicago farm system has been so bare for so long that all they've got is the three stalwarts from the mid-80's. In fact, Mark Grace is the last really good hitter the Cubbie farm has produced. Mark came up in 1988, and was overdue then. That means that the Cubs have gotten nothing from the farm, in terms of hitting, in five years. That's too long to assume anything about the offense.

Still, the pitching was just above average, with an Expected Winning Percentage of .507, or an 82/80 Expected record. And the offense was the same, with an Offensive Winning Percentage of .508. Altogether, that indicates that the team Supported Winning Percentage should be something like .510. But it's .474, with a Supported Won/Lost record of 77/85. Why? Well, the Cubs gave up 70 unearned runs, is what happened. A normal number is about 60 for an NL team. The good defensive teams kept it down to 50. The pitiful Dodgers gave up an absurd 91, but they were the only NL team worse than the Cubs. The culprits were who you'd expect. Derrick May was bad in left field, and Doug Dascenzo was not much better in center. The unlikely villain was Sammy Sosa, who was supposedly acquired to shore up the Cubbie glovework. He was just horrid, with six errors in only 67 games, and a Defensive Winning Percentage below Replacement Rate.

As for 1993, well, the future could look brighter. Greg Maddux is gone, and everyone is on the Cubs for letting him go. Everyone is right. Jose Guzman is not going to replace what Greg gave the team. Now, remember, I've not been a fan of Greg Maddux's workloads. Among analysts, I probably expect the least of Maddux over the next few years, as I think his arm will soon start showing the strain of too much work. But, if you're the Cubbies, and you're trying to squeeze another division title out of Ryne Sandberg, you've got to take short-term gambles. If Maddux does hold up, he is certainly the type of pitcher who can put a contending team over the top. Jose Guzman simply is not.

The rest of the pitching staff doesn't look all that great. Mike Morgan will be 33 in '93. He's coming off two years of over 235 innings. They are by far his hardest-working two campaigns. Now, Morgan had light workloads when he was young, and so may be able to handle that sort of work for a few years; I rate him a better bet to do that than Maddux is. But, still, I doubt he's suddenly become a pitcher who is legitimately going to win 2/3 of his decisions, year after year. I think 1991's 14/10 record is a much more likely indicator than this year's 16/8. 14/10 is also a reasonable guess for Jose Guzman, who is also off his career high in innings, and who also has never pitched really well before.

After these two men, it gets worse. No other Cubbie starter went over .500. Frank Castillo is probably the best of them, and he faded late in '92. Greg Hibbard, acquired from the White Sox, will someday recover from his 211 innings in 1990. But "someday" does not necessarily guarantee "1993". The bullpen is not really what you're looking for, although the Cubs have cornered the market on left-handed relief pitchers. Overall, the Cubs will be lucky to have an Expected Won / Lost record of .500 again this coming year, unless Randy Myers and Dan Plesac just go crazy or something.

The offense does have a chance to be better. Unfortunately, that chance's name is "Kal Daniels". Daniels might stage another of his injury-free recovery years. If he does, he's exactly the type of hitter that you want in Wrigley. He takes his walks, gets on base and lengthens the offensive sequence. He also has power, but it's a secondary concern. This assumes, of course, that the Cubs still have Daniels in 1993. He may be physically through, due to injuries, or someone else may sign him. If you've been reading the SABERMETRIC all along, you know that I've been talking about a hypothetical George Bell for Kal Daniels trade for the last two seasons. Essentially, that's what the Cubs did last year, Sammy Sosa or no Sammy Sosa. The problem may be that it's two years too late. Actually, neither Bell nor Daniels, nor Sosa, for that matter, played anything like they're supposed to be able to. But George Bell is not really the right type of hitter for Wrigley nor for the righty-laden Cubs, while Sosa is at least one class of hitter below either of the other two. It's like the Maddux / Guzman situation. Kal Daniels may be a bad bet to be healthy, but he can really help you if he is. Sammy Sosa can't really help, no matter how healthy he is.

As for the rest of the lineup, Steve Buechele will play all year, as will Rich Wilkins. Neither of them has to be as good as he was in 1992 to be better than anything the Cubs have had at their positions in years. Shawon Dunston will be back, apparently fully healed, and that will help. But remember, Dunston is another hitter who won't take a walk, and he has enough power to compensate only in odd years. Willie Wilson is the new center fielder; Jerome Walton and Doug Dascenzo are mercifully gone. Wilson is nowhere near his peak, and is in fact not a good center fielder any more. But he is still better than the 1992 fiasco.

If the Cubs do have Daniels, and he does perform, they're in good outfield shape, as the other slots will be manned by Derrick May and Candy Maldonado, with Sosa as a utility reserve. May is at least adequate as a hitter, and he, like Daniels, is a lefty. One of the biggest Cubbie lineup failings of the last few years is the insistence that Mark Grace is all the lefty hitting the team needs. A lineup with Grace, Daniels and May would be much more balanced than a normal Cubbie edition. At the least, it would keep the league from loading up the righty starters against the Cubs.

If Daniels is not available, or in games against lefties, Candy Maldonado will play right field, with May in left and Wilson in center. That's the most likely setup, as Daniels really is a question mark. Now, if you look at "May, Wilson, and Maldonado", what you'll say is "not much power". And that's a real problem for the Cubs. Derrick May has never hit double figures in homers in professional ball. Candy Maldonado sometimes hits 20 homers, but he also sometimes hits 12. It is quite possible that the three outfielders could produce fewer than 30 home runs among them, in Wrigley Field. That won't work, Ryne Sandberg or no Sandberg. Nor is a lineup with Willie Wilson batting leadoff going to help the Cubs in Wrigley. Wilson will simply make too many outs, especially for a team with Shawon Dunston in its lineup and Ryne Sandberg as its sole power source.

So, overall, while the offense might be better, it probably won't. The offensive sequence will likely be longer, just because Buechele and Wilkins will probably contribute. But, with Dawson and Bell gone, the Cubs are short of power. Without Daniels to augment Mark Grace, they're not going to get on base enough to compensate. They have removed the people who could hit, but were not the type of hitter that helps most in Wrigley. But they have not replaced them with people who can hit as well as the men they're replacing.

The biggest improvement in Chicago is very likely to be the defense. Both Buechele and Wilson are great improvements over what the Cubs started 1992 with. Wilkins is a better defensive catcher than Hector Villanueva, and Steve Lake is a Gold Glove backup. Dunston figures to return, and to be better than the backups were. Maldonado is not Andre Dawson, but he's the only minus. I expect the Cubbie defense to be average or a little below, not the worst in the league except for the Dodgers.

On balance, I don't expect the Cubs to contend. And that's sad. What we're seeing here is the waning days of Ryne Sandberg, being wasted by an organization that just won't spend the short-term money to go for the gold while they can. Sure, not signing Greg Maddux does save the Tribune some money over the next four years. But signing him could very well have produced a division title or two within that span. And there's no point waiting for the four years to end, because Ryne Sandberg will no longer be Superman by then. At that point, the Tribune could have jettisoned both Maddux and Sandberg and made up for the spent money with a couple of years of a skeleton team. As it is, they'd be doing both Sandberg and themselves a favor by trading the man now. They have no real use for him; they're not going to win anything and Wrigley Field sells out anyway. Might as well cash him in for a teamful of prospects who won't cost any money for at least five years, and who might be ready to win before then.

Chicago Cubs Home Park Performance Factors	Outs	Runs	Hits	2b	3b	HR	W	K	SH	SF	HBP	IBB	SB	CS	GDP
Home LH Batters	1.037	.994	1.046	1.125	2.077	1.102	.869	1.089	1.081	.748	1.438	1.009	.937	.918	1.002
Home RH Batters	.996	.909	.976	.876	.722	.819	.894	.949	1.053	.848	1.451	.725	.927	.938	1.050
All Home Batters	1.011	.944	.999	.936	.856	.891	.892	.989	1.041	.861	1.441	.815	.944	.946	1.047
Opp LH Batters	1.072	1.211	1.097	1.126	.966	1.095	1.116	1.092	1.220	1.041	2.186	1.216	1.384	1.145	.938
Opp RH Batters	1.017	1.066	1.067	1.078	.929	1.154	1.118	1.012	.935	.926	1.037	1.166	1.307	.901	1.015
All Opp Batters	1.029	1.108	1.067	1.113	.901	1.135	1.097	1.023	1.017	.978	1.276	1.130	1.275	.994	.988
All LH Batters	1.056	1.109	1.075	1.130	1.255	1.096	1.008	1.088	1.161	.907	1.823	1.122	1.202	1.047	.969
All RH Batters	1.004	.968	1.013	.958	.788	.926	.982	.974	.987	.880	1.198	.885	1.084	.909	1.035
All Batters	1.019	1.019	1.031	1.019	.878	.997	.993	1.004	1.023	.918	1.333	.969	1.110	.967	1.019

Sabermetric Batting Records for Chicago Cubs

	AB	Run	Hit	2B	3B	HR	RBI	W	SO	Avg	Slug	OBP	Ctd	Outs	27o	OW%	OG	OWAR	DWAR	TWAR
Arias	99	13	29	5	0	0	7	11	12	.293	.343	.375	13	74	4.74	.615	3	0.73	0.10	0.83
Buechele	241	24	67	8	2	0	21	18	43	.278	.328	.343	28	180	4.20	.556	7	1.37	0.25	1.62
Daniels	113	13	28	6	0	4	18	11	26	.248	.407	.320	14	89	4.25	.561	3	0.70	0.20	0.90
Dascenzo	384	37	99	13	3	0	20	26	32	.258	.307	.304	36	300	3.24	.427	11	0.85	0.27	1.12
Dawson	547	59	153	26	1	21	93	30	68	.280	.446	.319	76	413	4.97	.636	15	4.38	0.95	5.33
Dunston	73	7	23	2	0	0	2	3	12	.315	.342	.342	8	52	4.15	.550	2	0.39	0.22	0.61
Girardi	272	18	74	2	0	0	12	19	37	.272	.279	.322	24	207	3.13	.410	8	0.46	-0.01	0.45
Grace	638	79	198	41	7	9	86	71	39	.310	.439	.382	111	463	6.47	.748	17	6.83	0.94	7.76
Kunkel	29	0	4	1	0	0	1	0	7	.138	.172	.138	1	26	1.04	.071	1	-0.27	0.10	-0.17
May D	370	36	102	12	0	8	49	13	43	.276	.373	.309	41	281	3.94	.524	10	1.81	0.06	1.87
Pedre	4	0	0	0	0	0	0	0	0	.000	.000	.000	0	4	0.00	.000	0	-0.05	-0.01	-0.06
Ramsey F	25	0	3	0	0	0	2	0	5	.120	.120	.120	0	22	0.00	.000	1	-0.29	0.05	-0.23
Salazar L	257	19	54	6	1	4	25	11	33	.210	.288	.240	16	218	1.98	.218	8	-1.07	0.59	-0.47
Sanchez R	257	23	65	13	2	0	19	10	16	.253	.319	.288	23	204	3.04	.396	8	0.35	1.66	2.01
Sandberg	618	98	190	31	6	25	90	68	71	.307	.498	.374	118	451	7.06	.780	17	7.18	2.02	9.19
Scott G	96	7	15	1	0	1	11	5	13	.156	.198	.198	3	84	0.96	.062	3	-0.90	-0.09	-0.99
Smith Dw	229	30	64	11	4	3	26	12	43	.279	.402	.317	29	174	4.50	.589	6	1.54	0.14	1.69
Sosa	264	40	69	6	1	7	25	19	61	.261	.371	.319	32	209	4.13	.548	8	1.53	-0.02	1.51
Strange	95	7	15	1	0	1	5	9	15	.158	.200	.231	5	84	1.61	.155	3	-0.61	-0.03	-0.63
Villanueva	112	8	17	5	0	1	13	11	23	.152	.223	.228	5	99	1.36	.116	4	-0.86	0.12	-0.74
Vizcaino	291	25	66	10	3	1	17	13	35	.227	.292	.260	22	234	2.54	.314	9	-0.32	1.06	0.74
Walker C	26	2	3	0	0	0	2	2	4	.115	.115	.179	1	23	1.17	.089	1	-0.22	0.04	-0.19
Walton	55	6	7	0	0	0	1	9	12	.127	.127	.273	3	52	1.56	.147	2	-0.39	-0.01	-0.40
Wilkins R	257	22	70	10	1	8	24	27	57	.272	.412	.342	36	195	4.98	.638	7	2.08	0.22	2.30
TOTALS	5718	608	1466	226	36	105	588	414	820	.256	.364	.310	641	4538	3.81	.508	168	26.49	8.83	35.32

	G	AB	Run	Hit	2B	3B	HR	TB	RBI	W	K	IW	HB	SB	CS	BRng Eff	GI DP	SH	SF	Avg	Slug	OBP	Runs Ctd
Girardi	91	270	19	73	3	1	1	81	12	19	38	3	1	0	2	.242	8	0	1	.270	.300	.320	25
Grace	158	603	72	185	37	5	9	259	79	72	36	8	4	6	1	.392	14	2	8	.307	.430	.380	102
Sandberg	158	612	100	186	32	8	26	312	87	68	73	4	1	17	6	.457	13	0	6	.304	.510	.371	117
Buechele	65	239	25	66	9	3	1	84	21	18	44	2	5	1	1	.233	5	2	1	.276	.351	.338	29
Sanchez R	74	255	24	64	14	3	1	87	19	10	17	1	3	2	1	.450	7	5	2	.251	.341	.285	24
May D	124	351	33	96	11	0	8	131	45	14	40	4	3	5	3	.500	9	2	1	.274	.373	.306	38
Dascenzo	139	376	37	96	13	4	0	117	20	27	32	2	0	6	8	.443	3	4	2	.255	.311	.304	36
Dawson	143	542	60	150	27	2	22	247	90	30	70	8	4	6	2	.432	13	0	6	.277	.456	.316	76
Vizcaino	86	285	25	64	10	4	1	85	17	14	35	2	0	3	0	.362	4	5	1	.225	.298	.260	23
Sosa	67	262	41	68	7	2	8	103	25	19	63	1	4	15	7	.611	4	4	2	.260	.393	.317	33
Salazar L	98	255	20	53	7	2	5	79	25	11	34	2	0	1	1	.281	10	3	4	.208	.310	.237	17
Wilkins R	83	244	20	66	9	1	8	101	22	28	53	7	0	0	2	.235	6	1	1	.270	.414	.344	34
Smith Dw	109	217	28	60	10	3	3	85	24	13	40	0	1	9	8	.447	1	0	2	.276	.392	.318	26
Villanueva	51	112	9	17	6	0	2	29	13	11	24	2	0	0	0	.400	4	0	0	.152	.259	.228	6
Daniels	48	108	12	27	6	0	4	45	17	12	24	0	1	0	2	.600	3	0	1	.250	.417	.328	14
Arias	32	99	14	29	6	0	0	35	7	11	13	0	2	0	0	.455	4	1	0	.293	.354	.375	13
Scott G	36	96	8	15	2	0	2	23	11	5	14	1	0	0	0	.333	3	1	0	.156	.240	.198	4
Strange	52	94	7	15	1	0	1	19	5	10	15	2	0	1	0	.500	2	2	0	.160	.202	.240	5
Maddux G	35	88	6	15	3	0	1	21	8	1	22	0	0	0	0	.333	1	13	0	.170	.239	.180	4
Morgan M	34	74	1	8	0	0	0	8	5	2	16	0	0	0	0	.375	1	11	1	.108	.108	.130	2
Dunston	18	73	8	23	3	1	0	28	2	3	13	0	0	2	3	.385	0	0	0	.315	.384	.342	9
Castillo F	33	65	3	6	0	0	0	6	1	3	21	0	0	0	0	.333	2	5	0	.092	.092	.132	1
Walton	30	55	7	7	0	1	0	9	1	9	13	0	2	1	2	.385	1	3	0	.127	.164	.273	3
Jackson Dan	19	36	0	3	0	0	0	3	1	0	19	0	0	0	1	.667	0	4	0	.083	.083	.083	0
Kunkel	20	29	0	4	2	0	0	6	1	0	8	0	0	0	0	.500	1	0	0	.138	.207	.138	1
Boskie	23	27	1	5	1	0	0	6	1	2	9	0	0	0	0	.000	0	3	0	.185	.222	.241	2
Walker C	19	26	2	3	0	0	0	3	2	3	4	0	0	1	0	.333	0	0	1	.115	.115	.200	1
Ramsey F	18	25	0	3	0	0	0	3	2	0	6	0	0	0	0	.000	0	1	0	.120	.120	.120	0
Bullinger	39	20	3	5	0	0	1	8	2	1	7	0	1	0	0	.000	0	1	0	.250	.400	.286	3
Harkey	8	15	4	4	0	0	0	4	0	0	3	0	0	0	0	01.000	0	0	0	.267	.267	.267	1
Robinson JD	49	12	0	0	0	0	0	0	0	0	3	0	0	0	0	.000	0	2	0	.000	.000	.000	0
McElroy	72	6	2	4	2	1	0	8	1	0	0	0	0	0	0	.500	0	0	0	.6671.333	.667		5
Slocumb	30	4	0	0	0	0	0	0	0	0	3	0	0	0	0	.000	0	0	0	.000	.000	.000	0
Scanlan	69	4	1	0	0	0	0	0	0	0	1	0	0	0	0	.000	0	0	0	.000	.000	.000	0
Assenmacher	70	4	1	0	0	0	0	0	0	1	1	0	0	0	0	.000	0	2	0	.000	.000	.200	0
Pedre	4	4	0	0	0	0	0	0	0	0	1	0	0	0	0	.000	0	0	0	.000	.000	.000	0
Hartsock	4	2	0	0	0	0	0	0	0	0	1	0	0	0	0	.000	0	0	0	.000	.000	.000	0
Patterson K	32	1	0	0	0	0	0	0	0	0	1	0	0	0	0	.000	0	1	0	.000	.000	.000	0
Smith Dv	11	0	0	0	0	0	0	0	0	0	0	0	0	0	0	.000	0	0	0	.000	.000	.000	0
Rasmussen D	3	0	0	0	0	0	0	0	0	0	0	0	0	0	0	.000	0	1	0	.000	.000	.000	0
Hollins J	4	0	0	0	0	0	0	0	0	0	0	0	0	0	0	.000	0	0	0	.000	.000	.000	0
TOTALS	2258	5590	593	1420	221	41	104	2035	566	417	816	49	31	77	51	.410	119	78	40	.254	.364	.307	621

Pitching Records for Chicago Cubs

	ERA	W	L	Pct	G	GS	CG	ShO	GF	Sv	IP	R	ER	H	2B	3B	HR	BB	IW	SO	HB	WP	BK
Maddux G	2.18	20	11	.645	35	35	9	4	0	0	268.0	68	65	201	36	5	7	70	7	199	14	5	0
Morgan M	2.55	16	8	.667	34	34	6	1	0	0	240.0	80	68	203	39	3	14	79	10	123	3	11	0
Castillo F	3.46	10	11	.476	33	33	0	0	0	0	205.1	91	79	179	42	4	19	63	6	135	6	11	0
Jackson Dan	4.22	4	9	.308	19	19	0	0	0	0	113.0	59	53	117	21	4	5	48	3	51	3	1	2
Boskie	5.01	5	11	.313	23	18	0	0	2	0	91.2	55	51	96	25	0	14	36	3	39	4	5	1
Harkey	1.89	4	0	1.000	7	7	0	0	0	0	38.0	13	8	34	6	3	4	15	0	21	1	3	1
Scanlan	2.89	3	6	.333	69	0	0	0	41	14	87.1	32	28	76	13	1	4	30	6	42	1	6	4
Bullinger	4.66	2	8	.200	39	9	1	0	15	7	85.0	49	44	72	9	5	9	54	6	36	4	4	0
McElroy	3.55	4	7	.364	72	0	0	0	30	6	83.2	40	33	73	19	3	5	51	10	83	0	3	0
Robinson JD	3.00	4	3	.571	49	5	0	0	12	1	78.0	29	26	76	15	3	5	40	7	46	2	8	1
Assenmacher	4.10	4	4	.500	70	0	0	0	23	8	68.0	32	31	72	18	1	6	26	5	67	3	4	0
Patterson K	3.89	2	3	.400	32	1	0	0	4	0	41.2	25	18	41	9	2	7	27	6	23	1	3	1
Slocumb	6.50	0	3	.000	30	0	0	0	11	1	36.0	27	26	52	3	0	3	21	3	27	1	1	0
Smith Dv	2.51	0	0	.000	11	0	0	0	4	0	14.1	4	4	15	1	1	0	4	2	3	0	0	1
Hartsock	6.75	0	0	.000	4	0	0	0	0	0	9.1	7	7	15	1	0	2	4	0	6	0	2	0
Rasmussen D	10.80	0	0	.000	3	1	0	0	1	0	5.0	6	6	7	3	0	2	2	1	0	1	0	0
Hollins J	13.50	0	0	.000	4	0	0	0	3	0	4.2	7	7	8	1	0	1	5	0	0	0	1	0
TOTALS	3.39	78	84	.481	534	162	16	5	146	37	1469.0	624	554	1337	261	35	107	575	75	901	44	68	11

Sabermetric Pitching Records for Chicago Cubs

	Adj ERA	Expected W	Expected L	Pct	BFP	Opp Avg	Opp Slg	Opp OBA	RC/G	GDP	SB	CS	PK	PKE	SH	SF	RSup	RSp/G	W	L	Pct
Assenmacher	4.10	3	5	.422	298	.271	.414	.340	5.28	3	9	2	0	1	1	2	36	4.77	4	4	.524
Boskie	5.01	5	11	.329	393	.284	.482	.354	5.65	11	2	1	2	1	9	6	34	3.34	4	12	.266
Bullinger	4.66	4	6	.361	380	.233	.382	.350	4.86	7	8	2	0	0	9	4	27	2.86	2	8	.235
Castillo F	3.51	10	11	.500	856	.232	.371	.294	3.84	6	18	9	0	0	11	5	79	3.46	9	12	.443
Harkey	1.89	3	1	.774	159	.243	.414	.316	4.38	2	3	3	0	0	1	2	30	7.11	4	0	.920
Hartsock	6.75	0	0	.212	46	.375	.550	.422	8.78	0	1	2	0	0	1	1	4	3.86	0	0	.210
Hollins J	13.50	0	0	.063	27	.400	.600	.481	13.35	0	0	0	0	0	0	2	0	0.00	0	0	.000
Jackson Dan	4.30	5	8	.399	501	.270	.371	.343	4.48	11	15	9	0	5	11	5	42	3.35	4	9	.331
Maddux G	2.22	22	9	.714	1061	.210	.279	.272	2.50	19	26	13	1	1	15	3	118	3.96	22	9	.723
McElroy	3.55	5	6	.493	369	.237	.367	.341	4.63	2	4	3	0	0	5	5	30	3.23	4	7	.403
Morgan M	2.59	16	8	.647	966	.234	.334	.298	3.09	29	6	9	1	1	10	5	110	4.13	16	8	.675
Patterson K	3.89	2	3	.448	191	.268	.490	.373	6.51	1	2	3	0	2	6	4	12	2.59	1	4	.266
Rasmussen D	10.80	0	0	.095	24	.350	.800	.417	12.06	0	1	1	0	1	0	1	2	3.60	0	0	.083
Robinson JD	3.00	4	3	.577	335	.263	.388	.354	4.56	8	9	8	0	0	2	2	23	2.65	3	4	.390
Scanlan	2.89	5	4	.596	360	.235	.319	.301	3.23	8	6	3	0	0	4	2	30	3.09	4	5	.484
Slocumb	6.50	1	2	.225	174	.351	.432	.430	7.22	2	4	4	0	1	2	2	14	3.50	1	2	.191
Smith Dv	2.51	0	0	.661	61	.273	.327	.317	3.92	1	2	0	0	0	1	1	2	1.25	0	0	.169
TOTALS	3.46	82	80	.507	6201	.246	.366	.320	4.00	110	116	72	4	13	88	52	593	3.63	77	85	.474

Batting 'Splits' Records for Chicago Cubs

SPLITS for Grace

	G	AB	Run	Hit	2B	3B	HR	TB	RBI	W	K	IW	HB	SB	CS	DP	SH	SF	Avg	Slug	OBP	RC
vs LHP	97	225	21	63	11	1	3	85	29	17	19	0	2	3	0	6	2	5	.280	.378	.329	29
vs RHP	158	378	51	122	26	4	6	174	50	55	17	8	2	3	1	8	0	3	.323	.460	.409	74
Home	78	285	43	80	17	0	5	112	40	45	18	4	1	4	1	5	2	7	.281	.393	.373	46
Away	80	318	29	105	20	5	4	147	39	27	18	4	3	2	0	9	0	1	.330	.462	.387	56
Grass	111	418	57	120	22	3	6	166	54	56	31	6	2	5	1	8	2	7	.287	.397	.369	66
Turf	47	185	15	65	15	2	3	93	25	16	5	2	2	1	0	6	0	1	.351	.503	.407	37
April/June	73	266	39	87	17	4	4	124	37	42	12	3	1	1	1	8	1	1	.327	.466	.419	53
July/October	85	337	33	98	20	1	5	135	42	30	24	5	3	5	0	6	1	7	.291	.401	.347	50

SPLITS for May D

	G	AB	Run	Hit	2B	3B	HR	TB	RBI	W	K	IW	HB	SB	CS	DP	SH	SF	Avg	Slug	OBP	RC
vs LHP	44	76	6	19	2	0	2	27	9	3	13	0	1	0	1	3	1	0	.250	.355	.287	7
vs RHP	110	275	27	77	9	0	6	104	36	11	27	4	2	5	2	6	1	1	.280	.378	.311	31
Home	62	202	21	59	8	0	3	76	28	10	19	3	1	4	1	2	2	1	.292	.376	.327	26
Away	62	149	12	37	3	0	5	55	17	4	21	1	2	1	2	7	0	0	.248	.369	.277	13
Grass	87	260	25	76	10	0	4	98	34	14	26	4	2	4	2	4	2	1	.292	.377	.332	33
Turf	37	91	8	20	1	0	4	33	11	0	14	0	1	1	1	5	0	0	.220	.363	.228	6
April/June	50	138	13	36	4	0	3	49	17	7	16	1	0	2	1	3	1	0	.261	.355	.297	14
July/October	74	213	20	60	7	0	5	82	28	7	24	3	3	3	2	6	1	1	.282	.385	.313	24

SPLITS for Sandberg

	G	AB	Run	Hit	2B	3B	HR	TB	RBI	W	K	IW	HB	SB	CS	DP	SH	SF	Avg	Slug	OBP	RC
vs LHP	89	206	31	70	13	4	4	103	24	23	19	2	0	1	2	2	0	2	.340	.500	.403	43
vs RHP	157	406	69	116	19	4	22	209	63	45	54	2	1	16	4	11	0	4	.286	.515	.355	75
Home	80	300	57	92	19	6	16	171	46	41	35	2	0	8	2	2	0	4	.307	.570	.386	70
Away	78	312	43	94	13	2	10	141	41	27	38	2	1	9	4	11	0	2	.301	.452	.357	48
Grass	110	423	73	127	23	7	20	224	62	49	50	4	0	12	3	7	0	4	.300	.530	.370	85
Turf	48	189	27	59	9	1	6	88	25	19	23	0	1	5	3	6	0	2	.312	.466	.374	32
April/June	74	282	42	79	16	3	10	131	44	31	35	2	1	6	5	7	0	5	.280	.465	.348	45
July/October	84	330	58	107	16	5	16	181	43	37	38	2	0	11	1	6	0	1	.324	.548	.391	73

SPLITS for Chicago Cubs (all batters except pitchers)

	G	AB	Run	Hit	2B	3B	HR	TB	RBI	W	K	IW	HB	SB	CS	DP	SH	SF	Avg	Slug	OBP	RC
vs LHP	991	2008	199	525	92	17	25	726	194	132	262	17	8	18	19	48	35	18	.261	.362	.307	217
vs RHP	1730	3582	394	895	129	24	79	1309	372	285	554	32	23	59	32	71	43	22	.250	.365	.308	404
Home	1106	2768	315	711	120	25	59	1058	297	238	411	31	10	41	27	56	38	23	.257	.382	.316	335
Away	1152	2822	278	709	101	16	45	977	269	179	405	18	21	36	24	63	40	17	.251	.346	.299	288
Grass	1553	3907	427	990	155	32	77	1440	405	305	578	43	17	56	36	81	51	26	.253	.369	.308	442
Turf	705	1683	166	430	66	9	27	595	161	112	238	6	14	21	15	38	27	14	.255	.354	.305	179
April/June	1031	2554	274	618	96	19	43	881	260	195	386	23	11	36	25	49	39	22	.242	.345	.296	262
July/October	1227	3036	319	802	125	22	61	1154	306	222	430	26	20	41	26	70	39	18	.264	.380	.317	360

New York Mets

Brock J. Hanke

NEW YORK										
YEAR	1983	1984	1985	1986	1987	1988	1989	1990	1991	1992
W	68	90	98	108	92	100	87	91	77	72
L	94	72	64	54	70	60	75	71	84	90
WPCT	0.420	0.556	0.605	0.667	0.568	0.625	0.537	0.562	0.478	0.444
R	575	652	695	783	823	703	683	775	640	599
RA	680	676	568	578	698	532	595	613	646	653
PWPT	0.417	0.482	0.6	0.647	0.582	0.636	0.569	0.615	0.495	0.457
PythW	68	78	97	105	94	103	92	100	80	74
PythL	94	84	65	57	68	59	70	62	82	88
LUCK	0	12	1	3	-2	-3	-5	-9	-3	-2

Defensive Efficiency Record: .6898

Perhaps the most enlightening thing I can think of to write about the New York Mets is to do an analysis of their starters according to the Contender Profile method discussed in detail in the Philadelphia essay.

That method divides the world of Major League baseball players into five classes: superstars, stars, championship-quality players, bulk players, and holes. Then it places each of team's starters into one of these classes. What I mean by "starters" is the eight front line position players, the four starting pitchers who are actually in a real rotation, and the closer.

In general, a superstar will finish first or second at his position in his league. The 3-5 guys are the stars. 6-9 are the championship-quality players. Numbers 10 and 11 are bulk players, and #12 is a hole. Here is a listing of where the New York starters finished in 1992:

POS	NAME	RANK	CLASS
c	Todd Hundley	11	bulk
1b	Eddie Murray	6	c-q
2b	Willie Randolph	7	c-q
3b	Dave Magadan	7	c-q
ss	Dick Schofield	7	c-q
lf	Daryl Boston	6	c-q
cf	Howard Johnson	9	c-q
rf	Bobby Bonilla	7	c-q
s1	Sid Fernandez	13	star
s2	David Cone	15	star
s3	Pete Schourek	30	c-q
s4	Doc Gooden	31	c-q
rc	John Franco	1	super

Now, the model profile for a postseason team seems to be about 2 / 5 / 4 / 1 / 1 superstars / stars / champs / bulk / holes. That profile was obtained by estimating how good the postseason teams' players "were", which is partially subjective. The actual average of the four postseason profiles for 1992 was about 3 / 4 / 5 / 1 / 1, indicating that the teams that actually make the postseason are those contenders who get a little lucky or who really are dominant.

I want to say a couple of things about this before you figure them out, in about a minute or so. First, the theoretical profile for an "average" NL

Position	92 Starter	TWAR	93 Starter	TWAR
Catcher	Hundley	0.07	Hundley	0.07
First base	Murray	4.64	Murray	4.64
Second base	Randolph	2.04	Kent	0.63
Third base	Magadan	2.55	Johnson, H.	2.25
Shortstop	Schofield	2.56	Fernandez	3.79
Left field	Bass	2.74	Orsulak	3.96
Center field	Johnson, H.	2.25	Coleman	2.10
Right field	Bonilla	4.73	Bonilla	4.73

team is 2.17 / 3.25 / 4.33 / 2.17 / 1.08. This is because there are twelve ranking slots at each playing position, and thirteen playing positions. Second, and dependent on the first, is that the difference between a contending team and an average team is the replacement of one bulk player by one star or superstar. This is not entirely true, of course, as contending teams also have better-than-average benches, but it does point out how thin the line is separating the good from the mediocre. I'm sure this does not serve to console fans in Cleveland, but even the Indians aren't that far from contention.

The Mets, however, don't have exactly that conversion to perform. Their profile is, as you can see, 1 / 2 / 9 / 1 / 0. That's a unique team makeup, and it indicates some very important things about the Mets' current management, and also about the team history.

First, and most important for the Mets' immediate future, there is a paucity of star quality players. Since the Mets spend any amount of time talking about acquiring superstars, and planning to acquire them, and bragging about acquiring them, let's first consider if the Met profile is simply wrong, a one-year aberration soon to be forgotten in a rush of giant home run totals and microscopic ERAs from the superstars that the Mets actually have.

To start, here is a list of players on the Mets' roster who have, at one time or another, been superstars:

Murray

Randolph
Hojo
Bonilla
Gooden
Franco
Saberhagen

No, before you ask, Tony Fernandez has never had enough power nor taken enough walks to be a superstar. He's been a star, but no better. Actually, the main thing signing Fernandez does for the Mets is make up for the loss of Cone. They're about even as players, though Cone has a higher top end in the career year. And no, Vince Coleman has never been any better than a star, either. He is a left fielder, remember, and one with no power, as well. He has some flashy one-year stats, but flash isn't substance, and this is sabermetrics, not fandom.

Anyway, what can we say about these players' chances to turn in another superstar season? Well, we can start by saying that Willie Randolph and Eddie Murray are far too old to expect to do that again. Neither one of them is quite the caliber of Dave Winfield, and Winfield is who you're talking about if you're contemplating 38-year-old superstars.

We can also say that Dwight Gooden has shown no signs of returning to real superstardom for six years now. That's not a misprint, that's "six". National League superstar starting pitchers turn in ERAs below 2.75. Doc hasn't done that since 1985, although he was still showing signs of it in '86. Face it, Met fans, Davey Johnson blew out Gooden's arm in his first two years, with those ridiculous workloads he had to give the kid because his pitching staff was so thin overall.

We can say that Bret Saberhagen has had three separate and documentable arm injuries in his career, and that he hasn't turned in an ERA in the superstar category since 1989. That he came bouncing back from the first two arm collapses does not really indicate that he will fully recover from the third. The cause, of course, is the same as for Gooden. Bret was given brutal overloads of work as Kansas City attempted to cover for a thin middle relief corps.

That leaves John Franco, Howard Johnson and Bobby Bonilla. Of the three, Franco is the best bet to be a superstar in 1993. He showed every sign of being able to turn in that kind of season last year. He has had a durable arm; this is his first real trouble with it. Hojo is getting a little long in the tooth to be topping out again. Still, he's been a force before, and he's not all that old. If the competition at third base weren't so stiff, he'd be a decent bet to star. But third is a rough position right now, and Hojo apparently does not like playing the outfield.

Bobby Bonilla is fighting two facts in any attempt to turn in a superstar year. One is age; he's turning 30 now. The other is his real ability. Given his power drop since his age-27 career year, I have to doubt whether this is a real superstar candidate. What I think is that he's a solid star, unless he gets in media trouble again, but that he's not what we mean by a superstar. He's not Barry Bonds; he's just a man who can look really good if he's surrounded by Bonds and Andy Van Slyke.

So, in general, the profile is real. The team is not just loaded with superstars and stars on off years. They might have two of those, in Bonilla and Hojo, and Bret Saberhagen might have another miracle left, but that's all, and it's likely to give them stars, not superstars. Overall, the Met profile is what it looks like: a team full of championship quality ballplayers, with no holes, and no real top end.

Why is this so? Well, there are two reasons: one involving current management strategy and one involving history. The current management problem is the insistence on trying to fix a problem with stars by signing free agents. In doing this, they run into the following difficulties. First, most free agents are older than 27, which is to say that they're down from their peaks. The Mets just won't get the cream of Bobby Bonilla's seasons. Second, most teams that have young superstars tend to sign them as free agents, rather than letting them go. The Barry Bonds phenomenon is pretty rare; Ryne Sandberg and Robin Yount and George Brett are more typical of superstar players. And third, the real, hot, young superstars have no troubles with money; instead they have a pretty free choice of where to go. Then don't have to go to New York to get top money. Occasionally, a Bobby Bo will come along, who is actually from New York, but that's rare, too. Barry Bonds seems to never have considered New York, although he may have used a Yankee offer to get the price bid up. In any case, the New York teams did not get him, and they didn't get Greg Maddux, either. They got the second string, like Bobby Bo or Eddie Murray.

The history problem is that the Mets think they have a good farm system that will churn out superstars for them, while in fact they have nothing of the sort. So far, their system has only produced superstars when they had superstar draft picks to use. Darryl Strawberry, Dwight Gooden, even Tom Seaver was a product of a "can't miss" draft pick. The only real claim to fame that the Mets player development system can make is that they saw the value of Gooden after some teams had actually passed on him. Given the inconsistency of pitchers, I tend to call that "luck" rather than "skill".

What's more the success of the Mets of 1986 and 1988 was not built entirely on the farm. The Cardinals essentially gave Keith Hernandez to the Mets. Keith had a cocaine problem, and challenged Whitey Herzog about it, and was gone. The Mets got him not because Neil Allen looked so good, but because Whitey wanted to dump him on a team so bad that Keith couldn't come back to haunt the Cards. At the time, the Mets were awful. Howard Johnson, Sid Fernandez, and David Cone were trade acquisitions, not farm products. You can justly praise the Met front office for the trades, but you can't really put too much faith in the Met player development system.

What happens to the Mets is that the media gets to them with all that overwrought hype. Every Grade B prospect that hits Tidewater is touted as the next Straw or Doc. But none of them have been, nor have their MLEs suggested that they would be. So the Mets are always thinking that they are on the verge of contention, because the farm is about to crank out a dominant player or two. But it never happens, and no one give them a Keith Hernandez, either, because they don't look safe any more. Thus, the actual sources of the Mets' superstar talent of the late '80s are denied them. And so the Mets waste their money and energy acquiring championship-quality talent at superstar prices to fill out positions that the Mets think they need to shore up to win the division.

The result is a team of not-quite-superstars on the wane, and some young kids who aren't stars, either. The advantage this gives the Mets is that they don't tolerate true holes for very long; the disadvantage is that they don't have much top end. And thus, this profile, too diffuse and unfocused to actually win, but talented enough to look good to New York scribes, because it has no obvious holes.

The other fallout from this is that the Lords of Baseball think that this is what happens if you actually spend money. A lot of owners think that the Yankees of the late '80s and these Mets are the best you can do with bucks. But it's not true. Money has a very strong relationship to winning. Here are the eight highest payrolls in baseball for 1992:

Toronto
Oakland
New York Mets

Boston
Los Angeles
Pittsburgh
Atlanta
Cincinnati

years, except for the Mets and the Dodgers. And the Bums have finished second, by one game. What's more, of the division champions since 1990, the only one that is not on this list is the Minnesota Twins. And the twins added $9 million to their payroll between 1990 and their winning season of 1991. On balance, you win with money. You just don't win by spending it like the Mets.

Every one of these teams has been a division champion in the last three

New York Mets Home Park Performance Factors	Outs	Runs	Hits	2b	3b	HR	W	K	SH	SF	HBP	IBB	SB	CS	GDP
Home LH Batters	.989	.988	1.024	1.076	.745	1.011	1.155	1.004	1.185	.867	.745	1.654	.831	.728	1.041
Home RH Batters	.982	.963	.971	.966	.745	.952	.898	.984	.873	.919	1.203	.735	1.354	.867	.917
All Home Batters	.973	.975	.984	.991	.792	1.009	.948	.975	.922	.895	1.121	.886	1.212	.848	.965
Opp LH Batters	.968	1.001	1.003	.910	1.311	.849	1.067	1.018	1.042	.859	.889	.795	1.264	.889	1.010
Opp RH Batters	1.002	1.151	1.037	1.081	1.080	1.158	1.141	.977	1.099	1.481	.769	1.032	1.204	.960	.997
All Opp Batters	1.001	1.099	1.031	1.020	1.129	1.039	1.109	1.004	1.102	1.262	.907	.871	1.212	.962	1.040
All LH Batters	.976	.998	1.013	.967	1.147	.910	1.102	1.010	1.105	.861	.847	.970	1.109	.837	1.023
All RH Batters	.992	1.061	1.005	1.028	.962	1.067	1.001	.977	.973	1.222	.924	.861	1.231	.915	.959
All Batters	.988	1.038	1.007	1.004	1.014	1.023	1.023	.989	1.007	1.074	.981	.877	1.205	.907	1.004

Conventional Batting Records for New York Mets

	G	AB	Run	Hit	2B	3B	HR	TB	RBI	W	K	IW	HB	SB	CS	BRng Eff	GI DP	SH	SF	Avg	Slug	OBP	Runs Ctd
Hundley	123	358	32	75	17	0	7	113	32	19	76	4	4	3	0	.512	8	7	2	.209	.316	.256	29
Murray E	156	551	64	144	37	2	16	233	93	66	74	8	0	4	2	.349	14	0	8	.261	.423	.336	80
Randolph	90	286	29	72	11	1	2	91	15	40	34	1	4	1	3	.446	6	6	0	.252	.318	.352	34
Magadan	99	321	33	91	9	1	3	111	28	56	44	3	0	1	0	.283	6	2	0	.283	.346	.390	47
Schofield	142	420	52	86	18	2	4	120	36	60	82	4	5	11	4	.380	11	10	3	.205	.286	.309	41
Boston	130	289	37	72	14	2	11	123	35	38	60	6	3	12	6	.366	5	0	4	.249	.426	.338	43
Johnson H	100	350	48	78	19	0	7	118	43	55	79	5	2	22	5	.411	7	0	3	.223	.337	.329	44
Bonilla B	128	438	62	109	23	0	19	189	70	66	73	10	1	4	3	.524	11	0	1	.249	.432	.348	67
Pecota	117	269	28	61	13	0	2	80	26	25	40	3	1	9	3	.421	6	5	2	.227	.297	.293	25
Coleman	71	229	37	63	11	1	2	82	21	27	41	3	2	24	9	.617	1	2	1	.275	.358	.355	33
Walker C	107	227	24	70	12	1	4	96	36	24	46	3	0	14	1	.385	8	0	4	.308	.423	.369	37
Gallagher	98	175	20	42	11	1	1	58	21	19	16	0	1	4	5	.485	7	3	7	.240	.331	.307	17
O'Brien C	68	156	15	33	12	0	2	51	13	16	18	1	1	0	1	.316	4	4	0	.212	.327	.289	15
Sasser	92	141	7	34	6	0	2	46	18	3	10	0	0	0	0	.417	4	0	5	.241	.326	.248	11
Bass K	46	137	15	37	12	2	2	59	9	7	17	2	0	7	2	.500	2	0	1	.270	.431	.303	18
Donnels	45	121	8	21	4	0	0	25	6	17	25	0	0	1	0	.400	1	1	0	.174	.207	.275	8
Kent	37	113	16	27	8	1	3	46	15	7	29	0	1	0	2	.684	2	0	0	.239	.407	.289	12
Thompson R	30	108	15	24	7	1	3	42	10	8	24	0	0	2	2	.333	2	0	1	.222	.389	.274	11
McKnight	31	85	10	23	3	1	2	34	13	2	8	0	0	0	1	.400	2	0	0	.271	.400	.287	9
Howell P	31	75	9	14	1	0	0	15	1	2	15	0	1	4	0	.667	0	1	0	.187	.200	.218	3
Fernandez S	32	74	8	15	3	0	0	18	0	0	25	0	0	0	0	.250	1	7	0	.203	.243	.203	4
Gooden	33	72	8	19	3	1	1	27	9	1	16	0	0	0	0	.385	1	4	0	.264	.375	.274	7
Cone	27	65	5	6	1	0	0	7	4	3	19	0	0	0	0	.250	1	7	0	.092	.108	.132	1
Noboa	46	47	7	7	0	0	0	7	3	3	8	0	1	0	0	.417	2	0	1	.149	.149	.212	1
Dozier D	25	47	4	9	2	0	0	11	2	4	19	0	1	4	0	.625	0	1	1	.191	.234	.264	4
Schourek	23	42	0	2	0	0	0	2	1	0	13	0	0	0	0	.000	0	2	1	.048	.048	.047	0
Saberhagen	17	28	0	3	0	0	0	3	0	1	9	0	0	0	0	.000	0	3	0	.107	.107	.138	1
Young A	52	27	2	3	0	0	0	3	0	1	13	0	0	0	0	.000	2	0	0	.111	.111	.143	1
Whitehurst	44	22	1	4	1	0	0	5	3	1	5	0	0	0	1	.000	0	0	0	.182	.227	.217	1
Elster	6	18	0	4	0	0	0	4	0	0	2	0	0	0	0	.000	1	0	0	.222	.222	.222	1
Baez	6	13	0	2	0	0	0	2	0	0	0	0	0	0	0	.000	1	0	0	.154	.154	.154	0
Hillman	11	13	0	1	0	0	0	1	0	0	7	0	0	0	0	.000	0	5	0	.077	.077	.077	0
Gibson P	43	6	0	0	0	0	0	0	0	1	3	0	0	0	0	.000	0	1	0	.000	.000	.143	0
Springer	4	5	0	2	1	0	0	3	0	0	1	0	0	0	0	.000	0	0	0	.400	.600	.400	1
Filer	9	3	0	0	0	0	0	0	0	0	1	0	0	0	0	.000	0	0	0	.000	.000	.000	0
Innis	76	2	0	0	0	0	0	0	0	0	0	0	0	0	0	.000	0	0	0	.000	.000	.000	0
Guetterman	43	2	0	0	0	0	0	0	0	0	2	0	0	0	0	.000	0	0	0	.000	.000	.000	0
Birkbeck	1	2	0	0	0	0	0	0	0	0	0	0	0	0	0	.000	0	0	0	.000	.000	.000	0
Franco Jn	31	1	0	0	0	0	0	0	0	0	1	0	0	0	0	.000	0	0	0	.000	.000	.000	0
Dewey	20	1	0	0	0	0	0	0	0	0	1	0	0	0	0	.000	0	0	0	.000	.000	.000	0
McCray	18	1	3	1	0	0	0	1	1	0	0	0	0	2	0	.571	0	0	0	1.000	1.000	1.000	2
Burke	15	0	0	0	0	0	0	0	0	0	0	0	0	0	0	.000	0	0	0	.000	.000	.000	0
Jones Ba	17	0	0	0	0	0	0	0	0	0	0	0	0	0	0	.000	0	0	0	.000	.000	.000	0
Vitko	3	0	0	0	0	0	0	0	0	0	0	0	0	0	0	.000	0	0	0	.000	.000	.000	0
TOTALS	2343	5340	599	1254	259	17	93	1826	564	572	956	53	28	129	52	.424	114	74	45	.235	.342	.310	588

Batting 'Splits' Records for New York Mets

SPLITS for New York Mets (all batters except pitchers)

	G	AB	Run	Hit	2B	3B	HR	TB	RBI	W	K	IW	HB	SB	CS	DP	SH	SF	Avg	Slug	OBP	RC
vs LHP	1015	1916	221	462	95	8	26	651	206	191	308	13	8	40	18	42	26	20	.241	.340	.310	208
vs RHP	1796	3424	378	792	164	9	67	1175	358	381	648	40	20	89	34	72	48	25	.231	.343	.310	380
Home	1178	2585	288	599	123	10	42	868	270	288	465	29	11	46	29	55	39	24	.232	.336	.309	277
Away	1165	2755	311	655	136	7	51	958	294	284	491	24	17	83	23	59	35	21	.238	.348	.311	311
Grass	1621	3707	418	880	165	14	70	1283	393	388	647	35	15	76	43	83	54	29	.237	.346	.310	406
Turf	722	1633	181	374	94	3	23	543	171	184	309	18	13	53	9	31	20	16	.229	.333	.309	182
April/June	1064	2507	298	582	120	5	45	847	283	313	439	22	19	64	25	58	34	19	.232	.338	.320	286
July/October	1279	2833	301	672	139	12	48	979	281	259	517	31	9	65	27	56	40	26	.237	.346	.301	302

Sabermetric Batting Records for New York Mets

	AB	Run	Hit	2B	3B	HR	RBI	W	SO	Avg	Slug	OBP	Ctd	Outs	27o	OW%	OG	OWAR	DWAR	TWAR
			Ball Park Adjusted						Runs		Run/									
Baez	12	0	2	0	0	0	0	0	0	.167	.167	.167	0	10	0.00	.000	0	-0.13	-0.01	-0.14
Bass K	135	15	37	12	1	2	9	7	16	.274	.422	.308	18	102	4.76	.603	4	0.96	0.20	1.15
Bonilla B	433	64	109	23	0	19	72	67	72	.252	.436	.353	68	338	5.43	.664	13	3.93	0.80	4.73
Boston	284	36	72	13	2	10	33	42	60	.254	.419	.350	45	224	5.42	.663	8	2.60	0.41	3.01
Coleman	226	38	63	11	0	2	21	27	40	.279	.354	.359	34	175	5.25	.648	6	1.93	0.17	2.10
Donnels	118	7	21	3	0	0	5	18	25	.178	.203	.287	8	99	2.18	.242	4	-0.40	0.06	-0.34
Dozier D	46	4	9	2	0	0	2	4	18	.196	.239	.255	4	38	2.84	.351	1	0.00	0.03	0.03
Elster	17	0	4	0	0	0	0	0	1	.235	.235	.235	1	13	2.08	.224	0	-0.06	0.05	-0.01
Gallagher	173	21	42	11	0	1	22	19	15	.243	.324	.305	17	151	3.04	.382	6	0.18	0.36	0.54
Howell P	74	9	14	1	0	0	1	2	14	.189	.203	.221	4	62	1.74	.169	2	-0.42	0.26	-0.16
Hundley	354	33	75	17	0	7	33	19	75	.212	.319	.259	29	296	2.65	.319	11	-0.34	0.41	0.07
Johnson H	346	49	78	19	0	7	44	56	78	.225	.341	.334	46	282	4.40	.565	10	2.25	0.00	2.25
Kent	112	16	27	8	0	3	16	7	28	.241	.393	.286	12	87	3.72	.482	3	0.42	0.21	0.63
Magadan	316	32	92	8	1	2	27	62	44	.291	.342	.407	49	232	5.70	.685	9	2.88	-0.33	2.55
McCray	1	3	1	0	0	0	1	0	0	1.000	1.000	1.000	2	0	??????	.000	0	???????	0.01	???????
McKnight	84	10	23	3	0	2	13	2	7	.274	.381	.291	9	63	3.86	.499	2	0.35	0.07	0.42
Murray E	546	66	145	37	1	16	96	67	73	.266	.425	.341	81	424	5.16	.641	16	4.56	0.07	4.64
Noboa	46	7	7	0	0	0	3	3	7	.152	.152	.200	1	41	0.66	.028	2	-0.49	0.15	-0.34
O'Brien C	155	15	33	12	0	2	13	16	17	.213	.329	.287	15	128	3.16	.401	5	0.24	-0.39	-0.14
Pecota	267	29	61	13	0	2	27	25	39	.228	.300	.293	25	219	3.08	.389	8	0.31	0.40	0.72
Randolph	284	30	72	11	0	2	16	40	33	.254	.313	.352	34	224	4.10	.529	8	1.49	0.55	2.04
Sasser	138	6	34	5	0	1	17	3	10	.246	.304	.255	10	112	2.41	.280	4	-0.29	-0.13	-0.42
Schofield	417	54	86	18	1	4	38	61	80	.206	.283	.311	41	356	3.11	.393	13	0.57	1.99	2.56
Springer	4	0	2	1	0	0	0	0	0	.500	.750	.500	2		227.00	.980	0	0.05	0.01	0.06
Thompson R	107	15	24	7	0	3	10	8	23	.224	.374	.276	11	86	3.45	.444	3	0.30	0.25	0.55
Walker C	224	24	70	12	0	4	37	24	45	.313	.420	.373	38	166	6.18	.719	6	2.27	0.12	2.39
TOTALS	5296	620	1263	260	16	95	583	588	945	.238	.347	.315	611	4316	3.82	.495	160	23.11	5.74	28.85

Pitching Records for New York Mets

	ERA	W	L	Pct	G	GS	CG	ShO	GF	Sv	IP	R	ER	H	2B	3B	HR	BB	IW	SO	HB	WP	BK
Fernandez S	2.73	14	11	.560	32	32	5	2	0	0	214.2	67	65	162	37	9	12	67	4	193	4	0	0
Gooden	3.67	10	13	.435	31	31	3	0	0	0	206.0	93	84	197	43	7	11	70	7	145	3	3	1
Cone	2.88	13	7	.650	27	27	7	5	0	0	196.2	75	63	162	24	7	12	82	5	214	9	9	1
Schourek	3.64	6	8	.429	22	21	0	0	0	0	136.0	60	55	137	28	5	9	44	6	60	2	4	2
Saberhagen	3.50	3	5	.375	17	15	1	1	0	0	97.2	39	38	84	14	4	6	27	1	81	4	1	2
Hillman	5.33	2	2	.500	11	8	0	0	2	0	52.1	31	31	67	10	1	9	10	2	16	2	1	0
Birkbeck	9.00	0	1	.000	1	1	0	0	0	0	7.0	7	7	12	3	0	3	1	1	2	0	1	0
Young A	4.17	2	14	.125	52	13	1	0	26	15	121.0	66	56	134	23	9	8	31	5	64	1	3	1
Whitehurst	3.62	3	9	.250	44	11	0	0	7	0	97.0	45	39	99	25	4	4	33	5	70	4	2	1
Innis	2.86	6	9	.400	76	0	0	0	28	1	88.0	32	28	85	11	3	4	36	4	39	6	1	0
Gibson P	5.23	0	1	.000	43	1	0	0	12	0	62.0	37	36	70	17	3	7	25	0	49	0	1	0
Guetterman	5.82	3	4	.429	43	0	0	0	15	2	43.1	28	28	57	9	1	5	14	5	15	1	3	0
Franco Jn	1.64	6	2	.750	31	0	0	0	30	15	33.0	6	6	24	6	1	1	11	2	20	0	0	0
Dewey	4.32	1	0	1.000	20	0	0	0	6	0	33.1	16	16	37	5	0	2	10	2	24	0	0	1
Filer	2.05	0	1	.000	9	1	0	0	1	0	22.0	8	5	18	3	1	2	6	2	9	0	1	0
Burke	5.74	1	2	.333	15	0	0	0	9	0	15.2	15	10	26	3	1	1	3	0	7	0	2	0
Jones Ba	9.39	2	0	1.000	17	0	0	0	7	1	15.1	16	16	20	4	0	0	11	3	11	0	1	0
Vitko	13.50	0	1	.000	3	1	0	0	1	0	4.2	11	7	12	2	0	1	1	0	6	0	1	0
Pecota	9.00	0	0	.000	1	0	0	0	1	0	1.0	1	1	1	0	0	1	0	0	0	0	0	0
TOTALS	3.68	72	90	.444	495	162	17	8	145	34	1446.2	653	591	1404	267	56	98	482	54	1025	36	34	9

Sabermetric Pitching Records for New York Mets

	Adj ERA	W	L	Pct	BFP	Avg	Slg	OBA	RC/G	GDP	SB	CS	PK	PKE	SH	SF	RSup	RSp/G	W	L	Pct
		-Expected-				Opposing Batters											Supported				
Birkbeck	9.00	0	1	.132	33	.387	.774	.406	10.87	2	1	0	0	1	1	0	4	5.14	0	1	.210
Burke	5.74	1	2	.271	76	.371	.486	.392	7.80	1	1	0	0	1	3	1	3	1.72	0	3	.068
Cone	2.97	12	8	.581	831	.223	.324	.307	3.73	8	34	6	2	1	6	6	100	4.58	13	7	.659
Dewey	4.32	0	1	.397	143	.280	.364	.331	4.00	3	1	3	0	0	1	0	14	3.78	0	1	.385
Fernandez S	2.81	15	10	.609	865	.210	.328	.273	3.10	5	17	9	0	3	12	11	105	4.40	17	8	.667
Filer	2.05	1	0	.746	88	.222	.358	.276	3.35	1	3	1	0	1	1	0	3	1.23	0	1	.227
Franco Jn	1.64	7	1	.821	128	.209	.304	.273	2.22	6	2	3	0	2	1	1	7	1.91	4	4	.526
Gibson P	5.37	0	1	.299	273	.287	.467	.352	5.91	4	7	3	0	1	3	1	18	2.61	0	1	.162
Gooden	3.80	11	12	.459	863	.255	.371	.317	3.95	20	22	11	2	3	10	7	82	3.58	10	13	.420
Guetterman	6.02	2	5	.253	196	.324	.472	.371	6.21	7	4	1	0	0	2	3	25	5.19	3	4	.378
Hillman	5.50	1	3	.288	227	.318	.502	.353	5.84	6	4	5	0	2	3	1	27	4.64	1	3	.368
Innis	2.97	9	6	.583	373	.266	.357	.348	4.00	14	8	5	0	1	7	4	41	4.19	9	6	.620
Jones Ba	9.39	0	2	.122	76	.317	.381	.413	6.73	2	4	0	0	0	1	1	11	6.46	1	1	.278
Pecota	9.00	0	0	.132	4	.250	1.000	.250	9.17	0	0	0	0	0	0	0	0	0.00	0	0	.000
Saberhagen	3.59	4	4	.487	397	.233	.344	.292	3.40	4	6	5	3	0	3	3	32	2.95	3	5	.355
Schourek	3.77	6	8	.463	578	.261	.385	.319	4.29	12	15	5	0	2	4	4	48	3.18	5	9	.367
Vitko	13.50	0	1	.063	29	.444	.630	.448	14.22	2	0	1	0	1	0	1	0	0.00	0	1	.000
Whitehurst	3.71	6	6	.471	421	.264	.384	.328	4.38	11	9	3	0	0	6	3	27	2.51	3	9	.271
Young A	4.31	6	10	.397	517	.285	.423	.328	4.76	10	10	6	1	0	11	4	52	3.87	6	10	.396
TOTALS	3.81	74	88	.458	6118	.256	.379	.318	4.16	116	148	67	8	18	72	52	599	3.73	71	91	.438

Philadelphia Phillies

Brock J. Hanke

PHILADELPHIA										
YEAR	1983	1984	1985	1986	1987	1988	1989	1990	1991	1992
W	90	81	75	86	80	65	67	77	77	70
L	72	81	87	75	82	96	95	85	83	92
WPCT	0.556	0.500	0.463	0.534	0.494	0.404	0.414	0.475	0.481	0.432
R	696	720	667	739	702	597	629	646	629	686
RA	635	690	673	713	749	734	735	729	680	717
PWPT	0.546	0.521	0.496	0.518	0.468	0.398	0.423	0.44	0.461	0.478
PythW	88	84	80	84	76	65	68	71	75	77
PythL	74	78	82	78	86	97	94	91	87	85
LUCK	2	-3	-5	2	4	0	-1	6	2	-7

Well, hell. For a couple of years now, the Philly management has insisted that the team was going to move into contention for the NL East crown. Any year now, that was going to happen. Never mind that it hasn't happened yet, and that nobody seems to believe it is going to happen any time soon. The Phils are gonna be a contender; just ask them. So guess what? We're going to do an analysis here of the Phillies as though they were a real and true contender.

What we're going to do is to divide the world of Major League baseball players into five classes: superstars, stars, championship-quality players, bulk players, and holes. We're going to see how many of each the Phils have got among their starters, and how those numbers compare to what last year's contenders have. Then we're going to take a look at the three components of a bench: the bullpen, the pinch hitting, and the backups at the skill positions.

First, you need to understand what I mean by "starters". I figure that a National League team has 13 of these, while AL teams have 14. The eight front line position players, plus the DH in the AL, are obvious, as is the closer on the pitching staff. Then, I figure that each team has four starting pitchers who are actually in a real rotation. The #5 guy gets swapped in and out, according to the vagaries of the schedule, and so is not given regular work, in the sense that the front four are. In support of this, I offer that, when I compile the player rankings section, I rank only those starters who have had 20 or more starts. In both leagues, that number is very close to four times the number of teams; teams have four real rotation starters.

All right, let's talk superstars. In this class, I include only those position players and relief closers who can regularly be counted upon to finish in the top two at their position, if they get a full year's play. For starting pitchers, the top ten. At shortstop, for example, Barry Larkin, Ozzie Smith and Cal Ripken, Jr. are the superstars. Jay Bell is not, though he could finish ahead of either Larkin or Smith in any given year. But to do that, Ozzie or Barry would have to get hurt or have an off year. Bell really isn't in their class of player, injuries being equal. No one but Ripken is really like that in the American League, so there are only three real superstars at shortstop. At second base, there are rather more.

SUPERSTARS:

I figure that the Phillies have only one superstar, Dave Hollins. Dave finished third at third in 1992, but one of the men ahead of him was Gary Sheffield, who has not exactly established himself at that level, at least not yet. Darren Daulton finished first among catchers, but that's not his

Position	92 Starter	TWAR	93 Starter	TWAR
Catcher	Daulton	4.29	Daulton	4.29
First base	Kruk	5.33	Kruk	5.33
Second base	Morandini	1.62	Morandini	1.62
Third base	Hollins	5.80	Hollins	5.80
Shortstop			Bell, Ju.	0.20
Left field	Duncan	2.02	Incaviglia	3.32
			Thompson	1.89
Center field	Dykstra	3.83	Dykstra	3.83
	Javier	2.04		
Right field	Chamberlain	1.22	Chamberlain	1.22
	Amaro	0.97		

normal level of play. Yes, he could stay healthy and develop dominance, but it hasn't happened yet. He's a lot more like Sheffield than Hollins. Not, you understand, that Dave Hollins is established in the sense that Larkin, Smith and Ripken are. But his 1992 is consistent with his 1991 partial season, and also with his minor league projections. Besides, he's going to turn 27, and so should at least hold his value for this one "contending" year.

As to the four postseason participants for 1992, they all have two or more superstars. Toronto has Roberto Alomar and Juan Guzman. Last year they had Dave Winfield, and they've replaced him with Paul Molitor. The Oakland A's have Rickey Henderson, albeit on an off year, and they had Jose Canseco, not to mention Dennis Eckersley. The Braves have, as a minimum, Terry Pendelton and Tom Glavine. And the Pirates used to have Barry Bonds and Doug Drabek. That's not to mention the Pittsburgh catching platoon. If you rate the entire catching position for each team, that's the top combo in the league. However, it's not one superstar player, so let's count the 'Rats in for only the two superstars. It' doesn't matter, after all; the Phillies can't compete.

STARS:

The Phillies have two legitimate stars in John Kruk and Mitch Williams. I define a star as someone who will usually finish in the top five at his position, and who has a chance to enter the superstar ranks in a given year. Kruk and Williams certainly fit that definition. We probably ought to include some grouping of Darren Daulton, Lenny Dykstra and Curt Schilling, as well. Dykstra is a clear star, if he keeps his head on straight. Unfortunately, he can't always do that. Daulton is a superstar if he's healthy, but he seldom is. Schilling is, in my mind, a star starter. But he has only one year of support for that. Let's count the Phillies in for four stars; that's probably about what's fair. With Hollins, they have five players who are stars or better.

The Blue Jays have four stars. Their names are Carter, Olerud, Henke and Key, now replaced by Stewart. Candy Maldonado was just on a hot year. Jack Morris did not pitch as well as his Won / Lost record. Duane Ward will probably be a star next year, now that Henke is gone. That gives the Jays a total of seven stars and superstars. The A's had five stars: Steinbach, McGwire, Dave Henderson, Dave Stewart, and whichever of Bob Welch and Mike Moore was healthy in a given year. You don't count both Ruben Sierra and Jose Canseco. Nor do you count Pat Bordick, on the basis of one career year. In any case, the total of stars and superstars is eight. That's how you win 96 games.

The Braves have Smoltz, Avery, Justice, Nixon, and Gant. No wonder they win. And they've added Greg Maddux, too. Well, the 1992 total is, one more time, seven stars and above. the Pirates have Jay Bell, Andy Van Slyke, and Zane Smith. You count Smith for the same reason you count Dave Henderson but not Pat Bordick or Tim Wakefield. We're talking about the talent core of the team, not it's unproven luck. The total, given that we've already counted the catchers, is six stars or above. Again, every postseason team has more of these players than the Phillies have.

CHAMPIONSHIP-QUALITY

A championship-quality player will finish somewhere in the middle of the pack of starters at his position in his league. That's still a good player. Remember, only about half the league's players are starters. If you're in the middle there, you're at about the 75% point in talent over the whole league. You're helping your team, not hurting it. The Phillies have, in my opinion, exactly two such players. They are pitchers Terry Mulholland and Jose De Leon. They are going to have platoons that will produce this much, though. The platoon of Milt Thompson and Pete Incaviglia will certainly turn in that much. In fact, Thompson would be a championship-quality player all by himself, if someone would give him a full-time job. And, among Jim Eisenreich, Wes Chamberlain, Stan Javier, and all the other Phillie outfielders, they will probably get championship-quality play out of the other outfield spot as well. We also have the left over position from the stars count above. So, let's count the Phillies in for five positions filled with this level of play. The total at this level or above is ten positions out of thirteen.

The Jays have, or had five championship-quality players. They are Pat Borders, Candy Maldonado, Devon White, Jack Morris, and Manny Lee backing up Eddie Zosky. The cumulative total is 12. The A's have Borders / Blankenship, Baines and Ron Darling, for a total of 11. The Braves have the first basemen, the catchers, and Charlie Leibrandt, for a total of ten. That's if you don't count the shortstop platoon. The Pirates have, or had, the right field group, Steve Buechele, Randy Tomlin, and the committee bullpen. That's ten again.

BULK

The Phillies have no positions manned by bulk players. They have real holes at the #4 starter spot, and both middle infield positions. Only ten out of their 13 starting spots have bulk play or better.

The Blue Jays have 12 positions manned with championship quality or above. That leaves third base and #4 starter. I'm sure that the Jays were expecting at least championship quality from Kelly Gruber, but they didn't get it. They got a hole. The #4 starter was either Todd Stottlemyre or Dave Stieb, and both were awful. But the Jays reacted in mid-season, with David Cone. That upgrades the hole to at least bulk. One bulk starter, for a total of thirteen-bulk-or-above out of fourteen starters altogether. The A's have three places left. Walt Weiss was awful. The #4 starter, Mike Moore, was certainly bulk. The Lansford / Browne platoon was, too. That's 13 for 14, with the only hole being at short.

The Braves have a hole at second base, with the collapse of Jeff Treadway. Their bullpen was a hole as well. But the shortstops were certainly at least bulk players. That's 11 positions out of 13. The Pirates had at least bulk play out of every position other than Jose Lind's absent bat at second base. That's 12 out of 13.

STARTERS OVERALL:

You can see part of what the Philly problem is contending. They lack people at the top end, and they have some unfilled holes. All the real contenders have more superstars than the Phillies have, and they have no holes or only one. The Phillies, to be blunt, are missing one big-time free agent, and the decent ballplayers necessary to get the middle infield under control. They could also sure use a complete bill of health for Jose De Jesus, and they need for Jose De Leon to avoid his previous problems with winning ballgames.

I want to emphasize this. All the 1992 contenders, all four of them, share a basic profile. They have a couple or three true superstars, about five stars behind them, and mostly championship quality everywhere else. They just don't have holes. The basic profile of superstars / stars / champs / bulk / holes is 2 / 5 / 4 / 1 / 1. Let's check this against reality. Instead of discussing who "is" a superstar, let's say a team had a superstar in 1992 if the player finished first or second in his league at his position, or the equivalent for starting pitchers. Third through fifth, he was a star. Sixth through tenth was championship quality. Eleventh or twelfth was bulk play, and thirteenth or fourteenth was a hole. In the NL, bulk was 10-11, and only 12 was a real hole. Remember, this is tough criteria; Dennis Eckersley is only a "star" here, as he finished third among AL closers in our rankings. So is Rickey Henderson, and Willie Wilson is the Oakland center fielder.

Using this mechanical system, Toronto had a ridiculous four superstars: Roberto Alomar, Joe Carter, Dave Winfield, and Juan Guzman. They had only two regular stars: John Olerud and Candy Maldonado. But they had five championship-quality ballplayers, only two bulk players, and only Kelly Gruber was a hole. The profile is 4 / 2 / 5 / 2 / 1. Oakland's profile is 2 / 4 / 6 / 1 / 1. In the NL, with only 13 starters, the Braves are 3 / 4 / 4 / 2 / 0, and Pittsburgh fielded 2 / 4 / 3 / 3 / 1. If anything, these profiles are even stronger than the theoretical ones developed above.

The Phillies, on the other hand, figure to be more like 1 / 4 / 5 / 0 / 3. So let's take a look at the bench, and see if they can make it up.

PINCH HITTING:

The Phillies are going to have some pinch hitting, the result of all those platooning outfielders. In any given game, only two of Thompson, Eisenreich, Incaviglia, Javier, and Chamberlain can start. The Phils also have Ricky Jordan, who can hit, but not enough to beat out John Kruk and who cannot play the outfield. Pinch hitting, they've got.

Of the contenders above, only the Pirates had the sort of hitting bench the Phils will be sporting, because only they had the sort of outfield platoon the Phils have. The Jays traded all their bulk outfielders away, and so were a little thin on the bench. The A's didn't have much behind Willie Wilson, but Wilson was supposed to be on the bench. The Braves platoon in the infield, where the hitters are few, but they do have Deion Sanders and a couple of backup first basemen. Francisco Cabrera you may recall.

BULK BULLPEN:

The Phils take a pasting. They were using bulk bullpen pitchers in the starting rotation. Every contender above had better middle relief than the Phillies do or will.

SKILL REPLACEMENTS:

The Phils do OK. They have Milt Thompson, who can play a fine reserve center field. They also have just a raft of decent good-glove infielders. The problem, like in the bullpen, is that they have to start them. But they do have enough such people that they won't have troubles with injuries to the keystone combination. The one thing they don't have is a real backup for Darren Daulton. They let Steve Lake go, which a real contender shouldn't do.

However, the Phils don't really get an edge over the contenders here. The Jays and A's actually lived off their infield replacements, and the A's had to play their backup center fielder all year. They still won 96 games. The Braves have deep platooning at the keystone, and Deion Sanders in center and Damon Berryhill behind the plate. They didn't lose a step in defense up the middle. Only the Pirates were questionable. They had Cecil Espy behind Andy Van Slyke, and a platoon at catcher,

but not much to try around the keystone. On balance, though, the Phils don't look any better than the contenders do.

FINAL ANALYSIS:

Pending some big free agent signings, the Phillies are not going to contend. The need a real keystone combination, a real pitching staff, and a backup catcher. Somewhere, they need a superstar to augment Hollins. Don't be fooled by the hot year Darren Daulton had. This is not a contending team. The management is blowing smoke. The real use of this essay is to take a look at how similar the profiles of the contenders were. Use that info the next time someone tells you his favorite team is on the verge of winning. 2/5/4/1/1. One hole, no more, and the team shouldn't really be expecting it. That's the ticket, and nothing else.

Philadelphia Phillies Home Park Performance Factors	Outs	Runs	Hits	2b	3b	HR	W	K	SH	SF	HBP	IBB	SB	CS	GDP
Home LH Batters	.996	.870	.942	.989	.895	.781	.923	.978	.788	.889	1.169	.919	.918	1.031	1.437
Home RH Batters	.995	1.006	1.000	.996	.961	.950	.913	.957	1.047	1.174	1.040	.951	.912	1.755	1.118
All Home Batters	.991	.923	.976	.958	.927	.864	.925	.968	.949	1.033	1.002	.926	.933	1.343	1.139
Opp LH Batters	.951	1.114	.982	.987	.801	1.074	.988	.922	1.150	.869	1.602	.856	.935	.983	1.068
Opp RH Batters	1.023	1.100	1.073	1.173	.770	1.246	1.034	.954	1.206	.873	1.350	.999	1.058	.946	.913
All Opp Batters	1.004	1.104	1.043	1.111	.831	1.171	1.032	.942	1.194	.919	1.277	.985	1.085	1.015	.948
All LH Batters	.976	.952	.958	.988	.858	.858	.943	.955	1.038	.881	1.271	.898	.926	1.010	1.243
All RH Batters	1.009	1.052	1.035	1.077	.851	1.096	.978	.959	1.116	.967	1.165	.972	.968	1.122	1.026
All Batters	.997	1.006	1.008	1.029	.874	.993	.976	.958	1.068	.966	1.097	.953	.998	1.113	1.043

Conventional Batting Records for Philadelphia Phillies

	G	AB	Run	Hit	2B	3B	HR	TB	RBI	W	K	IW	HB	SB	CS	BRng Eff	GI DP	SH	SF	Avg	Slug	OBP	Runs Ctd
Daulton	145	485	80	131	32	5	27	254	109	88	103	11	6	11	2	.323	3	0	6	.270	.524	.385	108
Kruk	144	507	86	164	30	4	10	232	70	92	88	8	1	3	5	.404	11	0	7	.323	.458	.423	104
Morandini	127	422	47	112	8	8	3	145	30	25	64	2	0	8	3	.500	4	6	2	.265	.344	.305	46
Hollins	156	586	104	158	28	4	27	275	93	76	110	4	19	9	6	.607	8	0	4	.270	.469	.369	107
Bell Ju	46	147	12	30	3	1	1	38	8	18	29	5	1	5	0	.429	1	0	2	.204	.259	.292	13
Duncan	142	574	71	153	40	3	8	223	50	17	108	0	5	23	3	.462	15	5	4	.267	.389	.292	64
Dykstra	85	345	53	104	18	0	6	140	39	40	32	4	3	30	5	.380	1	0	4	.301	.406	.375	61
Amaro	126	374	43	82	15	6	7	130	34	37	54	1	9	11	5	.381	11	4	2	.219	.348	.303	40
Jordan	94	276	33	84	19	0	4	115	34	5	44	0	0	3	0	.395	8	0	3	.304	.417	.313	34
Javier	74	276	36	72	14	1	0	88	24	31	43	0	2	17	1	.418	4	2	2	.261	.319	.338	34
Chamberlain	76	275	26	71	18	0	9	116	41	10	55	2	1	4	0	.500	7	1	2	.258	.422	.285	32
Batiste K	44	136	9	28	4	0	1	35	10	4	18	1	0	0	0	.467	7	2	3	.206	.257	.224	7
Sveum	54	135	13	24	4	0	2	34	16	16	39	4	0	0	0	.273	5	0	2	.178	.252	.261	9
Marsh	42	125	7	25	3	2	2	38	16	2	23	0	1	0	1	.714	2	2	2	.200	.304	.215	8
Mulholland	32	83	1	8	1	0	0	9	3	3	35	0	0	0	0	.200	0	6	0	.096	.108	.128	2
Millette	33	78	5	16	0	0	0	16	2	5	10	2	2	1	0	.214	8	2	0	.205	.205	.271	3
Castillo Br	28	76	12	15	3	1	2	26	7	4	15	0	0	1	0	.556	1	1	0	.197	.342	.237	6
Grotewold	72	65	7	13	2	0	3	24	5	9	16	0	1	0	0	.400	4	0	0	.200	.369	.307	7
Schilling	42	64	3	10	1	0	0	11	3	1	22	0	0	0	0	.500	0	8	0	.156	.172	.169	2
Murphy Dl	18	62	5	10	1	0	2	17	7	1	13	0	0	0	0	.250	3	0	0	.161	.274	.175	2
Lake	20	53	3	13	2	0	1	18	2	1	8	0	0	0	0	.000	1	0	1	.245	.340	.255	4
Backman	42	48	6	13	1	0	0	14	6	6	9	1	0	1	0	.500	3	1	0	.271	.292	.352	5
Pratt	16	46	6	13	1	0	2	20	10	4	12	0	0	0	0	.111	0	0	0	.283	.435	.340	6
Lindeman	29	39	6	10	1	0	1	14	6	3	11	0	0	0	0	.375	1	0	0	.256	.359	.310	4
Rivera B	20	32	1	3	0	0	0	3	2	2	10	0	0	0	0	.000	0	2	0	.094	.094	.147	1
Abbott K	31	29	1	2	1	0	0	3	2	1	18	0	0	0	0	.250	0	6	0	.069	.103	.100	1
Greene	13	24	1	3	0	0	0	3	0	0	12	0	0	0	0	01.000	0	0	0	.125	.125	.125	0
Robinson D	10	18	0	7	3	0	0	10	1	0	5	0	0	0	0	.250	1	0	0	.389	.556	.389	3
Brantley C	28	14	1	3	0	1	0	5	1	1	4	0	0	0	0	.000	0	7	0	.214	.357	.267	2
Mathews	14	14	0	0	0	0	0	0	0	1	8	0	0	0	0	.000	0	0	0	.000	.000	.067	0
Scarsone S	7	13	1	2	0	0	0	2	0	1	6	0	0	0	0	.500	0	0	0	.154	.154	.214	0
Brink	8	12	0	1	0	0	0	1	0	0	5	0	1	0	0	.000	0	1	0	.083	.083	.154	0
Cox	9	11	0	1	0	0	0	1	1	0	7	0	0	0	0	.091	0	0	0	.091	.091	.091	0
Ashby A	10	11	0	1	1	0	0	2	1	0	7	0	0	0	0	.000	0	2	0	.091	.182	.091	0
Williams M	5	10	1	4	0	0	0	4	2	0	4	0	0	0	0	.000	0	1	0	.400	.400	.400	2
Peguero	14	9	3	2	0	0	0	2	0	3	3	0	0	0	0	.667	0	1	0	.222	.222	.417	1
Combs	4	8	1	1	1	0	0	2	2	1	1	0	0	0	0	.250	0	1	0	.125	.250	.222	1
DeLeon J	3	5	2	2	0	0	0	2	1	0	1	0	0	0	0	.000	0	1	0	.400	.400	.400	1
Williams Mitch	66	4	0	1	0	0	0	1	0	0	2	0	0	0	0	.000	0	0	0	.250	.250	.250	0
Hartley	46	4	0	0	0	0	0	0	0	0	1	0	0	0	0	.000	0	0	0	.000	.000	.000	0
Jones Ba	44	2	0	0	0	0	0	0	0	0	1	0	0	0	0	.000	0	0	0	.000	.000	.000	0
Weston	1	2	0	0	0	0	0	0	0	0	2	0	0	0	0	.000	0	0	0	.000	.000	.000	0
Ritchie	40	1	0	0	0	0	0	0	0	1	1	0	0	0	0	.000	0	0	0	.000	.000	.500	0
Searcy	10	1	0	0	0	0	0	0	0	0	0	0	0	0	0	.000	0	0	0	.000	.000	.000	0
Chapin	1	0	0	0	0	0	0	0	0	0	0	0	0	0	0	.000	0	0	0	.000	.000	.000	0
Ayrault	30	0	0	0	0	0	0	0	0	0	0	0	0	0	0	.000	0	0	0	.000	.000	.000	0
Baller	8	0	0	0	0	0	0	0	0	0	0	0	0	0	0	.000	0	0	0	.000	.000	.000	0
Shepherd K	12	0	0	0	0	0	0	0	0	0	0	0	0	0	0	.000	0	0	0	.000	.000	.000	0
TOTALS		2121	5500	686	1392	255	36	118	2073	638	509	1059	45	52	127	31	.422	111	64	46	.253	.377	.320	687

Sabermetric Batting Records for Philadelphia Phillies

	AB	Run	Hit	2B	3B	HR	RBI	W	SO	Avg	Slug	OBP	Ctd	Outs	27o	OW%	OG	OWAR	DWAR	TWAR
Amaro	373	43	82	15	5	7	34	36	51	.220	.343	.305	39	312	3.38	.378	12	0.32	0.64	0.97
Backman	46	5	12	0	0	0	5	5	8	.261	.261	.333	4	37	2.92	.312	1	-0.05	0.09	0.04
Batiste K	137	9	29	4	0	1	10	3	17	.212	.263	.224	7	120	1.58	.117	4	-1.04	-0.22	-1.25
Bell Ju	146	12	30	3	0	1	8	17	27	.205	.247	.291	12	118	2.75	.287	4	-0.28	0.47	0.20
Castillo Br	76	12	15	3	0	2	7	3	14	.197	.316	.228	5	63	2.14	.197	2	-0.36	0.07	-0.29
Chamberlain	278	27	73	19	0	9	44	9	52	.263	.428	.286	33	215	4.14	.478	8	1.02	0.20	1.22
Daulton	469	79	125	31	4	25	99	84	97	.267	.510	.383	101	354	7.70	.760	13	5.37	-1.08	4.29
Duncan	582	74	158	43	2	8	54	16	103	.271	.393	.295	66	452	3.94	.453	17	1.73	0.29	2.02
Dykstra	334	52	100	17	0	5	35	38	30	.299	.395	.375	57	243	6.33	.681	9	2.98	0.85	3.83
Grotewold	62	6	12	1	0	2	4	8	15	.194	.306	.296	5	55	2.45	.243	2	-0.22	0.01	-0.21
Hollins	585	105	159	28	3	27	94	74	105	.272	.468	.372	107	444	6.51	.693	16	5.64	0.16	5.80
Javier	275	36	72	14	0	0	24	30	41	.262	.313	.338	33	211	4.22	.487	8	1.07	0.92	2.00
Jordan	280	34	87	20	0	4	37	4	42	.311	.425	.317	35	204	4.63	.534	8	1.39	0.13	1.52
Kruk	490	85	157	29	3	9	64	87	83	.320	.447	.420	96	357	7.26	.738	13	5.13	0.20	5.33
Lake	53	3	13	2	0	1	2	0	7	.245	.340	.241	4	42	2.57	.261	2	-0.14	-0.18	-0.32
Lindeman	39	6	10	1	0	1	6	2	10	.256	.359	.293	4	30	3.60	.409	1	0.07	0.01	0.08
Marsh	125	7	25	3	1	2	17	1	21	.200	.288	.209	7	107	1.77	.143	4	-0.82	0.04	-0.78
Millette	78	5	16	0	0	0	2	4	9	.205	.205	.262	3	72	1.13	.063	3	-0.76	0.37	-0.39
Morandini	408	46	107	7	6	2	27	23	60	.262	.324	.301	40	315	3.43	.385	12	0.41	1.21	1.62
Murphy Dl	62	5	10	1	0	2	7	0	12	.161	.274	.161	2	55	0.98	.049	2	-0.61	-0.09	-0.70
Peguero	8	3	2	0	0	0	0	2	2	.250	.250	.400	1	7	3.86	.442	0	0.02	0.03	0.06
Pratt	46	6	13	1	0	2	10	3	11	.283	.435	.327	6	35	4.63	.533	1	0.24	-0.08	0.15
Scarsone S	13	1	2	0	0	0	0	0	5	.154	.154	.154	0	11	0.00	.000	0	-0.14	0.00	-0.14
Sveum	134	13	24	4	0	2	16	15	37	.179	.254	.260	9	116	2.09	.190	4	-0.69	0.41	-0.28
TOTALS	5502	694	1405	263	31	120	649	497	1011	.255	.380	.321	692	4360	4.29	.495	161	23.38	4.48	27.86

Pitching Records for Philadelphia Phillies

	ERA	W	L	Pct	G	GS	CG	ShO	GF	Sv	IP	R	ER	H	2B	3B	HR	BB	IW	SO	HB	WP	BK
Mulholland	3.81	13	11	.542	32	32	12	2	0	0	229.0	101	97	227	43	3	14	46	3	125	3	3	0
Schilling	2.35	14	11	.560	42	26	10	4	10	2	226.1	67	59	165	30	4	11	59	4	147	1	4	0
Abbott K	5.13	1	14	.067	31	19	0	0	0	0	133.1	80	76	147	16	8	20	45	0	88	1	9	1
Rivera B	2.82	7	3	.700	20	14	4	1	4	0	102.0	32	32	78	16	4	8	32	2	66	2	5	0
Greene	5.32	3	3	.500	13	12	0	0	0	0	64.1	39	38	75	14	2	5	34	2	39	0	1	0
Mathews	5.16	2	3	.400	14	7	0	0	1	0	52.1	31	30	54	13	0	7	24	2	27	1	1	2
Robinson D	6.18	1	4	.200	8	8	0	0	0	0	43.2	32	30	49	10	1	6	4	0	17	1	0	0
Brink	4.14	0	4	.000	8	7	0	0	0	0	41.1	27	19	53	8	2	2	13	2	16	1	0	0
Cox	5.40	2	2	.500	9	7	0	0	0	0	38.1	28	23	46	8	1	3	19	1	30	0	0	0
Ashby A	7.54	1	3	.250	10	8	0	0	0	0	37.0	31	31	42	7	2	6	21	0	24	1	2	0
Williams M	5.34	1	1	.500	5	5	1	0	0	0	28.2	20	17	29	9	1	3	7	0	5	0	0	0
Combs	7.71	1	1	.500	4	4	0	0	0	0	18.2	16	16	20	5	1	0	12	0	11	0	1	0
DeLeon J	3.00	0	1	.000	3	3	0	0	0	0	15.0	7	5	16	1	0	0	5	0	7	0	0	0
Weston	12.27	0	1	.000	1	1	0	0	0	0	3.2	5	5	7	2	0	1	1	0	0	1	0	0
Williams Mitc	3.78	5	8	.385	66	0	0	0	56	29	81.0	39	34	69	16	3	4	64	2	74	6	5	3
Brantley C	4.60	2	6	.250	28	9	0	0	6	0	76.1	45	39	71	9	1	6	58	4	32	4	4	1
Hartley	3.44	7	6	.538	46	0	0	0	15	0	55.0	23	21	54	12	2	5	23	6	53	2	4	0
Jones Ba	4.64	5	6	.455	44	0	0	0	10	0	54.1	30	28	65	15	2	3	24	4	19	2	1	2
Ayrault	3.12	2	2	.500	30	0	0	0	7	0	43.1	16	15	32	9	2	0	17	1	27	1	0	0
Ritchie	3.00	2	1	.667	40	0	0	0	13	1	39.0	17	13	44	10	2	3	17	3	19	0	0	0
Shepherd K	3.27	1	1	.500	12	0	0	0	6	2	22.0	10	8	19	6	0	0	6	1	10	0	1	0
Baller	8.18	0	0	.000	8	0	0	0	4	0	11.0	10	10	10	1	0	5	10	0	9	0	1	0
Searcy	6.10	0	0	.000	10	0	0	0	3	0	10.1	9	7	13	2	1	0	8	0	5	0	0	0
Chapin	9.00	0	0	.000	1	0	0	0	0	0	2.0	2	2	2	1	0	1	0	0	1	0	1	0
TOTALS	4.13	70	92	.432	485	162	27	7	135	34	1428.0	717	655	1387	263	42	113	549	37	851	27	43	9

	Adj ERA	Expected W	L	Pct	BFP	Avg	Slg	OBA	RC/G	GDP	SB	CS	PK	PKE	SH	SF	RSup	RSp/G	W	L	Pct
Abbott K	5.13	5	10	.318	577	.283	.460	.338	5.35	11	9	7	0	2	6	5	41	2.77	3	12	.192
Ashby A	7.54	1	3	.178	171	.290	.490	.379	6.79	3	4	2	0	0	2	2	23	5.59	1	3	.310
Ayrault	3.12	2	2	.558	178	.209	.294	.287	3.14	1	3	0	0	0	4	3	21	4.36	2	2	.615
Baller	8.18	0	0	.155	51	.250	.650	.392	8.87	0	3	2	0	0	0	1	1	0.82	0	0	.008
Brantley C	4.60	3	5	.367	353	.251	.353	.382	4.99	9	10	5	0	0	5	3	51	6.01	5	3	.583
Brink	4.14	2	2	.418	187	.308	.413	.360	5.36	5	3	2	0	0	1	0	8	1.74	1	3	.126
Chapin	9.00	0	0	.132	8	.250	.750	.250	6.83	0	0	0	0	0	0	0	0	0.00	0	0	.000
Combs	7.71	0	2	.171	88	.278	.375	.376	5.64	1	4	1	0	1	3	1	17	8.20	1	1	.480
Cox	5.40	1	3	.296	178	.299	.422	.371	6.11	2	4	1	0	0	3	2	21	4.93	2	2	.405
DeLeon J	3.00	1	0	.577	63	.281	.298	.339	3.42	1	0	1	0	0	1	0	9	5.40	1	0	.726
Greene	5.32	2	4	.303	298	.291	.419	.371	6.07	6	13	1	0	1	4	2	44	6.16	3	3	.523
Hartley	3.44	7	6	.510	243	.255	.401	.332	4.99	2	8	2	0	0	5	1	28	4.58	8	5	.592
Jones Ba	4.64	4	7	.363	243	.305	.437	.378	5.72	8	1	1	1	0	2	3	23	3.81	4	7	.355
Mathews	5.16	2	3	.316	228	.270	.440	.350	5.30	4	3	3	0	1	2	1	21	3.61	1	4	.286
Mulholland	3.81	11	13	.458	937	.261	.365	.298	3.67	14	2	5	15	2	10	7	127	4.99	14	10	.583
Ritchie	3.00	2	1	.577	174	.288	.438	.359	5.48	6	3	0	0	0	4	0	14	3.23	1	2	.486
Rivera B	2.82	6	4	.606	409	.211	.341	.277	3.22	7	13	2	1	0	5	1	66	5.82	8	2	.776
Robinson D	6.18	1	4	.243	183	.290	.467	.300	5.29	1	7	0	0	0	3	6	20	4.12	1	4	.266
Schilling	2.35	17	8	.690	895	.201	.288	.254	2.43	10	7	7	0	2	7	8	86	3.42	16	9	.634
Searcy	6.10	0	0	.248	50	.325	.425	.429	6.68	1	0	1	0	0	1	1	4	3.48	0	0	.210
Shepherd K	3.27	1	1	.534	91	.247	.325	.291	3.18	0	3	3	0	1	4	3	6	2.45	1	1	.315
Weston	12.27	0	1	.075	19	.412	.706	.474	13.52	1	1	0	0	0	0	0	1	2.45	0	1	.032
Williams M	5.34	1	1	.301	121	.259	.438	.300	4.35	3	1	0	1	0	1	1	24	7.54	1	1	.619
Williams Mitch	3.78	6	7	.462	368	.240	.359	.386	5.17	3	9	6	2	6	8	3	30	3.33	5	8	.389
TOTALS	4.15	67	95	.416	6113	.257	.384	.326	4.39	99	111	53	19	17	81	53	686	4.32	76	86	.470

Batting 'Splits' Records for Philadelphia Phillies

SPLITS for Daulton

	G	AB	Run	Hit	2B	3B	HR	TB	RBI	W	K	IW	HB	SB	CS	DP	SH	SF	Avg	Slug	OBP	RC
vs LHP	110	202	33	52	16	0	11	101	40	30	45	1	4	6	2	1	0	1	.257	.500	.363	40
vs RHP	139	283	47	79	16	5	16	153	69	58	58	10	2	5	0	2	0	5	.279	.541	.399	68
Home	70	229	47	73	17	4	17	149	63	46	51	6	3	6	2	0	0	3	.319	.651	.434	71
Away	75	256	33	58	15	1	10	105	46	42	52	5	3	5	0	3	0	3	.227	.410	.339	40
Grass	40	144	21	30	8	0	5	53	26	19	24	1	2	1	0	2	0	3	.208	.368	.304	18
Turf	105	341	59	101	24	5	22	201	83	69	79	10	4	10	2	1	0	3	.296	.589	.417	93
April/June	68	225	36	66	17	2	12	123	55	43	51	5	1	7	1	0	0	4	.293	.547	.403	56
July/October	77	260	44	65	15	3	15	131	54	45	52	6	5	4	1	3	0	2	.250	.504	.369	52

SPLITS for Hollins

	G	AB	Run	Hit	2B	3B	HR	TB	RBI	W	K	IW	HB	SB	CS	DP	SH	SF	Avg	Slug	OBP	RC
vs LHP	104	245	49	79	16	3	17	152	45	23	44	3	6	2	3	4	0	2	.322	.620	.391	59
vs RHP	156	341	55	79	12	1	10	123	48	53	66	1	13	7	3	4	0	2	.232	.361	.355	49
Home	81	291	62	77	19	2	14	142	48	46	54	4	11	5	1	5	0	1	.265	.488	.384	59
Away	75	295	42	81	9	2	13	133	45	30	56	0	8	4	5	3	0	3	.275	.451	.354	48
Grass	38	152	23	41	5	1	8	72	27	13	36	0	5	1	4	3	0	1	.270	.474	.345	24
Turf	118	434	81	117	23	3	19	203	66	63	74	4	14	8	2	5	0	3	.270	.468	.377	83
April/June	74	277	46	74	12	2	10	120	38	39	51	0	9	6	4	3	0	2	.267	.433	.373	48
July/October	82	309	58	84	16	2	17	155	55	37	59	4	10	3	2	5	0	2	.272	.502	.366	59

SPLITS for Kruk

	G	AB	Run	Hit	2B	3B	HR	TB	RBI	W	K	IW	HB	SB	CS	DP	SH	SF	Avg	Slug	OBP	RC
vs LHP	103	210	29	66	9	1	1	80	18	37	42	1	0	0	2	5	0	2	.314	.381	.414	35
vs RHP	142	297	57	98	21	3	9	152	52	55	46	7	1	3	3	6	0	5	.330	.512	.430	69
Home	72	248	48	76	11	1	7	110	37	46	39	4	0	2	2	2	0	4	.306	.444	.409	50
Away	72	259	38	88	19	3	3	122	33	46	49	4	1	1	3	9	0	3	.340	.471	.437	54
Grass	38	134	23	43	8	1	3	62	17	29	29	3	1	0	2	3	0	1	.321	.463	.442	29
Turf	106	373	63	121	22	3	7	170	53	63	59	5	0	3	3	8	0	6	.324	.456	.416	75
April/June	69	253	45	93	15	2	5	127	37	42	39	5	0	1	3	7	0	3	.368	.502	.453	59
July/October	75	254	41	71	15	2	5	105	33	50	49	3	1	2	2	4	0	4	.280	.413	.395	46

SPLITS for Philadelphia Phillies (all batters except pitchers)

	G	AB	Run	Hit	2B	3B	HR	TB	RBI	W	K	IW	HB	SB	CS	DP	SH	SF	Avg	Slug	OBP	RC
vs LHP	1101	2286	275	589	110	12	53	882	255	189	428	16	21	50	15	47	25	17	.258	.386	.318	286
vs RHP	1677	3214	411	803	145	24	65	1191	383	320	631	29	31	77	16	64	39	29	.250	.371	.321	401
Home	1050	2685	369	688	133	19	67	1060	342	269	526	24	26	65	10	47	34	21	.256	.395	.328	366
Away	1071	2815	317	704	122	17	51	1013	296	240	533	21	26	62	21	64	30	25	.250	.360	.312	323
Grass	544	1463	189	377	65	7	33	555	173	118	282	10	17	21	13	32	18	13	.258	.379	.318	177
Turf	1577	4037	497	1015	190	29	85	1518	465	391	777	35	35	106	18	79	46	33	.251	.376	.321	510
April/June	988	2528	319	643	128	13	52	953	303	245	491	22	25	55	17	52	23	24	.254	.377	.324	319
July/October	1133	2972	367	749	127	23	66	1120	335	264	568	23	27	72	14	59	41	22	.252	.377	.317	368

III

Player
Season
Rankings

Starting Pitchers

Brock J. Hanke

		ADJ ERA	GS	ACTUAL			EXPECTED			SUPPORTED		
				W	L	PCT	W	L	PCT	W	L	PCT
1.	Clemens	2.34	32	18	11	.621	21	8	.738	21	8	.730
2.	Appier	2.38	30	15	8	.652	17	6	.732	16	7	.702
3.	Mussina	2.54	32	18	5	.783	16	7	.705	17	6	.745
4.	Guzman Juan	2.64	28	16	5	.762	14	7	.688	15	6	.738
5.	Abbott	2.69	29	7	15	.318	15	7	.681	10	12	.444
6.	Perez M	2.80	33	13	16	.448	19	10	.663	18	11	.636
7.	Nagy	2.82	33	17	10	.630	18	9	.659	18	9	.663
8.	Smiley	3.17	34	16	9	.640	15	10	.604	15	10	.618
9.	Welch	3.20	20	11	7	.611	11	7	.600	12	6	.694
10.	McDowell J	3.31	34	20	10	.667	18	12	.584	21	9	.691
11.	Wegman	3.34	35	13	14	.481	16	11	.580	17	10	.635
12.	Erickson S	3.35	32	13	12	.520	14	11	.578	15	10	.584
13.	Viola	3.37	35	13	12	.520	14	11	.576	12	13	.490
14.	Fleming	3.39	33	17	10	.630	15	12	.573	16	11	.574
15.	Brown Kev	3.42	35	21	11	.656	18	14	.568	20	12	.613
16.	Navarro	3.48	34	17	11	.607	16	12	.560	17	11	.596
17.	Key	3.53	33	13	13	.500	14	12	.553	17	9	.655
18.	Langston	3.54	32	13	14	.481	15	12	.552	13	14	.473
19.	Valera	3.59	28	8	11	.421	10	9	.544	9	10	.490
20.	Stewart D	3.61	31	12	10	.545	12	10	.541	13	9	.573
21.	Darling	3.62	33	15	10	.600	14	11	.540	15	10	.600
22.	Cook D	3.65	25	5	7	.417	6	6	.537	6	6	.511
23.	Johnson R	3.77	31	12	14	.462	14	12	.521	14	12	.521
24.	Bosio	3.77	33	16	6	.727	11	11	.519	13	9	.611
25.	Guzman Jose	3.78	33	16	11	.593	14	13	.519	17	10	.633
26.	Pichardo	3.82	24	9	6	.600	8	7	.513	10	5	.647
27.	Finley C	3.83	31	7	12	.368	10	9	.512	8	11	.440
28.	Ryan	3.83	27	5	9	.357	7	7	.512	7	7	.488
29.	Tapani	3.93	34	16	11	.593	13	14	.500	18	9	.662
30.	Dopson	3.95	25	7	11	.389	9	9	.497	8	10	.460
31.	Morris Jk	4.04	34	21	6	.778	13	14	.486	17	10	.644
32.	Moore M	4.08	36	17	12	.586	14	15	.481	16	13	.550
33.	Hough	4.08	27	7	12	.368	9	10	.480	8	11	.407
34.	Hesketh	4.24	25	8	9	.471	8	9	.462	9	8	.537
35.	McDonald	4.24	35	13	13	.500	12	14	.461	13	13	.496
36.	Kamieniecki	4.26	28	6	14	.300	9	11	.459	9	11	.468
37.	Gullickson	4.30	34	14	13	.519	12	15	.454	15	12	.557
38.	Tanana	4.34	31	13	11	.542	11	13	.450	11	13	.446
39.	McCaskill	4.35	34	12	13	.480	11	14	.449	12	13	.494
40.	Witt B	4.38	31	10	14	.417	11	13	.450	11	13	.438
41.	Krueger	4.38	29	10	8	.556	8	10	.443	11	7	.599
42.	Armstrong	4.43	23	6	15	.286	9	12	.440	9	12	.421
43.	Fernandez A	4.46	29	8	11	.421	8	11	.436	8	11	.419
44.	Sutcliffe	4.47	36	16	15	.516	13	18	.435	13	18	.422
45.	Stottlemyre	4.50	27	12	11	.522	10	13	.432	13	10	.586
46.	Blyleven	4.53	24	8	12	.400	9	11	.428	7	13	.357
47.	Hibbard	4.60	28	10	7	.588	7	10	.421	6	11	.376
48.	Bones	4.79	28	9	10	.474	8	11	.401	7	12	.380
49.	Hanson	4.82	30	8	17	.320	10	15	.398	9	16	.351
50.	Sanderson	4.84	33	12	11	.522	9	14	.396	13	10	.578
51.	Scudder	5.04	22	6	10	.375	6	10	.378	6	10	.366
52.	Milacki	5.84	20	6	8	.429	4	10	.311	5	9	.375

1. Roger Clemens (BOS)

I do the occasional call-in show here in St. Louis, and probably the most-asked question is, "Who is the best player in baseball?". My answer varies, depending on whether I think the caller is asking about the current year's performance, the current established level of play, a prediction for the coming year, a prediction for the whole career, or a prediction for the next few years. If you think about it, those are all different questions, but they're all asked with the same words on call-in shows.

At any rate, sometimes my answer is "Ryne Sandberg", and sometimes "Barry Bonds", and sometimes "Ivan Rodriguez", and sometimes "Cal Ripken, Jr.", but it's never a pitcher. That's because, in general, callers don't want to know about pitchers. They think pitchers are inconsistent, and they're right. They also think that pitchers can't affect a team's overall record as much as an everyday player, and they're wrong. Mostly, though, it's the consistency.

Well, I have this to say. If I were to ask that question, what I would mean is, "Who would you pay the most money to sign to what is currently referred to as a long-term contract?". That is, given what contracts are like now, "who do you think will win the most games for a team in the next six years, compared to a good replacement?". And the answer to that is "Roger Clemens". The biggest difference between Clemens and Bonds or Ripken or Sandberg or Rodriguez or any other position player is that Roger Clemens has the consistency of a position player, and he's a pitcher. That has added value, because it redefines what "good replacement" means.

But there's another difference. That's the innings Roger can handle per year. In effect, Roger plays 170 games in a 162-game season. No position player can do that. But Roger can, because the available work is open-ended. The rules allow Roger to pitch as much as he can take. It's similar to the added value Ripken gets from being a shortstop, and thereby having more defensive responsibility than any other hitter of his caliber. But Roger gets even more extra opportunity, and that, to my mind, makes him THE MOST VALUABLE PLAYER IN BASEBALL.

2. Kevin Appier (KC)

I'll bet no other analyst has Kevin ranked this high. After all, he only won 15 games, and he plays for the Royals, and they have the much-flashier Tom Gordon for sportswriters to write about. And, to be honest, I'd rather have Juan Guzman than Kevin, because I think Juan can handle more innings per year. Still, Juan had some arm trouble, and Kevin didn't. And the difference in the two Won/Lost records is mostly due to the difference in the teams behind the pitchers. And therefore, I can't really justify putting Juan first; it's just a gut feeling. In any case, unless your fantasy league counts wins highly, Kevin Appier is FANTASY LEAGUE BEST BUY. If wins count big, you have to factor in the ability of the Royals to score runs and field ground balls.

3. Mike Mussina (BAL)

Mike doesn't strike enough batters out to indicate that he has a strong enough arm to handle 241 innings of work. Also, his hits, walks, and homers allowed don't really support the ERA. And therefore, I rate Mussina a BAD FANTASY BUY and a likely candidate for a big drop in the coming campaign. In the long term, I like him, and think he might turn out to be a top-ten pitcher in the American League, but not next year.

4. Juan Guzman (TOR)

He's only 26. This was supposed to be his Sophomore Slump. He only pitched 181 innings, and that's his career high by 50. He has monster strikeout totals. With all that, you might think I'd start the comment with "Superman here...." And I was tempted to do that. But there was that little bit of time lost with - shudder - arm trouble. I've got to wait and see if that has a long-term effect.

My bet is that it won't. My bet is that this is, in fact, Superman. And I certainly bet that his team is going to help his Won/Lost record. And, therefore, I've got to rate him as THE FANTASY PITCHER MVP, given what the Red Sox are likely to support Roger Clemens with.

I also have this to say. Cito Gaston got a lot of good press for being laid back and letting the talented Blue Jays just do their winning thing. And, in general, that press was deserved. But the idea of installing Jack Morris, off the season he had, as the Jays' starting postseason ace, when Cito had Juan Guzman available, is just a joke. I told everyone who would listen that Morris would bomb, and I only wish I'd gone to Las Vegas with a few hundred dollars to gamble. Juan Guzman, and no one else, is the Blue Jay ace.

5. Jim Abbott (CAL - NYY)

If you read my comments on the Angels last year, you know that I wasn't surprised when Whitey Herzog traded Jim Abbott away. Whitey simply doesn't believe in starting pitchers as the center of a team. He doesn't trust their consistency, and I am pretty much in agreement with that. Still, Abbott is not the pitcher I'd have given up. He's pitched great, and his 1992 Won/Lost record is in fact the joke that everyone thinks it was.

As you might imagine, I watched with interest to see what would happen the year after Abbott pitched 243 innings. He held up just fine, even though his strikeout totals don't support the idea that he can handle quite that much load. Here's what I have to say about that. I don't like using Jim Abbot in arm analysis at all. That's because his disability is, in this case, an advantage. As opposed to everyone else, Jim Abbott has had to use his one arm for everything. That may have built strength that no one else has. And therefore, I don't like to make workload comments about Jim.

6. Melido Perez (NYY)

I'm sure the Chisox are kicking themselves right now, after trading Melido for Steve Sax. In general, I agree, it was a lousy trade. That's not because I think that Melido was an obvious star in the making, though. It's because I don't think that much of Steve Sax, and regarded his 1991 season as a fluke.

In any case, I think Melido is a little over his head here in the rankings. I also note that his workload went up over 100 innings, to a career high by over 50. Do I need to write the rest of the comment? BAD FANTASY GAMBLE.

7. Charles Nagy (CLE)

Looks great to me, but 1) he pitches for the Indians, and 2) he put in over 250 innings.

8. John Smiley (MIN - CIN)

A very good pitcher, but he did set a big fat career high in workload, and he's changing teams for the second straight year. If he gets settled with one team, I expect him to return to a consistent (for a pitcher) and high level of play.

9. Bob Welch (OAK)

He's 36 years old, he's been brutally overworked by Tony LaRussa, he had an arm problem in 1992, and his strikeout totals went south in 1991. Against that is that his arm got some rest last year. He might put on a last big hurrah this year, when he's the acknowledged staff ace, but I think he'll be all but finished by 1994.

10. Jack McDowell (CHA)

Has led the league in complete games the last two years, with workloads over 250 innings, and he wants to campaign for the Cy Young award on the basis of how many games he wins. He's also on a team that has little else in the rotation, and whose closer - Bobby Thigpen - has completely collapsed from overwork. All this means that his manager is going to give him the ball as often as he'll take it and leave him in for as long as he can stand up out there. And he's going to refuse not one inning of it. BAD GAMBLE for anything but arm collapse.

11. Bill Wegman (MIL)

I like everything but the workload. The last time this man got 200 innings, his arm collapsed for THREE YEARS. I just cannot imagine what his mangler was thinking, to ask him to do that again.

12. Scott Erickson (MIN)

I think this is about his real level of ability. On the other hand, his ERA has gone up every year he's been in the Majors, and he's had two straight years of more than 200 innings. He may not have bottomed out yet.

13. Frank Viola (BOS)

Frank was able to sustain a very high level of ability for as long as his Strikeout to Inning ratio held at about 4/5. That stopped in 1991, and he really isn't the same pitcher. He can sustain a very high workload without injury, but I doubt his ability to keep the innings up and the quality up without the strikeout arm. Since the Bosox are doubtless going to overwork him again, and since they don't have anything like the offense to back him up with what he's used to, I expect him to step backwards in 1993. After that, we'll see what his team and his manager do to and for him.

14. Dave Fleming (SEA)

In the minors, he struck out many more batters per inning than he did last year. That's a sign that he probably needed the year in AAA ball that he was promoted past. Also, he took a career shot to the old innings pitched total. With all that, and Sophomore Slump as well, I'm not too sanguine about 1993. In the long run, well, his minor league stats certainly do support the idea that he'll be able to pitch in the Majors. Until we get some more big league results, I'll have to go with that.

15. Kevin Brown (TEX)

This looks like the age-27 career years that position players put in. Except, of course, that position players can't get overworked like this. If Kevin can handle this sort of inning load, he's Superman. Given his previous stats, I figure that to be a 1% bet at best. He might hold up for one year, just because he seems to

have finally found a strikeout pitch, but I'd be astonished if he hasn't regressed mightily by 1994.

16. Jaime Navarro (MIL)

Navarro, Bill Wegman, and Chris Bosio had very similar seasons, for three pitchers on the same team. Wegman was the best, and Bosio the luckiest. In couple of ways, though, Jaime was the oddest. His Strikeout / Walk ratio is really bad for a pitcher with this low an ERA. His Opposition Batting Average is low, but not low enough to really compensate for the walks. What he does have is the ability to keep the ball in the ballpark.

Now, a low Home Run total is usually linked to low Strikeouts, but it is also usually linked to low Walks. That is, it's the characteristic of the junkballer who throws down, and who lives by his control. That Jaime doesn't have that control is an indicator that he might get better. On the other hand, that he doesn't strike out that many indicates that he's living on the edge, and could fall apart over a comparatively minor problem. Like both Bill and Chris, he's getting much more work than I would like to see, and so I'm wary of all three of them. But I'm wariest of Jaime, despite his young age.

17. Jimmy Key (TOR - NYY)

If I were running the Jays, I'd have ponied up for both Dave Winfield and Jimmy Key. To a large extent, Jimmy saved the Series for the Jays with that one good game he did pitch. What was happening was that Jack Morris wasn't worth his uniform, as any damn fool could have figured out by looking at his 1992 ERA, instead of his Won / Lost record. This was placing a lot of stress on the staff, leaving them with little margin to work with if Juan Guzman, say, got himself in a tight ballgame. Then Jimmy rose up and pitched his game. That gave the Jays' bullpen rest, and gave Cito - and Guzman - a rotation tempo to work with. That was all they needed. Of course, what Cito should have done was replace Morris with Key in the rotation as soon as the ALCS was over.

For those of you who haven't read the earlier SABERMETRICs, and who aren't yet tired of workload comments, Jimmy is one of the obvious cases. He was given 261 innings in 1987, and his arm didn't recover until 1991. I think he's right on the edge of what he can do right now. His next manager has to be careful, or he's going to get one sore-armed starter for his trouble.

18. Mark Langston (CAL)

If you want to see what happens to Superman when he gets Superworkload, here it is. Mark

hasn't struck out 200 batters since he reached the Angels, and they won't let up on the work, and so here he is, rather than in the Top Ten, where his talent would place him. That he can keep answering the bell at all, much less at any level of ability, is what marks him as Superman.

19. Julio Valera (CAL)

A Grade B rookie prospect who pitched about as well in the Major Leagues as he could have. The question isn't, "Is Julio going to get better?". The answer to that one is, "Why would you think that, if you've looked at his minor league stats?". The question is, "How did Mark Langston fall so far as to pitch no better than Julio Valera?". The answer is, "Julio pitched over his head."

20. Dave Stewart (OAK - TOR)

Those of you who haven't read the earlier SABERMETRICS need the following information. Dave Stewart, for one reason or another, got a very late start as a full time pitcher. This allowed his arm to handle workloads that would have destroyed appendages that had suffered more early stress. Finally, though, in 1991, even Dave's wing went down.

The result has been much less work for Dave. This is not because Tony LaRussa has learned anything about arms, though. It's just that Dave has pitched badly enough that he keeps getting pulled out of games sooner than he used to. I do think, however, that a year of fewer than 200 innings is probably all the man needs to recover to what he used to have. I don't think he can keep it up, if Cito insists on returning him to 230-inning loads, but for one year, this is a VERY GOOD FANTASY BUY, as everyone has figured out that he has gone down, and no one is going to expect a recovery. Also, the Jays aren't going to let him down on offense.

21. Ron Darling (OAK)

This was an odd year for Ron. His Strikeouts went down, but so did his Home Runs. The result was an improved ERA without any real substantive improvement in reliable supporting stats. If his homers return to normal, and they probably will, his ERA could jump right back up to 4 again. On the other hand, if he can keep the ball in the park - and Oakland's stadium will help him - and regain the Strikeout arm, he could move up a little from this and become a very good pitcher again. I give him a 50% chance of moving back down, a 20% of staying where he is and a 30% chance of moving up.

22.   Dennis Cook (CLE)

Respectable bulk starting pitching. If the Indians field the team they think they will field, he will help, just as he would help the Expos, or any other team with a thin starting staff. If, on the other hand, the Indians are no better than I think they will be, he won't make any difference. If his manager goes crazy, and gives him 200 innings or something, he'll fall apart. That could happen, if the Indians have a good team or a lucky start, and they are very thin in pitching.

23.   Randy Johnson (SEA)

If Randy Johnson can stop leading the league in Walks allowed, he'll be a Top Ten pitcher. If not, this is it. One thing in his favor is that his managers in Seattle have not overworked him so far. Of course, this is because of the large number of games from which he has to be removed in the second inning or so, but it's still not overwork. For a while last year, Don Malcolm grumbled incessantly about Randy Johnson. This is because the Bill James game includes this feature of "bonus points" for bizarre performances, like very high strikeouts in one game. Johnson, while no better a pitcher than Don thought he should be, had turned in some bonus point performances for Don's top rival in his league. Don was seriously worried that he might lose his league by fewer points than those bonus points. In fact, that race was very close. I guess that does mean that Randy has some extra value in the Bill James game, but the reason that he's a GOOD FANTASY BUY is that he won't be any worse than this, while he could any year get his act together and win you a pennant singlehandedly.

24.   Chris Bosio (MIL - SEA)

The last time Chris got 230 innings of work, his ERA went up the next year by over a run. The last time he got 200 innings, his ERA went up by over a third of a run. That was in 1991. The Brewers apparently thought they were going to ride Chris', Bill Wegman's and Jaime Navarro's arms to sweet, sweet victory. If they were trying to conquer the Disabled List, they were right. As it is, the Mariners may need to have a two-year plan to get what they expect out of Chris.

25.   Jose Guzman (TEX - CHN)

Bulk starting pitching. The important thing to remember about him is that he is not Juan Guzman. This is the tall one, the old one, and the bad one. You know, the typical Cubbie pitcher. Now, Juan Guzman, HE might have really replaced Greg Maddux.

26.   Hipolito Pichardo (KC)

An interesting experiment by Hal McRae and the Royals. Hipolito here was at Memphis (AA ball) in 1991, where he got 99 innings as a spot starter of some sort. He was awful. Then, last year, he turned in two outstanding starts for the Chicks and the Royals promptly promoted him to the big club. He slipped into the rotation, and was never removed. As to results, well, he's ranked in the middle of the pack here. He didn't strike anybody out, and he walked a normal number, so that's a minus. He gave up some hits, but not too many home runs, which is no surprise given Royals Stadium. He's so young (23) that he could turn into almost anything, but his minor league stats, frankly, indicate mediocrity. A GREAT FANTASY BUY, as you'll get him for almost nothing, and the Royals will give him a rotation spot, and he'll probably be no worse than this again.

27.   Chuck Finley (CAL)

He got 236 innings in 1990, and his ERA went up a full run the next year. His load hasn't come down, so neither has his ERA. The worst thing that happened to him is that he got a fluke 18/9 Won/Lost record in 1991 without pitching anything like that well. Neither Buck Rodgers nor Whitey Herzog is any good at figuring this sort of thing out, so I expect Chuck won't get any better than this for a while yet. But, if somebody does figure out that he should be pitched about 180 innings a year, he's a Top Twenty pitcher and maybe more.

28.   Nolan Ryan (TEX)

At 319 / 287, his Won / Lost record is right up to the standards of the Hall of Fame. Of course, it's a foregone conclusion, since he has pitched well into his mid-40s. Actually, this was his worst year for ERA since 1985 in Houston. Given that, I can't say he's through yet.

29.   Kevin Tapani (MIN)

You know what would help with these comments? It would help if I had a macro. The macro would insert "got over 220 innings and his ERA went up a full run or more" into a comment with one keystroke. I also need another: "his mangler did it again, so he won't be getting any better next year".

30.   John Dopson (BOS)

About what you expect from Boston's #5 starter. This is completely consistent with every other year he's ever had. That includes his season in Montreal; the difference in ERA is mostly league and ballpark.

31.   Jack Morris (TOR)

Pitched about as well as John Dopson. How could anyone be fooled by his second-in-the-league run support? How could anyone ink him in as the post-season ace starter? How could someone who did that WIN the World Series? What's more, since he's pitched this bad or worse four of the last five years, I have no choice but to list him as FINISHED again.

32.   Mike Moore (OAK - DET)

Overworked again, unlikely to improve, worthless on the free agent market. Fits right in with the rest of Sparky's staff.

33.   Charlie Hough (CHA - FLA)

Finished. Now, I'm not going to guess how long it will take the White Sox to acquire five starters who are better than this, but this man is FINISHED. If I didn't have five better starters, I'd start signing guys from the Mexican League. Florida signed him to a minor league contract, which means he's a coach.

34.   Joe Hesketh (BOS)

Has had two good seasons as a spot starter, and is a ridiculous ten games over .500 for his career. Since every Major League manager believes in superstitious luck, he should be able to find work for at least five more years.

35.   Ben McDonald (BAL)

Has yet to recover from Sophomore Slump, which is a bad sign. He also pitched over 220 innings. Still, if there is anyone who can buck those innings and take a stride forward, it's this raw talent that apparently lacks a brain.

36.   Scott Kamieniecki (NYY)

He pitched OK in 1991, but that was the first time, and he's 29 now. Still, the Yankees have to pitch something, and this is all they've got. A GOOD FANTASY BUY, as he'll probably start again, and you'll pay nothing for him.

37.   Bill Gullickson (DET)

Oh, look! Oh, look! Sparky Anderson gave a 32-year-old pitcher 220 innings of work in 1991! And then the Detroit offense gave the man so much support he actually won 20 games, so Sparky did it again! You don't suppose the man's ERA went up a run in 1992, do you? You don't suppose he's not going to recover until his workload goes down, do you? Where's that macro?

38. Frank Tanana (DET - NYM)

Frank has put in roughly a decade of bulk starting pitching, and I have no idea how long he can keep it up. But I do know that he will continue to be employed for as long as he can. Lo, how the Metty have fallen.

39. Kirk McCaskill (CHA)

Either this guy was never any good, and his 1986 season was a complete fluke, or his arm has never recovered from the 246 innings he worked then, despite numerous opportunities. I vote for "mediocre pitcher who had a lucky year".

40. Bobby Witt (TEX/OAK)

This ranking is based on his composite Adjusted ERA with both the Rangers and the A's. The Rangers were waiting for his Walks to come down; instead, his Strikeouts did. Of course, that's what happens after an arm injury. Did you notice that the injury followed his one 200-inning season? What I think is that the A's should try to turn him into a reliever. Surely he could be as entertaining a closer as Mitch Williams.

41. Bill Krueger (MIN/MTL - DET)

This ranking is based on his composite Adjusted ERA with both the Twins and the Expos. There probably ought to be a tiny adjustment to that figure for the difference in base ERAs between the two leagues, but it wouldn't move Bill any in the rankings here, since I've been careful to list him after Bobby Witt. An old pitcher with a big fat arm injury in the middle of his career. Still, he's right at .500, and most teams don't have five guys better than that. This was an off year. Bill is better than Charlie Hough right now. Hell, he might turn out to be the Tiger ace.

42. Jack Armstrong (CLE - FLA)

Yes, it is time to write the All-American Boy off. He is still young enough to become a Major League pitcher, but he is demonstrably not one now. He'd have to be one of those surprises in his 30s that do happen.

43. Alex Fernandez (CHA)

Still young enough to become a Major League pitcher, but he's not one yet. As the Chisox have no one else to gamble upon, he'll be out there again in '93. Consequently, he's a GOOD FANTASY GAMBLE.

44. Rick Sutcliffe (BAL)

I can't believe the O's signed this guy again. Get it through your head, he was finished three years ago, when his arm went out again. Finished, finished, finished. Now, of course, he'll go out there and have a miraculous recovery.

45. Todd Stottlemyre (TOR)

This year was right about on his career average. That means that he's in the same category as Jack Armstrong. To be blunt, Todd has done nothing to indicate that he's anything more than a career AAA pitcher on a team with a hot offense.

46. Bert Blyleven (CAL)

A pitching coach that the Angels activated for some reason. The reason he went out there when they called, of course, is that he only needs 13 wins to reach 300 and secure his spot into the Hall of Fame. If I were the BBWAA, I'd waive the rules and vote him in, rather than watch another two years of this.

47. Greg Hibbard (CHA - CHN)

The hitters adjusted to him after a year, and he hasn't counter-adjusted back. Whether he can adjust is another question, but he's shown more than Armstrong or Stottlemyre, so I can't write him off just yet.

48. Ricky Bones (MIL)

I see nothing in his minor league record to suggest that he should be inserted into a starting Major League rotation.

49. Eric Hanson (SEA)

I predicted this would happen when he pitched 236 innings in 1990. Now I predict that he's had enough time to recover, and might get his act back together. Lord knows, the Mariners could use a break like that.

50. Scott Sanderson (NYY)

It took two years, because he was getting only a few over 200 innings, but the arm did go under. If you don't think that was it, look at the drop in the Strikeout column. His arm's just tired, that's all.

51. Scott Scudder (CLE)

Whitey Herzog thought this guy was a hot prospect a few years back. In fact, Whitey's last attempt to trade for someone to replace Jack Clark (Eric Davis) fell apart over the Reds' refusal to include Scott here. That's all I can think of to say about Scott at the Major League level.

52. Bob Milacki (BAL)

His rookie season introduction to the Major Leagues was 243 innings at the age of 24. He wasn't all that good then, and he's never recovered. I'd be astonished if he ever got enough back to be a respectable big league pitcher again. Right now, he'd have trouble with AAA ball.

Starting Pitchers

Brock J. Hanke

		ADJ ERA	GS	ACTUAL			EXPECTED			SUPPORTED		
				W	L	PCT	W	L	PCT	W	L	PCT
1.	Swift	2.08	22	10	4	.714	10	4	.740	11	3	.756
2.	Martinez De	2.19	32	16	11	.593	19	8	.720	20	7	.734
3.	Tewksbury	2.20	32	16	5	.762	15	6	.717	16	5	.738
4.	Maddux G	2.22	35	20	11	.645	22	9	.714	22	9	.723
5.	Schilling	2.35	26	14	11	.560	17	8	.690	16	9	.634
6.	Hill K	2.39	33	16	9	.640	17	8	.682	19	6	.742
7.	Rijo	2.47	33	15	10	.600	17	8	.667	18	7	.712
8.	Swindell	2.57	30	12	8	.600	13	7	.650	15	5	.750
9.	Morgan M	2.59	34	16	8	.667	16	8	.647	16	8	.675
10.	Glavine	2.68	33	20	8	.714	18	10	.631	21	7	.763
11.	Drabek	2.77	34	15	11	.577	16	10	.615	16	10	.621
12.	Smoltz	2.77	35	15	12	.556	17	10	.615	18	9	.659
13.	Fernandez S	2.81	32	14	11	.560	15	10	.609	17	8	.667
14.	Cone	2.88	34	17	10	.630	16	11	.607	19	9	.659
15.	Nabholz	2.95	32	11	12	.478	13	10	.585	15	8	.633
16.	Candiotti	3.05	30	11	15	.423	15	11	.569	12	14	.477
17.	Smith Z	3.06	22	8	8	.500	9	7	.567	9	7	.544
18.	Benes	3.11	34	13	14	.481	15	12	.559	12	15	.437
19.	Avery	3.12	35	11	11	.500	12	10	.558	12	10	.564
20.	Gross K	3.21	30	8	13	.381	11	10	.544	10	11	.495
21.	Leibrandt	3.26	31	15	7	.682	12	10	.535	13	9	.585
22.	Tomlin R	3.41	33	14	9	.609	12	11	.514	12	11	.525
23.	Lefferts	3.42	27	13	9	.591	11	11	.513	14	8	.616
24.	Castillo F	3.51	33	10	11	.476	10	11	.500	9	12	.443
25.	Hurst	3.60	32	14	9	.609	11	12	.486	11	12	.477
26.	Ojeda	3.68	29	6	9	.400	7	8	.476	7	8	.478
27.	Cormier	3.73	30	10	10	.500	9	11	.469	9	11	.475
28.	Belcher	3.76	34	15	14	.517	13	16	.465	16	13	.536
29.	Hershiser	3.76	33	10	15	.400	12	13	.465	10	15	.385
30.	Schourek	3.77	21	6	8	.429	6	8	.463	5	9	.367
31.	Gooden	3.80	31	10	13	.435	11	12	.459	10	13	.420
32.	Mulholland	3.81	32	13	11	.542	11	13	.458	14	10	.583
33.	Harris GW	3.81	20	4	8	.333	5	7	.458	6	6	.515
34.	Osborne	3.82	29	11	9	.550	9	11	.457	8	12	.423
35.	Burkett	3.84	32	13	9	.591	10	12	.454	12	10	.549
36.	Gardner M	3.86	30	12	10	.545	10	12	.452	11	11	.510
37.	Jackson Dan	3.89	34	8	13	.381	10	11	.453	9	12	.446
38.	Olivares	3.93	30	9	9	.500	8	10	.443	8	10	.444
39.	Black	3.97	28	10	12	.455	10	12	.438	8	14	.376
40.	Hammond	4.03	26	7	10	.412	7	10	.430	7	10	.427
41.	Harnisch	4.05	34	9	10	.474	8	11	.428	9	10	.475
42.	Martinez R	4.06	25	8	11	.421	8	11	.427	7	12	.381
43.	Wilson Tr	4.21	26	8	14	.364	9	13	.409	6	16	.266
44.	Kile	4.31	22	5	10	.333	6	9	.398	5	10	.315
45.	Jones Jim	4.39	23	10	6	.625	6	10	.389	8	8	.478
46.	Henry B	4.40	28	6	9	.400	6	9	.388	5	10	.324
47.	Clark M	4.53	20	3	10	.231	5	8	.375	4	9	.287

1. Bill Swift (SF)

The most predictable item in the entire 1992 season was that Bill Swift's arm would go south if Roger Craig used him as a rotation starter. There was no reason to think that Swift could adjust to that role without damage. To recap Bill's previous career: he had been awful for years as a Seattle starter. Then, in 1990, he was converted to relief and suddenly found his control in an environment where he wasn't asked to push his arm. Does that say anything to you? If I add that he strikes out very few hitters, and can thereby be presumed to throw very soft, does that help? How about if I just put it bluntly, "Bill Swift has a weak arm, for a Major League pitcher"?

The sad thing is that Roger Craig has gone all these years with a reputation as a pitchers' manager. Nothing could be further from the truth. Roger Craig, like so many of his contemporaries, tries to respond to the decreasing numbers of innings that pitchers can handle by ignoring the event. Or, rather, he treats it as some sort of group mental disorder, wherein modern pitchers are weak-willed, compared to the icons of his own playing career. If you give a manager like that a pitcher like this, you're just asking for trouble.

The sadder thing would be that Bill Swift managed to come back and have a good 4/5 of a year. It would be a lot sadder if Roger were returning to the Giants, where he would surely ask Swift to start again, and pitch as many complete games as Juan Marichal used to do. As it is, no one knows what sort of manager Bill will get. But I'll tell you this: either the man returns Bill to the bullpen, or he uses one of the inning-saving strategies I recommend in my pitcher article, or Bill goes down again. And, this time, the chances of his returning to complete form are greatly reduced.

And, therefore, Bill is NOT THE BEST FANTASY BUY.

2. Dennis Martinez (MTL)

BUT DENNIS MARTINEZ IS. There's no arguing with this consistency. There's also no arguing with the fact that he's going to get more offense than normal in 1993. Although Dennis has demonstrated conclusively, in 1979 and 1982, that he cannot handle 250 innings, he has also established that he can handle 220, even at age 38. And by the way, if you look at the whole career, you can see how he can do that. His second arm collapse, following the second overwork year of 1982, lasted so long that Dennis spent the peak of his career receiving very light workloads. Let's call that "Nolan Ryan Syndrome" and look for it if it crops up again. That is, if you see a good

pitcher getting underworked in his mid or late 20's, predict that he'll last long as a full time player. That's what Nolan and Dennis have done.

3. Bob Tewksbury (STL)

Now here we have a ballpark that favors the power pitcher. It forgives the long fly ball, keeping it in the ballpark. It has fast turf, so those grounders scoot right through. And so what sort of pitcher thrives here? Why, it's John Tudor and Bob Tewksbury, of course. I have no real explanation for this. Whitey Herzog thought Tewks would turn out to be bulk relief, if that. The ballpark isn't helping him. Yes, the infield defense is good, but it's not Pendelton, a young Ozzie and Herr or Oquendo any more.

Essentially, what Tewksbury has is that he doesn't walk anyone, and his hit totals are good. That's certainly the ticket. As for reasons why, the only explanation I can think of is that Tewks knows what sort of ballpark he's got, and just throws it in there when he gets behind, daring the hitters to jack it out. They try, only to find that Tewks throws so slow that he doesn't help them, and the ballpark is huge. I don't know that this is true, but it does fit the facts, including that Tewks gives up more home runs than his sort of pitcher usually does. That would support the idea that he throws a few gophers up there. It's just that you can't punish this type of pitcher in this ballpark for that particular sin.

4. Greg Maddux (CHI)

First off, understand that I agree completely with the Cy Young Award. The one weak point in ranking the pitchers by Ballpark-Adjusted ERA is that there is no factor for playing time. That's unlike the TWAR system for position players, and so leads to less accurate season rankings. It's clear that Greg, with his league lead in innings pitched, helped the Cubs more than any of the three guys above him here.

Second, understand that I have no explanation for how Greg's arm stood up to that workload two years in a row. I know that Roger Clemens can do that, but no one else has been able to for years, except for Dave Stewart, who was blatantly underworked when he was young. Now, I've always thought that the reason Roger could handle the tremendous loads was because he could throw so hard. Or, rather, that the fact that he can throw like that is a result of an arm so strong that it can take more-than-mortal loads. And Greg Maddux just doesn't strike out that many hitters. He's a good strikeout man, but he's no Rocket.

And so, until he does it a third straight year, and I absolutely have to revise my theories to account for him, I have to rate Greg Maddux a BAD FANTASY BUY. Unless Bobby Cox gets his workload under control immediately, I have to question whether he can take any more. Of course, Bobby Cox not only has the intelligence to figure this out, but also the starting rotation to take the heat off Greg....

5. Curt Schilling (PHI)

The guy Don won his league with. I just have two quick repeats of what Don told me about Curt when he crowed about picking him up:

1. In the Bill James league, you only need one relief pitcher if he's a top closer. So, if you have someone like Doug Jones, you should try to get a man who started off as a relief pitcher and ended up in his team's rotation. That's what happened to Curt here, and he was able to pile up starter points for Don while occupying a "reliever" slot in the game that Don had no other use for.

2. Of much more use to the general reader of this here book, a low Hits per Inning ratio is a VERY, VERY GOOD indicator of how good the pitcher is. If you've got some guy who has been untested, or worked erratically, you should consider using that ratio rather than ERA, or something else that is affected by work regularity.

6. Ken Hill (MTL)

In both 1989 and 1991, Ken Hill pitched like this for the Cardinals for half a season. Then he just seemed to run out of gas, lose his control and finish badly. What happened with the Expos is that he didn't fade. What I expect as a reason is that ol' Felipe Alou knows something about pitching arm use. In any case, Ken seemed to be worked intelligently. Since he did pitch over 200 innings, I can't exactly be sanguine about his 1993 year, but I think that Alou may respond early to any Ken Hill arm difficulties and salvage a decent year. We'll see. It's a good test, both of Alou and of Hill.

7. Jose Rijo (CIN)

A top of the line player if he doesn't get hurt. That puts him on the same team with Barry Larkin and Eric Davis and Chris Sabo and Paul O'Neill and....

8. Greg Swindell (CIN - HOU)

This season is not nearly as big an improvement over Greg's 1991 as it appears. First, there's about a half-run per game difference between the NL and the AL, fueled by the Designated

Hitter. Thus, Greg's 3.48 ERA of 1991 should be adjusted to 2.98 just for the league change. And, of course, Greg's huge Won / Lost improvement should be at least partially attributed to the equally huge difference between the quality of the teams he played for.

You can see this one in the Sabermetric Pitching lines we print in this here book. 1991 had Greg down for an Expected Won / Lost record of 14-11. That's the record he should have had, according to the Pythagorean Method, if he had pitched for an average team, rather than for the Indians. His Supported ERA was only 12-13, reflecting his lousy 3.63 Runs per Game of support. This year, his Expected Won / Lost was 13-7. That's better than 14-11, but it's nothing like the difference between Greg's actual Won / Lost records of 9-16 and 12-8. The difference does show up in the Supported Won / Lost. The 1992 Reds scored 4.93 R/G for Greg, and his Supported W/L is 15-5.

Now, if that looks like a negative comment, it isn't. What I have to say about Greg Swindell is that he's been consistent, as starting pitchers go. Consistent and good. The Indians' woeful offenses have concealed that quality, but it's there if you make the necessary adjustments. Not only that, but Greg is one of the very few pitchers who actually can handle 200+-inning workloads. He was pitched right in the middle of his normal range last year, and is not likely to collapse. There are not ten pitchers in baseball who I can call a GOOD, SOLID, RELIABLE FANTASY BUY, but Greg is one of them.

9.   Mike Morgan (CHN)

I want another year before I make any comment about what kind of pitcher Mike Morgan "is". He received very light workloads when he was young, and so has a chance to develop into the Nolan Ryan type of pitcher who pitches well in his late 30's. On the other hand, he's never been anything like as good as Ryan, and he's just off two years of 230+-inning loads. That's stiff for anyone other than Roger Clemens, and so Mike also has a chance to watch his arm completely collapse in 1993. That he held out for two years is nice, but not a real indicator of consistency. If Mike gets through '93 unscathed, though, I'd have to say he's proved he can handle the work. As it is, he's age 33, and he's not Nolan Ryan, and I'd be a bit anxious if I were the Cubs.

10.   Tom Glavine (ATL)

A lot of the Mike Morgan comment might look like it applies here, too. But there are three big differences. First, Bobby Cox backed off some on Tom's workload this year. Second, Tom's 27, not 33. Third, and most important,

Tom has pitched as well as Nolan Ryan. I have a lot of reason to think that Tom might be able to handle 220-inning loads with top quality performance. On the other hand, his body was showing some wear and tear last year. If I were Bobby Cox, I'd try to get another real good rotation starter, to help take some of the load off Tom's shoulder.

What's that? You say Bobby picked up Greg Maddux? Well, now, that's a completely different story. That means that Bobby can afford the luxury of pacing Tom Glavine early, to see how the injuries have healed. Bobby is certainly bright enough to do that, too. That takes Tom from a 75% bet to continue as a top starter and moved him right up into the 90% category. Just another reason that you should rate those teams' managers before you try to rate their pitchers.

11.   Doug Drabek (PIT-HOU)

This is the other side of the coin. Doug's 30, he's not really as good a pitcher as Tom Glavine, he's had four full years of huge workloads, he's going to a team that won't score as many runs as he's used to, he's going to a manager who has no real track record in handling a pitching staff, and the staff at hand has no depth to back him up with. All that means that Doug Drabek IS ABOUT HALF AS LIKELY AS TOM GLAVINE TO CONTINUE AS A TOP PERFORMER.

To put it bluntly, I regard those four years of 200+-inning loads as a fluke. With the leads he's often had, Doug has been able to pace himself during a lot of games. One of the biggest factors in the constant decrease in workload is that pitchers keep working harder on every pitch, year after year, decade after decade. If a guy has a break from that, like Doug's been getting, he really doesn't suffer the same effect. Jim Leyland has used that fact to get more work out of Doug than I think he really can give. The Astros won't give Doug that help, while both he and the manager will probably think of 220 innings as his normal workload. That's the worst possible recipe.

12.   John Smoltz (ATL)

Your basic monster gamble. On the one hand, John seems to have settled down mentally. He pitched a lot, and he pitched great. In particular, he improved his strikeout percentage and also decreased his walk percentage. It's a big, big stride forward, and, except for one thing, I'd rate John the best gamble for a sleeper super-star pitcher. That one thing, though, is the giant workload he was given. I just do not want to trust a man who has finished up a year of 247 innings and nine complete games. In the long run, I think John will be fine. Actually, I think

he will probably be the best of the Braves rotation, partially because he has the strongest arm. But, for just 1993, I have to worry about overwork and arm collapse.

13.   Sid Fernandez (NYM)

Clearly a better pitcher, right now, than Dwight Gooden. On the other hand, he has never responded well to a 200-inning season, and he's going to be counted on for more of the Met load than he ever has before. I THINK HE'S VERY LIKELY TO BLOW UP IN 1993. I also simply do not understand how any manager could pitch this man more than 180 innings in a year, unless the team were right up there in a tight pennant race. This will cause me not to trust Met starters in general, because I don't trust the manager.

14.   David Cone (NYM/TOR - KC)

This ranking is based on his composite Adjusted ERA with both the Mets and the Blue Jays. There probably ought to be a tiny adjustment to that figure for the difference in base ERAs between the two leagues, but it wouldn't move David any in the rankings here. Basically, this is a VASTLY OVERRATED pitcher. He is not now, nor has he ever been, one of the top ten starters in the game. He throws hard, and he gets media attention for his antics, but he's like Rob Dibble. A few games a year, his head goes south over some trivial matter, and he blows up. That drags his season down.

Now, you may be thinking that what is needed here is a little psychiatric help. You might cite John Smoltz as a reference for that idea. But the cases are different. Smoltz just had a general phobia or so, not a looseness in the head that occasionally exploded. And I think that looseness is part of David's talent, just as it is a part of Rob Dibble's. I may be pushing the envelope of amateur psychology here, but what I think is that both Cone and Dibble throw as hard as they do precisely because they're a little loose mentally. It's sort of like a very minor-league version of Rube Waddell. Waddell was what we used to call "retarded", with the mentality of a child. But he could throw harder than anyone, and it was partially attributed to the lack of complication in his mind. That's how Cone and Dibble strike me, and so I think neither one of them will ever really hit the absolute heights.

15.   Chris Nabholz (MTL)

The Expos' pennant ambitions could sure use another stride forward from Chris Nabholz, and I think he may be poised to make it. He's young, he was not overworked, he throws hard, and his biggest weakness is that he could use a little improvement in control. That's a good recipe. I'm not going to guarantee that Chris will fine-tune his use of the plate, but that's the most likely skill for a 26-year-old to develop.

If you're in a fantasy league, the prospects are even better. That's because your league won't ballpark-adjust anyone's stats, and the Expos' park was unusually favorable to hitters in 1992. That means that Chris' projected ERA for 1993 is even better than normal. The ballpark is, after all, likely to return to form. All things concerned, IF I WERE IN A FANTASY LEAGUE, I WOULD BE LOOKING TO PICK THIS MAN UP.

16.   Tom Candiotti (LA)

This is not really the kind of pitcher you're looking for in Los Angeles. Dodger Stadium, a true pitchers' park, favors the guys who throw it up there and let you hit it, because ht's hard to get the ball out of the yard. A knuckleballer tends to walk people, rather than challenging them. Still, it's worked out OK so far, I guess.

Tom is another guy who didn't get to be a starter in the Majors until he was 28, and so his arm can handle a bit more work than most men's. No, he can't handle the 238 innings he got in 1991, and so he was a little off this year. But he can handle 203, and so should come back fully for 1993. On the other hand, Tommy Lasorda can overwork anyone, and may not be able to make himself keep Tom down to right at the 200-inning mark. So check the innings pitched column early next year. If Tom is on a pace for 210 or less, he's probably going to be fine. But if Lasorda is penciling him in for 220 or more, I doubt he'll finish the season healthy.

17.   Zane Smith (PIT)

All right, so we know Zane can't handle 200 innings. We also know there's not much else in his team's rotation, so the temptation to overwork will be there. Now we get to see just what sort of manager Jim Leyland is.

18.   Andy Benes (SD)

All I ask you to do is to show me one stat - any one stat - that indicates that this man can handle 200 innings of work in a season. Unless his manager has a religious experience, look for a BIG COLLAPSE IN 1993.

19.   Steve Avery (ATL)

See above. The Braves scored 5.39 Runs per Game for Steve in 1991, and everyone knows that Fulton County is a hitters' park, so Steve's ERA got overlooked. But he really didn't pitch that well then, and he didn't get any better with another fine old helping of overwork. He's awfully young to predict a collapse next year, but he's not going to get any better as long as he gets this much work. And eventually, HE'S GOING TO SUFFER THE FATE OF DWIGHT GOODEN.

20.   Kevin Gross (LA)

Not really this good. The ballpark is helping him keep his homer totals down, and his ERA has followed. Still, 1992 saw a career year for low hits per inning. I have doubts about that feature holding up at Kevin's age. A sudden command of the strike zone, I would buy. But not a sudden ability to keep people from hitting the pitches. His best bet to stride forward would be for him to get a 180-inning year, and see if it would help his arm. Oh, he pitches for Tommy Lasorda? Well, forget that.

21.   Charlie Leibrandt (ATL - TEX)

I would hesitate, and hesitate a lot, before I let this fine, fine insurance policy go. On the other hand, if you tell him you've signed Greg Maddux, and you want Charlie to be insurance, he's going to leave. Just one of the reasons why the best teams do eventually move back to the center.

22.   Randy Tomlin (PIT)

The best bet for the Pirates to contend is for Randy Tomlin to take a big step forward and head a rotation including Zane Smith and Tim Wakefield. It's possible. This year may have been nothing more than Sophomore Slump. And Randy didn't get too many innings, either. Still, with as little offense as the Pirates are likely to have, he could take a real big stride out there and have no one notice.

23.   Craig Lefferts (SD - BAL)

Making this man into a starter at the age of 34 was one stupid idea, but I guess the Padres thought they were going to contend or something. Now he's with a team that already has a closer, and that closer is about a decade younger than Craig. Makes no sense. None at all.

24.   Frank Castillo (CHN)

Helped the Cubbies quite a bit early in the year, and then seemed to wear down. Previous to 1992, Frank's highest professional workload was 197.1 innings in 1989. That year, his highest level was AA Charlotte. You can imagine what I think of that information.

25.   Bruce Hurst (SD)

Bruce's ERA has gone up each year since he joined the Padres. What he needs, of course, is a manager who can keep his workload down to a reasonable level for a 35-year-old who did not get a late start in the Majors. Can you imagine how hard it is for me to stay awake writing this kind of comment? Can you imagine what it is like trying to find yet another way to say this thing?

26.   Bob Ojeda (LA - CLE)

If you look at his career, what you see is yet another workload case, though at a lower level than 200 innings. Essentially, when Bob gets more than 175 innings, his walks go up and his strikeouts down and his ERA goes up. When the load goes down, so do the ERA and walks, while the strikeouts increase. Since he got a light load last year, I figure him for an improvement over this season. On the other hand, he is 35, and this won't hold forever.

27.   Rheal Cormier (STL)

The Cardinals have a trio of young pitchers who are all real close in these rankings. OF THE THREE, CORMIER IS THE ONE I LIKE LEAST. For one thing, he's getting the latest start; Omar Olivares has three years in the Majors already and is only 25, while Donovan Osborne was a 23-year-old rookie. Rheal was 26. There's a lot of difference between the potential of a 23-year-old and a 26-year-old who pitch the same. For another, Rheal's minor league record does not suggest that he has been held down unfairly. In fact, I think he's been rushed. If he has a ten-year career as a serious starter, it will be a result of expansion.

28.   Tim Belcher (CIN)

I still don't think a whole lot of this guy, and I don't care what his Won/Lost record has been pitching for good teams. He's 31, and he's never pitched really well for any length of time. One thing I know: every time Tim's been given over 200 innings, his ERA has exploded, including 1992. Since he pitched 227 innings this year, I don't expect him to get any better. DITCH HIM IN YOUR FANTASY LEAGUE.

29.   Orel Hershiser (LA)

This is the kind of thing that my pitcher analysis is designed to avoid. For a while, at the peak of his athletic ability, Orel could handle brutal overloads of work. But when he finally went down, he went down completely. What this means is that he wasn't really able to cope with all the work; he was able to stave off the effects for a limited time with willpower and work ethic. But that only lasts so long. Essentially, I regard Orel's arm as irreparably ruined, and I doubt he'll ever rise above average again.

30. Pete Schourek (NYM)

Pete could probably use a whole year at Tidewater, just to get himself settled down. But the Met pitching staff isn't deep enough to afford that. In any case, he doesn't have the strikeout arm to be more than a Grade B prospect. He is that good, though, and I'D CONSIDER HIM IN FANTASY BALL, just because he seems real likely to pitch a full year, and, with two partial seasons already in, probably won't have a Sophomore Slump.

31. Dwight Gooden (NYM)

This year, Doc's career ERA will go over 3. Now, take a look at that 1985 season. Read the innings pitched. And now, remember, they DIDN'T WIN. And in 1986, they didn't really need all that work from Doc.

Now, look at Joe Magrane's career. Now, tell me why the players shouldn't bargain hard for a reduction in the years needed to reach arbitration and free agency. If your team is allowed to blow you up in three years, then you should be entitled to be paid for those three years.

32. Terry Mulholland (PHI)

A consistently mediocre pitcher that the Phillies got all worked up over because they didn't have anything better.

33. Greg W. Harris (SD)

Pitched great in relief in 1989 and '90. Then the Padres decided they just had to have him in the rotation. One year of that, and his ERA jumped almost two runs. Have they learned anything? No; they have him penciled in as a starter for 1993 as well. I expect him to finish the year on the DL, is what I expect. Write him off, unless some bright team trades for him and returns him to the pen.

34. Donovan Osborne (STL)

Age 24, good strikeout stats, didn't fall apart when promoted to the Majors from AA ball. You just have to like all that; it spells Grade A prospect. In addition, he didn't get over 200 innings, so he shouldn't be worked out. Against that, you have the Sophomore Slump. He's a hot discussion topic in fantasy leagues, because he's the hot rookie. What I say is this: with the Sophomore Slump factored in, he's not a good bet for 1993. Someone is going to bid too high. On the other hand, he's a Grade A long-term prospect. Whether you want to acquire him

this year depends on how hard the competition bids and whether you have holdover lists.

35. John Burkett (SF)

Take a good long look at this career. Now, recall that this is the best starting pitcher that Roger Craig has ever developed. Now, tell me again what a pitching genius ol' Humm Baby is. John has a chance to move up, now that his Mangler is gone.

36. Mark Gardner (MTL - KC)

Bulk starting pitching, which the Expos need. I'm not sure I understand giving him up, rather than cornering the garden on Gard(i)ners.

37. Danny Jackson (PIT - PHI)

Neither you, nor I, nor Bill James, nor anyone else has any idea what sort of season Jackson will turn in for 1993. Or 1994, or 1995, or....

38. Omar Olivares (STL)

Had a tiny little Sophomore Slump, completely fueled by a couple of bad outings in May, and the St. Louis management and press are on his case for "attitude". That's the frustration showing with the unwillingness of ownership to acquire the free agent slugger that is all the Cardinals need to contend. THERE IS NOTHING WRONG WITH OMAR OLIVARES. He'll be fine in '93 and beyond. What is wrong is that the Cardinals did not move up, and everyone knows why, and no one can do anything about it, so they get on the case of innocent victims like Omar and Todd Zeile. Just one more reason why badly managed teams don't win.

39. Bud Black (SF)

Bulk left-handed starting pitching, which is much, much better than just bulk starting pitching, of course. And, also of course, you will surely note how his ERA dropped like a stone and his home run total plummeted to nothing just as soon as he got in the hands of that miracle worker Roger Craig.

40. Chris Hammond (CIN)

A career AAA pitcher who the Reds just had to keep in the rotation because otherwise they'd have had to give a chance to Mo Sanford.

41. Pete Harnisch (HOU)

He's only had the one good year, but he's also only 26. The Astros will certainly be giving him another chance, and they've got an offense to score him some runs, so he's NOT AN UNREASONABLE CHEAP FANTASY

GAMBLE. As you probably have guessed, if you've looked at his career stats, I doubt that he can handle 200 innings of work in a season.

42. Ramon Martinez (LA)

Don Malcolm and I have probably gotten more laughs out of Ramon Martinez than out of any other real player (as opposed to our fiction constructs). Its is not because Ramon is funny, but because Tummy Lasorda is. I mean, we were joking about how long it would take for Tummy to destroy Ramon's arm in 1989, when it became obvious that he would be in the rotation the next year. Sure enough, Ramon led the league in complete games in 1990, and his ERA has never been the same. On the other hand, GAMBLE ON HIM IN YOUR FANTASY LEAGUE FOR ONE YEAR. He's off a light load, and his arm should improve. If it does, Tummy is going to throw him right back into the breach, because Tummy never learns anything. And that would mean another 18-7 season before the arm collapses again in 1994.

43. Trevor Wilson (SF)

Another brilliant Roger Craig protégé.

44. Darryl Kile (HOU)

Development arrested by an unwarranted promotion to the Majors in 1991. He's only 24, and might come around, but he sure could use a whole year at the AAA level.

45. Jimmy Jones (HOU - MTL)

Has never had a good year, unless you count his 18 innings in 1986. This is the guy sportswriters are thinking about when they talk about there not being enough pitching for expansion.

46. Butch Henry (HOU)

Development arrested by an unwarranted promotion to the Majors in 1992. He's only 24, and might come around, but he sure could use a whole year at the AAA level. What? You say I already wrote this comment? And it too was for a Houston pitcher? Well, whaddaya know about that?

47. Mark Clark (STL)

Unlike the Houston guys, Mark actually pitched well enough at Louisville in 1991 to earn a chance with the Cardinals. But I just do not understand staying with him as long as they did. It became obvious in July that Mark was worn out from the stress of full-time rotation duty in the Majors. The Cards are talking about sending him back down to Louisville, and I do think it would be for the best.

American League

Relief Closers

Brock J. Hanke

		ADJ ERA	SV	ACTUAL			EXPECTED			SUPPORTED		
				W	L	PCT	W	L	PCT	W	L	PCT
1.	Farr	1.38	30	2	2	.500	4	0	.889	2	2	.563
2.	Russell Jf	1.63	30	4	3	.571	6	1	.840	3	4	.495
3.	Eckersley	1.80	51	7	1	.875	7	1	.826	4	4	.538
4.	Olson Gregg	2.05	36	1	5	.167	5	1	.785	0	6	.063
5.	Montgomery	2.07	39	1	6	.143	5	2	.783	1	6	.186
6.	Olin	2.24	29	8	5	.615	10	3	.754	7	6	.572
7.	Henke	2.26	34	3	2	.600	4	1	.750	1	4	.254
8.	Aguilera	2.70	41	2	6	.250	5	3	.679	2	6	.200
9.	Reardon	3.10	30	5	2	.714	4	3	.617	2	5	.276
10.	Grahe	3.33	21	5	6	.455	6	5	.582	5	6	.479
11.	Henneman	3.84	24	2	6	.250	4	4	.511	1	7	.070
12.	Henry D	4.15	29	1	4	.200	2	3	.472	0	5	.022
13.	Schooler	4.70	13	2	7	.222	4	5	.410	2	7	.224
14.	Thigpen	4.91	22	1	3	.250	2	2	.390	1	3	.134

1. Steve Farr (NYY)

People aren't supposed to find their control in their mid-30s. They are not supposed to thrive on a mix of starting and relieving. In short, they are not supposed to do anything that Steve Farr has done the last three years. All I know is that it's been three years now, and he shows no sign of stopping, and I'D SURE LIKE HIM ON MY FANTASY TEAM.

2. Jeff Russell (TEX-OAK)

As soon as he hit Oakland, people started talking as though he'd been throwing Home Run Derby all year. But it wasn't anything like true. What was true is that the Oakland brain trust decided they didn't want to risk overworking the Eck and so they picked up a fine closer along with Ruben Sierra in exchange for a slugger who was causing clubhouse problems. Given how Eckersley pitched in the ALCS, I can hardly argue with the strategy.

3. Dennis Eckersley (OAK)

As noted above, Eck got into more innings than he likes last year. He has said publicly that his idea of a closer workload is 70 innings. I agree with that analysis. Eck got 80, and he wasn't sharp in the post season. But he did pitch there, and that means he got more than 80 innings, if you're dealing with predictions or fantasy leagues or that sort of stuff. LAY OFF HIM. At his age, it should take a year to get his arm back in shape.

As regards the MVP thing, Dennis Eckersley saved 51 games and blew a grand total of three save opportunities. He also went 7-1 in Wins and Losses. That gives him 58 successes out of 62 trials, a 58/4 success ratio. Steve Farr went 32/8 (30 + 2 vs. 6 + 2). Jeff Russell went 34/12. Gregg Olson went 37/13. The total for those three, who are the top end of the competition, was 103/33. That's a .757 "success percentage". In a sample of 62, that's 47/15. The implication is that Eck was about 11 games better than the best of the other closers. I doubt that's really accurate, but it is an impressive number. It is consistent with the idea that he was 9 games better than replacement rate. Over in the NL section, I talk about how closers really don't have any more impact than players at any other position. But they don't have any less, either. Eck is a legitimate MVP candidate, as long as you're going to admit pitchers into the competition at all.

4. Gregg Olson (BAL)

The best established young closer in the game. I read this season as a complete return to the form of his first year. Yes, I know all the comments about workload are boring, but look at the record. Gregg couldn't handle 80 innings, but he can handle 70 or so. The Orioles have learned their lesson.

Gregg is to be joined by Craig Lefferts for 1993. Lefferts has been starting for the Padres, but that was a silly move. Craig has really only shone as a closer. Now, I don't want to take the luster off Gregg as a fantasy prospect, but the possibility does exist that the O's will figure Craig out, and try to split the closer load between him and Gregg. That's the only reason I can think of to not regard Gregg as YOUR #1 LONG TERM FANTASY LEAGUE CLOSER.

5. Jeff Montgomery (NYY)

What it looks like is that Jeff has found a magical way to handle 90-inning workloads as a closer. That's wrong. What has been happening is that he hasn't been used exclusively as a closer, and so his innings pitched have been deceptive. I rate this year, with its 80 innings, as far more dangerous to Jeff than the preceding three years were. As a consequence, I'm none too sanguine about his prospects. And this is the Yankees, after all. And they do have Steve Howe, after all.

Given that Howe is loose again, JEFF IS NOT THE BEST FANTASY BUY.

6. Steve Olin (CLE)

Probably has as much ability as Gregg Olson, but the Indians are not exactly using him perfectly. He's been switched off and on the closer role before this year, which probably explains 1992's big improvement in ERA. You probably can figure out that I don't like the 88 innings of workload, either. The odd thing about Steve is that he had a much better ERA in a year when his Homers Allowed went way up. The reason the ERA went down is that his Hits Allowed just collapsed. I don't know exactly what to make of this. Maybe he's figured out that Cleveland has a huge outfield right now, and has adjusted to pitching high in the strike zone. That would make more sense if his Strikeouts had gone up, too, from throwing high fastballs. But they didn't. Steve still doesn't strike many people out, so, if he's throwing high, it's junk he's throwing there. That's not supposed to be a recipe for success.

I'm sure we'll know more after 1993 is over; until then, all I can say is to wait and see.

7. Tom Henke (TOR - TEX)

Here's another guy who didn't get started in the Majors until he was way into his 20s. Therefore, I don't rate the 35 years of age as big a factor as I might. I imagine that Tom will pitch about this well until he's at least 38, and maybe into his 40s. As a consequence, I question the Blue Jay decision to let him go. Yes, Duane Ward can handle the closer job, but I'd sure like to have both of them around if I were defending a World Championship. But, then, I'd like to have Dave Winfield around, too.

8. Rick Aguilera (MIN)

There's a big drop here to Rick from the pack of Olson, Montgomery, Olin and Henke. In general, that's a real drop in ability. Rick is just not as good as the other four guys are. On the other hand, Tom Kelly is a lot better about understanding pitching arms than any of the other managers are. As a consequence, Rick is consistent and reliable. A VERY GOOD FANTASY BUY, because you get as close to a guarantee as any relief pitcher will give you except Eckersley.

9. Jeff Reardon (BOS/ATL - CIN)

Despite the hot month for the Braves, I think he's through. I mean, he hasn't had a real good year since 1988. I also don't think his record will last at all. I don't mean just that Lee Smith will pass him. I mean that Jeff was one of the first pitchers to get settled in as a closer at a young age. He piled up a lot of saves simply because he piled up a lot of years in the job. But everybody now is ahead of his pace at his age.

10. Joe Grahe (CAL)

Another big drop here from Rick Aguilera. What that means is that we're running out of the real good closers and getting into the guys whose jobs are in danger. That doesn't really apply to Joe here, though. Bryan Harvey is gone, and Whitey Herzog likes a one-closer team. Joe's young, and he was not that bad. The job is certainly his to lose. Since 95 is not too many innings for a man who was not strictly a closer, I expect Joe to improve, and regard him as a FANTASY GOOD BUY, AT A LOW LEVEL.

11. Mike Henneman (DET)

Arm reamed out by Sparky, whose idea of workload was developed in the '50s. I don't expect him to recover in 1993, and he may well be through overall. If you look at his last five years, it's clear that Sparky just hadn't gotten the whole idea of a specialist closer. There is no excuse for a team's ace reliever finishing that small a percentage of his appearances.

12. Doug Henry (MIL)

I read this as just a real big Sophomore Slump. Doug's Strikeout and Walk stats didn't move much; he just gave up a pile of hits per inning. That's a sign of batter adjustment, not arm trouble or anything like that. I don't mean to imply that he's going to have another ERA of 1, though. His minor league stats just don't support a Hits per Inning ratio of 1/2. The support something more like 4/5. But that's not 1992's even-up ratio, and so his ERA should go down to, say, 3 or so. That's not great, but it's not awful, either. It'll rank in the middle of the pack.

13. Mike Schooler (SEA)

The keystone of the trade for Kevin Mitchell was the gamble that the Mariners could trade away their entire 1991 bullpen, and Mike Schooler would come back and plug the hole. That didn't happen, nor did anything else the Mariners thought might occur. The Woody Woodword response - to unload Mitchell for a closer - accomplishes nothing except to put the M's right back where they were at the end of the 1990 campaign. Well, that's not true. It's easier to find a cleanup man than a closer. As for Mike Schooler, his arm is still in trouble. As opposed to Doug Henry, Mike's Strikeout stats are down, and his Walks are up. That's not the sign you want.

14. Bobby Thigpen (CHA)

While I was writing these here closer comments, I got a letter from a reader who wants me to cool it with the workload notes. He claims they're boring to read. Well, I can imagine. They're boring to write, too. But, to be honest, they're also hard to avoid. I really believe that the dominant issue confronting baseball management today is how to get pitcher workloads under control. I can predict pitcher increases in ERA with tremendous regularity just by looking at role and innings. Nothing else gives me any such handle on how pitchers are going to do in the future.

And, if you want a demonstration, remember this: one of the first predictions I made was that Bobby Thigpen's arm had been destroyed by his absurd record-setting season of 1990. And yes, for you new readers, I made that prediction at the end of the 1990 season.

Relief Closers

Brock J. Hanke

		ADJ ERA	SV	ACTUAL			EXPECTED			SUPPORTED		
				W	L	PCT	W	L	PCT	W	L	PCT
	Rojas	1.25	10	7	1	.875	7	1	.887	7	1	.909
	Howell Jay	1.54	4	1	3	.250	3	1	.838	3	1	.683
1.	Jn Franco	1.64	15	6	2	.750	7	1	.821	4	4	.526
2.	Beck	1.76	17	3	3	.500	5	1	.798	4	2	.721
	Perez Mk	1.84	0	9	3	.750	9	3	.784	10	2	.827
3.	Jones D	2.02	36	11	8	.579	14	5	.751	10	9	.540
4.	Wetteland	2.59	37	4	4	.500	5	3	.646	4	4	.508
5.	Charlton	2.88	26	4	2	.667	4	2	.597	2	4	.369
6.	Scanlan	2.88	14	3	6	.333	5	4	.596	4	5	.484
7.	Dibble	2.94	25	3	5	.375	5	3	.586	3	5	.382
8.	Smith Le	3.12	43	4	9	.308	7	6	.558	1	12	.056
9.	Belinda	3.15	18	6	4	.600	6	4	.552	5	5	.540
10.	Williams Mitch	3.78	29	5	8	.385	6	7	.462	5	8	.389
11.	Pena A	3.86	15	1	6	.143	3	4	.452	1	6	.083
12.	Myers R	3.95	38	3	6	.333	4	5	.440	1	8	.130
13.	McDowell R	4.20	14	6	10	.375	7	9	.411	5	11	.340
14.	Young A	4.31	15	2	14	.125	6	10	.397	6	10	.396

1. John Franco (NYM)

John finally paid for all the overwork he got with the Reds. I read the injury as temporary and the recovery as complete. Consequently, I rate John as highly as any closer in the league. I know I'd rather have him than Rob Dibble, who will probably command the highest price in your fantasy league.

Certainly, Anthony Young is no threat to John's position. The only reason both of them are listed here is that the rule for this section is "20 saves or the most saves on the man's team". Both John and Anthony got 15 saves. Unless John gets hurt again, Anthony won't get 15 saves in 1993. He won't get two.

2. Rod Beck (SF)

Normally, I would rant and rave about the 92 innings of work. But Rod Beck was not a closer for a good part of the season, and innings in middle relief don't count like those pitched in the closer role. Rod is 24, and I hope is established as the Giants' closer for 1993. I don't know that he'll pitch this well again, but I would expect him to be near the top of the NL closer list. The NL closers are not a winner lot any more. All this makes Rod Beck, not John Franco, the FANTASY LEAGUE BEST BUY. He has no reputation, he's going to have the full-time job, and he has little competition for the top spot in the league. Pick him up. The Giants have already announced that, if Bill Swift has to return to the 'pen, one of the relievers will have to move into the rotation. Trust me, it will be Rod Beck.

3. Doug Jones (HOU)

Given that John Franco and Rod Beck did not work full time as closers, Doug is clearly the best of the lot, and should have won whatever award is given to the best closer in the National League. That he did not win the Rolaids award is a sad tale told under "Lee Smith".

This is one of the side effects I've noticed in studying pitchers and workloads. It is not at all uncommon for a good but overworked hurler to have his arm fall apart for a couple of years, and then stage a full comeback. The question in these cases is how long it takes the comeback team's manager to get greedy and overwork the arm again. Each time this happens, the comeback is to a lower level of performance. In Doug's case, he didn't start the year as the Astro closer, but he won the job comparatively quickly. He led the league in games finished, and pitched 112 innings. I doubt he can handle that, and I am sure he can't handle two years of it. If the Astros think they are going to move into contention based on the idea that they have shored up their rotation and that Doug is going to prove a reliable top closer, they have another think coming. BAD FANTASY GAMBLE.

4. John Wetteland (MTL)

I got into a horrible argument in the St. Louis pressbox about this guy. It was May or so, and the other writers were talking about what a wonderful year John was having as a closer.

At the time, his ERA was in the 4's somewhere. I noted that this was not what I meant by a great season closing. The opposition amounted to "I don't care what his ERA is, if he gets the saves, he's a great closer". That led to a study that had a lot more impact when I did it, because John Wetteland managed to get his ERA down to the point where he had a good year overall, by any standards. Still, here's a summary of the results of the study.

First, the ERA a closer posts does have a relationship to his save record. I don't imagine that's any surprise to this book's readers, but you'd be astonished how hard it is to get sportswriters to believe it. Here's a summary of the save and blown save record for each of the closers on this list:

	NAME	ADJ. ERA	OPS+DEC	SAVES+WINS	PERCENT
	Rojas	1.25	19	17	.895
	Howell Jay	1.54	10	5	.500
1.	Jn Franco	1.64	25	21	.840
2.	Beck	1.76	29	20	.690
	Perez Mk	1.84	15	9	.600
3.	Jones D	2.02	61	47	.770
4.	Wetteland	2.59	54	41	.759
5.	Charlton	2.88	40	30	.750
6.	Scanlan	2.88	27	17	.630
7.	Dibble	2.94	38	28	.737
8.	Smith Le	3.12	64	47	.734
9.	Belinda	3.15	34	24	.706
10.	Williams Mitch	3.78	49	34	.694
11.	Pena A	3.86	25	16	.640
12.	Myers R	3.95	55	41	.745
13.	McDowell R	4.20	38	20	.526
14.	Young A	4.31	36	17	.472

You don't need any formal statistics to see that a relationship is there, but you also don't need them to see that it's anything but perfect. If you think about it for a minute, the reason should be clear - there isn't enough variance among closers for a perfect relationship to hold up. There are only two pitchers here with success percentages over 80%, and only three under 60%. Now, the average number of opportunities here is 36.4. 80% of that is 29, while 60% is 22. That is, the difference between a "good" relief pitcher and a "bad" one is about 29-22, or 7 games. Does that make sense? Well, of course it does. If Barry Bonds is an "8-win" player, and John Franco is really worth 15 games or so, then he's twice as valuable as Bonds. No reliever is paid like that, which means that no team really believes that. Seven games of difference is about what you should expect from such an analysis. And so, when some sportswriter wants to tell me that John Wetteland is having a good year up to May, because he has only lost one more game and blown one more save than the top men in ERA, I just say, "That's not good. That's bad. That's what 'bad' looks like in relievers".

5. Norm Charlton (CIN-SEA)

I would not trade Norm Charlton for Kevin Mitchell, and I like Kevin Mitchell more than most analysts. Handled correctly, as he was last year, Norm could be a top closer for several years. That's more than Kevin has left in him. Sure Norm's 30, but he's had little use to date, and isn't suffering from undue arm wear. On the other hand, if Norm is handled correctly, Rob Dibble will go ballistic. The Reds chose to go with Dibble. That, in my opinion, is a mistake. Yes, Dibble's got a world-class fastball, but he's also got a world-class ego, and he's not what I call sane about it.

If you keep Norm Charlton as your top closer, you can get a good righty closer and platoon them and Norm won't blow up. On top of that, righty pitchers are much easier to find than lefties. And worst of all, Dibble's so nuts that he messes up his arm on his own, without managerial intervention. In three years, I expect Dibble to be all but out of the game, while I expect Norm still to be a top closer, if some Seattle manager doesn't destroy him.

6. Bob Scanlan (CHN)

This is the reason the Cubs picked up Randy Myers. They think that Bob might be effective as the righty half of a platoon, but they know perfectly well that he can't handle the closer job on his own. Given that he's not going to have more than half a job in 1993, I have to rank him a BAD FANTASY BUY.

7. Rob Dibble (CIN)

Did you read the Norm Charlton comment? If not, do so now. As baseball fans go, I think I'm exceptionally tolerant of screwball behavior.

For example, I am one of Steve Howe's last defenders in the fan community. But this sort of guy - the self-destructive madman - is more than I can handle. If I were the General Manager of his team, he wouldn't be on the roster for more than a month. I'd fire sale him if necessary. He doesn't help you in the clubhouse, he's going to undermine your manager's authority, and then he's likely to blow his game up just when you need him the most. Not the personality I want to entrust with the last inning of my last World Series game.

8. Lee Smith (STL)

I do not understand at all the lack of fan response to the means by which Lee won his Rolaids award. I mean, I tried to submit a little article on the oddities of the save rule by which this happened, and I got universally told that nothing could be worse than rewriting the save rule. I can't agree, so you poor readers get to put up with my argument here.

First, the facts. It was the bottom of the eighth inning in St. Louis, the last game of the year, and the Cardinals had a three run lead and the bases loaded with nobody out. Lee Smith was warming up, but there was some doubt as to whether he'd be used in the situation this seemed likely to turn into. Then the Busch Stadium scoreboard posted that Doug Jones had saved his game in Houston. That put Jones exactly one point up on Smith for the Rolaids award.

Now, the rules clearly state that you cannot get a save if you come into a game with more than a three-run lead. This was an amendment put into the rules to get rid of the annoying cheap saves that people used to pile up by coming in to pitch the ninth innings of blowouts. That is, it was designed in the first place to avoid pitchers padding their stats - and winning awards - with cheap saves.

Well, the first Cardinal batter at least tried. He hit a sharp liner to shortstop, and it in fact took a good play to keep the ball from going into left field and driving in one more run at least. But Rich Gedman managed to strike out, albeit he did swing at a couple of pitches. Milt Thompson never took the bat off his shoulder. To my complete astonishment, he actually took two balls among the five pitches thrown at him, but the other three were certainly strikes. The last one was a pitch I could have hit, grooved right down the middle.

So Lee Smith went into the ninth inning with only a three run lead, and saved his game and won the Rolaids award.

Now, I have no problem with the Cardinal

batters, not even with Milt Thompson. You've got to protect your teammates. If you can get them awards, you've got to do that. But what if the game were not meaningless in the standings? What if the Cardinals had been tied for, say, second place, and winning the game meant a few hundred dollars of World Series money? That's nothing to the players, but what about the clubhouse guy? Or worse, what if the tie is for first place? Do you make that automatic out, and trust the three-run lead, or do you score as much as you can? I mean, Lee Smith was laughing and joking out there in the bullpen, but what if he has a bonus dependent on the Rolaids thing?

I don't think baseball players should be put into this sort of situation. I think the rule needs changing. The question is how? That damn save rule is a big fat pain to deal with. Actually, we'd probably be better off to do away with the thing altogether. It is like the RBI, after all. That is, the save is one of those stats that is very dependent on things other than the ability of the pitcher. How many games does the team win, in general? Do they tend to win them by blowout, because their offense is so strong, or do they win close, because their starters are good?

And then there's the setup man. Wonder why I've got those guys listed at the top of this list who don't qualify as closers? It's to give you an idea of what effect the setup man can have. Look at the top man, Mel Rojas. Do you know what his job was all year? It was to pitch the seventh and eighth innings of Expo games, so that John Wetteland could come in with a lead. Think of the advantage that was for John, given Mel's stats. Not only did Mel blow virtually no leads for John, but he usually gave up no runs at all. That means that he turned a disproportionate number of one-run leads into bigger ones, so that John had more room to work with. That is a lot of why John had good-looking save stats with a weak ERA, early in the season. He'd give up a run, but the Expos would have a two-run cushion, so he'd get the save.

At any rate, here's what I came up with. If we're going to keep the save stat at all, let's add at least these to the rules:

1. If the last pitcher in a game enters with a lead, pitches one full inning, and does not give up even one earned run, and his team wins the game, then he gets a save regardless of how much lead he had. That covers the Lee Smith situation. All Lee has to do is pitch his scoreless inning and he gets his save. The Cards can score all the runs they want; it doesn't matter.

2. If the last pitcher in a game does not have the lowest ERA, within the game at hand, of all the game's relievers, then he doesn't get a save no matter what. That is, if Mel Rojas comes into the game with a one-run lead, and pitches two scoreless innings, and the Expos score two more, and then John Wetteland comes in for the ninth and gives up a run, John don't get no save.

The idea, in both cases, is to make the save more dependent on pitching well, and less dependent on the rest of the closer's team. That's what we're after with baseball stats, isn't it? To make them actually reflect the abilities of the players at hand?

9. Stan Belinda (PIT)

Let me get this straight. The Pirates have denuded themselves down to the bone at several positions. They figure to have the worst left fielder, right fielder, second baseman and first baseman in the league. Their rotation doesn't have a whole lot left, either. And they think that what they need to stay in contention is a name reliever with no consistency (Alejandro Pena) because Stan Belinda was only in the middle of the pack? Why didn't they think they needed a closer when they had Barry Bonds? I don't get it at all.

10. Mitch Williams (PHI)

Whee! Another Mitch Williams season to write about! But you know what? It was mediocre! I don't believe it! I'd have believed great. I'd have believed horrible. I'd have believed injured all year. I would easily have believed an all-time record for walk percentage. But mediocre?? Mitch, Mitch, Mitch, you've let a legion of fans down.

11. Alejandro Pena (ATL - PIT)

The Pirates have no use for him, but the Braves probably do. Go figure. What I figure is Alejandro for a comeback. Yes, it's exactly what you've come to expect from me. Alejandro's arm broke down from overwork, but the rest he got last year should lead to a comeback. Not to belabor the point, but here are Alejandro's Innings Pitched and ERA figures from 1988 through last year:

YEAR	IP	ERA
1988	94.1	1.91
1989	76	2.13
1990	76	3.20
1991	82.1	2.40
1992	42	4.07

Do these numbers say anything to you other than "This man can handle about 70 innings a year but no more."?

12. Randy Myers (SD-CHN)

Not my #1 choice for Wrigley Field. Randy tends to pitch high and hard, and the stadium does not forgive that sin. Doug Jones is more the Wrigley Field type. You know, early in the year, Randy here wasn't doing any better, really, than John Wetteland. But everyone saw him blow a huge lead on TV, and he didn't improve like John did, so everyone thinks they know what a bad closer season looks like. But they're wrong. A bad closer season does not consist of one spectacular collapse. It consists of a whole year's bad ERA.

13. Roger McDowell (LA)

If you think Roger can really handle 80+-inning workloads, you think like Tummy Lasorda. And, as long as you and Tummy think like that, Roger's going to pitch like this.

14. Anthony Young (NYM)

No, he had no business with this job. But, then, he wasn't supposed to have it. At age 27, he's no prospect beyond bulk middle relief, but it's not his fault John Franco got hurt. I guess what I'm trying to say is that I do feel guilty when someone like this gets ranked at the bottom of the pile. It's not fair. This wasn't supposed to be his job. He might do fine at the middle relief job he should be given.

Catchers

Brock J. Hanke

		OWAR	DWAR	TWAR
1.	Tettleton	4.13	-.42	3.72
2.	Hoiles	3.41	.13	3.54
3.	Steinbach	2.66	.35	3.01
4.	Harper B	3.02	-.25	2.76
5.	Macfarlane	2.49	.04	2.53
6.	Surhoff BJ	1.14	.80	1.94
7.	Karkovice	1.48	.18	1.66
8.	Borders	.75	.31	1.06
	Stanley M	1.30	-.26	1.03
	Nilsson	.54	.14	.68
	Webster L	.43	.22	.64
	Parrish Ln	.63	-.12	.50
	Fisk	.46	.01	.47
	Tackett	.01	.32	.34
	Melvin	.35	-.05	.30
	Parent	.24	-.05	.18
9.	Fitzgerald	.09	.06	.14
10.	Rodriguez I	.10	.03	.13
	Tingley	-.27	.24	-.03
11.	Nokes	.22	-.31	-.09
	Orton	-.11	-.05	-.16
	Myers G	-.08	-.14	-.22
12.	Pena T	-.85	.59	-.26
13.	Valle	.49	-.75	-.26
	Merullo	-.26	-.03	-.29
	Mayne	-.62	.33	-.30
14.	Alomar S	-.60	.30	-.30
	Flaherty	-.44	-.17	-.61
	Marzano	-.57	-.09	-.66
	Quirk	-.37	-.42	-.78
	Kreuter	-.34	-.55	-.89
	Petralli	-.76	-.29	-1.05
	Ortiz	-.89	-.42	-1.31

1. Mickey Tettleton (DET)

Mickey was plodding along as a mediocre platoon catcher, when the Orioles decided to try him out full time in 1989. Both his home runs and his walks just exploded, and he's been Gene Tenace on a good year ever since.

So what happened? Well, some of it, no doubt, was getting out of Oakland's ballpark. The progression from Oakland to Baltimore to Detroit is going to lend confidence - and stats - to anyone. The other factor probably is the full-time regular work. As any glance at pinch-hitting stats will show, it's hard to keep hitting skills up without regular work. Mickey had shown some sign of real strike zone judgment in 1986, when he took 39 walks against only 211 At-Bats. But he'd never been able to keep it up until he got to play every day.

As to future predictions or fantasy league evaluation, I see no reason not to expect him to CONTINUE AT THE TOP OF THE PACK. He's not that old, and hardly overworked. He hasn't been injured, which is the usual bane of catchers. The skills he's relying on are not speed-based, so the wear and tear that catching produces is not going to affect him for a while. Pending the development of Chris Hoiles or Ivan Rodriguez, Mickey is the best catcher in the game.

2. Chris Hoiles (BAL)

Sophomore Slump met the Age-27 Career Year, and age 27 won. Chris' raw totals don't look like that much of an improvement over 1991, but his Slugging Average improved from .384 to .506, and his On-Base Percentage went from .304 to .384. In slugging, that's from "OK" to "outstanding". In getting on base, it's from "not good enough" to, again, "outstanding". The only reason this season didn't rank first at the position is that Chris was hurt, and therefore only got into 96 games.

So, is he The Man at catcher? Well, I want to see another year. Specifically, I want to see 1) Chris go a whole year without an injury, and 2) these averages hold up in a year when he's not 27. If he can keep up these averages, and get into 120 games or so, he's a better player than

Catchers	G	PO	A	Er	TC	DP	PB	SB	CS	CS%	FPct	DI	DG	DW%	DWAR	ERA
Alomar S	88	477	39	2	518	5	3	43	35	.449	.996	729.2	5.0	.410	.30	3.81
Borders	137	784	88	8	880	7	11	116	51	.305	.991	1160.2	7.9	.388	.30	3.82
Fisk	54	252	26	2	280	2	4	41	20	.328	.993	429.2	2.9	.355	.01	3.98
Fitzgerald	74	291	20	3	314	4	3	41	18	.305	.990	468.0	3.2	.372	.07	3.73
Flaherty	34	102	7	2	111	2	0	16	7	.304	.982	195.1	1.3	.224	-.17	4.19
Harper B	133	744	58	13	815	8	12	118	52	.306	.984	1114.0	7.6	.317	-.25	3.85
Hoiles	95	500	32	3	535	7	4	87	22	.202	.994	817.1	5.6	.373	.13	3.83
Karkovice	119	533	53	6	592	9	6	69	33	.324	.990	915.0	6.3	.377	.17	3.77
Kreuter	62	271	22	5	298	6	4	26	22	.458	.983	475.2	3.3	.183	-.54	4.75
Leyritz	18	88	13	1	102	2	2	15	10	.400	.990	121.2	.8	.295	-.05	4.51
Macfarlane	104	527	43	4	574	7	9	67	28	.295	.993	845.0	5.8	.357	.04	3.93
Marzano	18	81	8	3	92	0	0	15	5	.250	.967	134.0	.9	.252	-.09	3.82
Mayne	62	277	23	3	303	1	3	26	18	.409	.990	458.1	3.1	.437	.27	3.30
Melvin	21	77	7	0	84	2	2	14	6	.300	1.000	144.0	1.0	.297	-.05	4.75
Merullo	16	64	3	2	69	0	3	10	3	.231	.971	107.0	.7	.314	-.03	3.28
Myers G	26	125	15	1	141	1	2	27	8	.229	.993	189.1	1.3	.510	.21	5.45
Nilsson	46	224	16	2	242	1	0	21	12	.364	.992	388.0	2.7	.401	.14	3.60
Nokes	111	552	47	4	603	6	7	108	33	.234	.993	903.0	6.2	.300	-.31	4.24
Ortiz	86	402	39	5	446	2	5	59	27	.314	.989	652.2	4.5	.255	-.42	4.44
Orton	43	238	22	5	265	3	1	22	18	.450	.981	344.1	2.4	.328	-.05	3.79
Parent	16	73	7	1	81	1	1	7	4	.364	.988	100.0	.7	.275	-.05	4.32
Parrish Ln	56	290	20	4	314	6	4	59	23	.280	.987	416.0	2.8	.576	.64	3.98
Pena T	132	786	55	6	847	11	7	80	39	.328	.993	1084.0	7.4	.429	.59	3.49
Petralli	54	263	21	3	287	6	3	22	20	.476	.990	367.2	2.5	.238	-.28	4.63
Quirk	59	258	24	8	290	3	1	41	20	.328	.972	384.2	2.6	.189	-.42	4.27
Rodriguez I	116	764	84	15	863	10	10	53	57	.518	.983	982.2	6.7	.355	.03	3.81
Stanley M	55	266	27	6	299	2	7	41	19	.317	.980	427.2	2.9	.256	-.27	4.10
Steinbach	124	579	70	10	659	6	7	68	53	.438	.985	998.2	6.8	.398	.33	3.50
Surhoff BJ	109	546	59	6	611	7	5	57	39	.406	.990	926.0	6.3	.458	.69	3.16
Tackett	64	311	32	1	344	4	9	33	18	.353	.997	516.2	3.5	.442	.33	3.73
Tettleton	113	475	47	2	524	10	4	74	39	.345	.996	943.0	6.5	.285	-.42	4.52
Tingley	69	270	35	4	309	3	0	28	23	.451	.987	412.2	2.8	.434	.24	3.42
Valle	122	608	61	7	676	10	4	84	40	.323	.990	972.1	6.7	.238	-.75	4.68
Webster L	49	190	11	1	202	4	2	29	9	.237	.995	315.0	2.2	.450	.22	3.31
TOTALS		12825	1183	154	14162	164	158	1704	860	.335	.989	1460.1	10.0	.969	6.19	3.95

Tettleton. For one thing, he has some defensive value. However, if he can only play 100 games a year, or if his averages retreat just a little, he's no better than Mickey, and will probably be eclipsed by Ivan Rodriguez sometime soon.

3. Terry Steinbach (OAK)

Terry has a reputation for being a journeyman catcher. That's accurate. There have been recent decades where he wouldn't be in the top 5 at the spot. But catchers are at a premium now, and reliable journeymen are hard to find. Hence, this ranking, which is pretty much the result of getting into 128 games behind the plate. RELIABLE FANTASY BUY, as he can do this year after year.

I don't mean to demean the skill of consistency at catcher. Terry Steinbach helps the Oakland effort a lot, just by insuring that the team won't have to spend resources backing him up. Most catchers, even the good ones, can't guarantee that. A consistent journeyman is still a journeyman, but insurance does have value.

4. Brian Harper (MIN)

In a normal year for catchers, relying on Brian Harper would be questionable. He's not really a catcher, but a designated hitter. If there were any people around who could play behind the plate and hit even a little, Brian's lack of defense would hurt his team. But, when nobody else can hit at all, Brian makes up for his glove with the bat. The Twins understand that, and it has helped them win one division title.

In addition, Brian, like Terry Steinbach, is consistent. That, too, has added value. Frankly, if I were running a team that thought it was going to be in contention, I'd rather have Brian or Terry than Chris Hoiles. Chris' top end is much higher, but contenders shouldn't be looking for top production out of the catching spot. They should be looking for someone who doesn't hurt them, and that's Brian or Terry. Chris Hoiles can leave you with some AAA player behind your plate all year. That can cost you a division title you would have won with Brian Harper.

By the way, according to his minor league stats, Lenny Webster can hit enough doubles and play enough defense to compete for this job.

5. Mike Macfarlane (KC)

A couple of years ago, I ranked this player under the name "Todd". For those of you who want to know, Todd Macfarlane is a comic book artist whose current title is "Spawn". Reportedly, Todd Macfarlane is also a baseball fan. In fact, it is rumored (unreliably) that, if he weren't making so much money drawing comic books, he'd be playing in the minors.

At any rate, Mike Macfarlane can't draw, at least as far as I know. But he can catch a little, and he does help the Royals. He's not going to help them as much as he did in 1991, when he was 27, but he can probably do a little more than this year showed. I wouldn't be surprised to see him keep the homers and walks of 1992, while regaining the batting average of 1990 (.255). The thing I question most is his ability to stay healthy. He's only played over 100 games twice in his life. Consequently, I have to WARN YOU OFF HIM IN FANTASY LEAGUES, as he just is not reliable.

There's a lot of talk in Kansas City about Brent Mayne. Brent's young, and he got bit by Sophomore Slump, so he's better than he looked in 1992. But he doesn't seem to be anything special. If Macfarlane is healthy, Brent Mayne can't beat him out.

6. B. J. Surhoff (MIL)

Here's an age-27 situation that deserves commenting upon. As you probably know, the turning date for baseball "age" is considered to be July 1. B. J. was born early in August, and so is always one of the oldest players of his "age". If you look at his career, the 1991 season, when he was "age 26", but actually 27 most of the year, looks like his career year. That would put B. J. in his decline phase, and suggest that this season is about as good as it's going to get. Supporting that theory is that his doubles total - where all his power lies - have been going down since he entered the league. That, in a catcher, is a standard sign of the wear and tear the position causes to the legs. All things concerned, I think the Brewers will be looking for a replacement in a couple of years.

Or maybe earlier. Right now, they have a kid catcher named Dave Nilsson who looks pretty good. He was probably not ready for the big time in 1992, but he'll be 24 in 1993, and by then, he should be hitting .265 or more. That's enough to run B. J. off the job, for sure.

7. Ron Karkovice (CHA)

Unlike Mickey Tettleton, Ron Karkovice was not helped by regular work. This is essentially the same sort of season he was putting in before, except that he played twice as much, because Carlton Fisk is finally proving to be mortal. Don't expect anything else, either from Ron or from Carlton.

8. Pat Borders (TOR)

Another guy who put in his normal season. If you're a catcher, and you play 138 games, and you can't rank any higher than 8th, you're in trouble. That's because some of the people who rank behind you are there only because they didn't play full time. Your actual rank within the position is probably more like 11th. In this case, the men who would clearly outrank Pat if they played full time include Mike Stanley, Lenny Webster, Lance Parrish (still), and Carlton Fisk platooned with any warm body. In addition, Ivan Rodriguez will very likely shoot straight up in the rankings this year, as he turns an age at which people actually play Major League baseball.

9. Mike Fitzgerald (CAL - SEA)

As those of you know who have read past SABERMETRICs, I thought Mike Fitzgerald was one of the most underrated players of the last '80s. I thought the Expos' refusal to just give him their catching job was absolutely ridiculous. Now he's on the Angels, who would be delighted to give him his shot. And so what happens? He can't recover from an injury, and plays terribly.

Please note that "plays terribly" means a #9 ranking in 95 games featuring only 189 At-Bats. If Fitz should recover, he can really help the Mariners, whither he has wandered. When healthy, he gets on base and has some line drive pop. He plays decent defense. That's a lot, from a catcher. It's sure more than Dave Valle gives you. You should also note that he is going to outlast Hubie Brooks and Gary Carter and everyone else involved in that trade.

10. Ivan Rodriguez (TEX)

I thought he'd take a stride forward this year, just because he'd be a year older. Instead, he got bit by the Sophomore Slump bug. Does that change my opinion of him? Not a bit. Ivan is one of the prize young players in baseball. Look for him to leap forward in 1993. As it is, he's got that cannon of an arm, so he's going to get to play. GREAT LONG-TERM PROSPECT.

11. Matt Nokes (NYY)

Your basic designated hitter, who got locked into the catching job because he doesn't really have the home run power people want to see in their DHs nowadays. As a consequence, he's always battling little injuries, and his concentration is sapped by trying to do things like call pitches and throw out runners, that he is not really suited for. That makes for one inconsistent player, and that's Matt. Mike Stanley hit a little in 1992, which means that Matt is also no lock to have a starting job at all.

12. Tony Pena (BOS)

He can still catch, and catch well, but he has lost all ability to hit. If you look back at his career, you could see this coming. His hitting was, for a catcher, speed-based, which is a bad sign for catchers' legs. Tony also loved those weird catching stances, exacerbating the problem. If the Bosox had anyone else, or if the position were rich enough to free up some free agents, Tony would be out of baseball. As it is, he's finished, but the Sox don't have anyone else who's even that good.

13. Dave Valle (SEA)

Lance Parrish, even at his age, is a much, much better player. Hell, Bob Melvin is a better player than Dave Valle. As for Mike Fitzgerald, well, see above.

14. Sandy Alomar, Jr. (CLE)

He's turning 27, and he better get with the program. As young as he is, and as good as he was supposed to be, he's no more than two years from being finished. Or maybe less. The Indians have come up with a catcher named Jesse Levis, whose MLEs are just outstanding. That's what happens when you hit .364 in AAA ball.

Catchers

Brock J. Hanke

		OWAR	DWAR	TWAR
1.	Daulton	5.37	-1.08	4.29
2.	Oliver	2.62	.14	2.76
3.	Slaught	2.67	-.33	2.35
4.	Wilkins R	2.08	.22	2.30
5.	Pagnozzi	1.17	.59	1.75
	LaValliere	.92	.65	1.57
6.	Olson Greg	.85	.34	1.19
	Berryhill	.53	.61	1.14
7.	Manwaring	1.00	.07	1.07
8.	Carter G	.38	.30	.68
9.	Scioscia	.17	.39	.56
	Girardi	.46	-.01	.45
	Fletcher D	-.04	.40	.35
	Walters D	.34	.01	.34
	Hernandez C	.58	-.33	.26
10.	Taubensee	.47	-.29	.19
	Piazza	.14	-.05	.09
	Gedman	.14	-.06	.08
11.	Hundley	-.34	.41	.07
	Cerone	.03	-.06	-.04
	Servais	-.21	.16	-.05
	Mcnamara	-.21	.08	-.14
	O'Brien C	.24	-.39	-.14
	Laker	-.29	.05	-.23
	Decker S	-.25	.00	-.25
	Lake	-.14	-.18	-.32
	Sasser	-.29	-.13	-.42
	Colbert	-.45	-.04	-.49
	Prince	-.53	-.07	-.61
	Tucker	-.57	-.10	-.68
	Villanueva	-.86	.12	-.74
12.	Santiago	-.21	-.61	-.82

1. Darren Daulton (PHI)

There are two important things to say about Darren Daulton. The first is that he has had the archetypal catcher's career: good, healthy seasons alternating with injury-riddled, awful ones. There is just no point in trying to predict what sort of season Darren will have next. The second is that the big difference between this season and his last healthy one in 1990 is the home run total. And those homers were a deliberate decision, made in 1991. In 1990, Darren acquired 459 At-Bats, and posted 12 homers (2.6 per 100 AB), 72 strikeouts (15.7 / 100 AB) and a .268 Batting Average. That was consistent with his history to date. In 1991, his average dropped to .201, but he had 4.2 homers per 100 AB, and 23.2 strikeouts. This year, his ratios were 5.6 HR / 100 AB and 21.2 SO / 100 AB. That's the true sign of uppercutting, and it paid off big, since Darren paid nothing in Batting Average, with .270. Obviously, if the NL pitchers don't adjust to the new batting style, and Darren doesn't get hurt, he's a force behind the plate. But those are two big if's for a catcher.

On the other hand, should Darren be a catcher at all? His Defensive WAR are the worst in the league at any position, and he surely can hit enough to play elsewhere. My usual position on this is that you play a man at the most valuable defensive position he can play without hurting him at the plate. But here, Darren really is a lousy catcher, and he loses enough production to injury that the Phillies might be better served by moving him out from behind the plate. The usual move for a catcher would be to first base, but Darren's base stealing stats suggest that he might be mobile enough to handle the outfield. He's not going to run Dave Hollins off third base, though.

2. Joe Oliver (CIN)

Lord mercy, but this is a lousy season to come in #2 at a position. If I were the Cardinals or the Astros, I'd take one look at this and move Todd Zeile and Craig Biggio back there so fast.... What's worse, there is nothing worthwhile at all to say about Oliver. His season, both on offense and on defense, is your basic jour-

Catchers	G	PO	A	Er	TC	DP	PB	SB	CS	CS%	FPct	DI	DG	DW%	DWAR	ERA
Berryhill	84	427	30	1	458	6	9	71	20	.220	.998	661.0	4.5	.484	.61	2.86
Carter G	85	482	50	6	538	3	1	98	38	.279	.989	665.0	4.6	.414	.29	3.14
Cerone	28	106	7	0	113	0	1	15	4	.211	1.000	143.2	1.0	.286	-.06	4.51
Colbert	35	140	13	1	154	4	6	16	9	.360	.994	217.0	1.5	.288	-.09	3.98
Daulton	141	760	69	11	840	8	12	88	49	.358	.987	1200.2	8.2	.221	-1.06	4.17
Decker S	15	94	4	0	98	1	1	2	2	.500	1.000	118.2	.8	.355	.00	3.87
Fletcher D	69	360	32	2	394	3	3	70	24	.255	.995	518.0	3.5	.462	.40	2.97
Gedman	40	227	12	3	242	2	2	37	3	.075	.988	291.0	2.0	.317	-.07	3.46
Girardi	86	370	51	4	425	6	8	46	32	.410	.991	651.1	4.5	.348	-.01	3.61
Hernandez C	63	295	37	7	339	4	5	44	15	.254	.979	434.0	3.0	.241	-.32	3.86
Hundley	121	701	47	3	751	2	6	89	33	.270	.996	892.1	6.1	.417	.41	3.31
Lake	17	71	8	2	81	1	0	14	4	.222	.975	125.2	.9	.150	-.17	4.37
Laker	28	102	8	1	111	1	4	13	2	.133	.991	127.1	.9	.412	.05	3.18
LaValliere	92	421	62	3	486	7	4	71	44	.383	.994	767.0	5.2	.474	.65	2.97
Manwaring	108	563	68	4	635	12	8	46	47	.505	.994	874.0	6.0	.361	.07	3.64
Mcnamara	30	131	8	1	140	1	1	11	5	.313	.993	198.2	1.4	.406	.08	3.17
O'Brien C	64	288	43	7	338	4	1	36	30	.455	.979	427.1	2.9	.219	-.38	4.15
Oliver	141	924	63	8	995	10	6	87	47	.351	.992	1199.2	8.2	.367	.14	3.42
Olson Greg	94	522	43	1	566	9	4	70	45	.391	.998	754.2	5.2	.415	.34	3.43
Pagnozzi	138	688	53	1	742	10	6	87	36	.293	.999	1189.0	8.1	.423	.59	3.36
Piazza	16	94	7	1	102	1	1	10	4	.286	.990	139.1	1.0	.301	-.05	3.68
Prince	19	76	8	2	86	0	1	8	4	.333	.977	114.0	.8	.255	-.07	3.63
Santiago	103	584	53	12	649	6	0	73	42	.365	.982	885.1	6.1	.249	-.61	3.73
Sasser	27	84	5	1	90	0	3	23	4	.148	.989	127.0	.9	.182	-.15	4.68
Scioscia	108	642	74	9	725	9	14	87	43	.331	.988	864.2	5.9	.415	.39	3.14
Servais	73	386	27	2	415	5	3	48	15	.238	.995	524.0	3.6	.394	.16	3.38
Slaught	79	365	32	5	402	3	6	45	25	.357	.988	598.2	4.1	.269	-.33	3.79
Taubensee	103	557	66	5	628	6	9	67	35	.343	.992	804.1	5.5	.298	-.28	3.99
Tucker	19	75	6	2	83	0	1	14	4	.222	.976	131.0	.9	.235	-.10	3.57
Villanueva	28	155	20	4	179	1	3	21	11	.344	.978	222.0	1.5	.411	.09	2.68
Walters D	55	328	25	3	356	5	2	47	18	.277	.992	432.0	3.0	.352	.01	3.50
Wilkins R	73	408	47	3	458	5	3	49	29	.372	.993	589.0	4.0	.405	.22	3.41
TOTALS		11853	1111	120	13084	140	138	1560	741	.322	.991	1461.0	10.0	.938	5.88	3.51

neyman catcher year. It's got the typical ten homers, an ordinary batting average, few walks, not many doubles. I mean, it's just so, so - AVERAGE. And it's the same story on defense. Joe throws out about the league average in base stealers and doesn't do anything else out of the ordinary, either. The Cincy pitchers do a bit better with him out there than with the replacement, but that's normal for a starter. Remember, when you're reading the rest of these comments, that this is an average catcher season, and everyone else did worse.

3. Don Slaught and Mike Lavalliere (PIT)

Well, actually, not everyone else did worse than Joe Oliver. The Pirate platoon came in just fine, thank you. In fact, Slaught and Lavalliere together should be ranked ahead of Oliver. But that would lead to the horrible question of whether these rankings should be done by player or by position. If I did them by player, as I have done in the past, this platoon would be ranked #4, under the Lavalliere name. That's because Mike had more playing time than Don, although Don had the better individual year. If I were to just rank the platoon, I'd then have to go back and add up the position totals for all the teams. And then, not only the Cub grouping of Rick Wilkins and Joe Girardi, but also the Braves' Olsen and

Berryhill, would move ahead of Tom Pagnozzi, who would lose the credit for his durability. What I eventually decided was to rank each team at the highest position any of its individual catchers achieved. Thus, the Pirates are ranked #3 because Don Slaught was the #3 player. And the Cubs will be next, because Rick Wilkins came in ahead of Pagnozzi all by his lonesome, in spite of playing less than Girardi did.

If you've read the Pirate comment, or the Atlanta one, you've already seen what I think of this platoon. When it comes time to pass around managerial kudos to Jim Leyland, this is where you start. The catcher position goes into a temporary decline, so Leyland just gets himself a steady left/right platoon and rides it to victory.

Here's an argument for all you people out there who place so much value on a catcher's intangibles in handling the pitching staff, and who therefore defend receivers who can't hit on the grounds that they save the pitching staff more runs than the guys who can hit get with their bats: 1) Mike Lavalliere is a true Gold Glove catcher, with tremendous defensive credentials, while 2) Don Slaught is naught. Pirate pitchers had a 2.97 ERA with Lavalliere behind the plate, and a lousy 3.79 throwing to

Slaught. 3) But, overall, the Pirate staff performed over its predicted head, despite having the two platooning receivers. 4) Now, does the Pirate staff seem to you to be overloaded with superstars? No? Than just how did it survive the horribly inconsistent catching it got? Could it be that switching catchers around does not really affect pitcher stability?

I mean, sure, the staff did better with Lavalliere out there. But, if you just benched Slaught, Lavalliere would have to hit lefties, which he cannot do. Mike would also wear out real soon there, and then he'd stop hitting righties, too. Even his defense would suffer from exhaustion. I'm beginning to believe that the catching position is one that truly should be platooned. The never-ending search for that elusive man who can catch 150 games without ever getting hurt is, frankly, not worth it.

4. Rick Wilkins and Joe Girardi, (CHN)

Again, the ranking is Rick Wilkins' place, although Girardi played more. I guess you can figure out that Wilkins now has the job, since Girardi is gone to Colorado. Now here's a bizarre stat: one of the Chicago catchers has the best ERA with/without Ratio in baseball this year. And guess what, Paul White, it's Hector Villanueva! And if you think that

Villanueva's turned into a top receiver, I have a team in Cleveland that I'll sell you a 49% share in. What happened, of course, is that Hector started out with a big share of the Cubbie catching job, and played his way out of it. Thus, all his playing time was early in the year. Well, I guess that tells us when the weather effects happened that made Wrigley Field into a pitchers' park. Gee, I wonder whether Hector's batting woes were related to the park effects. Maybe the Cubs gave up too fast on him. See what sabermetrics is good for?

5. Tom Pagnozzi (STL)

One thing for Pagnozzi, you get to see a lot of him. This year, only Darren Daulton played more, while Pags had a 30-game edge on the rest of the field. Yes, you have to admire Tom's ability to stay healthy, but you don't have to admire the 63-point drop in batting average between his worst month before the All-Star break (May, .289) and his best of the second half (July, .226). Bluntly put, Pags cannot handle the workload he's getting. But, with Rich Gedman as the only backup, nothing's going to change, is it?

I wonder what it's like to be Todd Zeile and watch Tom Pagnozzi strike out from August 1 to September 30, inclusive. I wonder what it's like to be Luis Alicea and watch Zeile get all the playing time at third base. I wonder what it's like to be Jose Oquendo....

6. Greg Olsen (ATL)

Not a whole lot better than Damon Berryhill, who ranks just behind Greg. The platoon was real effective, though I'm sure it's not what Bobby Cox had in mind. Still, it has the same effect as the Pirates' true platoon does. Olsen doesn't have to catch all the time, and so the things that happen to Tom Pagnozzi's bat in July don't happen to Greg.

7. Kurt Manwaring (SF)

The Giants exposed Steve Decker and lost him to the Marlins. That leaves Manwaring with the job to himself. I doubt that 's what the Giants had in mind, but you can hardly protect two catchers of this ability in your top 15. My take on Manwaring is that he's roughly a replacement-level player. That means that half the teams in the league are, or should be, looking for catching.

8. Gary Carter (MTL - ret.)

Darren Fletcher and someone named Tim Laker now have the job to share. Since the Expos think they are in contention now, I presume they are in the market for catching. Makes you appreciate Nelson Santovenia, much less Mike Fitzgerald.

9. Mike Scioscia (LA)

I got to see a little of Mike Piazza while out in LA. He's raw at the plate, but looks like he can catch. Carlos Hernandez, on the other hand, can hit some, but looks like a first baseman to me.

10. Ed Taubensee (HOU)

There were times last year where Taubensee looked about as much like a Major League ballplayer as I do. Still, he did hit some in the minors, and he's only 24, and he has an absolute cannon for an arm, even if it didn't pay off in the Caught Stealing stats. In general, his defensive numbers are awful for the possessor of that arm, and he's going to need work. I do know that, if I had Craig Biggio, he'd be back there and Taubensee would be a 40-game per year reserve. On the other hand, I'd probably trade Kenny Lofton for that good a backup catcher.

11. Todd Hundley (NYM)

Has a chance to develop into Tom Pagnozzi.

12. Benito Santiago (SD-FLA)

If you judge catchers only by their arms, this is what you end up with. As occasionally happens, Benito ended up dead last in the catcher rankings. That's because all the guys who were this bad or worse got themselves benched early and often. If I'd followed the rule about rankings that I applied to the Pirate catchers, I'd have ranked Dan Walters at #9 at the position. Walters, though, got too little playing time for even me to rank the entire team's catching corps under his name. He's 26, and probably is Tom Pagnozzi, as opposed to having a chance to develop into Pags. But he's no better than that and, at 26, he's not going to get any better. Still, he's what the Padres have got.

First Basemen

Brock J. Hanke

		OWAR	DWAR	TWAR
1.	Thomas F	7.44	0.19	7.63
2.	McGwire	5.81	.29	6.10
3.	Palmeiro	5.02	.91	5.94
4.	Joyner	4.44	.72	5.17
5.	Olerud	4.40	.36	4.75
6.	Milligan	3.48	.35	3.83
7.	Mattingly	2.91	.82	3.73
8.	Fielder	3.07	.37	3.43
9.	Sorrento	2.98	.20	3.18
10.	Hrbek	2.27	.42	2.69
11.	Vaughn M	1.92	.03	1.95
12.	Stevens	1.19	.29	1.48
13.	Stubbs	.90	.12	1.02
14.	Martinez Tino	.45	.37	.82
	James D	.58	.18	.77
	Jaha	.48	.14	.63
	Jefferson R	.54	.05	.59
	Conine	.28	.14	.43
	Segui	.02	.40	.41
	Oberkfell	.12	-.06	.06
	Bergman	-.91	.03	-.88

1. Frank Thomas (CHA)

It's hard to decide which was worse: putting Mike Sharperson on the All-Star team or leaving Frank Thomas off. That's not to say that the All-Star selections are usually perfect, but this was an unusually bad job. I mean, it's not as though this was the first year that Frank was the best hitter in the American League.

Last year, I made a comparison of Frank Thomas to Ted Williams. Well, not really; what I said was that Frank Thomas was the only hitter currently in baseball who reminded me of Williams at all. That's fair, but it's also fair to recognize that Frank has no speed at all, while Ted did have some. He wasn't a great outfielder but he did have some speed. And therefore, it is likely that Frank Thomas will not have nearly as long a career as Ted did. Not to mention that he shows no signs of ever being really THAT good.

I've mentioned elsewhere that, when I do call-in shows on the radio, the question most asked is, "Who is the best player in the game?". The answer to that question is, "It depends". If you're talking about career value, it's Cal Ripken, Jr. or Ryne Sandberg, probably Ripken. If you're talking about the best completely proven player who is still younger than 27, it's Roberto Alomar. But, if you're talking about, "Who is likely to turn in the best season with the bat in 1993?", it's Frank Thomas.

2. Mark McGwire (OAK)

And if you're talking about who's the most likely player to have a big collapse next year, it's Mark here. This is a completely inconsistent player, for reasons I'm not sure of. He doesn't seem to get hurt much, at least according to the record of games played. And he doesn't look like Jose Canseco or Eric Davis or Dave Justice, who are the guys who have bodybuilt too much muscle onto their bone structures. Instead, he just looks like a big guy who should be able to hit consistently. But he's had the worst age-27 season in recent memory, and then staged a complete recovery to this cam-

paign.

The key to the struggle seems to be batting average. Unlike Frank Thomas, Mark doesn't hit for any more than an average average, if that makes sense. If he has a decline year, his average drops so low that he has to start winging defensively, to protect himself against the Mendoza line. That's when the power collapses. If Mark is having no trouble with his average, he swings freely, and the taters come. Now, what it is that causes the batting average swings, I don't know. For all I know, it may be just random luck. Or perhaps he lacks what I call "bat accuracy". That's the ability to swing the bat where your eyes tell you the ball should be going. Some batters - usually those known for good two-strikes hitting - have good abilities to do that. Some, perhaps like Mark, don't. I'll try to watch him a few times on TV this year, and see if that looks to be the case.

3. Rafael Palmeiro (TEX)

I'd still rather have Mark Grace. Nonetheless, even after the ballpark adjustments, here he is, and he's on a weak year. Actually, Rafael's career to date looks like he's a year older than he claims to be. 1991 was the season that should be attached to age 27; this year is the one that should have been the age 28 start of the decline phase. Well, he was an old 27 (September birthday), but that's not something I want to dwell on. Either batters do, in general, have peak seasons at age 27 or they don't. Rafael didn't. He had his at age 26.

The numbers give Rafael the Gold Glove at first base this year, and I don't see how you can dispute that. Don Mattingly has had his career slip away to injury, and is no longer the gymnast he used to be. Wally Joyner is OK, but nothing special. If you look at the AL first basemen compared to the NL men, what you see is that all the agile guys are in the senior circuit. That, most likely, is the result of the DH rule and the turf outfields prevalent in the National League. AL teams tend to acquire the big lumbering guys who can hit, because they have two lineup spots that such players can fill, and sometimes an outfield slot as well. NL teams, on the other hand, have to get outfielders who can run, and don't have the DH spot to

First Base	G	PO	A	Er	TC	DP	FPct	DI	DG	DW%	DWAR
Bergman	55	338	21	5	364	28	.986	338.0	.7	.392	.03
Brett	15	137	12	2	151	9	.987	133.0	.3	.495	.04
Brunansky	28	184	10	2	196	20	.990	164.2	.3	.410	.02
Cooper S	62	446	33	5	484	43	.990	420.1	.9	.457	.09
Davis A	22	191	11	1	203	21	.995	171.0	.4	.537	.07
Fielder	114	957	89	10	1056	98	.991	954.1	2.0	.534	.36
Gaetti	44	371	32	5	408	36	.988	368.2	.8	.473	.09
Hrbek	104	954	67	3	1024	76	.997	903.1	1.9	.575	.42
Jaha	38	286	22	0	308	22	1.000	290.1	.6	.588	.14
Jefferson R	15	129	13	1	143	9	.993	136.1	.3	.522	.05
Joyner	145	1239	134	10	1383	139	.993	1262.1	2.6	.626	.72
Lansford	18	112	5	2	119	13	.983	126.0	.3	.242	-.03
Larkin G	55	456	29	4	489	50	.992	431.2	.9	.456	.09
Maas	22	142	4	2	148	10	.986	140.2	.3	.323	-.01
Martinez Crl	37	263	20	1	284	40	.996	264.0	.5	.532	.10
Martinez Tino	78	678	58	4	740	63	.995	663.2	1.4	.620	.37
Mattingly	143	1212	115	4	1331	133	.997	1223.2	2.5	.675	.82
McGwire	139	1119	70	6	1195	119	.995	1181.2	2.4	.466	.28
Milligan	129	1009	75	7	1091	109	.994	1061.0	2.2	.510	.35
Molitor	48	461	26	2	489	45	.996	425.2	.9	.467	.10
O'Brien P	81	623	54	3	680	73	.996	625.1	1.3	.631	.36
Olerud	133	1057	81	7	1145	73	.994	1095.0	2.3	.507	.35
Palmeiro	156	1251	142	7	1400	130	.995	1382.2	2.8	.671	.91
Segui	95	374	34	1	409	42	.998	385.0	.8	.631	.22
Sorrento	121	997	75	8	1080	109	.993	1016.2	2.1	.448	.20
Stevens	91	764	49	4	817	87	.995	738.0	1.5	.543	.29
Stubbs	68	525	63	8	596	44	.987	550.0	1.1	.459	.12
Surhoff BJ	17	143	13	0	156	18	1.000	129.0	.3	.661	.08
Tabler	34	281	20	0	301	22	1.000	265.1	.5	.629	.15
Thomas F	158	1428	90	13	1531	113	.992	1406.0	2.9	.415	.19
Vaughn M	85	740	54	15	809	75	.981	720.1	1.5	.371	.03
TOTALS		20210	1622	156	21988	1996	.993	1460.1	3.0	2.896	7.64

use. And so, Rafael, who is good, but hardly great in the field, ends up as the top man in the league.

4.   Wally Joyner (KC)

Got off to a ramping stamping start, delighted in his freedom from the Anaheim Zoo. Spent most of May wandering about in bewilderment at the horrid start and the complete collapse of momentum it inspired in KC. The end result was one of Wally's worst seasons. A quick look at the home/road splits points out the trouble. One whole home run in Royals Stadium; a normal 8 on the road. Either Wally's got to find a home runs stroke that works on those faraway walls, or he's got to start hitting line drives for doubles. If he does neither, that ballpark will just kill him.

5.   John Olerud (TOR)

You'll be reading elsewhere my comments on the Blue Jay lineup dilemma. Briefly, the "trade" of Dave Winfield for Paul Molitor leaves the Jays with too many leadoff men and too few cleanup hitters. If they lead Molitor off (and he's much better at it than Devon

White is), they end up with White down about #6 in the order. And Devon White has sulked before. If they bat Paul third, they have to move Joe Carter down. That won't hurt them, as Carter is not an ideal #3 hitter, but it will raise the question of whether Joe or John Olerud should bat before the other. Olerud gets on base much more, and has much less power, so the technical answer should be to bat him ahead of Carter. But that puts the Jays in danger of Joe Carter pouting.

For what it's worth, I'd bat John Olerud cleanup. I think he can handle the job just fine. It's nice to have big homers in the four hole, but it's not necessary. Besides, John's homer stats are oddly split. The Skydome is rather a homers park overall, but it suppresses them for lefties. (That's just one of the fascinating things you can find out by reading out ballpark adjustment lines listed with the team essays.) Thus, John hasn't hit any in his home park yet. I expect that to change as John ages. With experience, he'll figure out how to use what little the park will give him. He'll also get stronger. The result should be a 20-homer guy, which is fine for cleanup.

6.   Randy Milligan (BAL)

There's a big dropoff from John Olerud to Randy here, rivaled only by the drop from Frank Thomas to everyone else. In this case, it's not the dropoff from The Best to The Rest, but it is from The Good Players to The Pack. Milligan has never been a first class first baseman, and this was a bad year for him. The ranking is abnormally high, the result of a bad year out of Cecil Fielder, and Kent Hrbek. A BAD FANTASY BUY, as he does not predict to improve much, while at least a couple of the guys below him should pass him up.

7.   Don Mattingly (NYY)

Don, never a sturdy guy, has simply not recovered from the injury of 1990. Frankly, I doubt that he will. He's had plenty of time, but has not responded. He's not "through" or anything, but I think this ranking accurately reflects his current level of ability. He's a middle-of-the-pack first baseman, nothing more. Since your fantasy league doubtless has someone left who expects him to come back to the grandeur of the '80s, he's A LOUSY FANTASY BUY.

8. Cecil Fielder (DET)

His monstrous home run spurt straddles right athwart his age 27 years. Since then, in two years, he's lost 10 homers on the road and then ten at home. His batting average has dropped 15 points each of the last two years. He just signed a monstrous contract that he can't possibly justify. That's a recipe for collapse, if I've ever seen one. I'd still rather gamble on him than on Randy Milligan, but neither one is a good gamble. UNLOAD HIM IN FANTASY BALL.

9. Paul Sorrento (CLE)

He'll be 27 this year, and he's been moving steadily up for the last three seasons. I expect him to turn in that career year, and thereby recommend him as a FANTASY BEST BUY. I am sure he will be better than Randy Milligan. In fact, if the Indians do turn in that competitive year that they keep talking about, it is Paul Sorrento's bat that is most likely to fuel it.

10. Kent Hrbek (MIN)

I do expect a further comeback from 1991, for a couple of reasons. First, his 1992 year looks like the beginning of a recovery from an injury, and 1993 should see it complete. And second, Kent got nothing out of his ballpark in home runs in 1992. That's unusual, both for Kent and for the ballpark. I wouldn't be surprised at all to see a return to the 25+ homers of the glory days. Now, how long a 33-year-old man who carries too much weight around can keep it up, well, that's another question. I give him three more good years, maybe only two.

11. Mo Vaughn (BOS)

Coming off a year much below expectation, and stuck in the middle of a horrid lineup when he was expecting to fill out a contender, I can't imagine Mo's morale is worth much right now. The Boston fans are likely to just go nuts when they realize how bad their 1993 edition is, which isn't going to help. I think Mo will eventually turn out to be the player his minor league stats suggest, but I don't want to gamble on him for this year alone.

12. Lee Stevens (CAL - MTL)

The Angels are doing everything they can to avoid putting Lee Stevens in the starting lineup for 1993. That's a sure sign that Whitey Herzog and Buck Rodgers have given up on the prospect. I have to trust their judgment on that one. Besides, this year was right on his career average. The only thing Lee has to recommend him is the very short stint of 1991. That and his age. I have to rate him NO PROSPECT, until he shows me something more. The Expos apparently think he's Ivan Claderon.

13. Cranklin Stubbs (MIL)

Job belongs to John Jaha. Apparently the only ballpark Cranklin can hit in is the Astrodome. I don't know what happened here - perhaps an injury - but I'm afraid Don Malcolm's favorite here is finished.

14. Pete O'Brien (SEA)
    or, more likely,
    Tino Martinez

Martinez clearly should have the job, as O'Brien is finished, but the Mariners are strangely unwilling to just put Tino out there and let him develop. If they were contenders, and/or if the alternative were a good ballplayer, I could see that, but this is the Mariners and that is Pete O'Brien at age 34. The only thing I can guess is that Bill Plummer either a) thought the Mariners would be in contention, or b) thought he had to win as many games in 1992 as he could to keep his job. Both premises, I might add, are concepts that I agree with. I thought the M's could contend in 1992, if they got lucky with the pitchers and if Plummer could organize the bench. Neither happened, and they didn't happen in spectacular fashion, but I stand by the analysis. As for Plummer's job, well, by now you know where that went.

First Basemen

Brock J. Hanke

		OWAR	DWAR	TWAR
1.	Grace	6.83	.94	7.76
2.	Bagwell	6.37	.80	7.18
3.	Clark W	6.27	.40	6.67
4.	McGriff F	6.39	.13	6.53
5.	Kruk	5.13	.20	5.33
6.	Murray E	4.56	.07	4.64
7.	Karros	3.93	.59	4.52
8.	Bream	3.14	.10	3.24
9.	Merced	2.34	.60	2.94
10.	Morris H	2.31	.52	2.83
	Hunter B	1.91	.29	2.21
	Jordan	1.39	.13	1.52
11.	Galarraga	1.10	.16	1.26
	Redus	.97	.14	1.11
	Brewer R	.77	.17	.94
	McClendon	.87	.06	.93
	Benzinger	.65	.26	.91
	Litton	.32	.39	.72
12.	Cianfrocco	.31	.09	.40
	Colbrunn	.32	.08	.39
	Perry G	-.01	-.01	-.02
	Guerrero	-.24	-.04	-.28
	Donnels	-.40	.06	-.34

1. Mark Grace (CHN)

If you look at the stats of the first four men here, you'll be hard pressed to sort them out, and very unlikely to list Mark Grace first. That is, unless you've looked at this year's ballpark adjustments and seen that Wrigley Field was a neutral park for right handed hitters, and a decided pitcher's park for lefties. Couple that adjustment with Mark's exceptional playing time, and you get this ranking.

And I'm delighted to get to write about it. I've contended for some time that Mark Grace was exactly the type of player that the Cubs should concentrate on getting, rather than the Andre Dawson types they usually seem to want. In a normal year, Wrigley will be a hitters' park, and thereby inflate the value of on-base percentage relative to power. Mark, with limited power but many walks, is the right type of good hitter to get. Andre Dawson makes too many outs. A lineup of Dawsons won't get those long innings going that blow out ballgames. Mark Graces will.

2. Jeff Bagwell (HOU)

Actually, this was a very, very mild Sophomore Slump season for Jeff. On the other hand, his ranking requires some explanation. Mark Grace, Will Clark and Fred McGriff all outplayed Jeff on a per-out basis. But Jeff led the league in Games Played, and the WAR system fills in lost playing time with a .350 ballplayer. Thus, Jeff sneaks past Clark and McGriff. Is that fair? Well, Jeff probably won't keep playing all 162 games in a season. The workload will decrease as he ages, unless he's Cal Ripken's cousin or something. So, in the long run, that's not a real component of his value. But wait. Grace, Clark and McGriff are all 29, while Jeff Bagwell is 25. Will Clark led the league, playing every game, when he was 25, too. Fred McGriff played 161 at age 26. Mark Grace didn't, but he wasn't an established starter at that age, due to the oddities of the Chicago Cub player development system. It IS fair to credit Jeff with extra value for his ability to play every day.

This analysis also leads to a fantasy league point. All the other NL first basemen in Jeff's class are much older than he is. In fact, all the NL first basemen of any quality are older, except Eric Karros and Archi Cianfrocco. Neither of those two shows any signs of turning into Jeff Bagwell. That makes Jeff the MOST VALUABLE FANTASY LEAGUE FIRST BASEMAN, if you're in a league with hold-over lists. If you're just drafting for one year, pick Fred McGriff, as he is the most reliable hitter and plays in the most reliable hitters' ballpark.

3. Will Clark (SF)

I really don't think Clark is this good; I have him down as a slight dropoff from Grace, Bagwell and McGriff. But this year, with nothing behind him in the batting order, he was given 23 intentional walks. That's about twice what he was getting when Kevin Mitchell was around, and about 3 times as many as he'll get with Barry Bonds on board. Without the IBBs, Will's on-base percentage will suffer from his strike zone judgment. To be blunt, if Will didn't have power, he'd take fewer walks than average. As it is, he's at about the average with the power there to make pitchers cautious. Of course, none of that applies is a Rotisserie league, as opposed to a full-simulation fantasy league. In a Roti league, Will is probably the most valuable NL first baseman.

4. Fred McGriff (SD)

I wonder if he didn't try to throw the homer title to Sheffield for a while there. He just stopped hitting homers in September, until Gary was out of the Triple Crown run. Oh, well, who really cares? What I really want to say about Fred is that I think that he is the best of the NL first basemen in terms of one-year actual baseball (as opposed to fantasy) value. I'm not sure how seriously I want to take the defensive stats at first base, and they are the difference between Fred and the three guys above him. In any case, he's by far the best bet

First Base	G	PO	A	Er	TC	DP	FPct	DI	DG	DW%	DWAR
Bagwell	159	1334	130	7	1471	110	.995	1401.1	2.9	.628	.80
Benzinger	42	177	17	0	194	17	1.000	174.0	.4	.698	.12
Bream	120	855	72	10	937	70	.989	907.1	1.9	.405	.10
Brewer R	27	214	18	0	232	16	1.000	206.2	.4	.651	.13
Cianfrocco	56	373	40	3	416	25	.993	386.2	.8	.533	.15
Clark W	141	1277	103	10	1390	130	.993	1229.2	2.5	.510	.40
Colbrunn	47	363	29	3	395	23	.992	372.2	.8	.451	.08
Coles	21	146	7	0	153	7	1.000	134.0	.3	.540	.05
Doran	25	136	8	0	144	5	1.000	149.0	.3	.544	.06
Galarraga	90	778	62	8	848	72	.991	754.1	1.5	.453	.16
Grace	157	1578	141	4	1723	120	.998	1414.0	2.9	.675	.94
Guerrero	28	243	6	3	252	17	.988	241.1	.5	.263	-.04
Hunter B	92	528	48	2	578	36	.997	532.1	1.1	.568	.24
Jordan	54	415	27	2	444	33	.995	438.0	.9	.475	.11
Karros	143	1209	126	9	1344	98	.993	1201.1	2.5	.586	.58
King J	32	270	21	2	293	27	.993	266.1	.5	.521	.09
Kruk	121	980	58	7	1045	78	.993	958.0	2.0	.427	.15
Martinez Da	21	156	11	4	171	22	.977	161.1	.3	.292	-.02
McGriff F	151	1219	104	12	1335	95	.991	1334.2	2.7	.398	.13
Merced	114	882	73	5	960	73	.995	834.1	1.7	.585	.40
Morris H	109	840	84	1	925	66	.999	908.2	1.9	.626	.51
Murray E	154	1278	94	12	1384	111	.991	1308.1	2.7	.377	.07
Perry G	29	221	11	3	235	23	.987	214.1	.4	.321	-.01
Redus	36	280	16	0	296	16	1.000	247.1	.5	.615	.13
Snyder C	27	170	18	2	190	14	.989	196.0	.4	.476	.05
Wallach	71	630	61	6	697	42	.991	594.2	1.2	.506	.19
TOTALS		17478	1460	127	19065	1429	.993	1461.0	3.0	2.599	6.75

to hit 30+ homers, and he takes his walks to pump up his OB%, and if I can't have Frank Thomas, I'll take Fred.

5. John Kruk (PHI)

What I want to know is what took the Padres so long to promote John to the Majors. No, strike that, I know what it is: John Kruk does not look like a Major League ballplayer. Or, rather, he doesn't look like a 1980's ML ballplayer. What he looks like is one of those old dinosaur left fielders, like Greg Luzinski, that everybody used to have before the days of huge expanses of turf in the outfield. Of course, if John had hit homers like Greg Luzinski, he'd have been in the Majors much sooner. But no, he has to hit like Tony Gwynn, who, come to think of it, doesn't look like a Major League outfielder either.

The odd thing is that, with his looks, John has gotten no homer value out of his two home parks, both of which favor home runs. He's hit 20 homers twice, and both times it was fueled by a splurge of roadkills. Instead, he has milked the Philly ballpark for doubles, just like Tony Gwynn would try to hit.

6. Eddie Murray (NYM)

Well, whaddaya know. Eddie Murray really does have a media-proof personality. He goes to the Mets, the entire team blows up, and he turns in a fine, fine year, especially for his age. Actually, it was just about the same year as his 1991, except that Shea Stadium does not suppress doubles as much as Dodger Stadium does. Of course, the Mets, with the money they spend, don't want to win the pennant with a first baseman and cleanup man who is in the middle of the league's starters. No, they want to hire 37-year-old ballplayers and have them rejuvenate a decade to age 27. I mean, if they had enough other hitting that they could bat Willie Randolph 7th and Eddie here 6th, it would make sense to pay them the millions. As it is, forget it.

7. Eric Karros (LA)

I dunno. He's a decent hitter, but this is first base, and he can't play anywhere else. He's Jeff Bagwell's age, which makes his Rookie award just a tad suspect there. The Cardinals have three players about the same age (Lankford, Zeile and Pena) who all three figure to turn in much better careers. What the media focus on Karros indicates is just how far the Dodger farm system has fallen. They used to be able to do better than this, and so people expect the best Dodger prospect to be better than this. Then he sneaks in 20 homers and everybody loses their perspective. I WOULDN'T TAKE HIM IN A FANTASY LEAGUE, not at the price he'll probably command.

8. Sid Bream (ATL)

Klesko, that's the name. Ryan Klesko. That's who has the Atlanta first base job. And no, I don't think Sid, who cannot play the outfield, after all, can beat out Brian Hunter for the backup job. Real good candidate to be in Japan soon unless the Pirates get desperate.

9. Orlando Merced (PIT)

Which they might. Orlando here figures to end up in the Pirate outfield, which leaves them without a first baseman at all, I mean, Alex Cole, Gary Redus, Cecil Espy and Gary Varsho are all gone, aren't they? That leaves Lloyd McClendon in right and Merced in left, right? And so Jeff King goes to first, and John Wehner plays third. Sid Bream is better than that is. Hell, Ted Simmons can reactivate himself and play better than that. Or maybe they'll move Slaught to first and let Spanky catch every day. I don't know what the Pirates are going to do. It's one thing to lose your starting left fielder. It's another to lose all your backups, too.

10. Hal Morris (CIN)

This was supposed to be his big age-27 career year. But then, you can't play when you're hurt. But, then, if you never have played 140 games in your life, everyone ought to expect you to get hurt. But, then, the Reds have the league corner on injured ballplayers (Sabo, Larkin, etc., etc. Used to have someone named "Davis", didn't they?). But, then, do you expect Marge Schott to hire a competent conditioning coach? Do you expect Lou Pinella to install a calm, reasonable body development program?

11.   Andres Galarraga (STL - COL)

I don't believe this. There is actually one starter at this position ranked lower than Andres. Oh, no there's not. That's the Expos' first base corps. They have to rank Cianfrocco at first because Tim Wallach, who played the most games there, also played the most games for them at third. Yes, of course Wallach's a third baseman.

All kidding aside, Andres' season was just about what everyone should have expected. His current level of ability would indicate a season of about .265 Avg., with about 16 homers. That, though, is assuming he stays healthy, and that's not reasonable. Will he help the Rockies? No, not in any real sense. But that's not his job. His job is to make the Colorado batting order respectable enough to make Don Baylor look like a real Major League manager. Remember, Baylor can't afford to just fall on his face and lose 120, like Casey Stengel could. Don's trying to prove he's a championship-quality skipper. He's got to look at least decent, even with an expansion crew. Andres Galarraga's job is to provide Don Baylor with something at least remotely resembling a power center for his offense. That he can probably do.

By the way: at the SABR convention this summer, there was a little calculator being shown around with a database of Major League stats that you could look up. You could also do some simple computational lists. I had them compute the Top Twenty players in Weight/ Height ratio; that is, I had them list the 20 fattest ballplayers in their database. The leader, of course, was Jumbo Brown. But Andres Galarraga was the only active player in that top 20. If you think that's odd, look at Andres' rear end some time. And yet, he's a nimble first baseman, an honest infielder. He just can't run fast enough to play the outfield.

12.   Archi Cianfrocco (MTL)

The Expos, you see, were going to start the year with Tim Wallach at first base, Ivan Calderon in left field, and Bret Barberie at third. Then Calderon got hurt for the year, and Barberie had the Sophomore Slump of all time, and the manager who wanted to play Wallach at first got himself fired. That left Tim with about 2/5 of the playing time here, and the remaining 3/5 were split among Archi and Greg Colbrunn and about 18 other guys, who were also sharing the left field job. Archi was the one who got the plurality of the time at first.

That's not to imply that Archi would move right up in the rankings if he were to play 150 games here. He's a 15-homer guy with no big deal in Batting Average and no strike zone judgment at all. He's also already 26. I doubt that I will ever write about him in this section again.

Second Basemen

Brock J. Hanke

		OWAR	DWAR	TWAR
1.	Baerga	4.93	2.22	7.16
2.	Alomar R	5.57	.69	6.26
3.	Knoblauch	4.39	1.82	6.21
4.	Bordick	3.37	2.22	5.60
5.	Fletcher S	2.14	2.36	4.50
	Blankenship L	2.67	1.45	4.12
6.	Whitaker	3.27	.84	4.11
7.	Miller K	3.13	.61	3.74
	Browne J	2.03	.47	2.50
8.	Reed Jd	.36	2.13	2.49
9.	Sojo	.20	1.34	1.53
	Gallego	.57	.77	1.34
	Cora	.85	.43	1.28
10.	Kelly P	.56	.69	1.25
	Wilkerson	.20	.92	1.12
	McLemore	.13	.86	.99
	Kent	.96	-.08	.88
11.	Reynolds H	-.34	1.18	.84
12.	Ripken B	-.70	1.43	.73
	Samuel	.57	.14	.71
	Frye	.24	.39	.63
	Ready	.27	.20	.47
	Rose	.12	.27	.39
13.	Sax S	-.13	.45	.32
	Hill D	.20	.07	.27
	Franco Ju	.32	-.08	.24
	Brosius	.01	.13	.14
	Turner	-.02	.04	.02
14.	Newman	-.65	.57	-.08
	Amaral	-.51	.26	-.25
	Boone B	-.79	.17	-.62
	Shumpert	-.88	-.05	-.93

1. Carlos Baerga (CLE)

There's a temptation to just go crazy here. Carlos has risen to the top of a tough heap at the age of 23. He blew past Sophomore Slump like he'd never heard of it, and then found a way to adjust to his ballpark and get a few home homers. He's even an efficient base stealer, though the volume isn't much. The one offensive hole is the horrid walk total.

Carlos has talked about this to reporters. Basically, he's of the "you can't walk off the island" school of Latin players. That is, he believes in being super-aggressive and swinging at everything you think you can hit. The theory is that the scouts for the big league clubs aren't going to look at your walk totals, and they're not going to care about your strike zone judgment.

Now, all this may be true, but the American pitchers do care. Carlos was down to only 25 unintentional walks last year, which is absolutely pushing the envelope. It means that, very soon, American League pitchers are not just going to stop throwing him strikes, they're going to start throwing him wild pitches. I

can't believe that's never going to catch up to him.

As it is, the #1 ranking is currently a result of Roberto Alomar's lousy defensive stats and Julio Franco's one-year absence. At 24, Carlos certainly has the growth potential to catch those two, but he hasn't done it yet. And he could very easily take a step backwards, as the pitchers of the league catch on. Consequently, I want to see another year BEFORE I RANK HIM A GOOD FANTASY BUY.

2. Roberto Alomar (TOR)

He's still only one year older than Carlos Baerga, and much more established. Every year, it seems he adds another skill onto the resume. Either his batting average goes up, or he adds some line drive power, or, as this year, he develops a new high in strike zone judgment. Right now, the only thing he lacks as a hitter is home run power. As it's still a couple of years before some of the heaviest hitters have developed their homer pop, I'm not at all ready to write that skill off.

The only negative is the defense. This is the second year in a row where Roberto's defensive stats have been mediocre. It's not just some ratings fluke, either. Roberto trails all the good defensive keystone men in both Assists per Game and Double Plays. Those are the keys to the keystone, and Roberto just doesn't have them. Later on down the line, this might suggest that Roberto will end up in the outfield, like Robin Yount. For now, though, he's still the BEST PROVEN YOUNG PLAYER in baseball.

3. Chuck Knoblauch (MIN)

Took the whole concept of Sophomore Slump and just punted it down the road. With the big increase in walks, he's left with only one weakness, lack of power. That keeps him out of the offensive class of Alomar, Baerga, and Franco, but his defense keeps him in that class overall. Surely you can live with no power from a second baseman.

Those of you who have read Don Malcolm's Fantasy Diary have seen what offense at sec-

Second Base	G	PO	A	Er	TC	DP	FPct	DI	DG	DW%	DWAR
Alomar R	150	286	377	5	668	67	.993	1276.0	7.0	.448	.69
Baerga	160	400	475	19	894	137	.979	1434.0	7.9	.635	2.24
Blankenship L	78	160	222	3	385	57	.992	613.2	3.4	.730	1.28
Boone B	32	71	93	6	170	22	.965	277.2	1.5	.455	.16
Bordick	95	202	267	6	475	58	.987	733.2	4.0	.662	1.25
Cora	28	51	71	2	124	19	.984	210.1	1.2	.659	.36
Fletcher S	106	206	319	4	529	70	.992	855.1	4.7	.767	1.95
Frye	67	120	196	7	323	43	.978	555.2	3.0	.478	.39
Gallego	40	85	111	2	198	31	.990	330.1	1.8	.664	.57
Gantner	68	136	179	2	317	42	.994	511.1	2.8	.777	1.20
Gonzales R	42	78	91	1	170	28	.994	322.1	1.8	.586	.42
Huson	47	69	83	0	152	22	1.000	313.2	1.7	.465	.20
Kelly P	101	204	296	11	511	63	.978	864.0	4.7	.496	.69
Knoblauch	154	308	416	6	730	104	.992	1339.2	7.3	.597	1.82
McLemore	70	127	186	7	320	46	.978	519.1	2.8	.652	.86
Miller K	93	189	250	13	452	60	.971	786.1	4.3	.480	.56
Naehring	23	54	66	1	121	11	.992	170.1	.9	.656	.29
Newman A	72	118	168	5	291	31	.983	465.0	2.5	.500	.38
Oberkfell	21	34	34	1	69	5	.986	147.2	.8	.270	-.06
Phillips	57	110	167	4	281	40	.986	437.1	2.4	.657	.74
Reed Jd	142	304	471	14	789	113	.982	1256.0	6.9	.658	2.12
Reynolds H	134	301	361	12	674	89	.982	1107.1	6.1	.543	1.17
Ripken B	108	218	317	4	539	65	.993	893.2	4.9	.643	1.44
Rose	28	49	94	7	150	18	.953	212.0	1.2	.580	.27
Sax S	141	305	391	20	716	73	.972	1251.1	6.9	.416	.45
Shumpert	33	50	76	4	130	16	.969	260.0	1.4	.320	-.04
Sojo	96	188	267	7	462	73	.985	761.0	4.2	.658	1.28
Stankiewicz	34	52	89	1	142	20	.993	238.0	1.3	.636	.37
Whitaker	119	258	312	9	579	70	.984	978.1	5.4	.503	.82
Wilkerson	39	70	106	2	178	29	.989	295.2	1.6	.698	.56
TOTALS		5007	6850	204	12061	1578	.983	1460.1	8.0	6.957	52.86

ond base can do right now. I'm not completely sure all the kids will hold up, but if Alomar, Baerga and Knoblauch are for real, this position may be in for historic highs of hitting. THAT DECREASES THE FANTASY VALUE OF THE SECOND BASEMEN, but it doesn't decrease their quality overall. Coming in third or fourth at this position at Chuck's age is a badge of distinction, not a sign that something is lacking.

4. Mike Bordick (OAK)

He was 26, and has never done anything like this before, so you have to wonder if it's for real. In any case, he's not at the top of the second base heap, not in this league. For one thing, his defensive stats are padded by the playing time at shortstop, where the extra defensive responsibility expands the DWAR. For another, he has no power and he takes no walks. That's at least one more strike against him than the top three guys - and Julio Franco - have. Overall, I give him no more than a 25% chance to hold all this newfound value for more than a year or two. The fact that he's turning 27 is the biggest positive I can list. I WOULDN'T PICK HIM UP FOR MORE THAN ONE YEAR.

5. Scott Fletcher (MIL - BOS)

Now, let's not get all excited here. Yes, this season is not that far above Scott's career average, but it is a big gain over his recent experiences. And a lot of the ranking is fueled by the extraordinary defensive stats. Scott had more double plays in 106 games than Roberto Alomar did in 150; you can't expect that to keep up. And Scott is a decade older than practically everybody ranked above him.

Still, Scott's a valuable player, and nobody in your fantasy league knows it. If you're looking for a good player who'll go late and/or cheap, SCOTT'S YOUR MAN. That's particularly true if defensive stats count in your league, as they do in the Bill James game.

6. Lou Whitaker (DET)

Still a good second baseman, who is still performing over his career averages, particularly in power. In a normal collection of second basemen, he'd be a top guy. But this league is infested with really hot 24-year-olds, and Lou can't compete with that any more. I know this: he's playing better than Alan Trammell, and he's younger, and he hasn't

been hurt.

7. Keith Miller (KC)

The vagaries of our computer system ended up ranking placing Gregg Jeffries as a second baseman. He finished right ahead of Keith Miller, with 3.79 TWAR to Keith's 3.74 Does that seem obviously wrong? I mean, Gregg started all year, got himself 604 At-Bats, and accumulated 36 doubles and 10 home runs. Keith only played in 106 games, had only 416 At-Bats, and accumulated only 24 doubles and 4 homers. They had the same batting average (.285 to .284). The defensive stats give Keith the edge, but by less than a third of a run. Well, here's what happened. Gregg Jeffries did outpower Keith Miller. The Slugging Averages were .404 to .389. That's a 15-point margin. But Keith got on base .352 to Gregg's .329, which is a 23-point difference. Gregg walked only 43 times in all those At-Bats. Keith not only walked 31 times, but he was hit by 14 pitches as well. Gregg was hit only once.

On balance, I agree with the rankings. Keith Miller is, right now, a better player than Gregg Jeffries is. If they both played the same amount of time, Keith would rank about a WAR higher.

Keith Miller can play the infield, and Gregg Jeffries can't. Keith can get on base some, and Gregg is not what you want. The power differential is there, but it doesn't amount to as much as the defense and the on-base skills do.

Here's what I wrote before the Royals picked up Jose Lind. "Keith Miller is, also, A REAL GOOD FANTASY SLEEPER. He's got the job sewed up now; his new shortstop, Greg Gagne, is going to help his defense, and nobody has any idea of how much stats he'll pile up in full time play." Now, of course, Miller may find himself on the bench. That's silly - he's better than Jose Lind - but it still may happen.

8. Jody Reed (BOS - LA)

I really do not know what the Bosox are thinking in letting this man go. Sure, this year was a downer, but is that any reason to write the man off? And just who do the Sox think they have who's going to do the job Jody was doing? Did they forget that they were giving up Wade Boggs too? Do they think Mo Vaughn is going to lead off?

On the other hand, while Jody is certainly better than what the Dodgers were playing at second, I don't think that position was really Tommy Lasorda's problem. I have perfect faith in the Sharperson / Harris platoon. Well, there is this to say: the Dodgers are sure backed up against failure now. If Tim Wallach fails, they have Cory Snyder to try. Then it's the platoon. Then, if they are really against the wall, it's back to Dave Hansen. But don't worry about it; one of the other three options will come through. The Boston option is Tim Naehring, who isn't as good as either Sharperson or Harris.

9. Luis Sojo (CAL)

If Luis actually does break through with a big age-27 career year, he may keep a starting job. But right now, he's buried in this league's deep crowd of second sackers. He's also going to have to beat out Damion Easley just to get a chance to prove himself.

10. Pat Kelly (NYY)

For once, I don't laugh at the big New York hype. The Yankees had no way of knowing that Carlos Baerga and Chuck Knoblauch were going to rise up and dominate. As it is, Pat Kelly still might make a decent keystone man. If the Yankees just leave him alone with the job, he could gain some confidence and turn into someone as good as Scott Fletcher. But he's never going to be an Alomar or Baerga, and the Yankees may not be able to live with that. If they can't, and keep trying out people like Andy Stankiewicz, they're going to mess up both of them. I take that back. Stankiewicz would have ranked 8th at this spot, and he can play shortstop. It's much more important for the Yankees to develop Stankiewicz than Kelly. But, of course, they could have both....

11. Harold Reynolds (SEA - BAL)

This is the one decision Don Malcolm made in his fantasy league that I didn't like: the freezing of Harold Reynolds. Don thought talent at second base would be scarce; I didn't think so. I also thought Harold was well into his decline phase, whereas the good second basemen were all young enough to grow. Actually, it's hard to argue with Don's decision, given the competition that existed on his roster for freeze players, but the analysis of Harold, I'll stick to. He's just bulk infield help now, nothing special. The only reason I can think of for the Orioles to pick him up is that they have to have someone with a reputation to appease all the Ripken family loyalists out there who won't forgive them if Billy's replacement doesn't immediately perform noticeably better than Billy would have.

12. Billy Ripken (BAL - TEX)

Good field, no hit. Wrong position and wrong decade for that. Needs to go to winter ball and play shortstop. Now in the minors behind Julio Franco and Jeff Frye, who is no worse and two years younger.

13. Steve Sax (CHA)

Did anyone outside of the Chisox organization really think that 1991 was anything else but a fluke year for Steve Sax? Oh, well, he'll probably turn in his career average for the Sox next year, which will be an improvement. On the other hand, it won't be good enough to bat second in a lineup that could read:

Raines
Ventura
Thomas
Bell
any random outfielder or DH

14. Al Newman (TEX)
or maybe Jeff Frye
but soon to be
Julio Franco (yay!)

Jeff Frye would have come in right behind Billy Ripken, in very little playing time, and is a reasonable prospect at second base. Of course, he's not going to beat out Julio Franco, but he does solve the backup problem. Newman is a time server. And now, Ripken is here, in case Franco and Frye both die.

Second Basemen

Brock J. Hanke

		OWAR	DWAR	TWAR
1.	Sandberg	7.18	2.02	9.19
2.	Biggio	5.87	.70	6.56
3.	Thompson Ro	3.45	2.15	5.60
4.	DeShields	4.19	.51	4.70
	Sharperson	3.08	.47	3.55
5.	Pena G	2.41	1.12	3.53
6.	Doran	1.86	.77	2.64
	Alicea	1.49	.68	2.17
7.	Randolph	1.49	.55	2.04
	Duncan	1.73	.29	2.02
8.	Harris L	1.13	.65	1.78
9.	Morandini	.41	1.21	1.62
10.	Lemke	.47	.57	1.04
	Amaro	.32	.64	.97
	Kent	.42	.21	.63
11.	Lind	-1.52	1.97	.44
	Candaele	-.55	.94	.39
	Teufel	.12	.16	.29
	Young E	.14	.14	.28
	Treadway	-.26	.48	.22
	Bell Ju	-.28	.47	.20
	Samuel	.11	.05	.16
12.	Stillwell	-.44	.39	-.04
	Patterson J	-.61	.29	-.32

1. Ryne Sandberg (CHI)

As some of you know from elsewhere in the book, Ryne Sandberg here turned in the single best season of 1992, according to the TWAR method. Does this seem wrong? Are you looking at Ryne's 1991 and 1992 seasons together and wondering in just what way we think they are different? Well, the answer is the ballpark. For some combination of reasons, Wrigley Field was much less a hitters' park this year than it has been in the past. Maybe it was the wind direction. Maybe it was temperature. I don't know. But I do know that this was a wonderful Ryne Sandberg season, disguised by a one-year aberration in Chicago. I also know that, if Ryne keeps this up, he's going to get serious as a contender for the best second baseman ever.

2. Craig Biggio (HOU)

So far, I'm sure the Astros think they made a great move in converting Craig to a second baseman. Not only did his Defensive WAR promptly turn positive (the gain to Craig's ranking is over a Win, from -0.52 to +0.70), but his OWAR also improved by another Win and a Half, from 4.19 to 5.87. Altogether, Craig picked up 2.9 WAR, which is a ton. If that keeps up, even I am going to like the move.

And in truth, a lot of the gain looks like the effect of giving up the Tools of Ignorance. Craig's level of hitting performance did not really change all that much, but he was able to play 161 games, as opposed to the 149 which constituted his high as a catcher. He was also able to extend the impact of his good base stealing. His 70%+ success ratio used to produce only 20 or so SB; this time, it was almost 40. That should be attributed to stronger legs, from less squatting. His offensive production did go up, but not in the hitting department. The increase was in walks, which makes no sense as a product of moving to second base. It was a big jump. Previously, Craig had established himself as an average cager of free passes, with almost exactly one Walk for each ten At-Bats. Last year, though, he took 94 Walks against only 613 AB, which, again, is huge.

So what does this mean for the Fantasy Fan? Well, Craig's turning 27, which means his production does not figure to go down. No one year wonders here. The 1992 level of value is, for the next couple of years, real. He's a BEST BUY, unless everyone in your league has figured this all out.

3. Robbie Thompson (SF)

After a rare collapse year at age 27, Robbie has reestablished himself at a steady, excellent level of play. He's going to hit about .260, get on base about .330 and slug about .400. He won't steal you any serious bases, but no big deal. He will play big deal defense.

If you've read Don Malcolm's Bill James Fantasy League diary, you may have noticed that he beat his league with an offense loaded with second basemen. I imagine that's not what you were expecting. It sure wasn't what I thought I'd see on his roster. But, looking at the strategy, it made perfect sense. First, the second base position has some horses right now. Robbie Thompson is awfully good to be the #3 man at this position, and he's likely to be #4 next year, behind Geronimo Pena. The American League is no less fully stocked. There are five guys above 4 TWAR out there this year, and Julio Franco isn't one of them. But the real key is an odd bias in the Bill James game. The defensive stat that counts most is double plays. As you doubtless can figure out, that weights the league toward second sackers. Don worried a lot about his double play count last year, and the keystone emphasis on his team came from that concern. At any rate, if you're playing the Bill James game, Thompson has extra value. His 99 DPs led the NL, though you might check out Carlos Baerga over in the AL.

Second Base	G	PO	A	Er	TC	DP	FPct	DI	DG	DW%	DWAR
Alicea	75	130	227	4	361	36	.989	635.2	3.5	.544	.67
Barberie	26	29	59	1	89	6	.989	167.0	.9	.405	.05
Benavides	37	48	61	0	109	9	1.000	200.0	1.1	.479	.14
Biggio	161	343	412	12	767	81	.984	1407.2	7.7	.440	.70
Blauser	21	32	42	5	79	8	.937	136.0	.7	.380	.02
Branson	33	45	61	6	112	20	.946	179.2	1.0	.583	.23
DeShields	134	253	360	15	628	71	.976	1183.1	6.5	.429	.51
Doran	104	170	242	5	417	55	.988	792.0	4.3	.514	.71
Duncan	52	94	126	7	227	27	.969	420.2	2.3	.362	.03
Harris L	81	161	205	14	380	40	.963	541.0	3.0	.538	.56
Hudler	16	28	39	3	70	6	.957	107.1	.6	.481	.08
Jones Tim	28	35	47	1	83	14	.988	151.0	.8	.685	.28
Kent	34	61	84	3	148	18	.980	265.0	1.5	.934	.85
King J	32	49	68	0	117	16	1.000	201.2	1.1	.722	.41
Lemke	145	236	324	9	569	57	.984	1065.0	5.8	.442	.54
Lind	134	311	425	6	742	79	.992	1190.2	6.5	.655	1.99
Litton	31	52	69	1	122	18	.992	217.2	1.2	.643	.35
Morandini	124	236	332	5	573	64	.991	944.1	5.2	.577	1.17
Patterson J	22	42	53	4	99	15	.960	166.0	.9	.561	.19
Pecota	38	46	95	4	145	16	.972	230.2	1.3	.507	.20
Pena G	57	126	185	5	316	40	.984	470.0	2.6	.790	1.13
Randolph	79	151	194	8	353	53	.977	651.2	3.6	.502	.54
Roberts Bip	42	51	83	1	135	7	.993	277.2	1.5	.334	-.02
Samuel	38	75	77	4	156	13	.974	254.1	1.4	.945	.83
Sandberg	157	283	539	8	830	93	.990	1379.1	7.6	.619	2.03
Sharperson	63	104	134	5	243	26	.979	331.2	1.8	.655	.55
Stillwell	111	251	265	16	532	63	.970	938.1	5.1	.427	.39
Teufel	52	95	125	3	223	20	.987	390.1	2.1	.447	.21
Thompson Ro	120	298	381	15	694	99	.978	1051.0	5.8	.723	2.15
Treadway	45	54	83	1	138	24	.993	252.2	1.4	.695	.48
Young E	43	85	114	9	208	20	.957	311.0	1.7	.431	.14
TOTALS		4199	5864	194	10257	1178	.981	1461.0	8.0	5.969	44.96

4. Delino DeShields (MTL)

Certainly the worst defensive player among the good second basemen, but that's no real reason to move him, as the Expos are rumored to be considering. He's still better than Bip Roberts, who should, and probably will be playing second in 1993. Actually, Delino probably won't move, now that Bret Barberie is gone, but the point is still worth making. "If the man can hit, play him at the most valuable defensive position he can handle at all." I've said it before and I'll say it again. Delino DeShields can handle second base. Now, shortstop....

Supposedly, the Expos are proud of themselves for switching Delino and Marquis Grissom in the leadoff and #2 lineup holes. I have no idea why. It's true that Marquis hit better leading off, but so did Delino, and by about as much. What actually happened, of course, is that Marquis had a little hot streak in June, right after the switch was made. That got instant press attention, but the writers failed to follow up. Overall, Delino lost what Marquis gained. I wouldn't artificially support a left fielder's stats over a second baseman's.

5. Geronimo Pena (STL)
and Luis Alicea
and Jose Oquendo, too.

I will always have a warm spot in my heart for Luis Alicea. Last year, the Cardinals started the year with Jose Oquendo at second, Geronimo Pena on the bench and Luis Alicea at AAA Louisville. That was silly, as Pena is better than Oquendo, but those Cards were not about to trust those minor league numbers, nor were they about to admit that playing Todd Zeile at third base made no sense given the makeup of the ballclub. Actually, Pena was on the DL with a spring training injury, but it wouldn't have made any difference.

Anyway, Oquendo got hurt in the first game of the year, and, with Pena down too, Alicea got a freak chance to play. I write a column for a St. Louis weekly paper, THE RIVERFRONT TIMES, which gave me a chance to do a basic MLE prediction for Alicea. I figured he'd hit about .270 or so, with enough power and walks to make him the offensive equal of - Willie McGee. Now, remembering that Alicea had hit .212 and .191 in his previous Major League trials, you can imagine the shit I got in the press box for that column. Then Luis hit .116 for over a month. Just imagine.

The Cardinals had actually sent Luis back to Louisville and given the job to Rex "Hurricane" Hudler when Hudler hurt himself playing like, well, like Rex Hudler. Given a reprieve, and a week in AAA ball to get his stroke back, Luis returned and just beat the bejeezus out of the ball. I mean, a .349 average and 6 triples in the month of May alone. Excluding that April, Luis hit right at .271, and even the sportswriters couldn't ignore that triples total. Slowly, one by one, they came up to me and said "Well, I guess you did know what you were talking about, after all. How'd you do that, anyway?" So I told them about the MLE system, and they listened for a change. Thanks, Luis. I'd have written this article about you (you did, after all, have more playing time than Pena got), except that Pena came in 5th at second base, and you would have come in 7th.

So, now for GERONIMO PENA. I have Pena down for my ABSOLUTE BEST FANTASY BUY, in any league. I have him down for the #2 second baseman in the National League, behind only Sandberg. I have him down for about .295, with 15-20 homers, 35 doubles, decent walks and good baserunning. The system already has him down for the best Defensive Winning Percentage in the league, at any position, at .790. Sure, some of that is turning double plays with Ozzie Smith, but Geronimo's DWAR is better than Ozzie's, too. The system also has him down for the #5 man at second base in 1992, and he only played 57 games all year. And so, best of all, I have Pena down for full-time play at second base in 1993. Yes, the Cardinals have already had Jose Oquendo talking on the radio about how he doesn't mind being a "secret weapon" utility man again.

I have my doubts as to whether JOSE OQUENDO really means that. I think he's probably waiting for one of two things: Ozzie Smith to finally fall apart, or free agency. When he returns to full time play, he's likely to also return to being the #4 or 5 second baseman in the league. Until then, though, UNLOAD HIM IN A FANTASY LEAGUE. He's not going to play.

6. Bill Doran (CIN - MIL)

Bip Roberts would have come in #3, behind Sandberg and Biggio. At t his point in their careers, Roberts is not that much worse on defense than Doran is. Doran has escaped to the Brewers, where he certainly is no worse than Scott Fletcher was.

7. Willie Randolph (NYM)

Did anyone who lived anywhere but in New York really think Willie had discovered the Fountain of Youth? I mean, take a look at the Brock2 system. There's this odd anomaly where the batting average is actually adjusted upwards for age 37. This is because a lot of really good ballplayers get scared at that age, and put on one last hurrah. There is no such effect for age 38, much less for age 39. Willie still might help the Braves, or some other good team with a real hole at the keystone, but that's about it.

8. Mickey Morandini (PHI)

He's coming up on age 27, and so is due for his career year. And you know, if he has it, and hits .280, he still won't be an above-average player here.

9. Lenny Harris (LA)

I still don't know why Tummy Lasorda won't just install Lenny here, fix Mike Sharperson at third base and quit playing around with Dave Hansen. No, Lenny's not Dave Lopes, but he's good enough to win with, if you give him some stability. If he got full-time play, he'd be a real good bet to move into the top half at this spot. But, then, why am I bothering? Jody Reed has the job.

10. Mark Lemke (ATL)

As you've read elsewhere, I think Lemke is a cog in an overall Bobby Cox plan for winning without breaking the budget. That's the only real reason for playing him here on a contending team. Bobby figures that you can platoon at second and short, and get enough out of the platoons that you can win if your offense down the lines is strong enough, and your pitching is strong enough. Obviously, Bobby is right. Still, unless Mark has his age-27 career year, Bobby needs to find the other half of the platoon. Mark isn't really good enough to play full time.

11. Jose Lind (PIT - KC)

Of all the snakebit things to happen to the Pirates in the post season. First, Barry Bonds develops a hitting block after October 4, and then Jose Lind makes an error. I wonder what sort of hex Syd Thrift used on this franchise, anyway?

I also wonder whether the Royals plan to convert Jose to shortstop? His defensive stats suggest that he could do the job. They already have Keith Miller to play second. Jose's bat isn't enough to run Keith off the job. On the other hand, who knows what the Royals are using for a plan nowadays?

12. Kurt Stillwell (SD)

Well, I guess we can see who won the Alomar / McGriff trade now. Toronto has a World Championship, and Eddie Zosky may not yet be through as a shortstop prospect to replace Tony Fernandez. The Padres don't have those Championship rings. They also don't have Fernandez any more. And, to fill Roberto Alomar's spot, they have this. Say "Uncle", guys. The Blue Jays win.

Third Basemen

Brock J. Hanke

		OWAR	DWAR	TWAR
1.	Ventura	5.17	1.50	6.66
2.	Martinez E	5.88	.45	6.33
3.	Gomez L	3.65	.31	3.95
4.	Jeffries	3.50	.79	3.79
5.	Seitzer	2.79	.81	3.60
6.	Boggs W	2.88	.46	3.34
	Velarde	1.72	1.11	2.83
7.	Palmer Dn	2.60	.11	2.71
	Cooper S	2.18	.37	2.55
8.	Lansford	2.36	-.02	2.34
9.	Hayes C	1.22	.73	1.95
	Leyritz	1.08	-.03	1.05
	Hulett	.64	.37	1.00
	Gantner	-.37	1.35	.98
10.	Gaetti	.21	.56	.77
	Barnes	.28	.25	.52
11.	Livingstone	.11	.36	.47
12.	Leius	-.09	.34	.25
	Jorgensen	-.06	.13	.07
13.	Jacoby	-.45	.39	-.06
	Sprague	-.18	.07	-.11
	Blowers	-.53	.23	-.30
	Thome	-.31	-.21	-.52
14.	Gruber	-.83	.29	-.54
	Pagliarulo	-.79	.14	-.65

1. Robin Ventura (CHA)

Well, well, so the little devil sneaked in there ahead of Edgar Martinez. Of course, that wouldn't have happened if Edgar hadn't been hurt at the end of the year. Or if he could play good defense, like Robin can. I'm not really sure where Robin Ventura got so underrated. Maybe it was the Curse of the Hot College hitter. You may remember that, from Robin's senior season. It was all the rage to suggest that Robin would turn out to have no power, and to only have bat speed if the bat were aluminum, and to just strike out in job lots if he tried that "strike zone judgment" nonsense of Major League pitching. And then, Robin wasn't immediately great at the age of 21, and didn't have a real hot season when he was 22, and that was his rep.

But, of course, it's nonsense. Strike zone

judgment does in fact pay off in the Majors. In fact, the Chisox have made a whole offense out of drafting college hitters who took their walks. And those college skills do translate into the professional game. Sure, the occasional Jeff Ledbetter will fall apart as soon as he gets out of his friendly college ballpark. But the occasional high school #1 draft pick bombs, too. Actually, the only real surprise about Robin is the defense. He has top range, particularly on grounders. He turns more than his share of DPs. He has plenty of arm. This is not just another hitter who is carrying his infield glove with his bat.

A FANTASY BEST BUY, if your league counts either walks or defense; that means the Bill James game. He'd only be a Good Buy, except that most of your league probably still doesn't believe he's for real. They see that his home run totals dropped, and don't see that he

made up for it with a bunch of extra walks. They don't see the whole value of the walks, or don't know he can play defense, or both. They also probably think he's older than 25, and has less growth potential than he does.

One final note: I have no idea why the Sox insisted on batting Steve Sax in the second slot, when they had Robin available, and were batting him #5 for half the year. Robin is a horrid choice for #5. He doesn't have a ton of power, and he gets on base constantly. That's a top-of-the-order man, not a RBI vulture. Steve Sax, by contrast, takes few walks and makes a lot of outs unless he hits .330. He doesn't have much power - even less than Robin - but he does sport a high batting average to drive in those runners from scoring position. That is, he is much more like Felix Jose or even George Bell than Robin Ventura is. Well, with any luck, Sax will move way down in the order, and Robin will get his chance to bat behind Tim Raines, where he belongs.

2. Edgar Martinez (SEA)

A very good hitting season, but not what I mean by MVP Candidate. I'd really like to see a Slugging Percentage in the .600's, as well as that .400 OBP. Either that, or I'd like to see better defense; or at least defense somewhere a bit more valuable than third base.

What's going on here, of course, is that the sportswriters of America are finally catching up to Edgar's performance level of three years ago. Then they see that he's improved on that the last two seasons, and they go nuts with shame and guilt. Well, the guilt, they deserve. I know Seattle's not the media hotbed of the sports world, but there were more people on the Mariners than Ken Griffey, Jr. It was not impossible that one of them could have been a good player.

In case you've looked at his career stats and his age and are wondering, no, his career makes no sense so far. He was installed in the Majors at least two years too late. This is most odd, considering that the incumbent Seattle third baseman was the immortal Jim Presley. Then, he finally got his big chance at age 27, and piled his first regular chance to play on top of

Third Base	G	PO	A	Er	TC	DP	FPct	DI	DG	DW%	DWAR
Amaral	17	10	32	2	44	3	.955	116.1	.5	.582	.11
Barnes	39	34	68	9	111	7	.919	266.1	1.1	.512	.18
Blowers	29	19	41	1	61	8	.984	193.1	.8	.615	.21
Boggs W	117	70	230	15	315	22	.952	993.2	4.1	.461	.45
Browne J	58	40	70	4	114	7	.965	370.0	1.5	.484	.20
Cooper S	47	26	102	4	132	5	.970	375.0	1.5	.528	.27
Easley D	45	28	99	4	131	13	.969	373.1	1.5	.633	.43
Fermin	17	10	24	2	36	2	.944	105.1	.4	.448	.04
Fryman T	27	15	46	2	63	4	.968	220.0	.9	.431	.07
Gaetti	67	51	163	17	231	16	.926	563.1	2.3	.549	.46
Gantner	31	17	28	1	46	3	.978	150.0	.6	.599	.15
Gomez L	137	106	244	18	368	19	.951	1221.2	5.0	.411	.31
Gonzales R	53	32	112	7	151	9	.954	445.0	1.8	.484	.25
Gruber	120	104	214	17	335	11	.949	1021.2	4.2	.417	.28
Hayes C	139	95	251	13	359	31	.964	1211.2	5.0	.493	.71
Hulett	27	16	69	6	91	7	.934	219.1	.9	.638	.26
Jacoby	111	46	175	10	231	17	.957	731.1	3.0	.476	.38
Jefferies	146	96	302	26	424	23	.939	1288.1	5.3	.405	.29
Kent	49	33	74	10	117	3	.915	372.1	1.5	.253	-.15
Lansford	119	86	159	9	254	8	.965	963.1	4.0	.350	.00
Leius	125	58	257	15	330	12	.955	1025.1	4.2	.428	.33
Livingstone	112	67	189	10	266	15	.962	841.1	3.5	.451	.35
Martinez Crl	28	13	37	3	53	6	.943	213.1	.9	.360	.01
Martinez E	103	72	208	17	297	23	.943	869.2	3.6	.472	.44
Newman A	28	12	28	1	41	8	.976	167.1	.7	.457	.07
Pagliarulo	37	11	65	3	79	3	.962	232.0	1.0	.499	.14
Palmer Dn	150	124	253	22	399	24	.945	1272.0	5.2	.372	.11
Phillips	20	11	24	1	36	4	.972	104.0	.4	.633	.12
Reboulet	22	11	32	0	43	3	1.000	117.1	.5	.794	.21
Seitzer	146	99	271	12	382	18	.969	1265.0	5.2	.503	.80
Thome	40	21	61	11	93	3	.882	308.0	1.3	.185	-.21
Turner	18	8	29	5	42	5	.881	121.0	.5	.372	.01
Velarde	26	14	35	5	54	7	.907	219.2	.9	.274	-.07
Ventura	157	141	371	23	535	27	.957	1395.1	5.7	.609	1.48
TOTALS		1679	4591	331	6601	394	.950	1460.1	6.0	5.986	33.81

what sure looked like his career year. But that was wrong, too. He's stepped forward both of the last two years, which makes no sense at all. For his career to work out according to form, he's have to be 28 now, not 30. The only thing I can figure is that his late promotion to the Majors left him with some adjusting still to do after the form's peak year. At any rate, he had no Sophomore Slump at all, and has established himself as a consistent offensive force, at the very least. And, at last, his reputation has caught up to him. Now, if we can just get those writers to figure out about Robin Ventura.

3. Leo Gomez (BAL)

On the other hand, the same gang of sportswriters has been waiting for Leo to turn into Godzilla since he was in AA ball. That's what a reputation for hitting home runs will do for you, as opposed to one for taking walks.

Despite the #3 ranking here, Leo is not there yet. The drop from Martinez to Gomez is huge, and somewhat artificial. Both Travis

Fryman and Tony Phillips would be in there somewhere, and one of them is very likely to be the Tiger third baseman in 1993. Wade Boggs figures to recover at least somewhat; enough anyway to overtake Leo. And that's not counting the collapses of Gary Gaetti and Kelly Gruber. In short, the overall quality of this position stands to make a comeback over the next couple of years, and Leo will have to step forward to stay near the top of the heap.

There is also the problem with defense. Leo is not proving to be a real third baseman, and the Orioles may feel pressure to move him. They probably shouldn't, as long as he hits enough to carry the glove, but that will stop sooner or later. As a first baseman, Leo is only a Grade B prospect, unless he completely breaks loose with about 30 taters. I give that about a 30% chance. If it does happen, it will be this year or next; Leo's 26.

4. Gregg Jeffries (KC)

Another guy who really shouldn't be playing

third, although this year's defensive stats aren't that bad. He's also really not hitting well enough to be ranking fourth. That does not mean he's finished. He's only 25, which is younger than, say, Leo Gomez. He doesn't hit lefty pitching at all, and ground ball pitchers chew him up, too. In both cases, he has no strike zone judgment against these types of pitching. That leaves a clear path for growth; Gregg has to learn how to lay off the lefty curveball down. Of course, some guys never do learn that, but Gregg at least has enough other skills to induce a team to give him several years in which to try.

I DON'T FANCY HIM IN FANTASY PLAY. What I think is going to happen to Gregg is that he's going to move down in the Royal batting order as the team improves. If he starts hitting 6th and 7th all the time, as I think will happen, he will get maybe 60 fewer plate appearances than he has been getting. Even if he maintains this level of ability, that's going to hurt his fantasy stats, which are based on raw accumulation.

5. Kevin Seitzer (MIL - OAK)

It was the Mets who lost the Battle of the Headcase Third Basemen. To examine the chain reaction: The Padres disposed of Jack Howell, and then had to gamble on the benighted Gary Sheffield. You know what happened there. The Brewers, having given up on Sheffield, tried Kevin Seitzer, in trouble in the Kansas City clubhouse. Kevin promptly got back what he'd had in 1990. The Royals picked up Gregg Jeffries from the Mets, and he's doing OK. The Mets, though, never do anything by half measures. They not only let Gregg go, they moved Howard Johnson off the hot corner as well. They tried Dave Magadan. They lost.

I figure this to be Kevin Seitzer's true level of play. The .300 batting averages are gone with the legs of youth, but the other skills do remain. He doesn't have much power, but he will hit 35 doubles or so and take his walks. I don't think he can quite hold this ranking, as I think the overall position will improve, but he's a solid middle-of-the-pack man. Between Kevin and Jerry Browne, the A's are set here.

6. Wade Boggs (BOS - NYY)

FAIR WARNING: ANOTHER MAN WITH AN EGO JUST WENT TO NEW YORK. Now, it's true that Wade might prove to be the next Reggie Jackson or Dave Winfield. He might respond to pressure by turning up the heat. On the other hand, he's got the public personality weaknesses, and the New York press is not going to let him forget Margo. If he doesn't hit in April, they're going to get on him about the chicken. Face it, he's a walking target who has some skills to regain, and who will be, after all, 35. Mean while, the Worms in the Big Apple are expecting him to hit .360 again.

7. Dean Palmer (TEX)

THIS IS THE FANTASY GAMBLE. Dean could go either way, and is unlikely to remain in the middle of the pack. If he doesn't improve, the position is likely to pass him by, as Gaetti and Gruber either come back or get replaced. That could happen; Dean made a big stride forward in power, without enough batting average to protect it. The AL pitchers are very likely to figure out what he's hitting over the fence and just stop throwing it. On the other hand, Dean could learn to hit everything else for average. If he does that, his average is going to go to .270 or so, and the power will not drop drastically. That's a big time player. What I don't expect is for Dean to keep hitting .230, but with 25-homer power. That's a very hard combination to maintain.

8. Carney Lansford (OAK)

Jerry Browne would have ranked higher, despite playing only 111 games. Browne has probably resurrected his career. I fully expect him to hold his value in the middle of the pack at this position. He may bat second for the A's, and is a FANTASY BEST GAMBLE, if you don't get one of the top guys. Carney Lansford, you may have heard, has retired.

9. Charlie Hayes (NYY - FLA)

No one seems to be able to figure out what possessed the Yankees to expose Charlie Hayes to the expansion draft. I'm not sure I want to say that I understand how the New York management thinks, if any or at all, but Hayes' defensive stats were way down. Previously a monster Gold Glove infielder, Charlie had a big drop in range, although he did lead the league in DPs. Perhaps the Yankee brain trust noticed that, and decided to let him go on the grounds that defense is all he's worth. On the other hand, he left Philadelphia under odd circumstances, too; and his problem may simply be that he's no fun to manage as a person.

AT any rate, since he's surely going to play full time on his new team, and will probably bat near the center of the batting order, too, he's a GOOD FANTASY BUY.

10. Gary Gaetti (CAL)

This was a bad analysis I made several years ago, that I wouldn't make now. Essentially, what happened to Gary is that he had his big peak right on schedule, from age 27 through age 29. Then he dropped off. I, like most dumb sportswriters, thought it was just a fluke and he would surely recover. But, no, it really was the decline phase. A little steeper than most, but not all that out of the realm of possibility.

Now, in deep trouble, Gary may be close to finished. He is finished at the level of salary he is used to. In fact, his previous contracts may be a problem here. He can't command anything like what he used to, and teams may be afraid to sign him at a greatly reduced pay rate, for fear of a power outage in the morale. In any case, his job is gone to Kelly Gruber, who finished even lower.

11. Scott Livingstone (DET)

Don't got no power; don't take no walks. With that against him, he has to hit .300 to play. Even at that rate, he's not going to beat out Travis Fryman. Might help the Tigers as a utility man if he could learn to play shortstop and if Tony Phillips dies or something.

Speaking of Tony Phillips, who should be the one ranked here, I do not understand how Sparky could have decided not to install the man full time at third. I mean, why play Scott Livingstone at third base and Tony Phillips at DH, when you could play Tony at third and get a real bat into the order? But, as Don Malcolm discusses in complete detail in his article, no one respects those guys who take a lot of walks. Phillips has been a utility man on two teams now, when it was clear in both cases that he should have been installed in one position and batted regularly at the top of the order. Milt Cuyler or Tony Philips at leadoff? It's no contest, right?

12. Scott Leius (MIN)

Based on the signing of Dave Winfield, I have to think that the Twins think that they're going into contention in 1993. If they do, this is the spot that could hurt them. Scott Leius was no better than he should have been, and Mike Pagliarulo looks done. By far the Twins' best hope is for Scott to turn in that age-27 career year. But, with this season as a base, Scott Leius could take a big leap forward and still finish tenth at this spot in this league.

I still don't believe that I heard that Scott Leius is going to be moved to third base. Just who do the Twins expect to play at third?

13. Brook Jacoby (CLE)

Came back some, but not nearly enough. Still, third base is where he should be, as he can still play defense there. If he can't hit enough for third, he sure can't handle first base. Clearly, the Indians would like to improve here, as they think they're going into contention. Me? I'd give the job to Carlos Martinez. He's going to turn 27, and last year may have been an odd version of Sophomore Slump, where a player who's never played full time finally gets seen enough for the pitchers to figure him out. Jim Thome looks like he needs another year at AAA.

14. Kelly Gruber (TOR - CAL)

Just like Gary Gaetti. He had his peak at age 27, and came down off it hard. Also like Gary, Kelly takes few walks, and so has little margin for error when things get tough. Also, the only season Kelly hit 30 homers, he hit 23 of them at home. I'm not altogether confident in saying this about a man this young, but Kelly may really be finished. Not the best news for the Angels, is it?

Third Basemen

Brock J. Hanke

		OWAR	DWAR	TWAR
1.	Pendleton	5.75	1.26	7.01
2.	Sheffield	6.04	.86	6.90
3.	Hollins	5.64	.16	5.80
4.	Caminiti	4.70	.41	5.11
5.	Buechele	3.15	.64	3.79
6.	Zeile	3.04	.66	3.70
7.	Magadan	2.88	-.33	2.55
8.	Williams MD	1.62	.83	2.46
	Johnson H	2.25	.00	2.25
	Walker C	2.05	.12	2.17
9.	Wallach	.81	1.04	1.85
10.	King J	.81	.96	1.77
11.	Sabo	1.48	.19	1.67
	Barberie	.91	.30	1.21
12.	Hansen	.66	.30	.95
	Wilson C	.76	.14	.90
	Vizcaino	-.32	1.06	.74
	Pecota	.31	.40	.72
	Greene W	.62	.05	.68
	Berry	.29	-.10	.19
	Guerrero J	-.20	-.12	-.32
	Salazar L	-1.07	.59	-.47
	Wehner	-.77	.28	-.49
	Strange	-.61	-.03	-.63
	Scott G	-.90	-.09	-.99

1. Terry Pendelton (ATL)

Unless Terry Pendelton is your very favorite player, and you turned directly here as soon as you opened the book, you've already read about the similarities between Bobby Cox-built teams and those captained by Earl Weaver. You've seen the listing of shared qualities: strong starting rotations, soft bullpens, offense down the lines and defensive strength and offensive softness up the middle, trouble spots addressed by platooning.

Now, if you think about it, that collection of characteristics puts quite a stress on the third base position. You can easily find hitters to play first base, left field, and right field. You can find good defensive players to put at second base, shortstop, center field and catcher. But, to make the system work completely per specs, you have to find a third baseman who can field, for the infield defense, and who can hit for the down-the-lines offense. And so, if the given list is actually characteristic of Cox and Weaver teams, you should expect to see a collection of top third basemen. In fact, looking at the hot corner was the first test I put this theory to.

Here is the list of third basemen that Earl Weaver played between 1968 and 1981:

Brooks Robinson
Doug DeCinces

A short list, but sweet. In 1982, which was Earl's retirement year, you may recall that he had a kid third baseman set to take the place of the traded DeCinces. But, "What the hey?" thought Earl. "This kid's got range, as well as quick hands. Let's try him at shortstop." And so Earl played someone named Glenn Gulliver

at third for a half season while Cal Ripken got settled in at short. But, remember, the original plan was to play Ripken at third. And, in case you're wondering whether this was a Baltimore thing rather than an Earl Weaver thing, when Earl came back in 1985, the third baseman he inherited was Wayne Gross, who was promptly platooned with Fat Floyd Rayford. By the end of 1986, Earl had tried Juan Beniquez and Tom O'Malley in an attempt to get the position to produce.

When Bobby Cox took his first managerial post, with Atlanta in 1978, his most controversial move was the installation of some 20-year-old kid right out of college at the hot corner, which rhymes with "Bob Horner". When he left for Toronto, Bobby inherited a horrid third base crew. The nominal incumbent would have been Danny Ainge, but he had left for basketball. Bobby responded by setting up a lefty/righty platoon of Rance Mulliniks and Garth Iorg. By 1984, when the Jays started winning for Cox, the platoon was productive. Mulliniks was hitting .290 or .300, and Iorg contributed in off years. They were usually good for 60+ Runs Scored and 60+ RBI between them. Still, this is the least productive third base setup that either Earl or Bobby ever used for any length of time.

As you know, as soon as Bobby Cox took over as manager of the Braves, the team picked up Terry Pendelton as a free agent. Before the signing of Greg Maddux, this was the only big-money free agent the Braves had acquired for Cox. I think the message is clear: Bobby Cox and Earl Weaver place tremendous importance on the third base position. They know they have to have offense and defense from the spot, if they're going to win. Neither one of them has ever settled for anything as bad as an average filling of the spot. Mulliniks and Iorg, the weakest combination, were far above average for the league.

I also think that Bobby Cox may have helped Terry Pendelton as much as Terry has helped Bobby. Obviously the main difference between Terry now and Terry in St. Louis is that he has enough power for The Launching Pad, but not enough for Busch Stadium. There is one other factor involved, though. Whitey Herzog, who

Third Base	G	PO	A	Er	TC	DP	FPct	DI	DG	DW%	DWAR
Anderson D	26	13	24	1	38	3	.974	143.1	.6	.431	.05
Barberie	63	37	126	12	175	10	.931	508.2	2.1	.460	.23
Berry	20	10	18	4	32	1	.875	124.0	.5	.153	-.10
Buechele	143	102	285	17	404	16	.958	1240.1	5.1	.951	3.06
Caminiti	129	103	208	11	322	19	.966	1140.2	4.7	.436	.40
Candaele	29	24	52	4	80	3	.950	218.1	.9	.498	.13
Cianfrocco	19	7	27	5	39	1	.872	128.2	.5	.212	-.07
Coles	23	8	34	0	42	1	1.000	147.0	.6	.508	.10
Donnels	29	15	50	4	69	3	.942	203.2	.8	.400	.04
Greene W	25	16	40	3	59	5	.949	216.1	.9	.411	.05
Hansen	108	61	183	8	252	14	.968	832.1	3.4	.435	.29
Harris L	33	12	26	5	43	5	.884	127.1	.5	.347	-.00
Hollins	156	120	253	18	391	22	.954	1367.2	5.6	.378	.16
King J	73	44	140	9	193	14	.953	565.1	2.3	.579	.53
Magadan	93	41	135	11	187	10	.941	755.0	3.1	.243	-.33
Pecota	48	12	51	5	68	6	.926	228.1	.9	.363	.01
Pendleton	158	133	322	19	474	28	.960	1389.0	5.7	.570	1.26
Roberts Bip	36	20	68	5	93	6	.946	271.2	1.1	.504	.17
Sabo	94	60	158	9	227	12	.960	790.0	3.2	.409	.19
Salazar L	40	19	68	6	93	6	.935	260.1	1.1	.522	.18
Scott G	30	17	42	5	64	3	.922	237.0	1.0	.247	-.10
Sharperson	60	15	85	8	108	5	.926	335.0	1.4	.287	-.09
Sheffield	144	99	299	16	414	25	.961	1247.2	5.1	.519	.86
Snyder C	14	7	22	2	31	2	.935	112.0	.5	.333	-.01
Strange	33	19	34	6	59	2	.898	186.0	.8	.263	-.07
Teufel	26	13	34	4	51	1	.922	162.0	.7	.250	-.07
Vizcaino	29	18	51	2	71	6	.972	226.2	.9	.607	.24
Walker C	38	14	58	3	75	2	.960	251.1	1.0	.766	.43
Wallach	85	56	184	9	249	17	.964	700.2	2.9	.646	.85
Wehner	34	15	58	3	76	8	.961	199.1	.8	.686	.28
Williams MD	144	104	287	23	414	32	.944	1247.2	5.1	.512	.83
Wilson C	18	9	23	1	33	2	.970	140.2	.6	.396	.03
Woodson	26	17	35	3	55	4	.945	226.0	.9	.352	.00
Zeile	124	81	235	13	329	19	.960	1079.0	4.4	.500	.67
TOTALS		1369	3811	263	5443	321	.952	1461.0	6.0	5.022	28.03

also had dreams of Terry batting third, was on the man constantly to develop some strike zone judgment. I mean, this is a player who is a home run threat, and who plays full time, and whose last two years' walk totals have been 43 and 37. Whitey didn't want to live with that, not in the #3 slot. And so, under pressure from the manager, Terry's walk totals in St. Louis ranged as high as 83. But that's not Terry's game, and it appears to have cost him in the batting average and power categories. When he takes pitches, he hits tentative. Bobby Cox lets him swing away. I'll admit, I wasn't a big fan of this tactic last year. Terry consumes an awful lot of outs for a #3 hitter. Still, the move has obviously paid off, and paid off big. I might bat Ron Gant #3 and Terry #4 or #5, but I wouldn't ask Terry to go back to taking walks.

Oh, yeah, for you guys in fantasy leagues. In a normal fantasy league, Terry is worth what he appears to be worth. BUT HIS VALUE INCREASES IN A ROTISSERIE LEAGUE. In the Roti game, no one is going to count

walks. Everything Terry does pays off for you. And so his Roti value, relative to other players who have his actual baseball value, is extra.

2. Gary Sheffield (SD)

Needless to say, I have no sabermetric explanation for this. I yield the field to the insider guys. They can tell you all about racism in Milwaukee and the wonders of Fred McGriff's personality. I have nothing to add.

3. Dave Hollins (PHI)

The anchor of Don Malcolm's San Antonio Trotters. Don predicted Dave for this sort of season, picked him up early, and rode him to victory. Dave is real near the cutoff for baseball ages (birthday in May), and so this may have been his age-"27" career year. Still, he probably won't drop off all that much. Given Pendleton's age and Sheffield's instability, I'd rather have Dave Hollins than any other NL third sacker.

4. Ken Caminiti (HOU)

A fine, championship quality player, on a team that might finally have a real use for one. Actually, the preceding is probably not fair to Todd Zeile, and maybe Chris Sabo, but they've got to prove it consistently. Ken Caminiti is very consistent. His raw stats seem to be getting better and better, but I'm not sure whether that's Ken or changes in the Astrodome. The Astros are trying to damp down the Dome's extreme effects on hitting. I do know this: a player who hits as many homers in the Dome as on the road is a big help, adding an extra dimension to the Astro offense.

5. Steve Buechele (PIT/CHN)

Despite his reputation, Steve's defensive stats don't jump out and dance in front of you. Terry Pendleton's do. And, as a batter, Steve is just another starter. I think he's overpaid, but that's free agency for you. As to whether he can help the Cubs get into contention, well, I don't know. He's certainly better than anything the Bruins have had at third in quite some time, but I really don't think the Cubbies are one bat, much less this bat, away from contention. I mean, you can tell me that it turns the two-man offense of Grace and Sandberg into a threesome, but so did Andre Dawson. And you're not going to win a division with a three-man offense, anyway. The Cubs are, in my opinion, at least two big-time free agents away from real and true solid contention.

6. Todd Zeile (STL and LOU)

What happened here is that Todd Zeile got sick; bronchitis, to be exact. Unfortunately, he picked a time to do that when all the other Cardinal infielders were hurt. Todd played through the illness, but never recovered his strength. Also unfortunately, he developed a personality conflict with hitting coach Don Baylor, who likes his players a bit more intense. Rather than resting Todd, Don recommended that the man be sent down to AAA Louisville to straighten himself out. That worked about as well as you'd expect.

Bottom line: expect a full comeback in 1993. Normal expectation might be .280, with 15 homers and 35 doubles. On the other hand, he'll be turning 27, and might be due for that legendary career year. Todd almost certainly belongs with the first four guys here as the cream of the NL third base crop, and is a GREAT FANTASY GAMBLE.

7. Dave Magadan (NYM - FLA)

Might help the Marlins at first base. In fact, he'll probably bat third there. On the other hand, the laughable decision to move Dave to third, so that Hojo could be moved to the outfield, so that Eddie Murray could be signed, sure exposed the Met braintrust, didn't it? Your assignment, as a sabermetrician, is to devise a set of 1992 seasons for the Met players, all within reason, that would beat the Pirates if Murray were at first, and which would not if he were not signed. I'll print the most reasonable with the Met comment next year. Remember, you have to have one player for each position and one position for each player. No fair playing five outfielders with no shortstop or catcher.

8. Matt Williams (SF)

This is the sort of hitter who is most vulnerable to pitcher adjustments. Essentially, all Matt can do is hit home runs. If the pitchers don't have a good book on him, they're going to give him a reasonable batting average just out of respect for the power. But, once they figure out that he will swing at anything, they can just trash him, force him out of his game, and get him flailing.

For Matt to return to being an offensive force, he's got to get command of the strike zone. It's either that or learn to hit line drives instead of never-ending fly balls. I have to have my doubts. He's only established one weapon, and so has a limited toolkit to use. Next year will be the test that makes or breaks his career. He's coming up on that magic age 27, and is due for his big year. If he doesn't have it, I figure him to be on his way out. If he does, he's probably over the hump.

In either case, I still don't understand the decision to play this man at third base, when he can handle the shortstop job. I mean, if you had shortstop covered, don't you think you could find a third baseman who is better than Jose Uribe, if you tried just a little? Than Royce Clayton?? Mike Benjamin???

9. Tim Wallach (MTL-LA)

At Tim's age, there is considerable reason to question his ability to perform at the level the Expos need to win the division. I agree with the decision to trade him. But there does remain a hole in the Expo infield, and therefore I rate the loss of Bret Barberie to expansion as the greatest hit taken by any team. Among other things, Barberie was the only real backup for Delino DeShields and Marquis Grissom if either one were to get hurt. I also wince whenever I look at the power core of the Expo lineup. Last year, it looked great: Calderon, Walker and Wallach. Now, Ivan's gone, and Tim's questionable. The Expos don't need just Moises Alou to come through, they need Alou AND John Van Der Wal.

10. Jeff King (PIT)

Well, so that was the age-27 "career year". Compared to his lifetime totals, it was one batting point under, 8 on-base points over and 9 slugging points above average. That is, it was a lifetime average season. And a bad one. After the Exodus, the Pirates are weak enough they'll have to play him one more year, but even they will be looking elsewhere if he doesn't produce by the All-Star break.

11. Chris Sabo (CIN)

If you're wondering who's going to challenge the Braves, consider how much latent value is here for the Reds. Chris turned in about 4 wins fewer than his normal season is worth, and yet he did nothing to make anyone think he won't be back at full speed for 1993. On the other hand, the Reds have had a bunch of players like this for several years now. The one year no one got real hurt, they won. But you have to question whether, if Chris comes back fully, Barry Larkin or Bip Roberts or Jose Rijo or somebody won't go down just as hard, and keep the team from pushing over the top.

12. Dave Hansen (LA)

Cory Snyder is, if nothing else, a Dodger Stadium sort of player. Dodger suppresses offense in general, which favors power over on base. Snyder, as you surely know, has one of the highest homer / walk ratios in the game. The only question is how much he's going to play. The Dodgers already have Jody Reed on board, which leaves Lenny Harris and Mike Sharperson nowhere to take their platoon except the same third base Cory was supposed to have been signed to play. That's not to mention Tim Wallach, who will probably go into spring training with the job his to lose.

Oh, good grief! Look at that! The name on this comment is Dave Hansen! Don't tell me Tommy Lasorda actually moved Dave Hansen ahead of both Harris and Sharperson on the depth chart. Why, that would mean that Sharperson would be a utility man. How's he supposed to get to the All-Star game playing utility? You say he did WHAT? Well, I guess that would explain why I don't remember writing a Mike Sharperson comment yet.

Well, here's the Sharperson comment: anyone who can get on base .376, .355, and .387 three years in a row, bucking Dodger Stadium the whole time, deserves a chance to start. I don't care if he has no power at all. And any time you get a chance to platoon that with a lefty like Lenny Harris, you just HAVE to give that platoon a starting job to fill up. I don't care if you have to bench Snyder and release Hansen, you just can't ignore that forever.

Shortstops

Brock J. Hanke

		OWAR	DWAR	TWAR
1.	Listach	4.04	2.59	6.63
2.	Ripken C	2.72	3.07	5.79
3.	Fryman	2.33	1.73	4.07
	Gonzales R	2.19	.82	3.01
4.	Vizquel	.71	2.28	3.00
5.	Grebeck	1.67	1.22	2.90
	Huson	1.58	1.06	2.65
6.	Stankiewicz	.97	1.60	2.57
7.	Lee M	.96	1.48	2.44
	Valentin	1.28	.86	2.14
8.	Gagne	-.73	2.36	1.63
	Naehring	.45	.83	1.27
9.	Disarcina	-.88	2.15	1.27
10.	Thon	.83	.15	.98
	Reboulet	-.18	1.08	.91
11.	Howard D	-.62	1.28	.67
	Easley D	.21	.44	.65
12.	Lewis M	-.24	.75	.51
	Trammell	.14	.36	.49
	Fermin	-.10	.53	.42
	Rossy	-.29	.70	.41
	Sveum	.27	.09	.36
13.	Rivera L	-.92	1.24	.32
	Guillen	-.12	.24	.12
14.	Weiss	-.84	.47	-.37
	Griffin Alf	-.53	.14	-.39
	Colon	-.39	-.01	-.40
	Schaefer	-.86	.01	-.85
	Beltre	-.85	-.16	-1.01

1. Pat Listach (MIL)

This is the first time in the history of this book that anyone has outranked Cal Ripken, Jr. at this position. Now, true, it was a collapse year for Cal, evening out his 1991 MVP campaign, but it's still an achievement. So, is it a fluke?

Well, it is Pat Listach's career high in batting average. The rest of his career, you understand, has all been spent in the minors. It is also within one point of his career high in Slugging Percentage. But there are two important categories in which it is not his high point. First, he's been able to steal bases with great success for three years now. That looks real. Also, and most important, it is nothing like his career high in getting on base. Pat Listach once posted a .403 On-Base Percentage, in 1990, in a full season with Stockton. True, it's A ball, but it was also 105 walks. In fact, this 1992 season is his worst for taking walks since he broke in in 1988.

What I expect, then, is for Pat's batting average to drop down some, but for him to take enough more walks to make up the difference in OBP. That's not quite as valuable a player, and it's certainly not Cal Ripken's career average, but it's still no less than the Brewers need at the leadoff spot and at shortstop.

2. Cal Ripken, Jr. (BAL)

Please note that four of Cal's last six batting averages have been in the .250's. The real drop in this year, as compared to his recent career, was in home run power. Now, that could be the ballpark, for all we know. Cal did once turn in fewer road homers than he did this time. Nonetheless, and until some real data about the new stadium comes in, you really should just pencil in Cal's career average for a next year prediction. AND THAT STILL DOMINATES FANTASY BALL.

3. Travis Fryman (DET)

Forced to switch positions by the injury to Alan Trammell, Travis didn't miss a beat. Yes, his defensive stats aren't what you really want in a shortstop, but he really isn't supposed to be a shortstop. His bat held up just fine.

If Trammell fails to recover from the injury, which is a real probability at his age, the Tigers need to make a decision. Travis has demonstrated that he can play short. His glove is just good enough. It's a lot easier to pick up a third baseman who can play than it is someone who can play short. On the other hand, Travis will probably not hold up well in the job. His glove will likely become too weak for his bat to carry in three or four years. I guess it all depends on who the Tigers think they can afford, and how close to winning the division they think they are.

4. Omar Vizquel (SEA)

Yes, Omar Vizquel. The Man Who Was Born Without a Bat rose up and hit .294. Given his glove - he should start winning the Gold one of these years - he ranks right up there at the top. As to whether the new batting prowess will hold, well, I don't know. Omar did not develop any new power, and his walks went down. He just started hitting the ball where the fielders weren't. I have to question the stability of that, given that the pitchers have so many weaknesses to work with. It's not like Jose Oquendo, who won't swing at a pitch that isn't a strike. Nor is it like any of the people who have power and can threaten you with that. No, Omar has little to defend himself with if the pitchers of

Shortstop	G	PO	A	Er	TC	DP	FPct	DI	DG	DW%	DWAR
Amaral	17	17	37	1	55	8	.982	108.0	.8	.516	.14
Beltre	43	53	91	12	156	13	.923	307.1	2.3	.280	-.16
Bordick	70	108	185	10	303	50	.967	577.2	4.4	.568	.95
Colon	14	17	36	3	56	5	.946	102.0	.8	.339	-.01
Disarcina	157	250	485	25	760	110	.967	1376.1	10.4	.555	2.13
Fermin	55	64	134	6	204	36	.971	420.2	3.2	.491	.45
Fletcher S	22	29	64	5	98	14	.949	159.0	1.2	.684	.40
Fryman T	137	205	443	20	668	88	.970	1202.2	9.1	.530	1.63
Gagne	141	207	438	18	663	82	.973	1146.1	8.6	.622	2.35
Gallego	14	26	41	4	71	11	.944	119.0	.9	.567	.19
Grebeck	85	110	276	8	394	45	.980	728.2	5.5	.570	1.21
Griffin Alf	48	45	108	3	156	13	.981	335.2	2.5	.388	.09
Guillen	12	20	38	0	58	7	1.000	107.1	.8	.650	.24
Howard D	74	124	203	8	335	52	.976	616.0	4.6	.625	1.28
Huson	82	109	167	9	285	45	.968	507.0	3.8	.578	.87
Lee M	128	186	330	7	523	68	.987	1079.1	8.1	.529	1.46
Lewis M	121	184	333	25	542	72	.954	1017.1	7.7	.448	.75
Listach	148	238	451	24	713	89	.966	1279.0	9.6	.619	2.59
Naehring	30	36	86	1	123	18	.992	224.0	1.7	.659	.52
Reboulet	36	37	97	4	138	22	.971	222.0	1.7	.750	.67
Ripken C	162	287	445	12	744	117	.984	1440.0	10.8	.633	3.07
Rivera L	93	118	285	14	417	56	.966	732.0	5.5	.571	1.22
Rossy	51	60	135	8	203	37	.961	381.0	2.9	.578	.65
Schaefer	33	28	67	8	103	7	.922	177.0	1.3	.314	-.05
Stankiewicz	81	132	252	11	395	54	.972	696.0	5.2	.582	1.22
Sveum	37	39	97	8	144	19	.944	292.1	2.2	.389	.09
Thon	87	117	225	15	357	38	.958	678.2	5.1	.380	.15
Trammell	28	46	80	3	129	16	.977	229.0	1.7	.553	.35
Valentin	58	78	181	10	269	44	.963	491.1	3.7	.581	.85
Velarde	75	129	212	9	350	42	.974	606.1	4.6	.573	1.02
Vizquel	136	224	403	7	634	93	.989	1152.0	8.7	.610	2.26
Weiss	103	144	269	19	432	56	.956	859.2	6.5	.421	.46
Wilkerson	69	73	143	7	223	27	.969	449.1	3.4	.443	.32
TOTALS		3638	6987	339	10964	1486	.969	1460.1	11.0	8.632	91.11

the American League should find out what it is he has learned how to hit and start throwing him something else.

On the other hand, Omar's batting splits are consistent. He was not just exploiting something he found out about lefty pitching, or his home ballpark, or day games, nor did he just have one hot month. He wore down some late in the year, but that's probably workload, not a drop in hitting ability. Overall, Omar's maybe a 65% gamble to hold the hitting. Still, unless your fantasy league has defensive stats included, Omar's a poor gamble. If the league does count defense, as the Bill James game does, then Omar has value, as his defense is overlooked by most analysts. In the real game we're supposed to be analyzing here, Omar's a certified star, having come in second and fourth two years in a row.

5. Craig Grebek (CHA)

I think he can play. His totals and averages were both down for age 27, but he missed about half the season. If he can keep anything like the value he had when he was 26, he's a top player at the spot. I think he can do that, assuming he isn't permanently injured or anything. As a consequence, I rate him a FANTASY GOOD BUY. Most people don't know he ever did have a decent year. You may have noted in the Fantasy Diary that Don Malcolm liked him and wanted him. Don's an awfully good player analyst. I'd trust his opinion long before I'd trust an off year with a bunch of missed playing time.

6. Andy Stankiewicz (NYY)

At age 28, and with just these numbers for age 27, he's a Grade B prospect. Nonetheless, his progress through the minors supports the idea that this is in fact his true level of ability and not some fluke age-27 season he'll never duplicate. As I said under Pat Kelly, I'd worry about developing Andy before Pat. Andy won't be great, but he could fill that shortstop hole for the Yankees for seven or eight years with quality play. That team isn't chock full of players of that caliber.

7. Manny Lee (TOR - TEX)

If nothing else, Manny will always have a warm spot reserved for him in the hearts of Blue Jay fans for not completely dropping the ball when Eddie Zosky did not turn into Cal Ripken, Jr. Instead, Manny came through with a good, solid journeyman year, which was all Dave Winfield and crew needed to bring the bacon home.

The Blue Jays will doubtless try Zosky again, and I have to agree with that move. But, instead of signing Manny Lee, they've picked up Dick Schofield to fill in if Eddie should fail again. I have two things to say about that. First, Eddie Zosky is supposed to be a world-class head case, full of ego and rife with bullshit. That makes him a much worse gamble than just his playing stats indicate. The other thing I have to say is that I'd rather have Manny Lee in the hand then Dick Schofield in the minors.

As for fantasy play, well, Manny's going to the Rangers, where the ballpark will help his stats.

That makes him a FANTASY GOOD BUY. Schofield and Zosky, between them, don't make as good a purchase as Manny.

8. Greg Gagne (MIN - KC)

A quick look at the Twins' roster locates only Jeff Reboulet as a replacement for Greg. Reboulet showed a real hot glove there in his limited trial, but he also hit .190. He's also 28, and has done nothing in the minors to indicate that he's a Major League shortstop. Since the Twins act like they think they're going to contend (Dave Winfield), I assume they have some other plan for the position. Rumor has it that the plan is to move Scott Leius and hope they can come up with a third baseman. Personally, I'd rather have one position in trouble than two, but it's Tom Kelly's decision.

Kansas City will be happy to have Greg Gagne. They won't mind the lack of power, and they sorely need the glove, between Keith Miller (OK) and Gregg Jeffries (not OK). Oh, you say they've traded for Jose Lind, and Miller's now a utility man? Hah. I'll believe that after I see Jose Lind do some hitting. Until then, Miller's the second baseman and Lind's the bench warmer. After all, Hal McRae's already carrying his son's bat to get his glove. You have to generate some offense somewhere.

9. Gary Disarcina (CAL)

He's only 25, and a lot of the guys above him are a lot older, so he could move up. Right now, he's another "good field, no hit" shortstop. The Angels, though, are so bad that they can't really be worrying about that. They'll take what Gary can give them, at least until they get better.

10. Dickie Thon (TEX - MIL)

If you take Dickie Thon's career through 1983, until he got beaned, and plug it into the Brock2 prediction system, the chart below is what you get. Just wanted to print that somewhere, and I doubt I'll ever be writing about Thon as a starter again.

11. Dave Howard (KC)

Good field, no hit. Age 26. A fine backup for Greg Gagne. I suppose I should write more, as I don't think I'll ever be writing about him again, but what else is there to say?

12. Mark Lewis (CLE)

He's 23; he'll get better. He's never going to be really good, not with those power and walk totals. But he'll be OK. You never know, he might even help the Indians if they should ever get a good team together. I assume you know the Indians think they already have gotten that team together. They also think that they should hand the shortstop job to Felix Fermin to lose in spring training. Well, it might light a fire under Mark Lewis, but it also might make him demand a trade.

13. Luis Rivera (BOS)

At long last, he might be the best middle infielder on the Red Sox. I don't mean to imply that he's any good, but Tim Naehring? Actually, he's still not up there. John Valentin has probably won the shortstop job, and Scott Fletcher is still better than Luis Rivera.

14. Walt Weiss (OAK - FLA)

Lo! How the mighty have fallen! Lo, how the mighty have not recovered from injuries. Lo how the mighty are in trouble for playing time. Lo, how the mighty are eligible for arbitration. Lo, how the mighty have been left unprotected in the expansion draft. Lo, how the mighty will still bat seventh or eighth, even for Florida.

Dickie Thon Projection

Age	G	AB	R	H	D	T	HR	RBI	BB	AVG	TB	RC	RC25
20	0	0								0.000	0	0.0	0
21	35	56	6	19	3	0	0	8	5	0.339	22	8.7	5.85
22	80	267	32	68	12	2	0	15	10	0.255	84	23.7	2.97
23	49	95	13	26	6	0	0	3	9	0.274	32	10.8	3.90
24	136	496	73	137	31	10	3	36	37	0.276	197	64.3	4.48
25	154	619	81	177	28	9	20	79	54	0.286	283	97.1	5.49
26	154	588	73	167	31	9	14	75	49	0.284	259	87.7	5.21
27	154	597	86	180	31	8	20	88	56	0.302	289	104.4	6.26
28	154	583	69	164	29	7	15	75	48	0.281	254	84.9	5.06
29	158	596	68	165	29	7	16	77	53	0.277	256	85.9	4.98
30	155	591	66	166	29	6	14	73	51	0.281	251	84.6	4.97
31	156	578	62	160	28	6	13	69	51	0.277	239	80.2	4.79
32	155	573	55	153	26	5	11	64	51	0.267	223	72.7	4.32
33	154	560	52	147	25	4	10	60	55	0.262	212	69.3	4.19
34	153	552	49	145	25	4	9	58	47	0.262	206	66.0	4.05
35	152	543	44	138	23	4	8	53	50	0.254	192	60.9	3.75
36	152	536	41	133	23	3	7	50	48	0.248	184	57.2	3.55
37	151	529	35	124	21	3	6	45	49	0.234	168	50.1	3.09
38	81	257	20	66	11	1	3	24	23	0.257	89	28.5	3.75
39	102	312	17	67	11	1	3	24	29	0.215	89	25.1	2.56
40	24	56	4	14	2	0	0	5	5	0.248	18	5.5	3.22
41	14	29	2	7	1	0	0	2	3	0.239	9	2.5	2.74
TOTAL	2524	9015	949	2421	426	90	176	984	783	0.269	3554	1170.1	4.44

Shortstops

Brock J. Hanke

		OWAR	DWAR	TWAR
1.	Larkin B	5.61	1.86	7.46
2.	Smith O	4.16	3.04	7.20
3.	Bell Jay	3.59	2.95	6.55
4.	Fernandez T	2.83	.96	3.79
5.	Blauser	3.50	.27	3.78
6.	Owen S	2.63	1.14	3.77
7.	Schofield	.57	1.99	2.56
8.	Offerman	2.92	-.55	2.37
9.	Sanchez R	.35	1.66	2.01
	Uribe	.44	.91	1.35
10.	Clayton	-.20	1.12	.92
	Arias	.73	.10	.83
	Cordero	.81	-.14	.67
	Branson	.43	.21	.64
	Dunston	.39	.22	.61
	Anderson D	.39	.08	.47
	Shipley	-.27	.55	.29
	Benavides	-.06	.32	.26
11.	Bell Ju	-.28	.47	.20
	Ramirez R	-.16	.11	-.04
	Stillwell	-.44	.39	-.04
	Garcia C	-.27	.19	-.08
	Jones Tim	-.68	.52	-.16
	Benjamin	-.56	.30	-.25
	Sveum	-.69	.41	-.28
	Millette	-.76	.37	-.39
	Belliard	-1.46	1.05	-.41
	Foley T	-.90	.33	-.56
12.	Cedeno A	-.80	.01	-.79
	Batiste K	-1.04	-.22	-1.25

1. Barry Larkin (CIN)

Leader of the Cincy Suicide Squad, now that Eric Davis is gone. Actually it's down to Larkin and Sabo now, isn't it, with O'Neill and Braggs gone, too. Ooops, nope, I forgot Bip Roberts. And, oh yes, the pitchers. Sorry about that. If Barry gets in 3/5 of the season, he's going to rank #1 here, but that's no sure bet. If he gets in 90% of the season, he's a MVP candidate, but that's a horrid bet. And if all the Reds got in full time play for a season, they'd win the division again....

Most of the guys like this - Eric, Jose Canseco, Dave Justice - have obviously overbodybuilt.

That is, they have too much muscle for their bone and ligament structure. That's how come they're hurt all the time. Unless Barry has some weird bones, though, that's not his problem. Nor does he play silly, like George Brett. He's just fragile.

Of course, if you're in a fantasy league, you've got to take Barry Larkin if you can get him. If your league has a "minor league" system, like Bill James Fantasy Baseball does, you can also hide whoever Larkin's caddie is, figuring that he's going to play when Barry's on the DL. You wanna know how bad the shortstop position can get? Well, Freddy Benevides was Barry's caddie last year. He got into 34 games

total, 20 as a starter. And he actually beat out two starters in the rankings here.

2. Ozzie Smith (STL)

The strain of age is such that the Brock2 system only gives Ozzie two more years of full-time play. What it says is that Ozzie is down to one offensive skill: getting on base. His power is gone (20 doubles), and he's old. He figures to lose about 20 batting points in 1993, and 20 more in '94. That '94 average - around .250 - just isn't enough to keep him playing. In case you're wondering about defense, I deliberately loaded the system to compensate. What you're supposed to do in Brock2 is enter a factor based on playing position. The highest is "the league average of runs per game minus .8". That's for shortstop and second base. I entered league average - .9.

You may have read something about Ozzie's contract problems. Here's the situation. Ozzie wanted two guaranteed years, and the Cards wouldn't give them. That's because they have Jose Oquendo and no place to play him, with Geronimo Pena now established at second base. What finally happened is that the contract calls for Ozzie to get his millions as long as he gets 400 plate appearances. Now the sportswriters will tell you that this is injury protection for the Cardinals. Bunk. It's Oquendo protection. What the contract says is "Ozzie gets his $3 million per year as long as he can beat out Jose Oquendo". Of course, sportswriters don't think Oquendo is any good, because they can't count walks. But he's about as good as Ozzie right now, and he's 8 years younger.

3. Jay Bell (PIT)

Now clearly the MVP of the Pirates. And make no mistake, having a player this good at shortstop is one hell of a bonus. Still, if Jim Leyland can win a division with an offense consisting of Bell, Andy Van Slyke and a platoon of rookie outfielders, he's a magician.

4. Tony Fernandez (SD - NYM)

Tony really figures to help the Mets. As you no doubt recall, former Met manager Dave

Shortstop	G	PO	A	Er	TC	DP	FPct	DI	DG	DW%	DWAR
Arias	30	44	74	4	122	7	.967	244.0	1.8	.406	.10
Batiste K	41	69	85	13	167	17	.922	336.2	2.5	.266	-.21
Bell Jay	159	268	527	22	817	94	.973	1411.1	10.6	.631	2.99
Bell Ju	46	82	129	6	217	22	.972	390.1	2.9	.507	.46
Belliard	139	150	287	14	451	48	.969	860.1	6.5	.509	1.03
Benavides	34	33	68	6	107	18	.944	213.0	1.6	.462	.18
Benjamin	33	34	71	1	106	12	.991	211.2	1.6	.543	.31
Blauser	106	87	182	9	278	28	.968	587.2	4.4	.406	.25
Candaele	65	79	137	7	223	30	.969	391.1	2.9	.606	.75
Cedeno A	70	83	175	11	269	27	.959	563.0	4.2	.352	.01
Clayton	94	142	256	11	409	52	.973	787.2	5.9	.539	1.12
Cordero	35	40	71	6	117	11	.949	255.1	1.9	.293	-.11
Duncan	42	37	80	5	122	15	.959	231.0	1.7	.457	.19
Dunston	18	28	42	1	71	9	.986	143.2	1.1	.556	.22
Fernandez T	155	241	403	11	655	65	.983	1348.1	10.2	.445	.96
Foley T	33	37	81	4	122	14	.967	237.2	1.8	.505	.28
Guerrero J	19	15	35	1	51	5	.980	133.1	1.0	.255	-.10
Jones Tim	34	40	66	3	109	16	.972	237.1	1.8	.492	.25
Larkin B	140	232	405	11	648	69	.983	1207.2	9.1	.553	1.84
Millette	26	32	82	3	117	14	.974	205.2	1.5	.574	.35
Offerman	149	208	398	42	648	75	.935	1290.0	9.7	.295	-.54
Owen S	116	188	300	9	497	45	.982	972.0	7.3	.507	1.15
Pecota	39	34	71	3	108	11	.972	202.0	1.5	.474	.19
Ramirez R	57	60	113	7	180	17	.961	357.0	2.7	.391	.11
Sanchez R	68	143	198	9	350	52	.974	593.1	4.5	.719	1.65
Schofield	141	204	390	7	601	79	.988	1144.2	8.6	1.021	5.79
Shipley	23	29	41	1	71	11	.986	108.2	.8	.838	.40
Smith O	132	231	418	10	659	82	.985	1156.1	8.7	.704	3.08
Sveum	34	56	91	8	155	18	.948	252.2	1.9	.925	1.09
Uribe	62	75	157	7	239	37	.971	444.1	3.3	.622	.91
Vizcaino	50	73	143	7	223	29	.969	386.2	2.9	.634	.83
TOTALS		3173	5753	283	9209	1070	.969	1461.0	11.0	7.245	75.84

Johnson didn't really believe in the middle of the infield. In this, as in so many things, he showed himself a true Earl Weaver disciple. Historians talk about the Met weaknesses at third base, but they haven't had a decent shortstop since, well, they had Roy McMillan in his mid-30s, when he couldn't hit at all, but could still field Gold Glove. They had Bud Harrelson, who was the same type as McMillan, only worse. They had Frank Taveras, who at least could keep his batting average over .250. Hell, let's face it, the Mets have NEVER had a good shortstop. Now they do, and their outfield and third base spots, where Earl always had players, are a mess.

5. Jeff Blauser (ATL)
    instead of Rafael Belliard

Belliard had more playing time, which tells you two things. First, Blauser must really be a butcher out there in the field, to lose playing time to Belliard. Second, Blauser should rank higher, if you're considering the overall quality of the player, because the TWAR system weights playing time, and Jeff played less than half, and it wasn't injuries.

As it is, the indicated adjustments would place Jeff between Tony Fernandez and Jay Bell, which is only a one-spot move. That's fair. If Jeff played a full season, he'd probably hit enough to make up the defensive difference between him and Tony.

Now, the question is, will Bobby Cox, who I have elsewhere touted as a genius (well, a baseball genius), figure this out and bench Belliard? I doubt it. See the Earl Weaver comment above. Cox builds his teams like Earl did. His offense is supposed to come from the players down the foul lines. The middle of this infield is for defense. Rafael Belliard can't hit at all, but he is a better defensive player than Jeff Blauser is. As long as the Braves' offense holds up, Belliard is going to play. The only way Jeff Blauser is going to get the job is if the Braves start losing too many 2-1 and 1-0 games.

In fantasy league terms, what this means is that you should never pick up Jeff Blauser unless you get Belliard too. If you can carry both of them, in some "minor league" scheme like the Bill James game lets you have, you can main-

tain one full-time player out of the deal. But, if you only have one of them, you're gambling that the Braves are going to have the kind of offense that gives that player the majority of the time. Bad gamble, if you ask me.

6. Spike Owen (MTL - NYY)

When the Expos acquired Spike Owen from the Red Sox, I thought it was a horrible deal. I didn't see that he was any big margin better than Tom Foley, and I didn't think the Expos would still have him when they got around to contending. I guess I get half credit for that one, and now I have to say that, if I were the Expos, I'd have kept Spike around. With Bret Barberie gone to expansion (and there's something funny going on there - like an alcohol problem), the Expos are Exposed. As of right now, they do not have a Major League third baseman, and they're supposed to win their division. They can't cover with Wil Cordero, as he's got to play short. Ya gotta keep that bench full if ya wanna contend, eh?

7. Dick Schofield, Jr. (NYM - TOR)

There's a big gap in TWAR between Owen and Schofield. And it's no illusion, either. Basically, Owen is the last of the good shortstops. Schofield and Offerman head the rest of the list because they're the ones who got full playing time. Remember, Owen and Blauser did not have that advantage, either. Essentially, Dick Schofield, Jr. is a journeyman, "good field no hit" shortstop. His Defensive Winning Percentage, .579, is not tremendous for a shortstop. But, applied over his 8.7 Defensive Games played, gives him the 1.99 DWAR.

Let's rephrase that: any good - not great - defensive shortstop who gets full playing time will pile up about 2 WAR on defense alone. A minimal performance at the plate will add half a WAR on offense. Dick Schofield's Offensive Winning Percentage is .393 which is, well, not quite .400. The total player, with a TWAR of 2.56, is just good enough to keep a Major League job. He's good enough for Cleveland. But he's not good enough to start on the contender that the Mets think they have paid for. Remember that, when you're evaluating shortstops. Anything less than 3 TWAR is really just marking time. A contender should try to do better.

As for the Toronto Blue Jays, they should have kept Manny Lee to back up Eddie Zosky.

8. Jose Offerman (LA)

Essentially the same value as Schofield, but completely opposite in emphasis. What the numbers say is that Jose can hit well enough to move to second or third, and that his defense is bad enough to suggest the move.

I want to emphasize that defensive ranking. The second basemen on the Dodgers - Lenny Harris and Mike Sharperson - had good defensive stats, with Defensive Winning Percentages, at second, of .538 and .655. Part of the reason was that the Dodgers' pitching staff had a ground ball / fly ball ratio of 1.58, which was the second highest in the league. The Cubs, as usual, were first, because their hitters' ballpark forces them to accumulate a ground ball staff to avoid getting killed by fly ball home runs. Dodger Stadium, on the other hand, is a pitchers' park that forgives fly balls. Usually, the Dodger staff has a low grounder / fly ball ratio and high strikeouts. This year, they finished fifth in K's. Along with the lack of flies, that produced an unusual number of ground balls for infielders to handle. For Offerman to turn in stats this lousy (Defensive Winning Percentage of .295) in this environment strongly suggests that he is just as hopelessly out of position as he looks.

The Dodger solution to this was to acquire Jody Reed. Now, I like Reed. I think he will likely prove the best middle infielder the Dodgers have. But I don't see that he adds anything to the team that Offerman, Harris and Sharperson don't. They can all hit, and they're all suspect at short. The Dodgers can hardly play all four of them. Well, at least that gives Jose Offerman another chance.

Late developments make Offerman a BAD FANTASY BUY. The Dodgers picked up Kevin Elster from the Mets. What that means is that Jose is going to be removed for a pinch hitter every time the Dodgers lead or are in a close one late. Elster will then go in to play defense. That will cost Jose a lot of plate appearances; maybe as many as 75.

9. Rey Sanchez (CHN)

Did an OK job of holding the fort for Shawon Dunstan. His DWAR may be a bit high, for the same reasons given above for the Dodgers; but even so, he played better than anyone had any reason to expect.

10. Royce Clayton (SF)
    instead of Jose Uribe

In this case, I went with the guy who got the most playing time, rather than the one who ranked highest. That's because there is only one interesting thing left to say about Jose Uribe, at his age. That is that anyone who can't outrank him in more playing time has not established himself as a really good AAA player. Well, I guess that's the only thing to say about Royce Clayton, too. Well, at least he's got the job. Uribe's gone to the Astros.

11. Juan Bell (PHI)
    not Kim Batiste

Juan Bell can't hit, but he can play a little shortstop. Kim Batiste can't do anything. They were both 24, which is young, but still too old to be playing like this. I guess the difference is that I consider Batiste to be completely through, while Bell might make five years as a backup. The Phillies, who like to pretend they are in contention, need to go shopping.

12. Andujar Cedeno (HOU)
    or Jose Uribe
    or even Casey Candaele

Sigh. If you're a Cardinal fan, or even just a weird player fan, you've got to root for Andujar Cedeno. I mean, it's a perfect name, just perfect. It evokes everything. Still, what it evokes most is "unstable personality". And, sure enough, there are rumblings in Houston about their erstwhile prize rookie. Does it surprise you that ol' AC took all of 14 walks in 220 At-Bats? Why? Do you think he OUGHT to have patience?

Left Fielders

Brock J. Hanke

		OWAR	DWAR	TWAR
1.	Anderson B	7.25	.97	8.21
2.	Raines	5.49	1.40	6.89
3.	Mack	5.95	.73	6.69
4.	Henderson R	4.87	.71	5.58
5.	Maldonado	3.58	.89	4.48
6.	McReynolds	3.60	.27	3.87
7.	Polonia	3.23	.49	3.72
8.	Reimer	3.46	.17	3.63
9.	Vaughn G	2.80	.77	3.56
	Belle	3.13	.01	3.14
11.	Mitchell K	2.42	.48	2.91
	Koslofski	.79	.56	1.36
	Cotto	.60	.55	1.15
12.	Gladden	.18	.79	.96
	Bell D	.19	.58	.77
13.	Howard T	.25	.52	.77
	Gwynn C	.46	.08	.54
	Hulse	.39	.03	.42
	Thurman	-.51	.63	.13
	Briley	.02	.07	.09
	Bruett	-.10	.16	.05
	Fariss	-.10	.15	.05
	Cochrane	.02	-.01	.01
	Ducey	-.26	.09	-.17
	Carreon	-.67	.49	-.18
	Mercedes	-.36	.17	-.18
	Daugherty	-.25	.04	-.21
	McIntosh	-.46	.11	-.35
	Greenwell	-.67	.23	-.44
14.	Hatcher B	-.81	.18	-.63

1. Brady Anderson (BAL)

Just exploded, given a full time job. It was a year late for the age-27 theory, but that's really supposed to apply to people who were playing full time for a couple of years before they turned 27. As to whether this level of ability is real, I doubt it. I do think there's a career year factor going on here, and I also think that the American League pitchers are going to concentrate hard on adjusting to this particular batter. BAD FANTASY BUY, as at least one player in your league will pencil him in for another such year, while Sophomore Slump is what is due.

On the other hand, Brady should stabilize at a good level of play. I wouldn't be surprised to see him up here in the Top Five for some years to come. The improvement was over all the spectrum of skills. He hit more, and he hit for more power, both home runs and doubles. He took a lot more walks, which is a learning skill that won't disappear with the dropoff from his physical peak. That broad a base of improvement looks real to me; I just don't think he's going to turn out to be better than Tim Raines or Rickey Henderson.

2. Tim Raines (CHA)

Finally outranked Rickey Henderson, even if for only one season. The reasons were: 1) Tim had a little bit better year than normal, though not exactly out of the range of luck, 2) Rickey had a bad year, for Rickey, although it was better than 1991, and 3) Tim played in 27 more games than Rickey did. That last factor is the one that did it. In general, Tim Raines is not the player that Rickey Henderson is, and they should return to their accustomed ranking spots next year.

What are the chances of Tim Raines making the Hall of Fame, given that Rickey Henderson is there to skew the curve? Well, to make it to 900 Stolen Bases should take Tim about five more years, if he doesn't get badly hurt. He needs 170, and has been stealing over 40 each year. Five years is conservative. To get to 3,000 hits will take maybe 8 years. He needs 1077. 1077 divided by 8 equals 135. That's a lot to average from age 33 through 40, but Tim does look like the sort of player who will play full time for all eight of those seasons.

If he plays the 8 years, he'll get the 3,000 and also be over 1,000 SBs. That will surely do it. If he plays only 6 full seasons, he'll be struggling for it. The thousand stolen bases would have done it if Rickey weren't around, but he is. I don't think there's any doubt that Tim will play until he's 38, so the first benchmark is a lock. It's just a matter of how well he plays in his late 30's - whether he can hold a full time job at ages 38, 39, and 40. But, then, that's the usual test of the Hall candidate, isn't it?

3. Shane Mack (MIN)

What's amazing is not that the Twins could figure out that Shane Mack had long since bypassed Dan Gladden. What's amazing is that they were able to find anyone who would take Gladden off their hands.

As for Shane Mack, he's had this sort of value for three years now, he just hasn't been played full time. That is to say, this is not some age-27 career year. This is Shane Mack. This is what he's going to do. Do the people in your fantasy league know this? Of course not. That's why Shane Mack is a FANTASY BEST BUY.

4. Rickey Henderson (OAK)

I always rank Rickey as a FANTASY BEST BUY if he's been hurt at all. That's because:

1) Most fantasy players don't understand the

Left Field	G	PO	A	Er	TC	DP	FPct	DI	DG	DW%	DWAR
Anderson B	148	359	10	7	376	4	.981	1330.0	3.6	.618	.98
Bell D	24	49	2	0	51	0	1.000	208.0	.6	.771	.24
Bell Geo	15	27	0	1	28	0	.964	124.0	.3	.361	.00
Belle	52	94	1	3	98	0	.969	423.2	1.2	.362	.01
Blankenship L	22	32	0	0	32	0	1.000	114.2	.3	.669	.10
Briley	27	32	0	0	32	0	1.000	133.0	.4	.583	.08
Browne J	17	36	0	1	37	0	.973	108.0	.3	.556	.06
Carreon	64	136	5	2	143	1	.986	527.0	1.4	.648	.43
Cole	18	29	1	1	31	0	.968	130.1	.4	.473	.04
Conine	22	39	1	0	40	0	1.000	178.2	.5	.602	.12
Cotto	63	114	2	0	116	0	1.000	402.1	1.1	.686	.37
Curtis C	48	71	2	3	76	0	.961	352.0	1.0	.324	-.03
Ducey	20	31	2	2	35	1	.943	153.0	.4	.889	.23
Eisenreich	24	48	0	0	48	0	1.000	195.0	.5	.606	.14
Fariss	28	34	0	0	34	0	1.000	182.2	.5	.444	.05
Gladden	95	202	9	3	214	2	.986	754.2	2.1	.715	.75
Gonzalez Juan	31	68	3	2	73	0	.973	229.0	.6	.700	.22
Greenwell	41	85	1	0	86	0	1.000	360.0	1.0	.584	.23
Hall M	99	218	9	2	229	1	.991	860.0	2.4	.712	.85
Hamilton	30	49	2	0	51	0	1.000	231.0	.6	.736	.24
Hatcher B	63	116	5	4	125	0	.968	545.2	1.5	.492	.21
Henderson R	108	229	8	4	241	1	.983	883.1	2.4	.641	.70
Hill G	50	108	5	6	119	2	.950	460.0	1.3	.515	.21
Howard T	68	115	3	2	120	0	.983	453.0	1.2	.544	.24
Howitt	14	29	1	1	31	0	.968	112.1	.3	1.194	.26
Kelly	47	103	2	2	107	0	.981	391.1	1.1	.511	.17
Mack	150	306	7	4	317	1	.987	1265.0	3.5	.530	.63
Maldonado	129	257	13	6	276	2	.978	1123.0	3.1	.635	.88
McReynolds	94	184	4	2	190	0	.989	818.0	2.2	.498	.33
Miller K	16	41	0	2	43	0	.953	117.0	.3	.494	.05
Mitchell K	69	130	4	0	134	0	1.000	570.2	1.6	.655	.48
Orsulak	14	25	1	1	27	0	.963	105.0	.3	.560	.06
Phillips	14	42	0	2	44	0	.955	111.0	.3	.511	.05
Polonia	99	191	8	4	203	2	.980	841.0	2.3	.561	.49
Raines	129	312	12	2	326	0	.994	1118.1	3.1	.805	1.39
Ready	22	33	1	0	34	0	1.000	124.2	.3	.770	.14
Reimer	110	197	7	11	215	1	.949	840.2	2.3	.426	.17
Vaughn G	131	288	6	3	297	0	.990	1147.0	3.1	.594	.77
Winningham	36	61	4	1	66	1	.985	228.2	.6	.805	.28
Zupcic	32	39	4	1	44	1	.977	216.1	.6	.607	.15
TOTALS		5005	159	100	5264	24	.981	1460.1	4.0	3.267	11.67

value of a top player. In all fantasy leagues, the talent is compressed. That is, there are fewer players used in the fantasy game than there are in real baseball. So, to some extent, the fantasy managers get to skim the cream of quality. What that does is raises the Replacement Rate of performance. Now that does reduce Rickey's Wins Above Replacement locally for the fantasy league. Let's say he loses 2 WAR, and is only a 4-WAR man for fantasy play. But that also means that the man who is a 4-WAR player in real baseball, say Kevin McReynolds, is only a 2-WAR player in fantasy. And the 2-WAR real player, like Jim Eisenreich, is right at the Replacement Rate. All three players lose the same number of WAR, but not the same percentage of their value. And Rickey Henderson loses the least.

2) The media doesn't like Rickey Henderson, for the reason that he takes no bullshit from them and so they're always crowing when he shows any sign of weakness. When he gets hurt, it's all over the media. Some of your fantasy competitors believe this stuff, and have Rickey down for only 100 games in 1993. But that's nonsense; Rickey is not usually hurt. Rickey usually dominates this position.

3) Some people, including some of your fantasy competitors, just can't get it out of their heads that the top outfielder does not have to hit 30 home runs. No matter how many analyses Bill James, or I or anyone else does, they aren't going to believe Rickey can help them as much as he can. So they'll underbid for him, or draft him later than they should.

By the way, Rickey Henderson already has 1,000 Stolen Bases. And he only needs 1,000 hits exactly to reach 2,000. And he's going to play longer than Tim Raines is, in all likelihood. Rickey Henderson is the best leadoff man in the history of the game, and of course he's going into the Hall of Fame.

5. Candy Maldonado (TOR - CHN)

Taking into account playing time, as well as production per game, 1992 was Candy's greatest season. That's partially the result of his injury in 1987, when he was 26 and on his way to establishing his peak performance. It's also partially the ballpark; the Skydome is a better hitters' park than anyplace Candy has played before. Still, there's no taking away from the achievement, nor from the sense of timing that placed it right when Candy's team could use it the most.

Now with the Cubs, Candy is not going to get much help maintaining the pace. Sure, Wrigley Field is likely to inflate his stats, but he's also likely to be asked to bat cleanup and compete with the memory of Andre Dawson. The memory of Dawson, of course, will compete much better than Andre himself ever did. Also, Candy's likely to be the end of the Cubbie offensive sequence, which means that people will be pitching around him. He's never been in that situation before, and may be slow to adjust. Also, the Cubbie management is known to be erratic, and what Candy needs is stability. Against all this is the amount of money the Cubs will pay him. Well, I'd sure put up with the Cubs for that much money.

6. Kevin McReynolds (KC)

Generally known as a consistent player, Kevin does have one area of complete chaos. His strike zone judgment varies as wildly as any I've ever seen. Most of the time, he's bad at taking walks. He's only had 465, against 4892 At-Bats. The average would be 489. Kevin's had full-time seasons of 34, 38 and 39. On the other hand, he's had three seasons way over the average, much less his norm. In 1986, he took 66 walks against only 560 AB, and 1990 saw 71 against 521. And then, this last year, when his power decline continued, and he played in a ballpark that suppressed what power he had left, he took 67 walks against only 373 AB. And, in case you're wondering, only three of them were intentional.

If the 1990 and 1992 seasons represent a conscious adjustment to Kevin's decline phase, I have to give him big points for intelligence. Most hitters don't try to do that; they try to hold up their home run power as they age. That's a losing battle, whereas the battle to develop on-base skills is winnable, since the abilities required are mental, rather than physical.

Obviously, Kevin is a BAD FANTASY BUY. Not only is he clearly in decline, but he also is emphasizing a skill that is undervalued in most fantasy leagues.

7. Luis Polonia (CAL)

This was supposed to be Luis' age-27 peak year; instead it was his second step backwards in a row. It's always possible that this speed-based player peaked early, and it's also possible the moving up to full time play has not helped. Luis could be tired, or it might have been that he was being protected from pitchers he couldn't hit, and now must bat against them. In support of the "worn out" theory is the fact that his worst month by far was September, with August coming in second. In support of the "protected" theory is that he doesn't hit lefty pitching at all.

In any case, Buck Rodgers needs to reassess his use of Luis. My guess is that he will try to use the man as a starting center fielder, unless Whitey Herzog picks up a known defensive whiz for the spot. Junior Felix is gone. Last year, Luis did some DH work, but Chili Davis has that spot sewn up now. All the Angel prospects seem to be first basemen. The holdovers would have been Von Hayes and Hubie Brooks. That certainly leaves Luis to play center. Now, I have doubts about Luis' defensive skills in the first place. He's not exactly the Gold Glove in left field. And center field requires more physical exertion than left does, for a player who seems to tire as the season wears on. All in all, I have doubts that Luis' decline will reverse itself.

8. Kevin Reimer (TEX - COL - MIL)

The home run drop does represent a power outage, but I do prefer a home run / doubles balance of 16 / 32 to 20 / 22. What I basically have to say here is that Kevin was fighting the drop from age 27 to age 28, and also Sophomore Slump, and held his own pretty well. I can't rate him as more than a Grade B prospect, because of his age, but he might pick up a bit and move to, say, the top of the middle of the pack, instead of the bottom of the middle, if that makes any sense.

No, I can't imaging why wou'd expose him to expansion. No, I can't imagine why you'd trade him for Dante Bichette. No, I can't imagine why you'd think he can replace Paul Molitor in you batting order. But, then, that's not what Bud Selig thinks. Bud thinks that he has to pay less for players so he can negotiate tough with the union. Well, I'd pay less for Kevin than for Paul, too.

9. Greg Vaughn (MIL)

Coming up on age 27, and he and the Brewers could sure use a big step forward. Milwaukee's fans would like to move up into pennant contention, and they need a power center to do that. The only player they have who might provide that big power surge is Greg. John Jaha is not quite that hot. I give Greg a 70% chance to come through. It wouldn't take a whole lot for him to move up. He needs, basically, to develop a real ability to put the bat soundly on the ball. That would move his batting average up into the .270 range. At that level, the pitchers have to throw their best stuff at him, even if it's the stuff he can hit out of the park. Then his homer totals could just explode. On the basis of that possibility, I rate Greg a FANTASY GOOD BUY.

10. Mel Hall (NYY - Japan)

Early in his career, Mel took the occasional walk, and looked like he might turn out to be a Grade A player. But his troubles of 1985 seem to have robbed him of either his eyes or his brain, and he's been hamstrung by terrible strike zone judgment since. By now, the American League pitchers know that he'll swing at anything, so they wean him away from the pitches he can hit with any authority. The result is this, a tolerable starter, but not a championship quality ballplayer.

11. Kevin Mitchell (SEA - CIN)

I think the Reds are right to expect a comeback. For one thing, Kevin didn't really play all that badly, even including his horrid start. If Bill Plummer had just lived with him, so he could have played full time, he would have leap-frogged most of the pack ahead of him here, and been at the top of the middle of the pack. I don't know that he's going to replace Paul O'Neill, but he should help the Reds.

On the other hand, there is the Cincy management "team", headed by Magnificent Marge. If that crew can't find a way to get Kevin's fragile psyche to blow up, no one outside of New York can. At least Kevin will get one break, as compared to being in New York. The Cincy press won't spend all year comparing him to Norm Charlton, a comparison he can't possibly win.

12. Dan Gladden (DET)

Finished as a serious starting outfielder or leadoff man. One of the worst of Detroit's recent acquisitions.

13. Thomas Howard (CLE)

After all the hype about all the wonderful outfielders the Tribe had picked up, it came down to this: a man who was run out of San Diego by Jerald Clark. And yet, the Cleveland Indian publicity machine would have you believe that those outfielders are certain to power the team into contention any year now. I'd rather have Swindell and Candiotti, thank you.

14. Billy Hatcher (BOS)

Do you believe the Red Sox actually re-signed this man? I mean, it was only $700,000 a year, but still.... I mean, I'd be happy to play backup outfielder for the Sox, and I'd only take half that money, and I'd do at least half as well as Billy Hatcher will do.

Left Fielders

Brock J. Hanke

		OWAR	DWAR	TWAR
1.	Bonds	6.98	.66	7.63
2.	Roberts B	5.66	.43	6.08
3.	Gant	3.94	.48	4.43
4.	Gilkey	3.64	.74	4.38
	Incaviglia	2.76	.56	3.32
5.	Alou	2.76	.42	3.18
6.	Boston	2.60	.41	3.01
	Felder	2.45	.36	2.81
	Javier	1.11	.92	2.04
7.	Duncan	1.73	.29	2.02
8.	Gonzalez L	1.23	.74	1.97
9.	May D	1.81	.06	1.87
	Thompson M	1.77	.04	1.82
10.	Clark Je	.60	.98	1.57
	Smith Lo	1.36	.12	1.48
	Braggs	1.56	-.11	1.45
11.	Davis E	1.61	-.18	1.44
	Chamberlain	1.02	.20	1.22
	Vanderwal	.98	.22	1.20
12.	James	1.04	.15	1.19
	Calderon	.84	.15	.99
	Leonard M	.78	.15	.92
	Daniels	.72	.15	.87
	McKnight	.35	.07	.42
	Hatcher B	.34	-.04	.31
	Rodriguez H	.18	-.01	.17
	Dozier D	.00	.03	.03
	Jones Chris	.02	-.00	.01
	Gibson K	-.16	.14	-.01
	Hudler	-.25	.10	-.15
	Ashley	-.04	-.16	-.20
	Hosey	-.24	-.04	-.28
	Marsh	-.82	.04	-.78
	Ward K	-.95	.08	-.88
	Azocar	-1.09	.04	-1.05

1. Barry Bonds (PIT-SF)

As you may have already read, the TWAR system disagrees with the National League MVP for the second straight season. It's an odd situation. I don't think anyone really thought that Terry Pendelton had a better 1991 than Barry Bonds did. It was just thought that 1) Terry had been the player who put his team over the top, and 2) the award should be given to a player on the team that won by one game over the man on the team that won by 14.

As for 1992, I don't think anyone seriously considered the TWAR choice, Ryne Sandberg, for three reasons. First, I think the voters figured they owed Barry Bonds one, to make up for 1991. If nobody's season stood out clearly ahead of Barry's, he was going to get it. Second, Ryne's 1992 does not stand out even

within his own career, if you look at raw stats. It's the ballpark adjustment for Wrigley Field, which was nothing like its normal hitters' park, that makes Sandberg's value rise to the top. And third, all the attention focused on Gary Sheffield's Triple Crown chase hurt Sandberg. Nobody but Sheffield and Bonds got any serious attention at all.

With regard to the "Barry Bonds is the best player in baseball" stuff you hear on the TV, well, the above applies there, too. As long as Cal Ripken Jr. and Ryne Sandberg are still in good health, still under 38 years old, and still playing the middle infield, they are better than Barry Bonds. For Bonds to take over, either they've got to decline, or he's got to prove he's a top defensive center fielder. And I don't think Darren Lewis is going to let him have the chance to do that.

2. Bip Roberts (CIN)

If it were my team, I'd just install Bip at second base and be grateful I had him. On the other hand, he does seem to hit better when relieved of the big defensive responsibility. It's a difficult question.

What Lou Pinella seemed to be doing was making a true utility starter out of Bip. His job was to fill in for whoever was injured at the time. That would make sense, given the recent Cincy history of player collapse, except that the vulnerable guys were not at the positions Bip plays. What Lou needed was someone who could play third base, shortstop and left field - and pitch, of course. Now, as there is no such player, you might think that Lou was doing the best he could. But consider. The real weakness on the Reds is that injury problem on the right side of the infield. If Eric Davis, or one of the other outfielders, went down, there was going to be at least a decent replacement. You have to have decent replacement outfielders, just to get your pinch hitting in order. But, if Chris Sabo or Barry Larkin goes down, there's, well, Freddy Benevides. The drop is huge, and it's that disruption of the Red batting order that causes the problems.

What the Reds really need to acquire is a decent-hitting reserve shortstop, or third-baseman-who-can-play-short. Someone like

Left Field	G	PO	A	Er	TC	DP	FPct	DI	DG	DW%	DWAR
Alou	79	118	4	2	124	0	.984	578.0	1.6	.504	.24
Amaro	27	66	1	0	67	0	1.000	188.0	.5	.778	.22
Azocar	31	55	1	4	60	0	.933	206.2	.6	.372	.01
Bass K	84	137	1	2	140	0	.986	603.2	1.7	.907	.92
Benzinger	18	40	0	1	41	0	.976	137.2	.4	.472	.05
Bonds	139	310	4	3	317	0	.991	1240.2	3.4	.545	.66
Boston	66	95	5	1	101	1	.990	472.2	1.3	.596	.32
Braggs	56	65	2	1	68	0	.985	401.2	1.1	.312	-.04
Calderon	46	79	2	1	82	0	.988	371.1	1.0	.497	.15
Chamberlain	28	48	2	3	53	1	.943	202.2	.6	.476	.07
Clark Je	115	241	9	3	253	2	.988	958.0	2.6	.654	.80
Coleman	42	54	2	1	57	2	.982	314.2	.9	.319	-.03
Daniels	49	59	4	1	64	0	.984	357.1	1.0	.944	.58
Davis E	69	108	0	4	112	1	.964	573.0	1.6	.228	-.19
Dozier D	17	33	0	1	34	0	.971	120.2	.3	.441	.03
Duncan	65	123	1	3	127	0	.976	514.0	1.4	.423	.10
Felder	53	49	1	0	50	0	1.000	214.2	.6	.618	.16
Gallagher	22	30	2	2	34	1	.941	123.2	.3	.546	.07
Gant	138	236	3	4	243	0	.984	1096.2	3.0	.432	.25
Gilkey	110	216	8	5	229	3	.978	814.0	2.2	.678	.73
Gonzalez L	111	259	5	2	266	1	.992	859.1	2.4	.665	.74
Goodwin	35	34	0	0	34	0	1.000	145.2	.4	.555	.08
Hatcher B	23	29	0	1	30	0	.967	156.0	.4	.756	.17
Incaviglia	57	115	3	3	121	1	.975	401.0	1.1	.611	.29
James C	60	106	2	3	111	1	.973	430.0	1.2	.458	.13
Javier	42	78	2	0	80	0	1.000	272.2	.7	1.391	.78
Johnson H	16	25	1	1	27	0	.963	124.0	.3	.414	.02
Jordan B	27	42	3	1	46	0	.978	206.1	.6	.646	.17
Leonard M	33	56	2	1	59	2	.983	244.0	.7	.560	.14
Marsh	25	44	0	1	45	0	.978	183.0	.5	.426	.04
May D	98	134	3	5	142	0	.965	667.2	1.8	.362	.02
Roberts Bip	69	115	1	1	117	0	.991	496.1	1.4	.493	.19
Rodriguez H	17	26	6	2	34	2	.941	104.0	.3	.653	.09
Salazar L	33	46	2	0	48	0	1.000	206.1	.6	.770	.24
Sanders R	53	57	3	0	60	1	1.000	275.2	.8	.729	.29
Smith Dw	20	24	1	1	26	0	.962	116.2	.3	.482	.04
Smith Lo	35	61	2	3	66	0	.955	241.1	.7	.525	.12
Snyder C	22	33	0	0	33	0	1.000	134.0	.4	.620	.10
Thompson M	35	61	1	1	63	1	.984	252.1	.7	.502	.11
Vanderwal	55	97	2	2	101	0	.980	370.2	1.0	.537	.19
Walton	22	34	0	2	36	0	.944	144.2	.4	.343	-.00
Ward K	36	45	2	1	48	0	.979	203.1	.6	.568	.12
Webster M	36	46	0	0	46	0	1.000	198.2	.5	.552	.11
TOTALS		4088	103	88	4279	21	.979	1461.0	4.0	2.798	9.79

Luis Alicea would be good. Jose Oquendo would be perfect. How about Mike Sharperson? It's not like those guys aren't available. They are. But you have to focus on getting them rather than acquiring another big-time starter. That inability to fill in the holes is what's costing the Reds right now. They have enough stars to win, if they can cover for the injuries. Give Bip a regular spot, I say. He's not the utility man you need.

3. Ron Gant (ATL)

In technical terms, Ron Gant and Terry Pendelton are batting out of position. Terry, with his complete lack of plate discipline and his high RBI potential, is a textbook #5 hitter.

Ron takes many more walks and, homers or no homers, does not quite have Terry's RBI power. In addition, Ron runs fast and well, while Terry would like to believe he does, and so hurts you on the basepaths. In short, Ron Gant is a complete hitter, while Terry Pendelton is a RBI vulture.

So, big deal, you say. The Braves are winning, and Terry Pendelton is putting up much better numbers than Ron Gant. In fact, with the difference between their batting averages, Terry actually gets on base more often than Ron. And you're right. But look at Ron's walk numbers. He took 71 in 1991, which is a fine number and right about what you'd expect of his development. In 1992, though, he only

took 45. On top of that, his big age-27 year did not materialize. Is it possible that he's messing up his natural batting game trying to swing at too many pitches in an effort to finish off the offensive sequence? Remember, the man batting behind him is Sid Bream. In terms of top production, the Brave offense ends with Ron Gant. I don't think that pressure helps Ron at all. I think I'd move both men to the batting order spot that most suits their respective offensive emphases.

4. Bernard Gilkey (STL)

A surprise ranking, until you look at his cup of coffee in 1990. What happened is that the Sophomore Slump bit him early, during his nominal rookie year. Now he's back to what he showed at the beginning.

I have questions whether he can keep this up. Bernard has little strike zone judgment and marginal power. Nobody's going to be afraid to throw him anything, anywhere. Therefore, he's going to have to learn to hit everything there is to keep his batting average anything like this high. Willie McGee, of course, is the pattern for this sort of hitter. But Bernard hasn't shown Willie's two patented skills yet. Willie has these two swings, you see. One is a helicopter flail above his head that, for reasons physics has yet to explain, stays level and hits the ball on a line. The other is a true golf swing, where Willie swats the ball off his shoetops, on the ground but very hard. Those swings are how Willie was able to stay consistent without forcing anyone to throw strikes. Bernard doesn't have anything that looks like either of Willie's swings, and consequently has a lot still to prove.

And, yes, you're right. Hitters with this collection of characteristics do not make for good leadoff men. But Ozzie Smith, who can push around his manager, absolutely refuses to bat first.

5. Moises Alou (MTL)

Sometimes an old rookie (Moises was 25 this year) will turn in a season that looks awfully good for a rookie, but which would raise more questions for a veteran player of that age. This is one of them. Essentially, Moises is like Bernard Gilkey. He has marginal power and no strike zone judgment. The pitchers are going to adjust to that, and start throwing him garbage all over the place. He's going to have to prove he can hit that garbage. I'm afraid he looks like a GOOD SOPHOMORE SLUMP CANDIDATE to me, and I wouldn't gamble much on him in a fantasy league.

6. Darryl Boston (NYM-COL)

If you'll take a look at the TWAR numbers, you'll see that there are two superstar left fielders in the NL, and then there's this nosebleed drop to Bernard Gilkey. For Darryl Boston to rank in the middle of the pack just puts emphasis on the fact that this position is undermanned right now. The reason, oddly enough, is that few teams are doing what the Mets did here. Darryl Boston, you see, is fast enough, and his glove is good enough, that he can easily play center. To start him in left indicates that you don't think you need a good backup center fielder. The Mets, of course, were silly to think that, but then, their whole team was a mess of injuries and bad decisions last year.

Now, what used to happen was that there were these giant dinosaur hitters who were no way fast enough to play center. They got to play left field, and ranked high, because of their bats. But those guys get better training now, and can run better. Either that, or they go to the AL and play DH. Those turf outfields in the NL, you see, require more speed than Greg Luzinski ever had. And so, the only two real good left fielders are Barry Bonds, who is really a center fielder, but whose team had Andy Van Slyke, and Bip Roberts, who can play center as well. If Eric Davis had a healthy year, he'd probably rank up there, too.

By the way, I assume Darryl will be back in center for his new team.

7. Mariano Duncan (PHI)

The job now belongs to Milt Thompson. That's my idea of an outstanding mid-level free agent signing. Milt is surely better than Mariano Duncan, who ought to be the Phillies' shortstop, anyway. In addition, he can play center field; a useful quality in the face of Lenny Dykstra's style of play - on the baseball field, as well. I rate Pete Incaviglia as the backup left fielder / first baseman, by the way. If the Phillies actually install Inky in left and leave Thompson on the bench, they might as well not have signed Milt.

8. Luis Gonzalez (HOU)

Sophomore Slump. Younger than Moises Alou. PAY MORE FOR HIM THAN FOR MOISES. Likely to be the #4 man or so at this position in 1993. No, I don't think that Kevin Bass can take the job. I think the Astros think they're in contention, and have picked up Kevin and Jose Uribe as insurance.

9. Derrick May (CHI)

Very young, and the Cubs certainly have a place for him to play. On the other hand, he can't spell the term "take a pitch", and so I have him down for a SOPHOMORE SLUMP IN 1993. After that, though, he could turn out to be real good. Actually, I think I'd rather have him than either Moises Alou or Luis Gonzalez.

10. Jerald Clark (SD - COL)

Not to dis the man or anything, but Jerald Clark did just as much to hurt the Padre lineup as Fred McGriff did to help it. Having a hitter this bad in left field is the sort of thing that contenders, which the Padres thought they were, just don't do. Now, they've picked up Phil Plantier, and at least tried to fix the problem. But it's too late; the team's fire sale has clearly dragged them out of contention.

11. Eric Davis (LA)

If you've been reading these books for a couple of years now, you've gotten acquainted with my idea that there are some players who have just bodybuilt too much muscle onto their bone structures. By this, I don't mean that they've become musclebound or that they lack flexibility. On the contrary, modern bodybuilding techniques are well up to the task of producing a monstrously strong individual who is still completely loose in the joints. No, what I'm talking about is that a person's bones and ligaments and tendons can only take so much stress. If a person packs too much muscle onto that superstructure, he's eventually going to get injured. The more time his body spends in that condition, the more injuries he's going to get. That's what I'm talking about.

In case you're wondering why I'm writing this here, instead of under "Jose Canseco", it's because Eric Davis was the germ of this idea. The first time I looked at that body, the first thing that sprang to mind was "he's going to hurt himself with all those muscles on that tiny frame". Then I listened to the announcers talk about how he was going to be the next Mickey Mantle, and about how hard he plays and how he's willing to crash into walls to field fly balls. I shuddered in terror then, and his managers have been shuddering ever since.

Having said that, I stand by my opinion that Fred Claire was right to sign Eric Davis. Fred has to win now, to justify his job in that organization. His farm system isn't giving him the players it used to. He doesn't have the bats in the system to win, nor does he have the trade goods to get them. Yes, if he picks up Eric Davis, there's a chance this season will happen to him, and the Dodgers will be bad. But, if Eric lucks out, he and Darryl Strawberry can win the division for Fred. If Fred doesn't sign Eric, the Dodgers won't finish last, but they won't win either. Mitch Webster's best possible season just isn't going to do the trick. Eric Davis' best season will, and Fred Claire has to take that gamble.

12. Chris James (SF)

And to think that Roger Craig was crowing and trumpeting to the last about those mighty Cory Snyders and wonderful Mike Felders that he had acquired to take over Kevin Mitchell's job. It came down to this: Chris James. And a one-year blowout of Bill Swift's arm, spent starting when he could have had a fine career as a reliever. Let's face it. The last guy to have the same self-promotion to talent ratio that Roger Craig had was Ronald Reagan.

Center Fielders

Brock J. Hanke

		OWAR	DWAR	TWAR
1.	Puckett	6.11	1.40	7.51
2.	Griffey Jr	4.56	1.31	5.88
3.	Lofton	4.41	1.39	5.80
4.	Devereaux	4.51	.98	5.49
	Hamilton	3.54	1.70	5.24
5.	Yount	3.59	1.37	4.95
6.	Gonzalez Juan	4.06	.50	4.56
7.	White D	2.51	1.25	3.76
	Curtis C	2.51	.79	3.30
8.	Johnson L	1.84	1.41	3.24
9.	Kelly	2.05	.89	2.94
	Williams B	1.43	.77	2.20
10.	Wilson W	1.31	.87	2.17
11.	Felix	1.33	.83	2.16
12.	Zupcic	1.41	.65	2.06
13.	McRae B	.37	1.46	1.83
	Abner	.80	.66	1.46
	Burks	1.41	-.05	1.36
	Fox	.18	.38	.56
	Pettis	-.13	.52	.39
	Huff	-.51	.36	-.14
	Salmon	-.17	-.03	-.20
	Harris D	-.30	.08	-.22
	Cole	-.46	.05	-.41
	Winningham	-.83	.29	-.54
14.	Cuyler	-1.12	.43	-.69

1. Kirby Puckett (MIN)

Boy, it's hard to score 100 runs while walking only 44 times, 13 of them intentional. You either have to hit 40 homers or hit in a very bizarre position in the batting order. Kirby is, by distribution of talent, a #5 batter. But he's so good a hitter that he gets batted in spots where runs are scored, rather than just driven in. Of course, it didn't hurt that he played 160 games, either.

In general, what is happening to Kirby is that his skills are turning from those of a young man to those of an older player. His peak season occurred right on schedule, at age 27, in 1988. The next year, he dropped off badly, but posted a career high in doubles, which is the power/speed stat. Since then, his doubles have gone down and his homers have gone up.

Normally, a player will lose about 2 doubles for every homer, but Kirby has traded them even up. Actually, he's lost only 7 doubles from his peak, but has gained ten home runs from that low of 9 in 1989.

Now, as long as Kirby can do that, he's going to keep getting better, defying the whole concept of decline phase. At the rate he's going, he'll have his career year in 1994. But that's just not going to happen. What's going to happen, unless Kirby is not an actual homo sapiens, is that the power gain will level off, while the speed loss will accelerate. I would be very surprised if Kirby ever equals his 1992 season again. Since there are people in your fantasy league who think that he will one day equal 1988, he's a BAD FANTASY BUY. That's not because he's "bad", but because he can't be as good as some of your bidding competition think he is.

2. Ken Griffey, Jr. (SEA)

What appears to have happened here is that Junior decided to respond to being batted third instead of leadoff. He started swinging at more pitches, in an attempt to drive his RBI stats up. That accounts for his 27-walk drop, and probably the drop in Batting Average as well. As you can imagine, I don't think much of the decision. I expect that Junior will reverse it, and return to the steady gain in hitting quality that you expect of a man this young. In any case, Ken's power still seems on that steady rise, so he's going to continue to be a top player. I would be very surprised not to see him atop these rankings once again next year.

3. Kenny Lofton (CLE)

Sort of the mirror image on Ken Griffey, Jr. He's got Junior's normal walks, but the Batting Average and power are just not there. For him to rank up there with Griffey is a fluke of playing time; he's nothing like that good. That's not to mention that he's three years older, and very close to his peak.

I wouldn't be surprised to see him succumb to Sophomore Slump next year. He was promoted straight to AAA ball from Class A, and then to the Majors a year later. So far, he's handled it, but this is the first time a league's worth of pitchers has seen him two years in a row. Major League pitchers adjust, while Kenny has had no chance to learn to counter-adjust. I'm not going to guarantee that, though. Operating against the slump are two factors. First, Kenny will be 26, which is a year that usually sees a jump in hitting quality. And second, Kenny does have a batting eye. The pitchers may adjust to what he can hit, but they're going to have to adjust with strikes. Some of them won't be able to do that; the only pitches they can throw for strikes will be the ones that Kenny can hit. He'll still be able to hit those men, and that will soften the problems caused by adjustment.

Now, in terms of the Indians contending, they're going to need Kenny Lofton at full value.

Center Field	G	PO	A	Er	TC	DP	FPct	DI	DG	DW%	DWAR
Bell D	18	38	1	0	39	0	1.000	105.0	.4	.844	.21
Blankenship L	16	29	0	1	30	0	.967	108.2	.4	.274	-.03
Browne J	23	48	0	0	48	0	1.000	161.1	.7	.584	.15
Burks	63	122	3	2	127	0	.984	535.2	2.2	.326	-.05
Cangelosi	24	35	2	0	37	1	1.000	121.0	.5	.769	.21
Cotto	30	50	0	0	50	0	1.000	162.1	.7	.581	.15
Curtis C	35	78	3	2	83	0	.976	278.1	1.1	.479	.15
Cuyler	88	233	4	4	241	1	.983	733.2	3.0	.491	.43
Devereaux	155	431	5	5	441	3	.989	1396.0	5.7	.521	.98
Felix	125	334	9	6	349	3	.983	1076.2	4.4	.531	.80
Fox	19	45	1	1	47	0	.979	132.1	.5	.583	.13
Gladden	17	24	0	0	24	0	1.000	121.2	.5	.393	.02
Gonzalez Juan	123	309	6	8	323	1	.975	1023.1	4.2	.415	.28
Griffey Jr	137	358	8	1	367	4	.997	1187.0	4.9	.617	1.30
Hamilton	32	79	0	0	79	0	1.000	226.0	.9	.717	.34
Hatcher B	13	29	0	1	30	0	.967	106.1	.4	.266	-.04
Howard T	22	44	1	0	45	0	1.000	177.2	.7	.526	.13
Hulse	29	58	0	1	59	0	.983	194.0	.8	.383	.03
Johnson L	157	433	11	6	450	4	.987	1364.0	5.6	.601	1.41
Kelly	99	286	6	5	297	3	.983	877.1	3.6	.547	.71
Koslofski	18	53	1	1	55	0	.982	136.0	.6	.660	.17
Lofton	143	419	14	8	441	4	.982	1256.1	5.2	.621	1.40
McRae B	148	421	8	3	432	2	.993	1283.1	5.3	.624	1.45
Pettis	46	144	2	1	147	0	.993	389.1	1.6	.669	.51
Phillips	24	48	1	0	49	0	1.000	169.0	.7	.603	.18
Puckett	149	394	9	3	406	3	.993	1274.2	5.2	.616	1.39
White D	152	443	8	7	458	2	.985	1307.0	5.4	.579	1.23
Williams B	55	169	3	1	173	1	.994	485.1	2.0	.671	.64
Wilson W	118	351	2	7	360	1	.981	903.0	3.7	.576	.84
Winningham	32	51	3	2	56	0	.964	227.1	.9	.353	.00
Yount	139	371	6	2	379	0	.995	1196.0	4.9	.628	1.36
Zupcic	68	172	6	5	183	1	.973	575.1	2.4	.497	.35
TOTALS		6412	129	90	6631	37	.986	1460.1	6.0	4.829	26.87

Their backup center fielder is Thomas Howard, who ain't great. Their mass accumulation of left and right fielders hasn't produced the big power core they need yet. If they're to have a big time offense, they need to either get lucky with one of the outfielders, or to beat everyone to death with their strength up the middle. Since Sandy Alomar, Jr. isn't going to do that, and Mark Lewis is an unlikely candidate, that leaves it up to Carlos Baerga and Lofton. Carlos is going to come through, which makes the whole plan pivot on what Kenny is capable of.

4. Mike Devereaux (BAL)

What you've got here is a 30-year-old ballplayer who has been steadily improving since his age 27 year. Now, that 1990 season was a problem year, and Mike probably should have been in the Major Leagues a couple of years before he was promoted, but still, there's a limit to how long this can go on. Right now, Mike has more value than he did when he was 26, which was his previous career year. I think that's the sign that he's topped out. I think he will restart the

decline phase of his career in 1993. That makes him a FANTASY BAD BUY, and a likely disappointment to the Orioles, who are starting to expect Mike to get better every year, as if for all the world he'd been 20 years old when he was a rookie.

5. Robin Yount (MIL)

Just for fun, I thought I'd compute the approximate chance that Robin Yount will get 4,000 hits. The approved Bill James tool for this is called The Favorite Toy. Here's how it works:

1) List the hits needed to reach the goal. In this case, Robin has 3025 hits, and so needs 975.

2) Figure out how many seasons Robin has left to play by using the formula 24 - (.6 x age). Robin was 36 last year, so it's 24 - (.6 x 36) = 2.4

3) Establish how many hits we can expect each year from Robin. The formula is to take Robin's hits two years ago, add twice his hits

a year ago, and three times his hits this year, and divide the sum by 6. That's (145 + 2x131 + 3x147) / 6 = 141.3. We then have to check that this is over 75% of last year's performance, but it is far over, so 141.3 is what we use.

4) Compute Robin's projected remaining hits. That's computed as remaining years times established hit performance. In this case, that's 2.4 x 141.3 = 339. You can see immediately that 339 is a lot less than 975, so the chance is not going to be all that high.

5) To be exact, the chance is computed by the following formula: Divide the projected hits by the hits needed and subtract 0.5. Here, that's (339 / 975) - 0.5 = -.15. That's right, the chance is negative. On the off chance that the formula printed in the BASEBALL ABSTRACTs was wrong, I took the square root of the 339 / 975 figure. That's a standard procedure in statistics, and it gives .59. That would give Robin a 9% chance of getting the 4,000 hits.

Frankly, I prefer the negative figure. Robin is

coming up on age 37. If he does get 141 hits a year, it will take him almost exactly 7 years to get to 4,000. That would be ages 37 through 43. At age 43, Ty Cobb had just quit the game. He had averaged 131 hits per year in the preceding four years, which is the equivalent of 141 in a 162-game campaign, but he was gone, and he was Ty Cobb. Pete Rose was 43 years old in 1984. That was the year the Expos tried him and then traded him back to Cincinnati, where he insisted on playing himself despite the fact that he was clearly through. He did get 107 hits that year, but only 15 of them were doubles, and there were no homers. He was playing first base, and he was the worst in the league at it. The preceding four years, he had averaged 154 hits per year. And that's an underestimate; one of those years was 1981.

It is possible. Robin Yount could be the next Pete Rose. But he's going to have to want it bad. He's going to have to want it so bad he'll manage a team to get himself playing time. That's because, in 7 years, Robin is not going to be the #5 center fielder in his league. He's not going to be in center field, and he's not going to be #5 at the position he's at.

And he's probably not going to be getting 150 hits a year, either. When Pete Rose was 37, his established level of hits per year was 203. He was still hitting .300, and still getting 40 or more doubles a year. Robin's going to have to find the Fountain of Youth.

6.   Juan Gonzalez (TEX)

Juan would sure move up in the rankings here if he were played somewhere he could handle defensively. It would also help if he could get himself established. The Texas ballpark is supposed to help hitters, not leave them with a 19/24 home/road split in home runs. On the other hand, leading the league in road homers, when you play in a hitters' park, is a good leading indicator of improved performance. And there's more. You have to figure that a player who is hitting about .260 for average, and who never takes a walk, and who hits for big home run power, is either going to collapse or stride forward. Well, the AL pitchers have tried for two years now to figure out what sort of ball he can't hit, to no effect at all. I expect Juan's average to take a big step forward in 1993, and so rate him as a GOOD FANTASY BUY, as well as a top emerging hitter. If the Rangers move him to left or right, I'm even more sanguine, as I think the lessened defensive responsibility will help him concentrate at the plate.

7.   Devon White (TOR)

Back to reality. This and nothing else is Devon White's established level of ability. I would like to say here and now that Paul Molitor is a better leadoff man than this, and Roberto Alomar is a better #2 batter than this, and so on until Devon White is batting about #6 for the Blue Jays if I'm Cito Gaston.

8.   Lance Johnson (CHA)

Remains the Gold Glove in center. Also remains no offensive force; he's 29 now, and this is as good as it's going to get. The Chisox would probably be better off giving Warren Newson a chance, but they're probably going to play Lance here, Tim Raines, and Ellis Burks.

9.   Roberto Kelly (NYY - CIN)

Well, that was age 27. What I think is that he hasn't fully recovered from his difficulties of 1991. I wouldn't be at all surprised to see him return to his stats of 1989, with more power. That would be a decent hitter, but it still wouldn't crack the Top Five at this position. Basically, since he did not just move up from the '89 campaign, he's established himself as a middle-of-the-pack guy. With Cincinnati, that isn't enough to beat out Reggie Sanders, unless the management just decrees that it be so. Hmm. This is Cincinnati we're talking about here, and Roberto's a big name acquisition.

Well, between Roberto and Reggie, I don't expect either of them to play full time. That makes both of them BAD FANTASY BUYS.

10.   Willie Wilson (OAK)

Whee! What fun! Willie Wilson was through as a center fielder, and as a starting player for that matter, in 1991. Then Dave Henderson got hurt, and the A's had to play him full time, in center, for a division-winning year. Now, the Cubbies have had collective brain damage and, thinking that they're going to contend with a two-man offense, have picked up Willie for - you guessed it - starting center field. How long can this continue? How long can the Lords of Baseball conspire to keep Willie starting in center? There are these expansion teams....

11.   Senior Felix (CAL - FLA)

Whitey Herzog's team may have been bad, but he has his pride. Junior Felix in center field is beneath it, as Whitey let everyone know as soon as he hit Anaheim. Just in from the national media is a report that Junior has lied about his age. He's apparently at least 30, and maybe more. You know, his career would make sense if he were turning 30. That would place his best year, the 1990 season, at age 27.

12.   Bob Zupcic (BOS)

At age 26, a Grade C prospect. The Bosox will probably throw him out there again, though. What else do they have left?

13.   Brian McRae (KC)

Brian McRae has exactly one year left to avoid getting his father fired.

14.   Milt Cuyler (DET)

A Grade B prospect, playing in the Majors because Sparky got silly. At age 24, he should still be seasoning in AAA ball. It's not his fault he has to try to hit Major League pitching.

Center Fielders

Brock J. Hanke

		OWAR	DWAR	TWAR
1.	Lankford	6.72	1.57	8.29
2.	Van Slyke	6.69	1.43	8.12
3.	Butler	6.74	.84	7.58
4.	Finley S	5.14	1.33	6.47
5.	Grissom	4.66	.64	5.30
	Sanders R	3.81	.96	4.77
6.	Nixon O	2.69	1.36	4.05
7.	Dykstra	2.98	.85	3.83
	Sanders	2.98	.36	3.34
8.	Martinez Da	1.61	.70	2.31
9.	Johnson H	2.25	0	2.25
10.	Jackson Dar	.02	2.13	2.15
	Coleman	1.93	.17	2.10
11.	Lewis D	.63	.88	1.51
	Cole	.80	.40	1.20
12.	Dascenzo	.85	.27	1.12
	Thompson R	.30	.25	.55
	Gallagher	.18	.36	.54
	Carr	.20	.19	.39
	Goodwin	.02	.09	.11
	Howell P	-.42	.26	-.16
	Castillo Br	-.36	.07	-.29
	Young G	-.42	.10	-.32
	Walton	-.39	-.01	-.40

1. Ray Lankford (STL)

I confess that this ranking still astonishes me. I had absolutely no idea that Ray was turning in a season as good as Andy Van Slyke's. But checking the ballpark adjustment tells the tale. Busch Stadium was a virtually neutral park this year, due to the Cardinals' moving in the outfield fences. Ray Lankford's raw power stats are 40 doubles, 6 triples and 20 home runs. After adjustment, these become 40, 6 and 21. That's virtually no change. Three Rivers Stadium, on the other hand, was a hitters' park for lefties like Andy, and his 45 doubles, 12 triples and 14 homers convert to 41, 9, and 17. That looks much more like Lankford's totals. Overall, the two of them had close to the same number of Runs Created, and similar numbers of Outs made. That will produce a similar OWAR every time.

As for defense, Ray's numbers may be mis-leading. The raw stats have him down for huge quantities of putouts. Busch saw the highest total of fly balls and popups of any ballpark in the league. The actual ground ball / fly ball ratio was not the lowest NL figure, though it was one of the low ones. However, the Cards trailed the league in strikeouts, and so the fly ball raw total is the highest. What is suspicious is the STATS zone figures. All the while Ray was piling up those putouts, the zone method was not giving him great numbers in terms of percentage caught within his center field zone.

There could be two explanations for this. First, the ballpark could just be generating huge numbers of flies, and Ray's totals could be nothing more than the result of all the chances he had. The second possibility is that Ray plays center field oddly, and does not get his chances in a normal distribution. In the absence of other data, I have to go with the second, and treat Ray's defensive stats with respect. Not

all center fielders line up in the same place, and not all fly balls are equal. If Ray were confronting a lot of hard line drives within the zone, or if he were playing over in left center and right center a lot of the time, his zone totals would be artificially low. As long as we don't know what actually happened, I think we have to say that we don't care where the balls that Ray caught were hit. He caught them. They were outs. They helped the team just as much as flies caught in the zone would have.

Clearly, if Ray is for real at this level of play, he's one of the most valuable players in the league, especially since he's just now coming up on age 26. And in fact, no one of his totals seems unreasonable. He's just five doubles, a couple of triples and five homers better than all the predictions had him down for. Oh yes, and about 20 or 25 walks. Ray's never had much plate discipline before, but this year manager Joe Torre decided to start out with Ray leading off. The avowed purpose of this was to get Ray to learn to take pitches and get on base, so he could use his speed. Well, Ray's no base stealer, speed or not, but he did take some walks for a while. Unfortunately, his walking ability did wear off as the season wore on. His 41 in 1991 are a much better number to use in your predictions than this year's 72.

2. Andy Van Slyke (PIT)

Last year, I offhandedly remarked that we could forget about Andy's 1989 injury. I should have spent more time discussing the topic. What happened was this. Andy got hurt pretty bad, but insisted on playing through the pain. He was bad, and some people had him down for a quick decline phase. His 1990 comeback was only partial, and things did not improve in 1991. But this year, the comeback finally was complete. This year is not completely out of whack for Andy Van Slyke. It's completely consistent with his 1987 and 1988 years, before the injury. It just took him this long to get back to full speed. WORTH THE PRICE IN A FANTASY LEAGUE, IF YOU CAN'T GET LANKFORD.

Center Field	G	PO	A	Er	TC	DP	FPct	DI	DG	DW%	DWAR
Amaro	27	60	1	1	62	0	.984	203.1	.8	.452	.08
Butler	155	354	9	2	365	2	.995	1318.1	5.4	.502	.82
Coleman	21	58	0	0	58	0	1.000	174.1	.7	.624	.20
Dascenzo	80	177	1	3	181	0	.983	634.2	2.6	.412	.16
Dykstra	85	252	6	3	261	4	.989	750.2	3.1	.618	.83
Felder	58	106	1	1	108	0	.991	376.1	1.5	.474	.19
Finley S	160	417	8	3	428	3	.993	1352.1	5.6	.589	1.33
Gant	23	40	2	0	42	1	1.000	141.1	.6	.759	.24
Grissom	157	402	7	7	416	2	.983	1402.1	5.8	.462	.64
Howell P	28	66	0	0	66	0	1.000	176.2	.7	.700	.25
Jackson Dar	152	425	18	2	445	7	.996	1338.1	5.5	.733	2.10
Javier	51	148	5	3	156	1	.981	398.0	1.6	1.312	1.57
Johnson H	84	181	3	3	187	0	.984	713.0	2.9	.345	-.02
Lankford	153	439	5	2	446	1	.996	1369.0	5.6	.633	1.59
Lewis D	94	224	3	0	227	2	1.000	720.1	3.0	.648	.88
Martinez Da	105	212	5	2	219	1	.991	718.2	3.0	.560	.62
McGee	31	66	2	0	68	1	1.000	248.1	1.0	.627	.28
Nixon O	102	291	6	2	299	2	.993	826.0	3.4	.723	1.27
Sanders	60	137	2	2	141	0	.986	477.1	2.0	.465	.23
Sanders R	77	205	8	6	219	3	.973	600.2	2.5	.620	.67
Smith Dw	27	51	1	1	53	0	.981	198.0	.8	.395	.04
Sosa	67	145	4	6	155	1	.961	573.1	2.4	.341	-.02
Thompson R	26	62	1	1	64	0	.984	185.0	.8	.524	.13
Van Slyke	154	421	11	5	437	3	.989	1373.2	5.6	.606	1.45
TOTALS		5324	114	61	5499	36	.989	1461.0	6.0	4.158	22.85

3. Brett Butler (LA)

TO: The Sportswriters of America
FROM: Bobby Cox

No, no, you guys. It was a JOKE! I didn't mean to send a utility man to the All-Star game! I just wanted to point out that the Dodgers had lost their Bonds and Bonilla, so you can see what the Pirates are going to be like in 1993. I didn't mean for you to HOLD me to that list. Of COURSE Brett Butler's an All-Star. Do you think I could be blind to a man who has turned out the exact same season since he was operating under the name "Roy Thomas"? Just send him out there, and we'll use him to pinch hit when we need to get a man on base, or when we need to squeeze.

Thanks,
Your Pal,

Bobby

4. Steve Finley (HOU)

This was his age-27 year, and so I don't expect him to hold quite this value. Still, it's a lot better than I thought he would do when he came over from Baltimore. If you look at his career without ballpark adjustments, you'd think he was reading the Brock2 system ahead of time. His seasons just seem to chug right along, increasing just like the system says they should. But that's wrong. There's a big jump there, from Baltimore to Houston and the dreaded Dome. That increase in production Steve made back in 1991 was BIG. And it is the Dome. Steve's home/road splits this year are truly bizarre for some one in this ballpark. Simply put, Steve hits better in the Dome, and he hits for more power there as well. If the 'Stros do get into contention, he'll be a major cog.

5. Marquis Grissom (MTL)

For a lot of the year, the NL sportswriters compared the base stealing totals of the Cardinals and the Expos, as the two big running teams. Well, they couldn't be any more different. The Cardinals run out of some half-remembered compulsion left over from the Whitey Herzog era, when they actually had players like Vince Coleman and Tommy Herr. Everybody on the team runs, and they don't run well, except for Ozzie, who is Whitey's last holdover. Sure, they steal 208 bases, but they get caught 118 times, so it's not clear whether the effort helps or hurts the team. The success ratio, 64%, is below the theoretical break-even point. Actually, I think it hurts, as all that running causes some wear and tear on the Redbird legs.

The Expos, on the other hand, only have two men who run at all: Delino DeShields and Marquis here. And those two are great. Between them, they stole 124 bases, and only got caught 28 times. That's a combined 82% success ratio. The team as a whole stole 196, while getting caught 63 times. That's a fine 76% for the team; but more importantly, it's only 107 attempts total for the players other than DeShields and Grissom.

The Cardinals top two, meanwhile, were Ozzie Smith and Ray Lankford. Combined, they went 85 and 33, which is only 72%, or worse than the Expo team as a whole. Only Ozzie (43 and 9) is a serious base stealer by the standards of the Expos. And worse, the rest of the team attempted 208 steals, with a pitiful 59% success rate. The Expos are the only team in baseball that uses the stolen base as a real weapon.

6. Otis Nixon (ATL)

Otis would have ranked higher, if he'd played more, but whose fault is that? Essentially, the main difference between Nixon and Brett Butler is that Brett is a LOT more consistent, and bunts a little bit better. Frankly, Deion Sanders is better than either one, as long as he's healthy. Bo knows.

7. Lenny Dykstra (PHI)

I have to admit, I don't like this guy. He's exploiting his ballpark for what little power he has (17/5 home run home/road ratio in Philadelphia). His reputation is largely based on the age-27 career year. People just assume he's going to go back to that level as soon as he gets healthy. I've got two things to say about that. First, what makes you think he's ever going to be healthy? He plays crazy and he lives crazy - a lot crazier than Steve Howe lives, no matter how legal Lenny's addiction is. And second, what makes you think that career year is his sustainable level? There's no evidence for that except that he's never had a full healthy season since. That means you can't test the hypothesis that he's not that good, but it doesn't mean you should discard theory. In fact, if you can't test the hypothesis, you should go with theory. And theory says that the age-27 year was his peak, and he's past it.

All this is not to say Lenny's a bad player. He's probably capable of coming in as high as 4th at this position. But not usually. Center field is a strong spot right now, because everybody who can hit is getting put through good training programs, so all of them can run, too. If Lenny costs as much in your fantasy league as he does in most, AVOID HIM IN FANTASY BALL.

8.   Dave Martinez (CIN-SF)

FANTASY COMMENT: I THINK HE'S A RESERVE FOR THE GIANTS. Let's face it, he's not going to beat out Barry Bonds. And if the new management uses him as an excuse to stifle Darren Lewis, they're just being dumb. That leaves right field, where he gets to compete with Willie McGee. Now, I've seen Willie play his clubhouse politics. Dave's a reserve.

9.   Howard Johnson (NYM)

Will return to third base this year. Dave Magadan's gone. He should return to something like the average of 1988 through 1991. That's 33 homers, 35 doubles, a .260 average, 100+ runs, and 100+ RBI. I'll take it. A GOOD FANTASY BUY, because there will be some doubters who won't bid on him. Frankly, the Met power core is not the problem. Bobby Bonilla was not that far off form, and certainly didn't decimate the lineup. Eddie Murray is who he is and as old as he is and also does not hurt you. Hojo should be fine. The question is whether they will have Tony Fernandez leading off and consuming outs in job lots, or whether they can find someone who can really get on base.

The center field job apparently belongs to Ryan Thompson, acquired from the Blue Jays. Thompson's MLE calls for .260, with 12 homers, in the Skydome. He hit .222 in his cup of coffee with the Mets, with three homers, projecting to maybe 16 in a full season. Believe the MLE.

10.   Darrin Jackson (SD)

The sad thing is that Padre fans think this man's a star. The ballpark gives him a good bit of his home run power. Now that pitchers have adjusted to his pop, they've started throwing him sinking stuff, so he led the league in double plays. He won't take a walk. His average ain't that great and he don't hit doubles or triples. The only thing he does really well is steal bases, and he only tries that 20 times a year. Yes, his defense is outstanding, but hitting him #5 in your lineup is the same think as hitting Benito Santiago there. It assures you of a four-man offense.

11.   Darren Lewis (SF)

A perfectly respectable center field / leadoff man prospect, who deserves at least one full season without pressure to see what he actually has. Perhaps, now that Roger Craig is gone, the Giants won't think they're contending for the pennant without a full house, and will give him that chance. On the other hand, perhaps Barry Bonds will hypnotize them into thinking they can overtake the Braves without any pitching. In that case, Dave Martinez will get the job, and Lewis will be wasted. I guess you can figure out what I'd do. Dusty Baker thinks he's going to get a hundred Runs Scored out of Willie McGee leading off.

12.   Doug Dascenzo (CHN-released)

Right now, the Cubbie center fielder is Willie Wilson. If you had told me, two years ago, that I would be threatened with writing another comment on Willie Wilson, I'd have laughed in your face. If you'd told me he wouldn't be on an expansion team, well....

Ryne Sandberg should sue the Tribune for non-support.

Right Fielders

Brock J. Hanke

		OWAR	DWAR	TWAR
1.	Tartabull	4.86	.19	5.05
2.	Carter J	3.82	.82	4.64
3.	Brunansky	3.70	.53	4.22
4.	Buhner	2.67	1.54	4.21
5.	Sierra	3.81	.30	4.11
6.	Orsulak	2.99	.97	3.96
7.	Deer	3.10	.79	3.88
8.	Canseco	2.99	.63	3.62
9.	Whiten	1.64	1.30	2.94
10.	Bichette	2.08	.72	2.80
	Plantier	1.53	.53	2.05
11.	Eisenreich	1.55	.47	2.02
	Martinez C	1.46	.36	1.82
12.	Munoz P	.70	.82	1.52
13.	Hayes Von	1.01	.24	1.25
	Larkin G	.64	.40	1.05
14.	Pasqua	.75	.28	1.03
	Newson	.41	.42	.83
	Gonzalez Jo	-.34	.12	-.22
	Howitt	-.64	.26	-.38
	Bush	-.88	.13	-.75
	Barfield Je	-.95	.19	-.76
	Brooks	-.97	.01	-.96

1. Danny Tartabull (NYY)

Had his career year one season late, due to injury. But, then, "due to injury" is just about the story of Danny's life, isn't it? I expect him to hold this year's home run totals, as long as he doesn't go back to Kansas City or to some other similar ballpark. And I expect the doubles total to move back up into the 25 range. This year's injury doesn't seem to have done his running speed any good, but he should recover. On the other hand, Yankee stadium is not a good doubles park for right handed hitters, so 25 is all I really expect.

As far as value predictions go, the first thing you have to do is write him down for only 130 games. He's only been over 150 once in his life, and only over 140 one other time. His high for the last four years is 133. Actually, 120 would be a better average than 130, but you write 130 in because that's a full season to Danny. For those 130 games, he should per-

form at about this level or a little higher. If you're the real manager of the Yankees, what you've got to do is assure yourself of a good backup for the 30 or more games you know Danny's going to miss. If you're a fantasy manager, you can figure in some extra value, as you'll get at least 25 games of someone else, in addition to what Danny gives you himself.

Overall, Danny's probably going to help you, in reality or fantasy, about as much as any other AL outfielder can assure you, except Ken Griffey. Jr. The other people in this class are either old or injury-prone or both. A couple of them will surely produce more than this, but you don't know which two or three it will be. Betting on Brady Anderson, Tim Raines and Kirby Puckett to repeat is not a good idea. Since most people don't think of Danny as being in anything like this class, he's a GOOD FANTASY BUY, unless you've got a Danny Tartabull nut out there.

2. Joe Carter (TOR)

The second-highest TWAR among right fielders shouldn't be in the 4's. But Dave Winfield has moved to DH, and Shane Mack has moved to left, and so there we are. As I've said before in these comments, Joe Carter is my idea of an ideal #5 batter. Any reasonable look at his 1992 season next to Dave Winfield's will tell you that Dave should have been batting ahead of Joe. Of course, the question Cito has to face this year is whether John Olerud will really produce close enough to what Joe Carter does to be placed ahead of him regardless of the distribution of skills. I think he will. I don't see 3.82 OWAR as any big challenge. Joe Carter doesn't hit for any average, and he doesn't take any walks, and so he doesn't get on base much. That means he consumes an awful lot of outs. His offensive value is all in his power. Use it to drive in runs, I say. Bat the guys who take the walks in front of all those homers.

3. Tom Brunansky (BOS - MIL)

Usually, when Tom Brunansky has a good season, it's easy to find the hot streak that did the job. That didn't happen this year, although his power all came in one summer splash. Instead, Bruno just turned in a fine, fine year, given all expectations. Now, of course, you can't count on his repeating it; and, even if he did, it would not be enough to restore the vaunted Bosox offense to supremacy. What it did do, though, is make Tom a couple of million more dollars than he would have made had he continued his steady decline.

4. Jay Buhner (SEA)

This was the age-27 season. While it wasn't any big leap forward, it was compatible with his age-26 season, and can therefore be reliably assumed to represent Jay's peak. That is, he should not be quite able to maintain this level of play.

Right now, that's not really adequate. Jay needs to regain his ability to hit .270 for average, without losing the power. I give that about a 30% chance. The high averages of three years ago were likely due to platooning.

Right Field	G	PO	A	Er	TC	DP	FPct	DI	DG	DW%	DWAR
Abner	75	93	2	0	95	0	1.000	351.0	1.2	.703	.42
Baines	17	19	0	1	20	0	.950	100.0	.3	.234	-.04
Barfield Je	30	53	3	2	58	0	.966	236.0	.8	.580	.19
Bichette	101	186	6	2	194	3	.990	846.0	2.9	.597	.72
Blankenship L	20	29	1	1	31	0	.968	101.0	.3	.653	.10
Brunansky	92	189	6	4	199	2	.980	784.1	2.7	.537	.50
Buhner	150	312	14	2	328	4	.994	1325.1	4.5	.686	1.52
Bush	21	26	0	0	26	0	1.000	114.1	.4	.585	.09
Canseco	90	195	5	3	203	3	.985	766.2	2.6	1.060	1.86
Carreon	19	39	0	1	40	0	.975	138.0	.5	.479	.06
Carter J	123	246	10	8	264	2	.970	1043.2	3.6	.570	.79
Curtis C	62	101	11	1	113	3	.991	448.2	1.5	.783	.67
Deer	106	229	8	4	241	1	.983	919.0	3.1	.596	.77
Eisenreich	66	125	1	1	127	1	.992	499.0	1.7	.526	.30
Fox	16	22	1	0	23	0	1.000	109.0	.4	.690	.13
Gwynn C	14	21	0	0	21	0	1.000	115.1	.4	.462	.04
Hall M	37	63	1	1	65	1	.985	302.0	1.0	.395	.05
Hamilton	74	151	8	0	159	0	1.000	599.0	2.1	.890	1.11
Hayes V	85	169	1	3	173	0	.983	681.2	2.3	.445	.22
Howard T	13	26	1	0	27	0	1.000	106.0	.4	.763	.15
Huff	45	57	2	0	59	0	1.000	236.1	.8	.758	.33
James D	27	40	1	0	41	0	1.000	166.0	.6	.644	.17
Koslofski	23	35	3	0	38	0	1.000	149.0	.5	.910	.29
Larkin G	43	53	5	1	59	1	.983	286.0	1.0	.664	.31
Martinez C	52	104	4	3	111	1	.973	426.0	1.5	.597	.36
McReynolds	12	19	0	1	20	0	.950	109.2	.4	.179	-.06
Mercedes	13	34	2	2	38	0	.947	100.2	.3	.792	.15
Munoz P	117	214	8	3	225	3	.987	920.1	3.2	.608	.81
Newson	33	48	2	0	50	0	1.000	217.1	.7	.744	.29
Orsulak	98	203	8	3	214	1	.986	812.1	2.8	.678	.91
Pasqua	81	152	4	6	162	0	.963	622.0	2.1	.473	.26
Phillips	35	90	2	4	96	0	.958	259.2	.9	.608	.23
Plantier	63	128	6	2	136	1	.985	529.2	1.8	.661	.56
Salmon	21	40	1	2	43	1	.953	189.1	.6	.303	-.03
Samuel	18	26	2	3	31	0	.903	137.0	.5	.453	.05
Segui	15	27	1	0	28	0	1.000	103.0	.4	.825	.17
Sierra	144	284	6	7	297	0	.976	1269.1	4.3	1.032	2.97
Tartabull	68	135	3	3	141	1	.979	599.1	2.1	.434	.17
Thurman	59	122	5	2	129	0	.984	436.1	1.5	.732	.57
Whiten	144	321	14	7	342	2	.980	1278.1	4.4	.648	1.30
Winfield	26	52	1	0	53	0	1.000	217.1	.7	.637	.21
Zupcic	22	29	1	0	30	1	1.000	121.1	.4	.701	.15
TOTALS		4854	172	92	5118	38	.982	1460.1	5.0	3.191	14.21

It's an odd sort of platoon, in that Jay doesn't hit lefty pitching well, rather than the righties you think he'd have trouble with, but it's not the hand that makes the difference. The pitchers Jay can't hit are the fly ball pitchers. And that's really odd, since Jay is a marked fly ball hitter. Apparently, Jay hasn't got much accuracy in swinging at those high pitches, but he does have a good golf swing. Either that, or high heat is just too fast for him; he might lack bat speed.

The scouting reports don't tell me anything here. No one comments on his swing. They simply comment on the low average and high power combination. The result is that I can't

really judge if the one idea I have could help Jay. The idea is to use his batting eye to lay off high heat. Jay already takes a good number of walks; if he could get even better at it, his On-Base Percentage could go up without his having to learn how to hit any type of pitch. That would put him in the Jack Clark class of hitters, or perhaps the class beneath that one. As it is, he's at least two classes beneath Clark at the same age.

5. Ruben Sierra (TEX/OAK)

Believe it or not, Ruben is just now coming up on age 27. He was a 20-year-old rookie and a full time player at age 21. His big year came

when he was just 23. It was fueled by a ridiculous 21 homers in his home ballpark, and I think expectations ran too high. He's certainly unlikely to hit 30 taters in Oakland. But he might turn in a year that superficially resembles his 1991 season in Texas. In Oakland, that would be a monster. It would surely return him to the top of the heap at this position.

If you're in fantasy ball, you have to rate him a BAD BUY, because the switch from Texas to Oakland is such an uphill climb for a hitter that you can't expect his raw totals to hold up unless he does have the super year. And that's a slam on the fantasy games. Since they don't adjust for ballparks, they don't really rate players accurately. All the hitters in Oakland are rated too low, while all the men in Texas are overrated.

Of course that applies in reverse to Jose Canseco. Why wouldn't it?

6. Joe Orsulak (BAL - NYM)

Orsulak will certainly help the Mets, although he won't be Darryl Strawberry and Keith Hernandez combined. But he's been very consistent, and he's at that age - 30 - where consistency is most likely. The Mets could use some of that.

7. Rob Deer (DET)

Had the highest Batting Average he's had since age 27. Had the highest On-Base Percentage he's had since age 26. Had the highest Slugging Percentage he's ever had. If you think he's going to keep that up, I can't help you. Basically, Rob Deer is bulk outfielding, which is no more and no less useful than bulk pitching. If you start him, you're in trouble. If he's your bench, he helps. Says a lot about the Tigers, doesn't it?

8. Jose Canseco (OAK/TEX)

There's age-27 years, and then there are injury-prone ballplayers. If you've read much of this book before now, you know that I discuss Jose Canseco in a group with Eric Davis and Dave Justice. All three of them look to me like they have too much muscle on their bodies for their bone structures to support. This is the result of too much bodybuilding. None of the three is musclebound or inflexible, or anything like the opponents of weightlifting were expecting; they just keep tearing ligaments and tendons and cracking bones by putting too much stress on those body parts.

Does this mean that I want to write Jose Canseco off as an injury case? No, absolutely not. Jose has a wonderful record of recovery years. He probably has a peak of value that he didn't display last year that is waiting to burst forth. He's also just moved from Oakland to Texas; from one of the worst hitters' parks in baseball to one of the best.

THE ABSOLUTE BEST SUPER YEAR GAMBLE AVAILABLE.

It's no lock, but Jose Canseco is by far the best bet in the game to turn in some really extraordinary, record setting year in 1993.

9. Mark Whiten (CLE)

Cleveland loyalists were all over the press last year, expecting Mark Whiten to just explode all over the statistics of the game and carry them to newfound glory. Well, it didn't happen. If Mark makes a good stride forward, he reaches the middle of the pack. If he makes another at age 27 (1993), he'll get above average. But his chances of becoming a superstar are minimal. Face it, Indians fans, there just isn't a roster full of cleanup hitters waiting there for you.

10. Dante Bichette (MIL - COL)

Bulk outfielding. If you start him....

11. Jim Eisenreich (KC - PHI)

I admit to rooting shamelessly for this man to overcome his illness. Still, he never has had any power, and he never has taken any walks, and there's only so much of that you can stand for in the outfield. Jim has to hit at least .290 to really help your team. I expect him to be the Phillies' outfield bench in 1993; and I think that's a fair evaluation. If you've got him on a fantasy team, for some reason, get rid of him. He's not going to play in front of Milt Thompson, unless Lenny Dykstra gets hurt again and Milt has to play center.

12. Pedro Munoz (MIN)

A Grade B power prospect. If the Twins do get into contention, and a decent DH shows up available for trade, Dave Winfield may well end up in right field, with Pedro on the bench. That's not the best development plan for Pedro, but it may be necessary for the Twins to contend for that one year.

13. Von Hayes (CAL)

Well what did you think he was going to do? The only reason Whitey ended up with him was that Whitey had to try something after his owner's wife gutted the club's outfield / first base crew. He was still worth more than Kyle Abbott and Ruben Amaro.

14. Dan Pasqua (CHA)

Did not respond at all well to a reduced role as a platoon outfielder. Right now, I'd have him beneath both Ellis Burks and Warren Newson as a right fielder. Or, I suppose I should say, beneath Newson and Burks, as I'd rather have Warren than Ellis.

Still, there is more chance that Dan Pasqua will get a good chance to play than that Warren Newson will. The Chisox already have Tim Raines, Robin Ventura and Frank Thomas. I'm sure that they think that's quite enough patient hitters, thank you. They're wrong, but they probably think they need to get more power and more average out there than Newson will provide. Oh, well, maybe someone who understands about long-sequence offense will pick Newson up. You know, there are slots available in the Angel outfield, and the Chisox need pitching, and Whitey Herzog just loves to trade pitching for hitting....

Right Fielders

Brock J. Hanke

		OWAR	DWAR	TWAR
1.	Walker L	5.49	1.59	7.08
2.	Justice	4.81	.97	5.78
3.	Jose	4.52	1.13	5.65
4.	Dawson	4.38	.95	5.33
5.	Gwynn T	4.28	.79	5.07
6.	O'Neill	3.29	1.51	4.80
7.	Bonilla B	3.93	.80	4.73
8.	McGee	3.13	.90	4.03
	Snyder C	2.74	.70	3.44
	Bass K	2.41	.33	2.74
9.	Webster	2.55	.10	2.65
10.	Anthony	2.24	.15	2.39
	Martinez Da	1.61	.70	2.31
	Smith Dw	1.54	.14	1.69
	Sosa	1.53	-.02	1.51
	Coles	1.29	.17	1.46
	Strawberry	1.20	.04	1.24
11.	Amaro	.32	.64	.97
	Jordan B	.09	.42	.50
12.	Espy	.40	.09	.49
	Varsho	.04	.18	.22
	Wood	-.39	.06	-.33
	Murphy Dl	-.61	-.09	-.70

1. Larry Walker (MTL)

Last year, I rated him a Fantasy League Best Buy. He has done nothing to dispel that notion. The scary thing is that, at age 26, Larry should have two full years of growth left before he reaches his peak. And no, this 1992 season does not look like a fluke. It is completely consistent with steady growth from 1990 onwards. In fact, Larry has been one of the most consistent players around. What I fully expect to be doing, in a couple of years, is trying to sort him out from Frank Thomas and Roberto Alomar as to which one is the best young player in baseball. As for as hitter is concerned, it's no contest. Frank is better, by the margin of all those walks Larry doesn't take. But Larry is a real defensive star in right field, with the whole package of range, arm and brain. Roberto Alomar may have more defensive value, just because second base has more value than right field. But Larry has enough more power that he may turn out to be the better hitter.

Now, regarding whether he can provide the whole power core of a division winner, well, that's a different question. The Expos, by trading Ivan Calderon and Tim Wallach and losing Bret Barberie to expansion, have placed themselves in a situation where they're without both a power core and a third baseman. Larry's going to be awfully lonesome out there at cleanup. What will happen, of course, is what happened to Will Clark this year. Larry will start to pile up the intentional walks, even though he doesn't really have any plate discipline. That may make him look better as a hitter, in the short term, but it will hurt the Expos.

2. Dave Justice (ATL)

Well, last year I said, "He's about a 5.5 or 6 game player after the Fulton County gas is taken out of his stats". I guess 5.78 TWAR is in that range. On the other hand, I didn't think Dave would ever play more than 130 games in a season, so I rated him a bad fantasy buy. My reasoning was that someone would pencil Dave in for full time play and be willing to pay full value for the whole 5.78 WAR, and then he wouldn't play full time. I still think that reasoning is basically sound. Dave does seem to have too much muscle for his bone structure, and you know I don't like that. People still talk about him as injury-prone. On the other hand, he's about to turn 27. That might make a 6.5 or 7 win player for a year. That make him a GOOD FANTASY GAMBLE FOR ONE YEAR. But I still don't trust him, and I sure wouldn't pay more for him than for Larry Walker.

3. Felix Jose (STL)

Felix is a fine, fine player, but he shouldn't be ranking this high among the right fielders. This position should really generate at least three 6-win guys. The reason it doesn't is probably the same reason as for left field. It used to be that there were always several really good hitters who were too big and slow to play center field. Nowadays, though, they put those guys through the good conditioning programs, and they can run, and so they play center.

Also, as with Ray Lankford, it is possible that Busch Stadium is giving Felix some of his Defensive stats. The St. Louis ballpark saw the most fly balls of any NL park this season, and so Cardinal outfield range factors may be a bit inflated. On the other hand, Felix does have a tremendous arm and good range. To tell me that he's the third-best defensive right fielder is not any big surprise.

I said it last year, and I'll say it again: Felix Jose is the prototype for a #5 hitter. He has a high batting average, enough line drive power to get in those runs from first base, and he doesn't take walks, so you can bat him in the two-out slot without him wasting any more opportunities than the other guy.

4. Andre Dawson (CHN-BOS)

Well, we've finally done it. We've found a ballpark that Andre Dawson suits even less than Wrigley Field. In fact, if I had to evaluate a Boston management on one thing alone, it

Right Field	G	PO	A	Er	TC	DP	FPct	DI	DG	DW%	DWAR
Alou	15	28	0	2	30	0	.933	107.2	.4	.363	.00
Amaro	68	106	3	1	110	1	.991	451.1	1.5	.560	.33
Anthony	113	172	6	5	183	0	.973	900.1	3.1	.399	.15
Ashley	26	33	1	5	39	0	.872	206.0	.7	.121	-.16
Bass K	34	55	1	1	57	0	.982	227.2	.8	1.216	.67
Benzinger	33	47	1	0	48	0	1.000	257.1	.9	.452	.09
Bonilla B	121	238	7	2	247	1	.992	988.0	3.4	.588	.81
Braggs	29	37	1	5	43	0	.884	191.2	.7	.247	-.07
Castillo Br	16	35	0	1	36	0	.972	117.0	.4	.502	.06
Chamberlain	48	84	1	1	86	0	.988	388.0	1.3	.444	.12
Clark Je	22	40	1	0	41	1	1.000	167.0	.6	.626	.16
Cole	52	84	4	1	89	0	.989	398.1	1.4	1.250	1.23
Dawson	139	222	11	2	235	4	.991	1182.1	4.0	.585	.95
Espy	56	45	1	2	48	0	.958	210.2	.7	.369	.01
Gallagher	48	55	1	0	56	1	1.000	207.1	.7	.644	.21
Gibson K	13	25	1	0	26	1	1.000	112.0	.4	.731	.15
Gwynn T	127	270	9	5	284	3	.982	1127.2	3.9	.555	.79
Hosey	18	24	0	1	25	0	.960	128.0	.4	.262	-.04
Incaviglia	48	74	5	3	82	0	.963	351.0	1.2	.576	.27
Jordan B	21	36	1	0	37	0	1.000	178.2	.6	.602	.15
Jose	127	271	11	6	288	1	.979	1117.1	3.8	.648	1.14
Justice	140	313	9	8	330	3	.976	1198.0	4.1	.586	.97
Kruk	29	47	0	1	48	0	.979	225.2	.8	.368	.01
May D	14	19	0	0	19	0	1.000	112.0	.4	.460	.04
McClendon	50	70	0	2	72	0	.972	343.1	1.2	.361	.01
McGee	90	164	9	6	179	1	.966	721.0	2.5	.600	.62
Merced	17	23	3	0	26	1	1.000	112.2	.4	.879	.20
Murphy Dl	16	19	0	1	20	0	.950	121.0	.4	.143	-.09
Nixon O	16	38	0	1	39	0	.974	125.0	.4	.542	.08
O'Neill	143	291	12	1	304	2	.997	1209.2	4.1	.711	1.49
Reed D	21	31	1	0	32	0	1.000	132.2	.5	1.440	.50
Rodriguez H	31	39	1	1	41	0	.976	242.2	.8	.224	-.10
Snyder C	48	67	6	1	74	1	.986	332.1	1.1	.732	.43
Strawberry	40	63	2	1	66	0	.985	330.1	1.1	.376	.03
Varsho	28	43	0	1	44	0	.977	164.2	.6	.485	.08
Walker L	139	269	16	2	287	2	.993	1216.2	4.2	.734	1.60
Webster M	56	65	0	2	67	0	.970	300.2	1.0	.325	-.03
TOTALS		3900	137	85	4122	26	.979	1461.0	5.0	2.715	11.82

would be on their ability to leave this sort of player alone, while holding on to everyone they could find like Jody Reed and Wade Boggs.

As you may have read last year, one of the local sportscasters is a big Andre Dawson fan, and constantly asks me what I think of the man's chances of making the Hall of Fame. I always say the same thing: if he can really hold on for another 6 years, until he piles up 500 home runs, he's going to make it. Otherwise, he probably won't. He might make 3000 hits in four years, and that might get him in, but the competition is going to be tough. The problem, you see, is that the standards are going to have to rise, in terms of raw career stats. George Brett and Robin Yount are only the tip of what is going to be a Titanic iceberg of 3000-hit men. You're going to have modern medicine, and you're going to have careers composed entirely of 162-game seasons. Right now, the

writers who vote for the Hall are probably not aware that this is coming. But in nine years, they're going to see it coming. And it's going to take Andre four years to get the 3000 hits, much less the 500 homers. Add five years retirement wait, and it's nine minimum.

5. Tony Gwynn (SD)

The temptation is to say "will rank higher next year, when he won't be hurt". But that's a fallacy. Tony got into 128 games this year, while his last two years' totals have been only 134 and 141. And, when he was in there, he didn't play any worse than usual. What seems to be happening is that Tony is having an early decline phase. The last three years, he has performed comfortably under his lifetime averages in batting, slugging and on-base, too. He is also starting to lose walks. To me, that's a sign of what I call "retreating to the central skill". Tony Gwynn is going to go down

struggling, as all superstars do. And the center of the struggle will be his attempt to keep his batting average up. In trying to do that, he's going to swing at some pitches he used to take, because he thinks he can guide them for base hits. Thus the decline in walks, at an age when most players are taking more. NOT A GOOD FANTASY BUY, as I imaging his reputation is running some years behind his decline.

6. Paul O'Neill (CIN-NYY)

I'm sure that Yankee fans don't look at it this way, but the Pinstripes added defense in trading Roberto Kelly for Paul O'Neill. Kelly is an OK center fielder, but nothing outstanding, whereas O'Neill is Gold Glove material in right.

In fact, most of the national press seems to think that the Reds stole this deal; whereas the TWAR system objects violently. It says that

Paul is much the better player now, and 1992 was hardly a career year. On the other hand, this was supposed to be Roberto's age-27 big year, and he did not equal expectations. The questions are: 1) how much is the two-year age difference worth, and 2) is Roberto in the middle of a comeback from his 1991 season? I have my doubts about both. Essentially, what happened to Roberto is that his power fell apart, compared to all previous years. That's not the "middle" of anything. And neither player is old enough that his useful life is going to end before his contract does. All in all, I think the Yankees may prove to have stolen this deal.

7. Bobby Bonilla (NYM)

I expect a return to form. Of course, there is the question of what "form" is here. Is it the power totals he posted at age 27? Unlikely, but he should hit around 25 or so. Is it his excellent batting average and doubles total of 1991? Not in Shea Stadium, but I can easily see .270 and 35 two-baggers. That's a fine player, although the New York press will probably still gripe. I imagine it will help if the team around him improves, and I think it will. For one thing, Howard Johnson won't be in center field. And Dave Magadan won't be at third base. And there will be a real shortstop. On the other hand, the luster has gone from that pitching staff. Actually, what Bobby Bonilla probably needs most is for his team to sign an even more expensive free agent. But they didn't do that, and the Yankees only generated marginal help, for all their efforts. I guess I don't envy being the last of the New York free agent follies.

8. Willie McGee (SF)

I'm assuming that Willie will win the right field job from Dave Martinez. I'm assuming that Darren Lewis will be given a full-time chance in center field. On the other hand, if Lewis fails, or if the new management loses faith in him, Willie and Dave get to contend for center, not right. I'm not sure Willie can win that one, not at his age. Dusty Baker has announced that Willie will be the Giants' leadoff man. I expect that to last well into early May. By then, Dusty, who can't be that dumb, will have figured out that Willie won't take a walk and can't steal a decent percentage of bases, though he will surely try. Then Lewis will lead off.

9. Mitch Webster (LA)

If I had Darryl Strawberry, Mitch Webster is about what I'd pick up for an injury replacement. If Darryl plays his 140 games, Mitch won't bitch. And, if the big man goes down, as he did in 1992, you get this season, which ain't great, but which certainly is not what killed the Dodgers, not by itself, anyway. The Dodgers rewarded Mitch with a decent contract renewal, which is only fair. Of course, "only fair" puts the Fred Claire team well within the top five baseball managements.

10. Eric Anthony (HOU)

What I wanna know is what Bill James saw here; or, rather, what he didn't see. Back in 1989, when everybody and his great-grandson, myself included, had Eric down for Rookie of the Decade, Bill sort of passed him off with an "I really don't think he's going to make it big" comment. And, of course, Eric hasn't made it big, not yet.

I still think that a lot of what happened to Eric was that his early development was stifled by erratic use and lack of faith. The Astros basically gave him a month to prove himself; when he had a slump for that tiny amount of time, they sent him back to the minors, confidence no doubt at least shaken. Still, he ought to have recovered more than he has by now. He got 440 At-Bats last year, and just showed flashes of the power he was supposed to have. He hit for no average, and took no walks; both those qualities were in his minor league makeup.

I guess the final test is this year. He's going to be 25. He's had a full year of Major League play under his belt. He's got the job, and the team around him is not a disaster. If he's going to produce big, now is the time. And you know what? I still have enough faith in those minor league stats to say, "IF YOU'RE GOING TO TAKE A FANTASY GAMBLE AT THIS POSITION, TAKE THIS ONE".

11. Ruben Amaro (PHI)

And the Phillies thought they were going to score so heavy with that Von Hayes trade. Let the record show that Ruben Amaro had his big age-27 career year last season. I mean that; he'll never get anything like 300 At-Bats again.

12. Cecil Espy (PIT-CIN)

Now the #3 center fielder on the Reds, behind Roberto Kelly and Reggie Sanders. And you know what? He'd still be the starter here if the Pirates still had him.

Designated Hitters

Brock J. Hanke

		OWAR	DWAR	TWAR
1.	Molitor	6.68	.10	6.79
2.	Winfield	5.38	.22	5.59
3.	Phillips	3.53	1.33	4.86
4.	Brett	4.33	.04	4.36
5.	Davis C	3.91	.02	3.93
6.	Downing	3.09	.00	3.09
7.	Davis G	2.53	.01	2.54
8.	Baines	2.07	-.02	2.04
9.	Bell G	1.87	0	1.88
10.	Clark Jk	1.06	.03	1.09
11.	Maas	.97	-.01	.96
	Horn	.67	.00	.67
12.	Hill G	.37	.26	.62
	Davis A	.54	.07	.61
	Cangelosi	-.18	.35	.17
13.	O'Brien	-.21	.37	.15
	Tabler	-.23	.18	-.05
	Martinez Crl	-.17	.11	-.07
14.	Brooks	-.97	.01	-.96

1. Paul Molitor (MIL - TOR)

Another player who was injured at age 27, and so never did display his full peak potential. This has caused many people to underrate this magnificent hitter. At the ripe old age of 36, he is now established as a wonderful leadoff man who can hit third without hurting you. He may still be able to play third, as well; and the Blue Jays may give him a chance to prove it. I wouldn't do that, and the team, without Dave Winfield or Candy Maldonado, is not really set up to do it. However, Kelly Gruber's performance may be so weak as to tempt Cito Gaston.

What Paul really does is make Devon White expendable in the batting order. Paul is a much better leadoff hitter, and he does have enough base stealing speed that the Jays don't have to hit Devon first just to get that skill into their game. Now, whether Cito will actually hit Paul first is another question. If he does that, Devon White ends up batting sixth. He can't beat out Roberto Alomar for the #2 spot, and he doesn't have the power for 3, 4, or 5. It's just as likely that Cito will hit Paul third,

moving Joe Carter to cleanup, or John Olerud to cleanup and Carter to #5. That's technically worse, but it's not exactly a bad lineup. In any case, Paul does seem able to pick up the slack created by the loss of Dave Winfield.

2. Dave Winfield (TOR - MIN)

His perceive place in the game - cleanup man for hire - used to be filled by Don Baylor. Baylor made a sort of grand tour of pennant winners at the end of his career, and Dave may be on the same trail. I'm sure that's what the Twins have in mind, in any case.

3. Tony Phillips (DET)

Now, let's get this straight, Sparky. You've got a horrid left fielder, Dan Gladden, that the Twins ditched in order to play Shane Mack. Your center fielder was awful; by far the worst in the league. Your shortstop was hurt all year, and so your third baseman played short. Tony Phillips can play left, center or third base, and he spends most of the year doing DH duty. What was the problem? Could you not decide which starting spot to give him? I'll give you

a clue: your shortstop is coming back, and you can always find a left fielder. But Milt Cuyler is really not ready for prime time. Tony Phillips is a really good leadoff hitter. Is that enough?

4. George Brett (KC)

Still hits enough that he doesn't hurt you at DH. But remember, the DH rule is all that's keeping him in the game, now that he's got his 3,000.

You know, those 3,000 hits are related to the oddest feeling I've ever had about baseball. I was in Los Angeles when the Royals were in Anaheim, and I had this girl friend (as opposed to girlfriend; she's married to someone else) named "Ellie" who is a baseball fan, and who is from Kansas City, and who was out in the area too, and who I had already taken to a Dodger game. And, you know, if George had played even one of the preceding games in the series and gotten a hit, we'd have gone to the game he got the 3,000th in. But the chance that he'd get 4 hits was just so bad, and the distance to Anaheim so long, that we decided not to go. Oh, well, I did get to see Lou Brock's 3,000th hit.

5. Chili Davis (MIN - CAL)

Well, whaddaya know. Jean finally let Whitey have a cleanup man. It's not Dave Winfield, but it's the next best thing. You know, if Whitey only hadn't cut Big Dave, and had then signed Chili here, he'd have himself an offense, playing Chili at DH and Dave in right field.

6. Brian Downing (TEX)

Awfully good for a 41-year-old, but he has been reduced to bulk Designated Hitting. Doesn't help the Rangers much, but also doesn't hurt them.

7. Glenn Davis (BAL)

Glenn's power stroke still hasn't recovered from the injuries. Without it, he's in trouble. I give him one more year to prove he can still get the ball out of the ballpark. If not, he's expansion team bait.

8. Harold Baines (OAK - BAL)

Harold did not really help the A's this year. On the other hand, they've stretched themselves pretty thin to be letting him go. The Orioles are gambling that Glenn Davis can play some first base in 1993. That will allow them to get both Harold and Glenn into the batting order, and use Diego Segui as a backup.

9. George Bell (CHA)

Same story as Harold Baines. The Chisox need more. You just can't hit .255 and lead the league in double plays if you never take a walk. The Chisox will never make the replacement, but right now, Warren Newson is serious competition for George.

10. Jack Clark (BOS)

Jack would have probably been forcibly retired if the Bosox hadn't had a fire sale of hitters. As it is, he's going to need the money.

11. Kevin Maas (NYY)

He was never a great prospect, and wouldn't have been hyped so much if he hadn't been in New York. Still, he's not so bad as to deserve this treatment. He is certainly better than a platoon DH. A FANTASY LEAGUE SLEEPER, as he might get playing time, and he's overdue for that big peak season. On the other hand, it is a gamble. This is New York, after all.

12. Glenallen Hill (CLE)

The Indians were expecting some of those outfielders they got to become superstars and join Albert Belle and Carlos Baerga in a grand march to victory. So far, Hill and Mark Whiten have managed to resist assuming the role.

By the way, when you look at the Cleveland team essay, you'll see Albert Belle listed as the Indian left fielder. That's wrong; Thomas Howard got more playing time. Belle was platooned between LF and DH. On the other hand, if you're making predictions for 1993, it's probably correct. Either Belle or Hill will be the left fielder, the other will DH, and Thomas Howard will warm the bench.

13. Pete O'Brien (SEA)

A team with a real plan and a real budget would sign a real free agent.

14. Hubie Brooks (CAL - KC)

A team with a real plan and a real owner would have signed a real free agent. The difference between the Angels and the Mariners is that Whitey managed to get his owner a clue before anyone in Seattle arranged the feat. What the Royals want with Hubie, I do not know.

IV

Reference

American League

Total Wins Above Replacement

By WAR

NAME	OWAR	DWAR	TWAR	NAME	OWAR	DWAR	TWAR
Anderson B	7.25	.97	8.21	Canseco	2.99	.63	3.62
				Seitzer	2.79	.81	3.60
Thomas F	7.44	.19	7.63	Vaughn G	2.80	.77	3.56
Puckett	6.11	1.40	7.51	Holles	3.41	.13	3.54
Baerga	4.93	2.22	7.16	Fielder	3.07	.37	3.43
				Boggs W	2.88	.46	3.34
Raines	5.49	1.40	6.89	Curtis C	2.51	.79	3.30
Molitor	6.68	.10	6.79	Johnson L	1.84	1.41	3.24
Mack	5.95	.73	6.69	Sorrento	2.98	.20	3.18
Ventura	5.17	1.50	6.66	Belle	3.13	.01	3.14
Listach	4.04	2.59	6.63	Hall M	2.20	.91	3.11
Martinez E	5.88	.45	6.33	Downing	3.09	.00	3.09
Alomar R	5.57	.69	6.26	Gonzales R	2.19	.82	3.01
Knoblauch	4.39	1.82	6.21	Steinbach	2.66	.35	3.01
McGwire	5.81	.29	6.10	Vizquel	.71	2.28	3.00
Palmeiro	5.02	.91	5.94	Kelly	2.05	.89	2.94
Griffey Jr	4.56	1.31	5.88	Whiten	1.64	1.30	2.94
Lofton	4.41	1.39	5.80	Mitchell K	2.42	.48	2.91
Ripken C	2.72	3.07	5.79	Grebeck	1.67	1.22	2.90
Bordick	3.37	2.22	5.60	Velarde	1.72	1.11	2.83
Winfield	5.38	.22	5.59	Bichette	2.08	.72	2.80
Henderson R	4.87	.71	5.58	Harper B	3.02	-.25	2.76
Devereaux	4.51	.98	5.49	Palmer Dn	2.60	.11	2.71
Hamilton	3.54	1.70	5.24	Hrbek	2.27	.42	2.69
Joyner	4.44	.72	5.17	Huson	1.58	1.06	2.65
Tartabull	4.86	.19	5.05	Stankiewicz	.97	1.60	2.57
				Cooper S	2.18	.37	2.55
Yount	3.59	1.37	4.95	Davis G	2.53	.01	2.54
Phillips	3.53	1.33	4.86	Macfarlane	2.49	.04	2.53
Olerud	4.40	.36	4.75	Browne J	2.03	.47	2.50
Carter J	3.82	.82	4.64	Reed Jd	.36	2.13	2.49
Gonzalez Juan	4.06	.50	4.56	Lee M	.96	1.48	2.44
Fletcher S	2.14	2.36	4.50	Lansford	2.36	-.02	2.34
Maldonado	3.58	.89	4.48	Williams B	1.43	.77	2.20
Brett	4.33	.04	4.36	Wilson W	1.31	.87	2.17
Brunansky	3.70	.53	4.22	Felix	1.33	.83	2.16
Buhner	2.67	1.54	4.21	Valentin	1.28	.86	2.14
Blankenship L	2.67	1.45	4.12	Zupcic	1.41	.65	2.06
Sierra	3.81	.30	4.11	Plantier	1.53	.53	2.05
Whitaker	3.27	.84	4.11	Baines	2.07	-.02	2.04
Fryman T	2.33	1.73	4.07	Eisenreich	1.55	.47	2.02
Orsulak	2.99	.97	3.96	Vaughn M	1.92	.03	1.95
Gomez L	3.65	.31	3.95	Hayes C	1.22	.73	1.95
Davis C	3.91	.02	3.93	Surhoff BJ	1.14	.80	1.94
Deer	3.10	.79	3.88	Bell Geo	1.87	.00	1.88
McReynolds	3.60	.27	3.87	McRae B	.37	1.46	1.83
Milligan	3.48	.35	3.83	Martinez C	1.46	.36	1.82
Jefferies	3.50	.29	3.79	Karkovice	1.48	.18	1.66
White D	2.51	1.25	3.76	Gagne	-.73	2.36	1.63
Miller K	3.13	.61	3.74	Sojo	.20	1.34	1.53
Mattingly	2.91	.82	3.73	Munoz P	.70	.82	1.52
Polonia	3.23	.49	3.72				
Tettleton	4.13	-.42	3.72	Stevens	1.19	.29	1.48
Reimer	3.46	.17	3.63	Abner	.80	.66	1.46

NAME	OWAR	DWAR	TWAR	NAME	OWAR	DWAR	TWAR
Koslofski	.79	.56	1.36	Franco Ju	.32	-.08	.24
Burks	1.41	-.05	1.36	Parent	.24	-.05	.18
Gallego	.57	.77	1.34	Cangelosi	-.18	.35	.17
Cora	.85	.43	1.28	O'Brien P	-.21	.37	.15
Naehring	.45	.83	1.27	Fitzgerald	.09	.06	.14
Disarcina	-.88	2.15	1.27	Brosius	.01	.13	.14
Kelly P	.56	.69	1.25	Rodriguez I	.10	.03	.13
Hayes V	1.01	.24	1.25	Thurman	-.51	.63	.13
Cotto	.60	.55	1.15	Guillen	-.12	.24	.12
Wilkerson	.20	.92	1.12	Briley	.02	.07	.09
Clark Jk	1.06	.03	1.09	Jorgensen	-.06	.13	.07
Borders	.75	.31	1.06	Oberkfell	.12	-.06	.06
Leyritz	1.08	-.03	1.05	Bruett	-.10	.16	.05
Larkin G	.64	.40	1.05	Fariss	-.10	.15	.05
Stanley M	1.30	-.26	1.03	Turner	-.02	.04	.02
Pasqua	.75	.28	1.03	Cochrane	.02	-.01	.01
Stubbs	.90	.12	1.02				
Hulett	.64	.37	1.00	Tingley	-.27	.24	-.03
				Tabler	-.23	.18	-.05
McLemore	.13	.86	.99	Jacoby	-.45	.39	-.06
Gantner	-.37	1.35	.98	Martinez Crl	-.17	.11	-.07
Thon	.83	.15	.98	Newman A	-.65	.57	-.08
Gladden	.18	.79	.96	Nokes	.22	-.31	-.09
Maas	.97	-.01	.96	Sprague	-.18	.07	-.11
Reboulet	-.18	1.08	.91	Huff	-.51	.36	-.14
Kent	.96	-.08	.88	Orton	-.11	-.05	-.16
Reynolds H	-.34	1.18	.84	Ducey	-.26	.09	-.17
Newson	.41	.42	.83	Carreon	-.67	.49	-.18
Martinez Tino	.45	.37	.82	Mercedes	-.36	.17	-.18
Bell D	.19	.58	.77	Salmon	-.17	-.03	-.20
Howard T	.25	.52	.77	Daugherty	-.25	.04	-.21
Gaetti	.21	.56	.77	Harris D	-.30	.08	-.22
James D	.58	.18	.77	Gonzalez Jo	-.34	.12	-.22
Ripken B	-.70	1.43	.73	Myers G	-.08	-.14	-.22
Samuel	.57	.14	.71	Amaral	-.51	.26	-.25
Nilsson	.54	.14	.68	Pena T	-.85	.59	-.26
Horn	.67	.00	.67	Valle	.49	-.75	-.26
Howard D	-.62	1.28	.67	Merullo	-.26	-.03	-.29
Easley D	.21	.44	.65	Mayne	-.62	.33	-.30
Webster L	.43	.22	.64	Alomar S	-.60	.30	-.30
Frye	.24	.39	.63	Blowers	-.53	.23	-.30
Jaha	.48	.14	.63	McIntosh	-.46	.11	-.35
Hill G	.37	.26	.62	Weiss	-.84	.47	-.37
Davis A	.54	.07	.61	Howitt	-.64	.26	-.38
Jefferson R	.54	.05	.59	Griffin Alf	-.53	.14	-.39
Fox	.18	.38	.56	Colon	-.39	-.01	-.40
Gwynn C	.46	.08	.54	Cole	-.46	.05	-.41
Barnes	.28	.25	.52	Greenwell	-.67	.23	-.44
Lewis M	-.24	.75	.51				
Parrish Ln	.63	-.12	.50	Thome	-.31	-.21	-.52
				Winningham	-.83	.29	-.54
Trammell	.14	.36	.49	Gruber	-.83	.29	-.54
Livingstone	.11	.36	.47	Flaherty	-.44	-.17	-.61
Fisk	.46	.01	.47	Boone B	-.79	.17	-.62
Ready	.27	.20	.47	Hatcher B	-.81	.18	-.63
Conine	.28	.14	.43	Pagliarulo	-.79	.14	-.65
Fermin	-.10	.53	.42	Marzano	-.57	-.09	-.66
Hulse	.39	.03	.42	Cuyler	-1.12	.43	-.69
Segui	.02	.40	.41	Bush	-.88	.13	-.75
Rossy	-.29	.70	.41	Barfield Je	-.95	.19	-.76
Rose	.12	.27	.39	Quirk	-.37	-.42	-.78
Pettis	-.13	.52	.39	Schaefer	-.86	.01	-.85
Sveum	.27	.09	.36	Bergman	-.91	.03	-.88
Tackett	.01	.32	.34	Kreuter	-.34	-.55	-.89
Sax S	-.13	.45	.32	Shumpert	-.88	-.05	-.93
Rivera L	-.92	1.24	.32	Brooks	-.97	.01	-.96
Melvin	.35	-.05	.30	Beltre	-.85	-.16	-1.01
Hill D	.20	.07	.27	Petralli	-.76	-.29	-1.05
Leius	-.09	.34	.25	Ortiz	-.89	-.42	-1.31

Total Wins Above Replacement

By WAR

NAME	OWAR	DWAR	TWAR	NAME	OWAR	DWAR	TWAR
Sandberg	7.18	2.02	9.19	Merced	2.34	.60	2.94
Lankford	6.72	1.57	8.29	Morris H	2.31	.52	2.83
Van Slyke	6.69	1.43	8.12	Felder	2.45	.36	2.81
Grace	6.83	.94	7.76	Oliver	2.62	.14	2.76
Bonds	6.98	.66	7.63	Bass K	2.41	.33	2.74
Butler	6.74	.84	7.58	Webster M	2.55	.10	2.64
Larkin B	5.61	1.86	7.46	Doran	1.86	.77	2.64
Smith O	4.16	3.04	7.20	Schofield	.57	1.99	2.56
Bagwell	6.37	.80	7.18	Magadan	2.88	-.33	2.55
Walker L	5.49	1.59	7.08	Williams MD	1.62	.83	2.46
Pendleton	5.75	1.26	7.01	Anthony	2.24	.15	2.39
Sheffield	6.04	.86	6.90	Offerman	2.92	-.55	2.37
Clark W	6.27	.40	6.67	Slaught	2.67	-.33	2.35
Biggio	5.87	.70	6.56	Martinez Da	1.61	.70	2.31
Bell Jay	3.59	2.95	6.55	Wilkins R	2.08	.22	2.30
McGriff F	6.39	.13	6.53	Johnson H	2.25	.00	2.25
Finley S	5.14	1.33	6.47	Hunter B	1.91	.29	2.21
Roberts Bip	5.66	.43	6.08	Alicea	1.49	.68	2.17
Hollins	5.64	.16	5.80	Walker C	2.05	.12	2.17
Justice	4.81	.97	5.78	Jackson Dar	.02	2.13	2.15
Jose	4.52	1.13	5.65	Coleman	1.93	.17	2.10
Thompson Ro	3.45	2.15	5.60	Randolph	1.49	.55	2.04
Kruk	5.13	.20	5.33	Javier	1.11	.92	2.04
Dawson	4.38	.95	5.33	Duncan	1.73	.29	2.02
Grissom	4.66	.64	5.30	Sanchez R	.35	1.66	2.01
Caminiti	4.70	.41	5.11	Gonzalez L	1.23	.74	1.97
Gwynn T	4.28	.79	5.07	May D	1.81	.06	1.87
O'Neill	3.29	1.51	4.80	Wallach	.81	1.04	1.85
Sanders R	3.81	.96	4.77	Thompson M	1.77	.04	1.82
Bonilla B	3.93	.80	4.73	Harris L	1.13	.65	1.78
DeShields	4.19	.51	4.70	King J	.81	.96	1.77
Murray E	4.56	.07	4.64	Pagnozzi	1.17	.59	1.75
Karros	3.93	.59	4.52	Smith Dw	1.54	.14	1.69
Gant	3.94	.48	4.43	Sabo	1.48	.19	1.67
Gilkey	3.64	.74	4.38	Morandini	.41	1.21	1.62
Daulton	5.37	-1.08	4.29	Clark Je	.60	.98	1.57
Nixon O	2.69	1.36	4.05	LaValliere	.92	.65	1.57
McGee	3.13	.90	4.03	Jordan	1.39	.13	1.52
Dykstra	2.98	.85	3.83	Lewis D	.63	.88	1.51
Buechele	3.15	.64	3.79	Sosa	1.53	-.02	1.51
Fernandez T	2.83	.96	3.79	Smith Lo	1.36	.12	1.48
Blauser	3.50	.27	3.78	Coles	1.29	.17	1.46
Owen S	2.63	1.14	3.77	Braggs	1.56	-.11	1.45
Zeile	3.04	.66	3.70	Davis E	1.61	-.18	1.44
Sharperson	3.08	.47	3.55	Uribe	.44	.91	1.35
Pena G	2.41	1.12	3.53	Galarraga	1.10	.16	1.26
Snyder C	2.74	.70	3.44	Strawberry	1.20	.04	1.24
Sanders	2.98	.36	3.34	Chamberlain	1.02	.20	1.22
Incaviglia	2.76	.56	3.32	Barberie	.91	.30	1.21
Bream	3.14	.10	3.24	Vanderwal	.98	.22	1.20
Alou	2.76	.42	3.18	Cole	.80	.40	1.20
Boston	2.60	.41	3.01	Olson Greg	.85	.34	1.19

NAME	OWAR	DWAR	TWAR	NAME	OWAR	DWAR	TWAR
James C	1.04	.15	1.19	Goodwin	.02	.09	.11
Berryhill	.53	.61	1.14	Piazza	.14	-.05	.09
Dascenzo	.85	.27	1.12	Gedman	.14	-.06	.08
Redus	.97	.14	1.11	Hundley	-.34	.41	.07
Manwaring	1.00	.07	1.07	Dozier D	.00	.03	.03
Lemke	.47	.57	1.04	Jones Chris	.02	-.00	.01
Calderon	.84	.15	.99	Gibson K	-.16	.14	-.01
Amaro	.32	.64	.97	Perry G	-.01	-.01	-.02
Hansen	.66	.30	.95	Cerone	.03	-.06	-.04
Brewer R	.77	.17	.94	Ramirez R	-.16	.11	-.04
McClendon	.87	.06	.93	Stillwell	-.44	.39	-.04
Leonard M	.78	.15	.92	Servais	-.21	.16	-.05
Clayton	-.20	1.12	.92	Garcia C	-.27	.19	-.08
Benzinger	.65	.26	.91	Mcnamara	-.21	.08	-.14
Wilson C	.76	.14	.90	O'Brien C	.24	-.39	-.14
Woodson	.86	.02	.88	Hudler	-.25	.10	-.15
Daniels	.72	.15	.87	Jones Tim	-.68	.52	-.16
Arias	.73	.10	.83	Howell P	-.42	.26	-.16
Vizcaino	-.32	1.06	.74	Reed D	-.34	.18	-.16
Pecota	.31	.40	.72	Ashley	-.04	-.16	-.20
Litton	.32	.39	.72	Laker	-.29	.05	-.23
Carter G	.38	.30	.68	Decker S	-.25	.00	-.25
Greene W	.62	.05	.68	Benjamin	-.56	.30	-.25
Cordero	.81	-.14	.67	Guerrero	-.24	-.04	-.28
Branson	.43	.21	.64	Sveum	-.69	.41	-.28
Kent	.42	.21	.63	Hosey	-.24	-.04	-.28
Dunston	.39	.22	.61	Castillo Br	-.36	.07	-.29
Scioscia	.17	.39	.56	Lake	-.14	-.18	-.32
Thompson R	.30	.25	.55	Guerrero J	-.20	-.12	-.32
Gallagher	.18	.36	.54	Young G	-.42	.10	-.32
Jordan B	.09	.42	.50	Patterson J	-.61	.29	-.32
Espy	.40	.09	.49	Wood	-.39	.06	-.33
Anderson D	.39	.08	.47	Donnels	-.40	.06	-.34
Girardi	.46	-.01	.45	Stephenson	-.38	.03	-.35
Lind	-1.52	1.97	.44	Millette	-.76	.37	-.39
McKnight	.35	.07	.42	Walton	-.39	-.01	-.40
Cianfrocco	.31	.09	.40	Belliard	-1.46	1.05	-.41
Colbrunn	.32	.08	.39	Sasser	-.29	-.13	-.42
Candaele	-.55	.94	.39	Salazar L	-1.07	.59	-.47
Carr	.20	.19	.39	Wehner	-.77	.28	-.49
Fletcher D	-.04	.40	.35	Colbert	-.45	-.04	-.49
Walters D	.34	.01	.34	Foley T	-.90	.33	-.56
Hatcher B	.34	-.04	.31	Prince	-.53	-.07	-.61
Teufel	.12	.16	.29	Strange	-.61	-.03	-.63
Shipley	-.27	.55	.29	Tucker	-.57	-.10	-.68
Young E	.14	.14	.28	Murphy Di	-.61	-.09	-.70
Benavides	-.06	.32	.26	Villanueva	-.86	.12	-.74
Hernandez C	.58	-.33	.26	Marsh	-.82	.04	-.78
Varsho	.04	.18	.22	Cedeno A	-.80	.01	-.79
Treadway	-.26	.48	.22	Santiago	-.21	-.61	-.82
Bell Ju	-.28	.47	.20	Ward K	-.95	.08	-.88
Berry	.29	-.10	.19	Scott G	-.90	-.09	-.99
Taubensee	.47	-.29	.19	Azocar	-1.09	.04	-1.05
Rodriguez H	.18	-.01	.17	Batiste K	-1.04	-.22	-1.25
Samuel	.11	.05	.16				

Total Wins Above Replacement

Alphabetical

NAME	OWAR	DWAR	TWAR	NAME	OWAR	DWAR	TWAR
Abner	.80	.66	1.46	Fariss	-.10	.15	.05
Alomar R	5.57	.69	6.26	Felix	1.33	.83	2.16
Alomar S	-.60	.30	-.30	Fermin	-.10	.53	.42
Amaral	-.51	.26	-.25	Fielder	3.07	.37	3.43
Anderson B	7.25	.97	8.21	Fisk	.46	.01	.47
Baerga	4.93	2.22	7.16	Fitzgerald	.09	.06	.14
Baines	2.07	-.02	2.04	Flaherty	-.44	-.17	-.61
Barfield Je	-.95	.19	-.76	Fletcher S	2.14	2.36	4.50
Barnes	.28	.25	.52	Fox	.18	.38	.56
Bell D	.19	.58	.77	Franco Ju	.32	-.08	.24
Bell Geo	1.87	.00	1.88	Frye	.24	.39	.63
Belle	3.13	.01	3.14	Fryman T	2.33	1.73	4.07
Beltre	-.85	-.16	-1.01	Gaetti	.21	.56	.77
Bergman	-.91	.03	-.88	Gagne	-.73	2.36	1.63
Bichette	2.08	.72	2.80	Gallego	.57	.77	1.34
Blankenship L	2.67	1.45	4.12	Gantner	-.37	1.35	.98
Blowers	-.53	.23	-.30	Gladden	.18	.79	.96
Boggs W	2.88	.46	3.34	Gomez L	3.65	.31	3.95
Boone B	-.79	.17	-.62	Gonzales R	2.19	.82	3.01
Borders	.75	.31	1.06	Gonzalez Jo	-.34	.12	-.22
Bordick	3.37	2.22	5.60	Gonzalez Juan	4.06	.50	4.56
Brett	4.33	.04	4.36	Grebeck	1.67	1.22	2.90
Briley	.02	.07	.09	Greenwell	-.67	.23	-.44
Brooks	-.97	.01	-.96	Griffey Jr	4.56	1.31	5.88
Brosius	.01	.13	.14	Griffin Alf	-.53	.14	-.39
Browne J	2.03	.47	2.50	Gruber	-.83	.29	-.54
Bruett	-.10	.16	.05	Guillen	-.12	.24	.12
Brunansky	3.70	.53	4.22	Gwynn C	.46	.08	.54
Buhner	2.67	1.54	4.21	Hall M	2.20	.91	3.11
Burks	1.41	-.05	1.36	Hamilton	3.54	1.70	5.24
Bush	-.88	.13	-.75	Harper B	3.02	-.25	2.76
Cangelosi	-.18	.35	.17	Harris D	-.30	.08	-.22
Canseco	2.99	.63	3.62	Hatcher B	-.81	.18	-.63
Carreon	-.67	.49	-.18	Hayes C	1.22	.73	1.95
Carter J	3.82	.82	4.64	Hayes V	1.01	.24	1.25
Clark Jk	1.06	.03	1.09	Henderson R	4.87	.71	5.58
Cochrane	.02	-.01	.01	Hill D	.20	.07	.27
Cole	-.46	.05	-.41	Hill G	.37	.26	.62
Colon	-.39	-.01	-.40	Holles	3.41	.13	3.54
Conine	.28	.14	.43	Horn	.67	.00	.67
Cooper S	2.18	.37	2.55	Howard D	-.62	1.28	.67
Cora	.85	.43	1.28	Howard T	.25	.52	.77
Cotto	.60	.55	1.15	Howitt	-.64	.26	-.38
Curtis C	2.51	.79	3.30	Hrbek	2.27	.42	2.69
Cuyler	-1.12	.43	-.69	Huff	-.51	.36	-.14
Daugherty	-.25	.04	-.21	Hulett	.64	.37	1.00
Davis A	.54	.07	.61	Hulse	.39	.03	.42
Davis C	3.91	.02	3.93	Huson	1.58	1.06	2.65
Davis G	2.53	.01	2.54	Jacoby	-.45	.39	-.06
Deer	3.10	.79	3.88	Jaha	.48	.14	.63
Devereaux	4.51	.98	5.49	James D	.58	.18	.77
Disarcina	-.88	2.15	1.27	Jefferies	3.50	.29	3.79
Downing	3.09	.00	3.09	Jefferson R	.54	.05	.59
Ducey	-.26	.09	-.17	Johnson L	1.84	1.41	3.24
Easley D	.21	.44	.65	Jorgensen	-.06	.13	.07
Eisenreich	1.55	.47	2.02	Joyner	4.44	.72	5.17

NAME	OWAR	DWAR	TWAR	NAME	OWAR	DWAR	TWAR
Karkovice	1.48	.18	1.66	Polonia	3.23	.49	3.72
Kelly P	.56	.69	1.25	Puckett	6.11	1.40	7.51
Kelly	2.05	.89	2.94	Quirk	-.37	-.42	-.78
Kent	.96	-.08	.88	Raines	5.49	1.40	6.89
Knoblauch	4.39	1.82	6.21	Ready	.27	.20	.47
Koslofski	.79	.56	1.36	Reboulet	-.18	1.08	.91
Kreuter	-.34	-.55	-.89	Reed Jd	.36	2.13	2.49
Lansford	2.36	-.02	2.34	Reimer	3.46	.17	3.63
Larkin G	.64	.40	1.05	Reynolds H	-.34	1.18	.84
Lee M	.96	1.48	2.44	Ripken B	-.70	1.43	.73
Leius	-.09	.34	.25	Ripken C	2.72	3.07	5.79
Lewis M	-.24	.75	.51	Rivera L	-.92	1.24	.32
Leyritz	1.08	-.03	1.05	Rodriguez I	.10	.03	.13
Listach	4.04	2.59	6.63	Rose	.12	.27	.39
Livingstone	.11	.36	.47	Rossy	-.29	.70	.41
Lofton	4.41	1.39	5.80	Salmon	-.17	-.03	-.20
Maas	.97	-.01	.96	Samuel	.57	.14	.71
Macfarlane	2.49	.04	2.53	Sax S	-.13	.45	.32
Mack	5.95	.73	6.69	Schaefer	-.86	.01	-.85
Maldonado	3.58	.89	4.48	Segui	.02	.40	.41
Martinez Crl	-.17	.11	-.07	Seitzer	2.79	.81	3.60
Martinez C	1.46	.36	1.82	Shumpert	-.88	-.05	-.93
Martinez E	5.88	.45	6.33	Sierra	3.81	.30	4.11
Martinez Tino	.45	.37	.82	Sojo	.20	1.34	1.53
Marzano	-.57	-.09	-.66	Sorrento	2.98	.20	3.18
Mattingly	2.91	.82	3.73	Sprague	-.18	.07	-.11
Mayne	-.62	.33	-.30	Stankiewicz	.97	1.60	2.57
McGwire	5.81	.29	6.10	Stanley M	1.30	-.26	1.03
McIntosh	-.46	.11	-.35	Steinbach	2.66	.35	3.01
McLemore	.13	.86	.99	Stevens	1.19	.29	1.48
McRae B	.37	1.46	1.83	Stubbs	.90	.12	1.02
McReynolds	3.60	.27	3.87	Surhoff BJ	1.14	.80	1.94
Melvin	.35	-.05	.30	Sveum	.27	.09	.36
Mercedes	-.36	.17	-.18	Tabler	-.23	.18	-.05
Merullo	-.26	-.03	-.29	Tackett	.01	.32	.34
Miller K	3.13	.61	3.74	Tartabull	4.86	.19	5.05
Milligan	3.48	.35	3.83	Tettleton	4.13	-.42	3.72
Mitchell K	2.42	.48	2.91	Thomas F	7.44	.19	7.63
Molitor	6.68	.10	6.79	Thome	-.31	-.21	-.52
Munoz P	.70	.82	1.52	Thon	.83	.15	.98
Myers G	-.08	-.14	-.22	Thurman	-.51	.63	.13
Naehring	.45	.83	1.27	Tingley	-.27	.24	-.03
Newman A	-.65	.57	-.08	Trammell	.14	.36	.49
Newson	.41	.42	.83	Turner	-.02	.04	.02
Nilsson	.54	.14	.68	Valentin	1.28	.86	2.14
Nokes	.22	-.31	-.09	Valle	.49	-.75	-.26
O'Brien P	-.21	.37	.15	Vaughn G	2.80	.77	3.56
Oberkfell	.12	-.06	.06	Vaughn M	1.92	.03	1.95
Olerud	4.40	.36	4.75	Velarde	1.72	1.11	2.83
Orsulak	2.99	.97	3.96	Ventura	5.17	1.50	6.66
Ortiz	-.89	-.42	-1.31	Vizquel	.71	2.28	3.00
Orton	-.11	-.05	-.16	Webster L	.43	.22	.64
Pagliarulo	-.79	.14	-.65	Weiss	-.84	.47	-.37
Palmeiro	5.02	.91	5.94	Whitaker	3.27	.84	4.11
Palmer Dn	2.60	.11	2.71	White D	2.51	1.25	3.76
Parent	.24	-.05	.18	Whiten	1.64	1.30	2.94
Parrish Ln	.63	-.12	.50	Wilkerson	.20	.92	1.12
Pasqua	.75	.28	1.03	Williams B	1.43	.77	2.20
Pena T	-.85	.59	-.26	Wilson W	1.31	.87	2.17
Petralli	-.76	-.29	-1.05	Winfield	5.38	.22	5.59
Pettis	-.13	.52	.39	Winningham	-.83	.29	-.54
Phillips	3.53	1.33	4.86	Yount	3.59	1.37	4.95
Plantier	1.53	.53	2.05	Zupcic	1.41	.65	2.06

Total Wins Above Replacement

Alphabetical

NAME	OWAR	DWAR	TWAR	NAME	OWAR	DWAR	TWAR
Alicea	1.49	.68	2.17	Daulton	5.37	-1.08	4.29
Alou	2.76	.42	3.18	Davis E	1.61	-.18	1.44
Amaro	.32	.64	.97	Dawson	4.38	.95	5.33
Anderson D	.39	.08	.47	Decker S	-.25	.00	-.25
Anthony	2.24	.15	2.39	DeShields	4.19	.51	4.70
Arias	.73	.10	.83	Donnels	-.40	.06	-.34
Ashley	-.04	-.16	-.20	Doran	1.86	.77	2.64
Azocar	-1.09	.04	-1.05	Dozier D	.00	.03	.03
Bagwell	6.37	.80	7.18	Duncan	1.73	.29	2.02
Barberie	.91	.30	1.21	Dunston	.39	.22	.61
Bass K	2.41	.33	2.74	Dykstra	2.98	.85	3.83
Batiste K	-1.04	-.22	-1.25	Espy	.40	.09	.49
Bell Jay	3.59	2.95	6.55	Felder	2.45	.36	2.81
Bell Ju	-.28	.47	.20	Fernandez T	2.83	.96	3.79
Belliard	-1.46	1.05	-.41	Finley S	5.14	1.33	6.47
Benavides	-.06	.32	.26	Fletcher D	-.04	.40	.35
Benjamin	-.56	.30	-.25	Foley T	-.90	.33	-.56
Benzinger	.65	.26	.91	Galarraga	1.10	.16	1.26
Berry	.29	-.10	.19	Gallagher	.18	.36	.54
Berryhill	.53	.61	1.14	Gant	3.94	.48	4.43
Biggio	5.87	.70	6.56	Garcia C	-.27	.19	-.08
Blauser	3.50	.27	3.78	Gedman	.14	-.06	.08
Bonds	6.98	.66	7.63	Gibson K	-.16	.14	-.01
Bonilla B	3.93	.80	4.73	Gilkey	3.64	.74	4.38
Boston	2.60	.41	3.01	Girardi	.46	-.01	.45
Braggs	1.56	-.11	1.45	Gonzalez L	1.23	.74	1.97
Branson	.43	.21	.64	Goodwin	.02	.09	.11
Bream	3.14	.10	3.24	Grace	6.83	.94	7.76
Brewer R	.77	.17	.94	Greene W	.62	.05	.68
Buechele	3.15	.64	3.79	Grissom	4.66	.64	5.30
Butler	6.74	.84	7.58	Guerrero J	-.20	-.12	-.32
Calderon	.84	.15	.99	Guerrero	-.24	-.04	-.28
Caminiti	4.70	.41	5.11	Gwynn T	4.28	.79	5.07
Candaele	-.55	.94	.39	Hansen	.66	.30	.95
Carr	.20	.19	.39	Harris L	1.13	.65	1.78
Carter G	.38	.30	.68	Hatcher B	.34	-.04	.31
Castillo Br	-.36	.07	-.29	Hernandez C	.58	-.33	.26
Cedeno A	-.80	.01	-.79	Hollins	5.64	.16	5.80
Cerone	.03	-.06	-.04	Hosey	-.24	-.04	-.28
Chamberlain	1.02	.20	1.22	Howell P	-.42	.26	-.16
Cianfrocco	.31	.09	.40	Hudler	-.25	.10	-.15
Clark Je	.60	.98	1.57	Hundley	-.34	.41	.07
Clark W	6.27	.40	6.67	Hunter B	1.91	.29	2.21
Clayton	-.20	1.12	.92	Incaviglia	2.76	.56	3.32
Colbert	-.45	-.04	-.49	Jackson Dar	.02	2.13	2.15
Colbrunn	.32	.08	.39	James C	1.04	.15	1.19
Cole	.80	.40	1.20	Javier	1.11	.92	2.04
Coleman	1.93	.17	2.10	Johnson H	2.25	.00	2.25
Coles	1.29	.17	1.46	Jones Chris	.02	-.00	.01
Cordero	.81	-.14	.67	Jones Tim	-.68	.52	-.16
Daniels	.72	.15	.87	Jordan B	.09	.42	.50
Dascenzo	.85	.27	1.12	Jordan	1.39	.13	1.52

NAME	OWAR	DWAR	TWAR	NAME	OWAR	DWAR	TWAR
Jose	4.52	1.13	5.65	Samuel	.11	.05	.16
Justice	4.81	.97	5.78	Sanchez R	.35	1.66	2.01
Karros	3.93	.59	4.52	Sandberg	7.18	2.02	9.19
Kent	.42	.21	.63	Sanders	2.98	.36	3.34
King J	.81	.96	1.77	Sanders R	3.81	.96	4.77
Kruk	5.13	.20	5.33	Santiago	-.21	-.61	-.82
Lake	-.14	-.18	-.32	Sasser	-.29	-.13	-.42
Laker	-.29	.05	-.23	Schofield	.57	1.99	2.56
Lankford	6.72	1.57	8.29	Scioscia	.17	.39	.56
Larkin B	5.61	1.86	7.46	Scott G	-.90	-.09	-.99
LaValliere	.92	.65	1.57	Sorvais	-.21	.16	-.05
Lemke	.47	.57	1.04	Sharperson	3.08	.47	3.55
Leonard M	.78	.15	.92	Sheffield	6.04	.86	6.90
Lewis D	.63	.88	1.51	Shipley	-.27	.55	.29
Lind	-1.52	1.97	.44	Slaught	2.67	-.33	2.35
Litton	.32	.39	.72	Smith Dw	1.54	.14	1.69
Magadan	2.88	-.33	2.55	Smith Lo	1.36	.12	1.48
Manwaring	1.00	.07	1.07	Smith O	4.16	3.04	7.20
Marsh	-.82	.04	-.78	Snyder C	2.74	.70	3.44
Martinez Da	1.61	.70	2.31	Sosa	1.53	-.02	1.51
May D	1.81	.06	1.87	Stephenson	-.38	.03	-.35
McClendon	.87	.06	.93	Stillwell	-.44	.39	-.04
McGee	3.13	.90	4.03	Strange	-.61	-.03	-.63
McGriff F	6.39	.13	6.53	Strawberry	1.20	.04	1.24
McKnight	.35	.07	.42	Sveum	-.69	.41	-.28
Mcnamara	-.21	.08	-.14	Taubensee	.47	-.29	.19
Merced	2.34	.60	2.94	Teufel	.12	.16	.29
Millette	-.76	.37	-.39	Thompson M	1.77	.04	1.82
Morandini	.41	1.21	1.62	Thompson Ro	3.45	2.15	5.60
Morris H	2.31	.52	2.83	Thompson R	.30	.25	.55
Murphy Dl	-.61	-.09	-.70	Treadway	-.26	.48	.22
Murray E	4.56	.07	4.64	Tucker	-.57	-.10	-.68
Nixon O	2.69	1.36	4.05	Uribe	.44	.91	1.35
O'Brien C	.24	-.39	-.14	Van Slyke	6.69	1.43	8.12
O'Neill	3.29	1.51	4.80	Vanderwal	.98	.22	1.20
Offerman	2.92	-.55	2.37	Varsho	.04	.18	.22
Oliver	2.62	.14	2.76	Villanueva	-.86	.12	-.74
Olson Greg	.85	.34	1.19	Vizcaino	-.32	1.06	.74
Owen S	2.63	1.14	3.77	Walker C	2.05	.12	2.17
Pagnozzi	1.17	.59	1.75	Walker L	5.49	1.59	7.08
Patterson J	-.61	.29	-.32	Wallach	.81	1.04	1.85
Pecota	.31	.40	.72	Walters D	.34	.01	.34
Pena G	2.41	1.12	3.53	Walton	-.39	-.01	-.40
Pendleton	5.75	1.26	7.01	Ward K	-.95	.08	-.88
Perry G	-.01	-.01	-.02	Webster M	2.55	.10	2.64
Piazza	.14	-.05	.09	Wehner	-.77	.28	-.49
Prince	-.53	-.07	-.61	Wilkins R	2.08	.22	2.30
Ramirez R	-.16	.11	-.04	Williams MD	1.62	.83	2.46
Randolph	1.49	.55	2.04	Wilson C	.76	.14	.90
Redus	.97	.14	1.11	Wood	-.39	.06	-.33
Reed D	-.34	.18	-.16	Woodson	.86	.02	.88
Roberts Bip	5.66	.43	6.08	Young E	.14	.14	.28
Rodriguez H	.18	-.01	.17	Young G	-.42	.10	-.32
Sabo	1.48	.19	1.67	Zeile	3.04	.66	3.70
Salazar L	-1.07	.59	-.47				

Offensive Wins Above Replacement

All Players

NAME	OWAR	NAME	OWAR	NAME	OWAR	NAME	OWAR
Thomas F	7.44	Boggs W	2.88	Stubbs	.90	Leius	-.09
Anderson B	7.25	Vaughn G	2.80	Cora	.85	Fariss	-.10
Molitor	6.68	Seitzer	2.79	Thon	.83	Fermin	-.10
Puckett	6.11	Ripken C	2.72	Abner	.80	Orton	-.11
		Blankenship L	2.67	Koslofski	.79	Sax S	-.13
Mack	5.95	Buhner	2.67	Borders	.75	Pettis	-.13
Martinez E	5.88	Steinbach	2.66	Pasqua	.75	Martinez Crl	-.17
McGwire	5.81	Palmer Dn	2.60	Vizquel	.71	Reboulet	-.18
Alomar R	5.57	Davis G	2.53	Munoz P	.70	Cangelosi	-.18
Raines	5.49	White D	2.51	Horn	.67	O'Brien P	-.21
Winfield	5.38	Curtis C	2.51	Larkin G	.64	Tabler	-.23
Ventura	5.17			Hulett	.64	Lewis M	-.24
Palmeiro	5.02	Macfarlane	2.49	Parrish Ln	.63	Daugherty	-.25
		Mitchell K	2.42	Cotto	.60	Tingley	-.27
Baerga	4.93	Lansford	2.36	James D	.58	Rossy	-.29
Henderson R	4.87	Fryman T	2.33	Gallego	.57	Thome	-.31
Tartabull	4.86	Hrbek	2.27	Samuel	.57	Kreuter	-.34
Griffey Jr	4.56	Hall M	2.20	Kelly P	.56	Reynolds H	-.34
Devereaux	4.51	Gonzales R	2.19	Nilsson	.54	Quirk	-.37
Joyner	4.44	Cooper S	2.18	Davis A	.54	Gantner	-.37
Lofton	4.41	Fletcher S	2.14			Jacoby	-.45
Olerud	4.40	Bichette	2.08			Cole	-.46
Knoblauch	4.39	Baines	2.07	Valle	.49		
Brett	4.33	Kelly	2.05	Jaha	.48		
Tettleton	4.13	Browne J	2.03	Fisk	.46	Thurman	-.51
Gonzalez Juan	4.06			Martinez Tino	.45	Huff	-.51
Listach	4.04	Vaughn M	1.92	Naehring	.45	Amaral	-.51
		Bell Geo	1.87	Webster L	.43	Griffin Alf	-.53
Davis C	3.91	Johnson L	1.84	Newson	.41	Alomar S	-.60
Carter J	3.82	Velarde	1.72	McRae B	.37	Howard D	-.62
Sierra	3.81	Grebeck	1.67	Hill G	.37	Mayne	-.62
Brunansky	3.70	Whiten	1.64	Reed Jd	.36	Newman A	-.65
Gomez L	3.65	Huson	1.58	Franco Ju	.32	Carreon	-.67
McReynolds	3.60	Eisenreich	1.55	Barnes	.28	Greenwell	-.67
Yount	3.59	Plantier	1.53	Ready	.27	Ripken B	-.70
Maldonado	3.58			Sveum	.27	Gagne	-.73
Hamilton	3.54	Karkovice	1.48	Howard T	.25	Petralli	-.76
Phillips	3.53	Martinez C	1.46	Frye	.24	Boone B	-.79
Jefferies	3.50	Williams B	1.43	Nokes	.22	Pagliarulo	-.79
Milligan	3.48	Burks	1.41	Gaetti	.21	Hatcher B	-.81
Reimer	3.46	Zupcic	1.41	Easley D	.21	Winningham	-.83
Hoiles	3.41	Felix	1.33	Wilkerson	.20	Gruber	-.83
Bordick	3.37	Wilson W	1.31	Sojo	.20	Weiss	-.84
Whitaker	3.27	Stanley M	1.30	Bell D	.19	Beltre	-.85
Polonia	3.23	Valentin	1.28	Fox	.18	Pena T	-.85
Belle	3.13	Hayes C	1.22	Gladden	.18	Bush	-.88
Miller K	3.13	Stevens	1.19	Trammell	.14	Disarcina	-.88
Deer	3.10	Surhoff BJ	1.14	McLemore	.13	Ortiz	-.89
Downing	3.09	Leyritz	1.08	Oberkfell	.12	Bergman	-.91
Fielder	3.07	Clark Jk	1.06	Livingstone	.11	Rivera L	-.92
Harper B	3.02	Hayes V	1.01	Rodriguez I	.10	Barfield Je	-.95
				Fitzgerald	.09	Brooks	-.97
Orsulak	2.99	Maas	.97	Briley	.02	Cuyler	-1.12
Canseco	2.99	Stankiewicz	.97	Cochrane	.02		
Sorrento	2.98	Lee M	.96	Segui	.02		
Mattingly	2.91	Kent	.96	Tackett	.01		

Offensive Wins Above Replacement

All Players

NAME	OWAR	NAME	OWAR	NAME	OWAR	NAME	OWAR
Sandberg	7.18	Felder	2.45	Lewis D	.63	Patterson J	-.61
Bonds	6.98	Bass K	2.41	Greene W	.62	Jones Tim	-.68
Grace	6.83	Pena G	2.41	Clark Je	.60	Sveum	-.69
Butler	6.74	Merced	2.34	Hernandez C	.58	Wehner	-.77
Lankford	6.72	Morris H	2.31	Schofield	.57	Cedeno A	-.80
Van Slyke	6.69	Johnson H	2.25	Berryhill	.53	Marsh	-.82
McGriff F	6.39	Anthony	2.24	Taubensee	.47	Villanueva	-.86
Bagwell	6.37	Wilkins R	2.08	Lemke	.47	Foley T	-.90
Clark W	6.27	Walker C	2.05	Girardi	.46	Scott G	-.90
Sheffield	6.04	Coleman	1.93	Uribe	.44	Ward K	-.95
Biggio	5.87	Hunter B	1.91	Branson	.43	Batiste K	-1.04
Pendleton	5.75	Doran	1.86	Kent	.42	Salazar L	-1.07
Roberts Bip	5.66	May D	1.81	Morandini	.41	Azocar	-1.09
Hollins	5.64	Thompson M	1.77	Espy	.40	Belliard	-1.46
Larkin B	5.61	Duncan	1.73	Carter G	.38	Lind	-1.52
Walker L	5.49	Williams MD	1.62	Sanchez R	.35		
Daulton	5.37	Davis E	1.61	Hatcher B	.34		
Finley S	5.14	Martinez Da	1.61	Walters D	.34		
Kruk	5.13	Braggs	1.56	Amaro	.32		
Justice	4.81	Smith Dw	1.54	Litton	.32		
Caminiti	4.70	Sosa	1.53	Colbrunn	.32		
Grissom	4.66	Alicea	1.49	Pecota	.31		
Murray E	4.56	Randolph	1.49	Cianfrocco	.31		
Jose	4.52	Sabo	1.48	Thompson R	.30		
Dawson	4.38	Jordan	1.39	O'Brien C	.24		
Gwynn T	4.28	Smith Lo	1.36	Gallagher	.18		
DeShields	4.19	Coles	1.29	Rodriguez H	.18		
Smith O	4.16	Gonzalez L	1.23	Scioscia	.17		
Gant	3.94	Strawberry	1.20	Young E	.14		
Bonilla B	3.93	Pagnozzi	1.17	Gedman	.14		
Karros	3.93	Harris L	1.13	Teufel	.12		
Sanders R	3.81	Javier	1.11	Samuel	.11		
Gilkey	3.64	Galarraga	1.10	Jordan B	.09		
Bell Jay	3.59	James C	1.04	Varsho	.04		
Blauser	3.50	Chamberlain	1.02	Jackson Dar	.02		
Thompson Ro	3.45	Manwaring	1.00	Perry G	-.01		
O'Neill	3.29	Vanderwal	.98	Fletcher D	-.04		
Buechele	3.15	Redus	.97	Benavides	-.06		
Bream	3.14	LaValliere	.92	Ramirez R	-.16		
McGee	3.13	Barberie	.91	Guerrero J	-.20		
Sharperson	3.08	McClendon	.87	Clayton	-.20		
Zeile	3.04	Woodson	.86	Servais	-.21		
Dykstra	2.98	Olson Greg	.85	Santiago	-.21		
Sanders	2.98	Dascenzo	.85	Guerrero	-.24		
Offerman	2.92	Calderon	.84	Hudler	-.25		
Magadan	2.88	King J	.81	Treadway	-.26		
Fernandez T	2.83	Wallach	.81	Shipley	-.27		
Incaviglia	2.76	Cordero	.81	Bell Ju	-.28		
Alou	2.76	Cole	.80	Sasser	-.29		
Snyder C	2.74	Leonard M	.78	Vizcaino	-.32		
Nixon O	2.69	Brewer R	.77	Hundley	-.34		
Slaught	2.67	Wilson C	.76	Donnels	-.40		
Owen S	2.63	Arias	.73	Stillwell	-.44		
Oliver	2.62	Daniels	.72	Colbert	-.45		
Boston	2.60	Hansen	.66	Candaele	-.55		
Webster M	2.55	Benzinger	.65	Strange	-.61		

American League
Defensive Wins Above Replacement
All Players

Player	WAR	Player	WAR	Player	WAR	Player	WAR
Ripken C	3.07	Surhoff BJ	.80	Olerud	.36	Palmer Dn	.11
		Curtis C	.79	Trammell	.36	Martinez Crl	.11
Listach	2.59	Gladden	.79	Livingstone	.36	McIntosh	.11
Gagne	2.36	Deer	.79	Steinbach	.35	Molitor	.10
Fletcher S	2.36	Vaughn G	.77	Cangelosi	.35	Sveum	.09
Vizquel	2.28	Gallego	.77	Milligan	.35	Ducey	.09
Bordick	2.22	Williams B	.77	Leius	.34	Gwynn C	.08
Baerga	2.22	Lewis M	.75	Mayne	.33	Harris D	.08
Disarcina	2.15	Mack	.73	Tackett	.32	Sprague	.07
Reed Jd	2.13	Hayes C	.73	Borders	.31	Briley	.07
		Joyner	.72	Gomez L	.31	Hill D	.07
Knoblauch	1.82	Bichette	.72	Sierra	.30	Davis A	.07
Fryman T	1.73	Henderson R	.71	Alomar S	.30	Fitzgerald	.06
Hamilton	1.70	Rossy	.70	Stevens	.29	Cole	.05
Stankiewicz	1.60	Alomar R	.69	Jefferies	.29	Jefferson R	.05
Buhner	1.54	Kelly P	.69	Winningham	.29	Turner	.04
Ventura	1.50	Abner	.66	Gruber	.29	Daugherty	.04
		Zupcic	.65	McGwire	.29	Macfarlane	.04
Lee M	1.48	Thurman	.63	Pasqua	.28	Brett	.04
McRae B	1.46	Canseco	.63	Rose	.27	Rodriguez I	.03
Blankenship L	1.45	Miller K	.61	McReynolds	.27	Vaughn M	.03
Ripken B	1.43	Pena T	.59	Howitt	.26	Hulse	.03
Johnson L	1.41	Bell D	.58	Amaral	.26	Bergman	.03
Puckett	1.40	Newman A	.57	Hill G	.26	Belle	.01
Raines	1.40	Koslofski	.56			Fisk	.01
Lofton	1.39	Gaetti	.56	Barnes	.25	Schaefer	.01
Yount	1.37	Cotto	.55	Guillen	.24	Bell Geo	.00
Gantner	1.35	Fermin	.53	Hayes V	.24		
Sojo	1.34	Brunansky	.53	Tingley	.24	Maas	-.01
Phillips	1.33	Plantier	.53	Greenwell	.23	Colon	-.01
Griffey Jr	1.31	Pettis	.52	Blowers	.23	Cochrane	-.01
Whiten	1.30	Howard T	.52	Webster L	.22	Baines	-.02
Howard D	1.28	Gonzalez Juan	.50	Winfield	.22	Lansford	-.02
White D	1.25			Sorrento	.20	Merullo	-.03
Rivera L	1.24	Carreon	.49	Ready	.20	Salmon	-.03
Grebeck	1.22	Polonia	.49	Tartabull	.19	Leyritz	-.03
Reynolds H	1.18	Mitchell K	.48	Thomas F	.19	Shumpert	-.05
Velarde	1.11	Eisenreich	.47	Barfield Je	.19	Melvin	-.05
Reboulet	1.08	Browne J	.47	James D	.18	Parent	-.05
Huson	1.06	Weiss	.47	Karkovice	.18	Orton	-.05
		Boggs W	.46	Tabler	.18	Burks	-.05
Devereaux	.98	Martinez E	.45	Hatcher B	.18	Oberkfell	-.06
Orsulak	.97	Sax S	.45	Reimer	.17	Kent	-.08
Anderson B	.97	Easley D	.44	Mercedes	.17	Marzano	-.09
Wilkerson	.92	Cora	.43	Boone B	.17	Parrish Ln	-.12
Palmeiro	.91	Cuyler	.43	Bruett	.16	Myers G	-.14
Hall M	.91	Newson	.42	Fariss	.15	Beltre	-.16
Maldonado	.89	Hrbek	.42	Thon	.15	Flaherty	-.17
Kelly	.89	Larkin G	.40	Conine	.14	Thome	-.21
Wilson W	.87	Segui	.40	Pagliarulo	.14	Harper B	-.25
Valentin	.86	Jacoby	.39	Jaha	.14		
McLemore	.86	Frye	.39	Samuel	.14	Stanley M	-.26
Whitaker	.84	Fox	.38	Griffin Alf	.14	Petralli	-.29
Felix	.83	Martinez Tino	.37	Nilsson	.14	Nokes	-.31
Naehring	.83	Fielder	.37	Brosius	.13	Quirk	-.42
Munoz P	.82	Hulett	.37	Hoiles	.13	Tettleton	-.42
Mattingly	.82	Cooper S	.37	Jorgensen	.13	Ortiz	-.42
Gonzales R	.82	O'Brien P	.37	Bush	.13		
Carter J	.82	Huff	.36	Stubbs	.12	Kreuter	-.55
Seitzer	.81	Martinez C	.36	Gonzalez Jo	.12	Valle	-.75

Defensive Wins Above Replacement

All Players

Player	DWAR	Player	DWAR	Player	DWAR	Player	DWAR
Smith O	3.04	Zeile	.66	Howell P	.26	McClendon	.06
		Bonds	.66	Thompson R	.25	Donnels	.06
Bell Jay	2.95	LaValliere	.65			Greene W	.05
Thompson Ro	2.15	Harris L	.65	Dunston	.22	Laker	.05
Jackson Dar	2.13	Amaro	.64	Wilkins R	.22	Samuel	.05
Sandberg	2.02	Buechele	.64	Vanderwal	.22	Thompson M	.04
		Grissom	.64	Branson	.21	Marsh	.04
Schofield	1.99	Berryhill	.61	Kent	.21	Strawberry	.04
Lind	1.97	Merced	.60	Kruk	.20	Azocar	.04
Larkin B	1.86	Salazar L	.59	Chamberlain	.20	Dozier D	.03
Sanchez R	1.66	Karros	.59	Sabo	.19	Stephenson	.03
Walker L	1.59	Pagnozzi	.59	Garcia C	.19	Woodson	.02
Lankford	1.57	Lemke	.57	Carr	.19	Cedeno A	.01
O'Neill	1.51	Incaviglia	.56	Varsho	.18	Walters D	.01
		Shipley	.55	Reed D	.18	Decker S	.00
Van Slyke	1.43	Randolph	.55	Coles	.17	Johnson H	.00
Nixon O	1.36	Jones Tim	.52	Coleman	.17		
Finley S	1.33	Morris H	.52	Brewer R	.17	Jones Chris	-.00
Pendleton	1.26	DeShields	.51	Teufel	.16	Walton	-.01
Morandini	1.21			Hollins	.16	Girardi	-.01
Owen S	1.14	Gant	.48	Servais	.16	Perry G	-.01
Jose	1.13	Treadway	.48	Galarraga	.16	Rodriguez H	-.01
Clayton	1.12	Bell Ju	.47	Anthony	.15	Sosa	-.02
Pena G	1.12	Sharperson	.47	Leonard M	.15	Strange	-.03
Vizcaino	1.06	Roberts Bip	.43	Calderon	.15	Hatcher B	-.04
Belliard	1.05	Alou	.42	James C	.15	Hosey	-.04
Wallach	1.04	Jordan B	.42	Daniels	.15	Guerrero	-.04
		Sveum	.41	Smith Dw	.14	Colbert	-.04
Clark Je	.98	Hundley	.41	Gibson K	.14	Piazza	-.05
Justice	.97	Boston	.41	Redus	.14	Cerone	-.06
Fernandez T	.96	Caminiti	.41	Young E	.14	Gedman	-.06
King J	.96	Clark W	.40	Oliver	.14	Prince	-.07
Sanders R	.96	Pecota	.40	Wilson C	.14	Murphy Dl	-.09
Dawson	.95	Cole	.40	McGriff F	.13	Scott G	-.09
Candaele	.94	Fletcher D	.40	Jordan	.13	Berry	-.10
Grace	.94	Litton	.39	Walker C	.12	Tucker	-.10
Javier	.92	Stillwell	.39	Villanueva	.12	Braggs	-.11
Uribe	.91	Scioscia	.39	Smith Lo	.12	Guerrero J	-.12
McGee	.90	Millette	.37	Ramirez R	.11	Sasser	-.13
Lewis D	.88	Sanders	.36	Young G	.10	Cordero	-.14
Sheffield	.86	Gallagher	.36	Arias	.10	Ashley	-.16
Dykstra	.85	Felder	.36	Bream	.10	Davis E	-.18
Butler	.84	Olson Greg	.34	Webster M	.10	Lake	-.18
Williams MD	.83	Foley T	.33	Hudler	.10	Batiste K	-.22
Bonilla B	.80	Bass K	.33	Espy	.09	Taubensee	-.29
Bagwell	.80	Benavides	.32	Goodwin	.09	Slaught	-.33
Gwynn T	.79	Benjamin	.30	Cianfrocco	.09	Hernandez C	-.33
Doran	.77	Barberie	.30	Anderson D	.08	Magadan	-.33
		Carter G	.30	Colbrunn	.08	O'Brien C	-.39
Gonzalez L	.74	Hansen	.30	Mcnamara	.08	Offerman	-.55
Gilkey	.74	Duncan	.29	Ward K	.08	Santiago	-.61
Snyder C	.70	Hunter B	.29	Murray E	.07	Daulton	-1.08
Martinez Da	.70	Patterson J	.29	McKnight	.07		
Biggio	.70	Wehner	.28	Manwaring	.07		
Alicea	.68	Blauser	.27	Castillo Br	.07		
		Dascenzo	.27	Wood	.06		
		Benzinger	.26	May D	.06		

Trade Value

All Players

NAME	TRADE VALUE	NAME	TRADE VALUE	NAME	TRADE VALUE
Thomas F	12.446	Hoiles	3.915	Stankiewicz	2.354
Listach	12.033	Polonia	3.828	Whiten	2.338
Anderson B	11.239	Curtis C	3.770	Winfield	2.322
Knoblauch	11.005	Phillips	3.766	Whitaker	2.304
Baerga	10.824	Gomez L	3.701	Felix	2.277
Griffey Jr	10.343	Brunansky	3.691	Bichette	2.193
		Carter J	3.676	Yount	2.143
Lofton	9.466	Mitchell K	3.665	Steinbach	2.125
Ventura	9.331	McReynolds	3.631	Brett	2.074
Alomar R	9.244	Orsulak	3.584	Hall M	2.070
Puckett	9.133	Seitzer	3.403	Daugherty	2.054
McGwire	8.860	Kelly	3.401	Alomar S	2.014
Mack	8.593	Belle	3.384		
Palmeiro	8.406	Jacoby	3.373	Williams B	1.974
Bordick	8.332	Tettleton	3.331	Harper B	1.946
Martinez E	8.328	Vizquel	3.178	Macfarlane	1.938
Raines	7.014	Boggs W	3.155	Valentin	1.890
Greenwell	6.689	Deer	3.129	Huson	1.884
Gruber	6.507	Miller K	3.083	Zupcic	1.780
Henderson R	6.040	Hatcher B	3.069	Plantier	1.772
Ripken C	5.981	Reimer	3.068	Baines	1.726
Olerud	5.976	Vaughn G	3.052	Davis A	1.709
Hamilton	5.518	Davis C	3.036	Franco Ju	1.698
Devereaux	5.443			Lee M	1.697
Fielder	5.314	White D	2.986	Stubbs	1.690
Canseco	5.168	Grebeck	2.855	Vaughn M	1.654
Tartabull	5.128	Hrbek	2.810	Weiss	1.638
Sierra	5.083	Reed Jd	2.784	Surhoff BJ	1.548
Joyner	5.035	Johnson L	2.742	Martinez C	1.483
Gonzalez Juan	5.002	Palmer Dn	2.739	Brooks	1.483
		Mattingly	2.690	Myers G	1.447
Jefferies	4.961	Fletcher S	2.690	Cole	1.405
Barfield Je	4.851	Gonzales R	2.574	Hayes V	1.386
Blankenship L	4.712	Sorrento	2.560	Eisenreich	1.325
Fryman T	4.318	Velarde	2.526	Hayes C	1.305
Molitor	4.182	Davis G	2.501	Pasqua	1.289
Maldonado	4.072	Cooper S	2.480	Bell Geo	1.283
Buhner	4.053	Browne J	2.380	Maas	1.214
Milligan	4.033	Burks	2.366	McRae B	1.202

NAME	TRADE VALUE	NAME	TRADE VALUE	NAME	TRADE VALUE
Flaherty	1.201	Newson	.519	Rose	.178
Trammell	1.177	James D	.510	Gonzalez Jo	.177
Sojo	1.169	Hulett	.499	Barnes	.174
Stevens	1.116	Newman A	.497	Rivera L	.172
Abner	1.100	Gladden	.489	Melvin	.153
Karkovice	1.099	Cuyler	.487	Leius	.129
Downing	1.095	Thon	.487	O'Brien P	.087
Reynolds H	1.077	Petralli	.486	Cangelosi	.085
Marzano	1.072	Howard T	.476	Parent	.083
Carreon	1.065	Valle	.459	Brosius	.069
Kreuter	1.051	Tabler	.454	Thurman	.064
Pagliarulo	1.041	Bell D	.447	Rodriguez I	.040
Larkin G	1.037	Martinez Crl	.426	Jorgensen	.033
Clark Jk	1.021	Sax S	.422	Bruett	.025
Lansford	1.001	Hill G	.403	Fariss	.023
		Griffin Alf	.398	McIntosh	.023
Koslofski	.991	Howard D	.394	Oberkfell	.015
Orton	.983	Martinez Tino	.394	Turner	.010
Borders	.913	Frye	.374	Cochrane	.003
Disarcina	.895	Jaha	.369		
Ripken B	.884	Nilsson	.362		
Kelly P	.883	Quirk	.352		
Munoz P	.855	Easley D	.341		
Tingley	.855	Gwynn C	.336		
Merullo	.848	Pettis	.332		
Gagne	.845	Briley	.329		
Mayne	.815	Fox	.323		
Gallego	.806	Jefferson R	.323		
Naehring	.755	Pena T	.317		
Wilson W	.721	Webster L	.295		
Winningham	.720	Livingstone	.267		
Cora	.709	Bergman	.257		
Fitzgerald	.702	Ready	.256		
Ortiz	.691	Gaetti	.253		
Horn	.675				
Leyritz	.667	Ducey	.249		
Wilkerson	.664	Lewis M	.247		
Parrish Ln	.645	Fermin	.234		
McLemore	.645	Rossy	.228		
Cotto	.643	Segui	.228		
Stanley M	.633	Guillen	.226		
Reboulet	.579	Hill D	.222		
Bush	.576	Hulse	.216		
Nokes	.558	Gantner	.204		
Fisk	.554	Sveum	.196		
Samuel	.547	Tackett	.182		
Kent	.545	Conine	.178		

Trade Value

All Players

NAME	TRADE VALUE	NAME	TRADE VALUE	NAME	TRADE VALUE
Bagwell	14.158	McGee	3.750	Anthony	1.789
Lankford	13.494	Blauser	3.745	Javier	1.765
Bonds	13.114	Alou	3.441	Sanchez R	1.726
Grace	11.869	Snyder C	3.369	Gibson K	1.565
Sandberg	11.561	Smith O	3.315	Harris L	1.518
Larkin B	11.359	Magadan	3.259	James C	1.489
Sheffield	10.818	Murray E	3.185	Webster M	1.473
Walker L	10.774	Williams MD	3.131	Bass K	1.459
Van Slyke	10.204	Owen S	3.128	Slaught	1.444
McGriff F	10.115	Pena G	3.098	Sasser	1.428
		Merced	3.055	Galarraga	1.425
Clark W	9.734	Sharperson	3.034	Jackson Dar	1.363
Biggio	9.242	Morris H	2.988	Braggs	1.306
Hollins	9.141	Incaviglia	2.939	Walker C	1.263
Bell Jay	8.750	Bream	2.789	Gonzalez L	1.263
Pendleton	8.741	Buechele	2.762	Calderon	1.224
Roberts Bip	8.546	Sabo	2.710	O'Brien C	1.202
Justice	8.402	Dawson	2.658	Pagnozzi	1.195
Finley S	7.945	Strawberry	2.617	King J	1.174
Sanders R	6.858	Boston	2.613	May D	1.166
Jose	6.685	Guerrero	2.540	Walton	1.125
DeShields	6.612	Nixon O	2.534	Murphy Dl	1.124
Grissom	6.418			Colbert	1.123
Butler	6.393	Duncan	2.330	Smith Dw	1.121
Bonilla B	6.297	Doran	2.308	Prince	1.091
Karros	6.257	Johnson H	2.287	Smith Lo	1.079
Gant	6.213	Oliver	2.271	Lake	1.070
Dykstra	5.724	Coleman	2.270	Sosa	1.066
Thompson Ro	5.523	Davis E	2.239		
Kruk	5.516	Offerman	2.217	LaValliere	.999
O'Neill	5.276	Daniels	2.151	Coles	.987
		Wilkins R	2.115	Hudler	.986
Caminiti	4.973	Wallach	2.054	Cole	.979
Gwynn T	4.964	Martinez Da	2.047	Laker	.977
Daulton	4.511	Felder	2.003	Morandini	.963
Gilkey	4.438	Hunter B	1.989	Clark Je	.959
Zeile	4.073	Alicea	1.893	Tucker	.957
Fernandez T	3.800	Santiago	1.889	Thompson M	.914
Sanders	3.796	Schofield	1.825	Hatcher B	.876

NAME	TRADE VALUE	NAME	TRADE VALUE
Jordan	.876	Cordero	.302
Lewis D	.868	Jordan B	.279
Servais	.866	Anderson D	.279
Mcnamara	.862	Gallagher	.273
Barberie	.842	Espy	.272
Vanderwal	.840	Batiste K	.266
Berryhill	.760	Teufel	.236
Scioscia	.721	Carter G	.231
Manwaring	.721	McKnight	.228
Lemke	.693	Cianfrocco	.216
Uribe	.691	Cerone	.203
Chamberlain	.689	Girardi	.197
Olson Greg	.667	Carr	.195
Perry G	.653	Decker S	.192
Amaro	.633	Fletcher D	.190
Dascenzo	.616	Colbrunn	.187
Brewer R	.612	Walters D	.184
Candaele	.612	Shipley	.150
Ramirez R	.597	Young E	.148
Hansen	.590	Benavides	.137
Dunston	.578	Hernandez C	.129
Wilson C	.574	Azocar	.111
Randolph	.562	Varsho	.107
Benzinger	.561	Berry	.099
Redus	.540	Bell Ju	.093
Clayton	.538	Reed D	.087
Woodson	.533	Taubensee	.086
Belliard	.512	Rodriguez H	.080
Salazar L	.511	Gedman	.050
Arias	.507	Goodwin	.049
		Piazza	.039
Stillwell	.480	Hundley	.029
Villanueva	.452	Garcia C	.016
Leonard M	.451	Dozier D	.015
McClendon	.437	Jones Tim	.011
Litton	.435	Jones Chris	.006
Pecota	.434		
Treadway	.402		
Branson	.373		
Kent	.356		
Cedeno A	.352		
Stephenson	.339		
Vizcaino	.332		
Samuel	.323		
Greene W	.308		
Lind	.308		
Thompson R	.304		

Base Stealing Profit

$$SB + PkOE - 65(CS + PKO)/35 = \text{Net Bases Gained}$$

	SB	PkOE	CS	PkO	Net
Raines	45	5	6	0	38.86
Alomar R	49	6	9	1	36.43
Lofton	66	5	12	8	33.86
White D	37	3	4	0	32.57
Henderson R	48	4	11	1	29.71
Listach	54	4	18	0	24.57
Molitor	31	3	6	0	22.86
Johnson L	41	5	14	1	18.14
Kelly	28	1	5	1	17.86
Wilson W	28	4	8	0	17.14
Knoblauch	34	8	13	1	16.00
Anderson B	53	0	16	4	15.86
Thon	12	2	2	0	10.29
McRae B	18	3	5	1	9.86
Polonia	51	6	21	5	8.72
Martinez E	14	1	4	0	7.57
McReynolds	7	2	1	0	7.14
Puckett	17	3	7	0	7.00
Lee M	6	4	2	0	6.29
Miller K	16	3	6	1	6.00
Carter J	12	5	5	1	5.86
Sierra	12	1	4	0	5.57
Belle	8	1	2	0	5.29
Baerga	10	0	2	1	4.43
Sax S	30	0	12	2	4.00
Howard T	0	4	0	0	4.00
Yount	15	0	6	0	3.86
Palmer Dn	10	1	4	0	3.57
Jefferies	19	3	9	1	3.43
Lansford	7	0	2	0	3.29
Mack	26	3	14	0	3.00
Mattingly	3	0	0	0	3.00
Bichette	18	1	7	2	2.29
Deer	4	2	2	0	2.29
Bell Geo	5	1	2	0	2.29
Surhoff BJ	14	3	8	0	2.14
Curtis C	0	4	0	1	2.14
Cooper S	0	2	0	0	2.00
Cotto	0	2	0	0	2.00
Huson	0	2	0	0	2.00
Olerud	1	1	0	0	2.00
Huff	0	2	0	0	2.00
Allanson	0	2	0	0	2.00

	SB	PkOE	CS	PkO	Net
Amaral	0	2	0	0	2.00
Rb Williams	0	2	0	0	2.00
Bordick	12	1	6	0	1.86
Karkovice	10	1	4	1	1.71
Griffey Jr	10	1	5	0	1.71
Hrbek	5	0	2	0	1.29
Gaetti	3	0	1	0	1.14
Newman A	0	3	0	1	1.14
Pettis	0	3	0	1	1.14
Williams B	0	3	0	1	1.14
Bell D	0	3	0	1	1.14
Easley D	0	3	0	1	1.14
Greenwell	0	1	0	0	1.00
Downing	1	0	0	0	1.00
Browne J	0	1	0	0	1.00
Mayne	0	1	0	0	1.00
McIntosh	0	1	0	0	1.00
Gantner	0	1	0	0	1.00
Spiers	0	1	0	0	1.00
Ortiz	0	1	0	0	1.00
Velarde	0	1	0	0	1.00
Kreuter	0	1	0	0	1.00
Davis G	1	0	0	0	1.00
Mercedes	0	1	0	0	1.00
Wedge	0	1	0	0	1.00
Abner	0	1	0	0	1.00
Gonzalez Jo	0	1	0	0	1.00
Wilkerson	0	1	0	0	1.00
Nilsson	0	1	0	0	1.00
Jorgensen	0	1	0	0	1.00
Fox	0	1	0	0	1.00
Hulse	0	1	0	0	1.00
Joyner	11	1	5	1	.86
Rivera L	4	2	3	0	.43
Thomas F	6	0	3	0	.43
Weiss	6	0	3	0	.43
Gladden	4	0	2	0	.29
Hall M	4	0	2	0	.29
Gonzales R	0	2	0	1	.14
Thurman	0	2	0	1	.14
Martinez Tino	2	0	1	0	.14
O'Brien P	2	0	1	0	.14
Borders	1	1	1	0	.14
Hill G	9	2	6	0	-.14

	SB	PkOE	CS	PkO	Net
Fryman T	8	1	4	1	-.29
Whitaker	6	1	4	0	-.43
Fletcher S	17	1	10	0	-.57
Devereaux	10	6	8	1	-.71
Pena T	3	0	2	0	-.71
Maldonado	2	1	2	0	-.71
Tartabull	2	1	2	0	-.71
Maas	3	0	1	1	-.71
Blankenship L	0	3	0	2	-.71
Milligan	0	1	1	0	-.86
McGwire	0	1	1	0	-.86
Clark Jk	1	0	1	0	-.86
Cora	0	1	0	1	-.86
Winningham	0	1	0	1	-.86
Samuel	0	1	0	1	-.86
Diaz A	0	1	0	1	-.86
James D	0	1	0	1	-.86
Cuyler	8	2	5	1	-1.14
Stankiewicz	9	1	5	1	-1.14
Ripken C	4	0	3	0	-1.57
Fitzgerald	2	2	2	1	-1.57
Hamilton	0	2	0	2	-1.71
Zupcic	2	0	2	0	-1.71
Cangelosi	0	2	0	2	-1.71
Hayes V	11	2	6	2	-1.86
Melvin	0	0	0	1	-1.86
Pasqua	0	0	1	0	-1.86
Cole	0	0	0	1	-1.86
Nokes	0	0	1	0	-1.86
Harper B	0	0	1	0	-1.86
Valle	0	0	0	1	-1.86
Franco Ju	0	0	0	1	-1.86
Boone B	0	0	0	1	-1.86
Gruber	7	4	7	0	-2.00
Kelly P	8	1	5	1	-2.14
Seitzer	13	5	11	0	-2.43
Howard D	3	2	4	0	-2.43
Phillips	12	4	10	0	-2.57
Alomar S	3	0	3	0	-2.57
Brooks	3	0	3	0	-2.57
Frye	1	2	3	0	-2.57
Mitchell K	0	1	2	0	-2.71
Whiten	16	3	12	0	-3.29
Orsulak	5	1	4	1	-3.29
Leius	6	0	5	0	-3.29
Ripken B	2	0	3	0	-3.57
Gomez L	2	0	3	0	-3.57
Winfield	2	0	3	0	-3.57
Steinbach	2	0	3	0	-3.57
Palmeiro	2	0	3	0	-3.57
Hoiles	0	0	2	0	-3.71
Gonzalez Juan	0	0	1	1	-3.71
Barnes	0	0	0	2	-3.71
Griffin Alf	0	0	0	2	-3.71
Eisenreich	11	0	6	2	-3.86

	SB	PkOE	CS	PkO	Net
Stubbs	11	0	8	0	-3.86
Disarcina	9	0	7	0	-4.00
Ventura	2	1	4	0	-4.43
Reimer	2	1	4	0	-4.43
Vaughn M	3	0	3	1	-4.43
Boggs W	1	0	3	0	-4.57
Sorrento	0	1	3	0	-4.57
Baines	1	0	3	0	-4.57
Livingstone	1	0	3	0	-4.57
Brett	8	0	6	1	-5.00
Lewis M	4	2	5	1	-5.14
Hatcher B	4	2	6	0	-5.14
Davis C	4	0	5	0	-5.29
Munoz P	4	0	5	0	-5.29
Stevens	1	1	4	0	-5.43
Grebeck	0	0	3	0	-5.57
Jacoby	0	0	3	0	-5.57
Reynolds H	15	1	12	0	-6.29
Hayes C	3	0	5	0	-6.29
Felix	8	0	8	0	-6.86
Gagne	6	1	7	1	-7.86
Canseco	5	2	7	1	-7.86
Vizquel	15	3	13	1	-8.00
Brunansky	2	1	5	1	-8.14
Macfarlane	1	0	5	0	-8.29
Reed Jd	7	2	8	2	-9.57
Tettleton	0	1	6	0	-10.14
Buhner	0	0	6	0	-11.14
Sojo	7	0	11	1	-15.29
Vaughn G	15	1	15	3	-17.43

Base Stealing Profit

SB + PkOE - 65(CS + PKO)/35 = Net Bases Gained

NAME	SB	PkOE	CS	PkO	Net	NAME	SB	PkOE	CS	PkO	Net
Grissom	78	5	13	5	49.57	Espy	0	2	0	0	2.00
						Perry G	0	2	0	0	2.00
Finley S	44	2	9	1	27.43	Snyder C	0	2	0	0	2.00
Smith O	43	3	9	3	23.71						
Bonds	39	3	8	2	23.43	Bagwell	10	3	6	0	1.86
DeShields	46	9	15	3	21.57	Amaro	11	2	5	1	1.86
Dykstra	30	2	5	1	20.86	Barberie	9	2	5	0	1.71
Duncan	23	3	3	0	20.43	Olson Greg	2	1	1	0	1.14
						Sanchez R	2	1	1	0	1.14
Davis E	19	2	1	1	17.29	Lind	3	0	1	0	1.14
Lewis D	28	5	8	1	16.29	Manwaring	2	1	1	0	1.14
Roberts Bip	44	7	16	4	13.86	Bass K	0	3	0	1	1.14
Biggio	38	5	15	1	13.29	Berryhill	0	1	0	0	1.00
Alou	16	3	2	2	11.57	Hunter B	0	1	0	0	1.00
Johnson H	22	0	5	1	10.86	Smith Lo	0	1	0	0	1.00
Gant	32	1	10	2	10.71	Wilkins R	0	1	0	0	1.00
						Walton	0	1	0	0	1.00
Walker L	18	2	6	0	8.86	Benzinger	0	1	0	0	1.00
Nixon O	41	1	18	0	8.57	Cerone	0	1	0	0	1.00
Larkin B	15	1	4	0	8.57	Magadan	1	0	0	0	1.00
Jackson Dar	14	0	3	0	8.43	Teufel	0	1	0	0	1.00
Daulton	11	1	2	1	6.43	McClendon	0	1	0	0	1.00
Sandberg	17	2	6	1	6.00	King J	0	1	0	0	1.00
Bream	6	0	0	0	6.00	Guerrero	0	1	0	0	1.00
Hundley	3	2	0	0	5.00	Wilson C	0	1	0	0	1.00
Sosa	0	5	0	0	5.00	Ward K	0	1	0	0	1.00
						Uribe	0	1	0	0	1.00
McGee	13	3	4	2	4.86	Tucker	0	1	0	0	1.00
Schofield	11	1	4	0	4.57	Rodriguez H	0	1	0	0	1.00
Jose	28	4	12	3	4.14	Young E	0	1	0	0	1.00
Harris L	19	0	7	1	4.14						
Grace	6	0	1	0	4.14	Hollins	9	3	6	0	.86
Sanders R	0	4	0	0	4.00	Clayton	8	2	4	1	.71
Van Slyke	12	1	3	2	3.71	May D	5	1	3	0	.43
Caminiti	10	1	4	0	3.57	Bonilla B	4	2	3	0	.43
Clark Je	3	2	0	1	3.14	Taubensee	2	0	1	0	.14
Bell Ju	5	0	0	1	3.14	Boston	12	1	6	1	.00
Webster M	0	3	0	0	3.00	Clark W	12	1	7	0	.00
Gallagher	0	3	0	0	3.00						
Owen S	9	1	4	0	2.57	Gilkey	18	6	12	1	-.14
Morandini	8	0	3	0	2.43	Doran	7	0	4	0	-.43
Dawson	6	0	2	0	2.29	Pendleton	5	0	2	1	-.57
Stillwell	4	0	1	0	2.14	Sanders	0	3	0	2	-.71
Cedeno A	2	0	0	0	2.00	Scioscia	3	0	2	0	-.71
Young G	0	2	0	0	2.00	Strawberry	3	0	1	1	-.71
Javier	0	2	0	0	2.00	Vizcaino	0	1	0	1	-.86
Redus	0	2	0	0	2.00	Sharperson	0	1	0	1	-.86

NAME	SB	PkOE	CS	PkO	Net
Hudler	0	1	0	1	-.86
Pena G	0	1	0	1	-.86
Greene W	0	1	0	1	-.86
Marsh	0	1	0	1	-.86
Cole	7	3	4	2	-1.14
Butler	41	6	21	5	-1.28
Bell Jay	7	1	5	0	-1.29
O'Neill	6	0	3	1	-1.43
Galarraga	5	1	4	0	-1.43
Merced	5	1	4	0	-1.43
Wallach	2	0	2	0	-1.71
Belliard	0	0	1	0	-1.86
Walker C	0	0	0	1	-1.86
Scott G	0	0	0	1	-1.86
Benavides	0	0	0	1	-1.86
Varsho	0	0	0	1	-1.86
Azocar	0	0	0	1	-1.86
Coles	0	0	0	1	-1.86
Incaviglia	0	0	0	1	-1.86
Baez	0	0	0	1	-1.86
McCray	0	0	0	1	-1.86
Patterson J	0	0	0	1	-1.86
McGriff F	8	1	6	0	-2.14
Anthony	5	0	4	0	-2.43
Murray E	4	1	2	2	-2.43
Martinez Da	12	4	8	2	-2.57
Girardi	0	1	2	0	-2.71
Coleman	0	1	0	2	-2.71
Lankford	42	7	24	4	-3.00
James C	2	2	3	1	-3.43
Oliver	2	0	3	0	-3.57
Smith Dw	0	0	0	2	-3.71
Hansen	0	0	2	0	-3.71
Gonzalez L	7	4	7	1	-3.86
Sabo	4	1	5	0	-4.29
Justice	2	1	4	0	-4.43
Offerman	23	4	16	1	-4.57
Buechele	1	0	3	0	-4.57
Randolph	1	0	3	0	-4.57
Williams MD	7	1	7	0	-5.00
Sheffield	5	3	6	1	-5.00
Lemke	0	0	3	0	-5.57
LaValliere	0	0	3	0	-5.57
Kruk	3	0	5	0	-6.29
Alicea	2	1	5	0	-6.29
Felder	0	1	0	4	-6.43
Morris H	6	0	6	1	-7.00
Santiago	2	2	5	1	-7.14
Pagnozzi	2	0	5	0	-7.29
Carter G	0	0	4	0	-7.43
Gwynn T	3	2	6	1	-8.00
Karros	2	0	4	2	-9.14
Dascenzo	6	1	8	1	-9.71

NAME	SB	PkOE	CS	PkO	Net
Thompson Ro	5	1	9	0	-10.71
Zeile	7	0	10	0	-11.57
Fernandez T	20	2	20	0	-15.14

Earned Run Average

Ballpark-Adjusted

Name	ERA	Name	ERA	Name	ERA	Name	ERA
Rasmussen D	1.19	Rogers	3.20	Timlin	4.12	Alvarez W	5.38
Corsi	1.23	Monteleone	3.20	Henry D	4.15	Wells	5.40
Farr	1.38	Orosco	3.23	Cadaret	4.17	Berenguer	5.44
Lilliquist	1.61	Militello	3.30	Kipper	4.19	Delucia	5.49
Russell Jf	1.63	McDowell J	3.31	Hesketh	4.24	Ritz	5.49
Hernandez R	1.65	Grahe	3.33	Krueger	4.24	Banks	5.58
Eldred	1.79	Wegman	3.34	McDonald	4.24	Groom	5.59
Eckersley	1.80	Erickson S	3.35	Kamieniecki	4.26	Jones Cd	5.69
Austin	1.85	Viola	3.37	Gullickson	4.30	Milacki	5.84
Fetters	1.87	Frey	3.38	Tanana	4.34	Robinson JM	5.91
Ward D	1.95	Fleming	3.39	McCaskill	4.35	Boucher	5.93
Leach T	1.96	Plunk	3.39	Pavlik	4.36		
Kiely	1.96	Brown Kev	3.42	Nichols Rod	4.36	Robinson R	6.11
		Davis Storm	3.42	MacDonald	4.37	Mathews T	6.16
Quantrill	2.01	Nelson J	3.44	Witt B	4.38	Lancaster	6.23
Olson Gregg	2.05	Honeycutt	3.46	Aquino	4.39	Nelson G	6.27
Montgomery	2.07	Navarro	3.48	Armstrong	4.43	Johnson J	6.49
Olin	2.24			Gordon	4.44	Bohanon	6.50
Henke	2.26	Key	3.53	Young Mt	4.46	Bannister F	6.57
Horsman	2.28	Langston	3.54	Knudsen	4.46	Aldred	6.65
Clemens	2.34	Reed Rk	3.59	Fernandez A	4.46	Otto	6.72
Power	2.36	Valera	3.59	Sutcliffe	4.47	Davis Mrk	6.94
Appier	2.38	Stewart D	3.61	Mesa	4.48	Ruffin	6.98
Shifflett	2.42	Darling	3.62			Bailes	7.22
Harris GA	2.42	Rhodes A	3.63	Stottlemyre	4.50	Flanagan	8.05
Wayne	2.44	Gubicza	3.64	Fisher	4.53		
Frohwirth	2.46	Haney	3.64	Blyleven	4.53		
		Cook D	3.65	Powell	4.58		
Mussina	2.54	Habyan	3.71	Hibbard	4.60		
Cone	2.55	Young C	3.72	Gardiner	4.61		
Holmes	2.55	Lewis S	3.76	Schooler	4.70		
Gossage	2.61	Johnson R	3.77	Magnante	4.74		
Willis	2.61	Bosio	3.77	Swan	4.74		
Mills A	2.61	Guzman	3.78	Boddicker	4.78		
Guzman J	2.64	Haas D	3.79	Bones	4.79		
Meacham R	2.66	Doherty	3.80	Hanson	4.82		
Abbott	2.69	Pichardo	3.82	Sanderson	4.84		
Aguilera	2.70	Finley C	3.83	Thigpen	4.91		
Edens	2.71	Ryan	3.83	Mahomes	4.91		
Radinsky	2.73	Henneman	3.84	Crim	4.97		
Guthrie	2.76	Darwin	3.85	Fortugno	4.97		
Perez M	2.80	Heaton	3.86	Campbell K	4.98		
Munoz	2.81	Grant	3.89				
Nagy	2.82	Tapani	3.93	Nunez E	5.01		
Wickander	2.85	Burns	3.93	Hillegas	5.02		
Parrett	2.93	Wickman	3.93	Scudder	5.04		
Eichhorn	2.98	Dopson	3.95	Stieb	5.05		
				Pall	5.05		
Plesac	3.08	Morris Jk	4.04	King E	5.11		
Trombley	3.11	Reardon	4.04	Terrell	5.14		
Smiley	3.17	Moore M	4.08	Leary	5.30		
Downs	3.18	Hough	4.08	Slusarski	5.33		
Welch	3.20	Leiter M	4.10	Hentgen	5.36		

Earned Run Average

Ballpark-Adjusted

Rojas	1.25	Dibble	2.94	Hershiser	3.76	Scott Tim	4.78
Howell Jay	1.54	Brantley J	2.94	Schourek	3.77	Browning	4.86
Beck	1.76	Nabholz	2.95	Williams Mitch	3.78	Ruskin	4.86
Perez Mk	1.84	Innis	2.97	Gooden	3.80	Burba	4.97
Harkey	1.89	Carpenter	2.97	Mulholland	3.81		
Valdez	1.93	Cone	2.97	Harris GW	3.81	Boskie	5.01
Smith P	1.94	Rivera B	2.99	Osborne	3.82	Bolton	5.05
Astacio	1.98			Burkett	3.84	Righetti	5.06
		Robinson JD	3.00	Pena A	3.86	Abbott K	5.13
Jones D	2.02	Ritchie	3.00	Gardner M	3.86	Mathews	5.16
Swift	2.08	Deshaies	3.00	Patterson K	3.89	Crews	5.31
Worrell	2.11	Candiotti	3.05	Jackson Dan	3.89	Greene	5.32
Maddux M	2.15	Smith Z	3.06	Olivares	3.93	Gibson P	5.37
Wakefield	2.15	Freeman M	3.08	Myers R	3.95	Hillman	5.50
Rodriguez Rich	2.18	Andersen L	3.09	Stanton M	3.96	Jones Ba	5.68
Martinez De	2.19	Hickerson	3.09	Black	3.97	Guetterman	6.02
Tewksbury	2.20	Benes	3.11			Robinson D	6.18
Maddux G	2.22	Ayrault	3.12	Heredia G	4.03	Slocumb	6.50
Hernandez X	2.27	Henry	3.12	Hammond	4.03	Ashby A	7.54
Wohlers	2.29	Avery	3.12	Harnisch	4.05	Bowen R	11.76
Schilling	2.35	Smith Le	3.12	Martinez R	4.06		
Pugh	2.38	Belinda	3.15	Mason R	4.09		
Hill K	2.39	McClure	3.17	Assenmacher	4.10		
Bielecki	2.45	Walk	3.20	Brink	4.14		
Gott	2.45	Gross K	3.21	Wilson S	4.18		
Rijo	2.47	Leibrandt	3.26	McDowell R	4.20		
		Mercker	3.29	Br. Williams	4.20		
Fassero	2.52	Tomlin R	3.41	Wilson Tr	4.21		
Swindell	2.57	Seminara	3.41	Rogers K	4.24		
Morgan M	2.59	Lefferts	3.42	Palacios	4.24		
Wetteland	2.59	Hartley	3.44	Kile	4.31		
Barnes B	2.61	Downs	3.46	Young A	4.31		
Boever	2.67	Pena J	3.48	Blair	4.35		
Glavine	2.68			Murphy R	4.36		
Foster S	2.70	Castillo F	3.51	Jones Jim	4.39		
Sampen	2.70	McElroy	3.55	Henry B	4.40		
Melendez J	2.72	Saberhagen	3.59	DeLeon J	4.45		
Drabek	2.77	Hurst	3.60	Robinson JM	4.46		
Smoltz	2.77	Oliveras	3.63	Neagle	4.48		
Bankhead	2.80	Ojeda	3.68	Osuna	4.52		
Fernandez S	2.81	Hernandez Jer	3.68	Clark M	4.53		
Portugal	2.84	Whitehurst	3.71	Cox	4.60		
Charlton	2.88	Cormier	3.73	Brantley C	4.60		
Scanlan	2.88	Jackson M	3.73	Bullinger	4.66		
Patterson B	2.92	Belcher	3.76	Haney	4.74		

Top Tens

Ballpark Adjusted

Runs

Thomas F	113
Phillips	113
Raines	106
Puckett	105
Knoblauch	105
Alomar R	105
Mack	102
Martinez E	102
Anderson B	99
White D	98

Home Runs

Gonzalez Juan	45
McGwire	38
Fielder	33
Belle	32
Carter J	32
Deer	30
Tettleton	29
Palmer Dn	27
Tartabull	26
Griffey Jr	26

Slugging Pct

McGwire	.573
Thomas F	.548
Gonzalez Juan	.530
Martinez E	.527
Griffey Jr	.506
Tartabull	.492
Carter J	.490
Puckett	.488
Winfield	.484
Olerud	.481

Strikeouts

Johnson R	241
Perez M	218
Clemens	208
Guzman Jose	179
McDowell	178
Langston	174
Brown K	173
Nagy	169
Guzman Juan	165
Smiley	163

Hits

Puckett	211
Baerga	201
Molitor	192
Thomas F	191
Mack	190
Martinez E	183
Devereaux	181
Fryman T	179
Mattingly	179
Knoblauch	179

Runs Batted In

Fielder	123
Thomas F	122
Bell Geo	118
Carter J	118
Gonzalez Juan	116
Puckett	114
Devereaux	108
Winfield	107
McGwire	107
Belle	103

On-Base Ave

Thomas F	.450
Tartabull	.411
Martinez E	.403
Molitor	.402
Alomar R	.400
McGwire	.392
Raines	.391
Phillips	.387
Milligan	.386
Ventura	.386

Walks Allowed

Johnson R	150
Witt B	114
Finley C	102
Moore M	100
McCaskill	96
Perez M	91
Viola	90
Leary	87
Tanana	86
Erickson S	82

Doubles

Thomas F	52
Ventura	43
Yount	41
Martinez E	41
Puckett	38
Mattingly	38
Molitor	37
Seitzer	36
Joyner	35
Griffey Jr	35

Walks

Thomas F	126
Tettleton	117
Phillips	109
Milligan	108
Tartabull	107
Anderson B	95
Ventura	93
Henderson R	93
McGwire	88
Knoblauch	87

Offensive WPct

Thomas F	.830
McGwire	.790
Molitor	.774
Martinez E	.772
Anderson B	.758
Tartabull	.749
Raines	.715
Alomar R	.715
Puckett	.706
Mack	.706

Run Support/9 IP

Alvarez W	7.53
Doherty	6.67
Eldred	6.55
Sanderson	6.24
Tapani	6.05
Krueger	6.02
Morris Jk	5.98
Stottlemyre	5.90
Terrell	5.73
Pichardo	5.70

Triples

Anderson B	17
Johnson L	16
Lofton	11
Raines	10
Hamilton	9
Devereaux	8
Molitor	8
Sierra	7
Alomar R	7
Listach	7

Batting Ave

Martinez E	.341
Thomas F	.330
Molitor	.328
Puckett	.327
Mack	.314
Bordick	.313
Alomar R	.312
Harper B	.306
Baerga	.302
Raines	.301

Defensive WPct

Hamilton	.818
Raines	.806
Bell D	.796
Koslofski	.791
Reboulet	.765
Fletcher S	.750
Gantner	.745
Thurman	.733
Abner	.725
Williams B	.697

Catcher's Ratio

Surhoff BJ	.807
Mayne	.815
Rodriguez I	.819
Steinbach	.826
Merullo	.848
Tingley	.855
Alomar S	.866
Webster L	.869
Borders	.894
Pena T	.900

Top Tens

Ballpark Adjusted

Runs	
Biggio	110
Bonds	110
Hollins	105
Van Slyke	104
Bagwell	99
Sandberg	98
Pendleton	96
Butler	93
Bell Jay	91
Lankford	91

Home Runs	
Bonds	42
McGriff F	29
Karros	28
Hollins	27
Sheffield	27
Sandberg	25
Daulton	25
Justice	21
Dawson	21
Bagwell	21

Slugging Pct	
Bonds	.659
Sheffield	.528
McGriff F	.527
Daulton	.510
Van Slyke	.501
Sandberg	.498
Walker L	.488
Lankford	.471
Clark W	.470
Hollins	.468

Strikeouts	
Smoltz	215
Cone	214
Maddux G	199
Fernandez S	193
Drabek	177
Rijo	171
Benes	169
Harnisch	164
Gross	158
Candiotti	152

Hits	
Grace	198
Pendleton	195
Van Slyke	191
Sandberg	190
Finley S	184
Lankford	183
Biggio	175
Butler	175
Roberts Bip	173
Grissom	172

Runs Batted In	
Bagwell	106
Pendleton	102
Bonds	102
Daulton	99
McGriff F	99
Murray E	96
Hollins	94
Dawson	93
Karros	93
Sheffield	91

On-Base Ave	
Bonds	.443
Kruk	.423
Butler	.422
Roberts Bip	.396
Clark W	.394
McGriff F	.392
Larkin B	.383
Biggio	.380
Grace	.379
Daulton	.378

Walks Allowed	
Ojeda	85
Cone	83
Gross K	81
Smoltz	78
Morgan M	78
Belcher	77
Hill K	75
Jackson Dan	74
Nabholz	74
Hershiser	72

Doubles	
Duncan	43
Clark W	42
Grace	41
Van Slyke	41
Lankford	40
Pendleton	39
Murray E	37
Bagwell	35
Bell Jay	34
Sheffield	34

Walks	
Bonds	115
Butler	109
Biggio	103
Bagwell	92
Kruk	87
McGriff F	87
Daulton	84
Clark W	82
Justice	76
Hollins	74

Offensive WPct	
Bonds	.898
McGriff F	.790
Clark W	.788
Sandberg	.780
Van Slyke	.771
Butler	.763
Daulton	.760
Roberts Bip	.751
Grace	.748
Sheffield	.745

Run Support/9 IP	
Rivera B	5.91
Seminara	5.56
Walk	5.47
Hernandez X	5.43
Glavine	5.32
Mulholland	4.99
Swindell	4.93
Lefferts	4.79
Burkett	4.70
Jones Jim	4.65

Triples	
Sanders	14
Butler	12
Alicea	12
Finley S	11
Van Slyke	9
Gant	8
Grace	7
Larkin B	7
Sanders R	7
Bagwell	7

Batting Ave	
Roberts Bip	.328
Gwynn T	.321
Kruk	.320
Van Slyke	.318
Sheffield	.312
Larkin B	.311
Grace	.310
Butler	.310
Sandberg	.307
Pendleton	.306

Defensive WPct	
Pena G	.790
Walker L	.734
Jackson Dar	.734
Thompson Ro	.723
Javier	.717
Sanchez R	.716
O'Neill	.711
Smith O	.704
Nixon O	.703
Gilkey	.681

Catcher's Ratio	
Villanueva	.760
Hundley	.784
LaValliere	.789
Scioscia	.824
Berryhill	.845
Mcnamara	.862
Servais	.866
Fletcher D	.874
Oliver	.930
Carter G	.940

Ground Ball / Fly Ball / Strikeout

All Teams

American League

Groundballs, Flyballs, Strikeouts off Team

	Ground	Fly+Pop	G/F	K's
Baltimore	1931	1768	1.0922	846
Boston	2144	1370	1.5649	943
California	2054	1574	1.3049	888
Chicago	1994	1614	1.2354	810
Cleveland	1998	1671	1.1957	890
Detroit	2072	1623	1.2766	693
Kansas City	2040	1632	1.2500	834
Milwaukee	2017	1685	1.1970	793
Minnesota	1981	1591	1.2451	923
New York	2013	1697	1.1862	851
Oakland	1858	1801	1.0316	843
Seattle	1996	1648	1.2111	894
Texas	1946	1627	1.1960	1034
Toronto	1862	1634	1.1395	954

National League

Groundballs, Flyballs, Strikeouts off Team

	Ground	Fly+Pop	G/F	K's
Atlanta	1930	1523	1.2672	948
Chicago	2171	1335	1.6262	901
Cincinnati	1893	1556	1.2166	1060
Houston	1960	1565	1.2524	978
Los Angeles	2163	1365	1.5846	981
Montreal	2094	1419	1.4757	1014
New York	2006	1501	1.3364	1025
Philadelphia	1936	1629	1.1884	851
Pittsburgh	2205	1584	1.3920	844
St. Louis	2111	1653	1.2771	842
San Diego	1971	1433	1.3754	971
San Francisco	1956	1640	1.1927	927

Major League Equivalencies

for
Minor League Players

Brock J. Hanke and Brian Rodewald

What are Major League Equivalencies?

They are basic stat lines which approximate what AAA and AA players would have done had they been brought up by their Major League clubs.

How are they derived?

In the 1985 BILL JAMES BASEBALL ABSTRACT, Bill presented a method for doing MLE's. The method is functionally unchanged from Bill's original. Without going into screaming detail, the method does the following:

1. Adjusts for the minor league ballpark. Bill's original method didn't do this, because Bill had no access to home/ road splits for minor league parks, and so could not compute minor league ballpark adjustment factors. Well, I purchased the pertinent data from Howe, who now do all the AAA and AA stats, and got park adjustments made. That Bill doesn't do this, or that his adjustment method is different from mine, would explain why my MLEs are not exactly the same as those found in the STATS Inc. Minor League Handbook.

2. Adjusts for the relative levels of offense in the minor league and the Major League. That is, if the Texas League is scoring 10 runs per game, and the National League is scoring 8, that adjustment is made.

3. Deducts 18% for the difference in quality of play between the Majors and the minors. Oddly enough, this 18% is the same for AAA and AA stats. The varying qualities of the Class-A leagues makes translation from them impossible.

4. Using all the above, computes and uses mysterious "m" and "M" factors. See the Glossary.

Ballpark adjustments are made into the Major League ballpark the player would have moved into. This means that the MLE's are not strictly comparable to each other, any more than any other Major League stats in different ballparks are.

What use are these?

What MLEs do is give you a good handle on how close to ready for the big time a minor league player is.

Our MLE lines include two changes from Bill's. Instead of Slugging Percentage and On-Base Percentage, we have Runs Created and Runs Created per Game. Those of you who are old Bill James readers will realize that these are basic evaluative stats. They give you a good handle on how good a hitter this guy is. A team of him would score about this many runs in a game.

And another new twist. This is the PEAK line. That line is computed by feeding the MLE into Bill's old BROCK2 projection system. Then it's projected out to age 27, which is the strongest year in most careers. If you read a book I did a couple of years ago called THE TOP 150 MINOR LEAGUE PROSPECTS, you'll remember this method. It's experimental, as BROCK2 likes to use rather more than one year as a base, but there it is. It's designed to give you a handle on how good a prospect the man is, by eliminating the age bias. The Peak Line is the best he's ever likely to get.

By the way, for those of you who are sabermetricians yourselves, the MLE is placed into the BROCK2 system as though the player were one year older than he is. That is because MLEs are checked by comparing them to the player's performance the next year, in the Majors. That inherent aging factor is of little interest in just looking at the MLEs themselves, but it is very important to the BROCK2 system, which works by applying aging factors to the player's stats. Also, just in case you're particularly sharp, minor league players who are older than age 27 are assumed to be age 27 for purposes of the PEAK lines. This is because they are in their decline phases and don't figure to get any better.

ATLANTA BRAVES

RICHMOND

Name	Age	AB	R	H	D	T	HR	RBI	BB	AVG	RC	RC/27
Cabrera, Francisco	26	288	22	69	9	0	7	25	13	.240	26	3.21
PEAK		514	49	132	18	0	15	62	36	.257	60	4.24
Baraballo, Ramon	24	387	32	96	17	2	1	30	16	.248	31	2.88
PEAK		519	55	144	25	3	2	44	31	.277	58	4.18
Castilla, Vinny	30	431	37	95	25	1	6	33	16	.220	33	2.65
PEAK		530	46	117	31	1	7	41	20	.221	43	2.81
Klesko, Ryan	22	400	47	87	19	1	14	44	32	.218	39	3.36
PEAK		499	92	130	27	1	29	86	51	.261	81	5.93
Manto, Jeff	28	428	49	109	21	1	11	51	44	.255	50	4.23
PEAK		499	57	127	24	1	13	59	51	.255	62	4.50
Mitchell, Keith	23	387	34	75	16	1	4	38	51	.194	28	2.42
PEAK		479	61	113	23	1	8	46	71	.236	54	3.98
Moore, Bobby	27	303	31	66	11	2	0	18	16	.218	20	2.28
PEAK		522	53	114	19	3	0	31	28	.218	36	2.38
Rodriguez, Boi	27	265	30	64	7	2	13	30	24	.242	32	4.30
PEAK		504	57	122	13	4	25	57	46	.242	67	4.74
Tomberlin, Andy	26	389	51	93	14	3	7	35	32	.239	37	3.38
PEAK		499	79	128	19	4	11	55	51	.257	61	4.44

GREENVILLE

Name	Age	AB	R	H	D	T	HR	RBI	BB	AVG	RC	RC/27
Alicea, Ed	26	306	40	65	12	4	4	26	40	.212	28	3.14
PEAK		481	75	112	20	6	8	48	69	.233	55	4.02
Bell, Mike	25	409	45	95	20	7	2	52	48	.232	42	3.61
PEAK		489	68	127	26	2	12	57	61	.260	66	4.92
Giovanola, Ed	24	262	32	64	4	0	4	24	24	.244	24	3.27
PEAK		497	80	136	10	0	11	53	53	.274	62	4.64
Jones, Chipper	21	255	35	81	15	6	7	34	9	.318	42	6.52
PEAK		520	94	183	33	11	22	94	30	.352	118	9.45
Kelly, Mike	23	459	67	96	16	2	20	57	55	.209	50	3.72
PEAK		484	108	121	20	2	33	66	83	.250	83	6.17
Kelly, Pat	26	316	36	72	11	1	0	28	22	.228	23	2.55
PEAK		504	69	124	19	2	0	34	46	.246	45	3.20
Lopez, Javy	22	426	52	126	25	1	13	48	21	.296	61	5.49
PEAK		514	84	169	32	2	24	89	36	.329	103	8.06
Nieves, Melvin	21	338	49	87	20	2	14	61	44	.257	50	5.34
PEAK		475	102	142	30	3	32	97	75	.299	108	8.76
Olmeda, Jose	25	331	44	74	20	2	2	26	33	.224	29	3.05
PEAK		496	82	125	32	3	4	45	54	.252	57	4.15
Perez, Eduardo	25	268	22	56	14	0	5	33	21	.209	22	2.80
PEAK		504	55	120	29	0	13	58	46	.262	52	4.02
Tarasco, Tony	22	473	59	124	20	1	12	44	23	.300	83	6.22
PEAK		514	92	154	25	1	20	77	36			

BALTIMORE ORIOLES

ROCHESTER

Name	Age	AB	R	H	D	T	HR	RBI	BB	AVG	RC	RC/27
Gutierrez, Ricky	23	416	45	94	7	2	0	34	43	.226	30	2.52
PEAK		491	72	130	11	2	0	34	59	.265	50	3.74
Jennings, Doug	28	381	58	94	20	4	12	63	56	.247	57	4.09
PEAK		480	73	118	25	5	15	79	70	.246	68	5.07
Mercedes, Luis	25	391	51	110	13	1	2	24	36	.281	42	4.04
PEAK		499	77	152	18	1	3	46	51	.305	67	5.21
Parent, Mark	31	342	43	88	21	0	14	57	28	.257	45	4.78
PEAK		508	64	131	31	0	21	85	42	.258	71	5.08
Robbins, Doug	26	277	37	78	16	1	5	40	35	.282	38	5.16
PEAK		483	72	143	29	2	11	59	67	.296	80	6.35
Scarsone, Steve	27	392	46	95	22	9	9	50	24	.242	41	3.73
PEAK		518	61	126	29	12	12	66	32	.243	57	3.93
Shields, Tommy	28	413	48	112	20	2	8	49	30	.271	63	4.22
PEAK		520	60	141	25	3	10	62	24	.271	63	4.49
Voigt, Jack	27	426	61	109	20	5	13	62	32	.256	54	4.60
PEAK		495	71	127	23	3	15	53	47	.257	67	4.92
Yacopino, Ed	27	423	46	107	19	3	4	51	25	.253	40	3.42
PEAK		519	56	131	23	4	4	63	31	.252	51	3.55

HAGERSTOWN

Name	Age	AB	R	H	D	T	HR	RBI	BB	AVG	RC	RC/27
Alexander, Manny	22	480	55	110	18	4	2	33	21	.229	36	2.63
PEAK		516	85	140	23	4	3	46	34	.271	57	4.09
Buford, Damon	23	360	42	76	13	1	1	24	35	.211	25	2.38
PEAK		493	81	124	21	1	2	38	57	.252	50	3.66
Cairo, Sergio	22	392	35	98	10	2	2	36	28	.250	34	3.12
PEAK		503	62	145	16	2	4	46	47	.288	62	4.68
Devarez, Cesar	23	309	16	62	6	1	2	24	14	.201	17	1.86
PEAK		516	41	125	13	2	5	42	34	.242	45	3.11
Holland, Tim	24	254	23	53	7	1	2	17	12	.209	15	2.01
PEAK		516	64	125	17	2	5	39	34	.242	45	3.11
Miller, Brent	22	423	38	97	22	1	6	41	19	.229	33	2.73
PEAK		516	67	140	30	1	6	51	34	.271	60	4.31
Smith, Mark	23	452	41	116	25	3	3	49	37	.257	46	3.70
PEAK		500	59	146	30	3	5	51	50	.292	70	5.34
Tyler, Brad	24	247	33	48	7	1	2	16	28	.194	17	2.31
PEAK		488	89	112	16	2	6	41	62	.230	47	3.38
Washington, Kyle	23	372	34	93	10	1	2	33	30	.250	32	3.10
PEAK		500	61	143	16	1	4	45	50	.286	61	4.61
Wearing, Melvin	26	265	22	61	11	1	5	36	31	.230	26	3.44
PEAK		486	48	121	22	2	11	54	64	.249	61	4.51

BOSTON RED SOX
PAWTUCKET

Name	Age	AB	R	H	D	T	HR	RBI	BB	AVG		RCRC/27
Barrett, Tom	33	318	46	77	16	4	1	17	40	.242	32	3.59
PEAK		489	71	118	25	6	2	26	61	.241	52	3.78
Brumley, Mike	30	360	42	88	15	5	2	42	29	.244	35	3.47
PEAK		509	59	124	21	7	3	59	41	.244	50	3.51
Housie, Wayne	28	450	44	95	21	5	2	22	25	.211	32	2.43
PEAK		521	51	110	24	6	2	25	29	.211	38	2.50
Milstein, Dave	24	263	24	63	11	1	1	28	10	.240	21	2.83
PEAK		521	62	140	24	2	3	44	29	.269	54	3.83
Ross, Sean	25	384	39	89	13	5	7	40	12	.232	33	3.02
PEAK		523	71	136	20	6	13	62	27	.260	61	4.26
Shelby, John	35	462	47	91	26	4	11	52	36	.197	39	2.84
PEAK		510	52	101	29	4	12	57	40	.198	45	2.97
Snyder, Van	29	379	37	85	21	1	8	42	17	.224	33	3.03
PEAK		526	51	118	29	1	11	58	24	.224	47	3.11
Twardoski, Mike	28	383	46	107	22	4	8	41	70	.279	59	5.77
PEAK		465	56	130	27	5	10	50	85	.280	77	6.21
Valentin, John	26	326	39	81	16	1	7	24	36	.248	37	4.08
PEAK		489	69	130	25	1	13	59	61	.266	68	5.11

NEW BRITAIN

Name	Age	AB	R	H	D	T	HR	RBI	BB	AVG		RCRC/27
Beams, Mike	26	260	32	56	15	1	9	42	20	.215	27	3.57
PEAK		501	78	118	30	2	22	73	49	.236	66	4.65
Bethea, Scott	24	310	37	71	6	0	0	15	45	.229	25	2.82
PEAK		476	72	124	12	0	0	32	74	.261	49	3.76
Blosser, Greg	22	430	56	101	23	3	22	69	56	.235	62	5.09
PEAK		477	94	132	28	3	39	106	73	.277	105	8.22
Chick, Bruce	24	431	50	92	19	0	9	49	25	.213	35	2.79
PEAK		512	83	126	25	0	16	62	38	.246	59	4.13
Dekneef, Mike	23	405	49	89	10	4	3	32	24	.220	30	2.56
PEAK		510	88	132	16	5	6	47	40	.259	55	3.93
Dixon, Colin	24	264	22	54	6	1	1	25	13	.205	15	1.93
PEAK		516	60	123	14	2	3	38	34	.238	43	2.95
Graham, Greg	24	345	31	76	6	1	0	18	27	.220	23	2.31
PEAK		503	59	127	11	1	0	33	47	.252	44	3.16
Hatteberg, Scott	23	295	27	67	13	1	1	29	35	.227	26	3.08
PEAK		484	59	129	24	2	3	41	66	.267	59	4.49
McNeely, Jeff	23	259	29	55	8	3	2	10	23	.212	20	2.65
PEAK		497	79	126	18	6	6	47	53	.254	57	4.15
Norris, Bill	24	382	35	78	15	0	1	22	26	.204	24	2.13
PEAK		507	63	120	22	0	2	37	43	.237	44	3.07
Tatum, Willie	26	443	61	105	25	3	8	51	78	.237	55	4.39
PEAK		466	74	119	27	3	10	54	84	.255	67	5.21
Thoutsis, Paul	27	324	30	77	22	2	4	16	22	.238	33	3.61
PEAK		515	48	122	35	3	6	25	35	.237	52	3.57

CALIFORNIA ANGELS
EDMONTON

Name	Age	AB	R	H	D	T	HR	RBI	BB	AVG		RCRC/27
Barbara, Don	24	376	49	98	21	1	2	44	54	.261	41	3.98
PEAK		477	75	138	28	1	4	46	73	.289	69	5.50
Easley, Damion	23	409	43	104	13	2	1	31	21	.254	34	3.01
PEAK		514	72	149	19	2	2	44	36	.290	60	4.44
Martinez, Ray	24	270	30	71	16	1	1	25	19	.263	27	3.66
PEAK		506	69	147	32	2	3	47	44	.291	67	5.04
Salmon, Tim	24	385	72	118	32	2	16	74	21	.306	64	6.47
PEAK		513	120	170	44	2	29	102	37	.331	115	9.05
Van Burkleo, Ty	29	438	59	105	23	4	7	62	52	.240	46	3.73
PEAK		492	66	118	26	4	8	70	58	.240	56	4.04
Williams, Reggie	27	495	68	117	20	6	1	45	60	.236	44	3.14
PEAK		491	67	116	20	6	1	45	59	.236	48	3.46

MIDLAND

Name	Age	AB	R	H	D	T	HR	RBI	BB	AVG		RCRC/27
Correia, Ron	25	464	61	122	20	1	5	46	23	.263	45	3.55
PEAK		516	84	148	24	1	8	54	34	.287	66	4.84
Jones, Bobby	25	306	38	63	12	1	3	25	42	.206	25	2.78
PEAK		482	76	114	21	2	7	44	68	.237	53	3.89
Kipila, Jeff	27	402	53	93	19	2	25	64	40	.231	55	4.81
PEAK		500	66	116	24	3	31	80	50	.232	72	5.06
Phillips, J.R.	23	483	48	104	27	3	11	65	27	.215	42	2.99
PEAK		512	75	131	32	3	18	71	38	.256	69	4.89
Taylor, Terry	25	242	32	56	19	1	0	19	46	.231	26	3.77
PEAK		465	71	120	38	2	0	38	85	.258	60	4.70
Tejero, Fausto	24	260	18	44	9	0	2	25	10	.169	12	1.50
PEAK		521	55	107	21	0	6	41	29	.205	36	2.35

IOWA

Name	Age	AB	R	H	D	T	HR	RBI	BB	AVG	RCRC	RCRC/27
Arias, Alex	25	387	36	92	18	2	3	28	31	.238	33	3.02
PEAK		504	58	133	26	2	5	48	46	.264	58	4.22
Bates, Billy	29	245	21	50	6	1	1	13	20	.204	15	2.08
PEAK		508	44	104	12	2	2	27	42	.205	33	2.21
Bryant, Scott	25	300	24	64	17	2	11	36	18	.213	28	3.20
PEAK		511	56	124	31	3	2	83	39	.243	71	4.95
Chance, Tony	28	412	42	95	18	1	7	36	24	.231	35	4.00
PEAK		520	53	120	23	1	9	45	30	.231	47	4.33
Kunkel, Jeff	31	276	30	65	10	3	6	35	8	.236	24	3.07
PEAK		535	58	126	19	6	12	68	15	.236	49	3.23
Pedre, Jorge	26	282	22	61	13	1	3	24	19	.216	21	2.57
PEAK		505	49	119	25	2	7	46	45	.236	50	3.50
Ramsey, Fernando	27	456	43	105	7	5	1	26	17	.230	30	2.31
PEAK		530	50	122	8	6	1	30	20	.230	37	2.45
Schulz, Jeff	32	293	26	68	11	1	3	30	15	.232	23	2.76
PEAK		523	46	121	20	2	5	54	27	.231	43	2.89
Scott, Gary	24	337	33	76	20	0	6	33	27	.226	30	3.10
PEAK		502	66	129	32	0	13	60	48	.257	64	4.63

CHARLOTTE

Name	Age	AB	R	H	D	T	HR	RBI	BB	AVG	RCRC	RCRC/27
Crockett, Rusty	26	301	25	62	7	1	1	21	20	.206	18	2.03
PEAK		505	53	115	13	2	2	34	45	.228	40	2.77
Dauphin, Phil	24	492	62	108	20	3	7	31	46	.220	42	2.95
PEAK		496	84	125	23	3	10	54	54	.252	60	4.37
Ebright, Chris	25	386	46	85	18	1	13	58	43	.220	40	3.59
PEAK		492	77	122	25	1	23	75	58	.248	71	5.18
Franco, Matt	23	327	26	81	15	3	2	24	21	.248	30	3.29
PEAK		508	54	144	26	4	5	50	42	.283	65	4.82
Grace, Mike	25	307	31	66	13	3	5	26	22	.215	25	2.80
PEAK		507	67	124	24	5	12	57	43	.245	59	4.16
Grayum, Richie	24	320	35	67	20	0	9	38	37	.209	31	3.31
PEAK		488	73	118	33	0	20	70	62	.242	69	5.04
Jensen, John	26	381	48	86	13	0	10	40	46	.226	38	3.48
PEAK		485	74	119	18	0	16	59	65	.245	62	4.57
Walbeck, Matt	23	365	35	96	18	1	5	31	28	.263	39	3.91
PEAK		502	64	149	27	1	10	60	48	.297	75	5.74
White, Billy	24	385	42	84	10	0	3	25	38	.218	28	2.51
PEAK		494	72	124	15	0	6	42	56	.251	51	3.72

VANCOUVER

Name	Age	AB	R	H	D	T	HR	RBI	BB	AVG	RCRC	RCRC/27
Coomer, Ron	26	253	21	53	8	0	3	30	12	.209	16	2.16
PEAK		513	55	118	18	0	8	45	37	.230	45	3.08
Cron, Chris	29	479	55	118	23	0	14	66	66	.246	57	4.26
PEAK		483	57	119	23	0	14	61	67	.246	62	4.60
Denson, Drew	27	326	32	80	5	2	11	52	25	.245	34	3.73
PEAK		511	50	125	8	3	17	81	39	.245	57	3.99
Hall, Joe	27	351	33	88	15	5	5	41	42	.251	39	4.00
PEAK		491	46	123	21	7	7	57	59	.251	59	4.33
Jeter, Shawn	27	361	45	96	14	4	1	25	27	.266	36	3.67
PEAK		512	64	136	20	6	1	35	38	.266	54	3.88
Komminsk, Brad	32	397	53	96	19	5	9	51	45	.242	45	4.04
PEAK		494	66	119	24	6	11	63	56	.241	54	4.32
Lee, Derek	26	365	43	88	16	4	6	37	39	.241	38	3.70
PEAK		490	68	127	23	5	10	55	60	.259	65	4.83
Martin, Norberto	26	475	53	121	10	5	0	21	20	.255	38	2.90
PEAK		515	58	140	12	5	0	38	35	.272	52	3.74
Santovenia, Nelson	31	269	18	62	12	0	5	32	26	.230	25	3.26
PEAK		502	34	116	22	0	9	60	48	.231	49	3.43
Yelding, Eric	28	325	34	76	8	4	0	21	18	.234	24	2.60
PEAK		521	55	122	13	6	0	34	29	.234	40	2.71

BIRMINGHAM

Name	Age	AB	R	H	D	T	HR	RBI	BB	AVG	RCRC	RCRC/27
Bishop, James	30	306	24	72	11	0	6	41	27	.235	29	3.35
PEAK		505	40	119	18	0	10	68	45	.236	50	3.50
Castleberry, Kevin	25	377	53	93	8	4	3	24	42	.247	37	3.52
PEAK		492	84	134	12	5	5	46	58	.272	60	4.53
Cepicky, Scott	26	495	52	117	27	1	16	81	39	.236	55	3.93
PEAK		501	64	127	28	1	20	71	49	.253	69	4.98
Harris, Robert	27	279	37	66	11	1	4	23	9	.237	23	2.92
PEAK		533	71	126	21	2	8	44	17	.236	46	3.05
Jaster, Scott	27	321	42	86	21	2	8	32	39	.268	44	4.71
PEAK		521	59	138	27	2	11	55	58	.265	58	3.95
Lonigro, Greg	27	252	19	51	10	0	0	19	14	.202	18	2.42
PEAK		490	64	131	17	2	12	60	60	.267	65	4.89
Redington, Tom	24	252	19	56	7	0	6	27	24	.222	23	3.17
PEAK		496	39	105	21	0	8	39	29	.202	37	2.40
Tedder, Scott	27	424	51	96	16	3	0	44	57	.227	43	3.10
PEAK		485	58	110	16	3	1	50	65	.227	37	3.05
White, Charlie	26	260	27	53	9	1	1	16	14	.204	16	2.09
PEAK		511	67	115	19	2	2	37	39	.225	40	2.73

CINCINNATI REDS

NASHVILLE

Name	Age	AB	R	H	D	T	HR	RBI	BB	AVG	RC	RC/27
Berroa, Geronimo	28	434	53	124	32	2	16	64	23	.286	62	5.40
PEAK		522	64	149	39	2	19	77	28	.285	80	5.79
Capra, Nick	35	275	35	55	13	1	3	20	37	.200	22	2.70
PEAK		485	62	97	23	2	5	35	65	.200	41	2.85
Green, Gary	31	310	17	28	11	1	2	20	15	.90	6	0.57
PEAK		525	29	47	19	2	3	34	25	.90	10	0.56
Howie, Mark	30	331	25	70	19	1	3	30	15	.211	23	2.38
PEAK		526	40	111	30	2	5	48	24	.211	39	2.54
Morman, Russ	31	362	38	97	28	2	10	46	26	.268	47	4.79
PEAK		513	54	138	40	3	14	65	37	.269	72	5.18
Small, Jeff	27	478	47	115	28	2	5	33	15	.241	40	2.98
PEAK		533	52	128	31	2	6	37	17	.240	48	3.20
Wilson, Dan	24	349	20	75	15	1	3	25	23	.215	25	2.46
PEAK		508	39	126	24	1	6	47	42	.248	52	3.68

CHATTANOOGA

Name	Age	AB	R	H	D	T	HR	RBI	BB	AVG	RC	RC/27
Colvard, Benny	26	351	37	79	17	1	13	37	22	.225	35	3.47
PEAK		521	67	124	26	1	23	76	43	.245	67	4.72
Costo, Tim	24	507	50	85	16	1	23	56	40	.209	48	4.02
PEAK		495	89	120	22	1	26	114	55	.242	91	6.55
Cox, Darren	25	318	23	71	17	1	1	23	12	.223	22	2.40
PEAK		521	49	131	30	2	2	42	29	.251	50	3.46
Diaz, Kiki	29	452	57	102	10	1	0	36	60	.226	34	2.62
PEAK		486	61	110	11	1	0	39	64	.226	39	2.80
Greene, Willie	21	334	37	82	17	1	14	53	38	.246	43	4.61
PEAK		482	82	140	27	1	34	97	68	.290	102	8.05
Griffin, Ty	25	314	39	77	20	3	5	22	15	.245	29	3.30
PEAK		517	80	140	35	5	5	51	33	.271	63	4.51
Hernandez, Cesar	26	314	39	77	17	3	2	22	15	.245	29	3.30
PEAK		513	76	135	34	5	4	49	37	.263	60	4.29
Kremblas, Frank	26	272	23	55	14	1	0	22	14	.202	16	1.99
PEAK		511	54	114	28	2	0	34	39	.223	41	2.79
Pose, Scott	26	497	68	151	20	5	2	36	52	.304	64	4.99
PEAK		491	74	155	21	5	2	47	59	.316	75	6.03

CLEVELAND INDIANS

COLORADO SPRINGS

Name	Age	AB	R	H	D	T	HR	RBI	BB	AVG	RC	RC/27
Aldrete, Mike	32	440	51	126	36	1	6	61	46	.286	59	5.07
PEAK		498	58	143	41	1	7	69	52	.287	73	5.55
Allred, Beau	28	415	58	106	21	6	13	56	40	.255	53	4.63
PEAK		502	70	128	25	7	16	68	48	.255	69	4.98
Cockrell, Alan	30	250	23	52	5	1	5	28	15	.208	18	2.45
PEAK		519	48	108	10	2	10	58	31	.208	38	2.50
Davidson, Mark	32	296	42	74	15	2	4	32	22	.250	30	3.65
PEAK		512	73	128	26	3	7	55	38	.250	55	3.87
Espinoza, Alvaro	31	461	47	123	31	3	6	58	14	.267	48	3.83
PEAK		534	54	142	36	3	7	67	16	.266	59	4.06
Kirby, Wayne	29	445	74	137	16	8	7	54	25	.308	61	5.35
PEAK		521	87	160	19	9	8	63	29	.307	76	5.68
Levis, Jesse	25	239	29	78	18	1	4	32	26	.326	39	6.54
PEAK		493	68	170	38	2	11	68	57	.345	101	8.44
Liriano, Nelson	29	345	53	93	17	5	4	36	34	.270	41	4.39
PEAK		501	77	135	25	7	6	52	49	.269	64	4.72
Rohde, Dave	29	428	61	112	15	7	3	39	40	.262	45	3.84
PEAK		503	72	132	18	8	4	46	47	.262	58	4.22
Worthington, Craig	28	304	34	79	21	0	4	42	23	.260	32	3.84
PEAK		511	57	133	35	0	7	71	39	.260	59	4.21

CANTON-AKRON

Name	Age	AB	R	H	D	T	HR	RBI	BB	AVG	RC	RC/27
Colombino, Carlo	28	299	29	73	15	0	6	32	22	.244	31	3.70
PEAK		512	50	125	26	0	10	55	38	.244	54	3.77
Epley, Daren	26	286	38	88	21	1	2	51	31	.308	42	5.73
PEAK		489	71	156	36	2	4	53	61	.319	82	6.65
Flores, Miguel	22	448	39	115	21	3	1	36	29	.257	42	3.41
PEAK		506	59	149	27	3	2	46	44	.294	66	4.99
Hernandez, Jose	19	397	50	96	17	3	2	40	31	.242	37	3.32
PEAK		498	90	143	25	4	6	52	52	.287	69	5.25
Ramos, Ken	26	430	82	138	24	4	5	36	70	.321	73	6.75
PEAK		470	96	156	27	4	6	56	80	.332	90	7.74
Sanders, Tracy	23	375	57	85	11	2	21	77	66	.227	54	5.03
PEAK		462	103	123	16	2	40	102	88	.266	101	8.04
Stinnet, Kelly	23	290	32	78	9	0	16	68	35	.269	31	3.95
PEAK		515	77	156	19	0	16	68	35	.303	77	5.79
Tinsley, Lee	24	341	57	92	9	6	5	33	35	.270	42	4.55
PEAK		493	102	146	15	8	10	59	57	.296	76	5.91

DETROIT TIGERS

TOLEDO

Name	Age	AB	R	H	D	T	HR	RBI	BB	AVG	RC	RC/27
Allaire, Karl	29	469	57	112	18	1	5	37	53	.239	45	3.40
PEAK		494	60	118	19	1	5	39	56	.239	49	3.52
Brogna, Rica	23	379	37	93	19	3	7	49	28	.245	40	3.78
PEAK		503	67	142	28	4	14	66	47	.282	76	5.68
Carter, Steve	28	457	47	128	23	1	8	49	23	.280	53	4.35
PEAK		524	54	147	26	0	7	56	26	.281	63	4.51
Clark, Phil	25	265	24	70	20	0	8	32	14	.264	33	4.43
PEAK		514	59	149	41	0	18	76	36	.290	82	6.07
Decillis, Dean	25	263	19	61	7	2	2	13	13	.232	19	2.54
PEAK		516	49	134	16	0	5	44	28	.260	49	3.46
Ingram, Riccardo	26	402	37	95	15	4	7	34	28	.236	50	3.53
PEAK		504	56	128	20	5	11	56	46	.254	60	4.31
Rosario, Victor	26	331	22	62	9	1	2	13	7	.187	16	1.61
PEAK		524	47	110	16	2	4	37	26	.210	35	2.28
Rowland, Rich	26	464	63	102	19	1	21	80	57	.220	53	3.95
PEAK		490	83	117	21	1	28	80	60	.239	72	5.21
Smith, Greg	26	437	47	96	15	2	6	38	57	.220	40	3.17
PEAK		481	62	115	18	2	8	46	69	.239	54	3.98

LONDON

Name	Age	AB	R	H	D	T	HR	RBI	BB	AVG	RC	RC/27
Cornelius, Brian	26	289	27	67	12	3	4	30	20	.232	26	3.16
PEAK		504	57	126	22	5	9	52	32	.250	58	4.14
Cruz, Ivan	25	505	55	125	21	1	11	82	46	.248	51	3.62
PEAK		510	71	140	23	1	15	65	40	.275	69	5.04
DeButch, Mike	29	307	50	74	9	3	3	20	30	.241	30	3.48
PEAK		478	78	115	14	2	5	46	50	.241	50	3.72
Frazier, Lou	28	461	67	104	14	0	0	27	82	.226	40	3.03
PEAK		467	68	105	14	3	0	27	83	.225	43	3.21
Hurst, Jody	26	258	37	74	15	2	10	41	33	.287	43	6.31
PEAK		482	78	145	29	3	23	81	68	.301	96	7.69
Kingwood, Tyrone	27	363	44	93	12	1	5	36	24	.256	35	3.50
PEAK		516	63	132	17	1	7	51	34	.256	52	3.66
Madsen, Lance	24	321	31	65	15	1	4	31	28	.202	28	2.95
PEAK		499	68	118	26	2	9	70	51	.236	46	3.21
Makarewicz, Scott	26	331	30	85	14	0	4	30	30	.257	31	3.40
PEAK		510	55	139	23	0	8	51	40	.273	61	4.44
Mendenhall, Kirk	25	351	42	77	14	2	3	29	45	.219	31	3.05
PEAK		486	73	120	22	3	6	45	64	.247	56	4.13
Miller, Orlando	24	364	38	86	26	4	3	40	13	.236	32	3.11
PEAK		522	71	139	39	6	6	55	28	.266	63	4.28
Reimink, Rob	26	396	43	106	20	1	3	35	56	.268	46	4.28
PEAK		478	58	135	25	1	4	72	56	.282	63	5.12
Sellers, Rick	26	318	29	77	15	1	7	40	31	.242	27	3.81
PEAK		493	54	128	24	1	13	59	40	.260	53	4.81
Sparks, Greg	29	372	44	77	16	1	20	57	50	.207	45	4.12
PEAK		485	100	115	21	1	26	74	65	.206	60	4.21

HOUSTON ASTROS

TUCSON

Name	Age	AB	R	H	D	T	HR	RBI	BB	AVG	RC	RC/27
Booker, Rob	34	266	40	55	4	1	1	23	22	.207	16	2.05
PEAK		508	76	105	8	2	2	44	42	.207	33	2.21
Cedeno, Andujar	23	260	29	62	12	2	4	60	12	.238	22	3.00
PEAK		516	81	142	27	4	12	62	34	.275	68	4.91
Cooper, Gary	28	431	71	106	22	1	7	79	31	.246	41	3.41
PEAK		513	85	126	26	2	8	94	37	.246	53	3.70
Hubbard, Trent	29	389	75	99	11	2	2	36	29	.254	33	3.46
PEAK		512	99	130	14	3	3	47	38	.254	49	3.07
Lyons, Barry	33	257	35	63	17	0	6	48	6	.245	21	2.92
PEAK		537	73	132	36	0	13	100	13	.246	49	3.27
Mota, Andy	27	299	36	58	10	3	5	35	10	.194	17	1.90
PEAK		532	64	103	18	5	9	62	18	.194	32	2.01
Parker, Rick	30	294	56	78	7	5	3	41	18	.265	29	3.62
PEAK		518	99	138	12	9	5	72	32	.265	57	4.05
Rhodes, Karl	24	309	68	73	11	5	2	58	36	.236	28	3.20
PEAK		487	134	130	20	7	5	46	63	.267	63	4.76
Simms, Mike	26	377	79	87	15	3	9	80	40	.231	37	3.44
PEAK		490	124	122	21	4	15	60	60	.249	65	4.77
Tucker, Scooter	26	267	39	66	11	1	1	31	18	.247	22	2.96
PEAK		505	87	134	22	2	2	41	45	.265	54	3.93

JACKSON

Name	Age	AB	R	H	D	T	HR	RBI	BB	AVG	RC	RC/27
Ball, Jeff	24	271	21	46	12	1	3	18	16	.170	14	1.68
PEAK		511	59	105	25	2	9	47	39	.205	42	2.79
Eusebio, Tony	26	324	25	89	9	2	3	34	20	.275	33	3.79
PEAK		507	45	147	15	3	6	49	43	.290	64	4.80
Hajek, Dave	25	314	27	76	11	2	1	14	24	.242	26	2.95
PEAK		505	54	136	20	3	2	42	45	.269	55	4.02
Kellner, Frank	26	457	35	97	18	4	2	37	32	.212	32	2.40
PEAK		504	47	117	21	4	3	39	46	.232	46	3.21
Madsen, Lance	24	321	31	65	15	1	4	31	28	.202	28	2.95
PEAK		499	68	118	26	2	9	70	51	.236	46	3.21
Makarewicz, Scott	26	331	30	85	14	0	4	30	30	.257	31	3.40
PEAK		510	55	139	23	0	8	51	40	.273	61	4.44
Miller, Orlando	24	364	38	86	26	4	3	40	13	.236	32	3.11
PEAK		522	71	139	39	6	6	55	28	.266	63	4.28
Prager, Howard	26	314	27	72	12	0	5	37	35	.229	27	3.01
PEAK		488	50	121	20	0	6	43	62	.248	53	3.90
Sammons, Lee	25	265	25	54	5	1	2	12	30	.204	18	2.30
PEAK		491	60	115	11	2	5	40	59	.234	46	3.30

OMAHA

Name	Age	AB	R	H	D	T	HR	RBI	BB	AVG		RCRC/27
Berry, Sean	27	428	51	115	20	1	11	64	28	.269	51	4.40
PEAK		516	62	139	24	1	13	77	34	.269	64	4.58
Casillas, Adam	27	352	34	101	10	4	0	22	22	.287	37	3.98
PEAK		518	50	149	15	6	0	32	32	.288	58	4.24
Conine, Jeff	27	387	57	110	21	5	10	60	39	.284	56	5.46
PEAK		500	74	142	27	6	13	77	50	.284	77	5.81
Koslofski, Kevin	26	272	23	79	10	5	2	27	15	.290	33	4.62
PEAK		510	49	155	20	9	5	53	40	.304	74	5.63
Long, Kevin	26	305	23	64	14	4	1	23	21	.210	22	2.46
PEAK		504	47	116	25	6	2	40	46	.230	47	3.27
Medina, Luis	30	333	31	86	14	1	8	41	17	.258	36	3.94
PEAK		523	49	135	22	2	13	64	27	.258	59	4.11
Mota, Jose	28	460	38	99	9	0	2	23	30	.215	29	2.17
PEAK		516	43	111	10	0	2	26	34	.215	33	2.20
Pulliam, Harvey	25	351	46	89	10	1	8	50	23	.254	36	3.71
PEAK		509	85	142	17	1	16	65	41	.279	70	5.15
Spehr, Tim	26	328	40	77	20	0	8	35	44	.235	37	3.98
PEAK		480	69	122	30	0	15	60	70	.254	69	5.20

MEMPHIS

Name	Age	AB	R	H	D	T	HR	RBI	BB	AVG		RCRC/27
Burgos, Paco	25	274	21	52	8	0	2	21	6	.190	13	1.58
PEAK		527	59	116	18	0	6	41	23	.220	38	2.50
Garber, Jeff	26	321	35	68	17	1	5	36	22	.212	26	2.77
PEAK		505	69	117	28	2	10	52	45	.232	53	3.69
Hiatt, Phil	24	481	66	113	20	5	19	78	19	.235	52	3.82
PEAK		520	100	138	24	5	30	91	30	.265	80	5.65
Mota, Domingo	23	424	43	108	16	0	3	21	15	.255	36	3.08
PEAK		521	72	151	23	0	6	50	29	.290	63	4.60
Robinson, Darryl	25	349	38	80	18	2	8	40	14	.229	32	3.21
PEAK		520	76	133	29	3	17	68	30	.256	65	4.53
Rohrmeier, Dan	27	425	50	132	32	1	4	64	19	.311	59	5.44
PEAK		526	62	164	40	1	5	79	24	.312	76	5.67

ALBUQUERQUE

Name	Age	AB	R	H	D	T	HR	RBI	BB	AVG		RCRC/27
Barron, Tony	26	267	24	67	14	1	3	19	10	.251	23	3.10
PEAK		517	56	138	28	2	7	52	33	.267	59	4.20
Bournigal, Rafael	27	366	28	99	14	1	0	20	13	.270	31	3.13
PEAK		531	41	144	20	1	7	29	19	.271	49	3.42
Brooks, Jerry	26	439	46	96	27	1	7	47	24	.219	35	2.76
PEAK		510	67	122	33	1	10	54	40	.239	55	3.83
Goodwin, Tom	24	298	29	75	8	3	1	18	22	.252	25	3.03
PEAK		505	62	142	16	5	2	43	45	.281	59	4.39
Munoz, Jose	25	418	29	105	14	2	1	27	15	.251	32	2.76
PEAK		521	45	144	20	2	2	43	29	.276	55	3.94
Piazza, Mike	24	330	32	94	16	3	8	42	22	.285	41	4.69
PEAK		508	62	158	27	4	17	75	42	.311	89	6.87
Rodriguez, Henry	25	340	35	86	15	3	7	43	19	.253	34	3.61
PEAK		513	67	143	25	4	14	66	37	.279	71	5.18
Traxler, Brian	25	366	35	92	19	3	6	35	22	.251	36	3.55
PEAK		511	61	142	29	4	11	61	39	.278	70	5.12
Young, Eric	26	323	37	91	13	3	2	30	20	.282	34	3.96
PEAK		507	66	150	22	4	4	49	43	.296	67	5.07

SAN ANTONIO

Name	Age	AB	R	H	D	T	HR	RBI	BB	AVG		RCRC/27
Alvarez, Jorge	24	298	27	67	10	3	3	26	16	.225	23	2.69
PEAK		514	62	132	20	5	8	51	36	.257	57	4.03
Ashley, Billy	22	370	50	96	18	1	15	55	12	.259	44	4.34
PEAK		522	105	155	28	1	33	100	28	.297	94	6.92
Barker, Tim	25	341	39	86	14	2	1	21	26	.252	31	3.28
PEAK		505	70	140	23	3	2	43	45	.277	59	4.36
Busch, Mike	24	406	48	89	12	1	11	42	29	.219	36	3.07
PEAK		506	84	127	17	1	20	69	44	.251	64	4.56
Howard, Matt	25	336	33	84	10	4	2	28	22	.250	31	3.32
PEAK		509	62	141	17	6	4	47	41	.277	60	4.40

MILWAUKEE BREWERS

DENVER

Name	Age	AB	R	H	D	T	HR	RBI	BB	AVG	RC	RC/27
Allanson, Andy	31	250	28	63	12	1	3	20	18	.252	24	3.47
PEAK		513	57	129	25	2	6	41	37	.251	53	3.73
Diaz, Alex	24	431	43	98	13	1	1	27	19	.227	28	2.27
PEAK		518	69	134	18	1	2	39	32	.259	48	3.38
Guerrero, Sandy	27	241	25	66	15	1	4	29	12	.274	27	4.17
PEAK		524	54	143	33	2	9	63	26	.273	64	4.54
Jackson, Kenny	28	320	31	70	19	0	9	34	20	.219	29	3.13
PEAK		518	50	113	31	0	15	55	32	.218	52	3.85
Jaha, John	27	256	39	70	14	1	14	45	39	.273	43	6.24
PEAK		477	73	131	26	2	26	84	73	.275	89	6.95
Mieske, Matt	25	497	51	113	23	4	15	50	31	.227	48	3.38
PEAK		511	70	130	26	4	21	75	39	.254	70	4.96
Montoyo, Charlie	27	242	26	67	6	1	2	22	37	.277	28	4.32
PEAK		477	51	132	12	2	4	43	73	.277	60	4.70
Suero, William	26	262	28	57	8	3	1	16	24	.218	20	2.63
PEAK		496	64	118	17	6	2	38	54	.238	48	3.43
Valentin, Jose	23	468	51	94	15	4	14	29	41	.201	30	2.17
PEAK		497	78	121	19	4	21	41	53	.243	50	3.59

EL PASO

Name	Age	AB	R	H	D	T	HR	RBI	BB	AVG	RC	RC/27
Byington, John	25	449	45	124	30	2	4	49	28	.276	52	4.32
PEAK		511	61	153	36	2	6	56	39	.299	74	5.58
Caceres, Edgar	29	363	37	103	10	4	2	39	20	.284	39	4.05
PEAK		521	53	148	14	6	3	56	29	.284	59	4.27
Castaldo, Vince	25	396	46	103	25	5	3	37	42	.260	46	4.24
PEAK		494	68	141	33	6	5	52	56	.285	72	5.51
Diggs, Tony	26	272	35	52	5	1	0	15	25	.191	15	1.84
PEAK		496	80	106	11	2	0	28	54	.214	35	2.42
Dodson, Bo	22	323	35	71	15	4	4	34	63	.220	35	3.75
PEAK		452	68	119	24	6	9	52	98	.263	72	5.84
Finn, John	25	422	62	104	9	4	1	35	62	.246	40	3.40
PEAK		479	83	131	12	4	2	38	71	.273	58	4.50
Guerrero, Mike	25	248	27	54	8	2	1	21	27	.218	19	2.64
PEAK		493	67	121	18	4	3	39	57	.245	50	3.63
Lewis, Alan	26	315	31	76	16	4	4	33	34	.241	34	3.84
PEAK		490	56	127	26	6	8	52	60	.259	59	4.76
O'Leary, Troy	23	483	69	146	20	4	5	59	52	.302	66	5.29
PEAK		489	86	162	23	4	7	58	61	.331	87	7.18

MINNESOTA TWINS

PORTLAND

Name	Age	AB	R	H	D	T	HR	RBI	BB	AVG	RC	RC/27
Brito, Bernardo	29	541	64	129	23	4	21	77	26	.238	58	3.80
PEAK		525	62	125	22	4	20	75	25	.238	59	3.98
Bruett, J.T.	25	270	33	60	8	2	0	14	48	.222	23	2.96
PEAK		469	68	118	16	3	0	33	81	.252	51	3.92
Gilbert, Shawn	28	427	48	92	14	1	2	41	29	.215	29	2.34
PEAK		515	58	111	17	1	2	49	35	.216	36	2.41
Hale, Chip	28	453	62	114	20	5	1	42	59	.252	46	3.66
PEAK		487	67	122	21	5	1	45	63	.251	52	3.85
Jorgenson, Terry	26	481	62	125	27	1	11	57	44	.260	57	4.32
PEAK		496	75	137	29	1	14	63	54	.276	73	5.49
Lee, Terry	31	351	54	88	18	1	6	45	29	.251	35	3.59
PEAK		508	78	127	26	1	6	65	42	.250	53	3.76
Naveda, Ed	26	359	42	76	17	0	2	25	21	.212	24	2.29
PEAK		509	60	118	26	0	4	40	41	.232	45	3.11
Quinones, Luis	31	266	36	57	6	2	10	39	34	.214	28	3.62
PEAK		488	66	105	11	4	18	72	62	.215	54	3.81
Sheaffer, Danny	31	423	43	103	19	2	4	45	17	.243	36	3.04
PEAK		529	54	129	24	3	5	56	21	.244	47	3.17

ORLANDO

Name	Age	AB	R	H	D	T	HR	RBI	BB	AVG	RC	RC/27
Delanuez, Rex	25	424	58	104	35	1	10	48	60	.245	55	4.64
PEAK		481	80	131	42	1	16	68	69	.272	81	6.25
Delarwelle, Chris	25	288	24	70	11	2	2	25	25	.243	26	3.22
PEAK		501	52	135	21	5	4	46	49	.269	59	4.35
Lewis, Mica	26	369	49	92	13	1	4	30	41	.249	37	3.61
PEAK		488	75	130	19	1	7	47	62	.266	60	4.53
Masteller, Dan	25	355	34	86	24	1	6	34	19	.242	36	3.61
PEAK		514	63	138	37	3	12	63	36	.268	69	4.95
McCarty, Dave	23	443	62	110	16	1	14	65	47	.248	52	4.22
PEAK		490	96	139	20	1	23	78	60	.284	83	6.38
Meares, Pat	24	292	33	68	20	0	3	19	10	.233	24	2.89
PEAK		522	79	138	38	0	8	55	28	.264	60	4.22
Ortiz, Ray	25	259	33	63	16	1	8	39	18	.243	30	4.13
PEAK		508	84	137	33	2	22	78	42	.270	78	5.68
Owens, Jay	24	320	41	78	24	0	9	56	31	.244	34	3.79
PEAK		495	80	135	39	0	4	25	55	.273	69	5.18
Russo, Paul	23	409	52	96	13	1	18	61	41	.235	48	4.14
PEAK		492	92	134	19	1	33	93	58	.272	89	6.71
Bullock, Eric	33	295	41	83	20	1	4	33	29	.281	39	4.97
PEAK		501	70	141	34	2	7	56	49	.281	69	5.18

MONTREAL EXPOS

INDIANAPOLIS

Name	Age	AB	R	H	D	T	HR	RBI	BB	AVG	RC	RC/27
Eppard, Jim	33	248	30	59	15	1	2	22	29	.238	24	3.43
PEAK		492	60	117	30	2	4	44	58	.238	52	3.74
Fulton, Greg	27	283	23	54	9	1	5	23	13	.191	17	2.00
PEAK		526	43	100	17	2	9	43	24	.190	33	2.09
Goff, Jerry	29	302	30	63	16	1	12	31	21	.209	28	3.16
PEAK		514	51	107	27	2	20	53	36	.208	51	3.38
Mack, Quinn	27	289	27	73	18	0	3	29	13	.253	27	3.38
PEAK		526	49	133	33	0	5	53	24	.253	52	3.57
Munoz, Omer	27	361	27	80	11	1	1	25	6	.222	21	2.02
PEAK		541	40	120	16	1	1	37	9	.222	33	2.12
Natal, Bob	27	328	40	88	18	2	11	40	18	.268	41	4.61
PEAK		521	64	140	29	3	17	64	29	.269	69	4.89
Santangelo, F.P.	25	444	67	105	24	0	4	27	40	.236	39	3.11
PEAK		500	94	132	29	0	6	48	50	.264	59	4.33
Stairs, Matt	24	386	46	92	21	2	9	46	31	.238	39	3.58
PEAK		502	79	135	29	2	17	69	48	.269	73	5.37

HARRISBURG

Name	Age	AB	R	H	D	T	HR	RBI	BB	AVG	RC	RC/27
Hecht, Steve	27	262	40	62	12	3	1	16	26	.237	24	3.24
PEAK		500	76	118	23	6	2	31	50	.236	49	3.46
Hirtensteiner, Rick	25	439	60	108	17	3	4	45	28	.246	40	3.26
PEAK		510	87	139	22	3	6	50	40	.273	60	4.37
Kosco, Bryn	26	334	32	71	16	0	4	36	26	.213	26	2.67
PEAK		501	60	117	25	0	8	46	49	.234	50	3.52
Laker, Tim	23	401	49	91	18	2	13	60	33	.227	42	3.66
PEAK		500	89	133	25	2	25	81	50	.266	79	5.81
Lansing, Mike	25	471	59	123	18	4	5	48	43	.261	51	3.96
PEAK		499	76	143	21	4	7	53	51	.287	68	5.16
Martin, Chris	25	375	36	79	20	1	4	28	41	.211	31	2.83
PEAK		492	61	118	29	1	7	48	58	.240	54	3.90
Pennye, Darwin	26	303	34	77	9	4	1	21	18	.254	28	3.35
PEAK		508	67	138	17	6	2	43	42	.272	57	4.16
Siddall, Joe	25	283	23	62	12	0	2	25	23	.219	21	2.57
PEAK		503	53	125	24	0	5	43	47	.249	51	3.64
White, Derrick	23	482	56	125	18	1	11	72	34	.259	53	4.01
PEAK		505	80	148	22	1	17	70	45	.293	78	5.90

NEW YORK METS

TIDEWATER

Name	Age	AB	R	H	D	T	HR	RBI	BB	AVG	RC	RC/27
Baez, Kevin	26	343	22	74	14	1	3	24	10	.216	23	2.31
PEAK		521	43	123	23	1	6	45	29	.236	46	3.12
Bogar, Tim	26	468	40	121	28	1	7	28	11	.259	46	3.58
PEAK		523	54	144	32	1	10	58	27	.275	65	4.63
Burnitz, Jeromy	24	434	41	97	18	3	10	30	25	.224	39	3.12
PEAK		512	67	131	24	3	17	67	38	.256	65	4.61
Donnels, Chris	27	270	26	75	13	3	2	24	44	.278	41	5.68
PEAK		473	46	131	23	5	12	42	77	.277	76	6.00
Hansen, Terrel	26	385	32	88	15	0	16	35	19	.229	39	3.55
PEAK		512	54	127	21	0	26	80	38	.248	68	4.77
Howell, Pat	24	395	34	89	7	3	1	16	17	.225	26	2.29
PEAK		518	60	133	12	4	2	39	32	.257	48	3.37
Lyden, Mitch	28	292	25	70	11	0	19	39	10	.240	35	4.26
PEAK		532	46	127	20	0	35	71	18	.239	66	4.40
McKnight, Jeff	30	341	32	97	18	1	5	32	38	.284	44	4.87
PEAK		495	46	141	26	1	7	46	55	.285	68	5.19
Springer, Steve	28	415	42	112	14	0	21	52	17	.270	54	4.81
PEAK		528	53	143	18	0	27	66	22	.271	73	5.12

BINGHAMPTON

Name	Age	AB	R	H	D	T	HR	RBI	BB	AVG	RC	RC/27
Butterfield, Chris	25	469	45	94	18	2	12	39	43	.200	39	2.81
PEAK		499	65	115	22	2	18	64	51	.230	59	4.15
Dellicarri, Joe	26	319	25	72	10	1	2	22	24	.226	24	2.62
PEAK		502	48	123	17	2	4	40	48	.245	49	3.49
Fordyce, Brook	23	410	45	103	24	0	9	46	28	.251	44	3.87
PEAK		506	76	145	32	0	17	70	44	.287	78	5.83
Howard, Tim	24	489	52	121	18	5	4	59	31	.247	45	3.30
PEAK		509	69	141	21	5	6	51	41	.277	63	4.62
Hunter, Bert	25	395	46	84	16	3	5	27	29	.213	31	2.69
PEAK		506	77	122	23	4	9	51	44	.241	54	3.80
Katzaroff, Rob	24	433	49	110	16	4	0	22	32	.254	39	3.26
PEAK		505	71	143	21	4	0	41	45	.283	59	4.40
Saunders, Doug	23	420	35	94	14	1	4	29	40	.224	34	2.82
PEAK		494	58	130	19	1	7	48	56	.263	58	4.30
Zinter, Alan	25	419	48	84	11	3	13	39	54	.200	39	3.14
PEAK		485	75	112	15	3	22	68	65	.231	64	4.63

COLUMBUS

Name	Age	AB	R	H	D	T	HR	RBI	BB	AVG	RCRC/27
Ausmus, Brad	24	353	42	77	13	1	2	30	34	.218	27	2.64
PEAK		495	77	124	21	1	4	42	55	.251	52	3.78
DeJardin, Bobby	26	403	44	86	13	1	2	36	34	.213	28	2.38
PEAK		498	67	116	18	1	3	37	52	.233	44	3.11
Humphreys, Mike	26	393	72	100	16	4	5	40	50	.254	45	4.15
PEAK		483	101	131	21	5	8	51	67	.271	67	5.14
Lovullo, Torey	27	449	59	119	28	3	18	76	54	.265	67	5.48
PEAK		491	65	130	31	3	20	83	59	.265	78	5.83
Masse, Billy	26	345	45	83	12	1	11	52	43	.241	40	4.12
PEAK		484	75	125	18	1	19	67	67	.258	70	5.26
Meulens, Hensley	26	514	82	127	24	1	24	86	51	.247	67	4.67
PEAK		493	95	130	24	1	28	85	57	.264	82	6.10
Silvestri, Dave	25	405	72	102	21	3	12	62	49	.252	52	4.63
PEAK		488	108	136	27	3	20	74	62	.279	82	6.29
Snow, J.T.	25	472	70	134	22	2	13	67	59	.284	68	5.43
PEAK		487	86	149	24	2	18	72	63	.306	89	7.11
Williams, Bernie	24	348	58	96	19	4	7	43	44	.276	49	5.25
PEAK		483	99	146	28	5	14	67	67	.302	88	7.05
Williams, Gerald	26	526	79	135	26	4	14	74	33	.257	61	4.21
PEAK		507	91	138	26	4	17	69	43	.272	73	5.34

ALBANY

Name	Age	AB	R	H	D	T	HR	RBI	BB	AVG	RCRC/27
Barnwell, Richard	25	429	79	109	26	4	1	30	42	.254	46	3.88
PEAK		497	109	139	32	4	2	45	53	.280	65	4.90
Davis, Russ	23	486	75	134	23	4	22	70	43	.276	76	5.83
PEAK		497	104	153	26	4	33	101	53	.308	107	8.40
Hernandez, Kiki	24	324	46	88	18	0	3	40	34	.272	38	4.35
PEAK		492	86	147	29	0	6	52	58	.299	72	5.63
Obando, Sherman	23	377	70	103	19	3	17	55	28	.273	57	5.62
PEAK		503	128	154	28	4	34	102	47	.306	107	8.28
Rodriguez, Carlos	25	377	36	95	18	1	2	37	25	.252	35	3.35
PEAK		509	60	141	26	1	4	46	41	.277	60	4.40
Sparks, Don	27	498	63	150	32	5	13	71	26	.301	53	3.76
PEAK		523	66	157	34	5	14	75	27	.300	57	5.72
Vargas, Hector	27	411	63	119	26	7	1	41	42	.290	79	5.18
PEAK		499	76	144	32	8	1	50	51	.289	69	5.25

TACOMA

Name	Age	AB	R	H	D	T	HR	RBI	BB	AVG	RCRC/27
Carter, Jeff	28	363	46	86	11	4	1	28	52	.237	41	3.28
PEAK		481	61	114	15	5	1	37	69	.237	66	4.76
Grunhard, Dan	29	257	30	61	12	2	4	22	21	.237	25	3.44
PEAK		508	59	121	24	4	8	44	42	.238	52	3.63
Hill, Orsino	31	364	43	79	19	3	6	34	40	.217	34	3.22
PEAK		496	59	108	26	4	8	46	54	.218	49	3.41
Kingery, Mike	32	346	34	94	14	3	1	30	25	.272	35	3.75
PEAK		513	50	139	21	4	1	44	37	.271	55	3.97
Lockhart, Keith	28	348	34	86	18	2	4	29	22	.247	33	3.40
PEAK		517	51	128	27	3	6	43	33	.248	52	3.61
Neel, Troy	27	374	47	117	28	2	16	57	44	.313	70	7.35
PEAK		492	62	154	37	3	21	75	58	.313	100	7.99
Polidor, Gus	31	348	18	86	13	0	2	33	16	.247	27	2.78
PEAK		526	27	130	20	0	6	50	24	.247	44	3.00
Smith, Jack	28	277	34	62	9	0	11	32	24	.224	24	3.01
PEAK		506	62	113	16	0	21	58	44	.223	46	3.16
Witmeyer, Ron	26	481	43	100	19	2	4	42	41	.208	34	2.41
PEAK		498	55	114	21	2	5	42	52	.229	46	3.23

HUNTSVILLE

Name	Age	AB	R	H	D	T	HR	RBI	BB	AVG	RCRC/27
Abbott, Kurt	24	441	58	104	13	4	9	47	27	.236	41	3.28
PEAK		510	90	136	18	4	15	64	40	.267	66	4.76
Armas, Marcos	23	494	75	129	26	5	17	76	36	.261	65	4.81
PEAK		504	105	149	29	5	26	88	46	.296	94	7.15
Conte, Mike	25	283	29	62	8	3	1	24	34	.219	23	2.81
PEAK		488	62	121	16	5	2	39	62	.248	51	3.75
Dattola, Kevin	25	316	28	72	14	3	2	30	29	.228	29	3.21
PEAK		493	54	126	24	4	4	45	57	.256	57	4.19
Garrison, Webster	27	338	45	86	22	4	8	55	26	.254	41	4.39
PEAK		511	68	130	33	6	12	83	39	.254	65	4.61
Jacas, Dave	28	429	56	105	19	4	4	43	38	.245	43	3.58
PEAK		505	66	124	22	5	5	51	45	.246	53	3.76
Lydy, Scott	24	375	58	106	18	3	9	60	59	.283	57	5.72
PEAK		471	89	145	24	3	16	79	79	.308	91	7.54
Paquette, Craig	24	439	54	105	22	4	17	64	26	.239	51	4.12
PEAK		511	66	138	28	4	29	90	39	.270	84	6.08
Vice, Darryl	26	466	68	127	11	1	1	34	51	.273	51	4.06
PEAK		470	76	135	13	1	1	37	80	.287	60	4.84

PHILADELPHIA PHILLIES

SCRANTON WILKES-BARRE

Name	Age	AB	R	H	D	T	HR	RBI	BB	AVG	RC	RC/27
Alexander, Gary	28	388	37	68	21	1	8	37	30	.175	26	2.19
PEAK		511	49	89	28	1	11	49	39	.174	35	2.24
Batiste, Kim	25	258	21	59	9	3	1	20	5	.229	18	2.44
PEAK		529	56	135	21	6	3	44	21	.255	50	3.43
Castillo, Braulio	25	370	41	79	17	2	9	33	30	.214	32	2.97
PEAK		503	74	122	25	3	17	65	47	.243	63	4.46
Legg, Greg	33	279	25	56	9	1	1	20	32	.201	19	2.30
PEAK		493	44	99	16	2	2	35	57	.201	35	2.40
Lindsey, Doug	25	265	19	48	8	0	3	19	28	.181	16	1.99
PEAK		494	49	105	17	0	8	43	56	.213	43	2.98
Millette, Joe	26	246	16	58	9	1	1	16	11	.236	18	2.59
PEAK		514	41	131	20	2	3	41	36	.255	50	3.52
Peguero, Julio	24	277	28	62	11	1	1	15	18	.224	20	2.51
PEAK		509	68	130	23	2	3	41	41	.255	52	3.70
Schu, Rick	31	380	39	104	15	1	7	34	34	.274	44	4.30
PEAK		505	52	138	20	1	9	45	45	.273	62	4.56
Williams, Cary	26	359	27	69	15	1	4	28	11	.192	20	1.86
PEAK		520	52	111	23	1	7	45	30	.213	40	2.64

READING

Name	Age	AB	R	H	D	T	HR	RBI	BB	AVG	RC	RC/27
Escobar, John	24	292	23	60	13	1	2	21	15	.205	19	2.21
PEAK		515	56	123	25	2	5	45	35	.239	48	3.31
Lieberthal, Mike	21	293	23	73	15	1	2	28	15	.249	26	3.19
PEAK		511	57	150	29	2	6	53	39	.294	69	5.16
Lockett, Ron	23	385	31	76	16	1	3	27	13	.197	22	1.92
PEAK		522	64	125	25	1	7	47	28	.239	48	3.26
Neitzel, R.A.	24	258	23	42	6	0	0	13	27	.163	11	1.38
PEAK		492	63	98	14	0	0	26	58	.199	32	2.19
Ryan, Sean	24	338	22	79	17	1	4	43	30	.234	31	3.23
PEAK		498	42	132	27	1	9	53	52	.265	63	4.65
Taylor, Sam	24	335	31	72	17	3	6	41	27	.215	29	2.98
PEAK		502	63	124	28	4	13	60	48	.247	62	4.43
Trevino, Troy	28	271	24	54	9	1	1	16	18	.199	16	1.99
PEAK		516	46	103	17	2	2	30	34	.200	32	2.09
Waller, Casey	25	300	31	66	13	2	3	23	24	.220	24	2.77
PEAK		504	67	125	24	3	7	49	46	.248	55	3.92

PITTSBURGH PIRATES

BUFFALO

Name	Age	AB	R	H	D	T	HR	RBI	BB	AVG	RC	RC/27
Clark, Dave	30	243	32	67	16	3	8	40	25	.276	36	5.52
PEAK		499	66	138	33	6	16	82	51	.277	79	5.91
Dorsett, Brian	32	473	50	123	32	0	15	75	28	.260	57	4.40
PEAK		519	55	135	35	0	16	82	31	.260	66	4.64
Garcia, Carlos	25	409	54	112	25	5	9	51	18	.274	50	4.55
PEAK		518	85	154	34	6	15	73	32	.297	83	6.16
Martin, Al	25	403	62	111	14	8	15	43	26	.275	56	5.18
PEAK		510	98	152	20	9	26	88	40	.298	94	7.09
Richardson, Jeff	27	315	25	82	21	1	3	22	15	.260	32	3.71
PEAK		525	42	137	35	2	5	37	25	.261	56	3.90
Tubbs, Greg	30	413	50	109	19	2	5	31	43	.264	46	4.09
PEAK		498	60	131	23	2	6	37	52	.263	59	4.34
Young, Kevin	24	469	67	133	26	3	5	47	50	.284	59	4.74
PEAK		491	85	152	29	3	7	56	59	.310	80	6.37

CAROLINA

Name	Age	AB	R	H	D	T	HR	RBI	BB	AVG	RC	RC/27
Bullett, Scott	24	504	46	126	17	3	6	36	22	.250	45	3.21
PEAK		518	62	145	20	3	9	55	32	.280	64	4.63
De Los Santos, Alberto	23	346	27	84	7	4	1	19	14	.243	26	2.68
PEAK		519	55	145	14	4	2	43	31	.279	55	3.97
Edge, Greg	28	246	17	53	5	0	0	7	18	.215	15	2.10
PEAK		513	35	110	10	0	0	15	38	.214	32	2.14
Johnson, Mark	25	374	32	80	13	1	5	36	42	.214	31	2.85
PEAK		491	54	119	19	1	9	49	59	.242	54	3.92
Manahan, Austin	23	333	35	68	15	4	3	26	22	.204	24	2.45
PEAK		507	78	124	26	6	7	51	43	.245	56	3.95
Osik, Keith	24	414	32	99	15	1	3	36	41	.239	37	3.17
PEAK		494	49	133	20	1	5	45	56	.269	58	4.34
Ratliff, Daryl	23	403	36	89	12	2	0	21	31	.221	28	2.41
PEAK		502	62	131	18	2	0	36	48	.261	50	3.64
Romero, Mandy	25	263	22	52	14	0	2	21	22	.198	18	2.30
PEAK		502	56	115	29	0	5	43	48	.229	47	3.28
Schreiber, Bruce	26	250	11	62	4	3	0	12	7	.248	19	2.73
PEAK		521	28	138	10	6	0	38	29	.265	49	3.45
Shelton, Ben	23	360	44	78	15	0	8	39	53	.217	35	3.35
PEAK		473	83	121	22	0	16	62	77	.256	69	5.29

ST. LOUIS CARDINALS

LOUISVILLE

Name	Age	AB	R	H	D	T	HR	RBI	BB	AVG	RC	RC/27
Brewer, Rod	27	398	40	97	17	1	12	60	33	.244	42	3.77
PEAK		508	51	124	22	1	15	77	42	.244	58	4.08
Canseco, Ozzie	28	291	37	65	16	1	15	40	29	.223	34	3.03
PEAK		500	64	112	28	2	26	69	50	.224	65	4.52
Carr, Chuck	24	353	48	92	9	6	2	19	22	.261	33	3.41
PEAK		510	86	147	15	8	4	49	40	.288	65	4.83
Figueroa, Bien	29	301	30	73	9	1	1	17	23	.243	24	2.79
PEAK		511	51	124	15	2	2	29	39	.243	31	3.55
Ford, Curt	32	241	33	61	12	2	4	21	20	.253	24	3.07
PEAK		508	70	129	25	4	8	44	42	.254	53	3.75
Maclin, Lonnie	26	271	20	75	14	2	1	26	15	.277	28	2.44
PEAK		510	43	149	27	4	2	47	40	.292	55	3.86
Royer, Stan	25	418	39	99	26	1	7	54	22	.237	38	2.95
PEAK		514	62	136	34	1	12	61	36	.265	56	4.64
Woodson, Tracy	30	387	44	97	19	1	8	42	17	.251	37	3.44
PEAK		527	60	132	26	1	11	57	23	.250	54	3.69

ARKANSAS

Name	Age	AB	R	H	D	T	HR	RBI	BB	AVG	RC	RC/27
Beanblossom, Brad	25	371	33	73	9	2	0	9	26	.197	20	1.81
PEAK		507	60	115	15	3	0	32	43	.227	39	2.69
Brannon, Cliff	25	329	23	61	13	1	5	25	20	.185	20	2.01
PEAK		511	51	111	23	2	11	51	39	.217	47	3.17
Cromer, Tripp	25	326	21	69	13	4	5	20	18	.212	25	2.63
PEAK		513	44	124	23	6	11	56	37	.242	56	3.89
Martinez, Julian	26	290	14	42	12	1	2	16	22	.145	12	1.31
PEAK		502	34	86	23	2	5	34	48	.171	31	2.01
Mendez, Jesus	29	285	26	73	14	1	5	26	15	.256	29	3.69
PEAK		523	48	134	26	2	9	48	28	.256	56	3.89
Ross, Mike	27	384	29	93	24	2	5	30	24	.242	36	3.34
PEAK		518	39	134	26	2	9	48	28	.256	56	3.89
Selick, John	27	290	19	66	15	1	6	30	23	.227	27	3.49
PEAK		510	33	125	32	0	7	40	32	.241	51	3.50
Thomas, John	24	391	35	94	14	3	8	53	16	.240	35	3.18
PEAK		519	63	140	21	4	15	66	31	.270	67	4.77

SAN DIEGO PADRES

LAS VEGAS

Name	Age	AB	R	H	D	T	HR	RBI	BB	AVG	RC	RC/27
Faries, Paul	28	425	50	102	12	4	1	26	28	.240	33	2.76
PEAK		516	61	124	15	5	1	32	34	.240	44	3.03
Gardner, Jeff	29	405	52	113	23	3	1	33	47	.279	46	4.25
PEAK		493	63	138	28	4	1	40	57	.280	63	4.79
Higgins, Kevin	26	333	32	68	10	2	0	26	28	.204	20	2.04
PEAK		499	59	112	17	3	0	32	51	.224	40	2.79
Lampkin, Tom	29	316	29	80	13	2	2	31	37	.253	31	3.55
PEAK		492	45	125	20	3	3	48	58	.254	53	3.90
Lopez, Luis	22	373	29	80	13	3	3	20	13	.188	18	1.60
PEAK		521	45	136	26	3	3	48	58	.254	58	3.90
Pegues, Steve	25	354	33	77	16	2	7	36	39	.234	42	2.84
PEAK		531	65	122	27	7	6	60	67	.263	65	4.13
Sherman, Darrell	25	251	31	59	6	1	0	14	29	.247	25	2.44
PEAK		490	69	131	29	13	5	49	44	.267	55	3.71
Staton, Darrell	25	313	31	72	15	2	12	44	24	.230	32	2.59
PEAK		505	72	129	26	5	27	60	60	.263	56	4.19
Vatcher, Jim	27	262	27	59	12	2	6	22	27	.235	21	2.95
PEAK		499	51	112	23	4	6	49	45	.257	42	3.59
Velasquez, Guillermo	25	475	44	121	34	2	11	56	40	.255	47	3.58
PEAK		510	58	143	39	2	7	56	40	.280	69	5.08

WICHITA

Name	Age	AB	R	H	D	T	HR	RBI	BB	AVG	RC	RC/27
Bethea, Steve	24	249	29	59	12	3	1	29	29	.237	24	3.41
PEAK		487	71	130	26	6	3	44	63	.267	62	4.69
Gainer, Jay	26	370	50	92	12	1	19	88	39	.249	51	4.95
PEAK		491	80	130	17	1	31	88	51	.265	83	6.21
Gonzalez, Paul	24	426	52	104	18	2	13	76	40	.244	50	4.19
PEAK		496	80	136	23	2	22	76	59	.274	76	5.93
Holbert, Ray	22	299	41	81	7	3	2	20	35	.271	34	4.21
PEAK		483	87	148	15	2	22	76	79	.306	79	5.88
Hosey, Dwayne	26	421	49	102	22	5	7	49	67	.242	45	3.81
PEAK		501	69	130	27	7	10	60	73	.259	65	4.73
Lopez, Pedro	24	314	31	73	8	3	6	42	10	.232	26	2.91
PEAK		524	71	138	16	8	15	60	45	.263	62	4.34
Noland, J.D.	24	445	52	115	20	5	5	45	26	.258	48	3.80
PEAK		508	75	146	25	5	8	63	48	.287	70	5.22
Witkowski, Mat	23	424	53	111	12	3	6	42	28	.262	44	3.93
PEAK		507	85	150	17	3	11	59	43	.296	72	5.45

SAN FRANCISCO GIANTS

PHOENIX

Name	Age	AB	R	H	D	T	HR	RBI	BB	AVG	RC	RC/27
Decker, Steve	27	428	34	105	20	1	6	50	31	.245	40	3.34
PEAK		513	41	126	24	1	7	60	37	.246	51	3.56
Hosey, Steve	24	440	44	110	25	3	8	45	25	.250	44	3.60
PEAK		512	67	143	31	3	13	65	38	.279	72	5.27
Patterson, Dave	29	350	23	77	11	3	0	24	36	.220	25	2.47
PEAK		499	33	110	16	4	0	34	51	.220	39	2.71
Patterson, John	26	344	36	91	18	3	1	25	22	.265	34	3.63
PEAK		506	61	142	28	4	2	45	44	.281	62	4.60
Wood, Ted	26	396	49	105	22	3	5	44	31	.265	43	3.99
PEAK		501	72	141	29	4	8	55	49	.281	70	5.25

SHREVEPORT

Name	Age	AB	R	H	D	T	HR	RBI	BB	AVG	RC	RC/27
Bellinger, Clay	24	423	35	79	16	2	10	41	25	.187	29	2.28
PEAK		511	63	113	22	2	18	64	39	.221	53	3.60
Chimelis, Joel	25	268	38	78	12	1	7	26	13	.291	35	4.97
PEAK		516	90	162	25	2	18	75	34	.314	87	6.64
Christopherson, Eric	24	262	29	60	9	1	5	27	26	.229	24	3.21
PEAK		494	73	129	19	2	14	59	56	.261	65	4.81
Crowe, Ron	25	248	21	54	11	1	2	20	7	.218	17	2.37
PEAK		525	60	129	26	2	6	47	25	.246	50	3.41
Davenport, Adell	25	426	44	111	27	3	16	70	21	.261	54	4.63
PEAK		516	68	147	35	3	26	89	34	.285	88	6.44
Smiley, Reuben	24	305	31	71	11	3	5	28	15	.233	26	3.00
PEAK		516	70	136	21	5	12	60	34	.264	63	4.48
Weber, Pete	25	403	51	106	20	7	2	27	30	.263	43	3.91
PEAK		506	76	146	27	8	3	50	44	.289	68	5.10

SEATTLE MARINERS

CALGARY

Name	Age	AB	R	H	D	T	HR	RBI	BB	AVG	RC	RC/27
Amaral, Rich	31	377	53	102	17	4	0	14	47	.271	40	3.93
PEAK		489	69	132	22	5	0	18	61	.270	58	4.39
Blowers, Mike	28	281	38	76	22	1	6	45	34	.270	37	4.87
PEAK		491	66	133	38	2	10	79	59	.271	72	5.43
Bolick, Frank	27	258	23	63	16	4	9	36	27	.244	33	4.57
PEAK		498	44	122	31	8	17	69	52	.245	70	5.03
Boone, Bret	24	411	49	110	21	3	8	49	41	.268	49	4.40
PEAK		494	74	146	27	3	14	65	56	.296	81	6.28
Brundage, Dave	28	299	30	60	12	2	1	23	47	.201	22	2.49
PEAK		475	48	95	19	3	2	37	75	.200	39	2.77
Haselman, Bill	27	286	33	61	11	1	12	35	29	.213	29	3.48
PEAK		499	58	107	19	2	21	61	51	.214	55	3.79
Howard, Chris	27	303	20	60	13	0	5	30	10	.198	18	2.00
PEAK		532	35	105	23	0	9	53	18	.197	35	2.21
Howitt, Dann	21	299	36	76	18	4	4	40	24	.254	32	3.87
PEAK		497	84	148	32	7	11	64	53	.298	83	6.42
Pirkl, Greg	22	270	20	60	17	2	4	21	10	.222	22	2.83
PEAK		520	57	138	36	4	13	64	30	.265	68	4.81
Williams, Ted	28	237	24	48	3	3	1	12	9	.203	13	1.86
PEAK		530	54	107	7	7	2	27	20	.202	31	1.98

JACKSONVILLE

Name	Age	AB	R	H	D	T	HR	RBI	BB	AVG	RC	RC/27
Bowie, Jim	28	271	31	74	17	0	8	37	33	.273	39	5.35
PEAK		490	56	134	31	0	14	67	60	.273	73	5.54
Campanis, Jim	25	280	25	69	11	1	4	25	18	.246	27	3.45
PEAK		510	58	139	22	2	10	56	40	.273	63	4.58
Holley, Bobby	25	394	44	103	20	2	8	39	32	.261	46	4.27
PEAK		503	70	144	27	2	14	65	47	.286	75	5.64
Manahan, Anthony	24	495	60	120	26	5	6	42	32	.242	49	3.53
PEAK		509	80	139	29	5	9	57	41	.273	67	4.89
Maynard, Tow	27	398	47	107	12	4	1	25	27	.269	40	3.71
PEAK		515	61	138	16	5	1	32	35	.268	53	3.80
McDonald, Mike	24	305	42	75	17	3	6	28	27	.246	35	4.11
PEAK		499	88	137	30	5	14	65	51	.275	75	5.59
Merchant, Mark	24	374	36	86	9	1	10	40	31	.230	36	3.38
PEAK		501	66	131	15	1	19	68	49	.261	67	4.89
Tavarez, Jesus	22	385	33	94	9	2	3	21	19	.244	32	2.97
PEAK		513	63	146	16	3	6	50	37	.285	62	4.56
Turang, Brian	26	474	57	112	22	3	11	54	36	.236	49	3.65
PEAK		502	73	128	25	3	14	62	48	.255	64	4.62

TEXAS RANGERS

OKLAHOMA CITY

Name	Age	AB	R	H	D	T	HR	RBI	BB	AVG	RC	RC/27
Balboni, Steve	36	433	54	93	19	1	25	75	44	.215	51	4.05
PEAK		499	62	107	22	1	29	86	51	.214	63	4.34
Frye, Jeff	26	319	46	83	19	1	2	20	41	.260	35	4.00
PEAK		482	78	133	30	1	4	45	68	.276	65	5.03
Jackson, Chuck	30	436	48	98	17	5	9	38	50	.225	43	3.43
PEAK		493	54	111	19	6	10	43	57	.225	53	3.75
Maurer, Rob	25	468	55	117	25	1	9	60	61	.250	54	4.15
PEAK		485	70	134	28	1	13	60	65	.276	73	5.62
McGinnis, Russ	30	457	65	103	20	1	23	54	93	.225	69	5.26
PEAK		471	64	104	24	1	6	43	79	.221	43	3.40
Miller, Keith	30	438	60	97	22	6	6	40	74	.221	40	3.40
PEAK		314	45	71	14		16	37	64	.226	45	5.00
Peltier, Dan	25	426	47	109	22	5	6	38	48	.256	49	4.17
PEAK		491	65	138	27	5	9	57	59	.281	72	5.51

TULSA

Name	Age	AB	R	H	D	T	HR	RBI	BB	AVG	RC	RC/27
Belcher, Kevin	25	373	46	85	19	2	15	50	58	.228	48	4.50
PEAK		476	75	122	26	2	27	81	74	.256	83	6.33
Colon, Cris	24	406	30	100	16	2	1	37	13	.246	32	2.82
PEAK		523	50	144	23	2	2	44	27	.275	55	3.92
Greer, Rusty	24	478	65	134	30	4	8	31	49	.280	73	5.73
PEAK		351	39	88	21	3	4	49	42	.251	42	4.31
Harris, Donald	25	295	33	69	14	1	10	33	8	.234	28	3.35
PEAK		525	80	137	27	2	25	81	25	.261	72	5.01
Hulse, David	25	345	34	92	13	2	3	16	17	.267	34	3.63
PEAK		516	63	150	21	3	6	52	34	.291	65	4.80
Morris, Rod	27	358	31	88	12	6	0	24	24	.246	32	3.20
PEAK		515	45	127	17	9	0	35	35	.247	48	3.34
Oliva, Jose	22	435	48	110	27	4	13	63	32	.253	54	4.49
PEAK		502	79	146	34	4	24	85	48	.291	92	6.98
Sable, Luke	27	263	23	60	7	1	2	13	18	.228	20	2.66
PEAK		515	45	117	14	2	4	25	35	.227	41	2.78
Shave, Jon	25	442	48	119	22	4	2	30	30	.269	47	3.93
PEAK		508	66	149	27	4	3	49	42	.293	67	5.04

TONONTO BLUE JAYS

SYRACUSE

Name	Age	AB	R	H	D	T	HR	RBI	BB	AVG	RC	RC/27
Davis, Butch	35	534	57	138	29	7	7	64	29	.258	58	3.95
PEAK		522	56	135	28	7	7	63	28	.259	59	4.12
Martinez, Domingo	25	425	47	107	21	0	17	53	29	.252	52	4.42
PEAK		508	73	141	27	0	28	87	42	.278	84	6.18
Pederson, Stu	33	253	36	54	13	1	6	25	31	.213	25	3.39
PEAK		490	70	105	25	2	12	48	60	.214	51	3.58
Quinian, Tom	25	342	37	68	16	1	5	31	39	.199	28	2.76
PEAK		491	70	113	25	1	10	51	59	.230	53	3.79
Schunk, Jerry	27	406	34	98	16	1	6	22	18	.241	43	2.90
PEAK		527	44	127	21	1	3	29	23	.241	39	2.90
Sprague, Ed	25	359	42	92	17	1	13	43	39	.256	48	4.85
PEAK		493	73	139	25	1	24	81	57	.282	85	6.48
Thompson, Ryan	25	416	64	108	19	5	12	40	39	.260	54	4.73
PEAK		498	73	129	25	6	20	75	52	.260	84	6.37
Ward, Turner	28	274	35	61	9	1	8	25	39	.223	30	3.80
PEAK		481	62	107	16	2	14	44	69	.222	54	3.90
Zosky, Eddie	25	334	27	71	10	5	3	32	18	.213	25	2.57
PEAK		514	55	124	18	7	7	48	36	.241	51	3.53

KNOXVILLE

Name	Age	AB	R	H	D	T	HR	RBI	BB	AVG	RC	RC/27
Cedeno, Domingo	24	331	26	70	7	5	2	18	18	.211	23	2.38
PEAK		513	55	125	14	8	5	44	37	.244	50	3.48
Delarosa, Juan	24	493	59	152	30	8	11	46	14	.308	73	5.78
PEAK		525	77	175	34	8	16	80	25	.333	99	7.64
Henderson, Derek	25	416	32	98	11	2	2	33	24	.236	32	2.72
PEAK		512	50	135	16	2	3	42	38	.264	52	3.72
Mengel, Brad	25	288	18	64	8	1	1	19	8	.222	18	2.17
PEAK		525	44	131	16	2	2	38	24	.250	46	3.15
O'Halloran, Greg	25	399	34	101	19	3	3	29	29	.253	39	3.53
PEAK		506	59	141	26	4	3	47	44	.279	62	4.59
Perez, Robert	24	514	51	125	23	3	8	51	12	.243	45	3.12
PEAK		528	70	144	26	3	12	61	22	.273	64	4.50
Scott, Shawn	24	315	26	66	4	2	2	23	25	.210	21	2.28
PEAK		502	57	122	9	3	5	40	48	.243	47	3.34
Tollison, David	24	334	32	71	15	1	1	19	34	.213	25	2.57
PEAK		493	62	121	24	1	2	39	57	.245	50	3.63
Wilson, Nigel	23	508	73	130	32	5	23	60	31	.256	70	5.00
PEAK		509	103	148	34	5	35	104	41	.291	102	7.63
Yan, Julian	27	383	44	97	22	2	14	42	26	.253	48	4.53
PEAK		515	59	130	30	3	19	56	35	.252	67	4.70

Glossary

APPROXIMATE VALUE

This Bill James method computes the worth of a single player's single season. It relies on the rawest of stats, without ballpark adjustments. It also does not interpolate between its basic breakpoints. As a consequence, Approximate Values are, in fact, very approximate. They are only used for quick evaluations or when you have just the rawest of stats to work from. Bill used AV to get a quick handle on a player season for which he didn't or couldn't compute something more comprehensive.

BASEBALL SABERMETRIC Use

As it turns out, the range of Approximate Value figures is about the same as twice the range of Total Wins Above Replacement. Since TWAR is a much more reliable stat, and since a computer can calculate TWAR even faster than AV, BASEBALL SABERMETRIC uses 2xTWAR instead of Bill's AV. Actually, you won't see any AVs in the book; the only use we've made of AV was as a feeder stat for Trade Value (qv.).

BALLPARK ADJUSTMENT

This is the concept of adjusting a players' stats to reflect the biases of the home ballpark in which he plays half his games. The objective is to come up with a stat line that is "what the player would have done if he played the same number of games in each ballpark," or "what the player would have done in a neutral ballpark."

There are various methods of doing this, but the basic approach is always to compare the player's stats at home with his stats on the road. The ELIAS BASEBALL ANALYST does the silliest thing possible with this information, which is to compute the ratio of the two splits. This results in an adjustment not to a neutral ballpark, but to all parks EXCEPT the home park. I'm not sure what method PETE PALMER uses for his Linear Weights, but, knowing Pete, I'm sure they're much more reasonable than the ELIAS. What we do in the SABERMETRIC is to compute the following formulas for both the batting and pitching stats for a team, for the National and American Leagues:

NL: $(11R + H) / (6R + 6H)$
AL: $(13R + H) / (7R + 7H)$

where R and H are the road and home stats. Then we multiplied the results by each player's stats, to get a ballpark adjusted figure. This year and last, we did something a little more complicated with the formula. We made three sets of adjustment figures: one for lefty batters, one for righty batters, and one for the whole. The component stats were both the team's batters of the appropriate hand and also the team's pitchers' opposing batter lines for opposing batters of the appropriate hand. The only reason for generating the total figures was to work with switch hitters.

BILL JAMES HALL OF FAME METHOD (ORGANIC HALL OF FAME SYSTEM)

This method is used to evaluate a player's chance of making the Hall of Fame. it is NOT designed to determine whether the player "should" make the Hall; just whether he is likely to do so. That is, this is an evaluation of the apparent statistical criteria which the Hall of Fame voters do in fact use in determining who should be voted into the Hall.

PITCHERS

1. Wins

15-17	=	2
18-19	=	4
20-22	=	6
23-24	=	8
25-29	=	10
30+ =	15	

2. Strikeouts

200-249	=	2
250-299	=	3
300+	=	6

3. Winning Percentage of .700+ and 14+ Wins

   = 2

4. ERA (50+ games or 150+ innings)

   2.00-2.99 = 1

1.00-1.99 =	4

5. Saves

20-29	=	2
30+ =	5	

6. No-Hitter = 1

7. League Leader

ERA	=	2	
Games	=	1	
Wins	=	1	
Innings	=	1	
Winning Percentage	=	1	
Strikeouts	=	1	
Shutouts =	1		
Saves	=	1	
Complete Games	=	0.5	

8. Career Wins

150-174	=	5
175-199	=	8
200-224	=	10
225-249	=	15
250-274	=	20
275-299	=	25
300+	=	35

9. Career Winning Percentage (200+ decisions)

.550-.574 =		1
.575-.599 =		3
.600-.624 =		5
.625+	=	10

10. Career ERA Below 3.00 = 10

11. Career Saves

200-299	=	10
300+	=	20

12. Games Pitched

700-849	=	10
850-999	=	20
1000+	=	30

13. Career Strikeouts

3000-3999	=	10

4000+ = 20

14. World Series

   Game Started = 2
   Game Won = 2
   Relief Appearance = 1

15. LCS Win = 1

NOTE: Total Points for Post-Season play are limited to 20.

16. MVP = 8

17. Cy Young Award = 5

18. All-Star Game Pitched In = 3

19. Gold Glove = 1

20. Rookie of the Year = 1

NON-PITCHERS

1. Batting Average (only for seasons of 100+ games)

   .300-.349 = 2.5
   .350-.399 = 5.0
   .400+ = 15.0

2. 200+ Hits = 5

3. 100+ RBI= 3

4. 100+ Runs Scored = 3

5. Home Runs

   30-39 = 2
   40-49 = 4
   50+ = 10

6. Doubles

   35-44 = 1
   45+ = 2

7. 100+ Walks = 0.5

8. League Leader

   Batting Average = 6
   Home Runs = 4
   RBI = 4
   Runs Scored = 3
   Hits = 2
   Stolen Bases = 2
   Doubles = 1
   Triples = 1

9. Career Hits

   2000-2499 = 4

2500-2999 = 15
3000-3499 = 40
3500+ = 50

10. Career Home Runs

   300-399 = 3
   400-499 = 10
   500-599 = 20
   600+ = 30

11. Career Batting Average (1500+ games)

   .300-.314 = 8
   .315-.329 = 16
   .330+ = 24

12. Games Played at Catcher Only

   1200-1399=15
   1400-1599 = 30
   1600-1799 = 45
   1800+ = 60

13. Games Played at Shortstop

   1900-2199 = 15
   2200+ = 30

14. Games Played at Second Base

   same as #13

15. Games Played at Third Base

   2000 = 15

16. Games Played at Second, Short or Third Combined
   (in ADDITION to above)

   2500+ = 15

17. If the player has a career batting average of .275+ and has played 1500 games at either Second Base, Shortstop or Catcher (do NOT combine)

   = 15

18. MVP Award = 8

19. All-Star Game Played = 3

20. Gold Glove = 1

21. Rookie of the Year = 1

22. Regular Player on a World Champion

   Shortstop= 6
   Catcher = 6
   Second Base = 5
   Center Field = 5
   Third Base = 3

Left Field= 2
Right Field = 2
First Base = 1
DH = 1

23. Regular Player on World Series Loser

   Shortstop= 5
   Catcher = 5
   Second Base = 3
   Center Field = 3
   Third Base = 1

24. Regular Player on LCS Loser

   Shortstop= 2
   Catcher = 2
   Second Base = 1
   Center Field = 1
   Third Base = 1

MANAGERS

1. Managed 100+ Games = 2

2. World Champion = 8

3. World Series Loser = 5

4. LCS Loser = 3

5. EACH 200 Career Wins = 1

6. Team Won 100+ Games = 1

DEFENSIVE EFFICIENCY RECORD (DER)

This is the percentage of all balls in play that a team has turned into outs. Double Plays do NOT count twice. For seasons in which Play-by-Play data is available, this is a direct counting stat. For earlier seasons, the following computation is used to estimate the DER:

1. Compute:

   Putouts-Strikeouts minus Double Plays
   minus 2*Triple Plays
   minus Opposition Caught Stealing
   minus Outfield Assists

2. Compute:

   Total Batters Faced-Strikeouts
   -Hits-Walks-Hit by Pitch
   -.71*Errors

3. Average Computations 1 and 2 above. This is called Plays Made.

4. Compute DER=

Plays Made (#3 above) divided by
(Plays Made + Hits - Home Runs +
.71*Errors)

DEFENSIVE WINNING PERCENTAGE

This is an estimate made by Bill James on the basis of long analysis and observation. The chart is a little old and, therefore, out of date, but it is still the best estimate of defensive contribution available.

The Chart below is used to give the defensive player a number of Points, each of which converts into a hundredth (.01) in the winning percentage. The Chart contains, for each defensive position, four separate criteria, each with its own number of possible points. It is arranged so that each position has a "40-point" criteria, a 30-point, a 20-point and a 10-point. This gives a total possible of 100 points, each of which is worth .01. Therefore, a perfect score would be worth a Defensive Winning Percentage of 1.000. Naturally, the standards are set so that a perfect score is practically impossible. The Criteria at the various positions are:

CATCHERS

40-point Opposition Stolen Bases per Game
divided by the League Average.
30-point ERA when he is in the game minus
League ERA.
20-point Fielding Average.
10-point Assists per Game.

FIRST BASE

40-point Fielding Average.
30-point Assists per Game.
20-point Number of 363 Double Plays involving the player.
10-point Errors made at Third Base and
Shortstop.

SECOND BASE

40-point Compute:
Player's Double Plays / Games Played /
(Team (Hits + Walks) / Game).
30-point Compute:
Range Factor (qv.) - Double Plays per
Game.
20-point Fielding Percentage.
10-point Team Defensive Efficiency Record

THIRD BASE

40-point Range Factor (qv.)
30-point Fielding Percentage.

20-point Compute:
Player's Double Plays / Games Played /
(Team (Hits + Walks) / Game).

10-point Team Defensive Efficiency Record.

SHORTSTOP

40-point Compute:
Range Factor (qv.) - Double Plays / Game
30-point Compute:
Player's Double Plays / Games Played /
(Team (Hits + Walks) / Game).
20-point Fielding Percentage.
10-point Team Defensive Efficiency Record.

ALL OUTFIELDERS

40-point Range Factor (qv.)
30-point Fielding Percentage.
20-point Career Assists * 162 / Games Played.
10-point Team Defensive Efficiency Record.

DEFENSIVE WINS
ABOVE REPLACEMENT
(DWAR)

This process needs to be followed for EACH defensive position the player has played. Then, the various DWARs are added together to get the player's total DWAR.

1. Compute the Player's Defensive Winning Percentage (qv.) at the position.

2. Select the appropriate Game Assignment
from the following chart:

Shortstop = 11
Catcher = 10
Second Base = 8
Center field = 6
Third Base = 6
Right Field = 5
Left Field = 4
First Base = 3

NOTE: DH has no defensive value at all, and so will provide no DWAR component.

3. Compute the player's Defensive Games
at the position =

Defensive Innings at the position / 9

3. Compute DWAR =

Defensive Winning Percentage at the
position *
Game Assignment for the position *
Defensive Games at the position

EXPECTED WINNING PERCENTAGE

This is the winning percentage that a pitcher "should" have had in a perfect and completely just world. It is computed by applying the Pythagorean Method (qv.) to the Pitcher's Ballpark Adjusted ERA and the League's Average Runs Per Game. That is, it strips away the illusions of the pitcher's ballpark and his team's offensive contribution.

EXPECTED WINS / EXPECTED LOSSES

EWins are computed by multiplying the pitcher's Expected ERA (qv.) by his actual number of decisions, statistically rounding the result to an integer. ELosses are the actual decisions minus the EWins. Surely that is what you expected.

the FAR RIGHT END OF THE
NORMAL CURVE

As you may know, there is a statistics distribution called "normal"; you may have heard of it under the name "bell curve" or "normal curve". The normal curve represents the distribution of almost everything, provided that you are examining the whole possible population. Thus, the distribution of baseball talent among the whole of the human race is represented by the normal curve.

However, professional baseball players are not chosen randomly from the whole human race; they are chosen precisely for their ability to play baseball. They are the very best small part of the curve, the part that is on the "right end" of the "normal curve". The importance of this distinction is this: the whole normal curve has most of its people in the middle, with a small number of really great or really bad performers. The right end, on the other hand, has most of its people at the bottom (the left side of the right end, if you're following me), and can be turned on its side and treated as a talent pyramid.

There are a lot of consequences of the difference between a normal distribution and a pyramid distribution; you'll note several in this book. To keep things straight, remember that a talent will be normally distributed if the population you're talking about was selected by some method that is unrelated to the talent at hand. For example, the baseball talent of concert pianists is distributed normally. However, if your population is chosen by some method related to the talent to be examined, you will get the pyramid talent distribution, so the distribution of baseball talent among Major League baseball players is the pyramid. The distribution of talent in a minor league is the funny-looking trapezoid you get if you take a pyramid and lop the top (major leaguers) off.

FAVORITE TOY

This is a method for estimating the player's chance of attaining a goal, given whatever head start he already has. For example, Don Malcolm of the San Antonio Trotters wants to finish his career with 3000 walks (that hog - but that PATIENT hog). He is now 27 years old and has already accumulated 1492 walks (thereby officially discovering first base). He computes as follows:

1. Compute the number of the given event that has to happen before the goal is attained. For example, Malcolm needs 3000-1492=1508 walks.

2. Estimate the number of years remaining in the player's career as

    24 - .6*current age.

    For example, Malcolm, at age 27, has 24 - .6*27 = 24-16.2 = 7.8 estimated years remaining in his nefarious career.

    NOTE: Any player over 37 years old is automatically assumed to have 1.5 years left; that is, if he is still playing.

3. Compute the following:

    3 * this year's events +
    2 * last year's events +
    1 * two years ago's events
    divide the sum by 6.

Then compare that to 3/4 of this year's events. If the 3/4 figure is greater, use it instead. This gives you an estimate of how fast the player is proceeding towards his goal.

For example, Malcolm took 133 walks this year, 153! last year and only 98 the year before. The computation gives 3*133+2*153 +98 = 803, which, divided by 6, yields 133.8. Checking, 3/4 of this year's 133 is 99.75. That is less that 133.8, so 133.8 it is. Malcolm is taking, on the average, 133.8 walks per year, which means that he is roughly as lazy as Jack Clark.

4. Multiply #3 by #2. This gives you the estimated number of the event that will be attained before the career ends.

For example, Malcolm's #3 is 133.8 walks per year, while his #2 is 7.8 years left. Multiplying, we get an estimate of 133.8 * 7.8 = 1043.6 before Malcolm drops dead 3/5 of the way to

first (no doubt from being beaned by an irate catcher). Doesn't look like Malcolm's going to make it. BUT,

5. Compute:

    (#4 / #1) - .5. This gives you the estimated chance that the goal will, in fact, be reached.

For example, Malcolm computes (1043.6 / 1508) - 0.5 = .6921 - 0.5 = .1921. That is, there's almost a 20% chance that Malcolm will turn in a long, injury-free career, and get those 3000 free passes (not usable for special engagements).

MAJOR LEAGUE EQUIVALENCIES

A method devised by Bill James for deciphering what a minor league player's basic stats might be if he were to play in the majors. You start by adjusting Runs, Hits, Doubles, Triples, Homers, Walks and Strikeouts; from those you can compute the other basic stats. The method gets long and involved and works like this:

1. Adjust the minor league stats (R, H, D, T, HR, BB, SO) for the minor league ballpark.

2. Compute, but do not use yet, the minor league's Runs Per Game and divide by the Major League's R/G, to get the league context out of the way. In Bill's original presentation of this, in the 1985 ABSTRACT, he did not do this, because he didn't have minor league ballpark adjustments to work with. We got ours from Howe Sportsdata, which is now the official statisticians for all AAA and AA teams.

3. Multiply #2 above by .82 to adjust for the level of competition. Oddly enough, it's the same .82 for AAA ball as for AA ball. This gives you a factor called "m," which you'll use in the next step. You also need the square root of "m," which is called "M"."

4. Multiply each individual stat by a factor Bill determined, making use of "m" and "M" above. The factors are:

    Runs = "m"
    Hits = .98 x "M"
    Doubles = "M"
    Triples = .85 x "m"
    Homers = "m"
    Walks = "m"
    Strikeouts = 1.05

5. Adjust for the Major League ballpark.

6. Now, you can also compute At-Bats. This is done by taking the minor league At-Bats and subtracting the minor league Hits to get minor league Outs. Then you add those Outs back to the final, adjusted Major League Hits to get Major League At-Bats. That allows you to compute Batting Average, Slugging Percentage and On-Base Percentage.

OFFENSIVE GAMES (OG)

A player's offensive games are established by computing the portion of his team's games that he, personally, consumed. Remember, a team gets 27 outs in which to do its damage, not some set number of trips to the plate. Therefore, a player's Offensive Games are computed by looking at the number of OUTS that the player consumed and dividing by 27, which is the number of outs to a game. ("As it turns out," the extra-inning games just about exactly balance the rain-shortened games and the lost ninth innings of home teams that are already ahead.) The computation is:

    Player's Outs Created / 27.

OFFENSIVE WINNING PERCENTAGE (OW%)

A Bill James method designed to answer the question, "If all a team's players were just as good as this one is, what would that team's winning percentage be?" This is computed, as you might guess, by applying the Runs Created method to the Pythagorean method after ballpark adjusting the whole. It is done as follows:

1. Compute the player's Runs Created (qv.), and divide it by the player's Outs Made (including such things as sacrifice flies and caught stealings). Then multiply by 27 to get the players "Runs Created Per 27 Outs" or "Runs Created Per Game."

2. Compute the team's Runs Per Game as follows:

    Team Runs Scored + Team Runs Allowed
    divided by
    Twice the Team's Games Played (usually 162*2=324, but not always)

3. Divide #1 by #2 to get the ratio of what the player did to what the League's teams did in the player's ballpark.

4. Square #3 to start the Pythagorean ball rolling.

5. Compute:

$$\#4 / (1 + \#4)$$

to complete the Pythagorean process. This will give you the player's OW%.

OFFENSIVE WINS ABOVE REPLACEMENT (OWAR)

Compute:

(Player's Offensive Winning Percentage (qv.) - .350 (the Replacement Rate)) * Player's Offensive Games (qv.)

This gives you the amount by which the player is better than the hypothetical Replacement Player and multiplies that by the player's playing time in games. That gives you the number of games the player won for his team in his personal offensive window of opportunity.

PETE PALMER'S LINEAR WEIGHTS

Linear Weights is not a baseball concept, but a normal method of mainline statistics. In statistics, linear weights means assigning a value to each part of a whole and evaluating the whole by summing up the parts. So, to evaluate the runs contributed by a hitter, Pete assigns a value (called a "weight") to a home run, another to a triple, a double, a single and so on. Some values, like that for a strikeout, are negative. Then Pete sums all the values up and gets his answer.

Pete gets the weights he gives each event by correlating the sums for teams to the actual number of runs the team scores. That is, he applies the same standard that Bill James does, standard deviation of formula runs against actual team runs. Then, Pete applies a curve fitting formula. This method involves applying a multiplier to his original linear weights such that the final formula generates the very best correlation to actual team runs for an individual year.

You can find a much fuller explanation of Pete's methods in the book he produced with John Thorn, TOTAL BASEBALL. You can find early Thorn and Palmer in their two books THE HIDDEN GAME OF BASEBALL and THE PITCHER.

POSITIONAL ADJUSTMENT

A portion of Pete Palmer's Linear Weights method for evaluating the overall contribution of players. Pete evaluates their offensive con-tribution, and then their defense, and then adds in this factor, based on the individual player's defensive position. The adjustment involves finding out what the average player at the position hits and comparing it to what the average player overall hits. Pete figures that a shortstop who hits well is worth more than a first baseman who hits the same.

While no one argues with Pete's premise here, there are arguments against this method. The one I tend to bring up is that, during certain periods in baseball history, the very best superstars - the great hitters who could play anywhere on the diamond - were loaded up at one key position, and therefore had to "compete" with each other for positional adjustment. For example, in the dead ball era, superstars were loaded into the shortstop slot, with the result that Honus Wagner and his crowd get very small positional adjustments for playing this very valuable position. The same thing happens to the Willie Mays / Mickey Mantle / Duke Snider / Richie Ashburn / Larry Doby crowd in center field in the fifties, an era in which shortstops didn't hit much.

PYTHAGOREAN METHOD

A method for finding out what the winning percentage of Team A against Team B should be, given the number of runs per game that Team A scores against Team B pitching is and what the number of runs per game that Team B scores against Team A pitching is.

This concept is often applied with "the league as a whole" in the place of Team B, and a player's record instead of Team A. Thus, this method gives us such useful results as batters' Offensive Winning Percentages and Pitchers' Expected Won/Lost Records.

The method is:

1. Divide Team A's Runs/Game (against Team B) by Team B's R/G against Team A.

2. Square #1 to start the "Pythagorean" concept.

3. Compute:

$$\#2 / (1 + \#2)$$

to complete the Pythagorean process. This will give you Team A's winning percentage against Team B.

For example, let's say that the Cardinals score 5 runs per game against the Mets, and that the Mets score only 4 per game against the Cards (yeah, right, Hanke):

1. $5/4 = 1.2$

2. 1.2 squared $= 1.44$

3. $1.44/(1+1.44) = 1.44/2.44 = .590$

Thus, if these Cardinals got to play those Mets for 162 games, the Cardinal wins should total .590 x 162 = 95.58, for a probable record of 96 and 66. This should give you an idea of what sort of advantage it takes to win 100 games.

PYRAMID DISTRIBUTION OF TALENT

See "Far Right End of the Normal Curve".

RUNS OF SUPPORT PER GAME

The number of runs that a pitcher's team scored for him, per game.

STOLEN BASES PROFIT METHOD

A method devised by Brock J. Hanke for evaluating the actual contribution of base stealers. It relies on the fact that the positive value of a stolen base is almost exactly half the negative value of a caught stealing. In the method, stolen bases and bases gained on errors made while trying to steal bases are summed and caught stealings and pickoffs are subtracted at double value. The result is the "profit" the base stealer made for his team, expressed in bases. Please note that bases are not of that much value themselves; it takes about 4 1/2 of them to make a run.

SUPPORTED WINNING PERCENTAGE

Computed by applying the Pythagorean Method (qv.) to the pitcher's ERA (NOT ballpark adjusted) and his Runs of Support Per Game (qv.). This gives you the winning percentage the pitcher "should" have had, given the support his team's batters gave him. It is NOT as good a measure of pitching quality as Expected Winning Percentage (qv.). However, comparing the Supported record to the Actual record does give you a good handle on what the pitcher's actual pitching luck (or clutch ability, if you must) was like, as opposed to his luck in getting runs scored for him.

For example, Jack Morris had an ERA of 4.04, but a Won/Lost record of 21-6 in 1992. That looks like astonishing clutch pitching, until you see that he received 5.98 Runs of Support per game. His expected Won/Lost record, which reflects the poor ERA, was only 13-14. But his Supported record was 17-10. Morris did win four more games than his support should have given him, but not eight.

SUPPORTED WINS / SUPPORTED LOSSES

SWins are computed by multiplying the Supported ERA (qv.) by the pitcher's actual number of decisions, and statistically rounding to an integer. SLosses are the actual decisions minus the SWins.

TRADE VALUE

This is computed by combining the concepts of Approximate Value (qv.) and the Favorite Toy (also qv.). The idea is to estimate how much value the player would have left to give his new team if he were traded. The computations are:

1. Estimate the number of years left in the player's career by the method used in the Favorite Toy, which is

   24 - .6*Player's Age.

   If the player is over 37 years old, he still gets 1.5 years minimum.

2. Estimate the player's established Approximate Value Per Year. You can do this by the following computation:

   3*this year's AV +
   2* last year's AV +
   1*two years ago's AV
   all divided by 6.

   If the player you're dealing with doesn't have 3 years in yet, just use this year's AV. The whole process yields an estimate, after all. NOTE: We use 2x TWAR for AV (see Approximate Value in this Glossary).

3. Compute Trade Value as:

   a. (#2 - #1) squared
   b. #a * (#1 + 1) * #2 / 190
   c. #b + (#2 * #1 * #1 / 13)

TRUNCATED PYRAMID DISTRIBUTION OF TALENT

See "Far Right End of the Normal Curve". This is the distribution of talent in the minor leagues. It looks like a pyramid with the top lopped off. The top, of course, is the Major Leagues.

WINS ABOVE REPLACEMENT (WAR)

A Win Above Replacement represents one game won that a player contributed to his team's efforts that a "replacement" player would not have. We estimate "replacement" to be a player who's personal winning percentage would be .350. That's an expansion player, and is therefore a reasonable approximation of what a normal player would be replaced with if he left the lineup. The computation methods for WAR vary. See Offensive WAR and Defensive WAR. Total Wins Above Replacement (TWAR) is just the sum of OWAR and DWAR. TWAR is our "grand stat": what we use to rank players by and what we would use to identify our SSABERMETRIC MVP.

Mad Aztec Press
Order and Response Sheet

On the last page is our 1993 Order and Reader Response Sheet. There are spaces for backordering all five years' worth of this book. Please note the price increase on the 1989 ABSTRACT. What has happened is that I've almost sold out of that book. I want the few that remain to get into the hands of the people who REALLY want them. And, of course, I don't mind making a little extra money.

In addition to the order boxes, there are boxes to check if you think you'd buy a different format of book from us. Veteran readers will notice that these are the same books we've been touting for the last couple of years. Well, I'm still trying to sell them to a publisher. If you know of any, PLEASE HELP. And thanks!

If you want to participate in our Sabermetricians' Hall of Fame balloting, check that box, and I'll send you a ballot. A WARNING, though. That ballot will take literally weeks or months to fill out. So send the order in fast, so you'll have plenty of time.

I want to take this opportunity to thank all our veteran readers. We have several hundred people who have ordered all five books, all five years. It's you who have kept me going, through bad times (last year's finances) and good. I thank you, and I hope I'm justifying your contribution more each year. Thanks!

Regarding the two books on the order sheet. The BALLPARK BOOK is designed to combine the general fan's interest in pictures and stories about old ballparks with the sabermetrician's desire for information. The idea is to give each ballpark a picture or two and a general essay, and then discuss the effects it has had on the players who played there.

The other one is just what it's title says, a HANDBOOK for people who want to know what baseball statistics amount to, both the traditional ones and the sabermetric. In addition, I'll write real honest journalism essays on the important developers in the field, from Bill James, Pete Palmer and Dick Cramer right back into the 19th century.

Well, enough of the hard sell. thanks for joining us this year, and welcome back in advance for 1994.

Yours for an exciting year, full of the sort of outrageous fun you've come to expect from those clowns, the Lords of Baseball. And also, for a year where your favorites finish first,

Brock J. Hanke

Mad Aztec Press
1215 Willow View Drive, Kirkwood, MO 63122
(314) 965-9789

ORDERS

_____ copies of Baseball Sabermetric 1993   = _____
@ $15.95 per copy

_____ copies of Baseball Sabermetric 1992   = _____
@ $15.95 per copy

_____ copies of Baseball Sabermetric 1991   = _____
@ $15.95 per copy

_____ copies of Baseball Sabermetric 1990   = _____
@ $15.95 per copy

_____ copies of The 1989 Baseball Abstract   = _____
@ $19.95 per copy (only 25 left)

+ $2.00 postage to Canada, $5.00 foreign   = _____
NOTE: All monies in U. S. funds ONLY

TOTAL = _____

I WOULD AT LEAST CONSIDER ORDERING:

Conditions of the Game   ☐
(the sabermetric Ballpark Book)

The Encyclopedia of Baseball Statistics   ☐

I Want a Hall of Fame Ballott (it's free)   ☐

My Name and Address (send ordered books to):

Name: _____

Address: _____

_____

City: _____

State: _____ Zip: _____ Country: _____

Don't cut this sheet out! XEROX it! Keep your book in good condition!